EXTRA!

1929   1945

as recorded in

The Evening Capital

ANNAPOLIS, MARYLAND

Credits:
We gratefully acknowledge the cooperation of **The Capital** for their assistance in putting this book together, as well as the tireless efforts of the **Historical Briefs** staff for bringing it to life.
Cover Design, **Denise Murray and Brian Henley for The Capital.**
Microfilm Archives, **Maryland Hall of Records and The Capital**
John H. Vargo, Director, **Historical Briefs, Inc.**

Developed under agreement with **Historical Briefs, Inc.,**
Box 629, Sixth St. & Madalyn Ave., Verplanck N.Y. 10596

Printed by **Monument Printers & Lithographers, Inc.**
Sixth St. & Madalyn Ave., Verplanck, N.Y. 10596

FOREWORD

Dear Reader:

The Capital is proud to present the following pages of our newspaper, from the stock market crash in 1929 to V-J Day in 1945.

They make interesting reading, not only from a news standpoint, but also from an advertising standpoint. Don't forget to check some of the prices in the advertisements.

When William Parks cranked out the first edition of the *Maryland Gazette* in 1727—the forerunner of *The Capital*—on his hand press, little did he realize what a part of history he and his paper would become. Surely he could not envision a printing company which today produces four newspapers and two magazines.

On May 12, 1884, the first edition of Annapolis' daily newspaper—*The Evening Capital*—came off the presses owned by the *Maryland Gazette.* Thus was born a relationship that continues to this day: publications that preserve a link to the past yet serve the modern needs and interests of thousands of readers.

The Evening Capital was founded by William Abbott, a visionary man who felt the state capital needed a daily newspaper, even though the city's population was only 7,200 and Anne Arundel County's population was only 32,000.

The present chairman of the board, Philip Merrill, purchased Capital-Gazette Newspapers in 1968. Not coincidentally, the newspaper's greatest growth has been since 1968 to the present day.

In the following pages, you will experience some of the biggest news from 1929 to 1945.

You will move from the days of the Great Depression under President Herbert Hoover to victory in World War II under President Franklin D. Roosevelt, who died just days before V-J Day.

We hope you will enjoy rereading these historical moments in the life of the United States and in the life of your community.

Edward D. Casey

Edward D. Casey
Executive Editor
Capital-Gazette Newspapers

Associated Press
Dispatches of late news are published in the Evening Capital.

Evening Capital

Rain; Cooler
Probably rain tonight and Wednesday. Continued cool. Northeast and east winds.

PUBLISHED EVERY EVENING EXCEPT SUNDAYS. ESTABLISHED IN 1884 COMPREHENSIVE LOCAL AND GENERAL NEWS

No. 144 ANNAPOLIS, MD., TUESDAY, OCTOBER 29, 1929. PRICE TWO CENTS

STOCKS RALLY AFTER DECLINE

Hunting Season To Be Brisk, Licenses Indicate

NEARLY 1,300 PERSONS GAIN RIGHT TO SHOOT

Deputy Clerks In Courthouse Have Been Kept Busy—Ducks Are Reported As Plentiful—Rabbit Season Begins On November 10.

DAY'S BAG LIMIT AND OTHER RULES LISTED

From the number of hunting licenses issued in the local office of the clerk of the Circuit Court, wild fowl and animals such as rabbits are in for a tough fall. With the hunting season about to open, except for squirrel, which have been hunted for some time, 1,062 county licenses have been issued, according to Deputy Clerk Lawrence Merrill. These licenses net the county a goodly sum, a fee of $1.25 being charged for each.

Many Other Licenses

In addition 181 State-wide licenses have been issued here at $5.25 each, and 17 non-residence licenses to hunters from out of the State who wish to gun in Maryland. They paid $15.50 each. The duck season opens on November 1 and lasts until January 31 inclusive. This being the main sport in this section and with fowl reported plentiful along the shores a big season appears ahead.

The rail and reed bird seasons are closed indefinitely by federal regulations. The main troop of huntsmen will turn out on November 10, when the rabbit hunting season will open. This in spite of the report that hares are diseased. In addition to rabbit, woodcock, pheasant, grouse, wild turkeys and quail may be killed until December 31.

Rules to Observe

State Game Warden E. Lee LeCompte announces a few rules by which gunners must abide:

Non-Export—Unlawful to export any game (water fowl excepted) out of Maryland. Licensed sportsmen may carry out two days' bag limit.

Prohibited—Shooting wild fowl from a boat; shooting at night time; shooting on Sunday.

Unlawful to shoot muskrat at any time or kill in any manner, except by trapping.

Unlawful to have in possession any light for the purpose of hunting muskrats at night time.

Unlawful to gig muskrats.

Unlawful to sell, offer for sale, purchase, or offer to purchase, Bob-White quail, Chinese ring-necked pheasants, ruffed grouse, or wild turkey.

Bag Limits Wild ducks, 25 in aggregate of all kinds; geese, 8 in aggregate of all kinds; brant, 8 in aggregate of all kinds; wilson snipe or jacksnipe, 20 in aggregate of all kinds; railbirds.

ANNUAL MEETING OF ANNAPOLIS RED CROSS TO BE HELD THURSDAY

The annual meeting of the Annapolis and Anne Arundel County Chapter of the American Red Cross will take place on Thursday of this week at 4 o'clock in the House of Delegates' chamber of the State House. At this meeting the officers will be elected for the coming year and other necessary business will be transacted.

Any member who has paid the membership fee is entitled to vote at the meeting, and all interested are welcome. There's hardly a family in this vicinity who has not felt the help of the Red Cross in some of its manifold activities, especially in home service, public health nursing and civilian relief.

The Annapolis Red Cross demands the hearty support of every citizen.

ELKS TO CONDUCT ROLL-CALL NIGHT

Tomorrow night the local Elks Lodge will conduct roll-call night. Upon this occasion the name of each of the 311 members will be called and those present will be recorded on the minutes. As a report will also be made to the Grand Lodge, Exalted Ruler W. N. French urges a big attendance.

Named Chairman of Service, Community Welfare Com. of Elks

Chairmanship of one of the most important of the committees of the Maryland Delaware and District of Columbia State Association of Elks has been conferred upon E. M. Jackson Jr. secretary of the local Elks Lodge.

President John B. Berger, of the State association, announces the appointment of Mr. Jackson to head the Service and Community Welfare Committee of the association. Jackson, though not a past officer of the local lodge, was assistant secretary of the State association two years ago.

Eastern Star to Give Card Party Tonight at Masonic Temple

The Annapolis Chapter, Order of the Eastern Star, will have a card party at the Masonic Temple tonight at 8 o'clock. Both Bridge and "500" will be played. There will be prizes, and refreshments will be served.

MARRIAGE LICENSES

PARKS - BATES — Alvin Samuel Parks, 21, Deale; Virginia Marie Bates, 18, Washington.

FRENCH-GROLLMAN — Sydney W. French, 25, West Annapolis; Paula B. Grollman, 25, this city.

BARRETT-CRONE — Newell Austin Barrett, 22; Clemmie Estelle Crone, 21, both of this city.

JOHNNY GANNON IS EXPECTED IN LINE-UP COMING SATURDAY

With two more hard games coming in a row, Pennsylvania on Franklin Field on the coming Saturday, and Georgetown at Annapolis in the offing, there is little in the way of rest periods for the Navy football squad. However, the bad battering that most of the players received in the more or less rough game with Princeton Saturday moved the coaches to give most of the regulars only light work as they took the field yesterday afternoon to prep for the Red and Blue. And, according to the coaches, that is going to be a mighty stiff argument.

At least five players were badly used up in the fight with the Tigers, and two of these, Joe Clifton, the stalwart fullback, and Leo Crane, substitute end, did not see action at all yesterday. Clifton is suffering from a strained shoulder and bad bruises, while Crane's ailing from an organic injury which compelled him to remain in the Princeton infirmary over Saturday night, returning to the Academy Sunday "Moon" Chapple, guard, has two discolored optics, and Crinkley tackle, is bothered by one, and Art Spring, star back, is not in the best of shape. "Blimp" Bowstrom is a bit shaken up. All are expected to be in good trim for the Pennsy game, however. These casuals, as well as others hurt in a minor degree, were given only light work yesterday, such as passing and general limbering up exercises. But the rest of the squad went through a more strenuous session. Scrimmaging with the scrubs the latter using Pennsylvania formations, will be the order of the heavier work beginning today.

Good news was wafted into the Navy camp when it was announced by Commander Jonas H. Ingram, athletic director, that Johnny Gannon, veteran halfback, who has seen very little action this season because of a troublesome charley horse, will be in shape for the go against the Quakers. Whether he will start or substitute at some stage has not been determined. Gannon is not only a clever offensive and defensive back, but is also adept at field-goal kicking via the drop-kick route.

Navy and Penn are old rivals in virtually all branches of athletics, and it has asserted itself in good measure by the demand for tickets for Saturday's game made at the offices of the Navy Athletic Association.

Navy folk have always liked Philadelphia as a football town. This feeling is based to a large extent upon the fact that it was back in the early nineties, after a lapse of several years, that West Point and Annapolis resumed football arguments on Franklin Field, and for six years straight running the games were staged there. And there is no doubt but that a big naval contingent will be on hand Saturday.

PENN CENTER SPENT FOUR YEARS ON NAVY FOOTBALL ELEVENS

When Navy faces Penn in Philadelphia this week-end Whitey Hughes, the Middies great center, will be playing against a former fellow midshipman Warren now pivot man for the Quaker eleven.

Warren, it is recalled was a member of the Naval Academy team for three seasons. He reached his first class year only to resign and enter Pennsylvania. In his second and third years at the Academy he was a member of the "B" squad but in his final year was one of the three center candidates, namely Osborne and Hoerner, in addition to himself.

At the time "Whitey" Hughes was in the Academy but was unheard of. If Warren is able to stand up against Hughes a battle royal can be expected from the pivot men as the Tar regular is nine tenths whale bone and one tenth steel in the opinion of the Navy contingent.

W. M. HOLLADAY ILL IN BALTIMORE HOSPITAL; SUFFERS HEART ATTACK

Suffering from heart trouble, complicated with other ailments, W. Meade Holladay, president of the State Capital Bank of the Eastern Shore Trust Company, is under observation at a Baltimore hospital, it became known today. His condition is regarded as serious, according to friends and his attending physician states that he must be kept absolutely quiet for at least ten days. No visitors are being admitted to see him.

Mr. Holladay's health has not been of the best for some time, as he has been a sufferer of rheumatism. The heart affliction only became pronounced a few days ago, however, and on Saturday his condition became such that it was decided to remove him to a Baltimore institution to undergo special treatment. Mr. Holladay has a large circle of friends in the city and county, who hope for his speedy recovery.

HOOVER TO ATTEND RITES FOR BURTON IN SENATE TOMORROW

(By The Associated Press)

WASHINGTON, D. C., Oct. 29.—The White House announced today President Hoover will attend the public funeral services for the late Senator Theodore E. Burton, of Ohio, at the Capitol tomorrow. The decision of the President to do this was in keeping with the high respect in which he held the Ohio senator.

During Mr. Burton's illness, the chief executive called at his house three or four times, seeing him for the last time just prior to Mr. Hoover's trip to the mid-west last week.

The Senate today adopted a resolution expressing its "profound sorrow" over the death of Senator Burton and adjourned after a three-minute session out of respect for the dead legislator.

Adjournment was taken until 2:15 tomorrow. Two resolutions were adopted during the brief session. One called for funeral services in the Senate Chamber tomorrow beginning at 2:30 o'clock. The other authorized the Vice-President to appoint a committee of 19 senators to supervise the services and to accompany the body to Cleveland, where burial will take place.

Both were offered by Senator Fess, of Ohio, the late senator's colleague.

President Hoover, members of the cabinet, the diplomatic corps, high officials of the Army and Navy, members of the House and other prominent government officers were invited to attend the services.

Senator Burton died last night.

NAVY FINDS $47,000 LOOT OF SERVICE MAN, WHO HAS SURRENDERED

(By The Associated Press)

WASHINGTON, D. C., Oct. 29.—Navy Department officials announced today they had found $47,000 buried in a chickenyard in southeast Washington, by Lieutenant Charles Musil, who disappeared from Charleston, S. C., several weeks ago with a $54,000 payroll.

Lieut. Musil walked aboard the receiving ship Seattle in New York last week and surrendered. He turned over $1,500 in cash at that time. Officials have had little hope of finding the remainder of the money.

Musil told naval officials he had buried the money in the chickenyard located behind a vacant house once occupied by him and his family.

Armed with picks and shovels the officers succeeded in digging up the cash.

ARMY AND NAVY MAY NOT CLASH ON GRID BEFORE 1931 SEASON

(By The Associated Press)

WASHINGTON, D. C., Oct. 29.—Major-General William R. Smith, superintendent of the West Point Military Academy, conferred today with Secretary Good preparatory to his discussion tomorrow with Rear-Admiral S. S. Robison, superintendent of the Naval Academy, looking toward a resumption of athletic relations between West Point and Annapolis.

After the conference General Smith expressed the opinion that if the Military and Naval Academies were able to find a basis upon which to resume relations, the Army football schedules for 1929 and 1930 would not permit a game in those years. He said the prospects for a game would be favorable for 1931. The schedules for other sports are not yet closed.

DOGS KILL CHICKENS OF LEWIS H. KELLY

Among the business matters transacted by the Board of County Commissioners at their regular weekly meeting today was a discussion of a bill submitted by Lewis H. Kelly of Severn, asking $18 for the loss of 18 chickens, killed by dogs.

The Commissioners have been paying weekly bills to farmers whose chickens have been killed by ravaging dogs. While they do not blame owners for submitting the bills as the law permits, the board neverthless feels that the law is an injustice on the county and steps to have the measure repealed will be taken at the next session of the State Legislature.

NEGRO MAN HELD AFTER RAID; HAD LIQUOR IN BAER COURT RESIDENCE

A considerable quantity of liquor was found in the home of Wesley Johnson, Baer Court negro, when members of Sheriff Michael F. Carter's force swooped down on the premises.

Led by Chief Deputy Sheriff Charles Lewis, the officers found more than seven gallons of liquor, they reported to Police Justice John W. Anderson, before whom a preliminary hearing was held.

Following a hearing of testimony, Justice Anderson held Johnson under $500 bail for action of the grand jury. Morris Legum furnished bond.

ONE FIRM GOES UNDER IN STOCK MARKET PLUNGE

(By The Associated Press)

NEW YORK, Oct. 29.—The first casualty of the current break in the Stock Market was the firm of John J. Bell and Company, which was suspended from the New York Curb Exchange for failure to meet its engagements.

The Bell firm was not engaged in a general commission business, although Mr. Bell, a floor trader, is reported to have handled accounts for several of his friends.

MISTRIAL IN CASE OF GOVERNOR OF FLORIDA

(By The Associated Press)

TAMPA, Fla., Oct. 29.—A mistrial was declared here today in the case of Sidney J. Catts, former governor of Florida, who had been tried on a charge of aiding and abetting counterfeiting when the jury reported in federal court that it had been unable to agree.

EPISCOPAL CHURCHES OF NATION TO HONOR LATE BISHOP MURRAY

Services in memory of Bishop John G. Murray, who died October 3, will be held in every Protestant Episcopal Church in the country next Sunday. In that manner the churches of which Bishop Murray was the national head, by virtue of his office as presiding bishop of the church, will honor him.

In each a brief address prepared by Bishop William Andrew Leonard, of Ohio, who is now the acting presiding bishop by virtue of the fact that he is the senior bishop, will be read.

Bishop E. T. Helfenstein the Bishop of Maryland, has asked that the services in the churches in his diocese take the form of communion services held at 8 a. m.

On November 13 the National Council of the church will meet in Washington, at which time it is expected a presiding bishop to fill out the unexpired term of Bishop Murray will be named. The convention will also name a Bishop of Honolulu.

The Maryland Diocesan Convention will meet in Baltimore the last Tuesday in January.

DR. JOHN R. STRATTON, NOTED BAPTIST CLERIC, IS CLAIMED BY DEATH

(By The Associated Press)

CLIFTON SPRINGS, N. Y., Oct. 29—The Rev. Dr. John Roach Stratton noted militant sentimentalist, died at a sanitarium here today. He was 54 years old.

Although seriously ill with a nervous breakdown for the last month, death came unexpectedly at 5:50 a. m. after a heart attack. His wife was at his bedside when he died.

He suffered a slight paralytic stroke last April and immediately afterward went to a sanitarium at Atlanta, Ga. for a rest. He returned to his home a month ago, but soon suffered from a nervous breakdown and entered the sanitarium here.

He was pastor of Calvary Baptist Church in New York and by his aggressive campaign against modernism and especially evolution, he gained nationwide prominence. During the last presidential campaign he took an active part against the candidacy of Alfred E. Smith, attacking him from his pulpit and campaigning against him in the South.

Dr. Stratton is survived by his wife and four sons.

FATHER OF LIEUTENANT PRICE DIES IN HARFORD CO.; RETIRED FARMER

David E. Price, for many years a prominent farmer and canner of Harford county, father of Lieut. Harry E. Price, of the Navy, (retired), of this city, died at his residence at Darlington last night following an illness of several months.

Mr. Price was 78 years old. He was a life long Democrat. He never held public office, though he had been a frequent visitor to Annapolis during sessions of the General Assembly, manifesting a deep interest in affairs of the State's lawmakers. He was the son of the late Judge and Mrs. John H. Price of Harford county, and is survived by his wife, Mrs. Mary Miller Price and three sons, those in addition to Lieut. Price being Dr. L. M. Price, Washington, D. C., and John H. Price of Darlington, Md. A sister Miss Isobel Price also survives.

TODAY'S SALES GO WELL ABOVE 12,500,000 MARK

Morgan & Company And Other Big Banking Institutions Reported Doing All They Can To Relieve Situation — Demand Loans Cut.

NEW DECLINE EXCEEDS SLUMP OF FIRST DAY

(By The Associated Press)

NEW YORK, Oct. 29. Stock prices turned sharply upward shortly before 1:30 p. m. this afternoon after a steady stream of liquidation in the early trading had carried prices of active issues down $10 to $70 a share. General Electric rallied from $214 to $244 and American Can from $115 to $119 a share.

Sales Near 13,000,000

Sales on the stock market today up to 1 p. m., amounted to 12,651,000 shares which compares with the high record for a full session of 12,894,000 shares recorded last Thursday.

The mad scramble to get out of stocks had reached record breaking proportions as prices plunged downward under what appeared to be world wide liquidation of securities before the entire market turned for the better sharply before 1:30 p. m.

Extreme declines in most of the active issues ranged from 10 to 70 points, with more than half the general list in new low ground for the year. Total sales crossed the 8,000,000 share mark before noon.

The decline, like those which have preceded it, was not associated with anything in the day's news, but represented the closing out of speculative accounts weakened in the succession of crashes during the past week.

Bankers endeavored to relieve the situation by reducing margin requirements on street loans from 40 to 25 per cent, and providing occasional support to insure an orderly market, but this was not sufficient to stem the gigantic wave of selling.

The called money renewal was reduced from 6 to 5 per cent and time money was freely offered at the lowest rates of the year.

Failure of a member of the New York Curb Exchange increased the widespread uneasiness prevailing throughout the financial district, but New York Stock Exchange houses appeared to be weathering the storm in good shape.

Bankers Giving Support

NEW YORK, Oct. 29 Wall Street's most stalwart banking institutions were lending strong support to members of the New York Stock Exchange in order to keep in hand the financial crisis arising from the enormous liquidation of stocks, it was learned after another conference of executives at the office of J. P. Morgan and Company today.

Prices at New Low in Chicago

CHICAGO, Ill., Oct. 29.—Another selling stampede swept over the Chicago Stock Exchange today and forced prices down into new low territory with sales indicating a new record day was in prospect.

IRISH LOSE ROCKNE FOR REST OF SEASON

(By The Associated Press)

SOUTH BEND, Ind., Oct. 29.—Knute Rockne, famous Notre Dame football coach, probably will be lost to his team for the rest of the 1929 season, because of a dangerous infection in his right knee.

New Beauty
FOR THE NEW FORD

THE NEW FORD COUPE

Flowing grace of line gives style and distinction to new, roomy Ford bodies. Now on display at dealers' showrooms

THE NEW FORD CARS, shown last Tuesday for the first time, have been enthusiastically received throughout the country. Everywhere it is realized that now, more than ever, the new Ford is a "value far above the price."

One of the distinguishing features of the new Ford bodies is the carefully planned harmony of every detail of design. From the new deep radiator to the tip of the curving rear fender there is an unbroken sweep of line— a flowing grace of contour heretofore thought possible only in an expensive automobile.

LOOKING at the new Ford you are impressed instantly by its smart style and compact, substantial sturdiness. For there is about it a certain character or personality which sets it apart and gives it a fresh and lasting beauty. You will take a real pride in this beauty just as you find a real thrill in the alert, capable performance of the car.

All of the new Ford bodies are finished in a variety of colors, with new striping and new streamline moulding. Interiors have more leg room. Closed cars have adjustable front seats. The smaller wheels, with larger tires, bring the car closer to the road, with a consequent gain in riding comfort and safety.

An additional feature of importance is the Rustless Steel used for the radiator shell, head lamps, hub caps, cowl finish strip and tail lamp.

NOTE THESE LOW PRICES

Roadster	. . .	$435
Phaeton .	. .	$440
Coupe .	. .	$500
Two-window Fordor Sedan	. .	$600
Three-window Fordor Sedan	.	$625
Cabriolet . .	$645	

Tudor Sedan .	$500
Sport Coupe .	$530
Town Sedan .	$670

(F. O. B. Detroit, plus freight and delivery. Bumpers and spare tire extra.)

Universal Credit Company Plan of time payments offers you another Ford economy.

This Rustless Steel will retain its bright, gleaming luster throughout the life of the car. It will not corrode, rust or tarnish in any kind of weather. Its brilliance is permanent. There is no plate to wear off, crack or scale, for it is the same bright metal all the way through.

The use of this Rustless Steel on the new Ford is a reflection of the enduring quality that has been built into every part of the car.

AT today's low prices the new Ford is unquestionably an outstanding value. Check it over feature by feature and you will see that it brings you everything you want or need in a modern automobile:—beauty of line and color . . . safety , . . comfort . . . speed . . . power . . . quick acceleration . . . ease of control . . . economy of operation . . . low up-keep cost . . . typical Ford reliability and long life.

ST. JOHN'S HAS FINE 1930 FOOTBALL SCHEDULE

VIEWS and CHATTER on SPORTS

as seen by
E. M. Jackson, Jr.
Sports Editor

To know "Art" Shires is to love him. Few remember that statement made shortly after "The Great One" floored his boss, Lena Blackburne, pilot of the White Sox. It might be worth meditation.

If Shires can get away with a fortune for talking big, I personally would dub him a sap if he permitted the opportunity to slip by. Fans fall for chest. They may not like "such a guy" as they see Shires but at the same time they flow through the cash turnstiles to view and boo him.

At the worse, Shires appears a smart upright youngster, apparently too wise to fall by the wayside when he is on the good road to a fortune. One thing is certain "The Great One" is a mighty classy ball player and he is no wash-out as a fighter either.

Of course Art is in pretty bad right now, but I believe he can take it on the chin and come back for the decision. I agree with my friend Joe Malcomson (Captain Medical Corps U. S. N.) that Art is not guilty of the charges lodged against him by a jealous publicity seeker. Here's one who is pulling for the "bad boy."

Johnny Wilson's, crack out-of-bounds play under the opposition's goal, in which the center is featured, was given a rude jolt yesterday by Referee Jerry Voith.

Twice when Captain Colestock attempted the circling play which has bewildered all three teams the Tars have faced, Voith tooted his whistle and called blocking on forwards. Keyes and Reinhardt. The play is truly a great one and out of six referees the number would likely be divided as to whether the play is permissable. Personally I think it is, and at the same time it is undeniable that the play is the best of its sort that I've ever seen.

Navy showed signs of its Christmas leave yesterday, especially in the first half when Wake Forest had all kinds of shots. However, in the second half Navy according to the quint coach had a perfect defense which kept the Southerners shooting way out and without a point for 10 minutes.

This little midget, Keyes, showed up better than any of the other forwards yesterday. Wilson may find him valuable in the coming big battles with Duke and Penn, Saturday and Wednesday. Two such games in a row is a task and Wilson will be satisfied to divide, he reveals. In Lowrance and Campbell, Navy has a pair of good long distance shots and Blimp Bowstrom while not as finished as the others "is not so bad."

St. John's College's football schedule announced today is a pretty tough assignment, yet if the Johnnie players have the determination of their coaches, Tody Riggs and Bill Stromeyer, some of the big time foes are due for a flop.

Chalk up one for the movies. Kid Chocolate, a battling fool, credits the movies for much of his success. "I picked up much of my ring generalship from watching movies of the Gans-Nelson, Jeffries-Johnson and Leonard-Tendler battles," the kid credits.

A missionary with a punch, Earl Dunlap, will be quarterback of the Georgia Tech football team.

Old Dave Bancroft, although a slipping ball player is still good for an occasional story. His latest one is that prior to breaking into the big leagues in 1915, he had never seen a major league baseball team in action. As Dave made good right at the start his opinion of the big show must not have been too high, as is often the unfortunate case.

Publicity ideas are becoming more prominent than the sport itself. First the St. John's and Western Maryland football teams occupy the same bench, now the Yale University Athletic Association announces with expressed satisfaction that it has concluded separate and identical agreements with Princeton and Harvard for baseball games with these universities to be played with the coaches off the bench, the strategy and choice of plays throughout every game to be determined solely by the contesting players.

George H. Nettleton, chairman of the board of control of the Yale Athletic Association, said an effort was made by Yale more than four years ago to induce Princeton and Harvard to play all athletic contests without the presence and aid of the coaches during the actual competition.

Pirates Gamble On Gussie Suhr

If Gussie Suhr, Pittsburgh's recruit first baseman, has half as much confidence in himself as the Pirates have, he will easily make the big league grade.

By JAY VESSELS
Sports Editor
(Associated Press Feature Service)

NEW YORK, Jan. 8.—There's one sun-kissed rookie from California who won't have to worry about his big league job this year, even though he is a first-year man.

His name is Gussie Suhr and his home port is San Francisco.

Yes, sir, if Gussie gets insomnia it shouldn't be because of worry over his job.

For all he has to do is to get out there when April breezes begin to blow and play his usual game of baseball to be assured of the regular first base position with the Pirates.

You see Suhr's batting and fielding performance with the San Francisco Seals was so convincing to the Pirate scouts that they recommended his purchase at any reasonable sum. Then when the opening came for the Pirates to dispose of Earl Sheely, the regular first baseman, the scouts unhesitatingly assured the Pittsburgh management that Gussie could be depended upon.

This won't be the first time that a busher has picked up a regular assignment, but it will be one of the few times that a recruit shouldered great responsibility.

The statistics on the 1929 coast league season support the flowery reports forwarded by Pirate field men.

Playing his second full year with the Seals, Gussie batted .381 and fielded .989. He was up among the very leaders in batting and showed more than a mere wallop with the willow in checking in with 51 homers, six triples and 62 doubles. He made 299 hits, scored 169 runs and drove in 177 runs.

Haskell Indian Football Team To Play Strong Schedule Next Season

LAWRENCE, Kan., Jan. 8.—The football players from the Haskell Indian institution, the largest Indian school in the country, will renew gridiron relations with the University of Kansas next year and make their first trip in five years to the Pacific Coast, the 1930 schedule announced recently by Athletic Director F. W. McDonald revealed.

Travel Over 10,000 Miles

Traveling slightly more than 10,000 miles to the East, North, South and West, the Indians will ably uphold the reputation of being along with Notre Dame as the greatest travelers in the American collegiate gridiron. Six games will be played at night under the floodlights of stadiums scattered over the country.

The occasion of the game with Kansas University the night of October 11, in the Haskell stadium, will be used to celebrate a gigantic homecoming pow-pow of Haskell alumni and Indian braves of all tribes.

May Go West Twice

The Haskell trip to the Pacific Coast to meet Gonzaga University, at Spokane, Wash., will be the first game the Indians have played in that section since defeating Gonzaga in 1925. Probabilities are that the Indians will play another game November 15 with some western team between Spokane and Lawrnce, but McDonald has tentatively left the date open.

The Indians will invade the East in search of scalps against Butler College at Indianapolis and St. Xavier at Cincinnati. In the North Haskell will meet Creighton University, of Omaha, and in the South the redskins clash with Wichita University, Tulsa University and Oklahoma A. & M. College, at Stillwater, Okla.

Six Games At Night

The first six games of the schedule will be played at night, three on the Haskell gridiron and three away from home.

(Lone Star) Dietz, the Indians' head football coach, who led a young and green team through a tough season this year, with eight victories and two hair-breath defeats, regards the 1930 season as real test for his athletes.

BOWLING

Down the Alley with the Pin Spillers

ANNAPOLIS LEAGUE

Club Standings

	W.	L.	Pct.
Spa Gun Club	32	4	.888
Annapolis Buick Co.	25	8	.756
W. B. & A.	25	8	.756
Moose	21	12	.636
Rescue Hose Co.	21	15	.583
Annapolis Dairy	18	15	.545
Mayo	19	17	.528
Camp Parole	16	17	.485
Elks	17	19	.472
A. C. B. Power Co.	15	18	.455
Johnson Lumber	14	19	.424
H. B. Myers	14	22	.388
Capital-Gazette	12	24	.333
West End	11	25	.305
Coffee Pot Dome	10	26	.278
Edgewater	9	24	.273

This Week's Rollers

Thursday—Johnson Lumber Co. vs. Annapolis Buick; Annapolis Dairy vs. A. C. Bay Power Co.

Friday — Moose vs. Edgewater; Camp Parole vs. W. B. and A.

COMMERCIAL LEAGUE

Club Standings

	W.	L.	Pct.
Tri-City Sign Co.	25	5	[illegible]
Thomas & Co.	20	10	.667
A. and P.	17	10	.629
Severn Motor Co.	15	9	.625
Capital Fruit Co.	17	13	.567
Annapolis Buick Co.	15	12	.555
Colonial	15	12	.555
Tilghman & Co.	13	11	.542
Eastway Stores	16	14	.534
Coca Cola	16	14	.534
K. and S.	11	16	.407
Brownie's Garage	7	20	.258
Krause Chevrolet Co.	5	22	.185
Mutual Life Ins. Co.	3	24	.111

This Week's Rollers

Thursday—Chevrolet Sales vs. Severn Motor Co.; K. and S. Service vs. Mutual Life Insurance Co.

Friday—Brownie's Garage vs. A. and P. Stores.

MIDDY CAGERS CRUSH QUINTET FROM SOUTH

John N. Wilson's Outfit Off Color Themselves On The Defense — Nevertheless, Have High Power Attack Which Subdued Wake Forest.

AL DALTON, OF WAKE FOREST, SCORING THREAT

A fast passing five from Wake Forest College of North Carolina, failed to locate the rim despite their other good work and Navy yesterday rolled up win number three as the Southerners were tripped for the same number in a row. The score was 39 to 20, yet play was fairly interesting, the Southerners actually having more scoring opportunities than did the Middies.

At the start neither side could score, players on both sides rushing up and down the floor shooting at random. Coach John N. Wilson began his second team as is customary, but the visitors had so many scoring opportunities in the first eight minutes although they made but a lone foul, that the Middie mentor sent his first string in with the score of 5 to 1. At half time the count was 18 to 13, Albert Dalton, center making 8 points to keep his mates in the running. Dalton was high scorer of the game.

Navy kept its first combination in to start the second half, but again Navy was unable to stop the visitors thrusts which, however, aside for the flips of Dalton, high scorer of the day, were ineffective. Wake Forest did not score in the entire first 10 minutes of the second half. The underhand shooting of the entire team was somewhat of a novelty but lacked precision.

Most of Navy's scoring came from out of bound plays before which all opponents this year have been completely at bay. It was opportunity day for the Wake Forest quint but Navy made more of its scoring chances.

The summary:

WAKE FOREST	G	F	Pts.
Brogden, f	0	1-1	1
Allen, f	0	0-0	0
Hutchins, f	2	0-0	4
Webb, c	0	0-0	0
Dalton, c, f	5	3-3	13
Mills, g	0	0-2	0
Edwards, g	0	2-3	2
Quillan, g	0	0-0	0
Totals	7	6-9	20

NAVAL ACADEMY	G	F	Pts.
Keyes, f	3	2-2	8
Freshour, f	0	0-0	0
Reinhardt f	0	0-0	0
Rodgers, f	1	0-1	2
Allen, f	3	1-4	7
Bauer, c	1	0-0	2
Colestock, c	3	0-0	6
Holtzworth, c	1	0-0	2
Lucas, g	0	0-0	0
Bowstrom, g	0	0-0	0
Campbell, g	3	0-2	6
Lowrance, g	3	0-1	6
Totals	18	3-10	39

SCORE BY PERIODS

Wake Forest	13	7	20
Naval Academy	18	21	39

Referee—Voith, Loyola.
Umpire—Bowman, Ursinus.

BASKETBALL RESULTS

Army 50	Delaware 21
Navy 39	Wake Forest 20
Dickinson 58	Ursinus 32
Pittsburgh 24	Carnegie Tech 18
Dartmouth 52	Norwich 11
Duke 65	Virginia 32
Davidson 29	Wofford 15
Union 35	Albany Law 24
North Carolina State 44	High Point 24
Trinity 24	Clark 15
Colgate 34	Cornell 25
Penn 32	Haverford 13

The experts seem to be running into arithmetical difficulties in working out some system whereby the farmers can add several billions to their incomes without taking it away from anybody else. [illegible]

BABE WANTS $85,000 SALARY

Associated Press Photo

Jacob Ruppert (right), president of the New York Yankees, and Ed Barrow, secretary, barked an emphatic "no" when Babe Ruth, the slugger, demanded a three-year contract at $85,000 annually, a raise of $15,000.

Producing Margarine Delicate Job Process Calls for Constant Care

MAKING MARGARINE

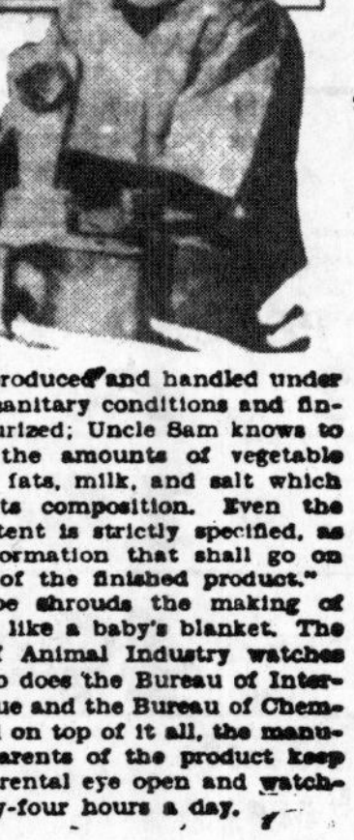

FULL MEASURE

WASHINGTON, D. C.—The most cared-for food in the world is margarine, the baby of the foodstuff family.

Not only do rigid laws govern every step taken in its manufacture and sale, but inspector-nursemaids, both those of the government and of the manufacturers, guard it from contamination as not one human infant in a million is guarded. From the farm and cocoanut groves to the housewife's door, the loving care of scores of persons is given to every pound.

"Government attention to the purity and wholesomeness of margarine begins in the great packing plants with an inspection of the beef and hogs, from which the wholesome fats contained in the product are obtained, and continues through the various phases of processing and handling until it has reached the stage where the label is applied to the container and the margarine is ready for shipment," it is disclosed in a bulletin of the Institute of Margarine Manufacturers, just made public here.

"The government sees to it that the milk used in every pound of margarine is produced and handled under the most sanitary conditions and finally pasteurized; Uncle Sam knows to a pound the amounts of vegetable oils, meat fats, milk, and salt which go into its composition. Even the water content is strictly specified, as is the information that shall go on the label of the finished product."

Red tape shrouds the making of margarine like a baby's blanket. The Bureau of Animal Industry watches over it. So does the Bureau of Internal Revenue and the Bureau of Chemistry. And on top of it all, the manufacturer-parents of the product keep a keen parental eye open and watchful twenty-four hours a day.

FIVE DIFFICULT EARLY GAMES WITH BIG FOES

Hard Group Attempted Because Sturdy Team Is Anticipated For Coming Season — Most Contests Are To Be Played Near Here.

MEET MARYLAND ON OCTOBER 18

The 1930 football schedule for St. John's College, announced today by Athletic Director M. Talbot Riggs, also head coach of the team, reveals that the Johnnies will play pretty much of a home card, in that games in Washington and Baltimore are considered on such a basis owing to their proximity.

The schedule will open on September 27th with Franklin and Marshal. Whether the game will be played here or in Lancaster has not been decided. On October 4 the Johnnies will meet Virginia Military Institute at Lexington, and on succeeding Saturdays, Western Maryland will be met in the Baltimore stadium and University of Maryland at College Park.

After the test with the Old Liners, which marks a renewal of athletic relations after a break of several years, the Johnnies will journey to Lexington again, this time to meet Washington and Lee. The campus of the Generals is adjacent to that of V. M. I. and the Johnnies in the meeting with each Lexington team has the other school's student body rooting for them and these games are high spots of the schedule.

With the hard games out of the way, the November 1st game has been given to American University. Normally Gallaudet of Washington had open one of the filler dates. The following week to the Hopkins game on November 15 is held open to allow injured men to recover. The Hopkins game, most important of the schedule, despite the Johnnies' 46-to-0 and 33-to-0 victories of the last two seasons, is nevertheless, most important of the schedule.

Saturday, November 22nd is also open, but on Thanksgiving Day, November 27th, the locals are slated to play Hampden Sydney College of Virginia. While definite arrangements have not been made tentative arrangements list the contest for Central High School stadium in Washington.

The Johnnies expect to have a fairly good team in 1930, according to Coach Riggs. University of Virginia was originally scheduled to meet the Johnnies on October 1, but the game was dropped by mutual consent when University of Pennsylvania offered the Cavaliers a big guarantee for that date. The University of Maryland scheduled for the opening game, through Athletic Director Curly Byrd, who formerly coached Riggs as a student at Maryland, then took the vacated date, and F. and M. was scheduled for the opener.

With Paul Casassa, star quarterback of the 1928 team expected back after a year's loss through injuries sustained in the Gallaudet game here last fall, Bob MacCartree, great broken field runner, Captain Willie Armacost, fullback, and Willis Lynch, halfback, completing the backfield, with Dulin and other capable substitutes, optimism for this hard schedule is held.

The schedule:

September 27—Franklin and Marshall.

October 4—V. M. I. at Lexington.

October 11—Western Maryland, Baltimore.

October 18—University of Maryland, College Park.

October 28—Washington and Lee, Lexington.

November 1—American University, here.

November 8—Definitely open.

November 15—Johns Hopkins, Baltimore.

November 22—Definitely open.

November 27—Hampden Sydney.

Want Basketball Games At 135 Lbs.

Annapolis Capital,
Annapolis, Md.

Dear Sports Editor:

The Original Mohawks of Baltimore desire to arrange basketball games with quints playing in the 135-pound class. Address Irving Gordon, 122 Jackson Place, Baltimore, Md.

Yours in sport,
IRVING GORDON.

January 8, 1930.

WORLD'S LARGEST SUSPENSION BRIDGE OPENED

New York and New Jersey joined in ceremonies opening the new $60,000,000 George Washington bridge across the Hudson, world's longest suspension structure. The giant bridge connecting New York City and New Jersey will have a capacity of 30,000,000 automobiles annually through its eight traffic lanes. Above is an air view looking up the Hudson and below a view of the giant tower from the New York side.

"AS HUSBANDS GO," THIRD PRODUCTION OF GUILD SUBSCRIPTION SERIES IN BALTIMORE

"As Husbands Go," a comedy of Paris and Dubuque which registered a six months run at the John Golden Theatre, New York, last season will be presented at Ford's Theatre, Baltimore, for one week beginning Monday, November 9, as the third production of the Theatre Guild's fourth subscription season. It will be the first production that John Golden has sent to Baltimore for eight years and with its original cast intact, Its coming its notable aside from its connection with the Guild subscription series. Among the players are Catharine Doucet, Jay Fassett, Gloria Holden, Geoffrey Wardwell, Marjorie Lytell and Roman Bohnen.

Rachel Crothers, for twenty-five years a contributor of brilliantly written comedies to the Broadway stage, has reached the pinnacle of her career with "As Husbands Go." It is her twenty-third play. Her twenty-fourth, entitled "Caught Wet," is now in preparation for Broadway.

The story of "As Husbands Go" deals with the adventures of two Dubuque, (Iowa) women who seek romance and adventure in Paris. One is a heart-hungry widow and the other the wife of a banker who is "fed up" with the humdrum of domestic existence in Iowa. Into the picture come a pair of boulevardiers who dance well and make love in true Prince Charming fashion. After a whirlwind double courtship the two couples depart for Dubuque. Two marriages are in prospect.

But the level-headed, money-grubbing husband whom Lucile Lingard left behind when she went to Paris senses the situation. Before Lucile can muster courage to ask his consent to a divorce the husband and the "boy friend" have gotten together over a bottle of Scotch and the cavalier departs for London. But the other visitor stays on to woo the widow.

Usual matinees are announced for Wednesday and Saturday during the engagement of "As Husbands Go."

SOUTH SEA CASTAWAYS RETURN TO CIVILIZATION

This camp on the Isle of Cocos was home to three Americans for six months after their yawl was shipwrecked off the lonely south sea island. The Crusoes built their hut from debris found on the beach. During their stay on the island their diet consisted principally of coconuts, fish and wild hog. They were rescued by an American gunboat.

The castaways looked well fed when they arrived at Balboa, Canal Zone, aboard the United States gunboat, Sacramento. Left to right: Leo Michelfelder, chief quartermaster of the Sacramento, Gordon Brewner of Springfield, Ill., Paul Stachwick of Huron, S. D., and Elmer Palliser of San Diego, Cal. Quartermaster Michelfelder was first to sight the men from the gunboat.

Associated Press Photo
Helen Kerr, blond junior at the University of Wichita, Wichita, Kas., has been chosen as the school's prettiest co-ed.

DANGEROUS TO LET COLDS LINGER ON

Mothers Urged To Safeguard Children From Diseases They Catch From Each Other.

Don't neglect the common cold or the digestive upset," is the advice of Dr. R. H. Riley, Director of the State Department of Health, to mothers of young children. "Mothers can help to safeguard their children from the diseases they catch from each other," he said.

"First—By building up the children's power of resistance to disease, by attention to their general health; by seeing that they have balanced meals; that they are dressed according to the weather; that they have some play out of doors on sunshiny days, and that they have plenty of sleep.

"Second—By taking the children to your family doctor at regular intervals for inspection and advice.

"Third—By taking your children who have not been protected against diphtheria to your family doctor to be immunized against that disease.

"Fourth—By observing danger signals; keeping the child who is not well, in bed and by having the family doctor come to see him; or her.

"Fifth—By keeping the well children away from the sick ones.

"Many of the diseases to which babies and young children are subject start with what seems to be 'only a cold' or 'just a digestive upset' and little attention is paid to these warning symptoms until measles, mumps, whooping cough, scarlet fever or one of the other 'catching' diseases has developed.

"Instead of ignoring these symptoms it is safer to regard every slight upset as a signal of possible danger and to act accordingly. Don't let them run on. Watch the child very carefully who develops the sniffles, who has a sore throat, who is droopy or otherwise under par; keep him or her in bed send for your doctor and follow his advice."

Feature Hits On Air Tonight

Conflict of Chinese rights and Japanese interests in Manchuria is endangering the peace of the Orient, James G. McDonald, chairman of the Foreign Policy Association, will say in his series "The World Today" over an NBC-WEAF network tonight from 6:30 to 6:45 o'clock, E. S. T.

"The Attitude of Japan," says McDonald, "dictated by military authorities, apparently against the will of the civil government, has united world opinion in support of China's contention that the immediate issues involved should be adjudicated by the League of Nations."

An international rebroadcast from London, presenting the Aga Khan, wealthy Indian ruler, proceedings at the rally of the girl reserves of Y. W. C. A.; and appearance of Belle Baker as guest artist with Rudy Vallee, will be among highlights on the schedule of the National Broadcasting Company tonight.

Andy Sannella and his orchestra will be heard tonight from station WEAF over a nationwide NBC network.

With Wayne King and his orchestra having played from Chicago on Tuesday evening, and Gus Arnheim playing from Los Angeles on Saturday evening, it has fallen to Andy Sannella to uphold the dance rhythms of the east on this inaugural week's series of broadcasts. Those who have followed Andy's career, not only as an orchestra leader, but also as one of radio's most versatile and popular soloists on every instrument from the steel guitar to the clarinet and saxophone, consider him one of the outstanding personalities in the music world.

NEW CITY TELEPHONE DIRECTORY ISSUED

Annapolis' latest telephone directory, just off the press, is now being delivered to the users of the 3,477 telephones in the city and its suburbs. Directories are also being delivered to telephone subscribers in North Beach, Prince Frederick and West River.

In making the delivery of this new book, every effort is being made to have the old directories returned, so that they can be destroyed. This is necessary because of the large number of changes made in numbers and listings of new subscribers to telephone service since the last directory was delivered, according to L. H. Cheek, manager of the company. Unless the old directories are recovered, users will obviously get wrong numbers in making calls.

Denison university at Granville, O., has celebrated its 100th anniversary.

Ohio is thirteenth among the states in agricultural productions.

Ninety per cent of Ecuador's population is estimated to be dependent in some measure on agriculture for their living.

BEWARE THE COUGH OR COLD THAT HANGS ON

Persistent coughs and colds lead to serious trouble. You can stop them now with Creomulsion, an emulsified creosote that is pleasant to take. Creomulsion is a new medical discovery with two-fold action; it soothes and heals the inflamed membranes and inhibits germ growth.

Of all known drugs, creosote is recognized by high medical authorities as one of the greatest healing agencies for persistent coughs and colds and other forms of throat troubles. Creomulsion contains, in addition to creosote, other healing elements which soothe and heal the infected membranes and stop the irritation and inflammation, while the creosote goes on to the stomach, is absorbed into the blood, attacks the seat of the trouble and checks the growth of the germs.

Creomulsion is guaranteed satisfactory in the treatment of persistent coughs and colds, bronchial asthma, bronchitis and other forms of respiratory diseases, and is excellent for building up the system after colds or flu. Money refunded if any cough or cold, no matter of how long standing, is not relieved after taking according to directions. Ask your druggist. (adv.)

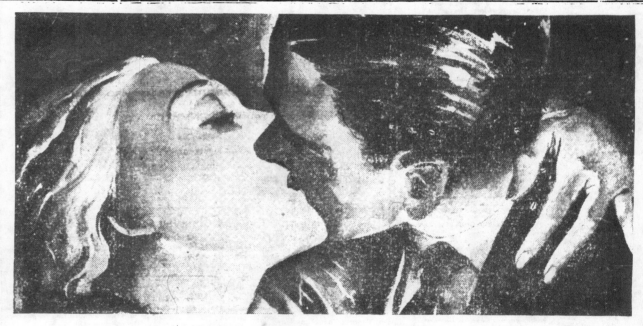

WAS THIS LOVE A SIN?

IS MONEY everything? Is it all that counts? This woman thought so. Poverty had thwarted her every ambition. Now, one hope alone was left—her daughter must have all the comforts of the world—her daughter must marry wealth.

But in spite of all her sacrifices to keep her daughter at a wealthy finishing school among "rich" folks—her daughter fell in love with a poor man.

Was fate to cheat this mother again—or should she break up this mad infatuation? She was still passionately alluring. Did she dare pit her enticing charms against her own daughter to lure away the love of a man—to satisfy her desire for a rich son-in-law?

This strange triangle—a mother, her daughter, and her daughter's sweetheart—makes one of the most dramatic true stories in the December issue of True Story Magazine. Read "Was This Love A Sin?" You'll find in it a thrill and a warning you'll never forget!

Throbbing dramas from life!

You'll find in this same issue of True Story many more pulsating true stories. The strange predicament of a frantic friend who was faced with the problem of meddling in the family life of another or allowing a physician's plot to mutilate a lovely girl. The stirring revelations of what happened to a mother who dared to dictate whom her son should love. The astonishing problem that confronted a girl when fate placed her seducer at her mercy. The answer a minister hurled at his cold, hide-bound congregation when the happiness of the woman he adored was at stake. These are a few of the many absorbing stories in December True Story.

And every word of these stories is *true*—every word has lived! Here, in these exciting pages, life is stripped—tortured souls lay bare their temptations, their mis-steps and hard-won victories—that other troubled hearts may take counsel and find new courage.

Get True Story to-day. Read it—and thrill!

Listen to the True Story Hour! Tune in on any of these stations every Monday night at 10 o'clock New York Time

New York City......	WEAF	Pittsburgh, Pa......	WCAE
Boston, Mass......	WEEI	Cincinnati, O......	WSAI
Providence, R. I...	WJAR	Cleveland, O......	WTAM
Worcester, Mass...	WTAG	Detroit, Mich......	WWJ
Portland, Me......	WCSH	Chicago, Ill......	WENR
Philadelphia, Pa...	WLIT	St. Louis, Mo......	KSD
Washington, D. C...	WRC	Davenport, Ia......	WOC
Schenectady, N. Y.	WGY	Des Moines, Ia......	WHO
Buffalo, N. Y......	WBEN	Baltimore, Md......	WFBR

DECEMBER ISSUE AT ALL NEWS-STANDS TO-DAY!

TRUE STORY

25c

the magazine for people who aren't afraid of life

Serving a trading population of over twenty-five thousand.

Evening Capital

Rain
Rain tonight and Thursday, probably changing to snow in extreme west portion tomorrow. Colder Thursday night.

PUBLISHED EVERY EVENING EXCEPT SUNDAYS — ANNAPOLIS, MD., WEDNESDAY, NOVEMBER 9, 1932. — ESTABLISHED IN 1884 — PRICE TWO CENTS.

ROOSEVELT'S SWEEP MOUNTS

County Joins Nation In Record Democratic Majority

Roosevelt and Garner Roll Up Plurality of 4,347 in Anne Arundel

Sweep of Democratic Standardbearers Set Record For Annapolis and County—Gambrill Given Huge Majority of 6,100 Votes to Lead Ticket—Tydings Follows With 5,110 Plurality—Constitutional Amendment Carries By 246.

Annapolis and Anne Arundel county contributed their share toward the Democratic triumph at the polls yesterday, the final returns today showing that the Democratic candidates were swept to victory by record-breaking county majorities that far exceeded the most optimistic hopes of the party leaders.

The vote throughout the county was unusually heavy, about [illegible]500 ballots being cast, as compared to slightly more than 13,000 in 1928. In many districts more than ninety per cent of the registered vote was cast. This was particularly true of the voters affiliated as Democrats.

County Presidential Vote

With the exception of the "A-J" voting place at Arnold, in the Third District and the Fourth Ward of Annapolis, the Negro section of the city, the Republican Presidential ticket was swamped by the huge Democratic vote. All of the remaining thirty-three polling places in the county were carried by the Democratic standard bearers.

The total vote for President and Vice President in the county was:

Roosevelt and Garner	9,181
Hoover and Curtis	4,834
Foster and Ford	10
Reynolds and Aiken	17
Thomas and Maurer	223

Roosevelt Given 4,347 Majority

Roosevelt and Garner, the Democratic standard bearers received a majority of 4,347 votes, setting a record in the county for a Persidential election.

In many cases the vote cast for the [illegible] ran ahead of the party candidates. This trend existed throughout the county and in Annapolis.

Tydings Wins By 5,110

United States Senator Millard E. Tydings, Democratic candidate for re-election defeated Wallace Williams, his Republican opponent by a majority of 5,110 votes in the county. The total [illegible] for the Senatorial candidates was:

Tydings	8,969
Williams	3,859
[illegible]	171
Twigg	34
Bradley	23

Gambrill Leads Ticket

Representative Stephen W. Gambrill, Democratic candidate for re-election from the Fifth Congressional district, led the Democratic ticket in the county, piling up the record breaking majority of 6,100 votes over A. Kingsley Love, Republican. The total county vote was Gambrill, 9,633; Love, 3,533. The voters of the county approved the amendment to the State Constitution proposed to take from the Legislature the authority to extend the term of Judges beyond the 70 year age limit. The total county vote, with [illegible] places unreported, was [illegible] for the amendment and 1,102

(Continued on Page 2)

THIRD CHURCH OF CHRIST, SCIENTIST,
Baltimore, Md.,
[illegible] a Free Lecture on
Christian Science
[illegible] Davis, C. S., of Chicago, [illegible] of the Board of Lectureship of The Mother Church, The First Church of Christ, Scientist, in Boston.
AT FORD'S THEATRE
W. Fayette Street
FRIDAY, NOVEMBER 11, 1932.
At 12:10 Noon.
[illegible] cordially invited to attend.
s-23

Harvest Home Supper
[illegible] Eastport Baptist Church
THURSDAY, NOV. 10—5:30 P. M.
Church Building
MENU
[illegible] and Roast Pork
Mashed Potatoes — Sweet Potatoes
[illegible] Turnips — Peas — Carrots
Tomatoes
Apple and Pumpkin Pies
Coffee
TICKETS 50 CENTS
Ice Cream and Cake on Sale
n-9

Roosevelt Replies To Pres. Hoover

New York, Nov. 9.—President-elect Franklin D. Roosevelt today telegraphed the following message to President Hoover at Palo Alto, California:

"I appreciate your generous telegram for the immediate as well as for the more distant future. I join in your gracious expression of a common purpose in helpful effort for our common country."

SENATE RESULTS

Associated Press returns compiled to 8:05 a. m. Eastern standard time, on contests for the 34 seats in the United States Senate showed:

Democrats elected, 24; hold overs 31; total, 55.

Republicans elected, 4; hold overs, 30; total, 34.

Farmer - Labors elected, none; hold overs, 1; total, 1.

Still doubtful, 6.

Necessary for a majority, 49.

HOUSE RESULTS

Associated Press returns compiled at 11 a. m., Eastern standard time, today on contests for the 435 seats in the new House of Representatives showed:

Democrats elected, 219; present Congress, 218.

Republicans elected, 68; present Congress, 209.

Farmer-Labor elected none; present Congress, 1.

Still doubtful, 148. Necessary for a majority 218.

Dress Rehearsal For Washington Pageant To Be Held Tonight

A dress rehearsal for the George Washington pageant will be held tonight, at 8 o'clock, at the High School.

Card of Thanks

Congregation Kenneseth Israel Of Annapolis, Md.

The officers of this congregation wish to thank all the Hebrews of Annapolis for their splendid donations towards the new cemetery—which made it possible to obtain the beautiful site at Three Mile Oak; also for their support and good work in helping to make the dedication of the new cemetery a real success.

By the Officers
Congregation Kenneseth Israel.
(Signed)
LOUIS SHANKER, President.

FOR RENT
Star Confectionery
CALVERT STREET
Apply at Star Theatre
n-9

Given Nation's Most Flattering Vote

FRANKLIN D. ROOSEVELT

FAMILIES IN COUNTY NEED FOOD AT ONCE

Central Relief Committee Investigator Reports That Many Unemployed Men And Their Wives And Children Are On Starvation Rations In County.

COMMUNITY CHEST FUND NOW TOTALS BUT $6,021.23

The Central Relief Committee is investigating some of the cases of unemployment in and around Brooklyn Park and Linthicum Heights. Dr. John H. Janney, chairman of the committee, announced today. A number of families have been visited and the investigator reports that every family seen—the children and adults—are on starvation rations. Requests for aid are coming into the various relief agencies daily and great difficulty is being experienced in meeting these needs.

Still Far From Quota

Although contributions to the Community Chest fund on the whole have been satisfactory, the quota is still far from reached and the public again is urged to do everything in its power to make individual donations as large as possible.

Six thousand and twenty-one dollars and twenty-three cents is the grand total of Community Chest contributions to date, Dr. Janney announced to-

(Continued on Page 4)

Chicken Salad Supper and Bazaar
Auspices
Ladies' Bible Class, College Avenue Baptist Church
THURSDAY, NOV. 10—5:30 P. M.
CHURCH BASEMENT
SUPPER 50 CENTS
Ice Cream, Cake and Candy on Sale
n-9

ELECTION FLASHES

HOOVER MAY RETURN TO WASHINGTON TONIGHT; MAY REST ABOARD BATTLESHIP

Palo Alto, Calif., Nov. 9.—Herbert Hoover, the first president of the United States defeated for re-election since 1912, has promised Governor Franklin D. Roosevelt, the newly elected Democratic president, "to dedicate myself to every possible helpful effort."

The chief executive, who conceded his defeat last night was uncertain today as to his plans for the immediate future.

He was considering seriously boarding his special train tonight for a record-breaking trip back to the White House.

Several of his aides, one of whom described the President as "the tiredest man in America," have urged Mr. Hoover to take a rest. A battleship trip through the Panama Canal has been suggested, but the President's plans remain uncertain.

Straggling returns from the heavy vote in favor in of Roosevelt were still coming into the Hoover home this morning when the President arose.

WISCONSIN GIVES ROOSEVELT 300,000 LEAD

Milwaukee, Wis., Nov. 9.—An unprecedented Democratic landslide hit Republican Wisconsin yesterday, piled up a majority that looks like 300,000 or better for Governor Franklin D. Roosevelt and assured the election of a Democratic governor and senator for the first time in many years.

The LaFollette progressive Republican vote, defeated in the September primary, contributed substantially to the Democratic victory.

Walter J. Kohler and John B. Chapple, conservative Republican candidates respectively for Governor and United States Senate, appeared to have been defeated.

In five of the ten Wisconsin congressional districts, it appeared that 4 Democrats and possibly 5 would be elected. In the remaining districts, four Progressive Republicans and one conservative Republican were in the lead.

With 2,072 of the state's 2,[illegible] precincts reported, the vote was: Hoover, 248,259; Roosevelt, 494,599.

ROOSEVELT SLEEPS IN AFTER NIGHT WATCH

New York, Nov. 9. — Franklin D Roosevelt, president-elect of the United States, took his ease this morning after the long hard fight for the country's highest office.

From his town house came word that he was still in bed at 9 o'clock and there were indications he would not appear in public until afternoon.

About that time he was expected to visit his national headquarters and there it was believed, he would make public his reply to the congratulatory message sent him last night by President Hoover.

PENNSYLVANIA REMAINS SAFE IN G. O. P. RANKS

Philadelphia, Nov. 9.—Pennsylvania, stronghold of Republicans since the Civil War, held steadfastly to the Hoover cause today in the face of the heaviest Democratic vote in its history.

Returns from three-quarters of the state's 8,199 districts gave Hoover 1,277,454 votes, a lead of 165,634 over Governor Franklin D. Roosevelt, whose 1,111,820 vote surpassed even the record-breaking total polled by Alfred E. Smith in his losing battle in 1928.

United States Senator James J. Davis, running for re-election, held a safe 1,139,476 to 968,726 lead over Lawrence H. Rupp, his Democratic opponent, on the face of returns from 6,336 districts.

ROOSEVELT'S MARGIN MOUNTS IN W. VA.

Charleston, W. Va., Nov. 9.—Governor Roosevelt's lead over President Hoover continued to mount steadily in normally Republican West Virginia today.

Returns from 911 of the state's 2,348 precincts gave him a majority of 21,828. The vote was: Roosevelt, [illegible]783; Hoover, 134,965.

Meanwhile H. G. Kump, [illegible] nominee for Governor of West Virginia, piled up a majority of 1[illegible] over his

(Continued on Page [illegible])

Drys and G. O. P. Beaten As Wets and Democrats Control Senate and House

Republican Casualty List In Congress Terrific As Smoot, Watson, Moses, Bingham and Jones "Old Guard" All Are Defeated—Democrats Gain 4 To 1 In House Members—Democratic Candidates for Governor Win In 30 of 35 States.

(By the Associated Press)

Marching resolutely in the parade which takes Roosevelt to the White House and Garner to the vice-presidency, Democrats continued to mow down their opponents in numbers whch became startling as the count of yesterday's election wore on today.

With the Democratic triumph for congressional control went mounting gains for anti-prohibitionists, and referenda on liquor legislation in eleven states showed the wet side ahead.

Out of Congress, out of governors' chairs and minor offices Republicans tumbled from coast to coast.

President Hoover, apparently more decisively defeated than was Alfred E. Smith in 1928, clung to a bare six states, indicating the possibility of an all-time record electoral vote of 472 for Roosevelt.

The latter's popular vote in 72,000 of the country's 119,000 election districts was 14,600,000 out of 25,000,000.

DEMOCRATS WIN GOVERNORSHIPS, TOO

Of the thirty-five governorships involved in yesterday's election, Republicans had won but two definitely and appeared likely to win no more than another four. Of states not electing governors this year, only four have Republcan chief executives.

The Republican casualty list in Congress was terrific. Smoot, Watson, Moses, Bingham, Jones—names to conjure with in the Senate—all were defeated. These men were the heart of the party's "old guard."

The House toll was but a repetition.

Hoover Loses Home State

The presidential vote was such that in Iowa, Herbert Hoover's birth state and traditionally a Republican stronghold, the Democrats were leading by more than 100,000.

Of the six states in which Hoover was ahead he had but 150,000 lead in Pennsylvania and Connecticut and New Hampshire gave him but 6,500 and 2,500 margins of victory.

The sweep appeared to have carried Roosevelt into office with 472 electoral votes, a record piled upon the unprecedented total of 444 given Hoover four years ago.

Incomplete returns compiled by the Associated Press at 8 a. m., Eastern Standard time, still inconclusive, if borne out by later returns will give the folowing electoral vote:

Hoover, 59; Roosevelt, 472.
Necessary to elect 266.

Beer Amendment

LITTLE ROCK, Ark., Nov. 9.—Senator Robinson, of Arkansas, the Democratic Senate leader, said today that he saw "no reason why Congress, during the short session should not consider the submission of a referendum relating to the modification or repeal of the Eighteenth Amendment as well as

(Continued on Page 2)

ROOSEVELT LEAD IN STATE NOW 128,391 VOTES

Democratic Standard Bearer Increases Lead, With 23 Polling Places Unreported — Tydings Defeats Williams For Senate By 151,848.

SIX DEMOCRATS WIN SEATS IN CONGRESS

(By The Associated Press)

BALTIMORE, Md., Nov. 9.—Late returns from yesterday's national election vote in Maryland today only served to emphasize the sweeping victory for the Democrats.

The State by a big majority gave its eight electoral votes to Roosevelt, the first time since 1916 a Democratic candidate has captured the State's presidential vote: gave Senator Millard E. Tydings an even bigger majority over his opponent, Wallace Williams, and elected six Democratic congressmen.

Holds 128,391 Lead

Roosevelt's lead over Hoover was shown in the following returns from 1348 out of 1871 polling places in the State: Roosevelt 311,704; Hoover 183,313.

While the total vote cast for United States Senator was not as large as that cast for president, Tydings' plurality was greater than that enjoyed by Governor Roosevelt. The count in the same polling places gave:

Tydings 287,596; Williams 135,738.

Democrats to Congress

Th constitution amendment prohibiting the Legislature from extending the term of judges who retire from the bench at the age of 70 years was carried although the total vote was not large.

The congressional races found the Democrats with safe majorities for

(Continued on Page 2)

FOR SALE
5½ Acres at Wellsville; large road front, $1000.
5 Acres on Annapolis Boulevard, $1250.
CHAS. F. LEE
Phone 608

Fire Insurance
D. J. Thompson
ANNAPOLIS, MD.
TELEPHONE 873-J

IF YOU ARE SEEKING A NEW WIFE, COME AND SEE
"New Wives For Old"
a One-Act Comedy
Given by
EPWORTH LEAGUE OF EDWARD'S CHAPEL
Friday, Nov. 11, 8 p. m.
EDWARD'S CHAPEL HALL
Adults 25c — Children 15c
n-10

KNIGHTS OF COLUMBUS DANCE
ST. MARY'S HALL
FRIDAY, NOVEMBER 11, 1932
9 TILL 1 — $1.00 PER COUPLE
McNEW'S ORCHESTRA

[illegible] Churchill Murray
Insurance
Exclusively
Phone 130

'BOY HAVEN' CAMP IN GOOD CONDITION

Season's Opening June 26—Two Skiffs To Be Built For Use Of Campers

Prof. Reginald C. Lamb, business manager of "Boy Haven," the camp of the Annapolis Young Men's Christian Association, returned last night from a week-end spent in Calvert county and at the camp. He reports that the camp is in excellent condition; that the depredations of weather or transient occupants are small; in fact, negligible, and that there will be but little labor required to put the camp in shape for the season's opening a week from today.

When in Prince Frederick, Professor Lamb made arrangements for the building of two fourteen-foot cypress skiffs so that the campers will have a patrol boat during swimming periods, a skiff for rowing exercise, for crabbing and for fishing for hardheads and rock, if the bait, the tide, the stars, and the fish themselves are agreeable. A start will be made this week toward clearing away the pines for a baseball diamond and athletic field. This will require about a hundred pounds of dynamite, two Calvert county oxen and a few handlers of oxen and explosives, but as the trees are not fixed very firmly, no trouble is expected in tearing them loose from virgin territory.

Two Periods

Some of the good people of Prince Frederick who helped secure the campsite last year have asked if the boys of the county seat of Calvert county are eligible to go to the camp, and the answer has been in the affirmative, so that it is expected that a few boys from Southern Maryland will be campers this season. This will not cut down the number expected to attend from Annapolis and vicinity, because two periods are to be run—the first from June 26 to July 10 and the second from July 10 to July 24. Applications are being received daily for the camp and are being acted on by the business manager and the director, Prof. J. B. Eppes. Any of last year's campers who know of boys desirous of attending camp should get in touch with either of the abovementioned officers, who can be reached by conversation, a letter with 3-cent postage via the Mercurys of Uncle Sam, or via the mysterious working of the C. and P. Telephone Company.

Southern High Graduates 22; Dr. Paul E. Titsworth, Speaker

The graduation exercises of Southern High School, Lothian, Md., were held in the auditorium last week-end. Twenty-two, the largest number in the history of the school, received their diplomas. The graduates were:

Laura Lyons
Jane Welch
Sue Smith
Iva Fern Proctor
Theresa Leitch
Henrietta Hopkins
Annie O. Sansbury
Eleanor Cunningham
Lillian Armiger
Martha Peake
Edna Norfolk

Audrey Grimes
Eudora Perry
Mildred Cox
Kenneth Gostin
Charles Hardesty
Hampton Dorsey
Grover Trott
Ronald Taylor
Ashby Shepherd
Allen Mason
Drury Plummer

Dr. Titsworth Speaker

The invocation was given by Rev. W. B. Dent, of the St. James Episcopal Church at Tracy's Landing, while the benediction was pronounced by Rev. A. M. Newall, of the Methodist Church at Mt. Zion.

The principal speaker of the afternoon was Dr. Paul E. Titsworth, of Washington College, Chestertown, Md. He delivered a most interesting address, taking for his subject "Coordination." Dr. Titsworth is soon to give up his present position to become president of Alfred University in New York.

The valedictory address was delivered by Sue Smith. The salutatory speeches were given by Laura Lyons and Henrietta Hopkins, who tied for the honor. Frank A. Munroe, president of the Anne Arundel County School Board, presented the diplomas.

Sue Smith Honored

The presentation of a scholarship certificate by Mr. Purvis, dean of Strayers' Business College in Washington, was an honor to both the school and pupil who received it. This award was made on the basis of a competitive examination and representatives from seven high schools took the test. The recipient was Sue Smith. The Maryland Society, Sons of the American Revolution, citizenship medal was awarded to Annie Owings Sansbury.

The speakers of the afternoon were introduced by Anthony Bisnoff, principal of the school.

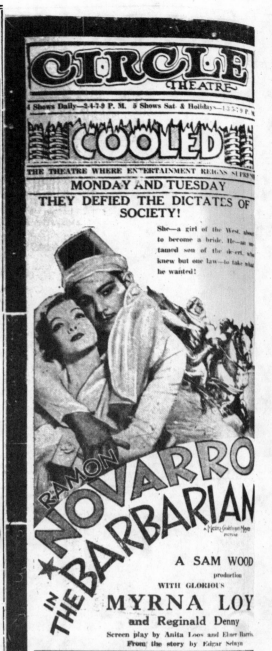

THE DRAMATIC STORY OF 1934 IN PICTURES

RECOVERY ADMINISTRATION

STRIKES

REVAMPED NRA

DEMOCRATIC OFF-YEAR VICTORY

THE RECOVERY ADMINISTRATION, with President Roosevelt at the helm, still smiling and carefree, weathered a year of turmoil in which the San Francisco and other widespread strikes, the midwestern drought, and the off-year Democratic landslide played an important part in the news. The exit of General Hugh Johnson from the scene in the revamping of the NRA and the rising star of Donald Richberg also captured the headlines. (Associated Press Photos)

INTERNATIONAL

KING PETER

KING ALBERT'S DEATH

NAZI PURGE

ALEXANDER ASSASSINATION

DOLLFUSS' ASSASSINATION

A CHAIN OF TRAGIC events cast threatening war clouds over Europe in a year during which foreign events figured more in the news month after month than at any time since the World War. The saddening death of King Albert of Belgium and the ascension of his son, Leopold to the vacated throne; Hitler's "blood purge"; assassination of Premier Dollfus of Austria and King Alexander of Yugoslavia studded the year with dramatic events. (Associated Press Photos)

SOCIAL

ASTOR-FRENCH WEDDING

GEORGE-MARINA WEDDING

TWO SOCIAL EVENTS, both weddings, found their way into the big news of 1934. The wedding of the Duke of Kent to Princess Marina of Greece assumed the proportions of a world-heralded romance. The marriage of John Jacob Astor to Ellen Tuck French was the highlight of the Newport season. (Associated Press Photos)

KIDNAPING

HAUPTMANN ARREST

PROBABLY NO OTHER single story claimed the place in the public eye that was given to the arrest of Bruno Richard Hauptmann, itinerant German carpenter, on charges of the murder of Charles Lindbergh, Jr., a tragedy that inspired the sympathies of the entire world. The finding of the Lindbergh ransom money and the chain of evidence disclosed leading up to Hauptmann's trial captured an unceasing hold upon the headlines. (Associated Press Photos)

ROBLES

STOLL

THE KIDNAPING of Mrs. Berry Stoll of Louisville, Ky., and the manhunt instigated by federal authorities for her abductor, Thomas Robinson, Jr., covered the front pages of the nation's newspapers, as did the kidnaping of June Robles. (Associated Press Photos)

PERSONALITY

DIONNE QUINTUPLETS

OF UNIVERSAL APPEAL was the birth of five girl babies to an obscure couple, the Dionnes, in the Ontario north woods. The quintuplets became the most widely discussed babies in the world and the mild-mannered, gray haired country doctor who kept them alive, Dr. Allan Roy Dafoe, shared the spotlight with them. (Associated Press Photos)

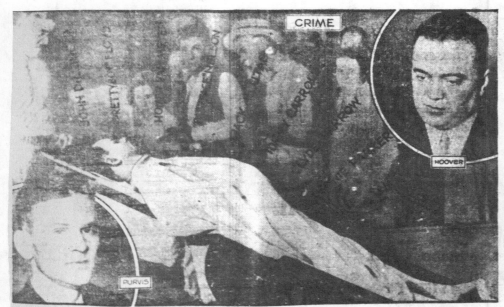

CRIME

HOOVER

PURVIS

THE KILLING OF PUBLIC ENEMIES occupied the spotlight throughout 1934 as the federal law enforcement agents, with J. Edgar Hoover (right), head of the bureau of investigation of the department of justice, and Melvin Purvis (left), his Chicago chief, playing the leading roles, staged the greatest drive on crime in modern American history. The year saw John Dillinger, Bad Man No. 1, stretched out on a morgue slab (as shown above) with "Pretty Boy" Floyd, George "Baby Face" Nelson and a host of other notorious outlaws brought down by government guns. (Associated Press Photos)

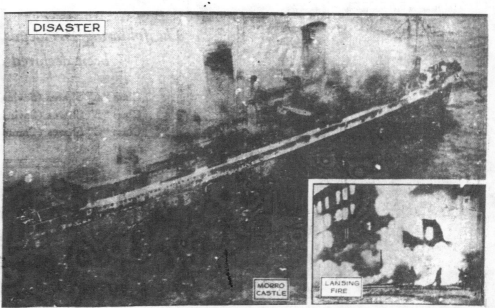

DISASTER

MORRO CASTLE

LANSING FIRE

FIRE AND A TREACHEROUS SEA combined forces to enact principal roles in one of the greatest disasters in history, the burning of the S.S. Morro Castle off the coast of New Jersey, with a death toll of approximately 124 persons. The above photo of the burning vessel serves to recall the stark tragedy, the flames of which have not entirely died down as investigators seek to determine the responsibility for the blaze. Fire struck late in the year at Lansing, Mich., snuffing out some 30 lives as a hotel filled with people was burned to the ground. (Associated Press Photos)

$8,415 COLLECTED IN TRAFFIC FINES

Annapolis Had Usual Quota Of Arrests During Week Ended October 2.

The State Automobile Commissioner, in his weekly report of fines collected throughout Maryland for violations of the traffic laws, listed $8,415 for the period from September 25 to October 2. Of this amount, $1,096 represented the Baltimore City collections, and $7,319 those from the counties of the State.

Annapolis reported its usual quota of arrests, as follows:

Enoch Abram, $10, no license; Howard Hall, $1, failing to pay rent for hired car; Thomas Hawkins, 2 years H. C., unauthorized use; Robert Henson, $10, no license; George Hopkins, $1, reckless driving; Lorenzo A. Laza, $10, improper markers; Wm. M. Norwood, $5, reckless driving; Charles Spencer, 9 mos. H. C., operating under influence of liquor, 10 days H. C., no license; Louis Stellar, $25, unauthorized use, $10, no license; John W. Trott, $25, unauthorized use; Rudolph W. Whittington, $10, reckless driving.

Glen Burnie Fines

At Glen Burnie, the following were fined:

Martin J. Andre, Jr., $2, exceeding 35 miles; Edward Jenkins, $8, reckless driving; Fred L. Kess, $5, failing to keep to right; Vincent R. Machis, $5, passing on top of hill; Henry B. Poehler, $15, speed too great; John F. Schmelder, $1, parking without lights; Millard Schreck, $5, failing to keep to right; Virgil V. Sharp, $100, operating under influence of liquor.

Jessup had a large number of arrests, including:

Maurice D. Bowman, $10, overweight; Paul P. Braungart, $10, expired chauffeur license, $5 no muffler; John Cimino, $10, no license to operate; Wise N. Clark, $15, exceeding 45 miles; O. C. Clayton, $5, overweight; Raymond Cohen, $20, overweight; Wm. S. Cook $10, markers issued to another; Robert T. Cortell, $1, no registration; Harry Feinberg, $5, overweight; Mamie Glassman, $1, reckless driving; Joe Goodman, $10, markers issued to another; Frank T. Gueras, $5, reckless driving; E. B. Henry, $5 overweight; markers issued to another; Richard Hayes, Henry, $10, no license, $10, markers issued to another; Richard Johnson, $10, no license; W. S. Jones, Jr., $10, markers issued to another; $1, no registration; Thomas, Murphy, $15, overweight; Fred Murray, $10, markers issued to another; $1, no registration; William H. Poole, $10, exceeding 45 miles; Frank R. Roberts, $5, failing to keep to right; John A. Smith, $5, no lights; Paul B. Story, $20, exceeding 45 miles; Joe Piepolopourno, $5, failing to keep to right; H. A. Yelder, $25, failing to stop after collision; A. A. York, $10, markers issued to another, $1, no registration.

Other County Fines

One fine was reported at Millersville, Joseph L. Galloway being assessed $10 for alleged reckless driving.

At Pasadena, two fines were reported. William Bailey being as-

---

sessed $5 for failing to stop at a boulevard intersection, and Carl Wagner $1 for exceeding 25 miles.

OFFICERS ELECTED BY COLLEGE WOMEN

(Continued from Page One)

zabeth Nitchie, of the English department of Goucher College; Mrs. Felice Ferraro, widow of Dr. Felice Ferraro, the brilliant Italian scholar and noted international correspondent; and Miss Isabella T. McNair, President of Kinnaird College, Lahore, India.

The musical programs, club dinners, and the reception to the high school girls of the city and county were pleasantly recalled.

Talk By Miss Magruder

Loath to forget happy vacations, various members contributed amusing and interesting accounts of their Summer activities. All parts of the United States were traversed.

In a general, humorous vein Miss Louise Magruder, registrar and genealogist for the Society of the Ark and the Dove, addressed the group on "Substantiating Family Tradition." Helpful hints were given for beginning and carrying through a search of one's family tree. Miss Magruder aptly illustrated the fact that such research would lead to many interesting slants on Maryland and Colonial history and that it might throw some astonishing light on some of the traditions that are generally accepted as facts.

Annual Meeting of Navy Relief Society Monday Afternoon

The annual meeting of the Naval Academy Auxiliary of the Navy Relief Society will be held at the home of the president, Mrs. D. F. Sellers, Superintendent's Quarters, at 4:30 o'clock on Monday afternoon, October 7.

Reports will be made of the activities of the past year and plans made for the future. Officers will be elected and committees appointed for the coming year.

The meeting is open to all who are interested in the work of the Society.

MRS. G. B. LAWTON SPEAKER AT MEET OF GERMANTOWN P.T.A.

The Germantown Parent-Teacher Association held its first session of the year yesterday afternoon, at 2:30 o'clock, at the school. A special feature of the program was a talk by Mrs. Glen B. Lawton, President of the Eastport P.T.A., who gave a most interesting report of the State Summer Conference of P.T.A. held at the University of Maryland, College Park. This conference was educational, having for its purpose the increased efficiency of Parent-Teacher Associations, and a better understanding of the aims of the organization. Mrs. H. Ross Coppage, Maryland State President, and Mrs. J. K. Pettingill, one of the national vice-presidents, shared the executive duties of this conference.

Mrs. Lawton announced the State convention of P.T.A., to be held at the Emerson Hotel, Baltimore, November 19, 20 and 21, and stated that the national president, Mrs. B. F. Langworthy, will be present on that occasion.

The new principal, Miss Eleanor Brice, was introduced, and spoke to the members of the P.T.A., of "Our mutual need and desire to cooperate for the good of the school."

It was decided to continue the dental clinic this year, as it is thought to be of great service to the community.

Tag Week will be planned soon, with the object of getting funds for books for the school library.

Appreciation of the work of the Safety Patrol boys was expressed, and a desire that this system continue in effect at Germantown.

Much interest is being shown in the annual membership drive, which is now on.

The first grade won the prize for attendance.

SEVERN RIVER ASS'N IN HIGHWAY PLEA TO FEDERAL RELIEF HEAD

The executive committee of the Severn River Association is meeting in Baltimore today, having arranged a conference with Arthur Hungerford, National Emergency Relief official, concerning the Annapolis-Baltimore Boulevard.

The federal office has disapproved of the desired improvements to the highway declaring that they cannot see the need.

The executive committee of the association is composed of Dr. Amos F. Hutchins, John W. Sherwood, H. G. Riggs, James D. Garrett, Edward N. Rich, James A. Walton, Phillip S. Morgan, B. D. Frese, and Charles M. Gosnell.

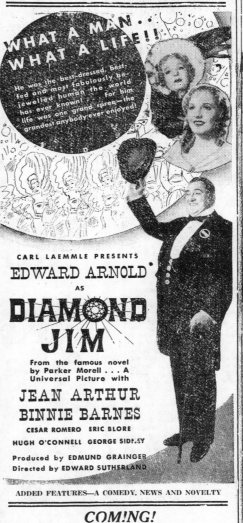

THREE OFFICERS OF NETHERLANDS NAVY VISIT THE ACADEMY

Three officers of the Netherlands Navy today inspected the departments, equipment, plant and aviation department of the Naval Academy.

Capt. H. Ferwerda, Lieut.-Comdr. J. N. Kramer and Lieut. B. Vroon, an aviator, were received by the guard of the day, a platoon of Marines, when they arrived at the institution. They were accompanied by Lieut. Comdr. John A. Gade, United States Naval Reserve, formerly naval attache in Brussels, Belgium.

Upon their arrival the visitors were greeted by Capt. H. K. Hewitt, head of the Department of Mathematics and Lieut. Comdr. C. M. McFall, commanding the aviation squadron at the Academy.

The officers, wearing the blue uniform of the Netherlands Navy were taken through the departments and points of interest on the reservation, paying particular attention the aviation training of midshipmen.

After luncheon as guests of Admiral Sellers they returned to Washington.

ANNAPOLIS
Evening Capital

Serving a Trading population of more than 25,000 in Annapolis and Anne Arundel County. Delivered in four of every five city homes.

Weather Forecast
Occasional rain, with mild temperature tonight and Tuesday, followed by colder Tuesday afternoon or night.

VOL. CI—No. 155. | ESTABLISHED IN 1884—PUBLISHED EVERY EVENING EXCEPT SUNDAYS | ANNAPOLIS, MONDAY, NOVEMBER 11, 1935. | THIS PUBLICATION IS PRINTED ON PAPER MADE BY LABOR IN THE UNITED STATES OF AMERICA | PRICE TWO CENTS.

SEEK WOMAN IN SLAYING OF BRIDE-ELECT

Mt. Rainier Police Assert Female Held Victim While She Was Beaten To Death—Bloody Fingerprints Found On Paper.

LARGE INSURANCE DECLARED INVOLVED

(By The Associated Press)

MT. RAINIER, Md., Nov. 11.—A prediction that "more than likely" the next arrest in the investigation of the murder of Corinna Loring, 27-year-old bride-elect, would be a woman, was made today by Police Chief Eugene Plummer.

He did not give any further details. As he spoke, two men were held—Auburen Hampton, 30, former suitor of the young woman, and Richard Tear, 29, who was to have married her last Wednesday, two days after she disappeared from her home here.

Plummer did say, however, that investigators had learned Miss Loring had been heavily insured. He would not give the amount nor the number of policies, and declined to name the beneficiary.

Diamond Ring Missing

He revealed that an expensive diamond engagement ring, given Miss Loring by Tear, was missing. Whether the girl was wearing it at the time of her death is not known.

Plummer said hair had been taken from Tear and Hampton for comparison with hair found on the girl's coat.

Asked For Novels

Tear was visited in his cell at the Hyattsville jail by two brothers, Theodore and H. E. Tear. They would not discuss their visit afterward except to say their brother had asked for some detective magazines. His request was granted.

The Loring family made arrangements for funeral services Wednesday if the body is released by authorities.

Mrs. Lillian Botkin, one of Washington's seven women taxicab drivers, made a futile effort to visit Hampton.

"Why doesn't someone help him?" she cried.

"He jilted her; she didn't jilt him. He is a very sensible boy."

Student At Night School

Mrs. Botkin said she came to

(Continued on Page Six)

TURKEY DINNER
Given by
LADIES' AID OF EASTPORT BAPTIST CHURCH
THURSDAY, NOVEMBER 14TH
At The Church Hall
MENU
Roast Turkey — Mashed Potatoes
Dressing — Cranberries
Candied Sweet Potatoes — Slaw
Rolls — Coffee
TICKETS 50 CENTS
Homemade Cake and Candy on Sale

BINGO PARTY
Given by
ANNAPOLIS REBEKAH LODGE No. 73, I. O. O. F.
TUESDAY, NOV. 12, 8 P. M.
Maryland Hotel
ADMISSION 35 CENTS
Prizes and Refreshments
n-11

LOTS
For Sale, at Cedar Park, and on the Baltimore-Annapolis boulevard.
Julian Brewer & Son
9 School Street — Telephone 815

City Championship Tournament
Open to All Bridge Players
TUESDAY, NOV. 12, 8 P. M.
At
CARVEL HALL
Entrance Fee 50 Cents
n-11

MARY HELEN'S Riding Academy
¼ Mile From 3-Mile Oak
On General Highway
Horses and Ponies for hire by hour
Horses 75c hour — Ponies 50c hour
Bridle path with jumps (off Highway)
Telephone—1835F6
n-11

FOR SALE
¼ acre near water, west of Eastport, with 5 room bungalow. Price $700.
Attractive wooded lot at Wardour with 90 ft. of waterfront. Price $1,500.
Chas. F. Lee
LEE BLDG. — PHONE 603

Bride-To-Be Slain

On the eve of her marriage, Corinna Loring, 27-year-old Mt. Ranier, Md., woman, was beaten to death near Washington, D. C., where she was a secretary. Her fiance, Richard Tear, 29-year-old hospital attendant, was taken into custody "for investigation," but was unable to shed any light on the murder. (Associated Press Photos)

Find Part Of Lt. Marple's Plane In Bay

The wing tip of an airplane found at Plum Point, today was indentified as a part of the plane flown by Lieut. Mathais M. Marple, Navy pilot, who has been missing from Dahlgren, Va., since October 30.

Lieut. Marple took off from Dover, Del., at 9:30 A. M. on October 30. At 10:10 A. M. during a fog oystermen and the crew of a tug heard a crash in the Chesapeake Bay off Hacketts Point. The tug recovered half the bottom wing of a Navy land plane and two wheels.

The tip of the right upper wing was found at Plum Point yesterday, with the starboard running light intact. It bore the number 9049. This was the number of Marple's plane as sent to the Naval academy authorities here when he first became overdue at Dahlgren.

A thorough search of the area off Hacketts Point which is still being made, has failed to locate the wreckage of the plane or the pilot's body.

—NOTICE—
Emergency Hospital

The annual meeting of the Hospital Association will take place on Monday, November 11th, 1935, at 8 P. M. in the Assembly Room of the Nurses' Home.

All persons interested in the welfare of this very necessary and useful institution, and who wish to have a vote in its management, are invited to become members by the payment of not less than $2.00 annually, and the enrollment of their name by the treasurer, Mrs. Edgar Basil, care of the Emergency Hospital, at once, as all donations to the hospital to be included in this year's reports, must be in before the meeting.

Every grown person in Annapolis who is interested in the Emergency Hospital is invited to attend this meeting, whether a subscriber or not. But only those who have subscribed to the amount of $2.00, or more, are invited to vote for managers.
(Signed)
BY ORDER OF THE BOARD.

RUMMAGE SALE
Given by
ST. MARGARETS GUILD
Tuesday, Nov. 12th
AT 39 WEST STREET
Sale begins at 9 A. M.
n-11

FOR SALE
6 Room Semi-bungalow, Garage, Lot 100 ft. x 150 ft. in West Annapolis, 2 minutes walk to P. G. School $3,750
Triple corner lot in Eastport, Size 128 ft. x 165 ft. .... $ 800
9 Room, 2 Story Dwelling with Hot Water Heat, Green Street .. $4,750
Bernard J. Wiegard
Hotel Maryland Bldg. — Phone 9

Would Stock City Reservoir With Game Fish

Committee Of County Fish And Game Association To Confer With Water Company And State Board Of Health Regarding Proposal.

MAYOR PHIPPS TO HEAD NEW GROUP

A committee of the Fish and Game Conservation Association of Anne Arundel County is communicating with the State Department of Health and the Annapolis Water Company, to determine if it is advisable and possible to stock the local water works reservoir with fish.

William J. Vanous, one of the directors of the association brought the question on the floor of the association meeting in which he pointed out that the Baltimore reservoir and practically all other reservoirs have been stocked with fish. He said he was advised that fish bring about certain purification of the water, rather than make it distateful.

Reservoir Two Miles Long

"The Annapolis reservoir proper is nearly two miles long and would make a wonderful place for bass and other game fish. We have practically no fresh water fishing here now, and the Water Company would allow angling at certain times under proper supervision. Loch Raven

(Continued on Page Four)

MIDDIES STAGE REAL COMEBACK BEFORE 75,208

Navy Shakes Jinx Which Has Been Trailing Them And Toss Heavy Penn Team For 13-to-0 Loss At Franklin Field On Saturday.

GAME MOST EXCITING AND BEST OF YEAR

By E. M. Jackson, Jr.

Returning to winning form a brilliantly determined and hard tackling Naval Academy football team, held the upper edge all the way in humbling Pennsylvania's ponderous eleven on Franklin Field, Philadelphia, on Saturday before 75,208 spectators.

The Tars won 13 to 0 by capitalizing on some of the breaks—such as have gone against them in the past three contests.

Hamilton Springs Surprise

Head Coach Tom Hamilton pulled a surprise at the outset on Saturday as he sent his third team, including two men newly up from the "B" squad, into action against Penn's huge and experienced machine. These third stringers battled the Quakers on fairly even terms for 12 minutes after which the first team came into action with the ball in Penn's possession, on first down way back on their own 20 yard line. After that Hamilton used the second stringers to re-inforce the first combination. The third team had done its job.

The first score came in the second quarter when a long punt by Midshipman John Schmidt, which rolled to the 10 yard line, was given to Navy, as Fike, Navy end, who

(Continued on Page 5)

5 ARE ARRESTED OVER WEEK-END

Five arrests featured the police activities in the city during the week-end. None of them were of a serious nature.

Those arrested were: Frank Green, colored, assault, ten days in jail; Asbury Colbert, colored, disorderly conduct, $6.75; John Jones, colored, assault and battery, $7.50; Bud Brady, white, drunk, $3.75; Samuel Day, colored, drunk and disorderly, five days in jail.

Armistice Day, An Occasion For Peace

As the conclusion of the World war is celebrated today, America, through President Roosevelt, proclaims it an occasion for an expression of "our determination to remain at peace with all nations." Numerous observances are scheduled for the day, including parades, as depicted below, and memorial addresses, the highlight of which will be a talk by President Roosevelt at Arlington National cemetery. War veterans' graves in Arlington are shown above. (Associated Press Photos)

COMMEMORATIVE ARMISTICE DAY SERVICE TONIGHT

Colonel Woodcock To Deliver Main Address At Joint Celebration Of Veterans' Groups.

At 8 o'clock tonight, a joint commemorative Armistice Day service, followed by a social session, will be held in the Ladies' Auxiliary of the V. F. W. Headquarters, Hotel Maryland, under the auspices of Annapolis Post, No. 304, Veterans of Foreign Wars and its Ladies' Auxiliary. The occasion is open to all veterans and their friends.

The first half of the program will be devoted to memorial observances, honoring the memory of the boys who sacrificed their all, during the World War, that their country might maintain its honor, and its rightful place among the nations of the world.

Program Planned

The principal address will be given by Col. Amos W. W. Woodcock, President of St. John's College, and the religious and ritualistic work, under the direction of Commander W. N. Thomas, Chaplain of the U. S. Naval Academy; the Rev. James J. Coale, pastor of the First Presbyterian Church, Duke of Gloucester street; Prof. Paul A. Lajoye, of the D. A. V.; Commander David S. Jenkins, of the American Legion; Com-

(Continued on Page 4)

COLORED BOXER ADMITS SLAYING

Held In Jail In Rockville For Torch Death Of Spanish Ship's Carpenter.

(By The Associated Press)

FREDERICK, Md., Nov. 11.—Albert Brown, 25-year-old colored boxer, who fought under the ring name of Young Bobby Burns, was in jail here today, named by police as the torch slayer of Manuel Silva, 44-year-old Spanish ship's carpenter.

Sheroff Roy Hiltner said Brown confessed the slaying. The confession cleared up a mystery killing which police at first believed to have been one of gangland vengeance.

Trail In Frederick

The colored man, a resident of Doub's, near here, will be brought before the Frederick County Circuit Court—the actual slaying having occurred in this county, though the charred body of Silva was found in Montgomery county. The grand jury is not scheduled to meet again until next Monday, but State's Attorney Sherman P.

(Continued on Page Six)

CHINESE RISE AGAINST JAPS IN SHANGHAI

Nipponese Land 2,000 Marines As Result Of Slaying In Native Quarters—Window Glass Of Shop Is Broken—General Uneasiness Is Felt.

WAR DEMANDED BY CELESTIALS

(By The Associated Press)

ROME, Nov. 11.—Italy's two grat armies in Ethiopia drove menacingly today toward that empire's "life line"—the railroad from Addis Ababa to Djibouti, French Somaliland.

The southern army sprang forward in a swift advance through desolate Ogaden Province during the week-end to seize Sasa Baneh—half way to its immediate objective to Jijiga, where the Ethiopians would have to defend their only railway.

Near to Railway

Italian press dispatches reported that the main Somaliland army then thrust forward an advance guard to Daggah Bur, 30 miles northwest of Sasa Baneh, less than 100 miles from Jijiga and little more than 150 miles from the railway itself.

The northern army, while making secure its new positions about Makale, also sent forward outposts. But between them and the ultimate objectives of Jijiga and the city of Diredawa on the railroad arose new evidence of a first Ethiopian stand.

The possibility of serious resistance, postponed after every previous alarm, came to the fore again as Italian land and air patrols reported more than 200,000 Ethiopian troops concentrating near Amba Alaji, immdiata objective on the north. The northern advance

(Continued on Page Four)

Street Widening Not Confined To City

Annapolis isn't the only town which is widening its main street.

Those who drove to Philadelphia on Saturday for the Navy-Penn game saw at least two construction jobs where workmen were busily engaged reducing the size of the sidewalks in order to widen the streets.

At Swarthmore, Pa., half the sidewalk is being removed on the main street.

Here at home, in addition to the city, the Naval Academy has widened certain drives.

NATION OBSERVES WAR CESSATION

(By The Associated Press)

With martial display the nations of Europe today celebrated the 17th anniversary of the end of the war to end war.

While Fascists legions pushed deep into Ethiopia, cutting at the country's "lifeline" railroad, Premier Mussolini told the Italian people their armies were ready "to defend Italy's interests in Europe, Africa or anywhere."

King Emanuel's Birthday

Properly it was a celebration of King Victor Emmanuel's 66th birthday. the nation celebrated its own Armistice November 4, anniversary of the peace with Austria.

The Italian consul in a celebration to Egyptian war dead at the British Memorial Cemetery.

Detachments from the British fleet, strongly concentrated in Mediterranean water because of the Italo-Ethiopian war, formed a guard of honor.

Guns Boom Out

In London, the booming of a gun from the Horse Guards parade stilled traffic for a two minute silence which spread over the far-flung empire. Members of the royal family participated in the ceremonies at the cenotaph of Britain's unknown soldier.

The "Death's Head" legions of the Nationalistic Croix De Feu demonstrated in strength at the Paris commemoration.

President Albert Lebrun officially reviewed the nation's armed forces as they filed past the tomb of the unknown soldier and the Arc De Triomphe.

The United States stood silent for two minutes while the official ceremony at the tomb of America's unknown soldier in Arlington Cemetery paid tribute to the dead.

President At Tomb

President Roosevelt laid a wreath on the tomb. Military organizations added their tribute to that of the nation.

The poppies of the American Legion were prominent in the service at the tomb of Belgium's unknown soldier, where the nation's observance centered.

The two-minute Armistice silence at Dublin was broken with shouts of "Up, Irish Republic."

Groups of young men cheered the Irish Republic and a British flag was sprinkled with gasoline and carried, burning, through the streets.

1,754 COUNTIANS IN ADULT EDUCATION

Maryland's adult education program, which will be operated this year on the same scale as last season, will care for about 24,000 pupils.

Anne Arundel County has 1,754 pupils in addition to 829 male and 67 female students at the Maryland House of Correction.

Editorial

WE CHALLENGE THE GOVERNOR

This morning the **Baltimore Sun** carried a lengthy statement of the Governor's, dealing with generalities. Such statements are being printed, we believe, to evade the issue of explaining specific instances under Governor Nice's regime, having to do with the critical mishandling of the State's affairs and the pointed evasion of the principles underlying the State Merit System.

"I must and shall uphold the law; there is no alternative, and I have accordingly issued to every governmental agent an executive order to the effect that the Merit System law must be observed in spirit and in letter. I believe that the public understands my position, and that those deserving of recognition must seek it through and under the law."

We point to the case of Daniel Armiger. All interested persons throughout the State have read about it. After four or five transfers from his original position, and after a slash in salary of more than 40 percent, Mr Armiger may be forced to leave the service of the State in order to support his family. His last check was held up five days. It was stated at the time that the head of his department would act in accordance with the manner in which Governor Nice wishes the people of the State to believe he would act. The case remains unadjusted.

We challenge Governor Nice to say that his regime has abided by the rules of the Merit System. To be more specific, we will appreciate printing his explanation of the failure of the State Roads Commission to deal justly with Daniel Armiger.

BALLOON SETS WORLD RECORD FOR ALTITUDE

Official Mark Broken As Bag Soars Beyond Unofficial High Made By Russians In 1934—Stevens Reports 74,000 Feet.

WILL TAKE CRAFT 3 HOURS TO LAND

(By The Associated Press)

RAPID CITY, S. D., Nov. 11.—After reaching an unofficial world record altitude computed by the ground crew at 74,000 feet, slightly over 14 miles, the stratosphere fliers of the balloon "Explorer II" radioed at 2:05 P. M. (Eastern Standard time) today, "We're starting down now."

When this report was made the two-man expedition into the thin air, composed of Capt. Orvil Anderson and Capt. Albert W. Stevens, had been up five hours and seven minutes.

Reached Its Goal

The lofty level of 74,000—34,000 feet out in the stratosphere—was the balloonists' fondest goal. If authenticated from their instruments it will mean a world altitude record far beyond that unofficially credited to three Russian balloonists who last year soared to 72,176 feet.

The Russians were killed when their craft collapsed.

To Land In 3 Hours

"It will take about three hours to get down," Captain Stevens told his ground crew by radio. "We're going to try to come down very slowly."

The balloon was then over the vicinity of Valentine, Neb.

Officials believed the landing would be made somewhat southeast of Valentine.

ROMANS PUSH TOWARD RAILS IN NEW DRIVE

Italians Announce Capture Of Sasa Baneh, But Ethiopians Make Denial—Trucks Are Bombed — Natives Gather Behind Mountain Range.

SERIOUS RESISTANCE IS NOW EXPECTED

(By The Associated Press)

SHANGHAI, Nov. 11.—Anti-Japanese terrorism flared anew today when a group of Chinese threw bricks and bottles through a plate-glass show window of a Japanese-owned store after 500 Japanese Marines had disembarked here.

The Japanese landing party strength reached more than 2,000 with the arrival of the new force, although Japanese Navy officers asserted they were merely replacements for an equal number of bluejackets who will sail to Japan Nov. 13.

The situation arising from the unsolved slaying of a Japanese Marine, Hideo Nakayama, which Japanese authorities said was "serious," was considered to be increasingly threatening by the outbreak of new terrorism.

Chinese Escape.

Hundreds of persons saw the Chinese break the window of the store, at one of Shanghai's busiest street corners, but the perpetrators escaped after scattering handbills emblazoned with the characters: "War on Japan to Save China!"

The slain Nakayama, was was scheduled to return to Japan with the departing contingent Nov. 13, was buried with full naval honors after Japanese Gen. T. Ishii called on Gen. Wu Teh-Chen, mayor of Greater Shanghai, urging an intensified hunt for the killer.

Feeling ran high in Shanghai's Japanese community, where a resolution was adopted by the Japanese Amalgamated Street Federation, asserting the Nakayama case "caused great uneasiness among our residents."

Repeated assurances by Japanese officials that no military measures were contemplated to force settlement of the issue served, however, to quiet somewhat the nervousness in the adjacent Chinese district of Chapei.

Investigation Is Made

Japan's consular spokesman asserted investigations indicated strongly that Nakayama was slain in the demilitarized native quarter Saturday as a Chinese demonstration against the presence of Japanese bluejackets.

Chinese officials insisted, however, that the assailant had not been proved to be Chinese, and asserted

(Continued on Page Six)

MRS. JAMES COLLINS BURIED YESTERDAY

The funeral of Mrs. Kate Collins, widow of James Collins, who died on Thursday at the residence of her son, John P. Collins, 41 Glenn avenue, took place at 2:30 o'clock yesterday afternoon, from Saint Anne's Church, the service being conducted by the Rev. James L. Smiley.

The following served as pallbearers: Edward Jones, George Jones, James Ivey, Preston Cantler, John Downey and Andrew May.

Interment was in St. Anne's cemetery, John M. Taylor being the director in charge of the funeral.

Postage Due

Dear Walter:

Even though you had to wait a year for the job, you look mighty important sitting in the back seat of the State car with a colored chauffeur. Politics pay, eh?

Yours,

Noe Zee

To: WARDEN
W. E. QUENSTEDT,
Md. House of Correction.

Big Family Of Pinks Can Furnish Whole Garden

It would be easily possible to grow a garden composed entirely of pinks and produce a grand show of color from early spring until hard freezing checked the parade. There are pinks for rock gardens, pinks for edging, pinks for bedding, pinks for pots, pinks for cutting and pinks good only for garden color. It is a general purpose plant and there are a great number of species, hybrids and varieties.

The colors run through all shades of red, pink rose to white, with some almost black. There are one or two pale yellow pinks, but blue is absent in the genus dianthus. For immediate display the same season, we have the annual Japanese and Chinese pinks, perennial if protected. For the pinks, the grass pinks, clove pinks, hardy carnations and the alpine pinks for the rock garden.

The mainstays are the annuals and the grass pinks known as Diane, the plumarums, also often known as June pinks, clove scented, fringed with blue green foliage and a wealth of bloom in their season.

The pink enjoys the distinction of being about the quickest of all flowers to germinate from seed. With good growing conditions the plants come up inside a week.

The annual pinks made fine masses of color with flakings and edgings, the prevailing colors being reds and pink. They come in double and single forms. Sow seed now and transplant eight inches apart. In a few weeks they will be in gorgeous bloom, developing new stems all summer if seed is kept cut.

The giant single-fringed, lacinia-

Pinks Come in a Great Number of Species, Hybrids and Varieties. You Cannot Have Too Many of Them.

tus, is one of the showiest of the annual pinks. They can be bought in single colors or mixed. The self-colored rich reds make most effective plantings. Plant plenty of annual pinks and at the same time start perennials for next year and the handsome biennial Sweet Williams, which are also pinks. You won't have too many pinks and they fit all situations in the garden. They, fortunately, are one of the easiest growing of all the garden plants.

SCENE OF FIERCE FIGHTING IN SPANISH REVOLT

The summer resort on the Bay of Biscay, San Sebastian, became one of the focal points in the heavy fighting between troops of the leftist Spanish government and revolting forces for supremacy of the country. First rebels, then loyal troops, were reported in control of the city where U. S. Ambassador Claude G. Bowers is maintaining a summer residence. This is a general view of San Sebastian. (Associated Press Photo)

DALLAS EXPOSITION SUFFERS IN WIND STORM

A torrential rain and windstorm caused damage estimated at a million dollars in central-northwest Texas, and wrecked a portion of the Texas exposition at Dallas where the midgets lost their homes temporarily. Workers are shown surveying damage inflicted on the abodes of the tiny folk. (Associated Press Photo)

TOPEKA DRESSED UP FOR LANDON

A huge picture of Gov. Alf M. Landon, measuring 40 by 60 feet, was hung on the side of Topeka's largest building as the city assumed festive garb in honor of the ceremony at which he will be notified of his selection as the Republican presidential nominee. (Associated Press Photo)

Loyal To Spain

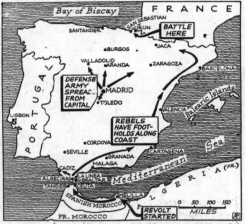

Catalonia proclaimed its loyalty to the Spanish leftist government by setting up a military regime against rightist revolutionaries, in accordance with directions issued by Luis Companys (above), president of the autonomous province. (Associated Press Photo)

REBELS HARASS SPANISH TROOPS

Control of some northern and eastern provinces was reported wrested from loyal leftist troops by Spanish insurgents, whose revolt spread northward from Spanish Morocco. A major engagement was reported fought at San Sebastian, where the United States summer embassy is located, and at nearby Irun. Developments in the tense situation are shown on this map.

SOCIAL and PERSONAL

This column is conducted for the pleasure of the subscribers and readers of the Evening Capital. Information regarding happenings of a social nature among the residents of Annapolis and vicinity—parties, marriages, births, trips, and visitors—is always most acceptable, and may be inserted by telephoning Annapolis 330, and asking for the editor of the Social and Personal Column.

Captain and Mrs. McBride Hosts at Luncheon Today.

Captain Lewis B. McBride, U. S. N., and Mrs. McBride, of 12 Porter Road, Naval Academy, entertained at luncheon today for Mrs. W. Fairlie Dabney, of Baltimore, and her guest, Miss Adele Ford, of New Orleans, La.

Leave for Visit at Blue Ridge Summit.

Captain Robert C. Giffen, Director of Athletics at the Naval Academy, Mrs. Giffen, and Captain F. A. L. Vossler left today to spend a few days with Captain and Mrs. Jules James, at their cottage in Blue Ridge Summit.

Mrs. Terwilliger to Give Bridge-Luncheon.

Mrs. Charles V. O. Terwilliger is entertaining tomorrow at a bridge-luncheon for Mrs. Charles N. Tyndell, of Niagara Falls, New York, who is visiting her brother-in-law and sister, Mr. and Mrs. Robert L. Burwell.

Visiting Relatives On Eastern Shore.

Mr. and Mrs. William B. McCready, of this city, are spending two weeks with relatives in Crisfield, Md.

Annapolis Youth Visiting in Richmond.

Robbin King, of 479 West street, is visiting his aunt, Mrs. Fred Moore, of Richmond, Va., for several weeks.

Mrs. Bernard Wells Home from Hospital.

Mrs. Bernard Wells, who underwent an operation last week, at the Emergency Hospital, has returned to her home in Prince George street. Her many friends will be glad to know that she is getting along nicely.

Miss Magruder to Visit Brother in New England.

Miss Mary Randall Magruder is leaving Annapolis Friday to be the guest of her brother, the Rev. Daniel Magruder, in Hingham, Mass.

Miss Strickland Spending Summer in Roanoke, Va.

Miss Dorothy Strickland is spending the Summer with her father, Dr. J. T. Strickland, at his home, "Miramont," Roanoke, Va. She will return to Annapolis in September.

Mrs. Philip Weaver, of Roanoke, Va., and Lakeland, Fla., was the recent guest of her mother, Mrs. N. M. Strickland, at the old Rawlings-Brewer home, in Green street. Mrs. Weaver was the former Jeannette Brewer Strickland.

Her daughter, Miss Jeannette Strickland Weaver, is traveling in Europe this Summer with a party of schoolmates, under the chaperonage of Mrs. Boyte Brown, of Charlotte, N. C. They are registered at the Hotel Royal Danieli, in Venice, Italy, and will return on the "Europa" late in August.

Miss Weaver is the seventh Jeannette in direct line of descent from Jeannette Gaston, wife of John Brewer, III, of Annapolis, and daughter of Captain Gaston, of the French Navy, who came to aid the American Revolution with the Marquis de Lafayette.

Recent Guests of Lieut. and Mrs. Moore.

Mr. and Mrs. Payne Bingham, of Philadelphia, came here Sunday by airplane and were guests of Mr. Bingham's brother-in-law and sister, Lieutenant and Mrs. Edward Moore, at their home in King George street.

To Spend Ten Days at North Carolina Resort.

Mrs. John M. Maukert, of this city, with her son-in-law and daughter, Captain and Mrs. W. W. Holler, and their two children, of West Point, New York, who have been visiting her here, left Monday for Lake Junaluska, North Carolina, where they will spend ten days.

Returns to New Jersey After Visit Here.

Miss Margaret Houston, of Fanwood, N. J., who has been visiting Miss Priscilla A. Hall, of Wardour, returned to her home yesterday.

Here from New Jersey for Granddaughter's Christening.

Mrs. Burton P. Hall, of New Jersey, was a guest this week-end of Mr. and Mrs. Clifford A. Hall, of Wardour.

Mrs. Hall came to attend the christening of her granddaughter, Eleanor Brooks Hall, infant daughter of Mr. and Mrs. Hall, which took place on Sunday at St. Anne's Church.

Visiting Relatives At Blue Ridge Summit.

Mrs. Samuel Brooke and her stepson, Mr. Samuel Brooke, of Southgate avenue, Murray Hill, are the guests of Mrs. Brooke's brothers-in-law and sister, Doctor and Mrs. Legh Reid, of Haverford, Pa., at their Summer home at Blue Ridge Summit.

Miss Kitty Hopkins In New York.

Miss Catherine Hopkins, daughter of Dr. and Mrs. Walton H. Hopkins, has gone to New York, where she will spend a week attending classes in design and knitting.

Miss Doris Maddox Guest of Aunt.

Miss Doris Maddox, of Glen Burnie, is spending some time with her aunt, Mrs. Frank H. Thompson, of this city.

Here from Alabama to Visit Son and Family.

The Rev. J. E. McCann, a retired Methodist Episcopal minister, has arrived from Alabama to spend a few months with his son and daughter-in-law, Mr. and Mrs. Irving G. McCann, of Edgewater.
— Use the Want Ads —

Kenesrael Society To Meet Tomorrow At Local Synagogue

The Kenesrael Society will hold its regular meeting tomorrow night, at 8:30 o'clock, at the local synagogue.

It is hoped that all members will attend, as matters of importance are to be discussed.
— Use the Want Ads —

Miss Riordan to Tell Stories at Library Tomorrow

Another of the Summer storytelling periods conducted by Miss Josephine Riordan, at the Public Library, will be held tomorrow morning at 9:30 o'clock. This feature of the Library service is open to all children, and is becoming increasingly popular with the young folk of Annapolis.
— Use the Want Ads —

HITLER CONGRATULATES VICTOR

Reichfuehrer Adolph Hitler is shown as he congratulated Tilly Fleisher of Germany, victor in the Javelin throw for women at the Olympics in Berlin. At his left is Air Minister Hermann Goering, who is not often seen in civilian clothes. The picture arrived on the airship Hindenburg.
(Associated Press Photo)

"Swing" Lines Newest Note In Lingerie Styles For Fall

NEW YORK, Aug. 12.—A "swing skirt" for your nightgown, inspired by the new swing music; and a new color called "lovebird," for slinky pajamas are the latest style notes in lingerie.

What's even more important in this field of apparel is the fact that frail-looking expensive underwear is back in the picture.

The gay days when women sometimes slapped down $79 for a nightgown and $49 for a slip—and husbands liked it—are slowly but surely returning, lingerie-makers said today.

One said a Texas oil man's daughter had bought a $3,000 negligee and underwear trousseau this year, and that "ew get more demand for the luxury type of thing every day."

The "swing-skirted" nighties in which you may swish to bed often have a three-yard circumference below the knee.

Even nightgowns have empire lines this season.— accented bust, slim-fitted waist, and diaphragm.

Women could get by with some of them at formal parties. (Lingerie-makers say some women have been appearing in public in their nightgowns occasionally for several years.)

A smart lingerie house, (Chevette) where even panties are specially designed, further describes the mode, saying "lingeries is 95 per cent satin.

"It is very lacy—but never 'plastered' with lace, as it was two years ago. The laces are Val, Binche, and fine, hand-run Alencon.

"American women are wearing many more sheer nightgowns, such as French women always have worn, of high colors: lipstick red, black, citron, which is like chartreuse, and French blue."

Most lingerie, however, is lustrous satin in pale pink and the "off-white" shades which are more flattering than dead white. New colors are "opaline," a white with a delicate pink tinge, "honey," "lamplight," and "crushed rose."

Those "lovebird" color pajamas, which one house is showing in satin, are, in plain English, green. Another new shade of green approved for pajamas is "spinach."

Sow Pansies For Bloom Next Year

Early August is a fine time to sow seed of pansies for bloom during tulip time next spring. It seems a long way off to be preparing for now, but the brilliant pansies, with their warm colors are a welcome sight in the spring, and if you are to have the latest and best varieties you must grow them yourself.

Pansies are really members of the viola family, the only distinction between them being that pansies have "faces." Be sure to get some of the giant strains. Compared to the pansies of a few years ago, they are enormous giants, practically all colorful flower, where the foliage hardly shows at all. There are also smaller types called the ruffled or Scotch pansies.

They are easy to grow if you prepare a proper bed for them. In cases where this is impossible, sow seed in boxes or flats. They can be placed in a shady situation outdoors, and if kept well watered the seedlings will appear in short order.

When sowing spread the seed thinly. If necessary mix a small quantity of sand with the seed to prevent overcrowding. If the seeds grow up too thick it is difficult to disentangle them, and space for individual growth is very important. As soon as the seedlings break ground they should be given full light and fresh air. But do not let them dry out, especially when planted in flats where the quantity of soil, and the consequent rate of evaporation is rapid. During midday, protect them from the sun with

Pansy Seedlings in a Cold Frame. When Cold Weather Sets in Cover Them With Leaves.

a piece of cheesecloth or a newspaper canopy.

Transplant them when the first rough leaves appear, either into other flats or another row in the cold frame. This process is called "pricking out," and they should be set about 2 inches apart. Sometimes another transplanting is practiced, although this is not absolutely necessary. In any case for the final setting out, see that they are 4 to 6 inches apart, and let them grow in the cold frame until it begins to freeze. Then, fill up the frame with dry leaves, and cover it with the sash or boards. In severe weather the sash can be covered with straw mats or any such covering, but this is not usually needed.

In the spring as soon as frost begins to come out of the ground, the leaves should be taken off the pansy plants and the sash put on the frame. Treat them from now on the same as any other planting in the spring. They will bloom under glass much earlier than outdoors, and you will have pansies to set out in the border when the tulips begin to bloom.

ELAINE BARRIE BREAKS BARRYMORE ROMANCE

(By The Associated Press)

HOLLYWOOD, Aug. 12.— Dark-eyed Elaine Barrie, 21-year-old actress, broke her "engagement" to Actor John Barrymore, but kept the veteran screen lover's 8½-carat diamond ring today.

Barrymore, ill with a serious heart ailment, lay in a sanitarium secluded and silent, while the brunette New Yorker announced at her apartment:

"Recent events have shown conclusively that it would be impossible for us to plan a happy married life together. With this realization, I would infinitely prefer to terminate our blessed relationship at this time rather than when we married."

GIANTS LOSE TWIN BILL AS CARDS WIN

New Yorkers, Four And One-Half Games Ahead, Need Two Victories, Or One Triumph And One Defeat Of St. Louis, To Clinch Pennant.

LEAGUE LEADERS BOW TO PHILLIES

By Orlo Robertson
(Associated Press Sports Writer)

It may be all over but the shouting as far as the Giants' fans are concerned but they would breathe a lot easier if their boys would do something mighty soon about getting rid of those pesky Cardinals, who are hanging like leeches to their fading National League pennant hopes.

The Giants still hold a four and a half game lead over the Gas House Gang. They need only two victories or one triumph and a Cardinal defeat to clinch the pennant but things don't look so rosy following yesterday's happenings at Philadelphia and St. Louis. Jimmy Wilson's men rose in all their might, belied their last place rating, and smote the league leaders in both games of a doubleheader, 11-7 and 6-2. At the same time the Cards trimmed the Reds 6-3 while even the Cubs retained their mathematical chance to tie for the pennant by hitting the third-place hopes of the Pirates with a 11-4 victory.

Hubbell Ignored

As the result the standings today were:

Club	W.	L.	Games behind	Games to play
Giants ...	89	59	..	6
Cards	85	64	4½	5
Cubs	85	64	5	4

Only Carl Hubbell, slated for his 16th straight victory today, and Fred Fitzsimmons were not called on as Bill Terry sent six pitchers into the games in an effort to stop the Phils. The Phillies blasted Ag Smith and Clydell Castleman for seven runs in the second inning of the first game to pave the way to victory and then collected enough runs off Frank Gabler and Dick Coffman in the first five innings to win the second before being stopped by Gumbert and Hal Schumacher.

Don Gutteridge, rookie third baseman, and Mike Ryba, "jack-of-all-positions," combined to give the Cards their victory. Gutteridge drove in five runs with a single, double and triple while Ryba relieved Henry Pippen on the mound in the second after the Reds had taken a 3-0 lead and held them scoreless and to two hits the remainder of the game.

Hoyt Taken Out

The Cubs pounded Waite Hoyt from the mound in the sixth to break a 4-4 tie and then scored six more runs off Mace Brown in the eighth to whip the Pirates and keep alive their pennant hopes.

The Detroit Tigers turned in a pair of shutout victories over the Browns, 12-0 and 14-[illegible] to run their string of consecuti[illegible] victories to nine and [illegible]trengthen their hold on second [illegible]ace in the American League.

The other two contestants for runner-up honors—the White Sox and Indians—battled 12 innings to an 8-8 draw after Earl Averill had tied the score in the ninth with his 27th circuit drive.

The Yankees had no trouble beating the Athletics 10-3 although Pat Malone was touched for 15 hits. Joe Cascarella outpointed Rube Walberg as the Senators whipped the Red Sox 4-0. In the other National League encounters, the Boston Bees took two close ones from the Dodgers, 4-3 and 3-2.

Yesterday's Stars

(By The Associated Press)

Elden Auker and Tommy Bridges, Tigers—Blanked Browns with five and three hits, respectively.

Don Gutteridge and Mike Ryba, Cards—Gutteridge drove in five runs with single, double and triple; Ryba held Reds to two hits in 7 2-3 innings of relief pitching.

Earl Averill, Indians—His ninth inning homer tied game with White Sox as teams played 12 innings to draw.

Joe Bowman, Phillies — Checked Giants in first game as relief hurler.

Ruppert Thompson and Bill Warstler, Bees—Drove in deciding runs that gave Bees double triumph over Dodgers.

Racing Today
Havre de Grace
SEVEN RACES DAILY
Penna. R. R. trains leave Penna. Station, Baltimore, 12:30 and 12:58 P. M. Direct to track.
FIRST RACE AT 2:30 P. M.
(Eastern Standard Time)

With steam up, the New York Yankees' "powerhouse" was ready for World Series battle—most probably a "subway" series with the Giants across the Harlem River. The likely choice of Manager Joe McCarthy (right) for a starting pitcher to oppose Hubbell rested between Vernon ("Goofy") Gomez (left), Charlie ("The Red") Ruffing (lower left center), and Monte Pearson (lower right center). Regardless of starting pitchers, the opposition has always to worry over the famous "Murderers' Row"—(left to right, top) Bill Dickey, Lou Gehrig, Joe Di Maggio and Tony Lazzeri. (Associated Press Photos)

Johnnies Backfield Heavier Than Forward Positions; Prep For Maryland Fracas

St. John's College will put a football team averaging 173 pounds on the field Saturday for the opening game with the University of Maryland at College Park.

Valentine (Dutch) Lentz, head coach, picked a team today made up of 7 veterans. The line averages a little over 172 pounds and the backfield slightly more than 173 pounds.

Len Delisio, veteran, and William Stallings, substitute tackle last season, will be at end; Stuart Christhilf and Frank Townsend, veterans, at tackle; Willard Todd, converted from a substitute tackle, and Richard Snibbe, sophomore, at guard. Robert Snibbe, veteran, will be at center.

Starting Backfield

The starting backfield will consist of John Lambros, quarterback; Fred Buck and Warran Hammann, halfbacks, and Ned Lathrop, fullback. Lambros, passer and kicker, Hammann and Lathrop are veterans from last year. Buck, who spells Lambros at kicking, played twice last season.

Belden Burns, veteran, will alternate with Lambros; William McMillian, playing his first year on the squad, will alternate with Hammann. Ted de Disse will spell Latrop.

21 Experienced Men

Lentz said he had 36 players on his squad including 15 who never played football before. He is shy of reserves and has no seasoned ends to relieve DeLisio and Stallings. Stallings will be playing his first game in the wing position.

"We have a fair small college football team," Lentz said. "It has prospects of developing into a good team, provided no one is hurt. Injuries would wreck us.

"In facing Maryland I'm like a man with a dime gambling with a man with $1,000."

Sands On Squad

For the rest of the week Lentz will concentrate on offense and defense. He will have dummy line scrimmage, but will not send his team into a hard scrimmage before the game because of the possiblity of injuries.

Spriggs Sands, veteran guard, reported back to school today but will not be in shape for action for some time. Lentz said he might send him in the Maryland game for a short period, but that later he would likely replace Todd at guard.

Mike Levely, a likely looking freshman player from Landon School, is showing well in practice, and will alternate with Richard Snibbe at guard. He was a back while attending prep school.

The Fish and Game Conservation Association Of Anne Arundel

By Gordon Fleet

The necessity for organization for the protection of our fish and game has been recognized for a number of years and such organizations existed 'way back to the "good old days." Those days when such things as bag limits were hardly even thought of and, in many instances, there was no closed season on many species of game. The hunter of today cannot visualize conditions where upland game was so plentiful, and yet, if we read the records of some of the sportsmen's clubs of those days, we cannot help but feel some resentmenet that our ancestral hunters did not do more to preserve for us the abundance of game that existed in their time.

However, credit must be given to those far-seeing sportsmen who did make an effort to preserve for us, as far as possible, the sport they so much enjoyed. Seth E. Gordon, president of the American Game Association, in an article appearing in the 1932 Fall issue of the "Maryland Conservationist;" tells of the "New York Sportsmen's Club," organized on the 20th of May, 1844. This club, the author states, was the earliest attempt to maintain a conservation organization in the United States, as far as he was able to learn. Mr. Gordon tells us that the immediate objective of this club was "to stop the loss of many valuable sporting dogs in the city of New York." It was soon suggested however, that they form an association for game and sporting generally."

From the foregoing we can readily see that there were far-seeing sportsmen nearly a hundred years ago who realized that unless some curb was placed on indescriminate killing, the day would come when our supply of game would be exhausted entirely. Unfortunately, for us, these far-seeing men were unable to accomplish as much as could be wished but it is a source of serious wonder to the writer just what our hunting conditions would be today had they not, at least made the effort.

With all this in mind the extreme necessity for more and better organization is certainly plain to us all. Our job of conserving our game supply, and of increasing it, has increased the necessity for organized effort a thousandfold. Increased population, modern firearms, automobiles, to name only a few of the problems which have contributed to the depletion of game, all these—if compared with conditions 92 years ago—certainly should be decisive proof (if conservation was considered necessary in 1844), that all persons interested in Wildlife should organize and work together for a sane management of one of our most valuable natural resources.

The word "sane" in the foregoing paragraph should receive special stress as it is a well known fact that there are certain organized groups preaching a form of conservation who declare all sportsmen simply destroyers of game. No authentic data is at hand at this moment but, I venture to say, that upon research it would be found that the very first effort to conserve and preserve our birds and animals was made by sportsmen. There are, without a doubt, plenty of hunters masquerading as sportsmen who would and do destroy game down to the last bird or animal. Just as there are plenty of dishonest persons in any community but they certainly do not represent the majority and it therefore, behooves the real sportsmen to strengthen their ranks and present a solid front for the proper conservation and management of our wildlife.

Let's look out for Anne Arundel county NOW and give our organization real support and cooperation the year 'round.

SOUTHERN HOLDS 1-HOUR SCRIMMAGE

The Southern Athletic Club held a one hour scrimmage last night. Coach Leo Hantske and his assistant Richard Stone are pleased at the progress the squad is making. The line and backs are clicking fine and dandy and it looks as though the downtown boys are out to win and bring back the State title to Annapolis once held by the Cardinals.

The Southern line will average around 155 pounds and the backfield about 150. The Southern football fans of last season will see a new fast moving backfield this year with plenty of new faces.

Henry Pastrana the hard running half-back of last year's team is improving with every practice and much will be expected from him this fall. H. Reynolds, Macy and Paterson, three nifty runners, have been showing up well in the last two drills. Atwell the hard blocking center of last year's team has been shifted to the backfield along with Jerrell who has plenty of power at guard.

On the Southern line will be Short, White, McNew and Stevens at ends, all bigger and better and ready for the opening whistle. The tackles will be Charles Pastrana, Sears, Bruce and Levy, all big and rangy boys. Coming to the guard position will be Frengel, Mitchell, Thomas.

The center job will be turned over to Schekles and Trott who played tackles last season. Thursday night the squad will hold another long scrimmage at the West Annapolis field.

HUNTINGTOWN TAKES LEAD IN BALL SERIES

	W	L	Pct.
Huntingtown	2	0	1.000
Greenock	0	2	.000

The playoff for the Southern Md. League championship started last Saturday at Huntingtown between Greenock and Huntingtown, the two league leaders.

Huntingtown jumped right in and took the first game to the tune of 14-6. Tucker and R. Turner pitched for Greenock and D. Tucker and Norfolk for Huntingtown. On Sunday Huntingtown journeyed to Greenock for the second game and took that game by the score of 18-7. M. Turner, R. Turner, J. Howard pitched for Greenock and Norfolk and Bowen for Huntingtown.

The next games will be played at Huntingtown Saturday and at Greenock on Sunday. The fifth game will be played at Galesville on Oct. 4, at which time the championship flag will be presented to the winner. The prospect of the next game will be much better than the last two. Huntingtown is not expecting such a walk-away as last week.

The two umpires are being furnished by the D. C. Umpires Ass'n of Washington.

FRIGIDAIRE
Annapolis Utilities, Inc.
126 West Street Phone 123
SALES & SERVICE

Major League Leaders

(By The Associated Press)

National League

Batting—P. Waner, Pirates, .375; Phelps, Dodgers, .370.

Runs—J. Martin, Cardinals, 120; Vaughan, Pirates, 119.

Runs Batted In—Ott, Giants, 134; Suhr, Pirates, 114.

Hits—Medwick, Cardinals, 215; P. Waner, Pirates, 2[illegible]3.

Doubles — Medwick, Cardinals, 62; Herman, Cubs, 54.

Triples — Medwick, Cardinals; Camilli, Phillies, and Goodman, Reds, 13.

Home Runs—Ott, Giants, 33; Camilli, Phillies, 27.

Stolen Bases—J. Martin, Cardinals, 22; S. Martin, Cardinals, and Galan, Cubs, 17.

Pitchers—Hubbell, Giants, 25-6; Lucas, Pirates, 14-4.

American League

Batting — Appling, White Sox, .384; Averill, Indians, .377.

Runs — Gehrig, Yankees, 165; Gehringer, Tigers, 142.

Runs Batted In—Trosky, Indians, 153; Gehrig, Yankees, 148.

Hits—Averill, Indians, and Gehringer, Tigers, 223.

Doubles—Gehringer, Tigers, 56; Walker, Tigers, 55.

Triples—Averill, Indians, and Di Maggio, Yankees, 15.

Home Runs—Gehrig, Yankees, 48; Trosky, Indians, 41.

Stolen Bases—Lary, Browns, 34; Powell, Yankees, 25.

Pitchers—Hadley, Yankees, 13-4; Pearson, Yankees, 19-6.

SANDLOT GRID INJURY FATAL

(By The Associated Press)

COUNCIL BLUFFS, Ia., Sept. 23. Raymond L. Harrod, Jr., 11, of Council Bluffs, died at a hospital here yesterday of a blood clot on the brain. His father said the injury was the result of playing sandlot football Friday.

School Days
AND
Cool Days
ARE
Hard Days
On the Family Purse
BORROW
ON YOUR
SIGNATURE
And Repay
The New, Easy Way
EQUAL PAYMENT PLAN
$2.60 a month pays $40.00
$5.28 a month pays $75.00
$10.55 a month pays $150.00
$18.29 a month pays $260.00
The above payments include both principal and interest.
Other amounts in same proportion.
BEFORE BORROWING ON ANY PLAN CALL, WRITE OR PHONE
It is no longer necessary to go elsewhere for your loan requirements. We supply a loan service complete in every detail.
LINCOLN
Loan Service Inc.
15 School Street Annapolis 1491

Bowling

ANNAPOLITAN LEAGUE

Team	Won	Lost	Pct.
Myers Co.	3	0	1.000
Elks	3	0	1.000
Skipper Electric..	3	0	1.000
Thomas & Co.....	2	1	.667
N. A. Printers...	1	2	.333
French's Garage..	0	0	.000
Bladen Hotel.....	0	0	.000
N. A. Five.......	0	0	.000
St. Margarets....	0	0	.000
Smith Bros.......	0	0	.000
Arundel Laundry	0	0	.000
Taylor's Store....	0	0	.000
Kiwanis	0	0	.000
Coco-Cola	0	3	.000
Annapolis Dairy..	0	3	.000
K. of P..........	0	3	.000

LAST NIGHT'S ROLLERS

COCO-COLA			
R. Easterday ..	124	109	120
R. Stanley	96	93	94
C. Suitt	100	99	100
J. Brown	101	99	89
J. Easterday ...	126	150	117
Totals	547	550	520

SKIPPER			
J. Beranck	118	107	126
J. Arnold	108	106	106
E. Hartge	117	112	138
E. Ford	109	111	117
E. Deale	121	123	97
Totals	573	559	580

N. A. PRINTERS			
Tarleton	131	125	148
Lewnes	99	..	101
Jons	104	..	112
Clow	108	116	148
Newton	112	114	111
Engelke	..	112	..
Basil	..	92	..
Totals	554	559	620

THOMAS & CO.			
Rogers	115	116	111
Jons	105	100	104
Martin	117	105	136
Zerhusen	114	132	130
Scible	138	111	124
Totals	589	564	605

THIS WEEK'S ROLLERS

Thursday — French's Garage vs. Bladen Hotel; N. A. Five vs. St. Margaret's A. C.

Friday — Smith Brother vs. Arundel Laundry; Taylor's Store vs. Kiwanis Club.

LEAGUE STANDINGS

NATIONAL LEAGUE

Scores Of Yesterday

Philadelphia, 11-6; New York, 7-2.
Chicago, 11; Pittsburgh, 4.
St. Louis, 6; Cincinnati, 3.
Boston, 4-3; Brooklyn, 3-2.

Where They Play Today

New York at Philadelphia.
Pittsburgh at Chicago.
Cincinnati at St. Louis.
Brooklyn at Boston.

Standing Of The Clubs

	W.	L.	PC.
New York	89	59	.601
St. Louis	85	64	.570
Chicago.	85	65	.567
Pittsburgh	82	68	.547
Cincinnati.	71	78	.477
Boston	69	79	.466
Brooklyn.	63	86	.423
Philadelphia.	52	97	349

Sloan, Big Tackle, Moved To Guard On Navy Team

Lieut. Thomas J. Hamilton, head coach of the Naval Academy football team preparing for his opening game with William and Mary today shifted David Sloan, 196 pounder, from tackle to left guard.

Sloan, a powerful six-footer, won his major letter last year as a reserve tackle, playing in the Army game. At left guard he will be grouped with Rivers J. Morrell, Jr., captain of the Navy team, Richard D. Gunderson, and Kenneth B. Hysong, who play in the position.

Fleps Advanced

C. J. Fleps, a tackle, who has been playing with the "B" squad has been advanced to the "A" squad to bolster the varsity strength in this position.

"In general the work to date has shown that we are not up to our usual standards," Hamilton said, discussing the progress of his practice. "We need a little bit of everything. The practice has been spotty.

"I expect a tough ball game with William and Mary College. I expect to use a lot of men."

Hamilton worked the squad yesterday on offensive assignments with blocking for the backs and ends. Later he staged a defensive scrimmage. He said he planned a similar program through tomorrow.

Gophers, Buckeyes, Irish Look Best In Midwest

By William Weekes
(By The Associated Press)

CHICAGO, Sept. 22.—It looks as though the grid machines of the central states — long rated as college football's toughest neighborhood — will have to put up with another season of pushing around at the hands of Minnesota, Ohio State and Notre Dame.

Minnesota and Ohio State, co-champions of the Big Ten conference, face problems in the replacement of stars who were graduated or riddled by ineligibility, but both appear to have enough talent to keep them up there another season, at least — provided Northwestern doesn't upset them.

Notre Dame lost 19 lettermen but retained 16 for its 9-game campaign which harbors no "breathers." Michigan State and Marquette, rapidly gaining stature in the football scheme, also are primed for victory marches.

The loss of such Minnesota greats as Glenn Seidel, George Roscoe, Sheldon (Shotgun) Beise, Dick Smith and Dale Rennebohm might wreck some elevens, but at Minnesota, Coach Bernie Bierman's biggest worry appears to be time. He has Sam Hunt to move in at quarterback where Seidel starred last fall, Rudy Gmitro for Beise's fullback post, and Earl (Bud) Svendsen as Rennebohm's successor at center — along with typical Gopher talent for the other spots.

Ohio State Strong As Ever

However, Bierman had less than a month to get his machinery tuned up for the opening battle with the University of Washington, ranked as the Pacific Coast's standout, on September 26 at Seattle.

Ohio State, which must face New York university and Pittsburgh in its first two games, has 16 lettermen, at least one for every position, to man Francis Schmidt's highly-specialized forward and lateral passes. This list includes "Jumping Joe" Williams, one of 1935's prize sophomore backs, Capt. Merle Wendt, all-Big Ten end, William Harrison (Tippy) Dye at quarterback, and Inwood Smith, outstanding guard.

Thoroughly broken into Coach Lynn Waldorf's methods, Northwestern has the makings of a misery-dealing eleven. For his second season in the Big Ten, Waldorf will start off with 20 lettermen, and a fine sophomore crop. Northwestern upset Notre Dame last year.

Michigan On Comeback Trail

Every other team in the conference, with the exception of Chicago and Iowa, promises to be stronger than last year. Purdue, hurt by the loss of Ed Skorokski, center, in last midseason, has 17 letter winners. Michigan, slowly moving back toward the top since the disastrous 1934 campaign, has 18—and its best sophomore group since 1931. Wisconsin, with 19 varsity veterans, is expecting a revival under Harry Stuhldreher, who succeeds Dr. Clarence Wiley Spears, in the Big Ten's only major coaching shift.

For the first time in five seasons Bob Zuppke, dean of Big Ten coaches, will have a few heavyweights on his Illinois squad.

Iowa will rely on its spectacular Negro fullback, slippery Oze Simmons, and 17 other lettermen. Indiana figures to be troublesome if the injury jinx doesn't attack Coach Bo McMillin again.

With Jay Berwanger as assistant coach instead of playing, Chicago appears doomed to last place in the final standing. Coach Clark Shaughnessy has only 10 lettermen.

AMERICAN LEAGUE

Scores Of Yesterday

New York, 10; Philadelphia, 3.
Detroit, 12-14; St. Louis, 0-0.
Washington, 4; Boston, 0.
*Cleveland, 8; Chicago, 8.

*Twelve innings, darkness.

Where They Play Today

St. Louis at Detroit.
Philadelphia at New York.
Chicago at Cleveland.
Boston at Washington.

Standing Of The Clubs

	W.	L.	PC.
New York	99	49	.669
Detroit.	83	68	.550
Chicago	78	69	.531
Washington.	79	70	.530
Cleveland	76	72	.514
Boston.	73	77	.487
St. Louis	55	92	.374
Philadelphia. ...	51	97	.345

IS EPILEPSY INHERITED? CAN IT BE CURED?
A booklet containing the opinions of famous doctors on this interesting subject will be sent FREE, while they last, to any reader writing to the Educational Division, 551 Fifth Avenue, New York, N. Y., Dept. S-680

Power in Every Stroke

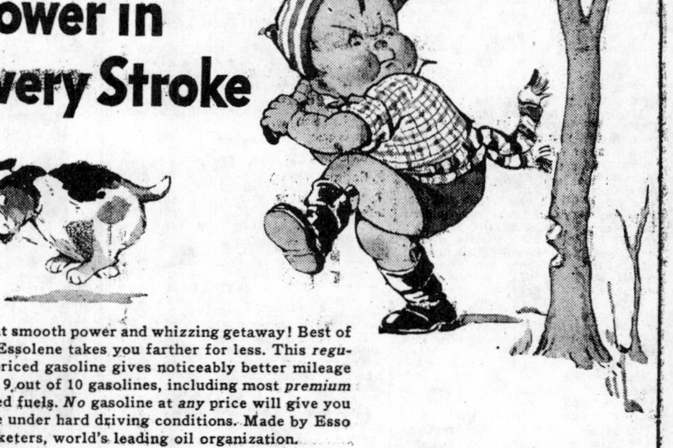

What smooth power and whizzing getaway! Best of all, Essolene takes you farther for less. This *regular* priced gasoline gives noticeably better mileage than 9 out of 10 gasolines, including most *premium* priced fuels. *No* gasoline at *any* price will give you more under hard driving conditions. Made by Esso Marketers, world's leading oil organization.
STANDARD OIL COMPANY OF NEW JERSEY
Essolene MOTOR FUEL
BUY AT THE ESSO SIGN
for Happy Motoring
LAST CALL . . $15,500 Prize Contest Closes Sept. 30th SEE YOUR ESSO DEALER TODAY
Copr. 1936, Esso, Inc.

LIBELED LADY

ADAPTED BY LEBBEUS MITCHELL from the METRO-GOLDWYN-MAYER Picture.

SYNOPSIS — *Bill Chandler, engaged by Warren Haggerty, managing editor of the New York Star, to quash a $5,000,000 libel suit brought by Connie Allenbury, marries Haggerty's sweetheart, Gladys Benton, as a temporary affair so that she can bring suit for alienation of affections against Connie, thereby causing her to drop the suit. The paper had charged her with husband-stealing, erroneously. Chandler falls in love with Connie and she with him, and he persaudes Haggerty not to start the alienation suit. But Gladys falls for her temporary husband and Haggerty accuses him of double dealing. When Haggerty finds Chandler at the Allenbury residence, he 'phones to Gladys to come with a detective, but Chandler makes a getaway.*

Chapter Eleven

A POSER FOR BILL CHANDLER

Warren Haggerty gloated over the headline proof to go over the Allenbury story: "Connie Allenbury Being Sued for Alienation of Affection by Mrs. William Chandler," and exuberantly poured himself another drink as Allen hurried in.

"Do we hold the press for the Allenbury yarn?" he asked.

"Go ahead — next edition. The longer we wait the better it gets! I can see 'em now — the Allenburys trying to buy Gladys off! I wish I was there — to see Chandler's face! First, he lies about the Allenbury case — seeing that girl every day! Then he lies to Gladys so *she* won't make trouble! Then he lies to me — tells me he loves Gladys, so I'll step in and clear the road to Connie."

"You got to hand it to Chandler — he always did think fast."

"But I think faster! He's played right into my hand! I settle the case, get my girl back and give him a kick in the pants! Here's to

"Will you marry me?" asked Connie.

the triple-crossing Chandler!"

"I hope it's not *quadruple*!" said Allen in a low voice, with a glance at the door of Haggerty's office. Bill and Gladys, arms lovingly entwined, stood there. Haggerty saw them, exploded:

"Where have you been, Gladys?"

"Dancing," she replied with a happy smile at Bill.

"Do you mean to say, you didn't go to the Allenburys?"

"No, we decided against it."

"Kill that story, Allen!" commanded Haggerty. When his secretary had departed he turned angrily on Bill and Gladys. "Now — what have you got to say for yourselves? What happened?"

"Well, Haggerty," said Bill, "what would you say if I told you I've practically gotten Connie Allenbury to agree to drop the case?"

"I'd say you were a dirty, double-crossing liar!"

"Come, William," said Gladys, placing a hand on Bill's arm, "I won't stay and listen to you being insulted."

"Oh, is that so!" shouted Haggerty. "Well, listen to *me* — not four hours ago I heard your two-timing Romeo cooing sweet nothings into Connie Allenbury's ear!"

"Bill told me all about that," said Gladys pityingly. "That was technique. But you wouldn't know about that."

Haggerty had a difficult time swallowing his rage. "Bill, why didn't you tell me you'd been seeing Connie Allenbury? All Gladys had to do was to bust in that house—"

"Yes! And get our names smeared all over your paper!" said Gladys.

"If I'd told you, you'd have spoiled all my good work," explained Bill — like you did tonight, barging in after I'd almost convinced her to drop the suit. Believe me, Warren, this is the best way. The Allenburys are giving a party tomorrow night, and I'll be there and get her to drop the suit — unless you decide to break in again."

"You're too obvious, Warren," said Gladys. "Bill knows best."

Haggerty's jealousy was more enflamed than ever at Gladys's championship of Bill against him, and he set himself to out-think Bill and outsmart him. The result appeared in but a single copy of the Star. At the head of the society column was an item to the effect that J. B. Allenbury and his daughter Connie were sailing after the party for a four months' tour of the world." Accompanying them on this cruise," continued the item, "will be Connie's favorite, William Chandler. Do we hear wedding bells?"

In his anxiety to show Gladys the item, he sought her out in a booth in a beauty parlor where she was having a permanent wave. She seized the paper from his hands. After watching the rage spread over her face, as she read, Haggerty left hurriedly. At the Star office, he ordered reporters to cover the Allenbury charity bazaar that night.

Madame Pardona, the fortune-teller the Allenburys had engaged to amuse their guests, looked up from Connie's palm. "I see a dark man — "

"Wonderful!" exclaimed Connie, with a fond glance at Bill. "I've been seeing one for four days!"

"Do you, by chance, see the lady ...ing what the dark man wants her to do?" asked Bill, dropping a dollar-bill upon the table.

At a glance from Connie, Madame Pardona replied: "It all depends—upon the lady."

Connie took his arm and led him out of the tent. "Serves you right — trying to get an answer on the libel suit!"

"Young woman, you're a hussy—luring me here under promise of an answer!"

"You'll get it when my last guest leaves."

"You're a hard woman, Connie Allenbury."

"Only when I'm crossed . . . "

Mrs. Van Arsdale and her daughter Babs bursting with news, cornered Mr. Allenbury in the midway which he had constructed on the lawn of his home for the amusement of his guests at the charity bazaar.

"Oh, Mr. Allenbury, where's Connie? We're dying to tell her all about Mr. Chandler's wife!" gushed Mrs. Van Arsdale. "You know, Chandler, the fish-man we met on the boat. We've met his wife."

"I'm sure you're mistaken, Mrs. Van Arsdale."

"Oh, no we're not! We saw him this afternoon coming from a hotel. We called to him, but he was getting into a taxi and didn't hear us. We stopped to leave a message at the hotel and the clerk said, did we wish to speak to his wife, and I said 'Naturally' — and he said she was in the beauty parlor shop. And we saw her!" She laid a hand on Mr. Allenbury's arm. "And, my dear, she's a *case* — a psychopathic case!"

"She was in a booth," added Babs, "and kept screaming 'Let me out of here!' And before we could even *speak* to her, she *rushed* past us—"

"Oh, look, there's Connie and Mr. Chandler now in that tin-type booth being photographed!" exclaimed Mrs. Van Arsdale.

"You wait here," said Mr. Allenbury hastily. "I'll get them. We'll make a party of it. I'll be right back." He ordered champagne cocktails from a passing waiter, and made his escape.

While Bill was paying the tin-type photographer, Mr. Allenbury took his daughter's arm.

"Connie, I must see you. I can't talk to you here. Come. Never mind Bill; he'll keep." He led her to a secluded spot in a corner of the yard where they were partly hidden by bushes.

"How much does Chandler mean to you, Connie? Are you in love with him?"

"Not jealous, are you, Dad?" She patted his cheek fondly, but at the serious look in his eyes, dropped her lightness. "Terribly in love with him, Dad. More than I ever dreamed I could care for anyone. Why? You like him, don't you?"

"Of course."

"Then stop being mysterious! *Tell* me what's worrying you!"

"The Van Arsdales say he's married."

For a moment she couldn't utter a word, then rallied to his defense. "I don't believe it! You know the Van Arsdales!"

"I'm afraid it's true, Connie. They've even met the woman."

"No, I *don't* believe it! I *won't*— Yes, it would explain so much. Why we always met alone — why . . . Oh, it's *hideous* suspecting him, and yet . . . "

"We've got to know — ask him point blank — "

"Let me ask him, father — in my way. Go please, darling. I'll ask him so he can't misunderstand . . . "

She found Bill on the terrace, hunting for her. "I'm glad you ran out, it's nicer here," he said unreproachfully.

"Bill, there's . . . I've got something to ask you . . . it's just . . . there's a question . . . the most important I'll ever ask! Just answer 'Yes' or 'No' . . . but don't explain! If it's 'No', don't explain . . . Bill, have you been proposed to much?"

Completely astounded, he murmured: "'Have I been' — What?"

"You know, proposed to — your hand in marriage . . ." She was breathless.

"What are you talking about?"

She was almost hysterical. "I'm asking you to *marry* me!"

"But you said a question." Bill was bewildered.

"*That's* a question: *Will you marry me?*"

He turned, without answering, to take her in his arms. She pushed him away.

"But will you?"

© 1936—Metro-Goldwyn-Mayer Corp.

(*To be concluded.*)

Try A Want Ad.

Many Women Entered In Life Of Prince Of Wales

(Editor's Note: Scented love letters have poured into Edward VII's quarters ever since he was a youth. His secretaries show him only a few—the funniest ones. That is not saying, however, that he has remained alooft from women. His current friendship with Mrs. Wallis Simpson is the strongest of all. In the following article, the last of three, DeWitt MacKenzie contrasts the Monarch's attitude toward the former Baltimore Belle and his previous women friends.)

By Dewitt MacKenzie
(By The Associated Press)

NEW YORK, Oct. 28—America's Mrs. Wallis Simpson, whose friendship with King Edward VIII has the world feverishly excited, does not represent his first romance, by a long stretch of imagination.

There have been others of considerable duration, and there have been many passing flirations.

Never before, however, has there been such talk of marriage. British society and officialdom, which have watched the progress of this friendship for a long time, admit privately to being worried. They fear that the prestige of the throne might be harmed irreparably were Edward to make a divorcee his queen.

Newspapers Silent

The general public there knows little or nothing about the affair. The English newspapers have been discreetly silent.

The fascinating Baltimore woman seems to have cast an extraordinary spell over the bachelor monarch. The grand passion appears to have hit him at last at the age of 42, and it is a woman of 40 who has inspired it.

The former Maryland society belle is said to possess those qualities which in past history have made and unmade kings. She is exceptionally clever in addition to being wholly attractive and charming—undoubtedly a striking personality.

Edward is an individualist and a hard man to handle, as his advisers and aides could testify. But Mrs. Simpson has no difficulty where so many others have failed.

It takes a super-woman to make him wait patiently for an hour or more outside a hairdresser's for her. He probably never did such a thing for anybody else.

Upset Engagements

He used to put gray hairs into the heads of his staff by abruptly upsetting engagements they had made for him. I have known his to send word in advance to a arge dinner party that he would stay as long as he was amused, and no longer. Nobody ever made him step about as does Mrs. Simpson.

She has the reputation of being exceedingly popular in English society. There is only one point in debate at all—whether it would be politic for the King-Emperor to marry a woman twice divorced.

The fact that she is American born does not enter into the proposition. The British public has let it be known that it would welcome an alliance with this country—but the people want their King to pick an unmarried girl.

Had Mrs. Simpson met Edward before she had been twice married, she perhaps would have been queen of England by now. She may still be queen, if Edward feels that it is wise to challenge public sentiment.

The King was introduced to her several years ago, and the fates decreed that he should be presented by another American-born woman who also was his good friend—Lady Furness, the former Thelma Morgan and twin sister of Mrs. Reginald Vanderbilt.

Another Divorce Suit

As Prince of Wales, Edward was frequently in the company of Lady Furness, and people speculated about romance there. Coincidentally, she obtained a divorce from Viscount Furness, just as Mrs. Simpson sued her husband this week.

Soon after this first meeting the Prince began to invite Mr. and Mrs. Simpson to affairs as his guests. This went on for some time. When the King asked them to accompany him on his now famous yachting holiday in the Adriatic this Summer, Simpson could not go, having a pressing business engagement on the continent. The wife went without her husband.

The Prince of Wales' first big love was Mrs. Dudley Ward, attractive daughter of a wealthy manufacturer. He met her while he was still in his teens, shortly before the war, and she was five years older than he.

He joined the colors in France, and she married a man 20 years her senior. When the war was over, Edward, making no secret of his admiration, met her frequently with friends. There seemed to be no question of their deep affection for each other.

Affair Was Ended

She became his favorite dancing partner and companion. This continued until about 1930, when she started suit for divorce. From that time they ceased to be seen so much in each other's company, and a real love match came to an end.

There was, among others, a vivacious French girl whom Edward liked. He used to go to France often and saw her on those trips.

London assumed that he made the journeys specially to visit her, but people always were assuming things about the Prince, as they now are assuming that he may contemplate marriage with Mrs. Simpson.

"David, the lady killer," was the characterization once applied to Edward by his sister, Princess Mary. That was years ago, before he had even heard of Mrs. Simpson.

The Princess was referring jokingly to the innumerable newspaper photographs showing the Prince (his family always called him David) in the company of beautiful women in various countries. But the ancient saw that many a true word is spoken in jest never was better exemplified.

The statistical chaps say that Edward has been the most publicized man in history. Certainly nobody ever has come anywhere near challenging his position as the world's most-sought-after bachelor. Great millionaires, screen stars and matinee idols have been also-rans.

Kept His Head

Attractive Women of many nations, including the United States, have been throwing themselves at him for years. It is a wonder he did not lose his head in the face of all the feminine adoration. But he showed common sense; and he is a gentleman. He never has displayed the characteristics of some of the woman-hunting Royalty on the Continent.

The King has been a paragon, compared to his august grandfather, Edward VII, who had the reputation of being one of the great lovers of all times.

Stories about Edward VII still enliven male conversation in England's club-land. The ladies get a pleasurable shudder of disapproval as they gossip over the tea-table about his mixed parties aboard Sir Thomas Lipton's yacht.

Lipton and Edward were great pals, but the famous sportsman and tea-merchant was a thorn in the side of the austere Queen Victoria. She used to read the riot act to her son for his wanderings, and she hated the ground that Lipton stood on.

Ever since Edward VIII was a mere youth, fascinated women and girls have followed him about in droves. Many times he has been the center of demonstrations of thousands of near-hysterical females who literally fought to get near him.

Prince Nearly Mobbed

A typical example was seen in November, 1927, when 5,000 women waited outside a motion picture theatre in London until Prince Charming came out. As he appeared the police could not hold back the frenzied hero-worshippers battling to get near enough to touch the Prince.

Many women fainted before police reinforcements finally cleared a path for His Royal Highness to his car.

The writer has seen a similar though milder demonstration on a ballroom floor when the Prince appeared. The other dancers would mill about him and his partner so that the slim young man and his lady would all but be swept off their feet—to say nothing of being unable to dance a step.

He was, of course, appearing in his capacity as Prince of Wales. When he was "off-duty" as royalty and wanted to dance, he was treated as an other private citizen, and people refrained from paying any attention to him.

Photographs Sent

Mash notes from lovesick girls all over the world have poured into Edward's headquarters daily. Frequently she of the palpitating heart sends her photograph in the hope that he may fall for a pretty face or figure.

A battery of male secretaries have handled these scented missives, and the King rarely has seen any of the notes. Occasionally some particularly choice bit may be handed on for his amusement. The letters go into capacious waste-baskets, and the great bulk is unanswered.

One eager and ambitious Texas girl wrote me in London and asked for the correct address of His Royal Highness so that she could indite an espistle to him. I gave her the address, but she might have had better luck if se had directed her attentions to a mere newspaperman.

In special cases girls have sometimes received autographed pictures of Edward. One such rare picture went to Anna Novotna, a Prague shop-girl. She sent the Prince a long love-letter in Czech, and she wrote so charmingly that her romantic letter got by the ordinarily hard-boiled secretaries to their chief. The photo was her reward.

It will be interesting to see what attitude King Edward's mother, Queen Mary, adopts in the present situation. She always has been so opposed to divorcees that she never would allow one to be presented to court.

Expect Queen's Backing

When Edward was young, the Queen used to stand between him and his father's displeasure. She has been a loving and loyal mother, and perhaps now she will thrust aside her own feelings and lifelong principles to back up her son.

It will also be interesting to see what the venerable Archbishop of Canterbury, head of the church of England, will do if he is called on to marry Edward to a divorcee. The church does not forbid such marriages, but it does not like them. The Archbishop would be rather "on the spot."

As far as English law is concerned, there is nothing to prevent the King's marriage to Mrs. Simpson. It is entirely up to him to decide whether such a move might harm his throne.

He might go to the extreme of abdicating in order to marry her, in which case the Duke of York would become King. If one wants to carry speculation to a somewhat absurd extreme, it is probable that Parliament could force his abdication, if it disapproved his marriage sufficiently. There has been no parallel case to provide precedent.

Beware Coughs from common colds That Hang On

No matter how many medicines you have tried for your cough, chest cold or bronchial irritation, you can get relief now with Creomulsion. Serious trouble may be brewing and you cannot afford to take a chance with anything less than Creomulsion, which goes right to the seat of the trouble to aid nature to soothe and heal the inflamed membranes as the germ-laden phlegm is loosened and expelled.

Even if other remedies have failed, don't be discouraged, your druggist is authorized to guarantee Creomulsion and to refund your money if you are not satisfied with results from the very first bottle. Get Creomulsion right now. (Adv.)

REVEL IN GOLDEN SUNSHINE

Keep tuned up! A week-end or longer does it at famous Colton Manor. Enjoy bracing fall air atop fascinating Ship's Deck overlooking ocean. Superb surroundings, luxurious accommodations, finest food. Rates no higher than ordinary hotels

ONE OF ATLANTIC CITY'S FINEST HOTELS

Colton Manor

Pennsylvania Ave. Paul Auchter, Mgr.

250 Rooms, each with bath

SPECIAL WEEK-END OFFER

As Low As $10 Room, Bath, All Meals — Friday after Breakfast thru Sunday — or Saturday thru Monday.

An Investment in WARMTH

HERE'S HEALTH, COMFORT AND HAPPINESS!

You get "all three" when you buy one of these heaters from the Henry B. Myers Company, now so low priced.

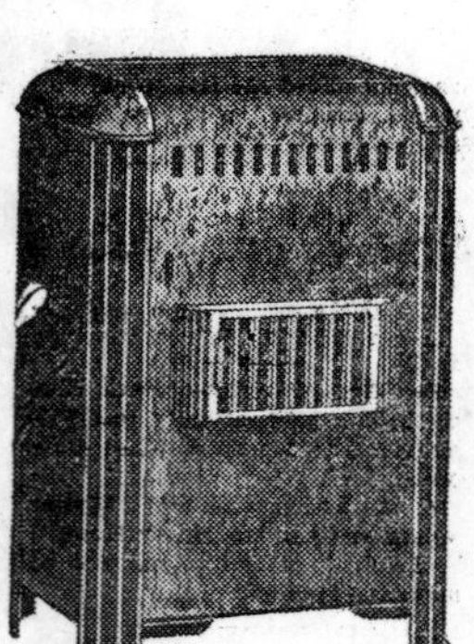

46x10 inch Firebox

Heaters $43.00

13x16 Firebox $53.50

A medium size Heater of astonishing efficiency. Burns inexpensive fuel perfectly. Radiates plenty of cheerful, healthful heat at smallest cost. Our low price brings the BEST in comfort within the reach of the modest purse. Mahogany finish.

Oil Heaters . . . . $5.50 to $12.75

Airtight Heaters . . . . $1.50 to $7.00

45-47-49 West St. THE HENRY B. MYERS CO. Phone 108

Bellwether for '37

WITH automobiles as with everything else, there has to be a leader of the flock.

All right then, step this way and feast your grateful eyes now on the authentic motor car bellwether for 1937!

Look at the size of it, the keen clean line of it, the streaming sweep of it, its neat fleet beauty.

It so perfectly captures in its beautifully contoured metal the dash and spirit of its buoyant action that it looks fast even when it's standing still!

Sure it's a Buick — the most stunning, sizeable, satisfying Buick that ever gladdened your startled gaze — but its good looks are literally the least of it.

Behind that massive radiator grille and under that gorgeous bonnet is an even bigger, smoother, valve-in-head straight-eight Buick engine, fed by an all-position aerobat carburetor that does thrifty things with gasoline.

And control of this magnificent performer — from thrilling take-off all through the range of speeds and including sure-stop hydraulic braking—is soft and easy as a fork in pie.

You can't describe it, so why handicap language this way — come in, *now*, see for yourself.

**Safety glass included — accessories slightly extra. Prices subject to change without notice. General Motors terms to suit your liking.*

"It's Buick again!"

YOUR MONEY GOES FARTHER IN A GENERAL MOTORS CAR

ANNAPOLIS BUICK COMPANY
240 WEST STREET
ANNAPOLIS, MD.

WHEN BETTER AUTOMOBILES ARE BUILT, BUICK WILL BUILD THEM

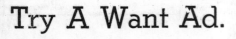

UNOFFICIAL TABULATION OF COUNTY BALLOTS

	First District				Second District								Third District								Fourth District					
	1st Prec.		2nd Prec.		1st Prec.			2nd Prec.		3rd Prec.			First Precinct				2nd Prec.				1st Prec.		2nd Prec.			
	A-J	K-Z	A-J	K-Z	A-F	G-Q	R-Z	A-J	K-Z	A-F	G-Q	R-Z	A-C	D-J	K-R	S-Z	A-C	D-J	K-R	S-Z	A-J	K-Z	A-C	D-J	K-R	S-Z
Roosevelt & Garner.	166	164	224	219	236	290	255	239	256	221	303	274	214	324	301	340	166	225	225	228	211	219	176	223	258	219
Landon & Knox.....	194	110	118	189	186	213	190	208	182	156	235	185	98	192	173	153	172	276	208	222	125	130	84	150	147	120
Gambrill...........	147	158	189	207	208	255	231	221	245	181	259	245	167	284	273	274	135	188	204	202	196	211	156	209	224	197
Rowe..............	166	96	108	181	159	194	162	217	166	157	255	184	83	151	134	114	158	265	196	202	106	98	67	139	128	92

	Fifth District									Annapolis									7th Dist.		8th Dist.		Totals	Annapolis
	1st Prec.			2nd Prec.			3rd. Prec.			1st Ward		2nd Ward		3rd. Ward			4th Ward							
	A-F	G-Q	R-Z	A-F	G-Q	R-Z	A-F	G-Q	R-Z	A-J	K-Z	A-J	K-Z	A-G	H-Q	R-Z	A-J	K-Z	A-J	K-Z	A-J	K-Z		
Roosevelt & Garner.	232	360	333	290	391	257	244	324	286	242	269	321	360	306	248	198	53	38	176	241	182	320	11,847	2,035
Landon & Knox.....	128	213	138	174	231	140	140	153	143	113	98	145	192	192	154	104	305	254	222	244	169	227	8,295	1,557
Gambrill...........	189	294	298	266	341	254	220	302	262	211	253	300	344	274	238	202	33	27	187	233	168	279	10,641	1,882
Rowe..............	106	173	111	148	194	100	118	135	102	100	88	144	179	176	133	96	259	215	172	191	142	194	7,254	1.390

ANNAPOLIS

Serving a Trading population of more than 25,000 in Annapolis and Anne Arundel County. Delivered in four of every five city homes.

Evening Capital

Weather Forecast Rain tonight and probably Thursday morning, changing to snow in west portion. Much colder tonight and tomorrow.

VOL. CIII — No. 150. ESTABLISHED IN 1884—PUBLISHED EVERY EVENING EXCEPT SUNDAY ANNAPOLIS, WEDNESDAY, NOVEMBER 4, 1936. THIS PUBLICATION IS PRINTED ON PAPER MADE BY LABOR IN THE UNITED STATES OF AMERICA PRICE TWO CENTS.

PRESIDENT ROOSEVELT TAKES ALL BUT TWO STATES FROM LANDON

Democrats Sweep City And County

President Roosevelt Easy Victor In Annapolis And Anne Arundel County — Congressman Gambrill Holds Big Edge Over Roscoe C. Rowe.

VICTORY DINNER FOR STATE SET FOR CITY

President Roosevelt's victorious sweep carried him to the front in Anne Arundel county, but a final check of the unofficial returns today showed that his majority was smaller than when he carried the county in 1932.

The President defeated Gov. Alfred M. Landon in the county, 11,847 to 8,295, a plurality of 3,552. In 1932 he rolled up a majority of 4,334 over former President Hoover.

The county electorate cast approximately 20,300 votes yesterday, compared to 15,933 four years ago.

COLORED VOTE SOLID

The colored voters of the county stood steadfast under the Republican banner. In the Fourth Ward of the city, in the heart of the colored section, Landon received 559 votes to 91 cast for Roosevelt, a Landon majority of 468. In 1932 the vote in the ward was Hoover 235, Roosevelt 69, a majority of 166 for the Republican candidate.

Rep. Stephen W. Gambrill (D-5th Md.) carried the city, home of his Republican opponent, State's Attorney Roscoe C. Rowe, of Anne Arundel county, by a 492 majority, but his county plurality dropped below his 1934 mark.

Vote In A. A. County

Gambrill took the county by a majority of 3,387, receiving 10,641 votes to 7,254 for Rowe. In 1934 the Democratic congressman won the county by a 4,296 majority, defeating Joseph A. Wilmer, 9,701 to 5,405.

The Young Democratic Club of Anne Arundel County will hold a state-wide victory dinner late this month, it was announced today by [illegible]ner M. Jackson, Jr., club president.

Mr. Jackson said that the execu-

(Continued on Page 6)

SPECIAL SALE

Large Chrysanthemums $2.00 doz.
Large Boston Ferns.......75c each
Philodentron ....35c each

CAPITAL CITY FLORIST
20 Murray Ave. Phone 942-J.

FOR SALE

Very desirable, modern dwelling on Southgate Avenue. 10 rooms, 2 baths, hot water heat, 3 car garage. Lot 78' x 135'. Inspection by appointment only.
BERNARD J. WIEGARD
Hotel Maryland Bldg. Phone 9

FOR RENT OR SALE

9 Room Dwelling on Duke of Gloucester Street. Hot water heat.
SERVICE AGENTS, INC.
H. H. LITTLE—F. E. VOGES
47 Maryland Avenue Phone 1477

FOR SALE

Dwelling on Prince George street with three apartments. Reasonably priced.
For particulars apply to
CHARLES F. LEE
Lee Bldg. Annapolis, Md.
Church Circle Phone 603

WM. MARTIN BRADY DIED AT HOME HERE; ILL SEVERAL MONTHS

Former Clerk Of Court Is Survived By Two Sisters, Two Brothers.

William Martin Brady, 69, former Clerk of the Anne Arundel County Circuit Court died yesterday at his home here. He had been ill for several months.

He was a member of the court house staff for 38 years, holding the office of Chief Deputy Clerk most of the time. He was appointed Clerk of the Court on the death of William N. Woodward, filling the office until the election of Frank S. Revell.

He was a power in Democratic ranks in the county for many years. His brother, former State Senator A. Theodore Brady, of Anne Arundel county, died 20 months ago.

He is survivey by two sisters, Miss Elizabeth Brady, and Mrs. Anna B. Wilson, and two brothers, Walter L. Brady, and Francis J. Brady, of Baltimore.

Mr. Brady was the son of the late John W., and Annie M. Revell Brady.

The funeral will take place at 10 o'clock Friday morning, from Saint Mary's Church, with interment in Saint Mary's cemetery.

OFFICERS ELECTED BY KIWANIS CLUB

Benjamin Michaelson Is New President, Succeeding Dr. Lyman F. Milliken; Dr. Coale, Vice-President.

At the well-attended luncheon meeting yesterday of the Annapolis Kiwanis Club, officers to serve for the ensuing year were elected as follows: president, Benjamin Michaelson, who will succeed Dr. Lyman F. Milliken; vice-president, Dr. J. J. Coale, pastor of the First Presbyterian Church: secretary-treasurer, Dr. William Y. Kitchin.

The directors elected were Judge Linwood L. Clark, Stephen W. Duckett, Harry S. Kenchington,

(Continued on Page 4)

Philip H. Dorsey Named to House

(By The Associated Press)

LEONARDTOWN, Md., Nov. 4.—Philip H. Dorsey, Jr., was elected to represent St. Mary's county in the House of Delegates by a vote of 3,130 to 1,692 for A. Kingsley Love, his Republican opponent.

Dorsey has represented the county in the House before. He and Love contested for the seat left vacant by the resignation of A. J. Lomax, who resigned after he was appointed State tobacco inspector.

NOTICE ELKS

Funeral services for our late Brother Wm. Martin Brady will be held Thursday, November 5th at 8 o'clock.

All members requested to meet at Elks Home at 7:45 P. M.

1t EXALTED RULER.

JULIAN BREWER AND SON
JOSEPH D. LAZENBY
3 School Street Tel. 815
Insurance of Every Kind
REAL ESTATE, SALES, RENTALS

REDS PIN HOPE ON ATTACK IN SOUTH SECTOR

Believe Fascists May Be Forced To Remove Madrid Besiegers To Relieve New Danger Point—Guns Thunder Within 3 Miles Of City.

HALT IS CALLED ON BOMBINGS

(By The Associated Press)

MADRID, Nov. 4.—Madrid, amid the crash of heavy cannonading and the continuous wail of air raid sirens, virtually completed today a long-expected cabinet shake-up to give the syndicalists a share in the government.

The government reorganization, 22nd since the fall of the Monarchy in 1931, came at the most critical moment in the history of the Republic.

Droves of insurgent planes circled back and forth over the Capital in continued assault on the morale of the civil population. Artillery fire on the battlefronts, a few miles to the South and West, echoed in the city streets.

Citizens Indoors

Most of the citizenry remained indoors. Occasionally, anti-aircraft guns blasted at the invaders when they ventured within range, but for the most part the planes stayed well out of reach, showing no immediate intention of beginning a bombardment.

The cabinet change involves the entry into the administration Premier of Francisco Largo Largo Caballero of four Syndicalists, one Ezquerra, or provisional automonist, and one Left Republican.

When the Largo Caballero cabi-

(Continued on Page 8)

BERNARD CRUTCHLEY DIED YESTERDAY IN EMERGENCY HOSPITAL

Bernard A. Crutchley, a former resident of Frederick, Md., and an employee of the Western Union Telegraph Company, died yesterday at the Emergency Hospital, where he had been a patient following a lingering illness of several months.

Mr. Crutchley, who was the son of Milton and Katharine Crutchley, of Frederick, is survived by his widow, Mrs. Edith A. Crutchley.

The funeral will take place at 11 o'clock Sunday morning from the Funeral Parlor of John M. Taylor, 147 Gloucester street, with interment in Woodlawn cemetery, Baltimore.

Prof. Robert Is Expert On Elections

It is interesting to note that Annapolis has an expert election prognosticator of its own. He is Prof. Henry M. Robert, of the Naval Academy faculty.

Professor Robert, co-author of Robert's Rules of Order, by which Congress and other official bodies of the country operate, said in advance of the election that he predicted an easy sweep for Roosevelt. In the 1932 election, Professor Robert had only one State wrong in his estimate of how the electoral vote would go. He was 100 per cent correct this year: also in 1928 and 1924.

Last night, at the Annapolitan Club, Professor Robert tabulated figures to bear out this prediction in every State.

Again The Choice Of The People

PRESIDENT FRANKLIN DELANO ROOSEVELT

ROOSEVELT IS GIVEN STATE'S BIGGEST VOTE

Unofficial Returns From 1,431 Of Maryland's 1,453 Precincts Give President 382,645 Votes To 226,070 For Landon — Democratic Congressmen Win.

FOUR COUNTIES IN G. O. P. COLUMN

(By The Associated Press)

Swelled by a record-breaking army of more than 600,000 voters, President Roosevelt's Maryland majority today passed the 155,000-mark—the greatest ever given a presidential candidate in this State.

Unofficial returns from 1,431 of 1,453 polling places gave Roosevelt 382,645, Landon 226,700, and a total of 608,715. The Roosevelt majority on that basis was 156,775, as compared with the 130,130 margin he received in the 1932 Democratic landslide.

The size of this year's vote compares with the 1932 total of 498,-

(Continued on Page 5)

Nice Will Give Roosevelt His Support, Aid

Governor Harry W. Nice today pledged his support to President Roosevelt, who, he said, faces a task for the next four years that will "try his soul."

In a statement issued today the Governor said:

"We made the best fight of which we were capable and offer no alibi for the result.

Must Have Support

"The election is over and it now becomes the duty of all American citizens to stand by the President. His task for the next four years will be one to try his very soul, and he must have the moral support of the people of this country.

"I feel that the work done by Mr. William P. Lawson should challenge the admiration of the Republicans of this State. From early morning until late at night he devoted his every hour to the accomplishment of Republican success. That he failed, as did we all, was not due to any lack of ability, cessation of activities, or absence of intelligent generalship, but due entirely to a nation-wide intention to re-elect Mr. Roosevelt.

Sent President Message

"Last night I sent the President

(Continued on Page 6)

ROOSEVELT FACES DIFFICULT TASKS IN NEXT 4 YEARS

President Expected To Take Definite Stand With Right Or Left.

By Byron Price
(By The Associated Press)

WASHINGTON, Nov. 4 — After the devastating triumph of President Roosevelt's party in the congressional elections of 1934, many wise observers felt that the returns left the most important questions unanswered. The same can be said of the election of 1936.

Again Mr. Roosevelt has won a tremendous victory. Again he has rallied to his support a multitudinous company of Americans who do not agree among themselves on many subjects, but whose philosophy of government and society spans a wide range. And again he has been vested with vast responsibilities, such as few men have known before him.

Hatreds Are Deep

The matter of first importance now is what Mr. Roosevelt will do with his responsibilities, what he will do with his victory. This has been no ordinary campaign. Its

(Continued on Page 5)

Kansas Governor Holds Lead In Vermont, Maine In Today's Late Returns

(By The Associated Press)

A Roosevelt landslide that shook the Nation today left but two States clinging to Republicanism.

Maine and Vermont alone clutched the beaten banner of Alf M. Landon. New Hampshire, after marching with him all night, finally turned into the victorious columns of Roosevelt in the morning returns to give the President a narrow lead.

All the other States already had given the Democratic presidential ticket-shouting majorities in the electoral college, sent new recruits to the previously top-heavy list of Democratic Senate and House members. The apparent electoral vote stood at 523 for Roosevelt, eight for Landon.

SMALLEST SINCE TAFT

The final thinning of the Republican ranks left the with the smallest electorial vote the party has had since the Taft debacle in 1912. Taft had eight votes; 88 had gone to Theodore Roosevelt, and the rest to Woodrow Wilson. Not since 1820, when James Munroe was re-elected, with only one dissenting vote in the electoral college, has there been so close an approach to unanimity of electors.

The New Deal plurality of popular vote seemed likely to approach 9,000,000.

Of the prize packages, heavily stuffed with electoral votes, California came to Roosevelt by half a million; Illinois by 600,000; Michigan by 100,000; New York by more than a million; Ohio by 300,000; Pennsylvania, the strong fortress of Republicanism, by 500,000.

Democrats Control Senate

In the Senate, the Democrats bade fair to hold 75 of the 96 seats. Senators Borah of Idaho and Norris of Nebraska, Independent Republicans, appeared to be escaping the landslide. Senator McNary of Oregon, the Republican leader, was having a hot fight and the veterans Hastings of Delaware and Metcalf of Rhode Island were beaten.

More Democratic House members instead of fewer seemed in prospect. In many states the issue was in doubt, however. The veteran Rep. Florence P. Kahn of California was beaten.

Of the governorships at stake, the Democrats had captured twelve, were leading for 14 others; the Republicans took two, were leading for three more.

While the President, smiling happily received the plaudits of supporters at Hyde Park, a message sped to him over the telegraph wires from the defeated governor of Kansas:

Landon Sends Wire

"The nation has spoken," Landon wired from Topeka. "Every American will accept the verdict, and work for the common cause of the good of our country. That is the spirit of democracy. You have my sincere congratulations."

After spending seven hours in receiving election returns—interrupted once to tell celebrating neighbors that it looked like "one of the largest sweeps" in history, Mr. Roosevelt received the Landon mes-

(Continued on Page 6)

Gambrill Defeats Rowe By 21, 617 In District

(By The Associated Press)

County	Pps.	Rptd.	Gambrill	Rowe
Anne Arundel..	49	48	10,641	7,254
Calvert	10	10	1,549	1,960
Charles	13	13	2,018	2,193
St. Mary's	13	13	1,957	1,587
Howard	14	14	3,606	2,064
Prince George's	45	45	13,133	6,066
Baltimore City.	55	55	15,037	4,218
Total	198	198	46,941	25,324

Fifth District congressional vote:

The vote by districts in the other Maryland congressional races:

First—169 of 186 polling places gave Goldsborough (D), 35,312; Lloyd (R), 24,062.

Second—374 of 420 gave Cole (D), 89,629; Whiteford (R), 53,175.

Third—157 (complete) gave Palmisano (D), 37,496; Hill (R), 23,945.

Fourth—234 of 235 gave Kennedy (D), 45,912; Ellison (R), 39,728.

Sixth—186 of 257 gave Lewis (D), 36,275; Legore (R), 28,027.

Rowe Congratulates Congressman Gambrill

State's Attorney Roscoe C. Rowe, Republican, Anne Arundel county, today congratulated his successful Democratic rival, Rep. Stephen W. Gambrill (5th. Md. Dist.) on his re-election.

In a telegram sent to Representative Gambrill in Washington, Rowe said:

"Congratulations on your re-election. We Republicans in the Fifth District fought our best cleanly. We join in wishing you success."

Card and Bingo Party

Given by
ST. MARY'S P. T. A.
FRIDAY, NOVEMBER 6, 8 P. M.
ST. MARY'S HALL
Bridge, 500, Bingo
ADMISSION 50 CENTS
Prizes and Refreshments
Please bring cards

Postage Due

DEAR EVERETT:

Is it true that you were on the Annapolis Public Library board for eleven months before you learned that you were the Association vice-president?

Yours,

Noe Zee

To: MR. B. EVERETT BEAVIN, Annapolis Dairy Products Co.

FEDERAL HOUSING LOANS
FOR REPAIRS AND EQUIPMENT
FOR LONG TERM MORTGAGE LOANS TO BUILD, BUY OR REFINANCE.
The Annapolis Banking & Trust Company
MAIN STREET AT CHURCH CIRCLE

Serving a Trading population of more than 25,000 in Annapolis and Anne Arundel County. Delivered in four of every five city homes.

ANNAPOLIS

Evening Capital

Weather Forecast
Cloudy, probably occasional light rain tonight and Sunday; somewhat colder Sunday.

VOL. CIII — No. 153. | ESTABLISHED IN 1884—PUBLISHED EVERY EVENING EXCEPT SUNDAY | ANNAPOLIS, SATURDAY, NOVEMBER 7, 1936. | THIS PUBLICATION IS PRINTED ON PAPER MADE BY LABOR IN THE UNITED STATES OF AMERICA | PRICE TWO CENTS.

HIGH SOCIALIST OFFICIALS FLEEING MADRID TODAY

State Garden Group Will Assist Restoration Society

Federated Garden Clubs Of Maryland Interested In Restoring Colonial Aspects Of Annapolis — Directors Of Company For Restoration Meets—Will Show Map On December 9.

At the meeting of the Board of Directors of the Company for the Restoration of Colonial Annapolis held yesterday afternoon in the Brice House business of unusual interest was transacted.

A letter was read from Mrs. Edward H. McKeon, President of the Federated Garden Clubs of Maryland, to the effect that their Pilgrimage Committe had voted to make "the object of their annual pilgrimage the Restoration and Preservation of Colonial Annapolis."

First Outside Recognition

This is the first recognition the company has received from an organization outside of Annapolis

It is most gratifying to know that the Company will have the support and interest of such a large and powerful organization, composed of thirty-four Garden Clubs, representing all parts of the State and having a membership reaching into the thousands.

New Member of Board

Mrs. Duncan K. Brent, a member of the Pilgrimage Committee was unanimously elected a member of the Board of Directors of the "Restoration Company," as was also John Churchill, well known architect of New York City, who has given much of his time and effort in the interest of the Company.

Plans are geing made for an open meeting to be held on Wednesday, December 9th for the purpose of showing the new map of old Annapolis which has recently been completed by Arthur Trader, Chief Clerk of the Hal of Records, in collaboration with B. Everet Beavin, formerly assistant enginer of the Annapolis Metropolitan Sewerage Commission.

To Be Shown By Forbes

This map, together with several old maps of Annapolis will be shown on the screen by George Forbes, former Annapolitan and for years an enthusiastic student of the History of Annapolis.

All citizens are cordially invited to attend this meeting and are especially urged to bring information and if possible documents and photographs relating to the early history of our ancient city.

Suggestions will be welcomed as to additions or corrections which should be made to the map.

The place of meeting, which has not yet been decided upon, will be announced later.

DANCE
Sponsored by the
NURSE'S CLUB
TUESDAY, NOV. 10TH, 1936
At Crownsville Hospital
ADMISSION 50 CENTS
n-7

NOTICE
Emergency Hospital

The annual meeting of the Hospital Association will take place on Monday, November 9th, 1936 at 8 P. M. in the Assembly Room of the Nurses' Home.

All persons interested in the welfare of this very necessary and useful institution and who wish to have a vote in its management, are invited to become members by the payment of not less than $2.00 annually, and the enrollment of their name by the treasurer Mrs. Edgar Basil care of the Emergency Hospital at once as all donations to the hospital to be included in this year's reports must be in before the meeting.

Every grown person in Annapolis who is interested in the Emergency Hospital is invited to attend this meeting, whether a subscriber or not. But only those who have subscribed to the amount of $2.00, or more, are invited to vote for managers.

(Signed)
BY ORDER OF THE BOARD.
xx

FOR SALE
Large on story building on East Street. Suitable for gagare and repair shop. Excellent central location for warehouse, shop or storage. Reasonably priced.
BERNARD J. WIEGARD
Hotel Maryland Bldg. Phone 9

PROFESSOR VASQUEZ TELLS COLLEGE WOMEN OF SPANISH REVOLT

Professor Angel C. Vasquez gave an interesting address to the College Womens Club Thursday evening at the Y.W.C.A. on the subject of Spain. Professor Vasquez talked chiefly of the change that had been wrought in Spain in the last few years and the reasons for the revolution. He told of his experiences in Spain just before the revolution and as interpreter on the Oklahoma during its maneuvers in Spanish waters to pick up Americans who were in Spain.

A lively discussion followed the address.

OLD-AGE PENSION REGISTRATION SOON

(By The Associated Press)

WASHINGTON, Nov. 7. — The long-planned registration of 26,000,000 workers for old-age pension accounts under the Social Security Act will begin November 16.

Making the announcement, the Security Board said 45,000 postoffices would distribute to employers on that date a form known as the "employer's application for identification number."

Local Legion Post To Hold Armistice Night Card Party

The Guy Carleton Parlett Post of the American Legion will hold an Armistice Day card party on Wednesday evening, November 11, at 8 o'clock, in St. Anne's Parish House, Duke of Gloucester street. There will be prizes and refreshments.

John Martin Green, of Acton Place, is Commander of the Post.

TO ENFORCE CULL LAW

(By The Associated Press)

BALTIMORE, Nov. 7. — Maryland's three-inch oyster cull law will be strictly enforced this year.

TWO HUNTERS KILLED

(By The Associated Press)

HARRISBURG, Pa., Nov. 7.—Death took a half-holiday at the opening of the Pennsylvania hunting season, and with the help of a game commission safety ruling cut its usually high toll of lives to two. At least 20 persons were wounded.

DEATH WON

(By The Associated Press)

WHEELING, W. Va., Nov. 7.—Among the victorious candidates in the election was Charles Schultz, chosen constable of Washington district. But Schultz never will take office. He died three months ago.

SEVERN TIED BY TOME GRID TEAM

Cashing in on their only chance to score, which came in the third quarter, the Tome football players yesterday deadlocked with Severn, 7 to 7, in a hard-fought contest at Severna Park.

The Tome squad was outplayed, but managed to stave off several scoring chances twice in the second quarter within the five-yard line. Tome was inside the Severn 40-yard line only once, and scored on that occasion.

STRAYED
SMALL FOX BEAGLE
Brown and white
Reward of $5.00 for its return
Call 1837F12
n-9

JULIAN BREWER AND SON
(JOSEPH D. LAZENBY)
3 School Street Tel. 815
Offers for sale a duplex apartment at 16-18 Franklin Street. Two 6 room apartments, large lot, best neighborhood. Price $8,500.

JUNIOR RED CROSS TEACHES SERVICE

Fundamental Precepts Taught To Youth Of Nation—Is Children's "Own Show."

A nationally known educator has said: "The Junior Red Cross builds character by teaching the youth of our nation the fundamental precepts of service to others. It builds for a deeper friendship among nations tomorrow through a better understanding between the youth of nations today."

But perhaps the Juniors themselves can best sum up the greatest single factor in the formation and maintenance of an organization which, in this country alone, boasts a roster of 8,350,000 boys and girls. As one boy put it, "The Junior Red Cross is our own show and we know it!"

Pick Own Project

The Junior Red Cross IS the children's own show. An able leadership coordinates its effort, but it is not led. In service, the Juniors pick their own projects; in organization, they choose their own leaders. The Junior Red Cross is an alignment of the home, school and child with particular emphasis upon the CHILD. It is adults who are led—who are privileged to follow, with pardonable pride, the selfless community, national and international efforts of these youngsters to help the other fellow.

It is significent, I think, that in this great program of service the child learns to attach less importance to himself. The first person "I" is sublimated to the symbol of community effort. When the Junior member speaks of his part in service to others he invariable says "We". To me, this is an important commentary on the direct benefits to the child through active association with the organization.

Local Organization

The organization of the Junior Red Cross is grouped by schools. Since each community offers different economic problems, each group of children must use initiative in effecting a solution.

Mrs. Roderick S. Merrick is chairman of the Junior Red Cross organization for the Annapolis and Anne Arundel County Chapter of the Red Cross. Active Junior Red Cross units are now in operation in a number of the local schools.

LOCAL SERVICE IN CONNECTION WITH PREACHING MISSION

Annapolis is to have a share in the nation-wide Preaching Mission in the latter part of November.

More than that, the place where the local service is to be held is suggestive of the national scope of the movement; for, it is arranged for it to take place in the Naval Academy Chapel.

While under the auspices of the Ministers' Association, the service is intended for all the people of Annapolis and the county who care to attend, whether connected with the churches represented by the Association or not.

Fuller particulars will be given later, but it is already settled that the service will be held on Monday November 23, at 8 P. M. The speaker will be the Right Rev. Henry Wise Hobson, Bishop of Southern Ohio.

Ladies' Sewing Circle Of Eastport Church To Present Play

A three-act play, entitled "Clubbing A Husband," will be presented by the Ladies' Sewing Circle of the Eastport M. E. Church, on Tuesday, November 10, at 8 P. M. in the church basement, at the corner of Chesapeake avenue and First street.

Ice cream and homemade candy will be on sale.

This entertainment is open to the public.

"Old Bill" Navy's Goat Mascot To Be Ousted If Team Don't Win Today

Naval Academy Mascot Who Came From Stockyards Will Be Returned There Unless He Gets Middies Out of Their Losing Streak

Ole Bill's nose is figuratively out of joint.

Ole Bill has been doing the mascoting for the Naval Academy football team since he helped win the Army game of 1934, but his powers have been diminishing ever since.

And now he has a rival in the person of a nobody from Texas. Advices from Dallas, Texas, today said that an Angora goat had been presented to the Naval Academy by a rancher, and that he would be in the line of march for the Army-Navy game, November 28.

MAY LOSE HIS LUXURY

Captain Robert R. Giffen, director of athletics, said today he was going to give Ole Bill another chance, and if the animal did not do his stuff, he was going before the selection board and would be passed over in a big way.

"We took Ole Bill from the Baltimore stockyards, dirty and unkempt," Captain Giffen said. "We bathed him, combed his hair, gilded his horns, and made him the pampered pet of the midshipmen.

"He better produce today, or else he leaves his life of luxury and returns to the humble surroundings of the stockyard," Giffen added.

When interviewed today, Ole Bill sneered goatishly at his alleged rival.

"Why I could out-butt, out-mascot that sissy from Texas with one leg tied behind me," he said.

WANT A GIANT GOAT

"Whoever heard of Texas in connection with naval affairs. They produce cowboys, long-horn steers and Rangers. All very fine in their places, but they know nothing of deep water sailors."

"Did you come from seafarin' goats, Bill?" he was asked.

'Ba-a-a-a," was the disgusted answer. "When a man joins the Navy, do not ask too much about his past.

"You just watch me with those Irishmen!"

And the Navy says Bill will be watched. The Captain added as a final threat: "He wins today or out he goes. The kind of goat I want is as big as a yearling steer with fire in his eye."

BILL NEEDED HELP LAST WEEK

Navy has lost three games in a row—Yale and Princeton winning on breaks, while Penn last week had too much power. In Philadelphia last Saturday, Penn students nearly pulled Old Bill apart. They surrounded the goat and attempted to pull the Navy blanket from his back. Middie cheerleaders and a handful of future admirals were obliged to rush from the stands and rescue Bill.

(By The Associated Press)

OFFER OF A NEW GOAT

DALLAS, Tex., Nov. 7.—An Angora goat, registered as "Admiral Halbert," became a mascot of the Naval Academy today to parade at the Army-Navy football game in Philadelphia November 28.

The goat was a present to the Navy from the Texas Centennial Exposition at ceremonies today. Lieut. C. H. Anderson, head of the naval company stationed at the exposition, represented the Academy at the exercises.

D. M. Halbert, of Sonora, Tex., gave the goat to the exposition to present to the Navy for the game.

Amelia Earhart Academy First Woman Speaker

Mrs. Amelia Earhart Putnam, aviatrix, shattered another record last night when she became the first woman to address a graduating class at the Naval Academy in the series of lectures that are included in the course in English and history.

She described her 1935 solo flight from Honolulu to Oakland, Calif., to an audience of midshipmen, officers and instructors at the Naval Academy, who, with their friends and families, filled Mahan Hall to capacity. Dr. Carroll S. Alden, head of the Department of English and History, announced she had set a precedent.

Guest Of Admiral

Mrs. Putnam, with her husband, George Palmer Putnam, is the house guest of Rear-Admiral David Foote Sellers, superintendent of the Academy, and Mrs. Sellers. They will be the Admiral's guests today in his box at the Navy-Notre Dame football game in Baltimore.

Shattering a record is nothing unusual for Mrs. Putnam. The list of her "firsts" includes:

First woman to fly the Atlantic.

First woman to fly the Atlantic solo.

First woman to fly the Atlantic twice.

First woman to fly an autogiro.

First woman to receive the Distinguished Service Cross.

First woman to receive the special gold medal of the National Geographic Society.

First woman to make a transcontinental non-stop flight.

First woman licensed in United States to carry passengers for hire in cabin planes weighing up to 7,700 pounds.

First person to make a solo flight from Honolulu to California.

Describes Flight

Last night she described this Pacific flight in detail. She declared she had no reason for making any flight "except my own wish to do so."

She said all worrying about a flight should be done two months before it gets underway; that, after hazards were considered, if the goal is not worth the hazards, then the expedition should be abandoned.

After Zioncheck

That's a smile of victory on the face of Warren G. Magnuson of Seattle, Wash., who succeeds his friend, the late Marion Zioncheck, in the House of Representatives at Washington. He was elected on the Democratic ticket, and was county prosecutor. (Associated Press Photo)

BERNARD CRUTCHLEY LAID TO REST TODAY IN WOODLAWN CEMETERY

The funeral of Bernard A. Crutchly, a former resident of Frederick, Md., and an employee of the Western Union Telegraph Company, who died Tuesday at the Emergency Hospital, where he had been a patient following a lingering illness of several months, took place at 11 o'clock this morning from the Funeral Parlor of John M. Taylor, 147 Gloucester street. The services were conducted by the Rev. Harry Yaggi, pastor of St. Martin's Evangelical Lutheran Church, assisted by the Rev. Dr. E. D. Johnson, rector of St. Anne's Episcopal Church.

The following served as pallbearers: Charles Talley, Louis E. Milton, Charles, Marion and Edgar Crutchley.

Interment was in Woodlawn cemetery, Baltimore, Md.

Mr. Crutchley who was the son of Milton and Katharine Crutchly, of Frederick, is survived by his widow, Mrs. Edith A. Crutchly.

BARRETT IS ELECTED D. A. V. COMMANDER

The Annapolis Chapter No. 3 Disabled American Veterans of the World War held their regular monthly meeting at the residence of Stewart U. Patton 11 Franklin street last evening.

The following officers were elected for the ensuing year of 1937: Commander, James H. Barrett; senior vice-Commander, Edgar A. Vey; Junior vice-commander, John Nicol; chaplain, George J. Crowley; quartermaster, Stewart U. Patton. Appointed officers will be announced later.

Report of "Forget-Me-Not Week" Nov. 7th to 11th Armistice Day inclusive" by committee stating that the public who wish to buy one of these flowers may do so at Harry M. Tongue's shoe store located at 36 Market Space.

A delegation from local chapter will attend the meeting to be held in Washington, D. C. Monday Nov. 9th in honor of National Commander M. Froome Barbour at the Army and Navy Club 1526 L St., Northwest, he will give a radio address over Station WMAL National Broadcasting blue network from 10:15 to 10:30 P. M. from coast to coast. All chapters not in this vicinity will hold meetings to listen to the commander.

HIGH SCHOOL P. T. A. TO BEGIN SERIES OF PANEL DISCUSSIONS

Beginning Monday night, at its regular meeting, the Parent-Teacher Association of the Annapolis High School will start a series of panel discussions on the general topic: "What Should A Parent Know About the School." Under this, there are numerous sub-topics, one or two of which will be taken up at each meeting.

The parents participating in Monday night's discussion will be: Mrs. C. C. Bramble, Mrs. W. A. Conrad, William A. Darden, the Rev. Paul R. Diehl and Mrs E. J. Klein, of Annapolis, and Mrs. Home Winchell, of Severna Park. The teachers taking part include: Miss Lorene Marking and Miss Kibler, of the English Department, and Edwin MaDan, of the Athletic Department, of Annapolis High School.

The leader of the discussion will be Mrs. G. R. Clements.

Henrietta Himberg Died This Morning; Funeral on Monday

The funeral of Henrietta Mary Himberg, daughter of Mr. and Mrs. Henry L. Himberg, who died this morning at the Emergency Hospital here, will take place at 2 P. M., Monday, from the residence of her parents, with interment in St. Andrew's cemetery, at Mayo

MARYLAND FARMLANDS SHOW GAIN IN VALUE

(By The Associated Press)

WASHINGTION, Nov. 7—The Department of Agriculture said today that farm land values in Maryland in 1936 showed an increase of three per cent over the preceding year.

An average value per acre for the nation as a whole rose four per cent above the 1935 figure, from 79 per cent of the pre-war level to 82 per cent.

The deparment did not estimate the increase in value on a dollar basis.

O'CONOR OVERRULES GORDY

(By The Associated Press)

BALTIMORE, Nov. 7.—Attorney-General Herbert R. O'Conor held invalid yesterday a regulation by the State Comptroller requiring printers to furnish information regarding disposition of tickets or admission cards, for use in determining the levy of admission taxes.

FOOTBALL
SOUTHERN A. C.
vs.
Hampden Badgers, of Baltimore
at the
West Annapolis Field
Sunday, Nov. 7th
Time 2:30 ADMISSION 25c
*A League Game

FOR RENT OR SALE
9 Room Dwelling on Duke of Gloucester Street. Hot water heat.
SERVICE AGENTS, INC.
H. H. LITTLE—F. E. VOGES
47 Maryland Avenue Phone 1477

FOR SALE
Dwelling on Prince George street with three apartments. Reasonably priced.
For particulars apply to
CHARLES F. LEE
Lee Bldg. Church Circle Annapolis, Md. Phone 603

FEAR OF MOORS GRIPS REDS AS END IS NEAR

Flesh-torn Women, Militiamen And Workers Stream Back Into Capital Whispering Terror Of Advancing Mohammedans — Shells Rock City.

FOOD GONE; MANY SEEKING HAVENS

(By The Associated Press)

LONDON, Nov. 7.— Foreign diplomats were informed today that members of the Spanish government had fled from Madrid to Valencia.

Only Premier Francisco Largo Carallero remained at the capital, the diplomats were told.

The exchange telegraphic agency said it had received word from Madrid at 12:56 P. M., that the "government retired in order that the lives of civilians might be saved."

Madrid still was occupied by government troops, the agency said.

Madrid was isolated from telephone communication to the outside world today.

London telephone officials said a call from the Associated Press bureau in Madrid to the London bureau, at 4:25 A. M. was the last connection before communications were cut off.

(Editor's Note —The following dispatch from an Associated Press correspondent is the message referred to in the dispatch from London

By James C. Oldfield
(By The Associated Press)

MADRID, Nov 7—Spain's Leftist government decided to abandon Madrid today. Terrified thousands fled eastward out of the capital.

The quaking populace that remained heard the ever nearing din of battle as fierce Moorish hordes of the Fascist attackers invaded the outskirts of the city.

Fear-stricken women and children, even men, voiced the dread question paramount in every mind of those remaining in the seemingly doomed capital:

Fear Moors

"What will the Moors do? Will they kill us all?"

As mounting panic swept the city,

(Continued on Page 4)

Postage Due

DEAR MISS SHEA:

Did you know that at least one of your nurses is a zealous voter, for, after she used a pen to mark her ballot, she then read it would be thrown out, which caused her to hurriedly return to the polling house, where she asked for a new ballot and her old one back—which, of course, couldn't be done?

Yours,

Noe Zee

To: MISS KATHERINE V. SHEA, Superintendent, Emergency Hospital.

FOOTBALL
GERMANTOWN RED RAIDERS
Vs.
METROPOLITAN POLICE BOYS' CLUB
SUNDAY, NOV. 8TH—2:30 P. M.—At Annapolis Ball Park

FEDERAL HOUSING LOANS
FOR REPAIRS AND EQUIPMENT
FOR LONG TERM MORTGAGE LOANS TO BUILD, BUY OR REFINANCE.
The Annapolis Banking & Trust Company
MAIN STREET AT CHURCH CIRCLE

MERCY on a WIDESPREAD FRONT

Red Cross Public Health Nurses engaged in a typhoid epidemic in Kentucky start for their rounds of visits. Red Cross nurses, besides year around work in almost 700 communities, are called for disaster relief and in epidemics.

The stork brought this youngster during the height of Johnstown, Pa., flood, but Red Cross nurses and hospitals were ready for such emergencies.

Through its varied services the Red Cross aids disaster stricken; safeguards life; helps the needy; trains for safety; protects public health. Your Membership in the Red Cross supports this free service.

Canteen workers organized on a volunteer basis give such vital help as this in time of disaster. These are members of Springfield, Mass., Canteen Corps who fed thousands during 1936 Spring floods.

Through the Home Hygiene and Care of the Sick courses of the Red Cross thousands learn better health. Here is a Junior Red Cross member learning hygiene for the baby.

When you see this sign it means there is a Red Cross First Aid station close by, where first aiders are trained to treat the injured. This new service of the Red Cross has dotted the nation's highways with first aid posts, in a drive against the huge death toll from motor accidents.

Junior Red Cross boys and girls of Toledo, Ohio, devote spare hours to repairing and making toys for other children. Eight million children are enrolled under the banner "I Serve" for such volunteer work.

During 1936 floods and tornadoes the Red Cross rescued, fed, clothed, housed and gave medical aid to 131,000 families. Rescue workers shown at Wilkes-Barre, Pa.

Army bombers dropped food on flood isolated sections of Pennsylvania for the Red Cross during 1936 Spring floods—a dramatic phase of Red Cross disaster relief.

Hundreds of Red Cross volunteers write books in braille for blind readers. Photo shows W.P.A. worker brailling a book under direction of Red Cross.

High on the mountainside the Red Cross first aider is prepared to treat the injuries of the ski jumper. More than a million persons have been trained in this aid to the injured work, and approximately the same number in water life saving.

COAST STRIKERS TAKE IT EASY

All was quiet on the San Francisco waterfront when this picture was taken. Shipyard picketers amused themselves the best they could while labor leaders and employers strove to end the deadlock that threatens to tie up shipping on both seaboards. (Associated Press)

SPANISH CHURCH DESTROYED

Here is the wreckage of a church at Getafe, Spain, pulverized in artillery bombardments as insurgents marched on Madrid. This picture was rushed to Paris by courier, transmitted to London by wire and radioed to New York. (Associated Press Photo)

Tank Captured By Spanish Insurgents

Insurgent soldiers are shown inspecting a Loyalist tank captured outside of Madrid during fighting near the suburbs. This picture was sent to Paris by courier, transmitted to London by wire and radioed to New York. (Associated Press Photo)

HEROES OF AMERICAN HISTORY

"GIVE ME LIBERTY, OR GIVE ME DEATH!" ... PATRICK HENRY

Patrick Henry was a very lazy youngster. He preferred hunting and fishing to school, and often sneaked away to the woods when he was supposed to be in class. However, he had the marvelous gift of oratory and became a famous lawyer. In court he once made a mistake and argued in masterly fashion on behalf of his opponent. Told of his error, Henry brilliantly answered his own arguments, and won the case!

Patrick Henry was the father of seventeen children. He was very popular and was later governor of Virginia for many terms. In 1775, with the revolution at a critical stage, he made his famous "speech against the tyranny of England, ending with the immortal words: "I know not what course others may take, but as for me, give me liberty or give me death!"

© Grosset & Dunlap.—WNU Service.

CHAPLIN REPORTED MARRIED

(By The Associated Press)

LOS ANGELES, Nov. 10.— The Examiner, in a copyrighted story, today said the marriage of Charlie Chaplin and his protege, Paulette Goddard, has been confirmed by Randolph Churchill, son of the British Chancellor of the Exchequer.

A CARGO OF CULTURE

A vast cargo of culture is daily carried over the ether waves of the United States. Loaded in Washington, the cargo is delivered through the radio loud speakers to thousands of American citizens, reaching those in the most remote outposts of our national life.

Behind this, the most famous school of the air, is the enterprise of the Federal Government. Making use of the discoveries of its vast research staff, the Government, through the Office of Education, disseminating information and instruction on a scale never before attempted. The story of the venture, one of the most novel ever undertaken in a field of education, is told in an illustrated article in the feature section of The Evening Star, Saturday, November 14.

GREAT DISASTERS IN AMERICAN HISTORY   The Johnstown Flood, 1889

HEAVY SPRING RAINS STARTED THE DEBACLE. FOR WEEKS THE DOWNPOUR DELUGED JOHNSTOWN AND VICINITY, BUT THE CONEMAUGH DAM ABOVE THE CITY WAS THOUGHT SAFE.

WITHOUT WARNING, ON A FRIDAY AFTERNOON, THE DAM BURST. A WALL OF WATER ROARED DOWN ON THE UNSUSPECTING CITY AT A MILE-A-MINUTE CLIP.

WHEN THE WATERS RECEDED, FRANTIC SEARCHERS FOUND MORE THAN 2,200 PERSONS HAD BEEN DROWNED—OTHER THOUSANDS WERE BADLY INJURED.

IN WASHINGTON, CLARA BARTON, ORGANIZER OF THE AMERICAN RED CROSS, GATHERED HOSPITAL SUPPLIES, FOOD, CLOTHING AND LUMBER AND HASTENED TO THE STRICKEN CITY.

SHE BUILT SHELTERS FOR HOMELESS REFUGEES, CLOTHED AND FED THE DISASTER VICTIMS AND AIDED IN BRINGING ORDER OUT OF CHAOS.

Associated Press Picks St. John's To Lose, Middie Team To Win

(By The Associated Press)

NEW YORK, Nov. 13 — Totally disregarding the vaunted evil influence of Friday the 13th on the theory that things could not be any worse, this football guesser arises from the resin and leads again with the chin.

Princeton-Yale: Slow to get under way this year, the Tigers apparently are ready to roll along now while Yale, with not much reserve strength, has looked tired in its last two engagements. Princeton's impressive 41-13 rout of Cornell was enough to swing this ballot to the Tigers.

Army-Notre Dame. Notre Dame teams habitually reach their peak against the Cadets. Army's first team, possibly, is more effective than any single combination the Irish have put together this season but Notre Dame's tremendous store of reserves more than counter-balances that advantage. The nod, not too emphatic, goes to Notre Dame.

A Dog Fight

Nebraska-Pitt: A real dog-fight in prospect here. Nebraska has many scores to settle with the Panther and Husker teams notoriously are hard to beat at Lincoln. Despite all this and with a hasty glance at the nearest shelter, Pitt.

Minnesota-Texas: The Texans have no luck and they'll need that and plenty more here. Minnesota.

Washington-Southern California. Somebody, perhaps, is going to catch up with Washington before the Pacific Coast Conference season is over. Maybe Southern California will tomorrow but Washington gets the call until then.

Auburn-Louisiana State: Auburn's plenty tough but the Plainsmen seem to have done entirely too much traveling the last three weeks for their own good. Louisiana to maintain its undefeated status.

Georgia Tech-Alabama. There's danger for the Crimson Tide here but Alabama must be picked.

Navy Is Choice

Michigan-Northwestern: They're all aiming at Northwestern now but Michigan seemingly doesn't have the weapons to stop the undefeated, untied Wildcats. Northwestern, decisively.

Marquette-Mississippi: Marquette partisans still shudder over that narrow escape with Creighton last week. With that one out of its system, the Golden Avalanche to roll over unlucky Mississippi.

Harvard-Navy: Navy but it should be close.

Cornell-Dartmouth: Cornell will be tougher on its own battlefield but Dartmouth rates the call.

Columbia-Syracuse: The Lions aren't the same without Sid Luckman but we'll take 'em over Syracuse.

A Tough One

Duquesne-Carnegie: We'd settle for a tie but Duquesne seems to have the offensive edge and gets the nod.

Illinois-Ohio State: Ohio State but the Illini will be fresh after a week's layoff.

Iowa-Purdue: Iowa lacks cohesion and seems to be having internal trouble in the bargain. Purdue.

Chicago-Indiana. Indiana but the Hoosiers had better do a better job than they did against Syracuse.

Southern Methodist-Arkansas: No rhyme or reason to the Southwest Conference. Out of the hat. S. M. U.

Texas Christian-Centenary: Christian in pieces Centenary's tough defense.

Kansas-Michigan State: Michigan State.

Oklahoma-Missouri: The coin says Oklahoma.

Kansas State-Iowa State: Kansas State.

Baylor-Oklahoma A. and M.: Baylor.

Santa Clara-St. Mary's: Throw out past performances in this one but it still looks like Santa Clara.

Harvard-Navy: Navy but it should be close.

U.C.L.A.-Washington State: Hoping for the best, U.C.L.A.

California-Oregon: California's finally playing up to expectations and rates a clear-cut edge in this one.

Oregon State-Stanford: Two big come-back teams meet in this one. On sheer guess-work, Stanford.

North Carolina-Duke: The objective game for both and the winner is almost certain to annex the Southern Conference championship. On the records, Duke looks the more powerful and gets the nod.

Tulane-Georgia: Tulane on the rebound after the Alabama disaster.

Vanderbilt-Tennessee: The Volunteers look too tough for Vanderbilt.

Kentucky-Clemson: Kentucky.

Penn Has Punch

Penn-Penn State: Penn's too strong for the Nittany Lions.

Temple-Villanova: One of those traditional things. Spinning the coin, Temple.

Boston College-Western Maryland: The Bostons.

Brown-Holy Cross: Holy Cross' Crusaders.

Catholic-North Carolina State: It's time for Catholic to win one.

Manhattan-Georgetown: Close, Georgetown narrowly.

New York University-Rutgers: N. Y. U.

Amherst-Williams: Williams to win the "Little Three" title.

Wisconsin-Cincinnati: The Badgers of Wisconsin.

Xavier-Detroit: Likewise Detroit.

Florida-Sewanee: Sewanee's football luck's all bad.

Maryland but it's a near toss-up, close one, Furman.
close on, Furman.

Washington & Lee-William & Mary: The Generals, safely.

Virginia Tech-Virginia: Not much to choose. Tech.

Montana-Idaho: Out of the hat, Montana.

Utah-Texas Aggies: Two games in four days for the Aggies but we'll take 'em anyway.

Utah State-Colorado University: Nobody's scored on Utah State yet but Colorado's dangerous. Utah State.

Greeley-Colorado State: On a coin flip, Colorado State.

Denver-Brigham Young: Denver.

Swarthmore Is Chosen

Western State-Colorado College: The College.

St. John's and Swarthmore should provide good entertainment at Annapolis. The Johnnies are a hard-fighting lot but Swarthmore seems more than a match for the eleven which tied Hampden-Sydney last week and has lost but one game all season. Swarthmore.

This is the time of the year that the best programs are on the air. Have your radio checked today, the cost is low.

Universal Sound Service

32½ West Street.   Phone 959

Maryland Should Win

Maryland-Virginia Military:

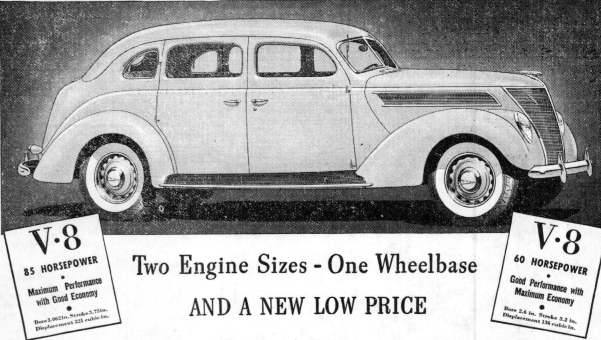

Evening Capital

ANNAPOLIS, MD.

1884 -:- 1936

Published Daily Except Sunday by
THE CAPITAL-GAZETTE PRESS, INCORPORATED

TALBOT T. SPEER, President
DAVID S JENKINS, Vice-President and Treasurer
E. M. JACKSON, JR., City Editor

You can have the EVENING CAPITAL mailed to you when away from the city by leaving your name and address at the office, for 45 cents per month: $5.00 per year payable in advance, to any postoffice in the United States or Canada.

Delivered in Annapolis, Eastport, Germantown and West Annapolis by Carrier for 45 cents per month. On sale at all newsstands.

Foreign Advertising Representative
J. J. DEVINE & ASSOCIATES, Inc.
New York—1932 Chrysler Bldg. Atlanta—206 Palmer Bldg.
Chicago—307 N. Michigan Ave. Pittsburgh—438 Oliver Bldg.
Detroit—817 New Center Bldg. Syracuse—State Tower Bldg.

Entered as Second Class Matter May 28, 1933, at the Post Office of Annapolis, Maryland under the Act of March 3, 1879.

MEMBERS OF THE ASSOCIATED PRESS

The Associated Press is exclusively entitled to the use for re-publication of all news credited to it or not otherwise credited in this paper and also the local news published herein. All rights of re-publication of special dispatches herein are also reserved.

TUESDAY, DECEMBER 1, 1936.

WARNING FROM THE FOREST'S CHILDREN

It seems advisable at this time to prepare for the worst. The storm windows and doors should be hung and the house should by all means be insulated. In addition, it would be well to get out the woolens. Charley Big Knife, Chippewa weather prophet from the Huron Mountain country, up in Michigan, who says he hasn't been wrong in forty years, reminds his public that all of the signs point to a long and hard winter.

"Ketch 'um big snow and plenty cold before next moon," Big Knife predicts. "Bear, muskrat, beaver, mink, loon and wild goose—him all say so and no tell 'um lie." And that isn't the whole story. "Muskrat build 'um house hurry-up and bear come out of swamp to look for place to sleep—everything no good." Furthermore, forest animals have thicker coats; the wild bees have begun their intensive gathering of honey weeks earlier than usual; the geese have gone South, and the snow-shoe rabbit is beginning to change his coat from brown to white, a transition which usually is reserved until later.

"Fish tell 'um same thing, too," Big Knife says. "Brook trout run up stream to spawn—him no wait for cold weather—and frog bury himself two feet in mud like winter 1917-1918. Everything plenty bad. Gitchi Manitou (Great Spirit)—him on warpath. Punish white people for talking all the time about election."

The prophet seems to have a great deal of evidence to support his dire forebodings. Surely, all of the bears and muskrats, beavers and mink, loons and wild geese, fish and bees can't be wrong.

ADVICE TO THE LOVELORN

Young people, pardon me this once for giving you advice,
I know it's very daring, but I'll finish in a trice,
Don't think a happy married life is just a throw of dice.

For:—Whatever other qualities, make sure your mate has three,
First tolerance, then humor, then adaptability.

Young man, a girl may lovely be, or then again not fair,
She may be crowned with Titian curls, or straight and mouse-like hair,
She may have soft and melting orbs, or give a squint eyed stare.

But:—Whatever her appearance is, make sure of virtues three,
First tolerance, then humor, then adaptability!

Young girl, a man may brilliant be, or eke a little dumb,
His mind with knowledge may be crammed, or mostly dazed with rum,
Success may stamp his noble brow, or he may look a bum.

Yet:—Whatever his intelligence, make sure of these traits three,
First tolerance, then humor, then adaptability.

And so, young people, fall in love, but heed experience,
Discriminate along these lines, and reap the recompence
Of happiness not only now, but twenty long years hence,

If:—Whatever other attributes, you make sure of these three,
First tolerance, then humor, then adaptability!

—D. A. C.

LETTER To The EDITOR

This column is provided by the Evening Capital to give its readers an opportunity to express their viewpoints. The Evening Capital reserves the right to reject any letters, or part of letters, and accepts no responsibility for the opinions contained therein.

OPPOSES SUNDAY BLUE LAWS

Editor The Evening Capital,

Dear Sir—I would like to express my opinion on closing the moving picture theatres in Annapolis on Sundays and the beer taverns. Can ministers tell me, that the Holy Bible states that moving pictures, which are shown on Sundays with the proceeds given to charity, are a sin? I say no, it is not a sin. God loves those who help others.

Does a person (HAVE TO GO TO CHURCH TO BE ON THE RIGHT SIDE OF GOD?) No they don't have to. Can't a person stay at home and have the pleasures that they like? Such as enjoying a clean decent moving picture and enjoy a bottle or a glass of beer in the taverns. Every tavern that you visit you will find clean, decent and respectable. The people who are in the beer business that sell beer on Sundays are not committing a sin, because they are making a living.

As for the closing of the beer taverns in Annapolis and Anne Arundel county, I think it is very UNJUST to the proprietors of business places. I will tell you the reasons why they should not be closed. The people in the beer business have a large overhead (heavy expenses) such as: Beer License, Trader's License, Restaurant License, etc. Rent, bartenders, waiters, ice, electricity, water bills, gas, coal and oil. And many other small items which make up the stock in their places of business. The proprietors order new stock on Mondays and Tuesdays, pay for it on Wednesdays and Thursdays. So they have to rely on Friday and Saturdays and Sundays to regain the money that they paid out the third and fourth day of the week and to live off the profits they make. The first four days of the week business is very slow. So they MUST depend on the last three days which business is very good.

Must we let a group of fanatics tell us "WHAT TO DO" and "WHAT NOT TO DO?" No we must not.

Yours sincerely.
A LAW ABIDING CITIZEN OF EASTPORT, MD.

Claiborne - Annapolis Matapeake Ferries

SAVE 100 MILES

FALL AND WINTER SCHEDULE

Effective September 29th, 1936

DAILY AND SUNDAY
Eastern Standard Time

BETWEEN ANNAPOLIS AND MATAPEAKE

Leave Annapolis	Leave Matapeake
9:00 a. m.	7:25 a. m.
11:00 a. m.	10:00 a. m.
1:00 p. m.	1:00 p. m.
2:00 p. m.	2:00 p. m.
3:00 p. m.	3:00 p. m.
4:00 p. m.	4:00 p. m.
6:00 p. m.	5:00 p. m.
8:00 p. m.	7:00 p. m.

BETWEEN ANNAPOLIS AND CLAIBORNE

Leave Annapolis	Leave Claiborne
8:00 a. m.	10:00 a. m.
5:00 p. m.	7:00 p. m.

THE CLAIBORNE-ANNAPOLIS FERRY COMPANY
Annapolis, Maryland

Washington Daybook
CAPITAL *Ins and Outs*

By Herbert Plummer

WASHINGTON—After a month's tour, Senator Thomas of Oklahoma has decided that Alaska is a good Pacific defense, useful as a safeguard for seals, rich in salmon and large scale mining, but no place for disheartened midwestern farmers.

Thomas toured Alaska in company with Senators Frazier of North Dakota and Shipstead of Minnesota. They were concerned with Indian welfare. A trip to the noted Matanuska valley settlement project was thrown in as a sideline but turned out to be one of their most impressive experiences.

* * *

Sees Project Folding

JUST how forcefully Thomas can impress congress with his findings is problematical, but he is against spending much more money on Matanuska. The project won't work, is already folding up, he said, and is valuable only in that it showed that Alaska is not a fit country for farming.

When white-haired red-faced Senator Thomas has a subject on his mind, he recites it to interviewers almost as if he had prepared it as a lesson. Here are some of the things he considered bad about Matanuska:

The sun shines practically 24 hours a day during July. Much of the rest of the year is winter, or nearly so. Garden crops mature so fast under such a flood of sun (from seed to table in two weeks) that they are nothing much but water. Radishes are flavorless as icicles. Potatoes won't keep. To permit storage, settlers have to heat their potatoes to steam off some of the water and that leaves them shriveled and ugly, unmarketable.

Oats can't mature, the season is so short, and when cut for hay turns black, he says. The same with grass.

The ground is frozen for 500 feet down, and thaws out only about 14 inches during the short summer. To an Oklahoman seasoned to much heartening sunlight, that is just like farming on an iceberg.

He predicts the settlers won't stay, once the federal government stops paying for the roads, schools and other civic needs. Already 75 families have gone, leaving about 250 in the valley. The cost of providing them with homes, machinery, livestock, schools and incidentals has mounted to $14,000 a farm, Thomas says, whereas the cost was supposed to be held to about $3,500.

* * *

Found No Side Line

THAT is about all from Senator Thomas about Matanuska except to add that he found no side line the settlers can follow. There are no fur-bearing animals in the vicinity, salmon fishing requires a large investment and mining even larger.

He saw a bright spot. Anyone in Alaska who wants a reindeer can go shoot one and haul it home without more ado, he says. That is easiest farther north, where there are more of them than around Matanuska. Reindeer meat is good to eat, but already the cattle-growing states are enacting laws to prevent it competing with beef. So as an industry he lists that, too, as limited.

He would vote for an appropriation bill to establish an air base in Alaska as good protection against Asiatic invasion.

The "Great" Pyramid is believed by many students to be a record of prophecy, and not a tomb.

AROUND THE RADIO DIAL

By BOB KAY, RADIO EDITOR

Editor's Note: Programs originating at WEAF may be heard over WFBR; those over WABC over WCAO, and those at WJZ over WBAL. This applies except when local programs interfere.

(By The Associated Press)

NEW YORK, Dec. 1.—One of the programs planned for the week-end in connection with the Inter-American Conference at Buenos Aires is an hour drama on WJZ-NBC for Saturday night, to be short-waved also toward South America. Called "New World," it is to depict in narrative and drama events leading up to the conference. On Sunday night WABC-CBS will have the second of its salutes in music and speech to the conference.

Tuning in tonight (Tuesday): Inter-American Congress — WJZ-NBC, 10—Secretary of State Hull and Dr. Carlos S. Lamas, Argentine Foreign Minister.

WEAF-NBC—7:15, Voice of Experience; 8, Leo Reisman Show; 9, Sidewalk Interviews; 9:30, Fred Astaire Revue; 10:30, Jimmy Fiddler; 11:45, Rudy Vallee Orchestra.

WABC-CBS — 8, Hammerstein Music Hall; 8:30, Ken Murray; 9, Pennsylvanians; 9:30, Rupert Hughes Caravan; 10:30, Mark Warnow Orchestra; 12:30, George Duffy Music.

WJZ-NBC—8, Dude Ranch; 8:30, Eddie Guest; 9, Ben Bernie Lads; 9:30, Husbands and Wives; 10:30, Eddy Duchin Orchestra.

What to expect Wednesday: Inter-American Congress — WABC-CBS, 3:30—program from Buenos Aires; WEAF-NBC, 6:20—Edward Tomlinson Resume; WABC-CBS, 6:35—H. V. Kaltenborn comment. Departure of President Roosevelt from Buenos Aires also is to be described by NBC and CBS at a time to be announced.

WEAF-NBC—2, Walter Logan's Musicale; 4, Henry Busse Orchestra. WABC-CBS—2:15, School of the Air; 3, Verdi's Requiem from Milan, [illegible] WJZ-NBC—10:45 A. M. and [illegible] M., National Council of Women: [illegible] Diesel Power luncheon. Speakers: David Sarnoff, Charles F. Kettering and others.

Some Wednesday short waves: TPA4, Paris—5:15 P. M., Concert; 2RO, Rome—6, American Hour; GSP, GSD, GSC, London—6:30, Visit to Cambridges; RAN, Moscow—7, Russian Operas; PCJ, Netherlands—7, Happy Program; DJD, Berlin—8:30, Musical Play; CJRO, CJRX, Winnipeg—9:30, Music to Remember; JVH, Tokyo—12, Overseas Program.

An Ordinance

AN ORDINANCE to repeal and re-enact with amendments Section 14 of Article 6 of the Charter and Code of the City of Annapolis, Annotated, (1935 Edition), title "Licenses," subtitle "Alcoholic Beverages," establishing the qualifications for applicants for liquor licenses in the City of Annapolis.

SECTION 1. BE IT ESTABLISHED AND ORDAINED, by the Mayor, Counselor and Aldermen of the City of Annapolis, that Section 14 of Article 6 of the Charter and Code of the City of Annapolis, Annotated (1935 Edition), title "Licenses, sub-title "Alcoholic Beverages" be and the same is hereby repealed and re-enacted with amendments to read as follows:

Sec. 14. Every person applying for a license to sell alcoholic beverages in said City shall file with the said Mayor, Counselor and Aldermen his, her, their or its petition for such license. Said petition for such license shall conform with the requirements of Article 2-B of the Code of Public General Laws of Maryland, and in addition said petitioner or petitioners shall be a resident of the City of Annapolis, and a voter therein.

SECTION 2. AND BE IT FURTHER ESTABLISHED AND ORDAINED, That this Ordinance shall take effect from the date of its passage.

APPROVED November 25, 1936.
ATTEST: (SEAL)
LOUIS N. PHIPPS, Mayor.
KATHERINE E. LINTHICUM, Clerk.
d-7

ORDER NISI

Upon the aforegoing Report, Affidavit and Certificate, it is, this 13th day of November, 1936, by the Circuit Court of Baltimore, City, ORDERED that the private sales of the property mentioned in these proceedings, made and reported by Harry Friedenwald and Julian S. Stein, Trustees, be ratified and confirmed unless cause to the contrary thereof be shown on or before the

16TH DAY OF DECEMBER, 1936.

Provided a copy of this order be inserted in some newspaper printed in Baltimore City and in Anne Arundel County, once in each of three successive weeks, before the 9th day of December, 1936.

ROBERT F. STANTON.
True Copy—Test.
CHAS. R. WHITEFORD, Clerk. d-1

M. Clare M. Green and Noah A. Hillman
Solicitors
Annapolis, Maryland

TRUSTEE'S SALE
OF VALUABLE
FEE SIMPLE PROPERTY
Situate in the Second Election District (Eastport) in Anne Arundel County.

By virtue of decree of the Circuit Court for Anne Arundel County, Maryland, dated the nineteenth day of November, 1936, and passed in a cause in said Court depending wherein Harwood G. Frazier et al, are Plaintiffs and Samuel R. Frazier, Jr. et al, are defendants, No. 6887 Equity, the undersigned, Trustees, will sell at Public Auction, at the Court House door in the City of Annapolis, Maryland, on

TUESDAY, DECEMBER 15 1936,
AT 11 O'CLOCK A. M.,

the following described property: An improved lot of ground on the east corner of Chester Avenue and Fourth Street fronting on Chester Avenue 82 feet 6 inches with a depth of 132 feet. Being Lot No. 112 on the Plat of Horn Point recorded among the Plat Records of Anne Arundel County in Plat Book G. W. No. 1, Section 1, folio 11, which was conveyed to Samuel R. Frazier by Thomas S. Beall and wife by Deed dated November 30, 1889, and recorded among the Land Records of Anne Arundel County in Liber S. H. No. 36, folio 72, Improved by 5 small frame dwellings.

TERMS OF SALE AS PRESCRIBED BY THE DECREE:—A deposit of one third part of the purchase money at the time of sale, the balance to be paid in two equal payments, the one to be paid in six months and the other in one year from date of sale, with interest at 6 per cent from date of sale, and to be secured by the notes of the purchaser or purchasers, with security to be approved by the Trustees, or all cash at the option of the purchasers.

All expenses, water rent, fire insurance and taxes to be adjusted to date of sale.

M. CLARE M. GREEN,
NOAH A. HILLMAN,
Trustees.
WM. H. MOSS & CO., Auctioneers.
d-14

CLASSIFIED ADS

SERVICE
(Phone 330)

RATES 2c PER WORD

This size type (6 point), Minimum ad 50c

Additional consecutive insertions 1c per word.

TELEPHONE SERVICE

If you are listed in the telephone directory we will accept your Want Ad over the phone and charge it to you. Charges must be paid 5 days after date of expiration of ad.

The Evening Capital will be responsible only for the first incorrect insertion of any advertisement and then only to the extent of a make good insertion.

Read your ads carefully and report any error immediately. The Evening Capital reserves the right to properly classify, revise, or reject any advertisement according to its option.

OUT-OF-TOWN ADS

All mail orders from advertisers outside of Annapolis must be accompanied by remittance.

FOR SALE

FOR SALE—Small girls used bicycle, see-saw. Apply Queen Anne's Cupboard, Maryland Avenue. d-2

FOR SALE—Boys' bicycle; in good condition. 13 German Street.

FOR SALE—Large stock of toys of all kinds. LOWEST PRICES! For real values see us. ANNAPOLIS FURNITURE CO., 96 West Street. d-5

WANTED

WANTED—Two or three room unfurnished apartment. Civilian couple (no children). Apply 52½ West St. d-3

WANTED—Maid for general housework. Apply 43 Southgate Ave. tf

FEMALE HELP WANTED

HELP WANTED—Colored girl, part time. 12 to 7 o'clock. $5.00 per week. Must be healthy and neat. Box 73, Evening Capital. d-1

Application For Oyster Ground

Jerome Nick Shady Side, Md.
About 3 Acres

Located in South Creek, on the easterly side thereof, a tributary of West River, and being the same ground formerly leased to Benjamin O. Crowner, in the waters of Anne Arundel County as shown on Published Chart No. 3.

The fourth and last insertion of this advertisement will appear in the issue dated December 1 1936. Protests must be filed with the Clerk of the Circuit Court for Anne Arundel County within thirty days thereafter.

CONSERVATION DEPARTMENT OF MARYLAND. d-1

FOR RENT

FOR RENT—Furnished apartment, oil heat and all conveniences. 376 Severn Avenue, Eastport. tf

FOR RENT—Six room bungalow, bath, and garage. Spa View Heights. Write Box 72, Evening Capital. tf

FOR RENT—House, corner 3rd and Chesapeake Avenue, Eastport. Apply 206 3rd Street, Eastport. Phone 759-J. d-1

FOR RENT—Apartment Maryland Avenue. Frigidaire, hot water, tile bath. $45. Phone 313. tf

FOR RENT—Two apartments, 2 and 3 rooms, private bath and entrance, 126 Main Street. Apply 200 Prince George Street. tf

FOR RENT—Bungalow, five rooms, bath. Two porches. Hot water heat. Located in Homewood. Mrs. George Rogers. Phone 875-R. tf

FOR RENT—6-room house, bath, gas, electricity. Apply 238 West Street. tf

FOR RENT—Two furnished rooms. One with private bath. 129 Monticello Ave. Phone 233. tf

FOR RENT—Unexpectedly available, attractive apartment, furnished, fireplace. Apply 205 Hanover St. tf

FOR RENT—Four room unfurnished apartment, heated; private bath. Available Nov. 20. Phone 195-J. tf

FOR RENT—Modern 3 room furnished apartment. 5 Murray Avenue. Call 356-J. tf

LOST

LOST—Child's blue knit skirt, Monday afternoon, near Naval Hospital, or State Circle at Randall Court. Reward if returned to Mrs. Pearson, 3 Acton Place. Phone 1073. d-1

An Ordinance

AN ORDINANCE to repeal and re-enact with amendments Section 10 of Article 10 of the Charter and Code of the City of Annapolis, Annotated, (1935 Edition), title "Public Safety," subtitle "Disorderly Conduct," regulating the laws for dancing in the City of Annapolis.

SECTION 1. BE IT ESTABLISHED AND ORDAINED by The Mayor, Counselor and Aldermen of the City of Annapolis, that Section 10 of Article 10 of the Charter and Code of the City of Annapolis, Annotated, (1935 Edition), title "Public Safety," subtitle "Disorderly Conduct," be and the same is hereby repealed and re-enacted with amendments to read as follows:

Sec. 10. Dancing or the playing of music of any kind shall not be permitted in any licensed public place within the limits of the City of Annapolis between the hours of 1 A. M. and 8 A. M. The owner, manager or licensee of any place where dancing is permitted between such hours shall be deemed to violate this section, and upon conviction thereof shall be fined not less than one dollar nor more than ten dollars, together with the cost of the prosecution, and the Mayor, Counselor and Aldermen of the City of Annapolis, shall, in their discretion, revoke the license of any person convicted for violation of this section, or may revoke such license under any circumstances if satisfied that this section is being violated.

SECTION 2. AND BE IT FURTHER ESTABLISHED AND ORDAINED, That this Ordinance shall take effect from the date of its passage.

APPROVED November 25, 1936.
ATTEST: (SEAL)
LOUIS N. PHIPPS, Mayor.
KATHERINE E. LINTHICUM, Clerk.
d-7

BUSINESS DIRECTORY

The services offered by the following Annapolis firms have been investigated by THE EVENING CAPITAL and found to be satisfactory.

TRANSFER

HAULING, done carefully and cheaply. Ernest Parker, Camp Parole, or Phone 330 Evening Capital. tf

*Jerome Bituminous
Colonial Anthracite
(Smokeless, High B. T. U.)
Fuel Oil Wood
"More heat per dollar"
ANNAPOLIS DAIRY
* Egg Size Oil Sprayed

Order your winter's supply of coal or fuel oil NOW.
H. B. MYERS CO.
47 West Street—Phone 108
Complete line of General Electric Refrigerators, Hardware, Feeds, Seeds, Farm Supplies and Sporting Goods. tf

PRINTING

Phone 330 and our representative will gladly call to give you prices on fine business printing.
CAPITAL-GAZETTE PRESS, INC.
3 Church Circle tf

AUTOMOBILES

ARUNDEL MOTORS
DeSoto—Plymouth
Sales and Service
28 West Street Phone 71
1y-25

ANNAPOLIS BUICK CO.
240 West Street
BUICK — OLDS
Used cars all makes and models
Phone 103 - 1085 tf

MEMORIALS

W. W. SULLIVAN
72 Northwest Street
Estimates cheerfully given on memorial markers.
Cemetery work a specialty

ORDER NISI

In the Circuit Court for Anne Arundel County

No. 6367 Equity

In the Matter of the Trust Estate of Folger McKinsey and Fannie H. McKinsey, his wife.

Ordered this 30th day of November, 1936, that the private sale of the property mentioned in these proceedings made and reported by Orlando Ridout, Jr., Trustee, be ratified and confirmed, unless cause to the contrary thereof be shown on or before the

31ST DAY OF DECEMBER, NEXT

Provided, a copy of this order be inserted in some newspaper published in Anne Arundel County, once in each of three successive weeks before the 31st day of December, next.

The report states that the amount of sales to be $600.00.

FRANK A. MUNROE, Clerk.
True Copy,
Test: FRANK A. MUNROE, Clerk.
d-15

CALL 123
GILBARCO
ESSOBURNER
ESSO FUEL OIL
SALES & SERVICE
ANNAPOLIS UTILITIES, INC.

SCORCHY SMITH — By John C. Terry

DOROTHY DARNIT — By Charles McManus

A.A.U. CONTROL BY GROUP HIT BY BRUNDAGE

Olympic Chieftain Says Organization Will Wither And Die Unless Democratic Principles Are Maintained—Fight For Presidency Resumed.

RETAIN SYSTEM OF MEAASURING

By Alan Gould

HOUSTON, Tex., Dec. 5 — After two days devoted to side-tracking Olympic controversies, shadow-boxing for political control, and wrestling with its 1937 sports program, delegates to the 48th convention of the Amateur Athletic Union faced a final, sharp warning today against a "divided house" from President Avery Brundage of Chicago.

The American Olympic chieftain, in a report marking his "farewell to A. A. U. arms," as he prepared to wield the convention gavel for the seventh and last time, declared the organization "will continue to grow and prosper if it confines itself to amateur sport alone."

'Tight Group Control

He added: "Once it is made the tool of some individual group or is used to serve political ambitions, for personal profit or for any other purpose alien to the objects as set forth in its constitution, it will, wither and die."

The statement to the first general session, reviving echoes of the Olympic fight which nearly disrupted the A.A.U. a year ago, followed committee struggles to whip the main business program into shape for final action.

Chief developments included:

1. Tightening of opposing lines in the contest between Jeremiah T. Mahoney and Major Patrick J. Walsh, two New York lawyers, for the presidency, with the indications the Mahoney forces were holding their pre-convention lead and that the Brundage-led group would lose control of the A.A.U. simultaneously with the retirement of their leader.

Retain Metric System

2. Committee recommendations to retain the metric system of measurement for national A.A.U. track and field championship, despite widespread dissatisfaction with this international standard. The proposal, however, involved "local option" for district or sectional "meets, which would have a choice between the metric or yardage system.

3. A major setback for the "Olympic tax" idea as a consequence of the track and field committee's rejection of the administration scheme to collect five cents per admission, on all A.A.U. events, as long-term means of building up funds for America's Olympic teams. The wrestling committee favored such a tax on all admissions of 75 cents or over. Brundage's report suggested collecting five cents for all admissions up to $1, ten cents on all tickets of higher value.

Would Liberalize Rules

4. A proposal by Lorrin Andrews of Los Angeles, president of the Southern Pacific Association, to "liberalize amateur rules" by naming a committee to study the situation, eliminate "rut-worn complications" and recommend a clarified amateur code for adoption at the 1937 convention.

Brundage's report prefaced its sweeping admonishment to the delegates by citing the organization's growth from a membership of 24 to 38 district associations since he first was elected president in 1928. It hailed the prospective affiliation of two new national groups, the Junior Chamber of Commerce of the United States and the Catholic Youth Organization, as allied members, with working agreements similar to those already established with the National Collegiate A. A. and the Y.M.C.A.

STAR THEATRE

CASH NITE
TONIGHT
"Elks Convention Of 1936"

ALSO

Adolph Zukor presents

"A SON COMES HOME"

— Also Added Attraction. —

FEW LOCAL FINES REPORTED BY STATE AUTO COMMISSIONER

Although the total fines collected throughout the state for violations of the motor vehicle traffic laws amounted to $7,030 during the week from November 25 to December 2, inclusive, no Annapolis arrests and few from other Anne Arundel county communities were listed in the State Automobile Commissioner's report for the period.

Of the state-wide total, $3,818 represented the Baltimore City fines and $3,212 those turned in from the counties of Maryland.

At Glen Burnie two fines were reported, Andrew Jackson, Jr., having been assessed $5 for failing to stop at a boulevard intersection, and George J. Miller $1 for not having his registration card in his possession.

At Jessup, the following were fined:

Burch, John H., $5, exceeding 35 miles; Kinney, H. S., $25, exceeding 45 miles; Preston, Gunner F., $100, operating under influence of liquor; Zimmerman, Chas. J., $5, failing to carry flares.

Need cash? Advertise those odds and ends. Someone wants them. Phone 330.

SPECIAL SALE
Xmas Toys

AND GIFTS FOR THE HOME. OUR STOCK IS NOW COMPLETE. WE ARE OFFERING SEASONABLE GIFTS OF ALL KINDS

—AT THE—

Lowest Prices
In Our History

Come In! Let Us Show You!

Annapolis Furniture Co.

94-96 WEST STREET

Open Late Every Night

CONSERVATION LAWS COMMITTEE FORMED

(By The Associated Press)

BALTIMORE, Dec. 5—T. H. Hubbard, a member of the State Planning Commission, announced the formation of a steering committee to guide legislative proposals looking to improvement of the State's oyster and crab resources. The steering committee will coordinate the recommendations of conservation and industrial leaders with those of the Planning Commission.

HUNTER KILLED

(By The Associated Press)

OAKLAND, Md., Dec. 4.—Elwood Orenders, 17-year-old hunter, who was killed by a shotgun blast while walking along a mountain trail. is Maryland's first 1936 hunting victim.

CIRCLE THEATRE
The Show Place of Broadway Entertainments

CONTINUOUS DAILY
1:30 'TILL 11 P. M.

FEATURE PRESENTATIONS 1:30, 3:30, 5:30, 7:30, 9:30 P. M.

TODAY—LAST SHOWINGS

TARZAN, KING OF THE JUNGLE!

Matching his Herculean strength with the Beasts of the Jungle!

TARZAN Escapes

with
Johnny WEISSMULLER
Maureen O'SULLIVAN

COMING—MONDAY AND TUESDAY

EDNA FERBER'S

"COME and GET IT"

with
EDWARD ARNOLD
JOEL McCREA
Frances FARMER

THRILLING DRAMA OF THE NORTH WOODS

Republic Theatre

—TODAY—

ROMANCE! RHYTHM-M-M! SONGS! SWINGOPATION!

Bing's best! As he rolls down the open road with a guitar and a yen for a gorgeous gal who done him wrong!

Pennies from Heaven

BING CROSBY

MADGE EVANS
EDITH FELLOWS
LOUIS ARMSTRONG
and His Famous Swing Band

From the story by and An Emanuel Cohen Production
A COLUMBIA PICTURE

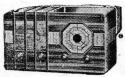

HEAR . . HEAR . .
"Let's Call a Heart a Heart"
"One, Two, Button Your Shoe"
"Skeleton in the Closet"
"Pennies From Heaven"
"So Do I"

—Added Features—
A NOVELTY AND NEWS

Special Pictures Of The
ARMY-NAVY GAME
Now Showing

MONDAY AND TUESDAY
Double Feature
"LADY FROM NOWHERE" and "STAMPEDE"

COMING SOON
"3 MEN ON A HORSE"

CHANUKAH STARTED AT SUNSET TUESDAY

At sunset, on the twenty-fourth of "Kislev," which corresponds this year to Tuesday, December 8, the Jews the world over usher in Chanuka, the Festival of Lights. This holiday lasts eight days, ending this year at sunset, on Wednesday, December 16. On the first evening one candle is lit, and every evening an additional candle is lighted until, on the eighth evening, eight little candles shed their light from the window of every Jewish home.

The Chanukah candles signalize the victory of the Jews more than two thousand years ago over the tyranny and despotism of the Syrian Antiochus. The semi-insane Antiochus, relying on his military power and the promises of the Jewish Hellinists, tried to force idol worship upon Judea.

A terrible time came upon the Jews who remained steadfast in their faith. Syrian soldiers were stationed in all important towns of Judea, altars were erected to the Greek idols and the Jews under the penalty of death were forced to worship them. Even the Temple of Jerusalem was defiled by idol worship. Naturally, the truly pious Jews did not yield. Many Jews sacrificed their lives and many more sought refuge in caves.

Perhaps the most heartrending instance of the martyrdom of that time is the death of Hannah and her seven sons. Every one of the young men met death bravely, rather than worship idols or do anything which would give the impression that they were doing so. The youngest, a mere child, was ordered to pick up a ring which was dropped near the altar of the idol, in order that the bystanders should think that he bowed to the idol. Even this child refused to do so whereupon he was executed.

The name "Chanukah" means dedication and is applied here to the rededication of the Second Temple after its profanation by the heathens. During the purification of the Temple a miracle took place. When the heathens entered the Temple courts they defiled all the oil they found there. But it so happened that one small cruse of oil remained undefiled as the unbroken seal upon it proved. It, however, contained oil enough for one day only and to prepare another supply of oil required at least eight days. A miracle then occurred which caused the small cruse of oil to last eight days.

The main lesson of Chanukah is the power of faith, which the Chanukah event proves. What enabled the Jews to endure privations, sufferings and even death, if not faith? What encouraged the Jews to fight their enemies, who exceeded them in numbers and military strength, if not faith? What enable the little Chanukah candles to survive many empires, if not faith?

WOMEN OF MOOSE ENJOYED VISIT OF GRAND RECORDER

At last night's meeting of the Women of the Moose 50 members were present. Thirteen candidates were initiated in honor of Grand Recorder Katharine Smith. The drill team put on the work at this meeting for the first time, and it was very well done. The Senior Regent presented half a dozen beautiful handkerchiefs to the Grand Recorder, on behalf of the Chapter and she expressed appreciation of the gift.

Co-Worker Bouchal sent in books for the library. Co-Workers Harder, Golcher, Collier, Earl and Wisner were remembered by their Capsule Sisters. Co-Worker Hilda Linton won the entrance prize.

On December 16 a Bingo party open to the public will be given for the benefit of the Christmas baskets. No refreshments will be served.

Tomorrow night, Moose Lodge No. 296 will hold a dance at the home from 9 P. M. to 1 A. M. for the benefit of Christmas cheer.

The ladies will hold their Christmas party December 27, and an exchange of Christmas presents will take place then.

The Grand Recorder complimented the drill team and chapter on its work and said that no woman should stay home from meeting as all play a vital part in the order. She said that in the ten years she has been Grand Recorder, the women sent $1,000,000 to Mooseheaven, and a little over $2,000 to Moosehaven.

After the meeting all were called to the spacious dining room where Chairman Collier and her committee had decorated the table beautifully with flowers. The menu served was chicken salad, shrimp salad, potato salad, slaw, bread and butter, coffee, tea, cup cakes with whipped cream, pickles and mints. Everyone enjoyed the social and the dancing which followed it.

FLANK ATTACK
(By The Associated Press)
CAMDEN, N. J., Dec. 10.—Earl Foy, a huckster, was returning to his wagon when he saw a man casually lift a bag of potatoes from the cart and place it in an automobile. Foy yelled. The man jumped into the car and sped away. Foy chased after for several blocks, then gave up.

He walked breathlessly back and in dismay found six more bags of potatoes missing.

NEW WRINKLE
(By The Associated Press)
COLUMBIA, S. C., Dec. 10.—Police reported they arrested a man with 11 mule and uncomplaining hens he had stolen from a suburban coop.

The chickens were silent because their beaks were clamped with clothes pins.

FED. GOVERNMENT AIDS MD. HIGHWAYS

Road Reports Show State Benefitted By U. S. Help On About 285 Miles.

(By The Associated Press)

BALTIMORE, Jan. 4.—Two reports on Maryland highways showed today that the Federal Government has provided financial aid for approximately 285 miles of roads and the State legal staff has been busy scouring rights-of-way for road building and grade crossing eliminations.

Arthur E. Hungerford, State Director for the National Emergency Council, made public a report of the Federal Bureau of Public Roads, pointing out that $11,399,404 has been assigned Maryland to furnish jobs and aid business recovery.

Thomas M. Jenifer, special assistant assistant to the State Roads Commission, in his annual report to Attorney General Herbert R. O'Conor, said the expenditure of Federal funds and highway damage caused by the floods of last March had increased the work in his office during 1936.

Federal Benefits

The Federal funds, supplemented in some cases by State aid, provided for 159.2 miles of completed roads, 30.2 miles under construction and 36.1 miles approved for construction. The balance of $2,652,221 was estimated sufficient for the construction of 60 miles more of roads.

Hungerford reported that seven grade crossing eliminations were under construction and three more and 15 grade crossing signals and gates were approved for construction. A balance of $547,689 was available for additional grade crossing projects. Most of these have been planned by the State Roads Commission.

List Annapolis Boulevard

Jenifer listed as the major projects handled in his office as: Relocation of the Frederick-Hagerstown road, Annapolis Boulevard construction, Edmonson avenue extension near Baltimore, Philadelphia road completion, Franklin street-Wilkens avenue route in Baltimore and Hagerstown-Conococheague road improvements.

Jenifer said the legal staff handled the right-of-way problems for all the projects and also those affecting the elimination of 20 grade crossings and installation of 13 flashing light signals. His office instituted 18 condemnation proceedings in connection with right-of-way clearances.

The report stated that "the disastrous flood which occurred in the State, and particularly in the Potomac river valley in March, 1936, led to great legal difficulties and many negotiations concerning the various bridges destroyed.

Replace Bridge

Jenifer pointed out in particular the negotiations for utilizing the Baltimore and Ohio Railroad bridge to replace the bridge destroyed at Harper's Ferry. He said agreements were sought with Virginia and West Virginia for replacing, relocating and repairing other bridges destroyed and damaged by the flood.

Efforts of the State Roads Commission in balancing the accounts of the various counties in which the State maintained the county roads also was mentioned in the report. It pointed out that bond issues were approved by his office for Talbot and Allegany counties in an effort to balance the accounts.

Telephone 123

Don't LET HIM IN!

Keep Your Home Warm With CLEAN COAL!

Your best protection against old man Winter and all his frigid blasts is a warm, evenly-heated home and a bin full of our coal. It holds a steady, even heat and gives complete warmth throughout the house.

Order Your Supply TODAY!

ANNAPOLIS DAIRY

O'CONNOR, RAYBURN BOTH CLAIM VICTORY

(Continued from Page 1)

the huge Democratic majority to split into blocs and become difficult to control.

One hundred five new Congressmen, many of them appearing self-conscious in fresh cutaway coats, will take their seats in the House and Senate tomorrow.

Thirteen Democrats, two Republicans and one Farmer-Laborite form the Senate's freshman class. Besides the 89 newcomers in the House, six former Representatives will start the comeback trail.

The new Republican Senators—H. Styles Bridges of New Hampshire and Henry Cabot Lodge, Jr., of Massachusetts—are comparative youngsters.

Bridges Is Now Gov.

Bridges, who plans to resign the governorship of his state at midnight, is 39, a one-time county farm agent and school teacher who carried New Hampshire twice in the midst of Roosevelt landslides.

Husky and blunt-spoken, he is known as a "liberal" Republican, a snappy dresser, rarely getting more than five hours sleep a night. He can doctor a sick pig and draft complex legislation with equal deftness. Lodge, 34, is a member of a top-flight family in Massachusetts society and politics. A grandson of the late Senator Henry Cabot Lodge, he once wrote Washington news for a New York newspaper.

New Democrats

Among the new Democratic Senators are Josh. Lee, once known to his Oklahoma neighbors as a boy orator; Gov. Clyde L. Herring of Iowa, former cowpuncher, jewelry clerk, and auto salesman, and Gov. Edwin C. Johnson of Colorado, who spent his boyhood as a railway section hand.

Rep. Ernest Lundee, 58, of Minnesota, who opposed American entry into the World War, is the new Farmer-Laborite, joining Senator Shipstead of the same state.

Like that in the Senate, the Democratic majority in the House will be the heaviest of any party since the Civil War.

The two youngest newcomers there — Representatives O'Connell (D-Mont) and Boren (D-Okla) are bringing brides to Washington. The bridegrooms are each 27.

Other New Arrivals

Among other new members are Frank R. Havenner, lone California Progressive, who has done newspaper work in San Francisco and Washington; 50-year-old Clyde L. Garrett of Eastland, Texas, who defeated Rep. Tom Blanton (D-Tex) long known as the "watch-dog of the treasury," and William S. Jacobsen of Clinton, Iowa, who takes the seat of his late father, Rep. Bernard M. Jacobsen.

Emporia, Kans., hometown of publisher William Allen White sent a Republican to succeed Rep Carpenter, a Democrat. He is Ed H. Rees, a lawyer-banker-stockman promoted from the Kansas Senate.

Among the old-timers starting comeback careers are Rep. Ross Collins (D-Miss), who attracted attention as an advocate of a motorized army, and Rep. Dowell (R-Ia), noted as a parliamentarian.

Many other familiar figures returned by their constituents include Rep. Sabath (D-Ill), dean of the House, who is beginning his 16th consecutive term, and Rep. Taylor (D-Colo) who has seen 27 years service. William E. Borah (R-Idaho), Senate Dean, is starting his 31st year.

BUZZ BORRIES' BROTHER CAGE STAR AT W. AND L.

(By The Associated Press)

LEXINGTON, Va., Jan. 4.—Washington and Lee's basketball squad, leading contender for the Southern Conference crown worn by North Carolina, ended its holiday period today and resumed training for a heavy schedule.

Coach Cy Young is building his offensive this season around one of the South's tallest basketball combinations—Bob Spessard, 6-foot 7-inch center, and Bill Borries, 6-foot 4-inch forward.

DOGGED

CHICAGO—Police were on the lookout for a patient robber after listening to August Gaydos' complaint.

The robber rode on the same street cars with his prospective victim from the far northwest side of the city to the south side, making two transfers, before taking $15.93 from him at the point of a pistol.

666 TABLETS for COLDS and

LIQUID-TABLETS SALVE-NOSE DROPS

HEADACHES

Price 25c

CALL 123

FRIGIDAIRE

SALES & SERVICE

Annapolis Utilities, Inc.

STATE FARMERS HAD FINE CROPS IN 1936

Harvests Valued At $55,465,000, An Increase Of Nine Million Over 1935.

(By The Associated Press)

COLLEGE PARK, Md. Jan. 4—Maryland farmers harvested crops valued at $55,465,000 during 1936—an increase of more than $9,005,000 over the value of 1935 crops.

J. A. Ewing, agricultural statistician for the Maryland crop reporting service, said today the total 1936 acreage harvested — 1,697,610 acres—was about two percent smaller than that harvested in 1935, but crop values were 20 percent higher.

In 1935, State farmers had a total harvested crop acreage of 1,735,420, valued at $46,283,000.

Ewing said field crops made up about 90 percent of the 1936 acreage. Truck crops accounted for the remaining 10 percent. Of the total farm value, field crops accounted for 15 percent, fruit four percent and truck crops for the remainder, or 21 percent.

Corn Led All Crops

Corn led all other crops in farm value and amounted to about 30 percent of the total value of crops. Wheat was second with 16 percent and tobacco third with 11 percent. Tame hay ranked fourth at nine percent, tomatoes were fifth at about the same percentage, Irish potatoes sixth, apples seventh, sweet potatoes eight, sweet corn ninth and snap beans tenth.

Crop yields in 1936 varied more than usual, Ewing reported, as a result of weather conditions. Yields of strawberries and canning peas were cut almost in half by the Spring drought. Tame hay production was reduced sharply by the dry weather, while clover and timothy ran about 40 percent under the 1935 crops.

Early Irish potatoes, however, were favored by weather conditions, he said, with yields much higher during the year just ended than for 1935. The price was more than three times as high.

Good Crop Of Wheat

A good crop of wheat sold at prices considerably above those of the previous year. A large volume of tomatoes brought good prices on the fresh market and all mid-season and late truck crop yields were "considerably above expectations."

Ewing said tobacco production ran about six percent above 1936, with the crop of good quality. Fruit production, however, was generally lighter than for 1935, and the clover seed crop is expected to be only half as large for 1936 as for the previous year.

Total corn production was about five percent above that of last year. Of the total 511,000 acres in corn, Ewing estimated 484,000 acres were used for grain, 20,000 for silage, and 7,000 for forage.

CCC AIDS UNEMPLOYED

(By The Associated Press)

WASHINGTON, Jan. 4.— The Civilian Conservation corps reported today that of 608 young men enrolled for the emergency conservation work program in Maryland, starting last October, 112 had not been employed previously.

New Battle Force Chief Congratulated

ADMIRAL CLAUDE C. BLOCK ... VICE-ADMIRAL F. J. HORNE ... VICE-ADMIRAL W. T. TARRANT

SAN PEDRO, CAL.—Admiral Block, aboard his flagship, the California, is shown receiving congratulations of Admiral Tarrant, commander of the scouting force, and Admiral Horne, commander of the fleet's aircraft, on taking command of the battle force.

JAMES M. MUNROE IS VICTIM OF PNEUMONIA

(Continued from Page 1)

Mrs. Mathilda Walter Munroe. His mother was a daughter of George Walter, of Gettysburg, Pa.

A Doctor Of Law

He received his early education from a private instructor and entered St. John's College in 1873, being graduated with a Bachelor of Arts degree four years later. He received his Bachelor of Law degree from the University of Maryland. Later, he was given the degree of Doctor of Laws by the university and by Washington College.

He began the practice of law in Annapolis in 1875 and at his death he was dean of the local bar, having served several times as president of the County Bar Association. A Republican, he was first elected State's attorney in 1883 and later served two other terms.

He was a member of the American Bar Association in addition to the State association.

Was Married In 1885

In 1885 he was married to Miss Mary A. Chase, of New Orleans, a daughter of Charles Lott Chase, one time acting Governor of Minnesota.

He is survived by his widow, four daughters, Mrs. Golda Hill, wife of Capt. Charles Hill, U. S. N., of Washington and Newport, R. I., head of the naval mission to Brazil; Mrs. Emily McNair, wife of Capt. M. N. McNair, U. S. N. commander of the battleship Tennessee; Mrs. Louise Reifsnider, wife of Commander Lawrence Reifsnider, U. S. N., of Washington, and Mrs. Adele Henry, widow of Lieut. Walter O. Henry, U. S. N., retired, a son. Walter Munroe, chief engineer of the Anne Arundel County Sanitary Commission; a brother, Frank A. Munroe, clerk of the Anne Arundel Circuit Court, and a sister, Mrs. Roland Brainard, of Washington.

Member Of Numerous Clubs

Munroe was a director of the Farmers National Bank, one of the seven oldest banks in the country, and of the Annapolis Savings Institution. He was counsel for both.

He was a member of the South River Club, reputed to be the oldest social club in the United States; a former president of the Annapolitan Club, social club of Annapolis; a member of the Maryland Historical Society and of the Masonic Order; a former circuit vice-president of the State Bar Association; a member of St. Anne's Protestant Episcopal Church and of the Churchmen's Club.

SLOW BUT SURE

(By The Associated Press)

BURBANK, Calif.—Mrs. Richard Reed can testify that mail service from the south seas is reliable—if a bit slow and devious.

She received a letter from Niuafoou Tonga, a tiny island 350 miles southwest of Samoa, where ships rarely call. Mailed by a friend on a world tour, the letter was floated out to a passing liner in a waterproofed bag.

Somewhere enroute it picked up Greek, French and Dutch cancellations. The letter took three months to reach Mrs. Reed.

LIPMAN'S QUALITY SHOP

174 MAIN STREET

JANUARY CLEARANCE

Sale! DRESSES

For right now when you really need a few extra dresses to tide you over ... we offer you some exciting buys at reductions.

STARTS TOMORROW

Sale! COATS

You owe it to yourself ... and your budget ... to come and see these coat values made possible by this early clearance.

All children's apparel greatly reduced!

Be sure to be here early tomorrow so that you may share in these

REDUCTIONS

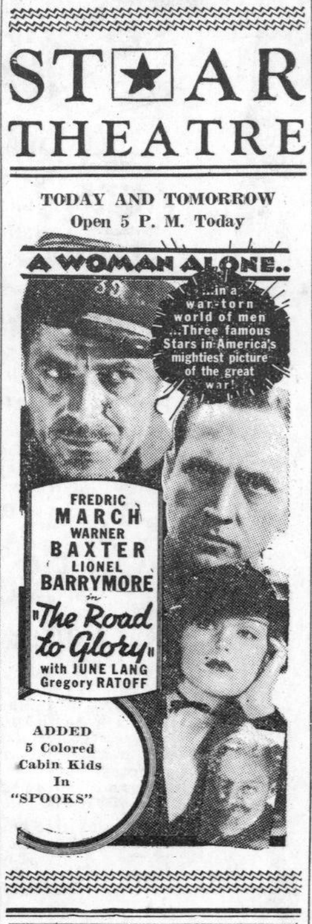

FOR SALE BROILERS and FRYERS

Dressed to order
Milk and Grain fed; Barred Rock and Rhode Island Reds.

Hillsmere Farm

Phone 1844F21

CIRCLE THEATRE

The Show Place of Broadway Entertainments

CONTINUOUS DAILY
1:30 'TILL 11 P. M.

FEATURE PRESENTATIONS 1:30, 3:25, 5:20, 7:15, 9:15 P. M.

TODAY, TUESDAY & WEDNESDAY

GRETA GARBO

TEMPESTUOUS... AS THE LADY OF THE CAMELLIAS

ROBERT TAYLOR

MAGNIFICENT... as the GENTLEMAN OF PARIS

ALEXANDRE DUMAS' IMMORTAL DRAMA!

"Camille"

with
LIONEL BARRYMORE
ELIZABETH ALLEN
JESSIE RALPH
HENRY DANIELL
LENORE ULRIC
Laura Hope Crews

An M-G-M Picture

STAR THEATRE

TODAY AND TOMORROW

Open 5 P. M. Today

A WOMAN ALONE!
...in a war-torn world of men...Three famous Stars in America's mightiest picture of the great war.

FREDRIC MARCH
WARNER BAXTER
LIONEL BARRYMORE

"The Road to Glory"
with JUNE LANG
Gregory RATOFF

ADDED
5 Colored Cabin Kids in "SPOOKS"

REPUBLIC THEATRE

MONDAY AND TUESDAY

PERRY MASON is on the spot!...

Unless He Can Tell a Doubting Jury ... How a Cat Can Commit a Murder! ... How a Dead Man Can Testify Against His Own Killer!

"THE CASE OF THE Black Cat"

By Erle Stanley Gardner with RICARDO CORTEZ JUNE TRAVIS

Jane Bryan • Craig Reynolds • Carlyle Moore, Jr. • Gordon Elliott • Directed by William McGann

A First National Picture

Added Features
A Comedy, News and Novelty

WEDNESDAY AND THURSDAY
"Happy-Go-Lucky"
With
Phil Regan and Evelyn Venable

Don't lay down your paper until you have looked over the classifieds.

Serving a Trading population of more than 25,000 in Annapolis and Anne Arundel County. Delivered in four of every five city homes.

ANNAPOLIS
Evening Capital

Weather Forecast
Rain with slowly rising temperature tonight; Thursday rain and warmer.

VOL. CIV — No. 57. | ESTABLISHED IN 1884—PUBLISHED EVERY EVENING EXCEPT SUNDAY | ANNAPOLIS, WEDNESDAY, JANUARY 20, 1937. | SOUTHERN MARYLAND'S ONLY DAILY PAPER | PRICE TWO CENTS.

PRESIDENT ROOSEVELT TAKES OATH OF OFFICE IN RAIN

County Avoids Loans For Current Expenses

Treasurer Reports Sufficient Money On Hand To Meet New Year Bills — Murray Praises Economy Move Of Commissioners.

With the 1936 taxes 86.4 percent collected, the county began the year 1937 with a built-up balance of ...,382.62 with which to meet first-of-the-year expenses without recourse to the usual borrowing of money to meet current expenses until the new year's tax collections begin.

These figures were released today by Joseph H. Pepper, county treasurer.

Mr. Pepper said that the county had collected $912,114.72 of the $1,-...3,315.18 cent 1936 levy. He also reported that all indebtedness to date had been paid and that for the entire year of 1936 the county was able to operate without resort to a short time loan for operating expenses.

Taxes Being Paid

Already the 1937 taxes are beginning to be paid and by the end of January it is expected the collections will be sufficient to take care of current expenses with the major portion of the taxes due paid by the end of the first six months in the year.

Despite an increase in the 1937 budget of approximately $18,000 over that of 1936 the county commissioners were able to effect an average tax rate cut of three cents on the one hundred dolars this year. This cut will mean approximately $15,000 to the taxpayers of the county.

The increased budget and tax rate cut were allowed by an increased in the assessable basis of the county.

Compared With 1937

In comparison with the 86.4 percent collections on December 31, 1936, it was pointed out that the county had collected but 78.7 percent on December 31 of the preceding year.

However, on December 31 of this year the collections of back taxes due in 1935 had increased the total collections for taxes due that year to 98.2 percent of the total levy.

In commenting on the financial status of the county at this time ... Churchill Murray, member of the Economy and Efficiency Committee, and president of the Better Government League, said:

Praises Work

It is most gratifying to see the results of business-like tax collections. I feel that Mr. Pepper should be commended and the county congratulated.

In regards to the avoidance of

(Continued on Page 4)

LIGHTING COST CUT PLAN GIVEN COUNTY

Eastport Civic Group Makes Recommendations To Commissioners.

Suggestions for changing county lighting system in the Second District, made by the Eastport Civic Association to the Board of County Commissioners Tuesday, would effect a savings of $682 a year to the county, if carried out, the Association reported Tuesday.

The changes sugested consisted of re-setting some light poles and changes in candle power of the lights. The recommendations were referred to the engineer, John A. Bromley and president of the Board Thomas J. Cullimore, from the Second District. Each commissioner will work out a plan for reduced lighting costs in his own district with the engineer.

Lack Police Protection

The Herald Harbor Citizens Association informed the Board they were without police protection and that as a result there had been several robberies in that section. The appointment of an officer was requested.

The Association also complained of the condition of the General's Highway, at Iglehart, where a small strip of the road belongs to the

(Continued on Page 4)

1,998 Treated At Emergency Hospital

The Annapolis Emergency Hospital treated a total of 1,998 patients during the year ending September 30, according to a report of the Board of State Aids and Charities, to be given to the Legislature tomorrow.

Of the number of patients treated, 643 were free patients and 1,355 were paid.

The hospital reported 15,750 total patient-days, with 5,897 free and 9,-853 paid.

The hospital reported an income of $76,387.95, with $11,500 from the State; $1,400 from the city or county; $168.94 from private income, and $63,819 from other sources.

St. John's College reported incomes of $63,000 in 1935 from the State and $65,000 in 1936. There were 55 scholarships given at the college, 25 of them full scholarships and 26 for tuition only.

What Congress Is Doing

(By The Associated Press)

TODAY

In recess for inauguration.

YESTERDAY

Passed legislation extending President's powers to devalue the dollar and continuing the stabilization fund.

84 MILLIONS IS STATE NEED, SOLONS TOLD

Relief Program To Call For $16,178,671.01 For Next Two Years—Budget Will Be Fixed At $64,000,000 By Governor Nice.

TWO BOND ISSUES ARE REQUESTED

Requests for funds totalling more than $84,000,000 face the Maryland legislature.

Yesterday's hearing on requests for relief funds for the next 30 months brought the record total into bold relief as the legislature continued its third and longest week of the current session. The Board of State Aid and Charities requested a $27,170,353.51 program, of which the State would furnish $16,-178,671.01.

The budget for the two years beginning next October 1 has not yet been submitted and will not reach the legislature until next week. However, it will call for approximately $64,000,000. Already before the legislature are these requests.

Want Bond Issues

A bond issue of $2,302,500 for construction and repairs of prisons.

A bond issue of $1,932,000 for construction and repairs of institutions for care of the insane.

Those requested bonds issues, the budget itself, the request for relief funds bring the total past the $84,000,000 mark.

Just what will happen to those requests cannot be told until the legislature has completed its consideration of the budget. The law does not allow consideration of any

(Continued on Page 4)

MD. INTELLIGENCE TESTS EXPLAINED

Miss Julia Wetherington Is Speaker At Grammar School Parent-Teacher Meeting.

The Parent-Teacher Association of the Annapolis Grammar School held its regular monthly meeting last night, in the Music Room. Mrs. Adam K. Backer, president, presided.

Reports were made by the members of the various committees. Mrs. Charles Rawlins announced the course in Adult Education. Mrs. Bob Orr Mathews explained the 40-minute lectures to be given February 5 by Dr. William French; February 12, by Dr. G. E. Moore; February 19 by Dr. Paul Padget, and February 26 by Miss Margaret Wohlgemuth, at 2 o'clock, in the Old Senate Chamber of the State House, on the control of spread of the most prevalent comunicable diseases, including syphilis. These lectures are open and free to all interested.

Instruction for Leaders

Mrs. Backer announced an after-

(Continued on Page 6)

"30 Governors Enough To Ruin Any Town"-Nice

(By The Associated Press)

WASHINGTON, Jan. 20.—Governor Harry W. Nice, of Maryland, here to see the inauguration of President Roosevelt and "attend everything I can get to," thinks a lot of governors can create a lot of excitement.

The State's Republican chief executive, at a reception given for him and Mrs. Nice, asked how many governors were in the Capital for the inauguration and was told "about thirty."

"Thirty governors," Nice repeated. "That's enough to ruin any town."

The President Begins His Second Term

This new picture of President Roosevelt shows the chief executive at his desk, preparing to lead the nation for another four years. The New Deal rode into a second term on a landslide which put congress strongly behind its leader. (Associated Press Photo)

BALTIMORE CITY OBLIGED TO PAY DAMAGES IN SUIT

Municipality Charged With Negligence And Woman Gets $7,500 Award.

The Court of Appeals today affirmed a judgment of the Baltimore City Court awarding Mrs. Hedwig Thompson damages of $7,500 against the Mayor and City Council of Baltimore, for injuries sustained in an automobile accident on the Eager street bridge.

The bridge runs over the tracks of the Pennsylvania Railroad company and the Jones Falls valley in Baltimore. It has a center girder, 5 feet high and 20 inches wide, covered with concrete, dividing the bridge into an east and west thoroughfare.

Car Hit Girder

On the night of Jan. 21, 1935, in

(Continued on Page 6)

John C. Gates, Jr. To Be Buried Here Friday Afternoon

The funeral of John C. Gates, Jr., aged 4½ years, son of Mr. and Mrs. John C. Gates, of 23 Jefferson street, who died yesterday, will take place at 9:30 A. M., Friday, from the residence of his parents, with interment in St. Mary's cemetery.

The boy's father, Corporal John C. Gates, formerly on duty here, is widely known throughout Southern Maryland.

Capt. Bruce Is Civitan Speaker

Capt. Bryson Bruce, head of the Department of Engineering at the Naval Academy, today addressed the Civitan Club at its weekly luncheon at Carvel Hall.

Captain Bruce told several interesting stories on the introduction of steam into the ships of the American Navy. He also gave the Civitans an insight into the new construction at the Naval Academy, which will provide the midshipmen with steam laboratories.

Middies Carry Rifles In Parade

Wearing rain clothes and carrying rifles, the regiment of midshipmen left here today to march in the inaugural parade of President Roosevelt.

The midshipmen traveled on special trains by way of Baltimore. Capt. Forde A. Todd, U. S. N., commandant of midshipmen, was in command.

As they splashed through a pouring rain to the railroad station, the midshipmen shielded the rifles under their raincapes. The Academy and national flags were in waterproof cases.

LAKE IN MOUNTAIN

(By The Associated Press)

BALTIMORE, Jan. 20 — A 55 acre artificial lake, in the heart of Garrett county mountains, is included in the 1937 construction plans of the State Department of Forestry and the Civilian Conservation Corps.

Gov. Nice Urges People To Get Behind Pres. Roosevelt

(By The Associated Press)

WASHINGTON, Jan. 20.—Maryland's Republican Governor, Harry W. Nice, said today the "people should get behind the President" preserving freedom to make "constructive criticism."

"We shall adjourn politics," said Nice, here to attend President Roosevelt's second inauguration. "The election is over. The people should get behind the President and give him all the assistance they can, but reserve to ourselves the right to criticize, providing that criticism is constructive.

Business Improving

"I hope the time will soon arrive when industry will absorb the unemployed. It hasn't arrived yet, but I think that it is on its way."

The Governor said any public works program should be of a permanent nature, such as bridges and highways, and referred to several bridges swept away by Potomac river floods last Spring.

Money In Circulation

Nice said he thought that in recent years there had been "marked recovery," but that was "more or less a natural result when you spend billions of dollars and put them into circulation."

PAROLED CONVICT SLAYS POLICEMAN; ESCAPES IN WOODS

Michigan State Officer Abducted By Man He Was Taking To Jail.

(By The Associated Press)

MONROE, Mich., Jan. 20—The bullet-pierced body of Michigan State policeman Richards F. Hammond was found handcuffed to a mail box on a lonely country road today, five hours after he was abducted by a former convict he had taken into custody.

A posse of more than 200 officers from Indiana, Ohio and Michigan combed wooded areas for Alcide (Frenchy) Benoit, alias Joe La Rue, who was paroled from the Michigan State Reformatory at Ionia a year ago.

Airplanes piloted by Detroit police and Indiana State Police joined the search and Michigan State Police issued radio appeals for farmers to arm themselves and search their out buildings for the fugitive.

Blockade Highway

Hammond, a husky, six-foot trooper, with a fellow officer, Sam Sineni, halted two men while bloc-

(Continued on Page 6)

LEE IN LITERATURE THEME OF ADDRESS

Prof. Charles L. Lewis Tells U. D. C. Chapter Of Works Depicting His Character.

"Lee in Literature," a comprehensive survey of the part the great Southern Leader has played in fiction, drama and poetry, by Professor Charles L. Lewis, of the Naval Academy Department of English and History, was the outstanding feature of the celebration of the one hundred and thirtieth anniversary of Lee's birth by the William H Murray Chapter, United Daughters of the Confederacy.

The meeting was held at the home of Senator and Mrs. Ridgely P. Melvin, the historic "Peggy Stewart House," 207 Hanover street, with Mrs. Melvin, Mrs. Robert L. Burwell, and Mrs. S. S. Hepburn as hostesses.

Next Meeting February 5

Mrs. Charles L. Lewis, president of the Chapter, presided. Dr.

(Continued on Page 4)

Executive Pledges Self To Eradicate Economic Evils Within Four Years

Oath Taken In Open and Bareheaded Despite Inclement Weather—Crowd Packs Plaza to Hear Address—Middies March in Parade.

(By The Associated Press)

WASHINGTON, Jan. 20.—President Franklin D. Roosevelt formally opened his second administration today with a demand for more and stronger government consecrated to "provide enough for those who have too little."

In militant phrases which left specific details to the future, he spoke to a rain-drenched, attentive crowd on the Capitol plaza of the need for government "to solve for the individual the ever-rising problems of a complex civilization" and to control "blind economic forces and blindly selfish men."

Moments before, in words repeated solemnly after Chief Justice Hughes, the President had taken his oath of office and been cheered with a warmth that belied the cold, forbidding day. For once "Roosevelt weather luck" did not hold.

Stands Bareheaded

Gusts of rain blew into Mr. Rosevelt's face. He stood bareheaded, looking out now and again over the black mass of umbrellas which confronted him. Nearby sat the newly-sworn Vice President Garner, members of their families, Justices of the Supreme Court, the Congress and the diplomatic corps.

The oath-taking completed constitutional inaugural requirements, but ahead lay festivities customary to the quadrennial ceremony.

Returning to the White House for them, Mr. Roosevelt chose an open car despite the rain.

After a buffet luncheon for party officials and visiting dignitaries at the White House, the President's place was in "The Hermitage"—a reproduction of "Old Hickory" Jackson's home in Tennessee—fronting the White House. The ornate face of this reviewing stand, decorated with artificial magnolias and roses, presented a bedraggled appearance in the constant downpour.

Middies In Line

A spirit of "the parade must go on" enlivened the numerous parties of Governors, the ranks of the West Point and Annapolis officers-to-be, companies from the Civilian Conservation Corps trim in khaki and the military units or marchers. Their route lay from the Capitol, along Pennsylvania avenue which has seen the inaugural parades since 1801 and by the Presidential reviewing stand.

Extolling democracy in his address, but making no mention of dictatorship abroad, Mr. Roosevelt said the American method had been made more powerful in the last four years.

"For we have begun," he said with deliberation that emphasized a beginning, "to bring private autocratic powers in their proper subordination to public government."

While the chill rain fell ever

(Continued on Page 2)

MARYLAND WELL REPRESENTED AT INAUGURATION

Governor Nice And Democratic Leaders Head Big Delegation.

(By The Associated Press)

WASHINGTON, Jan. 20.— Marylanders from every section of the State, headed by their Republican chief executive, Governor Harry W. Nice, and a group of Democratic party leaders, came to the Capital today to see President Roosevelt begin his second term.

Senator Millard E. Tydings, of Maryland, and Mrs. Tydings included among their guests for the inaugural ceremonies and a buffet luncheon at the Capitol "all the prospective gubernatorial candidates" in the State.

All Have Guests

Senator George L. Radcliffe, of Baltimore, and Mrs. Radciffe, and

(Continued on Page 6)

GOVERNOR NICE PAROLES SEVEN

Pardon Also Granted Another —One Countian Gains His Freedom.

Gov. Harry W. Nice announced today the granting of paroles to seven prisoners and the pardoning of a former convict, all effective immediately.

The pardon issued by the Governor restored the citizenship of Nevin W. Crouse, who completed a term for embezzlement last October. The Carroll County Circuit Court had sentenced him to the House of Correction.

Those paroled were:

Goldsborough Truitt, convicted of unauthorized use of an automobile in Worcester county, May 28, 1936, and sentenced to 18 months in the House of Correction.

William Disney, convicted of larceny in Baltimore, June 12, 1936, and sentenced to one year in the city jail.

Harry Pitts, colored, convicted of assault in Worcester county April 14, 1936, and sentenced to two years in the House of Correction.

Countian Paroled

Chesterfield Burley, colored, convicted of assault and battery in Anne Arundel county, September 21,

(Continued on Page 6)

CIVIC FEDERATION OF COUNTY TO MEET AT GLEN BURNIE TONIGHT

Francis I. Mooney, attorney-at-law, Baltimore, will be the principal speaker at the annual meeting of the Civic Federation of Anne Arundel County, to be held at 8 o'clock tonight at the Community Hall, Glen Burnie. The subject of his address will be "Taking the Profit Out of Politics."

A large delegation, representatives of the various civic and improvement associations throughout the county, is expected to be present at the meeting, at which time nomination and election of officers will be held, and proposed legislation will be discussed.

Robert E. Kindred, attorney of Glen Burnie, is the present president of the Federation.

PROBLEMS OF INTERVENTION NOW MOUNTING

Great Britain Stiffens Attitude Toward Germany — Italy Abandons Plan For Four-Power Pact—Nazi Annoyed By British Stand.

PORTUGAL VETOES BORDER SUGGESTION

(By The Associated Press)

Great Britain stiffened toward Germany today and Italy gave up her plans for a four-power pact with Germany, Britain and France.

Spanish interevention problems mounted. In Spain, itself, Fascist air bombers killed 20 or more Madrilenos.

Italians, holding fast to their new German alliance, decided Spanish tension. France's insistence on retaining her Soviet alliance, and British reluctance had killed the idea of a four-power accord which they hoped would combat Communism.

Eden Speaks Out

Foreign Secretary Anthony Eden's British House of Commons speech was interpreted as refusing responsibility for a Fascist-Communist showdown and putting Europe's future up to Germany.

Berlin called the speech "untimely" and unfair.

Portugal turned down a scheme to have international observers on her Spanish border to curb war shipments to the fighters. New German and Italian expressions on the question of stopping Spanish volunteers were awaited by the British.

Control Of Vounteers

An Italian government spokesman reiterated Italo-German willingness to accept international control of volunteers. But he said the two nations would insist that such "indirect intervention" as alleged Bolshevist propaganda and financial aid to the Spanish government cease forthwith.

3 COLORED BOYS HELD FOR ROBBERY

Three colored youths today were held in $500 bail each for grand jury action in connection with the burglary of the home of B. Bettman, 11 Munroe Court, Saturday night.

The Bettman home was entered through a side window, and watches, old coins, pennies and cigars and cigarettes valued at $94 was stolen.

Charles Sims, 17; Jerome McGowan, 17, and Edward Pinkney, 16, were arrested by Sergeant William Owens and Patrolmen Frank Cornell and Norman Finkle.

The three youths were arraigned before Police Magistrate Joseph M. Armstrong, who held them for grand jury action.

PHILATELIC SOCIETY MET IN CITY LIBRARY

The Annapolis Philatelic Society held its second meeting of the month at the public library last night. Four new members were present. After the business meeting a small auction was held and stamp trading carried on among members.

The club will meet the first and third Tuesdays of each month at 7:30 P. M. at the library. The active membership of 17 men and women is planning a program that will come to the attention of the majority of stamp collectors in Annapolis.

GOVERNOR NICE PAROLES SEVEN

(Continued from Page 1)

1936, and sentenced to six months in the House of Correction.

Carlton Hastings, convicted of being habitually disorderly in Wicomico county July 17, 1936, and sentenced to one year in the House of Correction.

Wilbur Lorschbaugh, convicted of forgery in Washington county Mar. 4, 1936, and sentenced to 18 months in the House of correction.

Governor's Opinion

Edward Boyer, colored, convicted of manslaughter in Baltimore, November 14, 1936, and sentenced to three and a half years in the House of Correction.

In accompanying statements on each case, the Governor said reliable sponsors had recommended the paroles and that most of the offenders had employment awaiting them.

Don't lay down your paper until you have looked over the classifieds.

NAVY WOMEN'S CLUB PRESENTS 3 PLAYS

Large Crowd Enjoyed Dramatics Under Mrs. Tillson's Direction.

Dramatic talent among Navy women here was uncovered last night at the annual play presentation of the Naval Academy Women's Club at Mahan Hall. Three one-act plays were presented during the evening under the capable direction of Mrs. E. M. Tillson, dramatic chairman of the Club. Much credit is due Mrs. Tillson for the smoothness and punctuality, with which the plays went off and for the many rehearsals of the casts which showed to such advantage last night.

"Overtones" the first play, proved to be the most entertaining. Billed as a "Fantasy" by Gertrude Gerstenberg it turned out to be a very clever satire on civilized woman's struggle to subdue her primitive self. Both the "real" and "primitive" selves of the characters appeared on the stage and the resulting dialogue was most amusing. Mrs. E. M. Jackson, Jr., as the "primitive self of Margaret" and "Margaret" as played by Mrs. Carl Hensel carried off acting honors in this presentation, although both Mrs. H. M. Zemner and Mrs. L. J. Knight, Jr., were excellent in their parts.

Spoiled Daughter Pleases

Pretty Mrs. Frank Johnson made a splendid spoiled daughter in "Smoke-Screens" by Harold Brighouse. In fact, we preferred her as the flip Miss rather than as the serious lady in love which she later became. Mrs. C. R. Todd failed to lose a Southern accent to play an English aunt, but in all other respects was very convincing. Mrs. B. P. Ward and Mrs. Elliott Parish were adequate, the former in a difficult role. The play showed a modern treatment of the old theme of mother love and child reaction.

The last play "Uplifting Sadie" had possibilities for comedy which we could not help feeling were never carried out. The fault, however, lay with the script and not with the players, all of whom were exceptionally well-cast in this production. The play was a satire on women's culture clubs—perhaps the reason that the actresses felt so at home in their roles. Mrs. C. W. Humphreys deserves mention for her characterization of the Club's president, while both leading roles, those of "Sadie" and "Lady FitzRoy," the visiting speaker, were ably portrayed by Mrs. R. N. Norgaard and Mrs. William Marshall, respectively. Mrs. D. R. Osborn was flustered and vague by turns as Mrs. Splurge, a club member with a Rolls Royce but little brain. Mrs. C. R. Todd and Mrs. B. P. Ward added a neat touch of comedy as the rival tea pourers.

Others in "Uplifting Sadie" were Mrs Paul J. Kiefer, Mrs. B. W. Decker, Mrs. Jackson, Mrs. P. E. McDowell, Mrs. Zemmer and Mrs. G. Bannerman.

Costumes Pleasing

Makeup and costumes were far above what is expected from amateur plays. Credit is due Mrs. Hensel for make-up and Mrs. Zemmer and Mrs. Knight for the costumes.

Others assisting were: Stage manager, Mrs. Stanley Leith; assistant stage manager, Mrs. C. E. Olsen; properties, Mrs. G. M. Dusinberre; stage hands, Mrs. W. E. Miller, Mrs. M. A. Anderson, Mrs W. E. Lankenau; prompter, Mrs. W. J. Suits; program, Mrs. W. M Downes.

(Reviewed by Mrs. Howard L. Collins.)

INTELLIGENCE TESTS EXPLAINED TO P. T. A.

(Continued from Page 1)

noon session devoted to an institute for instruction of P. T. A. leaders on February 21, at 1:15 o'clock, at the State House.

Miss Josephine Riordan, library chairman, told of an additional purchase of 70 books for the school library.

Awards Presented

George W. Norris reported on school patrol activities, and introduced Professor Harry F. Sturdy, who presented the awards given by the Rotary Club of Annapolis to the two most efficient school child patrolmen, May Hall and David Ansel.

The speaker of the evening was Miss Julia Wetherington, who gave instructive information on the State Intelligence tests, with demonstrations on charts.

Miss Maude Roberts, principal of the school, also gave a short talk on the same subject pertaining to the younger school children.

Professor R. C. Lamb read some articles in regard to the teachers' salaries, and spoke of the efforts being made to restore to them the full pay cut. Letters were read which expressed sympathy with this movement, and a great participation in a mass meeting before the Governor during next week was urged.

Roars Across Continent In 7½ Hours

Burning the wind at an estimated average speed of 332 miles an hour, Howard Hughes, flying movie producer, drove his special monoplane from Los Angeles to Newark, 2,490 miles, in seven hours and a half. He is shown climbing from the plane at the end of his record-shattering flight, most of which was made in the sub-stratosphere. (Associated Press Photo)

BALTO. CITY MUST PAY DAMAGE SUIT AWARD

(Continued from Page 1)

foggy weather, Mrs. Thompson was riding in an automobile driven by her husband west on Eager street from Greenmount avenue. The machine collided with the center girder of the bridge, Mrs. Thompson being knocked unconscious and otherwise injured.

She filed suit in the Baltimore court for $35,000 damages against the municipal government and the Pennsylvania railroad. The court granted a demurrer prayer to the suit filed by the railroad, but returned the verdict of $7,500 damages against the city.

Judge Offutt's Ruling

Judge T. Scott Offutt, speaking for the Appellate court, pointed out that it "seems obvious" that a wall of concrete 20 inches wide and 5 feet high in the center of an otherwise open highway is an obstruction, when under certain conditions the color blends with the street surface. It was pointed out that fogs occur in Baltimore and vicinity with sufficient frequency to justify an expectation of their reoccurrance from time to time.

"Therefore," the opinion continued. "The Appellant (city) should have anticipated their occurrence and have placed a warning light or other device which under fog conditions would have permitted a traveller approaching the bridge to have discovered the location of the center girder in time to avoid colliding with it."

MARYLAND WELL REPRESENTED AT CAPITAL TODAY

(Continued from Page 1)

the six representatives and their wives also had a number of guests for the inaugural ceremonies.

The "prospective gubernatorial candidates" invited by Senator and Mrs. Tydings included Mayor Howard W. Jackson, of Baltimore; Attorney-General Herbert R. O'Conor, of Baltimore; President Lansdale G. Sasscer, of the State Senate, and William Preston Lane, of Hagerstown, former State Attorney-General.

Other Guests Of Tydings'

The Tydings' guests also included Mrs. Jackson, Mrs. O'Conor, Mrs. Lane, Mrs. Sasscer; Howard Bruce, Democratic National Committeeman for Maryand, and Mrs. Bruce; William S. Gordy, Jr., Comptroller of Maryland, and Mrs. Gordy; State Senator S. Scott Beck and Mrs. Beck, of Chestertown; M. Hampton Magruder, Collector of Internal Revenue for Maryland, and Mrs. Magruder; Gilbert Dailey, Collector of Customs, and Mrs. Dailey, and former Judge William C. Walsh and Mrs. Walsh, of Cumberland.

Governor and Mrs. Nice, honored at a reception given by Brig.-Gen. John Philip Hill, were to be guests at a White House luncheon after the inaugural ceremonies; a tea at the White House following the inaugural parade this afternoon, and at the California Democratic Society's inaugural ball tonight.

Nice And Staff In Parade

The Governor, General Hill and other members of his staff had places in the inaugural parade.

666 SALVE for COLDS
Liquid - Tablets Salve - Nose Drops
price 5c, 10c, 25c

BABY CHICKS
Barred and White Rocks, N. H. Reds, White Leghorns, Barred Cross Breeds
Officially State Blood Tested
Custom Hatching
Milford Hatchery
Pikesville P. O., Rockdale, Md.
Pikesville 36-R

PAROLED CONVICT SLAYS POLICEMAN; ESCAPES IN WOODS

(Continued from Page One)

kading the highway at Monroe shortly before last midnight in search of two gunmen who abducted Fred Williams, a used car salesman in Detroit, and left him tied to a tree in Toledo.

Hammond took Benoit in the state police patrol car while Sineni entered a car operated by the second suspect, John Smith, alias Mike Delberto, formerly of Flint, and also a former convict.

Enroute to the state police barracks at Erie, Mich., Benoit suddenly overpowered trooper Hammond and sped away with him in the motorcar.

Trooper Sineni pursued the fugitive patrol car for ten miles, exchanging shots with Benoit until the pursuing car was ditched.

Escapes Into Woods

Two Monroe county deputies sheriff, Joe Dansard and Robert Navarre, came upon the hunted car near Lulu, Mich., and again a gunbattle ensued with Benoit finally abandoning the patrol car. He escaped on foot into nearby woods.

In the blood- stained car was the uniform coat of Trooper Hammond. It was saturated with blood.

At 5 A. M. officers patrolling roads in the area came upon the body of the missing trooper. Hammond had been shot through the head. His body was slumped against a rural mail box and his wrists were shackled with his own handcuffs to a steel post.

Captain Lawrence A. Lyon, of the Michigan State Police, who is directing the search, identified Benoit as the man sought. He said Trooper Sineni brought Smith to the Erie barracks after the gunbattle and then joined the search for the former convict.

State Police Identification Bureau records show that Benoit was first arrested in Nashville, Tenn., Nov. 7, 1930, on a charge of transporting a stolen automobile across the state line. Because he was a juvenile, Benoit was committed to the Michigan Boys' Vocational School at Lansing for two years. In 1933 he was sentenced to the State Reformatory at Ionia after conviction in Detroit of carrying concealed weapons and of receiving stolen property. Benoit was released on parole on Jan. 2, 1936.

Smith was sentenced at Flint, Mich., in 1932 to serve 2½ years to 7½ years in the state reformatory. Both Benoit and Smith had resided in Detroit in recent months.

Captain Lyon said the motorcar in which Benoit and Smith were arrested last night was stolen from Williams, the Detroit used car salesman, in Toledo last night.

Capt. Lyon said State Trooper Phil Paulson and Sheriff's Deputy Nadeau, of Monroe county, discovered Hammond's body.

Hammond, whose home was in Hanover, Mich., had been a member of the state police for 18 months.

Roosevelt Prays Before Ceremony

(By The Associated Press)

WASHINGTON, Jan. 20.—Franklin D. Roosevelt selected today, as he did four years ago, a biblical tribute to charity upon which to place his hand during the administration of the presidential oath.

He chose Chapter 13 in Paul's First Epistle to the Corinthians. Of the chapter's 13 verses, these are best known:

Cites Scripture

"Though I speak with the tongues of angels and have not charity, I am become as sounding brass or a tinkling cymbal. And "though I have the gift of prophecy and understand all mysteries and all knowledge; and though I have all faith so that I could remove mountains, and have not charity, I am nothing.

"When I was a child I spake as a child, I understood as a child, I thought as a child; but when I became man, I put away childish things.

"For now we see through a glass darkly; but then face to face; now I know in part; but then I shall know even as also I am known.

"And now abideth faith, hope, charity, these three; but the greatest of these is charity."

ATTENDS CHURCH

President Roosevelt went to church for prayer and blessing today before taking his second presidential oath.

The Rev. Endicott Peabody, of Groton, Mass., under whom the President studied as a boy at Groton School and by whom he was married, officiated.

HOBO ON LOCOMOTIVE FOUND ELECTROCUTED

(By The Associated Press)

BALTIMORE, Jan. 20.—A Pennsylvania Railroad train arrived here last night carrying on top of its electric locomotive the body of a man believed to have been electrocuted while stealing a ride.

Police sought to identify the man, who was about 25, lame in one foot, and tattoed on his hands and arms with "DOOD," "D. A. D.", and the picture of a woman. The body was carried to the morgue, after its discovery at Pennsylvania Station.

It is believed the man came in cocntact with the power line or the locomotive's pantograph.

FOR SALE
BROILERS and FRYERS
Dressed to order
Milk and Grain fed; Barred Rock and Rhode Island Reds.
Hillsmere Farm
Phone 1844F21

VISIT NEW YORK
$3.75 ROUND TRIP TO NEW YORK
FOR A DAY OF THRILLS
Take your family and friends
SUNDAY, JANUARY 24
From Baltimore
Lv. Baltimore (Camden Sta.) 1:00 A. M. or 7:58 A. M.
Lv. Baltimore (Mt. Royal Sta.) 1:05 A. M. or 8:04 A. M.
Ar. New York . . . . 5:50 A. M. or 11:38 A. M.
If you leave on the 1:00 A. M. train, you have a full day and evening in New York. Or if you take the morning train, you have an afternoon and evening.
Returning: Leave New York 6:08 P. M. or Midnight.
What a trip! What a day! What a grand time you'll have seeing the sights of New York. Glamorous Broadway — Radio City — Rockefeller Center—Fifth Avenue—Statue of Liberty—movies, theatres, night clubs — all the thrilling sights and scenes of America's greatest city — you'll have something to remember for years. A grand trip at very small cost. And only when you go B & O do you get a view of the famous skyline and the great ocean liners.
FAST TRAINS—COMFORTABLE COACHES
Similar excursions Sundays, February 7 and 21 and March 7.
BALTIMORE & OHIO Railroad

Indian Boy, 6, Escapes From Living Death

(By The Associated Press)

MUSKOGEE, Okla., Jan. 20.—At the age of six, black-haired Adoniram Judson Iglesias, a San Blas Indian boy from Central America, has escaped burial alive and being sold into slavery.

A waif of undetermined parentage condemned to die by tribal custom, he was adopted by Mrs. A. Iglesias, an American missionary who had married an Indian.

She sent him to Brooklyn for safekeeping until he was five. When he returned, however, the tribal leaders had not forgotten him and they asked that his life be forfeit.

Mrs. Iglesias appealed for aid, and Dr. B. D. Weeks, president of Bacone Indian School here, offered a haven for the lad. As Mrs. Iglesias prepared to send the boy to this country, he was kidnaped by Indians. Three months later he was rescued as he was about to be sold into slavery.

With his foster-brother, Claudio Iglesias, the boy was sent to New York. Immigration laws did not provide for admittance of Indians, but Oklahoma legislators in Washington persuaded immigration authorities to grant the boys' entrance.

Frank Thompson, Bacone literary instructor said the boys learned quickly the customs of the United States.

Describing his studies, Adoniram said:

"Study, write and read. No spell."

He likes ice cream, football—and blonde hair.

WOMEN OF MOOSE TO MEET TONIGHT

The Women of the Moose, Chapter No. 661, will have their regular meeting tonight, at 8 o'clock, at the Moose Home, West street. The chairmen of the various committees will be expected to bring in their reports, so that they can be mailed to the Grand Recorder.

A Three Days' Cough Is Your Danger Signal
No matter how many medicines you have tried for your cough, chest cold or bronchial irritation, you can get relief now with Creomulsion. Serious trouble may be brewing and you cannot afford to take a chance with anything less than Creomulsion, which goes right to the seat of the trouble to aid nature to soothe and heal the inflamed membranes as the germ-laden phlegm is loosened and expelled.
Even if other remedies have failed, don't be discouraged, your druggist is authorized to guarantee Creomulsion and to refund your money if you are not satisfied with results from the very first bottle. Get Creomulsion right now. (Adv.)

YOUR DOLLAR REACHES FARTHER NOW
MANY LONG DISTANCE TELEPHONE RATES REDUCED JAN. 15

STAR THEATRE
TODAY AND TOMORROW
MILLIONAIRE or PAUPER?

"Spendthrift"
with HENRY FONDA
PAT PATERSON

Added—Serial and Comedy

NEW CONFERENCE TO END AUTO STRIKE

(By The Associated Press)

DETROIT, Jan. 20.—Rival leaders in the automotive industry's labor conflict traveled to the East today to confer with associates on means of terminating the widespread strike.

A few hours after William S. Knudsen, executive vice-president of General Motors Corporation, entrained for New York, Homer Martin, president of the United Automobile Workers of America, said he would fly to Washington.

Those who know values are well acquainted with the Evening Capital Want Ads.

CIRCLE THEATRE
The Show Place of Broadway Entertainments
CONTINUOUS DAILY 1:30 'TILL 11 P. M.
FEATURE PRESENTATIONS—1:40, 3:40, 5:40, 7:40, 9:40 P. M.
TODAY—LAST SHOWINGS

ALL IN COLOR
It sweeps you into Love-Land!
Marlene DIETRICH
Charles BOYER
in "The GARDEN OF ALLAH"

COMING—THURS, FRI. and SAT.
COLLEGE HOLIDAY
starring JACK BENNY
George BURNS Gracie ALLEN
Mary BOLAND Martha RAYE

REPUBLIC THEATRE
CONTINUOUS PERFORMANCE—1:30 P. M. TO 11:00 P. M.
WED., THURS., FRI. & SAT.

You've Got a Heavy Date with a Light Moment!
She thumbed her way to the U.S.A. on a ship that carried wildcats!
The mad romance of a girl from France. Heart trouble set to music!
Lily PONS
Gene RAYMOND
Jack OAKIE
Where has she been all your life?
That's all you'll want to know
THAT GIRL FROM PARIS
With HERMAN BING
MISCHA AUER
LUCILLE BALL
FRANK JENKS
5 Palpitating New Song Hits and "The Blue Danube" in Swingtime!

ADDED FEATURES—A NOVELTY AND NEWS

ANNAPOLIS
Evening Capital

Serving a Trading population of more than 25,000 in Annapolis and Anne Arundel County. Delivered in four of every five city homes.

Weather Forecast
Fair and warmer today; fair tomorrow.

VOL. CIV — No. 92. | ESTABLISHED IN 1884—PUBLISHED EVERY EVENING EXCEPT SUNDAY | ANNAPOLIS, TUESDAY, MARCH 2, 1937. | SOUTHERN MARYLAND'S ONLY DAILY PAPER | PRICE TWO CENTS.

MILLION DOLLARS SOUGHT FOR NAVAL ACADEMY

$526,555,428 APPROPRIATION FOR U. S. NAVY

House Committee Approves Allotment For Navy Department For Next Fiscal Year —Budget Cut Under Record Sum Requested.

WILL START 8 NEW DESTROYERS, 4 "SUBS"

(By The Associated Press)

WASHINGTON, March 2.—The House Appropriations Committee approved today a $526,555,428 allotment for the Navy Department for the next fiscal year.

The appropriation included funds for the Navy's huge ship and airplane construction program for the year, beginning July 1.

The committee ignored budget demands that would have shot the supply measure to a new peacetime high of $562,425,709. It lopped $35,870,281 from the budget figures. That kept the amount $1,547,104 less than the record peacetime appropriation for the current year.

Cut New Ship Construction

The committee cut $27,000,000 from the $157,000,000 requested for the new ship construction program, but his was described as merely a "deferment," warranted on grounds that $56,000,000 of current funds to be unexpended June 30 will be carried over into the next fiscal year.

The $130,000,000 additional appropriation recommended by the House group compares with $168,000,000 additional appropriated for the current year.

New Destroyers, Submarines

The money will be used to start eight new destroyers and four submarines and to continue work on two battleships, three aircraft carriers, eleven cruisers, forty-eight destroyers, sixteen submarines and a gunboat.

For naval aviation the committee approved $49,500,000—an increase of nearly $11,000,000 over the present appropriation.

ITALY PREPARES FOR MILITARY STRIFE

(By The Associated Press)

Italy answered the challenge of the world armament race today with an order for virtual lifetime military readiness of all her men and strengthening of her war preparations.

Answerng Great Britain's recently announced $7,500,000,000 defense program, the Fascist Grand Council decreed the "integral militarization of all active forces between the ages of 18 and 55 with periodical recalls of the mobilizable classes."

The Maryland Upholstery Co.

Mr. C. H. Davis, Jr., will be in Annapolis to give estimates on furniture upholstering with new spring coverings, on Wednesday, March 3rd.

Write Box 21, Capital Office or send postcard to

The Maryland Upholstery Co.
2217-19 N. Fulton Ave., Baltimore, Maryland. m-2

FOR SALE

Modern dwelling on McKendree Avenue in excellent condition. 4 bedrooms, hot water heat, laundry tubs, fireplace, weatherstripped, 2 car garage. Lot 50' x 200'. Reasonably priced. F. H. A. terms available.

BERNARD J. WIEGARD
Hotel Maryland Bldg. Phone 9

FOR SALE

Dwelling No. 157 West Street, 8 rooms and bath. Hot water heat. $3700.00.

JULIAN BREWER & SON
(Joseph D. Lazenby)
9 School Street Telephone 815

FOR SALE

Residence of the late James M. Munroe, opposite St. John's College and known as 67 College Avenue. For full particulars apply

CHAS. F. LEE
Church Circle Phone 603

MUNSHOWER BACKS MELVIN POLICE BILL INCREASING POWER

Senator Says He Drew Measure As Outgrowth Of Defense Of Garey.

Senator Ridgely P. Melvin (D-Anne Arundel) announced today that Lieut.-Col. Elmer F. Munshower, superintendent of State police, has approved his bill to take the police department out of the State Merit System and place it under the sole charge of the superintendent.

The Senator had the bill prepared as the Legslature met for the ninth week of the biennial session and prepared to continue its probe of the police department.

Defended Garey

Senator Melvin said the bill grew out of the defense he made of Major Enoch B. Garey, deposed State police superintendent, on February 6, when he was successful in having a bill designed to take away certain of the superintendent's powers sent back to the Senate Committee on Judicial Proceedings. He said the bill was drawn before the police investigation began, and was not a result of developments during the inquiry.

After the speech, Melvin said Walter H. Buck, a leading advocate of Civil Service in the State, had written him suggesting that the police be put under the superintendent and removed from the Merit System. He said he asked Buck to draft such a bill. When it was received Melvin made a few amendments.

Under the terms of the measure the superintendent would have full power and authority to appoint officers, promote or demote, or to remove "any employee of the department."

Must File Charges

In the case of removals, the super-

(Continued on Page 4)

WEST ANNAPOLIS P. T. A. COMMITTEE TO HOLD CARD PARTY

The ways and means committee of the West Annapolis P. T. A. will hold a card party at the Firemen's Hall on Friday, March 5. Cards and other games will be played. Prizes will be awarded to all winners. A number of atractive prizes have been secured, and refreshments will be served.

The committee in charge includes Mrs. H. Willet (chairman), Mrs. L. Steuart, Mrs. J. Guy, and Mrs. A. Parkinson.

Transportation will be furnished from and to the Community Store, Eastport, the cars leaving there at 7:30 o'clock and the Annapolis postoffice at 7:45.

D-A-N-C-E
Moose Home—West Street
FRIDAY, MARCH 5TH
Time 9:30 To 1
Music by The Ramblers
45c Per Person xx

OYSTER SUPPER
Auspices
LADIES' AID SOCIETY
Of Mayo M. E. Church
THURSDAY, MARCH 4TH—5 P. M.
At Mayo Hall
Menu:—Oysters, Fresh and Smoked Ham, Salads, Slaw, Hot Rolls, Pickles, Coffee.
SUPPER 50 CENTS
Ice cream and cake on sale m3

DANCE
TUESDAY & FRIDAY NIGHTS
AT THE
BRASS RAIL
Music by The Syncopators
Ice Cold Beer Eats
WESS ATWELL Prop. m-2

FOR QUICK SALE
106 WEST STREET
Store and 8 room dwelling—all conveniences. Must be sold at once—good business opportunity.
SERVICE AGENTS, INC.
(F. E. Voges — H. H. Little)
47 Maryland Avenue. Phone 1477

Mrs. Roosevelt Tells Navy Club That Women Must Aid Gov't With Housing Plan

Wife of President of the United States Speaking Before Large Audience Yesterday Blamed Early Home Life for Many Crimes —Contends Many Mothers are Handicapped—Some Have Such a Bad Start That They Learn to Live During Prison Term, She Declares.

(By Anne Dorsey Beall)

Mrs. Franklin D. Roosevelt, who was the guest speaker of the Naval Academy Women's Club yesterday afternoon, told the members that "impossible" housing conditions under which large groups live is, perhaps, "one of the basic reasons for so many things that go wrong in our modern civilization."

The meeting was held in the auditorium of Mahan Hall, with a very large attendance of members and guests, both the balcony and main floor being filled. The club enjoyed hearing of the speaker's many interesting experiences and was impressed with the purposes expressed. The charm and naturalness of Mrs. Roosevelt's narration found a most sympathetic audience. She was introduced by Mrs. Harry W. Need, president of the club.

LUNCHEON GUEST OF MRS. SELLERS

Mrs. David Foote Sellers, wife of the Superintendent of the Naval Academy, and honorary president of the club, entertained at luncheon for Mrs. Roosevelt preceding the meeting. Her guests included the members of the executive board and chairmen of committees.

Announcing "housing" as her subject, she said she would discuss it "in not exactly the way that you have in mind."

Home Environment Important

"When you study the young criminal of today, go back to the home and invariably that home was a crowded tenement or a rural tenement (they are as bad in the country as in the city), where privacy is impossible and living conditions are very bad.

"So we who are interested in the progress of modern civilization have come to think of housing in this country and other countries as one of the things requiring our attention."

Subsidized Projects Necessary

Pointing out that it is impossible to have good housing if the cost is far above the income of the wage earner, Mrs. Roosevelt said that the whole question narrows down to whether it pays the people, who are the taxpayers, on whom the cost eventually comes, to subsidize a certain kind of housing to the extent of having only decent living quarters, or whether they would rather pay for it in the other way.

She urged the women to go into the slum areas and see for themselves, as she has done in the tenement districts of New York and elsewhere throughout the country, the conditions under which people live. "And I think you will see if you do that it will be a very wise economy to attack the thing that seems to be basic."

Urged Personal Interest

Mrs. Roosevelt said that the

(Continued on Page 3)

GROUNDS FOR DIVORCE

(By The Associated Press)

CAMDEN, N. J., March 2.—Advisory Master Alexander Trappe granted a divorce to a man who complained that his wife was tattooed with a Cupid and three initials. They weren't his initials, the husband said, and his wife was not tattooed when they were married.

UNIVERSITY CLUB MEETS TOMORROW

Two interesting addresses are scheduled for the meeting of the University Club, to be held at 8 o'clock tomorrow evening, in Carvel Hall.

Dr. L. R. Alderman, director of the Educational Division of the Works Progress Administration, Washington, will speak on "Why Adult Education?", and Paul D. Kalachov, formerly a lieutenant-colonel in the White Russian Army, will give a talk on "The March of the White Army Through Frozen Siberia."

The meeting is open to all college men and graduates of the two service academies.

Miss Esther King Begins Duties As Librarian

Miss Esther King assumed her duties yesterday as librarian at the Annapolis Public Library, in the old Reynolds Tavern Building.

Miss King has lived in Annapolis since she was five years old and was educated in the public schools of the city. She attended Goucher College and was a member of the class of 1926.

She is the daughter of Mr. and Mrs. William F. King and lives in Southgate avenue. She brings to her new post a considerable practical library experience. She resigned her post as manager of the circulating library of Hichschild, Kohn and Company, Baltimore, to accept the local post.

Miss King met last night with President B. Everett Beavin and other members of the library board at the regular monthly meeting of the governors of the library. The report of Acting Librarian Mary Belle Poole shows that the library is being used by more citizens every week.

JOHN THOMAS JONES, OLD RESIDENT HERE BURIED YESTERDAY

The funeral of John Thomas Jones, an old resident of Annapolis, who died February 26, at the home of his son, in Baltimore, took place at 1:30 o'clock yesterday afternoon, from the residence of another son in Raspburg, Baltimore county.

Mr. Jones is survived by two daughters, Mrs. William Davidson, Sr., of Charles street, this city, and Mrs. Mabel Tawef, of Easton, Md.; three sons, Edward, Claude and Clifton Jones, of Baltimore, and one brother, Edward Jones, of Charles street.

WALLY TO BE WELL DRESSED

(By The Associated Press)

PARIS, March 2—Wallis Warfield Simpson has ordered five new creations from the establishment of British Captain Edward Molyneux, Parisian dressmaker, it was disclosed today.

RESTORATION CO. HEADED BY ADM. SELLERS

Superintendent Of The Naval Academy Elected President Of Company For Restoration Of Colonial Annapolis At Recent Meeting.

SUCCEEDS GEN. AMOS WOODCOCK, OF ST. J.

At the meeting of the Board of Directors of the Company for the Restoration of Colonial Annapolis, held recently, Rear-Admiral David Foote Sellers, Superintendent of the Naval Academy, was elected president of the company.

The following other officers were named: first vice-president, Mrs. Theodore W. Johnson; second vice-president, George Forbes; secretary, Peter H. Magruder; treasurer, Albert H. MacCarthy; counselor, Senator Ridgely P. Melvin.

The Board of Directors represent the various men's and women's civic and patriotic organizations of the city, with the exception of Mrs. Duncan K. Breut, of Baltimore, who represents the Federated Garden Clubs of Maryland, and John Churchill, New York architect, son of Winston Churchill, author, who is well known here, and who has given much of his time to the company.

The directors, named at the first anniversary dinner of the company, on George Washington's birthday are: General A. W. W. Woodcock, F. M. Lazenby, Mrs. T. W. Johnson, P. H. Magruder, A. H. MacCarthy, R. P. Melvin, Governor H. W. Nice, Rear-Admiral D. F. Sellers, Mayor L. N. Phipps, Mrs. F. V. McNair, Mrs. J. M. Green, Mrs. L. P. Muster-

(Continued on Page 6)

Income From Football Aids All N. A. Sports

Admiral Sellers Reports That Receipts From 1935 Campaign Totaled $379,612—Expenses Amounted To $248,111—Paid All Bills And Left Surplus.

GRID INCOME $131,501 IN EXCESS OF EXPENSES

Navy's football team pays big dividends.

Rear-Admiral David F. Sellers, superintendent of the Naval Academy, told a House Appropriations subcommittee the Navy Athletic Association's total income from football during the fiscal year ended June 30, 1936, amounted to $379,612.

Returns from 13 other sports amounted only to $1,366.

The figures do not represent profits, however, for expenses, including salaries of coaches, instructors and other employes, material and equipment claimed $248,111 of the total.

U. S. Steel Controversy

(By The Associated Press)

C. I. O. wins wage bargaining right with Carnegie-Illinois Steel Corporation, employer of 120,000 of industry's 550,000 workers.

Six companies grant pay boosts expected to average $200 a year each to 190,000 workers, along with 40-hour week and time and a half for overtime.

Industry's annual payroll to jump $110,000,000 if other producers follow, on top of $75,000,000 boost four months ago.

Deadlock over Navy's steel contracts appears broken.

Price boost looms in all steel products.

Annapolitan Club To Hold Bridge Tourney

Second Annual Duplicate Bridge Invitation Competition To Begin March 11 —Prof. A. B. Cook, Chairman.

More than 100 invitations have been issued by the Board of Governors of the Annapolitan Club to bridge players of the community to participate in the Second Annual Tournament to determine the Men's Pair Championship.

The success of last year's play has created a keen interest in the coming series of four duplicate games to be played on Thursday nights, March 11 and 18 and April 1 and 8. The highest total percentage score for the best three out of four evenings of play will determine the new local men's championship pair. Each pair will be allowed one substitution during the series.

'36 Champion Gone

The holder of the 1936 championship, Commander Christopher C. Miller and Lieutenant A. B. Clarkson, both of the Navy, are now both serving sea duty and the field for the coming event is wide open.

A committee composed of Prof. Allen B. Cook, chairman; F. Marion Lazenby, Comdr. John T. Bowers and Lieut. C. W. Humphreys has been named to operate the tournament. Peter H. Magruder will be chairman of the club's reception committee. He will be assisted by Clarence L. Clemson, Lieut. Parke H. Brady and Carl S. Thomas.

Fire Caused Postponement

The tournament was originally planned for the month of February but the disastrous fire suffered by the Annapolitan Club caused a postponement to the date now scheduled.

The Annapolitan Club is one of the city's most representative organizations. Comdr. Francis M. Furlong retired, is president; Hamilton Gale, is vice-president and E. M, Jackson, Jr., is secretary-treasurer.

JAPAN WAR UNITS WORRIED BY U. S.

(By The Associated Press)

TOKYO, March 2.—Japan's Army and Navy ministers disclosed to the Diet today a program of stress on chemical warfare and vigorous plans to meet the "menace" of increased United States air units in the Pacific.

When Japan's Navy and naval air force rearmament program is finished, said Navy Minister Mitsumasa Yonai, Japan need not "fear" the United States for three years.

KILLS COYOTE BY 'DROPPING' PLANE

(By The Associated Press)

ANCHORAGE, Alaska, March 2.—Pilot Jack Elliott, nettled because he and a game warden carried no arms with which to shoot a coyote from the air, swooped earthward and struck the animal with one of the plane's skis, breaking the coyote's back.

Lecturer's Fund Found Small

Unless Congress comes to the rescue with $800, visiting clergymen may be "frozen out" again at the Naval Academy.

A House Naval Appropriations subcommittee learned from Admiral David F. Sellers, superintendent of the Academy, that last year's appropriation was not sufficient to defray the expenses of lecturers and visiting clergymen.

"At the present time the clergymen down there have been somewhat frozen out," Sellers testified. "There is not enough to pay the expenses of the visiting clergymen."

City May Get Radio Station

Group Of Interested Business Men Making Survey And Optimism Is Cited.

Annapolis soon may have a radio station.

A group of Annapolitans and Prof. G. R. Giet, of the Navy Postgraduate School, are making a survey of the city, and if the plan is found to be feasible a group of Annapolis merchants will be asked to pledge themselves to support a station for a period of five years.

Local Group Of Sponsors

The interested local citizens who are making the survey are Mayor Louis N. Phipps; F. Marion Lazenby, president of the Annapolis Dairy Products Company; R. P. Hall, of the Automotive Service of this city; Frank P. Sherman, manager of the Claiborne - Annapolis Ferry Company; Albert H. MacCarthy, owner of Carvel Hall Hotel, and City Counselor William J. McWilliams.

Preiminary surveys, including a study of the experiences encountered by the stations at Hagerstown, Frederick and Salisbury, has made the committee optimistic that a station can be established in Annapolis.

SEEK 12-YEAR-OLD YOUTH IN CAPITAL

(By The Associated Press)

WASHINGTON, March 2 — Justice Department agents and police searched today for 12-year-old James T. Brady, Jr., son of the Veterans' Administration Solicitor.

Brady expressed fear that his son, who has been missing since he left home yesterday for school, might have been the victim of a disgruntled client.

As solicitor, Brady explained, he signs letters denying applications for veterans' compensation.

He said a tramp at the Brady home last week mentioned that he was a former service man. Brady's son was present at the time.

MUD DOESN'T STOP CO. SCHOOL BUSES

Whatever tribulations school bus drivers in some sections of the State may experience from muddy roads, the Anne Arundel county drivers escape, their buses moving on schedule.

George Fox, superintendent of Anne Arundel county schools, said the county school buses had not been held up by muddy roads for 10 years.

"Our buses go through and carry a full load all the time," he said. "We consider the cooperation of the Board of County Commissioners responsible for this record. They watch the roads used by the buses, and if a hole develops have it fixed immediately."

DORMITORY TO BE ENLARGED BY TWO WINGS

Admiral Norman R. Smith Tells Subcommittee Increase In Number Of Midshipmen Results In Overcrowding—Three To One Room Seen.

ADMIRAL SELLERS LISTS OTHER NEEDS

Provision of $1,000,000 for extension of Bancroft Hall at the Annapolis Naval Academy is recommended by Navy officials for inclusion in the department's appropriation bill for the fiscal year starting next July 1.

Rear-Admiral Norman R. Smith, chief of the Bureau of Docks, in testimony before a House subcommittee, published today, said the construction was needed to relieve overcrowding at the Academy.

Dormitory Crowded

Admiral Smith said any increase above 2,278 in the number of midshipmen at the Academy "represents a definitely unsatisfactory condition of overcrowding." There are 2,315 midshipmen enrolled now, he said, and next year there will be 2,342. He estimated there would be 154 midshipmen in excess of the Naval Academy dormitory capacity by next October.

At a high point, Admiral Smith said, there would be 2,550 men, which would result in 1816 men being crowded three to a room in two-man rooms.

"This situation is by no means temporary but is permanent, unless and until at some future date a decrease in the officer strength of the Navy is to be attained by diminishing the output of the Naval Academy, a prospect surely not envisioned at present," he said.

Build Two Wings

Admiral Smith told the subcommittee the new project contemplates construction of two additional wings to accommodate 600 students. The department asked $750,000 last year for the project, and said the increased figure of $1,000,000 for the 1938 fiscal year was due principally to increased cost of construction.

Rear-Admiral David F. Sellers, superintendent of the Academy, recommended an increase of $166,404 over the 1937 total appropriations for the Academy.

From this amount he proposed that $50,000 be used for equipment for the new Marine Engineering Building; $27,797 for new employes; $9,500 for material for physical training; $15,000 for repairs to Bancroft Hall and quarters, $40,900 for increased costs due to complying with present laws in regard to leave for civil employes.

The estimated total for current and miscellaneous expenses for 1938, including purchase of materials peculiar to the Academy, such as text and reference books, stationery and equipment, was placed at $72,000. Sellers estimated $1,080,000 would be needed for maintenance and repairs at the Academy in 1938, including maintenance and operations of structures and grounds of the Academy.

SCHMELING DUE TODAY

(By The Associated Press)

NEW YORK, March 2.—Max Schmeling, the former heavyweight champion, who is scheduled to fight Jimmy Braddock for the title in June, if Madison Square Garden can convince everyone concerned that his contract is good, arrives today on the Berengaria to put in his words on the heavyweight situation.

W. T. SHAWN, Inc.
ANNOUNCES
Mr. Leslie Klakring
AS THEIR SALES REPRESENTATIVE
Oil Burners -- Heating -- Plumbing

Evening Capital

ANNAPOLIS, MD

1884 -:- 1937

Published Daily Except Sunday by
THE CAPITAL-GAZETTE PRESS, INCORPORATED

TALBOT T. SPEER, President
DAVID S JENKINS, Vice-President and Treasurer
E. M. JACKSON, JR., City Editor

You can have the EVENING CAPITAL mailed to you when away from the city by leaving your name and address at the office, for 45 cents per month: $5.00 per year payable in advance, to any postoffice in the United States or Canada.

Delivered in Annapolis, Eastport, Germantown and West Annapolis by Carrier for 45 cents per month. On sale at all newsstands.

Foreign Advertising Representative
J. J. DEVINE & ASSOCIATES, Inc.

New York—1932 Chrysler Bldg. Atlanta—206 Palmer Bldg.
Chicago—307 N. Michigan Ave. Pittsburgh—438 Oliver Bldg.
Detroit—817 Nsw Center Bldg. Syracuse—State Tower Bldg.

Entered as Second Class Matter May 28, 1933, at the Fost Office of Annapolis Maryland under the Act of March 3, 1879.

MEMBERS OF THE ASSOCIATED PRESS

The Associated Press is exclusively entitled to the use for re-publication of all news credited to it or not otherwise credited in this paper and also the local news published herein. All rights of re-publication of special dispatches herein are also reserved.

FRIDAY, APRIL 30, 1937.

ENCOURAGING SIGNS

Among many reports indicating an improvement in retail trade throughout the country, one of the most significant was the declaration of a large merchandising enterprise that the time had come to anticipate their needs a little farther in advance, and that in many staple lines it was desirable to make more advanced commitments.

In substance this means that this particular group has gained sufficient confidence in the continuing demand for goods to move away from the hand-to-mouth policy in buying, and that they must anticipate demand for their specialties to insure delivery and can and should carry larger inventories in the staple lines.

Retail sales over the United States are reported to have shown a gain of from 10 to 22 percent over corresponding periods of last year. Industrial operations following Easter show a greater increase than last year, a condition reflected in the improved figures of freight car loading. Buying is more prominent in the more ordinary consumer goods and shows in seasonal lines, but there is increasing confidence that it is now on a continuing upgrade, which enables the retailer to look ahead with greater surety.

Given this confidence in the future, even though at first it may not be very far-extended, the retailer is able to send his orders in to the wholesaler, or directly to the manufacturer, with the result that industrial production starts up, the call for workers goes out, wages are paid and new purchasing power for the support of retail trade is created.

This is the way the wheels of prosperity turn and any acceleration in this direction is hopeful and encouraging.

"A-L-L-'S .... W-E-L-L!"

When as a child in Navy Yards, I loitered years ago,
On summer nights, along the docks where ships rocked to and fro,
I loved to hear resounding every hour like a bell,
The voices of the sentries calling out that all was well:—
"Post Number One, and A-L-L-'S .... W-E-L-L!"

In groups we'd skirt the seawall's edge and leap upon the floats,
And when we seemed not too observed, climb into tethered boats;
Then suddenly, amidst our play, a silence on us fell,
While listening to some sentry calling out that all was well:—
"Post Number Two, and A-L-L-'S .... W-E-L-L!"

It ever made us feel protected, guarded and secure,
Someone was looking out for things . . . Life's happiness was sure;
Someone was watching over us—for by this we could tell—
Each sentry from his little box, called out that all was well:—
"Post Number Three, and AL-L-'S .... W-E-L-L!"

Ah me, that was so long ago . . . They do it now no more—
In colorless and colder ways they keep guard of the shore;
But how I long to hear again a voice that would dispel
The fear and dread of coming days by calling all was well!
"Posts down Life's road, and A-L-L-'S .... W-E-L-L!"

D. A. C.

GOV. NICE DEBATES LOCAL POLICE BILL

(Continued from Page 1)

as a bookie place is closed another springs up it is said.

34 Local Measures

Fifty-one bills were introduced by the county representatives in the Senate and House. So far, Gov. Nice has signed only six of the 34 local measures which passed. In this classification is the bill granting the B. and A. railroad tax exemption.

The Governor has signed the bills for a State office building here, another dealing with the Episcopal Church, one providing for a 4-year election term for members of the Annapolis city council, one providing a three-man Board of County Commissioners subject to referendum, and a bill allowing Sunday movies here and another measure allowing movies in Glen Burnie, also subject to referendum. In Glen Burnie movies can be held on Sundays as a benefit until the referendum is held.

"Lord of all pots and pans and things,
Since I've no time to be
A saint by doing lovely things,
Or watching late with Thee,
Or dreaming in the dawn light,
Or storming heaven's gates,
Make me a saint by getting meals
And washing up the plates.
"Although I must have Martha's hands,
I have a Mary mind,
And when I black the boots and shoes,
Thy sandals, Lord, I find.
I think of how they trod the earth
Each time I scrub the floor;
Accept this meditation, Lord,
I haven't time for more.
"Warm all the kitchen with Thy love
And light it with Thy peace;
Forgive me all my worrying
And make all grumbling cease.
Thou who didst love to give men food
In room, or by the sea,
Accept this service that I do—
I do it unto Thee."

NOTICE TO CONTRACTORS

Bids will be received in the office of the City Clerk, and opened Saturday, May 1, at 10:30 A. M., for remodeling Police Headquarters, Municipal Building.

Plans and specifications may be obtained from the City Commissioner Harry E. Bean.

The right is reserved to reject any and all bids.

JESSE A. FISHER,
Chairman, Public Property Committee.
a-30

NOTICE TO CREDITORS

Notice is hereby given that the Subscriber, of Anne Arundel County, has obtained from the Orphans' Court of Anne Arundel County, in Maryland, Letters Testamentary on the personal estate of

WALTER H. HART

late of Anne Arundel County, deceased. All persons having claims against the deceased, are hereby warned to exhibit the same, with the vouchers thereof, to the subscriber, on or before the

27TH DAY OF SEPTEMBER, 1937.

They may otherwise, by law, be excluded from all benefit of said estate. All persons indebted to said estate are requested to make immediate payment.

Given under my hand this 23rd day of March, 1937.

MERCANTILE TRUST COMPANY OF BALTIMORE, MD.
Executor.
a-30

PROCLAMATION

Know All Men, Women and Children By These Presents:

THAT, Whereas the health, happiness, life, safety and general welfare of each citizen are dependent upon existing living conditions, and,

WHEREAS, the lives and property of our people are endangered by fire, caused by rubbish accumulations in homes, factories, alleys and streets, and

WHEREAS, a city is judged largely by its general appearance of cleanliness, freshness and beauty, and

WHEREAS, we can benefit the unemployed by creating needed jobs for needed improvements,

NOW, THEREFORE, I, Louis N. Phipps, Mayor of the City of Annapolis, Maryland, do hereby designate the week of April 30th to May 8th, 1937, as FIRE PREVENTION CLEAN UP WEEK, and most respectfully call upon all departments of the City, the Chamber of Commerce, civil clubs, schools, all other clubs and associations, and our people in general to take active part in the constructive program planned to make our city, clean, healthful, thrifty, safe and beautiful.

In Testimony Whereof I hereby affix my name and the Seal of the city of Annapolis, this 15th day of April, in the year Nineteen Hundred and Thirty-seven.

(SEAL)

LOUIS N. PHIPPS, Mayor.

Attest:
KATHERINE E. LINTHICUM,
City Clerk.
a-30

—NOTICE—

Notice is hereby given that the following applications for Beer, Wine or Liquor licenses have been filed with the City Clerk, and will be considered at a Special Meeting of the Mayor, Counselor and Aldermen:

Raymond J. Swallow, 25 College Avenue, Off Sale Beer.

L. A. Ellison, 54 Cathedral Street, Off Sale Beer.
xx

MORTGAGEE'S SALE
—OF—
VALUABLE REAL ESTATE
Situated on the South East side of Randall Street, in the City of Annapolis, Maryland.

Under and by virtue of a power of sale contained in a mortgage from Joseph C. Droll and Carrie Droll, his wife, dated July 7, 1926, and recorded among the Land Records of Anne Arundel County in Liber W. M. B. No. 32, folio 451, default having occurred, the undersigned as Attorney named in said mortgage, will offer at Public Auction at the Court House Door in the City of Annapolis, Maryland, on

SATURDAY, MAY 1, 1937,
AT 11 O'CLOCK A. M.,

all those two lots or parcels of ground situate on the Southeast side of Randall Street in the City of Annapolis, Anne Arundel County, Maryland, and described as follows:

Fronting 40 feet on Randall Street having an even depth of 103 feet, being the same lots which were conveyed to the said Joseph C. Droll and Carrie Droll, his wife, by Ellsworth C. Burt, and wife, et al, by deed dated July 7, 1926, and recorded among the Land Records of Anne Arundel County in Liber W. M. B. No. 32, folio 450.

This property is improved by a modern two story dwelling.

TERMS OF SALE:—A deposit of $350.00 will be required of the purchaser at the time of the sale, and the balance of the puchase money with interest thereon at the rate of 6 per cent per annum to be paid in cash upon final ratification of sale.

Taxes and other expenses to be adjusted to the day of sale.

Signed:

BENJAMIN MICHAELSON,
Attorney-named-in-mortgage.
GEORGE W. SCIBLE, Auctioneer.

SPECIAL NOTICE: This property will positively be sold on the day of sale.

**BENJAMIN MICHAELSON,
Attorney-named-in-Mortgage.**
a-30

—NOTICE—

Application is made under Ch. 2, Acts Extraordinary Session 1933, General Assembly of Maryland, by

JOSEPH PHILLIPS

of Hanover, Md., for a Class D Beer License, to expire April 30, 1938, permitting him to sell the aforesaid beverage on the premises known as Phillip's Tavern, located on Ridge Road, three hundred feet east of same, opposite the home of Edward Adams, Hanover, Maryland.

Any one may speak for or against the granting of this license at a meeting to be held by this Board on May 10, 1937, at 8:00 p. m., at 21 West Street, Annapolis, by filing a written protest, signed by ten or more reputable citizens seven days prior to the aforesaid hearing.

BOARD OF LICENSE COMMISSIONERS OF ANNE ARUNDEL COUNTY.
STEWART LANDERS, Chairman.
JOSEPH H. GRISCOM, Clerk. a-30

NOTICE TO CREDITORS

Notice is hereby gien that the Subscriber, of Anne Arundel County, has obtained from the Orphans' Court of Anne Arundel County, in Maryland, Letters Administration d. b. n. c. t. a. on the personal estate of

MOLLIE HAYES HENRY

late of Anne Arundel County, deceased. All persons having claims against the deceased, are hereby warned to exhibit the same, with the vouchers thereof, to the subscriber, on or before the

23RD DAY OF OCTOBER, 1937.

They may otherwise, by law, be excluded from all benefit of said estate. All persons indebted to said estate are requested to make immediate payment.

Given under my hand this 20th day of April, 1937.

J. WILLIAM GRAHAM,
Administrator c. t. a.
m-28

Notice of Registration

TO THE VOTERS OF ANNAPOLIS:

Under provisions of Article 33 of the Annotated Code of Maryland Notice is hereby given that the Registration Officers for the several precincts will sit for the purpose of Revising the Registration Lists of Annapolis, Maryland, by adding the names of new voters, making transfers, etc., between the hours of 8 o'clock A. M. and 8 o'clock P. M. (see instructions of Attorney General. Registration and Election Laws) on the following dates and at the several polling places named below:

FIRST SITTING:
MONDAY, MAY 10TH, 1937,
SECOND SITTING
(Revision Only) No New Names Added
MONDAY, MAY 17TH, 19377

First Precinct—Polling House—East Street.

Second Precinct—Municipal Building (First Floor).

Third Precinct—Polling House—Second Street.

Fourth Precinct — Polling House—Calvert Street.

By Order of the Board of Supervisors of Elections for Annapolis.

CHARLES C. TAYLOR,
President.
JOHN J. STEHLE,
J. HENRY BROWN.
KATHERINE E. LINTHICUM, Clerk.
m-10

—NOTICE—

Notice is hereby given that the City Clerk will be prepared, on and after April 21st, 1937, to issue licenses for billiard, pool and bagatelle tables, legal slot machines, hucksters, wagons, poles, bill boards, amusement houses, milk permit, and all other city licenses required by law.

All such licenses expire on April 30th, and must be renewed on or before May 1st, under penalty of the law.

**KATHERINE E. LINTHICUM,
City Clerk.**
a-30

MISCELLANEOUS

MISCELLANEOUS — Kentucky mammoth jack, 16½ hands high, weight, 1,150 lbs. Will send this jack anywhere for 3 mares, or more. Raise mules and make money. Poplar Neck Stock Farm, P. F. Tippett, Mgr., Cheltenham, Md. xx

CLASSIFIED ADS

SERVICE

(Phone 330)

RATES

2c

PER WORD

This size type (6 point), Minimum ad 50c. Additional consecutive insertions 1c per word.

TELEPHONE SERVICE

If you are listed in the telephone directory we will accept your Want Ad over the phone and charge it to you. Charges must be paid 5 days after date of expiration of ad.

The Evening Capital will be responsible only for the first incorrect insertion of any advertisement and then only to the extent of a make good insertion.

Read your ads carefully and report any error immediately. The Evening Capital reserves the right to properly classify, revise, or reject any advertisement according to its option.

OUT-OF-TOWN ADS

All mail orders from advertisers outside of Annapolis must be accompanied by remittance.

FOR SALE

FOR SALE—37 foot Deadrise, 35 H. P. Gray motor, cabin, toilet, sheet copper bottom, bronze rudder and skag. In good condition. Phone 912-J. m-3

FOR SALE—Epping Forest 2-story house, 5 rooms, bath, open fireplace, screened porch. Owing to illness will sacrifice for $1,600. Easy terms. Address P. O. Box 352, Annapolis, Md. m-1

FOR SALE—40 Horses and Mules, 25 Belgian Colts, 2 to 5 years old. 10 Belgian Mares, some in foal. All A-1 workers. Some extra good tobacco planter horses. Poplar Neck Stock Farm, P. F. Tippett, Mgr., Cheltenham, Md. xx

FOR SALE—Old English Boxwood. Fine plants. Price 10c up. J. Margaret Heller, Boxwood Gardens, 88 Sixth Street, Eastport. m-5

FOR SALE—Year round 6-room home, on waterfront. Double garage, chicken house. Cheap. J. S. Enzinger, Priest Farm, Weems Creek. m-1

FOR SALE—House, 9 Locust Avenue, modern conveniences, oil burner. Apply above address. m-1

FOR SALE OR RENT

FOR SALE OR RENT—Garage one mile from Galesville. Apply L. Michaelson, Harwood, Md. tf

ROOM AND BOARD

ROOM AND BOARD — At Sylvan Shores, 15 minutes from Annapolis. Call 1837F22. m-1

Your Rental Ad in the Evening Capital will secure a tenant—quick!

FOR RENT

FOR RENT—Bungalow, all conveniences, fireplace, garage. One acre, two, miles from Annapolis, concrete road. 434½ West Street. m-4

FOR RENT—Two unfurnished apartments; one available May 1st, one June 1st. Apply Lipman's Bootery, 172 Main Street. tf

FOR RENT—DESIRABLE FURNISHED ROOM. Quiet neighborhood. Family with no children. Rent reasonable. Gentleman only. 134 Conduit Street. a-30

FOR RENT—Six room apartment. Can sublet part. 100 West Street. a-30

FOR RENT—8 room furnished house during summer. 3½ miles from Annapolis. Phone 1858-F-3. a-30

FOR RENT — Suburban apartments, furnished or unfurnished. Ranging in price and size, $40, $60, $90. All conveniences, delightfully liveable for year round. Will show by appointment. Box 59, Evening Capital. m-1

FOR RENT—Bungalow, two bedrooms, all conveniences, completely furnished. (Adults.) Directly on Chesapeake Bay. Seven miles from Annapolis. Available May 15th. Write Box 56, Evening Capital. a-30

FOR RENT—Furnished house in country, 4 bedrooms, 2 baths, and servant's quarters. On Main Road, 10 minutes from Naval Academy. Phone 458-W. m-6

FOR RENT—Large furnished room, private bath, in Colonial home. 112 Gloucester St. Phone 736. tf

FOR RENT—Three room heated apartment, furnished or unfurnished, electricity included. Phone 366 or 393-MX. tf

FOR RENT — Furnished apartment, five rooms, screened porch, heat, hot water, garage. Phone 521. tf

FOR RENT—Furnished apartment. Adults only. Apply 147 Prince George street.

FOR RENT — Apartment 3 rooms, kitchenette and bath. Furnished. Kelvinator, oil heat. 376 Severn avenue, Eastport. tf

FOR RENT—Houses, furnished and unfurnished, in new residential section. Naval officers moving out in May and June. Phone 178-R. tf

FOR RENT—Bungalow at Wardour. All modern conveniences including garage. Also have privilege of using private waterfront. Phone 1310. tf

FOR RENT—At Riva, 7-room house with sleeping porch; furnished, modern improvements. Good bathing beach. Large grounds. Apply E. W. Bassford, Harwood, Md. Phone West River 23F14. tf

FOR RENT — Unfurnished apartment, Heated. Apply Oscar Shacks, 37 West Street. tf

HELP WANTED MALE

MALE HELP WANTED — Energetic truck salesman, about 25. Capable of taking care of truck. Good opportunity for right man. Box 60, Evening Capital. a-30

WANTED

WANTED—Colored salesman by local concern. Apply 41 West Street. tf

WANTED—June to Sept., small furnished apartment, 1st floor. Rental not to exceed $35.00. Evening Capital, Box 61. m-4

Paint-Up and Clean-Up Campaign April 30th to May 8th.

BUSINESS DIRECTORY

The services offered by the following Annapolis firms have been investigated by THE EVENING CAPITAL and found to be satisfactory.

TRANSFER

HAULING, done carefully and cheaply. Ernest Parker, Camp Parole or Phone 330 Evening Capital. tf

COAL—FUEL OIL

Jerome Oil Sprayed Soft Coal
Colonial Cone-Cleaned Anthracite
Fuel Oil Wood
ANNAPOLIS DAIRY
Tel. 123
"More Heat Per Dollar"

PRINTING

Phone 330 and our representative will gladly call to give you prices on fine business printing.
CAPITAL-GAZETTE PRESS, INC.
3 Church Circle tf

AUTOMOBILES

ARUNDEL MOTORS
DeSoto—Plymouth
Sales and Service
28 West Street Phone 712
jy-23

ANNAPOLIS BUICK CO.
240 West Street
BUICK — OLDS
Used cars all makes and models
Phone 103 - 1685 tf

INSTALL NOW
Gilbarco
Essoburner
Automatic Oil Heat
As Low as $1.87 Per Week
Monthly Budget Plan
NO MONTHLY PAYMENTS BEFORE SEPTEMBER 15TH
Call 123
SALES & SERVICE
ANNAPOLIS UTILITIES, INC.

NO LONGER is it necessary for bereaved families to feel that they must accept inferior funeral services due to inability to pay a high price. T. A. Hardesty & Son offer a complete funeral, limousine, embalming, hearse and all, for as little as $75. The world's finest guaranteed steel vault may be had from Hardesty for $85. When death occurs call T. A. Hardesty & Son—one of the finest equipped funeral directors in the county—Galesville, Md. W. Riv. 201-F-2.

FOR SALE OR RENT
Bay Drive Bay Ridge
ALL-THE-YEAR HOME
Modern equipment, attractive, convenient, comfortable.
Moderate cost with small upkeep.
Will finance liberally.
Open Sundays or by appointment.
Phone Gilmor—5882
F. M. MILLER

Call 123
FRIGIDAIRE
SALES and SERVICE
ANNAPOLIS UTILITIES, INC.

Radio

Editor's Note: Programs originating at WEAF may be heard over WFBR; those over WABC over WCAO, and those at WJZ over WBAL. This applies except when local programs interfere.

NEW YORK, April 30.—The list of stations making up the two units of the NBC chain continues to undergo alteration and addition.

One important change, just announced for early Fall, takes place at Cleveland. WHK, oldest station here, is to join the network in lace of the present WGAR. WHK now is a part of the CBS chain, and is owned by the Radio Air Service Corp., an affiliate of the Cleveland Plain Dealer and The Cleveland News.

The newest addition is WJTN, of Jamestown, N. Y., which goes on the network May 15, to increase the station total to 126.

More and more pre-coronation broadcasts are being placed on the schedules. U. S. Ambassador Robert W. Bingham is to provide one a coronation eve talk, for NBC May '. He speaks just before midnight . London (5:40) here, the broadast to close with Big Ben's striking the hour that ushers in Coronation Day.

Another, "Dancing Around London," is for WABC-CBS, May 7, to originate from various night spots in the British capital. A third, for May 8 on NBC, is a microphone preview of the line of march for the coronation procession, to contain numerous interviews with the man on the street.

(Daylight Saving Time One Hour Later)

Listening tonight (Friday): Talks: WEAF-NBC, 6:30—Aldous Huxley on the Coronation; WJZ-NBC, 9:30—Lawyers Guild Dinner for John D. Devaney.

WEAF-NBC — 6:15, Uncle Ezra; 7, Lucille Manners Concert; 8, Waltz Time; 9, First Nighter, "Love Flies High"; 9:30, Varsity Varieties from Washington; 10:30, Cotton Land Musical Festival.

WABC-CBS—7, Broadway Varieties; 7:30, Hal Kemp Dance; 8, Hollywood Hotel; 9, San Francisco Symphony; 9:30, Babe Ruth; 10:30, Red Norvo Orchestra.

WJZ-NBC—7, Irene Rich; 7:30, Death Valley Days; 8, Harlem Revue; 8:30, Deems Taylor Program; 9, Jack Pearl; 10, Chicago Symphonic Hour.

What to expect Saturday: WEAF-NBC—11:30 A. M., Child Health Program; 12:30 P. M., Olivet College Orchestra; 3, Salute to Youth; 4:30, Kaltenmeyer's Kindergarten. WABC-CBS—10 A. M., Cincinnati Musicale; 1:15 P. M., Child Health Day Program; 4:30, Davis Cup tennis matches; 5, E. Robert Schmitz, piano; 5:45, Dr. Paul B. Sears on "Progress in the Dust Bowl." WJZ-NBC—12 Noon, U. of Cincinnati Glee Club; 2, Concert from Vienna; 3:30, Spelling Bee, Smith College vs. U. of Pennsylvania.

Paint-Up and Clean-Up Campaign April 30th to May 8th.

SELL! Through the WANT-ADS

SCORCHY SMITH

By John C. Terry

LET'S TAKE A WALK ON THE BEACH, SCORCHY-
-SORRY, KAY- I'VE PROMISED MR. TALLEY I WOULD SEE THE BROADCASTING STATION WITH HIM - WOULD YOU---
-MAY I OFFER TO ESCORT YOU, MISS KIMBERLEY?-
-WELL--ER-- MAYBE I'D BETTER GO IN AND LISTEN TO THE RADIO WITH THE OTHERS -
BUT THIS IS YOUR ONLY EVENING ON MIDWAY- YOU SHOULDN'T MISS THE MOONLIT BEACH - SHOULD SHE MR. TALLEY ?-
-OF COURSE NOT - WORTH SEEING -
-I ORDERED THAT MOON ESPECIALLY FOR YOU, KAY -
-SO CONSIDERATE OF YOU -

DOROTHY DARNIT

By Charles McManus

HOW DO YOU DO MISS JOHNSON IS SAL HOME?
NO SHE'S AT SUNDAY SCHOOL
WELL I'LL GO AND LOOK FOR HER GOOD BYE
GOOD BYE DOLLY
WELCOME LITTLE GIRL. DID YOU COME TO GET SALVATION?
NO SIR
I CAME FOR SAL JOHNSON
CHAS McMANUS

VICTIM OF HINDENBURG DISASTER

HINDENBURG BURSTS INTO FLAMES

LAKEHURST, N. J., May 6.—The giant German Zeppelin Hindenburg is shown as it burst into flames over the Lakehurst airport late today and plunged to earth, where it crumpled into a blazing mass of debris. An undetermined number of passengers and crew members lost their lives. This picture was taken by Murray Becker, Associated Press staff photographer, and is Copyright, 1937, by the Associated Press.

LAKEHURST, N. J., May 6.—His clothes gone, an unidentified passenger on the German dirigible Hindenburg leaped to safety as the giant airliner plunged to earth in a flaming mass late today. His clothing was burned from his body. He is shown being led to safety by rescue workers. This picture was taken by Murray Becker, Associated Press staff photographer, and is Copyright, 1937, by the Associated Press.—Associated Press Photo.

ST. JOHN'S GLEE CLUB TO PRESENT ANNUAL SPRING CONCERT

Edward C. Sommer, president of the St. John's College Glee Club, has announced the selection of the following patrons and patronesses for the Annual Spring Concert to be held in the Great Hall on May 12, at 8:30 o'clock; President Amos W. W. Woodcock, of the College; Major E. A. Harrson, Dr. and Mrs. V. J. Wyckoff, Dr. and Mrs. H. Bernhard, Dr. and Mrs. Richard Kuehnemund, Dean and Mrs. Paul Allen, Jr.

The guest soloist will be a student of the Peabody Conservatory of Music in Baltimore, Edward Silkman.

The concert will be given with his aid. Several additional features on the program are done by a quartet and a double quartet made up of students in the Glee Club.

St. John's College Glee Club has extended an invitation to friends, alumni, or other people interested to attend this concert.

N. A. Women's Club Book Review Group To Meet on Monday

The Book Review Section of the Naval Academy Women's Club will hold its final meeting of the year on Monday, May 10, at 2:30 P. M., at the Y. W. C. A. Building, on State Circle. Mrs. Hermann Bernhard will review Voltaire. Mrs. W. R. Thayer will speak on her travels in

Tea will be served.
South America this past winter.

Eastport Group to Hold Strawberry Festival Tonight

The Ladies' Sewing Circle of the Eastport M. E. Church will hold a strawberry festival in the basement of the church this evening, beginning at 6:30 o'clock. The menu will consist of strawberries, ice cream, and homemade cake.

At 8 o'clock an entertainment will be given, which is included in the price of the ticket.

The event is open to the public.

Keep in daily touch with the Want Ads and save time and money of Buy-Quick Bargains.

BLAZING ZEPPELIN ON THE GROUND

AS ZEPPELIN HIT THE EARTH

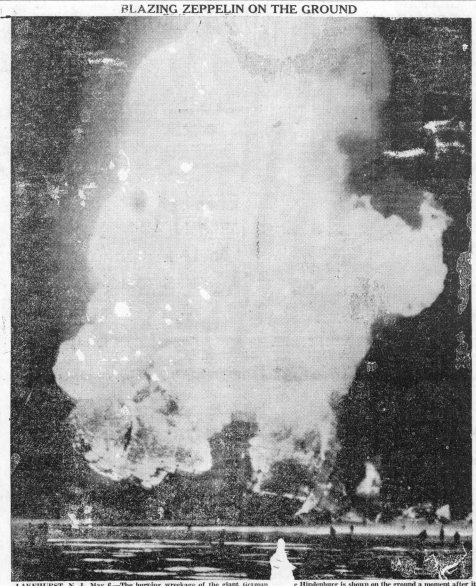

LAKEHURST, N. J., May 6.—The burning wreckage of the giant German Hindenburg is shown on the ground a moment after it crashed with many of its passengers and crew still aboard. Some saved their lives jumping. This spectacular picture was taken by Murray Becker, Associated Press staff photographer, and is Copyright, 1937, by the Associated Press.

LAKEHURST, N. J., May 6.—This picture was taken at the moment the giant German dirigible hit the earth, a flaming pyre, a few minutes after it had burst into flames over the Lakehurst airport. This picture was made by Murray Becker, Associated Press photographer.

ANNAPOLIS

Home of the
U. S. NAVAL ACADEMY
and
ST. JOHN'S COLLEGE

Evening Capital

Weather Forecas
Fair tonight and Tuesday. Little change in temperature.

VOL. CV — No. 11. | ESTABLISHED IN 1884—PUBLISHED EVERY EVENING EXCEPT SUNDAY | ANNAPOLIS, MONDAY, MAY 24, 1937. | SOUTHERN MARYLAND'S ONLY DAILY PAPER | PRICE TWO CENTS.

10 MARYLAND MIDDIES IN FIRST CLASS

Annapolis, However, Does Not Furnish Single One Of 328 Graduates This Year—June 3 Graduation Day—Students Celebrate End Of Exams.

COMPLETE LIST OF GRADUATING CLASS

Rear - Admiral Adolphus Andrews, chief of the Bureau of Navigation, Navy Department, will be the principal speaker at thet graduation of 325 midshipmen at the Naval Academy on June 3, it was announced today at the Academy.

Admiral Andrews also heads the personnel bureau of the Navy, which is charged with the training of all naval personnel.

Eight of the 12 midshipmen companies today began competition for the honor of naming the "color girl" for the June Week ceremonies. The other four companies will drill tomorrow. Platoons will compete on Wednesday and the four battalions on Thursday.

The first class at the Naval Academy which will graduate on June 3, includes 10 Marylanders among its 328 members. None of the Marylanders are from Annapolis, however, the official list discloses.

The Marylanders are: C. A. Burch, C. R. Dodds and W. P. Lowndes of Baltimore; H. H. Barton of Bethesda; W. D. Brinckloe, Jr., of Easton; C. H. Meigs, of Have De Grace; R. . Erly of Hyattsville; C. E. Lae, of Rockville; J. Dalton of Sparks and R. H. Northwood of Sparrows Point.

New York with 26 and California with 25 leads the list of graduates.

Studies Are Ended

The regiment of Midshipmen finished their studies for the year on Saturday and celebrated the event in accordance with time honored tradition of the institution.

The third (sophomore) class started things off by observing the "burial of math," to mark the end-

(Continued on Page 3)

Lindberghs Have 3rd Son

(By The Associated Press)

CLEVELAND, May 24.—The birth of a third son to Colonel and Mrs. Charles A. Lindbergh —on coronation night, May 12— was announced today by Miss Anne S. Cutter, Mrs. Lindbergh's aunt.

The baby presumably was born in the rambling English house, "Longbarn," Seven Oaks, Kent, in which the Lindberghs have sought solitude for more than a year. They fled there in December of 1935, before Bruno Richard Hauptmann died in the New Jersey electric chair for the kidnap-murder of Charles Augustus Lindbergh, Jr., their first-born.

JUDGE BENJ. WATKINS, 97, DIED YESTERDAY

Funeral Will Take Place Tomorrow From All Hallows Chapel Davidsonville.

Judge Benjamin Watkins, one of the oldest and most widely known residents of the Davidsonville section of Anne Arundel county, died last night at "The Locusts," the old Watkins homestead near Davidsonville, where he was born in 1840. Judge Watkins married Miss Anne Elizabeth Welsh of this county, who died twelve years ago.

He is survived by three children, Miss Katherine W. Watkins, Miss Eleanora E. Watkins and Benjamin Watkins, Jr., and two grandchildren, Miss Marion B. Watkins and Benjamin Watkins, 3rd.

Judge Watkins served as deputy tobacco inspector some years ago, was judge of the Orphans' Court, a member of the Board of Education, and president of the Bureau of Immigration. He was a member of the old South River Club, serving as chairman until he retired from active participation on account of his age. He was a life-long member of All Hallows Parish and vestryman for more than 70 years.

His funeral will take place tomorrow, at 11 A. M. from All Hallows Chapel, Davidsonville. The Rev. Victor S. Ross will officiate.

Catholic P. T. A. To Hold Important Meeting on May 26

The Parent-Teacher Association of St. Mary's Parochial School will have a special meeting on Wednesday evening of this week, at 7 o'clock, in the rectory of St. Mary's Church.

The meeting, which will precede the Wednesday night services in St. Mary's Church, is a most important one, and it is hoped that it will be well attended.

AN EMINENT AMERICAN FROM YOUTH TO OLD AGE

This group of photos shows John D. Rockefeller, Sr., who died at Ormond Beach, Fla., at various stages of his long life. 1—A young man. 2—In middle thirties, early in his career as president of the Standard Oil Company. 3—About peak of his active career, 1911. 4—When oil trust was dissolved in 1911, leading to his retirement. 5—On his 97th birthday in 1936 at his Lakewood, N. J., home. 6—Believed to be last picture of Rockefeller, showing him arriving at Ormond Beach, October 9, 1936.— (Copyright by Englebrecht from Associated Press).

C. L. WIEGAND AGAIN HEADS U. S. WORKERS

Maryland State Federation Holds Annual Convention Here Saturday — McCarran Addresses Delegates At Banquet Held At Armory.

NEXT MEETING AT EDGEWOOD

Representatives of five states and the District of Columbia assembled here Saturday for the convention of the Maryland Federal Employes Union and elected Charles L. Wiegand, of Baltimore, local 21, as its president for another term.

The Convention closed with a banquet at which places were set for 275, in the Bladen street National Guard Armory.

McCarran Speaker

The principal speaker of the evening was Senator Pat McCarran, Democrat, Nevada, who praised the work of the federal workers and urged that they remain contented in their work.

(Continued on Page 4)

Slayton Files For Alderman In 2nd Ward

Retired Navy Commander Announces Candidacy After Conversation With Mayor Louis N. Phipps And Other Friends, He Reports.

3 OTHERS ALREADY SEEK TWO OFFICES

A fourth candidate for alderman in the second ward subject to the Democratic primaries filed today The latest candidate is Comdr. Charles C. Slayton, U.S.N., retired, now in the insurance business in Maryland avenue. He lives at 112 Duke of Glocester street.

Mr. Slayton said: "I reached the decision to file after conversation with Mayor Phipps and other friends. I have nothing to say at the present time relative to issues."

Incumbents File

The two incumbent aldermen Arthur T. Elliott and J. William Graham have filed for re-election and Charles Bernstein who nearly won two years ago, again is a candidate.

Four candidates have filed in the

(Continued on Page 6)

WM. B. GARDINER DIES SUDDENLY OF HEART MALADY

Attack Occurs At Home Yesterday Following Motor Trip With Family.

William B. Gardiner, 67, of 50 Southgate avenue, died suddenly at his home Sunday afternoon as the result of a heart attack.

Mr. Gardiner had just returned to his home from an automobile ride with members of his family. He was seated on the porch of his home when he succumbed.

Born In Annapolis

Mr. Gardiner was born in Annapolis and was the son of William Brewer Gardiner and Evelyn Benjamin Gardiner. He has lived in this city all of his life. He was a lifelong member of the Presbyterian Church.

He was an architect and was a member of the Maryland Architectural Club. At one time he was building inspector for the city of Annapolis. He also was a member of the Elks, Red Men, and was a charter member of the local lodge of the Knights of Pythias. At the time of his death he was a county property assessor.

Survived By Wife

He is survived by his wife, Mrs. Stella Wright Gardiner, whom he married thirty years ago. Other survivors are: Mrs. Carrie Gott, of Annapolis; Miss Edith Gardiner, of Frederick, sisters; Mrs. Helen White, of Annapolis, and Mrs. Frank Kulp, of Washington, neices, and

(Continued on Page 6)

ROCKEFELLER SUCCUMBS TO HEART ATTACK

Founder Of One Of World's Largest Fortunes Died Comparatively A "Poor Man"—Valet Hears Last Words—Millions Given Away.

OIL MAGNATE IN HIS 97TH YEAR

(By The Associated Press)

ORMOND BEACH, Fla., May 24—John D. Rockefeller, Sr., the founder of the world's greatest "dollar dynasty," lay stiled in death today—just 26 months short of his cherished desire to live to be 100.

He would have been 98 years old July 8.

The aged capitalist died Sunday morning at 4:05 o'clock, E.S.T., at his winter home, "The Casements," drifting peacefully off to his final sleep after complaining that he felt "very tired."

His physician, Dr. Harry L. Marryday, attributed death to sclerotic myocarditis, a hardening of the heart muscles.

Died "Poor Man"

The Nonagenarian Croesus, who rose from a $4.50-a-week clerk to mastership of a fortune estimated as high as $2,400,000,000, died a

(Continued on Page 6)

PREMEDICAL GROUP HOLDS 'OPEN HOUSE'

Osler Club Of St. John's College Had Exhibit In Biology Laboratory Yesterday.

A number of people of Annapolis, as well as the faculty and students, attended the "open house" of the Osler Premedical Club in the biology laboratory of St. John's College yesterday afternoon. Among the exhibits were several old microscope slides made of bone and mica rather than of glass which is now employed, and an old microscope made by Dollond of London about 1800.

The 42 compound microscopes and six dissecting microscopes owned by the Biolodgy Department were employed to demonstrate standard laboratory material, as well as living and preserved native to Anne Arundel county. The department has also a very excellent micro-projector by aid of which living microscopic organisms of ponds and streams were projected onto the lecture room screen. In tanks and aquaria were living salamanders, frogs, turtles, crayfishes, and other forms which students have collected and classified outside the work of regular courses.

Exhibits were set up under the direction of a special committee composed of Professor William H. Bayliff, Thompson F. Dow and Norval Kemp, president of the Osler Premedical Club.

Mrs. Bayliff and Miss Elisabeth Ridgely served refreshments.

MISS R. M. FREEMAN DIED YESTERDAY AT HOME IN EAST STREET

Miss Rosie May Freeman, an invalid for some time, died yesterday at the residence of her mother, Mrs. Rebecca Freeman, 89 East street, this city.

Miss Freeman is survived by four sisters, Mrs. Helen Johnson, of California, Mrs. Henry Olson, Mrs. Bessie Morgan, and Mrs. Amanda Parkinson, of Annapolis, and four brothers, Horace, William H., S. Elmer and Edward Freeman, also of this city.

The funeral will take place at 3:30 o'clock on Wednesday afternoon, from the residence, with interment in St. Anne's cemetery.

Chamber Will Meet On Thursday

The regular monthly meeting of the Chamber of Commerce will be held Thursday evening in the Chamber rooms at Carvel Hall at 8 o'clock, instead of this evening.

PARLEY SET FOR TOMORROW ON MD. REFERENDA

Local Committee Will Sit With State And Baltimore Officials At City Hall At 4 O'clock Tomorrow Afternoon.

INVITATIONS SENT OUT FROM HERE OVER WIRE

Mayor Louis N. Phipps today revealed that his purpose in sponsoring a meeting of State leaders here tomorrow to discuss the referenda on the State office building and the State $9,052,000 bond issue, was to place the responsibility for "whatever happens squarely on their shoulders."

He issued invitations to the meeting Saturday night after the general committee had found it had enough names to force a referendum on the $9,000,000 bond issue, which carries funds for a variety of State purposes. This referendum move was launched in reprisal to the Baltimore referendum against the bill to construct an office building here.

Petitions Are Ready

"We wish to announce to those invited that the referendum petition on the $9,000,000 bond issue is ready to file," Phipps said. "We are merely inviting them to give them a chance to say the last word and if they do not act then the responsibility of what happens in the State is up to them.

"I know those who have been invited can stop the State office building referendum if they desire, and we are willing to drop our referendum when Baltimore drops the office building move. Four of those invited are candidates for Governor and are strong enough to stop the dispute.

Leaders' Responsibility

"If the leaders do not act, then what follows is their responsibility. If they are not interested enough to come its also their responsibility. We are giving them the chance.

Tomorow's meeting will be held at 4 P. M. in the city hall. The general committee consisting of Mayor Phipps, William U. McCready, David S. Jenkins, Alfred A. Erickson, John F. Martin, Elmer M. Jackson, Jr., Clarence Tyler, Robert Kucera, Jr., BenJamin Michaelson, John M. Maukert, Joseph M. Armstrong, William H. Labrot, William J. McWilliams, Noah A. Hillman and Harry S. Kenchington will attend.

The Invitations Read

The invitations read:

"You are invited to attend an important conference between the Mayor of Baltimore and the Annapolis committee on the State office building referendum at the City Hall, Annapolis, on Tuesday, 4 P. M. Our committee has sufficient names to petition for referendum on the State-wide bond issue. We would welcome your suggestions."

List Of Those Invited

Among those invited to the meet-

(Continued on Page 6)

Admiral Sellers Will Purchase First Stamp

President Roosevelt Makes Arrangements To Buy Memorial Issue On Sale Here May 26—Many Notables On List — Arrangements Are Completed.

The Annapolis post office is being swamped with orders for "first-day covers" and Postmaster William A. Strohm stated this morning that over 100,000 of these covers have already been received. The entire post office force, with six additional temporary appointments, have been working day and night for the past week in order to have these covers ready for dispatch on May 26 which will be the first day of sale of the new five-cent Naval Academy stamp.

These covers represent envelopes sent in to the post office already addressed and accompanied with remittance for the new stamps to be affixed, so that the "covers" can be postmarked on May 26. On that

(Continued on Page 6)

GEN. WOODCOCK TO BE MEMORIAL DAY SPEAKER IN CITY

Gen. Amos W. W. Woodcock, president of St. John's College, will be the principal speaker at the Memorial Day services to be held here on Monday, May 31, it was announced today by officials of the local Veterans of Foreign Wars post, which is sponsoring the program.

General Woodcock will speak at the Naval Academy cemetery. Services will also be held at the National Cemetery.

Maj. Charles E. Myers will be marshal of the Memorial Day parade, which will begin at 9 A. M. on Monday, starting from Amos Garrett boulevard and West street. Organizations and the public have been invited to participate in the parade.

Jobless Aid Act Is Held To Be Valid

(By The Associated Press)

WASHINGTON, May 24.—The Supreme Court held constitutional today the unemployment insurance provisions of the Social Security Act.

Justice Cardozo delivered the momentous opinion which affirmed a ruling in favor of the legislation by the Fifth Circuit Court of Appeals and gave the administration another major victory.

Justices Butler, McReynolds, Sutherland and Van Devanter—four of the nine justices—objected to at least part of the majority opinion.

MRS. W. B. ENNIS, SR. DIED SATURDAY AT HOME OF DAUGHTER

Mrs. Emma May Ennis, widow of William B. Ennis, Sr., a former resident of Annapolis, died Saturday at the home of her daughter, Mrs. Harry C. Lane, 20 Wetherspoon Road, Baltimore, after an illness of two weeks. She was 83 years old.

The funeral took place at 2 o'clock this afternoon, with burial in the Western cemetery. The Rev. Frank R. Bayley, D.D., Superintendent of the East Baltimore District of the Methodist Episcopal Church, conducted the services.

Mrs. Ennis is survived by three daughters: Mrs. H. C. Lane, and Mrs. Fred S. Hall, of Baltimore and Miss Nell Ennis, of Washington, D. C., and three sons, the Rev. Dr. Daniel L. Ennis, of Washington, D. C.; Robert S. Ennis, of East Orange, N. J., and William B. Ennis, Jr., of this city.

BELGIAN VETERANS PROTEST AMNESTY FOR GERMAN FRIENDS

(By The Associated Press)

BRUSSELS, June 10—Embittered Belgian war veterans caused a cabinet crisis today by their angry opposition to a government proposal to pardon all Belgians convicted of treason during the World War.

Mounted troops and tanks were thrown about the parliament buildings and strategic points in the capital to prevent a repetition of demonstrations such as one yesterday in which 400 veterans hurled their war decorations on the tomb of the unknown soldier.

The government received a delegation of the veterans in an effort to modify them, but feared a new outburst when the amnesty measure comes up for action before the Senate today.

Veterans who forced their way to the Speaker of the Senate swore to kill any 'traitor' who profited by the bill.

The government supported measure, already passed by the lower House 95 to 75, affects principally Flemings living in the north of Belgium who sided with Germany during the war in the hope of establishing an independent Flemish state if Germany won.

Many of these were convicted of treason and citizenship rights were taken from them. Some are still in prison.

POLICE, STRIKERS CLASH; SEVENTEEN SUSTAIN INJURIES

(Continued from Page 1)

lation of the Wagner Act was submitted to the National Labor Relations Board by S.W.O.C. Officials at Chicago. The unionists contended refusal of Inland to negotiate demands for a written contract guaranteeing collective bargaining constituted violation of the law.

Plan Civil Suits

Union leaders announced they were preparing civil suits against and Republic Corporation, alleging $500,000 damages for the deaths of eight men and injury to scores of others in the Memorial Day steel strike riot at Republic's South Chicago plant. They also disclosed John L. Lewis, C.I.O. chief, would address a mass meeting at Chicago June 17.

Electric light and power were restored to 192 cities in Michigan's Saginaw valley after settlement of a strike of Consumers Power company employes which plunged 80,000 workers into idleness. Members of the United Automobiles Workers Union pulled switches yesterday, disrupting service in the highly industrialized area. An official announcement said the agreement terminating the strike provided for wage increases.

At Washington, President William Green of the American Federation of Labor called for immediate payment of extra assessments by member unions to augment funds to be used in fighting the Committee for Industrial Organization. The groups split less than a year ago.

BRITAIN MAKES CLAIM

(By The Associated Press)

LONDON, June 10—Britain advanced her claims to territorial sovereignty in the Antarctic today, seeking eventual domination of the Southern Polar wastes where the United States, too, has staked out an ice-bound domain.

DECISION TO BUILD UP MERCHANT MARINE PRAISED BY KENNEDY

(By The Associated Press)

WASHINGTON, June 10—Chairman Joseph P. Kennedy of the Maritime Commission jubilantly said today that the administration's proposal to build 95 new merchant ships means the United States is "going places" on the high seas.

"We have no selfish ambition to become queen of the seven seas." he added, "but we do want our fair share of commerce—and we mean to get it."

President Roosevelt has asked Congress to provide $10,000,000 for an immediate start on construction of new vessels, and to authorize the Maritime Commission to contract for $150,000,000 additional construction next year.

"The large appropriation was requested because we have to act in a hurry." Kennedy explained.

F. D. R. ASKS AID FOR THOSE WITHOUT FUNDS NEEDING MEDICAL CARE

(By The Associated Press)

ATLANTIC CITY, N. J., June 10—A personal message from President Roosevelt asking cooperation in plans to give medical care to those unable to pay for it, was delivered to the House of Delegates of the American Medical Association here today by U. S. Senator J. Hamilton Lewis of Illinois.

Methodist Church School Group to Hold Lawn Fete

The members of the Intermediate Department of Calvary Methodist Episcopal Church School are giving a lawn fete Saturday, June 12, at 6:30 p. m., at the home of Miss Naomi Brewer, corner of Market and Union streets.

Miss Brewer is chairman with the following assistants: Mrs. E. Cranston Riggin and Miss Dorothy Lyons, with their classes have charge of the sale of home-made frozen custard and cakes; Miss Evelyn Stokes and class will sell candies and Miss Esther Garrett and class have a very interesting feature in the grab bag.

The young men of Prof. George Fox's class will arrange the lighting effect thereby enhancing the natural beauty of the garden, making it an ideal spot for the occasion.

PROPERTY TRANSFERS IN CITY AND COUNTY RECORDED IN COURT

From The Bay Beach Realty Company to The Holloway Company—5 lots of ground at Deale Beach in Seventh District.

From William A. Deeck and wife to Jesus J. Fugle and wife—2 lots of ground at Wodland Beach in First District.

From Walter Hagemeyer and wife to Jane Tupper Caul—lot of ground at Broadwater Beach this county.

From The Dunbar Heights Development Company to Mary L. Downs—3 lots of ground in this county the first lot containing 31 acres, the second lot containing 25¼ acres, the third lot containing 3¼ acres.

From C. Albert Hodges, late County Treasurer and others to William M. Leibold and wife—lot of ground in Third District containing 1.75 acres.

From C. Albert Hodges, late County Treasurer and others to James P. Sanders and wife—2 lots of ground in the Third District the first lot containing 1 acre, the second lot containing 10 acres.

From County Commissioners of Anne Arundel County to William Brelsore—2 lots of ground at North Beach Park in Eighth District.

From County Commissioners of Anne Arundel County to Harold Norton—2 lots of Ground at Brooklyn Park, in Fifth District.

OH HAPPY DAY.
It was a gay moment of informality after the wedding when this was snapped. It caught the new Duchess in a laugh, the Duke in the middle of a chuckle, and Major Dudley Metcalfe, best man, joined in the mirthful moment.

MISSED THE KING. An illness kept J. P. Morgan, American capitalist, from the coronation of King George VI. He is shown upon his arrival in New York.

BIG BOY.
Fondness for fried chicken has pushed Louis' weight up to 205 in spite of a rigid training program at his camp in Kenosha, Wis. Here he relaxes under the shower after a long, hard workout. He says he's ready for the champ.

NOSEGAY. YEAH? As a flower the Krubi, from Sumatra, appeared very much alive, but aromatically, quite the opposite. It reached a height of eight feet in a New York botanical garden. Most people preferred seeing it through a glass.

JOE.
In this corner—Joe Louis of Detroit; one-time auto plant worker, who gets a crack at Braddock's title June 22 in Chicago. Just 23, his star rose early, only to be dimmed by Schmeling's knockout blow a year ago.

IT'S JUNE.
And here is one of the most famous love matches in history. David of Windsor, who, rather, would be a husband than a king, and Wallis Warfield, American-born, who could not be a queen, are shown as bride and groom.

THREE KINGS. Monarchs of peaceful Scandinavian countries had a great time at the silver jubilee of King Christian of Denmark. Here they acknowledge the ovation of crowds at Amalienburg castle, left to right, Haakon of Norway, Gustav of Sweden and Christian.

HE HOLDS MADRID. It was a charity bullfight where this picture of Gen. Jose Miaja (in glasses and beret) was taken. He is the supreme commander of Spanish Loyalist forces and is credited with the stout defense of Madrid.

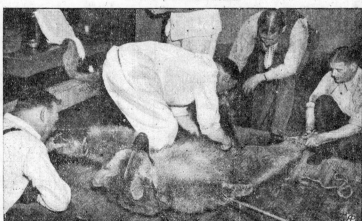

GRIN AND BEAR. Hurt and inquisitive, Rahjah, Syrian brown bear in a New York circus, failed to appreciate the work of a veterinarian whom he watched perform a major operation.

FRENCH TOAST.
And why not? The Chateau de Cande will be a landmark of posterity because there came the sequel to the romantic abdication of Edward VIII. Among the many townspeople who celebrated the wedding were the lodge-keeper and the towncrier of Monts, who are shown here drinking a toast to the newlyweds.

ANNAPOLIS Evening Capital

Home of the U. S. NAVAL ACADEMY and ST. JOHN'S COLLEGE

Weather Forecast
Generally fair and warmer today; fair and warmer tomorrow, except some probability of local thunder showers in afternoon.

VOL. CV — No. 46. | ESTABLISHED IN 1884—PUBLISHED EVERY EVENING EXCEPT SUNDAY | ANNAPOLIS, SATURDAY, JULY 3, 1937. | SOUTHERN MARYLAND'S ONLY DAILY PAPER | PRICE TWO CENTS.

Annapolis Faces Glen Burnie Tomorrow And Fort Meade On Monday

Winner To Get 60 Percent Of Gate Tomorrow, And Exciting Game Between Two Brilliant Teams Is Anticipated.

The biggest baseball week-end that Annapolis has known in some moons is in store for local fans over the holidays that begins tomorrow. On the Fourth of July Glen Burnie furnishes the opposition and on the following day Fort George Meade will be cast in the role of enemy. Both of these games will be played at the local ball yard and will start at 2:30 P. M.

These pair of games are naturals. Not only are the rivalries of long standing, but in addition both Glen Burnie and Fort Meade are to bring their own delegations of rooters. Glen Burnie in particular boasts a particularly rabid group of supporters who follow their choices everywhere.

60 Percent To Winner

The winner will take 60 percent of the gate tomorrow and both sides will fight for the added money.

Glen Burnie has announced that Steve Gerkin will take the hill on Sunday against Annapolis. Gerkin knows the local hitters having appeared here often for Eastport. If ... right he will be in the hair ... Hillearymen all day because ... has demonstrated before, he ... the locals at times. ... Gerkin will be efty Mc... Hilleary chose Mac over ... because of the unusual number of southpaw batters in the Glen ... array. Watt will work on ... drawing the tough Fort ... assignment. However, on the ... that he has shown his last two times out, Watt will be more than an even bet to annex another victory.

Monday's Line-Up

The lineups for the Glen Burnie game:

Annapolis: Stevens, ss; Myers, 3b; Zahn, 2b; Johnson, lf; Townsend, rf; Rolf, 1b; Wynne, c; MacIntyre, p.

Glen Burnie: Rutter, 2b; Brown, rf; Blades, lf; Oeschler, 3b.; Hess, 1b; Rock, ss; Solly, cr; Williams, ... Gerkin, p.

... the Fort Meade game Annap... will present the same lineup with the exception of MacIntyre. Watt will pitch. The Fort Meade array: Tedesco, rf; Miller, 1b; Kocher, ss; Krasliki, lf; Patton, c; Keller, 2b; Roser, 3b; Uffaslekey, cf; Solomose, p.

Idlewilde Hotel
ON CHESAPEAKE BAY
A Beautiful, Healthful Summer Resort
CHICKEN DINNER 85c
DANCE ORCHESTRA SATURDAY
Boating, Bathing, Fishing, Dancing
HARRY SALUS, Proprietor
Shady Side, Md.

Gray's Crab House
FRESH CRAB MEAT
DEVILED CRABS
STEAMED HARD CRABS
Foot Prince George Street
Phone 996-J
WE DELIVER IN CITY
WE WILL BE OPEN ALL DAY MONDAY

CALL 503
Between 9 A. M. and 11:30 P. M.
—FREE—
Immediate delivery on all kinds
WHSKEY—WINE—BEER
"DIXIE" LIQUOR STORE
58 Washington Street

FOR SALE
DESIRABLE DWELLING
Duke of Gloucester Street
Price $5500. Easy Terms
CHAS. F. LEE
Real Estate and Insurance
Church Circle Phone 603

—FOR SALE—
Suburban property—one and one-half acres on Severn River. Owner's house and guest house—both under lease.
Excellent opportunity—Terms
See F. E. Voges or H. H. Little
SERVICE AGENTS INC.
47 Maryland Avenue Phone 1477

WINES, LIQUORS AND CORDIALS
Gritz Liquor Store
32½ WEST STREET
Phone 641-J
FREE DELIVERY

FATAL MISHAP HELD TO BE UNAVOIDABLE

Magistrate Fowler Holds Inquest Into Automobile Death Of Two.

A coroner's jury last night returned an unavoidable accident verdict in the death of two colored women, drowned Thursday night when the automobile in which they were riding plunged from the Riva bridge into South river.

The jury convened by Police Magistrate Joseph O. Fowler, acting coroner, exonorated Wayman Reese, colored, driver of the machine that went through the wooden guard rail of the bridge and Franklin B. Sames, driver of a truck and trailer.

Grace Smothers, Camp Parole and Ruth Johnson, Annapolis, drowned in the crash. Reese and his wife, Helen, were rescued.

Sames said he felt something hit the trailer behind his truck, as he was passing the car driven by Reese on the 16 foot wide bridge.

SLADE CUTTER HERE AS FOOTBALL COACH

Ensign Slade D. Cutter, U.S.N., former Naval Academy football player and undefeated heavyweight boxer, has joined the academy football and boxing coaching staffs.

Cutter, a tackle on the varsity football team, in 1934, kicked the winning goal to give Navy a 3-0 victory over the Army. It was the first Navy victory in 13 years.

He will be one of the group of assistants to Lieut. Harry J. Hardwick, U.S.N., head football coach, and will aid Coach H. M. (Spike) Webb, with the Navy boxing team.

JUSTICES ARE NAMED

Gov. Harry W. Nice yesterday appointed 11 Justices of the Peace for Baltimore city to fill vacancies caused by the failure of previous appointees to qualify.

Those appointed were Jesse D. Rose, Harry Rifkin, Isadore Paserew, Joel J. Hachman, Joseph Leiter, Fillmore Cook, John W. Pariz, Samuel R. Zetzer, Jacob Schfartzman, Herman J. Gerber, Henry W. Schultheis.

FOR SALE
Hupp Six Sedan
$97.50
EXCELLENT RUNNING CONDITION
GOOD TIRES
May be seen at Atlantic White Flash Gas Station, West Street Extended

ALL-YEAR-BUNGALOW FOR SALE
Five rooms, gas, electricity, water, fireplace, furnace, porches, waterview. Near Arnold Station.
L. G. TURNER
Pines-on-Severn
PRICE $2,500. WORTH $4,000
jy-7

FOR SALE
5,000 GAL. CYPRESS TANK
$50.00
L. G. TURNER
Pines-on-Severn, Arnold, Md.
jy-7

NOTICE

There will be no collection of garbage on Monday, July 5th. Collection will be made on Tuesday, July 6th.

STREET COMMITTEE.

RESTAURANT
Old established restaurant on Main Street. Complete new equipment and booths, long lease, low rent, living quarters on second floor.
For sale at a bargain price.
JULIAN BREWER AND SON
Joseph D. Lazenby
9 School Street Tel. 815

NAVY JOINING IN SEARCH FOR MISS EARHART

Woman Flier Last Heard Of 100 Miles From Goal—Gasoline Reported To Be Low—Coast Guard Cutter And Mine Sweeper Hunt Plane.

RADIO S.O.S. SIGNALS REPORTED PICKED UP

(By The Associated Press)

HONOLULU, July 3 — Distress signals signed with the call letters of Amelia Earhart's monoplane flashed over the Pacific today in the midst of a feverish sea and sky hunt for the famed aviatrix missing in equatorial waters surrounding tiny Howland Island.

Amateur radio operations in Los Angeles heard repeated calls of "S O S—KHQQ" shortly before 1:30 A. M., Pacific time, (4:30 A. M. Eastern Standard Time) this was more than 14 hours after the intrepid flier said her gasoline supply would last but 30 minutes on her flight from distant New Quinea.

Signals Weak

The amateurs, Walter McMenamy and Carl Pierson, said the signals were so weak they could hardly heard them through dense static, and that once when they caught the letters "L-A-T" for latitude, the signals were blotted out by interference.

"KHQQ" is the call of Miss Earhart's plane, last heard from in the air yesterday at 2:12 P. M. EST when she reported she and her navigator, the veteran Fred Noonan, could not sight land and were nearly out of gas.

Another message signed with the plane's call letters and seeking radio contact was picked up in the south seas earlier by the New Zealand warship Achilles, the San Francisco Coast Guard reported.

Asked For Flashes

The Achilles, many miles south and east of Howland, messaged:

"Unknown station heard to make: 'please give us a few flashes if you get us. 7 signal on 3105 kiloeycles. This station made KHAQQ twice and disappeared. Nothing more since then."

The Achilles' message said the radio was heard on 3105 kilocycles, which is the frequency assigned to Miss Earhart's plane for night communication.

Miss Earhart was generally believed to have come down in shark-infested waters within a radius of 100 miles northwest of Howland Island after having overshot the tiny target on a 2,570 mile hop from Lae, New Quinea.

A heavy smoke belched from the funnels of the 250-foot cutter Itasca, visible for nine miles from its Howland Island anchorage, as it ploughed forward on a smooth sea in quest of the $80,000 Earhart "flying laboratory."

Navy Joins Search

While the cutter hunted by sea the woman who started a world

(Continued on Page 2)

SCHEDULE FOR BUS TO FLEET RESERVE ASS'N PINIC
SUNDAY, JULY 4, 1937
Beachwood Grove
Leaves corner of Severn Ave. and Third Street, Eastport, at 10:15, then to Postoffice to pick up passengers.

GAME PARTY
Benefit of
Owensville and Davidsonville Catholic Churches
Church Grounds at Owensville
JULY 3, 1937—8 P. M.
Free Bus leaves Postoffice at 7:30 P. M.

FOURTH OF JULY
DANCE
RUSTIC INN
Jones Station
SATURDAY & SUNDAY NITES
Three Tempo's Orchestra

Personal

JOE:

We will not guarantee to cure your rheumatism but we will help you forget your troubles if you spend an evening at SOUTH RIVER BEACH. Dance in Davey Jones Locker, swim in soft lighted waters. QUACK

ANNAPOLIS Independence Day Program

Monday July 5th, 1937

2:00 P. M.—WAGON RACE down Main Street for boys and girls under 12 years of age.

3:15 P. M.—PARADE—Forming at foot of Main Street
ROUTE—Main Street, Churc Circle, West Street to Baseball Park.

4:30 P M.—Address by Mayor Louis N. Phipps.

4:35 P. M.—Address by Thomas J. Cullimore, President County Commissioners.

4:40 P. M.—Mutt Dog Show at Baseball Park, Defense Highway. Dogs entered by children under 14 years. S. P. C. A. in charge of event, Junior Militia assisting.

5:30 P. M.—Athletic Contests for Boys and Girls, at Ball Park. Various types of races. Grand climax—"Pie-eating" contest with hands tied. Prof. Frank Sazama heads the committee in charge.

6:30 P. M.—Sandwiches and lemonade for all children at Ball Park. Carl Ortman, chairman.
Address by Walter H. Wooding, President Greater Annapolis Recreation Association.
Musical selections followed by comunity singing of patriotic songs. Herman L. Smith in charge of committee.
First Aid demonstration by firemen, in charge of Afred J. Fisher.

8:45 P. M.—Reading of Declaration of Independence by Hon. Linwood A. Clark, Judge of the Circuit Court.

9:00—10:00 P. M.—Fireworks display of 98 pieces. Set off by the firemen under approved safety methods.

Navy Man Wins First Prize In National Home Contest

Lieut. Richard F. Armknecht, Annapolis 1923, Wins Six-Room, Completely Air Conditioned House.

Fourth of July congratulations are in order for Lieut. Richard F. Armknecht, a Naval Academy graduate in the class of 1923, and now on shore duty at the Brooklyn Navy Yard. Lieutenant Armknecht was awarded first prize in the national Kelvin Home "missing word" contest in a radio presentation made Saturday night over a coast-to-coast network.

The prize was a six-room, completely air-conditioned home, to be built any place in the United States that Lieutenant Armknecht chooses. It was first in more than a thousand prizes distributed throughout the country in a contest that attracted over 140,000 entries. The contest was conducted to acquaint American consumers with the advances made in the past few years in the design and manufacture of household equipment that "cut the cost of better living."

Lieutenant Armknecht was a prize-winner in another line of literary endeavor while at the Academy, being given the Henry Van Dyke award for the best essay on a naval or patriotic subject. He was active in his class activities, being a member of the Glee Club, of the baseball and football squads. He was a platoon commander during his last year at Annapolis.

MRS. ZORA E. CADLE DIED YESTERDAY AT HOME IN EDGEWATER

Mrs. Zora Ellen Cadle died yesterday at her residence, at Edgewater, after a lingering illness.

Mrs. Cadle is survived by three sons, John R., William A., and G. A. Cadle, and two daughters, Mrs. Harry Stallings and Mrs. Josephine Galloway.

The funeral will take place at 2 o'clock tomorrow afternoon, from the Funeral Parlor of John M. Taylor, 147 Duke of Gloucester street, with interment at Taylorsville, this county.

RESTRAINS PICKETING

(By The Associated Press)

CUMBERLAND, Md., July 3.—An injunction signed by Chief Judge D. Lindley Sloan restrained strikers today from picketing a restaurant here.

THE EVENING CAPITAL will not be published on Monday, July 5th

FIREWORKS VIOLATIONS HERE SCORED

Prof. Henry F. Sturdy Calls Upon City Officials To Enforce Law Prohibiting Sale Or Firing Of Explosives—Points To Public Display On Monday.

STURDY REVEALS HE RESIGNED SAFETY POST

Holding that the general use of fireworks in the city creates a serious fire menace, endangers children and seriously disturbs the ill, Prof. Henry F. Sturdy, chairman of the Rotary Club's Boy Work Committee, today urged city officials to confiscate all fireworks now on sale within the corporate limits of Annapolis.

Professor Sturdy said sale and firing of fireworks in Annapolis is in violation of laws now on the city books. "It is time that city officials enforce the law. Flagrant violations of law are damaging to the youth of the city, and should not be tolerated by citizens in general," Professor Sturdy added.

City's Contribution

"I don't feel that merchants should lose what they have paid for their fireworks. The city should buy all on hand at the wholesale price and contribute the explosives, etc., to the Greater Annapolis Recreation Association, which is sponsoring a public display at the baseball park next Monday night. That would be a safe and sane way to observe Independence Day, and the city could afford to make the contribution involved," the Rotary committee chairman continued.

Professor Sturdy said that complaints were filed with the police from all sections of the city last night. "If so many firecrackers are exploded on July 2, we can expect much worse on July 4 and 5, and we haven't a sufficient number of police to regulate the situation. I would recommend the police hiring a cruise car between now and Monday to tour the city and, if necessary, make arrests, but at least warn residents that they are violating the law," Professor Sturdy continued.

Complaints Filed

It is reported that the police did receive nine complaints within 25 minutes last night. One woman left town to take her children into the country because she could not stand the noise. It is said that an officer was stationed near the hospital to prevent the firing of explosives in that vicinity. "However, the police cannot patrol the entire town fre-

(Continued on Page 3)

DEMOCRATS IN HARMONY AT BIG MEET

More Than 300 Enthusiastic Party Men And Women Attend Crab Feast And Beer Party At Elktonia Beach—Several Speakers Heard.

MAYOR PHIPPS AMONG THOSE MAKING TALKS

More than 300 Democrats gathered at Elktonia Beach last night and participated in one of the most enthusiastic party rallies held here in a long time. Last night's gathering, following on the heels of the big and successful card party held by Democratic women last Thursday night, encouraged the Democratic candidates over the election on July 12.

In addition to the crab feast and beer, last night's rally was marked by comment by Mayor Louis N. Phipps; his campaign manager, George B. Woelfel; George Wentworth Haley, candidate for city counselor, and by Mrs. George Abram Moss, chairman of the women's Democratic organization.

Mrs. Mess Confident

Mr. Woelfel, following his personal comment on the campaign, introduced Mrs. Moss, who spoke of the work the women of the party are doing. She predicted that the candidates would go on to victory. She promised, too, that the women would conduct a "dignified campaign."

Mayor Phipps spoke briefly, stating he was relying upon his friends to re-elect him. He said he was confident of re-election, and cited several accomplishments of his regime which he felt had been beneficial to the town.

Haley's Comment

The active and extensive law practice which he has enjoyed in several States was stressed by Mr. Haley. He promised a decent and conscientious administration of the duties of the office of counselor, if elected.

EASTPORT PLAYS MT. RAINIER TOMORROW

Game Set For Horn Point Diamond At 2:30 P. M.—Liggett To Toe Mound.

EASTPORT	Mt. Rainier
Bland, 2b.	Gren, 3b.
Ford or Tucker, 3b.	Merrello, 1b.
	Shipps, cf.
Woytych, ss.	Luckett, ss.
Felt, c.	Moxley, lf.
Wood, 1b.	Ciomei, rf.
Landrum, rf.	Lanrick, 2b.
Liggett, p.	Wise, c.
Belcher, lf.	Moore, p.
Hause, cf.	Pohl, p.
Catlin, p	
McArdle, p.	
Deale, utility.	

Staring time of game: 2:30 P. M. Umpire, Miles.

The Eastport baseball team will meet the Mt. Rainier Grays tomorrow on the Eastport diamond. Starting time has been set for 2:30 P. M.

The Mt. Rainier club is playing an excellent brand of ball in the National City league of Washington and are determined to lower the Eastport colors tomorrow for two reasons. In the first place they still remember how the Villagers came from behind to eke out a thrilling 5-4 victory in the last inning of their game a year ago. Secondly, Bill Liggett, star twirler for the Grays last season, is now wearing an Eastport uniform and the Grays claim they will bombard him from the box if he pitches tomorrow. Liggett claims that he will have something to say about that.

Pitchers In Trim

The Eastport nine will be ready for the visitors tomorrow with Liggett, Southpaw Newby Catlin and Hause to go to the mound and Felt to do the catching. Hause, who starred with Eastport last season, is the leading pitcher for the Buck Glass nine of the Baltimore Semi-Pro League. Last Sunday he defeated the heavy-hitting Glen Burnie team.

The Mt. Rainier team has three

(Continued on Page 3)

Mrs. Clements Poses Sixteen Questions For Phipps To Answer

Woman Candidate Makes First Political Speech Last Night—Refers to Mayor Taking Part in Aldermanic Race in Third Ward —Hillman Outlives Career.

Mrs. Mildred M. Clements, Republican, opening her campaign for the mayoralty of Annapolis, declared that a woman is serving her home best when she moves out into the community and inquires into its ways.

Speaking at a public mass-meeting in the House of Delegates chamber of the State House last night, she propounded 16 questions to her Democratic opponent, Mayor Louis N. Phipps. She said he could answer them in any way he choosed, "from a platform or through the press." The questions dealt with city government and administration.

Former Mayor Walter E. Quenstedt, warden of the House of Correction, and the Republican campaign manager, introduced Mrs. Clements, the first woman to seek the office of mayor since the city was incorporated. Her speech followed addresses by the Republican aldermanic candidates

"I am here tonight to advocate myself as Mayor of Annapolis because

"I m here tonight tcadvocate myself as Mayor of Annapolis, because I am a woman and a Republican," she said. "I am not apologizing for either of these things. If I had been a Democrat and a woman I could not possibly have had the nomination when Mr. Phipps was so eager for it.

"Women have come a long way from the days of Elizabeth Cady Stanton and Susan B. Anthony. . . There is still a lingering echo of the old refrain sung during the years when the woman suffrage movement was being agitated — a woman's place is in the home.

Work Must Be Done

"I agree with that too. Her plac is in the home, and so is her hus band's when his day's work is do and so is the child's place, in home. And it is the common tice to maintain their rela

Mrs. Clements pointed o "the home is going out to enric community" and declared that a man "is serving her home be when she moves into the communi and inquires into its ways."

"The conduct of her commun is dependent in many ways on government," she said. "Since th schools are part of government o who works in their behalf m enter the domain of politics."

"Woman have found they ca a great deal. They are good ers, and persistent—as some well know—and when they held by the conviction th side is just and right th stronger in their personal their influence is increased.

Men Are Gossips

"Women used to be spoken on gossips. I don't know why th have been singled out this way, cause I have never seen m thoroughgoing gossips then m who gather in bunches in one pla or another to guess what someb else is going to do and why.

"There is no question that ma women have the ability to carry such a job as that of mayor but n many have both the ability and t interest in the dommunity to after an elective office."

Turning to the pol is Mrs. Clements pointe "Mr. Phipps is the o this city with whom repeatedly into confli her first conflict was for the new high sch Parent-Teacher committee was to make a report.

"Mr. Phipps joined the P.-T.A. a few days before the meeting at which the committee was to report." she said. "Many strangers attended that night. A suggestion for a roll-call was discouraged and the ball park site which Mr. Phipps was urging with great dtermination, received a majority on a vocal vote. Rumors had been circulating for weeks that Mr. Phipps had a financial interest in the ball park, and that day the rumors were confirmed. The action of the P.T.-A was rescinded at the next meeting, when there was not such a large attendance."

Mrs. Clements said that when the Better Government League of Anne Arundel county was formed, the plan of organization for the first meeting was thoroughly understood and agreed upon by all.

Phipps Broke Rule

"But when the evening came it was Mr. Phipps who tried to break the rule and introduce a gentleman for the sort of speech that had been specically barred from that

(Continued on Page 3)

LOCAL YACHTSMEN IN SAILING RACES FROM GIBSON ISLE

Boats Leave City Early Today Forty Entries Expected In Gala Event.

Annapolis yatchtsmen who will compete in the race from Gibson Island to Annapolis left early today for the rendezvous at Gibson Island.

Among the boats making the trip was the Doris II, with Mayor Louis N. Phipps acting as skipper, which will bring the list of entries in the race from Gibson Island to Annapoils.

Local Boats Entered

Other boats from here included the Sewanna, owned and sailed by James Roosevelt; the Vamarie, famous racing ketch recently given to the Naval Academy, sailed by Captain John F. Shafroth, U.S.N., and a crew of midshipmen and enlisted men; the Mars, a six meter boat from the Academy sailed by Midshipman Herbert Denison Remington and a crew of midshipmen; the High Seas, owned and sailed by William H. Labrot and the Salabar, owned and sailed by Sylvester W. abrot.

The race is scheduled to start at 1 P. M. from the Baltimore light.

(Continued on Page 3)

NAVAL RESERVE TO MAKE TRIP ON TEXAS

Battleship Anchors Off Annapolis Roads — Sea Scouts Pay Visit.

The battleship Texas, off the Naval Academy today, was ready to take members of the Maryland and Virginia Naval Reserve on a summer training cruise.

Sixteen officers and 180 men of the Maryland Naval Reserve, together with contingents from Richmond, Norfolk and Newport News, will go for a cruise to Boston, Mass., and return.

Three hundred and sixty-five Sea Scouts arrived at the Academy for a tour of inspection shortly before the battleship steamed into Annapolis Roads yesterday. They came from the Sea Scout camp established

(Continued on Page 3)

PASTEURIZED MILK
IN CREAM TOP BOTTLES, PROTECTED BY SEALKAPS
The Annapolis Dairy Products Co.
126 WEST STREET TEL. 123
VISITORS ALWAYS WELCOME

ANNAPOLIS DEFEATS G-MEN FOR TENTH STRAIGHT WIN SUNDAY

LOCALS PILE UP 8-3 SCORE AGAINST FOES

Frank Watt Chalks Up Sixth Victory Of Year—City Gets Six Runs In First Inning—Visitors Failed Miserably In Pinches.

RALLY IN NINTH PROVES FAILURE

Annapolis rolled on to their tenth straight win yesterday, crushing the Bureau of Investigation G-Men 8-3. The game, which saw Frank Watt annex his sixth victory of the year, was won in the first frame, when the Hillearymen leaped on Ray Davidson for a half-dozen game-deciding runs.

The G-Men will never forget that first inning. Bobby Stevens started it all by scratching a hit through Walter Morris. Lefty Jewett by drawing a base on balls advanced Stevens to second. Oscar Johnson fanned for the first out. And when Feet Myers' terrific drive was caught by Pepco Barry, far out in center field, it looked as though the local rally was not to be.

Rolf Scores Stevens

Al Rolf had other plans. He lifted a honey of a single to center, scoring Stevens. On the throw in both Rolf and Jewett flashed plenty of speed and advanced to second and third. Fred Wahler proceeded to drive them both in by singling briskly to left.

Bill Townsend then drove hard to Morris who failed to hold the ball, putting Wahler on second and Townsend on first. Huck Wynne chose this point to get his first homer for Annapolis. The hefty catcher drove the ball on a line to left, clearing the garage sign with plenty to spare. Watt grounded out to end the inning but the damage was done.

Ahead 610 Watt coasted to an easy win. Even so he gave the local fans many a heart-throb. While he allowed but six hits, he was as wild as an African Bushman, issuing 9 bases on balls, and making a pair of wild throws to the bases. Only a happy combination of his own nerve in the pinches, tight fielding by his mates and inability to hit on the part of the Sleuths, tided him over the rough places.

Failed In Pinches

The G-Men left the astonishing total of fifteen men stranded on the paths. That bespeaks eloquently their inability to get to Watt when the chips were down. Twice they had the bases loaded and twice they had two men on. Out of it all they got but three runs.

Those three came in the seventh when two hits combined with the generosity of Watt, who passed two and made a wild throw, accounted for the entire crop of enemy tallies.

Jim Tennant, who replaced Davidson in the fifth, fared better than his predecessor. Annapolis could get but three hits off the big right-hander, but they bunched them all in the one inning, scoring twice in the seventh.

Myers Is Walked

Feet Myers walked and after Rolf and Wahler had rolled out, Bill Townsend singled Myers across the plate. Townsend took second on Tennant's wild toss, and came home on clutch man Huck Wynne's scorching one-baser. Wynne's hit delighted the fans for Tennant had dusted the local backstopper off on the first two pitches. Thus were the tosses that were intended to unsettle Wynne the cause of Tennant's own discomfort.

Trailing 8-3 the G-Men made a last futile rally in the ninth. Watt—liberal to a fault—walked Colliflower and Morris. As usual, however, he tightened up, forcing Shapiro to hit into an easy force play. On the play, Colliflower took third but Xander took a third strike and the game was over.

Bring on Easton.

The line-up:

Annapolis	Ab.	R.	H.	Po.	A.	E
Stevens, ss.	4	1	1	2	3	0
Jewett, cf.	2	1	0	1	0	0
Johnson, lf.	5	0	0	3	0	0
Myers, 3b.	3	1	1	0	4	1
Rolf, 1b.	4	1	1	13	0	0
Wahler, 2b.	4	1	1	0	5	0
Townsend, rf.	4	2	2	1	0	0
Wynne, c.	4	1	2	6	0	0
Watt, p.	4	0	1	1	0	2
Totals	34	8	9	27	12	3

G-Men	Ab	R	H	Po	A	E
Routon, ss.	4	0	0	2	2	0
Giovanetti, 3b.	4	0	0	2	0	0
Barry, cf.	5	0	1	2	0	0
Colliflower, lf.	3	0	1	0	0	1
Beall, 1b.	5	1	1	7	1	1
Morris, 2b.	3	0	1	3	3	1
Shapiro, rf.	3	1	0	1	0	0
Xander, c.	4	1	0	6	1	0
Davidson, p.	2	0	1	0	0	0
Tennant, p.	2	0	1	0	2	0
Totals	35	3	6	24	9	3

Annapolis .. 600 002 00x—8
G-Men ..... 000 000 300—3

Runs Batted In—Rolf, Wahler 2, Wynne 4, Townsend, Tennant 2. Two-Base Hits—Beall, Davidson. Home Run — Wynne. Double Plays—Routon, Morris and Beall; Tennant, Routon and Beall; Stevens and Rolf. Hits—off Davidson, 6 in 4 innings, off Tennant 3 in 4 innings. Base On Balls—off Watt, 9; off Davidson, 3; off Tennant, 3. Struck Out—By Watt, 4; by Davidson, 3; by Tennant, 4. Winning pitcher — Watt. Losing pitched — Davidson. Umpires — Sipple and Brockman.

'I'LL BEAT LOUIS.'
Over the tea cups, this fighting young Welshman unsmilingly asserted, "I'll beat Louis because I never have been knocked out . . . and am not afraid of anyone but God." Fighter Farr further elaborated, "If I didn't expect to lick him I wouldn't be here. All Louis has to do is stick his chin out once and he'll be gone."

RED BIRDS LOSE TO DAVIDSONVILLE NINE

The Red Birds lost to Davidsonville in a five-inning game by a score of 4 to 1 Sunday.

Both teams played good ball for the first two innings with neither scoring a run. The Red Birds opened the game in the last of the third when Thomas got on base on an error by Shepherd then Green followed and reached first on an error by Suitt. Thomas went to third and Green going to second. Shepherd then singled to left field and Thomas scored the first run of the game.

Davidsonville scored in the fourth inning when Welch walked both Beard and Shepherd. M. Thompson singled and Beard scored tieing the score. G. Thompson also singled and scored Shepherd. Duckett followed with a double and scored both the Thompson boys. Davidsonville then led by a score of 4 to 1. Both teams failed to score in the fifth. Davidsonville was making good headway in the sixth inning but rain stopped the game.

These two teams which have drawn the largest crowd at Davidsonville this year, will probably meet again in September.

Welch pitched for the Red Birds and allowed seven hits and four runs. He walked two men. "Whitey" Tucker pitched for Davidsonville and alowed but three hits and one run.

The Red Birds will hold a practice game Tuesday and Friday at the Annapolis Ball Park at 6:15 P. M. They will play the Fire Stone nine from Washington this Sunday at Camp Parole.

Box Score

Red Birds	Ab	H	Po	A	E
Thomas, lf, c.	3	0	2	0	0
Green, 3b.	3	0	1	1	0
Shepherd, 1b.	3	2	6	0	0
Gantt, rf.	3	1	0	0	0
Kirby, ss.	3	0	2	0	0
Brewer, 2b.	2	0	1	1	1
Miller, c. lf.	2	0	2	0	0
Spriggs, cf.	1	0	1	0	1
Welch, p.	2	0	0	3	0
Totals	22	3	15	5	2

Davidsonville	Ab	H	Po	A	E
Grimes, c.	3	2	3	1	0
Suitt, rf.	3	0	0	0	0
J. Beard, ss.	2	1	2	2	0
Shepherd, lf.	2	0	1	0	1
M. Thompson, 2b.	3	2	2	0	0
G. Thompson, 3b.	3	1	1	2	0
Duckett, cf.	2	1	2	1	1
C. Beard, 1b.	2	0	4	0	1
Tucker, p.	2	0	0	1	0
Totals	22	7	15	7	3

Earned runs — Red Birds, 1; Davidsonville, 2. Base On Balls—Off Welch, 2; off Tucker, 1. Strike Outs—By Welch, 0; by Tucker, 2. Double Play—Welch to Brewer to Shepherd. Two-Base Hit—Duckett.

Score by innings:
Red Birds .... 001 00—1
Davidsonville .... 000 40—4

NAVAL ACADEMY TRACK TEAM IS VICTOR, 79 - 29

Defeats Stonewall Democratic Club Of Baltimore Saturday Afternoon — McGuire And Hahnfeldt Rank High As Promising Track Athletec.

Led by as promising a pair of Plebe track and field men as has been seen in Thompson Stadium in some time the combined Second and Fourth class track team defeated the Stonewall Democratic Club of Baltimore on the local cinders last Saturday by the score of 79 to 29. Navy scored twelve firsts out of the same number of events and combined five seconds and four thirds for their total. The Plebes won ten of the events.

The "promising pair" is made up of Robert McGuire and Edward Hahnfeldt and offer speed and power. McGuire being a sprinter and the latter a weight man.

McGuire Ranks High

McGuire was ranked at the top of the Nation's schoolboy sprinters in 1935, having a 9.7 hundred and a 21.6 220 to his credit. Since that time, however, he has been busy preparing for the Naval Acaemy and has had little competition in the past two years. He showed a tremendous getaway from his marks last Saturday and won his races with yards to spare. He needs, however, considerable polish in latter part of his races before he will hit the top flight in collegiate competition.

Ed. Hahnfeldt is a three "weapon" man with the weights. He tosses the shot, discus and javelin with almost equal dexterity and has beaten the Plebe records in the first two events twice in the last two Saturdays. He was termed "the best looking freshman weight man I have ever seen" by Marshal Boone, Baltimore track official and former Intercollegiate point winner in the shot for Stanford University.

Other Promising Men

Besides these two men the first year men offered a likely looking hurdler in C. M. Hart who doubles in brass with the broad jump, Richard Opp a weight man who bettered the Plebe shot mark Saturday, T. T. Walker, L. C. Savage, H. H. Montgomery and R. W. Otto runners of promise. If these boys can stay up with the parade in academics, Navy track looks safe for a few years yet.

The two Second Classmen to win were A. J. Gardner and R. B. Neal, winners of the high jump and broad jump respectively in the Army feet last May.

The Company track meet was held a week ago last Saturday with the Second Company winning handily. The meet last Saturday closed the Summer work and many of the fourth class will report for football next week.

The summary:

Mile—Won by T. T. Walker (N); 2nd. V. W. Cox (S); 3rd. Morrison (S). Time 5:01.7.

100 Yards—Won by R. E. McGuire (N); 2nd. E. A. Kerins (S); 3rd. R. B. Neol (N). Time 10.1.

440 Yards—Won by H. H. Montgomery (N); 2nd. L. C. Savage (N); 3rd. J. Miller (S). Time 57.5.

220 Yards—Won by R. E. McGuire (N); 2nd. B. P. Seaman, Jr., (N); 3rd. E. A. Kerins (S). Time 23.5.

880 Yards—Won by R. W. Otto (N); 2nd. J. L. Schnepp (N); 3rd. B. McElroy (S). Time 2:15.7.

120 High Hurdles—Won by C. M. Hart (N); 2nd. J. Devlin (S); 3rd. J. W. Hart (S). Time 16.6.

220 Low Hurdles—Won by C. M. Hart (N); 2nd. J. R. Thomson (N); 3rd. R. E. Foster (N). Time 27.8.

Discus—Won by E. F. Hahnfeldt (N); 2nd. M. Sharretts (S); 3rd. R. D. Opp (N). Distance 137' 8".

Shot—Won by E. F. Hahnfeldt (N); 2nd. R. W. Opp (N); 3rd. M. Sharretts (S). Distance 51' 1". (12 pound shot).

Javelin—Won by E. F. Hahnfeldt (N); 2nd. G. M. Summers (S); 3rd. R. W. Op (N). Distance 173' 4".

High Jump—Won by A. J. Gardner (N); 2nd. F. Keavney (S); 3rd. F. Hayès (S). Heighth 6'.

Broad Jump—Won by R. B. Neal (N); 2nd. E. Fineblatt (S); 3rd. G. M. Summers (S). Distance 20' 9".

League Standings

AMERICAN LEAGUE

Scores of Yesterday

New York, 6; Cleveland, 5.
Detroit, 5; Washington, 1.
Boston, 7-0; Chicago, 6-13.
Philadelphia, 5-7; St. Louis, 4-3.

Where They Play Today

(Open date.)

Standing of the Clubs

	W.	L.	Pct.
New York	67	29	.698
Boston	57	38	.600
Detroit	56	40	.583
Chicago	58	43	.574
Cleveland	43	51	.457
Washington	41	53	.436
St. Louis	32	64	.333
Philadelphia	29	65	.309

NATIONAL LEAGUE

Scores of Yesterday

New York, 10-0; Pittsburgh, 2-3.
Chicago, 3-3; Boston, 0-2.
*St. Louis, 3-6; Philadelphia, 2-6.
Cincinnati, 6-1; Brooklyn, 4-1.

*Second game 12 innings, tie.

Where They Play Today

(Open date.)

Standing of the Clubs

	W.	L.	Pct.
Chicago	64	35	.646
New York	58	41	.586
St. Louis	53	44	.546
Pittsburgh	51	46	.526
Boston	47	54	.465
Cincinnati	41	55	.427
Brooklyn	39	57	.406
Philadelphia	40	61	.396

The Public Library can use the books that you wish to discard when house cleaning.

VILLAGE NINE DEFEATED BY ROSS SUNDAY

Catlin Fails In Ninth Inning—Visiting Catcher Leading Batsman Of Two Teams—Final Tally Was 5-3 After Nip-and-Tuck Affair.

HAUSE MADE RELIEF PITCHER

Ross A. C. defeated the hard-hitting Eastport team in the ninth inning yesterday by the score of 5 to 3. Catlin pitched fine ball until the ninth allowing only five hits which amounted to three runs.

Ross was held scoreless until two hits and two errors netted three runs. With two out the Villagers sent Hause to the mound who became the losing pitcher.

Joyer of the visitors pitched excellent ball allowing only six hits which resulted in three runs. Phelps, the visitor catcher, led both teams at bat with three hits out of four trips at the bat.

Hause caught a fine game behind the plate until he was called for mound duty in the ninth.

Ross Country Club	Ab	R	H	A	E
Glass, 2b.	4	0	0	2	1
Whittle, 1b.	4	1	0	0	0
Joyner, p.	4	1	1	3	0
Phelps, c.	4	1	3	2	0
M. Disney, lf.	4	0	0	0	0
R. Disney, 3b.	4	1	1	0	0
Shomper, rf.	4	1	1	0	1
Wilcar, ss.	4	0	1	5	0
Protenic, cf.	4	0	0	1	0
Totals	36	5	7	13	2

Eastport	Ab	R	H	A	E
Bland, 2b.	4	0	0	2	0
Tucker, lf.	4	0	0	0	0
Woytych, ss.	4	0	1	2	1
Felt, cf.	4	2	1	0	1
Rause, c.	3	0	1	2	0
Wood, 1b.	3	0	1	1	1
Welde, rf.	3	0	1	0	0
Belcher, 3b.	3	1	1	4	0
Catlin, p.	3	0	0	5	1
Totals	31	3	6	16	4

Hause pitched in ninth inning and Felt caught.

Two Base Hits—Joyner, Belcher. Three-Base Hit — Phelps. Strike Outs—Catlin, 11; Hause, 1. Joyner, 7. Left On Base—Eastport, 1; Ross A. C., 5.

Winning pitcher—Joyner. Losing pitcher—Hause.

DOWN THE TRACK.
Here is a typical crowd at the Hambletonian race. Last year it was Rosalind who took the coveted trophy for three-year-old trotters. Between 45,000 and 50,000 are expected to be in the stands at Good Time Park for the 1937 race on August 11, during the Grand Circuit meeting at Goshen, N. Y.

COLUMBIA BEATS GREEN HAVEN NINE

Columbia won the first game of a twin bill from Green Haven by a score of 10 to 4. Lefty McNally was on the hill for the home boys. He turned in what is believed to be a record by striking out 22 batsmen. Loose play gave the Green Haven boys their runs.

Skipper led the hitting by getting three hits in a row. "Inks" had to leave the game in the fourth inning due to an old injury. He will be lost to the team for the rest of the season.

Elliott, working behind the plate, came through with two hits.

Columbia was ahead in the nightcap, 1-0, when rain broke up the game. Holidayoke was on the mound, with Elliott receiving.

Joe Louis Booed As He Retains Title By Decision Over Gallant Tommy Farr

Welshman Was Winner In Eyes Of Admiring Fans; Louis Frightened

Colored Champion Puzzled by Tommy's Style, Was Hurt and Badly Frightened Number of Times—Louis Finished Strong as Blood Interfered With Challenger's Vision—Even Fight Until Last Three Rounds.

EXPERTS CONFESS FARR WOULD HAVE WON BY A KNOCKOUT IF HE HAD SCHMELING'S PUNCH

Farr Offers No Alibis Nor Does His Manager and Gains Praise of Everyone—Was Able to Hit Louis Whenever He Wanted to But Lacked Wallop—Champion Looked Like Second Rate Fighter—Farr Badly Cut.

By GAYLE TALBOT
(By The Associated Press)

NEW YORK, Aug. 31.—Joe Louis still has his heavyweight championship, and he also has a new and round-eyed respect for Tommy Farr.

So have 37,000 fans who sat in the lights and shadows of Yankee Stadium last night and watched the old carnival fighter, half-blinded at the finish, jab and jimmy it out with the alleged colored thunderbolt for 15 rounds.

Although they are without doubt hollering "robbery" around Fleet Street today, and the hotheads in The Mall are assuring each other over the matutinal Scotch and splash that a Britisher hasn't a chance of winning anything in America, there wasn't much doubt that the brown ex-bomber deserved the decision.

LOUIS LOOKED DUMB AND SCARED

He did, as badly scared as he looked in spots. In fact, he looked as dumb as a dime detective most of the evening, and he took a lot of fancy punches, first and last. He never learned how to fight Farr. Yet he was the better man, and Tommy will be the last to deny it. Tommy didn't deny it last night, even as he sat and tried to look out between battered eyes and listened to the "raspberries" that echoed and re-echoed across Yankee Stadium after Louis had been declared the winner.

Farr is a big man in the boxing game today, even though a loser. He can stay around—as he plans to do—and make himself a lot of money. He put up a great fight against a foeman who was expected to knock him spraddle-legged, and when his best wasn't good enough he accepted defeat like a soldier.

Got A Cold Reception

At that it must have been a thrill for the hard-boiled battler from the desolate mining district of Wales. No fighter who ever came to these shores received a sorrier reception. He was tabbed strictly a second-rater, a fighter who didn't belong in the same ring with the ebon assassin, Louis. He must have felt good last night when, after he had given his stout-hearted best for fifteen rounds, he groped his way toward he dressing room through thousands of Americans demanding the blood of referee, judges and anybody else who thought Louis had won.

But it didn't fool Tommy. He knew he had tried and failed, and he wasn't sore at anybody. The fight-writers expected him to rail at the decision, and to castigate them for the things they had written about him. Tommy didn't do either. He looked out between eyes that were swollen almost shut and said simply: "I gave them a good go, didn't I?" Tommy, then and there, made himself a lot of friends.

Spectators Viewpoint

Referee Arthur Donovan credited the Welshman with only two rounds, that Louis won eight, and that there wasn't anything in the other two. The spectators from ten rows on back thought Farr won the championship, by a country mile. It just goes to shown.

This much is certain: The old carnival scrapper put up a whale of a fight; he carried the carnage to Louis most of the way, and he undoubtedly would have won by a knockout if he had possessed a fight-hand wallop to compare with Schmeling's.

Louis Puzzled, Frightened

It's also true that Louis, though he was puzzled at Tommy's style all the way and was hurt and badly frightened a couple of times when Farr clouted him, had what it took to collect himself and jab out a victory with his left.

There wasn't a knockdown. In the fifth round, after the crowd had done some booing, Louis whipped over a quick right to the jaw and followed with a left that staggered Farr, but the bell saved the Welshman from serious trouble. Those were perhaps the most damaging blows of the fight. Farr hurt Louis with several rights, but the champ never looked like he was going down.

Farr's Eyes Spouted Blood

In the last two or three rounds, long, jagged cuts under Farr's eyes were spouting blood and he couldn't properly line up his sights. He couldn't locate Louis with the stabbing left that had piled up so many points in the early rounds, and he was trying desperately to land a telling right. That was when Joe piled up his decisive margin.

"I couldn't see him," said Farr, plaintively, in the dressing room. His face looked like it had been caught in a thresher. The middle finger of his right hand was broken and swollen, but he wouldn't alibi a nickel's worth.

Rest For Louis

Louis naturally was disappointed with his showing. He had to admit that Farr was a tough hombre to hit. Farr, to give an idea, was able to lead with a swishing right whenever he wanted to, and to miss, and suffer no ill effects. He has been at the game a lot longer than Louis.

Farr was back at Long Branch today, trying not to catch a glimpse of himself in the mirror. He looks pretty bad. Louis and his entourage still plan to visit London and Paris right away. What Joe needs, he figure, is a good, long rest.

Schmeling Unimpressed With Louis; Praises Farr The British Champ

FARR PUTS UP FIGHT, BUT LOUIS WINS DECISION.

Joe Louis (left), heavyweight champion, and challenger Tommy Farr of England, were taking their work pretty seriously when this remarkable photo was made in the first round of their title bout at Yankee Stadium, New York. The Brown Bomber met unexpected competition in the Englishman and the fight went the full 15 rounds, Louis being awarded the decision on points. (Associated Press Photo).

GIANTS BEAT REDS TO TAKE LEAGUE LEAD

Hubbell Rushed In By Terry After Two Others Fail To Hold Enemy — Trio Who Played Under McGrow Are Given Credit For Rise.

DETROIT TIGERS DEFEAT YANKS

By Sid Feder
(Associated Press Sports Writer)

Old John McGraw, who's probably managing a pennant winner in whatever Valhalla baseball men go to, looked down on his New York Giants today and found the view well nigh perfect.

They were leading the National League—by a margin thin as a dime, but leading nevertheless—and a trio of McGraw men showed the way.

Led By Terry

First, there was Bill Terry, who can take a bow himself for the way he's handled the reins since old Graw gave them up in '32. Then there was Master Melvin Ott, the veteran youngster of the National League, the little fellow who lifts up his front foot, swings at those high, hard ones, and deposits them where they do the most good—for his side. And last, but far from least, there was King Carl Hubbell, the master of the screwball.

These three, and the fight that was McGraws heritage to the Giants, made it appear today that the Giants are on the way to their second straight pennant, their third under Terry. At the moment, here were the statistics on the two clubs still in the red-hot pennant parade:

	W.	L.	Pct.	To Play
Giants. . .	71	46	.607	37
Cubs. . .	72	47	.605	35

Good Money Team

They're a remarkable collection, these Giants. They don't play great ball; sometimes they don't even play good ball. But they're a money team, and they play those breaks for all they're worth.

Right now, such other powers as the Cubs, Cardinals and Pirates appear to be quietly falling apart. So, the Giants, putting together timely hitting and good pitching, are making the most of it.

Yesterday, with the Cubs idle, the Giants had a chance to go into the lead. They turned the trick with a 4-3 decision over the Cincinnati Reds, and that's where McGraw's boys came in.

Of course, they had a lot of help from Terry's new Terriers. But Ott, pulled in from the outfield and now playing as good a third base as any in the league, belted his 28th homer with a mate aboard.

Hubbell To Rescue

Things were fine until Rookie Cliff Melton and Relief Flinger Dick Coffman couldn't stand prosperity in the seventh. Then Terry came up out of the dugout with a rush and waved wildly for Hubbell. Old Squarepants sauntered in—in the memory of the oldest residents he's never been known to hurry—and had the Reds begging for mercy. Six men went down in order before he gave up a dinky little scratch single and then retired the last batter.

The Giants' game was the only one in the National League. In the American League the Detroit Tigers tripped the Yankees, 5-4, with Hank Greenberg belting No. 30 and Roundhouse Rudy York poking No. 28, and the Cleveland Indians pushed over a ninth-inning run for a 7-6 win over the Senators.

FIGHT LITTLE MORE THAN PAID EXPENSES

NEW YORK, Aug. 31. — Promotor Mike Jacobs, who thought he might go "in the red" on the Louis-Farr fight, apparently cleared enough to pay his expenses and a little more.

After paying off the fighters, the rental on the Yankee Stadium, and the ten per cent. "cut" of the milk fund, Mike had about $65,000 left to pay all the other costs of promoting the battle and for his own share.

Here are the figures on attendance and receipts for last night's fight:

Total Attendance	36.903
Gross receipts	$265,753.11
Federal tax	28,409.29
State tax	14,880.02
Net receipts	222,463.80
Radio and movie rights	60,000.00
Total income	282,463.80
Louis' share (40 per cent of total)	112,987.52
Farr's share (guarantee)......	60,000.00
Stadium rental (10 per cent of net receipts)	22,246.38
Milk fund (10 per cent of net)	22,246.38
Promoter's hare	64,983.52

LOUIS CLAIMS HE HURT RIGHT HAND IN THIRD ROUND

(By The Associated Press)

DETROIT, Aug. 31.—Joe Louis, back in Detroit today after his 15-round decision victory over Tommy Farr, said that he "didn't feel good about being unable to knock him out," but explained he was handicapped by an injury to his right hand in the third round.

Wearing colored glasses that partly concealed a slightly puffed eye and nursing the aching right hand, Louis said he came here mainly to get a couple of days rest.

"I hurt my right swinging on Farr in the third," he said. "He was coming in, bobbing at me, and I swung. That bobbing made me miss the jaw and I landed on the top of his head. It felt as though my hand had been cut off."

Louis said he used his left almost exclusively after the third round. "I tried to use my right to set him up for a good punch a couple of times, but the pain was too much and I got scared that I might be doing serious damage to the hand," he continued.

"I kept feeding him the left, and I gave him so much that my left hand is all bruised. He's tough, that fellow is. He's the toughest fellow I've ever seen. He can't hurt with his punches, but he can take it like no man."

Major League Leaders

(By The Associated Press)

NATIONAL LEAGUE

Batting — Medwick, Cardinals, .390; P. Waner, Pirates, .380.

Runs—Medwick, Cardinals, 95; Galan, Cubs, 89.

Runs batted in—Medwick, Cardinals, 128; Demaree, Cubs, 96.

Hits—Medwick, Cardinals, 187; P. Waner, Pirates, 182.

Doubles — Medwick, Cardinals, 49; Mize, Cardinals, 31.

Triples — Vaughan, Pirates, 12; Handley, Pirates, 11.

Home Runs—Ott, Giants, 28; Medwick, Cardinals, 27.

Stolen Bases—Galan, Cubs, 18; Hassett, Dodgers, 13.

Pitching — Root, Cubs, 12-4; Hubbell, Giants, 17-6.

AMERICAN LEAGUE

Batting—Gehringer, Tigers, .383; Gehrig, Yankees, .369.

Runs—DiMaggio, Yankees, 121; Greenberg, Tigers, 113.

Runs batted in — Greenberg, Tigers, 141; DiMaggio, Yankees, 124.

Hits—DiMaggio, Yankees, 171; Walker, Tigers, 169.

Doubles—Vosmik, Browns, and Greenberg, Tigers, 41.

Triples — Stone, Senators, and Kreevich, White Sox, 13.

Home Runs—DiMaggio, Yankees, 38; Foxx, Red Sox, 32.

Stolen Bases—Chapman, Red Sox, 29; Walker, Tigers, 19.

Pitching — Murphy, Yankees, 13-3; Ruffing, Yankees, 17-4.

FARR'S MINER FOLKS SOB IN NIGHT WATCH

Bonfire On Trealaw Mountain To Have Been Lighted Only If Farr Was Victor, Burns Anyhow As Welshmen Celebrate All Night Before Going To Work In Pits.

FERVENT SINGING BY COAL-SMUDGED FACES

By Scotty Reston
(By The Associated Press)

TON - Y - PANDY, Wales, Aug. 31.—A high lonely flame on Trealow Mountain today illuminated the strangest scene ever inspired by a professional boxer.

It had been arranged that the bonfire should be touched off only if Tommy Farr, Ton-y-pandy's own, should win his fight with Joe Louis in New York. Tommy lost but the bonfire flared just the same.

The manner of his losing was so magnificent and the pride of his countrymen so deep that 5,000 miners and their weeping wives climbed the steep slopes of Trealaw just before dawn and touched off the fire of "victory."

Welshmen Sing

In the flickering flamelight over the desclate, coal-pitted valley of the Rhondda river, the Welshmen sang as only Welshmen sing, "Land of Our Fathers . . ."

The music echoed down in the dreary valley, where half the men are on the dole and the other half earn the equivalent of $12.50 a week in the mines.

So fervent was the song, so intense were the coal-smudged faces that it was difficult to comprehend the significance of the gathering. It seemed like a solemn religious ceremony.

Signal Of Victory

Miners all over the valley had waited for sight of the bonfire as a signal of victory. When the flames burst, little bands in other communities started up the slopes of their own hills and soon fires plumed every pinnacle for miles.

Before the fight Ton-y-pandy was tense. Court street, where Tommy lived when he was a pit boy, was decked with flags, and one huge banner said "Tommy Farr . . . Our Champion."

Absolute Quiet

Those who had tickets went to Judge's Hall for singing and dancing, which lasted until the radio broadcast of the fight started early today. Others milled through the streets and finally closed in a series of loudspeakers brought into town for the occasion.

An almost churchly hush settled upon Ton-y-pandy when the clipped tones of a British broadcaster at ringside in New York started his picture of the fight. His words and the voices of women at prayer were the only things to break the listening silence.

After the decision, Dick Farr, Tommy's brother, who had a private radio party at his home, said: "Tell Tommy we're proud of him. At least he proved British boxers have grit."

Stayed Up All Night

Dawn broke cold and gray. It was fully daylight when the crowd finally started down from Trealaw Mountain. The women went ahead to fix breakfast. The men stoically drank their morning tea and went back to the mines. The tea was bitter and the pits were deep and black.

Yesterday's Stars

(By The Associated Press)

Johnny Droner, Indians—His single in ninth drove in winning run to beat Senators, 7-6.

Charley Gehringer, Tigers—Singled winning run across in seventh to whip Yankees, 5-4.

Carl Hubbell and Mel Ott, Giants—Hubbell pitched one-hit ball in 2 1-3 inning relief trick to save 4-3 victory over Reds after Ott's homer brought in two runs.

Paulus Thinks Farr Won

NEW YORK, Aug. 31.—Although Tommy Farr himself has made no knick over the decision, several sports writers who were pro-Louis feel that Farr won from the Brown Bomber. Paul Paulus, sports editor of the Washington Post, said in part: "Tommy Farr stood across the ring and cried. For Tommy knew he had beaten the champion. And 35,000 fans crowded into the Yankee Stadium agreed with him."

After speaking of the jeering and booing Louis got as one of the worst in ring history, Paulus states, however, that "championships aren't lost by fights as this one." He said that Louis looked nothing like a champion, and neither did Farr, but it was one of the most savage fights of recent years, with Farr willing to take everything Louis had. He did, but neither fighter had a punch.

Sports Round-Up

By Eddie Brietz
(Associated Press Sports Writer)

NEW YORK, Aug. 31.—Boys, paste this one in your kellys: Fight experting is gone forever . . . Tommy Farr, the surprising gent from Wales, saw to that . . . That big crash you heard along about 11:15 P. M. was the well-known limb going down with all experts aboard . . . The scribes are a shame-faced lot today . . . Some of the out-of-towners are afraid to go home . . . Joe Jacobs, manager of Max Schmeling, rubbed it in hard . . . "All them experts," he snorted contemptuously, "should of stood in bed" . . . Anyway, Farr gaves 'em a licking even if he couldn't quite get past Joe Louis . . . So we hold the telegrams of ridicule in one hand and reach for the headache powders with the other.

Louis looked bad . . . For a while the fans told themselves he merely was holding back for an opening . . . But as the fight went on, Farr disproved this . . . Joe could not find an opening against the teasing bobbing, weaving style of the Britisher . . . Louis admitted after the fight he was able to land only one good punch and it took him 13 rounds to do this . . . It was the first of Joe's major bouts in which somebody didn't get knocked down . . . Max Schmeling again saw "somedings."

Tommy Farr wore the Welsh dragon on the back of his bathrobe . . . If Farr had had any punch at all he would have had Louis on the deck in the eighth . . . This corner scored seven rounds for Farr and eight for Louis . . . Referee Arthur Donovan gave Louis 13 of the 15 . . . He didn't credit Farr with a heat until the eighth . . . Bill Farnsworth, vice-president of the 20th Century, came in wearing green glasses so he couldn't see the empty seats, but took 'em off when the crowd began to gather . . . Horace Stoneham, president of the Giants, sat in the press box and rooted for Farr.

Fifteen past and present ring champs were introduced and photographed in the ring . . . Present title-holders were Marcel Thil, European middleweight king; Sixto Escobar, ruler of the bantams, and Barney Ross and Lou Ambers, heads of the welter and lightweight divisions . . . Former champs were Jack Johnson, Jack Dempsey, Gene Tunney, Max Baer, Jimmy Braddock, Max Schmeling and Jack Sharkey, all heavies; Mickey Walker, middleweight; Johnny Dundee, featherweight; Tony Canzoneri and Benny Leonard, lightweights . . . Braddock got the biggest hand.

Several times between rounds it looked like a puzzled Joe Louis was about to cry . . . Reports in Farr's dressing room said Tommy had bet $7,500 on himself—$2,500 at 2 to 1 and 7 to 2 that he would win . . . At that rate, he broke even . . . At 6 P. M. there were 350 cops on the job at the stadium to maintain order among 300 fans outside the bleacher windows . . . Farr used the Yankee dressing room at the Stadium, Louis the one occupied by the visitors.

'IF ONLY HE COULD PUNCH,' MAXIE MOANS

(By The Associated Press)

NEW YORK, Aug. 31.—Max Schmeling said it as early as the second round.

"He iss not more the same Louis."

At the time, even though Tommy Farr, the tough tomato from Ton-y-pandy, was cuffing the fuse - less Brown Bomber up against the ropes, it seemed a rash statement. Louis hadn't warmed up, hadn't had time to size up his man.

Took Louis' Best Blows

But as the fight progressed, and Tommy, blood dripping from his nose and from gashes under both eyes, stubbornly refused to buckle under the world's heavyweight champion's best licks, it looked better and better.

At no point in the surprising 15 rounds did Max appear impressed by the man he belted out in twelve rounds a year ago last June. At the end, when Louis' hand was raised in victory, Max was impressed rather by the durability of the Welsh miner who had gone into the ring an even-money shot to go out in less than six rounds.

Farr Proves Tough

"That Farr," said Schmeling, whose rugged good looks are marred only slightly by his battle scars—two puffed eyes and a dented nose—"he iss a good, tough fighter. He fought a brave fight. But you cannot win on a brave fight. If he only could punch. . ."

League Standings

NATIONAL LEAGUE

Scores of Yesterday

New York, 4; Cincinnati, 3.
(Other clubs not scheduled.)

Where They Play Today

St. Louis at New York.
Chicago at Brooklyn.
Pittsburgh at Philadelphia.
Cincinnati at Boston.

Standing of the Clubs

	W.	L.	Pct.
New York	71	46	.607
Chicago.......	72	47	.605
St. Louis	64	54	.542
Pittsburgh. ...	62	57	.521
Boston........	57	62	.479
Philadelphia ..	50	68	.424
Brooklyn	48	68	.414
Cincinnati. ...	46	68	.404

AMERICAN LEAGUE

Scores of Yesterday

Detroit, 5; New York, 4.
Cleveland, 7; Washington, 6.
(Other clubs not scheduled.)

Where They Play Today

New York at Cleveland.
Washington at Detroit.
Boston at Chicago.
Philadelphia at St. Louis (2).

Standing of the Clubs

	W.	L.	Pct.
New York.	80	37	.684
Detroit	69	49	.585
Chicago	68	53	.562
Boston	64	51	.557
Cleveland.	59	57	.509
Washington. ..	54	61	.470
St. Louis	37	80	.316
Philadelphia ..	36	79	.313

SOCIETY

This column is conducted for the pleasure of the subscribers and readers of the Evening Capital. Information regarding happenings of a social nature among the residents of Annapolis and vicinity—parties, marriages, births, trips, and visitors—is always most acceptable, and may be inserted by telephoning Annapolis 330, and asking for the editor of the Social and Personal Column

Miss Mary Spear Bride of Lieutenant R. S. Rooney.

One of the most beautiful and largely attended weddings of the late Summer took place at 4 o'clock Saturday afternoon, in the Naval Academy Chapel, when Miss Mary Mowry Spear, daughter of Captain and Mrs. Ray Spear, of Washington, was married to Lieutenant Roderick Shanahan Rooney, U. S. N., son of the late Judge John Jerome Rooney and Mrs. Rooney, of New York City. The ceremony was performed by the Rev. Father Joseph T. Casey, a Catholic Chaplain of the U. S. Navy, now on duty at the Philadelphia Navy Yard.

While the guests were assembling Prof. J. W. Crosley, organist of the Naval Academy, played a program of music. The altar was decorated with white flowers and the pews were marked with white flowers and white tulle bows.

The bride, who was given in marriage by her father, wore an ivory satin gown with a lace redingote which was buttoned from the neckline to the knees, and had a round collar and a long train. She wore a long lace veil which was worn by her grandmother, Mrs. Louis Piollet, of Towanda, Pa., at her wedding.

Miss Dorcas Tuck, of this city, was the maid of honor, wearing a turquoise blue chiffon gown with matching satin bands on the skirt, and a matching jacket. With this she wore a satin turban and a matching veil. The bridesmaids were the Misses Augusta Melvin, Cary Burwell and Anne Howard, of Annapolis, and Miss Anne Turner, of Washington, whose gowns and hats were like that of the maid of honor. All of the attendants carried bouquets of Talisman roses.

Mr. John Jerome Rooney, brother of the bridegroom, of New York, was best man and the ushers were Lieut. William Brown, Lieut. C. B. Laning, Mr. Otis J. Earle, Lieut. John Williams, Lieut. Robert McCoy, of Annapolis, and Midshipman Louis P. Spear.

A reception followed the wedding at the Naval Academy Officers' Club. Later Lieut. and Mrs. Rooney left on a wedding trip, the latter wearing a three-piece gray suit with a gray fox collar and satin blouse and black accessories.

Among the out-of-town guests were the chief of naval operations and Mrs. William D. Leahy, Rear-Admiral and Mrs. Emory Scott Land, Rear-Admiral and Mrs. W. M. Garton, Admiral and Mrs. Christian Jay Peoples, Rear-Admiral and Mrs. H. E. Lackey, Capt. and Mrs. Charles W. Fisher and Capt. and Mrs. Frank T. Watrous, all of Washington.

Lieutenant Rooney is on duty at the Naval Postgraduate School here, and he and his bride will occupy an apartment at 217 Hanover street.

Mr. and Mrs. Valiant Return From N. Y. Visit

Mr. and Mrs. Joseph W. Valiant have returned to their home, "Valiants' Cottage," at Wardour, after spending a fortnight in New York City as guests of Mr. and Mrs. Walter N. Walmsley, at the Fifth Avenue Hotel.

County Resident Bride Of Mr. George W. Wolf

Mrs. Louise H. Williams, of Bristol, this county, and Mr. George W. Wolf, of Baltimore, were married on Thursday, September 9, at Towson, Md., by the Rev. Dr. George E. McDorman.

After their return from a wedding trip to the North, Mr. and Mrs. Wolf will reside in Baltimore.

Miss Thelma Mae Jewell's Engagement is Announced

Mr. and Mrs. Harry I. Jewell, of Franklin street, announce the engagement of their daughter, Thelma Mae, to Mr. George W. Haughton, Jr., of this city.

The announcement was made at "The Anchorage," on Saturday night, during a party given in honor of Miss Jewell's birthday.

No date has been set for the wedding.

Entertained Guest Over the Week-End

Mr. Worthington Campbell, of Short Hills, N. J., was the week-end guest of Captain and Mrs. Walter D. Sharp, at their quarters in Porter Road.

Commodore and Mrs. Lloyd Return From New England

Commodore and Mrs. Edward Lloyd have returned to their home here, after spending the Summer at York Harbor, Maine.

On the way back to Annapolis, they stopped in New York for a visit to their son and daughter-in-law, Mr. and Mrs. Edward Lloyd, and little daughter, Joanna Leigh Lloyd.

Mrs. Redgrave Visiting Mr. and Mrs. Fowler

Mr. and Mrs. Clarence Vernon Fowler, after a two months' absence spent between the seashore and the mountains, have returned for the Winter to their home, 12 Maryland avenue.

Mrs. Fowler's sister, Mrs. Redgrave, of Los Angeles, California, widow of Commander DeWitt Clinton Redgrave, U. S. Navy, will be their guest through the month of September.

Mrs. Annie Brown Married to Mr. William C. A. Sands

Mrs. Annie Myrtle Brown and Mr. William C. A. Sands, both of this city, were married on Sunday evening, September 12, in St. Martin's Lutheran Church, the Rev. Harry G. Yaggi, pastor of the church, officiating.

Mr. Sands is a lifelong resident of Annapolis, while the bride, who was the widow of Mr. John H. Brown, has resided here for a number of years.

Mr. and Mrs. Sands are at home to their many friends at 73 Prince George street.

Miss Kitty Strange Visiting in Richmond

Miss Kitty Strange is spending a few days in Richmond, Va., as the guest of her brother-in-law and sister, Mr. and Mrs. Verbert Hayward, the latter formerly Miss Margaret Esther Strange, of this city.

Mr. "Jack" Taylor Student At University of N. C.

Mr. "Jack" Taylor, eldest son of Mr. and Mrs. John M. Taylor, df Duke of Gloucester street, has entered the Sophomore class of the University of North Carolina, at Chapel Hill.

His mother, Mrs. John M. Taylor; Mrs. William T. Barber and Mr. Kendall Barber motored to Chapel Hill with Mr. Taylor, and will spend a few days there.

Mr. John C. Hyde In Atlantic City

Mr. John C. Hyde, of 2 Maryland avenue, has been spending some time at the Chalfonte-Haddon Hall Hotel, in Atlantic City.

Married on Saturday In Naval Academy Chapel

Miss Marion Mannhart, daughter of Mr. and Mrs. H. J. Mannhart, of Berkeley, Calif., and Lieutenant (j. g.) Hugh MacKay, United States Navy, son of Mr. and Mrs. O. C. MacKay, of Lawrenceburg, Kentucky, were married at 5:30 o'clock on Saturday afternoon in the Naval Academy Chapel.

Chaplain William N. Thomas, of the Naval Academy, officiated.

The bride, who was given in marriage by Captain Oscar C. Smith, of the Naval Academy Department of Electrical Engineering, wore a lovely wedding dress of white satin, with a tulle veil held in place by a lace cap. Her shower bouquet was of gardenias, lilies-of-the-valley, and white orchids.

Miss Harriet MacConaughey, of Alameda, Calif., was the maid of honor and only attendant of the bride. She was gowned in pink net, with pink net hat, and carried an old-fashioned bouquet of mixed flowers in shades of pink, blue and lavender.

Lieutenant (j. g.) William B. Moore was best man, and the ushers included: Lieutenants (j. g.) W. T. Hines, R. W. Johnson, P. H. Brady, A. B. Roby, J. A. Robbins and W. L. Dye.

The ceremony was followed by a bridal supper at Carvel Hall.

Upon their return from a wedding trip, Lieutenant MacKay and his bride will make their home at 183 Prince George street, where they will be at home after September 20.

Lieutenant MacKay is now stationed at the Naval Postgraduate School here.

BALTO. COUPLE ASSAULTED

(By The Associated Press)

BALTIMORE, Sept. 13. — A young man and woman, attacked by a colored man as they sat in a parked car on the outskirts of town, managed to beat off their assailant early today.

Charles Boecker, 22, and Miss Vera Noweck, 18, reported to police the door of their car was jerked open without warning.

STEWARDESS DEATH IS COAST MYSTERY

(Continued from Page 1)

may have succumbed to a heart attack but said also they learned from friends that she was subject to fits of melancholia and was a "moody type."

Missed Flight

Chief stewardess of Western Air Express, Miss Gilligan missed her scheduled flight Thursday night.

Rumors linking her name romantically were frequent. She was once reported the sweetheart of Leroy King of Cedar Rapids, Ia., dubbed "Iowa"s most eligible bachelor."

Her mother, Mrs. Ed Gilligan, was due here today by plane to return the body to their home in Dunlap, Ia

FATAL CRASH

(By The Associated Press)

CUMBERLAND, Md., Sept. 13—James Woodrow O'Hara, 18, gasoline station operator, was fatally injured early this morning when the automobile which he was driving collided with an east bound Baltimore and Ohio passenger train No. 14, at Knox street crossing here.

The Public Library can use the books that you wish to discard when house cleaning.

Hitler Drinks Only Milk And Water; Eats No Meat; 5 Hours Sleep His Routine

By MELVIN K. WHITELEATHER

(By The Associated Press)

Nurnberg, Germany, Sept. 13.—I kept pace with Adolf Hitler five hours yesterday, and I wanted to sleep till noon today.

It's a killing pace the vegetarian bachelor Fuehrer sets his people at the annual Nazi Party Congress, a strenuous tempo that left me fatigued from following his heels only part of the crowded day.

The day started soon after midnight.

Aroused at 1:15 A. M.

A rap on my door roused me at 1:15 A. M., and a strange voice called: "We wanta word with you."

"The secret police" I asked myself.

Sure enough a black-uniformed guard was with a civilian at the door. In the face of my obvious nervousness the guard said he was "sorry, but orders are orders."

"You are invited to go to the Stormtrooper rally with Der Fuehrer and to lunch with him in Burg Castle today," the guard announced.

Promptly at the appointed hour of 7 A. M., I was walking with a black-uniformed guard through tightly guarded lines to Hitler's hotel which he commandeers entirely for his Nazi leaders.

We rode to Luitpold Arena ahead of Der Fuehrer through solid lines of guards and were in the stands when he arrived to speak to 100,000 Stormtroopers.

Well Guarded

Hitler spoke for half an hour and consecrated his party standards with the Nazis' sacred "Blood Flag" stained in the abortive Munich beerhall putsch in 1923. This ceremony lasted two and a half hours.

Then we rushed out and rode in open cars to the Hilltop Castle through three miles of the wildest cheering.

Behind us were three cars loaded with husky black-uniformed guardsmen.

Save for his eyes Hitler looked fresh and rested after the long public appearance. His eyes, however, always look as though he needed sleep.

At lunch in Burg Castle I saw beside Rudolf Hess, Hitler's thick-eyebrowed confident and quickly discovered he had a sense of humor.

"Don't you have a hat, Herr Reichsminister?" I asked him. Hess smiled.

"In Hamburg, which is a bit stiff socially, they used to say when I was in business, 'Oh yes, you're the man who never wears a hat!'"

Hess talked of the Fuehrer's personal habits and said Hitler never sleeps more than five hours. He usually goes to bed at 1:30 or 2 A. M. and reads an hour before dropping off to sleep.

Doen't Read Novels

Natural science, military history and memoirs are his principal literary fare and he never gets into novels.

In the morning the Reichsfuehrer reads the newspaper in bed, keeping in touch constantly with what the world is saying about him.

He eats carefully, drinking only milk and water. He hasn't tasted meat in six years, and this his fatithful adjutant believ is able to maintain his stren life.

On matters of state Hess was cagey conversationalist. It did not matter about his bareheaded proclivities, but when it came to discussing Reichsminister of Economics Hjalmar Schacht's reportedly impending resignation, that was another matter.

Reviewed Troops

"Yes, I too have heard rumors about Schacht's resignation," he said in reply to a question. "They are frequently running around."

We rode back to the patient cmowds ahead of Hitler, who descended from the Hilltop Castle to review the 100,000 troops in the marketplace.

It was a party congress day for Der Fuehrer, but it wore down an American newspaperman.

ONE POLIO CASE

Only one case of infantile paralysis is active in the county at present, the County Health Department reported today. The case is in the lower end of the county and is now under quarantine.

The Public Library can use the books that you wish to discard when house cleaning.

SOCIETY

This column is conducted for the pleasure of the subscribers and readers of the Evening Capital. Information regarding happenings of a social nature among the residents of Annapolis and vicinity—parties, marriages, births, trips, and visitors—is always most acceptable, and may be inserted by telephoning Annapolis 330, and asking for the editor of the Social and Personal Column.

EXILED

When I was a child, I lived by the
ocean
And shared each day its mysteri-
ous motion;
The tide rose high, the tide eb-
bed low—
It takes twelve thousand tides
for a child to grow—
Catching starfish or sailing a boat,
Putting to sea whatever would
float;
But now I have only a river.
I miss the dank smell of the tide-
flats, the booming
Of breakers, the miraculous silver
pluming
The tips of the oars when we
rowed at night;
The whirring of wings when the
sea-gulls took to flight;
O fresh water! running fast,
Close my mind to that which is
past,
For now I have only a river.
JANICE BLANCHARD
In "The New York Times".

**Admiral and Mrs. Sellers
Giving Two Luncheons.**

The Superintendent of the
Naval Academy, Rear-Admiral
David Foote Sellers, and Mrs. Sel-
lers will give a luncheon on Sun-
day for Rear-Admiral Thomas
Washington, U. S. N., Retired, and
Mrs. Washington, who will be
house guests this week-end of
Captain and Mrs. Howard H.
Crosby, at their quarters, 6 Porter
Road, Naval Academy.

Before the Navy-Columbia University football game tomorrow,
Admiral and Mrs. Sellers will entertain at luncheon for a number
of guests here from out-of-town
for the game. Their guests on
this occasion will include: Rear-
Admiral and Mrs. Hutch I. Cone,
Rear-Admiral and Mrs. Ralston S.
Holmes, Rear-Admiral and Mrs.
Emory S. Land, Captain William
D. Puleston, Rear-Admiral and
Mrs. H. H. Christy, Mrs. W. F. M.
Sowers, and Mrs. Albert P. Nib-
lack, all of Washington, and Lieutenant Basil Rittenhouse, Jr., aide
to Admiral Sellers.

**Captain and Mrs. Woods
Giving Tea Tomorrow.**

Captain and Mrs. Edgar Woods
will entertain at an informal tea
tomorrow afternoon, after the
Navy-Columbia University football
game, in honor of Admiral William H. Leahy, Chief of Naval
Operations, and Mrs. Leahy, who
will be their week-end house
guests.

**Local Debutantes to be Honor
Guests at Tea in Baltimore.**

Mrs. Frederic Jay Cotton, of
"San Rocco," and Mrs. A. G.
Cooke, of "Spring Hill," Waterbury, have issued invitations to a
tea at the Mount Vernon Club,
Baltimore, on Thursday, November 18, in honor of Miss Mary Burwell Melvin, debutante daughter
of Senator and Mrs. Ridgely P.
Melvin, of Annapolis, Miss Margaret Douglas Handy, debutante
daughter of Mr. and Mrs. D.
Claude Handy, also of this city,
and Miss Martha Tyson Chilton
Hopkins, daughter of Mr. and Mrs.
Samuel Harold Hopkins, of Baltimore.

**Lieut. and Mrs. Walton Hopkins
To Spend Week-end Here.**

Before leaving for Panama,
Lieutenant and Mrs. Walton Hop-
kins will spend this week-end with
Lieutenant Hopkins' parents, Dr.
and Mrs. Walton H. Hopkins, 15
Maryland avenue.

Lieutenant and Mrs. Hopkins
have been living in Norfolk, Va.,
since their marriage last Summer. He has recently been ordered to duty on the U. S. S.
"Erie."

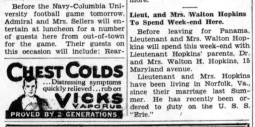
**Coming Here for
Week-end Visit.**

Lieutenant James D. Ferguson,
U. S. N., who is now in Norfolk,
Va., will spend the week-end with
his mother, Mrs. James F. Ferguson, at her home in King George
street.

Mrs. Ferguson's daughter, Miss
Polly Ferguson, will have as her
week-end guest, Miss Marguerite
Louise Williams, of New York.

**St. John's To Have
Alumni Dance Tomorrow**

The St. John's College Cotillion
Board is sponsoring the "Alumni
Dance" to be held tomorrow night
in Iglehart Hall, the college gymnasium, as the climax of "Homecoming Day" at the College.

**Zonta Club to Celebrate
Birthday of Order.**

The birthday of Zonta International will be celebrated by the
Annapolis Zonta Club at its November dinner, to be held on Monday evening, November 8, at 7
o'clock, at "The Blue Lantern
Inn," in King George street.

**Miss Vanderkloot Participant
In Celebration at School.**

Miss Isabell Vanderkloot, daughter of Commander and Mrs. Elroy
L. Vanderkloot, of 35 Upshur
Road, Naval Academy, represented
1930 in "The Parade of The Hundred Years," at the centenary
celebration held today at Mount
Vernon Seminary, in Washington.

**Game Party Tonight
At The Maryland Hotel.**

A game party will be given tonight at the Maryland Hotel. Very
attractive prizes will be
awarded.

**Annapolis Club Officers Guests
At Luncheon in Riverdale.**

Miss Jennie Waddy, District
Deputy of Maryland, yesterday
entertained ten officers of the
Woman's Benefit Association, at her
home in Riverdale, Md. A delicious luncheon was served by the
hostess.

Mrs. Lola E. Coles, State Field
Director of Maryland, and Mrs.
Viola Rice, of the Cumberland Re-
view, were guests at the luncheon.
Mrs. Coles gave an interesting
talk on the good of the order.

PROPERTY TRANSFERS IN CITY AND COUNTY RECORDED IN COURT

From George Freitsch and wife
to Sidney Shapiro, 2 lots of ground
at Holladay Park, Fourth District.

From Donald R. Roberts and
wife to Alpheus M. Sullivan and
wife, 2 lots of ground at Glendale
Terrace, Fifth District.

From The Kentview Land Company to Creed S. Sherwood and
wife, 2 lots of ground at Snug Harbor, Seventh District.

From H. H. Mancha to Theresa
Mancha, lot of ground in this
county, containing 15 acres.

From Southern Maryland Mortgage Company to Viola L. Still-
man and husband, lot of ground in
Third District containing 16 1-2
acres.

From Baltimore Company to
W. W. Farnandis, Inc., lot of
ground at Glen Burnie in the First
District.

From The Franklin Manor
Beach Company to Joseph H.
Bernheimer and wife, lot of
ground at Franklin Manor Beach,
Seventh District.

From Board of Education of
Anne Arundel County to John
Asquith, lot of ground in the First
District containing 1 acre.

From Caroline Pickert to Security Land Company, lot of
ground at Wardour, Second District.

From Lawson Ware to James
Chase and wife, 3 lots of ground
at Morris Hill, Fifth District.

From James H. Farren to Mary
Kathrine Fleming, 2 lots of
ground in the Third District.

CLARE TREE MAJOR GROUP TO PRESENT THREE PLAYS HERE

Annapolis Parent-Teacher Association Sponsoring Productions By Company Which Has Previously Appeared Here

The children of this community
who thrilled with delight at the
antics of the clown "Toby Tyler,"
who found Pinnochio's nose very
satisfactory—especially when it
grew perceptibly longer before
their incredulous eyes every time
poor Pinnochio lied, and whose
charmed "Oh's" and "Ah's" whenever Beauty stepped on the stage
in "Beauty and the Beast" showed
that they knew she had come
straight from fairyland—those
children will rejoice that again this
winter they will be privileged to
see three plays put on by the Clare
Tree Major Children's Theatre in
Annapolis.

These plays are sponsored in
Annapolis by the Parent-Teacher Association—by parents and
teachers who wish the best in
life for the children under their
care. Wholesome and charming
plays are presented by the experienced casts of the Children's
Theatre. An afternoon of enjoyment at one of these theatrical
performances may be the beginning of a lifelong love of plays
and of acting. Witnessing a play
based on a child classic such as
"Hansel and Gretel" is a delight
to the child who loves to read and
to whom the story is already familiar. The active non-reading child
is stimulated to read the story of
the play he has liked so much and
thus his approach to good books is
a natural one.

The undirected child is omni-
verous in his theatrical tastes. He
likes everything, good or bad, if it
is exciting, and will enjoy a movie
concerning gangsters or the under-
world whose influence may be distinctly harmful. The Clare Tree
Major plays are good theatre. They
have the action the child craves
but their effect is good. Their subject matter includes fairy stories
so worthwhile that they have become childhood classics, family
plays based on worthwhile children's books such as the Alcott
series, and historical plays.

Sweeten it with Domino

Crystal
Domino 2 lbs
Cane Sugar
Tablets
Crystallized by
Adant Process

Refined
in U.S.A.

Crystal 1 lb
Domino
Cane Sugar
Squares

American Sugar Refining Company

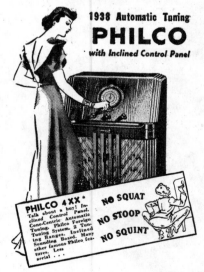

The new 1938 Chevrolet Master De Luxe Sport Coupe with rumble seat.

1938 Chevrolet Master De Luxe Four-Door Sedan

Hudson 8 Sedan for 1938

This luxurious model has a most striking interior, trimmed in modern style with two-tone upholstery and finished with chromium mouldings. The wheelbase is 122 inches; the horsepower, 122.

You'll MEET HUDSON
IN OUR SHOWROOM FROM NOW ON

New HUDSON Terraplane New HUDSON Six New HUDSON Eight
117-in. W. B., 96 and 101 H. P.   122-in. W. B., 101 and 107 H. P. with 5-Star Motor.   122 and 129 W. B., 122 H. P.

3 BRILLIANT NEW CARS
Built to Excel in Style, Performance, Long Life

When you come in, you'll meet three brilliant new cars . . . Hudson Terraplane, Hudson Six, Hudson Eight . . . built to excel in style, performance and long life.

You'll find new beauty and individual style outside . . . and new luxury inside. You'll meet performance that has won every worthwhile American official performance record . . . unmatched anywhere for smoothness.

Remarkable long life, built into every Hudson, gives you extra savings from low upkeep . . . together with unusually high resale value.

We're mighty proud to be selling these new Hudsons, for we honestly believe that they are America's No. 1 Value Cars.

Please regard this as your cordial invitation to come in and see our new Hudson headquarters and our special display of new 1938 Hudsons.

You'll find, too, that just as Hudson builds cars to excel, we have built an outstanding local sales organization, with modern facilities to service any make of car . . . an organization which aims to excel in service and customer satisfaction.

You'll be pleased, we're sure, when we show you how easy it is to own a beautiful new Hudson. Ask about the new low-cost Hudson-C. I. T. Time Payment Plan, with terms to suit your income. Come in today. See and drive the new 1938 Hudson.

Drive With
1938's GREATEST DRIVING FEATURE
HUDSON'S
SELECTIVE AUTOMATIC
SHIFT TRANSMISSION
Now . . . in Its Fourth Year
. . . Greater Than Ever

MEET HUDSON AT OUR GRAND OPENING ALL THIS WEEK
JESS MOTORS
270 WEST STREET   **ANNAPOLIS, MD.**
PRICES START DOWN CLOSE TO THE LOWEST

New Dodge Line Presents Its Claims to Public Approval

Forty-seven progressive improvements are embodied in this new Dodge 4-door touring sedan—and in the nine other models.

Beautiful, comfortable, and economical to operate—this new Dodge 2-door touring sedan will make many friends for itself.

The graceful, sturdy fender construction of the newest Dodge cars is seen here. Headlamps are embedded in the fender arches.

Twenty per cent more luggage space is achieved by carrying the spare tire vertically and by other changes in trunk construction.

Air-streamed beauty of an impressive and substantial order is noted in this head-on view of the new Dodge models.

---

5 NEW BODIES FOR LA SALLE IN 1938

La Salle introduces at the 1938 Automobile Show five new body styles.

Improvements and refinements in both bodies and chassis, smooth performances by the V-8 motor of 125 horsepower, refinement of lines and a new development in gear shifting feature the cars.

New Gear Shift

Leading this list of advances is the new gear shift, the lever of which has been moved from the floor to the steering column. A chief advantage of the application is said to be that it involves no problem of "relearning to shift."

There are five La Salle bodies — two-passenger coupe, convertible coupe, five-passenger touring coupe, five-passenger sedan and convertible sedan. The principal revision noticeable to the eye will be at the front, with the more massive grille, wider, higher catwalks between the hood and fenders and the new location for air-streamed headlamps.

The bodies proper, from the trunks to the headroom, are of generous proportions.

"Alligator" Hoods

The hood is of the "alligator type," hinged parallel with the windshield. It is raised by lifting the radiator ornament. The wider grille not alone lends itself to the style motif of the hood but also increases the radiator cooling area by nineteen square inches.

The 322-cubic-inch V-type, eight-cylinder motor is continued with numerous refinements.

Hydraulic brakes, self-lubricating rear spring inserts, unisteel bodies, are again specified. Carburetion has been improved by air-conditioned metering jet.

Generator drive belts have been given increased durability by large pulleys.

Minor changes in La Salle frames add to rigidity. Cross-type steering is continued along with the individual suspension of front wheels. The hypoid rear axle that proved so successful on the 1937 models will be continued.

DUAL EXHAUST PIPES

A Graham advance for 1938 is a dual arrangement of exhaust pipes. Three cylinder exhaust in each of two pipes instead of six cylinders into one, proving less restriction on power through the overlapping of exhaust impulses.

Home of the
U. S. NAVAL ACADEMY
and
ST. JOHN'S COLLEGE

ANNAPOLIS
Evening Capital

Weather Forecast
Generally fair today and tomorrow; not much change in temperature.

VOL CVI — No. 44. | ESTABLISHED IN 1884—PUBLISHED EVERY EVENING EXCEPT SUNDAY | ANNAPOLIS, WEDNESDAY, JANUARY 5, 1938. | SOUTHERN MARYLAND'S ONLY DAILY PAPER | PRICE TWO CENTS.

PRESIDENT ROOSEVELT BOOSTS BUDGET FOR NAVY

Sutherland To Quit Supreme Bench, Jan. 18

New Deal Foe Notifies President He Will Retire—Plans To Continue Living In Washington — Appointed In 1922

(By The Associated Press)

WASHINGTON, Jan. 5.— Justice George Sutherland of the Supreme Court today notified President Roosevelt he would retire from active service on that bench on January 18.

The retirement of Sutherland gives President Roosevelt his second opportunity to make an appointment to the Supreme Court.

His first came when Justice Willis Van Devanter retired last spring. To succeed Van Devanter Mr. Roosevelt named Senator Hugo L. Black, of Alabama. Disclosure that Black once had been affiliated with the Ku Klux Klan aroused a storm of controversy which lasted throughout the summer and provided one of the highlights of the 1937 battle over the President's move to increase the size of the Supreme Court.

Withholds Comment

Justice Sutherland refused to make any comment on his retirement. Friends said, however, that his action was based largely on his age. He has no serious ailment. They said he has reached the period when he feels that he cannot do his full share of court work without too much strain and that he is not willing to remain on the bench when he feels that he cannot carry his full burden of the work.

The Justice was expected to remain in Washington indefinitely and make himself available for such work on the lower Federal courts as may be agreeable to him. Such assignments by the chief justice are authorized by the retirement act and Van Devanter now is serving on a New York Federal Court.

The jurist was the first born on foreign soil of alien parents since 1806 and the fourth in history. He was born in Buckingham, England, March 25, 1862, but was brought to this country when 15 months old. His father became an American citizen in 1869.

Named In 1922

Sutherland was appointed an associate justice in 1922 by President Harding, after being defeated for re-election as Republican Senator from Utah by Senator William H. King, a Democrat, and his former law partner.

Since the inauguration of President Roosevelt in 1933, the Justice was one of the most consistent opponents of administration legisla-

(Continued on Page 6)

Mrs. Redfern Declared Widow by Court

Aviator Paul Redfern, who vanished on a projected non-stop flight from Georgia to South America in 1927, was declared legally dead by Circuit Court Judge Robert M. Toms in Detroit. Mrs. Redfern is shown above in her latest picture.

DR. HOPKINS' MOTHER DIES IN BALTIMORE

Funeral services for Mrs. Mary Hyde Hopkins, who died yesterday at the home of her daughter, Mrs. George Thomas Linthicum, 711 St. John's road, Baltimore, will be held at the residence at 10 A. M. tomorrow. Burial will be in Christ Church Cemetery, Owensville, West River, Anne Arundel County.

Mrs. Hopkins, the widow of the late John Henry Hopkins, was 85 years old. A native of West River, she had lived in Baltimore for thirty-seven years, the last ten at the home of her daughter, Mrs. Linthicum. Her husband, Mr. Hopkins, died in 1925.

Besides Mrs. Linthicum, she is survived by another daughter, Mrs. Albert B. Hall, of Dallas, Texas; six sons, Hastings Brown Hopkins, Baltimore; Dr. Walton H. Hopkins, Annapolis; George Hyde Hopkins, Miami, Fla.; Marion Byrd Hopkins, Elizabeth, N. J.; Dr. Philip Bird Hopkins, Bel Air, Md., and John Henry Hopkins, West River, and one brother, John F. B. Hyde, Baltimore.

Eastport Relief Group to Meet

The regular monthly meeting of the Eastport Relief Association will be held on Thursday at 7:30 P. M., at the residence of Mrs. John M. Mitchell, on Fourth street, at Eastport.

Card of Thanks

I wish to thank everyone for kindness and sympathy on the occasion of the death of my son Edward Jones, and also thank those persons who sent flowers or loaned automobiles.

EMMA JONES.

KIWANIS CLUB INSTALLS OFFICERS

Rev. James J. Coale Installed As President Succeeding Benjamin Michaelson

Sentiment and merriment combined yesterday at the regular weekly luncheon meeting of the Annapolis Kiwanis Club, held at the Cooper Grill, when the new officers to serve the present year were installed.

Officers Installed

The installation ceremonies were conducted by Clarence M. White, the club's first president, and Past President Albert Jerome Goodman. The following were installed:

President—Dr. J. J. Coale, pastor of the Presbyterian Church.

Immediate Past President—Benjamin Michaelson, local attorney and counsel to the Board of County Commissioners.

Secretary—Harry S. Kenchington, who succeeds Dr. William Y. Kitchin, who served three years.

Treasurer—Steve Duckett, manager of the Arundel Laundry.

In addition to the above officers, the board of directors this year will be composed of Herman Collier, Albert Jerome Goodman, S. Edwin James, John F. Martin and Charles E. Skipper.

Henry Zerhusen, manager of the Annapolis office of the Gas & Electric Company, was elected as a new member.

Tomorrow evening, at the Cooper Grill, at 6:15, a meeting of the officers and chairmen of the various committees will be held for the purpose of outlining plans of activities for the year.

MRS. CATES TO READ PLAY HERE JAN. 7

Mrs. John M. Cates, of Baltimore, will entertain the Play Readers Club and guests on next Friday, January 7, by reading "Yes, My Darling Daughter," an amusing play now running in New York.

The meeting this week will be held in the home of Mrs. Mason Porter Cusachs, Ogle Hall, at 2:30 P. M. The next reading will be on January 21.

REV. BEST PREACHES HERE THIS EVENING

The Rev. Dr. William H. Best, Presiding Elder of the Baltimore District of the Methodist Episcopal Church, South, will conduct the weekly prayer service at Trinity M. E. Church, South, tonight at 8 o'clock. After the service Dr. Best will preside at the first quarterly conference session of Trinity Church for the 1937-1938 church year.

Both services are open to the public.

$2,109,758 TO BE GIVEN ACADEMY HERE

Is Increase Over Past Year—Individual Expenditures Listed — Navy Construction Program To Get Endorsement Of Chief Executive.

HAMILTON DEMANDS BIG ATLANTIC FLEET

(By The Associated Press)

WASHINGTON, Jan. 5 — White House callers reported today President Roosevelt would send a special message to Congress very soon suggesting a new navy building program supplemental to the 18 ships provided for in the regular budget.

WASHINGTON, Jan. 5—President Roosevelt recommended today appropriation of $837,359 for maintenance and operation of the naval training stations at San Diego, Calif., Newport, R. I., Great Lakes, Ill., and Norfolk, Va., during the fiscal year starting July 1.

The estimate exceeded 1938 appropriations by $12,000, of which $8,500 was asked for the Norfolk station and $3,500 for the Newport station.

The estimates were: San Diego, $160,359; Newport, $152,000; Great Lakes, $256,500; and Norfolk, $286,500. Estimates for other naval shore stations and establishments were not detailed.

The lump estimate for maintenance and operation of shore stations was $34,246,339 for 1939 against 33,472,275 for 1938, and for repairs and improvements to shore stations, $6,404,430 for 1939 against $4,120,356 for 1938.

Boost In Budget

Estimates of Public Works Administration funds for the Bureau of Yards and Docks were $10,787,000, compared with $6,829,000 for 1938.

The message said major projects in the 1939 estimates included improvement of the channel and ship berthing and overhaul facilities at Pearl Harbor, Hawaii; development of the Alameda, Calif., air station; provision for quarters for naval personnel at Coco Solo and Balboa, Canal Zone, and the Norfolk, Va., air station; and start of construction of the naval medical center in the vicinity of Washington, D. C.

More Money For Academy

Estimates for the Naval Academy at Annapolis for 1939 were $2,109,758, against $2,023,282 for

(Continued on Page 6)

Co-Ed Elopes

Widespread search for Miss Gertrude Bennett, (above) 17-year-old daughter of Harry H. Bennett, head of the Ford Motor Company personnel bureau, was abandoned after word came of her marriage at Auburn, Ind. Her husband is Russell Hughes, 21, trap drummer and fellow student at Michigan State Normal College.

FIRST RETURNS STATE INCOME TAX FILED

The Maryland one-half of one percent income tax brought in a total of $14,427 from the time it became effective until December 31, it was learned today.

The payments were received from corporations, individuals and fiduciaries who conducted their affairs on a fiscal year basis. The returns from those who operate on a calendar year basis are payable on or before March 15.

Three hundred and thirty-seven corporations whose fiscal years ended prior to October 1 paid $14,161.31 in taxes; 19 individuals paid $261.76, and two fiduciaries paid $3.93. Seventeen partnerships and 205 corporations made returns but were non-taxable.

The income tax division has received about 150 returns from individuals on calendar year income during 1937. The payments on these have not been tabulated.

SKETCH CLUB PLANS EXHIBITION SHORTLY

The Annapolis Sketch Club is sponsoring an exhibition of the work of George Keester, local artist, at a private showing next Sunday, followed on Monday and Tuesday by an exhibition open to the public.

Mr. Keester is the son of Commander and Mrs. George B. Keester, of Duke of Gloucester street, and is now a teacher of design at the Maryland Institute in Baltimore. He started out as a pupil of Miss Jennie Richardson, then went to the Maryland Institute where he won a traveling scholarship in 1936. He is a member of Baltimore Water Color Club and has two lithographs in the club's exhibition at the Baltimore Museum of Art. He was represented in last year's show also, and had two pictures in the All Maryland Arts exhibition at the Baltimore Museum.

At his Annapolis showing he will display lithographs, water colors, etchings and commercial designs. The exhibition is open to the public without charge next Monday and Tuesday from 10 to 5 at the Calvert Studio on State Circle.

Funeral on Friday Of Mrs. M. Campbell

The funeral of Mrs. Mamie F. Campbell, wife of Henry C. Campbell, Jr., will take place on Friday at 3:30 P. M., from the funeral parlors of John M. Taylor, on Duke of Gloucester street.

Interment will be in Cedar Bluff cemetery.

Mrs. Campbell died on Monday, January 3.

JAPS INSTALL NEWS CENSOR IN SHANGHAI

Move Follows Threat To Assume Control Of International Settlement To Halt Chinese "Outrages" — Consolidate Captured Provinces.

AMERICANS AID CHINESE FORCES

(By The Associated Press)

HANGCHOW, Jan. 1, by courier to Shanghai, Jan. 5— After nine days of looting, disorder and fear Japanese military police today had succeeded in restoring a measure of peace and order and reassuring the terrified population of this capital of Chekiang Province.

SHANGHAI, Jan. 5—Japanese authorities announced today they had taken over all Chinese Government functions in the international city of Shanghai and other territory occupied by Japanese armies.

A final step in Japan's drive for dominance was projected censorship of news dispatches. Japanese officials were said to have notified cable companies that Japanese censors were moving in to prevent leakage of military information to Chinese.

For more than a month, dis-

(Continued on Page 6)

RITES HELD FOR MRS. WINCHESTER

The funeral of Mrs. Ella Kent Winchester, who died at the residence of her daughter, Mrs. Nancy Naughton, in Philadelphia, Pa., was held this morning from St. Mary's Church. The Rev. Father Fallon officiating.

Interment was in St. Mary's cemetery and the pall bearers were: J. Henry Zeller, John M. Green, Henry F. Sturdy, James A. Walton, Frank Ridout and C. Corner Ridout. Funeral arrangement were in charge of John M. Taylor.

Roosevelt's Budget Showing Deficits Of Above One Billion

Congress Asked to Increase Appropriation for National Defense—-Relief Costs May Go Over Estimate, President Says in Message.

(By The Associated Press)

WASHINGTON, Jan. 5—President Roosevelt sent Congress a budget message today which projected new billion-dollar treasury deficits and a new public debt peak despite estimates of lesser spending.

His forecast for the 1939 fiscal year contemplated a $539,000,000 cut in government outlays—"the most important fact of this budget," Mr. Roosevelt said—but conditioned the reduction on an upturn in business and national defense requirements.

The President's big volume of budget figures estimated a net deficit of $1,088,129,600 for the current fiscal year and $949,606,000 for the next twelve months which he noted would be successive declines. The public debt, he said, would reach a $38,528,200,000 high on June 30, 1939.

MAY SPEND MORE

In addition, Mr. Roosevelt left the treasury's doors ajar to the possibility of more spending for human relief and for armaments "due to world conditions over which this nation has no control."

The continued deficit was attributed to a sharp drop in expected revenue because of the business recession. President Roosevelt acknowledged that for the first time since he became Chief Executive he faced less, rather than more, governmental income.

To obtain next year's estimated spending slash of $539,000,000, the President cut his estimate for relief and recovery to $1,138,304,000 —down $841,356,600 from this year's figures. But he added:

"The economic situation may not improve and if it does not, I expect the approval of Congress and the public for additional appropriations if they become necessary to save thousands of American families from dire need."

Complete Budget

Nevertheless, for the first time in three years the President presented a complete budget, including relief estimates which previously had been left until later. He did so, apparently, on the basis of a treasury forecast that business would improve.

"We hope," he said, "that the calendar year 1938 will bring an improvement in business conditions, and, therefore, in tax receipts. The treasury, leaning to the conservative side, predicts some improvement over the present level but does not assume in its figures that business in the calendar year 1938 will reach as high a level as in the calendar year 1937."

Mr. Roosevelt asked an increase of $34,300,000 to bring national defense spending up to a record peacetime level of $991,300,000 in 1939. His message mentioned a $54,847,000 boost in regular defense funds, but part of this difference was offset by allocation of less emergency money for defense next year than in the current period.

Would Veto Items

Other important features of the budget message, which as usual was read to the two houses of Congress separately by their clerks, included:

A recommendation that Congress, either by legislation or a constitutional amendment, provide the Chief Executive with authority to veto individual items in an appropriation bill without returning the entire measure.

A renewed recommendation that Congress enact "at an early date such amendments to the revenue law as will maintain the revenue producing power of the present tax structure while correcting at the same time existing proven inequities."

Curtail Spending

Proposals to curtail spending on

(Continued on Page 6)

Trumpet Blast Heralds Phoebus' Filing Papers

Senator Harry T. Phoebus, State Commissioner of Labor and Statistics, his appearance heralded by trumpet blasts, today filed his certificate of candidacy for the Republican Gubernatorial nomination, at the office of E. Ray Jones, Secretary of State.

Harry T. Phoebus, Jr., 9-year-old son of the candidate, blew several blasts on a 2-foot trumpet as the Somerset county Senator arrived outside the State House. Mrs. Vera B. Phoebus accompanied her husband.

Accuser Watches Filing

Senator Robert B. Kimble (R-Allegany) who has filed charges of mal-administration against Phoebus in conducting his office of Labor Commissioner, was a witness of the arrival and filing. Kimble had just left the office of Gov. Harry W. Nice when the first blasts of the trumpet heralded Phoebus' arrival.

"I paid my respects to the Governor and laid my final demand before him for a hearing on my charge," Kimble said. "As I was leaving the office, by coincidence, I ran into Gabriel and his horn. I had the pleasure of witnessing the honorable gentleman file his papers."

Trumpet Was Gift

Young Phoebus received his trumpet as a Christmas present. He said he was practicing to play for his father's entrance when he was summoned from Princess Anne to come to Baltimore last night. He enjoyed his trumpeting and also a holiday from the Princess Anne school.

He said he would learn to play "Here comes the next Governor" by May. Senator Phoebus said he and his son would set the tune to music for his campaign which he plans to start within the next 60 days.

After the trumpeting outside the State House the Phoebus party

(Continued on Page 6)

Hard Tests For Navy Boxers, Wrestlers On Saturday's Program

Cagers Meet William And Mary and V. M. I. This Week—Swimmers Open On Saturday Against Penn — Gym Team Faces Temple In Philadelphia On Friday.

ST. JOHN'S TO PLAY TWO LOOP GAMES

Navy's big sports program of the week-end will be opened in Philadelphia when the Midshipmen face the Temple University gymnasium team, in the season's most important match for Navy, except for the clash with West Point, here later in the season. The Navy acrobats have been in action just once this year. On that occasion nearly two weeks ago they plastered at 45½ to 8½ decision on the inexperienced Penn State team. The meet was costly however, as Midshipman Robert K. R. Worthington of Philadelphia, was painfully injured in a fall from the flying rings. It is doubtful if Worthington, the No. 1 man in the event, will be able to compete either against Temple on Friday, or against Massachusetts Institute of Technology in Cambridge on Saturday. His period of hospitalization seems to have brought him back to first class physical condition, however.

Other Leading Sports

Basketball, swimming, wrestling and boxing will vie for top honors at the Academy on Saturday. The Tar cage team is almost certain to reach the game with Temple here on February 16, undefeated at home. Neither William and Mary to be met here at 4 P. M. on Wednesday, nor Virginia Military Institute, foe of Saturday, are expected to press the crack Navy quint seriously. Navy toyed with Columbia last Saturday getting a 20 points lead midway in the second half before resorting to defensive tactics.

The greatest interest this week centers in the boxing meet between the Navy and University of Virginia varsities. Virginia has been more successful against Navy than any other team, and the Cavaliers looked plenty tough in winning from Maryland last Saturday night. Coach Spike Webb, Comdr. O. O. Kessing and the Navy boxing squad went to College Park in a bus to witness the bouts, and Lieut. George Kosco, assistant Navy boxing coach, predicts a Navy triumph.

Wrestlers Meet Indiana

There will be no let-up for the Navy wrestling team which last Saturday bowed to Lehigh's powerful team. The Middies expect to be hard pressed on Saturday by Indiana. The wrestling meet will follow the basketball game which begins at 2:30 P. M.

Navy varsity and plebe natators will entertain like swimming teams from the University of Pennsylvania. The freshmen meet is set for 1:30 P. M. and the varsity splash for 3:30 P. M.

Also included on the Navy program are the following events:

1 P. M. — Wrestling between Navy plebes and V. M. I. freshmen.

1:30 P. M.—Varsity rifle between Navy and Lehigh.

2 P. M.—Varsity fencing between Navy and Yale.

4 P. M.—Basketball between Navy plebes and Eastern high school of Washington.

Two Games For St. John's

The St. John's College basketball team will play two games in the Maryland Collegiate League this week. Washington College will be met at Chestertown tomorrow night, while Hopkins will be hosts to the Johnnies in Baltimore, Saturday night.

St. John's looked mighty good in defeating Gettysburg 32 to 27 last Saturday night, which was the same margin by which Navy whipped the Battlefield boys.

On February 1c St. John's will play the Haviford quint at Haverford, then will return home on February 19 for a clash with the City College of New York five.

WAKE UP YOUR LIVER BILE—

Without Calomel—And You'll Jump Out of Bed in the Morning Rarin' to Go

The liver should pour out two pounds of liquid bile into your bowels daily. If this bile is not flowing freely, your food doesn't digest. It just decays in the bowels. Gas bloats up your stomach. You get constipated. Your whole system is poisoned and you feel sour, sunk and the world looks punk.

A mere bowel movement doesn't get at the cause. It takes those good, old Carter's Little Liver Pills to get these two pounds of bile flowing freely and make you feel "up and up." Harmless, gentle, yet amazing in making bile flow freely. Ask for Carter's Little Liver Pills by name. 25c. Stubbornly refuse anything else.

Bowling

ANNAPOLITAN LEAGUE

RED DIVISION

	W.	L.	Pct.
N. A. "5"	35	10	.778
Gas & Electric	26	19	.578
Taylor's Store	24	21	.533
Roger's Service Sta.	24	21	.533
French's Garage	23	22	.511
7-Up	22	23	.489
Coca-Cola	22	23	.489
St. Margaret's	22	23	.489
Metropolitan Life	21	24	.467
A. P. Tea Co.	20	25	.444
Happy "5"	17	28	.378
W. H. Thomas Co.	14	31	.311

BLUE DIVISION

	W.	L.	Pct.
Knesrael	32	13	.711
H. B. Myers Co.	29	16	.628
Smith Bros.	27	18	.600
Davis' Stationery	26	19	.578
Annapolis Dairy	25	20	.556
Variety "5"	24	21	.533
K. of C.	22	23	.489
Kiwanis	21	24	.467
Elks	18	27	.400
Arundel Laundry	17	28	.378
Universal Motors	15	30	.333
French's Studebakers	14	31	.311

High Single Game (Team)
Coca-Cola 681
High Three Games (Team)
Coca-Cola 1,969
High Individual Score (1 Game)
"Junie Easterday 178
High Individual Score (3 Games)
"Junie" Easterday 465
Coca-Cola

RED DIVISION

N. A. "5"

H. Zelko	136	123	116
F. Ecken	113	127	123
O. Jarosik	111	103	118
G. Duvall	130	121	104
G. Scible	110	91	129
Totals	600	565	590

FRENCH'S GARAGE

C. French	123	100	102
W. King	105	..	..
S. French	..	98	123
Anderson	117	123	122
T. Miller	122	130	110
M. French	107	103	111
Totals	574	554	568

W. H. THOMAS

H. Howard	124	116	135
A. Britton	105	..	..
R. Martin	111	112	99
C. Jones	125	127	116
E. Scible	109	122	100
S. Stokes	..	131	137
Totals	574	608	587

7-UP

Tomanio	135	127	132
Clark	125	93	117
Finky	111	140	99
Cranford	128	114	107
Myers	110	107	107
Totals	609	581	562

HAPPY "5"

Tarleton	114	120	106
Engelke	114	124	103
Clow	106	104	128
Jones	128	122	107
Newton	145	123	120
Totals	607	593	564

METROPOLITAN LIFE

Taylor	117	112	137
Jones	130	103	114
Krebs	118	99	..
Hartge	121	132	102
Tucker	119	111	119
Owens	..	..	113
Totals	605	557	585

A. & P. TEA CO.

E. Deale	101	125	124
F. Tomanio	103	112	115
E. Ford	93	118	129
B. Lamb	93	99	113
S. Fertitta	101	109	99
Totals	496	563	580

GAS & ELECTRIC CO.

Lacey	107	100	..
DiMaggio	152	123	130
Boteler	101	..	107
Galloway	109	104	115
Zerhusen	133	113	117
Hayes		125	111
Totals	602	565	580

COCA-COLA

Housley	96	119	122
Jones	100	95	108
R. Easterday	91	99	137
Lowman	103	114	110
J. Easterday	113	126	117
Totals	503	553	594

ROGERS' SERVICE STA.

L. Hoff	116	97	..
C. Lamb	106	137	107
Arnold	106	113	134
Rogers	111	136	108
A. Lamb	133	111	111
Sargnit	..	..	95
Totals	572	594	555

TAYLOR'S STORE

Cook	116	113	117
McCarter	139	123	117
Alvey	122	99	112
Gardner	127	106	..
Gaither	120	104	160
M. Collison	..	..	111
Totals	624	545	617

ST. MARGARET'S

Haneke	103	114	117
Hays	101	127	120
Mayer	114	109	131
Bryant	112	116	123
Campbell	115	96	115
Totals	545	562	606

BLUE DIVISION

SMITH BROS.

S. Dixon	118	113	116
G. Robbins	140	130	121
N. Smith	120	103	126
E. Mauk	100	103	125
D. Hartge	120	103	133
Totals	598	552	621

ARUNDEL LAUNDRY

Hopkins	108	139	115
Peterson	119	126	124
Duckett	107	103	..
G. Miller	109	116	125
O. Miller	108	148	122
Tucker	..	..	107
Totals	551	632	593

DAVIS STATIONERY

Tarleton	120	114	121
B. Britton	121	105	122
K. Davis	125	104	116
Weingarten	109	122	106
McKee	115	108	121
Totals	590	553	586

VARIETY 5

F. Sears	98	105	108
D. Ross	119	113	113
B. Ellers	99	122	97
B. Martin	100	130	106
J. Martin	121	122	142
Totals	537	592	566

ELKS

D. Howard	122	120	101
C. Smith	112	112	113
S. Young	112	101	98
M. Palmeria	122	119	107
O. Dawes	104	114	112
Totals	572	566	531

KNESRAEL

J. Cohen	127	118	128
D. Hyatt	127	129	129
S. Katcef	120	121	115
J. Katcef	126	109	87
L. Bloom	136	105	116
Totals	636	582	575

K. of C.

Brady	99	114	107
Pantaleo	100	100	107
Vallaningham	116	108	105
Haley	137	127	99
Brock	120	103	115
Totals	572	552	533

KIWANIS

Collier	113	100	112
Martin	100	103	135
Skipper	101	119	123
Phipps	101	109	119
Clark	121	152	131
Totals	536	583	620

FRENCH STUDEBAKERS

Rittenhouse	111	111	109
Loughead	127	111	116
Burford	122	124	110
Donovan	106	102	95
Pryce	101	..	..
Ward	..	96	..
Allen	..	..	138
Totals	567	544	568

H. B. MYERS

Myers	100	114	105
Milliken	141	104	144
Purdy	113	109	99
Stallings	106	115	97
Scible	122	138	128
Totals	582	580	573

ANNAPOLIS DAIRY

Sweeney	109	125	114
Blind	90	..	..
Hayman	113	106	108
Arnold	108	131	120
Buck	137	101	102
Winchester	..	115	106
Totals	557	578	550

UNIVERSAL MOTORS

Duvall	103	104	..
Cather	110	124	132
Huse	118	111	113
Beall	124	122	103
Green	144	113	120
Lee	..	..	99
Totals	599	574	567

Sports Round-Up

By EDDIE BRIETZ
(By The Associated Press)

NEW YORK, Feb. 8—Next week's Tony Galento-Harry Thomas fight promises to be one of those good old alley brawls from away back yonder . . . Any day now you can look for the Dodgers to make some news . . . Max Baer told Broadway hello and good bye in one hour yesterday, which is strange going ons for that guy . . . After Connie Smythe, coach of the Toronto Maple Leafs, had rushed across the ice and socked Referee Billy Boyd Sunday night, Connie explained he was only trying to straighten Boyd's necktie . . . Haw! . . . The Rideout and Brown twins on the North Texas Teachers' relay team made a smash hit with New Yorkers . . . Some of the smart boys are weakening on War Admiral in the $50,000 Widener Handicap race.

Plenty going on around here . . . Work is being rushed on Jack Dempsey's new Broadway bar . . . A few hours after Tommy Farr had left a taxi loudly bawling out a stunning brunette who remained inside, Tommy stepped on the stage at Billy Rose's new night spot and sang "Do You Remember Me?" in a not too bad tenor . . . (Customers gave him a hand) . . . Max Baer totes a picture of his kid around in his pocket and shows it off on the slightest provocation . . . Positively lovely the way Jack Dempsey and Jack Kearns are falling all over each other . . . Those pictures of them shaking hands couldn't have been purchased for any price ten years ago . . . It's Ruppert vs. Gehrig today and it's likely to be a draw.

Tarzan White, guard for the New York Pro Giants, has put on 30 pounds since he has been inhaling his own cooking . . . Pass that sausage, Tarzan . . . Gen. Critchley, the rich British promoter, hit town yesterday on his way to Palm Beach for a holiday . . . A reporter said: "Well, we got Tommy Farr over here," and the General replied: "Yes, and you can have him" . . . But mebbe that was because the General didn't get Tommy . . . Turns out that the "Roy Madison" who has been making hit records for one of the big concerns is none other than Bill Briordy, sports writer on the New York Times . . . My goodness, Bill—a crooner! . . . Bang, the Boxing Weekly recently taken over by Maurie Waxman, gets brighter with each issue.

Jack Kearns remains one of the best story tellers in the boxing biz . . . Get him to tell you the yarn of how the Dempsey-Willard fight was made . . . New York papers hear George Veeneker, who used to play with Michigan, will be announced as the new Wolverine coach any day now . . . Poppy Wingate, British woman professional golfer, is to tour the U. S. . . . Maxie Baer says playing golf with Lawson Little has cut ten strokes off his game . . . Pictures of Tony Galento smoking cigars and guzzling beer made the New York Boxing Commissioners mad, but when Tony obligingly posed with a glass of milk to the left, a book of bedtime stories in one hand and a lollypop in the other, the commissioners were infuriated . . . Joe Jackson, the old Major Leaguer, is running a liquor store in Greenville, S. C.

Isn't it a nice coincidence that a party measure always happens to agree with a good party man's conscience.

Navy Baseball Players Report To New Coach

Max Bishop, newly appointed coach of baseball at the Naval Academy, talked over the plans for the coming season with a squad of over 50 candidates who reported yesterday afternoon. Today, he will begin work in the armory.

Bill Ingram, captain of the team, was present at the conference, though he will, with Alan McFarland, delay reporting for baseball until the close of the basketball season.

Veterans of last year on hand included Lem Cooke, infielder, who developed as a pitcher during the summer; Jerry Bruckel and Joe Eliot, of the pitching staff; Jamie Adair, one of the catchers; Ralph McGuinness, Howard Thompson, Bill Pace and Al Sbisa, infielders, and Ralph Mann and Lucien Powell, outfielder. Powell has been shifted to first base.

During last summer, under Marty Karow, then coach, a fast infield was developed, with Powell at first base, Dick Cady, who developed finely during the period, at second, Thompson at shortstop and McGuinness at third.

The development of Cooke, also the Navy's ace football back, as a pitcher, was another happening of the summer season. Cooke, one of the best batsmen on the squad, is likely to play in the outfield when not on the mound.

VA. RINGMEN EXPECT CLOSE FIGHTS HERE

Coach Says Squad Came Through Meet With Western Maryland In Good Shape And Will Use Same Line-up Against Tars.

THREE VICTORIES SEEN AS CERTAIN

(By The Associated Press)

CHARLOTTESVILLE, Va., Feb. 8—Johnny Larowe, 71-year-old coach of the University of Virginia boxing team, said today his squad came through the grueling Maryland meet in good shape and no change in the lineup was planned for the Navy match at Annapolis Saturday.

The Cavaliers, unbeaten this season, holding a draw with Syracuse's Eastern Intercollegiate champions, were expecting a close scrap with the Middies. Virginia supporters expressed confidence of victories by John Simpson, veteran 115-pounder and former Southern Conference champion; Maynard Harlow, rugged 145-pounder who defeated Maryland's Benny Alperstein, national Collegiate titleholder; and Ray Schmidt, National Lightweight champion, who has never lost a bout in the college ring.

Other Virginia entries will be Kushner, 125, Williams, 135; Southall, 155, Mallard, 165, and Weeks, giant football tackle who was converted into a heavyweight ringman this year.

Virginia has beaten Navy four times in the past five years, more than any other school. The Middies won 4½ to 3½ last season.

The ticket allotment of 500 for Virginia students was over-subscribed some time ago.

The number of unemployed decreases but slowly. You see, so many men disagree with their boss about politics.

QUICK PRINTING SERVICE Modern Plant

The Capital-Gazette Press
3 Church Circle
Annapolis, Maryland

SASSCER DEMANDS PRIMARY BATTLE

"County" Candidate And Jackson Speak From Same Platform Last Night.

(By The Associated Press)

CLEAR SPRING, Md. Feb. 8—It became increasingly evident today, in the light of the most recent oratory, that at least one "county" candidate is conceding nothing to Baltimore's Mayor Howard W. Jackson in the Democratic gubernatorial campaign.

And, to judge by Jackson's remarks last night before the Clear Spring Women's Democratic Club, "most" of his three opponents for the party's nomination for governor are teaming up to eliminate him in the primary.

Sasscer Answers Charge

His prediction that any such move would fail drew from Senate President Lansdale G. Sasscer, Southern Maryland's hope, the assertion that the nomination was no one man's by "divine right," but a goal for all to fight for.

Both agreed, however, that an "open and vigorous primary"—to use Sasscer's words—would be wholesome for the party.

The other two candidates for the nomination, Attorney General Herbert R. O'Conor and State Comptroller William S. Gordy, Jr., failed to share the speakers' platform with Jackson and Sasscer last night. O'Conor is in Bermuda. Gordy is ill with a cold.

Run Against Jackson

"Most of the candidates in the field for the Democratic nomination for governor are busy explaining that they are not running against each other, but are running against me," Jackson said.

"This reason is extremely flattering. It means that, as matters stand, I am already the first choice of the great majority of the Democratic voters and that plans and schemes are under way for the express purpose of defeating the will of the Democratic voters.

"But such schemes do not alarm me. I know and you know that the Democratic party does not want and will not have any second or third choice candidate for the office of governor."

There still was time, he said, for "these minority groups to give up their efforts, doomed to failure anyhow, to nullify the people's choice."

Discuss Issues

To which Sasscer responded:

"All of us have a right to go in and fight out our cause in the primaries and discuss the issue before the great Democratic forum.

"No (individual candidate has any divine right to the nomination. We have no 'crown prince system' in Maryland."

He asserted there could be an "open and vigorous campaign" and "we do not have to get excited or angry," but "we can make a clean, aggressive fight within our party."

"I will adhere to the principles of sportsmanship and Democracy in my campaign," Sasscer said. "If the chips begin to fly and strike me in passage, I shall not whimper nor ask for quarter. I shall carry on the fight."

GIRL RESERVES HOME FROM CONFERENCE

The Girl Reserve Regional Midwinter Conference, held at the Baltimore Y. W. C. A., February 5-6, was voted a huge success by the 150 girls attending. Girls came from as far south as Richmond, Va., and as far north as Wilmington, Del.

Girls representing Annapolis included the following: Rosestelle Adams, Girl Reserve Advisor; the Misses Blanche Colbert, Snookie Elliott, Isabella Fowler, Mary Ann Hopping, Priscilla Hall, Olivia Hinton, Betty Joachim, Elma Kuchar, Evelyn Lee, Kitty Sarles, Florence Sears, Betty Kinchaloe, Marian Newton, and Dorothy Bean.

Some highlights of the conference were a talk by Mrs. Joseph D. Grisby, who took a very interesting and clever subject—"Vocations."

They held "Forums" which included: Service Work for Clubs, Federal and Civic Housing Plans, Child Labor and Anti-lynching Legislation.

The talk and discussion were led by Dr. George H. Preston on "Relationships," proved very enlightening to the girls.

Folk games and dances in the gymnasium added a note of gayety to the conference.

There was also a banquet—with Lieut.-Comdr. J. E. Johnson, Assistant Chaplain of the U. S. Naval Academy, as the guest speaker. "Peace" was the subject of Chaplain Johnson's message. He explained that, contrary to public opinion, the Navy is a peaceable group and does not enter actions only after everything possible to prevent war has been used. He touched on the present situation in the Far East and what is happening in our own country in the way of attitudes, propaganda, mob psychology, such as effectiveness or advisability of boycotting.

Louis and Farr, Braddock and Schmeling, all put together might make a Dempsey or a Tunney.

Raw Throat? Here's Quick Action!

Kill the cold germs that attack your throat and cause miserable colds. At the first sign of "raw" throat, gargle with Zonite.

Zonite is 9.3 times more active, by standard laboratory tests, than any other popular non-poisonous antiseptic. Kills all kinds of cold germs—*at contact!* And Zonite soothes your throat.

Get Zonite at once. Gargle immediately—1 teaspoon Zonite to half glass water. Kill cold germs before they spread UP into sinuses or DOWN into bronchial tubes. You'll feel relief after the first gargle with Zonite.
Advertisement.

SAFETY-TESTED USED CARS
"Means Safe Unused Transportation"
1936 Nash Ambassador 4-Door Sedan. Original Black finish, Clean Upholstery, Good tires, Super-Hydraulic Brakes, All steel Body, Safety glass windshield. Lowest finance charges. G. M. A. C. terms to suit . . . $495
Annapolis Buick Co.
240 WEST STREET 100 COLLEGE AVENUE
BUICK AND OLDSMOBILE—SALES AND SERVICE
PHONE 1030

Ten Chief Causes Of Traffic Accidents In Annapolis---No. 2, "Jaywalking"

Harmless enough is the chance meeting of these two young women, apparently homeward bound after a shopping trip.

Anxious to take advantage of the opportunity to chat for a while this diminutive blond leaves the sidewalk and starts over, intent on reaching her friend and glancing neither right nor left as she walks rapidly toward the other side.

Bearing down on his unintended victim before he has time to realize it, the motorist slams on the brakes in an attempt to avoid the collision. A quick stop is not quick enough and packages fly as the pedestrian topples.

Thrown over the fender and hurled to the street unconscious, the woman is immediately surrounded by a throng—a typical scene on Annapolis streets, where pedestrians are killed and injured through careless walking.—Washington Star Staff Photos, with co-operation of the American Automobile Association.

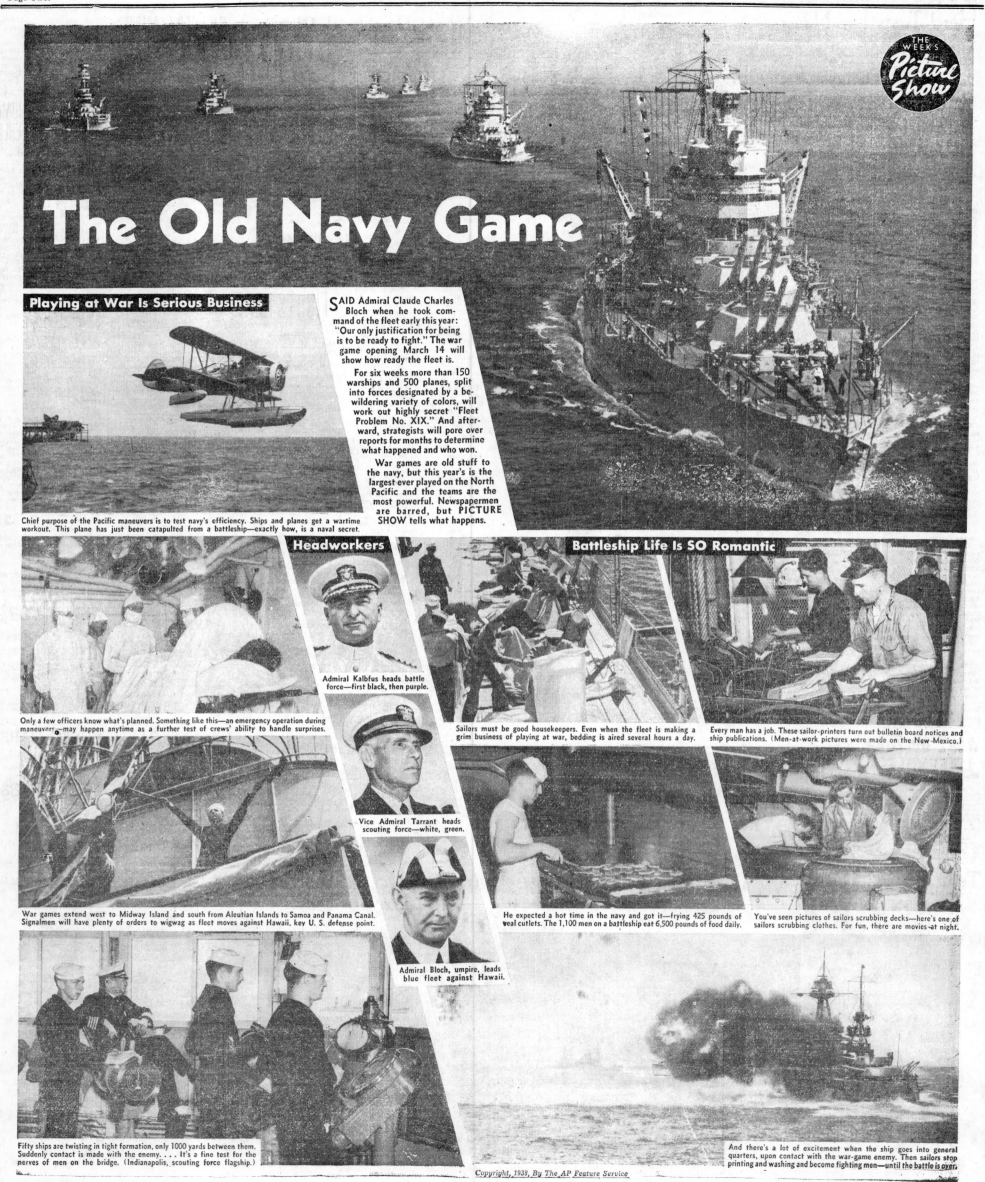

The Old Navy Game

THE WEEK'S *Picture Show*

Playing at War Is Serious Business

SAID Admiral Claude Charles Bloch when he took command of the fleet early this year: "Our only justification for being is to be ready to fight." The war game opening March 14 will show how ready the fleet is.

For six weeks more than 150 warships and 500 planes, split into forces designated by a bewildering variety of colors, will work out highly secret "Fleet Problem No. XIX." And afterward, strategists will pore over reports for months to determine what happened and who won.

War games are old stuff to the navy, but this year's is the largest ever played on the North Pacific and the teams are the most powerful. Newspapermen are barred, but PICTURE SHOW tells what happens.

Chief purpose of the Pacific maneuvers is to test navy's efficiency. Ships and planes get a wartime workout. This plane has just been catapulted from a battleship—exactly how, is a naval secret.

Headworkers

Admiral Kalbfus heads battle force—first black, then purple.

Vice Admiral Tarrant heads scouting force—white, green.

Admiral Bloch, umpire, leads blue fleet against Hawaii.

Only a few officers know what's planned. Something like this—an emergency operation during maneuvers—may happen anytime as a further test of crews' ability to handle surprises.

War games extend west to Midway Island and south from Aleutian Islands to Samoa and Panama Canal. Signalmen will have plenty of orders to wigwag as fleet moves against Hawaii, key U. S. defense point.

Battleship Life Is SO Romantic

Sailors must be good housekeepers. Even when the fleet is making a grim business of playing at war, bedding is aired several hours a day.

Every man has a job. These sailor-printers turn out bulletin board notices and ship publications. (Men-at-work pictures were made on the New Mexico.)

He expected a hot time in the navy and got it—frying 425 pounds of veal cutlets. The 1,100 men on a battleship eat 6,500 pounds of food daily.

You've seen pictures of sailors scrubbing decks—here's one of sailors scrubbing clothes. For fun, there are movies at night.

Fifty ships are twisting in tight formation, only 1000 yards between them. Suddenly contact is made with the enemy. . . . It's a fine test for the nerves of men on the bridge. (Indianapolis, scouting force flagship.)

And there's a lot of excitement when the ship goes into general quarters, upon contact with the war-game enemy. Then sailors stop printing and washing and become fighting men—until the battle is over.

Home of the
U. S. NAVAL ACADEMY
and
ST. JOHN'S COLLEGE

ANNAPOLIS
Evening Capital

VOL. CVI — No. 125. ESTABLISHED IN 1884—PUBLISHED EVERY EVENING EXCEPT SUNDAY ANNAPOLIS, SATURDAY, APRIL 9, 1938. SOUTHERN MARYLAND'S ONLY DAILY PAPER PRICE TWO CENTS.

Weather Forecast
Partly cloudy and slightly colder tonight, with snow flurries and freezing temperature in west portion.

SPRING BRINGS ANNUAL "FITTING OUT" TASK FOR ANNAPOLIS' PLEASURE BOATMEN

Covers are coming off the family cruisers as Annapolis' pleasure boat owners prepare for the 1938 season. Above is a typical early Spring scene. Seams must be recaulked (left) and bottoms painted (right) among other fitting out chores as the fleet once again is made ship shape.

Spring has returned to Annapolis and from boatyards there come traditional sounds heralding the approach of another Summer of record recreational boating activity.

All along the water here men and women are turning to their annual labor of love—the task of fitting out the pleasure fleet for the boating season. Canvas covers are coming off the family cruisers, blow torch and paint brush are being applied to boat bottoms, and interiors are being renovated as balmy weather, happily ahead of schedule this year, has stirred the boat enthusiasts from their Winter firesides.

Fitting out operations by pleasure boat owners will cost them a large sum. Much money will be spent with shipyards, and a considerable sum will go for labor, but the greater outlay will be for new marine motors, paints, varnish, rope, sail cloth, fittings, hardware and other nautical accessories. The average boat owner does the bulk of his own fitting out work, with the entire family and immediate circle of friends turning to with a helping hand. One of the supreme joys of boat ownership is the ability to properly care for one's craft.

Engines must be overhauled and tuned up in motor craft; topsides, decks and bottoms scraped, caulked and painted; brightwork and spars varnished, cabins cleaned and enameled, fittings buffed and polished, upholstery vacuumed, gear inspected and numerous other details attended to before the fleet is ready to go down the ways for the 1938 season.

Big Season Expected

The growing interest in recreational boating in Annapolis as well as in all parts of the country, indicates that this year will be one of the biggest in the history of the sport here. The activity of the 1937 season was easily the most brilliant in the past decade, with larger and gayer spectator fleets lining regatta courses, entire families turning to the water for full vacations afloat, and a sharp increase in the number of youngsters launching their nautical careers in outboards, sail boats and small play craft.

REFORM BILL DEFEAT BLOW TO ROOSEVELT

House Votes To Return Measure To Committee In Surprise Move Last Night Greatest Blow To Administration Since Court Bill Was Killed By Senate.

LEADERS' PLEAS ARE IGNORED

(By The Associated Press)

WASHINGTON, April 9 — The House sent to a stunning defeat last night the administration's Government Reorganization bill—the measure that prompted President Roosevelt to say he did not want to be a dictator.

Ignoring fervent pleas of party leaders not to proclaim to the nation a "lack of confidence" in the Chief Executive, 108 Democrats revolted and joined Republicans to bury the measure in a committee pigeonhole, 204 to 196.

Defeat Was Surprise

The death blow to the measure, which some foes asserted would make a dictator of the President, came as a surprise and a shock to Democratic chieftains.

Before the vote, Speaker Bankhead (Dem., Ala.), told members of his party, that rejection of the measure would be interpreted "in blazing headlines" as House "repudiation of the President of the United States."

The 204-to-196 vote returned the bill to the House Committee on reorganization.

Rebuff To President

The rebuff to the President was comparable only to that of the Senate's rejection of his Court Reorganization Bill last year.

On both issues, the administration made determined fights, only to suffer defeat. Whereas its attitude was "no compromise" in the Court struggle, this time it made concessions. The motion to recommit was offered by a Republican, Rep. Taber of New York.

SPECIAL MUSIC AT ON PALM SUNDAY

There will be special music at the Presbyterian Church on Palm Sunday. "Fling Wide The Gates" from "The Crucifixion" will be sung and a male quartet will render "God So Loved The World" from the same opus. A trio will give the Oratorio "The Creation" and the entire choir will present "Open The Gates Of The Temple."

J. W. ROBINSON, ASST. POSTMASTER, DIED YESTERDAY

Employee Of Postoffice For 40 Years Succumbs To Heart Attack At His Home

Annapolis' assistant postmaster, James W. Robinson, aged 60, died at 5 P. M., yesterday at his home in Murray avenue after an illness of several months.

Death was due to heart trouble.

Mr. Robinson served as assistant postmaster here for the past 20 years. He has been connected with the local post office for 40 years. He was a native of Annapolis.

Survivors include his widow, Mrs. Blanche D. Robinson and a sister, Mrs. Clara Croxton, of Baltimore.

Funeral services will be held on Monday afternoon at 2.30 o'clock, from the late residence with interment in St. Anne's Cemetery.

Postmaster William A. Strohm termed Mr. Robinson's death "the loss of a loyal public servant and outstanding citizen for both the post office department and the city." In addition Postmaster Strohm ordered the post office flag flown at half mast until after the funeral.

STATE TO IMPROVE ROAD AT ODENTON

(By The Associated Press)

BALTIMORE, April 9 — The State Roads Commission will receive bids until April 19 on the following projects:

Construction of approaches to the Odenton, Anne Arundel county grade elimination, including 1.38 miles of concrete surfacing.

Construction of 1.19 miles of concrete-surfaced highway along the Middletown-Jefferson road approaching the Frederick-Knoxville road, Frederick county.

Construction of a State Roads Commission garage at Westminster.

Mayor Jackson To Speak At Galesville

Mayor Howard Jackson, of Baltimore, has accepted an invitation from the Galesville Volunteer Fire Company to speak at an oyster roast sponsored by the firemen, tomorrow afternoon. The roast will be held at Zang's Pier, and plans are being made for the entertainment of an unusually large crowd.

Other political speakers are slated for addresses during the afternoon, so that those attending will have an opportunity to meet political aspirants.

FLIVVER AIRPLANES

(By The Associated Press)

NEW YORK, April 9—Dr. Alexander Klemin, head of New York University's School of Aeronautics, today forecast mass production of "Flivver" airplanes within five years which would incorporate revolutionary safety devices for the private owner.

LENTEN SERMONS AT ASBURY CHURCH

Special services will be held in Asbury Church during this week. Dr. James Magruder, Episcopal Church, preaches tonight. The Rev. Gordon Clews, Odenton, Md., preaches Monday night; Dr. James Coale, Presbyterian, Annapolis, Tuesday; Chaplain W. N. Thomas, U. S. N., Wednesday; the Rev. Harris Waters, Harmans, Md., Thursday; Chaplain J. E. Johnson, Friday.

The Lord's Supper will be administered on Thursday. All the services begin at eight o'clock.

The church has a new carpet given by a group of interested people who are not members of Asbury Church. They gave their money and asked their friends to give theirs. The carpet committee is as follows: Lt. Arthur Bryan, Mr. and Mrs. Walter Moon, Dr. Stoner, Mr. David Jenkins and Mr. Charles Lee. We also thank the women of the Church for laying the carpet.

For the new rest rooms Robert Stinchcomb gave more than five weeks' time and labor to their construction. Dr. John C. Joyce, Mr. Cyrus Joyce, Lt. Bryan and Mr. George Schaeffer also aided.

The members of the young people's class worked long and late at night to finish the interior decorating. Rodgers Joyce is teacher of the class. Albert Frantum and Franklin Spriggs donated the floor paint.

Mrs. Walter Monroe has given time and supervision to the landscaping. Dr. Joyce and Lt. Bryan contributed plants and labor.

Earl Harder measured and secured felt for the rung.

LAW ON DIVORCE UPHELD BY COURT

Appeals Judges Rule Voluntary Separation For Five Years Grounds For Action

A Baltimore court ruling holding the 1937 State law establishing voluntary separation for five consecutive years as a ground for divorce to be constitutional was upheld yesterday by the Court of Appeals.

The case, the first to reach the court under the law, was filed by George A. Campbell, seeking absolute divorce from Mrs. Elizabeth Campbell, in Baltimore Circuit Court No. 2 on June 1 last, the day the law became effective. Judge Hammond Urner, for the Appellate Court, affirmed the decree of the lower court granting Campbell the divorce.

Rejects Contention

The opinion rejected a contention that the title of the law was defective and held it "an exercise of the ample power of the legislature to determine the grounds upon which marriages may be judicially dissolved."

"If when the bill of complaint is filed, the parties 'shall have voluntarily lived separate and apart' for the designated period, and the separation has been complete and is probably permanent, the court is authorized by the act to decree an absolute divorce," the opinion continued. "There is no evidence in the act of an intention that the whole of the five year period of separation must be subsequent to its effective date."

Pay Counsel Fees

The case was remanded to the lower court with the direction that Campbell pay Mrs. Campbell's counsel fees and court costs. Judge T. Scott Offutt dissented from the ruling directing the payment of counsel fees.

The court adjourned until April 19, with eight pending opinions on cases argued during the January term. They include the right of Maryland to tax bank stock held by the Reconstruction Finance Corporation, and the validity of a Baltimore county law providing for public transportation of students to non-State aided schools.

FATAL MD. ACCIDENT

(By The Associated Press)

EASTON, Md., April 9—Robert Parks, 21, of Baltimore, was struck and killed by an automobile last night on the road between Elkwood and Beulah, near here.

Navy Jr. Boxing Pictures Will Be Shown At Circle

Scenes from the Navy Junior boxing bouts held at the Naval Academy last Saturday, will be shown Sunday, Monday, Tuesday and Wednesday at the Circle Theatre.

REV. DR. MAGRUDER AT ASBURY CHURCH

The Reverend James M. Magruder, D. D., will preach the Lenten sermon at Asbury Church, Arnold, Md., Palm Sunday evening at eight o'clock. The Reverend Dr. C. L. Fossett, rector, will conduct the services.

SACRED CANTATA AT ACADEMY CHAPEL

Tomorrow, Palm Sunday, Stainer's Sacred Cantata, "The Crucifixion" will be given at the Naval Academy Chapel, by the Chapel Choir.

The organist will be Professor J. W. Crosley and the soloists will be Midshipman J. F. Stevens, tenor; Midshipman E. Allen, baritone; Midshipman M. A. Berns, Jr., bass; Midshipman R. K. John, Jr., baritone; Midshipman W. S. Farrel, bass.

THE PSALMS TO BE SUNG AT ST. LUKES

"The Palms," by Faure, will be sung tomorrow evening at Saint Luke's Chapel, Eastport. Some of the representative members of St. Anne's choir will render the selection under the direction of Charles H. Sherman, choirmaster. The service begins at 7:30 P. M.

$897,211.31 Paid On State Incomes

The tabulation of 63,369 returns today brought to total of the Maryland ½ of 1 per cent income tax to $897,211.31.

The returns were submitted by 2,769 corporations, 59,721 individuals and 879 non-resident, fiduciaries and paid-at-source employers on salaries to out-of-State employes.

BASSFORD PRAISED AT CLUB MEETING

Candidates Make Short Talks At Session Held Last Night

Despite the bad weather, quite a large meeting of the Annapolis Democratic Club was held last night at Hotel Maryland, this being its regular meeting night. Representatives of the Fifth, Second and Eighth Districts were present. The meeting was presided over by the club's president, George Frank. Routine business was transacted and quite a number of new members were admitted.

Several candidates who are running for office were present, including Albert J. Goodman, candidate for State's Attorney and John H. Hopkins, candidate for Clerk of the Circuit Court. Each were introduced to the club, all of whom responded and gave short remarks regarding their candidacies for their respective offices. Mayor Louis N. Phipps, who is a candidate for State Senator, also spoke.

Ward Introduced

Others present and introduced were Robert Ward, of Glen Burnie, who has been endorsed by his friends to run for County Commissioner from the Fifth District; the president and secretary of the Lusby Democratic Club, and George Nutwell of the Deale Democratic Club.

Alderman Clarence M. Bassford was given a rousing greeting of confidence on having announced his candidacy for the office of County Commissioner from the Sixth District.

The club's board of directors announced they would unani-

(Continued on Page 4)

PURSE IS STOLEN WOMAN REPORTS

Mrs. Margaret Bentley, 321½ Burnside avenue, Eastport, reported to police that a colored man had snatched her pocketbook last night, while she was walking on Compromise street.

She said the pocketbook contained, besides a number of personal articles, about $20 in cash.

She was returning from Annapolis about 10:30 when the man suddenly grabbed the pocketbook and fled into the school yard. Police searched the neighborhood but were unable to find any trace of the culprit.

PROCESSING TAXES DELAY SENATE VOTE ON GENERAL LEVY

Defeat Of Reorganization Bill Brings Hopes For Measure Wanted By Business

(By The Associated Press)

WASHINGTON, April 9 — Debate of a proposal to levy processing taxes delayed today a Senate vote on the general tax bill.

Senator Pope (D-Idaho) offered an amendment to impose processing taxes on corn, cotton, wheat, rice, tobacco and synthetic fibers.

Pope asked that these levies be attached to the Senate Finance Committee's bill. He said they would add $121,000,000 a year to the $500,000,000 now available for farm benefits.

Reduce Exemptions

Another proposal to be disposed of before the final vote was that of Senator La Follette (Prog-Wis) to reduce income exemptions. He suggested they be cut from $1,000 to $800 for single persons and from $2,500 to $2,000 for heads of families.

Senate opponents of Administration tax proposals said the House vote shelving the Government Reorganization Bill increased the chances for final enactment of a measure more along the lines recommended by business leaders.

Kill Profits Tax

The Senate Committee threw out of the House approved tax bil the Administration-sponsored undistributed profits and capital gains taxes and substituted levies suggested by business spokesmen.

Proponents of the committee bill argued privately that the House reorganization vote exhibited a spirit of independence which argued well for House acceptance of it.

MARCH WAS MILD

March was the mildest in Maryland since 1935. The monthly precipitation, mostly in the form of rain, was about three-fourths of normal. Little snow fell.

In Maryland, 47 stations reporting, the mean temperature was 47.5 degrees, or 5.3 degrees above normal.

CHINESE SAY JAPS FACING ANNIHILATION

Defeat At Taierchwang Imperials Disorganized Forces — Defenders Converge On Foes From All Directions —Reports Denied By Nipponese.

"DELAY" IS ADMITTED

(By The Associated Press)

SHANGHAI, April 9—The Chinese army high command declared jubilantly today that defeat of Japanese forces at Taierchwang created a situation favorable for annihilation or capture of the disorganized Japanese units in that area of Central China.

Chinese troops were reported converging from all directions to cut off Japanese retreating from the war-devastated city of Taierchwang, in southern Shantung province.

Denied By Japs

These reports were flatly denied by Japanese army officers who asserted Chinese attacks on Taierchwang, as well as Yihsien, Tsaochuwang and Lincheng, had been repulsed.

Yihsien was reported in flames.

Japanese said they were holding these cities and that they had not retreated from the battle zones along the Grand Canal and the Tientsin-Pukow railway, which runs south to meet the Lunghai at strategic Suchow.

Offensive Delayed

Under questioning by correspondents, Japanese admitted their offensive in this area, designed to cut the Lunghai line and gain control of Central China, had been "delayed" due to the necessity of making extensive preparations for launching a large-scale drive.

Neutral observers, nevertheless, believed the Japanese had suffered a distinct setback.

BALL GAME OFF

The Naval Academy postponed today's baseball game between Navy and Princeton because of wet grounds.

CRAB SEASON OPENS WITH BANNER YEAR FOR BAY PREDICTED

(By The Associated Press)

Maryland crabbers moved in force today in Chesapeake Bay and Potomac river waters with Conservation Commission officials predicting the 1938 season catch would exceed the 183,507 barrels produced last year.

Commission Inspector William E. Robbins, said crabs this year were "looking fine".

"They're in good shape and large," Robbins reported. "I've heard the same report all over the Bay. On the Potomac, they tell me, they're catching as many as two-thirds of a barrel a night in a pound net."

Severe winter weather of 1933-34 was held responsible for holding crab production down in 1937, although the output of hard, soft and peeler crabs was regarded as satisfactory. Conservation officials warned watermen to respect laws prohibiting the taking of undersized crabs.

ROUND-UP COMMITTEE BEGINS VISITS TODAY

The Annapolis Grammar School P.-T. A. committee on the Summer Round-Up of the children, is beginning its rounds of visiting homes today. All parents who have children of less than school age may expect, within the next few days, one of these messengers who will explain the purpose of her visit. The heartiest cooperation with the roundup workers is sought.

JAPS LICKED IN BIG AIRPLANE BATTLE

(By The Associated Press)

SHANGHAI, May 2 — Reports from Peiping today said foreign sources there had confirmed the fact that the Japanese lost twenty-one planes in their raid on Hankow last Friday.

RAIN HALTS SPANISH WAR.

(By The Associated Press).

HENDAYE, France (at the Spanish Frontier), May 2—Spanish Civil War armies marked time today, awaiting a let-up in the rains which for more than a week have interfered with operations on all fronts.

ADVISORY BOARD TO HOLD MEETING

The final meeting of the Advisory Board of the Woman's Field Army for Control of Cancer, of Anne Arundel county, will meet Thursday afternoon at 2:30 P. M. in the Board Room of the old school building on Green street. Mrs. H. P. Levely will preside and the chairman of committees will make their reports.

VAN'S

POULTRY OF ALL KINDS

Killed On Order

Only Strictly Fresh Laid Eggs

From Hennery To You

Baking Chickens	lb. 32c
Frying Chickens	lb. 32c
Stewing Chickens	lb. 30c
Ducks	lb. 35c

BROILERS 35c—3 for $1.00

PHONE 307

Deliveries—Any Time—Any Day

PROVE FREE

Rheumatism Pains

Stop in 7 to 10 Minutes

It is now easy to end rheumatism pains. Seven to 10 minutes will prove it to you. The test will cost you nothing.

So why suffer another day from the agony of this painful ailment when you can secure MUSCLE-RUB, the new preparation that not only conquers the pains of rheumatism but also lumbago, sciatica, neuralgia, as well as the less serious lameness of muscles and joints? It is no longer necessary to dose the system with internal medicine. The entire MUSCLE-RUB treatment is a simple liquid, applied directly to the limbs, shoulders, neck, face, or back—wherever the trouble may be. There is no burning—no irritation. All pain stops as if by magic. Even chronic and severe conditions respond so amazingly that seldom is more than a bottle needed.

We urge only that you make this test. MUSCLE-RUB is now obtainable in the $1.00 large family size. Buy it today. Use one-half the bottle and if you are not amazed and delighted with the results, return the remaining half to your druggist and he will refund your money.

Get a Bottle of Muscle-Rub Today Special This Week at

Read's—Hopkins—Green's and West End Drug Stores

U. S. WARSHIPS BACK FROM NAVAL GAMES

Back from the far stretches of the Pacific where they took part in the United States navy's extended war games, some 30 destroyers are shown as they anchored in San Diego bay. Larger craft put in at San Pedro, Calif., to bring the maneuvers officially to an end.

BAPTIST CHURCH FETES BIRTHDAY

(Continued from Page 1)

the church building now stands at the corner of College avenue and St. John's street, was purchased in 1900. The Rev. Allard and Rehn were appointed to hold this property in trust until the organization could be effected.

Meetings In Y. M. C. A. Hall

Prayer services were held from house to house until the autumn of 1901, when the Y. M. C. A. Hall was secured for these meetings. In spite of slow progress and discouragements, this small beginning ripened into a permanent Baptist interest in the city, due largely to the untiring efforts of the Rev. Allard. He did not, however, remain in this vicinity until the organization was perfected. Dr. E. B. Hatcher, State Superintendent of Baptist Missions, directed affairs during the remaining time until the organization was complete.

On August 19, 1903, Articles of Incorporation were adopted, and the church became a corporate body under the provisions of the laws of the State of Maryland.

Visiting Ministers Served

The church was without a pastor until November, 1903, but the pulpit was supplied each Sunday by visiting ministers. The Rev. Thomas P. Holloway, of Baltimore, who at first declined the call, finally accepted, beginning his pastorate on November 29, 1903.

Dr. Holloway began immediately to take active steps looking toward the building of a meeting house. Sunday services were held in the City Hall Assembly Rooms, until the close of the year 1904. After that date they were held in the Red Men's Hall until the completion of the church building in April, 1906. The Thursday prayer meetings were held in the Presbyterian Church, of which the Rev. George Bell was pastor.

Building Dedicated

The church building, which is a monument to the successful efforts of Dr. Holloway, was dedicated on April 8, 1906. The cost of the building, together with the work which was donated, approximated $32,500. George E. Merrill, whose coming to Annapolis was occasioned by the building of the new Naval Academy after the Spanish-American War, served as chairman of the building committee. His keen foresight and knowledge of architectural design and construction contributed largely to the harmonious effect of the church edifice as a whole. His generosity and the unselfish giving of his time and means contributed a large part to the strength of the church during the pastorate of Dr. Holloway.

Growth Of Membership

Dr. Holloway resigned January 12, 1908. During the four years and two months of his services the church enjoyed a slow but steady increase in membership and interest. A total of 55 members were received during his pastorate, with 14 losses by death, letter, leaving a net gain of 41 and a total membership of 80.

The College Avenue Baptist Church will observe its thirty-fifth anniversary with special services on next Sunday and Monday, May 8 and 9. Memorial flowers given by the deacons of the church will bespeak for the membership their sincere appreciation of the consecrated efforts of its first leader, who passed to his reward while in active service in another field on March 24, 1922.

MOOSE LODGE INSTALLS NEW OFFICERS FRIDAY

Last Friday night the Moose Lodge No. 296, held their installation of officers for the year. District Deputy of the Supreme Dictator, Brother Bitters, of Highlandtown, was the Grand Installing officer.

Those installed were:

Past dictator, Edward Dougherty; dictator, J. A. Kramer; vice-dictator, Sidney Robinson; chaplain, Bruce Sothers; treasurer, James Lee; sergeant at arms, Alfred Sinclair; inner guard, J. Kendall; trustee, Irving Brown. Attorney General Herbert R. O'Conor gave a fine talk on Moose Haven and Moose Heart. Other speakers were: Brother Louis Phipps, Mayor of Annapolis, and Brother Albert Jerome Goodman. After the meeting a dance was held for the members, chapter members and friends. Congratulations were extended to the new dictator and success wished them for the ensuing year.

2 FATAL FALLS

(By The Associated Press)

BALTIMORE, May 2—Coroner Charles W. Wood began today an investigation of two fatal falls here. Leroy Timmons died of injuries suffered when he fell from the second to the first floor of his boarding house. Mrs. Rosalie Lazarewicz, 70, fell down a flight of stairs in her home and was found dead.

INJURIES PROVE FATAL

(By The Associated Press)

WASHINGTON, May 2—Mrs. Elizabeth Rice, 65, died today of injuries she suffered near Bacon Hill, Md., March 22. Her husband was killed in the automobile accident.

ROOSEVELT OFF FOR A VACATION

With the sailors of the cruiser U. S. S. Philadelphia standing at attention in the backround, President Roosevelt is shown as he boarded the ship at Charleston, S. C., bound for a sea-going vacation. With the Chief Executive are Col. E. M. Watson (center), and Capt. W. B. Woodson, his aides.

WE NOW GIVE AND REDEEM

"S.H." Green Stamps "S.H."

ON ALL PURCHASES

Oriole Cut-Rate Co.

PERFUME—PATENTS—COSMETICS

196 MAIN STREET ANNAPOLIS, MD.

Party To Mark Maiden Voyage Of Local Ferry

The new ferry boat, the Gov. Harry W. Nice, will make its maiden voyage tomorrow, leaving here at 10:30 A. M. with a group of guest, including Gov. and Mrs. Nice.

The ferry will go from here to Claiborne, thence to Kent Island, for the dedication of the Claiborne-Annapolis Ferry Company's new Romancoke terminal.

Former Governor Emerson C. Harrington, president of the ferry company, named the new steel ferry after Governor Nice. The vessel, designed and built by Koppers company's subsidiary, The Maryland Drydock Company, Baltimore, is 207 feet long and is capable of carrying 730 persons and 65 autos. Largest in the ferry company's fleet, this Fairbanks, Morse diesel-powered, double-ended ferry will provide transportation across the Chesapeake Bay between Annapolis and Claiborne.

U. S. IN WAR ON NARCOTICS IN WEST

(By The Associated Press)

SAN FRANCISCO, May 2—A world-wide drive against smugglers of narcotics has resulted in the seizure of contraband valued up to $1,000,00 on the Pacific Slope alone, it was learned on indisputable authority here today, and has more than trebled the price.

Eight major shore-side raids alone, including the frustration of a daring attempt to smuggle 81 tins of opium, worth $40,000, from the Navy transport Chaumont a month ago, have netted narcotics for which addicts would have paid more than $500,000.

The major hauls have captured 317 tins (132 pounds) of smoking opium, 32 pounds of morphine, and 54 pounds of heroin.

Opium is so rare it has jumped from $80 to $260 "wholesale" for a five-tael (6 2/3 ounce) tin; morphine has skyrocketed from $50 to $160 an ounce and heroin is scarcely available.

Narcotics are smuggled in double-lined oil cans, in innocent looking containers labelled everything from "ties" to "toys." The Chaumont's mail clerk was caught with 40 tins in a mail pouch as he went into a cafe to deliver his cargo. Another 41 tins were found on the vessel in a pouch not comingled with mail that was subject to customs inspection.

7 AMERICANS RESCUED

(By The Associated Press)

HONGKONG, May 2—Seven American passengers from the British steamer Thurland Castle were among the survivors brought to Hongkong today after the 6,372-ton vessel ran aground last night.

ANNE ARUNDEL STOPS DIRECT RELIEF, WORD

(By The Associated Press)

BALTIMORE, May 2.—State, county and city Welfare officials, meeting here to discuss Maryland's entire relief program, heard a report today that a lack of funds has already forced cessation of direct relief aid in at least five counties.

The report, based on a questionnaire distributed to county and city Welfare Boards, said that, in addition to these five, Frederick County "finds itself in a very serious situation with no funds available after this quarter."

Counties in which direct relief has already been stopped include Anne Arundel, Caroline, Carroll, Dorchester, and Queen Anne's. Five counties, Allegany, Cecil, Charles, Somerset, Washington, failed to reply officially to the questionnaire.

We Rent!

Cots, Beds, Bureaus, Furniture

FOR JUNE WEEK

Place Your Requirements Now

Annapolis Furniture Company

94-96 WEST ST. PHONE 214-W

NINETEEN ARE KILLED IN ITALIAN PLANE CRASH

(By The Associated Press)

ROME, May 2—The worst disaster in the history of Italian civil aviation, costing the lives of 14 airplane passengers and five aviators, was investigated today by the Italian Government.

General Aldo Pellegrini, chief of Italy's commercial aviation, went to Formia to conduct the inquiry.

The giant airliner of the Ala Littoria Company, en route from Tirana, Albania, to Rome, ran into defense clouds Saturday afternoon and hit a mountainside near Formia, 70 miles southeast of Rome on the Ryddhenian coast.

The United States Consulate at Rome said one of the victims was an American woman, Helen Lindheim, born in 1909. It said she carried a passport issued in Jerusalem and was on her way to Rome from Palestine, having boarded the plane at Brindisi.

GROUP FORMED TO SELL JACKSON TO VOTERS OF MD.

(Continued from Page 1)

fessional politicians, Mr. Bandiere said.

"In other words we want to contact the man who doesn't attend political meetings; who doesn't go to oyster roasts, and who doesn't go to a shore and drink beer," he said.

To accomplish this the group expects to utilize all the best features used in "selling" merchandise. "For," said Mr. Bandiere, "we want to 'sell' Howard Jackson to those who foot the bills of government by paying taxes."

Speeches Planned

There will be speeches made at public meetings, speeches to be broadcast, solicitation by direct mail, and person-to-person contacts.

Other officers named thus far include C. K. Oakley, William J. Fitzsimmons and Howard M. Kaplan, vice-chairman; Richard W. Bozell, treasurer, and Edwin A. Dempsey, secretary.

Permanent headquarters will be maintained at the Southern, with Mr. Bandiere or one of his aids in daily attendance.

RED CROSS PRAISED

(By The Associated Press)

SAN FRANCISCO, May 2—The American Red Cross, opening its annual convention here, was pictured today by speakers as a force for peace in a world where modern war's destruction was increased and endangered the Red Cross workers' task.

LIBRARY MEETING

The Annapolis and Anne Arundel county public library board will meet tonight at 7:30 P. M.

ANNEXATION

The Anne Arundel County Sanitary Commission will tonight present figures on the financial setup of the communities around Annapolis considering annexation, at a meeting at Eastport. The meeting to be held at the fire hall, is considered important.

TESTS LEGISLATIVE ACT

(By The Associated Press)

BALTIMORE, May 2.—A Maryland penitentiary guard instituted proceedings in the Superior Court today to test the validity of the 1938 Act reducing salaries of state employes.

William F. Listman asked the court to order the Board of Welfare to pay him $715, the amount he lost by the pay cut. The outcome of his suit will affect more than $50,000 in salary cuts made in the salaries of other guards.

STAR THEATRE

TONIGHT

Added—Mickey Mouse

HENLEIN DEMANDS CZECH PLEBISCITE

(Continued from Page 1)

was welcomed with cries of "We greet our Fuehrer" and Nazi salutes. He was, however, less fiery than some of his lieutenants, such as George Wollner, who declared that "national socialism knows no boundaries" and demanded that Germans be substituted for Czechs on the police force.

Another Nazi speaker, Franz Oberlik, said at Gablonz that the Nazis hoped "by next fall we shall have achieved our freedom." Both Oberlik and Wollner are deputies.

M. A. HANCOCK

Dealer in

FLAGSTONE, BUILDING and ROUGH STONE

Elkridge, Md.

Phone Elkridge 207-J-2

TODAY AND TUESDAY **REPUBLIC**

Broadway's Darling

The toast of the bright lights... hungry for Romance!

Irene DUNNE

Douglas FAIRBANKS, Jr

in

JOY OF LIVING

RKO RADIO

FEATURE PRESENTATIONS 1:30, 3:31, 5:32, 7:33, 9:34 P. M.

STARTS SUNDAY—ENTIRE WEEK

WALT DISNEY'S first feature

Snow White

AND THE SEVEN DWARFS

ONLY THREE MORE DAYS TODAY, TUES., WED. **CIRCLE**

I CAN'T Quit ... I'M A TEST PILOT

CLARK GABLE

MYRNA LOY

SPENCER TRACY

in

TEST PILOT

with Lionel Barrymore

M-G-M PICTURE

FEATURES:
1:30, 3:24, 5:18,
7:12, 9:18 P. M.

Starts Thursday
BURNS & ALLEN
In
"COLLEGE SWING"

ANNAPOLIS
Evening Capital

Home of the U. S. NAVAL ACADEMY and ST. JOHN'S COLLEGE

Weather Forecast
Cloudy, with showers tonight and probably in east portion Friday morning.

VOL. CVII — No. 19. | ESTABLISHED IN 1884—PUBLISHED EVERY EVENING EXCEPT SUNDAY | ANNAPOLIS, THURSDAY, JUNE 2, 1938. | SOUTHERN MARYLAND'S ONLY DAILY PAPER | PRICE TWO CENTS.

PRESIDENT ROOSEVELT PRESENTS NAVY DIPLOMAS

F. B. I. Chief Heads Search For Missing Cash Youngster

Hoover Sends Out Small Boats And Divers As Huge Posse Combs Area Near Home.

(By The Associated Press)

PRINCETON, Fla., June 2—J. Edgar Hoover, Chief of the Federal Bureau of Investigation, took charge of the James Bailey Cash, Jr., kidnaping case today while small boats and divers augmented a huge posse combing this area in the rain for a trace of the 5-year-old victim.

Arriving at Miami from Washington, Hoover hastened immediately to the FBI office in downtown skyscraper where agents have been questioning several suspects for 24 hours. He refused, like his subordinates, to discuss the case and indicated he expected to be here several days.

Men Are Armed

Hundreds of men, many with pistols at their belts, assembled at dawn and were taken out in farm trucks to the sectors assigned for the second day of the search.

The Senior Cash and his wife remained secluded in their frame apartment building, although the father came to the door to receive three telegrams.

It was learned that the anguished mother, who had been prostrated with grief, finally was sleeping.

The Federal men centered efforts on tracking down the abductors, who accepted a $10,000 ransom payment without returning the victim.

In their custody were several persons—no outsider knew exactly how many—and a number of finds regarded as clues.

Legionnaires Busy

Sam Bennett of Fort Pierce, District American Legion Commander, announced 1,000 Legionnaires would join the spreading hunt early today, augmenting the hundreds of armed men who yesterday beat over palmetto groves and truck lands.

An indication of what the F. B. I. men think the searchers might find was contained in final instructions of E. J. Connelly, head of the Justice Department forces, to the posses.

"We must face the strong pos-

(Continued on Page 4)

Question About Missing Child, 5

M. F. BRAXTON

Third District Group To Hear Mayor Jackson

Mayor Howard W. Jackson, of Baltimore, Democratic candidate for Governor of Maryland, will address the meeting of the Democratic Campaign Organization of the Second Precinct of the Third District on Monday, June 6. The meeting will be held at the old Arnold Beneficial Association Hall at 8 P. M.

Frank S. Revell Democratic chief of Anne Arundel county, and officials of the county government will be introduced at the meeting.

Mayor Jackson will be the only candidate for office to speak at the Arnold meeting. Members of the host organization will be entitled to bring ladies and friends.

Editorial

THE STATE OFFICE BUILDING BONDS

With all due respect to our mighty contemporary, the Baltimore "Sun", its editorial in this morning's issue entitled "Purely Fortuitous" about the sale of bonds for the State office building in Annapolis, makes it appropriate for us to comment on another phase of this situation which the "Sun" has evidently overlooked.

They have only to look at the record to see that one of the main points of attack on this measure, at the time when its author, Senator Ridgely P. Melvin, was in the midst of his uphill battle for it in the legislature, was that the bill was defective in failing to adequately finance the project. It was pointed out by its enemies in printed statements that the bonds could not be sold, according to the provisions of the bill, at a low enough interest rate to meet the sinking fund requirements, and that there were fatal miscalculations in other respects. Senator Melvin, however, stood his ground, and the measure was enacted exactly as he had first presented it, and it was finally upheld by the Court of Appeals.

Even after this had been accomplished, the chief spokesman for the opposition, Attorney Willis R. Jones, of Baltimore, kept harping on this alleged defect in the law and used it in his attacks in the court. It was insisted that the bonds would go abegging because the law showed on its face that the interest calculations were out of line and assumed a rate of interest entirely too low.

The rate at which the bonds were actually sold, the record-breaking low of 1.60 per cent, completely knocks the props from under the last leg upon which the law's opponents have tried to stand.

The "Sun" refers again to the law as "'Senator Ridgely P. Melvin's dream". Well, it is certainly most gratifying to all Annapolitans and true Marylanders that we have as a dreamer one who, at the same time, is practical and effective enough to see that when the dream does come true, the details of its substantial form have been taken care of. It took fight, as well as vision, to carry this measure through and to withstand the bitter attacks along the line. But now that the victory has been won, we suggest that it would be more gracious for our great metropolitan luminary "The Sun", to extend wholehearted congratulations on this latest proof of their mistaken attitude, and not ascribe the State's good fortune in the extraordinarily low interest to luck or call it "purely fortuitous."

Middies Embark At 1 P. M. Tomorrow

The undergraduate midshipmen of the Naval Academy of the classes of 1939 and 1941 will board the battleships tomorrow at 1 P. M. to begin the annual practice cruise to European waters.

PLANES HELP JAPANESE IN NEW ADVANCE

Important Gains Reported Made Along Lunghai Railway — Nipponese Occupy Kihsien—Plan Mass Offensive Against Hankow.

DOIHARA RELIEF IS DELAYED

By Elmer W. Peterson
(By The Associated Press)

SHANGHAI, June 2 — Warplanes of the army of Nippon again spread a trail of destruction today through towns and villages about the Lunghai railway and Japanese said this enabled their columns to make important gains.

The Japanese announced they had occupied a corner of Kihsien 20 miles south of Lanfeng, after an hour's fight. Chinese field gun positions north of Kihsien were damaged heavily.

Fight for Village

For two weeks, the Japanese have been fighting for staunchly defended villages about Lanfeng, railway station on the Lunghai on the westward route of Chengchow, whence they hope to turn southward in a mass offensive against Hankow, China's provisional capital.

Supporting the land forces on this Central China front, Jap-

(Continued on Page 4)

FESTIVAL TO HELP P.-T. A. OF EASTPORT

There will be a strawberry festival on June 3, at the Eastport school, for the benefit of the Parent Teacher Association. It will begin at 6:30. Ice cream, strawberries and cake will be served. At 7:30 P. M. the children of the fourth and fifth grades will present an entertainment. This is open to the public.

Roosevelt Greeted In City Today

Military pomp and ceremony today marked the reception of President Roosevelt at the Naval Academy, when he motored over from Washington to present diplomas to the graduating class.

Prior to his arrival a company of marines and the Naval Academy band, drawn up in front of the residence of Rear-Admiral Wilson Brown, superintendent of the academy, was kept busy giving honors to distinguished guests.

Senior Officer Here

When the President arrived the marines presented arms, while the band gave four ruffles and flourishes, and then swung in "Hail to the Chief," the presidential march. At its conclusion a 21-gun salute roared out and the flag of the president went to the fore of the station ship, Reina Mercedes, signifying that he was the "senior officer present."

The President was accompanied by his secretary-son, James; Captain W. B. Woodson, naval aide; Col. Edwin Watson, military aide, and Capt. R. T. McIntire (MC, USN). After receiving his honors he drove to the side door of the armory and took his place on the rostrum.

Edison Greeted, Too

Charles Edison, Assistant Secretary of the Navy, was received with four ruffles and flourishes by the band, and the playing of the "Admiral's March" as he arrived and joined the group at the superintendent's home.

GIVES NEW OFFICERS THEIR INITIAL ADVICE

FRANKLIN D. ROOSEVELT

Text Of President Roosevelt's Speech

The text of President Roosevelt's address to the midshipmen of the Naval Academy at graduation today follows:

A quarter of a century ago I began coming to graduation exercises at the United States Naval Academy. I find it a good custom and I hope to be following it occasionally when I have reached the age of the oldest Admiral on the retired list. As a retired commander-in-chief of the navy I could do nothing else.

Disgraced Himself

The only time I disgraced myself was, I think, during the World War. Because of the strenuous work in the Navy Department, I was a bit in arrears on sleep. The temperature in Dahlgren Hall was in the neighborhood of a hundred. There I was sitting on the right of the superintendent of the Naval Academy. The speaker of the occasion began his address. My eyes slowly but firmly closed. I think my mouth fell open. I slept ungracefully but soundly directly in front of the eyes of the entire graduating class. Could anything be more unmilitary, more humiliating—but more satisfactory?

You who are about to become officers of the navy of the United States have had four years of advice—kindly advice but firm advice. I do not propose to add to it except to make one friendly suggestion which is not addressed to you as officers but is intended to apply to you just as much as to this year's graduates of any other college or school in the country.

World Problems

No matter whether your specialty is naval science, or medicine, or the law, or teaching, or the church, or the civil service or public service—remember that you will never reach the top and stay at the top unless you are well rounded in your knowledge of all the other factors in modern civilization that lie outside of your own special profession.

That applies to all of world thought and world problems, but it applies, of course, with special emphasis to the thought and problems of our own nation.

Let me illustrate by quoting what Theodore Roosevelt once said to me. A bill for the conservation of natural resources, which he had strongly recommended, had been defeated in the Congress by a coalition of votes by members who saw in the bill no special advantage to their own Congressional districts. When he learned of the defeat he said: "I wish we could have a constitutional amendment requiring that no person could run for Congress unless he had visited every one of the forty-eight States in the Union."

Must Know Govt.

You who graduate today will fill many important Government posts during many intervals of shore duty. In these posts you will need national knowledge—knowledge of the problems of industry, knowledge of the problems of farming, knowledge of the problems of labor and knowledge of the problems of capital. You will need to know intimately the geography and the natural and human resources of the United States. You will need to know the current operations of Federal, State and local government. You will be called on for decisions in your line of duty where such knowledge will be of at least daily desirability—daily help to you in coming to your own conclusions.

Preliminary knowledge of this kind you have, but the best of it—the most important part of it—will come to you through the passing years.

It will come to you in two ways. First, by the experiences of your daily life and those experiences can be profitable to you or not in proportion to your ability to relate each experience to the whole field of experiences. Second you will have the opportunity constantly to widen your knowledge by your own individual efforts. You can confine your field of thought to your professional work or you can widen it to include a current interest in current events.

Govt. Certification

You graduate with the certification by the Government of the United States that you are gentlemen — and the fact that you have been able to graduate from the Naval Academy at all proves that you are scholars. I want to prove that you have another qualification—that you are also thorough-going, up-to-date, intelligent American citizens.

Now before you get your Bachelor of Science Degree, I must advise you not to put too much emphasis on the word bachelor.

I congratulate you on your graduation. Your commander-in-chief is proud of you. Good luck. Happy voyage.

TICK CAUSES DEATH

(By The Associated Press)

BALTIMORE, Md., June 2—The State Health Department reported today one death had resulted from a seasonal outbreak of Rocky Mountain spotted fever in Maryland.

Knowledge Of Modern Civilization Essential F. D. R. Tells Graduates

Commander-in-Chief Of Service Informs Midshipmen They Will Never "Reach the Top And Stay At The Top," Unless They Go Outside "Your Own Special Profession"—Rousing Exercises Held Today As June Week Ends.

President Franklin D. Roosevelt advised the Naval Academy's graduating midshipmen today to acquire a well-rounded knowledge of "modern civilization" in addition to their training as officers of the navy.

"That applies," the President said, "to all of world thought and world problems but it applies, of course, with special emphasis to the thought and problems of our own nation."

NEED WELL ROUNDED KNOWLEDGE

The President stood before the white-bloused graduates as their commander-in-chief and told them they would never "reach the top and stay at the top" unless they become well-rounded in their knowledge of all factors of civilization "that lie outside of your own special profession."

President Roosevelt presented diplomas to 435 graduates amid a roar of applause and cheering from the under-classmen, parents and friends of midshipmen who packed the huge academy armory. The throng was estimated at 15,000 persons.

Twenty-six graduates became second lieutenants in the Marine Corps, while 385 assembled in Bancroft Hall after graduation and were sworn in as ensigns in the line of the navy. Twenty-one were honorably discharged for physical disability, while two will be given physicals in the Fall to determine their status for commissions. M. S. Castillo, Filipino, graduated, but was not commissioned.

THE SPEAKING ROSTRUM

The white uniformed graduates were seated facing a rostrum, containing the President, Charles Edison, Assistant Secretary of the Navy; Rear-Admiral Wilson Brown, superintendent of the Academy, and high ranking naval officers, heads of academic departments and officers from the battleships New York, Texas and Wyoming, now at the academy. All the officers wore white.

The undergraduate midshipmen, in blue uniforms, flanked the group of parents, friends and sweethearts of the graduates. Many a mother or girl held new ensign's caps and shoulder markers waiting for the ceremony to end, so they could confer them on their midshipman.

The armory was decorated in blue and gold, with pendant lanterns of the same color. Navy signal flags spotted the balcony, and the flags of the 48 States hung from the walls.

The President saw the graduates follow the traditional ceremony of tossing their white midshipmen caps away to be scrambled for by the girls present. He heard the midshipmen give him a thunderous greeting, their famous "4-N" yell, that has resounded over athletic fields for many years.

President Greeted

The audience rose as the President entered the armory and remained standing until he took his place in the speaker's stand. The academy band signaled his entrance with four ruffles and flourishes and playing the President's march. His flag, as commander-in-chief, flew over the station ship, Reina Mercedes.

After an invocation by Comdr. William N. Thomas, chaplain of the academy, Admiral Brown conferred the degree of bachelor of science upon the graduates.

Presentation for F. D. R.

Mayor G. F. MacLaren, of St. John, New Brunswick, presented the President with the sextant of John Paul Jones, Revolutionary War naval hero, whose

(Continued on Page 4)

Middies Cheer Roosevelt On His "Bachelor" Comment

While his talk to the Naval Academy graduates, in the main urged the new officers to know their country and its problems, the President of the United States, Franklin Delano Roosevelt, caused waves of laughter to ripple through the big crowd during several points of his address.

The biggest laugh, and incidentally the most applause came when the President said: "Now before you get your Bachelor of Science Degree I must advise you not to put too much emphasis on the word bachelor."

President Roosevelt left Annapolis at 2:30 P. M. (EST) for Washington. He and other dignitaries were luncheon guests of Rear-Admiral Wilson Brown, superintendent of the Naval Academy.

CONDUCT CLINIC

Dr. C. H. Peckham will conduct a pre-natal clinic at the County Health Office, in the old high school building, on Green street, tomorrow at 10 A. M.

2,000 ATTEND ST. MARGARET'S TOURNAMENT

Horse Show Held Along With Jousting Events As Part Of Annual Labor Day Program —Glen Colleen Wins Show Honors.

PARRAN TAKES 12 RINGS FOR HONORS

(Continued from Page 1)

tors was preceded by a tournament, in which professional, amateur males and women riders participated. Douglas Parran, of Lusby, riding as the Knight of Frederick, took first place in the Professional class. He made a perfect score of 12 rings.

Thomas Weems, of Prince Frederick, the Knight of Lucky Strike was second, and William Weems, Prince Frederick, Knight of Luck, third. Ed Duckett, Davidsonville, was fourth.

The summaries.

Tournament

Other tournament results follow:

Local Riders—Won by J. B. Bourke, Knight of Severna Park: 2nd, Orlando Ridout, Jr., Knight of Woodlawn, and 3rd, Robert Ripley, Knight of Hope.

Amateur Women Riders — Won by Mrs. J. B. Bourke, Maid of Linthicum Heights; second, Mrs. Myra Lineberger, Maid of Marley, and third, Mrs. Robert Ripley, Maid of Four Winds.

Horse Show

Ponies (lead in) — Won by Queenie, Ann Chew Green entry, shown by Margaret Finney; second, Sugar Lump, Mrs. Graham Boyce entry, shown by Dorsey Meyers; third, Silver, Walter Murray entry, shown by Billy Carter.

Suitable to Become Hunters—Won by Dr. Oliver T. Brice entry, Boz Zindorf up; second, Gallant Pat, Miss Catherine Ridout up and owner; third, Rover, Mrs. Frances Ripley up and owner.

Ponies (under 12 hands)—Sugar, Mrs. Graham Boyce entry, Kelly Kilby up; Gypsy Queen, Walter Munroe entry, Elizabeth Merryman up; Queenie, Ann Chew Green up and owner.

Local Saddle Class—Won by Billy Sunday, W. O. Welch up and owner; second, Tammany, Arthur Jones up and owner; third, Moon Magic, Mrs. J. A. Lineberger up and owner.

Junior Hunter—Won by Billy, Buddy Thomas up; second, Midnight, Elmer Binswanger entry, Buddy Conrad up; third, Elzora, W. O. Welch entry, Billy Thomas up.

Pony Jumping Class—Won by Sugar Lump, Mrs. Graham Boyce entry, Jerry Kilby up; second, Gypsy Queen, Elizabeth Merryman up; third, Queenie, Ann Chew Green up and owner.

Handy Hunters—Won by Glen Colleen, Orlando, Jr., entry, Catherine Ridout up; second, Billy, Buddy Thomas entry, Billy Thomas up; third, Playful Arch, Mrs. Frances Ripley up and owner.

Ponies (12 Hands to 14.2 Hands)—Won by Miss Virginia, Ann Chew Green up and owner; second, Dr. Pepper, Eileen Smith up and owner; third, Windy Sylvester Labrot up and owner.

Local Jumpers—Won by Elzora, W. O. Welch up and owner; second, Glen Colleen, Orlando Ridout, Jr., entry, Catherine Ridout up; third, Tammany, Arthur Jones entry, Robert Ripley up.

Horsemanship Class (for children under 16)—Won by Nancy Beil, riding Outbound; second, Catherine Ridout, riding Billy Sunday; third, Eileen Smith, riding Dr. Pepper.

Ladies' Hunters—Won by Glen Colleen, Orlando Ridout, Jr., entry, Catherine Ridout up; second, Tammany, Arthur Jones entry, Mrs. Robert Ripley up; third, Seagram, Mrs. Ernest Smith, up and owner.

Pony Jumping Class (12 hands to 14.2 hands)—Won by Miss Virginia, Ann Chew Green entry, Barbara Tschudi up; second, Dr. Pepper, Eileen Smith, up and owner; third, Socks, Orlando Ridout, Jr., entry, Catherine Ridout up.

Open Hunter Class—Won by Tammany, Arthur Jones entry, Robert Ripley up; second, Billy, Buddy Thomas entry, Billy Thomas up; third, Chipmunk, Mrs. J. E. Lineberger entry, Mrs. Robert Tucker up.

Horsemanship Class for Adults —Won by Mrs. Ernest Smith, riding Seagram; second, Mrs. Robert Tucker, riding Chipmunk, entry of Mrs. J. E. Lineberger; third, Albert Martin, riding Little John.

Horsemanship Classes

Pairs of Hunters—Won by Midnight, Elmer Binswanger entry, Buddy Conrad up, and Elzora, W. O. Welch, owner and rider; second, Prince, Henry Thomas entry, Mrs. Murray Clark up, and Billy, Buddy Thomas entry, Bill Thomas up; third, Tammany, Arthur Jones entry, Robert Ripley up, and Playful Arch, Mrs. Frances Ripley, owner and rider.

Road Hack—Won by Seagram, Mrs. Ernest Smith, owner and rider; second, Tammany, Arthur Jones, owner and rider; third, Dunemar, Mike McCaffrey up.

Knock-Down-and-Out—Won by Glen Colleen, Orlando Ridout, Jr., entry.

Working Hunter Sweepstake—Won by Glen Colleen, Orlando Ridout, Jr., entry, Catherine Ridout up; second, Billy, Buddy Thomas entry, Billy Thomas up; third, Easter Morn, Harry Buckheimer, owner and rider.

Ladies' Hunters—First, won by Blue Cross, owned by C. C. Mickle, Mrs. Mickle up; second, Royal Prince, owned by C. Quigley, ridden by Marion G. Reib; third, Sonny Boy, owned by Edward Anderson, ridden by Joan Smith.

Hunter Hacks (under saddle)—Won by The Ghost, owned by A. Richardson, ridden by Alene Richardson; second, Marketry, owned by C. C. Mickle, ridden by Mrs. Mickle; third, Fisherman, owned and ridden by C. E. Lang.

Pairs of Hunters—First, Lady Howell and Royal Prince, owned by J. Williams (riders unknown); second, Pat O'Malley and Fisherman, owned by C. E. Lang, ridden by owner and J. E. Hector; third, The Ghost and King James, owned by Richardson, ridden by Richardson brothers. Trophies were silver sandwich plates.

Children's Horsemanship Class —First, Smoky, owned by C. C. Mickle, ridden by Ann Mickle; second, Nickey, owned and ridden by Nicky Burris; third, Tony, owned by C. C. Mickle, ridden by Pat Mickle.

Touch and Out—First, Royal Prince, owned by Quigley, ridden by Emory Bonwell; second, Cassius Belle, owned by C. Coleman, ridden by Eleanor Coleman; third, The Ghost, owned by Richardson, ridden by Miss Richardson.

Green Hunters—First, Cassius Belle, owned by Coleman, ridden by Coleman; second, Marquette, owned and ridden by Charles Hurtt; third, Red Wing, owned and ridden by James Taylor. Dudley G. Roe Trophy.

Pony Jumping Class—First, Tony, owned by C. C. Mickle, Jr., ridden by Pat Mickle; second, Smoky, owned by C. C. Mickle, ridden by Ann Mickle; third, Honey Boy, owned by Roy Downes, Earl Sutton up.

Open Hunters — First, Blue Cross, owned by C. C. Mickle and ridden by Mrs. Mickle; second, Fisherman, owned and ridden by E. Lang; third, Nancy, owned and ridden by E. Fox.

In the running races the small pony race was won by Terry Blackwood.

Large ponies, won by Queen, owned and ridden by Emory Bonwell.

Standard-bred—Won by Dancing Doll, owned and ridden by Earle Sutton.

Half-bred — Won by Royal Prince, owned by C. Quigley, ridden by Emory Bonwell.

Thorough-bred Race — Won by Wargold, owned and ridden by Emory Bonwell.

Major League Standings

AMERICAN LEAGUE

Scores Of Yesterday

New York, 5-6; Philadelphia, 2-3.
Boston, 14-8; Washington, 4-6.
*St. Louis; 3-3; Detroit, 2-9.
Cleveland, 6-4; Chicago, 4-2.

*Second game called, darkness.

Where They Play Today

Cleveland at Detroit.
St. Louis at Chicago.
Boston at Washington.
(Only games scheduled.)

Standing Of The Clubs

	W.	L.	P.C.
New York	89	40	.690
Boston	74	52	.587
Cleveland	73	53	.579
Detroit	65	62	.512
Washington	63	66	.488
Chicago	53	70	.431
St. Louis	45	80	.360
Philadelphia	45	84	.349

NATIONAL LEAGUE

Scores Of Yesterday

Chicago, 3-4; Pittsburgh, 0-3.
Boston, 5-5; Brooklyn, 4-3.
Cincinnati, 4-4; St. Louis, 3-2.
New York, 7-3; Philadelphia, 0-4.

Where They Play Today

Boston at New York.
Brooklyn at Philadelphia.
St. Louis at Cincinnati.
(Only games scheduled.)

Standing Of The Clubs

	W.	L.	P.C.
Pittsburgh	75	52	.591
Cincinnati	72	57	.562
Chicago	71	58	.550
New York	69	59	.539
Boston	65	61	.516
St. Louis	61	68	.473
Brooklyn	57	70	.449
Philadelphia	40	85	.320

Skipper Ten Wins Softball Honors

Defeat Naval Hospital Ten For Top Honors In Local League—Score 10 To 4.

Sunday morning on the St. John's College grounds the Skipper Electric softball team took undisputed possession of the city softball championship when they thumped the Naval Hospital ten by the score of 10 to 4.

Burton Bell, of the Skipper team, allowed only six hits and chalked up his 19th victory of the season. Howard Green, Tommy Linthicum, Erkey White and Daffy Russell led the Skipper attack with two hits apiece. Top honors for the Hospital team went to Joe Ash who hit a long home run in the second inning.

The Navy boys started the game by scoring three runs in the first inning on two hits and two errors. In the second Skipper put over five runs. After Daffy Russell hit safely, Mose Schleiche, the Hospital pitcher, lost control and walked three men. Green and Linthicum followed with sharp singles cleaning the bases. Joe Ash smashed a home run to left field in the second for the Navy team's fourth and last run.

In the fourth inning the Skipper boys got four more runs off of five hits and a walk. Erky White scored the Skipper's last run after he doubled to left and scored on Purdy Tucker's bunt.

This same team, entered in the league last year as the Capital-Gazette Press, took the championship for the 1937 campaign.

The summary:

Hospital	Ab	R	H	E
Schleiche, p.	4	0	0	0
Ratchford, c.	3	1	1	0
Thompson, lb.	3	1	1	1
Danbache, ss.	3	1	0	0
Coutruia, lf.	3	0	0	0
Kreamer, 2b.	3	0	1	0
Fitzpatrick, rf.	3	0	0	0
Ash, 3b.	3	1	1	0
Clay, sf.	3	0	0	1
Hamilton, cf.	3	0	2	0
Totals	31	4	6	2

Skipper	Ab	R	H	E
Green, lf.	4	2	2	2
Linthicum, sf.	4	0	2	1
White, 3b.	4	1	2	1
P. Hantske, 2b.	4	0	0	0
Tucker, ss.	4	0	1	0
Bell, p.	4	0	0	0
Russell, c.	3	2	2	0
Stuart, cf.	3	2	1	0
Lowman, rf.	3	1	0	0
Kent, 1b.	3	2	0	0
Totals	36	10	10	4

Scoring by innings:
Hospital ..... 310 000 0— 4
Skipper ..... 050 401 0—10

SWEENEY WINS FIRST PLACE IN SAIL RACE

Jack Martin Gets Second In West River Sailing Association Regatta Held Saturday And Sunday — Garnett Z. Clark Enters Affair.

TWENTY-SIX EVENTS HELD

Swash, a fourteen-foot International dinghy, owned and sailed by R. J. Sweeney, of Annapolis, took first place in both events for that class boat at the West River Sailing Association held on Saturday and Sunday.

Black Boy, owned and sailed by Jack Martin, also of Annapolis, took second place in both events.

Ju Jan, owned by Jane Martin and sailed by Garnett Y. Clark, of Annapolis, took second place in one race and third in another in the Hampton Class.

The summaries of the races were as follows:

Boys' Race (Somerville Trophy)—Won by Hawk, Billy Hartge, Galesville; second, Cardinal, Bill Hutchison, Shady Side; third, Gull, Frank Wallace, Washington.

Girls' Race (Somerville Trophy)—Won by Hawk, Katherine McReynolds, Washington; second, Whistler, June Peters, Galesville; third, Gull, Elsie Hartge, Galesville.

20-Foot Open Class—Won by Wings, Carroll Smith, Galesville; second Strut Away, Dick Hartge, Galesville; third, Vanity, Osburn Owings, Washington.

20-Foot Restricted Class — Won by Crickett II, H. C. Bush, Alexandria; second, Spray, Herbert Neily, Baltimore; third, Kandoo, Dr. Albert Pagan, Washington.

Albatross Class—Won by Raven, Arthur Fifer, Galesville; second, Gull, Hugh Irey, Washington; third, Hawk, Emile Hartge, Galesville.

14-Foot Knockabout—Won by U. S. 77, James Sweeney, Annapolis; second, Black Boy, Dr. Willis Martin, Annapolis; third, Flighty, Bob Cochrane, Richmond.

Moth Class—Won by Stepins, Buddy Elderkin, Mago-Vista, Md.; second, Indigo-Under, Jack Babcock, Washington; third, Aw-Wa, Robert Johnson, Mago-Vista.

Comet Class — Won by Frolic, William White, Washington; second, Sassy Too, Verner Smythe, Washington; third, Escapade, Ernest Covert, Washington.

18-Foot Knockabout Class—Won by Oriole, W. L. Lane, Tilghman Island, Md.; second, Intrepid, Joseph McDonald, Fairhaven, Md.; third, Hornet, Capt. Ed. Leatherbury, Shady Side.

16-Foot Knockabout Class—Won by Swan, Charles Walton, Fairhaven; second, Flying Cloud, Enos Ray, Fairhaven; third, Dot, Noah Hazard, Galesville.

Hampton One-Design Class—Won by number 48, John Wilson, Annapolis; second, Sea Biscuit, Dr. Harry Wilson, Annapolis; third, Ju-Jam, Jane Martin, Annapolis.

Snipe Class—Won by Shim Sham, Ernest Liskey, Baltimore; second, Shoo-Fly, Louis Coffin, Jr., Baltimore; third, Little Mae, Roger Gintling, Baltimore.

Twenty-Foot Open Class — Won by Wings, owned and sailed by Carroll Smith, West River Sailing Association; second, Vanity, owned and sailed by Osborne Owings, West River Sailing Association.

Twenty-Foot Restricted Class — Won by Cricket, owned and sailed by Twig Bush, Old Dominion Boat Club; second, Spray, owned and sailed by Herbert Neily, Jr., West River Sailing Association.

Albatross—Won by Raven, owned and sailed by Arthur Feifer, West River Sailing Association; second, Hawk, owned and sailed by Emile Hartge, West River Sailing Association; third, Gull, owned and sailed by Hugh Irey, West River Sailing Association.

Comet Class—Won by Frolic, owned and sailed by Bill White, Capital Yacht Club; second, Escapade, owned and sailed by Ernie Covert, Capital Yacht Club; third, Sassy Too, owned and sailed by Verner Smythe, Capital Yacht Club.

Ten-Foot Knockabout Class—Won by Intrepid, owned and sailed by Bill McDonald, Fair Haven Sailing Association; second, Oriole, owned and sailed by W. L. Lane, Bozman.

Sixteen-Foot Knockabout Class—Won by Swan, owned and sailed by Charles Walton, Fair Haven Sailing Association; second, Flying Cloud, owned and sailed by Enos Ray, Fair Haven Sailing Association.

Hampden One-Design Class—Won by No. 48, owned and sailed by L. D. Bagett, Annapolis Yacht Club; second, Jim Jam, owned by Jane Martin, sailed by J. J. Clark, Annapolis Yacht Club.

Snipe Class — Won by Shim Sham, owned and sailed by Ernest Liskie, Sparrows Point; second, Little Mag, owned and sailed by Rodger L. Gintling, Sparrows Point; third, Shoo Fly, owned an dsailed by Lewis and Elizabeth Coffin, Sparrows Point.

Fourteen-Foot Knockabout Class — Won by Swash, owned and sailed by R. J. Sweeney, Annapolis Yacht Club; second, Black Boy, owned and sailed by Jack Martin, Annapolis Yacht Club.

Moth Class—Won by Indigo Under, owned and sailed by Jack Babcock, Old Dominion Cllb; second, Stepin, owned and sailed by Buddy Elderkin, West River Sailing Association.

Cruising Handicap Class — First to finish, Grisle, owned and sailed by Albert Byrd, West River Sailing Association. Corrected Time — Won by Spin Drift, owned and sailed by Dr. Balls, West River Sailing Association; second, Grisle; third, Larna, owned and sailed by Wally Russell, West River Sailing Association.

Handicap Race—Won by Dot, owned by Noel Hartge, sailed by Lawrence Hartge, West River Sailing Association; second, My Ray, owned and sailed by Ralph Young, Capital Yacht Club; third, Strut Away, owned by Kenneth Smith and sailed by Dick Hartge, West River Sailing Association.

Free-for-All, 16-Foot or Under—Won by Shim Sham, owned and sailed by Ernst Liskie, Jr., Sparrows Point; second, Swan, owned and sailed by Charles Walton, Fair Haven Sailing Association.

Free-for-All, 20-Foot or Under—Won by Ranger, owned and sailed by J. S. Harding, West River Sailing Association; second, Vanity owned and sailed by Osborne Owings, West River Sailing Association; third, Strut Away, owned by Kenneth Smith and sailed by Dick.

Championship Softball Series Starts Tomorrow

Annapolis Juniors And Annapolis Cardinals In Junior League Playoff.

Twenty ambitious boys will meet on the softball diamond on Wednesday to decide the junior championship of Annapolis for 1938. The teams participating in this series will be the Annapolis Juniors and the Annapolis Cardinals. Both teams have enviable records for the season and, accordingly, should give an exceptional exhibition of team work and cooperation in their efforts to claim the title which will be awarded the winner of four out of the seven game series.

During the first half of the season the Annapolis Junior Club led the league undefeated and finished the entire season by winning 11 games out of 14. The Annapolis Cardinal Club, though 2nd at the end of the first half of the season, was undefeated during the second half and finished the entire season by winning 13 games out of 14.

The first game of the series is scheduled for Wednesday, September 7 and will be played on the St. John's College softball diamond beginning at 5:30 P. M. Subsequent games will be played on Fridays, Mondays and Wednesdays following. Time and place of all game will be as above.

Standing of teams at end of second half:

	W.	L.	Pct.
Annapolis Cardinals	8	0	1.000
Annapolis Juniors	5	3	.625
St. John's Juniors	4	4	.500
Germantown	3	5	.375

Standing of teams for season:

	W.	L.	Pct.
Annapolis Cardinals	13	1	.928
Annapolis Juniors	11	3	.785
St. John's Juniors	8	6	.571
Germantown Eagles	5	9	.357

Huge Crowd Hears President On Eastern Shore

—Associated Press Photo

Standing under the protecting shade of trees and beneath patriotic bunting, thousands of residents of the Eastern Shore of Maryland gathered at Denton Labor Day to hear President Roosevelt call for continued liberalism in the Democratic party. The President, speaking from platform at left, took the occasion to ask for the nomination of Representative Davis J. Lewis as the Democratic nominee for the United States Senate.

Ignores President

Mayor William E. Ward, of Crisfield, Md. (above) had no reception there when President Roosevelt arrived September 5 because "Mr. Roosevelt came as a politician and so I did not pay any attention to him."

Maryland's Welcome For Chief Executive

Several hundred Marylanders thronged the Maryland-District of Columbia line to welcome President Roosevelt on his way to the Eastern Shore to deliver a Labor Day address in support of the Senatorial candidacy of Representative David J. Lewis, Democratic primary foe of Senator Millard E. Tydings.

Politics and Weather Both Were Hot

On a trip into Maryland to deliver a speech for the candidacy of Representative David J. Lewis, who seeks the Democratic nomination in opposition to the veteran Senator Millard E. Tydings, President Roosevelt paused to mop perspiration at Laidlow's Ferry. Behind the big cigar is Representative Lewis.

McNair Defeats Bill Godfrey In Junior Matches

Freddie McNair defeated Bill Godfrey yesterday to the tune of 7-5, 4-6, 6-3, 6-3 to win the Annapolis Junior Tennis Championship for the third consecutive year. In 1936 Freddie trounced Bill Godfrey and in '37 Bob Crutcher met the same fate.

With the count a set apiece and three games all Godfrey seemed to have even chance to win but from there on McNair was master of the situation. His drives and overhead were too consistent for Godfrey's game at its best. It was another victory for probably the greatest tennis player Annapolis has developed.

In the semi-finals both McNair and Godfrey won straight set victories. McNair beating Gaver after the latter had nosed out Scott Slocum, while Godfrey beat Crutcher for the second time in the last three tournaments.

McNair, Godfrey, and Crutcher all hope to go to the Naval Academy. In matches with the plebe classes of the last two years these boys have scored five out of six victories. This certainly indicates that they should stand high on the Naval Academy varsity tennis team withi nthe next few years if they go to the Academy.

VAMARIE SECOND IN SAILING RACES

Vamarie, the big mahogany hulled ketch of the United States Naval Academy, added another "first to finish" to her season's record when she led the fleet of more than a score of crack yachts across the finish line in the 100-mile Cedar Point race of the Gibson Island Yacht Squadron Sunday.

Vamarie, scratch boat in Class A, finished at 5.46.03 A. M. but was unable to save her time. On corrected time White Cloud, George A. Whiting, which crossed the line at 6.21, was awarded first place in Class A, with Vamarie second and Egret, C. Porter Shutt, third.

Crying Dutch Lentz Wails For Beef, Brawn To Help Light Squad

Valentine ("Crying Dutch") Lentz, runnerup in last year's "moaning coach contest," looked at his St. John's College football team today and heaved another sigh.

"If we make a first down," he said, with tears popping out like electric light bulbs, "it will be a moral victory."

Lentz said his worries started when a squad of nine turned out for first practice. He talked Plato to them to make signals seem easier, and dug up enough men to fill out his line and provide substitutes. But weight is his trouble now.

Light Squad

"Look," he said, pointing eloquently at Striet Cunningham, 135-pound halfback. "And look ...." he added, showing off two of the 1937 regulars who are back. They were Ed Roache, 145, end,

and Skippy McWilliams, 142, halfback.

"I have to call off practice when it rains so they won't shrink any more," he said, "and we have to hold secret practice for two reasons.

"We've got one boy almost normal football size and the spectators would lynch the big bully for picking on the rest of the little tykes on the squad. Second, three of our opponents' scouts have laughed themselves into hysterics watching us."

De-Emphasized Football

St. John's recently "de-emphasized" football, scheduling only Swarthmore, Johns Hopkins, Delaware, Randolph-Macon and American University.

"De-emphasized football, did you say?" Lentz cried. "Listen, friend—my squad would de-emphasize football without any action of the college authorities."

LION KILLS MAN, OWNER IS JAILED

Manslaughter Charges Develops From N. J. Tragedy —Cop Slays Beast

(By The Associated Press)

WILDWOOD, N. J., Oct. 6—A manslaughter charge was lodged today against a boardwalk side show operator whose circus lion broke out of a cage, tore a man to death and for nearly three hours terrorized this resort city until slain by a policeman's bullet.

Recorder Leonard Byrne held Joseph Dobish, 50, without bail for the grand jury in connection with the death last night of Thomas Saito, 37, of Philadelphia, a Japanese auction room employe, whose mangled body was found in a maze of pilings under the ocean front boardwalk, nearly deserted in this off-season month.

Was Gentle Lion

Until five weeks ago the 300-pound killer known as "Tuffy" was one of two lions strapped to a motorcycle side car while the driver roared around a steep-walled bowl called the "wall of death." Since then "Tuffy" has been inactive.

Sometime last night in a manner as yet undetermined "Tuffy" escaped from the cage and roamed the nearby boardwalk.

Saito, about to enter his parked automobile when the lion pounced from the elevated boardwalk upon the man's back and dragged him into the darkened recesses under the walk. There Saito's body was found, clad only in a ripped shirt.

Police, informed by Dobish of the lion's escape, hurriedly formed a posse of officers, firemen and volunteers. An armed cordon was thrown around a four-block area.

Cop Slays Lion

As hours passed horror in the city increased and even distant streets became desolate. Police searchlights pierced the frightening darkness as the posse combed the labyrinth of piling.

Then Patrolman John Gares, crossing the boardwalk, spied the lion bounding toward him. He waited, pistol ready. When the animal came within ten feet he fired. "Tuffy" fell dead at his feet with a bullet through his right eye.

Series Facts

(By The Associated Press)

CHICAGO, Oct. 6—World Series facts:

FIRST GAME

Score—New York Yankees 3, Chicago Cubs 1.
Total attendance 43,642.
Total receipts $210,025.00.
Commissioner's share $31,503.75.
Players' pool $107,112.75.
Leagues and clubs $71,408.50.

DAVIDSONVILLE WOMEN'S CLUB AIDS GIRLS IN COLLEGES

(Continued from Page 1)

man; Mrs. St. George Barber, and Mrs. Burch Beard will submit names for officers at the next meeting of the club.

The annual Hallowe'en Frolic in the Davidsonville Hall will be held this year on October 27 at 12:30 P. M. Mrs. J. Mortimer Hayes is chairman, with Mrs. George Beall, Mrs. Gott Beard, Mrs. Burch Beard and Mrs. Norman Carr assisting.

ANNAPOLIS
Evening Capital

Home of the
U. S. NAVAL ACADEMY,
and
ST. JOHN'S COLLEGE

Weather Forecast
Fair tonight and Tuesday; colder tonight, with light to heavy frost.

VOL. CVIII — No. 2. | ESTABLISHED IN 1884 —PUBLISHED EVENING EXCEPT SUNDAY | ANNAPOLIS, MONDAY, NOVEMBER, 14, 1938. | SOUTHERN MARYLAND'S ONLY DAILY PAPER | PRICE TWO CENTS.

MIDDIES BY GREAT RALLY TOP COLUMBIA

Naval Academy Grid Team Keyed Up For Army Fracas Two Weeks Distant By 14 To 9 Win Over Fiery Lion Team In N. Y.

SUPERIORITY OF N. A. LINE DECIDED TILT

A fighting Naval Academy football team, with a never-say-die spirit, gained its most notable victory of the season on Saturday against an almost equally inspired Columbia University eleven. After spotting Columbia nine points the Middies came back with the two touchdowns needed for victory, and held the lead through a hair-raising fourth quarter which found the Lions' great Sid Luckman, pitching pass after pass against a Tar defense which refused to crack.

Navy's victory, 14 to 9, left the crowd weak. In fact excitement got so great that one fan dropped dead and two others fainted. Every one of the 34,000 seats in Baker Field, N. Y., were filled and those who attended were treated to the most interesting game the Middies have participated in this year.

Toughest Game Of Year

It also was the toughest game Navy had had this season. Columbia made 18 first downs to nine for the Annapolitans and gained almost as much ground against the Navy as Notre Dame did in Baltimore the week before. In the Notre Dame game Navy had some wonderful chances to score on passes, but bungled them all. Columbia had similar ideas but the Navy pass defenders were alert, with special honors going to big Harold Hansen, a lesser light of the squad heretofore. One time Hansen leaped several feet into the air to bat a touchdown pass from the hands of Arthur Radvilas. It is doubtful if any other back on the Navy team

(Continued on Page 5)

CARD PARTY
Given by
Annapolis Section
Nat'l Council of Jewish Women
WEDNESDAY, NOV. 16—8 P. M.
Synagogue—Tickets 45c
Prizes and refreshments

FRIED CHICKEN SUPPER
Given by
Ladies' Aid of Trinity M. E. Church, South
West St. and Amos Garrett Blvd.
TUESDAY, NOVEMBER 15th
Serving from 5 to 8
TICKET 50c

NOTICE

The annual meeting of the Hospital Association of the Emergency Hospital will be held Monday, November 14th, at 8:30 P. M., in the assembly room of the Nurses Home.

CHICKEN SALAD SUPPER
—given by—
SALVATION ARMY
TUESDAY, NOVEMBER 15
Beginning 4:30 P. M.
47 RANDALL ST.
TICKET 25c n-14

LOTS FOR SALE
N. Southwood Avenue (formerly Estelle Avenue) near West Street. Lots 50 by 150. Water, sewer. Reasonable prices. Terms.
JULIAN BREWER AND SON
Joseph D. Lazenby
9 School St. Dial 2685

FOR SALE
WARDOUR
Modern frame home, 2 baths, garage, oil heat, city conveniences available.
3 lots - - - $8,000.
SERVICE AGENTS, INC
SEE F. E. VOGES or H. H. LITTLE
47 Md. Ave. — Dial 4477

FOR SALE
Desirable residence on lot 100x450 ft.. Six rooms and bath. all conveniences. Oil burning heat; garage. For full particulars apply to
CHAS. F. LEE
LEE BLDG, DIAL 2461

ELKS WILL ASSIST WORTHY STUDENTS

National Foundation Offers Prizes In Addition To Local Fund

In addition to the $150 scholarship fund given by the local lodge of Elks to the Annapolis High School student who has the highest scholastic honors, the Elks' National Foundation has provided scholastic prizes totalling $1,500 for proficient students.

In this "Most Valuable Student Contest" for 1938-1939, prizes will be awarded as follows:
First prize—$600.00.
Second prize—$400.00.
Third prize—$300.00.
Fourth prize—$200.00.

Eligibility Rule

Any student in the senior or graduating class of a high or preparatory school, or in any undergraduate class of a recognized college, who is a resident within the jurisdiction of the Order, is eligible to enter this contest.

Character, citizenship, scholarship, exceptional courage, patriotism or service, and any notable action or distinguishing accomplishment are criteria by which the applicants will be judged.

Present Applications

The Foundation trustees do not furnish application blanks nor do they insist upon any special form of application or presentation. It is preferred that each applicant should use his own ingenuity in presenting his case. It is suggested, however, that each applicant should present, or have presented in his behalf, a printed or typewritten brief, or prospectus which sets forth all the data, with supporting exhibits, including a recent picture of the applicant and a certificate signed by the

(Continued on Page 6)

Grammar School P.-T. A, Meet Set For Tuesday Night

The Annapolis Grammar School Parent-Teacher Association will hold its meeting tomorrow at 8 o'clock, in the Annapolis Grammar school music room.

The speaker of the evening will be the Rev. E. Cranston Riggin who will discuss character education from the standpoint of "First Things First". Miss Vera Pickard, supervisor of elementary schools, will give a short talk on the new report card.

COLONIAL ANTHRACITE
RED ASH COAL + WHITE ASH COAL = COLONIAL BLENDED ANTHRACITE
A 7-STAR FUEL
The Annapolis Dairy PRODUCTS COMPANY
Dial 2345
ALSO JEROME SOFT COAL
Oil Treated for Dust Control

COMMUNITY
OYSTER SUPPER
Benefit Eastport Vol. Fire Co.
Methodist Church Hall
Eastport, Md.
THURSDAY, NOV. 17, 5:00 P. M
Salt Water Oysters

CARD AND GAME PARTY
Given by
ST. MARY'S P.-T. A.
FRIDAY, NOVEMBER 18, 8:15
St. Mary's Hall
Games, 500, Bridge
Prizes and Refreshments
ADMISSION 50c
x

Notice of Stockholder's Meeting

The annual meeting of the stockholders of the Workingmen's Building and Loan Association of Annapolis, Anne Arundel County Md., will be held at 8 o'clock P. M. at its office, 14 Church Circle, on Wednesday, November 16th, 1938 for the purpose of electing a Board of Directors for the ensuing year, and the transaction of such business as may be brought before it.

GEORGE T. FELDMEYER,
President.
GEORGE F. QUAID,
Secretary.

O'CONOR WILL NAME FISCAL STUDY GROUP

Governor-Elect Seeks Data On State Budget, Reorganization Of State Government To Eliminate Waste And Raise Revenue.

NICE IS ASKED FOR CONFERENCE

Governor-elect Herbert R. O'Conor will appoint three committees this week to study the State's financial problems.

The survey will be divided into three categories, one for each committee, O'Conor said, which will be:

1. Preparation of the State budget.
2. Reorganization of the State government to eliminate as much as possible unnecessary expenditures and useless jobs.
3. Problems of revenue raising.

Arrange Date

The Governor-elect planned to

(Continued on Page 4)

102,210 Service Game Seats In U. S. Mail Today

The Naval Academy athletic office today put in the mails, 102,210 seats for the Army-Navy football game to be played in the Philadelphia Municipal Stadium on November 26.

Comdr. Morris D. Gilmore, U. S. N., retired, in charge of the tickets said that all the pasteboards had left his office and were now in the hands of postoffice authorities.

As usual the game was more than a sellout an dthe applications of some unsuccessful fans who did not follow the Navy team throughout the season were returned unfilled.

Postmaster General James A. Farley should present the navy with a cruiser or something to balance the business Navy tossed the postoffice department by mailing the tickets.

All the pasteboards were sent out by registered mail. Registry fees alone were more than $1,800.

In addition, postage on more than 50,000 applications for tickets was upward of $1.500.

Navy Women Plan Dramatic Evening

A group of plays will be presented by the Drama Section of the Naval Women's Club at Mahan Hall, on November 16, under the direction of Mrs. R. M. L. Graham and Mrs. L. H. Thebaud.

The plays, three in number, will cover three phases of drama —comedy mystery and farce.

"None Of Them Perfect" holds up a mirror for husbandly foibles which the dear men themselves never suspected existed.

"Heard In Camera" unravels a gripping murder mystery in Shanghai.

"The Glamour Girl" shows the lighter — much lighter — side of politics, a phase which should prove most welcome at this date on the calendar.

The playbills for the three productions follow:

"None of Them Perfect": Amanda Bartlett, Crystal Tardy; Lucy Haines, Mrs. H. A. Renken; Julia Moore, Mrs. J. C. South; Amy, Mrs. W. C. Bailey; Cecile, Mrs. C. S. Manning; Eve, Mrs. J. R. Moore.

"Heard In Camera": Mrs. Tulane, Miss Katharine Lewis; Mrs. Surtees, Mrs. G. A. Lyle; Mrs. Katharine Vail, Mrs. Marcy M. Dupre; Mary Cameron, Mrs. J. C. Dempsey; Mrs. Fordyce, Mrs. J. E. O'Brien; Bijou Fordyce (Portia, Mrs. R. J. Woodaman; Tang Fong, Miss Margaret Bowman.

"The Glamour Girl": Marian Hardy, Mrs. W. H. Duvall; Jessie Hardy, Mrs. C. T. Logan; Mary Louise Spencer, Mrs. J. B. Weiler; Lizzie Wright, Mrs. A. A. Cumberledge; Mrs. Drexel Caldwell, Mrs. W. J. Giles.

Dress rehearsals for the plays will be held tonight at 8:30 P. M.

Hold First Conversation Over Dial Telephone System

Photo by Hayman Studio.

Above Mayor Louis N. Phipps is shown dialing the first call over the new dial telephone system and Governor-Elect Herbert R. O'Conor answering the call.

Mayor Phipps in the top picture, seated at his desk, is shown with his son and Roy C. Chambers, local manager of the telephone company.

Below is Governor-Elect O'Conor seated at his desk in his library answering the call. Lloyd Griffin, general manager of the Chesapeake and Potomac Telephone Company of Baltimore City, is standing.

Dial Telephone System Begins Operation Here

Change From Old Manual Method Effected By C. & P. Co. Before Midnight.

Mayor Phipps Makes First Recorded Call—Cutover Take Less Than Two Minutes As Officials And Visitors Watch

Almost in the twinkling of an eyelash Annapolis' telephone system was changed from manual to dial operation before the closing minutes of November 12 as a group of Chesapeake and Potomac Telephone Company officials, city officials, representatives of the Chamber of Commerce, civic groups, and a group of business men and others visitors especially invited for the occasion looked on in the new telephone building.

Mayor Louis N. Phipps represented the city in the change over operation which was accomplished with such dispatch that none of the visitors could have known anything that occurred had they not been informed in advance that the pulling of hundreds of wedges from banks of relays in the switch room by a group of employees acting under signal meant that the old manual system was out of date and that Annapolis had gone dial in reality.

The first dialed number was made by Mayor Phipps when on advice that the first line was ready he dialed and requested to talk to Governor-elect Herbert R. O'Conor. Mayor Phipps, after extending congratulations to Mr. O'Conor and welcoming him as a coming citizen of Annapolis, said, "We are proud of our city and we are proud of any company or individual that will do the things that this company has done to bring about improvement for Annapolis." Mayor Phipps also commented on the new colonial type telephone building. Mr. O'Conor expressed his pleasure in being the

(Continued on Page 6)

Editorial

ANNAPOLIS' NEW MAYOR

The City Council will, within the next seven weeks, name a new Mayor of Annapolis to succeed Mayor Louis N. Phipps who will become the Senator from Anne Arundel county.

While the City Council has the entire say as to who will govern the city for the next two and one-half years, it would seem a good plan for that body to ascertain who the citizens of Annapolis want to fill the Mayoralty, before anyone is selected.

A way to determine public sentiment is offered by this newspaper. The Evening Capital is willing to contribute a section of its front page for a limited time, for the publication of a ballot which the legal voters of the city can use in stating their choice for Mayor. This offer is made to the City Council in the hope that the gentlemen of that body will see fit to convass the city before the new Mayor is selected.

The result of such a poll would not be binding upon the members of the City Council, who are faced with the burden of selection, but the management of The Evening Capital believes that the right man will be selected if the straw vote is tried. The Council has nothing to lose by offering to cooperate with this newspaper in the straw vote. There is reason to believe, too that voters of the city will be better satisfied with the selection if the outstanding men of the city are given full consideration for the post.

No one in the city would object if either of the two veteran aldermen of the city. Jesse A. Fisher or Arthur T. Elliott would be named. Either of these men would serve the city well as Mayor. Their long records as aldermen are filled with outstanding service to the municipality. The selection of either would be a well deserved honor for meritorious service. However, it is reported that neither man is a candidate for elevation within the Council.

While other younger members of the Council might be able to fill the post most capably, too, it would seem advisable for the Council members to first subscribe to the poll idea before making a selection.

Until the last session of the Legislature a city election was held every two years. The Assembly at that time saw fit to make the Annapolis election term four years. The new Mayor will serve more than half of that term, or more than the total of the previous elective term.

The welfare of the city demands that the best man attainable be selected for this important post, and it would seem feasible for the Council to select a citizens committee. which in turn could nominate persons for the office. Those nominated, say half a dozen in number, could be placed on the ballot which The Evening Capital offers to run without charge. The vote could be tabulated and printed daily. By this means the City Council would have an expression from all the people. It might not be too far fetched for the city fathers to promise to consider the names of the first three in standing after the poll closes. Such a proposal seems to have its merits.

Without attempting to usurp the Council's prerogatives in naming possible nominees for the office The Evening Capital management nevertheless can-

(Continued on Page 4)

Deny Higher Education To German Jews

Rectors Of All Nazi Universities Ordered To Oust Jewish Students Immediately—Eliminates Jews From All State Schools—Jews Already Cut From Nazi Economic Life—Merchants Fined $60,000 To Repair Damage Done Shops.

(By The Associated Press)

BERLIN, Nov. 14—Minister of Education Bernhard Rust today expelled Jewish students from all universities, technical schools and other institutions of higher learning in the latest move toward separation of Jews and Germans.

The Minister of Education telegraphed the rectors of all universities ordering them to oust Jewish students immediately and not to permit any more to enter even for lectures which do not involve examination for degrees.

He said a decree embodying that order was being prepared and would be issued soon.

ELIMINATES JEWS FROM SCHOOL SYSTEM

This means final elimination of Jews of all ages from the German school system. Lower grade pupils from six to 14 years old were taken from German schools in 1936 and put into Jewish private schools. Jewish professors had previously been ousted.

Since 1935 admittance to higher institutions had been on a quota based on the population of Jews in the various university districts. Also Jews already enrolled had been permitted to continue their studies.

CUT OUT OF ECONOMIC LIFE

Now these students are thrown out with no prospects of completing their education, since no purely Jewish universities exist in Germany.

Rust's order follows Saturday's decrees by Field Marshall Hermann Wilhelm Goering and Propaganda Minister Paul Joseph Goebbels eliminating Jews from the nation's economic life, forbidding them to attend theaters and other public entertainments, and placing heavy fines on their wealth.

Merchants Fined $60,000

Special bills up to $60,000 each were presented to about 100 of the wealthiest Jews of Berlin payable today to repair damage done to Jewish shops by angry crowds in a wave of violence last Thursday.

These bills were in addition to the 1,000,000,000 mark ($400,-000000) penalty decreed upon Jews in general for the slaying in Paris of Ernest Vom Rath, embassy secretary, by a Jewish youth who once lived in Germany.

The assassination provoked the Thursday demonstrations, and rising resentment inspired government decrees compelling Jews to sell their shops by Jan. 1 and barring them from retail, mail order, commission and handicraft businesses.

Arrests Cease

Male Jews were arrested in general raids throughout Germany but today the arrest period apparently had ended. Many who had been jailed were released, if they were over 30.

Propaganda Minister Goebbels in a speech Sunday gave an indication there would be further action.

The Jewish problem would be solved very shortly, he told 500 social workers at a barley and beef stew dinner for the winter relief fund, "in a manner satisfactory to the nation's sense of what is right and just. The people will do it. And we are only executors of their will."

Anti-Catholic Feeling

Anti-Catholic feeling flared, meanwhile, in a brief demonstration Sunday before St. Mary's Square in Munich.

JAPS REJECT U. S. PROTEST IN NOTE TODAY

(By The Associated Press)

TOKYO, Nov. 14—The Japanese Government today rejected the protests of the United States, Great Britain and France against the closing of the Yangtze river to all but Japanese vessels.

In separate notes handed to Ambassadors of the three powers, the government declared military operations still made navigation of the Yangtze dangerous and for that reason foreign vessels must be barred.

Notes Summarized

A foreign office statement summarizing the notes said:

Although Japan has no intention of deliberately hampering commerce and navigation of third powers in the Yangtze, the Japanese Government holds the view that the time has not yet arrived to warrant a general opening."

The summary listed five reasons for Japan's refusal to open the river:

1—The blockade at Kiangyin,

(Continued on Page 4)

MISS ROSA E. CARR DIED ON SUNDAY

Miss Rosa Ellen Carr, daughter of the late Mr. and Mrs. Samuel Wilson Carr, died yesterday at her residence, 33 Jefferson street.

Surviving Miss Carr are two sisters, Mrs. Annie M. Trott, and Miss Laura B. Carr.

Funeral services will be held on Tuesday, November 15, at 3 P. M. from the residence, with interment at Cedar Bluff Cemetery. Arrangements for the funeral are in charge of John M. Taylor.

MRS. JULIA ROGERS SUCCUMBS SUNDAY

Mrs. Julia R. Rogers, wife of Frederick A. Rogers, of Deale, died yesterday at her residence in Deale, following a short illness.

Funeral services will take place tomorrow morning at 11 A. M from the Cedar Grove M. E. Church, with interment in Deale Cemetery.

Smoke Needed To Drive Bees From Office Bldg. Site

They had labor trouble and troubled labor on the $1,000,000 State Office Building project Saturday—a highly organized and militant local of bees "picketed" the work.

Gangs of workmen were clearing the site of the building. They felled a huge hardwood tree. The bees' union in the hollow upper half immediately passed a unanimous strike vote—and struck. The other workmen on the project saw the point, literally, and joined the walkout—but most of them ran.

Smoke finally cleared the picket line and work was resumed. Workmen removed approximately 75 pounds of honey from the bee tree.

LUXURIOUSNESS THE KEYNOTE IN DODGE LUXURY LINERS

Style Surprises And Mechanical Innovations Distinguish Cars Celebrating The Company's Silver Anniversary.

The 1939 line of Dodge passenger automobiles will be viewed with lively interest, partly because it presents a number of style surprises and mechanical innovations, and also because the newest of Dodge cars is the company's Silver Anniversary model to which engineers, style leaders and production experts, stimulated no doubt by extra pride and sentiment, are said to have devoted their utmost skill and effort.

So marked appears the regard which the manufacturers have given to the attainment of new streamlined beauty and exceptional luxuries, that there seems to be ample justification for announcing the new car as the "Dodge Luxury Liner."

To the show visitor examining the cars for the first time, only the nameplate and the familiar Rocky Mountain Ram which for years has served as Dodge radiator ornament, suggest the car's identity. Everything else is new and different — body contours, hood lines, front grilles, fenders, lamps, windshield, front wheel springing, running boards—even the tire pattern differs from that used on preceding Dodge models.

The gracefully proportioned rear sweep of the all-steel bodies completely conceals a 27 per cent larger luggage compartment. The driving compartment is clear of gear shift and parking brake levers. It is evident that Dodge designers have made a clean break with the past and now exhibit an entirely new, ultra-modern car of remarkable attraction.

New Model Is Larger

The new Dodge is longer in wheelbase and wider in body, two circumstances which have been turned to advantage in the interiors—in wider seats, increased leg and elbow space, and in markedly greater visibility.

In designing the chassi of the new Dodge Luxury Liner, engineers have provided a new frame with six-inch side members. The greatest change is noted in the heavier front end of the new frame, which now accommodates an individual-action front-wheel suspension using a pair of tough yet resilient coil springs of Amola, the sensational new steel also used extensively in the manufacture of Dodge wheel shafts, transmission and drive gears, and in many other vital parts. In securing the closest approach to ideal weight distribution, the front and rear seats are located in the cradled area between front and rear wheels.

The hood section of the new model expresses new beauty as well as aero-dynamic advantages resulting from extensive wind-tunnel studies. At the lower forward end or catwalk, artistically spaced transverse ventilating slots are delineated by polished chromium strips. In the gracefully tapering bow, lengthwise slots are separated by a broad chromium band curving upward toward the radiator ornament. The effect is one of grace and symmetry which have practical values in substantially reduced wind resistance and in fuel economy gains.

Front Suspension Changed

In the new Dodge individual-action front springing, road vibration is leveled out by sturdy, matched, rust-proofed coil springs of Amola steel. There is no front axle and therefore no common support for right and left front wheels. Each wheel is free to move up or down in conformity with the road surface, independent of the opposite wheel.

An important adjunct of the front suspension is a steering mechanism that has neither Pitman arm nor drag link, but employs a Y-shaped steering arm moving horizontally, crosswise to the frame. The steering linkage appears simple, extremely short and direct, so that the steering action is sure and steady, and free from vibration. The steering, basically of the worm-and-roller-tooth type, is said to be 28 per cent easier, due to mechanical features and to a change in steering ratio from 14.6 to 18.2.

The rear suspension of the Dodge Luxury Liner employs thin-leaf, semi - elliptic, squeakless springs of Amola steel. The spring suspension is augmented by four airplane type, double-action hydraulic shock absorbers.

The road wheels—pierced for four instead of three chain straps—are of new, thicker steel section. Hub caps are of new design and incorporate a variant of the Dodge Rocky Mountain Ram trademark. The tires have specially ribbed side walls and widened treads, with seven grooves in front and non-skid pattern in the rear.

Safety In Vision

The V-type "airplane vision" windshield also is of entirely new design: it is mounted between trimmed-down corner posts, is wider and higher, giving 23 per cent more glass area. The windshield wiper action is electric and constant in speed, regardless of engine vacuum.

The unusual visibility forward is matched by similar side visibility through wide wndows in the sides and rear. The entire body construction is without blind spots likely to interfere with unobstructed vision in all directions.

Slam Taken Out Of Doors

Several interesting details distinguish the doors. The front doors enhance the smoothness of the body structure by having the upper hinges completely concealed. The lower edges of the doors are provided with a flare. When the doors are closed, this flare increases the streamling effect by narrowing the running boards; it also acts as additional weather seal. When the doors are opened, the flared edge uncovers the full width of the rubber-sheathed running boards which then afford safe steps for entrance and exit.

The old-time slam has been taken out of the doors by equipping them with new-style rotary, self-tightening locks. Still another safety feature built into the doors consists of ingenious supplementary, button - operated door locks mounted in the window sills, through the garnish moldings. When the buttons are pushed down, the door handles are locked, inside and out. Only when the buttons are lifted can the door handles be operated. This detail is one sure to be appreciated by motorists transporting children who thus are effectively protected from dangers incident to accidental or playful opening of doors.

Light For Night Driving

In keeping with other features of streamlining, the headiamps of the new Dodge Luxury Liners are recessed in the forward curves of the front fenders, flush with the surface. The arrangement results in several advantages; one of these is that the driving lights are 13 inches farther apart and illuminate the entire width of the road; another advantage is that the lamps are closer to the ground where they give safer road illuminating in hazy or foggy weather and cause little or no glare. The bright driving beam may be modified for "passing" by a foot swith which cuts out the straight-ahead driving beam and substitutes a passing beam equal in brightness, but tilted downward and over toward the right shoulder of the road. Tail lamps are set flush into rear fenders.

A noteworthy service convenience is incorporated in the design of the hood which is unlocked by the conventional handle, but lifts only the top section, leaving the sides in place. The hood covers are provided with automatic stays, one on each side, which hold the lifted hood in locked position during servicing.

Dodge bodies are doubly insulated—against heat and cold, by the liberal use of linings of felt and other materials—and against road noises and operating vibrations by fourteen "hush points" of live rubber which keep chasis and bodies out of actual metal-to-metal contact.

Dodge Engine Improvements

The hydraulic brakes of Dodge have been further improved by relocating air-cooling ribs and redesigning the brake drums to give the brake action a better "feel".

Especially noteworthy among engine improvements are new auto-thermic pistons. Because these new pistons are lighter and also carry lighter piston pins, the loads on main and connecting rod bearings are reduced. The new pistons, of the steel-strut type and cam-ground for most effective expansion, are surface-coated with a low-friction metal of great durability. Because of the coating, the pistons close in upon the cylinder walls; because of the cam design and reduced friction, the pistons maintain their original clearances over greatly lengthened periods.

Two of the four piston rings, the compression rings, also are surface-coated, the coating serving as a lubricant as well as compression seal.

The Dodge engine itself, having a bore of 3-¼ inch, a stroke of 4-⅜ inch, and a compression ratio of 6.5 normally develops a maximum of 87 horsepower. The famous "floating power" engine mountings are used, with improvements making them still more effective. Other engine improvements are a new manifold riser, a new down-draft carburetor connected to a double-unit air cleaner and intake silencer—and tappet screws which are self-locking. The exhaust valve seats are formed by inserts of special alloy steel said to reduce the need for valve grinding to the very minimum.

Many Automatic Features

Dodge engineers have gone to considerable lengths in making the operation of their cars as free as possible from manipulations formerly calling for driving judgment and experience. Thus there are: automatic engine choke, automatic spark advance, automatic carburetor heat control, automatic regulation of cooling water circulation, etc.

The operation of the clutch has been further improved by equipping the clutch pedal with an over-center spring control, so connected that when the pedal is depressed and passes a certain midway point, the power of a balanced coil spring is added to the pressure of the driver's foot; clutch action is both eased and speeded up by these means.

Many Inside Luxuries

Inside its streamlined bodies, the Dodge Luxury Liner achieves a fine method of upholstering and trimming. Fabrics covering wider seats are attached with an attractive tailored effect. The front seats have wider range of adjustment forward and back, the front seats being arranged to tilt upward as they are moved toward the instrument panel.

The most intriguing feature of the instrument panel is the Dodge "safety-light" speedometer; its indicating member consists of a small bead which moves over an illuminated dial as the speed of the car goes up or down. For speeds up to 30 miles an hour, the color of the tell-tale bead is green; from 30 to 50 miles an hour the color of the bead is amber; for speeds above 50 miles the bead is red.

In the center of the instrument panel is a removable section to accommodate a radio receiver. The panel also features a tiny headlight annunciator light, a push button lock for the glove compartment; an ash tray on the top ledge of the instrument panel may be opened and shut with thickly gloved hands.

In the driving compartment one notes a wide expanse of unobstructed leg room. The parking brake lever, of the pistol-grip type, is located below the instrumental panel, at the left of the steering column. The gearshift affords a new, easy way to change speeds, with an inbuilt control near the steering wheel. As the arc of the gearshift handle coincides with the circumference of the steering wheel, the gearshift—which is of the H-pattern familiar to all motorists—is quick and extremely handy.

The transmission gears are cut from dropforged blanks of Amola steel. The ring gear, pinion and differential gears of the rear drive, also are of Amola steel, the drive itself being of the hypoid type, silent and of great strength.

The fuel system of the new Dodge Luxury Liner includes a new, larger carburetor, supplied through a mechanical fuel pump. The 18-gallon gasoline tank is fashioned of two steel sections, which are not soldered together, but welded in a manner preventing corrosion due to chemical action. The Dodge Luxury Liner offers three body styles—4-door sedan, 2-door sedan and coupe. The Luxury Liner deluxe series offers six body types—4-door sedan, 2-door sedan, coupe, coupe for four—and two 7-passenger models, one a sedan, the other a limousine.

In every 100 American families, 27 have two members, 45 have three or four, 19 have five or six, and nine have seven or more members.

A Royal Decree-Law published in the Italian Official Gazette requires that all new power plants be built so they can use gas, solid fuel, or electric power.

Buick Gear Control Is Feature

SIMPLICITY, with complete comfort and safety characterize the controls of the 1939 Buick cars. This photograph shows the Handi-shift transmission lever mounted on the steering column under the wheel, legible instruments directly in front of the driver, horn ring flush with steering wheel spokes, and hand brake lever mounted under the panel. Mounting of the gear shift lever under the wheel not only clears the front compartment, but adds greatly to the ease of shifting and the pleasure of driving. On the lever, close to the driver's hand, is a flip-switch that operates Buick's new safety direction signal.

New Plymouth "Roadking" 2-Door Sedan

Built on a bigger, 114-inch wheelbase, this Plymouth "Roadking" for 1939 introduces still greater luxury for the lowest price field. For improved lighting, headlamps are streamlined into bigger, more massive fenders. A new "Vee" windshield adds more than six inches to body length above the belt. Improvements this year include new, softer-acting coil springs of Amola steel; new high-torque engine performance; new "true-steady" steering and a new "safety-signal" speedometer with built-in warning lights. A green light turns to amber at 30 m.p.h., and above 50 shines a warning red. This is the "Roadking" Two-Door Touring Sedan.

1939 Pontiac De Luxe Six Four-Door Sedan . . . Styled in the modern manner with or without running boards . . . Curb-high floors, two inches lower than last year . . . Four inches greater over-all length than any previous Pontiac Six . . . 25 per cent greater visibility . . . Wider, roomier bodies . . . Silver Streak . . . Remote control gear shift standard equipment . . . New clutch . . . Duflex rear springs, newest Pontiac feature, that give one passenger the same easy riding comfort as six passengers.

Evening Capital

ANNAPOLIS, MD.
1884 -:- 1938

Published Daily Except Sunday by
THE CAPITAL-GAZETTE PRESS, INCORPORATED

TALBOT T. SPEER President
DAVID S. JENKINS Vice-President and Treasurer
E. M. JACKSON, JR., City Editor

You can have the EVENING CAPITAL mailed to you when away from the city by leaving your name and address at the office, for 45 cents per month; $5.00 per year payable in advance, to any postoffice in the United States or Canada.
Delivered in Annapolis, Eastport, Germantown and West Annapolis by Carrier for 45 cents per month. On sale at all newsstands.

Foreign Advertising Representative
J. J. DEVINE & ASSOCIATES, Inc.
New York—1332 Chrysler Bldg.   Atlanta—286 Palmer Bldg.
Chicago—307 N. Michigan Ave.   Pittsburgh—428 Oliver Bldg.
Detroit—617 New Center Bldg.   Syracuse—State Tower Bldg.

Entered as Second Class Matter May 28, 1903, at the Post Office of Annapolis, Maryland under the Act of March 5, 1879.

MEMBER OF THE ASSOCIATED PRESS
The Associated Press is exclusively entitled to the use for re-publication of all news credited to it or not otherwise credited in this paper and also the local news published herein. All rights of re-publication of special dispatches herein are also reserved.

THURSDAY, DECEMBER 15, 1938.

THE BENEVOLENT SEASON

During the Christmas season, citizens of Annapolis are called on to give generously to charity.

The Christmas spirit which prompts such generous activities is said to bring more happiness to the giver than to those who receive. But this does not mean that gifts should be planned to please the giver with little reference to the needs and hopes of the beneficiary.

Children look to their parents first for gifts at Christmas. For this reason it is usually best to give to needy children through their parents. It is well to remember that families in need on Christmas are likely to be in more dire need on other days of the year. For these families the gift that would be more appreciated and beneficial would be employment for the breadwinners, medical care for the sick and institutional care for those needing it.

A Christmas dinner is always a source of cheer, but if it is not backed up by some more permanent relief or effort at rehabilitation it proves to be shortlived comfort.

Toast To The King Marks Eden's Visit

(Continued on Page 2)

tyn Becket, and Ronald Free, Dr. Hugh H. Young and Mrs. John Garrett.

At the door of the Colonial mansion, built by Mathias Hammond in 1774, during the administration of Sir Robert, the British diplomat was greeted by Gov. Harry W. Nice, Rear-Admiral Wilson Brown, superintendent of the Naval Academy; Mrs. Harry R. Slack, former president of the Federated Garden Clubs. He received a "key to the city" from Mayor Louis N. Phipps, as he ascended the steps of the home.

Building Crowded

Every room in the mansion was crowded by representatives of the Pilgrimage committee of the Federated Garden Clubs, the Society of Colonial Wars, Society of the Ark and the Dove, the Historical Society of Maryland, and other historical groups.

After examining the dining room and the Colonial kitchen, the Eden party went to the ballroom on the second floor. Mrs. Slack presented Senator George Radcliffe, who introduced Eden to his radio audience. The Senator reviewed the career of Sir Robert and pointed out that the Provincial Governor was a friend of George Washington, who headed the Continental Army in the Revolution. He said that Sir Robert and Washington attended many horse races here.

Grateful For Welcome

"I am most grateful for your friendly welcome," Eden said. "I cannot feel altogether a stranger. In a measure it is like coming home, indeed this is an occasion in which any Englishman could take pride.

"I like to think that Maryland was a center of religious and political toleration.

"I like to think that my ancestor was a friend of those he was called upon to govern and they were his friends.

"I like to think that he understood the American point of view and in a large measure sympathized with it.

"I like to think of his friendship with George Washington, indeed a mutual love of horse racing is a pretty good basis of friendship.

"I like to think of those historic days of which we can both be proud."

Center of Society

Mrs. Slack pointed out that Sir Robert was a brother-in-law of the sixth Lord Baltimore, and during this rule of the colony from 1769 to 1776, with his wife, Caroline Calvert, was the center of the charming social life of Colonial Annapolis.

"Governor Eden possessed the confidence of the Colonists to a very unusual extent and the break between Maryland and Great Britain was attended with less feeling and disorder than in other colonies.

"Governor Eden dined frequently with some of the patriotic leaders. One of his hosts was Mathias Hammond, the builder of this house."

'Old Glasses Used'

The glasses from which the toasts to the King and President were drunk were early English.

Silver service used was made in 1750 by Paul LaMerie, while china plates on which cakes were served were brought from Worcester, England, by William Pinkney, first American minister to the Court of St. James. They were brought to the house for the occasion by Mrs. Miles White, Jr., of Baltimore.

After leaving the Hammond-Harwood House, the Eden party

Constipated?

"For years I had constipation, awful gas bloating, headaches and back pains. Adlerika helped right away. Now, I eat sausage, bananas, pie, anything I want. Never felt better." Mrs. Mabel Schott.

ADLERIKA
At All Leading Druggists.

drove through the Naval Academy and then went to Shipwright street to the Convent of the Sisters of Notre Dame. In a room in this house, built in 1765 by Dr. Upton Scott, Sir Robert Eden died in 1784. The room is now used as a chapel.

Views Communion Service

Mrs. Beauregard Clark, of Jessups, a descendant of Dr. Scott, attended the ceremonies. She said when Sir Robert died, Dr. Scott took the body at night to the old St. Margaret's church at Winchester, where it was buried beneath the chancel. It was located by Daniel R. Randall, former postmaster, and interred in the St. Anne's churchyard, in 1926.

The Rev. Dr. Darlington Johnson, rector of St. Anne's, met Eden and his party, as they arrived at the church. He exhibited the Colonial records of the church, including a silver communion service presented by King William III. He gave Eden and other members of the party souvenirs including a history of Annapolis and

Places Wreath

Standing bareheaded in the churchyard, Eden laid a wreath of evergreen at the base of his ancestor's tomb. With his wife he stood a few moments in silent reverence, before entering his automobile and leaving for Baltimore.

The wreath was presented by Mrs. Francis Beirne, daughter of Daniel R. Randall, and member of the Federated Garden Clubs.

Eden, after presentation of a scroll and emblem of the Society

recipes used in Colonial Days.

of the Ark and the Dove, was also presented with two volumes of Maryland history.

The area of Rumaria was more than doubled as the result of the Second Balkan war and the World war.

ORDER NISI

In Anne Arundel County Orphans' Court.

December 13th, 1938.
Ordered, That the Sale of the Real Estate of Carolyn L. Healy, infant, made by Carolyn L. Healy, Guardian, to the State Roads Commission, and this day reported to this Court, by the said Guardian, be ratified and confirmed, unless cause be shown to the contrary, on or before the 8TH DAY OF JANUARY, next. Provided, a copy of this order be inserted in some newspaper published in the City of Annapolis, Anne Arundel County, at least once a week for three successive weeks before the said 5th day of January, next.

The Report states the Amount of sales to be $460.00.

MAYNARD CARR, C. J.
GWAIN E. OWENS, A. J.
WILLIAM H. ELLIOTT, A. J.
Judges

True Copy Test:
R. GLENN PROUT
R. GLENN PROUT,
Register of Wills for Anne Arundel County   d-29

BUSINESS DIRECTORY

The services offered by the following Annapolis firms have been investigated by THE EVENING CAPITAL and found to be satisfactory.

ROOMS AND APARTMENTS

By Day, Week or Month
Desirable Rooms and Apartments
COOPER APARTMENTS CORP.
Dial 2251   2 Maryland Ave.

PRINTING

Dial 2332 and our representative will gladly call to give you prices on fine business printing.
CAPITAL-GAZETTE PRESS, INC.

BUILDERS & CONTRACTORS

BUILDERS AND CONTRACTORS
Save money on cinder and cement blocks. Delivered in Annapolis. Independent or exclusive contract. Write CINDECRETE CORP.
Halethorpe, Md., or Phone Arbutus 366   d-22

NOTICE TO CREDITORS

Notice is hereby given that the Subscriber, of Anne Arundel County, has obtained from the Orphans' Court of Anne Arundel County, in Maryland, Letters of Administration c.t.a. on the personal estate of

THOMAS D. GRIFFIN

late of Anne Arundel County, deceased. All persons having claims against the deceased, are hereby warned to exhibit the same, with the vouchers thereof, to the subscriber, on or before the 16TH DAY OF MAY, 1939. They may otherwise, by law, be excluded from all benefit of said estate. All persons indebted to said estate are requested to make immediate payment. Given under my hand this 16th day of November, 1938.

THOMAS C. GRIFFIN,
Administrator, c.t.a.   d-22

Texas cities estimate the State is losing $200,000 a year from people who ship their cigarettes into the State by parcel post to avoid paying the State cigarette tax.

Home of the
U. S. NAVAL ACADEMY
and
ST. JOHN'S COLLEGE

ANNAPOLIS Evening Capital

VOL. CVIII — No. 50. | ESTABLISHED IN 1884 —PUBLISHED EVERY EVENING EXCEPT SUNDAY | ANNAPOLIS, THURSDAY, JANUARY 12, 1939. | SOUTHERN MARYLAND'S ONLY DAILY PAPER | PRICE TWO CENTS.

Weather Forecast
Snow in west and rain or snow in east portion late tonight and Friday; colder tonight.

GOVERNOR O'CONOR TAKES HIS OATH OF OFFICE

Herbert R. O'Conor was sworn in as sixtieth Governor of Maryland by Chief Judge Carroll T. Bond yesterday while former Governor Harry W. Nice watched the audience impassively. The Associated Press

O'CONOR TO SPEED WORK ON MEASURES

Starts First Day By Appointing Commission To Study Magistrate's System — Will Send Budget To Legislature Early — Has Bills On Re-Organization Prepared.

HOPES TO STOP LEGISLATIVE JAM

Gov. Herbert R. O'Conor, calm and smiling after the stress of his inaugural and the victory acclaim of his supporters, today launched his administration with characteristic energy, taking up a number of the more important problems facing the State.

Showing no apparent effect from the strain of swearing in, with the strenuous schedule that included shaking the hands of thousands of well-wishers, he reported to the executive office in the State House at 9 A. M. and immediately launched upon his duties.

Has Bills Prepared

He took steps to have the Attorney-General's office begin preparation of measures necessary to carry out the State governmental re-organization plan recommended by the Bowman Commission. It is expected that several measures bearing on the plan will be ready for submission to the Legislature when it reconvenes at 8 P. M. Tuesday.

The new Governor said he had determined to have the bills prepared by the Attorney-General's office, because of his confidence in the personnel and the necessity of having the constitutionality passed on before submission to the Legislature.

Forms Commission

He also began the formation of a committee to make a complete study of magistrates' courts in the State, in line with his campaign pledge to reform the present conditions under which the Justices of the Peace are appointed and operate.

In addition to speeding these plans, he took steps to have the budget laid before the Legislature some time in advance of the limit he is allowed by the State Constitution. He said he would like to get the Legislative committees at work on the budget so that they can clear it as soon as possible, thus opening the way

(Continued on Page 2)

CONSERVATION PROGRAM

HANCOCK, Md., Jan. 12 — A statewide conservation program and proposals for a national or State park in the Blue Ridge Mountains of Western Maryland will be laid before business men and civic leaders of this section at a meeting here Monday.

HOUSEKEEPER AVAILABLE

Middle-aged woman desires position as housekeeper. Excellent cook. Will stay in. Write Box 96. Evening Capital.

Salt Water Oysters
FRESH FISH
Campbell Seafood Co.
DIAL 2814 CITY MARKET
We Deliver

WARDOUR
DESIRABLE HOME SITES
¼ To Acre Tracts
$100 Cash — Easy Monthly Payments
CHAS. F. LEE
Dial 2461 For Appointment

NEW BUNGALOW
HORN POINT, EASTPORT
Five rooms, finished basement, weather-stripping and storm windows, lot 53 x 125. Owner leaving city.
SERVICE AGENTS, INC
SEE F. E. VOGES or H. H. LITTLE
47 Md. Ave. — Dial 4477

FOR SALE
' Cherry Grove Avenue N. Bungalow. 3 bedrooms. Modern, with oil heat garage, large lot. Price reasonable.
JULIAN BREWER AND SON
Joseph D. Lazenby
9 School St. Dial 2685

PYTHIAN SISTERS INSTALL OFFICERS

Out-Of-Town Visitors See Ceremonies—Mrs. Frances Cantler Takes Post

The Pythian Sisters of Friendship Temple No. 6 of Maryland, had installation of officers on January 9. A large number of members were present, as well as out-of-town visitors.

Grand Chief, R. Buddemier, of Baltimore, gave a talk and wished the Temple success in the coming year.

Visitors Here

Among the out-of-town visitors were: Grand Keeper of Records, and Seals, Elwood Martak, Mrs. Martak and Mrs. L. Leary, of Cumberland. Other Grand Temple officers from the local Temple were: May Brooks, Grand Trustee, District Deputy Grand Chief, Alice Williams, and Grand Mistress of Records and Correspondence, Emma Parker.

Supreme Representative Joseph Parker, of the Knights of Pythias, was present also.

Install Officers

The officers installed were: Past Chief Frances Cantler, Most Excellent Chief, Mildred Wooding, Excellent Senior, M. Huth, Excellent Junior, Katheryn Stewart, Mistress of Records and Correspondence, Alice Williams, Mistress of Finance, May Brooks, Protector, Mary Russell, Guard Shirley Snyder.

Preceding the meeting, a delicious turkey supper was served. After the meeting a Christmas and Cheerio party was held when each member found out, through the exchange of presents, who had been their "Cheerio" for the past year.

INSTALL OFFICERS OF MASONIC ORDER ON MONDAY NIGHT

Preceded by a delicious dinner served under the direction of William H. Weaver, the officers of Mount Vernon Royal Arch Chapter were installed on last Monday evening at the Masonic Temple, the ceremony being performed by the grand officers with Grover L. Michael, of Frederick, presiding as Grand High Priest.

The officers installed were as follows: Edgar F. Donaldson, High Priest; Orville W. McNamara, King; Jacob P. Wohlgemuth, Scribe; John F. Brooks, treasurer; D. Ross Vansant, Jr., secretary; Roland R. Thomas, Captain of the Host; Edward G. Chaney, Principal Sojourner; Clint W. Ticknor, Royal Arch Captain; George W. Sullivan, Master of the 3rd Veil; John J. Flood, Master of the 2nd Veil; Norman B. Wells, Master of the 1st Veil and William H. Weaver, Sentinel.

Announcement at the meeting was made of the appointment of Hanford L. Sarles as Grand Inspector to succeed Clarence B. McCrane.

Fourteen of the eighteen living past presiding officers were present in addition to a large number of members and visitors.

Accountant
Will audit and prepare books or fiscal statements—including Federal and State Income Tax for 1938.
Will work evenings. Phone 2514

CARD PARTY
Given by
CAPITAL COUNCIL NO. 92,
DAUGHTERS OF AMERICA
Maryland Hotel
TONIGHT—8:15 O'CLOCK
Admission 35c

The Dixie Farm
On Defense Highway
POULTRY—EGG SERVICE
Choice Week-end Selection.
Our Meaty, Milk-cornfed
WHITE PEKIN DUCKLINGS
Wt. 4½ to 5 lb. ave.—30c lb.
BARRED ROCK BROILERS
Wt. 2 to 2¼ lb. ave.—35c lb.
(Both items only 11 weeks old)
—BAKING HENS—
Dial 2912

HOUSE GROUP VOTES TO CUT RELIEF MONEY

Appropriations Committee Contends Thousands On WPA Rolls Neither Rightfully Nor Justifiably—Roosevelt's Request Presages Condition Out of Harmony With Actuality.

REPUBLICANS ASK FURTHER SLASH

(By The Associated Press)

WASHINGTON, Jan. 12 — The House Appropriations Committee, contending that WPA rolls carry "thousands neither rightfully nor justifiably thereon," formally recommended today a $725,000,000 appropriation to keep the relief agency going until June 30.

The full committee thus went along with a subcommittee in a revolt against the Administration's spending program.

Out Of Harmony

President Roosevelt had asked $875,000,000 for WPA but that figure, the committee said, "presages a continued degree of unemployment out of harmony with general recovery indications."

Four Republican committeemen, asserting that "a national scandal requires immediate action," went even farther. They said in a minority report that funds should be

(Continued on Page 4)

P.-T. A. PLANNING STUDENTS' PARTY

A novel and amusing party will be given for the students of the Annapolis High School by the High School P.T.A. on Friday at 7:45 P. M. in the boys' gymnasium.

This party is called an Indoor Track Meet, but is quite different from any other track meet, in that, no special athletic ability is required, and a hilarious time is had by all.

Some of the Judges will be: Dr. Howard Kinhart, Judge Ridgely P. Melvin, R. C. Lamb, H. B. Winchell, Mrs. Charles Payne, George Beneze, Henry Ortland, A. Gordon Fleet, Joseph Sheff and Alfred Roth. All High School students have been invited.

A small admittance fee will be charged to pay for the prizes. Hot Dogs, pop corn, and other refreshments will be sold between halves

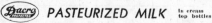

Tubercular Group To Meet Thursday

The Executive Committee of the Anne Arundel County Tuberculosis Association will meet on Thursday, January 19 at 10:30 A. M. in the Green Street building.

DUCE WILL DEMAND JUSTICE FOR PEACE

Mussolini Expected To Require Settlement Of Colonial Desires

(By The Associated Press)

ROME, Jan. 12—Premier Mussolini presents to Prime Minister Chamberlain today his demands upon Europe, constituting, in effect, a definition of the "justice" which he sets as the price of peace and likely revolving about control of the Mediterranean and colonial concessions.

Mussolini laid down the policy of "peace founded on justice" in a friendly toast at the banquet he gave the British minister last night.

Chamberlain, in an answering toast, said his way was for a "just and peaceful solution of international difficulties by the method of negotiation."

The two talked informally for 90 minutes yesterday. The chatted again after the banquet. The formal conference today included, as did the previous discussions, Foreign Ministers Lord Halifax and Count Galeazzo Ciano, Mussolini's son-in-law.

Count Ciano received Lord Halifax, Sir Alexander Cadogan, British Permanent Undersecretary of Foreign Affairs, and Sir Noel Charles, counselor of the British Embassy, an hour before the formal program started with a visit by Chamberlain and Viscount Halifax to leave wreaths at the pantheon of Italian Kings and the Unknown Soldier's Tomb.

The presence of Sir Alexander was believed to indicate that the preliminary talks dealt with Italian desire for concessions in French Africa and perhaps with the Spanish war.

COUNCIL TO HOLD SPECIAL MEETING ON MARKET RENTS

There will be a special meeting of City Council tonight for the purpose of determining what action will be taken regarding the occupants of the City Market who are in arrears in their rent.

Mayor Louis N. Phipps will preside and when asked today if he would tender his resignation to the Council in order to take his seat in the State Senate, he said he had not made any decision yet.

Navy Fleet In Canal Zone

(By The Associated Press)

CRISTOBAL, Canal Zone, Jan. 11—The first squadron of a United States navy fleet of 48 patrol bombers ended a 3,000-mile non-stop flight from San Diego today, landing at the Coco Solo military airfield.

They were the first of four squadrons winging their way down the Pacific Coast in a test flight.

The planes left San Diego yesterday at 2:12 EST.

PHIPPS, MRS. PAYNE TO ADDRESS LEAGUE OF WOMEN VOTERS FRI.

The League of Women Voters will hold a meeting with several points of interest Friday afternoon at 2:30 P. M. in the Old Senate Building of the State House.

Mrs. John M. Green, president of the League announces the following program, arranged by Mrs. St. George Barber, chairman of the committee on arrangements:

Talk by Mayor Louis N. Phipps, Senator-elect from Anne Arundel county, on his plans for legislation for Anne Arundel county and the State.

Comment by Mrs. Edna Payne on Legislation proposed by the local and State groups of Women Voters, together with comment on the Anne Arundel County School Board. Mrs. Payne is a member of the Board of Education.

JORDAN DORSEY IS NAMED CLUB HEAD

T. Jordan Dorsey, recent candidate for Sheriff, will head the West Annapolis Democratic club for the coming year.

Other officers elected were Alonzo Smith, vice-president; Robert Smith, secretary; Guy Frank, assistant secretary; C. L. Logan, treasurer.

The following were named to the Board of Directors: W. F. Casey, Thomas Jackson, Amos Lorens.

The House Committee was elected as follows: Howard Finkle, A. W. Phillips, Frank Reese, James Lorens, Jr., Adam Kornberger.

At the meeting the club arranged its program for the coming year.

YACHT CLUB WILL ELECT OFFICERS

The Annapolis Yacht Club will hold its annual meeting and election of officers at the club tonight at 8 P. M. Refreshments will be served following the election.

Current officers of the club are:
Commodore—Dr. J. Willis Martin
Vice-commodore—William H. Labrot
Rear-commodore—Louis N. Phipps
Fleet Captain—Peter H. Magruder
Secretary—C. C. Slayton
Treasurer—John C. Hyde

Mrs. Hall Hostess To Church Guild

The regular meeting of St. Margarett's Guild, was held yesterday afternoon, at the home of Mrs. Clifford Hall at Wardour.

Plans were made for a bake sale to be held Thursday, January 19 at Ridout's Store, beginning at 9 A. M. Miss Margaret Ridout is chairman and is being assisted by Mrs. Hall.

COMMITTEE HONORS GO TO A. A. MEN

County Delegation In Maryland Legislature Gains Most Important Committee Posts County Has Held In Number Of Years.

ALL LOCAL REQUESTS GRANTED BY SPEAKER

The Anne Arundel County delegation gained the most important committee appointments that the Speaker of the House has ever given to local representatives.

The county is represented on every important committee and gained two chairmanships. The delegation, with the support of Frank S. Revell, veteran party leader, requested certain committee appointments and Speaker Thomas E. Conlon granted all and added three others to the Anne Arundel group's allotment.

Delegation In Agreement

The local delegation had met and agreed among itself on committee requests, and being as large and solidly Democratic as any group in the Legislature, won its point. The Anne Arundel bloc was lined solidly behind Speaker Conlon in his fight for the presiding chair.

Speaker Conlon also announced that besides several State-wide appointments which will go to Anne Arundel county, that each Anne Arundel county delegate would have 20 days of patronage during the session. This will mean that the delegates can hire persons to their liking for door men and pages.

The Anne Arundel allotment in patronage was greater than the average given delegates in the Assembly, but is smaller than in pre-

(Continued on Page 4)

Democratic Women Assisted Visitors To City Yesterday

The Women's Democratic Club of Annapolis and Anne Arundel County entertained more than 100 visitors from Baltimore City and the counties of Maryland yesterday—inauguration day.

The club had rooms in State Circle open from 10 A. M. on and as they were attractive and warm and had a radio, many persons heard the complete inaugural ceremony there, while resting.

Mrs. George Abram Moss, president of the club, said that Miss Ethel Sullivan and her committee were busy during the day and more than 100 persons signed the guest book.

The windows of the club quarters proved an excellent vantage point from which to watch the parade.

Roosevelt Demands $552,000,000 For Defense Purposes

President Demands Big Sum Immediately To Build Up Army And Navy And To Strengthen Defense Positions—Fears "Offense Against Us."

(By The Associated Press)

WASHINGTON, Jan. 12—President Roosevelt asked Congress today for an immediate appropriation of $552,000,000 as the "minimum of requirements" for bulwarking the nation's defense against the "possibilities of present offense against us. Our existing forces are so utterly inadequate they must be immediately strengthened."

In a special message the President requested that the $525,000,000 be appropriated at once to be divided between the army and navy.

The fund would include $300,000 for a minimum increase of 3,000 in army plane strength.

He also asked for another $27,000,000 to provide an adequate "peace garrison for the Panama Canal," of which $5,000,000 would be for immediate use to begin necessary housing construction.

The total request, all of which would not be spent in one year, would boost the new budget for defense to $1,661,558,000, largest by far of any peace-time outlay.

MINIMUM REQUIREMENTS

"Devoid of all hysteria," the President said, "this program is but the minimum of requirements.

"I trust, therefore, that the Congress will quickly act on this emergency for the strengthening of the defense of the United States."

Mr. Roosevelt said that after entry into the World War the United States "had more than a year of absolute peace at home without any threat of attack on this continent" to prepare its fighting forces.

Not Ready In 1917

"Calling attention to these facts," the President said, "does not remotely intimate that the Congress or the President have any thought of taking part in another war on European soil, but it does show that in 1917 we were not ready to conduct large-scale land or air operations.

"Relatively we are not much more ready to do so today than we were then—and we cannot guarantee a long period free from attack in which we could prepare."

Of the $525,000,000 the President asked that $450,000,000 be allocated for new needs of the army, $65,000,000 for similar requirements of the navy, and $10,000,000 for training civil air pilots.

Army Fund

The $300,000,000 of the army should provide a minimum increase of 3,000 planes, he said, adding it was hoped that orders placed on a large scale will "materially reduce the unit cost and actually provide many more planes."

(The present authorized plane strength for the army is 2,3230.)

Of the $150,000,000 balance for the army, $110,000,000 would go for "critical items" of equipment such as anti-aircraft artillery, semi-automatic rifles, anti-tank guns, tanks, light and heavy artillery, ammunition and gas masks—all to equip regular army and national guard units.

A total of $32,000,000 would go for "educational orders" of the army—to "enable industry to prepare for quantity production in an emergency of those military items which are non-commercial in character and are so difficult of manufacture as to constitute what is known as 'bottlenecks' in the problem of procurement."

Continuing the President said:

"The balance should be used, I believe, for improving and strengthening the seacoast defenses of Panama, Hawaii and the continental United States, including the construction of a highway outside the limits of the

(Continued on Page 2)

CITY HAS TWO INAUGURATIONS ON SAME DAY

Samuel S. Stokes Installed As President Of Civitan Club At Ceremonies At Carvel Hall Last Night — Boy Scouts To Get Long Trip.

WILL VISIT WORLD'S FAIR AND CANADA

Governor O'Conor wasn't the only person inaugurated here yesterday.

The day's second inaugural ceremony took place at Carvel Hall last night as Samuel S. Stokes was inducted into the presidency of the Civitan Club.

With former District Governor George E. Rullman administering the ritual, Stokes, Main street merchant, took the presiding chair succeeding Robert L. Burwell, engineer of the Annapolis Metropolitan Sewerage Commission.

Burwell Lauded

The ceremony included comment by retiring President Burwell, a talk by Rullman who lauded the retiring officer's administration, and brief remarks by former Civitan president Dr. Robert S. G. Welch. Dr. Welch presented Burwell with a silver platter from the club members as a token of their esteem.

While the inaugural ceremonies in the State House were all Democratic, the Civitans were inaugura-

(Continued on Page 6)

Going South?
Naval Officer desires 5-passenger sedan equipped with radio and heater delivered to any point vicinity Florida after 22 January. Reference requested. Write Box 97, Evening Capital.

NOTICE TO FEDERAL EMPLOYEES
On Friday evening, January 13th, at 8:00 o'clock, in the Pythian Building, School street, the Federal Employees Union No. 124 will be addresed by Mr. A. F. Noyes, Director of Enrollment, Associated Hospital Service, of Baltimore, Inc. This Local is contemplating membership in this association and respectfully urges all members of the local and other Federal Employees interested in this Plan to be present to hear Mr. Noyes.

Dacro PROTECTED PASTEURIZED MILK In cream top bottles
BUTTERMILK COTTAGE CHEESE CREAM
LACTIC (Sour) CREAM CHOC-AU-LAIT (with vitamin D)
DAIRY ORANGEADE AND GRAPEADE
93 Score Anne Arundel Butter
The ANNAPOLIS DAIRY Products Co.
126 WEST STREET DIAL 2315
VISITORS ALWAYS WELCOME
Tune in "Annapolis News and Views"—WFBR—2 P. M. Sunday.

THIRTY-FIVE JOHNNIES ON STICK SQUAD

Donohue Prepares For Last Season With Five Veterans —First Game Set March 24 With Lehigh.

TEN CONTESTS SCHEDULED

St. John's College is prepared to open its last intercollegiate lacrosse season with approximately one fourth of the entire student body coming out for the squad.

Coach John Donohue said he has 35 men on the practice field, five of them veterans.

Game March 24

Facing a practice game with Lehigh on March 24 and a 10-game schedule beginning April 1, the Johnnies began practice last Monday and will continue through their impending spring vacation.

Fred Buck, all-Maryland player last year; Dick Snibbe and Les Medford, who have been playing together for three years, make up the close attack. Skip MacMillan, voted all-Maryland and third-team all-American in 1938, will be at midfield with Jim McQueen, converted attack man. Page Ball and Harry Hamilton, up from junior varsity, are fighting it out for the other midfield post.

Defense replacements are Donohue's biggest problem and he has tentatively picked Nelson Shawn, Mike Archie, and either Will Matz or Bill Hopps, with B. J. Todd tending goal. Shawn, who was captain of the basketball team, played varsity lacrosse in 1937 but was kept out last season with an injured knee, while Todd hung up a record for keeping the B squad net clean last year. Other promising B squad candidates include Bill King, Dannie Hill and Harold Reynolds.

Won Six Games Last Year

The Johnnies won six out of nine games last year and hope to better the record in what is to be their last season, since intercollegiate sports will be discontinued at the end of the school year.

Last year's stickmen handed the Mount Washington club its first defeat in five years and lost to B. A. C. by one point in the closing seconds of their game.

NAVY FENCERS WILL ENTER MEET FOR CHAMPIONSHIP

The Navy fencing team will compete in the Intercollegiate Fencing Championship Meet to be held in New York on March 31 and April 1.

The Navy fencers have a fine record so far this season having defeated all opponents to date, and having won the Epee, Sabre, and Three Weapon Championships in the Pentagonal meet competing against fencers from Army, Harvard, Princeton, and Yale.

HUGE SWAMP FIRE
(By The Associated Press)

FORT LAUDERDALE, Fla., March 15—A fire so huge that it generated rain slowly ate into nearly 15,000 acres of muck soil in the Everglades west of here today.

CRONIN SEEN BUILDING FOR FUTURE TEAM

Red Sox Gave Wealthy Owner Pleasant Surprise By Finishing Second Last Year—Had Tremendous Power At Plate.

LEFTY GROVE IS ON DOWN GRADE

By Gayle Talbot
(Associated Press Sports Writer)

SARASOTA, Fla., March 15—As a charter member of the group that thought Manager Joe Cronin of the Boston Red Sox took an outrageous gamble in turning loose Frank Higgins and Ben Chapman during the winter, I'm now about to relent to the extent of advising my fellow members to wait and see.

Maybe Cronin, who is preparing to start his fifth season as shortstop-manager of the gilded hose, knew exactly what he was doing. It's even highly probable that he knows more about baseball than any of the members of our club. But, still he's got to show me that he can send Higgins, a fine-fielding, .303-hitting third baseman to Detroit, and Chapman a .340-clubbing outfielder to Cleveland and still have as good an entry in the American League race.

Looking To Future

There is, of course, the probability that he was looking to the future, rather than to the 1939 flag race. Perhaps he feels, as several of his fellow pilots have been bold enough to admit, that the Yankees are a cinch for another season or two, anyway, so why not start cutting across to, say 1941 on the chance of nailing them there?

The Sox gave their wealthy young owner, Tom Yawkey, a pleasant surprise by finishing second last year, beating out the more favored Cleveland and Detroit clubs in the process. They won 88 games, only one less than Chicago needed to capture the National League pennant. But the Sox were a hopeless nine and one-half games behind the Yanks.

They had thunderous power at the plate: Jimmy Foxx, .349; Cronin, .325; Chapman, .340; Joe Vosmik, .324; Roger Cramer, .301; and Higgins, .303. But they didn't have enough good starting pitchers, so Cronin decided to give up some of their power to get the pitching he needed, and to gamble that he had replacements for Higgins and Chapman.

Veteran Pitchers

The pitchers he got were the veterans Elden Auker and Jake Wade from Detroit, and Denny Galehouse from Cleveland. The boys he hopes will make him forget the two stars he lost are Ted Williams, one of the most talked-of rookies of the year, who hit an impressive .366 for Minneapolis in 1938, and Jim Tabor, a promising young third sacker, also from Minneapolis, who hit .316 in 19 games with the Sox at the close of the season.

"The way I look at it," said Joe, "is that we still have everything we had last season, and have added pitching strength. I haven't any doubts about Williams and Tabor, and I know that Auker, Wade and Galehouse will improve our pitching."

Grove Is Failing

One thing that forced Cronin to reach out recklessly for pitchers was the indication that old Bob Grove's great left arm was headed for the last wind-up. The ageing wing cracked up in midrace last year, and there's yet no telling whether one of the game's outstanding pitchers will be ready to take his turn this season.

Other members of a staff that performed sensationally in streaks last year include Jack Wilson, Fred Ostermueller, Joe Heving and young Jim Bagby, who beat the Yankees in his first big league start. Outside of Woodrow Rich, who won 19 for Little Rock, there appear to be no outstanding prospects among the rookie moundsmen.

Gene Desautels is back to do the bulk of the catching, with John Peacock in support.

Hall of Fame

The Hall of Fame! The name has a magic sound. The Baseball Hall of Fame stands at Cooperstown, New York, where baseball was born, and designated by bronze plaques are those great men of the national game whose deeds will live forever in baseball memories. In this series, the story of what earned the great players their places in this Hall of Fame is told. As one of the features of Baseball's Centennial program this year, their plaques will be unveiled.

THE BIG BAM

Idols may come, others will go but there probably will never be another baseball idol like the Sultan of Swat — George Herman Ruth, "The Babe."

Babe Ruth was a pitcher with the Boston Red Sox, and a good one at that, when Ed Barrow, now head of the Yankees but then with the Sox, decided that there was a mighty hitter; one too good in

Babe Ruth

fact to get into the game on the infrequent occasions that a pitcher is called upon. And so Mr. Barrow converted the former Baltimore orphan boy into an outfielder. From that point on, most people forgot about Mr. Ruth's pitching. They just wanted to watch him slam home runs.

There weren't many at first, it is true. Four with Boston in 1915, three in 1916, just a couple in 1917, but in 1918 the total had climbed to 11, and in 1919 it was ascending still higher to 29. At this point, Col. Jacob Ruppert, owner of the Yankees, decided that New York wanted to see more of Ruth's batting prowess, so he bought the great hitter for a record price of $125,000.

Babe did not disappoint. In 1920, he knocked no fewer than 54 circuit smashes, and how the fans cheered as he took his bulky frame around the four bases. With his characteristic south-paw stance, the slugger connected for 59 homers in 1921, establishing a record, and giving American boyhood a brand new ambition in life. Ruth was now their unquestioned idol.

His years with the Yankees were marked with one triumph after another, culminated without any dispute in 1927 when he slammed a new all-time total of 60 home runs, a mark that still stands. Ruth became the great modern figure, an immortal along with Cobb, and Wagner and Lajoie.

He made a fortune for himself out of his homers. He reached his earning peak in 1930, when he signed a contract for $80,000. When Babe retired he still could hit them as hard as ever, but his legs were going back on him. He remains today one of the most popular and colorful figures the national game has ever had. And no wonder—he hit 729 home runs in his major league career, a mark far ahead of any other player.

He batted in 2,209 runs during his career; led the American League in homers for twelve years; hit 50 or more homers four seasons, and drew 2,056 bases on balls during his playing years, which certainly indicates how pitchers feared him. Ruth ranks with Ty Cobb as a record-maker, and he is tops as the Home Run King!

Yesterday's Results

At Tampa: Cincinnati (N) 9, St. Louis (N) 2.

SOFTBALL LEAGUE ELECTS M'NULTY

John F. McNulty, Jr., of Linthicum Heights, has been elected president of the Anne Arundel County Softball League.

McNulty has been active in sports for the past seven years, having been the youngest runner to place in the National Marathon a few years ago. In 1935 he won the Baltimore City 118-pound boxing championship and went on to be a finalist in the South Atlantic and National Guard championship bouts. In 1937 he won the award of being the best student in the C. M. T. C. training camp against a competition of 4,000.

Eight teams are to play in the league this summer and the winner of the playoff will enter for the P. A. L. championship in Baltimore.

There has been considerable interest shown in the league from all over the county.

FARR FINED $3,750 AND IS RE-INSTATED

(By The Associated Press)

LONDON, March 15 — Tommy Farr paid a fine of $3,750 and was reinstated today by the British Boxing Control Board. The fine was for failing to meet Max Schmeling, Oct. 14. Farr fights Red Burman of Baltimore at Harringay April 13.

Exhibition Baseball Today

At Tampa, Fla.: Cincinnati (N) vs. New York (A).

At St. Petersburg, Fla.: St. Louis (N) vs. Boston (N).

At New Baunfels, Tex.: Philadelphia (N) vs. St. Louis (A).

New Baseball Book Off Press

Centennial Edition Of Guide Offers Facts About Game In Convenient Form

Containing many new features in keeping with the observance of baseball's 100th anniversary, the Centennial Edition of The Dope Book, published by The Sporting News, St. Louis, Mo., has made its annual appearance as a prelude to the opening of the new playing season. Issued in handy vest-pocket size, this compact manual of the game, with cover printed in gold, is packed with facts and figures of interest to followers of the diamond sport.

Among the outstanding additions to The Dope Book, now in its twenty-third year of publication, are the following: Highlights of the game's 100-year history, the first written rules, changes in playing rules for 1939, box scores of Johnny Vander Meer's two successive no-hit games, yearly home-run leaders and players hitting home runs with bases filled.

Schedules of the larger leagues also are included, those of the majors being arranged in convenient day-by-day form. Other information embraces rosters of major league clubs, with ages, heights and weights, averages of major league leaders, World's Series facts and figures, 1938 All-Star game, All-Star team, No. 1 Men of the Year in 1938, and similar features giving fans a concise, authoritative record of the game.

The Dope Book is compiled from the official records as provided by the leagues. Copies may be obtained by sending 15 cents to C. C. Spink & Son, St. Louis, Mo.

REINA TAKES FIRST PLACE IN CITY LOOP

Station Ship Quintet Defeats Naval Hospital Last Night To Clinch Gold Trophy — Hyde Comes From Behind To Beat Columbia.

PLAYOFF SET FOR FRIDAY

The Reina Mercedes quintet took the City Basketball League title last night by defeating the Naval Hospital 42 to 32.

In the second game B. J. Hyde defeated Columbia 36 to 31 in an overtime game. Jack King's field goal in the last 40 seconds of play enabled Hyde to tie the score and go into an overtime period. Johnny Bland then shot two field goals to win.

Led All the Way

Reina experienced little trouble in defeating the Hospital five for they took the lead at the start and were never stopped. Once, in the early part of the second quarter the hospital men pulled up to within three points of their rivals. Baskets by Reagan and Pica, however, ended the threat and at the half Reina led by 25 to 16.

In the second half the Reina remained ten points ahead.

The Reina five will be presented with a gold trophy within the next two weeks.

Columbia Ahead At Half

In the Columbia-Hyde game the losers led all the way until the last quarter. Columbia took the lead at the start on Freeny's long shot from mid court and at the half were still leading, 17-12.

At the end of the third quarter Bland and Richard McNew pulled the plumbers to within five points of the leading Columbia.

In the last quarter Bland made a long shot to make the score 25-22. Bounelis fouled R. McNew and the throw was good. Bounelis then made a shot from the midcourt region to put the score at 27-23. With six minutes to play remaining Bland made another long one and Harry McNew made good a four shot. The plumbers then trailed by only one point.

Hyde Still Trailed

Joe Stehle fired a one-handed pivot shot from the foul line that pulled Columbia ahead. Jarrell shot one from under the basket and with 40 seconds remaining Hyde still trailed by two points.

The Hyde company is now tied for second place honors with the Henry B. Myers Company, for the second half of the league play. Hyde also was tied for second place in the first half of the season. This time they split honors with the Naval Hospital.

Friday night Hyde will play Myers and the winner of this game will meet the Hospital for the second-place trophy. Also on Friday Skipper Electric will play Columbia as a preliminary event.

Box scores:

Reina Mercedes	G	F	T
Bercaw, f	1	1- 2	3
Reagar, f	4	0- 0	8
Ruge, c	6	2- 5	14
Heminway, g	1	0- 0	2
Landrum, g	2	0- 2	4
Shuffler, g	1	0- 0	2
Pica, g	4	1- 2	9
Totals	19	4-11	42
Naval Hospital	**G**	**F**	**T**
Ratchford, f	2	2- 3	6

(Continued on Page 8)

Navy Seen As East's Best, But Harvard Remains In Picture

Middies, Near Record In New York On Saturday, Face Cornell Here On Saturday.

(By The Associated Press)

NEW YORK, May 1—From this early-season viewpoint, it begins to look as if the 1939 Eastern crew-racing season would come close to being a duplicate of last season with Navy and Harvard sharing the honors. But three regattas this week should make it clear whether such an indecisive duel is in prospect.

Those two were on top in 1938, with the Crimson edging out Navy for "sprint" honors by a very slight margin and each winning its climatic four-mile test, Navy at Poughkeepsie and Harvard against Yale at New London.

Navy Looks Best

So far this year, Navy looks the best. The midshipmen have conquered two fairly strong rivals, Princeton and Columbia, without much trouble. Harvard has had only one race, but showed all kinds of strength in breezing home ahead of Rutgers, M. I. T. and Boston University.

Victorious in their opening regattas last Saturday were Cornell and Pennsylvania, but neither had a real test.

This week Navy and Cornell come together in a dual test at Annapolis. Columbia, Pennsylvania and Yale clash in the Blackwell Cup race on the Housatonic at Derby, Conn., and the Compton Cup regatta at Cambridge brings together Harvard, Princeton, Massachusetts Tech and Syracuse. That accounts for all the "major" varsity eights in the East and should indicate the strongest.

Navy Has Class

After whipping a stubborn Princeton eight on the Severn's rough waters in its opener, Navy added to its prestige by breezing home a length and a half in front of Columbia on the smooth Harlem. Columbia, boating a number of veterans from the crew that was fourth at Poughkeepsie last June, was rated as a potentially strong eight, but it never could catch up. The midshipmen never raised their beat above 33 while rowing the mile and three quarters in 7:41.8, less than two seconds slower than the course record.

'MOVING DAY' FOR LAST OF NICE APPOINTEES

O'Conor Department Heads Prepare To Take Control

Officially, today was "moving day" for the last of former Gov. Harry W. Nice's Republican State department heads.

Actually, the change-over whereby Democrats took control was far from complete.

At 10 A. M., only one of Gov. Herbert R. O'Conor's May 1 appointees — Parole Commissioner Herman Moser—was at his desk.

Ezra Whitman, new chairman of the State Roads Commission, was "expected in some time today;" Daniel Clayland, incoming State Auditor, dropped in to see his office, but delayed his official oath-taking until 2 P. M.

Ober, Police Head

Miss Mary Risteau, former State Senator from Harford county, said she expected to take office as Loans Commissioner "as soon as I receive my commission." Her appointment was announced by the Governor last night.

Col. Beverly Ober, new commandant of State Police, will succeed Col. Elmer F. Munshower on June 1.

Although terms of the incumbent Labor Commissioner, Bank Commissioner, and Insurance Commissioner expired today, their successors have not yet been named. Governor O'Conor said he was still working on those departments.

"I want to avoid hurrying to fill these places," he explained. "I'm more anxious to get the right people by moving slowly and calmly."

Tax Commission

In June, he must fill a vacancy on the State Tax Commission. In July, the chairmanship of the State Racing Commission will be open to appointment.

Most of the important State posts carry terms dating from the first Monday in May, and uncertainty as to new department heads had lesser employes in a fret of conjecture and surmise. In past years, new appointees usually have taken office immediately, leaving no holdovers.

One Western Shoreman and one Eastern Shoreman are still be to named as Associate members of the State Roads Commission.

456 WEST POINTERS GRADUATE JUNE 12

WEST POINT, N. Y., May 1,—Graduation exercises at the United States Military Academy will be held on Monday, June 12, according to the June Week program published by Brigadier General Jay L. Benedict, superintendent. The June Week will extend from Monday, June 5 to June 12, this year, and will include the usual annual horseshow, presentation of awards, and alumni exercises, ending with the award of the Bachelor of Science degree and diplomas on Monday morning, at which time the graduating class will be sworn in as second lieutenants in the United States Army.

Included in the graduating class are cadets from forty-six states, the District of Columbia, Hawaii, Panama Canal Zone, Ecuador and Alaska. The states of Rhode Island and Arizona have no representative in the class this year.

The class of 456 cadets come from the following states:

Alabama, 3; Alaska, 1; Arkansas, 5; California, 21; Colorado, 3; Connecticut, 6; Delaware, 1; District of Columbia, 10; Ecuador, 2; Florida, 9; Georgia, 11; Hawaii, 5; Idaho, 4; Illinois, 22; Indiana, 12; Iowa, 6; Kansas, 11; Kentucky, 7; Louisiana, 10; Maine, 2; Maryland, 7, of the Marylanders two are from Annapolis and one each from Baltimore, Lutherville, Chevy Chase, Westminster and Chesapeake City; Massachusetts, 20; Michigan, 10; Minnesota, 10; Mississippi, 6; Missouri, 9; Montana, 2; Nebraska, 5; Nevada, 3; New Hampshire, 2; New Jersey, 16; New Mexico, 4; New York, 51; North Carolina, 7; North Dakota, 1; Ohio, 19; Oklahoma, 11; Oregon, 5; Panama Canal Zone, 3; Pennsylvania, 32; South Carolina, 7; South Dakota, 1; Tennessee, 9; Texas, 33; Utah, 5; Vermont, 2; Virginia, 7; Washington, 5; West Virginia, 5; Wisconsin, 5; Wyoming, 3.

FLEET RIDES IN FOR WORLD'S FAIR

Twenty-eight ships of the U. S. Navy's Atlantic squadron made an impressive sight as they cruised up the Hudson river in formation, to be on hand for the opening of the New York World's Fair. This aerial photograph was taken from above the New Jersey shore (foreground). Tall spire at right of center is the Empire State building; to the left of that are midtown skyscrapers, dominated by the thin tower of the Chrysler building. The fleet attracted thousends of sightseers.

Kidnaped?

Mrs. Edna Keil reported to Pittsburgh, Pa., police that her daughter, Ruth Luck, (above), 25-year-old stenographer, had been kidnaped by a jealous suitor just a week before her wedding to another man. The mother said bystanders saw the girl forced into an automobile and driven away while she screamed and struggled.

Old Homes Of City Open For Garden Tour

(Continued From Page One)

den House, Ogle House, Peggy Stewart House, Scott House and he Workman House.

The Texas group arriving here was somewhat smaller than expected as the train tour was not carried out. Due to the coal strike the special rates were withdrawn according to reports circulated here today.

Hitler

(Continued From Page One)

France's air force as a counterpart to Britain's expansion of her army and plans for military conscription.

In London, Foreign Secretary Viscount Halifax placed Poland's reaction to Hitler's speech before he Cabinet and was reported to have said British negotiations to bring Soviet Russia into the Anglo-French front were "making excellent progress."

Bills calling for military conscription of men aged 20 years for six months of training and enabling the government to call up reserve forces when it deems necessary were introduced in the House of Commons.

Germany And Italy Confer

Virginio Gayda, authoritative Italian editor, indicated Germany and Italy were working out a joint military plan to counter what he charged was an Anglo-English attempt at "encirclement."

The visit to Italy of Colonel-General Walther Von Brauchitsch, chief of staff of the German army, Gayda said, was for that purpose.

The possibility was raised in Warsaw that Poland might seek control of Danzig to block any German action toward forceful annexation. An article in the official Gazetta Polska was interpreted as meaning that Poland might ask the League of Nations—the nominal administrator to Danzig—to transfer certain of its rights to the Polish Government.

This followed reports that Hitler had backed up his demands for return of war-lost Danzig to Germany and a highway-railroad link through the Polish Corridor to East Prussia with specific details of what he wants.

Hitler made two May Day speeches, taking occasion to strike at American action against German goods.

WORLD FAIR OPENS; 600,000 PRESENT

NEW YORK, May 1 — New York's $160,000,000 World's Fair, which took three years to build, is here at last. Nearly 600,000 saw the opening yesterday.

The greatest international exposition in history—two square miles of Long Island embracing 300 gleaming buildings, 50 miles of roads and 35,000 employees—opened its gates yesterday to several hundred thousand visito s.

President Roosevelt headed a kaleidoscopic program of inaugural ceremonies, coming down from Hyde Park to proclaim the fair a token of America's spirit of friendship and peace toward all the world.

He spoke before about 40,000 special guests from a huge wooden stand on the steps of the $3,000,000 Federal Building which heads the fair's main avenue, "Constitution Hall," and dominates the "Court of Peace" formed by the imposing pavilions of a dozen nations.

At noon, two hours before, the fair's first ceremony took place in the dedication of the huge interdenominational "Temple of Religion" by leaders of several faiths.

There followed a parade down the mall with 25,000 announced participants — army, navy, marines, police, fair workers and foreign groups in an eye-filling array of variegated costumes.

After the President's address and speeches by Grover Whalen, the fair's dapper, top-hatted $100,000-year chief, Mayor Fiorello LaGuardia, and Governor Herbert Lehman, the throng of visitors scattered throughout the grounds for a multiplicity of other activities.

George Washington's inauguration, of which the fair opening marked the 150th anniversary, was re-enacted on the mall near a heroic statue of the first President, with cartoonist Denys Wortman, fresh from re-enacting Washington's inaugural journey to New York, in the leading role.

Four other huge statues, representing the freedom of speech, press, religion and assembly, were dedicated.

As night fell, the fair's unprecedented display of color illumination was snapped on by the impulse of a cosmic ray from a distant star.

ANNUAL COLORED METHODIST MEET AT MT. MORIAH

Final sessions of the annual conference of the African Methodist Episcopal Church were held last night at Mt. Moriah Church on Franklin street.

The conference began Wednesday and continued through to 11 P. M. yesterday, with approximately 5,000 in attendance. Divine services and financial reports were the main events of the sessions.

Rt. Rev. Bishop M. H. Davis, of Baltimore, presided. The Rev. S. R. Drummond is pastor of Mt. Moriah.

The next conference will be called by the bishop next April and will be held at the Metropolitan Church, Washington, D. C.

ROOSEVELT'S FAIR SPEECH

Flanked by Boy Scouts and standing behind the famed trylon and perisphere emblem of the New York World's Fair, President Roosevelt declares that America has "hitched her wagon to a star of good will." Among the listening thousands were visitors from many nations.

MRS. BUXTON FREED FROM SPRINGFIELD; IS DECLARED SANE

(Continued From Page One)

victim and Mrs. Buxton's husband, based his decision of the testimony on the physicians and the petitioner.

The jurist made her release conditional on the observance of regulations imposed by the court. He retained jurisdiction in the case. His conditions were concurred in by all parties.

Goes To Canada.

Judge Melvin directed that Mrs. Buxton remain permanently outside Kent County. She was released in custody of her sister, Mrs. Winifred M. Francis, of Montreal, Canada. The court stipulated that she live with her sister in her childhod home, as recommended by the psychiatrists. The expert witresses said such conditions would be conducive to her permanent recovery.

Judge Melvin also directed, on recommendation of Dr. Guttmacher, that Mrs. Buxton be under regular surveillance by psychiatrists.

Dr. Buxton is professor of chemistry at Washington College. His mother was killed in the Chestertown apartment she shared with her son and daughter-in-law.

Dr. Buxton testified at length in the hearing today, and urged his wife's release. Mrs. Bpxton was also present at the court session.

ROMANCE COMES TO DEATH VALLEY AS SCOTTY PREPARES CASTLE FOR MARRIAGE OF FRIENDS

By The Associated Press

THE CASTLE, Death Valley, May 1—Death Valley Scotty is dusting out the Castle for a wedding this week.

"The mules are shined up," the genial mystery prospector said. "We chased out the owls and bats. There's goin' to be a big time.

"Carrie Jacobs Bond is comin' up to sing 'Just A Wearying For You.' There'll be Indians and organists, preachers and movie stars, bankers and prospectors. All kinds of folks!

"My partner, Al Johnson, is goin' to give the bride away. I'll stand up fer the groom. Everything will be a 'bustin' with romance. Figure on feedin' and waterin' 80 or 90."

"Who are the lucky bride and groom?" Scotty was asked.

Lawyer, Groom

"Wal, the feller is my lawyer. He's some kin of old Joe Choate, who fought Boss Tweed in New York's old days and who uster tell them plain and fancy after dinner stories around New York, Washington and in the Court of St. James when he was ambassador to England. The lad is Joseph Choate of Los Angeles.

"He gits around a lot. Tells me he traveled 200,000 miles. Visited a Maharajah in India and then when he made a speech about him at some Salem college they gave him another degree.

"The gal is some kin of William Jennings Bryan, or William Cullen Bryant, one or the other, and her name is Dorothy Drew. She's quite a traveler, too.

Was In Jungles

"She says she was in the jungles of Cambodia when Joe cabled her to meet him in Greece. Joe tells me he popped the question on Mars Hills, in Athens. hat's where Saint Paul uster preach.

"The gal looked into his eyes when he told her about the Gods of Mt. Olympus. Then she looked over at Mt. Olympus when he askt her to marry him. They held hands and both said yes, or somethin.' That was a month ago.

"When I heard about it I told Joe he might as well come to the Castle to get hitched. 'There's lots of rocks 'round here and you kin call it Mt. Olympus or Mars Hill if you want,' I sez. He thought it a good idea, so we're gettin' ready."

The bride elect is a native of Boston. At one time she was secretary to Dr. Stewart MacClennan, Hollywood clergyman, who will perform the ceremony Wednesday. She is a talented musician and writer. Choate, native of Santa Ana, California, is an international lawyer.

Mrs. McCarter Dies

NEW YORK, May 1—Death at 55 came yesterday to Mrs. Maryon Andrews McCarter, mother of Ann Cooper Hewitt, the "sterilized" heiress.

Home of the
U. S. NAVAL ACADI
and
ST. JOHN'S COLLEGE

ANNAPOLIS
Evening Capital

WEATHER FORECAST
Generally fair tonight and Sunday; little change in temperature.

VOL. CIX — NO. 96. | ESTABLISHED IN 1884 PUBLISHED EVERY EVENING EXCEPT SUNDAY | ANNAPOLIS, FRIDAY, SEPTEMBER 1, 1939. | SOUTHERN MARYLAND'S ONLY DAILY PAPER | PRICE TWO CENTS

POLES RESIST INVADING GERMAN ARMY

NAVY VETS OPEN ANNUAL CONVENTION

Fifteenth Annual Convention Of Fleet Reserve Association Meets In House Of Delegates — Governor O'Conor, Admiral Brown Among Speakers.

LADIES' AUXILIARY ALSO IN SESSION

Discussion of the European crisis was interspersed with reminiscences today as Navy veterans, subject to immediate call if the United States goes to war, met in the fifteenth annual convention of the Fleet Reserve Association.

While delegates and members of their Ladies' Auxiliary registered at Carvel Hall, groups discussed the latest developments in Europe. "It's 1914 all over again," said one. "Well, I'm glad I just bought a new uniform," another commented. "Let her go, we're ready," a third interjected.

Wear Leis

L. S. Rothschild, Mr. and Mrs. John Subee, their son, Irving, 5, and niece, Miss Jane Subee, of Honolulu, representing the Honolulu branch and ladies' auxiliary unit traveled the longest distance to attend the convention. They wore the yellow leis of Hawaii as they met former comrades.

The white uniform of the ladies' auxiliary, with its blue trimmings was much in evidence as the delegates registered. The men wore civilian clothing.

Opening Session

The first session of the convention was held in the House of Delegates chamber of the State House, with Paul J. Dunleavy, of Annapolis, convention chairman, presiding. Alexander Steele, of

(Continued on Page Three)

Fish Stories In Reverse

Local Anglers Tell What They Didn't Catch — Even Hardheads Stop Biting—One And Two Fish A Boatload Reported.

The fishing season here seems to be at a stand still.

Even hardhead which were caught in the millions by line and net fishermen this Summer are getting scarce. Trout are not plentiful, rock aren't taking the lures and there is no indication that the big blues are ready to move into the bay.

Some Small Catches

Parties after catching hundreds of fish at one time a few weeks ago aren't having any luck at all. Recently the county's chief tax assessor, George T. Cromwell, caught the only fish in a large party.

This week E. C. Krueger of Pasadena, a member of the Board of

(Continued on Page Five)

COUNTY FISH AND GAME ASS'N TALKS ABOUT QUAIL HERE

Sentiment Seems To Favor Local Stock Rather Than Mexican Birds—Choose Bass Pond—Talk About Bag Limits.

At a meeting of the Fish and Game Conservation Association of Anne Arundel County, held at the Moose Home last night, the club members expressed disapproval of a proposal to purchase Mexican quail for stocking in Anne Arundey County, but passed a resolution to make the question a special order of business for the Septem-

(Continued on Page Five)

A. A. Democrats Silent About 1940 Election

Local Party Leaders Greet State Chiefs And Others But Refrain From Commitments At Party Given Yesterday By Former Delegate Philip Miller—Report That Tydings Will Support Radcliffe Revealed At Function.

O'CONOR AVOIDED ALL POLITICAL TALK

The Democratic nomination for United States Senator next year was the chief conversation at a big political party given yesterday by former Delegate Philip Miller at his estate Eu-De-So near Annapolis Roads.

The two leading candidates for the nomination, the incumbent, Senator George L. Radcliffe, and Howard Bruce, close ally to Governor Herbert R. O'Conor, were both present at the party as was the State's Chief Executive.

Candidates Are Pleased

Bruce confided to his friends that the situation looks fine for him. Senator Radcliffe's close associates dropped a bombshell in the happy afternoon for the Bruce forces, however, with the announcement that United States Senator Millard E. Tydings would soon come out supporting Radcliffe. Radcliffe was Tydings' campaign manager in the last election despite the fact that Radcliffe has been seeing almost eye to eye with President Roosevelt in Washington, and Tydings has

(Continued on Page Five)

GOVERNOR TO PICNIC

The fifth annual Tri State basket luncheon picnic will be held in Rock Creek Park on Sunday, September 10th, 1939, at Miller's Cabin. Gov. Herbert R. O'Conor will be the principal guest and speaker. All residents of Maryland, Virginia and West Virginia, residing in Washington and vicinity may attend.

4 LOCAL SPORTSMEN HAVE ROUGH TIME IN BAY JOURNEY

Four local sportsmen and Elks who left here at 1 A. M. recently for the B.P.O.E. convention at Crisfield had a rough journey, it was disclosed today upon the return here of one member of the crew.

Leon Lipman, Main street merchant, is home having returned on the ferry, and three others are due here tonight aboard the powerboat Elkay, if the rough water subsides. Setting out with Mr. Lipman were: Harry Klawans, also a Main street business man; A. Guy Miller, who works for Uncle Sam at the post-office, and is also Secretary of the local Elks, and Pete Macaluso, a convention-going Elk, who most of the time is busy with the Government's income tax duties.

The four Annapolitans ran into a northeaster soon after they got out of Annapolis' sheltered harbor—but they stuck it out to Crisfield, although the boat rolled and tossed like a cork most of the way. The return trip has been delayed, however, awaiting calm weather. Mr. Lipman said Mr. Macaluso was making his maiden voyage across the bay in a speed boat, and that he was particularly insistent that the return journey be delayed until the northeaster faded to a mere ripple.

Annapolis Gets 3 Prizes In Elks' Parade

CRISFIELD, Sept. 1 (AP)—Officials of the tri-State Elks' convention awarded the Annapolis lodge the prize for best appearance in parade. Frostburg Elks received a prize for the lodge coming from the greatest distance. Washington had the best band. Robert Davis of Crisfield took the prize for the tallest Elk; Ray Hare of Salisbury for the largest Elk, and George Hahn, of Annapolis, for the oldest Elk. Annapolis also won the award for having the largest number of Elks in the parade.

MRS. ALICE L. WELSH DIES AT HOSPITAL

Mrs. Alice Leakin Welsh, onetime State regent of the Daughters of the American Revolution and until recently manager of the Rising Sun, historic D. A. R. Inn on the General's Highway, died last night in Emergency Hospital after a long illness.

Funeral services will be held at 3 P. M. tomorrow in the Baldwin Memorial Church, Millersville. Burial will take place in the church cemetery.

The widow of Robert A. Welsh, Mrs. Welsh was the daughter of the Prof. Phil Moore Leakin of the agricultural school of the University of Maryland and the Anne Arundel Academy, of Millersville, and the late Juliet Woodward Leakin. She is survived by two sons, Robert I. and Woodward Leakin Welsh.

Mrs. Welsh was also a member of the Colonial Dames of America and was active in both patriotic societies.

75 LOTS IN NEW DEVELOPMENT NEAR RITCHIE MEMORIAL

Seventy-five lots on the Ritchie Highway, opposite the site of the Ritchie Memorial through to the Severn River, are available for sale through Charles F. Lee.

The Baltimore Asphalt Block & Tile Company has been contracted for the clearing, grading and building of more than a mile of macadam road into the property, which is owned by the North Severnside Realty Company.

HITLER STARTS WAR

ITALY NEUTRAL; FRANCE AND BRITAIN MOBILIZE

Poland today grimly battled successive waves of German bombers and three German armies which crossed her borders and formally appealed to Great Britain and France for assistance.

The invasion began at 5:45 A. M. (11:45 P. M. Thursday, E.S.T.) almost a quarter of a day before Adolf Hitler in an impassioned speech before the Reichstag declared he would enforce a settlement of the Polish question or die fighting. The Reichstag unanimously shouted its approval of a law annexing Danzig to the Reich.

Great Britain and France ordered general mobilization of all their defense forces. Prime Minister Chamberlain told the House of Commons that unless Germany would suspend aggressive action and withdraw from Poland Britain would unhesitatingly fulfil her obligations to the threatened nation. France took similar action.

The Italian Cabinet announced that Italy would refrain from starting any military operations. Hitler said that he did not count on Italian help. Rumors that Russia might follow up her non-aggression pact with a military agreement with Germany met with extreme skepticism in Moscow.

BOMB 19 POLISH CITIES

The Nazi troops drove into Poland in three main sectors—first, from East Prussia against Dzialdowo and Mlawa; second, from Pomerania against Chojnice at the narrowest part of the west border of the disputed Polish corridor, and third, from Breslau against Katowice, believed to have been evacuated.

German planes, attacking in waves throughout the day bombed 19 Polish cities and towns including Warsaw. Four attempts were made to bomb Warsaw before the German squadron broke through its defenses at 4:30 P. M. (10:30 A. M. E. S. T.). They dropped bombs near the United States Embassy and the bridges over the Vistula.

WOMEN, CHILDREN KILLED

Three German planes were shot down near Krakow and four others near Gdynia, which was reported bombed and bombarded by the German fleet. The first air raid by Germany was reported at Puck, near Danzig at 5:40 A. M. (11:40 P. M. E. S. T. Thursday).

A Polish communique said large numbers of women and children were killed when German planes bombed a refugee train from Pozan at the Kutho station, 70 miles west of Warsaw. It charged that German troops invading Pomorze (the Polish corridor) were "murdering the Polish population." Polish troops seized a German armored train at Chojnice.

Battle Near Grudziac

Polish officials placed the guilt of starting the war squarely on Germany. They said they had agreed yesterday to an act of mediation by the British Government, the aim of which was to start conversations between the Polish and German governments.

The German army high command in a communique said their army which advanced on Poland from East Prussia is "deep in Polish territory" and that the airforce is "controlling Polish air." Other advances were said to be well under way toward their objectives. German troops were reporting advancing toward Neumark and Sucha from Maerich-Ostrau. They crossed the Osla river. The communique said the troops reached the Nerze river near Nakel and that a battle was raging near Grudziacz. The "successful air raid" on Warsaw was announced by three German units, bombs being dropped on the Random military airdome.

Polish Air Raid

DNB, German news agency, said Polish airplanes attempted to raid the outskirts of Beuthen, in German Silesia and dropped six bombs in the Homestead settlement. Polish artillery also was reported as shelling the Beuthen railroad station. The Germans said there were no casualties and no damage of consequence.

Warning air sirens howled in Berlin, announcing the advance of enemy warplanes. The populace immediately rushed to cellars and other shelters.

No War Declaration

German authorized sources insisted there was no war — but merely a counterstruck in retaliation for an alleged Polish attack on Gliewitz and for border incidents. A complete "black-out" was ordered in Berlin. An army ambulance carrying wounded German soldiers arrived at the Emergency hospital at Gliewitz.

Hitler, in his address to the Reichstag, declared his intention of leading his forces at the front and named Field Marshal Goering as his first choice for succession to Nazi leadership if he were killed.

Chamberlain told the Commons that "we shall stand at the bar of history knowing that the responsibility for this terrible catastrophe rests on the shoulders of one man—the German Chancellor!"

King George VI signed the order for complete British army, navy and air force mobilization after the Polish ambassador had called on Britain to help Poland against Germany.

Italy Undetermined

The House of Commons approved a bill providing $2,110,000,000 to prosecute war for defense, and for maintenance of public order. The Ministry of Transport took over British railroads. The Canadian government placed all militia and naval and air forces on an active basis.

Italy seemed undetermined in the situation brought about by the swiftly moving events. The general tenor of newspaper articles was pro-German, but commentators were circumspect, making no definite commitments.

France, in addition to decreeing general mobilization tomorrow, also proclaimed a stage of siege bringing the country under military law. A total of 8,000,000 m-

(Continued on Page Two)

Marine Indicted For Holdup Of Local Bank

BALTIMORE, Sept. 1 (AP)—Wilbur Russell Davis was indicted by a Federal grand jury today on charges of holding up and robbing the Annapolis Bank and Trust Company.

Also indicted was Louise S. Brooks, a postal clerk at the Bowie, Md., post office, charged with misuse of funds entrusted to her care. She was the only woman among 43 persons indicted.

Hunt To Play Doubles Only; Pairings Noted

HAVERFORD, Pa., Sept. 1 (AP). Bobby Riggs, of the United States, will meet John Bromwich, Australian ace, in the first match of the challenge round for the Davis Cup at the Merion Cricket Club tomorrow afternoon as a result of drawings today.

The second singles match will pit Frank Parker of the U. S. team against Adrian Quist of Australia.

Non-playing Captain Walter L. Pate stuck by his previously indicated choice for the U. S. doubles team—Joe Hunt and Jack Kramer, youngest members of the team—to meet Australia's crack doubles pair, Bromwich and Quist, Sunday.

Monday's program will send Riggs against Quist in the first match, then Parker against Bromwich.

50 MIDDIES TAKE TESTS AT ACADEMY

Approximately 50 midshipmen today took re-examinations to make up scholastic deficiencies before going on leave.

Most of these taking the test returned from the summer practice cruise and remained at the academy for the purpose.

They will go on leave tomorrow, returning with the other midshipmen on September 29.

The only midshipmen remaining at the academy are the 785 members of the plebe class, formed during the summer.

F. D. R. BELIEVES U. S. CAN STAY OUT OF WAR

President Roosevelt Urges Co-Operation Of Press In Publishing Only Verified Accounts — Sends Message To European Powers To Avoid Bombing Civilian Population—Special Session Of Congress Likely.

U. S. UNDECIDED ON NEUTRALITY LAWS

WASHINGTON, Sept. 1 (AP)—Secretary Hull announced today Great Britain and France had agreed to refrain from bombing civilian populations in response to an appeal from President Roosevelt.

Great Britain made her acceptance conditional upon the understanding that all her opponents would also refrain from bombing civilian populations.

WASHINGTON, Sept. 1 (AP)—President Roosevelt told reporters today that he believed the United States could stay out of the European conflict and the administration would make every effort to keep this country out.

In response to a press conference question about whether America could keep from being involved the President authorized a direct quotation that "I not only sincerely hope so, but I believe we can and that every effort will be made by the administration so to do."

Ambassador Resigns

Mr. Roosevelt announced at the conference that Hugh Wilson, Ambassador to Germany, had submitted his resignation this morning, that it had been accepted, and that Wilson was being assigned to special duty in the State Department.

Developments abroad today and those that may be expected tomorrow, Mr. Roosevelt declared, would have an important bearing on what the administraion would do about invoking the neutrality act and summoning Congress to a special session.

He gave no hint, however, as to when steps along those two lines might be expected.

Asked whether his remarks meant definitely that Congress

(Continued on Page Four)

Home of the
. S. NAVAL ACADEMY
and
ST. JOHN'S COLLEGE

ANNAPOLIS
Evening Capital

WEATHER FORECAST
Fair tonight and Wednesday; cooler tonight; slowly rising temperature in the interior Wednesday.

VOL. CIX — NO. 98. | ESTABLISHED IN 1884 PUBLISHED EVERY EVENING EXCEPT SUNDAY | ANNAPOLIS, TUESDAY, SEPTEMBER 5, 1939. | SOUTHERN MARYLAND'S ONLY DAILY PAPER | PRICE TWO CENTS

F. D. R. PROCLAIMS UNITED STATES' NEUTRALITY

POSTMASTERS TO HOLD MEET IN OCEAN CITY

W. A. Strohm, Local Postmaster, Will Preside At Session.

William A. Strohm, president of the Maryland Chapter, National Association of Postmasters, today said many Postoffice Department officials and congressmen would attend the annual meeting of the chapter to be held at the Atlantic Hotel, Ocean City, on Friday.

Mr. Strohm, local postmaster, will call the convention to order at 2 P. M. An informal dinner will be held at 7 P. M.

Speakers at the convention include J. Austin Latimer, special assistant to the Postmaster General; Smith W. Purdum, fourth assistant Postmaster General; Senator George L. Radcliffe, (D-Md.); Rep. David J. Ward, (D-1st Md.); C. H. Buckley, Postoffice Inspection Service; George W. Purcell, postmaster, Bloomington, Ill., and president of the national association and Paul R. Younts, postmaster, Charlotte, N. C.

Other high executives from the Postoffice Department, Federal and State officials will be the guests of the Maryland postmasters at the dinner meeting.

Democratic Clubs Face Moonlight Excursion Tonight

The last moonlight excursion of the season, sponsored by the Democratic clubs of Annapolis and the county, will leave promptly at 8:30 tonight from the foot of Prince George street, on the S.S. Dixie.

Many distinguished guests are expected and tickets have been selling rapidly. Free dancing and movies will be provided on board.

FOR SALE
Modern eight-room dwelling in Murray Hill — $7,000
Convenient Terms Available
BERNARD J. WIEGARD
Hotel Maryland Building
Phone 3909

THOMAS G. BASIL
Insurance Of All Kinds
92 WEST STREET
Annapolis, Md.
DIAL 2161

NOTICE
The business of the late Charles E. Hicks, Jr., is being carried on by his widow Mrs. Ethel Hicks and a professional embalmer and funeral director. The same services are being rendered as when Mr. Hicks lived.
45 Northwest Street
PHONE 3851

WATERFRONT LOT
At Edgewater Beach
For Sale at Bargain Price.
JULIAN BREWER AND SON
Joseph D. Lazenby
9 School St. Dial 2685

FOR SALE
WARDOUR
3 lots with modern dwelling. Oil burner, 2 baths, 2 garages.
$7,500
SERVICE AGENTS, INC.
F. E. VOGES — H. H. LITTLE
47 Md. Ave. — Dial 4477

FOR SALE
No. 4 Randall Place. 5 bedrooms, 3 baths, very nice home in nice neighborhood — $8,000.00.
.84 acre with 5-room dwelling at Wellsview. Price $1200.00.
CHAS. F. LEE
Dial 2461
Lee Bldg. Church Circle

U. S. Liner With 539 Passengers Reaches Gotham

Ship Also Carried $21,000,000 In Gold And New Type Of Torpedo Boat—Followed Zig-Zag Course.

MYSTERY SURROUNDS LOCATION OF BREMEN

NEW YORK, Sept. 5 (AP)—With 539 passengers crowded into improvised quarters the United States liner President Roosevelt arrived from Europe today.

In addition to her 125 extra passengers she carried $21,000,000 in gold.

The Cunard White Star liner Samaria, a day late, followed with 693 passengers from Europe, 245 of them Americans.

Meanwhile whereabouts of the great North German Lloyd liner Bremen, which left New York last Wednesday night without passengers or cargo, continued a mystery. The $20,000,000 vessel announced her destination as Bremenhaven, but it was believed she may have turned southward, hoping to reach Vera Cruz, Mexico, where another German liner, the Columbus, docked yesterday instead of going to Germany.

To Be Demonstrated

The President Roosevelt had on her forward deck a new type of motor British torpedo boat carrying four torpedoes and quick-firing guns.

The torpedo boat was to be taken to the Brooklyn navy yard for demonstration to potential buyers, said Kenneth Perry, a retired British naval officer, who came over with it.

Perry said it cost about $200,000, weighed about 45 tons, had a range of over 1,000 miles and was considerably faster than the 40-knot maximum of previously built boats. It draws 4½ feet of water and can be used in mine-infested waters because mines are usually ten or fifteen feet below the surface, he said.

The Frech line offices said to-

(Continued on Page Four)

FOOD PRICES IN U. S. SOAR

CHICAGO, Sept. 5 (AP)—War in Europe today lifted hog prices $1 to a top of $8, a level they had not reached since last March. Cattle prices were mostly 50 cents higher and spring lambs 40 to 65 cents higher.

Buy Your
Colonial Anthracite
NOW
ANNAPOLIS DAIRY PRODUCTS CO.
Annapolis 2345

QUICK SALE
Attractive, modern 6-room house, 13 Thompson street. Reasonable price. Call at house or phone 4845.

Final Notice On Arrearage Taxes

All persons owing taxes under the five year Amortization Agreement Plan enacted in 1935 are hereby notified that the total amount still due must be paid by October 1st, 1939.

All open accounts will be advertised immediately after October 1st, 1939 and the properties sold to satisfy these taxes.

C. ALBERT HODGES,
Late County Treasurer.

11 Die In Md. Over Labor Day; 7 Auto Deaths

Three Drownings In State Over Long Week-End—2 Die At Prince Frederick

Maryland counted eleven dead today as the result of automobile crashes and drownings over the long Labor Day holiday.

Eight persons were killed in traffic accidents and three drowned over the holiday that began Saturday and ended yesterday.

Three of the automobile crashes claimed two lives each.

Auto Overturned

Two children, Louise Swann, 14, and Louis Thompson, 14, both of Pomfret, were killed yesterday when the automobile in which they were riding overturned near Chapel Point. James Thompson 22, the driver, was injured.

Mrs. Nora Reber, 66, of Reading Pa., died at Havre De Grace last night, second victim of a collision near Aberdeen Sunday in which Albert C. Dallas, 22, of Tamaque, Pa., was killed and ten others injured.

ELLIOTT ACTING MAYOR AS CUPID CLAIMS CITY'S MUNICIPAL EXECUTIVE

Dan Cupid's arrow having struck Mayor George W. Haley who today was honeymooning in the Chesapeake Bay, it was announced at the City Hall that Alderman Arthur T. Elliott would be acting Mayor until Mayor Haley returns to this city.

(Turn to the social page for details on Mayor Haley's wedding.)

Midshipman And Girl Hit By Automobile

CUMBERLAND, Md., Sept. 5 (AP)—Midshipman Burton Andrews, 23, of the Naval Academy, Annapolis, Md., and Miss Eurith Maynard, 19, Baltimore, were seriously injured Labor Day afternoon when struck by an automobile while they walked along the highway near Deep Creek, near Oakland.

Andrews, whose home is in Los Angeles, Calif., suffered a possible skull fracture and multiple bruises. Miss Maynard received severe cuts and bruises about the head and body. There condition was reported "fair" at Memorial hospital here.

They were struck by a car owned by Dr. Frank M. Wilson, this city, and driven by Hopwood J. Woodell, Oakland. Woodell told police the car skidded on loose shale and struck the couple.

ICKES HAS A SON

BALTIMORE, Sept. 5 (AP)—Mars took precedence over the stork last night and prevented Interior Secretary Harold L. Ickes from being present at the birth of a son to his young wife.

Ickes was detained in Washington at an emergency cabinet meeting for war news discussion called by President Roosevelt, and arrived several hours after the birth of his 7-pound, 11-ounce heir at Woman's Clinic, Johns Hopkins Hospital.

PASSENGER WANTED
To accompany driver 1939 Ford sedan to Los Angeles leaving immediately after Labor Day. Exchanged references required. Answer Box 26 care Evening Capital.

DEVILED CRAB SUPPER
Given by
LADIES' AID SOCIETY
Eastport M. E. Church
Church Basement
THURSDAY, SEPT. 7th, 5 P. M.
Tickets 35 Cents

ATHENIA'S SURVIVORS LANDED

POLES FLEE WARSAW; NAZIS ARMY CLAIMS CAPTURE OF KATOWICE AND CHORZOW

Captured Cities On Route To Krakow—Polish Cavalry Raid East Prussia And Silesia—Westerplatte Garrison Still Holding Out—French Claim Penetration Into German Territory—British Shower Germany With Propaganda Leaflets—Cunard Steamer Bosnia And German Ship Carl Fritzen Sunk—Two British Planes Shot Down Over Hamburg.

(By The Associated Press)

WASHINGTON—President Roosevelt prolaims United States neutrality in European war.

WARSAW—Thousands of Poles leave Warsaw for safety from German air aids and advancing army; United States Ambassador Biddle takes staff away; report Polish government officials may leave soon; Polish defense lines shortened.

LONDON—More than 1,400 survivors of torpedoed British liner Athenia land in Ireland and Scotland; Cunard Line announces steamer Bosnia sunk by submarine, crew saved; London informed German vessel Carl Fritzen sunk. Fliers drop leaflets over Germany.

BERLIN—Germany announces capture of Katowic and Chorzow, rich industrial cities on southwest front; reports 11 polish planes destroyed in air battle near Warsaw; German military machine pounds Poland as Hitler follows through Polish Corridor marking reported reunion of East Prussia with Germany.

NEW YORK—Financial and commodity markets swept by buying surge.

TOKYO—Japan gives formal notice of her intention to remain neutral toward European war.

BERLIN—Germans report ten of 12 British raiders shot down and deny any damage by aerial attack on German fleet; Hitler follows eastern troops across Polish Corridor marking consolidation of German territory. Germans report 15,000 Polish prisoners taken.

PARIS—French War Ministry says "movements develop normally" in campaign against Germany, but keeps secret actual operations; air raid warnings sound in Paris, but German planes turn back without dropping bombs.

GREENOCK, Scotland—Survivor declares German submarine torpedo sank British liner Athenia and fired two shells at sinking boat; Two boatloads of survivors reach Scotland reporting about 90 persons lost.

GALWAY, Ireland—Boatload of 430 Athenia survivors put ashore by Norwegian rescue ship.

BUENOS AIRES—Two British cruisers halt German shipping in South Atlantic after sinking German cargo vessel Olinda.

President Roosevelt proclaimed American neutrality today as thousands of Poles and several hundred foreigners, including Americans, left Warsaw after German planes made two raids on the city and Germany claimed the capture of Katowice and Chorzow, two rich Polish industrial cities, near the frontier in Silesia.

The President is expected to follow his neutrality proclamation by another putting an embargo on export of arms, ammunition and implements of war to the combatant nations. It also will place restrictions on travel of Americans on vessels of warring countries. The French liner-freighter Vermont, with 19 airplanes aboard, cleared the Mississippi river entrance a few hours before the neutrality act was invoked.

FRENCH PENETRATE GERMANY

The French Government announced that their forces had made contact with German troops on the Western front and had penetrated into German territory. A semi-official Paris radio reported trouble in Germany, and said there had been disorders in Cologne, Dusseldorf and Essen, as well as the areas of all Czecho-Slovakia.

The official German news agency, DND, announced that two of four British scouting planes that appeared over Hamburg were shot down by German fliers. It reported that an English bomber was shot down by a German seaplane over the Dogger Bank in the North Sea, and that a third Polish submarine had been sunk by the German navy in Danzig harbor.

PROPAGANDA RAID OVER GERMANY

The British Ministry of Information announced that Royal Air Force planes had dropped 3,000,000 additional pamphlet appeals to

(Continued on Page Two)

Cheering Crowd Of Adults And Children Watch Soapbox Derby

Several hundred adults and a milling crowd of enthusiastic boys and girls yesterday saw Webster Egbert, 15, take first honors in the initial Annapolis soap-box derby held on Lafayette avenue under the sponsorship of the Greater Annapolis Recreation Association.

Eleven white and two colored boys entered the contest. Their soap-box wagons surprised the adults by the ingenuity shown and their designs. Many had the appearance of racing automobiles, underslung and with complicated steering mechanism. Some were equipped with lights and horns. They were a far cry from the soap-box wagons many of the adults present had used in their younger days.

Raced In Heats

Charles Bissell, recreational director for the association, started the derby heats on a signal from Dr. A. K. Snyder, vice-president of the association. Chief William Curry, Harry S. Kenchington and Richard H. Elliott were judges.

The youngsters were raced in heats, but several times the excited children at the finish raced out in the street to see the contestants, and blocked racers who were attempting to pass leaders

(Continued on Page Six)

CAPTAIN SAYS SUBMARINE SUNK SHIP

Master Of Athenia Declares After Torpedo Was Fired Submarine Rose And Shelled Liner—Survivors Claim Two Shells Were Fired While Life Boats Were Being Lowered.

1,430 LANDED IN SCOTLAND, IRELAND

Shaken by their experience when the British liner Athenia was sunk Sunday, 1,430 survivors, including the captain, James Cook, landed today at Galway, Ireland, and Greenock, Scotland.

Captain Cook and 430 other survivors were brought to Galway by the Norwegian steamer Knut Nelson. The others were brought to Greenock, including 200 injured.

The survivors who landed in Scotland declared that the submarine which sent the liner to the bottom fired two shells while her life boats were being lowered.

In Berlin last night, State Secretary Ernst Von Wiesaeker, told Alexander Kirk, American Charge d'Affair: "German sea forces could not possibly have been responsible. Strict orders have been issued for the German sea forces to hold themselves within the prize law."

Describes Shelling

Captain Cook said that immediately after the torpedo was fired, the submarine rose to the surface and shelled the Athenia.

"One shell carried away the mast," he related. "It was evidently aimed at the wireless room, but missed its mark."

He called witnesses to tell newspaper men that the torpedo was fired at a range of 800 to 1,000 yards on the port side of the vessel. One officer said he saw the periscope of the submarine just before the torpedo struck. Other officers and members of the crew said they saw a line of smoke rising from the water off the port bow just before the disaster. The smoke described a complete circle over the surface of the water.

90 Reported Dead

Captain Cook said he did not know how many were dead and injured. He declared: "There was

(Continued on Page Two)

Paul J. Vazquez Drowned While On Fishing Trip

Paul J. Vazquez, 31, Washington, was drowned in Herring Bay Sunday while on a fishing trip His body was recovered yesterday by Capt. Samuel Manifold, of Deale.

Vazquez, a good swimmer, lost his line while fishing, and jumped overboard to retrieve it. He was swimming back to the boat when he suddenly sank in about 30 feet of water.

Dr. J. M. Claffy, Anne Arundel county medical examiner, gave a verdict of accidental drowning.

Milton Starlings, Davidsonville and John Jones, colored, Lothian were treated at the Emergency Hospital for accidental gunshot wounds received while hunting doves. Starlings was shot in the left foot and Jones in the left arm. They were hunting separately when their guns were discharged.

Substitute Trial Magistrate Albert J. Goodman fined Mariano Rossett, 41, Filipino, and John F Berger, 24 $6.75 each on assault charges. W. H. Boswell was fined $6.75 on a disorderly conduct charge.

Joe Leary Is New Annapolis Open Golf Ace

Worker At Experiment Station Turns In Fine Scores To Win Annapolis Open Trophy Known As Charles Denby Cup Last Played For In 1929, From 35 Rivals — Pick Scibles And Monty French, Of Annapolis, Also Play Well.

WASHINGTONIANS IN HANDICAP FIELD

While the main trophy, The Charles Denby Cup, went to Joseph P. Leary, of Annapolis, top honors in the handicap division for both men and women in the Annapolis Golf Open tournament today went to Washingtonians..

Ending a week-end of play on the sporting Annapolis Roads course, Mr. and Mrs. A. P. Sasscer, of Washington, made a clean sweep of net score honors. Mr. Sasscer won the men's handicap division with an 89—with a 24 handicap giving him a 65.

LeRoy Smith, local civilian employe of the Naval Academy, was second with 104, minus a 37 handicap for a 67, while third honors went to Gordon L. "Pick" Scibles, of Annapolis, generally better known athletically as a bowler. Scibles had 88 less a 20 handicap for a 68. He had low net in his division.

Mrs. Sasscer Wins

Mrs. Sasscer won the women's handicap tournament from Mrs. Harold S. Lewis, of Washington. The winner had a net 73, her score for the difficult course being 101.

Leary waltzed to top honors among 36 players in the Annapolis Open to cop the Denby trophy. He shot a 74 on Sunday and a 72 Labor Day to outdistance the field.

(Continued on Page Six)

Show Boat Here For Week's Stay

The famous Show Boat, background for the moving picture and Edna Ferber's novel, arrived here yesterday for a week's stay at Severn Beach on the other side of the Severn River Beach.

The boat will be here through Saturday giving a different play each night, as well as a musical revue.

T. C. RYAN HEADS FLEET RESERVE

Veteran Member Of Association Elected National President—E. M. Page, Annapolis, Elected National Chaplain.

MYRTLE MAYE HEADS LADIES' AUXILIARY

Thomas C. Ryan, Pacific Beach, Calif., today headed the Fleet Reserve Association as national president for the ensuing year.

Myrtle Maye, Vallejo, Calif., was elected president of the Ladies' Auxiliary of the association, succeeding Viola Harrington, Newport, R. I.

The sixteenth annual convention of the association and its auxiliary will be held in Long Beach, Calif.

Other Officers

Mr. Ryan, known as "Doggie" to members of the association, served last year as vice-president. He completed 22 years service in the navy and 3 in the army before entering the Reserve in 1925 by organizing Branch Number 9, of Pacific Beach. He was regional vice-president of the association for California for two years, and is a member of the national board of directors.

Other association officers elected are G. S. Corbein, Philadelphia, national vice-president; C. E. Lofgren, Washington, national secretary; P. G. Cronan, Washington, national treasurer; C. A. Tudge, Washington, national financial secretary; E. M. Page, Annapolis, national chaplain. The new regional vice-presidents are, northeast, C. F. Bunker, Newport, R. I.; R. F. Bonamarte, east coast, Washington, D. C.; W. H. Shoemaker, east central, Cleveland; J. C. Wilkins, mid-west, Chicago; J. H. Burch, California, San Leandro, Calif.; E. J. Braddock, north-west, Seattle, Wash., and J. L. Bent, Philippine Islands, Cavite, P. I.

Auxiliary Officers

Mae Burress West Somerville, Mass., was elected national vice-president of the Ladies' Auxiliary. Other auxiliary officers elected were Mildred Davidson, Long Island, N. Y., national recording secretary; Margaret Drobney, San Diego, Calif., national financial secretary; Amelia Anselm, Philadelphia, national chaplain; Mabel Sally, Alexandria, Va., national treasurer; directors, Viola Harrington, Jr., Newport, R. I.; Katherine Zeltman and Brainor. The regional vice-presidents elected are Teresa Davidson, Bay Shore, L. I., north-

(Continued on Page 2)

MR. CHARLES HOYES
IS PLEASED TO ANNOUNCE THE RE-OPENING OF HIS
Studio of the Dance
ADDRESS INQUIRIES CARE ST. JOHN'S COLLEGE
REFERENCES REQUIRED

MILLINERY OPENING
TUESDAY and WEDNESDAY
September 5 and 6
L. P. MUSTERMAN
197 Main Street
Dobbs Hats Gage Hats

MODERN PLUMBING—GUARANTEED HEATING
OIL BURNERS
INSTALL NOW PAY WHEN CONVENIENT
EASY TERMS
W. T. SHAWN, Inc.
DIAL 4187

Famous with Millions
A&P SOFT TWIST
BREAD

They've got that BAKED·JUST·NOW FRESHNESS

The loaf which has made A&P Bakers famous! Oven-fresh. Deliciously soft, tender texture — baked to a golden crusted brown.

2 18-oz. loaves **15¢**   A&P BREAD Soft Twist

A&P VIENNA TWIST
WITH POPPY SEEDS
Spicy and Original

Made from a master baker's recipe. Soft, smooth and generously topped with poppy seeds for that added "spice."

2 1-lb. loaves **17¢**

A&P 100% WHOLE WHEAT
Hale and Hearty

Giant wheat kernels especially milled give this loaf its delicious nut-like flavor and fragrance.

2 1-lb. loaves **17¢**   A&P 100% Whole Wheat

MOST SPECIAL!
A&P DE LUXE RAISIN

"Let 'em eat cake" said the Queen. She must have meant this great favorite . . . generous with raisins . . spread with icing . . . a hit!

2 1-lb. loaves **17¢**

For Extra ZEST
A&P SEEDED RYE

For giving the perfect touch to a tasty meal —you'll find this loaf absolutely tops!

2 1-lb. loaves **17¢**   A&P Seeded Rye

A&P CRACKED WHEAT
For that "Toasty" FLAVOR

You'll enjoy the nut-like flavor of this hearty loaf. It's tops when toasted. Hearty and substantial.

2 1-lb. loaves **17¢**   A&P Cracked Wheat

JANE PARKER
DO-NUTS
10¢

JANE PARKER
ICED RINGS
ASSORTED ICINGS
each **27¢**

LEGS of LAMB
SHOULDER ROAST FORE-QUARTER STYLE lb. 13c
lb. **21¢**

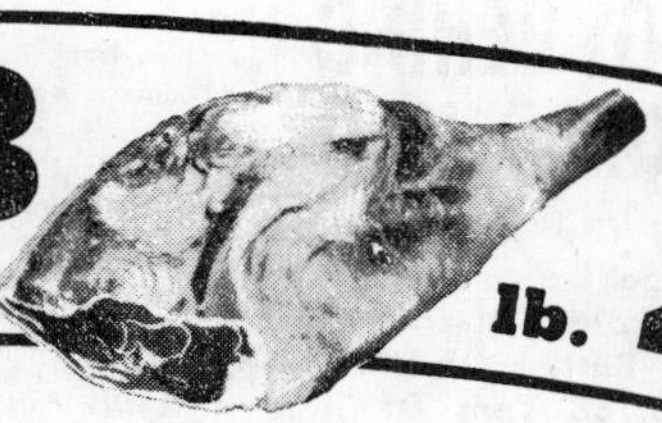

A&P
SELF SERVICE

SUPER MARKETS

Owned and Operated by The Great Atlantic & Pacific Tea Co.

A&P Guaranteed Quality Meats Are Hard To Beat!

Fussy about the quality of Meats? We don't blame you . . . so are we. From all of the meat offered our expert buyers only those grades which meet A & P's high standards of quality are selected. We insist that all of our meats must be tender, juicy and flavorful to assure complete customer satisfaction. The fine cuts you see in the spotless, white, temperature controlled cases in A & P Super Markets are Quality Meats. They have been skillfully cut and trimmed by our own expert butchers. You can buy them with confidence . . . they are sold on a money-back guarantee. Take a tip from those who recognize good meats . . Begin buying at an A & P Super Market today. Select your favorite cuts with the knowledge that you are getting dependable quality. Serve them on all occasions . . . win the praise of your family and guests. If the reasonable prices seem too reasonable . . . just remember, A & P has the values! Come in; buy with confidence.

STEAKS	ROUND OR SIRLOIN CUT FROM CHOICE STEER BEEF	lb. **25¢**
PORK LOIN	ROAST RIB END UP TO 3½ LBS.	lb. **15¢**
CHUCK	BEEF ROAST ALL CUTS—ONE PRICE	lb. **17¢**
CHICKENS	FRESH KILLED FRYERS BARRED ROCKS	lb. **23¢**

HAMS GOETZE'S BONELESS ROLLED—WHOLE OR HALF	lb. 27c	**SHOULDERS** FRESH PORK	lb. 15c
Potato Salad OR COLE SLAW	lb. 10c	Bacon	½-lb. pkg. 10c
Adam's Scrapple COUNTRY STYLE	2 lbs. 25c	Sausage Meat Sunnyfield Sliced U.S. No. 1 PORK	lb. 19c

SEAFOOD
FANCY BUTTERFISH or CROAKERS 2 lbs. 15¢

FANCY SHRIMP	....	2 lbs. 25c
PAN TROUT	....	2 lbs. 15c
Pollock Fillets	....	lb. 10c
OYSTERS SALT-WATER STANDARDS	....	qt. 35c

CAMPBELL'S TOMATO SOUP		3 cans	20c
DEL MONTE PEACHES SLICES OR HALVES	No. 2½ can		14c
PINK SALMON COLD STREAM		2 tall cans	23c
ANN PAGE BEANS TENDER COOKED	1-lb. can		5c
GARDEN PEAS STANDARD PACK		3 No. 2 cans	22c
GREEN GIANT PEAS		2 17-oz. cans	27c
CRUSHED CORN IONA		3 No. 2 cans	20c
SPRY SHORTENING	1-lb. can 19c	3-lb. can	49c
CRISCO SHORTENING	1-lb. can 19c	3-lb. can	49c
SALAD DRESSING ANN PAGE	pt. jar 15c	qt. jar	25c
IVORY FLAKES OR SNOW	2 sm. pkgs. 17c	lge. pkg.	20c
CHIPSO QUICK SUDS—RICH AND LASTING	sm. box 8c	lge. box	20c
RINSO WASHES CLOTHES WHITER	sm. box 8c	lge. box	19c
OXYDOL NO SCRUBBING NO BOILING	sm. box 8c	lge. box	19c
SUPER SUDS RED BOX	sm. box 8c	lge. box	15c
IVORY SOAP	med. cake 5c	3 lge. cakes	25c
FELS-NAPTHA SOAP		3 bars	13c
PALMOLIVE TOILET SOAP		3 cakes	17c
LIFEBUOY HEALTH SOAP		2 cakes	11c
P&G LAUNDRY SOAP		3 bars	10c
KIRKMAN'S BORAX SOAP		5 bars	17c
OCTAGON LAUNDRY SOAP		5 cakes	17c

IONA PEACHES
SLICES OR HALVES **2** No. 2½ cans **23¢**

PANCAKE FLOUR AUNT JEMIMA		pkg.	10c
SYRUP RAJAH MAPLE AND CANE		qt. bot.	25c
SHREDDED WHEAT N.B.C.		2 pkgs.	21c
PINEAPPLE DOLE OR DEL MONTE		No. 2 can	29c
TOMATO JUICE IONA		4 24-oz. cans	25c
CHERRIES SOUR PITTED FOR PIES		2 No. 2 can	19c
PINEAPPLE S'LTANA BROKEN SLICES		No. 2½ can	19c
MARSHMALLOWS RECIPE		cello. box	10c
MOTT'S CIDER	2 qts. 23c	gal. jug	37c
CORNED BEEF ARMOUR'S STAR		12-oz. can	16c
SAUERKRAUT SILVER FLOSS		2 No. 2½ cans	15c
HOMINY MANNING'S COOKED		3 No. 2½ cans	15c
VEGETABLES MIXED		No. 2 can	11c
OLIVES IONA PLAIN		10½-oz. can	19c
CORN FLAKES SUNNYFIELD		8-oz. pkg.	5c
COMET RICE	2 12-oz. pkgs. 15c	2-lb. pkg.	17c
BROOMS CLEAN SWEEP		each	25c
DAILY DOG FOOD		6 1-lb. cans	25c
THRIVO DOG FOOD		3 1-lb. cans	20c
ATLANTIC TOILET TISSUE		3 rolls	10c

GET A USEFUL
APRON FOR ONLY **1c**
WITH THE PURCHASE OF A GIANT BOX OF CONCENTRATED
SUPER SUDS
AT THE REGULAR PRICE OF 55c   BOTH FOR **56¢**

PURE CANE SUGAR
IN PAPER BAGS
10 lbs. **55¢**

STANDARD PACK STRINGLESS
BEANS or TOMATOES
No. 2 can **5¢**

CRESTVIEW
EGGS
doz. **22¢**
SUNNYBROOK EGGS doz. 37c

BUTTER	OUR FINEST CREAMERY TUB CUT	lb. **31¢**
SUNNYFIELD BUTTER	IN ¼-LB. PRINTS	lb. 33c
FLOUR	SUNNYFIELD FAMILY 12-lb. bag	**35¢** 24-lb. bag **69¢**
PILLSBURY'S	12-lb. bag 43c 24-lb. bag 85c	GOLD MEDAL 12-lb. bag 44c 24-lb. bag 87c
PURE LARD	BULK OR PKG.	2 lbs. 17c

Bisquick WITH Butter Dish	lge. pkg.	27c
Ann Page Ketchup	14-oz. bot.	10c
Preserves ANN PAGE MOST VARIETIES	1-lb. jar 15c 2-lb. jar	27c
Sparkle Desserts ANN PAGE	3 pkgs.	10c
Maxwell House Coffee	lb.	27c
Evap. Milk WHITE HOUSE	4 tall cans	23c
Nectar Tea ORANGE PEKOE	¼-lb. pkg. 13c ½-lb. pkg.	25c

110 DOCK STREET
Annapolis, Md.

STORE HOURS:
MONDAY THRU THURSDAY ...... 8 A.M. to 6 P.M.
FRIDAY ...... 8 A.M. to 9 P.M.
SATURDAY ...... 8 A.M. to 10 P.M.

Do it now!
Join the thousands who save up to 10¢ a lb. on fine, fresh coffee.
EIGHT O'CLOCK COFFEE
3 lb. bag **39¢** 1-lb. pkg. **14c**
AS ADVERTISED IN **LIFE**

Fruits and Vegetables

JUICY FLORIDA—MEDIUM SIZE
ORANGES 20 for 23¢
LARGE SIZE, DOZ., 21c

Cauliflower head **9c**

BRUSSELS SPROUTS	EMPEROR GRAPES
quart container **14¢**	lb. **5¢**
ONE PRICE—NONE HIGHER	ONE PRICE—NONE HIGHER

GRAPEFRUIT JUICY FLORIDA MED. SIZE	4 for	15c
BANANAS GOLDEN RIPE ONE PRICE—NONE HIGHER	doz.	14c
NEW CABBAGE 50-LB. BAG 75c ONE PRICE—NONE HIGHER	5 lbs.	9c
YELLOW SWEETS ONE PRICE NONE HIGHER	4 lbs.	9c
YELLOW ONIONS	10-lb. bag	18c

MISSISSIPPI IS LOW

NEW ORLEANS, La., Nov. 3 (AP). Salt water from the 110-mile distant Gulf of Mexico flowed through New Orleans city water mains today for the second time in more han forty years and speckled trout were being caught at the foot of Canal street for the first time in memory.

Due to prolonged drought through its entire watershed, the Mississippi has reached an almost record low and Gulf tides flowed into the long delta channel.

There are fewer pedestrian deaths in traffic accidents on holidays than on weekdays.

PRESENT WAR LAGS BEHIND WORLD WAR

First Two Months Lack Huge Casualty Lists, Swift Maneuvering And Big Battles Of 1914 — 433,168 Tons Of Shipping Sunk Exceeds 399,-947 Tons At Start Of World War.

EASTERN FRONT VICTORIES SIMILAR

Despite deadliest weapons in history—or perhaps because of them — the European war, two months old today, has lagged behind the World War.

The conflict on the Western front has lacked the huge casualty lists, battles with hundreds of thousands engaged and swift maneuvering that marked the corresponding period of 1914.

Only in the Polish campaign, starting Sept. 1, two days before Great Britain and France went to war against Germany, were there any large scale or decisive battles. Casualties there were vastly greater than on the Western front but less than on the Eastern front in 1914.

Dead and wounded in the opening days of the World War were counted in the scores of thousands; 1939 Western front reports count them in the low hundreds.

Few Killed

Germany reported only 196 killed and 356 wounded in the west up to Oct. 17. The Royal Air Force, only British service issuing casualty summaries, reported 122 dead up to last night. There have been no French casualty figures.

Since Great Britain declared war—

Germany has conquered Poland; sunk an estimated 433,168 tons of Allied and neutral shipping; admittedly destroyed a British battleship and an aircraft carrier and conducted a few scattered air raids on the British Isles and on British ships.

Britain and France have blockaded Germany by sea; France has made a shortlived invasion of the Reich along the Western front and Britain has carried out a few air raids on German naval bases.

During the first two months of the World War (Aug. 4-Oct. 4)—

World War

Germany dealt a terrific blow at Russia in the battle of Tannenburg; the Kaiser's armies swept through Belgium to drive within 40 miles of Paris before being stopped in the first battle of the Marne; on the seas, German submarines, surface raiders and mines sank 399,947 tons of Allied and neutral merchant shipping and seven British warships, including four cruisers; German warships spasmodically raided British seaport towns.

The British fleet bottled up the German fleet in the North Sea and the Russians repelled the Germans in the Baltic; Britain won a sea battle off Helgoland bight and British naval craft sank six German warships, including five cruisers.

One similarity in the two wars has been the quick German victories on the Eastern front.

Polish Campaign

The Nazi blitzkrieg on Poland brought heavy death tolls to armed forces and civilian population. A few days before Warsaw fell, Polish officials estimated the death toll of their armed force as between 50,000 and 100,000. No estimate was made on the number of civilians killed.

With Poland conquered, Adolf Hitler declared German military casualties were 10,752 killed, 30,-322 wounded and 3,404 missing. German army communiques estimated 600,000 Polish prisoners had been taken.

At the outbreak of the World War, two Russian armies invaded East Prussia and made rapid progress until the battle of Tannenburg Aug. 27-30, when the Russian armies were cut to ribbons. General Samsonoff, commander of one of the two Russian armies, was killed and of a total Russian forrce of 230,000 more than 70,000 were killed or wounded and 90,000 taken prisoner.

Warship Losses

Warship losses on both sides were heavier during the World War than they have been in 1939.

The British have lost the aircraft carrier Courageous and the battleship Royal Oak, both sunk by German submarines. The Germans have claimed the destruction also of the British battle cruiser Repulse and aircraft carrier Ark Royal, but the British have denied these claims.

In turn, the British Admiralty asserts that French and British warships have sunk or disabled a third of the Nazi submarine fleet, which at the outbreak of the war was said to total about 60.

During the first two months of 1914 the British warships Pathfinder, Aboukir, Cressy, Hague, Pegasus, Amphion and Speedy were sunk by submarines or surface craft. The Germans lost the warships Matnz, Koler, Ariadue, Kaiser Wilhelm Der Grosse, Madgeburg and Hela.

Armless Mother Uses Feet To Care For Baby

SAFFORD, Ariz., Nov. 3 (AP)—A six-day-old girl snuggled close to her armless mother, unaware that it was anything but normal to be juggled about for feeding and other care by feet instead of hands.

The mother, Mrs. Ruth Matthews, a transient, has eight other children. Despite dozens of offers for adoption, she expressed determination to keep the baby, born alongside a highway Saturday.

"It will not take much to feed the baby. It won't cost much," she added anxiously.

Because of the child's birth, Matthews has found a job on a nearby ranch and a house in which the family may live. Having a roof over its head, Mrs. Matthews related, is a new experience for her family.

At her insistence, Mrs. Matthews was released from the hospital to go to her new home, on the edge of one of the upper Gila Valley's many cotton fields.

Her armless condition is congenital. Asked how she managed a family and household duties under such a handicap, she said:

"I don't know. But I do manage. I get along. You can do an awful lot with your feet. I can thread a needle, sew, launder and iron, take care of the children and feed myself.

"I'll be able to take just as good care of my baby as you do in the hospital."

DIPLOMATS MUST PAY MARYLAND GASOLINE TAXES

BALTIMORE, Nov. 3 (AP)—State Department credentials notwithstanding, diplomats should be made to pay gasoline taxes in Maryland, a ruling by Attorney General William C. Walsh said today.

Walsh, in an opinion sent to Gov. Herbert R. O'Conor, held that certificates and identification cards which Secretary of State Hull proposes to issue to foreign diplomatic officers should not be honored.

The credentials would entitle their holders to gas tax rebates.

Walsh asserted no diplomats were entitled to exemption from various taxes unless such exemption was specifically provided for in treaties between the United States and nations they represent.

There was no provision in Maryland's law for recognizing exemption cards, his opinion said.

The First Presbyterian Church at Fayetteville, N. C., built in 1800, was designed by Christopher Wren.

EDUCATION WEEK TO BE OBSERVED HERE NOV. 6-11

American Education Week, celebrated annually since 1821, will be observed throughout the nation next week, Nov. 6 to 11.

Annapolis High School will have "open house" all week so that patrons and friends may visit classes and learn just how the school operates.

Essential purpose of American Education Week is to call to the attention of the public the importance of education in a democratic country. It has been estimated that during this yearly observance seven or eight million persons visit the schools of the nation to learn about modern methods of instruction and consult teachers about individual pupils.

Without the cooperation of the community, the schools are handicapped; for illiteracy cannot be eradicated, appreciations developed and ideals nurtured unless all groups responsible for and interested in the youth of the nation dedicate themselves to the cause of education and democracy, according to local educational leaders.

The high school will be open for visiting between the hours of 9 A. M. and 12 noon and 1 to 3 P. M. next week.

PANTS DEVICE

CHICAGO, Nov. 3 (AP)—Auburn Taylor has notified the National Inventors' Congress that it's no longer necessary for men to stoop over to pull on their pants.

From his home in Charleston, W. Va., he has dispatched plans and specifications for the Taylor Valet Chamber, or fireman's friend.

It shoots your pants on in a flash. An accessory also helps you with your shoes and socks, slipping them on or off with scarcely the requirement of a downward glance.

Children say IT'S FUN TO BUY POLL-PARROTS Here

Poll-Parrot SHOES

Come in ... and see! We know what growing feet need ... we know how to please both parents and children at the same time. Poll-Parrots add to the joy! They're thrilling to say the least. They're made with genuine leather in vital parts ... no paper or fibreboard. Bring in the children for their new Poll-Parrots.

$1.50 to $3.95

Frank Slama & Son
55 WEST STREET
Home of good shoes since 1869

ROOFING
DEPENDABLE LIFE TIME ROOFING
A Roof For Every Building
EASY TERMS, NOTHING DOWN
Write Mr. S. Hieatzman at
Enterprise Roofing Co.
2316-18-20-22 HARFORD AVE.
BALTIMORE, MD.

THE
Family Liquor Store
Is A Good Place For
Ladies To Shop
No Drinks Sold on Premises
NO BAR—NO NOISE
Our Prices Are Low
101-103 Main St.
For Delivery Call 2429

Special Benesch
89th Anniversary Sale
Value for Readers of the Evening Capital . . . .

A comfortable chair that's a wonderful bargain at this Special Anniversary Price for you! Sturdily constructed, with smart, durable covers.

Exactly as Illustrated

BIG LOUNGE CHAIR
just advertised at $12.95
50c a week! No carrying charge!
$9.95 WITH COUPON

This coupon entitles the undersigned to a regular $12.95 Lounge Chair for $9.95

Name......................

Address......................

CLIP COUPON AND BRING TO
BENESCH'S
549-557 N. Gay St., Howard and Mulberry Sts.
BALTIMORE
Open Saturday and Monday Nights, Free Parking
C

SERVICE RUGBY Flintwist DOUBLE-DUTY SWEATER

The most serviceable of all sweaters, is the famous "FLINTWIST" Sweater. That is the opinion of men who have put them to the most gruelling test of long, hard service, and are agreed nothing can equal their wonder wear.

If you want a sweater that will do year upon year of sturdy duty, that will give you warmth without weight or bulk, and will keep its shape for life, we guarantee all this in a "FLINTWIST".

Made in 8 colors and 4 models; button or zipper style.

At all Good Dealers

Buy your Flintwist Sweater at
W. H. Thomas Co.
143 MAIN STREET

"Shopping for Shoes?"

YOU GET VALUE SUPREMACY plus Style in STAR BRANDS

Cut your shopping time and worries by seeing Star Brands first. You're sure to find just the smart style you're looking for ... and Star Brands are known for value supremacy.

$2.95 to $5

Frank Slama & Son
55 WEST STREET
Home of good shoes since 1869

STAR THEATRE
TODAY AND TOMORROW

DARRYL F. ZANUCK'S
JESSE JAMES IN TECHNICOLOR
TYRONE POWER
HENRY FONDA
NANCY KELLY
RANDOLPH SCOTT
Directed by Henry King
A 20th Century-Fox Picture
Added—News of the Day

GUARANTEED SERVICE BY BONDED GARAGES
KEYSTONE AUTOMOBILE CLUB
The soundest business investment a motorist can make.
Phone or See Philip C. Woodward, District Manager
West and Lafayette Sts., Annapolis
Phone 2697 or 4362
Reciprocates with the Automobile Club Of Southern California

First Time In Annapolis . . .
Johns Hopkins Blue Jays Swing Band
New Annapolis Roads Club
Saturday, November 4th
9 'TIL 2
SUNDAY, NOVEMBER 5th
Opening Annapolis Sports Club
Trap Shoot 2 to 5
Clam Chowder—Oyster Roast
SPECIAL NOTICE
Club House reserved for private party Saturday, November 11th.

Cool Saving of $5.40
4 Year Old WYNBROOK
Straight Rye Whiskey

BOTTLED IN BOND
Wynbrook
Straight Rye Whiskey

Yes, Sir, a 100 Proof Straight Rye . . .
Our own private stock, mellowed to "bonding" maturity! One of our biggest repeaters!

Save $5.40 on Case of 12 quarts $18.00

Quart $1.95
Half Pint 53c
Full Pint 99c

Right Reserved to Limit Quantities! Sale Friday and Saturday Only!!

RUN RIGHT TO Read's
Drug Stores Worthy of Your Confidence

176 MAIN STREET
PHONE 2356

HEAR THE LATEST
VICTOR and BLUEBIRD Records
Jess Radio & Electric
Francis Street at Main Dial 3000
WE SERVICE ALL MAKES OF RADIOS

1940 DOG LICENSES

The 1940 licenses covering the period from November 1st, 1939, to December 31st, 1940, are now ready for issue at the regular annual license fee for all dogs that have 1939 licenses and for other dogs that have just been acquired or have become 4 months of age since November 1st.

The County Treasurer still has 1939 licenses for issue to all owners that are delinquent in taking out licenses.

All 1940 licenses must be procured not later than January 31st, 1940, otherwise a penalty will be imposed for delinquency.

S. P. C. A. OF A. A. Co.

TODAY AND SATURDAY
Republic
FEATURE PRESENTATIONS: 1:56, 3:55, 5:54, 7:53, 9:52 P. M.

YOUR NEW LITTLE Queen of the Ice
...in a romance fit for the Queen of Hearts!!
RKO RADIO
"Everything's ON ICE"
with
IRENE DARE
ROSCOE KARNS
EDGAR KENNEDY
LYNNE ROBERTS
ERIC LINDEN
MARY HART
BOBBY WATSON

"Somewhat Secret"
"Mutiny Ain't Nice"
Republic News Events

TODAY AND SATURDAY
CIRCLE
FEATURE PRESENTATIONS: 1:30, 3:28, 5:26, 7:24, 9:22 P. M.

1939's Happiest HIT!
IT'S GOT MICKEY!
IT'S GOT JUDY!
...IT'S GOT—
Everything
Mickey Judy
ROONEY GARLAND
in "babes in arms"
CHARLES WINNINGER
GUY KIBBEE
HUNDREDS MORE
M-G-M PICTURE

"FOOTBALL THRILLS"
CIRCLE NEWS EVENTS

SOCIETY

This column is conducted for the pleasure of the subscribers and readers of The Evening Capital. Information regarding happenings of a social nature among the residents of Annapolis and vicinity — parties, marriages, births, trips and visitors — is always most acceptable, and may be inserted by dialing Annapolis 2332, and asking for the editor of the Social and Personal Column.

Mrs. Melvin, Mrs. Handy Visiting In Norfolk

Mrs. Ridgely P. Melvin and Mrs. D. Claude Handy are spending some time at Norfolk, Va., with Mrs. T. A. Torgerson, wife of Lieut. Torgerson, U. S. N., who is on duty there.

Mrs. Torgerson is the daughter of Judge and Mrs. Melvin.

Mrs. Melvin and Mrs. Handy will return to Annapolis by way of Richmond where their daughters, the Misses Elizabeth Melvin and Elizabeth Handy, are pupils at St. Catherine's School. The young misses will return with their mothers to Annapolis for the Thanksgiving holiday.

The Rev. Mr. Magruder Here For Thanksgiving

The Rev. Daniel R. Magruder, of Hingham, Mass., is spending the Thanksgiving holidays with his sister, Miss Mary R. Magruder, of King George street.

To Give Thanksgiving Dinner For Midshipmen

Capt. and Mrs. H. A. Baldridge will entertain at Thanksgiving dinner tomorrow for eight midshipmen, among them their son, who is a member of the plebe class this year.

Thanksgiving Eve Dance Tonight at Yacht Club

The Annapolis Yacht Club will hold its annual Thanksgiving Eve dance from 10 P. M. to 2 A. M. tonight at the club house for members and guests.

Music will be furnished by the Rhythmonian orchestra and a large attendance is expected. Evening dress is requested, according to the committee in charge.

Mrs. Carr Winner In Garden Contest

Mrs. L. Warrington Carr was the winner in a contest sponsored by the Federated Garden Clubs to show improvement in a garden the beginning to date, it was announced at a board meeting and luncheon yesterday at the Emerson Hotel, Baltimore.

Trinity Church Aid To Hold Rummage Sale Friday

The Church Aid of Trinity Methodist Church will hold a rummage sale Friday, Nov. 24, at 98 West street.

Musical Party Planned For Dec. 11 In Owensville Hall

The annual musical party, for the benefit of St. Luke's Christmas Tree, will be held at 7:30 P. M., Monday, Dec. 11, at the Parish Hall, Owensville.

Mr. Slater Bryant and Mr. Hammond Cantwell are members of the committee in charge of which Mrs. William Shepherd is chairman.

The evening's program includes duets and solos by the children, musical selections by Mrs. Clyde Collinson, Mr. Cantwell and Mr. Bryant, and old songs and rounds by the audience.

BEFORE A COLD GETS A REAL START

Use a few drops of Va-tro-nol. It's a wonderful help in preventing colds from developing.

VICKS VA-TRO-NOL

Enjoy Your THANKSGIVING DAY DINNER at Carvel Hall

A truly fine Thanksgiving Day Dinner, served in the traditional Carvel Hall manner in the stately Colonial Room, will make this Thanksgiving Day a day of days for you and your family. It's the perfect way to celebrate this glorious American day of national thanksgiving.

DINNER MENU
Served from 12 noon 'till 9 P. M.

Hot Spiced Cider
Relish Platter
Seafood Cocktail

CHOICE OF
Green Split Pea Soup or Consomme

CHOICE OF
Filet of Sole with Tartar Sauce.... 1.25
Fricassee of Chicken, with
  Hot Biscuit 1.55
Broiled Filet Mignon with
  Mushroom Sauce 1.50
Roast Turkey with Chestnut Dressing, Giblet Gravy and Cranberry
  Sauce 1.50

Creamed White Onions
Baked Hubbard Squash
Buttered String Beans
Candied Sweet Potatoes
Whipped Potatoes
Hot Rolls   Butter   Jelly
Mixed Green Salad with Cheese Straws

CHOICE OF
Hot Mince Pie with Melted Cheese
Pumpkin Pie with Whipped Cream
Fresh Fruit Plate with Nuts and Raisins
Ice Cream or Sherbet
Demi-Tasse Served in the Lounge

Miss Nancy Barr Leaves Today For Charlottesville

Miss Nancy Barr, who has been visiting her uncle and aunt, Mr. Stringfellow Barr, president of St. John's College, and Mrs. Barr, left today to spend Thanksgiving at her home in Charlottesville, Va.

Her brother, Mr. William Alexander Barr, a student at the college, returned with her.

Miss Welch Arrives Home Today For Thanksgiving !

Miss Sarah Bond Welch will arrive today from Hood College where she is a freshman to spend the Thanksgiving holidays with her parents, Dr. and Mrs. Robert S. G. Welch.

Annapolis Cotillon Begins Season Tomorrow

The Annapolis Cotillon, under the direction of Mrs. Joseph D. Lazenby and Miss Virginia Lazenby, will open its season tomorrow with a Thanksgiving dance in the Carvel Hall Ball Room.

The younger group will meet at 7:45 P. M., and the older group at 9 P. M.

Mrs. F. V. McNair and Mrs. Amos F. Hutchins will be the chaperons.

Instruction in dancing will be given by Miss Martha Currier and Mrs. Hannah Stewart Taylor Hand, of Baltimore, representatives of the Arthur Murray Dance Studio, New York.

Mr. and Mrs. Borsodi To Spend Thanksgiving Here

Mr. and Mrs. Ralph Borsodi, of Dogwoods, Suffern, N. Y., arrived today with their infant daughter, Lorna, to spend the Thanksgiving holidays with Mrs. Borsodi's parents, Mr. and Mrs. C. H. Sherman, at their home on Conduit street.

Col. and Mrs. Taylor Have Week-End Guests

Col. James G. Taylor, U.S.A. (retired) and Mrs. Taylor, had as their week-end guests last weekend, Miss Mary Louise Hitt, daughter of Col. and Mrs. Parker Hitt; Mr. John Dempsey, of Philadelphia; and Mr. J. Ford Collison, of Baltimore.

Eastport Club To Hold Public Oyster Roast Sunday

An oyster roast, open to the public, will be given by the Eastport Democratic Club from 1 to 5 P. M., Sunday, November 26, at the clubhouse on State street, Eastport.

Mr. Charles Williams is the chairman in charge of the affair.

Auxiliary Sale Planned Dec. 2 By Christ Church

The annual auxiliary sale of Christ Church will be held Saturday, Dec. 2, at the Parish Hall, Owensville, beginning at noon.

Cake, flowers and toys will be for sale and a fancy table will display its wares. Luncheon will be served at 1 P. M. Miss Anne M. Cheston will be chairman.

Leave Today To Spend Thanksgiving In Pennsylvania

Mr. and Mrs. T. M. Heck and Mr. and Mrs. Shelley Palmer are leaving today to spend the Thanksgiving holidays with Mr. Heck's mother, Mrs. Earl D. Campbell, of Bethlehem, Pa.

Mr. Evans Initiated Into Society At Randolph-Macon

Mr. A. Paul Evans, of Arnold, was initiated into the Washington Literary Society of Randolph-Macon College at a recent meeting of that organization in its hall on the Randolph-Macon campus. Mr. Evans, a junior at the college, is a member of the Glee Club, a non-clerical member of the Clericus, and affiliated with the Randolph-Macon Players.

The Washington Literary Society, founded in 1853, trains its members in oratory, debate, extemporaneous speaking and other forms of public speaking as well as experience in the fundamentals of parliamentary procedure.

Miss Fowler In Business Office At St. John's

Miss Isabella Fowler, of Edgewater, has a position in the business office of St. John's College where she is secretary to Mr. John Winthrop Wright, college treasurer.

Miss Cantler's Marriage To Mr. Mayo Announced

Mr. and Mrs. Frank M. Cantler, of this city, announce the marriage of their daughter, Eutha Ellen, to Mr. George Mayo, of Nevada, Mo., on Nov. 17.

HOLIDAY SPIRIT AT SATURDAY ART CLASSES

Santa's holiday spirit already prevails in the Saturday morning art classes conducted by Miss Jennie Richardson at the Calvert Studio.

Unusually busy with pencil and paint brush, each student is working on a Christmas gift. Some are making nut bowls, painting an original design in vivid colors within its hollow surface. Others are using the same idea for tea trays.

Christmas Cards

Fay Acuff and Peggy Johnston, two members of the class, sketched informal groupings at a flower stall in the marketplace and are now portraying them in water colors. These familiar scenes will make their gifts of double significance to their parents.

Making Christmas cards by means of linoleum blocks occupies the two-hour sessions of several students. After sketching haphazardly in charcoal, the pleasing plan that gradually evolves is perfected and cut for reproduction.

Water Colors

Miss Richardson arranged a blue jug and a couple of yellow apples, one opened in half in mellow lusciousness for the boys in the class to portray in water colors. When Ben Warrington Carr began his study, he started with a small sketch and was encouraged to try one after another until he reached the actual size. By noon, his eight years may have prompted a better use of the paint.

Other young people being taught in these phases of art, as well as pastels, oils, modeling, and still life groups, are Annabelle James, Ella Malliard, Betty Anne Moore, D'Arcy Stephens, Charles Lamb and Kenneth Kirk Patrick. Miss Margaret Weems assists in the

---

instruction of the Saturday morning classes.

Model Sketching

Monday and Tuesday afternoons are scheduled for costume model sketching and painting by grownups.

Miss Richardson is a graduate of the Maryland Institute and a former teacher in its Saturday classes. She studied one season under Charles Hawthorne at Providencetown, Mass., and has exhibited her work in both the Museum of Art and Maryland Institute, Baltimore. Her present classes in Annapolis were begun sixteen years ago as a partner of Miss Katherine Walton.

New Gov't Farm Loan On Corn

WASHINGTON, Nov. 22 (AP)—Secretary Wallace announced today the government would make loans to farmers on surplus 1939-grown corn at the base rate of 57 cents a bushel.

Evening Capital

ANNAPOLIS, MD.
1884 -:- 1939

Published Daily Except Sunday by
THE CAPITAL-GAZETTE PRESS, INCORPORATED

TALBOT T. SPEER, President
DAVID S. JENKINS, Vice-President and Treasurer
E. M. JACKSON, JR., City Editor

You can have the EVENING CAPITAL mailed to you when away from the city by leaving your name and address at the office, for 45 cents per month. $5.00 per year payable in advance, to any postoffice in the United States or Canada.

Delivered in Annapolis, Eastport, Germantown and West Annapolis by Carrier for 45 cents per month. On sale at all newsstands.

Foreign Advertising Representative
J. J. DEVINE & ASSOCIATES, Inc.

New York—1932 Chrysler Bldg.   Atlanta—206 Palmer Bldg.
Chicago—307 N. Michigan Ave.   Pittsburgh—438 Oliver Bldg.
Detroit—817 New Center Bldg.   Syracuse—State Tower Bldg.

Entered as Second Class Matter May 28, 1933, at the Post Office of Annapolis, Maryland, under the Act of March 3, 1879.

MEMBERS OF THE ASSOCIATED PRESS

The Associated Press is exclusively entitled to the use for re-publication of all news credited to it or not otherwise credited in this paper and also the local news published herein. All rights of re-publication of special dispatches here also reserved.

SATURDAY, NOVEMBER 25, 1939.

PROTESTS FOR THE RECORD

Objections raised by European neutrals to Britain's plan to impose a blockade upon exports from Germany are mostly for the record. Most of the neutrals are of course not neutral, but they are in geographic positions that makes it compulsory to attempt to continue the illusion. None of these neutral states knows when its turn will come to join Poland, Czechoslovakia and Austria.

But for appearance's sake, they pretend to be annoyed by the British action. Actually, they know that their only salvation lies in British victory, regardless of the means necessary to bring it.

Germany's ruthlessness on the sea left England no alternative than to retaliate by every action possible. Sinking of 20 ships, flying the flags of seven nations, in one week has stilled all talk of a "phony" war for the time being, at least. Such destructiveness on the sea must be curbed speedily by England and France or the consequences could easily be dire.

Unless the ship lanes are held open, England will be seriously handicapped in moving supplies from the dominions and from the United States. No one seems to believe, however, that the havoc wrought by mines in the last week can be long maintained. In the end Germany will suffer more than Britain if, as a result, the latter energetically enforces its blockade of German exports. Exporting of goods is vital to Germany if she is to finance the war. Already the allied blockade of Germany is having its effect. That Der Fuehrer fears strangulation of his war efforts as a result is evident from the note of desperation to be seen in the latest campaign of sea frightfulness. Deserted by his supposed ally, Mussolini, and suspicious of his new pal, Stalin, Hitler is in a fix the like of which he never hoped to see.

LETTERS To The EDITOR

More About County Taxes And How County Officials Tried To Keep The Tax Rate Down.

Editor, The Evening Capital.
Dear Sir:—

The Anne Arundel County Budget for 1940 carries an average increase in the tax rate for all eight districts of 17¼ cents. Of this increase, 7 cents was imposed by the 1939 legislation enacted by the 1939 legislative Assembly, 2 cents was the increase required by the School Board, and 4 cents was necessitated to cover election costs, not incurred last year.

The increase levied by the Board of County Commissioners was, therefore, 4¼ cents. The principal items causing this increase were the County Health Officer's office, the County Welfare, and to avoid the deficit that has been incurred annually for some years.

The effort to get county finances on a pay-as-you-go basis is highly commendable, and should appeal to the business sense of everybody. I believe that business men generally will agree that any reorganization where waste has been the order will involve considerable first cost.

The total increase authorized by legislative acts would have represented an increase in the tax rate 8½ cents, but through the cooperation of five of the organizations benefitting by these acts, and the decision of the County Commissioners to cut $2,000.00 from the General Public Assistance appropriation requested, this was brought down to 7 cents.

The organizations that cooperated were as follows:

Organization	Amount Authorized	Increase Accepted	% reduction of Cut
County Police	$4,800	$2,280	47.50
1st Dist. Fire Dept.	1,440	600	41.67
4th Dist. Fire Dept.	2,125	1,450	68.25
Annapolis Library	3,500	500	14.25
Glen Burnie Library	700	100	14.25
Gen. Pub. Asst.	10,236.72	2,000*	19.53

*Imposed.

The representative of the fire companies of the Second District offered to cooperate provided the County Commissioners would accept a cut of 10% on their salaries. The County Commissioners each receive $600 a year for the responsibility of the economical expenditure of more than a million dollars of public funds. The salaries of the relief fire chauffeurs was fixed at $1,200.00 a year to start, with increases for longevity, as compensation for part time driving of a fire truck. To imply equality of value of public service between the two categories seems disproportionate. It is to be hoped the taxpayers of the Second District approve the stand taken.

The Budget Committee of the League for Lower Taxes in Anne Arundel County sat with the County Commissioners and the Budget Supervisor for about six evenings. They realized what an extremely difficult situation existed, and they were impressed with the sincere desire shown by the county officials to cooperate in order to bring about the very necessary reorganization of county affairs. It must be remembered that for years there has been no organized, systematic control of county expenditures, and in order to effect necessary and possible economies it is first necessary to establish a system that will show up needless expenditures and duplications of effort.

I will add that I do not wish to belittle the value of the work done and to be done by the County Health Office and the Welfare Board. It is merely a question of how much the people can afford to pay.

J. T. Bowers.

PRAISE FOR LOCAL S.P.C.A.

Editor, The Evening Capital.

Dear Sir—The unit of the Society for the Prevention of Cruelty to Animals for Annapolis and Anne Arundel county is probably equal to the best units in the country and superior to most of them.

The work is done systematically and efficiently and is maintained day in and day out with splendid steadfastness. Our community has never had anything like this good work for dumb animals before.

But, strange to say, it has been observed lately that there are a few persons who seek to change the operation of the society and in consequence seriously to reduce its effectiveness.

The purpose of this letter is to invite the renewed attention of all our citizens to the work that is being done by the S.P.C.A. in the belief that they will not forgive any interference with the society that will at all cripple it or check it.

Yours very truly,
RICHARD J. DUVAL.

DOROTHY DARNIT   By Charles McManus

Classified Ads

OAKY DOAKS   A Rising Young Inventor

The Great Balloon Ascension

SCORCHY SMITH   Wanted: A Happy Ending

Visiting Hour

ASSOCIATED PRESS
Review of 1939 Sports Events

YANKS MACHINE FLATTENS REDS Out of this home-plate confusion in 10th inning of final game at Cincinnati came a 7-4 victory for Yanks, giving them fourth series title in a row. The fun began when DiMaggio (rear) singled and Crosetti (1) scored. Thanks to a double error Keller raced in, bowling over Reds' Catcher Lombardi (left), who was still down when DiMaggio sprinted by. No. 8 is Dickey. Yanks took four straight games.

GOLF GLORY Make way for Pro Byron Nelson who bested Craig Wood to take National Open in two-day playoff of triple tie among Nelson, Wood, Shute. Bud Ward won U. S. Amateur; Betty Jameson won women's title.

CURB CONTROVERSY Sprint by Fenske (10) settled Princeton's June 17 "mile of century" but still unsettled is question over above turn into last stretch. Britain's Sydney Wooderson (28), whose stride broke when he stepped on curb, says he was bumped by Rideout when latter took lead. Race finish: Fenske, 1; Cunningham, 2; San Romani (24), 3; Rideout, 4; Wooderson, 5.

MUD IN THEIR EYES Fans who thought Johnstown (5), seen leading at above first turn in the May 13 Pimlico Preakness, would repeat his Kentucky Derby win over Challedon, who's hugging the rail, were disappointed. Challedon won Preakness, followed by Gilded Knight (2), 2nd; Volitant (4), 3rd; Impound (7), 4th; Johnstown, 5th.; Ciencia (6), filly that won $50,000 Santa Anita derby, last. In Nov. 1 Pimlico Special, Challedon defeated Kayak II, winner of $100,000 Santa Anita Handicap. Blue Peter won English derby.

TONY'S GOLDEN MOMENT Third-round triumph of Tony Galento, who floored Champion Joe Louis June 28, didn't last; Joe won by technical KO in Round 4, and Tony joined Lewis, Roper and Pastor in list of men who didn't beat Joe. Other fights: Nova stopped Baer, Ambers took lightweight title from Armstrong.

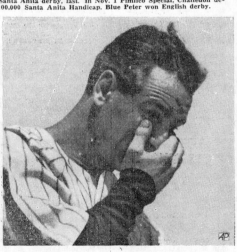

FAST Streaking over Utah's salt flats Aug. 23 in his 2,600-horsepower "Railton Red Lion" Britain's John Cobb set world records of 368.85 m.p.h. for measured mile, 369.74 for kilometer. This means better than six miles per minute.

U. S. LOSES CUP Pleased Australians hover 'round the Davis cup, symbol of world tennis supremacy which they won Sept. 4 at Haverford, Pa., John Bromwich defeating Frank Parker of California, 6—0, 6—3, 6—1, in final match. Left to right: Jack Crawford, Adrian Quist, Bromwich, Capt. Harry Hopman. Last year's tennis queen, Helen Wills Moody, made news by marrying Aidan Roark, polo star.

BEST To Nile Kinnick, Iowa's iron-man back who played 402 out of a possible 420 minutes in 7 major games went the Heisman trophy—annual award for nation's outstanding gridder. He helped pull Iowa out of 1938 cellar to second place in the Big Ten.

LAST PUTOUT Tears shook Yankees' Lou Gehrig July 5 when 61,000 N. Y. fans helped him say farewell to a career ended by infantile paralysis. He played 2,130 straight games, is now a N. Y. parole commissioner. Yanks also lost Col. Jacob Ruppert, their owner, who died in January. Another death: J. Louis Comiskey, White Sox owner.

TO THE LADIES! Wimbledon's July matches set beauty "high" when California Alice Marble (left) won the singles by defeating British Kay Stammers, 6—2, 6—0, and teamed with Mrs. Sarah Fabyan (right) to win women's doubles from Helen Jacobs, Billy Yorke. Bobby Riggs took men's singles, beating Elwood Cooke.

A RACE DEATH WON Beyond Bob Swanson's flaming car is auto in which Floyd Roberts of Van Nuys, Cal., last year's winner, suffered fatal injuries at May 30 Indianapolis Speedway. Roberts had collided with Swanson; a third car, driven by Chet Miller, overturned (foreground). Wilbur Shaw finished first, Jimmy Snyder, 2d.

CAGE TOPPERS Oregon won national collegiate basketball title from Ohio State, 46-33, at Evanston March 27. Above, John Schick (11), Ohio center, adds two points. Under basket is Lauren Gale (28), Oregon.

THE PUSH (BUT NOT) OVER Top football teams were Cornell, U.S.C., Tennessee, Texas A. & M.—to list a few—and this action shot shows at least one serious threat to Tennessee's uncrossed goal line: Vanderbilt Huggins hits a stone wall one foot from goal. Vols won, 13-0. The Cinderella team of season was Iowa, 1938 underdog that beat Notre Dame and enough Big Ten teams to finish second in conference with Ohio as No. 1. It was Coach Eddie Anderson's first year with Hawkeyes.

Navy Junior Boxers To Share Sports Program With Middies Who Compete In Seven Events

Baseball, Lacrosse, Tennis And Dinghy Races Scheduled For Afternoon — Juvenile Boxing Set For 9 A. M.

The 21st Navy Junior boxing tournament, with 60 participants ranging from 30 to 130 pounds, will begin at 10 A. M. tomorrow in the Naval Academy gymnasium.

The paper-weights, fly-weights and the "heavy-weights" of 100 or more pounds, will assemble at 9 A. M. for photographs. H. M. (Spike) Webb, Navy's veteran boxing coach, will run the tourney.

The officials will be Comdr. Charles L. Austin, (S. C.) head time keeper; Midshipmen Jess Worley and Jim Marion, referees, and Midshipmen John Williams and Jim Newsome, judges.

15 Defend Titles

Fifteen of the juniors will defend championships won last year, and there is much interest in juvenile ranks over the possible outcome of these bouts.

The enthusiasm of the youngsters has spread to the families and an array of mothers, fathers, sisters and other relatives will be on hand to back the battlers.

Varsity Ring

Motion picture photographers will snap the junior fighters in various poses beginning at 9 A. M. They will be shown punching light and heavy bags, skipping rope, and training in general. Mothers and fathers will come in for their share of the picture taking.

The bouts will be held in the varsity boxing ring. Bleacher seats have been installed to take care of the crowd.

There IS A War

BERLIN (AP)—The war is beginning to make itself felt where for most Germans it will hurt most. Beer production has been cut 25 per cent.

MILDNESS QUALITY TASTE —at a lower price

MARVELS The CIGARETTE of Quality

Your STOP in Baltimore **The ARUNDEL HOTEL** CHARLES ST. AT MONUMENT AVENUE **RATES FROM $1.50 UP**

Our Family's WHISKEY RECIPE Harry E. Wilken

PINT $1.00   QUART $1.99

THE WILKEN FAMILY BLENDED WHISKEY

At package stores and bars. Blended whiskey. 86.8 proof. 75% grain neutral spirits. Copyright 1940, The Wilken Family, Inc., Aladdin, Schenley P. O., Pa.

Navy Gymnasts At National Meet In Chicago

Midshipmen Attend National Championships—Locals Are Eastern Champs

Champion gymnasts from all parts of the country will participate in the national collegiate meet at the University of Chicago tomorrow night. The Naval Academy team, conqueror of the Army and winner of the eastern intercollegiate title, offers the greatest threat to Illinois's defending champions.

The Illini, whose captain, Joe Giallombardo, ends his years of intercollegiate competition this year, will be particularly anxious to repeat last year's intercollegiate title stand because of their photo-finish defeat by Minnesota's team in the recent Big Ten meet. Minnesota, with a small but efficient team, outpointed the Illini 105½ to 105.

Other institutions in the N. C. A. A. meet include Minnesota's Conference titleholders; the University of Chicago squad, Big Ten champions two years ago; Temple University, Eastern champions in 1938, and Dension University. A strong team from the University of California at Los Angeles, West Coast titleholders, also is expected to come to Chicago for the meet.

Giallombardo is the only defending champion who will compete in the 1940 meet; last year he won both the tumbling and the all-around performance crowns. The stocky Illinois captain also is Big Ten champion in tumbling and co-champion on the parallel bars with Bob Hanning, of Minnesota.

Navy's World's Champion

Outstanding individual competitor in the meet probably is Midshipman Stanley Ellison, of the Navy, who already holds two world records in the rope climb and may break one Saturday night. Ellison set a record in the 25 feet climb in the National A.A.U. meet in 1939, and in the Army-Navy meet this spring set a new record on the 20-feet rope, the length used in the N.C.A.A. meet. He ascended the distance in 3.6 seconds, .2 seconds under the old mark.

Injury of Dave Danser, Temple veteran (who was second in the flying rings competition) which kept him out of the Eastern intercollegiate meet, leaves the event open to a stiff battle among Jim Hafey, Minnesota's Big Ten titleholder; Midshipman Bill Butler, Navy's intercollegiate champion and Bob Weiss, of Illinois, Big Ten runner-up.

Ed Danser, younger brother of the Temple star, and winner of the eastern all-around championship in tumbling and also is an outstanding prospect to take the horizontal bar title vacated by his teammate Adam Walters. John Cress, of Illinois, Big Ten champion, will furnish Danser's stiffest competition.

Parallel Bars

On the parallel bars Sam Togel, wearer of the eastern crown, will tangle with four closely matched contestants, Bob Hanning, Gopher holder of the Big Ten title, and Hafey, Giallombardo, and Illinois' Paul Fina, second, third and fourth place winners respectively last year.

Leonard Bassett, the Navy's leading representative, is conceded an excellent chance of upsetting Harry Koehnemann, of Illinois, Big Ten champion, but Minnesota's Jim Ronning and Captain Glenn Pierre, of Chicago, also are considered dangerous.

FLEA HUNT

FOREST GROVE, Ore. (AP)—Dr. C. Anderson Hubbard's 5-year itch for a flea is over. He caught it. The Pacific university biologist, noted for his contributions to the British museum flea collection, found an unfamiliar "skipper" on a deer mouse. It was there by some mistake of nature, so he decided to look for the original carrier. Fvie years later he found another on a mole shrew. Several moles, all carrying the same strange flea, indicated they were the true hosts. Hubbard named the new flea "corypsylla Jordani" in honor of Dr. Karl Jordan, famous flea authority and curator of the British museum.

A species of Russian sturgeon is believed by scientists to attain an age of between 200 to 300 years.

Meet Ben Hogan, Golf's Winter Heat Wave

YOUNG BEN HOGAN, golf's latest scoring sensation, grins as he exhibits the irons he used to win three straight tournaments.

THE TEXAN who plays from White Plains, N. Y., is one of the straightest and longest drivers among the pros, hitting with a low trajectory.

HERE HOGAN SHOWS HOW he blasts out of traps and stops the ball near the cup. Ben won his first tournament at Pinehurst in mid-March and then repeated with victories at Greensboro and Asheville, N. C.

PHENOMENAL PUTTING has been a major reason for his recent triumphs. "I just keep the putter face dead upright," he explains.

BEN'S STRONGEST BOOSTER is—you guessed it—the Missus. She never lost faith in Hogan's game during the many months he played without winning. Now she can help him spend the $6,500 he won this spring.

BOWLING SCORES
By SAM STOKES

In a match replete with thrills the Tomanio Brothers, Fred and Ernie, scored their second straight triumph over the Zerhusens. Opening with a 243 set the Zerhusens, Hen and Len, quickly ran into an eleven pin lead only to find the Tomanios reversing the decision in the second game and themselves taking a five-pin advantage.

With Henry shooting a fine 126 together with Len's 117 the Zerhusens took a thirty-pin lead with the score reading 693-663 at the end of the third game. At this point the Tomanios, teaming together in fine fashion, came to life; picking up nine sticks in the fourth game to bring the deficit down to twenty-one. Here, Freddie inserted a powerful 154 and Ernie contributed a 112 game to quickly wipe out the Zerhusens' advantage, and breeze home the victors by eighteen pins.

Complete scores follow:

E. Tomanio	120	123	100	135	112	590
F. Tomanio	112	100	108	111	154	585
Totals	232	223	208	246	266	1175
H. Zerhusen	114	83	126	108	125	556
L. Zerhusen	129	124	117	129	102	601
Totals	243	207	243	237	227	1157

Commercial League

The Wednesday night section of the Commercial League resulted in three wins for Johnson Lumber over the American Stores, and the E. E. Anchors making a clean sweep of their match with Hopkins. Carroll Lee turned in a fine 386 set for Johnson, while A. Lowman's 349 was high for the losers. Brewer, Stine and Welsh were instrumental in the Anchors' three wins, and Davis deserves a hand for his splendid 376. The Commercial League standing to date:

	W.	L.
Sadler's Hardware	70	26
Strange and White	58	38
Tilghman Co.	58	38
Annapolis Buick	57	39
Exper. Station Anchors	57	39
Capital-Gazette	54	42
American Beer	53	43
B. & B. Nash	52	44
Experiment Station Jays	42	44
Carr Brothers	46	50
A. B. & T. Co.	45	51
Johnson Lumber Co.	54	51
Post Office	45	51
Hoff's Garage	41	55
American Stores	37	59
Hopkins Furniture Co.	36	60
Southern Dairies	31	65
B, and A. Railroad	27	69

Naval Academy League

The status of the leading teams in the Naval Academy League remained the same this week as all the top teams turned in two wins apiece. Crosby and McKee were the aces for Sheet Metal while Burns' 349 led the Carpenters team. Anderson's 381 was responsible for the Laundry's two wins although Back's 355 was creditable for the losers. Phillips led the Garage 5 to victory with a noble 377, as Heath's 347 topped the vanquished. Masons, with Smith's 341, took the odd game from Administration as Suit shot 348 for the losers. Brewer's 356 helped Electricians take all three from Supervisors despite a bang-up 350 set by Gomaljak. Tarleton's 336 was wasted as the Tree Doctors lost three for Luce Hall. Reynolds was tops for the winners with 337. E. E. Ramblers, with Williams 372, took the odd game from the Plumbers as W. McNew blasted a 357 set. Cliff French's gigantic 383 total was largely responsible for Marine Engineering's two wins over the Tailor Shop. Bouchal, with 340, was high man for the losers. Riggers captured three games from the Painters as Moreland's 360 was tops. Thompson and Green shot 329 and 328 respectively for the victims. Led by Barr, who rolled 150-114-149 for a beautiful 413 set, Armory shut the Power Plant out while Lamb totaled 346.

The bowling season is fast drawing to a close, so you teams that are just laying off the pace will have to apply the pressure if you expect to overhaul the league leading Sheet Metal.

Special Matches For Saturday

An attractive girls' match has been arranged for Saturday night which the Annapolis Buick quintette will bowl the American Nut Brown Ale five. Hostilities will get underway at 9:00 o'clock, and as the two teams are evenly balanced a good match should result.

Campbell's Distributing, composed of Phipps, Scible, Campbell, Easterday and Seim, will roll a return match with Park Circle of Baltimore on Saturday evening at the Severn Alleys. The first meeting of these two teams earlier in the season in Baltimore resulted in a win for Campbell's so Park Circle, made up of Hohman, Pace, Stetz, Hamilton and Rimbach, will be seeking revenge for the previous loss. Plenty of action is promised so come early and get a ringside seat.

Al Blozis Of Georgetown, World's Greatest Shot Putter, To Face Navy Opposition Tomorrow

AL BLOZIS

League Race Seen As Two Team Affair

NEW YORK, April 12 (AP)—Baseball "experts" as a whole are generally agreed that the 1940 National League race will be a two-team affair, but right there the general agreement stops. They are split almost 50-50 on whether the St. Louis Cardinals or the Cincinnati Reds will come home in front, with a slight edge going to the St. Louis entry.

Of the 76 sports writers taking part in the Associated Press poll all but three named either the Cards or Reds in the No. 1 spot, the Cards drawing 39 first-place votes to 34 for the defending champions. One long-shot addict picked the Pirates, and two strung along with the Cubs.

Point Bases

Second-place ballots also were pretty well cornered by the 2 teams, although nine voters picked the Cubs for the runner-up spot, six named the Giants, four the Dodgers and two the Pirates.

There the common agreement ceased, however, and it was every man for himself the rest of the way in, or at least down to the Bees and Phillies. The Phillies escaped being a unanimous last-place choice by three seventh-place votes, and the Bees escaped a similar seventh-place designation by drawing one fourth, one fifth, two sixth and three eighth-place votes.

On a point basis—eight for first, seven for second, etc.—the Cards edged out the Reds by seven points —557 to 550.

Sports Round-Up
By EDDIE BRIETZ
(Associated Press Sports Writer)

NEW YORK, April 12 (AP)—Among the things that hurt Billy Conn down was the 7,300 frogskins Uncle Sam nicked him for income taxes. (He can fight June 1 if he'll stop worrying) . . . Open Champ Byron Nelson will have to pass the $5,000 Goodall Tourney because he's needed back at Inverness, Toledo, his home base . . . Dizzy Dean ate a chicken dinner, topped it off with a beer or two and predicted Gabby Hartnett wouldn't last the season—a power-

ful lot of chattering on two glasses of suds . . . Patty Berg was among the golf teachers at a Minnesota golf clinic . . . Wake Forest has cropped Elon for Texas A. and M., and now you tell one.

Today's Guest Star

Dick Vullum, Minneapolis Times-Tribune: "Benny Leonard is reported in wrong with the big shots around New York because he sold them Johnny Paychek as an opponent for Joe Louis . . . I know Leonard was never really sold on Paychek and it's too bad he had to get himself in a spot where he was compelled to do the Paychek gang that favor."

This Screwy World

Missouri U. had to order size 13½ shoes for Raymond Phelps, 230-pound tackle from Montana . . . Bob Feller's closest pal on the Indians is that bad boy, Rolly Hemsley . . . Lew Tendler, the old lightweight, seldom goes to a fight, but never misses a ball game . . . Which is something since it is the A's and Phils he has to look at . . . Out in Minnesota a boxer apologized to another boxer for calling him a bum . . . A

rookie reported to the San Antonio club equipped with his own uniform, shoes, glove—and ball . . . And Lee Grissom has gone one up on Lefty Gomez for screw ball honors by picking the Dodgers to win the bunting.

Headline: "Frisch says two Waners will miss opener."

We pass along this item with mingled grief and pain. For it looks as if the Waners Are really on the wane.

Brietzkrieg!

A gent on the coast is writing a 24,000 word book on the life of Seabiscuit . . . Frank Loebs, new football coach at Washington U., pronounces it "Labes" but he had just as soon be called Butch . . . All the boxers Oklahoma sent to the A. A. U. tournament at Beantown were tobacco chewers . . . Most popular player on the Red Red Sox barnstorming tour was Jimmy Foxx . . . Runner-up: Ernie Lombardi . . . Horton Smith will do a bit of guest instructing at New York U. next Monday . . . Add holdouts: Herb Dana, who has been making $7,500 per as commissioner of football officials out west, was offered reappointment at $500 a year . . . Wow! . . .

One-Minute Interview

Frank Howard, Clemson coach: "I was all set to follow Jess Neely to Rice until I saw pictures of the Sugar Bowl antics . . . I changed my mind right quick when I saw John Kimbrough in action . . . I just couldn't stand the thought of having him come steaming my lines . . . So I stayed at Clemson where all we have to do is read about him."

Attention Europe!

Medina, Tennessee, is getting ready to open the outdoor checker season June 1 with a big parade, a brass band and the governor doing the orating.

2 Great New Gasolines!

ESSO PREMIUM QUALITY AT REGULAR PRICE!

ESSO EXTRA ALL-TIME HIGH IN PREMIUM PERFORMANCE!

STANDARD OIL COMPANY OF NEW JERSEY

FOR SMART ● ENTERTAINING

BUBBLES

The Crisp, Super-Carbonated Suburban Club Soda

LARGE BOTTLE 10c

Distributed by **Herman O. Collier** 270 West St. Dial 4271

Tide Calendar
FOR APRIL, 1940

Day	High Water A.M.	High Water P.M.	Low Water A.M.	Low Water P.M.	MOON Rise	MOON Set	SUN Rise	SUN Set
12	9:47	9:56	3:13	4:42	8:43a	11:17p	5:34	6:41
13	10:37	10:48	3:59	5:34	9:34a	....	5:33	6:42
14	11:37	11:47	4:55	6:31	10:31a	0:09a	5:31	6:43
15	....	12:30	6:03	7:38	11:32a	0:56a	5:30	6:45
16	0:51	1:31	7:19	8:22	12:37p	1:40a	5:28	6:45
17	1:57	2:31	8:32	9:11	1:45p	2:22a	5:27	6:46
18	3:00	3:28	9:41	10:00	2:54p	3:01a	5:25	6:47
19	3:57	4:24	10:42	10:44	4:06p	3:39a	5:24	6:48
20	4:52	5:14	11:41	11:28	5:18p	4:18a	5:28	6:49
21	5:42	6:04	....	12:36	6:29p	4:58a	5:21	6:50
22	6:33	6:52	0:13	1:30	7:40p	5:40a	5:20	6:50
23	7:22	7:41	1:00	2:21	8:47p	6:26a	5:19	6:51
24	8:11	8:30	1:46	3:12	9:51p	7:14a	5:17	6:52
25	9:00	9:24	2:36	4:04	10:47p	8:07a	5:16	6:53
26	9:50	10:16	3:29	4:57	11:37p	9:02a	5:15	6:54
27	10:42	11:12	4:26	5:52	....	9:59a	5:14	6:55
28	11:36	....	5:31	6:46	0:21a	10:56a	5:12	6:56
29	0:14	12:32	6:41	7:38	1:00a	11:53a	5:11	6:57
30	1:18	1:28	7:51	8:26	1:34a	12:49p	5:10	6:58

PLACE	DEDUCT FROM BALTIMORE TIME
Port Carrol	0:05
Sardy Point	1:35
Annapolis	1:55
Thomas Point Shoal	2:35

Moon's Phases: New 7th, 1st quar. 15th, Full 22nd, Last quar. 29th

ANNAPOLIS-MATAPEAKE ROMANCOKE-CLAIBORNE FERRIES

FALL & WINTER SCHEDULE Effective September 26, 1939 DAILY AND SUNDAY Eastern Standard Time

BETWEEN ANNAPOLIS AND MATAPEAKE

Leave Annapolis	Leave Matapeake
7:25 a. m.	7:25 a. m.
8:00 a. m.	8:00 a. m.
9:00 a. m.	9:00 a. m.
10:00 a. m.	10:00 a. m.
11:00 a. m.	11:00 a. m.
12:00 noon	12:95 p. m.
1:00 p. m.	1:00 p. m.
2:00 p. m.	2:00 p. m.
3:00 p. m.	3:00 p. m.
4:00 p. m.	4:00 p. m.
5:00 p. m.	5:00 p. m.
6:00 p. m.	6:00 p. m.
7:00 p. m.	7:00 p. m.
8:00 p. m.	8:00 p. m.

BETWEEN ROMANCOKE AND CLAIBORNE

Leave Romancoke	Leave Claiborne
10:00 a. m.	9:00 a. m.
2:00 p. m.	1:00 p. m.
5:00 p. m.	3:00 p. m.
6:00 p. m.	5:00 p. m.
8:00 p. m.	7:00 p. m.

THE CLAIBORNE-ANNAPOLIS FERRY COMPANY ANNAPOLIS, MARYLAND

Evening Capital

ANNAPOLIS, MD.
1884 -:- 1940

Published Daily Except Sunday by
THE CAPITAL-GAZETTE PRESS, INCORPORATED

TALBOT T. SPEER, President
DAVID S. JENKINS, Vice-President and Treasurer
E. M. JACKSON, JR., City Editor

You can have the EVENING CAPITAL mailed to you when away from the city by leaving your name and address at the office, for 50c per month. $5.00 per year payable in advance, to any postoffice in the United States or Canada.
Delivered in Annapolis, Eastport, Germantown and West Annapolis by Carrier for 50 cents per month. On sale at all newsstands.

Foreign Advertising Representative
J. J. DEVINE & ASSOCIATES, Inc.
New York—1932 Chrysler Bldg.   Atlanta—1265 Boulevard Drive, S.E.
Chicago—307 N. Michigan Ave.   Pittsburgh—438 Oliver Bldg.
Detroit—817 New Center Bldg.   Syracuse—State Tower Bldg.

Entered as Second Class Matter May 28, 1933, at the Post Office of Annapolis, Maryland, under the Act of March 3, 1879.

MEMBERS OF THE ASSOCIATED PRESS

The Associated Press is exclusively entitled to the use for re-publication of all news credited to it or not otherwise credited in this paper and also the local news published herein. All rights of re-publication of special dispatches herein are also reserved.

THURSDAY, MAY 2, 1940.

DECORATIONS

Annapolis people love a parade and local merchants several times each season decorate their stores with flags and bunting in compliment to the particular event at hand.

Usually these decorations are rented from some out of the city concern which owns a great quantity of fine flags. The cost of renting flags for one event isn't large, in fact, the decorating concerns probably make only a reasonable profit, yet if the local merchants got together they could, it would seem, save a considerable sum over a period of years.

If all the merchants who decorate would get together and buy their own flags and decorations they would have them on hand for years to come. Decorations lend a festive spirit to a city, and certainly by owning their own bunting local business men could decorate at the least provocation.

With Annapolis fast becoming a convention city, and several major events, headed by the annual conclave of the Elks, set here for late summer, a united decoration buying program guided by the Chamber of Commerce would seem to be in order.

WASTING LEAVES

It may have been the publicity given the recent meeting of the Chemurgic Society that prompts a Philadelphia newspaper writer to deplore the waste of burning leaves. He hints that chemists or other scientists ought to find a way to make better use of the tremendous leaf tonnage produced by shade trees and forests.

No doubt he has been properly coached, rebuked and instructed by his "To the Editor" letters from scientific gardeners, florists, foresters and hobby farmers. They have told him on excellent authority that "the accumulation of leaves as leafmold in forests is the explanation of the sustained soil fertility there even though no fertilizer is ever supplied." That quotation is from one of the best gardening authorities in the country. Also they warned him that he never should burn leaves, but should add them to a compost heap to be used for his garden.

But after making all these concessions to those who have use for leaves, it is still possible to back the Philadelphia writer in acknowledging that to millions of homeowners leaves are just a nuisance, and the quicker chemists find ways of making them into wall covering, ladies' stockings, automobile body finish or tires, the better said homeowners will be pleased.

The factor that dims such hopes for the near future is the present abundance. While man is wasting such a lot of stuff that could be used easily if he were a little hard pressed, he is not likely to go to a lot of trouble about leaves which can be gotten out of the way by scratching a match.

MOTHER'S CASH VALUE

Song and story through the ages proclaim the value of a mother's love. Some of the tenderest passages in all literature have to do with the sufferings, both physical and spiritual, of youth bereft of it.

It has been the central theme of great novels; the most poignant appeal in poems long remembered. But though the worth of mother love to offspring is recognized by all races and in all climes, it never has been a tangible, susceptible to yardstick measure or evaluation by troy weight.

Unable to find that New Jersey statute law had ever put a pecuniary value on a mother's life, Judge Barbour in the Bergen circuit court was willing to create a precedent in the case of a mother of five in "a typical American family of modest means," who had been killed in an automobile accident. This he did by refusing to set aside a verdict of $30,000 damages for her estate, saying:

"Certainly it would seem that if the jury is entitled to consider the intellectual, moral and physical training which a child is entitled to receive from its mother, one cannot very well say that it is not worth $5,000, and that the child, in fact, does not suffer a loss of pecuniary value to that extent. In view of the elements which the jury properly considered, the court cannot say that the verdict is excessive."

This is an interesting commentary in more respects than one. It should, among other things, stimulate parents whose eyes it meets to a little introspection as to whether they are worth as much to their children as they ought to be. And unless this reasoning is set aside in the event the case is appealed, there is a precedent for other jurists in dealing with damages alleged to be excessive. It can, though, scarcely affect the decisions of other juries. These have to be made on the basis of the facts in each case, and such awards as are determined will be not by court precedents, but by the jury's own reasoning.

RETIRING DIPLOMAT

Mr. Doris Duke Cromwell's appointment as United States minister to Canada, when it was made by President Roosevelt, was construed in political quarters as part of the build-up for his candidacy for United States Senator from New Jersey. If that is so, it the build-up will prove is controversial.

might be fairly said that he had a build-up, but how effective Mr. Cromwell stepped out of diplomatic character to make a pro-Ally speech which pleased Canadians, but provoked a public reprimand by Secretary Hull. Now Mr. Hull announces in Washington that the new minister will resign immediately after the May 21 primaries are run off in New Jersey.

Thus Mr. Cromwell will appear on the home grounds after May 21 not as a diplomat, but as a private citizen in quest of office—a private citizen who, with one section of the administration, at least, has lost his pulling power. His campaign manager says he is pleased with the turn of events. His candidate, he adds, needs no longer labor under "diplomatic limitations and restrictions" in the conduct of his campaign. After what Mr. Cromwell said at Toronto, it did not appear to Mr. Hull, for one, that the minister to Canada was unduly hampered by any officious "limitations."

But it cannot be, can it, that Mr. Hull's action presages the time when these diplomatic posts will no longer be shopped about as ... heavy campaign contributors? No, that would be too much to hope for.

Man About
Manhattan
By George Tucker

NEW YORK — Buddy DeSylva and Irving Berlin, two showmen of a kind, were cornered in the pit of the old empty French Casino. The idea was to learn why Victor Moore, Bill Gaxton, Zorina, Irene Bordini and a host of boys and girls were running around on the empty stage and trudging upstairs to the mezz, where somebody was lazily pounding a piano.

"A new show," said DeSylva. "A musical comedy," said Berlin. "A sort of political satire on Louisiana," added DeSylva. "We call it," said Berlin, "'Louisiana Purchase.'"

So that was it, Louisiana Purchase. And Vic Moore was a Senator from New England who went south to investigate alleged scandals down there.

"Please understand," said Berlin, "this is all in fun. Just innocent fun. Remember 'Of Thee I Sing?' That was a satire on the White House, on the incoming and the out-going Presidents. That was eight years ago. This is a satire on a state. But it's comedy. Musical comedy. Nobody points a moral. Nobody wants to reform anybody. We just turn the crank, and hop on, and let 'er go."

* * *

YOUR correspondent inquired whether these gentlemen thought anyone would take offense to anything in the show.

"Well," said DeSylva, "our first scene is a lawyer's office. The lawyer dictates a letter to Irving and me. He tells us we can't put the show on. He says we'll risk being sued. Then he tells us there's a way out. He says we mustn't name a real state, or a real city, or real people, but that we must write about a fictional state."

"That's right," broke in Irving Berlin, "so we built our first musical number around this idea, and we call it our 'Explanation to the Audience.' We carefully point out, in song, that:

"'The politicians we've investigated,
Could come from Maine, or Kansas or Montana;
So we've laid our story in a mystical state,
A mythical state we call Louisiana.'

"Because," Berlin went on, "there isn't really a state named Louisiana. Not really. It's one of those fictional Balkan Kingdom ideas. And then we had to make up a name for a city, too, and we incorporated it in the song like this:

"'We laid our scenes
In New Orleans.
A city we've named so that there would be no fuss.
If there is such a place, it's certainly news to us.'

"Which," broke in Mr. DeSylva, "certainly explains the case. It's just like a foreword in a novel, saying any similarity between the characters in the book and in real life is purely coincidental and a big surprise to us. We coined the words 'Louisiana' and 'New Orleans,' and I think we're going to have a lot of fun."

SO THERE it is. "Louisiana Purchase," a new musical comedy, is a fictional story laid in the mythical city of New Orleans in the entirely fictional state of Louisiana. Irene Bordini takes the role of the owner of a famous restaurant. Zorina will play a bankrupt countess who just has to get hold of $500. Vic Moore is the non-drinking, non-smoking, non-hand-holding senator who investigates conditions. Suddenly a guy named Westbrook Pegler shows up. He is fictional too. What happens from there on is the secret of the Messrs. Berlin and DeSylva, and will be until opening night, which will be sometime in May.

The
Literary
Guidepost
By John Selby

"BRITAIN AND FRANCE BETWEEN TWO WARS," by Arnold Wolfers (Harcourt, Brace: $3.75).

THERE IS a chill charm about the writing of Arnold Wolfers' "Britain and France Between Two Wars," which, for this reader, is the best possible approach to such a study. The author is neither ponderous nor pompous; nor is he knowledge-proud nor hopelessly clever. He skims along, neatly choosing the facts that support his thesis and eventually persuading his reader — sometimes against his reader's judgment it should be added.

Mr. Wolfers is a Swiss and at present is professor of international relations at Yale. It is possible to see traces of his background throughout his book, and particularly in his conclusion. It is this last which may annoy some readers, but these same readers may have difficulty refuting their author's reasoning. The conclusion is simply that after this war the only practical course will be a return to the "balance of power" theory in Europe.

The basic disagreement between the French and the British over Germany was, he shows, that France believed it imperative that Germany not rise above the limits imposed by the Versailles treaty, whereas Britain was not opposed to an increase of power for it. France could not see German influence extended, even to the east and southeast; Britain was for the most part quite willing that concessions be made in those directions, since they would improve the balance of power on the Continent and also might appease Germany to the extent that

a major explosion might be avoided.

Yet there was Franco-British harmony in spite of these different views, because after all Britain did not want Germany strengthened at the expense of Britain's really vital interests, and certainly not to the point of permitting Germany to dominate western Europe. Hence, when in 1939 the world faced Germany's threat of domination, it was possible for the two countries to unite against it.

There is not space to detail Mr. Wolfers' reasoning. He says, in the conclusion of his admirable book, that although the only alternative to domination by one nation or one group of nations is a balance of power, even this does not solve the problem of "peace." It would provide only a kind of platform upon which a course toward an ultimate (but as yet impracticable) federation of European states might be worked out.

Your Family Names
Their Origin And Meaning

Barton

Barton is in the "local class" of names and throughout various counties of England there are found some 37 parishes or places which bear it. The surname Barton signifies, "Dweller at the barley grange or barn," and is derived from the Old English, "bere," barley, and "tun," enclosure. This surname has its strongest representation in England, especially in Gloucestershire, Kent, Hampshire, and Lancashire, also in Sussex, Lincolnshire, and Wiltshire. In the West of England the demesnes of a manor or any large homestead were called bartons. Barton and Barten are other forms of this surname.

One of the earliest members of the family in America was Thomas Barton (1730-1780) who came about 1751 from Ireland, to Lancaster, Pennsylvania, where he was pastor of St. James Church for nearly twenty years. In 1753

he married Esther Rittenhouse, granddaughter of William Rittenhouse, who came from Holland to Germantown, Pa., and built the first paper mill in America in 1690. Bartons prominent in America today are: Albert Olaus, editor, historian, Madison, Wisconsin; Arthur James, minister, publicist, Wilmington, North Carolina; Bruce, author, New York City; Donald Clinton, geologist, Houston, Texas; Francis Brown, professor of Romance Languages at the University of Minnesota; George, author and journalist, Philadelphia, Pa.; George Lloyd, Jr., educator, Niagara Falls, New York; James Levi, clergyman, Brookline, Massachusetts; Loren Roberts, artist, New York City; Walter Elbert, lawyer, Washington, D. C.; William Edward, judge, Houston, Missouri.

The arms shown above are ascribed to Edward Rittenhouse Barton of Englewood, New Jersey, who was born at College Point, Long Island, July 24, 1847. The motto "Crescit sub pondere virtus" is translated: "Virtue thrives under oppressor."

- - And Tell Us, Too!

ALAN KLEIN

Washington Daybook
By Jack Stinnett

WASHINGTON—It's the easiest thing in the world to fight a war on a map on your library table.

Any ordinary fellow with a knack for strategy can beat any full fledged general, hands down. As Napoleon observed, anybody can map a masterful piece of strategy. But it takes a genius to carry it out.

The trouble with you and me when we map strategy is that we leave out factors, including the weather, and what it does to armies and navies, and the big surprise use for weather—water, air, and terrain.

More often than not, it's the weather that wins and loses battles, and not armed forces.

In this battle for Scandinavia, two extremely important weather factors don't appear on your map.

1. The North Sea is the foggiest area on the earth's surface in the spring, and,

2. Norwegian roads at this time of year look like the lane to the pasture after a spring rain.

That means the Germans have an ally in the Scandinavian weather, just as they had the weather for a friend in Poland, and just as the Russians tried to use the weather against the Finns—and darn near lost the war.

* * *

Weather Beat Poland

IN Poland, Germany wanted to stage a blitzkrieg with a mechanized army. So her generals took the weather map for 70 years back, picked the average driest month of year—August—and struck. Motorized armies run best in dry country. You know the rest of the story.

In Finland Russia chose December. Finland was invaded eight times, you see, and every time, the attacking force chose December. It's the one time the lake ice is frozen deep enough to hold up marching columns. At other times, an invading army could be cut up, and its units beaten by guerillas.

Dame Nature almost beat the Russians, because she sent the worst package of weather in 50 years to northern Europe.

In Scandinavia, the Germans are playing the weather to the hilt, and the law of averages, too.

Usually, the fog closes in 40 per cent of the time along the coast of Norway at this time of year. Add to that some 10 hours of darkness in every 24, and you have increased hiding time for German transports and naval units—perhaps up to 60 per cent of the time.

That's just what the Germans want to slip past the British fleet. German ships navigate along the Norwegian coast only during fog or darkness. When the weather clears they hide in fjords.

Fog Favors The Germans

NOW that Germany has her armed forces in command of land positions at Trondheim, Oslo, Bergen, Stavanger, Kristiansand, and other points, she has the drop on both naval and aerial forces because of the fog. And for an attacking army, the roads are terrific—all slush, now freezing, now thawing.

Victor Hugo, in Les Miserables, wrote: "If it had not rained on the night of June 17, 1815, the future of Europe would have changed." He meant the rain delayed units of Napoleon's armies. Subsequent historians think Napoleon's conflicting orders had something to do with Waterloo, too, but anyway, rain was an important factor.

At Jutland in 1916, the weather almost beat the British fleet, then suddenly changed, and helped the British gunners find their targets. Today the weather is more important than it ever was before. The weather man has a word for it. Visibility. He tells us what visibility is in his daily charts, and on his daily maps.

As visibility goes, so goes the war.

Did You Know That

The first boys' club in America was established at Hartford, Conn.

It is believed that the first fire insurance company in America was organized at Charleston, S. C. in 1736.

New oil reserves found in the last five years are equal to the total United States oil production of the first 70 years.

The cedars of Lebanon grow 6,000 feet above sea level, and reach a height of 50 to 80 feet.

Oystermen who "plant" their beds, cover the producing bottoms with layers of old shells. The young oysters attach themselves to these after passing the larval stage.

William Lloyd Garrison, the abolitionist at one time, was editor of the National Philanthropist, the first paper published in America for the promotion of total abstemption from liquor.

Rural free mail delivery in the United States was begun in a small way in 1896.

The first medical school in America was established in Philadelphia in 1751.

LITTLE SPITFIRE
By Jean Randall

YESTERDAY: To Brenda's surprise she learns that her friendship with Saltus is the subject of conversation of The Street. Mac advises her to drop Saltus and Eric tells her to stick to her guns. Resentful at first, Brenda later decides she likes the interest shown in her.

Chapter Eight
Alaine And Abner

BRENDA had seated herself to become An Author.

A good many preparations had been required but they were finished now. All that remained was to write the novel which was to bring her fame and fortune—but especially fame, Mac . . . this is, certain people would take her Work seriously when she became a really noted writer.

Her typewriter stood on a firm table. She had had to buy that table since nothing in the house seemed other than shaky. The typewriter had a new ribbon. On one side lay a package of yellow second sheets; on a shelf of her closet was a box of "good sixteen-pound paper," as recommended by more experienced writers. Close at hand were a dictionary, thesaurus and a book of familiar quotations. She had no intention of making use of the last two but they gave a professional air to her desk.

All that was lacking now was the row after row of little words, tripping along in proper procession to tell her story. As for the story itself . . . Brenda had worked out a real system about that.

On her bed lay a sheet of thin cardboard, a yard and a half long, three-quarters of a yard wide. It was marked off into thirty-two squares; squares which represented the chapters of the book. In each square was a brief outline of what was to be contained in the chapter it stood for. As for instance: "Chap. I. Margareth meets Brian in wood. She stumbles over root, and he helps her home. Dialog develops mutual friends and interests; ends with engagement Brian call next day for ankle."

It seemed a very simple and easy way of writing a book. Brenda marveled that she had never heard of anyone using it before. A square for each chapter, a chapter a day; in thirty-two days her book would be done, provided she felt it did not need revising.

She had made other preparations, too.

"I'm not to be interrupted when I'm writing," she said severely at the table. Supposedly she addressed the interested Grenadine but everyone present realized her warning included them all. "The fear of interruption is as bad as the interruption itself, you know, I must feel I'm safe when I'm writing."

Adelaide replied innocently: "Mae never minds how many people interrupt him. Sometimes I feel guilty, thinking how we use his room as a gathering place nights when he's writing."

"Oh, well, mine's not creative work," Mac said comfortably. "Anyhow, I'm used to being interrupted at the office. I know what Brenda means, though. We'll all have to listen for her typewriter and refrain from knocking at her door when it's going."

"Her door or the typewriter?" Eric inquired frivolously. He had made it amply clear that he considered it a waste of time for a girl as pretty as Brenda to spend her time picking away at a typewriter.

"Her door as the typewriter," Brenda said simply. With sentimental encouragement, Brenda sometimes thought she would seek other quarters.

'Neighborhood Matter'

HOWEVER, here she was; and here was Margareth and Brian, whose program clearly outlined for them, and neither one finding a word to say to the other. Their creator was acutely annoyed with them. This first chapter, consisting almost entirely of conversation and having little action, must sparkle! Indeed she had written at the top of the cardboard in the first square "sparkling! But how in the name of heaven was an author to make her characters sparkle if they refused even to speak to each other? It was all most discouraging.

All morning she wrote and tore up, wrote and tore up. In the afternoon, she laid away one completed page with a sigh. It was far from being what she wished but she had to make a start somewhere. She was fitting in a fresh sheet of paper when upon her outraged ears fell the sound of a knock.

"Grenadine!" she exclaimed sternly. "Didn't I tell you——"

But it was Adelaide's plaintive voice which said: "It's I, dearie! I'm so sorry to interrupt you but he said it was important, truly he did, Brenda! And when Judge Harper says anything is important——"

Brenda flung open the door. "Judge Harper? To see me? What for?"

Her landlady shook her head. "I haven't the slightest idea. He asked if you were in and I said yes but you were writing; and he said it was important and would you please come down——"

"Tell him I'll be with him in two minutes!"

Brenda powdered her nose and ran her comb through her curls. If there were bad news from Aunt Anne . . . but no, surely Dr. VanNess would have been selected as its bearer rather than Judge Harper.

"Good afternoon, Judge!" She gave him both her hands as he rose a little stiffly. Her apprehensions returned as she saw how troubled was his face. "Is — has Aunt Anne—"

Old Judge Harper might be stiff in his joints, but his mental faculties were as alert as ever. He said swiftly: "My dear child, I am not the bearer of bad news! I haven't had a word from your aunt. It's a—a neighborhood matter on which I've come to consult you."

"Me?" She spread one small hand over her heart and her dimples flashed. "Oh, Judge Harper, am I to be consulted about neighborhood matters already? I'm so flattered!"

He looked somewhat abashed. "I . . . you—it's partly because you're a stranger, my dear, and—and young. I must be honest with you. Isobel Burke is young, too, but she's too familiar with the situation. She thinks I'm forever crying 'wolf! wolf!' and perhaps I am." The old eyes under their wrinkled lids sought hers imploringly.

"Tell me about it," she invited.

He glanced toward the door. "If you don't object to my closing it—? Not that Adelaide and everybody else in The Street isn't aware of the facts, but I'd like to present them to you without—without comment."

When the door was safely shut, he began briefly.

"It's the Abernathy twins—Alaine and Abner. They've had one of their quarrels again—"

Brenda interrupted, despite her respect for the old man.

'Secrets Of The Street'

"BUT I thought they were so devoted to each other! I thought they hardly left the house except in each other's company!"

"Even the most devoted persons quarrel," was the somewhat dry answer. "And usually their quarrels are more bitter than those whose attachment is casual. Every now and then Alaine and Abner have really dreadful—well, one might as well call them rows, I suppose. When they were quite young it didn't matter; they threw things at each other, then kissed and made up. But now—"

"Now?" Brenda prompted.

"It's more serious. In fact, it's very serious. I . . . I feel disloyal, telling you about this, Brenda, but after all you're a Burnham—you have a right to know the secrets of The Street." He looked down at his hands, locked tightly on one knee. Suddenly aware of his evidence of agitation, he loosed them, let them drop at his sides.

"Alaine has a young man," he said simply. "A—a suitor. Abner detests him, whether with reason or from fraternal jealousy I don't know. Alaine pays little attention to him except when she quarrels with Ab. Then she sends for him—his name is Ned Barrow—and threatens to marry him. Eric and Isobel—in fact, practically everybody on The Street, insist it is merely bluff; that she will never do it. But Ab gets into a panic about it and comes to me; and I—I'm an old fool," he said, smiling, "but I get disturbed, too."

"Why?" she demanded. "Don't you want Alaine to marry? Or do you know something against this suitor?"

He shook his head. "Not a thing in the world! I don't want her to marry him because she doesn't love him. That's plain enough, isn't it? Or she'd see him when she's not quarreling with Ab. A marriage entered into out of revenge — in anger — has small chance of producing happiness, it seems to me."

"Of course. You're perfectly right, Judge. Alaine mustn't marry this Barrow—unless she decides to while she's at peace with her twin. But what can I do about it?"

"You can come and talk to her now," was the unexpected reply. "He's waiting while she packs."

"Waiting at the Abernathy house, you mean?" Her tone was incredulous.

"Yes. She and Ab had one of their worst rows right after lunch. I couldn't help hearing them—I never can help it in the summertime with the windows open," he said unhappily. "And when I saw young Barrow drive up a few minutes ago I was entirely prepared for Ab's dashing in to implore my help. I can't force my way into the child's bedroom, you know," he concluded trustfully, "I came right to you."

Brenda's eyes had been growing wider and wider as she listened to this preposterous tale. Now she exclaimed with a little gasp: "But, Judge, I've only met her once! She'd have every right to order me out—if I went barging into her house, let alone into her room!"

"Does that matter if we keep her from doing so foolish a thing?"

The sheer simplicity of the question caught her breath. He was right, of course. What did Alaine's attitude matter — what difference did it make if she ruined Brenda for all time—if interference just now could protect her happiness?

"I'll come with you," she said, and followed him out of the house without even stopping for her hat.

Continued tomorrow

Side saddles for women were first used in England by Queen Anne in 1388.

Motor transportation is rapidly replacing pack animals for hauling in Afghanistan.

Evening Capital

WEATHER
Cloudy with light showers tonight; Tuesday partly cloudy and warmer, local showers in afternoon.

VOL. LVI — NO. 138. EVERY EVENING EXCEPT SUNDAY ANNAPOLIS, MD., MONDAY, JUNE 10, 1940. SOUTHERN MARYLAND'S ONLY DAILY TWO CENTS

ITALY DECLARES WAR

BRITISH AIRCRAFT CARRIER GLORIOUS SUNK

LATE NEWS

HOLDS AMERICA HAS NOT GROWN SOFT

Canton, N. Y., June 10 (AP)—Industrialist Owen D. Young said today America can, "if necessary, fashion weapons of war equal to any in their deadly power."

"Let no one think that because we are rich and comfortable that we have grown soft and weak," the honorary chairman of the General Electric Company's board of directors told St. Lawrence University's graduating class.

BRITAIN LOSES AIR ACE

London, June 10 (AP)—Britain's first air ace of the war, Flying Officer E. J. "Cobber" Kain, unofficially credited with more than 40 German planes shot down in action, has been killed, it was disclosed today. His death resulted from a flying accident while on duty, not in action.

BRITAIN VISIONS NEW NATIONS AT WAR

London, June 10 (AP)—Lord Beaverbroke's Evening Standard predicted today that "this coming week will be the greatest in the history of the world * * * ."

"Never before," the Standard said, "did men extend their field of war across whole nations * * * and before the news is out fresh continents may be shaken by these terrific convulsions and perhaps themselves engulfed."

For the prize of Paris, the paper said, "the German Fuehrer would slit the throats of more than half the youth of Germany," while "in Rome a master opportunist waits for a chance to snatch his twardy gains from the furnace."

DEATH PLUNGE

Washington, June 10 (AP)—Mrs. Esther Schwartzman, 48, Brooklyn N. Y., plunged to her death today from the second-story of the home of a sister, with whom she had been staying. The coroner said he would issue a certificate of suicide.

TEACHERS HAVE JOB OF KEEPING DEMOCRACY ALIVE

Frostburg, Md., June 10 (AP)—Governor O'Conor rested upon the nation's teachers today the responsibility for "keeping alive and strengthening the ideals of democracy upon which this country was founded."

New totalitarian ideas of foreign nations, he told the Frostburg Teachers' College graduating class, were "inculcated into the young people, boys and girls, during their formative years in the classroom, and by the various other methods of propaganda that are available in profusion today."

F.D.R. SPEAKS TONIGHT

Washington, June 10 (AP)—President Roosevelt will discuss the European war and international relations early this evening in a hastily-planned address at the University of Virginia's commencement exercises.

BEE CAUSES TROUBLE

Cumberland, Md., June 10 (AP). Mrs. Sue M. Hixon, widow of William T. Hixon, narrowly escaped serious injury while returning from Hill Cres Burial Park, where she had placed flowers on the grave of her husband, when she lost control of her automobile while battling a bee.

The machine overturned and careened down an embankment.

Stock Market

By Victor Eubank

NEW YORK, June 10 (AP) Leading stocks fell 1 to more than 4 points—a few inactives were off as much as 10—in today's market as Italy took the long-debated step and plunged into the war on the side of the Germans. Steels then came back and cancelled losses and other groups stiffened near the final hour.

Quotations of selected stocks at close today follow:

Al Chemical	135½
American Can	87
American Radiator	5⅛
American Smelting	34¾
A. T. & T.	149
Anaconda	19⅞
Baltimore and Ohio	3
Bethlehem	67
Chrysler	54½
Consolidated Edison	23⅞
Corn Products	45
General Cigar	..
General Electric	28½
General Motors	38⅝
Goodyear	13⅛
International Harvester	39
Johns Manville	44
Kennecott	25¾
Montgomery Ward	33½
National Dairy	12¼
New York Central	9⅝
Packard	3¼
Penney (JC)	72
Penn. R. R.	16⅜
Republic Steel	14⅝
Sears Roebuck	62½
Southern Railway	8⅝
S. O. of N. J.	33
Texas Corporation	34⅜
Union Pacific	73
U. S. Steel	45⅛
Va-Car Chemical	..
Va-Car Preferred	14½
Western Union	14⅝
Woolworth	30¼

New Ministers Assigned To Local Churches

The Rev. E. Cranston Riggin Made Supt. Of Methodist Baltimore East District

New ministers were assigned to the Methodist churches in Annapolis and Eastport by Bishop Edwin Holt Hughes at the church conference which closed last night at Westminster.

The Rev. E. Cranston Riggin, for five years pastor of Calvary Church, was appointed superintendent of the Baltimore east district, succeeding the Rev. Dr. F. R. Bayley, who was assigned as pastor of Wilson Memorial Church, Baltimore.

Pierpont To Calvary

The Rev. William Pierpont, former pastor of the Calvary Church, Martinsburg, W. Va., was assigned as pastor of the local Calvary Church, succeeding the Rev. Mr. Riggin.

The Rev. R. A. Rice, pastor of Trinity Church, was assigned to Lingamore and Liberty. He was succeeded at Trinity by the Rev. J. J. Dawson.

The Rev. E. O. Otto was transferred from the Eastport church to Sparrows Point. The Rev. J. E. Stacks was assigned to Eastport.

Rev. Hoffman At Baldwin

The Rev. William M. Hoffman was continued as the pastor of Baldwin Memorial Church at Severn Crossroads.

Other ministers appointed were:
Ferndale-Pasadena—C. L. Felty.
Glen Burnie—J. A. Dudley.
Green Haven—W. R. Ruths (supply).
Linthicum Heights — W. A. Gbets.
Magothy—R. E. Armstrong.
Marley—L. E. Haddaway.
Mount Carmel—W. R. Harris (supply).
Odenton—William Schmeiser.
Patapsco-Dundalk—W. H. Stone.
Patuxent—S. J. L. Dulaney (supply).
Riviera Beach—T. H. Baker (supply).
Severn-Jesups—B. P. Moore.
Wesley Grove—H. M. Waters.

PAYS FINE FOR RECKLESS DRIVING

Emanuel T. Tople, 46, was fined $6.45 for reckless driving when he was brought before Trial Magistrate James G. Woodward.

C. H. McGarry, 23, was fined $6.75 for disorderly conduct. W. F. Johns, 38, colored, was given a suspended 30-day sentence for disorderly conduct.

Top Cadet

Harold Brown (above) of Concord, N. H., is the No. 1 graduate of the United States Military Academy in the June 1940 class. He and 28 classmates were on the list for the award of honors at the "Star" parade. For four years, he compiled the "highest standing in general order of merit."

Second Classmen Leave On Cruise

Will See Navy Crew Race At Poughkeepsie

Three hundred midshipmen, half of the new second class, left today on eight destroyers for a five-week training cruise along the Atlantic Coast.

The squadron will visit the Dahlgren Proving grounds, Indian Head, Key West, Pensacola, New York, Newport and West Point. The midshipmen will see the intercollegiate regatta at Poughkeepsie and cheer the Navy crew on June 18.

In previous years the second class has made three cruises of a month's duration each, one-third of the class going on the destroyers at a time. This year's schedule, with two cruisers, gives a week longer at sea.

WPA HELPS MD. GUARD

BALTIMORE, June 10 (AP)—National Guard facilities in all sections of Maryland have been expanded and improved by the WPA, State WPA Administrator Francis H. Dryden said today.

COUNCIL MAKES VANSANT ACTING CITY TREASURER

James Vansant today took office as acting city collector and treasurer, filling the vacancy created by the death of George F. Quaid.

The acting appointment was made by the Mayor, Counselor and City Council.

The Council will hold the regular monthly meeting tonight to dispose of routine business.

WEST ANNAPOLIS P.-T. A. TO MEET

The West Annapolis P.-T. A. will hold its final meeting of the year at 8 P. M. tomorrow at the school.

Mrs. Guy Clements, president of the Maryland Congress of Parents and Teachers, will install officers for the coming year. Plans for the annual school picnic will be made.

St. John's College Will Graduate 13 Tomorrow

Exercises Will Be Held Under Old Liberty Tree

Thirteen members of the graduating class of St. John's College will receive their diplomas at 11 A. M. tomorrow at exercises held under the Old Liberty Tree on the front campus. All took the old elective courses at the college.

Dr. Thomas Parran, Surgeon-General of the United States, a graduate of St. John's and member of the Board of Visitors and Governors, will present the diplomas and make the commencement address.

Board Meets

The Board of Visitors and Governors met today as the senior class picnic was held. During the afternoon a party was held at the boat house. Tonight the cotillion board will hold another boat house party and at 10 P. M. the "hellzapopping dance," with those attending wearing old clothing, will start.

The seniors, in academic caps and gowns, attended the annual baccalaureate sermon yesterday in St. Anne's Protestant Episcopal Church.

The Rev. Dr. Edward Darlington Johnson, rector of the church, used as his text part of the 50th Psalm, "these things hast thou done, and I held my tongue."

Baccalaureate Sermon

His theme was the seeming silence of God. He pointed out that some men live in a partial world, a half world—it may be a world of sports, or finance, or scholarship—to the exclusion of other things.

"To some, the world of religion is a closed world," he said. "God is thought of, if at all, as a silent person. But, impressive, beautiful and convincing are the beliefs and utterances of those who not at all bereft in this world of seeming silence.

"And God speaks through such persons to all of us, wherever a voice is lifted in behalf of moral personality and holy fellowship. In the words of Browning:
" 'Through such souls alone
God stooping shows sufficient of his light
For us in the dark to rise by. And I rise'."

Reception Planned

Graduates and their guests will be entertained at a reception and luncheon given by the college in McDowell Hall after commence-

(Continued From Page Six)

DISABLED VETERANS BACK DEFENSE MOVE

The local chapter of the Disabled Americans Veterans unanimously adopted a resolution commending President Roosevelt on his defense measures at the group's regular monthly meeting aboard the Floating Hotel, foot of Prince George street.

The resolution follows:

"Chapter No. 3 of the Disabled American Veterans of the World War of Annapolis, wishes you to know that they have, by resolution, unanimously endorsed your admirable and timely action in strengthening the defenses of our country.

"GEORGE J. CROWLEY,
"Commander.
"L. L. MERRILL,
"Adjutant."

Commander Crowley, was elected as delegate to the national convention of the organization, to be held August 24 to 31 at Green Bay, Wis.

4 DEAD OVER WEEK-END

3 Fatalities On Highway —Youth, 7, Drowns

HAGERSTOWN, Md., June 10 (AP)—Ralph Henson, 39, a railroad employee, died this morning at the Washington County Hospital of injuries suffered when he was struck by a car operated by Joseph E. Jones, Boonsboro, while crossing a street in Hagerstown Saturday night. Henson is survived by his wife, four sons and a daughter. An investigation of the accident is under way.

(By The Associated Press)

Highway accidents and a drowning claimed four lives in Maryland over the week-end.

Donald Kavanaugh, 7, son of Mr. and Mrs. Martin Kavanaugh, Baltimore, died in an iron lung yesterday after he slid from an inflated inner tube into five feet of water in Middle river.

Unconscious When Found

A companion summoned aid, and police pulled the unconscious boy from the water and took him to a hospital. Physicians worked in vain to revive him and said he apparently died in the iron lung.

Traffic victims were:

Roland J. Koller, 17, Baltimore, who died when a car plunged into a marsh near Prince Frederick.

Head-On Crash

Warren B. Cox, 71, hitchhiker from New London, Conn., struck by an automobile on the Philadelphia road, near Bush river.

Edward L. Smith, 29, Cambridge, fatally injured in a head-on collision of two automobiles near Cambridge.

BALTIMOREAN HURT IN BOAT CRASH

James C. Chambers, of Baltimore, today was recovering in the Emergency Hospital from injuries received in a crash between a motorboat and a rowboat yesterday off Horn Point.

Mr. Chambers was in the rowboat when it was struck by the motorboat. He was tossed into the river and bruised. After being brought to the foot of Third street, Eastport, in the motorboat he was taken to the hospital in the city ambulance.

LOCAL YACHTSMEN WIN AT WEST RIVER

Take Events In Initial Summer Races

Members of the Annapolis Yacht Club were winners in two of the three events in the West River Sailing Club's initial races in the summer series yesterday.

John Kramer's "Stormy," which won the 20-foot round bottom race at the local Yacht Club yesterday, came in first again in the 20-foot open event.

Second in the West River race was E. H. Hartge, West River, sailing "Chesapeake." "Wing," sailed by Carrol Smith, of the West River club, was third.

Sea Witch Wins

"Sea Witch 11," sailed by Vincent Kramer, of the Annapolis Yacht Club, won the 20-foot chine bottom race. In the similar event here yesterday morning, he came in third.

Carl Skinner, West River, sailed "Aelour 11" to come in second.

In the albatross race, Emil Hartge, West River, was the winner in the "Hawk," and John Narin, of Shady Side, was second in the "Wistley."

County Boys And Girls Star In W. Md. Meet

Anne Arundel Loses Championship But Ann Dorn And Lyle Parlett Star

Anne Arundel county boys and girls failed to successfully defend their 1939 Maryland Western Shore public school championships at College Park on Saturday, but they finished sixth, with just nine points less than the winning Allegany county squad.

The final standing for the counties follows:

Allegany	60
Washington	58
Baltimore	58
Frederick	55
Prince George's	52
Anne Arundel	51
Montgomery	28
Charles	28
Carroll	28
St. Mary's	25
Howard	20
Harford	19
Calvert	3
Garrett	2

Set Two Records

Countians were outstanding among the 1,850 children from the 14 competing counties. Among eight meet records broken during the day, the chief laurels went to Ann Dorn, of Anne Arundel, who leaped 9 feet in the standing broad jump to shatter her own existing mark of 8 feet 1½ inches.

Another record was turned in by

(Continued on Page Six)

FUNERAL RITES FOR GEORGE FRANCIS QUAID

Funeral services for George Francis Quaid, city treasurer, were conducted at 3:30 P. M. yesterday from St. Anne's Church by the Rev. Edward D. Johnson.

The pallbearers were Walter H. Myers, William G. Brewer, Charles Gates, D. Ross Vansant, John T. Basil, George Frank, Jess Russell and Edward Wild.

Burial was in Cedar Bluff Cemetery.

Mr. Quaid, who is survived by his widow, Mrs. Louise G. Quaid, died Thursday at his home, 94 Shipwright street, of heart disease.

John M. Taylor was in charge of funeral arrangements.

O. BOWIE DUCKETT FUNERAL SERVICES HELD

Funeral services for Oden Bowie Duckett, Register of Wills of Anne Arundel County for 20 years, were held at 3 P. M. today from All Hallows Chapel, Davidsonville.

The Rev. Victor Ross officiated and the pallbearers were Charles B. Bishop, Bernard Williams, Benjamin Watkins, 3rd, Ramsay Hodges, Jr., J. Irving Bird, 3rd, Rogers Israel, Frank A. Monroe and Jonathan Sellman.

Burial was in All Hallows, Davidsonville.

Mr. Duckett died at his Davidsonville home Friday after a short illness.

John M. Taylor was the funeral director.

POLICE BOYS' CLUB MEETS

Members of the Police Boys Club gathered recently at the Municial Building for a meeting and drill, under the direction of Policemen James Moreland, James Wilde and Melvin Covington.

Games were played and refreshments, donated by two Annapolis firms, were served.

JOINS GERMANY AND SENDS TROOPS AGAINST SOUTHERN FRANCE THROUGH RIVIERA

Mussolini Announces Decision To Italian People—Orders Soldiers Against "Reactionary Democracies Of The West"—Nearly 2,000,000 Nazis Hammer French Line Guarding Paris—British Troops Land To Aid French—Aircraft Carrier Lost In North Sea—Turkey Ready To Fulfill Mutual Assistance Pact With Allies

PARIS, June 10 (AP)—Premier Reynaud in a radio address to the French nation today said "our armies have retreated slowly, and only after destroying all points they have relinquished."

Italy plunged into the European war at the side of Germany against England and France today, and Berlin reported that Premier Mussolini's Fascist troops had marched into French territory through the Riviera at approximately 6:30 P. M. (11:30 A. M., E. S. T.).

Mussolini, speaking from the balcony of the Palazzo Venezia before a wildly cheering crowd of Fascists, announced the sending of his vaunted "9,000,000 bayonets" against the "plutocratic democracies and the reactionary democracies of the west." He said it was a struggle between young and progressive people as against the decadent people.

BRITISH AIRCRAFT CARRIER SUNK

As he spoke nearly 2,000,000 German soldiers were hammering at the French defenses guarding Paris from the north, while some German tanks had reached the Seine river, 35 miles northeast of the French capital. Fresh British troops landed in France to support the battling French troops stubbornly resisting the Nazi drive all along the front in the sixth day of continuous battle.

The British Admiralty announced that the British aircraft carrier Glorious, 22,500 tons, a converted cruiser, had been sunk along with the transport Orama in the North Sea. All allied forces were withdrawn from Narvik, Norway, to throw into the struggle in France.

Turkish officials, in first reaction to Italy's announcement, voiced Turkey's resolve to fulfill her mutual assistance pact with France and Britain.

Bourse Suspended

Trading was suspended on the world-famous Paris Bourse and there were indications that the French Government might remove from the capital as they did in 1914. A British news agency reported that Paris had been placed in a state of defense and that permanent staffs of ministries were removed to the provinces.

In the titantic struggle to save their homeland against the biggest Nazi offensive of the war, the French had dropped back yesterday to a main line along the heavily wooded Bresle river—a line extending through the Oise valley to the Marne plains south of the Aisne. Today the center of the Weygand line was falling back to meet the threat of its left flank from the Nazi tank column which

(Continued on Page Six)

FRANKLIN DELANO ROOSEVELT: The First Third-Termer In History

ROOSEVELT'S CAREER started at 28 in New York state senate. At 31, he took post of Assistant Secretary of Navy, which he held during World War. He's shown, left, as he looked in those days. In 1920, he ran for vice-president.

INTO PRESIDENCY, after two terms as New York's governor, FDR took over from Hoover in depression times. Started public works, farm relief, and inaugurated new system of press conferences and "fireside chats."

SECOND TERM found FDR still the adroit chief of state. He visited South American "good neighbors," panned dictators, found time to fish and play host in world's biggest social event entertaining Britain's monarchs.

THIRD TERM brings the President to another crossroads after depression and world crisis. Right, he's shown signing the conscription bill. With bi-partisan cabinet, he stresses national unit, strong defenses.

By MORGAN M. BEATTY
AP Feature Service Writer

WASHINGTON—President Roosevelt guessed right in 1938 and won a third term in 1940.

The Republicans guessed wrong in January, 1938, and lost in 1940!

That's the conclusion of many impartial observers. They base it on the general theory that the threat of war led voters generally to support experienced President Roosevelt despite the fact that he ran in violation of the third-term tradition.

The observers thumb back through 40,000 pages and almost three years of Congressional Record for their evidence.

The President guessed, on January 3, 1938 (page 6, Volume 83, part one, Congressional Record, 75th Congress) that world troubles would be uppermost in the critical western states, prevented a Republican slide there.

Wallace Vs. McNary

Ten days later, Bertrand Snell, speaking for the Republican party (page 184, Volume 83, Congressional Record appendix, 75th Congress), guessed exactly opposite.

There were, of course, other strong undercurrents that helped to spell victory for the Democrats.

Vice-Presidential candidates Henry Wallace and Charles McNary sort of cancelled each other out in the critical western farm states, prevented a Republican slide there.

New Deal publications may have played a part. For instance, the Federal Works Agency's "Millions for Defense" pictured New Deal relief spending for defense in the depression years, well ahead of the national alarm of 1939. "Technology on the Farm," by Henry Wallace's department of agriculture, outlined a 10-year program further accenting help for the poorer farmers of the nation. And a report by the Securities and Exchange Commission added up the hundreds of millions of dollars of family holdings by the Fords, duPonts, Rockefellers, Mellons, etc.

Then there was the relief vote, generally regarded as a reservoir of strength for the party in power, and votes from several big city political machines, like the Kelly-Nash setup in Chicago, and from the solid south.

But the big element still remains the threat of war.

Started In '37

The story of how the Democrats won begins with Christmas week in 1937. Another economic setback had the country by the throat. Steel production had dropped 70 per cent in a few months. Automobile sales were tobogganing. Business and government were alarmed.

Suddenly two New Deal minions, Utility-fighting Bob Jackson and general handy-man namecaller Harold Ickes, launched the Administration's bitterest attack on big business. Jackson accused the nation's tycoons of a sitdown strike against the New Deal. Ickes attacked the nation's "sixty-families."

"A-ha," said the experts, "the President's getting ready for another attack on business. Ickes and Jackson paved the way. The boss will follow up with the main onslaught in his speech to Congress on the state of the nation."

But the President surprised everyone, perhaps even Ickes and Jackson. He made no attack on big business on January 3. Instead, he opened up with a carefully-worded attack on aggressor nations. He supported the other democracies. He advocated "adequately strong self defense." And finally he appealed to business, labor, and agriculture "to demonstrate national unity in a world of high tension and disorder."

He Saw War Clouds First

The Republicans waited 10 days, then sent Snell to the radio for the official reply. Through 3,500 words, almost up to the last paragraph of his speech, Snell concentrated on the domestic scene—the "depression," the "11,000,000 unemployed," the $17,000,000,000 worth of Roosevelt public debt, the "hamstringing" reform laws.

Snell dismissed the clouds of war with one oddly-worded sentence:

"Above all, we oppose the continual preaching of war against and hate among our own people."

From then on out, the New Deal marked time on domestic issues, offered fewer and fewer reforms, more and more big defense plans. Republicans multiplied their attacks on spending, extravagance, and in a final splurge, took a business man to head their party ticket in 1940—the one big business man who had throughout the New Deal championed business against "big government."

As war spread, the Republicans supported defense and conscription, but charged the President with a slow administration of defense, and insisted he was leading the country toward war. Willkie also talked up to the dictators as the campaign swung into its climax.

The margin of Roosevelt victory was established in 1938 because he saw the war clouds first.

Women's Club To Give Play

The Women's Club of Linthicum Heights will present a three-act comedy "Correspondence Courtship," on the evening of Nov. 15, in the auditorium of the Fire House on Camp Meade Road.

As the proceeds from the play will be donated to the Red Cross, the committee on arrangement hopes for a large attendance.

"Correspondence Courtship" is under the direction of Mrs. E. W. Price, who has had college training in dramatics. Mrs. Price, in announcing the cast for the play, stated that she has a group of actors working with her whom she feels she can count on for an entertaining performance.

Those taking part in the play are Elizabeth Mateling as Bessie, Richard Hallam as Bill Gordon, Marinta Kelso as Ella Carlson, Ed Thompson as John Randolph, Sr., Walter Kay as Paul Jackson, Dorothy Reilly as Anne Gregory, Mrs. Thacker as Miss Ann Gregory, Mrs. Brown as Mrs. Sheffield, and Edward Cole as McGuire.

Last year, the Women's Club of Linthicum Heights contributed over $160 to the Red Cross, a sum representing the proceeds of a play and dance which the members sponsored.

Mrs. C. W. Reilly, chairman of the Red Cross roll call for the Linthicum Heights and North Linthicum district, has appointed as assistants Mrs. R. M. McAdam, Mrs. Edgar Grempler, Mrs. E. Hare, Mrs. Dorsey Owens, Mrs. Cleveland Shipley, Mrs. Charles Rice, and Mrs. Fred Lang.

CARD PARTY FOR HEALTH CENTER

The Magothy Health Center will hold a luncheon and card party Dec. 4 at the club studio of Madison apartments, Baltimore.

Mrs. M. S. Bullen and Mrs. F. G. Stroh are co-chairmen. Tickets may be purchased from any active member of the center. As only 70 persons can be accommodated, an early sellout is anticipated.

LADY O' LONDON

IDA LUPINO — lovely descendant of generations of English stage notables has already made an enviable screen record in America, among her latest successes being "The Light That Failed" and "They Drive by Night." She will be starred next in Warners' melodramatic romance "High Sierra" with Humphrey Bogart.

Dogs Love That Moon

DANVILLE, Va. (AP)—Residents here agree the hunter's moon is a lovely sight, but they wish their canine friends were less appreciative. Police have received scores of complaints this fall about baying dogs.

Detective Finds Spiritualism Boring

OROVILLE, Calif. (AP)—Harry Cohen, who has been practicing as a spiritualist under the name of the Rev. George Baker, is going back to his old job as a detective

He explains it's simply too boring sitting there and listening to all your consultants' private troubles.

No Mercy

LOS ANGELES (AP)—Mme. Elsa Schiaparelli, Paris apparel designer, told the Los Angeles Junior League:

"All of us in Paris are impressed with the generosity of American men regarding their women. American men have a world wide reputation for the money they spend on their women.

"I say bravo to you. Go right ahead!"

She Hurried Back

DURHAM, N. C. (AP)—Two days after Mrs. Elizabeth Fisher underwent an appendectomy she taught her Sunday school class. It was the 781st time she had attended Sunday school without an absence.

Anne Arundel Bldg. Permits

Building permits totaling $12,145 were issued during the week by the Board of Anne Arundel County Commissioners. Those receiving permits were:

James F. Hartley, near Severn, addition to dwelling, $300; Goldin Nickelson, Furnace Branch, garage, $95; James T. Groh, Pasadena, dwelling addition, $600; Charles Reichel, Pasadena, dwelling addition, $100; Dr. Roger P. Batchelor, Gibson Island, bungalow, $3,000.

Roy Moyston, Point Pleasant, bungalow, $150; John Segelton, Parkwood-Eastport, 4 bungalows, $4,000; William Ackney Offer, Parole, bungalow, $900; James B. Thomas, Patapsco Station, dwelling addition, $100; Lorey Green, General's Highway, shed, $100.

Charles W. Sorenson, Arundel Gardens, $2,500; August C. Sauerwald, Shoreacres, cabin, $200; Sarah M. Hallock, Boucher street, garage, $100.

Crab Lives Five Days Out Of Water

MORGANTOWN, W. Va. (AP)—"King crab," commonly known as a horseshoe crab, rules the collection of marine animals at West Virginia university.

Prof. A. M. Reese was given the crab by a friend. Caught in Florida waters, it was not placed in water for five days, but didn't take long to get back into the swing of life.

PA. DEMOCRATS SMILE

HARRISBURG, Pa., Nov. 7 (AP) Tuesday's election had some ironic twists, principally at the expense of the Republicans who lost the Pennsylvania House of Representatives.

Speaker Ellwood J. Turner, who had a legislative appropriation of $100,000 passed when the Republicans held the House in 1939 to redecorate the Speaker's office, expand committee rooms, bring the Legislative Reference Bureau into the main control, and provide a new House caucus room, now must watch his work being turned over to the Democrats.

Ann Thomas, attractive NBC dramatic actress currently featured Tuesday evenings on the "Johnny Presents" show over the NBC-Red Network, ponders her sudden turn of fortune. Two months ago A n was featured in her 35th Broadway stage production (she began at four) with scarcely a thought of radio stardom. Now look at her.

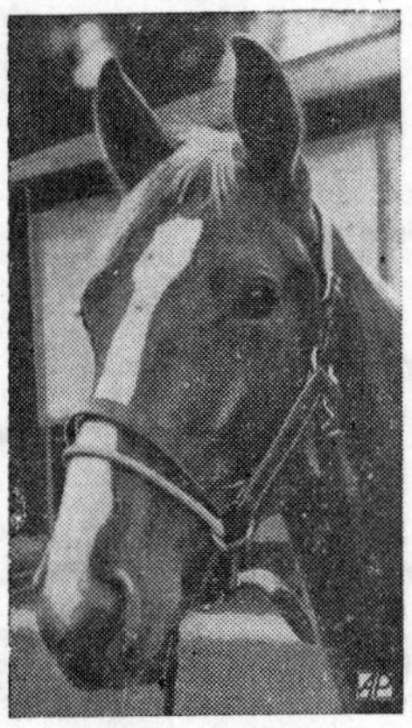

SOLD—Wher , the Hambletonian is run at Goshen, N. Y., in 1942, keep an eye on Archie Hanover, trotting horse yearling who brought $850 at recent Harrisburg, Pa., auction. Archie, by Mr. McElwyn, went to John Kelley of Bangor, Me.

Harvest "God's" Corn

DUNBAR, Neb. (AP)—They harvested corn from "God's acres" this fall. Each farmer member of the Presbyterian and Catholic churches planted one acre of corn and donated the yield to the church.

Confidential Dope, Right From The Coach

LINCOLN, Neb. (AP) — This is the pet story of Floyd Bottorff, University of Nebraska equipment manager who has seen the Huskers play 99 consecutive football games.

Some years ago Dr. Earl Deppen, team physician, made his first trip with the Huskers to Pittsburgh.

Dr. Deppen, related Bottorff, had always longed to sit on the bench and listen in on what the coaches talk about when the going is tough.

With a seat right behind Dana X. Bible, then Nebraska's coach, Dr. Deppen believed his day had arrived as Bible leaned toward Bunny Oakes, then line coach. Dr. Deppen, all ears, leaned forward.

Then Bible spoke:

"Bunny, we're sure getting the stuffin' beat out of us today!"

(P.S.—The final score was 40 to 0, Pitt.)

Hands Across The Sea

WINCHESTER, Va. (AP) — This city, namesake of an old English community and boasting of a friendship between the mayors of the two towns, also claims a draft registrant named Winston Churchill.

MARRIAGE LICENSES

The clerk of the Anne Arundel County Circuit Court issued the following marriage licenses during the week: Clarence White, 56, and Lora Dils, 54, Odenton, Md.

James H. Truitt, 65, and Gertrude Klein, 56, Lansdowne.

Bills Passed by County Commissioners

BILLS PASSED TUESDAY, OCTOBER 22ND.

Annapolis Banking and Trust Co., for payment of interest	$ 25.00
Frank Dawson, for labor	18.90
Maryland Training School for Colored Girls, for quarterly payment ending September, 1940	307.00
Remington Rand, Inc., for repairs to typewriters	3.00
Vernon Cockrell, for same	1.50
Underwood Elliott Fisher Co., for same	1.85
Annapolis Water Company, water for courthouse and jail and quarterly payment for fireplugs	422.27
The Postage Meter Company, for quarterly rental of postage meter	30.00
State Department of Health, for support of public health work for months of September and October and salary of bacteriologist	666.66
Carl Reynolds, et al, account of forest fires	13.75
Nelson Crandell, disposing of dead dog	2.00
Norman Stadiger, commission on dog license issued	.79
Gar Wood Industries, Inc., for repair parts	1.62
The Chesapeake & Potomac Telephone Co., for telephone service	27.52
Better Roads Corporation, for asphalt	580.96
Alan E. Barton, for gravel	202.06
Land Office of Maryland, for blueprints	7.50
State Department of Forestry, for tree permit	1.00
Sadler's Hardware Store, for supplies	19.63
Mabel Stevenson, et al, for salaries	40.00
John L. Steiff, et al, for services rendered on Fifth District road commission	6.00
Cecil A. Teal, et al, same, Third District	6.00
County Commissioners of Anne Arundel County, to transfer of funds to Shipley fire house account	50.00
Farmers National Bank, for payment of interest	23.75
Sidney's, supplies for Police Department	12.00
A. Jacobs & Sons, uniforms for Police Department	35.75
American Oil Company, gasoline and oil for same	302.17
Annapolis Banking & Trust Co., for payment of interest	25.00
E. D Tucker, et al. payroll, First District	141.05
William T. Jenkins, et al, same, Third District roads	247.16
William T Jenkins, et al, same, Third District roads	247.16
Clarence Whittington, et al, same, Third District roads	193.15
Morris Pumphrey, et al, same, Fourth District roads	215.00
George T. Chaney, et al, same, Fifth District roads	306.10
Norwood Wood, et al, same, Seventh District roads	95.40
W. Allen Moreland, et al, same, Eighth District roads	84.80
Frank G. Baldwin, et al, payroll, county garage	188.38
John C. Strohm, et al, payroll	266.99
John Evans, salary—charged to Eastport streets	18.90
West Disinfecting Co., for supplies	7.43
Emory S. and Basil Cromwell, garage rent from September 1, 1939, to August 30, 1940	300.00
Davis' Stationery, supplies for Treasurer's office	.90
Southern Oxygen Co., for acetylene and oxygen	8.00
The White Motor Company, for repair parts	20.71
Traffic and Road Equipment Co., for street brooms	2.00
The Electric Tool and Equipment Co., for supplies	3.60
The Chesapeake Supply and Equipment Co., for repair parts	9.35
Alban Tractor Co., Inc., for same	38.50
American Wiping Cloth Co., for wiping cloth	14.04
J. F. Johnson Lumber Co., for lumber	124.85
Caroline Foundry Co., for frames and covers	59.40
Charles W. Cox, for lumber	62.26
George T. Youngbar, glass installed in truck	4.75
O. Rossback, for lumber	6.67
The Chesapeake & Potomac Telephone Co., for service	2.60
Jenk[illegible] Stationery, for supplies	3.45
Charles A. Howard, for work at county jail	15.00
Joseph E. Campbell, for painting tin roof	36.00
The Corporation of Annapolis City, for 50 per cent of fines and forfeitures collected by police magistrate	20.12
James A. Walton, Treasurer, for Circuit Court expenses	40.50
D. S. Graham, et al, for services rendered Board of Supervisors	101.20
Wiylbur Stevenson, for transportation of workers	48.00
Jenkins Stationery, for lights	10.00

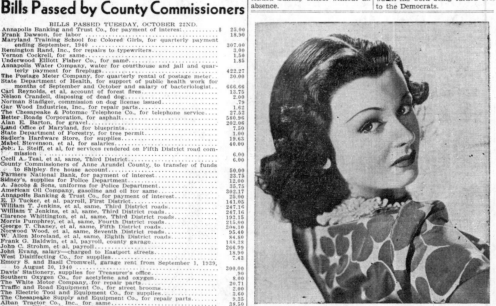

Beautiful Joan Bennett, of stage and screen fame, will make a radio stop-over as the guest star of "Lincoln Highway", to be broadcast over the NBC-Red Network on Saturday, October 26. The many films in which Miss Bennett has been seen include "Wedding Present", "I Met My Love Again", and "Private Worlds".

Navy Gridders Seek Prestige In Ivy League And Eastern Circles

Out Of U. S. Rating After Loss To Notre Dame; Middies Must Top Columbia And West Point

One Slipup In Tackling Enabled Irish To Score Decisive Points Before 63,000 In Baltimore

Tars Overcome Early Irish Touchdown Pass To Lead 7 To 6 Only To Lose In Final Minutes—Irish Take Ball From Middies On 1 And 10 Yard Lines, After Field-Goal Try, And On Fumbles To Remain Unbeaten—Take Advantage Of Own Chances To Tally—Grand Spectacle At Game's Conclusion—Irish Players Visit Annapolis, And Coaches Have Party, Too—Hun School Cancels On Plebes Holding Undefeated Local Club To Be Too Good

(Continued from Page One)

of the national grid spotlight due to two straight defeats.

Left on the schedule are Columbia to be met in New York on Saturday and Army three weeks distant. The local boys can yet win high eastern prestige although Cornell seems to have the district's highest honor sewed up along with the national crown. The Middies, however, can end the campaign with a better record than they had in 1938 and may rank among the East's first five if Columbia and Army are taken into camp.

Columbia Is Tough

Columbia, the immediate objective, is going to be a mighty tough opponent. The Lions have been improving with every game and are famous for winning the close ones. Last Saturday was no exception when the Lions defeated the huskies of Wisconsin, 7 to 6, on Baker Field. Navy is going to need more luck, and perhaps a sharper punch inside the 15-yard line in order to humble Lou Little's New Yorkers.

Saturday's tilt is to be played on Baker Field, New York, a rather unique stadium. The stands seem to be right on the playing field, and it takes a visiting team some time to get accustomed to the sensation that the spectators are almost right beside them. The Middies also are in the throes of examination week, a situation which makes football unimportant here for several days. Thus Saturday's fracas looms all the tougher.

Now getting back to last Saturday in Baltimore.

Irish Were Stopped

Navy stopped the Irish reverses, bucks and sweeps with great consistency. The Tar ends played soundly, the halfbacks covered well, which incidentally, probably accounted for the Irish success in passing and, except for brief moments in the first, third and fourth quarters the mid-westerners were bottled up behind their own 30-yard line on the offense. In no department did the Irish prove to be the great team they were in Cleveland a year ago although the score ended then 14 to 7. The writer has never seen a team run against Navy like the Irish did in Cleveland, but things were quite different on Saturday. Although Notre Dame got off to a first period touchdown, Navy kept knocking at the touchdown door and from the second period to the final minutes it looked like an ultimate Navy triumph.

Then came two "hope and pray" passes that clicked. Notre Dame probably could try the same plays a hundred times against any team on their schedule, including Navy, and they never would work again. Both were long, both were near the side line, both required the receiver to outrun the Navy defenders, and both were desperate rather than confident tosses. Even after their completion carried the Irish from deep in their own territory to Navy's scoring door, the visitors did not seem destined to score. Navy's 7 to 6 lead still loomed big; there was little time left to play, and once in possession of the ball Navy might keep it to the game's conclusion on short thrusts leading to a first down or two.

Navy Line Play

Just before the winning scores Navy's line surged through and smeared the Irish for losses, a pass failed, and then came fourth down with Notre Dame's Bob Saggau cutting wide around his right end. Big Gene Flathmann had Saggau, or so it seemed, yards behind the line of scrimmage. Saggau, however, faked a dodge and then headed straight through giant Gene as the Middie's hands slipped off the visitor's sleek silk pants. Three other Navy men were between Saggau and the goal and he still seemed sure to be tackled short of the goal with the result that the ball would go to Navy. However, through the three Navy men he went, Hargrave taking one out, and, although two Navy men were on their feet just inches from him, Saggau went over standing up. Navy's tackling was never worse than on this play, and while Irish luck and courage must be given due credit, the winning score must be placed in the column of a Navy error rather than Notre Dame skill for the Middies were not blocked out on the play. They simply fell down in the clutch.

Still Navy's young ball team made a creditable showing for the day. It looked mighty good most of the time and the game was exciting. It outplayed Notre Dame in the line, and the local backs out-plunged the South Benders. Although the Notre Dame's winning score was over Bob Froude, the Tar end was the best Navy flank on the field for the day with Bob Zoeller also standing out, and all the ends for that matter doing creditable work. Ed Svendson played great ball in backing up the line and Sherwood Werner plunged well. Howie Clark played brilliantly too during the short time he was in action, a kick on the jaw knocking him out for the day and West Gebert must be praised for his touchdown jaunt.

Irish Visit Annapolis

It was a typical Navy-Notre Dame game. It was hard fought, tackling was savage but clean, and, as is usually the case when the Tars and Irish clash, there were few injuries. Notre Dame was alert, and smart, and despite their poor running attack the Irish might conceiveably reach the end of the campaign undefeated. Their future foes do not look too tough. The South Benders have the wishes of the disappointed Navy clan to wind up unwhipped our Middies told the South Benders here Saturday night at a dinner in Bancroft Hall.

The Notre Dame coaches were entertained at a stag party at the Navy boat house. There Elmer Layden, Notre Dame coach got into several huddles with his old "Four Horseman" teammate, "Rip" Miller, Middie line tutor. The Layden-Miller conversations ended up in the new Miller home with Captain E. W. King, Navy's director of athletics, joining in the late snack. There Layden confessed: "Navy had the tickets to win, but not the Irish luck." And, although he won't come out and say so in as many words, Layden has had his fingers crossed all season and still isn't making any predictions about the future.

Great Closing Spectacle

The closing spectacle of the game in Baltimore on Saturday was just about as thrilling as the three touchdown plays. With the band blaring out the National Anthem 63,000 persons stood bareheaded in pleased satisfaction and the writer could not help but think of the well known lines: "Breathes there a man with soul so dead who n'er to himself hath said, this is my own, my native land." And as the Academy's largest regiment of all times fell into ranks, the picture of America's future seemed all the brighter. In the dressing rooms the Notre Dame and Navy players were fraternizing, forgetful of the bruising action of a short time before. There was proof that America isn't growing soft—that there is still the American way.

The game:

FIRST QUARTER

Vito Vitucci kicked off to Notre Dame. The Irish couldn't gain and Owen Evans (the Irish started their second team) punted to Bill Busik on the Notre Dame 48 Navy couldn't gain either so Busik punted out on the Irish 22.

Navy's tackling was poor on the second play of the next Notre Dame series as Steve Bagarus ran 21 yards around left end for the game's initial first down. The Irish, after a fine tackle by Froude who tossed Evans for a 7-yard loss kicked, Evan's great punt pushing the Middies back to the Navy 34.

The Middies still couldn't get going missing a fourth down by inches so Busik punted deep to Notre Dame's 19, Bagarus being smeared hard on the 25. After Cameron had thrown Evans for a loss, Chip missed Bagarus who ran 8 yards, and then hit the right side of the Navy line for 7 yards and a first down on the Notre Dame 38. After a short completed pass and three bucks Notre Dame punted, Evans hitting coffin corner as the ball went out on the Middies' 8-yard stripe At this stage the first Notre Dame team came into the fracas.

Notre Dame Scores

Busik immediately punted to Bob Hargraves on the Navy 34. Notre Dame was off sides on their initial play but three plays later Bob Saggau, who later made the winning score, passed almost down the middle to Bob Dove, end, in the end zone. Dove outran Busik to snatch the touchdown pass. Flathmann blocked Captain Milt Piepul's try for the placement.

Phil Gutting ran the Notre Dame kickoff back to the Navy 30. On third down Busik fumbled and Steve Juzwik recovered for the Irish on the Navy 49. At this stage the Navy second team entered the game.

Notre Dame had the ball as the first period ended:

SECOND QUARTER

On the first play of the quarter Saggau kicked, the ball being downed on Navy's 28. Navy immediately began to move. Clark, at right end, picked up 10 yards and Navy's first first down. Navy missed a first down in the next series and Sammie Boothe left-footed the ball out of bounds on the Irish 10, but the ball was called back and Navy given a first down on the penalty for running into the kicker. Clark picked up eight and Werner two yards for Navy's third consecutive third down. Clark picked up 6 more at right end but Navy then was penalized 15 yards for holding so Boothe kicked to the Notre Dame 10, Hargraves running back to the 23. Clark, blocking for Boothe, was kicked on this play and left the game for good, Wes Gebert replacing him.

Navy Near Touchdown

Notre Dame couldn't gain a yard and punted to Gebert who raced back 19 to the Navy 39. Werner, on consecutive bucks, carried to the Notre Dame territory. An end around play, Werner to Harrell to Zoeller, lost 4 yards but Werner then passed to Zoeller for 18 yards and a first down on the Irish 26 A beautiful block by Boothe helped Zoeller and it would have been a touchdown had Zoeller not been caught from behind.

On second down Notre Dame seemed to lose sight of the ball as Gebert, on a fake reverse, ran to the Irish 8 for a first down. There Navy bungled a glorious opportunity to score.

Bungled Opportunity

On first down Gebert failed at left end. Werner picked up 3 yards at right guard. On third down Gebert, back to pass, was smeared for a 3-yard loss. On fourth down the same thing happened. Gebert held the ball and was dropped for a two-yard loss and the ball went to the Irish on the 10.

Navy got a great break as Piepul, faking a kick, crashed into the line, fumbled and Werner recovered for Navy on the Notre Dame 13. It was a great break for the Middies and the crowd howled.

8 Chances At A Score

The fumble gave Navy four more chances to score. On first down Werner, back to pass, fumbled but recovered. At this stage Busik replaced Gebert. Busik passed to Harrell for a 3-yard gain on second down. On the third down Boothe was called upon to pass and he couldn't find a receiver and was thrown for a 10-yard loss. This was fatal. On fourth down Bob Leonard was rushed in to try a field goal. Werner held the ball for him on the 32, but the boot was short.

The half ended soon thereafter.

THIRD QUARTER

Notre Dame received the kickoff and after Bagarus picked up 8 yards, and Evans make just short of two more, the Navy line refused to yield an inch on third down and Evans kicked out on the Navy 32.

There was no holding Navy. Running plays by Cameron and Busik netted 12 yards and a first down. Leaping high into the air Busik passed to Froude on the Notre Dame 41 but the Navy was penalized 15 yards for holding instead.

Bad Break

Luck just would not come Navy's was for when Busik passed again, this time to Gutting, Evans intercepted. Navy got in a bad hole as Evans' punt went out of bounds on the Navy 1-yard line. Notre Dame's first team returned to the game.

Standing deep in his own end zone Busik got off the greatest kick of the game, a 75-yard boot which carried far over Hargrave's head, finally being downed on the Notre Dame 34. Juzwik was tossed for a 13-yard loss by Chewning and Piepul kicked to the Navy 29.

Navy again rolled. Busik passed down the middle to Froude for a first down on the Notre Dame 41.

In the next series Busik pushed Notre Dame back to their 6 with a punt.

Saggau promptly returned the boot Busik taking it on the Navy's 47 and running to the Irish 43. Busik's pass to Foster was wide as Foster couldn't shake loose. One to Froude was too high. Then after Cameron was stopped at center Busik kicked out on the Irish 14.

Saggau tried a quick-kick and it was very short to the Notre Dame 41. After Gutting had lost 4 yards on a reverse Busik hit left tackle for a first down on the Irish 30. On second down Busik fumbled for the second time during the game and John O'Brien recovered for Notre Dame on his 25, as the period ended.

FOURTH QUARTER

Navy's second team came in. Notre Dame couldn't advance and Saggau punted to Gebert who ran 13 yards to the Navy 39. Gebert then passed to Lars Wanggaard for a first down on the Irish 8- for a first down on the Notre Dame 46.

On Navy marched, Werner and Gebert alternating to plant the ball on the Notre Dame 8-yard line. Again Navy seemed sure to score. The team had marched 53 yards in a few plays. In one series the Middies made 3 first downs on 4 plays in this parade. Werner made 4 yards and reached the Irish 4 on first down, Gebert lost a yard at tackle but Werner gained that back and another yard to place the ball on the Irish 3. On fourth down Gebert went wide at right end, after faking a pass but was downed on the 1-yard line.

Gebert Scores

Evans kicked to Gebert on the Notre Dame 30. On second down Gebert, attempting to pass, couldn't find an opening and decided to run the ball. He leaped and hurdled past several Irish tacklers and weaved his way across the Notre Dame goal. The Middie blockers did a nice job for Gebert on this play. At this point Leonard came in to boot the placement and, with just 7 minutes to play, Navy seemed to have the game won.

Boothe kicked off and also made a great tackle to drop Saggau on the Notre Dame 22. On first down Juzwik passed to Saggau almost in front of the Notre Dame bench on the Irish 40. Saggau stepped out of bounds just after he caught the ball and for a moment the officials seemed in doubt. However, it was ruled good. Then the passing team reversed, and Saggau whipped a long heave to Juzwik who outraced the Navy secondary and took the pass on the Navy 25. Momentum carried him out of bounds.

Lucky Break

Juzwik fumbled on the next play and lost 9 yards, as Zoeller tackled him. Then Notre Dame got a break. Navy was penalized for holding and the Irish got a first down on the Navy 20.

Saggau passed down the middle to Ray Ebli who was downed on the 3-yard stripe, and another first down. Cameron stopped Juzwik at left end. Notre Dame was penalized for offsides. Juzwik then ran back 4 yards to the Navy 4. On third down Saggau's pass to Hargraves in the end zone was too long. On fourth down, Saggau outsmarted Flathmann, who had him for a loss, and scored at his own right end as Navy bogged down in tackling.

The game ended soon thereafter.

* * *

Navy's card tricks were impressive. So were the antics of the Middies gymnast cheer leaders. However, the tricks bring too many fans onto the field during the half to watch them. When the teams came back on the field they had to do the day's best broken field running to find the turf at all.

* * *

Injured Clif Lenz, Navy's best pass receiver for Busik since the Busik to Zoeller combination no longer is tried, sat in the press box. Joe Hunt, famous Middie tennis star, was in a varsity uniform on the bench but didn't get into the game.

* * *

Navy's head coach, Major "Swede" Larson, always plays square with the press on line-up announcements. When he says a player is out of action he means it. Talk that Notre Dame's Piepul wouldn't play and that the Notre Dame teams had been shaken up by Layden proved to be just so much taffy. Piepul didn't even have a limp.

* * *

One Navy wife, who carried her ticket in hand half a block from the stadium gate, was stopped six times by persons who offered to buy it. Pasteboards really were scarce. Next year Baltimore will have a chance to support two big time Navy games.

* * *

Next year more youngster backs will push those now on hand. Warren Montgomery, who is also an end, is the best of the crop, with Siegfried just about the best blocker in the Academy, or at least next to Johnny Harrell. Feden, plebe center; Tony Ploszay, who, like Siegfried, is spending his second year on the plebe team; George Studer, John Davis, Theodore Gilliland, fastest of them all; Bob Wood, Vince Anania and Oreal Crepeau, are great prospects.

* * *

The plebes have not lost since Hun School whipped them in 1938 Hun, due to be the last fore for the plebes this year, has cancelled the game holding themselves no match for Johnny Wilson's unwhipped team. Therefore, the plebe season is at an end except for working against the varsity in preparation for the Army tilt.

* * *

Zeke Zachella, who injured his ankle in varsity scrimmage before the season opened still isn't in form and isn't likely to play at all this year.

STATISTICS

	Notre Dame	Navy
First Downs	6	13
Rushing	2	8
Passing	4	4
Penalties	0	1
Net Yards Rushing	55	163
Yards lost	46	21
Net Yards Forwards	120	60
Forwards Attempted	8	16
Forwards Completed	6	5
Intercepted By	3	0
Punts, Number	13	7
Returned by	3	6
Blocked By	0	0
Punts, Average	35	38
Kickoffs, Number	1	3
Returned By	1	2
Kickoffs, Average	44	44
Yards Kicks Returned	50	103
Punts	25	77
Kickoffs	25	36
Fumbles	1	2
Recovered By	2	0
Penalties	6	7
Yards Lost On Penalties	48	45

Julius KOSHLAP
—SPARK-PLUG OF GEORGETOWN'S POWERFUL TEAM !!
MIX 'EM UP
30
1938
1939
1940
KOSHLAP TOSSES FORWARD PASSES ACCURATELY WITH EITHER HAND
GEORGETOWN HAS NOT BEEN DEFEATED IN 21 GAMES
PAP'

"HOYAS' HANDYMAN" ...by PAP'

NAVY-IRISH LINEUP

Notre Dame		Navy
Sheridan	L.E.	Foster
Brutz	L.T.	Flathmann
Laiber	L.G.	Vitucci
Brock	C.	Sims
Maddock	R.G.	Svendsen
Neff	R.T.	Chewning
Kovatch	R.E.	Froude
Hayes	Q.B.	Busik
Evans	L.H.	Gutting
Bagarus	R.H.	Chip
Crimmins	F.B.	Cameron

Score by periods:

Notre Dame	6	0	0	7	13
Navy	0	0	0	7	7

Scoring: Notre Dame—Touchdowns—Dove, Saggau. Tries for point—Piepul, 1 in 2 (placekicks).

Navy: Touchdown—Gebert. Try for point—Leonard (placekick). Field goal—Leonard missed placekick.

Substitutes: Notre Dame—Ends, Dove, O'Brien, Ebli; tackles, Gallagher, Ziemba, Rymkus, L. Sullivan; guards, Kelly, Gubanich; center, O'Reilly; backs, Hargrave, Saggau, Piepul, Juzwik.

Navy—Ends, Zoeller, Wanggard; tackles, Steen, Opp; guards, Rowney, Sliwka, Feldmeier; center, Harwood; backs, Leonard, Harrell, Boothe, Werner, Hurt, Clark, Rowse, Gebert.

Referee—J. R. Trimble (Dubuque); umpire, W. R. Crowley (Bowdoin); linesman, A. R. Lake (LaFayette); field judge, R. J. Barbuti (Syracuse).

HERE'S THE WINNING IRISH TOUCHDOWN

His team trailing Navy 7 to 6, Bob Saggau (34), Notre Dame back, slips out of reach of a Middie tackler and skirts right end for seven yards and a touchdown in the fourth quarter of the game in Baltimore, Md. Rushing in at right to assist Saggau is John O'Brien (47). Milt Piepul kicked the extra point and Navy was sunk, 13 to 7.

Sports Round-Up

By EDDIE BRIETZ
Associated Press Sports Writer

NEW YORK, Nov. 11—Smart baseball men say Bill Meyer of Kansas City is not the mysterious third man in the Cleveland managerial picture. Well, who is, then—Hornsby? . . . Winner of the Georgetown-Boston College game is a lead pipe cinch for one of the bowl games . . . Since Larry MacPhail took charge, the Dodgers have paid off $300,000 of a $400,000 debt besides investing a pile of lettuce in players . . . One man's opinion: Based on accomplishments, Minnesota is No. 1 in football circles. Just take a look at the class of opposition the Gopher have knocked off.

Names Is Names

Colorado's Quarterback, Click, makes his plays do just that . . . When Fred Shook tackles 'em for Maury (Norfolk, Va.) High, they stay that way . . . Halfback Quick of Franklin and Marshall is the fastest guy on the squad . . . Thrus is the backfield threat of the Mansfield (Pa) Teachers . . . And Romeo Popp pops 'em over for Mississippi U.

Short, Short Stories

Lou Nova's second victim in his comeback campaign will be Johnny Hanschen of the George Parnassus stable . . . Jimmy Dykes says he's willing to trade every White Sox player except Ted Lyons, Mike Kreevich, Joe Kuhel and Johnny Rigney . . . Tulane players voted Boston College the best team they've played this year . . . Harvard just about changed Penn's mind about putting in 7,000 extra seats for the Cornell game, Nov. 23.

Today's Guest Star

Edward T. Murphy, N. Y. Sun: "As soon as Alva Bradley names the new Cleveland manager tomorrow, he'll sit back and await developments . . . Some of the players ought to have their first batch of complaints in by Wednesday."

Spirit Of The Press

Tim Cohane, N. Y. World-Telegram: John Kimbrough is the toughest man to come out of Texas since the Lone Ranger . . . Gordie Spear, Billings (Mont.) Gazette: All this publicity the blockers are getting leads us to fear that one of these days the experts are going to put a blocker in the blocking spot on their All-Americas . . . Al Sharp, Atlanta Constitution: Down South the preferred method of signal calling in having the yardage chain holder relay the plays from the coach . . . John Mooney, Salt Lake City Telegram: Wyoming has been the conference door mat so long, the players are wondering if their "W" monograms stands for Wyoming or welcome.

Admiral King Gets Command Of Patrol Force

Captain Badger Assigned As His Chief Of Staff And Aide

WASHINGTON, Dec. 11 (AP)—The Navy announced today Rear Admiral Ernest J. King, member of the Navy General Board, had been ordered to duty as commander of the patrol force, effective about December 17.

He will relieve Rear Admiral Hayne Ellis, who has been ordered to the department as a member of the general board.

Captain Oscar C. Badger, secretary of the general board, has been assigned as chief of staff and aide of the commander, patrol force.

Home Here

Captain Robert R. M. Emmet, now chief of staff and aide commander, patrol force, will report for duty in the office of the chief of naval operations here after being relieved by Captain Badger.

Admiral King was born in Lorain, Ohio, November 23, 1876, and was appointed to the Naval Academy in 1897. His present home address is Annapolis, Md.

Admiral Ellis was born August 26, 1877, in Macon, Ga., and was appointed to the Academy in 1896. His present home address is Long View Farm, Lee's Summit, Mo.

Born In Washington

Captain Badger was born in Washington, D. C., June 26, 1890, and was appointed to the Academy in 1907. His present home address is Washington.

Captain Emmet was born in New Rochelle, N. Y., January 27, 1888, and was appointed to the Academy in 1904. His present home address is Rye, N. Y.

Council Approves State Home Guard

Legislative Group Sanctions Bill To Replace National Guard

Governor O'Conor said today emergency legislation providing for a home guard in Maryland, replacing the National Guard which goes on active duty in January, had been approved by the Legislative Council and would be given to the Legislature as soon as it convenes next month.

The bill was drawn by the State Law Department after a study of various "model" home guard bills approved by the War Department and would set up the "Maryland State Guard of approximately 2,000 officers and men."

"Private Armies'

One section of the measure applies to the much-discussed question of "private armies" in this fashion:

"No civil organization, society, club, post, fraternity, association, brotherhood, body, union, league or other combination of persons or civil groups shall be enlisted in such forces (the home guard) as an organization or unit."

Enlistment as individuals only will be permitted under the bill.

The Governor is given wide discretionary powers under the legislation, may determine the definite strength of the outfit, its commander, its uniform and its rules and regulations conforming "in so far as he deems practicable and desirable" with existing regulations governing the National Guard.

To Get Equipment

Equipment will be requisitioned from the War Department to whatever extent arms and ammunition can be spared. State armories and other State property will be utilized by the guard and school authorities are authorized "to permit" use of school buildings and grounds.

Enlistments will be for one year, with the right of re-enlistment.

Pay will be at the same rate as for the National Guard. While on duty, members of the State Guard will be invested with all the authority of sheriffs and deputy sheriffs in enforcing State laws.

War

(Continued from Page One.)

ed that up to December 10 thirty-seven British warships and 33 merchant vessels had been sunk against 23 Italian warships sunk. They said 56 British warships and 41 merchantmen had been damaged, compared with four Italian warships damaged.

It also was claimed that 667 "enemy" planes were shot down against a loss of 110 Italian planes.

From the beginning of the war Italian casualties were reported as 18,824, including dead, wounded and missing.

Windsors Welcomed In Miami

The Duke and Duchess of Windsor chat with Mayor Alexander Orr, Jr., as they arrived in Miami, Fla., for the duchess to undergo a dental operation. The Windsors reached American shores on the fourth anniversary of the duke's abdication from the British throne, for his first visit to the United States since he came here 16 years ago as Prince of Wales.

News From Our Neighbors

(Continued from Page Five)

bury Point to members of the National Farm Bureau Association then meeting in Baltimore. The hosts of the occasion were the Farm Bureau Associations of the five counties of Southern Maryland. The visitors were brought from Baltimore in busses and taken on a sight-seeing tour through Annapolis and the Naval Academy before going to the roast.

Farmers are busy now husking corn and butchering hogs, also taking advantage of damp days to strip tobacco. Many of them are also taking jobs at Camp Meade.

SEVERNA PARK ROUND BAY and VICINITY

John P. Hacker, of Detroit, spent the week-end with his mother, Mrs. Harriet B. Hacker and family at Tedshaven.

Robert Smith and children, Jean and Bobbie, have returned to their home at Cypress Creek following their unfortunate trip to visit Mrs. Smith's mother, Mrs. Lloyd, at Straudsburg, Pa. at Thanksgiving, when their car was demolished when hit from behind by a truck. Mrs. Smith is still in the hospital at Straudsburg recuperating from a broken arm and back injuries. Mrs. Lloyd returned with the family to take charge until her daughter's return.

A carol service will be held on Christmas eve at 11:30 at the Severna Park Presbyterian Church.

Mrs. Antrim McKay and Mrs. Thomas P. Kirpatrick were joint hostesses at the meeting of the Women's Guild on Tuesday.

The Girl Scout Troop 11 program of December 9 follows: A talk by Mrs. Frank J. E. Peters on conservation of Christmas greens for decorations; rehearsal of Christmas carols with Mrs. W. Holmes Davis in charge; writing of invitations to the Christmas party, Monday, December 23; Mrs. H. Claire Dees continuing work on cooking badge with Busy Bees Patrol; Mrs. Davis on metal craft work with the Poplar Patrol; Mrs. Peters in raffia work with the Clover Leaf Patrol; plans for the entertainment at Christmas discussed, namely a pantomime under the direction of Mrs. Matthew Strohm Evans.

All efforts and money previously expended by the girls in gifts at the Christmas party will be concentrated this year on the needy family selected for them by the County Welfare. The Senior Girl Scouts are knitting and collecting clothes for the children, and the younger Scouts are collecting toys and planning filling of the stockings. The Boy Scouts are doing any repair work needed on the toys.

MILLERSVILLE

Mrs. Marvin I. Anderson, president of the Diakonia Club, and Mrs. Nathan Childs, Jr., chairman of the supper committee, wish to thank all those who so willingly and competently helped in the recent supper for the Farm Bureau of Anne Arundel county.

At the annual banquet for the Farm Bureau, Oscar Grimes, president of the county organization, acted as toastmaster. He introduced Dr. Benjamin, of the University of Maryland, who made the address of the evening; president P. Z. Turner, ppresident of the State Farm Bureau; Wilbur Smith, field man for the Western Shore; Zach Turner, Jr., State insurance agent for the Farm Bureau Insurance, and Stanley Day, county agent. The Rev. W. M. Hoffman pronounced the invocation, Mrs. Calvin Miller played beautifully, and, among other selections, Mr. Linthicum, of Pasadena, sang "Jeannie With the Light Brown Hair," by Stephen Foster. The directors who will guide the policies of the Farm Bureau for 1941, were elected and at the next director's meeting the president and secretary will be selected.

Robert I. Welsh, president of the Indian Landing Boat Club, Eugene Scharf and James Campbell, attended the luncheon and meeting of the Chesapeake Bay Yacht Racing Association at the Potomac Yacht Club in Washington on Saturday.

Mr. Lemkey, who recently sustained an operation at the Naval Hospital, is improving and hopes to be home for Christmas.

The Gambrills Bridge Club met with Mrs. Edwin Cecil and Miss Blanche Virginia Cecil on Wednesday.

Mrs. Abbott Holmes entered the Union Memorial Hospital on Tuesday, where she expects to be for some time.

The Rev. W. M. Hoffman preached at Camp Chapel, Baltimore county, on Sunday night at their annual homecoming.

The Community Fair will be held on Friday, Dec. 13, at the Consolidated School.

Mr. Gottwals and the shop classes at Arundel High School will be glad to repair toys to be donated to the Diakonia Club Christmas baskets.

William Wigley recently underwent an operation at the Maryland General Hospital last week and is progressing satisfactorily.

Mrs. John Rice is also at the Maryland General Hospital after a relapse at her home in Glen Burnie.

The Ladies' Bible Class held their Christmas social at the home of Mrs. E. F. Joyce, on Thursday, December 19.

OWENSVILLE

Mr. and Mrs. Paul Ripley and small son, Louis, spent several days last week in Woodbine, Carroll county, Md., having been called by the death of Mr. Ripley's father.

Mr. and Mrs. Lester Phy and family, formerly of Millersville, recently purchased the home of Charles B. Smith of Gott.

Mr. and Mrs. Wilson Hance moved to Eastport last week.

Funeral services for James Jubb, Sr., father of Mrs. Mary Carter, of Gott, and Charles Jubb, Sr., of Millersville, were held on Sunday afternoon from the home of his son, James Jubb, Jr., Marley Neck Road. Services at Magothy Methodist Church, with burial in the adjoining cemetery.

Mrs. William Rice, of Millersville, was the guest on Monday of her sister, Mrs. W. D. Carr.

GAMBRILLS

The Gambrills Garden Club held its annual Christmas party at St. John's Chapel yesterday at 2 p. m. The hostesses were Mrs. Samuel Peters, Mrs. John McGill and Mrs. Edward Fink.

During the short business meeting, at which two new members were installed, and with two guests present, the following officers were re-elected: Mrs. J. C. Fleming, president; Mrs. Carroll Thomas, Jr., vice-president; Mrs. Leslie Maynard, treasurer; and Mrs. J. McEachern, secretary.

A gift was purchased by the club members for Mrs. Georgianna Linton Agent, who unfortunately was unable to be present.

Several prizes were given for Christmas floral decorations. Mrs. Samuel Watts won first prize for a table decoration, Mrs. Carroll Thomas, Jr., won second prize with a decoration for a door, and Mrs. Louis Schneider was the winner of the third prize with a hanging decoration.

There were most attractive favors and the refreshments were carried out in Christmas colors on tables gaily decorated in Christmas greens and trimmings, making a most festive occasion.

ARNOLD

The Woman's Day luncheon, held yesterday at Asbury Church, at the monthly meeting of the Women's Society of Christian Service, with Mrs. J. Edward Snyder as president, was very successful. A Christmas program was a feature of the occasion. Mrs. George Fast, a native of Norway, described Christmas in her country. Mrs. Clarence Fossett and Mrs. W. S. Evans also took part in the program.

DOUGHBOY DICTIONARY
(AP Feature Service)

Keeping up with the army's "slanguage":

Bootleg—coffee.
Bought another star—fined by court martial.
Brass—rank.
Brass hats—officers in general.
Browned-off—fed up.
Bucking—cleaning up.
Bull—roast beef.
Bumpkin—German balloon.
Bunk Fatigue—take a nap.
Busted—demoted.

Oysters and mushrooms blend together nicely for a stew or for an escalloped or soup mixture.

NEWLY-ARRIVED DETACHMENT DRILLS IN EGYPT

Leaving their camp for a route march is this detachment of British troops, described by British sources as newly-arrived in Egypt. It is part of a training program intended to accustom them to new surroundings. The British African command announced that Britain's armored desert fighters, striking against Marshal Graziani's Italian legion in the Sidi Barrani region, captured 1,000 prisoners, killed their commanding officer and captured his assistant. The region is 70 miles from Libya's frontiers.

AMERICA'S WAR

Your Life Expectancy Moves Up To 62 As Science Studies Affairs Of Heart

(This is the fourth of a series on what science is doing to combat the ten major causes of death in the United States.)

By JOHN GROVER
(AP Feature Service Writer)

WASHINGTON, Dec. 9—Doctors are becoming so expert that they are driving up the death rate of heart disease, kidney and brain ailments.

A contradiction? Not at all. The doctors are saving more people from death in infancy, youth and middle age. Since they live longer, deaths among the elderly, from "wearing out" of vital organs, are increasing.

Heart disease, with 380,000 deaths a year, is the No. 1 cause of death. Brain hemorrhage and cerebral embolisms stand fourth with 112,000, and nephritis (kidney inflammation) fifth with about 100,000.

Falls Off One-Third

Rheumatic heart disease, once a major killer of youth, is decreasing. Its rate has dropped off a third in 25 years. Cause of the decrease is obscure, but doctors are inclined to credit it to better diet, better home sanitation and better general health.

Treatment for heart ailments shows marked advances. New techniques are prolonging the lives of sufferers, and add to their comfort. Honest doctors admit, however, that these are merely postponements of the final reckoning. As more persons are saved for old age, more hearts will wear out. There is little hope that anything will change this inflexible picture—much. Likewise, they expect nephritis and brain hemorrhage deaths to increase. Both are natural associates of old age.

Life Expectancy 62

New drugs, new surgical techniques and better diagnosis can and do prolong the lives of those who inevitably fall victim to these diseases. Their last years are spent more comfortably because of science.

Public health authorities view the increases in the degenerative disease death rate with no alarm. They point out that half these who now die in old age would have died years and years before unless science had stepped in. It has added years to the life expectancy of the average American until it now stands at 62.

Hawaii is 4,665 miles from the Panama canal and 2,015 from the nearest point in Alaska.

Gibraltar has an area of only two square miles. Its population is 17,000.

Public school property in the United States is estimated at $5,000,000,000.

Phi Beta Phi has the largest membership of any college sorority.

The original circumnavigation of the globe by Magellan's fleet took 1,083 days.

U. S. NAVAL BASES

Washington, Dec. 11 (AP)—The United States Government was reported today to be insisting upon placing its new air and naval bases in Trinidad where it wants them, although local authorities of the strategic Caribbean island have objected to some of the locations.

Vibrations from a dynamite explosion have been detected 2,000 miles away.

The first point in the United States touched by the rising sun is Mount Katahdin, Maine.

The word "geography" is derived from Greek roots meaning "description of the earth."

There are 275,300 autos in Argentina.

There are ten colleges in the United States bearing the name "St. Mary" or "St. Mary's."

Only about one-tenth of the vast area of Soviet Russia is under cultivation.

American artichoke production is confined largely to a strip of coastland south of San Francisco.

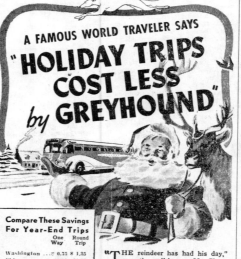

1940 SPORTS NEWS

A Picture Review by The Associated Press

GOLF UPSET. Playing on his home course, Winged Foot at Mamaroneck, N. Y., Dick Chapman (left) swamped W. B. McCullough, Jr., of Philadelphia, 11 and 9, to win national amateur golf title Sept. 14, plus trophy from Harold Pierce (center) of U.S.G.A. Lawson Little won national open at Cleveland; Byron Nelson won the P.G.A. at Hershey, Pa.

OUT OF HARMON'S WAY Not since Red Grange has praise so showered on a gridder as on Michigan's Tom Harmon, star back seen with ball in the Northwestern-Michigan game won by Wolverines, 20-13. An elusive breakaway artist, runner and kicker, Harmon scored 33 touchdowns in three years, registered 237 points to top Grange's Western conference record. Minnesota was rated nation's No. 1 team, and Nebraska is to meet Stanford in Rose Bowl.

SWAN SONG With no more tennis worlds to conquer, Alice Marble of California, seen at Forest Hills with Don McNeill after September matches which both won, turned pro in November. She wants money for a singing career, At Forest Hills she took her third straight singles title, and McNeill of Oklahoma upset Bobby Riggs for singles crown. Alice was last defeated in competition in 1938 at Wimbledon.

HERE'S THAT JOE AGAIN No one in 1940 jarred the heavyweight crown off Joe Louis, but Arturo Godoy (right) rocked that head with this punch June 20. Louis won in 8th by technical KO. In February, Godoy stayed 15 rounds, Louis took decision. In March, Louis disposed of Johnny Paychek in 44 seconds of Round 2.

HOPE Fistic shuffles of 1940 turned up Billy Conn (above), winner over Pastor and Savold, as most likely candidate for doubtful privilege of fighting Joe Louis. Henry Armstrong lost welter title—last of his three championships.

TURNOVER Chicago Cubs and Gabby Hartnett parted company after 19 years, and Jimmy Wilson (above), 40, former Reds catcher-coach, signed to manage Cubs for two years. In October Jimmy was hero of world series.

RUNNING INTO THE MONEY Gallahadion, a 25-to-1 shot, took the Kentucky Derby but a greater turf thrill was the comeback of Seabiscuit whose winning (above) of the $100,000 added Santa Anita Handicap March 2 in Los Angeles made him the greatest money winner of all time. Kayak II was 2nd and Whichcee, 3rd. Seabiscuit's owned by Charles Howard. Bimelech won Pimlico Preakness, and Our Boots, the rich Belmont Futurity.

SWIM Otto Jaretz (above), 18, Chicagoan, set 220-yard free style swim record July 4, 2:13.1 at Santa Barbara.

RETURN Fired by Cleveland Indians' prexy in 1933, Roger Peckinpaugh (above) got a two-year contract to manage the Indians, replacing Oscar Vitt against whom Redskins rebelled in June. The fiery Vitt signed to manage Portland, Ore., team.

'ALL OUT' BASEBALL WARS Wretched was the lot of umpires during a 1940 season marked by unusual scrappiness among baseball players and louder squawks from fans. Here's a July 19 free-for-all in Dodgers-Cubs game in Chicago with four Cubs hurrying into fray. Umps are J. W. Sears (masked), Lou Jorda.

SUCCESS Credit for Stanford's phenomenal rise from 1939 cellar to Rose Bowl in 1940 with a record of no defeats goes to Clark Shaughnessy, former Chicago coach who went to Stanford last spring after Chicago decided to abandon intercollegiate football.

Navy Fencers Triumph In Ivy League

Gernhart Top Man In Foils

NEW YORK, Dec. 23 — Navy, with victories in the foils and saber, gained the major portion of honors last night in the annual Christmas recess fencing tournament of the pentagonal Ivy League group at the Fencers Club. Allen Gernhardt won the top foils prize for the Middies, while his teammates, Richard G. Bienvenu, and Don F. Quigley, finished one-two in the saber.

Yale's James Hausman won the epee competition, shading big Jim McPherson, of Navy, with R. F. Sweek, another Annapolis swordsman, and Paul Stevens, of Yale, finishing in a tie for third.

Alfred Owre, of Yale, placed second behind Gernhardt in the foil, and Joseph Smith, another Blue fencer, finished third in the sabre for what amounted to almost a shutout for the swordsmen of Princeton, Harvard and Army. The best this trio of colleges could do was a third-place tie in the foil involving Darwin L. Wood, Jr., of Princeton, and B. W. Spore and W. B. Tichenor, both of Navy.

Aids To Beauty Can Serve Santa

By BETTY CLARKE
AP Feature Service Writer

It's easier than it used to be to give a girl a Christmas gift of makeup which you can be sure she will appreciate.

That's because such things as the three essentials on most American dressing tables—cleansing cream, skin fresheners and conditioning cream or powder bases—come in gift form at prices that are within range of the modest purse.

It's the same with the lipsticks, powder, rouge and eye-makeup. These give you a chance for real individuality, because you can get them in traveling kits, in a compact six inches in diameter or in specially-built pocketbooks and evening bags.

Another group of gifts to please her are the things she marks as luxuries in her beauty budget: the daytime perfumes which must be "informal fragrance," the heavier perfumes for evening wear, bubble bath preparations, wash cloths which come as condensed disks for the traveler and guest soap which looks like a set of checkers.

Among the new are the novel nail polishes in self-feeding tubes also containing the brush. There's a powder which includes its own base. And a good perfume which is a guaranteed deodorant as well.

The Mother Who Works

By SARA WINSLOW
AP Feature Service Writer

When a mother must work, who will care for her children? A relative, perhaps? A nurse, if the family income is sufficient? Or shall she place her children in the care of some social agency?

One solution, offered in many communities, is the day nursery.

The modern day nursery, which may be supported by private contributions or from public funds, often does a better job of child care than an unsuitable relative or nurse. It takes the child as early in the morning as is necessary to allow the mother to get to work, and it cares for him until she is free to come and call for him in the evening.

Its workers try to give the child more than routine care. They train him, guard his health, even give him the love and attention which may be inadequate at home. They attempt to help solve family problems through cooperation with other agencies.

Sloan Seals

Slogan seals of the National Tuberculosis Association are replaced this season by three seals in the upper left part of each sheet, showing a child and the inscription "Protect Us from Tuberculosis."

Lithographers inserted as identification marks one small letter in the yellow space under the book at the right on the sixth seal from the left side of the sheet. It's in the sixth horizontal row. By mistake a few sheets went out with an S on the blue field below the cross on the 56th seal.

C'MON, LET'S DANCE—Book learnin' gets a go-by when girls appear, to teach dancing aboard training ship, Illinois. Men are Chas. Ware (left), Pomona, Cal.; Robt. Ross, Robinson, Ill.

DEEP IN BOOKS—NOW!—Out of books as well as the sea do navy men get their training. These students are U.S. naval reserve midshipmen in New York aboard the naval training ship Illinois, before a call to dance came.

NEW YEAR BEGINS MORE THAN ONCE. BELIEVE IT OR NOT!

New Year's day isn't always New Year's day. The actual date varies among the Egyptians, Chinese, Jews, Romans and Mohammedans from September 6 to March 1.

January 1 was designated to be New Year's day when Julius Caesar established the Julian calendar in 46 B. C. However, the calendar year thus established was 11 minutes longer than the astronomical year.

To correct this discrepancy, Pope Gregory III suppressed 10 days in 1852 by order that October 5 be called October 15. England and its colonies, however, did not adopt this new calendar until 1752. For almost three centuries, therefore, New Year's was celebrated twice every year—both times on January 1.

New Year's never fell on the same day two years in succession in old China. The new year began on the first moon after the sun entered the sign Aquarius. This date varied from January 21 to February 18. Jewish New Year's, when translated into dates of the Gregorian calendar, varies from September 6 to October 4.

Mohammedans celebrated Muharram, or New Year's, on February 10 last year. But it wasn't the beginning of 1940 for them; it was the first day of 1359. Because the Mohammedan calendar is arranged differently from ours, the new year does not always fall on the same date according to the calendar in use by the Christian nations.

Happy New Year! When will YOU celebrate?

Don't Take Chance On Stomach Ache

By JOHN GROVER
AP Feature Service Writer

WASHINGTON—Poohpoohing a stomach ache kills thousands of Americans every year.

Digestive tract ailments, causing about 85,000 deaths annually, are the seventh largest cause of mortality. Appendicitis, the neglected stomach ache, is greatest killer in this category, digging 14,500-plus graves a year.

Paradoxically, expert surgery made appendicitis more dangerous. Once the appendicitis death rate was almost 100 per cent but surgery changed all that. Surgeons now cansave the great majority, so many that the public grows increasingly careless about appendicitis.

No Minor Ailment

Early symptoms are disregarded. Victims does with physics, the worst possible thing to do. The result is a rising appendicitis death curve. Failure to call a doctor soon enough results in a ruptured appendix, probable peritonitis and a good chance to meet the coroner professionally.

U. S. Surgeon General Thomas Parran emphatically warns that appendicitis is no minor ailment. When pooh-poohed, the ailment kills.

Diarrhea in infants is the second greatest killer among digestive tract ailments. Doctors resurrected an old remedy—just plain apples—to minimize this disease. Apple pulp, dried or fresh, controls the ailment. The death rate has been cut many times over since 1900.

Other major fatal ailments of the digestive tract are hernia and intestinal obstructions — 12,000 deaths; cirrhosis of the liver—10,000; and stomach ulcers—8,500. Surgeons are becoming more adept in repairing stomach ulcer damage, and the death curve is going down slowly. Surgery likewise is more successful in controlling hernia and intestinal obstruction deaths.

Hopeful Picture

Cirrhosis deaths are inching ahead since prohibition was repealed, alcohol receiving blame for one-tenth of them. Non-alcoholic causes of the disease exist, but have not been determined.

Some studies in the causes of cirrhosis and stomach ulcers are in progress, but have not made much headway. There seems to be a definit connection between worry and stomach ulcers.

But all in all, the fight against deaths from digestive system ailments presents a hopeful picture. Infant diarrhea is being conquered. Surgery is trimming the hernia, stomach ulcer and bowel obstruction death rate. Appendicitis can be held safe if only the public will take it seriously.

War

(Continued from Page One.)

Nazi dive-bomber. Today a few sporadic one-plane attacks were made on the east coast of England.

The British government announced that a German bomb fell in the Cloister court of the House of Parliament, wrecking one of the most ancient and architecturally beautiful parts of the building.

Blast Mannheim

RAF planes, in reprisal, blasted the German industrial center of Mannheim and the nearby suburb if Ludwigshaven again during the night and also attacked the invasion ports of Flushing, Dunkerque and Calais. The attacks capped a series of British raids on Germany, Italy and four Nazi-conquered countries.

Marshal Graziano blamed Italian reverses in Egypt and Libya on the failure of tanks and armored cars to reach him from Italy, thus preventing his forces from getting the jump on the British. He refused, however, to concede defeat in north Africa.

He attributed the Italian retreat from Egypt to the "crushing superiority" of British armored forces and added that his army was outnumbered.

Spies Executed

The Italian execution of two men as spies and the imprisonment of 220 other persons, two of them women, revealed the smashing of an alleged "network of informers" which some observers thought might have been related to the damaging British raid on the Taranto naval base.

Italy is converting an 18th century villa of the old Roman Orsini family into a prison residence deluxe for high ranking British officers near Fonte D'Amore where some 350 French and British captives are shivering in quarters built during the world war.

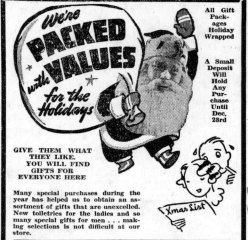

1940 AMERICA'S NEWS IN A WAR YEAR

An Associated Press Picture Review

'GALLOPING GERTIE' GOES Wind-blamed crackup of 2,800-foot center span of the new $6,400,000 Narrows bridge at Tacoma, Wash.—third longest single suspension in world—put an end Nov. 7 to the shimmying undulations that gave the bridge its nickname, "Galloping Gertie." Nature's fury in 1940 was also responsible for earthquakes: in Turkey (January); Peru (May); Rumania (November).

CHANGE Philip Murray (above) became CIO chieftain at Atlantic City convention where John L. Lewis on Nov. 18 formally resigned, sticking to a pre-election pledge that he'd quit if Franklin D. Roosevelt won.

'THIRD TERM' PRESIDENT Victor in a spirited election that broke even the Third Term precedent, President Roosevelt waved greetings from the White House Nov. 7, along with Mrs. Roosevelt (left), Vice President-Elect Henry Agard Wallace, Mrs. Wallace. F.D.R. accepted re-election as an endorsement of policies which in 1940 led to: Huge defense program, peacetime draft, trade of 50 over-age U.S. destroyers for British bases, western hemisphere defense collaboration with South and Central American republics, "all possible aid to the nations that still resist aggression."

THE WAX CASE Deprived by court action of a girl's wax-preserved corpse that he'd kept in his bedroom seven years while busy with life-restoring experiments, Karl van Cosel, 70, studies her death mask. Key West, Fla., commission found him sane, discharged him Oct. 10.

BOMBERS BY THE YARD Symbol of the faster tempo of U.S. production of planes and defense weapons are these four-motored, long-range bombers, so big they're assembled in yard at San Diego plant. Along with Sperry bombsight, planes like these were released to Britain in line with government's policy of giving aid.

HAVEN Foremost among war refugees who reached the Americas' hospitable shores was Crown Princess Juliana (above) of The Netherlands. U.S. greeted thousands of refugee children and such celebrities as Paderewski, Former Empress Zita of Austria.

SAFE RETURN But for alert Cecil Wetzel and Ellis Woods, two lumbermen who stumbled onto the kidnaper and boy, there might not have been this reunion between Count and Countess Marc de Tristan and their son, Marc, 3, Sept. 22 at Hillsborough, Cal. Wilhelm Muhlenbroich, an alien, is serving a life sentence at San Quentin on kidnap charge. The little boy was held captive for 48 hours.

GOOD NEIGHBORS Uncle Sam's courtship of western hemisphere nations pushed ahead when Vice President-Elect Henry Agard Wallace traveled to Mexico City for Dec. 1 inaugural of Pres. Avila Camacho, and paused en route for this chat with a Mexican farmer. Also entered in neighborliness ledger is granting by U.S. of millions in credit to Argentina, Brazil, Chile, Peru, Ecuador.

CAMPAIGN TARGET From this brush with an egg-tossing Chicagoan Oct. 22 Wendell L. Willkie, Republican presidential candidate, emerged to carry on a fight that netted him some 22,000,000 votes in the country's bitterest political battle. The campaign even set a new high for vegetables thrown.
© Chicago Daily Times

IT'S NO. 158 Eyes of 17,000,000 men who registered on Oct. 16 turned Oct. 29 to above drawing of first number in nation's first peacetime draft, in Washington. It was 158, drawn by blindfolded War Secretary Henry Stimson. Draftees are from 21 to 35, are being called according to drawing of serial numbers issued by local boards.

DEATH AT THE BEND Close to 30 persons were killed when a Chicago-bound express piled up at this bend near Little Falls, N. Y., April 19—the same month in which 212 Negro men and women burned to death in a flaming dance hall at Natchez, Miss. Heavy in death toll was the headon collision of a commuters' train and a freight July 31 at Cuyahoga Falls, Ohio, which killed about 40 persons. Sen. Ernest Lundeen of Minnesota was among 25 killed in Aug. 31 plane crash at Lovettsville, Va. Mine caveins at Bartley, W. Va., St. Clairsville, O., and in Pennsylvania cost the lives of several score miners.

GONE The death in January of Sen. William E. Borah (above), Idaho Republican, took a veteran legislator from Senate's ranks that before 1940 ended were to lose Sen. Ernest Lundeen, Minnesota; Sen. William Bankhead, Alabama; Sen. Key Pittman, Nevada.

SOLDIERS' LIFE FOR THEM Thousands of men shouldered arms as United States, bent on a bigger army, a two-ocean navy, an adequate air force, sent draftees and volunteers to army camps that mushroomed into being. The defense commission named by F.D.R. in May and including such leaders as William Knudsen, Sidney Hillman, Edward Stettinius, Jr., and Ralph Budd helped co-ordinate nation's defense efforts.

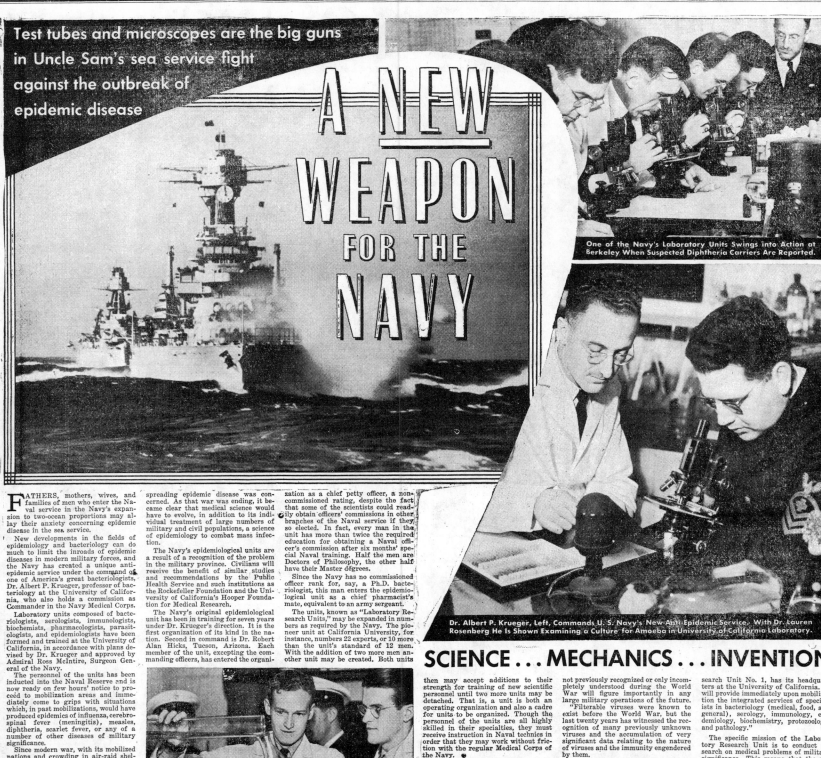

Test tubes and microscopes are the big guns in Uncle Sam's sea service fight against the outbreak of epidemic disease

A NEW WEAPON FOR THE NAVY

One of the Navy's Laboratory Units Swings into Action at Berkeley When Suspected Diphtheria Carriers Are Reported.

Dr. Albert P. Krueger, Left, Commands U. S. Navy's New Anti-Epidemic Service. With Dr. Lauren Rosenberg He Is Shown Examining a Culture for Amoeba in University of California Laboratory.

FATHERS, mothers, wives, and families of men who enter the Naval service in the Navy's expansion to two-ocean proportions may allay their anxiety concerning epidemic disease in the sea service.

New developments in the fields of epidemiology and bacteriology can do much to limit the inroads of epidemic diseases in modern military forces, and the Navy has created a unique anti-epidemic service under the command of one of America's great bacteriologists, Dr. Albert P. Krueger, professor of bacteriology at the University of California, who also holds a commission as Commander in the Navy Medical Corps.

Laboratory units composed of bacteriologists, serologists, immunologists, biochemists, pharmacologists, parasitologists, and epidemiologists have been formed and trained at the University of California, in accordance with plans devised by Dr. Krueger and approved by Admiral Ross McIntire, Surgeon General of the Navy.

The personnel of the units has been inducted into the Naval Reserve and is now ready on few hours' notice to proceed to mobilization areas and immediately come to grips with situations which, in past mobilizations, would have produced epidemics of influenza, cerebrospinal fever (meningitis), measles, diphtheria, scarlet fever, or any of a number of other diseases of military significance.

Since modern war, with its mobilized nations and crowding in air-raid shelters, produces the most rigorous herding to which mankind has ever been subjected, collateral with nervous and physical attrition over wide territories, the peril of epidemic disease has been intensified.

Epidemic disease has always claimed a heavy toll of armies and navies, often inflicting more casualties than those received at the hands of the enemy, but the transformation of the conditions of warfare, to include entire nations, caught the first World War nations completely off-guard so far as rapidly spreading epidemic disease was concerned. As that war was ending, it became clear that medical science would have to evolve, in addition to its individual treatment of large numbers of military and civil populations, a science of epidemiology to combat mass infection.

The Navy's epidemiological units are a result of a recognition of the problem in the military province. Civilians will receive the benefit of similar studies and recommendations by the Public Health Service and such institutions as the Rockefeller Foundation and the University of California's Hooper Foundation for Medical Research.

The Navy's original epidemiological unit has been in training for seven years under Dr. Krueger's direction. It is the first organization of its kind in the nation. Second in command is Dr. Robert Alan Hicks, Tucson, Arizona. Each member of the unit, excepting the commanding officers, has entered the organization as a chief petty officer, a noncommissioned rating, despite the fact that some of the scientists could readily obtain officers' commissions in other branches of the Naval service if they so elected. In fact, every man in the unit has more than twice the required education for obtaining a Naval officer's commission after six months' special Naval training. Half the men are Doctors of Philosophy, the other half have their Master degrees.

Since the Navy has no commissioned officer rank for, say, a Ph.D. bacteriologist, this man enters the epidemiological unit as a chief pharmacist's mate, equivalent to an army sergeant.

The units, known as "Laboratory Research Units," may be expanded in numbers as required by the Navy. The pioneer unit at California University, for instance, numbers 22 experts, or 10 more than the unit's standard of 12 men. With the addition of two more men another unit may be created. Both units then may accept additions to their strength for training of new scientific personnel until two more units may be detached. That is, a unit is both an operating organization and also a cadre for units to be organized. Though the personnel of the units are all highly skilled in their specialties, they must receive instruction in Naval technics in order that they may work without friction with the regular Medical Corps of the Navy.

Recognizing the extraordinary efficiency of the Navy's regular Medical Corps, Dr. Krueger has organized his epidemiological service to confront special problems of mobilization.

"New situations," he points out, "which cannot always be anticipated arise whenever war shifts about and alters the environment of large population masses. Laboratory studies of immunology and herd infections furnish data only partially applicable to these problems and of incomplete aid in their solution. Thus prior to the World War we could not predict the part to be played by trench fever and shell shock, to name only two diseases.

"It is fairly certain that phenomena not previously recognized or only incompletely understood during the World War will figure importantly in any large military operations of the future.

"Filterable viruses were known to exist before the World War, but the last twenty years has witnessed the recognition of many previously unknown viruses and the accumulation of very significant data relating to the nature of viruses and the immunity engendered by them.

"The medical, surgical, and laboratory facilities already provided and those which will come into being from reserve cadres upon, perhaps, a declaration of war may be expected to cope effectively with the great majority of the practical problems that will arise. Nevertheless it was clearly evident in 1917 that additional personnel and equipment for research purposes were needed.

"The need for such a supplementary service in the U. S. Navy has been recognized, and in 1934 Admiral Rossiter, then Surgeon General, encouraged and authorized me to gather together a group of specialists trained in various phases of laboratory research.

"This unit, known as Laboratory Research Unit No. 1, has its headquarters at the University of California. It will provide immediately upon mobilization the integrated services of specialists in bacteriology (medical, food, and general), serology, immunology, epidemiology, biochemistry, protozoology, and pathology."

The specific mission of the Laboratory Research Unit is to conduct research on medical problems of military significance. This means that the nature of the work will be essentially practical and investigations on subjects of only theoretical importance will not be undertaken unless there is a fair chance that the data obtained will be of immediate or eventual utility to the Navy Medical Service in its effort to "keep as many men at as many guns as many days as possible."

The respiratory diseases will receive major emphasis and attention will be focused on the isolation and identification of causal strains, use of vaccines and sera in their prevention and cure, the epidemiology of these diseases, etc.

As a secondary function the unit will attempt to provide Naval laboratories with a center to which problems in infection and immunity may be referred when the individual laboratories are unable to conduct the work themselves because of limitations of time and facilities. For example, if there occurred several simultaneous outbreaks of epidemic cerebrospinal meningitis the research unit could classify the meningococci isolated from patients in various organizations and could then determine which of the many sera available were active against these strains and could consequently be used to best advantage therapeutically.

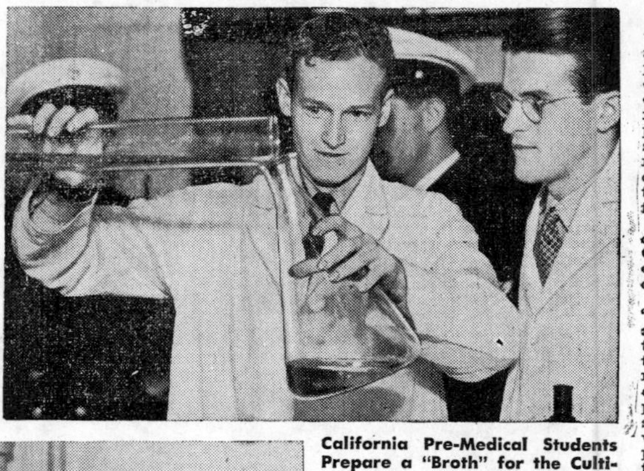

California Pre-Medical Students Prepare a "Broth" for the Cultivation of Organisms.

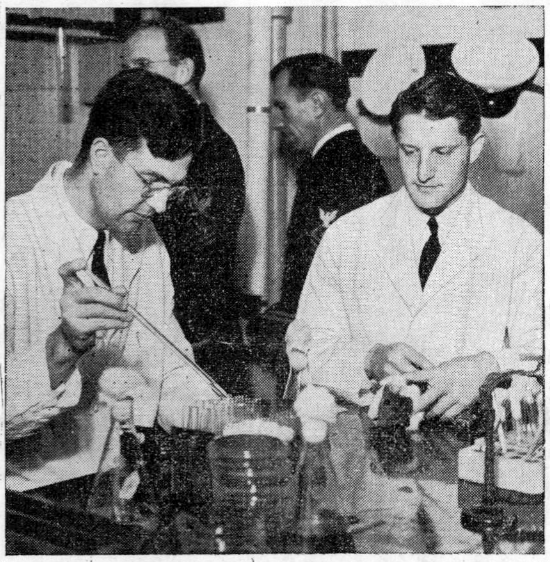

Immunologist Alcor Brown and Bacteriologist Orville Golub Are Shown Setting Up Fixation Tests with the Use of a Guinea Pig in the Laboratory. They Are Fighting the Influenza Epidemic.

SCIENCE . . . MECHANICS . . . INVENTION

THIS WEEK IN THE SKY

(Prepared by the Hayden Planetarium of the American Museum of Natural History in New York City)

Look due south after sunset on January 27th to find the planet Jupiter. On this date it is said to be in quadrature with the sun. That is, as observed from the earth, Jupiter is at a 90-degree angle to the sun in the sky. On Tuesday, the 28th, Saturn is in quadrature with the sun. This means that these planets will be visible only until about midnight, when they disappear in the west.

Mars climbs into the eastern sky about 3:37 A.M. Eastern Standard Time on February 1st, and Venus rises at about 6 A.M., E.S.T. As the months advance the rising time of Venus will become steadily later until it finally reaches a position too near the sun for observation. After passing to the east of the sun, this planet will become visible above the western horizon after sunset as an evening star.

Mars, however, will rise earlier each night and by next summer will appear well above the eastern horizon at midnight.

The moon is new on the 27th of January and throughout the remainder of the week it will appear in the west each night as an ever growing crescent which will attain its first quarter phase on the 4th of February.

Milestones of Science

WHEY, a byproduct of milk left over in the manufacture of cheese and casein, is now being converted into wine by a new chemical process. The wine can be made either in the sherry or sauterne type with about 15 per cent alcoholic content.

●

A new type of precision metal working machine capable of exerting a force of three million pounds in compression and one million pounds in tension, is being demonstrated at the Aluminum Research laboratories. It is the most powerful testing machine ever built.

●

Polonium, a metal with a commercial value of two million dollars an ounce, is now used, but only in minute quantities, in the new automobile spark-plugs. The polonium is said to ensure quicker starting and an appreciable saving in fuel.

●

According to the National Bureau of Standards, the cost of the cheapest commercial "synthetic" rubber on the market today, although about twice that of the natural product, is gradually being reduced to the level of real rubber through the introduction of improved methods of manufacture.

●

Three Cornell University professors, Paul F. Sharp, E. S. Guthrie and David B. Hand, have perfected a process of de-aerating pasteurized milk without taking away any of the valued vitamin C content. By taking air out of the milk they made it possible for one quart of the liquid to retain a vitamin content equal to the juice of a whole orange. The content of vitamin C in one quart of average pasteurized milk is said to be equal to the juice in one slice of orange. The Cornell scientists estimated that the operating cost of de-aerating 1,500 quarts of milk would be eleven cents, so that the process would not increase the price to the consumer.

●

War statisticians have estimated that during an average day's operation of a fleet of bombing and pursuit planes, more than two and one-quarter million gallons of high-test gasoline are consumed. This quantity of fuel would be sufficient to operate 3,000 American passenger automobiles for one entire year.

●

One of the newest pencils on the market not only writes, it also gives all the answers to simple mathematical problems as well. The pencil is equipped with a movable band which is turned until the two numbers to be multiplied coincide. The product is read through a hole in the band.

Around The Radio Dial Tonight

WCAO	600K
WFBR	1270K
WCBM	1270K
WBAL until 9.00 P. M.	1060K
WBAL after 9.00 P.M.	760K
‡WOR N. B. S. Key	710K
‡WEAF N. B. C. Red Key	660K
‡WABC—C. B. S. Key	860K
‡WJZ N. B. C. Blue Key	760K

(By C. E. Butterfield)

(Time is Eastern Standard)

NEW YORK, Feb. 28—Chances for a get-together leading to possible settlement of the radio music fee row are considered "pretty good." But when meetings are to start is another question.

Meanwhile, Broadcast Music, Inc., continues as the main source of music for most radio stations.

Apparently opening of conferences awaits an ASCAP proposal to the National Association of Broadcasters, with the price and method of payment the main questions to be threshed out.

In the meetings, it was said, BMI, which was organized by NAB, would be regarded as an established competitor of ASCAP.

Dialing tonight: The war—NBC-Red 7:15, 11:15; CBS 8:55, 10:45 East, 12; NBC-Blue 9:30; MBS 10, 12:30; NBC 12.

Talks—MBS 9:15, Assistant Sec. of War Patterson to Federal Bar Association; CBS 10, John Hay Whitney at School of the Air conference; CBS 10:15, Dr. Don Luis Quintanilla, Mexican minister, on "Steps Toward Pan-American Unity."

NBC-Red: 8, Lucille Manners Concert; 8:30, Information Please; 9, Waltz Time.

CBS: 7:30, (West 10:30) Al Pearce; 8, Kate Smith's Hour; 9, Johnny Presents.

NBC-Blue: 8, Broadcast from Ft. Bliss, Tex.; 9, Gang Busters; 10, Lightweight Fight, Lew Jenkins vs. Lou Ambers.

MBS: 7:15, Here's Morgan; 8:30, Laugh and Swing Club; 9:30, 2 I Want A Divorce.

5:00
WCAO: *The Goldbergs, sketch.
WFBR: ‡Girl Alone, sketch.
WBAL: Kiddie Club, variety.
WCBM: Talk, Nat Youngelson.
WOR: Superman, sketch.
WJZ: Irene Wicker, stories.

5:15
WCAO: *The O'Neills, sketch.
WFBR: ‡Lone Journey, sketch.
WBAL: Little Orphan Annie.
WCBM: Melodic Interlude; Talk.
WJZ: Bud Barton, sketch.

5:30
WCAO: Musical Varieties.
WFBR: ‡Jack Armstrong, drama.
WBAL: Streamlined Fairy Tales.
WCBM: Rhythm Rounders, music.
WOR: Mandrake, the Magician.
WABC: World Day of Prayer.
WJZ: Behind The News.

5:45
WCAO: *Scattergood Baines, sketch.
WFBR: Life Can Be Beautiful.
WBAL: ‡Tom Mix, sketch.
WCBM: ‡"Capt. Midnight," drama.

6:00
WABC: News; Edwin C. Hill.
WFBR: Baltimore Public Schools.
WBAL: News; Sports Parade.
WEAF: Story Behind the Headlines.
WCBM: News; WCBM Dinner Music.
WOR: Uncle Don's Children Prgm.
WJZ: News; Music; Quartet.

6:15
WCAO: Don Riley, sports; News.
WBAL: The Singing Cop.
WCBM: Around the Dinner Table.
WABC: Bob Hope's Hollywood.
WEAF: Music; Talk; News.
WJZ: Bill Stern's, sports.

6:30
WCAO: ‡Paul Sullivan, talk.
WFBR: Bob Hurleigh; Voice of Sports.
WCBM: News; Sports, Lee Davis.
WOR: Press Bulletins.
WEAF: Captain Tim Healy's Stamp Club.
WJZ: Dinner Date, orchestra.

6:45
WCBM: The World Today.

WFBR: Junior Bar Assn. Talk.
WBAL: ‡Talk, Lowell Thomas.
WCBM: Swing Music.
WOR: Meet Mr. Morgan.
WEAF: Gasoline Alley, sketch.

7:00
WCAO: *Amos 'n' Andy, sketch.
WFBR: ‡Fred Waring's Orchestra.
WBAL: ‡Happy Gordon's Rangers.
WCBM: ‡Fulton Lewis, Jr., talk.
WOR: Stan Lomax, sports talk.

7:15
WCAO: Lanny Ross, songs.
WFBR: ‡Newsroom of the Air.
WBAL: Radio Magic, sketch.
WCBM: The Polish Hour.
WOR: "Confidentially Yours."
WJZ: Radio Magic, sketch.

7:30
WCAO: Al Pearce's Gang.
WFBR: Fort Meade on Parade.
WBAL: ‡Abe Templeton Time.
WOR: The Lone Ranger.
WJZ: "Discoveries in 1941."

7:45
WCBM: The Polish Period.

8:00
WCAO: ‡Kate Smith Show; News.
WFBR: Lucille Manners and Orch.
WBAL: ‡Friday Night Army Show.
WCBM: "Take a Number," variety.
WOR: Symphonic Strings.

8:15
WCBM: Soldiers' Prospects, talk.

8:30
WFBR: ‡"Information Please."
WBAL: ‡Death Valley Days, drama.
WCBM: ‡Laugh and Swing Club.

9:00
WCAO: ‡Johnny Presents, Music.
WFBR: ‡Waltz Time, Frank Munn.
WCBM: Gang Busters, sketch.
WBAL: Ed Fenton Scholastic Sports.
WOR: Talk, Gabriel Heatter.

9:15
WCBM: ‡Twenty-first Annual Banquet

9:30
WOR: Press Bulletins.
WCAO: *The Playhouse, drama.
WFBR: ‡Every Man's Theatre.
WBAL: ‡News; Your Happy Birthday.
WCBM: ‡‡I Want A Divorce.

10:00
WCAO: Talk, John Hay Whitney.
WFBR: ‡Wings of Destiny, drama.
WBAL: ‡Jenkins-Ambers, fight.
WCBM: ‡Talk, Raymond Gram Swing.

10:15
WCAO: ‡Dr. Luis Quintanilla.
WCBM: ‡Sen. Robert R. Reynolds.
WOR: News; Paul Schubert, talk.

10:30
WCAO: News; John Varney Music.
WFBR: Alberta Dominguez & Orch.
WCBM: ‡Teddy Powell's Orchestra.
WOR: Talk, Fulton Lewis, Jr.
WABC: Back Where I Come From.

10:45
WFBR: ‡Deep Rhythm, orchestra.
WCBM: ‡Cats and Jammers, music.
WABC: News in the World.

11:00
WCAO: Film Facts; Denny Thompson's Orch.
WFBR: News; Movie Parade.
WBAL: ‡News; Mal Hallett's Orch.
WCBM: Press Bulletins.
WOR: Press Bulletins.
WABC: Sports Time, talk.
WEAF: Press Bulletins.

11:15
WCAO: Moonlight Serenade.
WCBM: The Music You Want.
WOR: Twenty-first Annual Banquet Federal Bar Assn.
WABC: Shep Fields' Orchestra.
WEAF: You Want Music.

(Continued on Page 6)

OAKY DOAKS

Double Indemnity

SCORCHY SMITH

Toni Has A Taking-Off Way With Her

OH, DIANA!

Practice Makes Perfect

DICKIE DARE

Birth Of A Brainthrob

THE ADVENTURES OF PATSY

HOMER HOOPEE

The Defense Rests!

NEIGHBORLY NEIGHBORS

PETERS DIDN'T BOTHER TO ANSWER MYRA—HE DIDN'T EVEN HEAR HER—HE'S TOO ENGROSSED IN HIS WALL THUMPING!—SNAPPING HIS FINGERS, HE JUMPED UP, SCURRIED OUT TO THE WOODSHED, GATHERED UP AN ARMFUL OF TOOLS AND HEADED BACK FOR THE HOUSE—!!

MODEST MAIDENS

"Haven't you something more doggy? I want to fascinate a gay old dog."

THE DOOLITTLES

MAMMA'S LIL' HELPER

Can Hitler's Forces Invade England This Year ... And Will They?

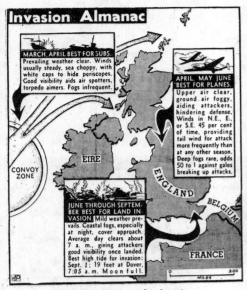

Invasion Almanac

MARCH, APRIL BEST FOR SUBS. Prevailing weather clear. Winds usually steady, sea choppy, with white caps to hide periscopes. Good visibility aids air spotters, torpedo aimers. Fogs infrequent.

APRIL, MAY, JUNE BEST FOR PLANES. Upper air clear, ground air foggy, aiding attackers, hindering defense. Winds in N.E., E. or S.E. 45 per cent of time, providing tail wind for attack more frequently than at any other season. Deep fogs rare, odds 50 to 1 against gales breaking up attacks.

JUNE THROUGH SEPTEMBER BEST FOR LAND INVASION. Mild weather prevails. Coastal fogs, especially at night, cover approach. Average day clears about 7 a. m., giving attackers good visibility once landed. Best high tide for invasion: Sept. 1; 19 feet at Dover, 7:05 a.m. Moon full.

Weather data suggest an order of events ...

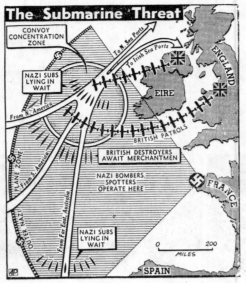

The Submarine Threat

CONVOY CONCENTRATION ZONE

NAZI SUBS LYING IN WAIT

To M. Sea Ports / To Irish Sea Ports

From N. America

BRITISH PATROLS

BRITISH DESTROYERS AWAIT MERCHANTMEN

NAZI BOMBERS SPOTTERS OPERATE HERE

NAZI SUBS LYING IN WAIT

EIRE / ENGLAND / FRANCE / SPAIN

0   200   MILES

1. Early spring is ideal for attacks on shipping.

The Air Threat

NORWAY / STAVANGER

COASTAL DEFENSE (HEAVIEST ON EAST)
- DEFENSE IN DEPTH
- HOME GUARD DEFENSES
- HEAVILY BOMBED AREAS

ABERDEEN / GLASGOW / NEWCASTLE / HULL / LIVERPOOL / BIRMINGHAM / COVENTRY / NORWICH / BRISTOL / LONDON / PLYMOUTH / DOVER / BOULOGNE

EIRE / THE HAGUE / NETHERLANDS / BELGIUM / FRANCE

0   200   MILES

2. Flying conditions improve as the season advances.

The All-Out Invasion Threat

SECONDARY OBJECTIVES: To divert and hold back large British forces while the main attack progresses. If a beachhead were won, Germans could shift main attack accordingly.

NORWAY

THIS LINE separates heart of England (London) from its industrial support. Main German objective in invasion would be to cut through here.

NAZI E BOATS, SUBS AND MINES GUARD CHANNEL AT BOTH ENDS

EIRE / DENMARK / INDUSTRIAL MIDLANDS / LONDON / NETHERLANDS / GERMANY / BELGIUM / LILLE

ZONE CLEARED FOR INVASION (22 MI. DEEP) POSSIBLE GERMAN PENETRATION ZONES

3. Finally, the best conditions for invasion.

Artist Previews Battle For a Beachhead

By MORGAN M. BEATTY

WASHINGTON—Canvass the best military, economic and diplomatic opinion on this side of the Atlantic and you get a picture of Germany attempting an all-out invasion of the British isles along a fairly definite pattern. And you also find odds about 3 to 2 against an all-out attempt this year.

If the Germans should try it, however, the first week in September affords the most auspicious combination of advantages from their point of view.

The odds as reckoned here are a little higher than 2 to 1 that the invasion attempt would fail.

Most experts accept the general thesis that the Germans will first loose their submarines and planes on the British. In fact the battle of the Atlantic already has started, and the stepped-up air Battle of Britain should begin about mid-April. Meanwhile, the Nazis use axis diplomacy and force along the British lifelines to divert as much empire strength as possible to those danger points.

In the opinion of observers here—

If the submarines and their helping plane eyes threaten the British isles with strangulation, AND

If air attack shows signs of breaking British morale, AND

If thrusts at empire lifelines succeed,

Then—and only then—should a prudent German high command consider all-out invasion.

But nevertheless, Hitler should be prepared for the odds, and have a huge army ready to spring from the invasion coast of France anytime between April 1 and September 30.

ON THE other hand there are three stark, compelling reasons why the Nazis might throw cautions to the winds and attack this summer.

1. Germany must feed several hundred millions of people in conquered Europe. Diet deficiency among these people already ranges close to 50 per cent by official Nazi reports. The Germans must break the blockade soon.

2. American aid is mounting fast.

3. Except for war industry, economic stagnation is admittedly general over Europe. Peacetime work must be resumed before people can receive money for work and afford the necessities of life.

The weather should go a long way to dictate the timing of the German attack. It has always been a major factor with German military leaders.

The battle of the Atlantic, in line with this weather factor theory, was launched about March 1. Prevailing weather is clear, white caps hide periscopes, torpedo wakes. Spring air attacks should start in April as land storms subside and generally milder conditions prevail.

The ideal period for land invasion is the first week in September. It's usually extremely mild, storms almost never occur, and night fogs, lifting with the sunrise, are the rule.

If and when invasion comes, the pattern of attack is foreshadowed by the known training methods of the modern German army and navy, and their equipment.

The Germans are training huge forces in embarkation and landing from all types of large and small air and sea craft.

They're concentrating on the art of loading the big freight of war—tanks, ambulances, staff cars, medium-sized guns, etc.—in both air transports and huge motorless gliders.

ALL this adds up to this kind of attack:

While subs and bombers are striking at England's transport, the convoy lanes, and her industrial centers, some 30-odd sudden attacks by air infantry might be launched. Relays of planes carrying complete miniature armies would continue to supply these points of penetration until they had succeeded—or failed—to establish defensible positions.

All along the countryside between the penetration points, thousands of parachute pioneers would drop, undermine defense, spread panic. This should make it easier for the penetration points to join forces, and lop off chunks of the English ciast (beachheads).

Finally, huge forces would cross the channel for the frontal assault.

THIS artist's conception of an all-out attack on the English coast is based on reports of actual preparations—of the Germans for the attack and of the British for the defense. The Germans are training huge forces in embarkation and landing and in transporting by air and by sea all the heavy equipment of an invading army. The British have ringed their beach areas with guns for throwing large drums of gasoline that will explode and spread flames among approaching craft, or set up a curtain of fire along the shore.

Barbed wire and tank traps also are important in the beach defenses, while farther back are big guns and the fields from which aircraft will take off to meet the invaders. The drawing depicts the battle for air supremacy as a part of the assault on the beachhead, a situation which observers agree must be expected unless the Germans knock out the Royal Air Force before they try to land troops. In the background is the city of Hastings, where William the conqueror won a battle in 1066.

All this sounds fairly easy, but nobody knows better than the German naval command the extreme military risk the invaders must run to hold a perch on the hostile shores of England. Besides the initial risk, the Germans have little naval strength to convoy and protect invasion troops.

Offense Vs Defense

By Land—

Parachutists   Parashooters

By Sea—

Secret Barges / Sea Forts   (Artist's version) (Actual photograph)

By Air—

New Bomber   Anti-Aircraft Gun

Conquerors And The Dreams Of Conquerors Have Harassed England Down Through The Centuries

Roman soldiers are depicted here in the first invasion of England. The legions of Julius Caesar landed in 55 B. C., subjugated the native Britons. The Romans ruled till 410, then withdrew. The Romans gone, the Picts and Scots came down from the north, and the Britons called for aid from the Teutonic Angles, Saxons and Jutes, who ended up with control of most of the country.

Danish raiders, shown here, came across the sea to harass the Anglo-Saxon kings and eventually to establish a line of Danish kings, of which the first was the Canute of legendary fame. The Danish and Anglo-Saxon elements gradually blended and in 1042 the Saxon line of kings was restored. Hero of wars with the Danes was Alfred the Great (871-901).

Second in the second line of Saxon kings was Harold, whose death in 1066 at the Battle of Hastings, pictured above, was followed by successful conquest by William the Conqueror and his Normans. William and his son and grandson became complete masters of the country, remodeled the church, made Norman-French the official language, compiled the first English census and survey.

Napoleon considered conquest of the island vitally important to his plans, and in the summer of 1805 he had his army poised at Boulogne ready for a dash across the channel. Failure of one of his admirals to carry out instructions forced abandonment of the plan and the emperor turned to other conquests. Defeat of the Spanish Armada was the frustration of another attempt on the isle.

Ted Williams, Hitting Over .400, Eyes Triple Batting Crown

The Beanville Beanpole is ready . . .   . . . and swings determinedly . . .   . . . as the ball whistles in . . .   . . . Swatto! The slugger connects . . .   . . . and then carries out . . .   . . . his perfect follow-through.

By DILLON GRAHAM
Sports Editor, AP Feature Service

NEW YORK—The beanpole who leads American league batters was burning.

"That dumb scorer," said Ted Williams, "he gave me an error yesterday. Didja see the game? Well, a guy hits one out my way and I come in fast to trap the ball on the bounce. The durn thing takes a bad hop and kicks me in the shoulder.

"And I get an error. Me, who never touched the ball. Am I sore! That scorer, he don't know a hit from a lilypad.

"Oh, hell," he said, with a shrug, "I don't give a damn about fielding anyway. They say I'm a bonehead fielder and maybe they're right. But, Bud," he said, aggressively, "I'm a hitter. I can bust 'em."

And Ted Williams of the Boston Red Sox outfield can. He can blast a ball a country mile. He was pacing the league at a better-than-.400 clip in early July.

Ted can't explain his high average. "Luck, I guess," he said. "Aw, it 's not all luck, y'know, you gotta be swinging good. But I'm hitting the ball just like I did last year, same grip, same stance, same swing. More of e'm are falling safe. 'Course, after a couple of years in the league I know the pitchers better and I guess that helps.

"But, shucks, a fellow can be hitting the ball fine and lose 20 points in his average in a week or so. It's just a matter of hitting 'em where they ain't."

Williams thinks the odds are all against his finishing the year with an average above .400: "Say, it's been 18 years since an American leaguer hit over .400 and we've had some pretty fair punchers up there during that time. I guess the odds ought to be about 25 to 1 against me, mebbe 50."

Tall Ted led the league in runs batted in—the real payoff on a hitter's value—in his first year, 1939, with 145. He said that during his career he'd like to be top man at least once in every department of hitting. His chief ambition is to win triple hitting honors—batting, homers, and runs-batted-in—the same year.

"But that's sorta hard to do. I'm leading in batting now and well up in homers and RBI. I've got a chance this year," he said.

Ted is hitting third in the Boston batting order and he says that's a handicap in knocking in counters. "It's better to be hitting fourth or fifth. You've generally got more men on base. That York, he's hitting fourth. Keller is batting fifth. See, Keller's got somebody on base almost every time he come up and he's liable to push somebody across every time he hits one.

"Hell," he said, "I haven't had but one chance this year to hit with the bases loaded. That was against the White Sox and Lyons walked me. Tension? Naw, there isn't no tension for me hitting in the clutch. Why should I tighten up? Jeepers, I'd like to have the bases loaded every time I came up. And say, don't forget, there's some tension on the pitcher, too."

Ted does look loose as a goose, as the ball players say, when he's up at the dish. He's 6 foot 3 and weighs only 175 pounds.

"Just a beanpole," he explains. "I drink gallons of milk and eat like a hoss but I don't get any heavier."

The 22-year-old California youngster wouldn't say whom he regarded as the toughest pitcher in the league to hit. "You know why?" he asked. "Well, it's this way: After my first year with Boston, folks asked me which pitchers were tough and I said that Ruffing of the Yanks was the easiest. Say, I murdered that guy all the time. He was meat. And, y'know what happened last year? Well, I couldn't buy a hit off the guy. So I ain't talking any more. They're all tough when you ain't swinging good.

Tedt thinks Joe DiMaggio is a great hitter but he believes Jimtimes I can't figure how a ball can go as far as he hits it. Looks like his blast would tear the cover off the ball."

Ted says he isn't superstitious, but—"I don't like black cats any too well."

Indians, Cards Battle Hard For League Flags

Both Teams Pressing For Leadership

By Bill Boni
(Associated Press Sports Writer)

Though they can turn out to be duds just as easily as high-explosive, there were definite indications today that the Cleveland Indians and St. Louis Cardinals aren't going to give up the pennant races without a struggle.

At the moment, the battles are just as they were before the All-Star contest, with the New York Yankees three and a half games up on Cleveland in the American League, the Brooklyn Dodgers three games to the good over the Cards in the National. But there's the hitch—the pace-setters didn't pick up any ground.

Rained Out

The Yanks, opening a swing through the West, got in five innings last night before it rained in St. Louis. That proved just enough for Joe Di Magio to run his batting streak to 49 straight games and for Lefty Gomez to blank the Browns, 1-0, on five hits. At the same time, though, the Indians were beating the Athletics 3-2, with Bobby Feller setting the A's down on six safeties and then climbing victory No. 17 by scoring the deciding run after belting a triple in the ninth.

In the other circuit the Dodgers also were kept from widening there margin. In one of the program's two afternoon games they tamed the Cincinnati Reds, 8-3, on Kirby Higbe's second straight five-hitter and timely hitting by Cookie Lavagetto, Billy Herman and Ducky Medwick.

Cards Win

The Cardinals stuck right on their heels. In a wild-eyed, free-swinging contest that involved five homers and eight pitchers, the Red Birds first ran up an 8-0 lead, saw it disappear in one inning, then came back with five more to blast the New Gaints, 13-9, and end their own five-game losing streak.

With one exception all of the night tilts were eloquent testimonials to the popularity of baseball under lights. The night's top crowd, 34,849, was at the Polo Grounds; 32,280 turned out to honor Feller and watch the kid win the 99th game of his career; 17,949 at Chicago saw the White Sox support John Dungan Rigney's seven-hit hurling with a 14-hit assault of their own to down the Washington Senators, 5-1, and the lure of the Di Maggio streak was strong enough to bring 12,682, second-biggest crowd of the year, into St. Louis' Sportsman's Park.

Big Crowd

Only the National League Phillies were unable to top 10,000. Winners of but two of their past 14 games, they were whipped, 6-3, by the Pittsburgh Pirates before a gathering of 4,630.

In the other day game, also in the National League, the Chicago Cubs Vern Olsen came out the winner, 3-1, over the Boston Braves' Al Javery, with Javery allowing only six hits to Olsen's seven but Olsen getting one of those six to drive in the deciding run.

In the American League the Boston Red Sox were rained out at Detroit.

Sports Round-Up
By EDDIE BRIETZ

NEW YORK, July 11 — (The Special News Service)—The name of Billy Conn's movie has been changed from "Kid Tinsel" to "The Pittsburgh Kid," which is more like it . . . Billy's opponent will be Jack Roper, the old heavy-weight, who is a Hollywood electrician . . . Don't let 'em tell you the gals at Elmira, N. Y., don't take their baseball seriously . . . One cutie tripod to bop Umpire Charlie Moore the other day . . . Pilgrims returning from Detroit say old Bobo Newsom was going around wondering right out loud why he wasn't on the all-star team . . . Is Joe Louis slipping? Well, last Sunday Mike Jacobs long-distanced Chicago and tried to get promotional rights to Booker Beckwith, sensational colored heavy with a string of 17 straight wins since turning pro. A year ago Mike turned down a chance to take r Beckwith because it would "detract from Louis." The Dan Toppings (you all know who she was) hit town today. Sonja was carrying her ice in platinum, while Dan had the signed contract of Dean McAdams, Washington U's great fullback, in his hip pocket.

The Anvil Chorus

The baseball writers are having a fine old time second-guessing Bill McKechnie's strategy in letting Claude Passeau pitch the ninth inning of the All-Star game . . . McKechnie said: "I wish I'd had Riddle." . . . Asked why he didn't call on Carl Hubbell, Bill said: "I didn't want to use any old men."

Short, Short Stories

Tom Stidham of Marquette will startle the Mid-West this fall with a four-man defense line . . . Joe DiMaggio says for his dough Bucky Walter was the best elbower he looked at in the All-Star game . . . Tommy Farr, due here soon.

may be sent against Billy Conn at Washington . . . A weakened tendon has thrown King Cole, the speedy three-year-old, out of training for the remainder of the season . . . If the Cubs ever get around to waiving on Johnny Rizzo, the Phils will ship him to Brooklyn for Blimp Phelps in a straight waiver exchange . . . Texas fans, some of whom drove 400 miles to see the bums, are blasting Tony Galento for running out on Kirg Levinsky. If you'll pardon us for horning in, the cowboys should have known better.

Some Fight!

We were not there, but the Mauriello-Mamakos brawl at Ebbets Field must have been one of those good old knock-down, drag-out affairs . . . The N. Y. Times reports: " . . . Mauriello came into his own when he flashed an effective left HOOF which found its mark often on Mamakos' head."

That's Right

Mebbe Deacon McKechnie did muff a few in the all-star game, but from the looks of the National League standings, he won't make the same mistakes next year.

G-Men Find Time For Songs

NEW YORK (AP)—G-men aren't too busy with spies to take care of other little matters.

For one thing, they swooped down on 11 men selling song sheets on Times Square. It was alleged the sheets contained copyrighted songs.

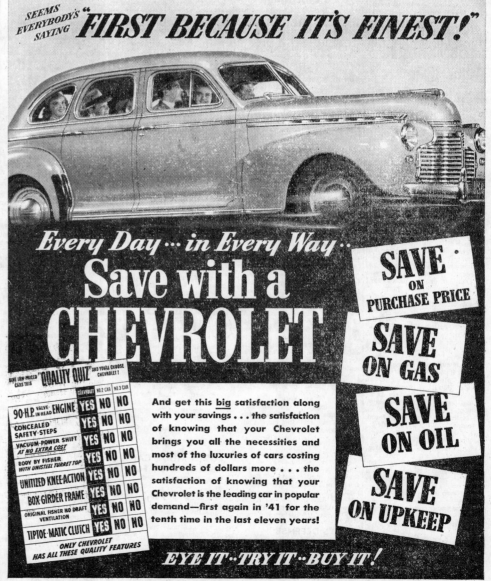

Evening Capital

VOL. LVII — NO. 170. EVERY EVENING EXCEPT SUNDAY ANNAPOLIS, MD., SATURDAY, JULY 19, 1941. SOUTHERN MARYLAND'S ONLY DAILY TWO CENTS.

WEATHER

Scattered showers and thunderstorms this afternoon followed by generally fair and cooler tonight.

Navy Asks $1,470,000 For Academy

LATE NEWS

VETERAN WINS HYDROPLANE RACE

Havre de Grace, Md., July 19 (AP)—Jack O. Cooper, 70-year-old race boat veteran of Kansas City, Mo., gave youthful drivers a lesson today in motor boat racing.

Cooper piloted his hydroplane Tops Pup to a hands down victory in the final heat of the 91 cubic inch race in the Havre de Grace Yacht Club's 12th annual regatta.

GIVES INDUSTRIAL PEACE FORMULA

(By The Associated Press)

An industrial peace formula—strike moratorium committees composed of representatives of labor, management and the public—was placed before the nation for consideration today by Albert W. Hawkes, president of the United States Chamber of Commerce.

He said local Chambers of Commerce could establish the committees and push voluntary mediation. In Toledo, said Mayor John Q. Carey of that city, the board of five labor, five industrial and eight public members, saved many millions of dollars in wages and man-hours of production.

FARM OFFICIALS FOR PRICE FIXING

Washington, July 19 (AP)—Administration officials were reported today to be favorable toward price-regulating legislation expected to be offered in Congress next week.

Such a stand would be opposite to that taken by a number of farm state Congressmen on proposal which would give the Government authority to establish maximum prices for commodities, both industrial and agricultural.

URGES PRIORITY FOR NAVY SHIPS

Washington, July 19 (AP) — Chairman Vinson (D-Ga) of the House Naval Committee complained today that although the country regarded the Navy as its first line of defense "others things" were given prior call on defense materials.

"The national policy is that nothing is more important than building these naval ships," he declared, adding that despite a wide-spread belief that the Navy was expanding fast his committee had found that scheduled dates could not be met without spending an extra $585,000,000.

58 Get Officers Authority In New Home Guard

Governor Makes Appointment Upon Recommendation Of General Mohr

Fifty-eight men today had gubernatorial approval of their commissions as officers in Maryland's State guard, recently organized to replace the National guard.

Governor O'Conor, upon recommendation of Brig. Gen. Dwight H. Mohr, commanding general of the State guard, and battalion commanders, yesterday approved the issuance of commissions to officers in eight battalions and a medical corps.

They are:

Second Battalion Engineers—Dr. Leon Arthur Kochman, Ellicott City, captain medical corps; E. William Fischer and Leroy C. Hubbard, both of Baltimore, 1st lieutenant.

Second Battalion Engineers—Dr. Leon Arthur Kochman, Ellicott City, captain, medical corps; E. William Fischer and Leroy C. Hubard both of Baltimore, 1st lieutenants.

Jessups Man Named

Third Battalion—Lee W. Tipton, captain; Howard F. Edmonston, captain; Edward J. Herman, captain; Paul J. Trinite, 1st lieut., all Baltimore; Charles B. Krimm, Jessups, 1st lieut., Lee W. Tipton, Jr., Baltimore, 1st lieut.; Frank J. Randall, Baltimore, 2nd lieut.; Carl M. Schneider, Jr., Baltimore, 2nd lieut.

Fourth Battalion—John E. Morris, captain; Alfred T. Truitt, captain; Dr. Philip A. Insley, major, medical officer; George Richard Long, 1st lieut.; Nicholas H. Hol-

(Continued on Page 6)

SONJA APPLIES FOR CITIZENSHIP

Sonja Henie, movie and skating star, is sworn in by George A. Saden, naturalization court clerk at the Fairfield County courthouse, Bridgeport, Conn., for a preliminary test for United States citizenship.

5 Elks Return From National Confab In Phila.

Patriotism Theme Of B.P.O.E. Gathering

Patriotism emerged as the central theme of the grand lodge convention of the Benevolent and Protective Order of Elks, which met this week in Philadelphia, birthplace of the nation's independence.

Attending from local lodge 622 were H. W. Russell, R. Taylor, F. C. Thompson, A. G. Miller and Frank Hladky.

Elaborate Parade

The six-day meeting ended Thursday night with an elaborate parade demonstrating "Defending America," which included an electrical display with State floats, units of the Philadelphia Mummers, Army, Navy and Marine Corps detachments and bands, a historical pageant by the New Jersey State Association, a "Gone With the Wind" motif by the Georgia State delegation, and an "United We Stand" spectacle by the Elks of America.

Brilliantly-decorated floats took three hours to pass through crowd-clogged streets in downtown Philadelphia. Eight thousand persons marched in the parade.

Gen. Pratt Speaks

In one of the convention's major sessions, Major-General Henry G. Pratt, commander of the Second Army Corps, warned that "our national defense effort is doomed to failure unless a spirit of complete cooperation and assistance is obtained throughout the United States."

He said he was thinking of "not only the extra energy and effort devoted to the production of the materials of war, but the extra efforts that must be devoted to the inculcation of this spirit in our people."

Navy View

Rear-Admiral A. E. Watson, commandant of the Philadelphia Navy Yard, told the more than 1,000 delegates that the Navy is ready to operate in any theatre of war.

Another feature of the convention was a water pageant on the Schuylkill river, complete with fireworks and patriotic floats. Boat races, fancy and comic diving, an aquacade exhibition and a 125-foot dive by Paul McDowell, former Olympic champion, were highlights of the party.

SAYS DEFENSE BOOM HASN'T AIDED RURAL POVERTY

WASHINGTON, July 19 (AP)—C. B. Baldwin, Farm Security Administrator, told a Congressional Committee today that the national defense program, with its re-employment of millions, has not yet made any substantial inroads into rural poverty.

Jehovah Witness Hearing Friday

Postponed At Request Of Attorney For Group

Trial Magistrate James G. Woodward postponed the hearings for 36 Jehovah's Witnesses yesterday afternoon until 11 o'clock Friday.

The members of the group were arrested Saturday night for obstructing the free passage of pedestrians on the sidewalk.

The postponement yesterday was granted at the request of counsel for the group.

Magistrate Woodward said new charges would be prepared, one under Section 6 of Article 10 of the code, charging the obstructing of traffic and another charging the selling or offering of merchandise for sale without a license.

TROOPS HEADED FOR SWIM LOSE PISTOL

Army troops from Fort George G. Meade, going to Bay Ridge on maneuvers and to swim, lost an automatic pistol while en route from Anderson's corner and Annapolis.

Police were informed that the pistol, bearing serial number 515-136, was in a leather holster which was attached to a web belt, along with a first aid packet.

The pistol and belt was issued to Company A, 191st Tank Battalion.

FUNERAL SERVICES FOR RAYMOND L. MOSS

The Rev. James L. Smiley conducted funeral services for Raymond L. Moss at 3 P. M. yesterday at the funeral home of John M. Taylor.

Pallbearers were Eugene P. Childs, Carey L. Meredith, Charles F. Lee, Arthur Moss, George A. Moss and Frank M. Duvall. Burial was in Cedar Bluff Cemetery.

Mr. Moss, who lived in Green street, died Wednesday in Catonville.

ROBIN MOOR CAPT. AGAIN READY FOR SEA DUTY

BALTIMORE, July 19 (AP)—The master of the torpedoed American freighter Robin Moor is ready for the sea again—when he gets his two weeks' vacation—but he hopes his next command will be a ship "with a slick little gun."

Home after a South Atlantic adventure that generated international repercussions, Capt. Edward W. Myers talked freely of the Robin Moor's destruction May 21, of his rescue after 13 days at sea in an open lifeboat, and expressed the belief that a submarine operating from Dakar, French West Africa, sent his ship to the bottom.

Plan Six New Projects Here Including Taking Over Of Ferry Space

$200,000 Recreation Center For Navy Enlisted Men Proposed — Plea For New Field House And Auditorium Not Presented At This Time — Move To Purchase City Property Near Number One Gate Also Delayed — Admiral Willson Learns Academy Setup Is Considered Satisfactory By Navy — Pay Recommendations

[Washington Bureau of The Evening Capital]

Washington, July 19—The House appropriations committee today prepared to make recommendations to the House on six construction projects for the Naval Academy at a total cost of $1,470,000.

The projects, recommended in the Naval Academy Board of Visitors' report which was made public today, includes $200,000 for conditioning the new land adjacent to the football stadium for recreational purposes but omits the proposed new auditorium.

LIST OF PROJECTS

Other projects to be acted on by the appropriations committee are:

Construction of a boat basin on the eastern shore of the Severn and a repair shop at a cost of $500,000.

A $200,000 rcreation center for enlisted men on the east shore to accommodate 850 men. The proposed center would have a gymnasium, bowling alleys, billiard and pool rooms, library, reading and writing rooms and a movie auditorium.

Purchase of 160 acres of Fort Severn property on the east shore, where the new boat basin is to be, at a cost of $300,000.

Would Purchase Slip

Purchase of a ferry and con-Academy side of the Severn and struction of two ferry slips on the one slip on the east side at a cost of $130,000. The ferry would be used to transport midshipmen, civilians and enlisted men from the Academy to the east shore developments.

Conditioning land in the vicinity of the Navy hospital to produce additional drill space and recreation fields and extension of the gun sheds to house new anti-aircraft fire control equipment, $140,000.

In addition to these projects, the board of visitors recommended a number of other items which either were not approved by the Navy Department as essential at present or were eliminated by the bureau of the budget.

Lose Expansion Plea

Most important of these was proposals for a new $2,000,000 auditorium to seat 3,000 and a new $1,250,000 field house to replace the present gymnasium. The board also recommended purchase of 1.8 acres of land bounded by Wagner street, Hanover street, College avenue and King George street as a site for the auditorium at a cost of $225,000.

Another item recommended by the board which was not approved was the purchase of 40 acres of land adjacent to the superintendent's garden at a cost of $40,000 for additional recreation space. The board also recommended $1,200,000 for construction of officers' quarters; an apartment building at the hospital for medical officers to cost $110,000; and an extension to Halligan Hall to cost $240,000, none of which were sent to Congress.

Cost Not Excessive

The board of visitors noted in its report that if all the projects recommended were appropriated for, the total cost of the Naval Academy over the 96 years of its existence would be less than the cost of the new air training station at Corpus Christi, Texas.

Requests by Rear-Admiral Russell Willson, superintendent of the Academy, made in a written statement to the board, for a direct comment on proposals to eliminate the Academy or for establishment of a second one on the West Coast were ignored by the board but the report indirectly sustained the establishment as it now exists.

In his statement Admiral Willson said:

"There are some who criticize our basic system for training young officers. Several alternate and radical plans have been put forth. Probably the best known would do away with the Academy as such and use it only as a post-

(Continued on Page 6)

Foreign Minsiter

Replacing the pro-Axis leader Yosuke Matsuoka, Teijiro Toyoda (above), a retired vice admiral is the new foreign minister of Japan in the cabinet newly formed by Premier Prince Fumomaro Konoye.

Scrap Aluminum Collection Will Start Monday

Plans Announced By Mrs. W. H. Diefel, Chairman

Complete plans for the collection of scrap aluminum to aid in national defense which will start Monday were announced today by Mrs. William H. Diefel, chairman.

A house to house canvass will be made throughout next week. On Monday morning, chairmen of every street in Annapolis will have with them volunteers from the Police Boys Drum Corps under the leadership of Police Commissioner Thomas G. Basil and Officer Melvin Covington.

Other chairmen will canvass the county districts. Every solicitor will be identified with a blue and white badge.

Receiving Station

The Court House will be the official receiving station here. Committees will serve from 9 A. M. to noon and from 1 to 3:30 P. M.

(Continued on Page 6)

County Seeks Federal Aid For Schools

Wants New School In Jacobsville-Solley Section

The Anne Arundel County Board of Education is preparing a $300,000 school improvement program to be submitted to the Federal government for financing from national defense funds.

George Fox, superintendent of county schools, said negotiations with the Federal authorities had been underway for some time.

Congress has made available a $150,000,000 appropriation for the construction of schools, recreation centers, sewerage plants, hospitals, recreation centers and similar construction made necessary in communities through the expansion of national defense agencies and work.

Must Show Need

Mr. Fox pointed out that it must be proven that the defense program has caused an increase in enrollments of schools in order to qualify for these defense funds.

He said the situation at the Jacobsville school was bad because of the crowding of pupils, caused by the settling in the vicinty of families working in the the ship yards at Curtis Bay. The Glen Burnie High school also is crowded with children of defense workers and service personnel stationed at nearby camps. The Bates High school falls in the same status. Mr. Fox said there was plenty of room in the Odenton school.

Conference Held

The applications being prepared for submission to the Federal authorities directing the expenditure of the fund call for a new school in the Jacobsville-Solley section, the enlargement of the Glen Burnie and the Bates High schools.

Mr. Fox said several conferences ont he subject have been held with H. S. Shyrock, chief engineer for the PWA in Maryland.

Great Progress In Navy Bldg. In Last 40 Days

Keels For 42 Vessels Laid, 22 Others Launched

The Navy Department today announced that in the forty-day period from June 1, to July 10, excellent progress in the naval construction program is reflected in the fact that keels have been laid for 42 naval vessels, and that 22 vessels have been launched.

Keels laid in the period include:

Three cruisers—the USS Boston, USS Sante Fe and USS Tallahase.

Five submarines — USS Barb, USS Blockfish, USS Wahoo, USS Whale and USS Peto.

Fifteen destroyers—USS Frankford, USS Parker, USS Frazier, USS Gansevoort, USS Gillespie, USS Hobby, USS Kalk, USS Doran, USS Earle, USS Halford, USS Leutze, USS Capps, USS David W. Taylor, USS Claxton and USS Dryson.

Six Minesweepers—USS Sheldrake, USS Pluck, USS Positive, USS Power, USS Radiant and USS Victor.

Two seaplane tenders — USS Rockaway and USS San Pablo.

Eight sub-chasers.

Three motor torpedo boats.

Ships launched in the period were:

One battleship—USS South Dakota.

One submarine — USS Flying Fish.

Two destroyers—USS Forrest and USS Fitch.

Eight minesweepers—USS Cha-Chalaca, USS Skimmer, USS Tapacola, USS Adamant, USS Defiance, USS Dominant and USS Endurance.

One minelayer—USS Terror.

Two sub-chasers.

Seven motor torpedo boats.

Germans Claim Way To Moscow Is Now Open

Report "Substantial Successes" East Of Smolensk — Have Driven A 140-mile Wedge Into Russian Lines — Furious Fighting Along Flanks Of Salient — Turkish Dispatch Declares Russia Has 4,000,000 Army Waiting Behind Moscow — Red Guerrillas Battle Germans

German sources declared the "gate to Moscow" was open today after the Nazi armies claimed substantial successes far east of Smolensk, but there was no indication that the Germans proposed to take immediate advantage of the reported vulnerability of the Russian capital.

How far the motorized troops had pierced beyond the historic city of Smolensk, 230 miles from Moscow, was not revealed by the German high command which reported simply that the wedge driven past the city was being widened.

U. S. EMBASSY FORCE MOVES

Part of the personnel of the United States Embassy moved from Moscow to Kazan, 450 miles, as the Red army fought stubbornly in the Polotsk-Nevel, Smolensk and Bobrisk areas.

The roar of cannon, planes and tanks came from the 140-mile-deep salient the Nazi mechanized forces and speed infantry drove to Smolensk and the areas on its flanks. The Soviet forces admittedly were suffering and inflicting very heavy casualties in the furious fighting along the broad marshy valleys of the Dnieper and Dvina rivers to the west and northwest of Moscow.

The German 140-mile-deep wedge apparently ran along the Dvina river on the north, with the Nazis launching a new offensive at Nevel to threaten the defenders of the northern bank with encirclement.

A dispatch from Istanbul, Turkey, quoting an Axis diplomat recently arrived from Moscow, said a Russian army of 4,000,000 is waiting behind Moscow, ready to be thrown forward at a critical moment.

Russian Resistance

The character of the Russian defense was indicated by the government newspaper Izvestia which said the Red troops were resorting to trench warfare, digging individual foxholes where the soldiers waited out the storm of German shell and mortar fire and dive bombings and then turned loose sweeping machine-gun fire when the Nazi infantry advanced. When Germans even then were not stopped the Red soldiers faced them with the bayonet, it was said.

The newspapeer indicateed these tactics were designed to slow up the Germans advance while the People's army, which Joseph Stalin has called into being from the rank and file of Soviet citizens, is being massed behind the front.

German Claims

The Russian command said the full fury of the blitz offensive was concentrated in the Smolensk and related sectors, with nothing of significance occurring on the rest of the front.

In a review of the first three weeks of the Russian war, the Germans said the Reds had lost 6,233 planes on all fronts, 324,000 prisoners, 1,800 cannon and 3,332 tanks.

Berlin declared German and Rumanian troops advancing from Bessarabia have forced a crossing of the Dniester river at several points.

A reliable source in London said the Russian war drain on the German military machine to such an extent that it would be improbable the Nazis could organize an attempt to invade Britain this year.

Northern Front

The Germans also claimed a breaking of "embittered enemy resistance" by Finnish-German advancing to the northern shore of Lake Ladoga in the flanking offensive north of Leningrad.

Big refineries in Rumani's Ploesti old fields and tanks containing 20,000 tons of oil have been destroyed by the Red air force, an authoritative source said at Ankara.

Russian guerrilla detachments behind the German lines were reported to have recaptured two cities identified only as "Sh" and "Z." The army newspaper Red Star said the guerrillas, originally 10 men, expanded by recruiting of "partisans," and armed themselves by breaking up a German armored column.

They seized three whippet tanks, several armored cars and bicycles as well as "considerable munitions," Red Star said, and then assailed the Germans holding the two towns.

Air War

In Germany's war with Britain, the Hitler command reported that a 1,500-ton freighter was sunk by bombs and two other merchantmen hit off England during the night; that no British planes penetrated German territory last night or yesterday and that the RAF lost 10 planes along the coast.

Sir Archibald Sinclair, Britain's secretary of state for air, told a Liberal party conference today that the RAF had sunk "no less than 300,000 tons of enemy shipping and damaged as much again" in the past four months.

French Somaliland

Progress in the British-Free

(Continued on Page 6)

Card of Thanks

Mrs. Lucy Brewer and family wish to thank their many friends for the lovely floral designs and kind expressions of sympathy and those who loaned cars in the bereavement of her husband Nathan Brewer. jy-19

How Movie Glamour Mothers Stay That Way

JOAN BENNETT and daughters. She dieted rigorously to bring her weight back to normal. Now she weighs 111 pounds.

BORING, says Marlene Dietrich of exercises. Diet? She doesn't, except to regain pounds lost during a filming.

ATHLETICS don't come too strenuous for Joan Blondell. In high school she was the captain of the gym team. Badminton is one of the favorite sports of this mother of two.

BOWLING helped Brenda Marshall regain her figure after birth of her daughter.

By ROBBIN COONS
AP Feature Service Writer

HOLLYWOOD—Have you ever wondered how the glamour mamas of Hollywood keep their figures? They have to do it, because any sacrifice figures to motherhood sacrifice their screen careers at the same time—but this is not a story of sacrifice.

Some — Marlene Dietrich, for example—have no secrets for post - maternity figure upkeep. Dietrich, 38 and the mother of a 16-year-old daughter, has a figure best described by an ecstatic studio designer who said, "She's the only star I know who never wears a girdle—and doesn't have to."

Exercises bore Dietrich. And diet? "I don't, unless you count my skipping lunch," she says.

Of those actress-mothers who have figure problems—and solutions—most are quite willing to pass along their "secrets."

There's Joan Blondell, who's the mother of two. Joan's a non-dieter but she goes for exercise. "I eat food combinations which dietitians consider both easy and natural for the system to handle, and good food," she says.

For Joan, there are no large quantities of proteins and carbohydrates at the same meal. Meat or potatoes with vegetables, but never meat and potatoes (or bread) with vegetables. She eats as much as she wants.

A Game With Cards

Mary Martin, expecting her second child, makes no claims to athletic prowess but enjoys dancing and swimming. Her favorite waistline - trimmer: "Sprinkle a deck of cards on the floor, then pick up one at a time without bending your knees."

Jane Wyman (Mrs. Ronald Reagan) went swimming six weeks after Maureen Elizabeth Reagan was born. Played golf, too. Her doctor-ordered exercises: (1) Begin each day with a walk before breakfast, swinging legs and arms and breathing deeply. (2) In late afternoon, before a beauty nap, lie flat on back, feet close together, and pull up slowly without bending knees. Touch toes, return slowly to count of ten. (3) Lie on back with knees drawn slightly up. Pull body up, allowing head to fall back easily.

Keep arms straight in front, return slowly to position. (4) Stand straight with feet apart, hands on hips, and bend back slowly as far as possible—stretching stomach muscles. In standing position drop slowly to squatting position and arise to count of ten.

Geraldine Fitzgerald, mother of Michael Edward Lindsay-Hogg, recommends deep breathing for 15 minutes, morning, noon and night, before an open window. Miss Fitzgerald is a stretching enthusiast.

The Fitzgerald post-maternity diet was similar to Jane Wyman's—except that Geraldine's included one day on milk and orange juice, rather than salads.

Ellen Drew took a few tips from Jim Davies, the studio athletic instructor and expert masseur, who has to keep watch on all contract "figures," maternal and otherwise.

"Never put on shoes the easiest way," says Ellen. "Sit erect on a chair and, pulling the leg close to the body, slip the shoe on. It's a definite waist-slimmer. And when applying make-up, try not to slouch over the dressing table. Instead, sit erect and stretch legs well forward. Apply powder, turn the body to left and right, holding the hand mirror far away. May not sound like exercise but it is—and a game of badminton helps, too."

Joan Bennett, mother of Diana and Melinda Markey, doesn't diet any more, and her exercise has been limited to mild forms because of an old injury during a movie—she fell off a horse. She gardens, however, swims, and plays golf.

"I was 'way off form after the children were born," she says, "and had to diet rigorously to get back in shape."

Brenda Marshall (mother of 4-year-old Virginia Gaines) credits her return to a normal figure mainly to an enthusiasm for bowling. Diet: lean meats, vegetables (including a head of lettuce daily), water, a pint of milk daily, no desserts except fresh or stewed fruit, one baked potato a week, melba toast, a daily cocktail of orange juice, beaten raw egg with a spoonful of wheat germ oil. She stayed on this nourishing, strengthening, but streamlining diet for a month after the baby was born.

Anne Shirley, mother of June Anne Payne, aged 11 months, says swimming brought her figure back to before-baby measurements more quickly than any other exercise she took. "But it's important," she emphasizes, "that all such exercises be taken only if your doctor approves."

Dorothy Comingore, only recently a mother, recommends "a snug girdle" as well as doctor-recommended exercises.

And she sums up the opinion of most of Hollywood's glamour mothers when she says: "Motherhood isn't as likely to ruin a woman's figure as is laziness and too much food!"

ANOTHER ODDITY FOR RECORD BOOK

BROOKLYN (AP) — Were the Chicago Cubs embarrassed on their last trip here!

Jimmy Wilson's club was subjected to two successive shutouts by the then high-flying Brooklyn Dodgers. That's an oddity, and perhaps a National League record. In each game the Cubs' total at bats in the box score added up to 27.

Kirby Higbe, winning the first game, faced only 30 batters, while Curt Davis threw to only 28 in the second contest.

"PEEPING TOM" BOVINE

CRISFIELD, Md., Aug. 14 (AP)—One of Crisfield's "Peeping Toms" has been caught.

Prowlers have been reported in various sections of town for about a month. When a "Peeping Tom" was reported one night, police and citizens formed a small posse and searched the area.

Standing near a window, close to the weeds and flowers from a window ledge flower box, was a cow.

So This Is How Sorority Girls Get To Be That Way!

AP Feature Service

TO ANNOY and humiliate—that's the idea of a sorority initiation. Here are initiation stunts as demonstrated by members of Delta Beta Sigma of San Jose (California) State College in anticipation of the school year just opening. Some of the hazing is new, most of it follows a pattern familiar on campuses throughout the country.

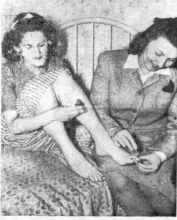

1. PLEDGES drop their books and salaam when a full member passes. Dorothea Bernsdorf, chapter president, is honored.

2. GREEN TOENAILS and fingernails are the order of the day. Gem March gets the treatment. This stunt isn't a hit with the boys.

3. MAKING FACES at all comers is a standby. Genevieve Gomes poses.

4. EATING FROM A BOWL affords the older sisters much satisfaction. The victim here, Mabel Gomes, is glad she won't be eating all her meals this way.

5. STAIRCASES are used. Earline Bailey slides down, as ordered by an upper classman.

GOLF (As A Golf Widow Knows It)

AP Feature Service

KAY ELLINGSEN, who had heard all the golf terms but didn't know what they meant, decided to go out and play the silly game just the way she had heard it. What happened wasn't exactly golf, but Kay seemed to have fun. She had fun, that is, until Harold Beer, pro at the San Francisco Ingleside course, decided to make a "nice approach" and wise her up on the game as it really is played:

SHOOTING A BIRDIE

SPOON SHOT

IN A TRAP

A SLICE

NICE APPROACH

Circle Schedules 'Charley's Aunt'

Jack Benny Plays Title Role In Classic Comedy

Jack Benny turns from heckling Rochester and his trials with the Maxwell to make his bow in Brandon Thomas' comedy, "Charley's Aunt," which 20th Century-Fox will present tomorrow through Saturday at the Circle theatre.

Jack has been cast in the title role of this long-time laugh favorite. He impersonates his friend's aunt to help out two college pals in this latest version of the ancient farce which has well nigh achieved immortality.

Benny Stars

Preview audience hailed Benny's performance and have called him the funnies thing in skirts. Kay Francis is the real aunt who turns up at the wrong time and James Ellison is the friend who needs the help.

Among the others in the cast are Edmund Gwenn, Anne Baxter, Reginald Owen, Arleen Whelan, Laird Cregar, Ernest Cossart, Richard Hayden and Morton Lowry.

"Charley's Aunt" will succeed "Whistling in the Dark," the Red Skelton comedy featuring Ann Rutherford which ends its engagement at the Circle today.

Current attraction at Republic is the latest of Arthur Lake as Blondie and Dagwood.

Damon Runyon Story

The Damon Runyon story, "Tight Shoes," which will play at the Republic tomorrow and Thursday, emerges as one of the brightest little pictures of the season.

John Howard and Binnie Barnes are featured.

Scheduled for Friday and Saturday is the newest Disney feature, "The Reluctant Dragon," which takes the movie-going public behind the scenes in the cartoon studio. Robert Benchley serves as guide and commentator.

603 ENGINEERS CALLED BY NAVY

The Navy Department announced today that a total of 603 reserve officers in the civil engineer corps of the navy had been called to duty to date, augmenting this branch of the service which has had a normal total of 133 regular officers on active duty.

The tremendous program of short developments in carrying forward the nation's defense plans has necessitated this multiplication of construction engineers. During the fiscal year ending June 30, 1941, a total of $656,659,000 was contracted for naval bases and other shore developments under the cognizance of the Bureau of Yards and Docks. During the 21-year period, uly 1, 1916, to December 1, 1937, the total so contracted for expenditure by this bureau was $361,265,000.

Australia has a shortage of doctors both in civilian and army life.

Score Injured In Work Stoppage

Police And Workers Hurt In Clash At Sparrows Point

BALTIMORE, Aug. 19 (AP)—Day shift workers went on duty without incident early today after a brief "protest work stoppage" injured a score of police and steelworkers during the night shift at the Bethlehem Steel Company's huge Sparrows Point plant.

Nicholas Fontecchio, district director of the Steel Workers Organizing Committee, CIO, said the "work stoppage" was called in protest against "various kinds of intimidation and threats to union men by sub-bosses and company police."

Eight Arrested

No official statement was available from the company immediately.

Eight men were arrested, and more than 20 company police and workmen were injured in clashes after union men threw up picket lines shortly before midnight. Windows of a dozen automobiles were broken and company police said some attempts had been made to pull workers from their cars.

This morning, however, a union sound truck at the entrance to the three Bethlehem mills affected urged union men to return to work as usual.

O'CONOR INVITED TO TOURNAMENT

CORDOVA, Md., Aug. 19—Gov. Herbert O'Conor, Attorney General William C. Walsh, and State Comptroller J. Millard Tawes have been invited to the Old St. Joseph's Church riding tournament to be held tomorrow. A horse show will be held in the morning with tournament competition in the afternoon.

Research at National Bureau of Standards, Department of Commerce, has more than doubled the life of currency paper.

Beauty
Everyone (Not Just The Men) Will Look At Legs Hereafter

By BETTY CLARKE

LOOKING at legs seemed to be a man's prerogative until the silk stocking scare.

Now everyone will be looking at your legs. You'd better, too.

If silk stockings or sheer-as-silk substitutes get plentiful again, you certainly won't look worse because you went in for leg-art lesson.

You can do your legs a daily good turn as simply as this: Be sure your shoes are long enough, and the heels for walking not too high. Use a brush to scrub both your knees and heels whether you think they need it or not. Rub a little greaseless lotion or cream over your entire leg but particularly into your knees, heels, and bottom of your feet—after the scrubbing.

Do some sort of magician act weekly to whisk away hairs. Maybe you think the glamour girls of moving pictures and model fame have been overemphasizing this, but it is still a thing for you to do if you want your legs considered chic.

If you think your legs could be smaller and smarter, study them in your full-length mirror. Get out your tape measure and compare your own inches with those suggested as standard. Make a chart before you begin either massage or exercising. Record weekly the measurements for your thigh, knee, calf and ankle. Then you can see if you are taking your exercises correctly enough, long enough and regularly enough.

Care of the legs and feet calls for a lot of things, of which none are more important than soap and water.

DO YOU ANKLE UP TO THIS?

"No ankle should be over 8 inches around," says Ann Delafield, director of a New York beauty school. She explains:

A perfect 34 girl 5 feet 5 inches tall, has legs like this:
  Thigh, 20½ inches.
  Knee, 13½ inches.
  Calf 12½ inches.
  Ankle, 7½ inches.

A perfect 36 who is 5 feet 7 inches tall can add either a half or whole inch to thigh, knee and calf measurements, but should have only an 8-inch ankle.

Otherwise why kid yourself into thinking you benefit from pinching, bending or bumping?

Whether your legs seem thick or thin, you can improve them by improving your posture. A simple check is to back up to a wall. If your shoulders, hips, calves and heels touch the wall, you're doing pretty well. If they don't, set yourself the daily task of trying to make them do it. It all amounts to an exercise well worth the effort.

Ceylon has about 1,100,000 acres, or 14 percent of the world cocoanut-palm acreage, the Department of Commerce reports.

RESERVE ENSIGNS TO TAKE P. G. COURSE

A class of from 50 to 55 ensigns in the Navy Reserve will arrive tomorrow at the Post-graduate

LATE NEWS

Evening Capital

WEATHER
Fair tonight; Wednesday considerable cloudiness; moderate temperature.

VOL. LVII — NO. 207. EVERY EVENING EXCEPT SUNDAY ANNAPOLIS, MD., TUESDAY, SEPTEMBER 2, 1941. SOUTHERN MARYLAND'S ONLY DAILY TWO CENTS.

10 PER CENT CUT IN SEPTEMBER GAS

Washington, Sept. 2 (AP)—A ten per cent over all curtailment of September gasoline deliveries to retail outlets in the East, which would mean an estimated 15 per cent cut for "nonessential" motorists, was announced today by Ralph K. Davies, acting Petroleum Coordinator.

A general stoppage of service at most of the eastern seaboard's 100,000 gasoline stations is held out as a possibility unless the government insures the dealers a "living margin," was predicted by Benjamin L. Jacoby, head of the Associated Gasoline Retailers of Philadelphia and vicinity.

LAVAL REPORTED SHOWING IMPROVEMENT

Vichy, Unoccupied France, Sept. 2 (AP)—Pierre Laval's physicians issued a bulletin this morning saying the former vice premier, who was gravely wounded by an assassin's bullet at Versailles last Wednesday, was showing "progressive improvement."

EQUADOR SEIZES NAZI AIR LINE

Guayaquil, Equador, Sept. 2 (AP). An army detachment took custody of the Guayaquil and Quito hangars and facilities of Aerea Sedta, subsidiary of Lufthansa, the German aviation concern.

The suspension followed similar action by Bolivia and Peru against German air lines.

THREE SOLDIERS DIE IN WRECK

Rainelle, W. Va., Sept. 2 (AP)—A truck loaded with soldiers returning to Camp Lee, Va., from a furlough overturned on U. S. Route 60 near here early today, causing the death of three and injury to 18 others.

The 21 men were spilled from the truck as it failed to make a curve on the mountain road.

TAX BILL APPROVED BY SENATE GROUP

Washington, Sept. 2 (AP)—The Senate Finance Committee formally approved the record-breaking tax bill today and sent it on to the Senate for debate tomorrow.

The bill, biggest in history, was estimated by the Treasury to produce $3,672,400,000 and by chairman George (D-Ga) of the Finance group to yield approximately $4,500,000,000.

DELAY PROBE INTO MOVIES

Washington, Sept. 2 (AP)—A Senate Interstate Commerce subcommittee decided today to delay until next Tuesday a projected inquiry into whether the motion picture industry has disseminated propaganda.

Record Crowds At County Shores Over Week-End

Riva Man Injured When Car Overturns; No Fatalities Here

The long Labor Day week-end brought out record crowds of pleasure seekers to Anne Arundel's shores and the holiday traffic glutted roads here. No fatalities occurred in the county, however.

Six traffic deaths were reported in the State, along with two drownings and four deaths by other causes.

John Sault, 31, Riva, is in Emergency Hospital as a result of injuries sustained when the car he was driving overturned yesterday near Bartgis' store, Davidsonville. George Brown, colored, a passenger in the car, was unhurt.

Ferries Crowded

The West Annapolis ambulance took Mr. Saulit to the hospital. The accident was the only serious one reported in the county.

Thousands of passengers and cars used the Claiborne-Annapolis ferries over the week-end. Traffic was particularly heavy Saturday night when cars were lined up for blocks on King George St. awaiting passage. The ferry company, which usually schedules only two trips after 8 P. M.—at 10 and at midnight—last night kept all their ferries in operation until 3 A. M.

Six hundred fourteen persons were killed in accidents or by other violence over the week-end in the nation, 416 of them in highway traffic, heavy with homebound vacationists and tourists on their final outing of the summer.

73 Drownings

Seventy-three were drowned and 125 died in shootings, stabbings, falls, fires, airplane accidents and by other violent means.

Deaths from all violent causes over the Labor Day week-end a year ago totaled 514.

The automobile fatalities included Robert L. Ramsay, Jr., son of Rep. Ramsay (Dem., W. Va.), who was thrown from a sideswiped car near Rockland, Md. He died Sunday of a broken neck.

California lead in traffic accident deaths with 46, Ohio had 28 and Illinois, 27. Michigan had the most drownings, 15, and Ohio the most fatalities from miscellaneous causes, 13.

GERMANY'S GAINS AS SECOND YEAR OF WAR ENDS

Territorial gains made by Germany since the start of the war, September 1, 1939, are marked on this map by various types of shadings as the second year ended. Blocked shading denotes German territory at the start of the war. The territory acquired by the end of the first year is designated by dotted shading, with cross-hatched shading denoting the territory acquired within the past year. The broken line designates the Russian border as it was on September 1, 1939.

Oyster Season Opens; Hampered By Hot Weather

Tongers Put Out Yesterday But Catch Was Small

Oysters are in season again, but Maryland watermen admitted today that the bivalve loving public won't be able to do much about satiating the palate as long as the mercury lingers way up there.

It was hot yesterday when the first oyster boats put out in the Chesapeake Bay, and catches were small, quality was just so-so and the price—about 50 cents a bushel.

About 5 bushels per boat was the average for oyster captains who stayed out half a day, then headed for shore as the sun beat down.

Four Licenses

Four tonging licenses have been issued at the court house, but more will be taken out on Saturday when the oystermen come into the city.

Local seafood dealers will have oysters during the day. Salt water oysters from Stockton, Md., are available.

The season in the Patuxent river will open on September 15. In the upper part of the river the oysters are reported in excellent shape for this season of the year. Reports received at the State Conservation Department from Tilghman's Island were that oysters were running about 4 shucked pints to the bushel. This was considered rather poor yield.

The season will get in full swing next month when many waterfront farmers finish their harvests and turn to the water. With the coming of cold weather the crab, who has held sway all summer, will make way for Maryland's best winter seafood product — King Oyster.

Reports from Kent Island were that oysters were shucking six pints to the bushel and were bringing from 55 to 60 cents a bushel. The price at Cambridge was 60 cents a bushel.

Report Dispute Over Policies Tears Japanese

Internal Struggle Between German-Goaded Extremists And Realistic Moderates—American Shipment Of Gasoline To Vladivostok Intensifies Crisis—Germans Reported Checked On Russian Front—Fighting Centers Around Leningrad

Japan was reported reliably today to be in the throes of an internal struggle between German-goaded extremists and realistic moderates over how best to achieve the unchallenged Oriental dominance which Japanese regard as their ordained world role.

According to reliable foreigners, including Axis nationals, arriving at Shanghai, the seething situation behind Tokyo's censorship may develop one or more of the following:

1. Japanese action in the Pacific or a new move on the Asiatic continent; the former might be a thrust against the Netherlands East Indies and the latter a move against Thailand or Vladivostok, Russia's Pacific gateway for receipt of war supplies from the United States.

2. Overthrow of the present Konoye government, possibly by force.

BREATHING SPELL

3. Rapprochement with the United States and Britain, desired by the realistic moderates as a breathing spell pending hope for eventual American-British acceptance of the Japanese expansionist policy.

The last would represent a victory for the present moderating influences in the Konoye Government; the first two a victory for the extremists, notably the military clique, which, according to the Shanghai arrivals, is under pressure and even demands from German advisers for a Japanese challenge to the United Stats, Britain and Russia.

Realistic Japanese leaders were pictured as sure that Japan would face a catastrophic defeat if she makes that challenge.

At Crossroads

Between the rival leaders in Japan lay the mass of panicky civilians, according to the Shanghai visitors, preparing for incendiaries and explosives with buckets of water and piles of sand outside their flimsily built homes and with sand mats under which to take refuge in their gardens.

The shipment of American war supplies to Russia via Vladivostok—the first shipload of aviation gasoline is now nearing that port—has brought Japan to the crossroads of her policy. What she will do beyond her present representations against the Vladivostok shipments is the big question.

With the battle of Russia again pivoting on Leningrad and with the Germans checked if not actually on the defensive along the rest of the sprawling front, international attention centered on Japan.

Russian Front

For the fifth consecutive day the Red army pictured the front as stabilized, Germany's deep-spearing Panzer divisions finally brought to heel. The Germans themselves shifted emphasis to their air force, reporting it had spanned far beyond the Dnieper for its first attack on Crimea while also helping to forge a ring of steel around Leningrad.

Berlin reports conveyed the im-

(Continued on Page 6)

POLICE TRAINING CLASSES PLANNED

Police Commissioner Thomas G. Basil today arranged for Police Training classes to be held in the City Council chamber beginning Sept. 18.

The basic course of training will consist of 16 lessons.

Day patrolmen will attend the classes at 7 P. M. each Thursday. Night officers will report at 1:30 P. M. on Thursdays.

EASTPORT LEAGUE TO MEET TONIGHT

The Epworth League of the Eastport Methodist Church will hold its first fall meeting at 7:30 tonight at the church.

A social hour at which refreshments will be served will follow the business session.

ROBERT WILLIAM TATE DIES IN NEW YORK

Robert William Tate, a native of Annapolis, died recently, at his home on Riverside Drive, New York City, recently, it was learned today.

Mr. Tate was an alumnus of St. John's College and a former Baltimore business man.

He is survived by his widow, the former Miss Katherine Manlon of Glascow, Scotland; two daughters, the Misses Katherine Brooke and Harriet Brooke Tate of New York City; two sisters, Miss Mary Brooke Tate of Washington, D. C.; and Mrs. Charles Montgomery of Dallas, Texas; and two nieces and a nephew.

MUSTERMAN INVITED TO F.B.I. SESSION

Sergt. J. Walter Musterman, of the Anne Arundel county Police Department, today was invited by J. Edgar Hoover, Director of the Federal Bureau of Investigation, to attend the annual Retraining Session of Reunion of the FBI National Police Academy to be held in Washington, D. C., during the week of October 6, according to E. A. Soucy, Special Agent in Charge of the FBI'S Office in Baltimore.

Those in attendance at the Retraining Session this year will receive specialized instruction in the investigative and technical aspects of espionage, sabotage and other internal security matters. Opportunity will also be afforded for advanced studies in various scientific law enforcement procedures.

The FBI National Police Academy was inaugurated by Mr. Hoover in 1935 and since that time there have been 591 graduates representing police personal of over 92,000. The graduates have received twelves weeks of extensive training in various phases of law enforcement work in order that they might instruct other members of their departments in the latest methods of scientific crime detection and investigation.

MRS. HUTH NAMES COMMITTEE MEMBERS FOR U.S.O. OUTING

Mrs. Frances J. Hutch, chairman of the Sixth District women's committee for the USO outing to be held at Beverly Beach on September 21 today appointed the members of her commitee.

Those appointed include Mrs. Herbert R. O'Conor, Mrs. William U. McCready, Mrs. Ridgely P. Melvin, Mrs. Louis N. Phipps, Mrs. George Abram Moss, Mrs. James A. Haley, Mrs. Edith Rawlings, Mrs. Bernard Hoff, Mrs. Charleton Evans, Mrs. Jesse A. Fisher, Mrs. Arthur Ellington, Mrs. Charles Bernstein, Mrs. Albert Crandall, Mrs. Edward G. Chaney, Mrs. Elmer M. Jackson, Jr., Mrs. Benjamin Hopping, Mrs. T. Thompson, Mrs. Malcolm DeConway, Mrs. Alice Williams, Mrs. Herbert Wilson, Mrs. John Kramer, Mrs. William Diefel and Mrs. John Engelke.

Mrs. Moss is chairman of the publicity committee of the women's committee. Mrs. Alice Duvall and Mrs. Amanda Teal are members of this committee.

The woman's group is working with the men's committe in arranging the all-day outing. A feature will be a baseball game between city and county teams with all players more than 40 years of age. High State and county officials will play on the teams.

THOMAS G. BASIL
INSURANCE OF ALL KINDS
92 West Street
Annapolis, Maryland
Dial 2161

Capital Bowling League

Vacancies will be filled at meeting Thursday, Sept. 4th, Moose Home. Last year's teams and teams desiring to join have representatives present.

RUMMAGE SALE
BENEFIT
British War Relief Society, Inc.
Thursday, Friday and Saturday
SEPTEMBER 4, 5 AND 6
10 A. M. TO 9 P. M.
17-19 WEST STREET
Annapolis, Md.

HOUSE AT EASTPORT CATCHES FIRE TODAY

A fire in a house in the 300 block, First street, Eastport, today did little damage.

Men from the American Oil Company worked with extinguishers and brought it under control by the time the Eastport fire department arrived. Firemen said the blaze apparently was started by an oil stove.

A small fire caused by a burning cigarette thrown into some rags under the Eastport bridge was put out before the Water Witch company could get to the spot yesterday morning.

Captain Picking Dies In Crash

Among 10 Lost In RAF Transport Ferry Plane

London, Sept. 2 (AP)—Two Americans and Count Guy de Baillet-Latour, son of the chairman of the International Olympic committee, Count Henri de Baillet-Latour, were among ten persons aboard a transport plane of the RAF ferry command given up for lost today by the Air Ministry.

The Americans were Capt. Sherwood Picking of the U. S. Navy, a passenger, and flight engineer Charles Alvan Spence, of Little Neck, L. I., a member of the crew.

The plane left North America (presumably Canada) yesterday for England.

One of the passengers on the missing plane was Dr. Mark Benjamin, of Wembley, England, of the central Scientific Office in Washington.

Captain Picking was a native of Baltimore, Md., and a resident of Falmouth Foreside (Route 4), Portland, Me.

Picking, 51, was in command of the submarine O-10 during the World War. For "heroic action" in this command he won the Navy Cross. He also holds the victory medal with submarine clasp. He entered the Naval Academy at Annapolis in 1907.

The Navy said Picking had been ordered to London as Assistant Naval Attache.

For Information Regarding DELIVERY SERVICE of the EVENING CAPITAL Call Annapolis 3881

"V FOR VICTORY" STICKERS ON SALE AT DOG SHOW

"V for Victory" campaign stickers will be sold as a feature of the Bundles for Britain dog show Thursday in the garden of Acton House, home of Captain and Mrs. W. Taylor Smith.

In a letter to Mrs. A. St. Clair Smith, president of the Annapolis branch, Mrs. Wales Latham, president of Bundles for Britain, Inc., announced that a valuable prize will be given the branch raising the most money in comparison to their population, for the "V for Victory" campaign.

This prize is a copy of Winston Churchill's book "Into Battle," autographed by the author and dated July 4, in commemoration of America's Independence Day. The money raised in the campaign will be cabled directly to Mrs. Churchill, who will give it to any war relief organization she may choose in England.

Mrs. Middleton C. Guest assisted by Mrs. Lawrence Stewarе and the Misses Margaret Larson, Betty Krebs, Nancy Sabalot and Patsy McCeney, will have charge of the "V for Victory" sticker sale a the dog show.

The benefit lawn fete in the historical old home on Franklin street is scheduled to start at 3 P. M. and continue on through the supper hour.

Ticket sale for the benefit is being sponsored by Mrs. Franklin

(Continued on Page 6)

Parsons, Bay Hunter, Wins O'Conor Challenge Trophy At St. Margaret's Horse Show; Towson Horse Second

Winner, Owned By Miss Pat Patrick, Baltimore County, Scores 25 Points—Sandrock, Reserve Champion, Makes 17—Ben Duckett And McKenzie Ridout Win In Tournament—Jackson Gives Charge To Knights

Parsons, big bay hunter owned by Miss Pat Patrick, of Baltimore county, scored 25 points to win the Gov. Herbert R. O'Conor challenge trophy and title of best horse in show yesterday at the annual St. Margaret's Church horse show on the farm of former Senator Frank M. Duvall.

Reserve champion was Sandrock, whose owner is H. O. Firor, of Towson, and who was ridden in most of his classes by young Hugh Wiley, of Towson, to amass 17 points.

Well-Matched Pair

Parsons and Sandrock, a well-matched pair, teamed up to take a second in the pair of hunters event which was won by Silver Cross and My Colors, both owned by Mrs. William O. Tucker, Davidsonville.

The champion took blues in junior hunter and working sweepstakes events; placed second in non-thoroughbred model hunters, hunter hack and handy hunter classes, and was third in the ladies' hunters division. Sandrock won the road hack, open hunter and ladies' hack events.

Tournament Rivalry

Rivalry was keen for the crowns in the two divisions in the 18th annual St. Margaret's tournament, which followed the show. McKenzie Ridout, the Knight of Eden Lawn, finally won over Elliott Pettibone, the Knight of Bay Head, after tying with him three consecutive times in the first event limited to local riders.

A no less obstinate tie in the amateur class was decided by the toss of a coin after two unsuccessful attempts to ride it off. Benjamin Duckett, the Knight of Davidsonville, emerged victorious over James Burke, Knight of Severna Park.

In his charge to the Knights which opened the tournament, Mayor Howard W. Jackson of Baltimore, recalled the long history of such sporting events, dating, he said, to the time of King Arthur.

Knightly Deeds

"The tournament is a healthy expression of the idea that modern life does not necessarily efface our thoughts of knightly deeds, queens of love and beauty and maids of honor in a chivalric

(Continued on Page Two)

BURNICE M. GOTT DIES IN BALTIMORE

Burnice M. Gott, for many years a resident of Annapolis, died Sunday afternoon in the Florence Nightingale Home, Baltimore.

While living here Mr. Gott was a regular attendant of the Calvery Methodist Church.

He is survived by one brother, Thomas O. Gott, Annapolis, and two sisters both living in Baltimore.

Funeral services will be held at 3 P. M. Wednesday from the Walter Brooks Bradley funeral home, 1022 W. North vaenue, at Monroe street.

CATOE'S CONFESSION CLEARS LIFE PRISONER

WASHINGTON, Sept. 1 (AP)—Jarvis R. Catoe, 36, colored, confessed sex slayer of Betty Strieff and six other women, has admitted one killing for which another man already has served five years of a life sentence, police announced today.

Children's School Dresses
JUNE PRESTON
All Sizes
also
LADIES' FALL DRESSES
Bergen's Dress Shop
522 1st St., Eastport Dial 2037
OPEN UNTIL 9 P. M.

ATTENTION
JUNIOR MOOSE PICNIC
THURSDAY, SEPT. 4
THURSDAY, SEPTEMBER 4
Cars leave Moose Home 10:30 a. m.
Anna Price, Governess

LOST
White female Boston Bull Terrier with black saddle on one side. Answers to the name of "Spunk." Liberal reward if returned to J. R. Williams, U. S. N. Golf Club. Phone Annapolis 4366.

Save Gas For Defense!
Governor O'Conor has made a 10-point program for the conservation of gasoline. Here's one of the ways he suggests:
Have ignition system and plugs checked regularly.
And here's another way you can help: Order all the milk, cream, coal, ice, and dairy products you need well in advance to avoid the necessity of a special delivery to your home.
ANNAPOLIS DAIRY PRODUCTS COMPANY

HIGH SCHOOL REGISTRATION

Pupils qualified to enter the Annapolis High School, and who did not register in June, should come to the school building on Thursday, September 4th, between the hours of 9-12 and 1-3 and register for the coming year.

Unregistered pupils will not be admitted on the opening day of school, because on that day the principal's full time must be devoted to the details of organization.

This announcement does not concern children from the public schools of Mayo, Davidsonville, Severna Park, Germantown, Arnold, Annapolis Gramar and the St. Mary's Parochial School. Children from these schools registered in June.

An examination will be given in the office of the Board of Education on Tuesday morning, September 9 at 9 o'clock, for all children who wish to enter high school and who did not take the examination in June. This is a placement examination and children from other school systems should take it.

HOWARD A. KINHART, Principal.

Around The Radio Dial Tonight

WCAO	600K
WFBR	1390K
WBAL	1090K
WCBM	1400K
WITH	1230K
WOR, M.B.S. Key	710K
WABC, C.B.S. Key	880K
WEAF, N.B.C. Red Key	660K
WJZ, N.B.C. Blue Key	770K

By C. E. Butterfield

Time Is Eastern Standard

NEW YORK, Nov. 3 (AP)—(The Special News Service) — Pittsburgh's KDKA today classifies itself as "of age." It is 21 years old.

The exact anniversary hour was at 7 P. M. Sunday, for it was at that time in 1920 when the station began broadcasting returns of the Harding election. Thereafter it maintained a regular program schedule.

The station then had a power of 500 watts, compared with today's 50,000. Most of the early listener, and they weren't so ferent orchestra, Kay Kyser numerous, had crystal sets.

Two program premieres are scheduled for tonight.

One for NBC-Blue will give Bert Wheeler and Hank Ladd, comedy team, their first crack at network entertainment after trying out their act of Pacific Coast radio. Herbert Marshall will be master of ceremonies, with Virginia Bruce as guest. The program is at 7.

The other, on at 10:15, carries the title of spotlight bands, it will be on six nights a week with different orchestras. Kay Kyser starts things off.

Programs tonight: The War—
7:00 MBS, 7:15 NBC-Red, 7:45 NBC-Blue, 8:00 MBS, 8:55 CBS, 10:00 MBS, 10:30 NBC-Blue, 10:45 CBS-East, 11:30 MBS, 12:00 NBC CBS.

NBC-Red—8 James Melton Concert; 8:30 Richard Crooks, Tenor; 10 Contented Concert.

CBS—8 Vox Pop Anniversary; 9 William Powell, Myrna Loy in "Hired Wife;" 10 Orson Welles.

NBC-Blue—8:30 True or False; 9 Radio Forum, Secretary Cluade Wickard on "Agriculture Will Do Its Part In Defense;" 9:30 For America We Sing.

MBS—8:0 Boy, Girl, Band; 9:30 Russell Bennett Notebook.

5:00
WCAO: *Story of Mary Marlin.
WFBR: †Little Orphan Annie.
WBAL: ‡When a Girl Marries.
WCBM: Sir Phillp Gibbs, talk.
WITH: News; Sports, Bill Bingham.
WJZ: Adventure Stories.

5:15
WCAO: *The Goldbergs, sketch.
WFBR: †Streamline Fairy Tales.
WBAL: ‡Portia Faces Life, drama.
WCBM: Talk, Nat Youngelson.
WOR: Mandrake the Magician.
WJZ: Secret City, sketch.

5:30
WCAO: *The O'Neills', sketch.
WFBR: ‡Jack Armstrong, sketch.
WBAL: ‡We The Abbotts, sketch.
WCBM: Five Strings, Music.
WJZ: The Flying Patrol.

5:45
WCAO: *Ben Bernie's Orchestra.
WFBR: ‡Capt. Midnight, drama.
WBAL: The Afternoon Show,
WCBM: ‡Tom Mix, sketch.
WEAF: Vagabonds—quartet.

6:00
WCAO: *Edwin C. Hill, news.
WFBR: Dinner Dance Rhythms.
WBAL: News; Sports Parade.
WCBM: Music Interlude; News.
WITH: News; Dinner Music.
WOR: Uncle Don, Children's Prgm.
WEAF: Music by Shrednik.
WJZ: Music; Talk; Sports.

6:15
WCAO: Sports, Don Riley; News.
WFBR: Special Edition of Sports.
WBAL: Around The Dinner Table.
WCBM: Bill Dyer, sports.
WITH: The Radio Dial.
WABC: Hedda Hopper's Hollywood.
WEAF: Robert St. John, news.

WJZ: Bill Stern, sports.

6:30
WCAO: *Golden Treasury of Song.
WFBR: Press Bulletins.
WCBM: Music A La Carte.
WOR: Press Bulletins.
WEAF: Talk, Dorothy Thompson.
WJZ: Lum and Abner, sketch.

6:45
WCAO: *The World Today.
WFBR: Dinner Dance Rhythms.
WBAL: ‡News, Lowell Thomas.
WITH: Sports Resume.
WOR: Here's Morgan, variety.
WEAF: Three Suns Trio.

7:00
WCAO: *Amos 'n' Andy, sketch.
WFBR: ‡News, Fulton Lewis, Jr.
WBAL: ‡Fred Waring's Orchestra.
WCBM: ‡Herbert Marshall, Bert Wheeler and orchestra.
WITH: News; Music Fun Time.
WOR: Stan Lomax, sports.

7:15
WCAO: *Lanny Ross, songs.
WFBR: El Gary and Orchestra.
WBAL: ‡News of the World.
WITH: Broadway Band Wagon.
WOR: Confidentially Yours.

7:30
WCAO: *Blondie & Dagwood, sketch.
WFBR: The Lone Ranger.
WBAL: ‡Cavalcade of America.
WCBM: ‡Schedastic Sports, Ed Fenton.
WITH: Calling With Dollars.
WJZ: Independent Citizens Comm.

7:45
WCBM: Lum and Abner, drama.
WJZ: John Gunther, from London.

8:00
WCAO: *Vox Pop, interviews.
WFBR: ‡Sizing Up The News.
WBAL: ‡James Melton & Orchestra.
WCBM: ‡I Love a Mystery.

(Continued on Page Four)

WITH: News; Night Life Reporter.

8:15
WFBR: 13th Birthday of Panama.
WITH: Phil Fine, pianist.
WOR: The Sky over Britain.

8:30
WCAO: *Gay Nineties Revue; News.
WFBR: ‡The Big Money Bee, quiz.
WBAL: ‡Richard Crooks & Orchestra.
WCBM: ‡True or False, quiz.
WITH: Swing Class Session.
WOR: Boake Carter, news.

8:45
WOR: Bert Shefter and Octette.

9:00
WCAO: *William Powell & Myrna Loy, "Hired Wife."
WFBR: ‡News, Gabriel Heatter.
WBAL: ‡Dr. I. Q. Quiz Program.
WCBM: Stumping the Sports Experts.
WITH: News; Music By The Stars.
WJZ: National Radio Forum.

9:15
WFBR: ‡Dick Rogers' Orchestra.
WITH: The Symphony Hall.
WOR: Mary Small & Orchestra.

9:30
WFBR: ‡Russell Bennett's Orch.
WBAL: ‡That Brewster Boy, drama.
WCBM: ‡For America We Sing.

9:45
WOR: Mary Small and Orchestra.

10:00
WCAO: *Orson Welles Theater.
WFBR: ‡Raymond Gram Swing.
WBAL: ‡Evelyn Ames & Orchestra.
WCBM: ‡Monday Night Merry-Go-Round.
WITH: News; Just Dance, music.

10:15
WCAO: ‡Kay Kyser's Orchestra.
WITH: The Korn Kobblers.

THE ADVENTURES OF PATSY

NEIGHBORLY NEIGHBORS

OAKY DOAKS

SCORCHY SMITH

OH, DIANA!

DICKIE DARE

HOMER HOOPEE

MODEST MAIDENS

"I'm going shopping, so I got Biff to run interference for me."

THE DOOLITTLES

LATE NEWS

Evening Capital

WEATHER
Cloudy tonight; Tuesday mostly cloudy and somewhat warmer.

VOL. LVII — NO. 283. EVERY EVENING EXCEPT SUNDAY ANNAPOLIS, MD., MONDAY, DECEMBER 1, 1941. SOUTHERN MARYLAND'S ONLY DAILY TWO CENTS

1 KILLED, 15 HURT IN GAS BLAST

Okmulgee, Okla., Dec. 1 (AP)—One man was killed and 15 others injured today as an explosion ripped through the gasoline plant of the Phillips Petroleum Company refinery.

The explosion and fire apparently centered in the accumulators and tanks of the gasoline department. The refinery normally employs 350 to 400 workers.

COAL PRODUCTION SHOWS BIG DROP

Washington, Dec. 1 (AP)—Secretary Iskes of the Interior Department announced today that there was a decline of 2,760,000 tons in bituminous coal production during the week ending November 22 as compared to the preceding week.

RAIL BOARD CONTINUES SESSIONS

Washington, Dec. 1 (AP)—President Roosevelt's special fact finding board continued sessions today in efforts to mediate the threatened strike of 350,000 rail-operating employes after a marathon session of nearly 23 hours brought no results.

CHARGE FILED IN DOG CASE

Mrs. Mary Jondreau, owner of the boxer dogs that attacked Carroll Cox, 7 years old, at St. Margaret's on Nov. 3, has been released under $500 bail for grand jury action on a charge filed by Anne Arundel county police.

Sergt. J. W. Musterman obtained a warrant from Trial Magistrate James G. Woodward charging Mrs. Jondreau with having "committed a nuisance by keeping unmuzzled and at large a pack of large boxer dogs which she well knew to be fierce, ferocious and dangerous and used and accustomed to bite mankind."

Mrs. Jordreau waived a preliminary hearing and was released on bail pending action of the April grand jury.

25 Midshipmen Selected For Marine Corps

Will Receive Commission Upon Graduation

Twenty-five members of the graduating class of midshipmen who will receive their diplomas on Dec. 19 have been selected for appointment as Second Lieutenants in the U. S. Marine Corps.

Those selected will receive their commissions following the graduation exercises.

Richard D. Opp, who captained the Navy's alternate football team this season is among those to join the marines.

Those selected are: Robert Carkeek Armstead, Medina, Wash.; Donald Dexter Blue, Wichita, Kans.; James Martin Callender, Beaumont, Tex.; Paul Elmo Caton, Fort Smith, Ark.; Thomas Madrye Coggins, St. Marks, Fla.; Wayne Lee Edwards, Ironton, O.; Sam Hal Fletcher, Normangee, Tex.; Bernard Wilfred Giebler, Hays, Kans.; Richard Alan Glaeser, Brighton, Mass.; Jacob Ezra Glick, Mount Carmel, Ill.; Harold Arthur Harwood, Los Angeles, Cal.; Alton Lucian Hicks, Medicine Mound, Tex.; John Thomas Hill, Akron, O.; Richard Dana Opp, Jr., Jamaica, N. Y.; Richard Lowe Pierce, Tulsa, Okla.; Herbert Dwight Raymond, Jr., North Hollywood, Cal.; Robert McKain Richards, Camden, S. C.; John Earl Shedaker, Jr., Burlington, N. J.; Walter William Stegemerten, East McKeesport, Pa.; Murray Lacock Thompson, Avalon, Pa.; Carleton Eli Tripp, Milford, Mich.; Donald James Van Oeveren, Grand Rapids, Mich.; Douglas Claude Whitaker, Castle Rock, Wash.; John Edward Williams, San Diego, Cal. and Henry John Woessner, 2d., Chicago.

CALVARY CHURCH BOARD TO MEET

The regular monthly meeting of the Calvary Methodist Chudch official board will be held tomorrow at 8 P. M. in the church parlor.

HELP WANTED, MALE

BELLINGHAM, Wash.—Promoter George Portiss is cancelling his dances for the duration.

He reached the decision after a count of the evening's customers showed 70 ladies and only 6 males.

NAVY ELEVEN WINS EASTERN AND IVY TITLES

Middies Expected To Get Lambert Cup Following Win Over West Point By 14 To 6 Tally Last Saturday—Busik Sparks Team To Third In Row Over Cadet Gridders—Locals Rank Among Nation's First Five Teams

The Naval Academy football team, outstanding Midshipmen grid outfit of the past fifteen years, today held a 14 to 6 triumph over their service rival West Point; possessed without dispute the Ivy League Championship; staked claim to the Lambert Cup, symbolic of the Eastern United States grid championship; and, at the end of a glorious campaign were ranked by practically all experts as one of the nation's five best football elevens. All of which ought to indicate that Annapolis had a brilliant team this year.

William S. Busik

Saturday's triumph over West Point at the Philadelphia Municipal Stadium marked the third time in a row that Navy had come out on the top, and equaled two previous triumphant streaks by Navy grid teams over the Army.

One Of The Best In Series

Last Saturday's game, 42nd, in the series, will stand out more vividly in the memories of most of the 98,900 fans there than most of the other Army-Navy games, however, for the spectacle was above par in thrills and chills, on the gridiron, and, on the sidelines. In the first half a surprising Army team rocked a jittery Navy eleven back on its heels and led 6 to 0 midway. Then an amazing Midshipmen outfit came back to write a new chapter in Army-Navy football history by keeping possession of the ball, for 13 minutes and 10 seconds, except for Army kickoffs, during which time the Tars became the "dream" team of all service conflicts. In this offensive they paraded 195 yards to two touchdowns and sewed up the contest in the victory bag,

West Point tried some surprises and fought gallantly but there was no stopping the Navy in the second half. First of all Army sprang a "T" formation for the initial time this season but it did not bother the home boys one bit. Greatest surprise of all by West Point, however, boomeranged into a "gift" for Navy. After Navy had forged ahead, 7 to 6, in the third quarter, Army had the choice of receiving or kicking off. Normally the team scored against elects to receive but not so West Point. It chose to kickoff to a Middie team which had taken the previous kickoff one yard behind its own goal line and paraded straight down the field to a touchdown. This time, counting the kickoff, and a five yard penalty, Navy marched 94 yards to another touchdown. It was almost unbelievable that the third quarter was about ended before the Cadets were permitted to get their hands on the pellet. Red Blaik, the Army coach, was somewhat puzzled by his team's decision to kickoff after Navy's first touchdown but he was not alarmed, stating he believed, just as his players did, that Navy couldn't march through them again for another Navy touchdown

Robert Zoeller

West Point Edge

The first half, however, was all West Point in flavor. Twice Navy drives were stopped by fumbles recovered by West Point, and on another occasion Bill Busik's pass intercepted by Bob Evans, Army's great center. Navy's luck was bad throughout the first half for even on the kickoff after Army's touchdown, Howie Clark took the ball on his five yard line, and slipped to the ground at that point, although

(Continued on Page Two)

ARMY-NAVY PACKS 'EM IN

There wasn't any room to spare in Philadelphia's Municipal Stadium as this airview well indicates, when 98,924 customers jammed the stands for the 42nd annual Army-Navy football game. The white section in the stands at right is occupied by white-capped midshipmen. The cadets' section is directly across the field.

Navy Players Autograph Ball Used In Game

Present It To Coach On Way Back To Annapolis

Major Emery E. (Swede) Larson, coach of the Navy football team that defeated Army Saturday, today had the ball used in the game, covered with signatures of Middie players, while Bob Froude, captain of the team, was wondering what to do with a goat made of white carnations.

The football players signed the ball on the way back to Annapolis yesterday and turned it over to Mrs. Larson. Major Larson went to New York for a coaches' meeting after the game.

The regiment of jubilant midshipmen arrived back in Annapolis from Philadelphia early Sunday morning, singing and cheering as they marched through the streets to the Academy.

Welcome From State

But the big celebration came last night when the football squad rolled into the Bladen street station shortly after 5 P. M. Three busses waited to take them to Bancroft Hall, where the regiment had assembled on the front terrace.

Gov. Herbert R. O'Conor joined in the welcome by havinlg an illuminated sign erected on the fence of the Government House facing the station. It read:

"Maryland Hails Navy, Victors Again.

Two small Navy pennants flew from the top of the sign. They flanked a small wooden figure of a mule, wearing crepe, and a triumphant goat, sporting the blue and gold ribbons of the Navy.

Large Crowd

A large crowd of residents had gathered at the station to see the team arrive and others were lined all along the route to the Maryland avenue gate of the Academy.

With the Academy band playing football songs, the massed midshipmen awaited the team, greeting the busses with a roar of cheering as they rolled to a stop.

A call for "Swede" came from the loudspeakers, and when it was announced that the coach had gone on to New York, cries arose for Busik and Clark.

Busik Speaks

Busik, responding, declared that Saturday was the "happiest day of my life."

"It was a happy day for all of us," he continued. "But especially to me. My parents were there to see us play and we won."

Clark thanked the regiment for the "grand support" given the team during the year. He paid a tribute to Major Larson for giving the squad his "time, ideals and good sportsmanship."

The Japanese bell, mounted on the steps of Bancroft Hall, had been rung continuously since the news of the Navy victory arrived on Saturday, and as Clark finished speaking the football players stepped up to ring out the 14

(Continued on Page Six)

NAVAL OFFICER DIES OF ACCIDENT INJURIES

Lieut. Comdr. Delos Parker Heath, U.S.N., 54, died last night in Philadelphia of injuries sustained when he was struck near Municipal Stadium by an automobile. The driver failed to stop.

Commander Heath was a prominent Detroit refrigeration engineer until his recall to active duty ten months ago. He was attached to the aircraft factory at the Philadelphia Navy Yard. The officer was graduated from the Naval Academy in 1906 and was retired from actice service in 1920. He won service medtals in Haiti, at Vera Cruz and in the World War. Mrs. Heath and a 10-year-old son live at Grosse Pointe Farms, Mich.

Vincent Vernacchio, 19, of Philadelphia, who was arrested a day after the accident as the hit-and-run driver, has been charged with aggravated assault and battery and with leaving the scene of an accident.

Fashion Show Planned Dec. 9

Junior Women's Club To Hold Show At Carvel Hall

Clothes of the Colonial and the present era will be modeled at 8 P. M. Dec. 9 when the Junior Women's Club holds its fashion show and card party at Carvel Hall.

Members of the club will wear clothes of the earlier period, including those of Colonial days. Then the modern clothing, sport, afternoon, evening and a complete wedding party will be exhibited.

Governor and Mrs. Herbert R. O'Conor head the patrons.

Mrs. O'Conor, Mrs. Louis N. Phipps and Mrs. William U. McCready will constitute the Fashion Congress to select the most attractive gowns.

The decorations will be symbolic of the Christmas season, complete with a Santa Claus. Every member of the club will take part.

Mrs. Elliott Cox is chairman of the ways and means committee Mrs. Albert Weirich heads the program committee.

MRS. GRACE MELCHER DIES IN EASTPORT

Mrs. Grace Elizabeth Melcher, widow of St. Louis Munroe Melcher, retired Navy man, died suddenly this morning at the home of her son, Claude D. Melcher, 331 Burnside avenue, Eastport.

Surviving are five daughters, Mrs. William H. Brown, Jr., Mrs Earl D. Evans, Mrs. Madeline Beaulieu, Mrs. Grace Kellenbentz and Mrs. Ruby Hunt, and two sons, Claude and Warren S. Melcher.

Funeral services will be held at 2:30 P. M. Wednesday from the Burnside avenue residence. Burial will be in the Naval Academy Cemetery.

John M. Taylor is the funeral director in charge.

Variety Club To Preview Musical

Selections From "Rational Defense" To Be Given Tomorrow In Easton

The Variety Club of St. John's College will give a "sneak preview" of some of the numbers from its new production, "Rational Defense," tomorrow night in Easton. The musical will be performed here Friday night, Dec. 12, in Iglehart Hall.

The Royal Oak Players are staging their first annual Follies and have invited the St. John's students to be their guests.

The feature number will be a swing ballet with the chorus "girls" being classical with Beethoven.

James Waranch will give his rendition of "Break the News to Mother," a timely hit number which has been revived for "Rational Defense." In keeping abreast with current events, the Variety Club members will do offerings apropos to the military motif. Charles Hoyes, director of the college production, will give "Marche Militaire," a tap dance. Albert Poppiti, who will be remembered for his impersonation of Mortimer J. Adler in last year's show, will do a take-off on Mussolini.

Two Men Injured In Auto Accident

James Wicks And Thomas Scott In Emergency Hospital

Two colored men are in Emergency Hospital today under treatment for injuries incurred in an automobile accident last Saturday night on the Muddy Creek road near Galesville.

James Wicks, 27, the driver of one of the cars involved, was admitted to the hospital with lacerations of the mouth. Several teeth were knocked out, Galesville police said. Thomas Scott, 47, sustained lacerations of the left eyelid. Both men are from Shady Side.

Galesville police said the northbound car driven by Wicks cut across the left side of the road and collided head-on with an automobile operated by Arthur Turner, colored, of Churchton, which was heading south toward Shady Side. Scott was a passenger in the car driven by Turner. The accident occurred about a mile north of the Galesville police station.

Both Wicks and Turner are charged with reckless driving.

PUTS OUT CHIMNEY FIRE ON SPA ROAD

A fire in the chimney of a house occupied by a colored family on Spa road was extinguished this morning by the West Annapolis fire department.

Minor damage was caused, firemen said.

Ferry Workers Reject Pay Boost

Attorney Assails "Fancy" Expenses Of Roads Commission

Pay raises of 15 to 16 per cent above present base levels which were scheduled to go into effect today for some 120 employes of the State-owned Annapolis-Matapeake ferry have been rejected by Leonard Weinberg, counsel for the employes.

Weinberg declared that if the ferry system were operated properly it would yield the State a profit of from $150,000 to $200,000 annually. He assailed what he termed certain "fancy" and "ridiculous" expenditures, citing the recently created post of public relations counsel for the State Roads Commission.

In his letter to Ezra B. Whitman, chairman, State Roads Commission, Weinberg declared that until the commission grants the employes a work schedule of not more than 60 hours a week, made up of five days of 12 hours each, they are not ready to accept the wage offer.

The new rates were adopted because "the way the employes have been paid was very unsatisfactory and we wanted to stabilize the pay," Mr. Whitman said.

No Overtime

No overtime pay will be given under the new rates, he explained, because each worker is expected to receive slightly higher pay than he received when overtime was added to his base pay.

Richard A. Bowie, of Local 1603, International Longshoremen's Union, who represented unlicensed ferry employes at the wage negotiations, termed the increases over and above what was offered about two months ago."

Ferry employes struck for a few hours last September, complaining they worked long hours and received less pay than comparable workers on privately-owned boats

FUNERAL TOMORROW FOR MRS. PEDDICORD

Funeral services for Mrs. Alice Marietta Peddicord, 86, who died Saturday morning at Edgewater, will be held at 9:30 A. M. tomorrow from the home of her daughter, Mrs. John T. Connell, Edgewater.

A requiem mass will be sung at 10 a. m. at St. Mary's R. C. Church of which Mrs. Peddicord was a member. Burial will be in St. Mary's Cemetery.

Mrs. Peddicord was born June 22, 1855, in Gettysburg, Pa., the daughter of William and Eleanor Freeberger Stauffer. She had been ill for 18 months.

Surviving are five daughters Miss Fannie Peddicord, Mrs. Connell, Mrs. Russell Whittington, Mrs. George Jones and Mrs. William Watts; three sons, Frank, Harry and William Peddicord; 32 grandchildren and 24 great-grandchildren.

B. L. Hopping is in charge of funeral arrangements.

Japanese Voice Preference For Further Parley

Negotiations Resumed In Washington—Situation Tense In Far East—Russians Claim Germans Still In Retreat In Rostov Sector—Soviet Attacks Reported To Have Stalled Nazi Offensive Toward Moscow—British Battle German Force That Penetrated Lines In Libya

Coinciding with Russian reports of the greatest German reversals since Adolph Hitler put 'blitzkrieg" into the world's vocabulary, Japan voiced a preference to day for further negotiations with the United States for peace in the Pacific in place of war.

Domei, authoritative Japanese news agency, said that the cabinet, weighing the issues at hand in the gravest crisis of long-troubled Japanese-United States relations, had decided to continue negotiations despite great differences in the viewpoints of the two governments.

The negotiations were resumed in Washington by Secretary Hull and the Japanese ambassadors, after which the Secretary hurried across the street to the White House to report to President Roosevelt, who had cut short a southern holiday.

Japanese Ambassador Grave

Ambassador Kichisaburo Nomura looked grave when he left Hull's office. When asked whether there was still a wide gap between the American and Japanese positions, he replied:

"I believe there must be wise statesmanship to save the situation."

United States army and naval forces in the Philippines were held in readiness for any emergency as war fears in the Far East were fed by the arrival of fresh British reinforcements in Burma, intense military preparations in Thailand and reports that the Japanese were pouring additional troops into neighboring French Indo-China.

The Governor General of the Dutch East Indies has ordered mobilization of the military and air force of the colony. Volunteers in Malaya were called up for service. A state of emergency was reported proclaimed in Singapore. American citizens in Thailand were advised to be ready to leave. The United States and Britain were reported cooperating in creating military bases between Hawaii and Australia.

Nazi Retreat

The Moscow radio declared severely battered German troops, hurled back though village after village in a retreat from Rostov that has become the biggest reversal of the Russian campaign, have been unable to stem the Red army's counter drive and are in danger of being cut off by a new thrust from the north.

The broadcast said the new Soviet thrust developed yesterday morning in the Dornets basin, northwest of Rostov, where the advance might open a corridor to the Sea of Azov which would cut off the hotly-engaged Nazi sea guard. Hard riding Red calvary were reported breaking up repeated German attempts to form a new line.

Russian counter-attacks in the battle for Moscow were said to have put 35 villages and towns back under the Russian banner and pulled the steel prongs of the German offensive against the capital.

The British radio reported that the German commander in the south, Field Marshal Ewald Von Kliest had moved his headquarters back to Mariupol two days ago and now was on the move further to the east.

Berlin declared the Russians had attacked at Rostov regardless of losses in men and material. A Berlin spokeman denied the Nazis had retreatde to Taganrog.

In London an authoritative source declared that the British had counter-attacked German forces which penetrated their positions around Rezegh, in the main Libyan war theatre, and that "our position is restablished once more." British general headquraters acknowledged that German forces had made a "penetration" into the British defense. British armored forces declared they had destroyed about half the remaining tanks in the Italian Ariete division.

Bomb Hamburg

The British reported yesterday reaching the Mediterranean coast along the Gulf of Sirte, between Bangasi and Agedabia, more than 300 miles west from the Egyptian frontier and across the Axis' one supply road from Tripoli. On that report and the hacking down of German-Italian strength, British observers confidently predicted Petain met in Orleans in occuin the Tobruk area within three days.

F. B. Hufnagle (above), board chairman of Crucible Steel Company of America, informed the "captive" coal mines arbitration board in New York he could not "agree blindly" to accept its decision as binding on his company.

LAUREL STABLEMAN DIES OF HEART ATTACK

Charles O'Keefe, 57, who was employed as a stableman at the Laurel race track, died suddenly Saturday afternoon at the track.

Dr. John M. Claffy, county coroner, pronounced the man died of a heart attack.

NOTICE

All members of Court Annapolis 326, Catholic Daughter of America, are requested to meet at the home of Mrs. John Connell, Edgewater at 7 P. M. tonight to recite the Rosary for her deceased mother, Mrs. Peddicord.

By Order Of
BERNADINE WILSON
Grand Regent

NOTICE

I will not be responsible for any bills contracted by anyone except myself.

Signed,
F. M. PATTERSON

ALL-MARYLAND 1941

YERKES Back—Wash. Coll.

DUDDERER Center—Wash. Coll.

BURLIN Tackle—Maryland

BRICKER Back—Western Md.

MORTON Guard—Maryland

ROGAN End—Mt. St. Mary's

FOY Tackle—Mt. St. Mary's

CONRAD End—Maryland

WRIGHT Back—Maryland

KITTNER Guard—Western Md.

CORDYACK Back—Maryland

BOWLING SCORES

By TIDLEY BASSFORD

The E. E. S. Anchors, who have been holding sway in the Commercial League, suffered a stunning setback on Monday night at the hands of the American Stores boys, the latter outfit taking three in stride as L. Englar shot a timely 385. A serious loss it was, too, because the Asco lads jumped atop the ladder from their third-place position as Sadler's Hardware and Carr Brothers could win but a single engagement. Sadler's fell victims twice to General Refining Company, Balderson hammering 387 for the oil crew, Charley Sadler, Sr., 385 for the paint dealers, and Carr faltered in a pair before the withering fire of an inspired Strange and White team, Jim Brady poured forth a 161 and 417 for the clothiers, while Earl Young chimed in with 383.

1,810 Total

An 1,810 total, climaxed by H. Curtis' 413, was more than enough for Southern Maryland Supply to swamp Thomas' Lumber Company, while Will Purdy's 378, aided by Berny Hoff's and Quinones' 373's for Hoff's Garage, was quite sufficient to smother the Hopkins Furniture Co. Automotive Service, paced by Joe Novesel's 394, took the odd fracas from Annapolis Buick, Francis Brewer clicking off 383 for the "straight eights";

the E. E. S. Jays won 2-1 from Johnson Lumber Company, Tilghman copped the first two but dropped the nightcap to B. and B. Nash as George Clark elbowed 374 for the jewelers, Brandenberg 388 for the Nash dealers, and Annapolis Banking & Trust Company and National Bohemian wound up in total pinfall, deadlocked at 1,802-1,802. However, in games won, the Brewers had a 2-1 edge, despite a nifty 393 by Velenovsky and a noteworthy 398 by Reynolds of the bankers.

Sweeney High

Sweeney of Southern Dairies posted the best set of the night when he turned in a 425 performance against American Beer, reeling off counts of 151, 136 and 149. Fate was with the bcermen though, and they took a double victory as the result of more consistent, rolling as a unit. Dick Deale batted out 383, Will Grimes 391 for John Martin's representatives.

Don't forget to sign up for the 225 men's doubles sweepstakes

Sports Round-Up

(By Hugh Fullerton, Jr.)

NEW YORK, Dec. 5—(Wide World)—Puzzle: Where will Jimmy Foxx play next season? ... After a couple of visits with Connie Mack it looked as if he might return to the A's, although some guessers said the Giants ... But now Al Flair is about to go into the army and that will leave the Red Sox with only Lou Finney, Ulysses Lupien (a doubtful quantity) and old Double-x to play first base ... Power of the press:

scheduled for Sunday night, Dec. 7. Bill Arnold, Dave Myers, or any of the floormen at the Severn will accept your entry, but hurry, as the field will be limited.

Tomorrow's Washington State-Texas A. and M. game stirred up so much interest that Graduate Manager Earl Foster of the Cougars ordered a new press box for the Tacoma stadium ... And the Texas State Fair Association plans to spend $4,000 improving the Cotton Bowl press coop ... The golf pros will have collected $202,000—an all-time high—after they round out the year with the $10,000 Miami Open next week and $5,000 tournaments at Harlingen and Beaumont, Texas.

Today's Guest Star

Walter Stewart, Memphis Commercial Appeal: " 'If' is a thin, two-letter word which is worn even thinner during the football season—used to soothe defeat and buttress the reputation of that

All-America tackle who served as a parade-ground for the Pickwick backfield that certain Saturday."

Hot Stove Warmup

Over in Jersey City they're not interested in how Mel Ott will make out, but whether Bill Terry now can find time to help the Little Giants ... One of the best greeters at Jacksonville was Lieut. George Earnshaw of the naval air station. The old Athletics' elbower sounded like another Waite Hoyt in airing interviews with the celebrities ... Hans Lobert hopes to sign Andy Tomasic, who pitches baseballs and footballs for Temple U. ... Andy can't lose much; his Temple footballers were given credit for a "moral victory" when they played a 1-1 tie with the girls' field hockey team the other

day ... When Rogers Hornsby signed to run the affairs of the Fort Worth Texas Leaguers, he was about to get a bid to manage St. Paul ... The Tigers' expensive Dick Wakefield is expected to spend the 1942 season at Buffalo getting more seasoning.

The Fort Story (Va.) grid team will get a crack at the Norfolk Shamrocks, Dixie League champs, December 14, and the soldiers figure they can win if they stop Pistol Pete Sachon ... The army has asked the National Ski Association to gather information on men subject to the draft who have skiing ability—for possible service in the 87th Infantry mountain regiment at Fort Lewis (Wash.). Join the army and ski the world, eh?

One-Minute Sports Page

Southern writers aren't pulling their punches replying to blasts from Los Angeles over the choice of Duke for the Rose Bowl ... Maybe they should toss the teams out and put the scribes in ... Bill Farnsworth of Mike Jacobs' publicity department was held up the other day—and not for tickets It cost him 20 bucks and a black eye ... The N. Y. U. wolves are really after Coach Mal Stevens. Even ran ads in yesterdays papers summoning grads to the letter club meeting ... Earl Sande's 16-year-old step-son, Alfred, is due to make his debut as a jockey at Hialeah this winter ... Ed Dudley will be the first P.G.A. president to make the winter golf tour as a player.

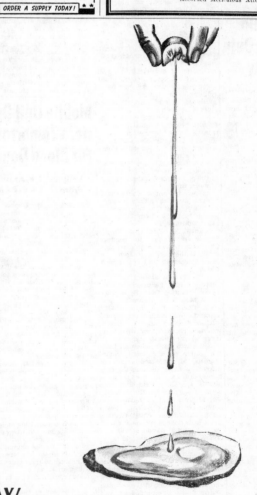

Evening Capital

VOL. LVII — NO. 290. EVERY EVENING EXCEPT SUNDAY ANNAPOLIS, MD., TUESDAY, DECEMBER 9, 1941. SOUTHERN MARYLAND'S ONLY DAILY TWO CENTS

WEATHER
Fair and somewhat co[ld] tonight; Wednesday [in]creasing cloudiness a[nd] moderate cold.

AIR ALARM IN NEW YORK CITY

LATE NEWS

SECOND AIR ALARM IN NEW YORK

New York, Dec. 9 (AP)—A second air raid alarm was sounded in New York city at 2:05 today, just 15 minutes after the all-clear signal had been flashed by the police department following a previous alarm at 1:25 P. M. (EST) prompted by unconfirmed reports of hostile planes off the east coast.

REPORT HOSTILE FORCES OFF BOSTON

Portland, Me., Dec. 9 (AP)—Authoritative sources here, which did not wish to be named, said it was reliably reported that "Hostile Forces" were an hour outside of Boston at 2:00 P. M., Eastern Standard Time.

NORFOLK ORDERED TO BE ALERT

Norfolk, Va., Dec. 9 (AP)—The small radio beam at the Norfolk municipal airport was shut down and all Norfolk police were ordered on the alert today following reports that enemy planes, possibly headed toward this important defense area were approaching the Atlantic coast.

PAVE WAY FOR A.E.F.

Washington, Dec. 9 (AP)—Legislation to permit use of the nation's land and naval forces, including Selective Service trainees, on foreign soil was approved swiftly today by the House Military Affairs Committee.

3 BELIEVED DEAD IN BOMBER CRASH

El Paso, Tex., Dec. 9 (AP)—Three men were reported killed and three burned severely today in the crash of an army bomber three miles east of El Paso.

Army officials went to the scene to investigate. The names of the crewmen were not announced.

PLANES LEAVE SEATTLE BASE

Seattle, Dec. 9 (AP)—Planes at Portland (Ore.) Air Base hopped off at 8:15 A. M., today, the 2nd Interceptor Command announced, to hunt 600 miles to sea for two or three Japanese aircraft carriers operating off coast.

Enroll Air Raid Wardens For Duty In City, County

Annapolis Divided Into 30 Air Raid Sectors

The enrollment of air raid wardens for duty in Annapolis and Anne Arundel county started today as the result of a conference held last night.

Thomas G. Basil, Chief Air Raid Warden, met with Deputy Chiefs William S. Bauer, Brooklyn, and R. Edward Dove, Brewer avenue.

Annapolis was divided into 30 air raid sectors with an air raid warden to be appointed in each sector. These wardens will appoint their assistants.

Mr. Bauer is organizing the Third, Fourth and Fifth Districts of the county, while Mr. Dove is organizing the First, Second, Seventh and Eighth Districts.

After the air raid wardens and their assistants are appointed they will attend classes for instruction in their duties.

J. H. BARRETT, JR. IN ARMY AIR CORPS

MONTGOMERY, Ala., Dec. 9—James Herman Barrett, Jr., og Annapolis, Md., is now pursuing his course in aerial navigation at the Air Corps Training Detachment, Coral Gables, Fla.

Cadet Barrett, the son of Mr. and Mrs. James H. Barrett, has been studying navigation at the replacement center at Maxwell Field, Ala., headquarters of the Southeast Air Corps Training Center, since September 18.

He attended St. John's College, Annapolis, and the University of Maryland, College Park. He was the assistant manager of the Annapolis airport before he entered the army.

Upon the completion of the navigation course, he will be awarded a commission as a second lieutenant in the United States Army Air Corps.

EASTPORT BRUSH FIRE EXTINGUISHED

The Eastport fire department yesterday afternoon extinguished a brush fire on Van Buren street, Eastport.

13 Shopping Days till Christmas
TO ALL TRAINS

COUNCIL REJECTS APPLICATION FOR FILLING STATION PERMIT

Oppose Station At King George Street And College Avenue

After hearing protests from property owners of the section, the City Council last night refused the Texas Oil Company a permit for a filling station at the northeast corner of King George street and College avenue.

The company asked permission to construct a station on the old Lutz property. It would have had two 1,000-gallon tanks and one 2,000-gallon tank.

Mayor William U. McCready announced that the city had acquired title to property at 63 Northwest street to be used as a recreation center for colored service men and others. He pointed out that a court decision in the injunction proceedings involving the proposed community recreation building on the market house site was expected by the end of the week.

Consider Airport

The Council empowerd the Mayor and Counslor Edward G. Chaney to borrow $30,000 for the proposed community building and $7,500 for the Northwest street premises from the Annapolis Banking and Trust Company, the low bidder.

On the motion of Alderman Harry England, the Council passed an order providing for the consideration of the Council of the acceptance of the tract offered by Albert H. MacCarthy and its development as a municipal airport.

Other business transacted by the Council was:

Sanctioned a request to Naval Academy authorities for the grant of 10 feet of property now being condemned in a strip along the southeast side of Randall street from King George street to Terry's alley. It was pointed out that the Council believes it possible to obtain a main artery of traffic through the city along Randall street from King George to Compromise streets.

Made Harry E. Bean, city commissioner, responsible for control of the city dump and the handling of dump fires.

Adopted the annual Santa Claus motion, made by Alderman England, directing that all city employes be paid their December salaries on Dec. 15.

Granted the Albright Sound Service permission to conduct Christmas programs in the city, provided they originate from the place of business and not from a trailer.

Protest Station

Mrs. James Ferguson, N. W. James, Maurice Ogle, S. B. Littauer, Miss Julia Trenholme and Lieut. Comdr. J. A. Hill, U.S.N., opposed the filling station permit.

They declared another station was not necessary as there are three at present in the section; that the area was residential; that the station would increase traffic hazards. Mr. Ogle said he had no interest in the station on the opposite corner and declared it was a pity it was there. He cited the many residences in the section. Mr. Littauer told of having his automobile struck several times while parked on King George street near College avenue and declared another station would increase the traffic volume and hazard.

Alderman Jesse A. Fisher declared it would be "a crime" to erect the station. He claimed that "any gas station is a fire hazard," and moved rejection of the permit. The motion was seconded by Alderman England and adopted unanimously.

Parking Meters

Counselor Chaney said that the

(Continued on Page Three)

PRESBYTERIAN GUILD MEETS TOMORROW

The regular meeting of the Presbyterian Guild will be held at the church tomorrow evening at 7:45 o'clock, with a short business meeting, followed by a Christmas program.

Gifts will be received for Christmas baskets.

The hostesses are Mesdames Franklin W. Slaven, C. Carroll Brice, Jr., Arthur S. Jensen, W. Randolph Church, Misses Anne Brewer, Mary M. Munroe and Elinore G. Girault.

Council Stresses Need For Civilian Defense Groups

Makes Full Resources Available To Federal Government

Citizens of Annapolis were urged to give their full and complete cooperation in the efforts of local Civilian Defense officials last night by the City Council.

The following resolution was adopted:

"Whereas, the United States of America has been subjected to dastardly military attack by a foreign power; and

"Whereas, the recent national emergency has now become a program of national defense in a state of war; and

"Whereas, it is now essential to effective national defense that all bodies politic as well as individuals join their efforts in united endeavor to defend our nation and our freedom.

"Now, Therefore, Be It Resolved by the Mayor, Counselor and Aldermen of the City of Annapolis, that its entire resources be readily available to the United States Government for the purpose of the defense of our nation in its present situation; and, further, that the Mayor, Counselor and Aldermen of the City of Annapolis urge the citizens of Annapolis to give their full and complete cooperation in the efforts of local Civilian Defense officials."

Mobile Unit Due Here Tomorrow For Blood Donors

Will Be At Armory From 2 To 6 P. M.

Reservations were made yesterday and today by residents of the city and county for donations of blood for the armed forces tomorrow afternoon in the State Armory, Bladen street.

The committee in charge of the Blood Donors Project will bring the mobile unit of the Baltimore Red Cross chapter here to receive the donations from 2 to 6 P. M. The 12-bed unit will be staffed with doctors and nurses.

Reservations were made at the Red Cross offices in the Court of Appeals building and in the Post Office. The local Motor Corps will furnish transportation to donors who need it, and the Canteen Corps will serve refreshments after the donations.

Minors Need Releases

Minors must procure releases at the Armory or at the Red Cross rooms, and all donors must refrain from eating fatty foods for seven hours before the donation.

The blood is processed into plasmas or blood serum, which are different in composition and method of processing, but when properly prepared there is little difference in the results obtained from the use of one or the other. They are employed to treat shock, burns and hemorrhage.

Traumatic shock is a condition

(Continued on Page Six)

LUBIN WILL SPEAK TONIGHT

Isador Lubin, economic advisor to President Roosevelt, will address the Town Meeting tonight in the gymnasium of St. John's College at 8 o'clock.

Mr. Lubin will talk on Price Control. The public is cordially invited to attend.

STANLEY B. TROTT NAMED TO OFFICE

Stanley B. Trott of the Annapolis Yacht Club is the new secretary-treasurer of the Chesapeake Bay Yacht Racing Association, which also has a county man, J. Miller Sherwood of Gibson Island, as president.

F.D.R. SIGNS WAR DECLARATION AGAINST JAPAN

Surrounded by Congressional leaders, President Roosevelt signs in Washington a declaration of war against Japan, the second war in which the U. S. has been embroiled in 24 years. Watching the Chief Executive are, left to right: Rep. Luther Johnson (D-Tex), Rep. Charles A. Eaton (R-NJ), Rep. Joseph E. Martin (R-Mass), Vice-President Henry A. Wallace, House Speaker Sam Rayburn, Rep. John McCormack (D-Mass), Sen. Charles L. McNary (R-Ore) and Sen. Alben W. Barkley (D-Ky).

EASTPORT CALLS MASS MEETING

Col. Douw To Address Session On Defense Plans

A mass-meeting of Eastport citizens will convene Thursday night in the Eastport school auditorium to draw up plans for the defense of the suburb and vicinity.

Col. John DeP. Douw, director of Civilian Defense for Annapolis and Anne Arundel county, will address the meeting.

A spokesman for the Eastport residents who called the meeting said today that cooperation on the part of the citizenry was needed.

ROY O. HAYES MADE CORPORAL

FORT BENNING, Ga., Dec. 9—Roy O. Hayes, of near Annapolis, Md., has been promoted to the grade of corporal in Company A, 20th Engineer regiment.

Commander

Admiral Thomas C. Hart (above) is commander-in-chief of the U. S. Asiatic fleet based at Manila, P. I.

NAVY CHECKING ALL CASUALTIES

The navy said today it had only meager information to date about casualties in Hawaii and that it was carefully checking all names to avoid mistakes.

Relatives of men will be notified as soon as names and numbers are determined, the navy said, and later the public will be informed through an official list.

WILLSON GIVEN NEW COMMAND

Admiral In Charge Of Newly Created Severn River Command

The Navy announced today establishment of the Severn River and Potomac River naval commands designed to protect all naval shores activities in the vicinity of the nation's capital and Annapolis, Md.

All shore activities in the Severn river area will be under the command of Rear Admiral Russell E. Willson, superintendent of the Naval Academy, while Rear Admiral George G. Pettengill, commandant of the Washington Navy Yard will command the Potomac river area.

In announcing the establishments of the commands for the purpose of military control, the Navy said that marine barracks at Quantico, Va., and Washington.

(Continued on Page Three)

LIQUOR DEALERS HOLD MEETING

Defense problems were discussed at a meeting of the Anne Arundel County Beer and Liquor Dealers Association last night at the Moose Home on West street.

The group decided to request the National Brewers Association to advocate the elimination of metal containers for beer in order to conserve metal.

Fred J. Tfingsten is president of the organization.

O'CONOR CALLS HOME GUARD

Assigned To Duty At Points In State

Governor O'Conor signed and presented to the Military Department today an order placing the Maryland Home Guard on active duty.

"These companies affected by the order will be on duty today, December 9. In order to avoid disclosure of locations considered by the United States army as sensitive points within the State of Maryland, no publication is being made of the places to which the State Guard is being assigned," the Governor said.

Precaution Taken

"Before issuing the order for active duty, every precaution was taken for the welfare, the health and comfort of the men being called into active service. In addition, compensation insurance has today been provided for all members of the State Guard on active duty."

Governors of a few States are

(Continued on Page Two)

NAVY RECRUITING OFFICERS BUSY

Will Be Here Again At 10 A. M. Friday

Recruiting officers in the office of the Capital-Gazette Press, 3 Church Circle, were kept busy today enrolling men in the U. S navy.

Before noon 20 men had applied to Comdr. John H. Bowers, U. S. N. (retired), navy editor of the Evening Capital and Chief Boatswain's mate, W. L. Thomas.

The recruiting officers will be at the office again at 10 A. M. Friday to confer with all men who wish to enlist.

THOMAS G. BASIL
INSURANCE OF ALL KINDS
92 West Street
Annapolis, Maryland
Dial 2161

SALE — NOW
CHRISTMAS GIFTS OF ENGLISH ARTICLES
Benefit
BRITISH WAR RELIEF, INC.
17 WEST STREET

SCHOOLS EVACUATED AS HOSTILE PLANE REPORT SWEEPS EASTERN COAST

Interceptor Aircraft Patrols Skies Of New England—American Forces Seek Japanese Carrier That Caused Air Raid Alarm On West Coast During Night—President To Address Nation At 10 P. M.—Manila Bombed Again

TOKYO, KOBE REPORTED BOMBED

Berlin Reports Japanese Landing In Philippines—Germany May Declare War On United States

All families were evacuated from Mitchel Field, headquarters of the First Air Force, today and "every plane was off the ground," after an "official warning from Washington that hostile planes were two hours out of New York.

The sirens roared as United States forces on the west coast were on the prowl for an enemy aircraft carrier which stirred three air-raid alarms in San Francisco during the night.

A few minutes later, a Panama radio broadcast said Japanese planes were reported flying over the Panama coast this morning—but no bombs were dropped.

In Washington, the White House, War and Navy departments said they knew nothing about the reported presence of planes off the east coast.

HULL WARNS OF ATTACK

Air raid listening posts throughout Long Island and in Massachusetts went into action as soon as the warning report came through.

A few minutes after Mitchel Field's original announcement Secretary of State Hull in Washington warned the nation to be on the alert for a surprise attack.

A DNB dispatch from Shanghai appearing in Berlin quoted the Japanese army spokesman as saying Japanese troops had landed in the Philippines. A radio report from Manila reported an air raid on the city at 8:55 A. M. The army announced that one U. S. soldier was killed and [illegible] red in a morning predawn raid on Fort Nicholas, near Manila. Two other soldiers were hurt.

Langley Safe [illegible]

Naval sources in Manila denied reports that the seaplane tender Langley was bombed during a Japanese attack on Davao yesterday.

When the New York warning came in all radio long range stations in the vicinity were shut down. Metropolitan police transmitted the warning throughout the city. All school children were sent home.

The huge new naval air base at Quonset Point, R. I., had an air raid alarm at 12:45 P. M.

There were reports that other Japanese forces were off the Aleutian Islands, in the narrow Bering Sea strait between Alaska and Siberia.

Tokyo Bombed?

Unverified reports of the bomb[ing] of Tokyo, Kobe and the Japanese island of Formosa were broadcast by CBS from Manila—the first such reports of aerial counter-blows against Japan since the war began. However, latest word from Imperial headquarters at Tokyo asserted there had been no air attack on Japanese territory up to this morning.

A Tokyo broadcast said Guam and Wake islands, American-owned stepping stones across the Pacific from Honolulu to Manila, were now under the Japanese flag.

In Tokyo, the Japanese navy's

(Continued on Page Eight)

Card Of Thanks

We wish to think our many friends for their expressions of kindness, sympathy and lovely floral tributes during our recent bereavement. Also for the use of their cars.

Grace Michaelson and Family

TONIGHT
GAME PARTY
Given by
Greek Ladies' Society of Annapolis
MOOSE HOME—8 P. M.
Prizes Admission 40c incl. tax

MAMMOTH GAME PARTY
given by
Waterwich Fire Company
FRIDAY, DECEMBER 12
20 Games Guaranteed
ADMISSION $1.00

TURKEY DINNER
ST. ANNE'S PARISH HOUSE
Thursday, December 11
MENU
Turkey, Cranberry Sauce,
Sweet Potatoes, Peas, Celery
Slaw, Hot Rolls, Pie, Coffee
TICKETS 75c 5:30 P. M.
Ice Cream, Cake, Candy on sale

WHY NOT
"PAY - AS - YOU - USE"
instead of
PAYING IN ADVANCE?
In Check Master, checkbooks are absolutely free. No worries about losing or spoiling blank checks. And no need to pay in advance for service you haven't received!
No Minimum Balance Ever Required
5c Per Check Drawn And Item Deposited
Start Your Account With A Deposit Of Any Amount—Even As Little As $1
Checkbooks FREE. No CHARGES in ADVANCE
Your Check Looks Just Like Any Other Check.
Annapolis Banking & Trust Company
ANNAPOLIS
Member Federal Deposit Insurance Corporation

The Assault On Pearl Harbor--An Artist's Conception

HANK BARROW, AP artist, reconstructs the battle at Pearl Harbor from information provided by Secretary Knox. One battleship, the U.S.S. Arizona, (right center), was sunk by a bomb that "literally passed through the smokestack." An-

other battleship, the U.S.S. Oklahoma, (left center), capsized. It can be repaired.

Three destroyers (one in right foreground), an old target ship, and a mine layer also went down. Other ships were damaged, many U. S. planes were destroyed on the ground. Almost

2,900 servicemen died. The attackers lost three subs (one midget sub at extreme right), 41 aircraft.

Knox said that after the initial surprise, American men fought with "magnificent courage and resourcefulness . . . The men's will to resist was tremendous."

WAMPUM WHIP UM!

WINDOW ROCK, Ariz. (AP) — Hosteen, Bahe, his wife and daughter, trudged into the office of the Navajo reservation superintendent and said they were ready to help the great white father in Washington.

Mrs. Bahe, opened a cigar box and counted out $350 in silver and currency. The Indians returned home to Manuelitao, N. M., their fists full of defense bonds.

STATE OF MARYLAND OFFICE OF THE SECRETARY OF STATE

Notice is hereby given that application has been made to the Governor of Maryland for the Pardon, Parole or Reduction of Sentence of the individuals named below, who were convicted of the crimes and who received the sentences specified.

CHARLES SHELDON (w), sentenced eight years, Maryland Penitentiary, Circuit Court for Prince George's County, Assault with intent to kill.

LAWRENCE BILLERBECK (w), sentenced eight years, Maryland Penitentiary, Circuit Court for Prince George's County, Assault with intent to kill.

FRED HARTONG (w), sentenced eight years, Maryland Penitentiary, Circuit Court for Prince George's County, Assault with intent to kill.

JOHN L. LAVEZZA (w), sentenced four months in the House of Correction, Criminal Court of Baltimore City, Non-Support.

CHRISTOPHER LANCIONE (w), sentenced twenty-one years, Maryland Penitentiary, Circuit Court for Baltimore County, Rape.

VINCENT FRACCI (w), sentenced twenty-one years, Maryland Penitentiary, Circuit Court for Baltimore County, Rape.

VETO BERTAZZON (w), sentenced twenty-one years, Maryland Penitentiary, Circuit Court for Baltimore County, Rape.

ANTHONY DOMICO (w), sentenced twenty-one years, Maryland Penitentiary, Circuit Court for Baltimore County, Rape.

JOSEPH DOMICO (w), sentenced twenty-one years, Maryland Penitentiary, Circuit Court for Baltimore County, Rape.

RICHARD KEYS (w), sentenced one year, House of Correction, Circuit Court for Prince George's County, Assault and Battery.

HARRY MILLER (w), sentenced three months, House of Correction, Criminal Court, Baltimore, Larceny.

JOHN SPEAKS (c), sentenced two years, House of Correction, Criminal Court, Baltimore, Bastardy.

WILLIAM TAYLOR (w), sentenced eighteen months, House of Correction, Circuit Court Frederick County, False Pretenses.

MAURICE W. HOMER (w), sentenced one year, Maryland Penitentiary, Criminal Court, Baltimore, Burglary.

OSTEN RILEY (w), sentenced one year, Maryland House of Correction, Criminal Court, Baltimore.

MAURICE W. HOMER (w), sentenced one year, Maryland Penitentiary, Criminal Court, Baltimore, Larceny.

GEORGE THOMPSON (w), sentenced eighteen years, Maryland Penitentiary, Circuit Court, Washington County, Murder 2nd Degree.

A. JAMES PERKINS (w), sentenced two years, Maryland Penitentiary, Circuit Court Prince George's County, Robbery.

GARFIELD HOOPER (c), sentenced eighteen months, Maryland Penitentiary, Criminal Court, Baltimore, Burglary.

HERMAN BAILEY (c), sentenced four years, Maryland Penitentiary, Criminal Court, Baltimore, Larceny.

WILLIAM HENRY FOSTER (w), sentenced seven years, Maryland Penitentiary, Circuit Court Prince Georges County, Robbery.

CHARLES WILLIAM LEWIS No. 2 (c), sentenced three years, Maryland Penitentiary, Circuit Court, Baltimore County, Rape.

BERNARD CHARNOCK (w), sentenced sixteen months, Baltimore City Jail, Criminal Court, Baltimore, Larceny.

HOWARD TURNER (c), sentenced eighteen months, Baltimore City Jail, Criminal Court, Baltimore, Deadly Weapon and Assault, Royston W. Jackson (w), sentenced one year, Baltimore City Jail, Traffic Court Baltimore City, Violation of the Motor Vehicle Code.

WILLIAM TAYLOR (w), sentenced one year, Maryland House of Correction, Criminal Court, Baltimore, Desertion.

JAMES MURDOCK (c), sentenced five years, Maryland House of Correction, Criminal Court, Baltimore, Manslaughter.

CHARLES KNIGHT (c), sentenced fifteen months, Maryland House of Correction, Magistrate's Court, Kent County, Larceny.

NATHAN FISCHER (c) sentenced one year, Maryland House of Correction, Criminal Court, Baltimore, Burglary.

ALLEN LEWIS (c), sentenced one year, Maryland House of Correction, Criminal Court, Baltimore, Burglary.

ARTHUR WILLIAMS (c), sentenced six months, Maryland House of Correction, Magistrate's Court, Prince George's County, Driving under influence of liquor.

DAVE JOHNSON (c), sentenced six months, Maryland House of Correction, Criminal Court, Baltimore, Assault.

RICCIORDIA MARTINI (w), sentenced thirty days and thirty days (consecutively), Baltimore City Jail, Magistrate's Court, Baltimore City, Violation of the Motor Vehicle Code.

HENRY KALETA (w), sentenced ninety days, Baltimore City Jail, Magistrate's Court Baltimore City, Violation of the Motor Vehicle Code.

FRED ALLEN (c), sentenced thirty days, Baltimore City Jail, Magistrate's Court, Baltimore, Larceny.

JESSE J. BRADFORD (c), sentenced sixty days, Baltimore City Jail, Criminal Court, Baltimore, Larceny.

WILLIAM GARNER (c), sentenced ten years, Maryland Penitentiary, Criminal Court, Baltimore, Rape and Burglary.

SPENCER MAY (c), sentenced six months, Baltimore City Jail, Criminal Court, Baltimore, Burglary.

THOMAS J. CONLON (w), sentenced six months, Baltimore City Jail, Criminal Court, Baltimore, Burglary.

CHARLES WITHERS (w), sentenced ninety days, Baltimore City Jail, Criminal Court, Baltimore, Larceny.

CHARLES E. JAMES (w), sentenced ninety days, Baltimore City Jail, Criminal Court, Baltimore, Violation Motor Vehicle Code.

CLYDE SLONAKER (w), sentenced three months, Baltimore City Jail, Criminal Court, Baltimore, Burglary.

THOMAS GRIFFIN (w), sentenced thirty days, Baltimore City Jail, Magistrate's Court, Baltimore City.

ARTHUR LOUIS CARNEAL (w), sentenced sixty days and costs concurrently, Baltimore City Jail, Magistrate's Court, Baltimore, Violation of the Motor Vehicle Code.

The Governor will take up the said cases for final decision on or after Tuesday, December 23, 1941, and until he said date protests against the granting of a Pardon, Parole or Reduction of Sentence in any of the above mentioned cases will be heard, and in the meantime the papers in the said cases will be open for inspection at the direction of the Governor.

By order of the Governor:

THOMAS ELMO JONES,
Secretary of State.

Japanese Attack
(Continued From Page One)

Chinese coastal cities forged the victim's greatest weapon, unity—this in a nation that in four thousand odd years of history had never been totally united in a common cause. For "vulture's eggs," as the Chinese called bombs, made no individual distinctions. All citizens were suddenly bound together in bonds of blood and pain and loss, and from that agony Free China was born.

Losing most mechanical equipment in the first months Chinese troops fought with whatever came to hand. Their tiny remaining air force staged regular cautious forays over enemy concentrations to provoke an expenditure of valuable munitions. As the Japanese advanced, Chiang's men retreated forcing the intruders to spread in dangerously thin lines.

Scorched Earth

That nothing useful might fall to the aggressor, civilian refugees destroyed everything they could not carry with them on the long heartbreaking trek toward safety in the West, personally laying the torch to homes, household possessions, and field crops.

In the occupied territory civilian men and women formed guerilla bands and terrorized isolated Japanese forces. Whatever enemy engineers accomplished in the daylight was destroyed at night, supplies were raided as soon as stored, messages intercepted, and fortified positions taken in surprise attacks. In 1937-38, for every Jap-

anese killed, five Chinese perished; in 1941, guerillas claim that for every man they lose, thirteen Japanese die. Farmers feed these guerilla bands, priests house them in temples, merchants clothe and arm them right under the conquerors' very eyes. No Chinese citizen today leads a private life in either free or occupied territory. All, both rich and poor, are involved in working, sharing, or fighting. When completely blockaded by sea, Chinese civilians built a highway through bleak deserts to Russia, and another across perilous mountain ranges to Burma, literally digging them out with bare hands.

Fight On

Summing up this effort, Madam Chiang Kai-Shek says, "Swept by flames, deluged by blood, stripped by looters . . . still we shall not cease to resist . . . China has come a long way from knitting socks and making occasional gifts. In the determination to fight on we give our lives, our livelihood, and al that we hold dear."

At present Annapolis and Anne Arundel County are asked to give largely to the Red Cross War Relief Fund. We are a fortunate people—sheltered, clothed, well fed, and still able to enjoy Christmas festivities. It may be that we shall never be called upon to suffer as has China in fighting our common enemy, Japan. One thing is certain—we shall win no war against the triple alliance of Germany, Italy, and Japan by halfway measures in either services or contributions. "Cheap things are not valuable," the Chinese remind us from ancient wisdom, "valuable things are never cheap."

LATE NEWS

Evening Capital

WEATHER
Fair and continued cold, except not quite so cold in extreme west portion tonight.

VOL. LVIII — NO. 4. EVERY EVENING EXCEPT SUNDAY ANNAPOLIS, MD., TUESDAY, JANUARY 6, 1942. SOUTHERN MARYLAND'S ONLY DAILY TWO CENTS.

HUGE ARMS PLAN OUTLINED

O'CONOR MEETS WITH EDITORS

Governor O'Conor asked for the assistance of daily and weekly newspaper editors, radio and motion picture theatre representatives today in an effort to give complete public information" to civilians in home defense matters.

At a luncheon conference at Carvel Hall attended also by Civilian Defense officials, O'Conor asserted:

"Because we realize only too well the difficulty of achieving complete distribution of such information, I have asked you gentlemen to come here today to consult with us and to help us in our efforts to achieve the desired, complete public information.

INJURED GIRL'S CONDITION UNCHANGED

The condition of Miss Rosalie Johnson, 216 King George street, was reported unchanged today at Emergency Hospital where she has been a patient since early yesterday morning.

Miss Johnson, an employee at the Naval Academy laundry, was found unconscious near the Navy Post-graduate School yesterday, with a possible fracture of the base of the skull, lacerations and brush burns. Dr. Claffy, county medical officer said her condition was serious.

Anne Arundel police made no report on the case today. The cause of Miss Johnson's injuries so far is unknown.

FOUR RIVERS CLUB PLANS BUSINESS MEET

The Four Rivers Garden Club will hold a business meeting at 3 P. M. Tuesday, Jan. 13, at the home of Mrs. Frank A. Munroe, 27 Franklin St.

Mrs. Munroe and Mrs. Samuel Brooke will be co-hostesses.

BLAZING XMAS TREE BRINGS FIRE COMPANY

A blazing Christmas tree at 3 Sleepy Hollow, Weems Creek, brought the West Annapolis fire department to the scene this morning. Practically no damage was caused by the fire.

YACHT CLUB WIVES FORM RED CROSS CLASS

The Red Cross class formed by wives of members of the Annapolis Yacht Club will have its first meeting Thursday at the club.

Sessions are planned from 10 A. M. to 3 P. M. each Thursday. Luncheon will be served at noon.

Sewing machines and other equipment have been loaned to the club for the class.

CITY SHIVERS IN COLD WIND; MERCURY DROPS

Annapolis shivered and shook last night and early this morning in its first real taste of winter so far this year.

Minimum temperature, recorded early today, stood at 11.5 above zero. Maximum was 14.5 in midmorning. Although the sun shone brightly, the wind was cold and piercing.

ASQUITH BABY DIES AT HOME

Doris Rosell Asquith, 19-day-old daughter of Peter P. and Doris R. Asquith, 219 Lockwood street, Eastport, died suddenly yesterday at the Asquith home.

Funeral services will be held at 10 A. M. tomorrow from All Hallows Church, Davidsonville. Burial will be in All Hallows Cemetery.

HOLD FUNERAL RITES FOR J. H. THOMAS

Funeral services for Joseph H. Thomas were conducted this afternoon from the Taylor funeral home by the Rev. James L. Smiley.

Burial was in Cedar Bluff Cemetery. Pallbearers were Daniel Wiggan, Charles Ford, Benjamin Leitch, Stewart Leitch, Robert Ellers and Samuel F. Cantler.

Mr. Thomas died suddenly Sunday at his home 520 First street, Eastport.

WAR RELIEF TO HOLD MONTHLY RUMMAGE SALE

The British War Relief Society will hold its monthly rummage sale from 10 A. M. to 6 P. M. Thursday and Friday at the organization's headquaters on West street.

JUNIOR BUSINESS CLUB TO MEET THURSDAY

The Junior Business Girls' Club will hold its first meeting after the holidays at 7:30 P. M. Thursday at the Y.W.C.A.

The president has requested that all members be present.

RECREATION BUILDING SITE ON COMPROMISE STREET SELECTED; HOUSING GROUP TAKES ACTION

Housing Authority Agrees To Purchase And Clear Property In Chestnut Street Section, Running Along Compromise Street—Will Sell Portion Near St. Mary's Street To City For Recreation Building Site—City Holds Option On Adjoining St. Mary's Street Lot—Council Accepts Proposal At Special Meeting

The purchase and clearing of all property bordering on Compromise street in the Chestnut street area and the location of the proposed community recreation building on part of the site so acquired was agreed upon last night by the Annapolis Housing Authority and the City Council.

Options on the property have been secured and the Finance Commission of the city was empowered to proceed to close the deal. The recreation building site, overlooking Spa Creek, has been approved by Army officials.

New Site Necessary

The selection of a new site was made necessary when Judge James E. Boylan, Jr., ruled that the community building could not be located on the present market site.

The Housing Authority, which plans to clear the property involved, made the first move at a special meeting held last night, shortly before the Council met in special session.

The Authority notified the Council that it would cooperate in clearing the buildings that exist in the Chestnut street area and would buy the property, selling the part needed for the recreation building site to the city for one-third of the cost of the whole.

Property Ownership

The property involved is owned by Mr. and Mrs. Harry Ivrey; the estate of James E. Abbott; Mr. and Mrs. Evelyn Peters, and Rachel Walker, George Woelfel, trustee.

The property lies along Compromise street and runs back to an alley which parallels this street. It extends from the boundary line of the public school playgrounds across Chestnut street to land owned by the Redemptorist Fathers, facing St. Mary's street. It takes in garages, houses on both sides of Chestnut street, a tenement building and a store on Compromise street.

Cost Of Land

The Housing Authority estimated that the total cost of its purchase of this property would be around $38,000 or $39,000. All of this land would be cleared of the present buildings.

The Housing Authority then offered to sell the city a portion of the land on the St. Mary's street

(Continued on Page Six)

The armed forces of our Country are offering their lives for our security. What are we offering? We can answer through the Red Cross War Relief fund, now.

Blood Donor Unit To Return Here

Armory Visits Scheduled For Jan. 13 And 14

The mobile unit for blood donors from the Baltimore chapter of the Red Cross will be in Annapolis three times during January.

Today this unit completed its work of receiving all the donors from the Engineering Expermient Station, who volunteered just before Dec. 10, adding probably another 80 donors to the already large list that Annapolis and Anne Arundel county have contributed to the "plasma bank," established for the armed forces of the United States. With this last visit the total for the county has risen to 312 units of plasma.

The mobile unit, consisting of 12 beds, staff and supplies, will return to Annapolis Tuesday and Wednesday, Jan. 13 and 14. It will be set up in the State Armory on Bladen Street for full day sessions. Beginning in the morning at 11, the unit will be open until 5 P. M.

Appoinments are rapidly being filled but if anyone is interested in being a donor he may call the volunteer services during business hours or Mrs. Richard West after 5 P. M.

Continued on Page Six)

Press Conference For Pacific Fleet Chief

Admiral Chester W. Nimitz, commander-in-chief of the U. S. Pacific fleet, and his staff stand at attention during the fleet chief's first press conference aboard a submarine at Pearl Harbor. Left to right (facing camera), Capt. W. W. Smith, assistant chief of staff; Admiral Nimitz; and Rear Admiral T. Withers, commander submarine scouting force.

CAPT. BEARDALL NEW HEAD OF NAVAL ACADEMY

First Captain Assigned To Post Since 1919

CAPT. JOHN BEARDALL

Capt. John Beardall, naval aide to President Roosevelt, will be the thirty-third superintendent of the Naval Academy, when he takes command of the institution the latter part of this month.

Captain Beardall, whose promotion to the grade of Rear Admiral is now before the Senate for approval was appointed to the post late yesterday. He will succeed Rear Admiral Russell Willson who was relieved two weeks ago to become chief of staff to Admiral Ernest J. King, commander-in-chief of the United States Fleet.

Twelfth Captain

He is the first navy captain to be appointed to the post since Capt. Archibald H. Scales became superintendent on Feb. 12, 1919. Captain Scales became a Rear Admiral on Jan. 3, 1921.

Since the Academy was founded on Oct. 10, 1845, six commanders, 12 captains and 13 rear admirals and two commodores have been superintendents. The commanders were assigned to the duty in the early days of the Academy.

Capt. John L. McCrea, now aide

(Continued on Page Six)

'Union Now' To Be Debate Subject

Stringfellow Barr, Comdr. Wise To Participate

Stringfellow Barr, president of St. John's College, and Lieut. Comdr. J. A. Wise, U. S. N. R., will debate the subject of "Union Now" at 8 P. M. tomorrow in the Carvel Hall Mirror Room.

Mr. Ball will take the side in favor of the proposed federal union of self-governed democratic nations, and Commander Wise will represent the opposition.

The program will be presented at the regular meeting of the University Club of Annapolis. The debate is open to all men, whether or not they are members of the club.

Form Committee On Birthday Ball

Dance To Be Given Here Jan. 30

Annapolis will join the nation again in the celebration of President Roosevelt's diamond jubilee birthday Jan. 30 with a ball at Carvel Hall as part of the drive which continues the fight against infantile paralysis.

Senator Louis N. Phipps is chairman of the organization for the 1942 campaign and Mayor William U. McCready is honorary chairman.

Other officials include Barney Berman, co-chairman; Clarence M. White, vice-chairman; Mrs. Carroll Lee, secretary, and W. W. Townshend, Jr., treasurer.

Heads Women's Group

Mrs. Francis J. Huth heads the women's division with Mrs. Edith Rawlings as co-chairman and Mrs. Malcolm E. DeConway as vice-chairman.

In Mrs. Huth's organization is Mrs. Amanda Teal as chairman of the prize committee consisting of Mrs. Wilmer Smith, Mrs. Bosley Myers, Mrs. Raymond Price, Mrs. Joseph Bouchel, Mrs. George B. Woelfel, Mrs. Emma Carter, Mrs. Eulalia L'Aigle, Mrs. Charles Tucker, Mrs. Ella Rogers, Mrs. Samuel Fertitta, Mrs. K. Collinson and Mrs. W. Hewell.

Other committee chairmen are Mrs. Charles Bove, card; Mrs. Wilbur Shawn, bridge; Mrs. Norbert Aubery and Mrs. William Owens, "500."

Assisting Mrs. Bove will be Mrs. Vincent Velna, Mrs. A. C. Morris, Mrs. Daniel Keller, Mrs. Charles Bernstein, Mrs. William Vanous, Mrs. Andrew Brown, Mrs. Arthur G. Ellington,, Mrs. Garnard Day and Mrs. John Kramer.

Clubs Pledge Help

Mrs. Carrie Dammeyer, as a representative of the Pythian Sisters, has offered her assistance. The Caravan Club, the Kiwanis Club and the Women's Democratic Club have pledged full support.

Senator Phipps named Harry S. Kenchington chairman of the ticket committee, Benjamin Michaelson chairman of the dance committee with Mrs. W. Henry French and Mrs. Lee to assist.

Serving on the reception committee will be Mrs Herbert R. O'Conor,, Mrs. Phipps, Mrs. Albert W. Woodfield, Mrs. W. U. McCready, Mrs. George Abram Moss, Mrs. St. George Barber and Mrs. Lena Smith.

There will be a meeting of the committees and their key workers at 2 P. M. Friday at Mrs. Huth's home, 125 Archwood avenue.

WAR RELIEF FUND PASSES HALF WAY MARK IN QUOTA

Now Totals $10,241.48; $20,000 Needed From City And County

The Red Cross war relief fund, now totaling $10,241.48, will be further increased by the contribution of $1,000 from the Johnson Lumber Company. The Glen Burnie office and the Annapolis plant of the company are making the contribution jointly.

Judge Ridgely P. Melvin, director of the drive, yesterday met with the district chairmen in order to give all sections of Anne Arundel county a more active share in raising the $20,000 quota.

Mrs. Herman Fiske will head the committee of the Third District; Mrs. Ernest Shepherd, the First, Seventh and Eighth; State's Attorney Marvin I. Anderson, the Fourth, and Edward N. C. Bradley, the Fifth. The district chairmen pledged an intensification of the war relief campaign, stating that vigorous and immediate action will be taken to over-subscribe the $20,000 goal.

New contributions:

Through St. Anne's Church	$16.00
Coca Cola Bottling Co.	500.00
Consolidated Gas and Electric Company	250.00
Mrs. Hugh Purvis	5.00
Mrs. Morris Smellow	10.00
Employees Annapolis Buick Company	30.00
A freshman home room	2.00
Cash through St. Anne's Church	2.24
T. Stanforth Shepherd	25.00
Mrs. J. W. Fisher	10.00
Mrs. Gertrude Dawson	1.00
Hal E. Owens	1.00
Thomas Simms	2.00
Dr. George T. Feldmeyer	5.00
Lieut. and Mrs. W. W. Fife	20.00
Mr. and Mrs. J. A. Murphy	10.00
Sigma Theta Pi sorority	25.00
Mrs. Michael Sachs	5.00
Mr. and Mrs. Max Schiff	1.00
Mrs. Ford A. Brown	100.00
Mr. and Mrs. A. F. France	4.00
Clarence E. Tyler	50.00
Anonymous	600.00
Anonymous	10.00
Anonymous	5.00
Anonymous	50.00

(The folowing amounts have been collected through the efforts of Mrs. Herman Fiske, Round Bay, and Mrs. Edwin F. Samuels, Severna Park):

Mrs. Birdie M. Rhodes	5.00
Frances S. Fellows	5.00
Dorothy P. Bartlett	5.00
J. A. Keller	5.00
Thelma S. MacCarthy	5.00

(Continued on Page Six)

WILL USE CITY SIRENS FOR FIRES

Air Raid Alarm System Changed—Firemen Were Handicapped

The use of sirens to sound fire alarms, discontinued several weeks ago in order to keep the sirens exclusively for air raid warnings, will be resumed at 4 P. M. Thursday.

Fire Marshal Jessie A. Fisher said the use of the sirens was necessary to get enough volunteer firemen to report to fight fires in the city. He said he would not be responsible for loss of life and property in the city unless they were put back in use.

New Signal

The City Council approved the use of the sirens for fire purposes and municipal officials, after conferring with Col. John deP. Douw, civilian defense director, said the following siren signals would be used for fires and air raid warnings:

Six long blasts of the sirens will be sounded for fires.

The air raid alert will be one long continous blast.

The air raid all-clear will be one short blast.

It was pointed out that as a further check on air raid warning, persons hearing the sirens could check the street lights. These are turned out for air raids on telephonic orders. If the street lights are extinguished while the sirens are sounding it means and air raid with all blackout orders in effect.

Air Raid Siren

Mayor William U. McCready last night informed the City Council that he had been informed by Colonel Douw that air raid signal equipment for Annapolis would cost from $1,600 to $1,800. The city had appropriated $600 for this purpose.

To Act Monday

Alderman Fisher said that he was opposed to spending that much money unless the city could get equipment that could be put to municipal uses in peace time.

He suggested that the city purchase an air compressor that could be used for street work, and equip the fire houses with air raid sirens that would work from tanks of compressed air. He pointed out that the air compressor could keep these tanks charged so the sirens could be used, and at the same time would be useful in city work.

It was decided to investigate and reconsider the air raid siren matter at the regular monthly meeting of the Council Monday night.

Fire Problem

During the discussion Alderman Fisher declared that the failure to use the sirens for fire purposes was crippling the fire fighting in the city.

"An air raid is possible but remote," he declared, "We have fires all the time."

He pointed out that the volunteer firemen did not hear the bells and therefore failed to report to the fire houses when an alarm was sounded. He also declared that it was practically impossible to get the fire trucks through traffic in the city speedily because motorists apparently failed to notice the bells on the trucks.

Alderman Fisher declared that "we lost three at Eastport because we are not getting enough people out."

Alderman Bernard Hoff also cited the difficulty the firemen have in hearing the bells, and pointed out how fire apparatus was being held up in traffic.

RECKORD GETS HIGH POST IN ARMY

BALTIMORE, Jan. 6 (AP)—Maj. Gen. Milton A. Reckord, a native Marylander who rose through the ranks in a brilliant military career spanning more than 40 years, assumes his most important post today—command of the army's Third Corps Area.

General Reckord was named yesterday to succeed Maj. Gen. H. Conger Pratt, retiring corps area commander, who was assigned to other duties, the nature of which was not disclosed. General Reckord was immediately relieved of command of the Twenty-Ninth Infantry Division.

PRESIDENT SETS PROGRAM OF ARMS PRODUCTION IN NATION FOR 1942-1943

Forecasts Victory In Long, Hard, Bloody War—Wants Nation To Produce 185,000 Airplanes And 120,000 Tanks By End Of 1943—Places Cost At $56,000,000,000 For Next Fiscal Year—Seven Japanese Bombers Downed At Corregidor—British Withdraw Again In Malaya

President Roosevelt, assuring the nation of ultimate victory in "a bloody war," told Congress today the war program for the next fiscal year would require $56,000,000,000 to help produce 185,000 airplanes and 120,000 tanks by the end of 1943.

Imperial Tokyo headquarters let slip what seemed an admission that Japanese troops have made little progress in attempting to drive Gen. Douglas MacArthur's forces back into the Batan peninsula, and more good news came with the reported arrival of American aerial reinforcements in the Philippine conflict.

U. S. anti-aircraft gunners were officially reported to have hit at least seven Japanese planes during a four-hour aerial assault yesterday upon Corregidor Island fortress and Mariveles. Fifty Japanese planes were reported as having participated in the attack.

GRIM-WORDED MESSAGE

In a grim-worded message to Congress, President Roosevelt pledged that "powerful and offensive actions must and will be taken in proper time" and disclosed a gigantic two-year program of production so that in:

1942—"We shall produce 60,000 planes, 10,000 more than the goal set a year and a half ago"; 45,000 tanks, 20,000 anti-aircraft guns, and 8,000,000 deadweight tons of merchant vessels.

1943—125,000 planes, 75,000 tanks, 35,000 anti-aircraft guns and 10,000,000 tons of ships.

"The militarists in Berlin and Tokyo started this war," the President said sternly. "But the massed, angered forces of common humanity will finish it."

Tokyo Claims

Tokyo claimed that military aircraft coperation with land forces on Batan peninsula have bombed enemy concentrations at Rimai, Balanga and Subic.

The key to the Japanese acknowledgement lay in the reference to Subic, which lies in Zambales province, six miles north of the Batan province border, at the head of Subic bay.

With General MacArthur's troops still holding Subic, it appeared to follow that the Japanese had failed to achieve any deep thrust into Batan, since a major advance would out-flank Subic's defenders and presumably force them to withdraw southward into Batan.

Malayan Front

On the Malayan front, grave new reverses marked the British stand against Japanese invasion columns driving toward Singapore. British Far Eastern headquarters acknowledged that hard-pressed British troops had yielded further ground at both ends of the front, under Japanese attacks by land and sea.

On the eastern side of the Peninsula, a communique disclosed, the British were forced to retreat from Kauntan, only 190 miles north of Singapore, while on the west coast British troops made their second withdrawal in three days to meet a flank threat.

Japanese bombers again attacked the $400,000,000 fortifications of Singapore, inflicting slight damage and pounding nearby Johore.

In the Philippines the Japanese reported the sinking of 10 ships and destruction of 146 trucks in aerial attacks.

U. S. Bombers

For Americans, however, these blows were more than offset by the exploit of U. S. army bombers in sinking a Japanese destroyer and scoring three direct hits on a Japanese battleship in Davao Bay, Mindanao island, 600 miles south of Manila.

The bombers returned safely to base.

The 840-ton Seaplane Tender Heron was safe in a Far Eastern port after shooting down a four-motored Japanese flying boat and damaging another during a seven-hour attack by 15 Japanese bombers. She suffered some damage herself.

Chungking claimed Japanese troops had been driven back ten miles from Changsha but the Japanese claimed they had occupied the city. A Chungking military dispatch said 40,000 Japanese troops were caught in a Chinese trap on the plains northwest of Changsha.

President Roosevelt told the Congress that the "Stars and Stripes will fly again over Wake and Guam . . .the brave peoples of the Philippines will be rid of Japanese imperialism; and will live in freedom, security and independence."

"The superiority of the United States in munitions and ships must be overwhelming that the Axis nations can never hope to catch up with it," he continued. "Let no man say it cannot be done.

(Continued on Page Three)

FOR SALE

WATERFRONT BUNGALOW
Open fireplace, large screened porch, double garage, 1½ acre of land, $1,000 boathouse. 2½ miles from Annapolis on Spa Road. $3,5000. Write Box 27, Evening Capital.

THOMAS G. BASIL
INSURANCE OF ALL KINDS
92 West Street
Annapolis, Maryland
Dial 2161

Watch For HERBERT'S January Clearance Sale

RUMMAGE SALE
Benefit
BRITISH WAR RELIEF
17 WEST ST.
Thursday — Friday
JAN. 8 AND 9
10 TO 6 P. M.

NOTICE

The Annual Meeting of the Shareholders of the ENTERPRISE FEDERAL Savings & Loan Association will be held at its Office at 15 School Street on Wednesday, January 21 at 7:30 P. M. for the election of Directors for the ensuing year and for the transaction of such other business as may properly come before said meeting.

EDWARD A. HESSELBROCK, Secretary.

GAME PARTY
Benefit
FIRST WARD DEMOCRATIC
WEDNESDAY
CLUB
JANUARY 7—8 P. M.
8 Martin Street Admission 40¢

Mothers' Health Guarded By State Group

2,500 Had Benefit Of Clinics Last Year

Emphasizing the need of every expectant mother for medical advice, continuous supervision and attention during the entire period before the baby arrives, skilled care at confinement, and for some time afterwards, Dr. J. H. M. Knox, Jr., Chief of the Bureau of Child Hygiene of the State Department of Health, said that last year over 2,500 mothers-to-be, in the counties of Maryland, had the benefit of supervision of this sort at the prenatal clinics held throughout the State.

Started in 1928, in a single county, for the benefit of mothers of limited means, the services has gradually been extended, Dr. Knox said, to other counties. It is available now to expectant mothers in twenty of the twenty-three counties of the State.

Clinics Arranged

In each county where they are held, the clinics are arranged by the County Health Officer, with the approval of the local physicians and the County Medical Society. They are conducted in cooperation with the Bureau of Child Hygiene by physicians with special training and experience in service of this sort and are held at some central place at a regular time, each month. Follow-up care, according to the instructions of the clinic physicians, is given to the expectant mothers in their homes, by the public health nurses.

The prenatal services are planned especially for expectant mothers who cannot afford the services of private physicians. They include a preliminary physical examination, measurements, blood tests, periodical tests of the urine, advice as to diet, personal hygiene and so to preparations for confinement. Return visits to the clinics are made by the mothers at regular intervals for further instruction and advice. Care at the time of confinement is not included, but advice and assistance are given in making the necessary arrangements for care at home, or if advisable, in a hospital.

Safeguard Lives

"Services of this sort," Dr. Knox continued, "safeguard two lives—the life of the baby as well as the life of the mother. Mothers come through the waiting period much more safely and the babies who have had a share in prenatal care have a much better start in life than do those of the mothers who drift along without medical supervision.

"It is the responsibility of the fathers as well as of the mothers to arrange for these prenatal services and to see that the advice and instruction of the doctor and the public health nurse are carefully followed.

"Information about the prenatal services, the dates and places where the clinics are to be held may be obtained by those who are interested, from the County Health Departments."

Neighborhood News

(Continued From Page Three)

February 12 at the Calvary Methodist Church in Frederick, Md., her previous home, and were conducted by one of the former ministers. Mr. and Mrs. Frank Churchill Woods and Mr. and Mrs. Robert H. Woods of The Park were among those attending.

Members of the Chess team of Western Maryland College, of which James Griffin is a member, were supper guests of his parents, Mr. and Mrs. D. W. Griffin, at their home in Round Bay Sunday night after their return from the game at the Naval Academy. Mr. and Mrs. Richard Sperry and children, Richard, Jr., Thelma and Glenn of Towson, and Mrs. Sperry, Sr., of Indianapolis, were also Sunday guests of Mr. and Mrs. Griffin.

Mr. and Mrs. W. Gordon Schreitz of the Park are receiving congratulations on the birth of a daughter on February 14 at Johns Hopkins Hospital.

Mr. and Mrs. Edgar Smith of the Park, entertained at a Valentine cocktail and dinner party on Sunday for Mr. and Mrs. George Golden, Mr. and Mrs. Albert Evans, Mrs. Edward Laib, Miss Nell Millar all of Baltimore, and Mr. and Mrs. Henry Trenka of the Park.

Shortage of coal and gas caused a recent partial shut-down of industrial operations in France, says the Department of Commerce.

Rationing of automobiles and tires points to deep changes in the structure of domestic transport, according to the Department of Commerce.

BATTLESHIP ALABAMA LAUNCHED AT PORTSMOUTH

Completed nine months ahead of schedule, the U. S. S. Alabama, 35,000-ton battleship, slides down the ways at Norfolk navy yard, Portsmouth, Va. It was the first battleship to be launched there in half a century.

Defense Plans

(Continued from Page Six)

them as self-sufficient as possible, and to educate them as to their duties, conduct, and behavior in the event of an aerial attack or some natural catastrophe.

The Seventh and Eighth districts and part of the First have been divided up into the following divisions with the boundaries set: Shady Side, Deale, Galesville, Cumberstone, Harwood, Polling House Road, Owensville, Mt. Zion, Tracy's Landing, Bristol and Friendship.

We, in the country, have several problems which those in the towns and cities do not have. First, the distances are greater, making notification and communication more difficult; second, the stock and crops in the stables and barns must be protected. This plan takes into account these exigencies.

Meetings Held

To set our plan in operation in each community, we have picked out key people in that section and asked them to call a meeting of their neighbors. Then the Air Raid Warden for our districts, J. Irving King of Davidsonville, and several of the defense workers have attended the meeting and explained the dangers which we are facing, and how disaster and destruction will ensue if the people are not organized for mutual help in their own and neighboring communities in the event of an attack. Then the actual organization is begun.

The first thing is to choose a central place, which is or can be manned twenty-four hours a day, as Communications Center. The person in charge here is the contact with the outside world. It is the duty of this person to pass on any information received to the deputy air raid warden of this particular section and to the other persons having a definite job to perform. After the Communications Center is settled upon, the people are asked to name that person in whom they have the most confidence and whom they would rather follow in a time of danger. When they have settled upon a person, who the District Air Raid Warden feels will be equal to the occasion, he appoints him officially. This neighborhood deputy air raid warden, in turn, appoints as many assistants as he thinks necessary to cover his territory. This deputy, also, appoints a group as messengers to carry information in case the telephones are out of order or to those people who do not have telephones; a second group, who will be responsible for the transportation of the injured and the crews needed for rescue or fire fighting work; a third group, who will be responsible for the evacuation of people and furniture from damaged or burning houses; a fourth group responsible for the evacuation of stock from damaged or burning stables; a fifth group, known as "free lance" to assist wherever the need is greatest. After these appointments are made, a suitable building or home in the section is chosen as a casualty station, where first aid may be administered before the injured are sent to an emergency hospital, which is to be set up at the Southern High School. The final point in the organization is to obtain homes for emergency food and housing for those who will be so unfortunate as to lose their dwellings.

Warning Problem

The greatest problem with us lies in the difficulty of spreading the alarm for an air raid. The only means of giving a warning at the present time would be by church and farm bells, which are inadequate, or by the telephone, which, in an attack, might be put out of order.

The response to Civilian Defense registration has been very good. If the people can understand that, when they sign these cards, it does not mean that they can be sent anywhere in Maryland for an indefinite length of time, but that they are only subject to call in their own and neighboring communities, they are ready and willing to register. We are very proud of the fact that there are about 125 people taking the standard Red Cross Course in First Aid, which is being given at the Southern High School twice each week.

Our organization is not perfect, but I feel that we have made a good beginning. The co-operation and spirit of the people in our communities have been good. Their morale is high and they are ready to do their part.

Navy Women

(Continued from Page Six)

plished student of literature but exhibited charming delivery.

Mrs. Alfred Chandler of the Music Group, displayed a voice of rare beauty in a solo group with Stanley McCusker accompanying at the piano.

Scribes of the Writers' Group proved gifted in the closing number of the afternoon. Mrs. Cleveland McCauley read an original story about an Irish setter pup, which completely won her audience. Mrs. Bertha Bare, chairman of the group, read a series of tabloids written in newspaper style.

Tea concluded the affair.

It is planned to make ammonia from natural gas in the near future.

NAVY TO WORK ON HOLIDAY

All bureaus, boards and offices of the Navy Department, the Commandants of the Marine Corps and of the Coast Guard have been informed by letter sent out by Assistant Secretary of the Navy Ralph A. Bard that Washington's birthday, due to the war emergency, will be a regular work day for all employees of the executive department of the Navy, Headquarters of the Marine Corps and U. S. Coast Guard.

Employees will receive their regular compensation for work performed or for authorized annual leave on February 22.

Washington's birthday will be a working day throughout the naval service.

ENGINEERS CLOSE OLD JUG BRIDGE

FREDERICK, Md., Feb. 17 (AP)—The old Jug Bridge built in 1808 and storied as a soldier's whiskey bank in the Cvil War, has has succumbed to time and travel.

The stone bridge spanning the Monocacy River on route 40 near Frederick has been condemned by the State Roads Commission, and closed to all traffic except passenger automobiles.

It takes its name from a stone demijohn at one end. And the story goes that Civil War soldiers hid their whiskey bottles n the jug to keep them from being found by their officers.

Wilson T. Ballard, Road Commission Chief Engineer, said the span had started to sag. Trucks and other heavy vehices will be diverted over Route 26 from Frederick to Baltimore.

Ballard said plans would be pressed for a dual highway bridge to be built at a nearby location.

Colbert Flim Here Tomorrow

"Remember The Day" Will Start Tomorrow At Circle

Claudette Colbert, on vacation from her recent comedy roles, will be seen tomorrow at the Circle Theatre in a serious part as the feminine half of a love story in "Remember the Day."

Chosen to play opposite the indefatigable Colbert is John Payne, recently seen here in "Sun Valley Serenade" and "Week-End in Havana."

Two juveniles — Douglas Croft and Ann Todd—are in the featured supporting cast, which also includes John Shepherd, Jane Seymour and Frieda Inescort.

"Remember the Day" will play through Saturday.

Now playing at the Circle is "All Through the Night," which purports to show American gangsterdom ranged against Nazi bundsmen and fifty columnists. Humphrey Bogart is, of course, the Dillinger of the piece and Peter Lorre may be seen as one of the more sinister characters. Kaaren Verne provides the heart interest.

Victor McLaglen and Edmund Lowe are back in circulation again, a bit creaky at the joints, in an epic titled "Call Out the Marines," today ending its run at the Republic. A ditty called "A Gentleman at Heart" is scheduled for tomorrow and Thursday, and the Republic will wind up the week with "Wolf Man" Friday and Saturday.

Huge War Bill

(Continued from Page One)

"Unquestionably, practices have crept in of a most reprehensible character, despite the care and diligence of those having over-all responsibility for the expenditure of funds."

Hits Strikes

"It is worse than unfortunate," it said, "that even a small number of men whose services are vitally useful in the prosecution of shipbuilding are not at work."

Referring to "the welders' strike on the Pacific Coast," which was terminated today, it declared:

"These disputes wear us out fighting with each other while the production of war materials languishes and the chief beneficiary is the Axis enemy.

"It is not fair to the men who are fighting the battles of the country; it is not fair to the people of the nation, it is not fair to the vast body of loyal workers who are giving their best efforts in industry to produce everything that is needed for the war effort."

Called "Appalling"

Even with the tremendous sums already authorized — "appalling" was the word used by the committee in describing them—the report said that additional appropriations would be forthcoming for further airplane expansion and for the pay of personnel.

The bill would bring the total of war appropriations voted since Pearl Harbor to $606 for every man, woman and child in the United States. It would provide arms for an army of 3,600,000, including an air force of 1,000,000 by the end of the year.

"There will be a strain on manpower," said Undersecretary of War Robert P. Patterson. His testimony before the House Appropriations committee along with that of War Production Chief Donald Nelson and Major General R. C. Moore army deputy chief of staff, accompanied the bill.

As sent up to Capitol Hill by the Bureau of the Budget, the new bill called for:

2,877 Ships

A. $22,888,901,900 for the War Department, including $13,252,200,000 designated for ordnance and $3,011,512,000 to expedite production. The Deficiency Appropriations Committee inserted a clause to prevent diversion of more than half of that amount to the Allies in the form of lend-lease aid.

B. $3,852,000,000 for the Maritime Commission. Rear Admiral Emory S. Land, commission chairman, disclosed that the construction program contemplated 2,877 ships with a 30,834,421 total tonnage and a total expenditure of $6,704,464,056, including the funds in the pending bill. He said that the 1942 schedules called for 783 vessels.

C. $5,430,000,000 for lend lease purposes, boosting the total appropriations for that form of aid to more than $17,000,000,000. Largest single item in the new allotment was listed as food—$1,300,000,000 — and Secretary of Agriculture Wickard said the emphasis would be on "more concentrated products, such as meat, dairy products and dried eggs, and less on such products as cotton and corn."

IT'S SAILOR McNEIL, NOW

NEW YORK (AP)—Don McNeil, former national tennis singles champion and ranked fourth last year, likely won't be around to compete in this year's tournament. He is awaiting a call to report as an ensign in the naval reserve.

BASEBALL BIG STUFF

OKLAHOMA CITY (AP) — Baseball goes big in high schools out this way. There were teams representing 120 high schools last year.

CEILING ZERO

SACRAMENTO, Calif. (AP) — A check to the state for 1 cent—to adjust a tax error—bounced back. the bank had written: "Insufficient funds.

Evening Capital

VOL. LVIII — NO. 84. EVERY EVENING EXCEPT SUNDAY ANNAPOLIS, MD., THURSDAY, APRIL 9, 1942. SOUTHERN MARYLAND'S ONLY DAILY THREE CENTS.

WEATHER

Occasional rain with slowly rising temperature tonight.

LATE NEWS

O'CONOR WATCHES STATE FINANCES

Sources close to Governor O'Conor said today he was awaiting further financial and civilian defense developments before deciding if and when a special General Assembly session should be called.

The Governor is keeping in close touch with State finances and revenue from the state income tax, due April 15, should clarify somewhat the financial picture, the sources said.

WOULD LEVY PROFIT TAX

Washington, April 9 (AP)—A special tax on the income from military production contracts was proposed today by Chairman George (D-Ga.) of the Senate Finance Committee to supplement congressional efforts to limit war profits.

TAX PROGRAM WILL STAND

Washington, April 9 (AP)—Secretary Morgenthau said today the Treasury's $7,000,000,000 tax program will stand unchanged "until there is a public announcement by the President that the amount is to be changed."

SENATOR ASSAILS PLANT CONTRACT

Washington, April 9 (AP)—Senator Bunker (D-Nev.) charged in a Senate address today that an agreement between the Defense Plant Corporation and Basic Magnesium, Inc., of Cleveland, O., for construction of a $53,000,000 magnesium refinery at Las Vegas, Nev., "is so sinster as to indicate that some officials of our government are guilty of malfeasance."

Fire Sweeps Melvin Property

All Outbuildings Destroyed At Aberdeen

Fire today swept all buildings at Aberdeen, the home of Judge Ridgely P. Melvin, with the exception of the house.

The blaze destroyed the stable, barn, garage and other outbuildings. An automobile and a small boat used as a yacht tender were destroyed. No livestock was destroyed.

Rotarians Plan Program At USO

Club To Entertain Service Men Tonight At Center

An evening of entertainment for service men at the USO club tonight will be sponsored by the Rotary Club.

Featured on the program will be Capt. Charles C. Slayton and his magic tricks. Rotarians and their wives will be guests of the club and will furnish the refreshments.

In charge will be F. Marion Lazenby, chairman of the community service committee, and the members of his group include Guy C. Hendry, USO director, Mayor William U. McCready, Senator Louis N. Phipps, David S. Jenkins, Walter H. Myers and William A. Strohm

Preceding the entertainment, club members will meet at 6:30 for dinner at Carvel Hall in place of the regular luncheon meeting Members will give talks on the various phases of Rotary as part of a program planned by the club service committee composed of George Fox, chairman, Joseph D. Lazenby, R. Tilghman Brice, Robley D. Roane, John Smearman and Jesse G. Simpson.

Prof. Earl W. Thomson is president of the club.

Civitans Hear Talk On Health Work In County

Dr. French Describes Activities Of His Department

The work of the Anne Arundel County Health Department was outlined by Dr. William J. French, county health officer last night, at the regular monthly dinner meeting of the Civitan Club.

He declared that the department was engaged in "big business," and listed the many services in which it is employed, including civilian defense work.

"The department is very complicated," he said. "It embraces a tremendous number of activities and we have taken in a large number of other agencies and large groups of lay people."

Lists Staff

He said the department had 15

(Continued on Page Six)

JUDGE MELVIN ENDORSED FOR CHIEF JUDGESHIP OF CIRCUIT BY STATE CENTRAL COMMITTEE

Assured Of United Democratic Party Backing By Action Of Party's Offical Governing Body—Democratic Committee Calls Upon All Party Members And Citizens To Support Judge At The Polls Both At Primary And General Elections

Judge Ridgely P. Melvin today was assured of the backing of the united Democratic party for election to the chief judgeship of the Fifth Judicial Circuit when the Democratic State Central Committee of Anne Arundel county adopted a resolution endorsing his candidacy.

The resolution, signed by John L. Stiff, chairman, and Thomas W. Wilmer, Mrs. Bessie Dorsey Moss, John Lipin, Thomas B. Williams and J. A. Ford, members of the committee, follows:

Text Of Resolution

"Whereas, the Democratic State Central Committee of Anne Arundel county is the official governing body of the party in this county, representing the Democratic party as a whole and not any faction or factions thereof; and

"Whereas, this year the voters of this county, along with the voters of Howard and Carroll counties, will choose a chief judge of the Fifth Judicial Circuit, and Anne Arundel county is presenting as its candidate Hon. Ridgely P. Melvin, present associate judge; and

Unanimous Endorsement

"Whereas, Judge Melvin has received the unanimous endorsement of the Bar Association of Anne Arundel County, pointing to his eminent qualifications for the chief judgeship, which is borne out by grand jury reports and others who have had dealings with the court, all speaking of him with the highest praise; and

"Whereas, the whole county has every reason to be proud of Judge Melvin and the record he has made while serving on our court, thereby fully earning the right to promotion to the highest court of Maryland, which this county has not been represented on since the time of Chief Judge Oliver Miller fifty years ago.

"Therefore, be it resolved by the Democratic State Central Committee of Anne Arundel county that we, officially speaking for the party as a whole, hereby heartily endorse Hon. Ridgely P. Melvin for the office of chief judge of the Fifth Judicial Circuit of Maryland, and call upon all members of the party and citizens to support him at the polls both at the primary and the general elections to be held this year."

United Front

Previously several elements of the Democratic party had endorsed Judge Melvin's candidacy, but the action taken by the central committee, the official governing body of the party, assures him of a united party front.

Judge Melvin's candidacy was launched in January by the Bar Association of Anne Arundel county, which unanimously endorsed him at a regular meeting and proposed him as the county's candidate for the chief judgeship of the circuit.

The Fifth Judicial Circuit consists of Anne Arundel, Howard and Carroll counties, and the voters of these three counties will choose the chief judge next fall.

The incumbent is Judge William Henry Forsythe, Jr., of Howard county, who was appointed in November, 1941, to succeed former Chief Judge Francis Neal Parke of Carroll county, who retired at that time because of the age limit. Judge Forsythe, an announced candidate this year, will reach the age limit in May, 1944.

Would Stay On Bench

Judge Melvin's friends declared that he has earned the elevation to the Court of Appeals through his career at the bar and on the county bench.

His election to the chief judgeship would not mean his retirement from the Anne Arundel county court or the appointment of a new judge for the county. Judge Melvin would continue to preside in the local court, except when his duties required his services in the Court of Appeals. At such times one of the associate judges from either Howard or Carroll counties would take over his duties in the Anne Arundel court.

This has been the established practice in the circuit courts of the State when the Court of Appeals is in session. The pressure of court work in Howard and Carroll counties is lighter than in Anne Arundel.

It also was pointed out that Anne Arundel county has not had a chief judge of the Fifth Judicial Circuit for 50 years, although the court business here is estimated to be at least double that of either of the other two counties.

State Guard Adopts New Service Plan

Men May Enlist In One Of Four Echelons

Reorganization of the Maryland State Guard has resulted in "a place for every man" to join the home-defense corps, Capt. T. Chattle Hopkins, commanding officer of Co. B, Annapolis company of the guard, said today.

Under the new plan, announced recently by Gov. Herbert R. O'Conor, the company will be formed of four "echelons," Captain Hopkins said three of the echelons, will be limited to either emergency-duty only, or to one or two-week periods of normal-duty service. The remaining echelon, limited to fourteen men, will be available for continuous duty if needed for usual guard purposes.

Allows More To Serve

"The new plan will allow more men to enlist and be trained as State Guardsmen," Capt. Hopkins explained, "because it will not take them from their regular employment unless an emergency develops. Under the former plan, all our men were subject to duty call at any time, and this resulted in many hardships, both to the men and to their employers.

"Now, our largest echelon will be composed of what might be termed reserves; those available only in case of an emergency which, in all probability, would disrupt normal employment, anyway."

Enlistments in any of the four echelons chosen by the applicant are now being received at the Annapolis Armory, on Bladen street, daily from 8 to 10 P. M., Captain Hopkins said.

War Films Will Be Show For Red Cross Benefit

Proceeds Will Go For Mobile Canteen Equipment

A showing of motion pictures of America and Britain at war will be given in the Calvary Methodist Church tomorrow.

The proceeds from the sale of tickets for this film entertainment will be used for the purchase of mobile canteen equipment under the local chapter of the American Red Cross.

Three separte showings of the war pictures have been arranged, including matinee performances for school children and students of St. John's college and others at 3:30 and 5:15 P. M. The evening showing starts at 8 P. M.

The motion picture showing is

(Continued on Page Six)

GIBSON ISLAND YOUTH SEEKS NAVY WINGS

Charles English Henderson, III of Gibson Island, is among the 440 fledgling pilots who reported in today to the Navy's two main flight training centers, Pensacola and Corpus Christi.

Products of United States Naval Reserve bases, the pilots are seeking their navy wings and commissions as ensigns in the Naval Reserve.

They have already successfully completed the one-month course in preliminary flight training and will embark immediately on the advanced flight training course given at the two big centers in Florida and Texas.

36,853 American-Filipino Defenders Of Bataan Facing Death Or Capture

ADMIRAL NIMITZ HONORS NAVAL HEROES

Admiral Chester W. Nimitz (right), commander in chief of the Pacific fleet, presents a navy cross to one of 24 officers and men so honored aboard a battleship at Pearl Harbor, T. H., for heroism during the Japanese assault on that American base December 7. This is the first newsphoto transmitted from Honolulu to San Francisco in a new radiophoto service.

HEROIC 3-MONTHS BATTLE ENDS; BRITISH LOSE TWO CRUISERS

American Troops Still Hold Manila Bay Forts—British Cruisers Cornwall And Dorsetshire Sunk By Japanese Bombers—British Submarine Sinks Italian Cruiser—Big Naval Battle Forecast In Bay Of Bengal—Understanding Reported Near In India Russians Claim Heavy German Air Losses—Berlin Admits Russians Broke Nazi Lines Near Orel—Battle In Libya Desert

Capture or death at the hands of invading Japanese hordes faced the bulk of 36,853 gallant American-Filipino defenders of Bataan peninsula today, closing an heroic three-months battle against numerically overwhelming forces.

Exhausted by short rations and disease, and virtually cut off from supplies despite costly efforts which provided some ammunition but did not relieve the food shortage, the doughty defenders fell back before the Japanese who already had overrun the rich Dutch Indies and Britain's Singapore and Malaya.

Secretary of War Stimson related the first details concerning the defenders today, after a special communique had announced that the defense of Bataan had probably been overcome, and said President Roosevelt had authorized the Philippine commander to make any decision he deemed necessary in the light of events.

BRITISH LOSE TWO CRUISERS

There was a round-about radio report from Berlin, quoting a Shanghai newspaper report that Lieut. Gen. Johnathan M. Wainwright, commander on Bataan, had sought an armistice, but this was not confirmed in any other quarter.

Latest reports, Stimson said, indicated that Corregidor and other fortresses guarding Manial Bay were still in United States hands, as was about half the area of the Philippines, but he declined to make predictions how long the forts could be held. He saw no reason why resistance by small, isolated forces would not continue.

Two British, 8-inch gun cruisers, the 10,000-ton Conwall and the 9,975-ton Dorsetshire, whose torpedoes finished off the German battleship Bismafk little less than a year ago, have been sunk by Japanese bombers ranging the Bay of Bengal and battering at thin-stretched British naval communications to India, the British Admiralty announced.

Italian Cruiser Sunk

From New Delhi, it was announced also that combined Japanese naval and air attacks had resulted in the sinking of several Allied merchant ships in the Indian Ocean area. From 400 to 500 survivors had landed on the Orissa coast.

The shock of the loss of the two powerful ships rubbed the gilt off the Admiralty's announcement two hours earlier that a British submarine had sent a 10,000-ton Italian cruiser to the bottom of the central Mediterranean.

Japanese broadcasts quoted Imperial headquarters' claims that, in addition to the cruisers, Japanese forces sank 21 Allied merchantmen in the Bay of Bengal up to last Tuesday, and badly damaged 23 other ships.

Expect Naval Battle

Heard, too, without confirmation, was a Berlin broadcast quoting dispatches purportedly from Tokyo that Japanese expeditionary forces, supported by cruisers and destroyers, landed last Sunday on the Burma west coast and were within 30 miles of the Bengal border of India. That would place them between the border and the big Burma port of Akyab Earlier roundabout reports that the Japanese were ashore at Akyab have been denied by the British.

Naval reporters in London said the "biggest naval battle in all history" seems about to blaze up in the Bay of Bengal between the Japanese and British fleets. Last week Axis reports declared a powerful British naval force had been sighted speeding around the Cape of Good Hope en route to the Indian Ocean and the Bay of Bengal.

The city of Trincomalee, where the British have a naval base, was bombed this morning. There were no civilian casualties.

A general understanding on the main points at issue between the British and politically articulate Hindus appeared to be at hand with reported assent by leaders of the All-India Congress party and the Hindu Mahassaba to the establishment of a national government in India.

Such a government would serve India pending the post-war dominion status offered by Britain.

Raid Tulagi

Five Japanese bombers flying at 5,000 feet raided Tulagi, in the Solomon Islands and dropped between 30 and 40 bombs. Japanese occupation of Lorengau on Manus island, largest of the Admiralty group, has been confirmed. A Reuters dispatch from Port Moresby, New Guinea, said that many aircraft were destroyed on the ground and others damaged in an Allied raid on Rabaul.

British headquarters announced

(Continued on Page Two)

Elks Lodge Ends Successful Year

Invests $2,000 In War Bonds; Postpones Building Improvements

Closing one of the most successful years in its history, Annapolis Lodge 622, B. P. O. E., met last night under the chairmanship of James P. Brock, new exalted ruler.

The installing of further improvements to the lodge building was indefinitely postponed and 2,000 was invested in war bonds.

It was announced that the grand lodge of the order will meet in July in Omaha, Neb. Mr. Brock will represent the local lodge.

Other recently installed officers include; Howard B. Pyle, esteemed leading knight; R. Edward Dove, esteemed loyal knight; J. Lloyd Young, esteemed lecturing knight; A. Guy Miller, P.E.R. secretary; T. Earl Duckwall, treasurer; Theodore Echterhoff, tiler; Charles

(Continued On Page Five)

KIWANIS DIRECTORS TO MEET TONIGHT

The Regular monthly business meeting of the board of directors of the Annapolis Kiwanis Club will be held at 8 o'clock tonight at the home of Linwood L. Clark, Horn Point.

The chairmen of the various committees will meet with the board.

FINED $27.50 FOR ASSAULT

Charged with assault and battery, Charles Ball. 27, colored, was fined $27.50 when he was arraigned before Trial Magistrate James G. Woodward.

Agnes Simms, colored, was fined $6.75 for disorderly conduct and given five days in default. Louis W. Harmon, 37, was fined $6.75 for disorderly conduct. Marie Simms. colored, was fined $2.75 for disorderly conduct.

VAN HOORN FUNERAL SET FOR TOMORROW

Funeral services for Albert W. W. van Hoorn, Eastport resident who died Tuesday in Washington, will be held at 2:30 P. M. tomorrow from the Taylor funeral home, 147 Duke of Gloucester street.

Burial will be at Sandusky. O.

Mr. van Hoorn, who was born in Batavia, Java is survived by his widow, Helen van Hoorn, and a daughter, Marianna van Hoorn. He lived at 607 Creek View.

HOLD HEARING ON NEW SPA CREEK BRIDGE

Army Engineers Hear Only Favorable Comment At Hearing Held In Court House

Officials from the U. S. District Engineer's office in Baltimore today heard arguments for the immediate construction of the proposed new bridge over Spa creek from Annapolis to Eastport without a dissenting voice.

Lieut. Col. Conrad P. Hardy, district engineer, who ordered the public hearing to be held today in the courthouse, was unable to be present. He was represented by Maj. Paul J. B. Murphy, Corps of Engineers; Lieut. Col. J. A. Doyle, principal engineer; C. C. Warner, senior engineer; H. E. Carmine, assistant engineer, and J. W. Davis, engineering aide.

832-Foot Structure

The State Roads Commission has asked War Department approval of the location and plans of a double leaf bascule bridge to run from Compromise street, Annapolis, to Sixth street, Eastport. The bridge would be 832 feet long, with a vertical underclear-

(Continued on Page Three)

Cross Saves His Life

Second Lieutenant Clarence Sanford (above) of Auburn, N. Y., reported from "somewhere in Australia" that his life had been saved by a silver crucifix from natives of a small Pacific island after he had bailed out of his fighter plane while chasing Japanese warplanes.

Party Tomorrow At Colored USO

G.S.O. To Sponsor Spring Social For Service Men

The Girls Service Organization of the colored USO club will sponsor a spring social tomorrow night at the College Creek social hall for sailors stationed on the U.S.S. Cumberland and soldiers from Fort George G. Meade.

The program will consist of dancing, table games, novelties and refrehments. Alden H. McAuley, director of the unit, will set up a new recording machine and the service men will be able to

(Continued from Page Five)

FIRE DAMAGES HOUSE AT ST. MARGARET'S

Fire, caused by chimney sparks, last night damaged the roof over one room of a house owned by Mr. and Mrs. F. E. Voges on the old Winchester road near St. Margaret's Church.

Earleigh Heights, Eastport and Riveria Beach fire departments responded to the call and extinguished the blazing roof.

The West Annapolis department put out a brush fire on Northwood road, Wardour, yesterday with a waterfront booster tank.

Held For Larceny Of Seven Autos

Harry A. Johnson Under $1,000 Bond For Grand Jury Action

Harry A. Johnson, 18, colored, was held for grand jury action in $1,000 bail. when he was brought before Trial Magistrate James G. Woodward charged with the larceny of seven automobiles.

Charges of the larceny of six automobiles filed against William Parker, 17, colored, were dismissed and he was held in $1,000 as a State's witness.

Police said Johnson was picked up on Mar. 26 and two automobile keys were found in his possession. Later they said he admitted taking two additional machines. Still later they said he admitted taking one more in the city and two in Eastport.

Parker was taken into cutody after police questioned Johnson.

Police declared all the automobiles involved had been recovered.

POLICE OFFICER SHOOTS OVER HEADS OF TWO FLEEING SAILORS

A local police officer fired a shot over the heads of two colored sailors on Conduit street last night when they fled as he was investigating a disturbance.

According to police the sailors and a colored girl were walking on Main street when four white sailors pushed them off the street.

A fight followed which attracted the attention of Patrolman Richard Johnson. Police said the officer talked to the four white sailors, seeking the cause of the trouble, but when he turned to talk to the colored sailors they ran up Conduit street. They said he fired in the air.

War

(Continued From Page One)

province remained stalled west of the Salween river, near the border with Burma. The Flying Tigers of the American Volunteer Group yesterday bombed Japanese positions and returned to their base without loss.

In the Australian theater, the long-range air duel between the Japanese in their island bases facing Australia on the north and the American-Australian airmen continued over the week-end.

On Saturday the Allies bombed Amboina in the Dutch East Indies —a 1,300 - mile roundtrip—and either by luck or suicide a Japanese plane, winged by anti-aircraft fire, struck an Allied vessel amidships, several hundred miles off Australia, and set her afire. An Allied destroyer removed 100 survivors, many of them injured.

Mexico Near War

Three allied planes were lost in the raids. Twenty Allied bombs fell among a group of about 20 grounded planes at Vunakanau airdrome, New Britain. Three

SONGS BUTCHERED NIGHTLY

You ought to hear how some of our girls mangle a piece of music. Who they don't know about singing would fill a library. But what they know about creating fun is what you're after and your laughs are waiting for you tonight. Swap a frown for a smile and a song for your cares. You'll feel better for it and your pocketbook won't even feel the difference.

OASIS CABARET
Baltimore Street at Frederick
Open Nightly and Sundays to 2 A. M.
Baltimore, Md.

Japanese Zero fighters were shot down.

Mexico moved slowly toward a formal declaration of war on the Axis powers.

Bern, Switzerland, reported that Germans critical of Pierre Laval's failure to bring France into full collaboration with them, had revived rumors that the Vichy chief of government might step out.

Air War

High-flying RAF fighters streaked over the British southeast coast in mid-morning apparently bound across the English channel for a resumption of daylight attacks on targets in occupied France.

German night raiders dropped bombs at several places along the coast of southern England and some damage and a few casualties were reported. One of the raiders was downed.

Observers in Moscow said the Kharkov battle appeared to have settled into an exchange of savage blows resembling a slugging match between two heavyweights. Masses of modern material, including medium and heavy tanks, the latest model planes and fast-firing guns were in action while the bulk of the infantry on both sides were locked in battle.

In the Izyum-Barvenkova sector the Russians said they were inflicting heavy losses on German infantry and mechanized forces.

TROLLEYS, BUSES HALT IN CLEVELAND

CLEVELAND, May 25 (AP)— Dozens of street cars and buses on city transit lines were halted today in what appeared to be a widespread strike. The stoppage occurred about 11 A. M., while many department store workers were starting downtown for the usual Monday noon opening of stores here.

The Marine band is fondly dubbed the granddaddy of American bands, for it dates back to 1800.

STRONG ARM OF THE UNITED NATIONS—This B-24 Consolidated heavy bomber is of the type used by the United Nations to blast Axis factories and ships. Gun in tail gives protection where bombers were once vulnerable. (U. S. Army Signal Corps Photo.)

Army-Navy Sport Teams Meet Wednesday

Baseball Game And Track Meets Will Be Held Here

The Navy spring sport squads will end their seasons on Wednesday when they meet Army teams in lacrosse, tennis, golf, baseball and track.

The baseball game will be played on Lawrence Field at the Naval Academy at 2:30 P. M. The track meet will be held in the Thompson Stadium, academy football field, at 3:30 P. M.

The Navy baseball team has won 14 games during the season and lost three. The Army team has won nine, lost five and tied one.

Army Team Undefeated

The midshipmen track and field team has four victories to its credit. It placed third in the quadrangular meet with Princeton, Pennsylvania and Columbia. The Army team also has four wins but is undefeated.

No special tickets will be required for admission to the baseball game and track meet. However, admission to the Naval Academy will be governed by the regulations in effect during war time. These regulations limit admission to officers, civilian instructors and midshipmen and guests accompanying them and to other members of the armed forces when properly identified.

Middies Leave Tomorrow

The Navy contingent going to West Point will leave here at 8:30 A. M. tomorrow, with Comdr. H. F. Cope, U.S.N., in charge of the party. They are scheduled to return to the Academy at 7:10 A. M. Thursday, in time for early morning classes.

The army track and baseball squads will arrive here at 2:40 P. M. tomorrow and will leave on the return trip to West Point Wednesday after the contests. The West Point athletes will be accompanied by Maj. J. E. Metzler, officer in charge of baseball; Maj. T. R. Stoughton, Jr., assistant to Major Metzler; Capt. H. P. Van-Ormer, officer in charge of track, and First Lieut. George Schwab, assistant graduate manager of athletics.

33 DIE IN FLASH FLOODS

HONESDALE, Pa., May 25.— This once-gay mountain resort town of 5,687, grieving for its dead and missing, waged a grim fight against disease today as the death toll in eastern Pennsylvania's week-end flash floods rose to 33.

Scores were still missing and feared drowned in a devastated area extending from Chester county on the south to Wayne county on the north as the Lackawaxen, Lehigh, Schuylkill and Delaware rivers receded over layers of bacteria-laden mud.

WEEK'S SAFETY TIP

The Maryland Traffic Safety Commission's slogan for the week is:

"It's not the car that runs wild, it's the driver. Drive under 40."

May Reclassify Family Men

WASHINGTON, May 25 (AP)— Congress considered today proposals to give President Roosevelt broad authority to revamp the selective service system by classifying family men into groups who would be called for army duty only after the rolls of those without dependents had been exhausted.

Explaining that the selective service hoped to set up general classifications based on family relationship and economic dependency, Senator Johnson (Dem., Colo.) predicted that the Senate Military Affairs Committee would amend a pending family allowance bill tomorrow to vest such authority in the President.

Linked with reports that an effort soon would be made to make men of 19 and 20 subject to the draft, legislation of this nature was expected to clear up the status of older men, and those with dependents, who now are subject to induction into active service at the discretion of local boards.

EXPECTED TO RETURN TO TRAILER CAMP

Five Who Left On Hearing Rumor Expected Back

Five defense workers who left a trailer camp at Riviera Beach, were expected to return after the scotching of a rumor that Anne Arundel county planned to levy a heavy tax on trailers.

Residents of the camp of trailers said the five pulled out with their trailers when they heard a rumor that the county had suddenly decided to tax all cars and trailers from $100 to $500, and that the tax must be paid in full by 8 A. M. today.

George Cromwell, county budget director, said the report apparently stemmed from misinterpretation of a plan under discussion to tax trailers for their use of public facilities, with trailers perhaps assessed as personal property at $100.

SWAIN SWOONED

SPOKANE, Wash. (AP)—Policeman M. A. Clinton dashed off on an emergency call—man reported stricken!

Chagrined but enlightened, he came back to headquarters and filed his report:

"False alarm. Young millworker fainted while embracing his girl."

O'Conor Sees

(Continued From Page One)

the State military police. The police group suffered two "casualties." These were tagged, taken to a Red Cross mobile unit and transported to the casualty station at the Woodland Beach club by the Red Cross Motor Corps.

Minute Men

The Mayo Minute Men, commanded by Darce Stonebraker, were acting as connecting files between the State military police advance guard and the main body of Minute Men. This main body was composed of the St. Margaret's company, commanded by Orlando Ridout, the Woodland Beach-Edgewater Company, commanded by William Wesley Stevens and the Riva unit, under command of Carl W. Riddick.

After the first contact the "enemy" troops fell back on their supports about 500 yards down the Camp Letts' road where another fire action took place as the Minute Men companies began building up the firing line in support of the advance guard. In this skirmish the Minute Men took three "prisoners" and suffered five "casualties."

Defenders Deploy

Then the "enemy" outpost troops fell back to the main line of the "parachutists" along the edge of a woods overlooking a field.

The advance guard of the Minute Men held them under fire until all the companies of Minute Men had deployed and formed a firing line. Then the actual "battle" joined when the State Guard company assumed to be in Annapolis was en route to join the defense forces.

Both combatant lines used smoke, the "parachutists" to mask their retreat to positions further back in the woods and the Minute Men to cover their deployment and advance.

Governor Speaks

D. W. Webber, commander of the Civil Patrol Squadron, led the airplanes that took part. Other aviators were Bill Shaab, Harry Gilden, J. Watson, H. Doepkins and W. Miller.

The "battle" was halted for a short time after the first contact and prisoner capture to allow Governor O'Conor to address the Minute Men.

He told them they were organized primarily for the protection of their homes, wives, children and loved ones.

He said the Minute Men would be used for home defense only.

"I promise you that nothing of a selfish, personal or political nature will be permitted to enter this organization," he declared.

BALTIMORE TO HAVE BLACKOUT

BALTIMORE, May 25 (AP)—The Baltimore committee on civilian defense today ordered a three-hour blackout, starting at 9 P. M. Wednesday, June 3, affecting all homes and buildings.

The test will be followed a few days later by an all-night dusk-to-dawn blackout.

NOVA-SAVOLD FIGHT TONIGHT

WASHINGTON, May 25 (AP)—The twice-postponed Lou Nova-Lee Savold heavyweight scrap comes up again tonight, weather permitting, with each fighter forecasting a victory that may lead to a shot at Joe Louis and the title of the boxing world.

STATE GUARD WILL COOPERATE WITH ARMY IN EMERGENCY

Maryland's State Guard would be used in cooperation with regular army forces in event of extreme emergency Governor O'Conor reported today.

The Governor said he has been advised by Maj. Gen. Milton A. Reckord, Third Corps Area Commander, that the War Department has adopted plans to have State Guards and regular army troops join hand in resisting threatened invasion.

Reckord has asked for approval of the use of State forces and, O'Conor said, reporting he replied "the fullest possible use of the Maryland Guard will be available and ready for a call whenever it might be issued by the War Department."

The War Department, O'Conor reported, assured him that under present plans it is not contemplated to use State Guardsmen out side state boundaries and they will not be commanded by Federal Military officers, but will continue to take orders from the Governor.

The State Guard also will receive increased training by the army and additional equipment to the extent it can be spared from Federal troops, the Governor said.

Army Corps Area commanders soon will make available instructors for the Guard and also will provide further training aids, O'Conor said. Frequent tests and alerts are planned for Guardsmen, he explained, to promote efficieny.

Maryland's Guard now numbers about 2,500, O'Conor said. Recently it was praised by War Department officials following a general inspection.

"This latest War Department move," the Governor added, "justifies the organization of 'Minute Men' companies of Reserve Militia in various state areas." There still is no plan to call the Minute Men for active Guard duty, O'Conor said.

FREIGHTER DAMAGED IN BALTIMORE

BALTIMORE, May 25 (AP)—Fire breaking out in the hold caused "considerable damage" today to a large freighter taking on cargo at Pennsylvania railroad pier No 1, Canton.

The blaze was brought under control by the fireboat Deluge and several pieces of ground equipment.

FDR CONGRATULATES JAP-SHOOTING PILOT

Lieut. George S. Welch of Wilmington, Del., gets a hearty handshake from President Roosevelt and congratulations for shooting down four Japanese planes in the attack on Pearl Harbor, Dec. 7. Left to right are: Sen. James H. Hughes (D-Del); Mrs. Hughes, Mrs. George Schwartz, Welch's mother; George Schwartz, his stepfather; and Lieut. Welch.

Report Rubber Out For Cars For Three Years

Would Conserve 1,000,000 Tons Now On Motor Vehicles

WASHINGTON, May 25 (AP)—The Senate defense investigating committee criticized the army and navy today for not paring their rubber requirements to the bone, asserting that if the production of synthetics did not come up to schedule the military forces "may find themselves without rubber at some future date."

In a 57-page report, the committee said:

National gasoline rationing on "a sensible basis" and the requisitioning of tires must be given serious consideration to conserve 1,000,000 tons of rubber now on the wheels of motor vehicles.

There will be no new or reclaimed rubber at all for non-essential users within the next three years.

The best that could be expected from a successful synthetic program would be to supply military needs and essential civilian requirements, such as tires for cars transporting defense workers.

Resources in this hemisphere offer little hope of adding substantially to United Nations supplies of crude rubber, which price Administrator Leon Henderson testified would be exhausted by May, 1943, even with the greatest possible curtailment of civilian uses.

The committee recommended that "some one person" be designated to assume full responsibility over the rubber program. Such a task recently was assigned by Donald M. Nelson, war production chief, to Arthur Newhall.

County Blackout

(Continued from Page One)

of conditions will be simulated: bomb damage, fires, casualties and refugees.

The chiefs of the emergency services, gatherd at the control center, will be assigned the problems falling within their divisions and will issue the orders to start their services operating.

Auxiliary police received full instructions for the blackout last night.

Tonight at 7 P. M. the air raid signal at the Independent Fire company will be tested.

SHRIVER HEADS ARSENAL BOARD

Samuel H. Shriver of Pikesville will begin a six-year term June 1 as chairman of the State Board of the Arsenal and Veterans Memorial Commission.

Appointment of Shriver, son of the late George H. Shriver, commission chairman, was announced by Governor O'Conor. O'Conor also reappointed Dr. W. P. E. Wyse of Baltimore to the board. Terms of the late Mr. Shriver and Wyse were to expire June 1.

O'CONOR ISSUES VOTE PROCLAMATION

Governor O'Conor today issued a proclamation providing that Marylanders in the armed services may vote by mail in State and Congressional elections this year.

The Governor said the army and navy had agreed to help distribute the ballots, which will be sent to about 110,000 Maryland soldiers, sailors, marines and nurses who were granted absentee voting privileges.

TWO KILLED IN PLANT EXPLOSION

LANSING, MICH., May 26 (AP)—At least two men were killed and three seriously injured in an explosion which shattered part of the Fisher Body Corporation plant here today.

The plant is engaged in war material production. Fire following the explosion was brought under control.

A plant official said one end of a building was "pretty badly damaged" but that he did not know the cause or how many men were working in the section.

The explosion occurred at approximately 8:35 A. M., and was heard throughout the west side of the city.

The dead were identified as Wallace F. Irish, 45, Grand Ledge and Roy H. Anderson, 29, Lansing.

FORT MEADE SOLDIER KILLED

A soldier, tentatively identified by papers in his clothing as Thurman McLamb, 25, of Florence, S. C., a private at nearby Fort Meade, was found dead at the Baltimore and Ohio railroad station at Laurel today, apparently the victim of a train.

No witnesses to the accident were found but authorities said the soldier apparently was struck by a through freight train while lying or sitting on the station platform near the rails.

Dr. James I. Boyd, Prince George's county medical examiner, issued a certificate of accidental death.

STRAWBERRY FEST.VAL CANCELLED - NO SUGAR

The strawberry festival planned for tonight at Trinity Methodist Church is a casualty of the war.

Members of the Women's Society of Christian Service, sponsor organization, were unable to get sugar for the event and the festival has been cancelled.

War

(Continued From Page One)

out to be the toughest battles this summer in Asia," the spokesman continued. "Our most urgent needs are for air forces and transportation."

The Japanese apparently also were preparing another campaign in the Fukis province which borders Chekiang province to the south.

Bomb Rabaul and Lae

Allied bombers again blasted Japanese airdromes at Rabaul, New Britain and Lae, New Guinea from Australian bases.

Gen Douglas MacArthur's headquarters said four Japanese planes were shot down. One Allied plane was lost.

London announced that British troops have withdrawn entirely from Burma.

At Recife, Brazil, the rescue ship Rio Iguazu, with survivors from an unidentified ship variously reported to number from 52 to 25, was expected almost hourly. Authorities were unable to confirm Axis broadcasts that the survivors were from a U. S. battleship of the Maryland class which the Italians have claimed was sunk by one of their submarines.

Brazilians officials said U. S. authorities had not communicated with port officers, the usual procedure when a vessel is arriving with U. S. survivors, and expressed doubt that the men aboard the rescue ship were from a U. S. vessel.

Claim Convoy Battered

Radio Berlin claimed Nazi bombers sank an 8,000-ton merchantman and damaged five others with bomb hits in an attack on a convoy between Iceland and the North Cape. Light German warplanes also were reported to have crippled a medium-sized merchant ship off the British east coast.

Paris newspapers said that fighter-escorted British bombers had bombed St. Omer in occupied France, killing six persons and wounding eight.

Rome announced that the Italian airmen had destroyed nine British planes without loss to themselves.

In the French situation, the Germans were portrayed as using the Italian territorial demands on France as a threat to force Vichy to give up the French fleet.

Laval was reported to have offered to negotiate the Italian demands with a disarming offer to discuss Tunisia. His reported agreement to allow German sailors to train in French navy yards was taken as a possibly placatory negotiating move with the Nazis.

A U. S. war mission, headed by Lieut. Gen. Henry H. Arnold, chief of the Army air force and Rear Admiral John H. Towers, chief of naval aeronautics, arrived in London.

Admiral Sir Andrew Browne Cunningham, until recently commander-in-chief of Britain's Mediterranean fleet, promised "complete victory" for the Allies in the Mediterranean once Britain and the United States meet the Axis' air and surface fleets on terms of equality.

Brownie Scouts To Give Program

Will Entertain Mothers Thursday At German-Town School

For the last meeting of the year, the Brownie Scouts of Germantown school will entertain their mothers Thursday at 3:15 P. M., in the auditorium.

In addition to play activities demonstrated by the pack under the leadership of Mrs. W. F. Treat and Mrs. Jack Wood, several Brownies will present dances in costume. An acrobatic number will be given by Jean Palmer, ballet by Patricia Hill, toe by Jane Carr, tap by Joan Donaldson, and song by Audrey Miller.

Refreshments are in charge of Mrs. J. L. Basil and Mrs. F. W. Harder.

TWO LOCAL SOLDIERS WIN COMMISSIONS AT FORT KNOX SCHOOL

FORT KNOX, Ky., May 26—Two Anne Arundel county soldiers have graduated from the Armored Force Officer Candidate School here and received commissions as second lieutenants, U. S. Army.

The two—Second Lieutenants Harry P. Levely, Jr., of Annapolis, and John S. Hunner, of Pasadena, were members of the first class to be graduated from this department of the Armored Force School. Most of the graduates will be assigned to duty with an armored division or tank battalion.

For the past three months these new officers have received detailed training regarding all eight branches of the armored force, including the actual maintenance and operation of the main types of vehicles. They also received training in shop practice and classroom work, tactical operations in the field and physical conditioning.

JEWISH COUNCIL TO ELECT OFFICERS

Officers will be elected at the annual meeting of the Annapolis Section, National Council of Jewish Women, at 8 P. M. tomorrow at the local synagogue.

Dessert will be served to the members prior to the meeting. Mrs. H. Reichel will preside.

Moose To Initiate

(Continued From Page One)

tary J. Allen Levay, of the local Moose lodges, No. 296, "nevertheless, it is now engaged in building a class in honor of our graduates of Mooseheart and those former graduates now in the armed services.

"Mooseheart is an educational and philanthropic enterprise supported by the 1,500 and more lodges of the Moose fraternity. All Mooseheart graduates belong to our lodge as much as to any other.

"This school class," concluded the secretary, "will exceed 1,500 candidates from the participating lodges alone. Including the number of candidates in this honor class from all the lodges, this number may reach 25,000."

Acquatic School

(Continued From Page One)

swimming, life-saving, accident prevention, first aid, and the handling of canoes and other small craft.

Serving with Mr. Zubrod as members of the faculty are six national representatives of the Red Cross, several chapter directors and a number of volunteers. National field representatives include: William H. Karl, Holman G. Marks, William B. Simpson, J. Roy Zoeller, Grant McCubbin and Max Rotc.

Chapter directors of First Aid and Water Safety participating are: Dudley Bradstreet, Richmond, V.; Clarence Frank, Reading Pa.; Oscar Hoar, Baltimore; Frank Holt, Philadelphia; John Komp, Pittsburgh; Len Pielmeier, Altoona, Pa., and Robert H. Duncan, Washington.

LATE NEWS

Evening Capital

WEATHER
Somewhat Cooler Tonight

VOL. LVIII — NO. 135. EVERY EVENING EXCEPT SUNDAY ANNAPOLIS, MD., MONDAY, JUNE 8, 1942. SOUTHERN MARYLAND'S ONLY DAILY THREE CENTS.

PLANE CRASHES; BOMBS EXPLODE

Fort Benning, Ga., June 8 (AP)—An airplane crashed on the Fort Benning reservation today and Lt. Russell Hammargren, Public Relations officer, said the craft's load of bombs exploded.

The plane fell some 15 miles from the post headquarters and it was not immediately determined whether there had been loss of life.

SENATE VOTES ON SERVICE PAY

Washington, June 8 (AP) —The Senate voted today to increase the minimum pay in the armed forces to $50 monthly, to raise that of first class privates and corresponding naval ratings to $54 and to make all pay increases effective as of June 1.

JEHOVAH'S WITNESSES LOSE COURT CASE

Washington, June 8 (AP)—The Supreme Court ruled today that a municipal ordinance requiring a license for peddlers may constitutionally be applied to a member of "Jehovah's Witnesses" engaged in distributing literature for which contributions were solicited.

College Seniors Told To Combat Evils Of World

Baccalaureate Sermon Distinguishes Between Martyrdom, Suicide

Members of the St. John's College graduating class, who will receive their diplomas tomorrow morning, were charged yesterday not to flee from the evils of the world and not to hate the world but to love it "in all its sin and misery, as God loves it."

The Rev. J. Winfree Smith, tutor at the college, who preached

(Continued on Page Six)

BRYANT FUNERAL HELD SATURDAY

Funeral services for Mrs. Marie C. Bryant, wife of Fred Bryant, of Crownsville, were conducted Saturday morning from St Mary's Catholic Church by the Rev. Cornelius Sullivan.

Serving as pallbearers were Joseph Grimes, William M. Feldmeyer, Charles Gates, William Dawson, John Bryant and F. L. Lyons. Burial was in Lorraine Cemetery, Baltimore.

Mrs. Bryant, who was 52, died Wednesday in Mercy Hospital, Baltimore. She was born in Baltimore on Jan. 19, 1890.

B. L. Hopping was the funeral director.

Motorists Will Get About Four Gallons Of Gas

WASHINGTON, June 8 (AP)—President Roosevelt, who has been surveying the possibility of nation-wide rationing of gasoline as a measure for conserving tires, invited three House members to the White House today to talk over the problems involved.

WASHINGTON, June 8 (AP)—East coast motorists will get an average basis ration of nearly four gallons of gasoline a week under the regular coupon-book system starting next month, Joel Dean, OPA fuel rationing administrator, said today.

Under the present temporary program, non-essential drivers are allowed about three gallons weekly.

Dean told reporters the additional ration would be permitted because of tightened controls made possible under the new plan. Considerably fewer "B" coupons will be issued, Dean explained, since motorists will be required to prove need for supplemental allowances.

To Be Model

They must show to the satis-

(Continued on Page Six)

ASSOCIATED DEMOCRATS WILL MEET AT FIRST WARD CLUB TUESDAY

The Associated Democratic Clubs of Anne Arundel county will hold their monthly meeting Tuesday night at the local First Ward Club.

The association monthly meetings are held at the club houses of the clubs enrolled in the organization.

John Lipin, president of the Associated Clubs, will preside.

Eevry Democratic candidate who has announced or filed for office will be invited to attend the meeting.

DR. HUTCHINS PRAISES SYSTEM OF INSTRUCTION AT ST. JOHN'S

Addresses Seniors At Class Day Exercises—Commencement Tomorrow

Dr. Robert Maynard Hutchins, president of the University of Chicago, told 17 St. John's College seniors today that he considers himself to be "on the educational level of a St. John's sophomore."

Nineteen students will receive their degrees at 11 A. M., tomorrow at graduation ceremonies to be held under the old Liberty Tree on th front campus. Stringfellow Barr, president of the college will make the address and present the diplomas.

The students, graduates, faculty and guests will march in academic procession from McDowell Hall to the stands under the tree for the ceremony. Two of the students will receive master of arts degrees.

Class Day Exercises

Speaking at Class Day exercises, Dr. Hutchins gave what he termed "the auto-biography of a boy who ever went to St. John's."

He described his own college life, which he said brought him to a college presidency after he had "closed my educational career a wholly uneducated man."

Dr. Hutchins, a member of the St. John's Board of Visitors

(Continued on Page Six)

Middies Start Final Tests

Companies Also Compete For "Color Girl" Honor

Final examinations—the jinx of many midshipmen—began today at the Naval Academy.

For some 615 first classmen, the exams are the last barrier to long-sought commissions as navy ensigns. For the remaining 2,500 midshipmen, they're a tedious problem that must be solved if they hope to be elevated in the regimental ranks.

The majority of midshipmen forsook week-end liberties to re-

(Continued on Page Three)

RED CROSS GROUPS TO FINISH COURSE

A class of approximately 75 members of the Red Cross Motor Corps, Canteen Corps and Staff Assistant Corps will graduate tonight at Linthicum Heights.

The classes for the different corps were arranged under the direction of Mrs. C. W. Reilly, chairman of Volunteer Services of the Red Cross for northern Anne Arundel county.

Certificates will be issued to members of the nutrition classes and the production groups.

V.F.W. Guests Of USO Tonight

Part Of Nation-Wide Observance

The Veterans of Foreign Wars and the Ladies' Auxiliary will be guests at a dance tonight at the USO Club.

This is a nation-wide observance in USO Clubs over the country to acquaint former service men with present day hospitality for men of the armed forces. For those who wish other activity than dancing, there will be games and cards on the "lower deck" of the club. The Strodusters will play for dancing. All girls must present guests cards for admission.

There will be an evening of square dancing tomorrow to the tune of USO director Guy Hendry's fiddle and the piano playing of bandsman Fred Magliano. D. W. Bell will call the dances. This may develop into a regular feature of USO Club program.

The Hendry home on Weems Creek will be the scene of a Port Watch picnic on Wednesday evening. Thse weekly picnics are drawing a group of young people who enjoy getting out in the open playing strenuous games, swimming, and cooking a meal over an open fire.

The group of ladies who serve regularly as hostesses for the club plan to hold a business meeting at the club on Thursday at 10 A. M. to make plans for their part in the dedication week for the new building. All chairmen of committees were urged to attend together with other regular hostesses who are interested in the plans.

(Continued on Page Three)

F. B. PICKERING WINS COMMISSION

Frederick B. Pickering, Ferry Farms, has been commissioned a second lieutenant upon graduation from the Coast Artillery Officer Candidate School of the U. S Army at Camp Davis, N. C.

Pickering, who was employed with an importing firm in New York city before he entered the army was a first class private when he was sent to the officer's school.

MUSIC STUDENTS GIVE PIANO RECITAL

Pupils of Mrs. Adrienne Ross gave a piano recital yesterday in Carvel Hall.

An outstanding performance was given by Allan Willey, of Bay Ridge, who played Chopin's "Military Polonaise" and Sibelius' "Romance." He has studied at Peabody Conservatory of Music, Baltimore.

Midway Victory Seen As Placing Jap Forces On Defensive In Pacific War

COLOGNE AFTER R. A. F. RAID

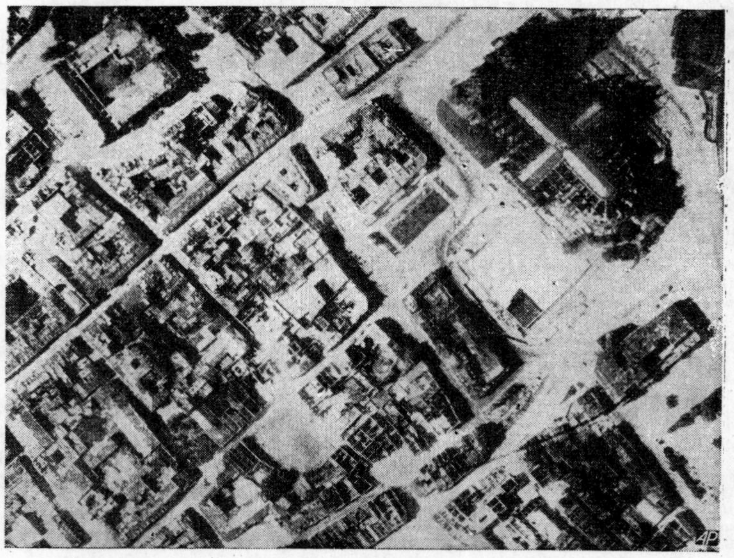

Following the R. A. F.'s 1,000-plane bombing raid on Cologne, a British reconaissance plane made the photo (above), which was cabled from London to New York. The section photographed is part of the city's old town in the heavily bombed business area. The British said the cathedral (top right) appears to have escaped all but superficial blast damage. The street running from left to top right of the photo is the Hohestrasse, described in Baedeker's guide book as the busiest street in Cologne. The famed cathedral's upper structure throws a heavy shadow. Most of the buildings at lower center and right are roofless, gutted by fire with only shells remaining, giving a honeycomb effect.

Test Case On Sunday Work Law

Arrest On USO Building Brings Up Question Of Jurisdiction

The arrest of seven men working on the new USO building yesterday for violation of the State Sunday work law today provided the basis for a test case.

The men were taken into custody by Chief William Curry and Patrolman Mose Rawlings. Later they were released on bond for a hearing at 3 P. M. Wednesday. Mayor William U. McCready furnished the bond.

The city purchased the site at St. Mary's and Compromise street, on which the USO building is being constructed. However, the project was leased to the Federal government, with the title retained by the municipality.

(Continued on Page Four)

WILL TEST AIR RAID WARNING

Col. John deP. Douw, civilian defense director, today gave notice that the air raid system of the community would be given a series of tests on Thursday after 2 P. M.

A factory representative will be in the city that afternoon to adjust the system, and signals will be given from time to time in the course of his work.

NEW RED CROSS SWIM COURSE PLANNED

A Red Cross course in junior and senior life-saving will begin Monday, June 15, from 9 A. M. to noon at Horn Point.

Miss Lillian Herold will be the instructor. Registration will be on the beach at 9 A. M.

Local Ministers Are Reassigned

Assignments Announced At Methodist Conference

Annapolis and Eastport ministers were reassigned to their churches yesterday at the Baltimore annual conference of the Methodist Church, in session at Westminster.

The Rev. Dr. J. Luther Neff was reassigned to Calvary church, the Rev. John J. Dawson to Trinity church, and the Rev. J. E. Stacks to the Eastport church.

Other assignments in the county were: Ferndale-Pasadena, C. L. Felty; Glen Burnie, E. T. Kirkley; Green Haven-Marley Park, W. R. L. Ruths; Marley-Arundel Cove, B. A. Bryan; Linthicum Heights, C. C. Knapp; Riviera Beach, T. H. Baker; Severn-Jessup, W. R.

(Continued on Page Three)

BATTERED JAPANESE FLEET LEAVES BATTLE GROUND; CONTACT LOST

Officials Look For New Japanese Effort To Break Might In Pacific—Situation at Dutch Harbor Still Obscure—Britain Calls On Residents Of German-Occupied Coast To Vacate Area Which Will Be Theater Of Operations—Roosevelt Asks $34,417,827,337 More For Army—British Apparently Hold Upper Hand In Libyan Fighting

A once mighty Japanese naval force, reported to constitute the bulk of that country's sea power, today limped westward in retreat from Midway Island, its units pounded by an American defense turned into a shattering offense.

"The enemy appears to be withdrawing," said Admiral Chester W. Nimitz, commander-in-chief of the Pacific fleet. "Contact was lost during the night."

But even should the Japanese make good their escape it will be only at the cost of at least three warships—two aircraft carriers and a destroyer—sunk, and 11 damaged—one carrier, three battleships, four cruisers and three transports. Against this enemy loss the U. S. Navy counted a destroyer lost and an aircraft carrier damaged. The destroyer was sunk by a Japanese submarine but nearby ships rescued the personnel with small loss of life.

JAPAN SEEN ON DEFENSIVE

With the victory the United States seems to have wrested the initiative from Japan in the battle of the Pacific, at the same time readying for active entry into the battle of Europe. The triumph, coming after the Coral Sea victory, means that a corner has been turned in the second phase of the Pacific war—much sooner than many expected.

Desperate new Japanese efforts to break the growing might of America's air and sea power in the Pacific was predicted in informed quarters in Washington as the only course left open to the enemy. It was pointed out that the Japanese must either initiate new operations somewhere along the sweeping defense line that runs from Alaska to Australia or else by inactivity admit their defeat even before the United Nation's grand offensive begins.

Might Decide War

In Washington, Admiral Ernest J. King, commander-in-chief of the U. S. Fleet, declared that the battle just ending might decide the course of the war in the Pacific, depending on the extent of damage inflicted on the enemy.

He said it would not be "well advised" for the American forces to rush into any territory where the Japanese could bring their land-based bombers and fighter planes in action. The gravity of the action at Midway for the United States was emphasized by the admiral with the assertion that Pearl Harbor, fleet base for which Midway is the most westernmost outpost, "must be held at all costs" because it is "the key to the Pacific."

King linked the Midway action with the bombing attack on Dutch Harbor, Alaska, where, he disclosed, battle maeuvers of an unspecified nature were still in progress.

Battle Began Thursday

The civilian population in Hawaii as well as Army and Navy officers and men were jubilant over the news of the American success.

The opening stage of the battle took place early Thursday in a raid by Japanese carrier-based planes on Midway. Army, Navy and Marine planes repulsed the raid, taking heavy toll of the attackers. American forces quickly took control of the air despite the fact that the invading force had at least four carriers. One battleship and one carrier were heavily damaged and other Japanese warships hit.

On Friday, the repulsed invaders were placed on the defensive and sought safety in retreat, their four or more battleships being ineffective against American air superiority. Several carriers, battleships, cruisers and troopships were heavily damaged as the retreat progressed.

By Friday morning American forces in full offensive had partially avenged Pearl Harbor, having inflicted losses and casualties upon the Japanese greater than those involved at Pearl Harbor in the sneak raid six months ago.

Hail "Splendid Victory"

Messages of congratulations began arriving at Admiral Nimitz headquarters. Gen. Douglas MacArthur declared "the splendid victory" has aroused "the greatest enthusiasm throughout" Australia. "We will not fail," he added.

Chinese newspapers hailed the battle. The Combined Daily declared it "marks the beginning of Japan's downfall." The New China Daily News said the Japanese navy "invincibility hoax has been blown to pieces by the American navy."

Lieut. Gen. Henry H. Arnold, Army Air Force chief, congratulated the army fliers and exhorted them to "Keep 'em fleeing."

Meanwhile, with what was perhaps a significant reference to the handicap which the presence of civilians sometimes imposed on operations of land forces, "particularly of friendly troops"—Britain called upon the population of the French coastal belt, from Belgium to Spain, to evacuate the zone at all costs.

Warn French On Coast

"We do not underestimate the difficulties of such an evacuation, nor the obstacles which will be presented," the British radio said in a notice beamed to the German-conquered Frenchmen in their own lauguage. "If we urge you to overcome them it is because it affects the success of operations of capital importance in the struggle for the liberation of France.

It was pointed out that the French coastal region would become "more and more a theater of operations."

President Roosevelt asked Congress for a new appropriation of $34,417,827,337 for the War Department for the fiscal year ending June 30, 1943. If granted it would boost to more than two hundred billions the war chest approved by Congress for the three years ending June 30, 1943.

Libyan Tank Battle

The great tank battle in the Libyan desert roared into its 14th day with the British and their Free French allies apparently holding the upper hand after repulsing new Axis attacks at Knightbridge and Bir Hachiem.

The British reported that their artillery fire had smashed another attempt by Field Marshal Erwin Rommel's columns yesterday to break through toward Tobruk, 15 miles northeast of Knightsbridge.

NOTICE
MT. VERNON R. A.
CHAPTER NO. 25
meets
TONIGHT — 7:30 P. M.

A HALF YEAR OF WAR IN THE PACIFIC

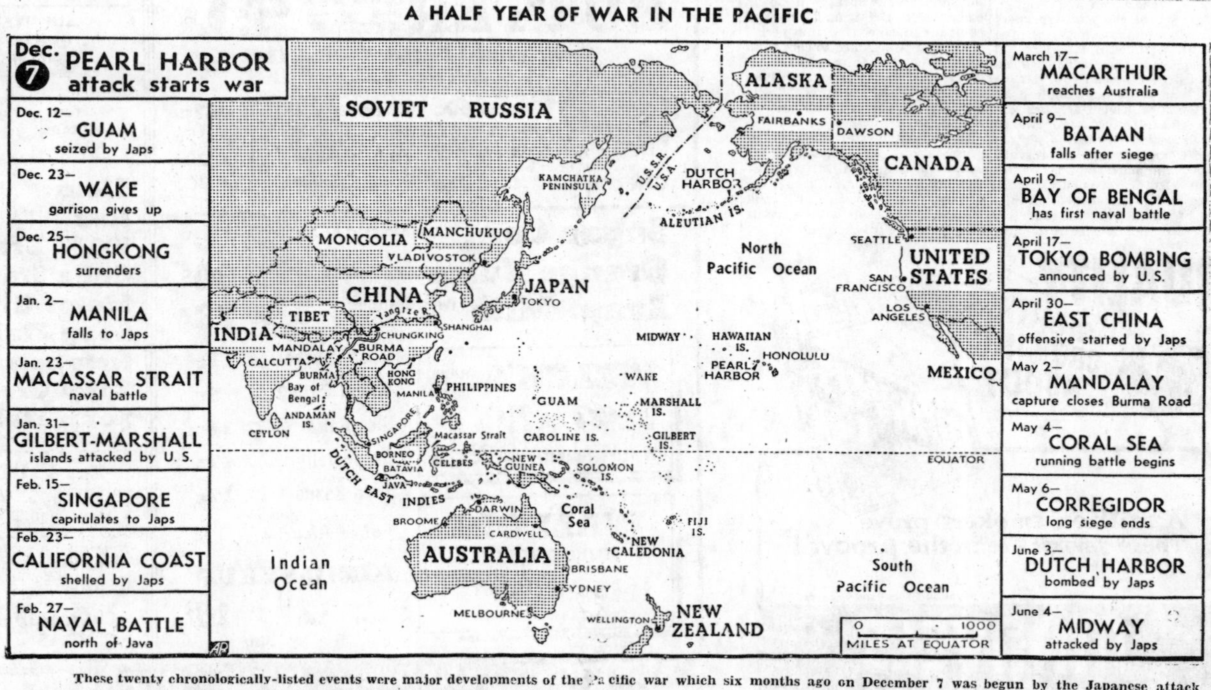
Dec. 7 PEARL HARBOR attack starts war
Dec. 12— GUAM seized by Japs
Dec. 23— WAKE garrison gives up
Dec. 25— HONGKONG surrenders
Jan. 2— MANILA falls to Japs
Jan. 23— MACASSAR STRAIT naval battle
Jan. 31— GILBERT-MARSHALL islands attacked by U. S.
Feb. 15— SINGAPORE capitulates to Japs
Feb. 23— CALIFORNIA COAST shelled by Japs
Feb. 27— NAVAL BATTLE north of Java
March 17— MACARTHUR reaches Australia
April 9— BATAAN falls after siege
April 9— BAY OF BENGAL has first naval battle
April 17— TOKYO BOMBING announced by U.S.
April 30— EAST CHINA offensive started by Japs
May 2— MANDALAY capture closes Burma Road
May 4— CORAL SEA running battle begins
May 6— CORREGIDOR long siege ends
June 3— DUTCH HARBOR bombed by Japs
June 4— MIDWAY attacked by Japs
SOVIET RUSSIA
ALASKA
FAIRBANKS
DAWSON
CANADA
KAMCHATKA PENINSULA
U.S.S.R.
U.S.A.
DUTCH HARBOR
ALEUTIAN IS.
MONGOLIA
MANCHUKUO
VLADIVOSTOK
CHINA
JAPAN
TOKYO
TIBET
Yangtze R.
SHANGHAI
INDIA
CHUNGKING
MANDALAY
BURMA ROAD
CALCUTTA
BURMA
HONG KONG
Bay of Bengal
MANILA
PHILIPPINES
ANDAMAN IS.
CEYLON
SINGAPORE
Macassar Strait
BORNEO
CELEBES
BATAVIA
JAVA
DUTCH EAST INDIES
NEW GUINEA
SOLOMON IS.
GUAM
CAROLINE IS.
WAKE
MARSHALL IS.
GILBERT IS.
MIDWAY
HAWAIIAN IS.
HONOLULU
PEARL HARBOR
North Pacific Ocean
SEATTLE
UNITED STATES
SAN FRANCISCO
LOS ANGELES
MEXICO
EQUATOR
DARWIN
BROOME
CARDWELL
AUSTRALIA
Coral Sea
NEW CALEDONIA
FIJI IS.
BRISBANE
SYDNEY
MELBOURNE
WELLINGTON
NEW ZEALAND
Indian Ocean
South Pacific Ocean
0 1000 MILES AT EQUATOR

These twenty chronologically-listed events were major developments of the Pacific war which six months ago on December 7 was begun by the Japanese attack against a United States at peace. The three dates representing United Nations triumphs — January 31, April 17 and May 4 — all are to the credit of American fighting men.

PATROLING ALASKAN COAST—On a routine patrol flight watching for a Jap stab, a navy bomber skirts a range of snow-covered mountains on the south coast of Alaska near the Aleutian Island chain. Frequent bad weather hampers these flights.

Gives Hints On Wartime Motoring

Local Auto Club Manager Discusses Gas, Tire Saving

Walton I. Howard, manager of the Annapolis Branch, A.A.A., today suggested ten war-time motoring hints. They are:

1. Accept restrictions cheerfully. Work with your government by planning the use of your car wisely.

2. By all means take a vacation. No roaming around, but carefully planned short vacations to give you the rest that you need.

3. Budget your mileage to save enough gas for essential short motor trips advocated in time of war.

4. Use your car at regular intervals to avoid rotting tires, sticky valves and engine trouble.

5. Don't make unnecessary trips in your car when you can walk or ride in public conveyances.

6. Where possible, ride busses and street cars at odd hours when they are not carrying peak loads of workers to and from their jobs.

7. Use the "share your car" plan. Ride alternating days with your neighbors.

8. Pick up fellow workers to relieve crowded busses and street cars.

9. Drive your car with consideration for tires. Avoid sudden stops and jackrabbit starts.

10. Drive at "patriotic pace"—stay below 40 M. P. H. and save gasoline.

Summer School

(Continued from Page One)

voted, for the first three weeks, to a close reading from the viewpoint of language study, of Plato's 'Meno" (in English translation); during the second three weeks the text for the tutorial will be the "De Magistro" of Augustine, also in English translation.

Open To Annapolitans

The summer course is open also to residents of Annapolis. For them, as for the students who live on the campus, it is possible to register for either the first or second three-week term.

In addition to the Resident Summer Course, the Adult School will carry on other courses. Nicolas Nabokov is offering a course in "Great Works of Music," a continuation of the course begun earlier in the year.

The summer term is, however, open to newcomers. The course is devoted to study of a few great compositions; the method is listening, reading the score, analyzing. The aim of the course is to increase understanding of all good music through close study of a few great works. The first meeting of the music course is scheduled for Wednesday, July 17, at 8 P. M. in the Reverdy Johnson House. It will meet once a week for eight weeks.

Basic Russian

A course in basic Russian is also offered by Mr. Nabokov, to begin Monday, June 22, at 5 P. M., in McDowell Hall, Room 22. The course will meet twice a week for a period of eight weeks. Its aim will be a quick reading and talking knowledge of the language for immediate practical purposes.

Announcement will be made shortly of a discussion course based on reading pertinent to the war and the peace.

Further information about the summer program is available at the Adult School office on the campus.

O'Conor Acts

(Continued From Page One)

industry was to "help the defense worker get enough gas to report for work."

To Ickes he said: "War production is being jeopardized in this area by the gasoline curtailment program. Already 500 workers in one defense industry have been affected, resulting in tremendous loss of man hours. I appeal to you to make possible greater gasoline allotments for workers in defense industries so that war production can be continued at maximum capacity."

The Governor said he received word today that "500 defense workers" were unable to report for work recently at one Baltimore factory and that executives had asked him to carry their appeals to Washington officials.

His message to Henderson read in part:

"Because of serious developments I request your cooperation, under the rationing program, to make additional gasoline available for defense workers."

Sunday Work

(Continued From Page One)

yesterday that under the lease the USO project was a Federal project which has been placed in an emergency classification. He contested the State had no jurisdiction to interfere with a Federal government agency or its work under present conditions.

He pointed out that if the work was stopped this coming Sunday an injunction would be filed in the Federal Court for Maryland to restrain local authorities from interfering with the construction.

He declared that, in the last analysis, the Federal government had the right to declare martial law covering the section, thus setting aside all State regulations. No one, he declared, wished to go to this extreme.

Orioles Defeat Navy Team

Bob Feller, Hurling For Sailors, Yields Five Hits

BALTIMORE, June 11 (AP)—The Baltimore Orioles shelled Sailor Bob Feller for three runs in the fourth inning last night to score a 3 to 2 victory over the Norfolk Training Station baseball team before a crowd of 10,000.

Feller, former Cleveland fireballer, was on the mound for five innings and yielded five hits, four of which came in the big fourth after the sailors had scored twice in their half of the inning.

Russ Niller went the route for the Orioles and parceled out six hits, while the International Leaguers eked out seven safeties off Feller and Freddy Hutchinson.

Sidelight of the contest was the induction of 107 youths into the navy. Gene Tunney, former world's heavyweight boxing champion, gave them the oath.

HOMEMAKER'S CORNER

"If the Victory Garden Campaign is to be a success, none of the foods produced can be allowed to go to waste," says Miss Margaret McPheeters, specialist in nutrition for the University of Maryland Extension Service. That means thinking now about the various methods of preserving these products—storing, drying, brining, freezing, and canning. Miss McPheeters offers the following suggestions for meeting a year-round food plan based on the Victory Garden:

Use as many fresh fruits and vegetables as possible during the growing season. Store everything that will keep in the cellar, or above ground in mounds, or in underground pits or trenches. Plan to dry corn, shelled peas and beans, cherries, apples, pears, and peaches. Brine purple-top fall turnips and cabbage for kraut, snap beans, and green tomatoes and cucumbers for pickles. If a freezer locker is used, keep it filled to capacity. Trim and prepare products properly for frozen storage.

Finally, consider home canning and look over all of the canning equipment on hand. An egg candling lamp or frosted electric lamp bulb used in a dark room will show defects in glass jars which should be discarded. She says there will be enough rubber jar rings to go around for reasonable amounts of home canning, also tin cans for those with experience in using them.

Miss McPheeters points out that if you have a pressure cooker you should take good care of it because the chances of getting a new one or having an old cooker repaired are exceedingly slim.

Miss Ruth Reed

(Continued from Page One)

Mr. and Mrs. S. J. Cowin of Orono, attended the Orono high school and the University of Maine before entering the Naval Academy. He took part in battalion gymnastics, was manager of the plebe boxing team, and participated in battalion soccer. He has been president of the Masqueraders, the dramatic club of the academy; circulation manager of the Lucky Bag, and vice-president of the Newman Club.

Presented Annually

The regimental flag is presented annually to the company of midshipmen winning the greatest number of points in the detailed competitions consisting of ordnance and gunnery, seamanship and navigation, athletics and infantry drills. The competition began in July, 1941.

All of the companies of the regiment were commanded by midshipmen of the 1942 class until the graduation of that class on Dec. 19 last, at which time the 1943 class became the senior midshipmen at the academy.

In accordance with the system now employed at the academy to enable the greatest number of midshipmen to exercise the responsibilities of command, the time since December was divided into three periods.

To Hold Rehearsals

During each of these periods the companies of the regiment were commanded by different midshipmen. Midshipman Cowin commanded the winning twelfth company during the first period and was again named to command for the current third period.

Midshipman George William Ringenberg, of Seattle, Wash., commanded the company during the second period.

A dress rehearsal of the color presentation for photographers will be held at 9 A. M. Wednesday. The regiment will not be present, but the "color girl" and Midshipman Cowin will be available for close-up pictures.

"If the Victory Garden Campaign is to be a success, none of the foods produced can be allowed to go to waste," and other problems resulting from present conditions. Miss Kellar points out that the decision to eliminate the short course was made only after very serious consideration of all factors and following statements by many farm women that they would not be able to attend this year for the full week.

Dr. Liu Chieh, Counselor of the Chinese Embassy in Washington, will be one of the main speakers who will address farm women from all sections of Maryland on "Homemakers' Day" which will be held at the University of Maryland, June 17. It is announced by Miss Venia M. Kellar, assistant director of the University of Maryland Extension Service.

The Homemakers' Day program will take the place this year of the regular Rural Women's Short Course which was called off because of the shortage of labor on farms, tire and gasoline rationing.

The name Paoshan, a small city in China's Yunnan province, means "precious mountain."

Evening Capital

VOL. LVIII — NO. 144. EVERY EVENING EXCEPT SUNDAY ANNAPOLIS, MD., THURSDAY, JUNE 18, 1942. SOUTHERN MARYLAND'S ONLY DAILY THREE CENTS.

WEATHER
Moderate Temperature Tonight

LATE NEWS

WAR COSTING BILLION WEEKLY

Washington, June 18 (AP)—Budget Director Harold L. Smith revealed today that America's arms factories are rolling so fast now that Government war expenditures have climbed to approximately $1,000,000,000 per week.

CURTAIL ACTIVITIES OF JOE LOUIS

Washington, June 18 (AP)—Secretary of War Stimson said today that Heavyweight Champion Joe Louis would make no more public appearances, except those strictly for the armed forces, until he completes his basic military training.

WILL REDUCE OFFICERS IN WASHINGTON

Washington, June 18 (AP)—The War Department announced today that it would reduce the number of officers assigned to duty in Washington, replacing many of them with members of the new army specialist corps, but made it plain that the new organization was no haven for job hunters or draft dodgers.

SEEK TEST ON RENT CONTROL LAW

South Bend, Ind., June 18 (AP)—The constitutionality of the rent control provisions of the emergency price control act were challenged today in a test suit in Federal Court here by a landlord.

POSTPONE HEARING IN WEINBERG CASE

Rockville, Md., June 18 (AP)—A three-judge court postponed hearings today on a citation to disbar Leo Weinberg, Frederick attorney, when advised that Weinberg is a patient in a Philadelphia sanatorium.

ST. JOHN'S TO HOLD SOLDIER SEMINARS AT FORT GEORGE G. MEADE

Two-fisted fighting men who have proved they like classic plays—and are not ashamed to show it—will get an opportunity soon to demonstrate whether the interest extends to reading.

Seminars for soldiers, featuring the experimental educational program of St. John's College, will be started next Tuesday. The seminars will last at least 10 weeks, with discussions patterned after college seminars.

No previous education will be required.

Ford K. Brown, St. John's faculty member who will conduct the course, said that only an interest in reading the great books and in "pursuing their ideas in conversation with others," is necessary to qualify.

The soldiers two weeks ago packed three performances of "Macbeth," given by Maurice Evans and Judith Anderson.

They'll get around to Shakespeare in the seminars, too, after studying Homer, Plato and Thucydides.

INCREASE VALUE OF SUGAR STAMPS

WASHINGTON, June 18 (AP)—The value of sugar stamps 5 and 6 has been increased to two pounds each, but each stamp will cover four weeks instead of two, so the weekly ration for each consumer will remain at a half pound.

Stamp No. 4, now valid for the purchase of a pound, will expire at midnight June 27, the Office of Price Administration announced. No. 5, good for two pounds, may be used at any time up to July 26, and No. 6 will then be valid until August 22.

Under the new plan grocers will have fewer stamps to handle.

Navy To Use State Yacht

Du Pont To Be Used In Coast Guard Service

Maryland's 185-foot State yacht, the duPont, is going to war again.

Governor O'Conor reported today the navy formally accepted loan of the State-owned steam yacht for the war's duration. He said the duPont, which won a naval service chevron in the first World War, would be put into Coast Guard service soon.

O'Conor received permission from the Public Service Commission to offer the duPont to the navy. Coast Guard officials, he said, offered to restrict its use to Maryland's and surrounding waters but were told they could sail the yacht wherever necessary.

The Governor said the ship would be pressed into active service as soon as Coast Guard and Tidewater Fisheries Department officials sign a pact containing terms for the duPont's return to the State at the war's end.

BOY SCOUTS BUSY COLLECTING SCRAP RUBBER IN COMMUNITY

Automobile Club Manager Urges Motorists To Cooperate To Help Nation And Themselves

The national campaign for rubber today found the Annapolis Boy Scouts busy ransacking nooks in garages, attics, backyards and farms for all reclaimable rubber articles.

Scouts from Troop 334 are working in the city, turning all the scrap rubber they find, over to filling stations. They helped to collect waste paper when the shortage developed.

In addition the scouts are assisting the civilian defense medical unit stationed at St. John's College and will work with the group this evening in a first aid and ambulance duty drill.

Road Workers

County road employes also are working in the rubber drive, collecting scrap rubber throughout the county.

Motorists were urged by Walton I. Howard, resident manager of the Annapolis Branch of the Automobile Club of Maryland, today to give fullest cooperation in the rubber collection program, which is to continue through June 30.

"Upon the success or failure of this drive," Howard said, "depend many far-reaching decisions that will vitally affect automobile op-

(Continued on Page Six)

Four City Youths In Air Corps School

Start Training As Pilots At Maxwell Field, Alabama

Taking the initial steps toward winning their wings as pilots and commissions as second lieutenants in the Army Air Forces, James O. Bush, Jr., Route 3, Annapolis; James A. Elder, Jr., 8 Hill street; George W. Ford, 30 Munroe Court, Annapolis, and John W. Siegert, 104 McKendree avenue, all of Annapolis, are now enrolled as aviation cadets in the Army Air Forces Pre-Flight School (pilot) at Maxwell Field, Ala., where they will undergo military, physical and academic training calculated to fit them for the job of learning to fly fighter planes expertly.

Cadet Bush is a former student of Randolph-Macon Academy and Washington College. He was accepted as a cadet in the Army Air Forces on March 9, at Baltimore.

Cadet Elder was educated at Annapolis and New London, Conn., and was employed as a proof-reader by the Capital-Gazette Press when accepted as a cadet on May 9.

Cadet Ford attended Annapolis Business College and was employed as an operations agent for Pennsylvania Central Airlines when he was accepted as a cadet in the Army Air Forces on May 7, at Baltimore.

Cadet Siegert was attending the University of Baltimore in 1942. He had civilian flight training before being accepted as a cadet on May 7, at Baltimore.

After completing their pre-flight course at Maxwell Field these cadets will be sent to one of the many primary flying schools located in the Southeast Army Air Forces Training Center for the first phase of their pilot training.

Navy Sport Captains Elected

McNamara Heads Baseball Team—Salsig, Crew

Comdr. L. S. Perry, graduate manager of athletics at the Naval Academy, today announced the election of captains and managers in seven sports.

W. J. McNamara, Hewlett, N. Y., was elected captain of the baseball team, with H. S. Barbour, Holly Bluff, Miss., as manager.

E. S. Salsig, Fort Bragg, Calif., will captain next year's crew. T. J. Christman, Orlando, Fla., is manager.

Others elected were:

Tennis—E. Wyatt, San Diego,

(Continued on Page Three)

Young Artists Hold Exhibit

Pupils Of Miss Richardson Show Compositions In Various Media

The art pupils of Miss Jeanette Richardson are holding their annual exhibition at the Calvert Studio on State Circle.

The ages of the entrants range from six to sixteen and some exceptional talent is found among them. The knotty pine panelling of the studio walls makes a mellow background for the vivid entries.

The students have expressed themselves in every medium. Among the oils is a misty grey-blue composition of hydrangeas and pottery by Ella Mallard. Annabelle James shows a lively arrangement of blackeyed susans and D'Arcy Stephens presents a number of still-lifes.

Water Colors Shown

Among the water colors are a spray of japonica, fresh and dainty, by Mary Elizabeth Hazelett and a farm yard scene by Mary Bess Treat, who has achieved a striking effect by combining water color and ink. One effective poster is shown by Carrie Lou Treat.

The favorite medium seems to be pastels. Robert Hefler achieves an oriental atmosphere with japonica in a jade vase handled with great sensitivity. Ella Mallard shows a feeling for line and color in her arrangement of magnolia leaves and a sea shell. Martha Smith offers a spray of pink dogwood in a black vase and Susan Talbot a gay bowl of daffodils. Others exhibiting pastels are Carol Brice, Sybil Godfrey and Alan Jackson.

Sketches

In the pencil and crayon sketches are two excellent drawings of costumed models by Robert Helfer and one by Bruce Boundy. Lottie Anne Reed presents a conventional design of pussy willow and a china frog. Claude Handy is at her best in her vivid character sketches, while Emily Stevenson's most appropriate picture is a view of the Naval Academy from Pendennis Mount. Helen Williams illustrates "house-cleaning" with vigor.

One of the walls carries entries for the monthly prizes for expression. Each month the pupils submit a picture showing what that season means to them. An

(Continued on Page Two)

John Bateson, 10, Killed In Crash

Was Riding Bicycle On Ritchie Highway

John Bateson, 10-year-old son of Mr. and Mrs. John T. Bateson of Pasadena, was fatally injured last night while riding a bicycle on the Governor Ritchie highway.

Dr. John M. Claffy, county medical examiner, said the boy was crossing the highway at the Pasadena road intersection when struck by an automobile driven by Mrs Virginia Bachmann, of Jones station.

The injured boy was taken to the Emergency Hospital by a passing motorist and was pronounced dead at 7:10 P. M.

O'CONOR TO ATTEND JUDICIAL MEETING

Governor O'Conor leaves today for Asheville, N. C., where he will attend a Federal judicial conference and the annual meeting of the State Governors throughout the nation.

O'Conor speaks before the judicial conference tomorrow evening. The governors' meeting opens Sunday.

PLAN RECEPTION FOR REV. JOHN J. DAWSON

A reception and pantry shower to welcome the return of the Rev. John J. Dawson and his family back to the Trinity Methodist Church for another year will be held at 8 P. M. Friday.

Members and friends of the church have been invited to attend the reception to be held in the social hall of the church.

Ickes Warns That Coal Bins Should Be Filled

Points Out That Coal May Not Be Available In Winter

WASHINGTON, June 18 (AP)—If Mr. and Mrs. America don't get busy and have their coal bins filled up, they're tempting the possibility of heatless houses next winter, with fuel not to be had for love nor money.

That was the warning of Fuel Coordinator Harold L. Ickes, who said today the nation was not providing itself with full protection against coal shortages despite the government's repeated urging that all consumers "buy coal now."

Ickes' aides already are at work on an emergency coal allocation program, against the possibility that the war haulage burden on transportation systems may cause coal shortages.

The coordinator said each householder should put in his entire winter's supply this summer, if possible, and he said he thought supplies adequate for 60 to 90 days were not too much for the ordinary industrial consumer to have on hand. Vital war industries and utilities, he added, ought to carry coal enough to last at least 120 days.

Yet coal stocks held by industrial plants, railroads and coal dealers rose from 57,221,000 tons on April 1 to 61,832,000 tons on May 1, according to estimates of the bituminous coal division of the Interior Department, representing an increase from an average of 38 days' supply in storage

(Continued on Page Six)

Organize More Minute Men

Pasadena And Severna Park Group Meet

Plans for the organization of another company of Minute Men in Anne Arundel county were made last night at a meeting of men from Severna Park and Pasadena at the Severna Park school.

The movement for the formation of the company was led by Orlando Ridout, acting captain of the St. Margaret's company, Commissioner Weems R. Duvall and former State Senator Frank M. Duvall.

Howard T. Albrecht, Severna Park, aided in arranging the meeting as the temporary leader of the group. Lieut. Colonels E. Leslie Medford, Paul E. Sutherland and Capt. Leslie Klakring and Lieut. Charles C. Tessier of the State Guard, attended.

Many of the men present enlisted in the new company to be designated No. 905. The Pasadena delegation enlisted in a body. Plans are being made to muster the company into the State service at a meeting to be held Wednesday. Captain Klakring will be in charge of the company instruction.

Led Mediterranean Raid

Major Alfred F. Kalberer (above), commanded the flight of U. S. B-24 Consolidated bombers which scored 25 direct bomb hits on two Italian battleships in the Mediterranean June 15. A former United Airlines pilot, he flew more than 1,300,000 miles as a commercial flier in the United States. His parents, Mr. and Mrs. Ernest I. Kalberer, live in Lafayette, Ind. His wife lives in North Hollywood, Calif.

British Fall Back On Tobruk Before Axis Libyan Offensive

Admiral Nimitz Congratulates Ensign

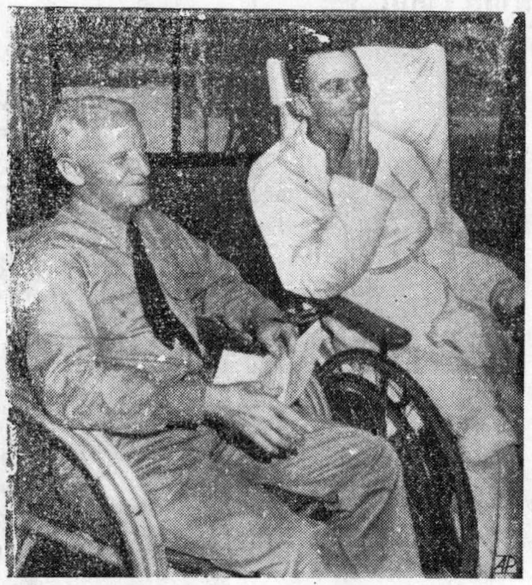

Admiral C. W. Nimitz, (left) paying a visit to the navy hospital at Pearl Harbor, T. H., congratulated Ensign G. H. Gay (right) for the latter's part in the battle of Midway. Gay, a torpedo plane pilot, saw much of the battle from the sea after being shot down after launching a torpedo at a Jap carrier.

SITUATION IS SIMILAR TO 1941 WHEN TOBRUK STOOD LONG SIEGE

British Give Up El Adem And Sidi Rezegh To Form New Defense Line—Moscow Press Claims Germans Beaten Back At Sevastopol—Berlin Reports Main Defenses Of Black Sea Naval Base Have Been Stormed—British Planes Batter Nazi Submarine Base At St. Nazaire—Nimitz Hints Of New Blows Again Japanese—Japanese Advance Continues In China

The British In Libya fell back to fortified positions near the Egyptian frontier today, leaving the famous fortress of Tobruk all but surrounded by Marshal Erwin Rommel's German and Italian divisions. Only a coastal road remained open to link Tobruk with the Egyptian border 80 miles eastward.

Apparently British Gen. Neil M. Ritchie's Eighth Army split into two forces, one remaining to man the defenses to Tobruk against imminent onslaught or a seige such as that which endured for nearly eight months in 1941.

British forces still were on the perimeter of Tobruk's south and southwest defenses, where they hurled back repeated Axis assaults last year and where they stood when relieved by a British westward offensive on Dec. 10, 1941. Thus the situation now was almost the same as during the long siege.

ALLIED AIR FORCE ACTIVE

Allied air squadron, supporting the ground forces, were declared to have broken all records for bombing and strafing as the Germans moved eastward and the British pulled out of El Adem and Sidi Rezegh. The desert trails were littered with vehicles wrecked or burned by the Allied pilots.

Berlin reported that the British Libyan army had been split into two parts. Rome declared the British were beginning a general withdrawal toward the Egyptian frontier. Cairo said new British lines had been set up between Tobruk and the Egyptian frontier.

Britons acknowledged that their tank strength had been reduced in the desert combat to that below that of the Axis. A heavy Axis assault on Tobruk was expected.

Sevastopol Fighting

On the Sevastopol front, Pravda, Communist party newspaper, reported in dispatches from the fighting lines that Red army and navy defense forces had beaten back every German attempt to smash through the shell scarred fortifications meeting tank led waves of attackers with point-blank artillery fire.

The newspaper said that since yesterday steadily reinforced German shock troops had battered almost unceasingly at the grimly held Crimean base from north and south, disregarding a toll of 1,500 killed in a single day.

"The enemy attempted by every mean to break through our defense, but failed," Pravda said. "Fighting continues in two directions, to the north and south."

United States built Consolidated Liberator bombers were reported unofficially in a Stockholm dispatch to London to be operating with the Red air force in defense of the Crimean base.

Bomb St. Nazaire Base

Moscow declared that on the Kharkov front "we destroyed 15 enemy tanks and annihilated nearly 1,500 German officers and men."

Berlin told a different story, claiming that its forces had stormed the main fortifications of Sevastopol, capturing the Maxim Gorky fort and driving to within two miles of the harbor entrance. Fort Gorky was described as "the most modern and strongest bastion of the whole fortress."

British warplanes attacked the Nazi submarine base at St. Nazaire on the occupied French coast last night, laid mines in enemy waters and attacked military targets in northern France and Belgium. One British fighter plane was reported lost. There was no German air activity over Britain during the night but two Nazi planes dropped bombs on the southwest coast early today, causing some damage and a small number of casualties.

Sea War

A picture of tremendously growing American strength in the Battle of the Pacific, where U. S. airmen have already exacted a 10-to-1 toll in Japanese men and planes, was drawn by Admiral Chester W. Nimitz, along with a hint of new sledgehammer blows against Japan in the offing.

Other heartening news came from War Secretary Stimson, who declared in Washington that losses inflicted on the Japanese in the Pacific had temporarily but substantially reduced the threat of an attack on the Pacific coast. Stimson has repeatedly said an attack on the West Coast might be expected.

The War Secretary said the Japanese so far had made only "a very small landing" in the Aleutian islands of Alaska, but he emphasized that fog and bad weather obscured developments in the north Pacific and that information was still incomplete.

"We are greatly increasing our battle strength," Admiral Nimitz declared.

"Our ships, planes and pilots are being added in constantly increasing numbers."

Carrier Forces

The commander-in-chief of the U. S. Pacific fleet told veterans of the two great air-sea battles of Midway Island and the Coral Sea that while American aircraft carrier personnel had suffered hard losses since the war began, with little rest or relief, "it will soon be possible to organize additional carrier groups and rotate them."

The news from the China fighting front was dark.

Chinese headquarters acknowledged that Japan's invasion armies now had seized all but 50 miles of the 450-mile Chekiang-Kiangsi railway which feeds supplies into the heart of China.

This offensive is an important

(Continued on Page 6)

Revival Services Will Continue

Vacation Bible School At West Annapolis Starts Monday

The old-fashioned revival services at the Full Gospel Assembly of West Annapolis will be continued through next week.

The services are being conducted by Miss Mary Warren, evangelist of San Francisco, Calif.

The sixth annual daily Vacation Bible School will open Monday at 9 A. M., in charge of Mrs. Vernon B. Stinchcomb, principal. She will be assisted by Miss Julia Tayman. Children from 5 to 15 years old will attend classes in the Bible, music, handiwork, character building and health.

The school has been well attended in the past and a heavy registration is expected.

USO COMMITTEE MEETS TONIGHT

The USO Committee of Management will meet at 8 o'clock tonight at the home of Mrs. A. Gordon Fleet, Edgewater.

GRADUATE'S FATHER FINDS CITY CROWDED

Lieut. L. R. Heselton, U.S.N. (retired), now on duty at San Diego, Calif., father of Leslie R. Heselton, Jr., second honor man at the Naval Academy, found a crowded city when he arrived here last night to see his son graduate tomorrow.

Unable to find quarters, he appealed to the USO club and the Navy Wives' Club took up the problem. They were successful and found him a place to stay despite his late arrival.

Lieutenant Heselton also plans to attend his son's wedding, which will be held after graduation.

CHILDREN'S DAY AT ST. MARTIN'S CHURCH

Children's day at St. Martin's Evangelical Lutheran Church will be celebrated Sunday with a combined Sunday school and church service at 10:30 A. M.

John Jensen and Rudolph Smith will read the scripture lesson for the day and the main Sunday school will lead the singing during the service. The beginners department, under Misses Eleanor Weaver and Barbara Windsor, and the primary department, under Mrs. R. M. J. Smith, will give children's day recitations. The two groups will combine to sing appropriate songs. Henry Weaver will lead the service.

Civitans Hear Talk On Russia

Nicolas Nabokov Discusses Situation On Russian Front

Nicolas Nabokov, of the St. John's College faculty, told members of the Civitan Club at the weekly luncheon that the belief that the only route into the oil fields of Russia was through the Caucasus was a fallacy.

He declared that the German armies now attacking in the Crimea and around Kharkov could aid their drive along the Caspin Sea and then down to Batum to the oil fields thus avoiding the difficult terrain of the Caucasus.

Pointing out that Russia had always overcome the invaders—including the Tartar after 300 years—he said that the winter had not stopped the Nazi drive on Moscow last year. He said the attack was stopped by the people of Moscow, men, women and children, who manned the trenches and barricades and hurled back the Germans thrust.

Great Spaces

Citing the difficulties of invading Russia, he pointed out the great spaces and the will of the Russian people to fight for their soil and homes. He said in the Crimea towns were 40 and 50 miles part with few good roads, making it difficult country to fortify and hold as well as to defend.

He pointed to the black earth of the Ukraine, its fine grazing land and bountiful crops, which make it desired by invaders.

The fact that the main railroads all run north and south, while the east west connections are not so good was pointed to as one of the reason for the failure of the Nazi invasion last year. Nabokov said as the German lines of communication grew longer this feature of the rail net threw a great burden on the supply lines, which also were hampered by gurerillas.

Four Offensives

He pointed out that the Germans last year mustered some four offensives, each in different parts of a 1,200 or 1,300 mile front, so

(Continued on Page Two)

DE MOLAY MOTHER'S CIRCLE TO MEET

The DeMolay Mother's Circle will hold their final meeting before the summer recess tonight at 8 o'clock.

LIBRARY STORY HOUR SCHEDULE

During the summer months the story hour at the Public Library will be held each Friday at 10:30 A. M. in the library garden.

Miss Josephine Riordan conducts the story hour.

Evening Capital

VOL. LVIII — NO. 163. EVERY EVENING EXCEPT SUNDAY ANNAPOLIS, MD., SATURDAY, JULY 11, 1942. SOUTHERN MARYLAND'S ONLY DAILY THREE CENTS.

WEATHER

Somewhat cooler tonight

LATE NEWS

MANY DOCUMENTS IN NAZI TRIALS

Washington, July 11 (AP)—Army officers prosecuting and defending eight accused Nazi plotters lugged armloads of documents into the Justice Department today, as the secret trial resumed for its fourth day.

WOULD USE CASH REGISTERS FOR FERRY

Baltimore, July 11 (AP)—Thievery or shortages in Chesapeake Ferry System toll charges can be prevented by installation of special cash registers at the Annapolis and Matapeake terminals of the system, Ezra B. Whitman, State Roads Commissioner, believes.

CONGRESS AGAINST PRICE SUBSIDIES

Washington, July 11 (AP) The administration was reported today to have decided against asking Congress for Price Control subsidies now, even though Leon Henderson has warned that present ceilings could not be maintained without them.

GRAND JURY FAILS TO ACT ON CHARGE AGAINST SAILOR

Meeting in special session yesterday, the Anne Arundel county grand jury ignored a rape charge brought against a 33-year-old second class navy pharmacist's mate, States's Attorney Marvin I. Anderson reported today.

Anderson said no action was taken against Harry Wright, the sailor, charged with rape June 22 by a 20-year-old Annapolis motion picture theater cashier. Wright had been held under $5,000 bond.

The State's Attorney also reported that testimony submitted by H. C. Jones, State Employment Commissioner, following a recent hearing in connection with Chesapeake Bay ferry system fund shortages was given to the grand jury for consideration.

The testimony was taken during a state hearing for William M. Thompson of Annapolis, dismissed last week by Jones as toll sergeant of the Annapolis ferry terminal, with Harrison H. Norris, Stevensville toll collector.

Anderson said the grand jury, which reconvenes for another special session July 22, either could ignore the testimony, return an indictment, launch a further investigation, or turn the matter over to the October grand jury.

Testimony taken during the State's hearing for Norris, June 30, was sent to State's Attorney John Palmer Smith of Queen Anne's county.

Aid Sought For Sub Victims

Mrs. R. C. Giffen Receives Letter Citing Needs

The following letter was received by Mrs. R. C. Giffen, wife of Admiral Giffen, from a relative in the service at a South American port. It is a plea for clothing for American survivors being landed at this port.

"We are getting a great many survivors in here now and getting them clothing is becoming quite a problem. We had last week a navy gun crew of a torpedoed merchantman, the ensign, a nice lad from Chicago, was here at the house quite a bit while waiting transportation home. They had just five minutes after being hit when he and his crew jumped (or rather slipped) overboard. They started to swim away from the ship—two boats had gotten away with merchant crew but they were at their guns trying to get a shot at the sub, and they left them.

"These boys, 10 in number, were swimming when suddenly a life raft drifted by—the ensign got it and they got nine aboard—one lost. He said undoubtedly God had sent it as it had to be cut loose from the ship and it floated directly to them. Five days later one of four ships picked them up and brought them in here. These boys saved nothing—escaped in underwear and had to be outfitted, and just two days ago the same ship came into port again with forty-two more. The captain and several of his officers said, 'We are going to have to join a nudist colony—we have no shirts, underwear or 'cervies' left.

"We have a real need for men's clothing here—do you think that you can do anything for us? We have no branch of the Red Cross here, too few Americans—the British have one and are very generous but they have their own survivors to look out for. If you could get together a box of underwear, shirts, suits of clothes, preferably light weight, though by winter these men will have to land home in whatever they have on—

(Continued on Page Two)

RENT REGULATIONS PROVIDE FOR ADJUSTMENT IN SPECIAL CASES

Grounds On Which Rent Director May Raise Or Lower Maximum Rent Are Limited

In order to provide for some flexibility in Federal rent control, under which rents in Annapolis and Anne Arundel county have been frozen at the April 1, 1941 level, the regulations set up machinery for adjusting maximum rents where conditions have changed since the maximum rent date.

The grounds on which Lucien E. D. Gaudreau, area rent director who has offices in the Baltimore Trust building, Baltimore, may raise or lower the maximum rent are limited.

Chiefly they cover substantial alterations in the housing accomodations, substantial alteration in the services or furnishings, and leases based on personal or special relationships between the landlord and tenant.

Ordinary Repair

The regulations will permit an increase in the maximum rent only if the alterations "bring about a substantial change in the housing accomodations by a major capital improvement as distinguished from ordinary repair and maintenance."

Painting and papering constitute ordinary repair and maintenance and are items generally provided by the landlord unless the rental agreement specifies otherwise.

If the alterations were completed between April 1, 1941, and the date on which the Federal regulations became effective, July 1, 1942, the maximum rent is the first rent charged for the remodeled quarters. However, the landlord must report this rent to the rent director within a month of the time Federal regulations became effective and the director may order a decrease.

Case Cited

In event the alterations were completed after July 1 last, the owner must petition the rent director a least 15 days before renting the property, to fix the maximum rent.

The following case was cited as an example of the method followed.

Since April 1, 1941, a large single-family house has been made into apartments for four families. How is the maximum rent for each apartment set?

If the remodeling in this case was completed before July 1, 1942, the maximum rent is the first charged for the new quarters. The owner, however, must file a report with the rent director, who has authority to lower the figure. If completed after July 1, 1942, the maximum rent must be set in advance by the rent director.

Services

All services provided by the

(Continued On Page Three)

Strong Pressure Develops Against Rent Control

Seattle Threatens Nation-Wide Protest By Landlords — Eviction Moves In New Haven

WASHINGTON, July 11 (AP)—The rent control sector of the government's stand against inflation was beset today by strong pressure from organized and individual landlords in many sections of the country.

Threats from Seattle of a nation-wide gathering of property owners to force rent ceilings upward reached the office of Price Administration here simultaneously with news of a threatened "rent strike" by 200,000 CIO unionists in Detroit if rents were raised.

Attempted wholesale evictions were reported from New Haven, Conn., and to top it off, a suit challenging constitutionality of the whole price control act was on file in Mobile, Ala., where a property owner petitioned Federal court to block enforcement of the rent freeze in that area.

Officials Silent

For the time being, top OPA rent officials were silent on the situation.

But aside from "almost innumerable" instances of OPA lawyers rushing to court to prevent evictions arising from rent-ceiling disputes, an OPA spokesman indicates that the reaction to rent controls—now covering 75 cities, was hardly more biter than anticipated.

Only two attacks on constitutional grounds—the Mobile case and one in South Bend, Ind.—are

(Continued On Page Three)

Moscow Admits Nazi Drive Toward Don River Is Meeting With Some Success

PACIFIC FLEET COMMANDER HONORED

Admiral Chester W. Nimitz (center), commander in chief of the U. S. Pacific fleet, stands before Admiral Ernest J. King, commander in chief of the entire U. S. fleet aboard a battleship at a west coast port. King reads the presidential citation awarding Nimitz the distinguished service medal for "exceptionally meritorious service."

NAZIS CLAIM TROOPS NOW HOLD 250-MILE FRONT ALONG RIVER

Timoshenko's Forces Fight Against Spearheads Jabbed Across Don At Voronezh — Rossosh Falls To Germans — Berlin Claims 88,689 Russian Prisoners — Great Air Fights Rage Over Desert In Egypt — British Drive Rommel Back Five Miles Along Railroad — Japanese Raid Port Moresby, Lose Two Bombers — Medium U. S. Vessel Torpedoed

NEW YORK, July 11 (AP)—The arrest of 158 German aliens, members of an organization which the government said furnished money for the return to Germany of one of eight submarine-borne saboteurs who recently landed on American shores, was announced today by the Federal Bureau of Investigation.

German divisions having captured Rossosh, pressed a three-pronged offensive toward the Don river with such vigor that the Russian army newspaper Red Star acknowledged their "developing success."

Marshal Semeon Timoshenko's Soviet field forces battled on against spearheads jabbed across the Don at Voronezh, and in the direction of the strategic river at Kantemirovka, 145 miles to the south; and near Lisichansk, 200 miles below Voronezh.

Red Star said the Germans fighting to expand their holdings on the east bank of the Don were finding rough going because of tank traps and heavy Russian artillery fire, but acknowledged "the area of fighting west of Voronezh is spreading."

BERLIN CLAIMS BIG ADVANCE

Berlin claimed "a great destructive defense" of the Russian armies in the south of Russia and claimed German troops now had reached the Don on a 220-mile front south of Voronezh, established several bridgeheads on the east bank and cleared the west bank of practically all Soviet forces.

A special Nazi announcement said that from June 28 to July 9 German and German-allied troops captured 88,689 Russian troops and destroyed or captured 1,007 tanks, 1,688 guns and other war materials and shot down 540 planes in the gigantic battle west of the Don.

In Egypt allied airmen thundered into action with the mightiest air assault ever witnessed in the desert in support of British ground forces which advanced five miles on the northern sector of the El Alamein front yesterday.

Many Dogfights

A greatly strengthened enemy air force rose to challenge the violent allied assaults and dogfights raged high above the desert. The axis appeared to be drawing mainly on the Italians for air reinforcements, losing many of them.

British General Sir Claude Auchinleck reopened the savage desert fighting yesterday in a thrust which began before dawn. A number of Axis prisoners were captured.

The five mile British advance was made along the railroad line leading westward from El Alamein.

Rome reported Axis troops had forced back the left flank of the British Eighth army in a surprise attack and stopped strong British thrusts in the central and coastal zones.

Fresh Supplies

That the German commander has fresh supplies for the struggle was a certainty, for British reports have told of Axis convoys moving across the Mediterranean toward Libya. Some of these supply ships have been sunk by British submarines and others have been attacked by U. S. bombers.

Axis aircraft were very active over Malta again yesterday with RAF fighters shooting down 19 enemy planes. The British lost 13 planes in the desert fighting. Cairo announced that an Italian destroyer and a 5,000-ton merchant ship were each hit twice Thursday night by RAF bombs.

American planes, raiding far into northern Burma from their Indian bases, repeatedly attacked the Japanese air field at Myitkyina during the week, preventing the Japanese from repairing or using the runways.

Twenty-one Japanese bombers, escorted by eight fighters, attacked the Allied outpost at Port Moresby, New Guinea, yesterday, but were kept at high altitude by anti-aircraft fire which brought down two bombers.

China Front

In China Allied planes blasted Japanese headquarters at Linchuan, main base of the enemy's drive into central Kiangsi province, "with satisfactory results," two planes failed to return.

Allied bombers sank a Japanese transport in the river at Nanchang, and destroyed 10 planes on

(Continued on Page 6)

Police Help Girl Scouts

Help Fix Camp At Truxtun Park During Heavy Rain

Police, responding to flashlight signals, went to Truxtun Park early today to aid the Girl Scouts on the day camp during the deluge of rain.

Stephen Duckett, 2 Spa road, called police headquarters at 1:13 A. M. and told night desk officer Derf Myers that he had noticed what were apparently flashlight signals coming from the scout camp. He said the girls might need aid because of the heavy rain.

Myers radioed Patrolman Anthony Howes in a cruise car. That officer went to the foot of Monticello avenue, noticed the lights, and called across the creek. The girls told him their camp had been washed out.

With Patrolman George Rawlings, Howes drove through Eastport to Truxtun Park. They were joined by Sergt. Brooke Meade of the county police. The officers found two tents down, but the girls had extra tents.

The three policemen helped them get things back in order. By that time the rain had slackened and the girls decided to stay through the night in camp.

MRS. CORDELIA FISHPAW BURIED YESTERDAY

Funeral services for Mrs. Cordelia Mae Fishpaw, 29, were held yesterday afternoon from the home of her parents, Mr. and Mrs John E. Stokes, Bay Ridge avenue, Eastport.

The services were conducted by the Rev. Clarence Fossett, former pastor of Asbury Methodist Church, Arnold; the Rev. David W. Charlton and the Rev. Nelson H. Henck. Burial was in Cedar Bluff Cemetery.

Serving as pallbearers were John Stokes, 3rd, Austin Stokes, Edgar Hall, Russell Hall, Samuel Stokes, Jr., and Leonard Wilson.

Mrs. Fishpaw, who lived at Arnold, died Wednesday of gunshot wounds. She suffered a nervous breakdown about six weeks ago.

Surviving are her husband, Charles B. Fishpaw, and an infant son, Charles B. Fishpaw, Jr.

John M. Taylor was the funeral director.

DR. MURPHY HEARS FROM SOLDIER

Robert Lee Sears, who is with a quartermaster training regiment stationed at Fort Francis E. Warren, Wyoming, in a letter to Dr. J. J. Murphy, chairman of the medical section of the Annapolis local board, describes his experiences since he entered the U. S. Army.

He wrote the that the troops were receiving the best of medical care and that the army "let nothing go for grant." He declared the army physicians and dentists "know their business" and said the medical and dental care he had received was more than he could have afforded in civilian life.

Sears, who graduated from the Supply School earlier this year has remained at the fort and is on duty in the office of a company commander.

SCOUTS LEAVE FOR CAMP LINSTEAD

Boy Scout Troop No. 366, headed by William A. Chambers, scoutmaster, left today for a two weeks period at Camp Linstead on the Severn river.

Several members of Troops 334, 335 and 378 accompanied them to the camp.

During their two week stay the scouts will receive instruction in handicraft, woodcraft and nature study and will enjoy boating, canoeing, swimming and game.

Accused As Spy

Herbert Karl Friederich Bahr (above), 29, an American citizen, was seized by FBI agents on charges of violating the espionage law. Bahr was on the Drottningholm when it docked June 30. He was born in Germany and came to the U. S. where he lived at Buffalo for a time. An honor high school student, Bahr was said by FBI agents to have been trained in Germany to return to the U. S. and obtain vital information for the Nazis.

LAST CHANCE TO REGISTER FOR GASOLINE

Schools Will Be Open Until 8 O'clock Tonight

Operators of passenger automobiles and motorcycles had their last chance today to register for the new gasoline ration books.

The registration rooms in 25 white schools of the county opened at 9 A. M. and will continue issuing ration books until 8 P. M. Only three schools—Glen Burnie high, Arundel high and Millersville high—were closed.

Many Seek More

The total number of registrants will not be known until the final

(Continued on Page Six)

PLAN COMMUNION AT PRES. CHURCH

The Sacrament of the Lord's Supper will be observed at the 10:45 A. M. service tomorrow at the First Presbyterian Church.

LORETTA YOUNG AUTOGRAPHED PHOTOS FOR BOND BUYERS

Loretta Young, motion picture actress who sold $14,500 in War Bonds and Stamps here yesterday afternoon, left a number of autographed photographs behind to be distributed to persons who buy a bond from a retail merchant during July.

After conducting the bond and stamp rally from the porch of the State House, she went to the offices of Gov. Herbert R. O'Conor where the photographs were taken and autographed.

Joseph D. Lazenby, county chairman War Bond and Stamp committee, said the photographs would be available for bond purchasers beginning Monday.

Gets Compact

Miss Young today had a gold compact as a souvenir of her visit to Annapolis. It was presented to her by Walter H. Myers, president of the Chamber of Commerce, on behalf of that organization.

Wearing a floral print dress, with the design in lavender-pink on a black background, and a large black straw hat with lavender pink flowers in front, Miss Young sold a $1,000 bond to Governor O'Conor. This was the largest bond sold. Meanwhile, young girls going through the crowd on the State House hill sold $1,000 worth of stamps and $12,500 in bonds.

Several hundred cards, autographed by Miss Young, were distributed to bond and stamp purchasers who bought more than $5 worth.

Luncheon Guest

After the rally Miss Young was a luncheon guest at Carvel Hall. In the party were Governor O'Conor, Mayor William U. McCready, Capt. Kemp C. Christian, USN, and Mrs. Christian; Postmaster and Mrs. William A. Strohm, Mrs. William T. Armbruster, Mr. and Mrs. Joseph D. Lazenby and Mr. and Mrs. Walter Ruth.

Following the luncheon the party went to the Naval Academy where Miss Young was greeted by Rear Admiral John R. Beardall superintendent. She was escorted on a tour of the Academy by Captain Christian.

RECOVER TWO STOLEN VEHICLES

Two motor vehicles, an automobile and a truck, reported stolen from Glen Burnie and Baltimore have been recovered by Patrolman Anthony Howes.

He found the automobile, reported stolen in Baltimore on July 8, yesterday parked on Gloucester street.

A trouble truck, reported stolen from Glen Burnie, was found last night on Division street.

Yacht Club Ready For 7th Regatta

Entrants To Register Tonight For Events Tomorrow

The Yacht Club, decorated with bunting, today awaited the beginning of its seventh annual regatta tomorrow.

Registration of entrants will take place at the club at 8 tonight followed by an informal dance in honor of the regatta sailors. The Chesapeake Bay Yacht Racing Association, sponsor organization of the event, will rendezvous at the club tonight following the commodore's cocktail party at 5 P. M.

Preliminaries

West River and Gibson Island skippers were expected to race their boats from their home ports to Annapolis, beginning at 5 P. M.

Events to take place tomorrow include two heats each for the 20-foot round and chine bottoms, Hamptons, knockabouts, whaleboats, comets, 14-foot international dinghies, National One and Severn One designs, penguins, D dinghies, moths and stars.

The racing cruising divisions and the Delta class boats will run one heat only.

Awards

Awards will be presented at 3 P. M. tomorrow at the club. Permanent trophies to be won are the Naval Academy Boat Club, W. T. Morris, Commodore's J. Willis Martin Memorial and Arturo Fernandez cups. The first three will go to winners in the cruising division; the Martin trophy is for the club Hamptons, and Fernandez award is for the international dinghy race.

Comdr. C. Covode Davis, U.S.N., and W. G. Sullivan head the race committee, and Judge Ridgely P. Melvin is chairman of the committee on rules and appeals. Peter H. Magruder is commodore of the club.

Club Active In War Service

Women's Club Adopts Red, White And Blue As Colors

"Red, white and blue" will be the theme for the program of the Woman's Club of Annapolis and Anne Arundel county during the coming year, adding to the club colors the third patriotic tint to signify the war service planned by its 150 members.

Doubling the membership is one

(Continued On Page Three)

Evening Capital

ANNAPOLIS, MD.

1884 -:- 1942

TALBOT T. SPEER, President and Publisher
FRANK L. McSHANE, General Manager
ELMER M. JACKSON, Jr., Editor
RICHARD H. ELLIOTT, Associate Editor

Published Daily Except Sunday by
THE CAPITAL-GAZETTE PRESS, INCORPORATED
Telephone 2332 Subscriptions 3881

SUBSCRIPTION RATES:

Delivered in Annapolis, the United States Naval Academy, Eastport, Germantown, Homewood, West Annapolis, Wardour and vicinity by carrier, or by mail in the United States and Canada, for $7 a year; $4 for six months; or 75 cents a month.

Price at newsstands, 3 cents a copy.

National Advertising Representatives
J. J. DEVINE & ASSOCIATES, INC.
New York—415 Lexington Ave. Atlanta—633 Boulevard, N. E.
Chicago—307 N. Michigan Ave. Philadelphia—900 Lincoln Liberty Bldg.

Entered as Second Class Matter May 28, 1933, at the Post Office of Annapolis, Maryland, under the Act of March 3, 1879.

MEMBERS OF THE ASSOCIATED PRESS
The Associated Press is exclusively entitled to the use for re-publication of all news credited to it or not otherwise credited in this paper and also the local news published herein. All rights of re-publication of special dispatches herein are also reserved.

SATURDAY, JULY 11, 1942

AMERICAN HEROES DAY

Annapolis, along with the rest of the nation, will observe American Heroes day on Friday—a day when the United States will make its all-out effort for the sale of War Bonds and Stamps.

The retail merchants of the city and nation, now engaged in the Retailers for Victory drive, and many organizations are planning to make the day one long to be remembered. Already the merchants have sold many bonds and stamps during their Victory campaign which began on July 1 and is being continued all month. But on Friday they hope, with the assistance of all residents, to set up a mark for bond and stamp sales that will be an all time high.

The day has been dedicated to the men of Annapolis and Anne Arundel county who are fighting now on every battle front to protect our freedom and the flag we live under.

The people of the city and county are called upon to honor their heroes in the best possible way—by redoubling their own efforts to win the war by buying U. S. War Bonds and Stamps.

It is planned to have an action tribute rather than a "word tribute." Words won't buy the gun the soldier needs to fight the enemy. Words won't buy the clothing that protects the service man's health. Words won't buy planes, guns, tanks, ships, gas masks, trucks, ammunition, bombs or the thousand and one items needed to insure victory.

But War Bonds and Stamps will buy them. War Bonds and Stamps will give the men fighting on the fronts the things they need, and, for this reason, the purchase of these bonds and stamps is considered the best way to honor the soldiers, sailors and marines of the community.

Give them the tools they need to do the big job facing them. Give them the aid and assistance that comes from the assurance that the people on the home front are behind them, not in words alone, but in a hard practicable way. Buy a bond and give a gun, buy more bonds and give a machine-gun.

That is the reason for American Heroes day. It is a call to every resident of Annapolis and Anne Arundel county to do their part and to march in spirit with the men in the ranks of the American armed services.

Hollywood Sights And Sounds

By Robbin Coons

HOLLYWOOD—Set-seeing: Comes the revolution. Time stops in its tracks. Nothing is the same. Andy Hardy is talking back to the judge.

For five years now, picture after picture, Mickey Rooney and Lewis Stone have shared those man-to-man talks. It's in "Andy Hardy's Last Fling"—and don't believe that title as long as the family series makes money—that it happens.

Andy is off to college, and the judge, an alumnus, wants to make the trip with him, introduce him to the dean. Andy knows that his college career will be "ruined" if the other boys see him being so sponsored, but he knows also that his father will be disappointed not to go.

* * *

SAYS Andy to the judge, "We've made a kind of habit of man-to-man talks, haven't we?"

"They've meant a great deal to me, Andy," says the judge.

Andy: "But they weren't really man-to-man talks. They were just a kid trying to hide that he only had a kid's troubles, but pretending he was grown up and trying to make it all seem important."

Then he goes on to say that this must be the real thing—man to man—and from then on Andy does all the talking.

After the scene Mickey Rooney mops his brow, turns to Stone, and says: "Gee, I didn't know whether I could get away with that or not. Me! Telling you! It just doesn't seem right!"

* * *

THE set of "Watch on the Rhine" is minus its star, Paul Lukas, and its principal supporting player, Bette Davis. Bette will be co-starred, of course, but the real starring role is Paul's. He played it for 11 months on Broadway, thus reviving movie interest in him. Bette chose the assignment, beginning work even before "Now, Voyager" was completed, just to get in her swat at the Nazis. The picture, like the play, is one of the most emotional and strongest of the anti-Nazi line, and at the same time one of the quietest.

If Paul and Bette are absent, an unforgettable character is decidedly present. George Coulouris. He's the villain.

George was the villain in the play, too, which makes Hollywood seem sort of quiet by contrast. Night after night, those 11 months and four more on the road, George got booed. Lukas and the others would get applause on the curtain calls, but George got only hisses.

"I guess it was a compliment, since I'm supposed to be an actor," he says. "But a man gets tired of hisses every night."

He figures, in compensation, that his villain will be remembered—as villains usually are. He wonders if movie audiences will boo, too. They may, he admits. But he won't be there, and he's glad of it.

HAVE YOU BOUGHT YOURS?
HOW DO YOU SUPPOSE WE ARE GOING TO RAISE THIS MONEY, HENRY?
HERE'S A STARTER, MR PRESIDENT. IF WE MAKE EVERY PAY-DAY A BOND DAY, WE CAN DO IT.
$59 BILLION WAR BUDGET
DEFENSE BONDS
—Courtesy Washington, D. C., Star

THE WAR TODAY

By DeWitt Mackenzie
(Wide World War Analyst)

The battle for Egypt patently has developed into a play for position and a race against time by both belligerents to bring up reinforcements and materiel, and the outcome of this conflict, which is a part of Hitler's win-the-war-this-year offensive, may easily depend on which side is the quicker with the reserves.

There is a fair amount of mystery regarding this extraordinary combat of the sands, which had been relatively quiet for 10 days until yesterday's pre-dawn flareup because both armies were too fagged out and weakened in equipment to carry on without repairs. However, the way things are going the fight seems likely to blow up in our faces in the near future. Certainly the present position is a package of dynamite.

If the fate of the Allied cause didn't depend so heavily on this battle, it would be fascinating to watch the contest of wits between Gen. Sir Claude Auchinleck, the shrewd and capable Scotsman, and Field Marshal Rommel, who perhaps is the greatest tactician of his day. The Scot is maneuvering cannily to trap the crafty Nazi against the Mediterranean coast and hold him there in a pocket while American and British bombers and British submarines try to cut the Axis supply lines. Rommel is moving his chessmen to keep his line of retreat open and hang on to his position until fresh equipment arrives.

Rommel's armored right wing originally had rested some 35 miles almost due south in the desert, while his left wing lay on the coast. He kept swinging at Auchinleck with that fast-moving armored force, like a prizefighter chopping with his right, hoping to swing the Scotsman back and outflank him—that is, put Auchinleck in the same kind of sack that the latter now is holding open as he punches at Rommel.

But Auchinleck wasn't having any, and then he began to show a retaliatory strength which indicated that he was beginning to receive badly needed reinforcements, both in men and equipment. At the same time Rommel's striking power apparently deteriorated because of lack of supplies due to the over-extension of his lines of communication.

Thus we see Auchinleck became the aggressor in a cautious sort of way—just enough to keep the initiative, make things uncomfortable for Rommel and be ready to take advantage of any opening without actually precipitating a renewal of the battle for which the British weren't ready. Yesterday, for instance, the British pushed that right flank of Rommel's back still further but Rommel rebounded there and the British struck his left for a five-mile advance.

Everybody realized that Rommel hadn't lost his cunning and that he was still that dangerous foe who more than once had turned almost certain defeat into victory. Whether he or Auchinleck is ready for full scale resumption of the battle is not known.

Rommel's need of help is confirmed by the appearance of a convoy headed across the Mediterranean for Libya. British headquarters announce that long-range United States bombers which were scouting for Axis ships, shot down two German fighter planes that tried to intercept the Yankees. At the same time a British submarine was reported as sinking an Axis cargo vessel and a naval auxiliary ship.

Reports from Ankara say that Hitler is moving reinforcements to Rommel from the Balkans. It is said that German troops are being pulled out of Yugoslavia and even Crete. While the dispatches don't mention equipment, it must be assumed that this also is being sent, since it's safe to assume that Rommel needs it even more than he does men. That Hitler places great store on a victory in Egypt is quite clear.

The appearance of the Axis convoys off the Libyan coast will be awaited with tense anxiety by both Allies and Axis. That the advent of these ships will result in a fierce air and naval attack by the Allies is probable. Meanwhile there is no indication whether Auchinleck is receiving further help, but presumably more is being rushed to him.

Doggie - Woogie

Wide World Features

LITTLE Tommy Tucker of the nursery rhymes song sang for his supper, but Mr. and Mrs. Ralph K. Smith's Irish setter at Richmond, Va., plays the piano for his. That's why they call him Mozart. When Mozart sights a cookie or other tidbit, he runs to the piano, rears on his hind legs and begins pounding the keys with his front paws. Then he collects the cookie.

THE UPHILL BATTLE

Man About Manhattan

By George Tucker

NEW YORK—There is a sign in the New York Museum of Science and Industry that says:

"Versailles — Here begins a story of how free nations fell into life and death peril. . . ."

After you read this sign, if you turn your eyes slowly to the right, you will see a pictorial display that is the accumulated steps—some of them political blunders, others historically important of a high dramatic quality — of the flow of events that began when the Versailles treaty was signed and ended with Japanese bombs falling over Pearl Harbor.

Then, at the end of the display, is another sign that is President Roosevelt's Prayer For Peace, and in it is the significant line: "Grant us faith and understanding to cherish all those who fight for freedom as if they were our brothers."

* * *

THIS is a sobering display. You didn't think so much of the pictures themselves, when they appeared back in the twenties, back in the early thirties, and now. But taken together, they add up to an awesome total.

You can see the signers of the Versailles treaty, who hoped for lasting peace, shaking hands with each other after their signatures had been affixed to the documents. . . . You can see crowds clamoring through the streets of Berlin. . . . You can see Hitler upon his election as Chancellor of Germany. . . . You can see the Kaiser fleeing to Doorn, the assassination of a Yugoslav king, a harassed Selassie pleading at Geneva, Franco leading his rebel army, King George dead in London, Hitler and Mussolini forming a pact, Hitler and Matsuoka forming another pact, the "impregnable" Maginot line, with its neat little cement pill boxes and its yawning guns. . . . It's all there, from Doorn to Dunkirk, from Russia to Rangoon. . . . I'd say maybe there are 50 pictures, certainly no more than fifty. . . . But, they tell a story. They make you think.

* * *

HERE'E a little personal note that can bear telling. I suppose, without anyone raising objection. . . . In Tommy Dorsey's orchestra are 30 men and a girl. That makes 31 musicians. But on Tommy's payroll are 32 names. It's explained this way: Bunny Berigan's name remains on the payroll, though Bunny himself, that ace of hot trumpet players, is dead. His salary goes on just the same, to his widow and two kids.

Dorsey, by the way, travels so constantly that he plays solos to his pack of hounds, just so they won't forget him. Everytime he gets home he surrounds himself with yelping mutts and gives them something sweet on the old slide trombone. Now, when someone puts on one of Tommy's records, the pack goes crazy. They think the "Old Massa" is just around the corner.

Washington In Wartime

By Jack Stinnett

WASHINGTON—Assuming that there are a few direct questions and answers which will reduce the manpower problem to its A-B-C's, the War Manpower commission has attempted to do same by giving the following replies:

Q. How many men will be required in the labor army—on and off the farms?

A. By the end of 1943 and early in 1944, we must have 20,000,000 workers in direct war production; 12,000,000 more on the farms.

Q. How many men will be taken by the armed forces?

A. There are slightly over 2,000,000 now under arms; there may be 4,500,000 by the end of the year; perhaps 6,000,000 to 7,000,000 by next year end; and if the war continues, at least 10,000,000.

Q. How many war workers will be women?

A. There now are close to a million and a half women doing war work. Probably 4,000,000 more will be needed in the next two years.

* * *

Q. Where is this war labor force coming from?

A. Conversion and suspension of peacetime industries will provide approximately 8,000,000; a half million more will come from the farms; around 400,000 from the professional ranks; a million and a half from the presently unemployed; and some 2,000,000 from the present reservoir of housewives, youths and over-age (retired) workers.

Q. Who is in charge of seeing that this is brought about in an orderly way?

A. The War Manpower commission, headed by Paul V. McNutt, which is working with the various government labor agencies in the Labor and Agriculture departments; Selective Service; the War Labor Board, and scores of training agencies and private industrial set-ups.

Q. Will there be a labor "draft"?

A. Probably not. In some specialized professional fields, such as the medical profession, it may be necessary if present trends continue. But at the moment, it is considered likely that the voluntary movement to place every man and woman in the job for which he or she is best fitted and most needed will be sufficient.

* * *

Q. What industries will need the most additional workers?

A. Civilian employment in navy yards, army arsenals and air depots will be increased at least five-fold; aircraft workers quadrupled; shipbuilding and army and navy ordnance tripled.

Q. How many "new" workers will be needed?

A. Approximately 11,000,000 in industry; 2,500,000 on the farms (during harvest periods).

Q. How many "trades" are short of manpower?

A. At least 100. For example, 50 tool designers are needed for every one now employed; 25 toolmakers for every one now working; 22 marine machinists, etc.

Q. Where does one apply for a wartime job?

A. At the offices of the United States Employment Service. These are located in all large cities, in all state capitals, and most of the county seat towns

The Literary Guidepost

By John Selby

"A NEW RUSSIAN GRAMMAR" AND "A FIRST RUSSIAN READER," by Anna H. Semeonoff (Dutton; each $1.95); "COLLOQUIAL JAPANESE," by William Montgomery McGovern; (Dutton: $1.85).

BISMARCK is said to have sneered one day that a talent for languages is a head waiter's talent. Whether because of that strange remark (comparable to "history is bunk" in the sublimity of its ignorance) or because of laziness, many people believe Americans are the worst linguists in the world. Perhaps we are.

I may be a little late for us to take up either Russian or Japanese, but if we want to try, the means are at hand. Three books of value have been re-issued in the light of Pearl Harbor.

Two are Russian books—Anna H. Semeonoff's "A New Russian Grammar" and the same teacher's "A First Russian Reader." The last is not really a re-issue. My review copy is from the first American edition and it was published in 1936. The grammar is the fourth edition published in this country.

The third book is William Montgomery McGovern's "Colloquial Japanese," and it is subtitled "a quick, easy way to learn Japanese" This grammar begins by insisting that Japanese is not really very hard—that, indeed, a fair student can get through the book and emerge with a workable command of Japanese in six months. Both grammars are designed for independent study as well as classroom work, and a brief survey indicates that this is not merely wishful thinking. But one day's experience is not enough for me to be sure!

For the amateur, the odd characters of both Russians and Japanese are forbidding. In Japanese there is a good deal of reason for fright, too, because actually there are a number of Japanese languages. The colloquial style of Japanese is the ordinary medium of exchange. The epistolary style is used for letters and post cars. There is a literary style for books and periodicals (about two-thirds Chinese and one-third Japanese). And finally there is the classical style which is actually Chinese, based on the Confucian Canon. In addition, Japanese may be written in either the ideographic or the phonetic way, and there are three ways of writing phonetcally.

Russian has its peculiar alphabet and distinctive orthography, but it at least stays put. Perhaps it would be better to start on Russian.

KING'S ROW KINFOLK

RONALD REAGAN and ANN SHERIDAN — starred in Warners' brilliant picturization of Henry Bellamann's best-selling novel, "King's Row." The characters above are Drake McHugh, happy-go-lucky small town boy and Randy Monaghan, daughter of a section boss on 'the other side of the tracks,' who marries him. Others in the distinguished cast are Robert Cummings, Betty Field, Charles Coburn, Claude Rains, Judith Anderson, Nancy Coleman, Maria Ouspenskaya, Harry Davenport and Kaaren Verne.

NEWS From Our NEIGHBORS

DEALE

Howard Parks is accompanying the Rev. George Stahl to the camp meeting to be held in Potomac Park, W. Va. on Wednesday, Thursday and Friday, July 15, 16 and 17.

The meeting is organized by the Pentecostal Assemblies of God of Potomac Park.

SEVERNA PARK ROUND BAY and VICINITY

Miss Marie Shiroky underwent an appendix operation at South Baltimore General Hospital on Monday, July 6.

Mrs. John L. Wilbourn's mother, Mrs. Lillie May Phelps, wife of the late Royal Lee Phelps, died on July 8 after an illness of several weeks. The funeral was held on Friday at her home in Larchmont at 3 P. M. with burial at Parkwood Cemetery. Mrs. Phelps is survived as well by a son, R. Gorman Phelps of New York City. Mr. and Mrs. Wilbourn have made their summer home at Westhaven for a number of years.

Warren Ensor Schaeffer, third class carpenter's mate, is home on a ten days' leave.

Supper party and barn dance guests of Nancy Kittinger on Saturday night from 6 to 9 at her home on the Severn were Araby Morgan, Irene Grakley, Priscilla Winchell, Marie Giddings, Teresa Cyr, Denny Morgan, Bill Coney, Ronald Giddings, Jimmie Mills, Hugh Auld and Donald Brown.

Francis Machin, son of Mr. and Mrs. Isaac Machin of Carrollton Manor left on July 1 to join the Navy at Norfolk.

Horace Potter has returned from Chicago where he was called by the serious illness of his father, Edward E. Potter who died the following Saturday after his arrival. Funeral services were held on Tuesday, July 7. Besides his son, Mr. Potter is survived by a daughter, Mrs. Helen Spiering of Chicago.

Mr. and Mrs. George B. Mosner have returned from a business trip of several weeks during which they stayed at Long View Farm, the home of Mrs. Mosner's brother, Charles E. Slade. They will soon leave for a sojourn on the Eastern Shore of Maryland and Virginia where Mr. Mosner will be occupied for some time.

Miss Janus Yentsch visited Mr. and Mrs. Norval Hahn of Westminster over the week-end. Mr. and Mrs. Charles Yentsch were guests of Mr. and Mrs. Carlton Gray of Baltmiore on the 4th.

Mr. and Mrs. Edward F. Mitchell were recent guests of their son-in-law and daughter, Mr. and Mrs. Herbert Brown of the Park.

Doctor and Mrs. John Skodowsky and son, John, Jr., are spending two weeks vacation at Carrollton Manor.

Mr. and Mrs. Ernest Turner of Manhattan Beach presented the defense organization there with an American flag.

Mrs. Edward Brinton and baby daughter, Norvell Pearson Brinton, are visiting Mrs. Brinton's mother, Mrs. Norvell F. Chapman, of Round Bay.

Miss Ruth Thopmson was hostess to a number of her friends a a dance at her home in the Park on Wednesday night.

DON WINSLOW OF THE NAVY by FRANK MARTINEK
HERE'S WHAT I MEAN, RED. EACH DEFENSE BOND WE BUY MEANS MORE SHIPS AND PLANES FOR OUR NAVY!
DON WINSLOW OF THE NAVY SAYS— SHIPMATES, LET'S GO ALL OUT FOR OUR EXPANDING NAVY—
BUY DEFENSE BONDS!
—Courtesy Bell Syndicate

CLASSIFIED ADS

For Rent 1

FOR RENT — Unfurnished two bedroom modern house. $40.00 per month. R. C. Riddick, Sylvan Shores, Riva, Md. Phone 5616. a-4

FOR RENT — Furnished three-room apartment. Private bath. Apply 63 East Street. Phone 2175. a-13

FOR RENT—Two unfurnished rooms, light good location. No cooking facilities. Phone 3446. tf

FOR RENT—Five and seven room cottages. Furnished or unfurnished, improved. Sale 7-room cottage and acre. Telephone West River 20-F-14. a-1

FOR RENT—Furnished bedroom in residential section. Phone 2923. tf

FOR RENT—Unfurnished apartment. Apply Oscar Shacks, 37 West St. tf

FOR RENT—Modern bungalow completely furnished 4920 County Road, Woodland Beach. Adults only. Call Sundays or after 6 P. M. during week. tf

FOR RENT—Rooms for gentlemen. Wally Hotel, 81 West Street. tf

FOR RENT—Furnished room, Centrally located. Phone 4194. tf

For Sale 2

FOR SALE

217 South Cherry Grove Avenue.
LOT—50 ft. x 150 ft.
HOUSE—Two bedroom bungalow, three years old. Has large second floor where additional rooms may be added.
FIRST FLOOR — Living room with fire place, dinette, kitchen with built-in cabinets, 2 bedrooms and bath. House in perfect condition. Was built to owner's specifications using finest materials. PRICE $6,590

FOR SALE

522 Burnside Avenue, Eastport.
LOT—100 ft. x 160 ft. Driveway in rear.
HOUSE, 7 ROOMS — Hot water heat, with coal burning furnace. Large porch. Convenient terms. PRICE $4,250

CARL S. THOMAS
REAL ESTATE & INSURANCE
221 Main St. Hotel Md. Bldg.
ANNAPOLIS 3336

FOR SALE—6-room house furnished or unfurnished in Wardour. Immediate occupancy. Phone 5097. a-1

FOR SALE—Sacrifice. New automatic oil heater for water tank. Call Severna Park 310-J. a-1

FOR SALE—Pipeless furnace in good condition. Phone for information 6248. a-4

FOR SALE—Small unfurnished cottage. Available bathing. Delightful location. Price $750. Write Box 87 Evening Capital. a-1

FOR SALE—4-room furnished bungalow, Harness Creek. All improvements. One hundred feet waterfront, 200 feet deep. Screen porch. Phone 6241. a-1

FOR SALE—Studio couch, walnut bedroom set, English perambulator, crib and mattress, play pen and bassinet. Phone 3683. a-3

FOR SALE—Buick 1937 Special Sedan. Four brand new tires, one spare. Price $495 cash. Box 86 Evening Capital. a-4

FOR SALE—Severn, Maryland. Bungalow, ¾ acre. New, 3 rooms and bath, fruit trees, schools, churches and bus service. J. Lindsey, Twin Oak Road, Severn, Md a-4

FOR SALE—House centrally located. Income producing. Reasonable. Apply Box 85 Evening Capital. tf

FOR SALE—Buick 1938 Special sedan. Five new tires, price $550 cash. Phone South Shore 2178. a-1

FOR SALE—Vacant lot. 40x192 feet on Jefferson St., city. Price $500. Dial 2461. Chas. F. Lee. a-1

FOR SALE — Waterfront year-round bungalow, 2 car garage, 90 foot frontage on Harness Creek. Price, $3,700. W. H. M. Smith Agenye, 11 School St. Telephone 4221. tf

FOR SALE—Oil Ranges, Refrigerators, Washing Machines, Slipcovers, Bedding, Strollers, Cribs, Congoleum and Summer Rugs. BOUGHT-SOLD-EXCHANGED-RENTED. Annapolis Furniture Co., 96 West Street. Phone 2110. tf

Help Wanted—Female 4

HELP WANTED FEMALE—White or colored. General housework, nice salary. Phone 4119. tf

HELP WANTED FEMALE — Colored girl for next few weeks. Cooking and general housework. Part time either afternoon or morning. Small family. Fares paid. References required. Dial 3188. a-4

HELP WANTED FEMALE—White and colored women. Apply Arundel Laundry. West street. tf

HELP WANTED FEMALE — Maid for general housework. Phone 2504, after 7 P. M. a-1

HELP WANTED FEMALE—First cook, good salary, steady employment. Apply Ortman's Restaurant. tf

HELP WANTED FEMALE — White waitress for week-end nights. Wally Cocktail Lounge. tf

Miscellaneous 12

MISCELLANEOUS—Tanglewood-on-the Bay. Picnic Grove cottages, outing dinners, Annapolis 5574. tf

MISCELLANEOUS — We deliver anything — anywhere. Personal Delivery Service. Phone 2781. tf

MISCELLANEOUS — Paper hanging, painting, stove and furnace repairing. Phone 4197. tf

Help Wanted—Male 4

HELP WANTED MALE — Night bar porter. Wally Hotel. tf

HELP WANTED MALE — Ambitious young man as stock clerk and salesman. Good salary, marvelous opportunity. Apply Herbert's Men's Shop. tf

Wanted 6

WANTED—To sub-lease an apartment or small house for month of August. Apply Box 88, Evening Capital. a-1

WANTED—U. S. N. A. instructor and wife want furnished apartment. Two to three-rooms, kitchen and bath. Call Annapolis 2474. a-4

WANTED—Two horse trailer, reasonable. Call 5451. a-4

WANTED—Unfurnished house or apartment by Navy couple. Phone 6427. a-4

WANTED—Unfurnished apartment or small house for officer and wife. Call 2780. a-3

WANTED—To buy antique secretary walnut or mahogany preferred. Phone 2720. a-1

WANTED—To rent for year or more two or three bedroom furnished house or apartment, prior to August 18 Phone 4755. a-3

WANTED—A mature woman to act as hostess and cashier for summer hotel. Phone Mr. Emory, Annapolis 5621. a-1

WANTED—Reliable nursemaid with some house work. Phone 4701. a-1

WANTED—Cook or short order cook. Apply Jack's Barbecue, 1803 West St. a-1

WANTED — Daily transportation to Navy Department, Washington. Hours 4-12, either as passenger or Share Your-Car Club. Phone 2139. a-1

WANTED—Will pay cash for your car William J. Meyers. Call Vernon 5320 or 1780 North Charles St., Baltimore Md. 1

Lost and Found 8

LOST — Ladies' sport model Bulova watch between Main and Cathedral streets. Phone 3751. a-3

ORDER NISI
In The Circuit Court For
Anne Arundel County
No. 8361 Equity

In the Matter of the Sale of the Mortgaged Real Estate of Belva Lord Ravenburg and Husband

Ordered, this 31st day of July, 1942, That the Report and Account of the Auditor, filed this day in the above entitled cause, be ratified and confirmed, unless cause to the contrary be shown on or before the

31ST DAY OF AUGUST, NEXT;

Provided, a copy of this Order be inserted in some newspaper published in Anne Arundel County, once in each of three successive weeks before the 31st day of August, next.

JOHN H. HOPKINS, 3rd, Clerk.
True Copy:
Test: JOHN H. HOPKINS, 3rd, Clerk. a-15

DIED

BLAXTON—On Friday, July 31, 1942, at her residence, 49 Washington Street, ANNIE E., beloved wife of the late Colbert Blaxton.

Funeral will be held Monday, August 3, 1942. Interment in Brewer Hill Cemetery. E. H. B. Parker, funeral Directoress. a-1

VANCOUVER ISLAND SET FOR EMERGENCY

Wide World Features

VICTORIA, B. C.—A civilian automobile reserve of nearly 500 vehicles and power boat squadrons of some 400 craft stand ready for any emergency on Vancouver Island, whether it be a sudden troop movement or the evacuation of civilians.

Harold Husband, of Victoria, recently appointed by Transit Controller George S. Gray to survey and organize all emergency transport facilities on the island, has indexed every motor vehicle on the records of provincial police. His staff has arranged to fit drivers into an emergency plan and organized a civilian sea force of ferries, tugs, barges and smaller power boats.

The island has been zoned and district controllers for the emergency service appointed in some cases. Car owners have equipped their vans and trucks with removable seats so the vehicles could be transformed into evacuee carriers at a moment's notice.

ON THE OFFENSIVE AMERICA!

★ ★ ★

Wars are won by attacking, not by sitting in a fort!

And today America is taking the offensive against the Axis with hard-fighting, non-stoppable men and materials!

We're taking the offensive, too, against the enemy at home—the inflationary 6th column that blows prices sky high.

You can help in both fights by saving at least 10% of your money in U. S. War Bonds every pay day. Attack the Axis with your dollars today.

You can start with as little as a 10c War Stamp and you can get a $25.00 War Bond (maturity value) for only $18.75—at your local post office, bank or other convenient sales agency.

U. S. Treasury Department

GOOD BREEDING STOCK NEEDED FOR LAYING HENS

In these days of relatively high feed prices, laying flocks must be secured from good breeding flocks in order to produce eggs at a reasonable profit, according to Charles S. Williams of the University of Maryland poultry extension staff.

At current prices, he says, the layers should average about 150 eggs per bird on a henhoused basis.

Most poultrymen calculate the average egg production of their flocks on a monthly basis, Mr. Williams says, and then add the 12 monthly averages. This method, he states, gives a higher average than is actually represented by the total production. Some poultrymen use the hen-housed basis of determining average production per bird, dividing the total number of eggs produced during the year by the total number of birds placed in the house in the fall.

This method, he says, is the fairest for determining average production because it takes into account mortality as well as birds culled. An average of 150 eggs on a hen-housed basis is equivalent to 167 eggs per hen when mortality amounts to 10 per cent., and 188 eggs per hen when mortality amounts to 20 per cent.

Mr. Williams says that mortality and culling are usually less among well-bred flocks than among poorly-bred flocks. For that reason, he advises that the breeding flock used to produce chicks from which the laying stock is secured be carefully selected. Vigor, body type, and other factors should be considered. Egg production, he points out, is inherited.

Training in the selection of breeding stock will be given, Mr. Williams says, at the Hatchery School to be held at the University of Maryland on August 11, 12 and 13. It is particularly important, he states, that flock-selecting agents who select hatchery flocks attend the school. Flock owners from all parts of the State are invited to participate.

Tragedy!

Enough To Break A Pitcher's Heart

Wide World Features

SEATTLE—The University of Washington baseball team was playing its old foe—Washington State, at Pullman.

It was the last of the ninth. Doug Ford, 215-pound sophomore hurler, was on the mound for Washington.

He hadn't allowed a single hit up to that point.

He got the first man. The second also went out. Just one more putout and Ford would have a perfect no-hit, no-run game.

The third man hit an infield roller. There was plenty of time, but the first sacker was pulled off the bag. Before the uprising could be quelled, Washington State scored two runs to tie the score, then went into the tenth inning to win, 3-2.

Ford can tell you that coming close just doesn't count.

SOLDIERS IN ALASKA GET FISHING TACKLE

Wide World Features

SEATTLE — Seattle sportsmen have turned the wartime motto to "keep 'em fishing."

An appeal for fishing tackle to provide recreation for service men in Alaska, where there's a heap more chance for fun at fishing than at night clubs, has brought in an array of tackle that would make a boy's—or a salmon-snagging sergeant's—eyes bulge.

Rods, reels, lines, plugs and leaders — just about everything but bent pins—are included in the collection that has flooded in since an appeal was issued to sportsmen.

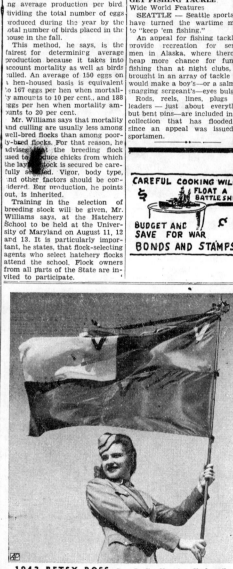

1942 BETSY ROSS—Joan Leslie, film star, displays the United Nations flag she designed, with fields of red, white, blue and green. From the top of the staff ripple streamers of varied colors symbolizing the United Nations.

MODEST MAIDENS

Trademark Registered U. S. Patent Office

"But what do you want with a mink coat in THIS weather?"

SCORCHY SMITH

Trademark Registered U. S. Patent Office

Welcome!

OAKY DOAKS

Trademark Registered U. S. Patent Office

A Nutty Affair

OH, DIANA!

Trademark Registered U. S. Patent Office

Flight Of The Jailbird

DICKIE DARE

Trademark Registered U. S. Patent Office

The Riot Act

HOMER HOOPEE

Trademark Registered U. S. Patent Office

Oh, Promise Me!

THE ADVENTURES OF PATSY

Trademark Registered U. S. Patent Office

Saved By The Bell

NEIGHBORLY NEIGHBORS

THE DOOLITTLES

WOMEN OF MOOSE TO HOLD PICNIC

The local chapter Women of the Moose and invited guests will hold a picnic, rain or shine, at 1:30 P. M. Sunday at the Moose Home on West street.

Members have been told to

come and bring picnic lunches. There will be dancing and games.

The Junior Moose will meet at the home at 7:30 P. M. Monday.

CALVARY GROUP TO MEET MONDAY

Group No. 1, Women's Society of Christian Service of Calvary Methodist Church, will meet at 8 P. M. Monday at the home of Mrs. A. W. Condell, 10 Monroe court.

German prisoners, captured by the Allies in action on the North African front, ride in a lighter to a vessel which will take them overseas to permanent prison camps for the duration of the war.

Local Tennis Club Tourney Holds Interest

Members Competing In Hard Fought Ladder Matches

(By Leonard Berman)

Another tennis season is slowly ebbing away, one which is bright-packed with its first wartime background in 25 years.

The current campaign opened in the midst of shortages and rationing caused by the war. Rubber, scarce essential product for war, was of course the worry of the players, since the balls are essential.

Ersatz Balls

As a result, a new kind of tennis ball was created, one in which reclaimed rubber is used in place of the crude rubber. Players all over the country eventually had to fall back on the ersatz balls, thankful that they have any with which to play.

Many tournaments have been discontinued for the duration on account of the shortage. However, this year as every year near the completion of its season, the Annapolis Tennis Club will stage its own tournament, consisting of five separate divisions. Champions will be crowned in men's singles, women's singles and junior singles and also men's doubles and mixed doubles.

Much Enthusiasm

Much enthusiasm is engendered annually over the A.T.C. tournament, which more or less supplements a municipal tennis tournament. Competition this year promises to be keener than in all of the club's history. An indication of the closely matched members is the hard fought ladder matches played almost daily on the St. John's new Har-Tru courts.

J. Calvin Rogers, president of the Annapolis Tennis Club, urged all interested tennis players in Annapolis to join the club for the final month of the season in order to be eligible to compete in the tournament and also to play a

full month on the courts from Aug. 15 to Sept. 15.

Players Invited

"I want present and prospective members to understand," Rogers remarked, "that this tournament will be run off differently than in former years in that the rounds of play will take from one to two days to be completed and not a whole drawn out week as was the former custom."

Plans are now being made for the A.T.C. tournament to begin within a week's time, so that new members will have time to join up at the St. John's business office and present ones to register at the courts.

WAR

(Continued From Page One)

one of claiming victories in order to get denials for the purpose of information.

Rioting Ebbs In India

Evidence of a quiet but troublesome boycott by the All-India Congress in its campaign for independence appeared as rioting and terrorism died down throughout India.

While Tokyo maintained silence on land operations in the Solomons, the Japanese War Ministry announced that Lieut. Gen. Masaharu Homma had been relieved of his post as commander-in-chief of Japanese forces in the Philippines to permit his assignment elsewhere. This might mean that Homma was being shifted to the Solomons to direct the defense of these strategic islands where American Marines, by latest accounts, are expanding at least three beachheads.

Tight official secrecy cloaked the progress of the Solomon battle with the navy in Washington announcing only that "operations are continuing." Unofficial reports in Australia, however, said the Marines were pushing deeper into the jungles of three key islands, believed to be Florida, Guadalcanal and Malaita.

Flying Fortresses Attack

Allied flying fortresses and medium bombers caught Japanese vessels in New Guinea waters, west of the Solomons, yesterday and drove home three separate attacks, General MacArthur's headquarters reported. Bad weather prevented the pilots from observing the full extent of the damage. Three Japanese fighter planes were shot down, and three were damaged. All the Allied planes returned to the bases.

The Japanese vessels presumably were heading toward the Solomons from Salamaua, their chief base in New Guinea, or from Rabaul or Gasmata, in New Britain.

Marshal Semeon Timoshenko's Red armies, according to Moscow, were reported to have crushed the first great Nazi onslaught toward Stalingrad, counter-attacking to drive back the Germans after they had broken through and reached

the Don river below Kletskaya, 75 miles northwest of the big Volga steel city.

Caucasus Front

In the Caucasus, the Russians acknowledged that German flying columns driving down the Rostov-Baku railway toward the Caspian Sea had advanced within 140 miles of the Grozny oil fields after a 50-mile thrust in 24 hours. The invaders were now leaving the flat plains on the northern side of the towering Caucasus range, a terrain ideally suited for tanks, and had come within sight of snow-capped Mt. Elborus rising 18,465 feet above the steppes. A bulletin from Adolf Hitler's headquarters emphasizing this new phase of the fighting said:

"The enemy, exploiting mountainous terrain which is particularly favorable for defense, is still putting up resistance in order to cover his retreat on the sea route from the north Caucasus front."

Moscow claimed that 3,000 Germans had been killed in two days of fighting near a point on Lake Ilmen. The Russians also were attacking in the Bryansk sector.

The British admiralty report on the battle of the Mediterranean convoy discounted the Axis claims that it had been smashed and dispersed. Axis reports declared three cruisers, two destroyers, 21 merchant ships, and the aircraft carrier Eagle had been sunk and other ships damaged.

Military Must

(Continued From Page One)

blackouts, including practice tests.

O'Conor was advised that the order also has been issued to all posts, camps and stations and to all military personnel in the Third Service Command.

Military Missions

Reckord stipulated that only officers and enlisted men engaged on military missions would move through civilian areas during blackout periods. All other military personnel in civilian areas, located there because of residence or for other reasons, would conform to the civilian blackout code when alarm signs were received, he said.

Officers, not in formation, but required to move through civilian areas, must present proper identification or challenged by civilian defense authorities, Reckord said. Enlisted men, besides carrying proper identification, also must bear another identification card, signed by their commanding officers, stating that they are authorized to move through the areas.

All military personnel, moving in formation, whether on foot or in trucks, must be passed unchallenged by civilian authorities, he told O'Conor.

SOLOMON ISLAND MARINES MAY HAVE TRAINED AT SOLOMONS

SOLOMONS, Md., Aug. 14 (AP) —Residents of this Chesapeake bay community today speculated whether U. S. Marines now fighting in the south Pacific may have gone from Solomons Island to the Solomon Islands.

The speculation was spurred by Lieut. Gen. Thomas Holcomb, commandant of the U. S. Marine Corps, who said last night that the marines had staged near Solomons a training operation "similar in most respects" to the Solomon Island invasion.

"Ships arrived off shore," General Holcomb said in a radio broadcast from New York describing the Chesapeake bay maneuver. "Marines shoved off in fast landing boats, and at the prearranged time sped shoreward. During the run to the beach and throughout the attack, guns of the fleet and planes pinned the enemy to the ground with their shells and bombs.

"Upon reaching the beach, the first wave of marines, quickly followed by others, began the slow, difficult process of cutting through enemy wire and infiltrating through enemy lines."

General Holcomb said that the offensive operation against the Japanese in the Solomon Islands is "something marines have been trained to do for the last 167 years."

Solomons Island, connected by a causeway with the Southern Maryland mainland, figured in the first World War, residents recalled.

It was here that four German vessels confiscated by the U. S. in 1917 were stored until the government ordered their sale in 1939, one, renamed the George Washington, in 1918 carried President Wilson to the peace conference at Versailles.

Around The Radio Dial Tonight

WCAO	600K	WCBM	Sweet and Mellow.	WCBM	Ted Straeter, songs.
WBAL	1090K	WITH	Sports Special.	WABC	Maudie's Diary.
WBBM	1000K	WJZ	Sweet and Low.		
WCBM	1400K			**7:45**	
WITH	1230K	**5:15**		WCAO	Spotlight News: Music.
WOR, M.B.S. Key	710K	WFBR	Talk, James McMillan.	WFBR	You're in the Army Now.
WBAL, C.B.S. Key	880K	WITH	Portia Faces Life, drama.	WEAF	Kaltenborn Edits the News.
WEAF, N.B.C. Red Key	660K	WCEM	Rhythm Rounders.	WJZ	Diane Courtney and the Jesters.
WJZ, N.B.C. Blue Key	770K	WJZ	The Sea Hound.	WOR	Dick Jurgens' Orch.

NEW YORK, Aug. 20 — (Wide World)—For something like 13 years Alfred Ryder has played the part of Sammy in the Goldbergs, Gertrude Berg's serial which has been on the air the same number of years. Now Ryder, who is 26 years old, is going in the army, and so is Sammy in the script.

Ryder's last broadcast via CBS is August 31, the day before his induction. In that same program Sammy will bid goodbye to the listeners. His character, except for references to him and letters home, will be omitted for the duration.

Topics tonight (Thursday):
NBC—8 Frank Morgan and others; 8:30 Aldrich Family; 9 Bob Crosby hour; 10 Rudy Vallee and Billie Burke; 10:30 March of Time.

CBS—8 Thirty Minutes to Play; 8:30 Death Valley Days; 9 Major Bowes amateurs.

BLU—7:30 Earl Wrightson, baritone; 8:30 Sur Les Boulevards, concert; 10:15 Tommy Dorsey's show.

MBS—8 Sinfonietta; 8:30 It Pays To Be Ignorant, quiz; 9:30 Chateau Horgan, variety.

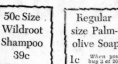
Japanese Beetle Season Near End

Use Milky Disease At 1500 Points In County

The 1942 season for Japanese beetles in Anne Arundel county is practically over according to County Agent Stanley E. Day.

A few stragglers, he said, may be seen until frost but the number will be so reduced that damage from feeding will be negligible.

In areas where adults were abundant this summer Mr. Day said he anticipated some damage to the roots of plants, lawns, and pastures this fall and next spring. The reason for this is that the females of the beetle that were flying this summer laid on an average of from 40 to 60 eggs. These eggs which are laid in the ground, usually in grassland, hatch into little grubs that feed upon and damage the roots of plants. Severe grub damage on the roots of strawberry plants has been reported from Somerset county.

In commenting upon the control work that is being conducted in Anne Arundel county by the County Agent, in cooperation with the Department of Entomology at the University of Maryland, and the Board of County Commissioners, Mr. Day explained that the main objective of the county program is to establish disease and parasites for the purpose of ultimately relieving present acute conditions and reducing the beetle to the status of an unimportant insect.

Definite Results

Indications are that definite results are being obtained. Notwithstanding the fact that beetles are increasing in certain formerly lightly infested areas—a condition to be expected—there is improvement in certain old, heavily infested areas throughout the State. Reports show where milky disease is being used in a concentrated way, beetle populations are diminishing. Areas in the State showing noticeably fewer beetles this year than last include Pocomoke City, Cecil county, the northern portion of Queen Anne's, Kent and Harford counties, the Patapsco Neck section of Baltimore, and certain sections in the metropolitan area of Prince George's county.

Mr. Day reported that the milky disease has been established on over 1,500 properties and farms in Anne Arundel county.

In discussing the milky disease Mr. Day cautioned that it must be remembered that before satisfactory results can be obtained

(Continued on Page Six)

SOCIETY

Ensign Robert Neff To Wed Miss Barbara Sanger Tomorrow

The marriage of Miss Barbara Sanger, daughter of Mr. and Mrs. Alan Bridgman Sanger of Old Greenwich, Conn., to Ensign Robert L. Neff, U.S.N.R., son of Doctor and Mrs. J. Luther Neff of Annapolis, will take place tomorrow afternoon in St. Paul's Episcopal Church, Riverside, Conn.

The Rev. John J. Hawkins will perform the ceremony, assisted by the bridegroom's father, who is pastor of Calvary Methodist Church.

Miss Sanger will be given in marriage by her father and will be attended by her sister, Miss Marcia Sanger.

Paul Neff, Annapolis, will serve his brother as best man. The ushers will be John Neff, Annapolis; Ensign Walter Neal, U.S.N.R., Frostburg; Richard Stephens, Washington, and Gordon Rennie, Greenwich, Conn.

* * *

Son Is Born To James O'Neills

Mr. and Mrs. James O'Neill of Flushing, N. Y., announce the birth of a son yesterday at Long Island College Hospital.

Before her marriage, Mrs. O'Neill was Miss Eleanor Hill, daughter of Mrs. Owen Hill, 86 Duke of Gloucester street, and the late Lieut. Comdr. Hill, U.S.N.

* * *

Miss Comp In Hospital

Miss Suzie Jane Comp, daughter of Commander and Mrs. C. O. Comp, is recuperating at Emergency Hospital following an appendectomy.

* * *

Frank R. Stewart Promoted In Navy

Frank Reid Stewart, son of Mr. and Mrs. N. F. Stewart, has been promoted to second class aviation machinist's mate and is at Ellyson Field, Pensacola, Fla.

He has been in service since December.

* * *

Maj. Gen. Colton Has Responsible Post

Maj. Gen. Roger B. Colton, assistant chief, Signal Corps, U. S. Army, is in charge of signal material for the army. He is a younger brother of Prof. M. A. Colton, retired Naval Academy professor.

* * *

Relatives Visit Prof. Darden

Mrs. H. E. Brewer and her daughter, Mimi, of Rocky Mount, N. C., are the guests of Mrs. Brewer's brother, Prof. William Darden, and his family of Thompson street.

* * *

Coale Back From New York

The Rev. Dr. James J. Coale, pastor of the First Presbyterian Church, has returned from a vacation trip to New York, where he spent two weeks.

Calendar Of The Week

SATURDAY, AUG. 29
Informal dance, USO building.
MONDAY, AUG. 31
Junior Hadassah rummage sale, 9-6, 439 Third St., Eastport.

Comdr., Mrs. Wright Christen Son

Comdr. and Mrs. W. D. Wright, of College avenue, had their son, Douglas Scott Wright, christened on Wednesday by Capt. William N. Thomas (Ch.C.) at 4 P. M., in St Andrew's Chapel, Naval Academy

Following the ceremony Comdr. and Mrs. Wright entertained the christening party at the Officers' Club.

* * *

Capt. and Mrs. Alden Honor Guests

The doctors on duty at the Naval Academy are entertaining at a farewell buffet supper tomorrow night at the Officers' Club, in honor of Captain George A. Alden (M.C.) and Mrs. Alden.

Oyster Season

(Continued From Page One)

construction, bleeding the industry of tongers, shuckers and packers.

Army engineers are constructing barracks at Solomons and are building at Cedar Point. To make it worse, the conversion of most of the bay's oyster boat construction facilities for the production of mosquito boats has deprived the industry of much-needed craft.

This year's product should be infinitely tastier than its predecessors, Mr. Woodfield said. The heavy rains of the past month have poured unprecedented amounts of fresh water into the bay and should make bivalves larger and less salty.

The outlook is not too dark, he said, except for the over-the-counter buyer of the half-shell variety. He must pay an estimated increase of 25 per cent.

Menus Of The Day

By Mrs. Alexander George

A Defense Dinner

(Lima beans, high in protein and carbohydrates, take over the main part of a dinner).

Serving 5 Or 6
Lima Stuffed Green Peppers
Baked Carrots
Blueberry Squares
Margarine or Butter
Sliced Pineapple (Fresh or Canned)
Molasses Crisps (Cookies)
Coffee for Adults
Milk for Children

Lima Stuffed Green Peppers

- 6 large firm peppers
- 1 cup cooked lima beans
- 2 tablespoons chopped pimientos
- 1 tablespoon chopped parsley
- ¼ teaspoon salt
- ⅔ cup boiled brown or white rice
- ⅛ teaspoon paprika
- 1 egg, beaten
- 3 tablespoons butter, melted
- 3 tablespoons cream

Remove tops and seeds from peppers. Rinse and cover with cold water. Slowly bring to boiling point and simmer 1 minute. Drain and rinse in cold water. Mix rest of ingredients and stuff peppers. Arrange in shallow pan and add ½ inch water. Bake 25 minutes in moderate oven.

Blueberry Squares

- 2 cups flour
- 4 teaspoons baking powder
- ¼ teaspoon salt
- 3 tablespoons fat
- ⅔ cup milk
- 1 beaten egg

Mix flour, baking powder and salt. Cut in fat. Add rest of ingredients and mix lightly. Pour into shallow pan and cover with berries.

Berries

- 2 cups blueberries
- 4 tablespoons honey
- ¼ teaspoon cinnamon
- 3 tablespoons soft butter

Mix ingredients and spread on top soft dough. Lightly press down with the broad side of a knife. Bake 20 minutes in moderate oven. Cut in squares

Modes Of The Moment

By Dorothy Roe

BLACK AND BLUE combine in this skillfully draped crepe dress and hat.

SEEK BOOKS FOR LIBRARY AT COLLEGE CREEK TERRACE

The College Creek Terrace Library is conducting a campaign to raise $200 to supply books for its shelves.

Names of organizations and individuals contributing $5 or more will be posted in the library.

A group of young people in the section have been offered a course in liberal arts, based on reading the "great books" of the St. John's College program. The college is helping by supplying two discussion leaders for the course, one a member of the faculty and the other a student of the college.

In order to supply the books needed and at the same time to build up the library, the committee for the library, headed by Summerfield Brown, chairman, is seeking contributions from civic organizations, churches, fraternities and individuals.

Because of their use both for food and oil, peanuts are being produced at a 155 per cent increase over 1941.

LOCAL AUTO CLUB OFFICIAL DISCUSSES GASOLINE PROBLEMS

Gas rationing brought to light certain factors which should serve as a warning to all motorists, Walton I. Howard, manager of the Annapolis branch of the Automobile Club of America, declared today. He pointed out that gasoline is dangerous to handle and is dangerous to hoard, not only to the owner but to the entire neighborhood.

"There has not been until recently any Federal regulation under the rationing program which prohibits the carrying of additional gasoline in containers in the Eastern rationed area," Mr. Howard continued.

New Regulations

"Under the new gasoline rationing regulations, though, no person shall consume gasoline unless such gasoline was acquired by him or on his behalf in exchange for valid coupons. Recent interpretation by OPA counsel has ruled that this applies to persons coming into the rationed areas. It does not apply to gasoline brought into the rationed area in the tank of the vehicle, including an auxiliary tank which is directly connected with the regular tank or the engine.

"Tourists entering Virginia may not carry extra gasoline in containers according to a ruling by T. Nelson Parker, chief state attorney for the Virginia office of the OPA.

"Maryland does not have a law prohibiting the carrying of gasoline although the Insurance Commissioner has prepared a code, not yet in effect. Some cities limit or prohibit carrying of gasoline in containers as a fire hazard. Baltimore city prohibits the carrying of more than one gallon in the car, even if it is in a safety can that is; an approved Underwriters ventilated can with automatic closure valve. Baltimore county will permit the carrying of gasoline providing it is in the safety can. Many other counties have similar laws.

States Differ

"Some states tax any gasoline brought in other than carried in the regular tank; others impose such a tax only when the additional amount is in excess of twenty gallons. Motorists should examine their insurance policies, although the standard form contract does not preclude such carrying of gasoline.

"Some motorists have installed a regular auxiliary gas tank in the back of their car, the work being done by capable mechanics, with a tubing connecting the auxiliary tank to the regular tank, and a vent running out under the fender to one side. Although they would not recommend such installations since they create quite a hazard in case of accident, Baltimore county and city fire authorities feel that such equipment already installed would be satisfactory as far as the law is concerned.

Storing Gasoline

"Storing of gasoline in or around the home is not prohibited by State law. The new regulations mentioned above will be very strict on this. In Baltimore city it is limited to one gallon in a safety container and in the county it must be in a safety can. Many other counties or towns limit the amount to five gallons in a safety can. Insurance policies for the home do not permit the storing of gasoline in the home, and the Insurance Commissioner will back up the companies in the voiding of claims where storage of gasoline can be proved.

"Because of the hazards involved, we do not feel it advisable to recommend the carrying of gasoline in containers, or storing it, but believe it is in order to point out the regulations governing such action and leave the decision to the individual's own judgment."

U. S. S. Iowa, Nation's Biggest, Slides Down Ways

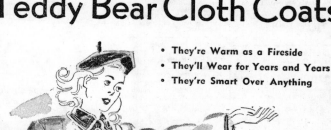

The 45,000-ton battleship Iowa, largest ever built by the United States, slides down the ways at Brooklyn navy yard seven months ahead of schedule. Assistant Secretary of the Navy Ralph A. Bard said the Iowa will "fire faster and farther than any other ship afloat."

RENT CONTROL

Area Rent Director, Lucien E. D. Gaudreau, in collaboration with the Chief Area Attorney, Risque W. Plummer, has released the following statement, which has to do with major capital improvements.

Major Capital Improvements

The term "major capital improvement" contemplates a substantial change in the housing accommodations such as would materially increase the rental value in a normal market where free bargaining prevails unaffected by a shortage in housing accommodations. It must be different from ordinary repair, replacement and maintenance. For the purpose of rent control the term has been liberally interpreted to the extent that a major capital improvement would fall into one of three categories:

(1) Structural Addition.
(2) A structural betterment,
(3) A complete rehabilitation.

(1) Structural Addition.

A structural addition is a clear addition to the housing accommodations, such as the construction of an additional room or a new porch or the installation of plumbing, heating or electricity where such facilities did not previously exist. The addition need not necessarily be a part of the structure, but might also include a new garage or the installation of sidewalks. If the improvement has resulted in some added feature which did not exist prior to the change of a kind which normally result in an increase in the rental value, then it would be a substantial change by a major improvement. provement.

(2) Structural Betterment.

A structural betterment is a qualitative improvement, even though such an improvement is in part a replacement. Within this group would be the modernization of an existing bathroom, the installation of a modern heating plant replacing an antiquated system, a change in the interior partitions such as would improve the layout, and all changes of similar character.

(3) Complete Rehabilitation.

A complete rehabilitation is a general modernization and reconstruction such as would make the property attractive in a different rental range. Even though the individual items involved would, if considered separately, be normal repair, replacement and maintenance, if, in the aggregate, there is a substantial change in the character of the housing accommodations, there would be grounds for adjustment. The difference between a rehabilitation which is a major capital improvement and ordinary repairs, is primarily a question of degree and extent. Only where the rehabilitation is so comprehensive that it would be expected to result in a comparatively high percentage adjustment in rental would it constitute a major capital improvement.

Even though a major capital improvement is made, it does not necessarily follow that an adjustment in the maximum rent is justified. Unless the improvement has resulted in an increase in the rental value of the housing accommodations, no adjustments should be granted. An example would be the installation of an automatic stoker in an apartment building where the landlord is obligated to furnish heat and hot water. Such an improvement does not give the tenants anything they did not previously receive and is made by the landlord solely for his own benefit. No increase in rental value would result, and no adjustment would be warranted.

It is important to note that where the landlord is now obligated to make and is making normal repairs, replacement and maintenance which the tenant was making on the date determining the maximum rent, this is not a major capital improvement but gives grounds for an adjustment based on an increase in services. Likewise, if a new stove or refrigerator not previously provided is now furnished by the landlord, there would be grounds for an adjustment based on Section 5 (a) (3) of the Maximum Rent Regula-
(3) of th eMaximum Rent Regula-

CLASSIFIED ADS

For Rent   1

OR RENT—Large furnished room for gentleman, or two. 424 Sixth Street, Eastport. Phone 2513 afer 4:30 P. M.   o-10

OR RENT—Nice comfortable rooms. 200 Gloucester Street. Phone 2214.   o-8

OR RENT—Barber shop with fixtures. Apply 435 Fourth St., Eastport.   tf

OR RENT—Three-room furnished cottage, electricity, running water in kitchen. Five minutes from Bus Line. Call 5007.   tf

OR RENT—Bedroom for one or two persons in residential section. Phone 2923.   tf

OR RENT—Rooms for gentlemen. Wally Hotel, 81 West Street.   tf

For Sale   2

OR SALE—Three rugs in good condition. One 9x12, others smaller. Phone 2720.   o-10

OR SALE—Chesapeake Bay puppies. Males, $15.00; females, $10.00. Norman ward, Shady Side, Maryland. Telephone West River 57-F-23.   o-8

OR SALE—Two small gas stoves for apartment. 110 Market St.   tf

OR SALE—1938 DeSoto coupe, six tires, new seat covers. $450. Telephone 4280.   o-13

OR SALE—1931 Chevrolet coupe, good tires. Call Annapolis 6401.   o-8

OR SALE—Cottage in West Annapolis. No reasonable offer will be refused. Apply Box 34, Evening Capital.   xx

OR SALE—Monarch electric range, like new. Phone 2854.   o-10

OR SALE—Unilow water softener. Little used. Complete fittings. Eliminates rust in Bunker type wells. Telephone 3133.   tf

OR SALE—Old country hams. Frederick R. Siegert, Galesville, Maryland. Phone West River 241-H.   o-16

OR SALE—Cookstoves, Coal Ranges, Cabinet Heaters, Fireplace Equipment, Bedding, blankets, cribs, Refrigerators, Congoleum Rugs BOUGHT-SOLD-EXCHANGED-RENTED. Annapolis Furniture Co., 96 West St. Phone 2140.

Help Wanted—Female   4

HELP WANTED, FEMALE—Experienced full time maid for general housework and cooking. Phone 2611 —Ext. 211.   o-10

HELP WANTED, FEMALE—Cleaning, hand laundry one day a week. Two adults—no children. Phone 1263.   tf

HELP WANTED, FEMALE—Maid for general housework. Must be experienced and reliable. References required. Phone 6211.   o-10

HELP WANTED FEMALE—Maid for general housework. Call 3070.   o-9

HELP WANTED FEMALE—Waitress, 6 day week, good wages. Apply The Annapolitan Tea Room, 48 Md. Ave. tf

HELP WANTED FEMALE — White waitress. Apply Wally Hotel, 81 West street.   tf

HELP WANTED FEMALE — Salesladies. Apply Oscar Shacks, 37 West street.

Help Wanted Male or Female   5

HELP WANTED MALE OR FEMALE. Colored waiters and waitresses for permanent employment. $40 per month. Apply Mr. Southerland, Carvel Hall.

Help Wanted—Male   4

HELP WANTED, MALE—Experienced white bartender for permanent position. Excellent salary. Write Box 69, Evening Capital, giving age, draft status, experience and references.   o-10

HELP WANTED, MALE—Full or part-time work in receiving room. Apply Sears-Roebuck & Company.   o-10

HELP WANTED MALE — Experienced stock man. Good salary, reasonable hours. Apply Evening Capital Box 56.   tf

HELP WANTED MALE — Night bar porter. Apply Wally Hotel, 81 West street.

Wanted   6

WANTED — ATTENTION — New and used civilian clothing bought. Cash at once. Phone 3070.   o-10

WANTED — Experienced bookkeeper. Permanent position. Excellent salary. Carvel Hall.   o-9

WANTED—To buy portable typewriter in good condition. Must have Elite type. Box 57. Evening Capital.   o-9

WANTED—To rent house or apartment furnished, two bedrooms or more in Annapolis or vicinity. Call Miss Sullivan 4139.   o-12

WANTED — Unfurnished two bedroom apartment or house in town or on bus line. Mr. Falkenstine, Maryland Hotel.   o-8

WANTED — Women to earn QUICK CASH. Sell Guild EMBOSSED Christmas Cards 50 for $1 with customer's name imprinted free. No experience necessary. 9 other beautiful assortments. You make up to 100% profit working full or part time. For free samples write to The Card Guild, 110 RU West 32nd St., New York City. xx

WANTED — Young couple wish to rent apartment or bungalow, furnished. Location within three miles of Academy. Roy L. Stephens, Arnold, Maryland. Phone 5172.   o-9

WANTED—Will pay cash for your car. All makes and models. Call 5629 after 7 P. M.

WANTED—Will pay cash for your car. William J. Meyers. Call Vernon 5320 or 1708 North Charles St., Baltimore, Md.

WANTED—Small furnished house or apartment in Annapolis or vicinity. Phone 6102.   tf

WANTED—Unfurnished room by elderly gentleman. Write Box 59, Evening Capital.   o-10

Lost and Found   8

LOST — "A" gasoline rationing book. Mary Margarete Kelly. P. O. Box 6, Annapolis.   o-9

LOST—In the vicinity of Eastport, four-month-old Pointer bird dog; brown and white. Reward. See George Libot'e, 415 Severn Avenue, Eastport.   o-9

Miscellaneous   12

MISCELLANEOUS — We deliver anything — anywhere. Personal Delivery Service. Phone 2781.   tf

MISCELLANEOUS — Paper hanging, painting, stove and furnace repairing. Phone 4197.   tf

---

Three countries in the western hemisphere have "United States" in their official name: the U.S.A., Brazil and Venezuela.

The U. S. could add two million women a year for 10 years to war production lines from today's reserve of womenpower.

In India, there are only thirty-six cities with a population of more than 100,000.

Most popular fiction among service men overseas is the western story.

NOTICE TO CREDITORS

Notice is hereby given that the subscriber, of Anne Arundel County, has obtained from the Orphans' Court of Anne Arundel County, in Maryland, Letters Testamentary on the personal estate of

ABRAM CLAUDE HOWARD

late of Anne Arundel County, deceased. All persons having claims against the deceased, are hereby warned to exhibit the same, with the vouchers thereof, to the subscriber, on or before the

18TH DAY OF MARCH, 1943.

They may otherwise, by law, be excluded from all benefit of said estate. All persons indebted to said estate are requested to make immediate payment.

Given under my hand this 15th day of September, 1942.

Margaret Vaulx Whitham Howard
Executrix   o-21

ORDER NISI

In the Circuit Court for Anne Arundel County,
No. 8418 Equity.

Louis M. Strauss, Assignee, versus
Leonard W. Cramblitt, et al.

Ordered, this 1st day of October, 1942, that the sale of the property mentioned in these proceedings, made and reported by Louis M. Strauss, Assignee, be ratified and confirmed, unless cause to the contrary thereof be shown on or before the

2ND DAY OF NOVEMBER, NEXT; provided a copy of this order be inserted in some newspaper published in Anne Arundel County, once in each of three successive weeks before the 2nd day of November next.

The report states the amount of sales to be $975.00.

JOHN H. HOPKINS, 3RD, Clerk.
True Copy, Test:
JOHN H. HOPKINS, 3RD, Clerk.

MODEST MAIDENS
Trademark Registered U. S. Patent Office

"Have you anything to remove the green marks left by engagement rings?"

Shark's liver, weighing ¼ of the total weight of the shark, contains as much as 80 per cent of vitamin-rich oil.

The last man to leave the burial vaults of Egyptians thousands of years ago left footprints still visible in the sands of time.

FLIGHT ENDS AT SCRAP HEAP—This 10-year-old plane was landed on a Philadelphia parkway and taxied to this scrap pile by Joseph Campbell, who contributed the plane as he was preparing to join the Marines.

SCORCHY SMITH
Trademark Registered U. S. Patent Office   **Merely A Matter Of Arithmetic**

OAKY DOAKS
Trademark Registered U. S. Patent Office   **Scotty's Late For School**

OH, DIANA!
Trademark Registered U. S. Patent Office   **Scorched Pan Policy**

DICKIE DARE
Trademark Registered U. S. Patent Office   **Something's Fishy!**

HOMER HOOPEE
Trademark Registered U. S. Patent Office   **That Remains To Be Seen**

THE ADVENTURES OF PATSY
Trademark Registered U. S. Patent Office   **Buckle Down, Jersey!**

NEIGHBORLY NEIGHBORS

THE DOOLITTLES

You Can Help Fight The War By Turning In Scrap Metal

Evening Capital

VOL. LVIII — NO. 239. EVERY EVENING EXCEPT SUNDAY ANNAPOLIS, MD., THURSDAY, OCTOBER 8. 1942. SOUTHERN MARYLAND'S ONLY DAILY THREE CENTS.

WEATHER
Somewhat warmer today and mild temperature tonight

Russians Break Into German Fortified Left Flank Northwest Of Stalingrad

LATE NEWS

SHUT DOWN BIG GOLD MINES

Washington, Oct. 8 (AP)—The War Production Board today orderer the shut down of 200 to 300 of the nation's largest gold mines, in order to release manpower for work in copper and other vital war metal production.

MAY DRAFT FOR LABOR POSTS

Washington, Oct. 8 (AP) — Congress was given blunt notice today that it soon may be called upon to tackle the job of recruiting the nation's manpower through national service legislation.

NAZIS WANT AMERICAN LABOR

Moscow, Oct. 8 (AP)—The Germans are hoping to use American prisoners for forced labor, the Communist party newspaper Pravda deduced today from a letter on the body of a German officer.

GORDON HELD FOR RATION VIOLATION

New York, Oct. 8 (AP)—Waxey Gordon, beer baron of Broadway in the prohibition era, was indicted today by a Federal Grand Jury on a charge of violating a rationing order regulating the sale of sugar.

CHECK ON POSSIBLE TIPS TO SUBS

Washington, Oct. 8 (AP)—The Federal Communications Commission is investigating reports that radio announcers have been tipping off enemy submarines through tricky song dedications and the juggling of prices in advertising.

GIANT FLYING BOAT IS HELD OBSOLETE

Washington, Oct. 8 (AP)—Congress was told today that the navy's 70-ton flying boat, the Martin Mars, already was "obsolete insofar as performance is concerned," but would be used upon delivery "in a few weeks" as a navy cargo transport plane.

F.B.I. SEIZES SHIP CAPTAIN

Baltimore, Oct. 8 (AP)—The arrest of a Spanish ship captain and four other men in Baltimore and New York on charges of conspiracy to export platinum valued at from $10,000 to $15,000 from the United States was announced today by the Federal Bureau of Investigation.;

E. A. Soucy, F.B.I. agent in charge, said these men were taken into custody simultaneously:

In Baltimore, Capt. Isidro Bilbao Ojinaga, master of the S. S. Motomar, and the handyman of that ship, Indalecio Sevillano.

In New York, Dr. Juan Tomas Bareno, Juan Gallego and Manuel Rodrigues.

ESTIMATE 1942 COTTON CROP

Washington, Oct. 8 (AP)—The Agriculture Department today estimated this year's cotton crop at 13,818,000 bales of 500 pounds gross weight each, based on Oct. 1 conditions.

ARMY CHANGES SAVING METAL

Washington, Oct. 8 (AP)—Changes in army building methods are saving about 26,000 tons of metal in the construction of camp facilities for every 100,000 men, Undersecretary of War Robert P. Patterson reported today.

CALL ON MINERS TO CEASE STRIKE

Cincinnati, Oct. 8 (AP)—President John L. Lewis of the United Mine Workers of America today asked and received a vote by the union's 37th annual convention, instructing more than 6,000 anthracite miners in Pennsylvania to call off what Lewis said were "totally unwarranted" strikes.

DECLARES ARMY NEEDS YOUNG MEN

Washington, Oct. 8 (AP)—Maj. Gen. James A. Ulio, adjutant-general of the army, asserted today that the army "wants and needs" for immediate training "every available young American 18 and 19 years of age."

Local Tides

TOMORROW

High water—5:01 A. M., 1.4 feet; 5:35 P. M., 1.4 feet. Low water— 11:22 A. M., 11:11 P. M.

Moon rises 6:24 A. M.; sets 6:42 P. M.

Sun rises 7:09 A. M.; sets 6:38 P. M.

Tides are given for Annapolis. For Sandy Point, add 15 minutes. For Thomas Point Shoal, subtract 30 minutes.

CONGRESS GETS BIG WAR BILL

$6,236,956,621 Measure Carries Funds For Navy

WASHINGTON, Oct. 8 (AP) — A $6,236,956,621 appropriation bill, swelling the country's cost of arms to more than six times the bill for World War No. 1, was sent to the House floor today with approximately 90 per cent of the new expenditures earmarked for the navy.

In approving the omnibus second supplementary national defense bill, the House Appropriations Committee authorized 14,611 new naval planes to complement an unprecedented aircraft carrier building program now under way.

Simultaneously, the bill would furnish fresh financial reserves for the war projects of a dozen different government agencies—rubber for the war machine to roll on, air lanes to carry the allies' message of victory, homes for war workers.

Navy Credits

The $5,559,974,309 set apart for the navy would raise its spending credits for the fiscal year of 1943 to $30,827,982,282, while the measure as a whole would in-

(Continued on Page Four)

MINUTE MEN PLAN DANCE TOMORROW

The local 900th Company of Maryland Minute Men will hold a dance, open to the public, from 9 P.M. to 1 A. M. tomorrow at the State Armory.

The event will be for the benefit of the company funds. Music will be furnished by the Stardusters.

BOARD PREPARES SOLDIER BALLOTS

The County Board of Supervisors of Election is having county ballots prepared to be sent to members of the armed forces.

The ballots are being prepared at the request of the Secretary of State. Men serving in the armed forces can secure the ballots from the Secretary of State by writing his office in the State House up to seven days before the Nov. 3 general election.

46 FIREMEN COMPLETE COURSE

Forty-six members of the Rescue Hose Company last night completed a five-hour course in war gases required by the Office of Civilian Defense.

Thomas G. Basil, civilian defense director, said the course covered all phases of detecting and combating gases.

Tonight at 7 o'clock the first session of a Civilian Protection Class will be held in the Municipal building.

Chiefs of all emergency services and first deputies will meet in the same building at 7:30 P. M. tomorrow.

Music Rehearsals Begin Next Week

Chorus And Orchestra To Hold First Practices

Rehearsals for the Community Chorus and Orchestra will begin next week on the top floor of Humphreys Hall, St. John's College.

The chorus will meet at 5 P. M. Monday and the orchestra at 8 P. M. Wednesday. The chorus will rehearse regularly at 5 P. M. Mondays and Fridays unless members of the group find another hour more suitable. Orchestra members will hold regular rehearsals at 8 P. M. Wednesdays.

There is room for new members in both organizations, according to Nicolas Nabokov, director. Mr. Nabokov today urged persons who would like to sing or play an instrument to come to the first rehearsals. Plans for the coming season's musical program will be discussed at the first meetings.

Clubwomen To Be USO Hostesses

Mrs. Albert J. Trageser Is Chairman Of Committee

Beginning next Tuesday night, the members of the Woman's Club of Annapolis and Anne Arundel county will serve as hostesses at the USO under the chairmanship of Mrs. Albert J. Trageser of Arnold.

Anyone wishing to help on that dates should get in touch with Mrs. Trageser by telephone on Friday. Committees wil change from month to month so that no member need obligate herself to serve regularly. Pumpkin and apple pies are being solicited by Mrs. Trageser, also, for the Hallowe'en party for service men on Oct. 31.

The surgical dressings group under Mrs. J. E. Greenwood and Mrs. Basil Moore is meeting on Thursday mornings from 10 to noon in the Red Cross rooms. Mrs. E. E. Perkins of Sylvan Shores, chairman of housing, will now accept postalcard registrations of beds available in case of disaster from members of the club.

Luncheon reservations for the Fourth District meeting on Oct. 20, 11 A. M., to be held at Calvary Church, must be received by Mrs. Joseph Peters of Linthicum Heights by Oct. 15, with check. Delegates from the local club are Mrs. Albert Krapf, Mrs. George E. Benedict and Mrs. A. Lee Creighton.

EASTPORT CIVIC GROUP TO DISCUSS GARBAGE BIDS

Pending bids for the collection of garbage in the Eastport section will be discussed at 8 o'clock tonight at a meeting of the Civic Association of Eastport.

The meeting will be held at the Eastport fire hall.

Under the bid submitted to the Board of County Commissioners for handling garbage next year the section faces a substantial increase in garbage taxes.

The Commissioners have requested expressions of opinion from residents.

Urge Draftees To Join Guard

Mohr Points Out Training Will Help When They Are Inducted

Men in the 3-A draft classifications were urged today to enlist in the Maryland State Guard by Brig. Gen Dwight H. Mohr, its commanding general.

"Such enlistment," he pointed out, "is a splendid opportunity for the men to gain military experience during their spare hours which will be of great benefit to them if and when they are inducted into the regular army."

"Basic training in the State Guard already has helped numerous volunteers and draftees secure ratings and quicker promotions in the army."

In Annapolis, applications will be received at the Bladen Street armory on Monday evenings between 7:45 and 10:00 P. M.

NO. 8 SUGAR STAMP GOOD UNTIL OCT. 31

Housewives were reminded today the No. 8 stamp in the sugar ration book is good until midnight Oct. 31.

Canning sugar applications must be filed with the ration board by Oct. 15.

DANCING SCHOOL RESUMES TOMORROW

Its fall recital having been given at the USO for the service men and public last Friday, the Hoffman School of Dance will resume the regular classes tomorrow at Carvel Hall.

With the baby group at 1:45 and pre-school at 2:45, the older children receive instruction as follows: beginners, 3:45; intermediates, 4:45; advanced, 6:00 P. M. More than fifty students have enrolled for the season.

STRUGGLE GROWS FOR CONTROL OF GUADALCANAL

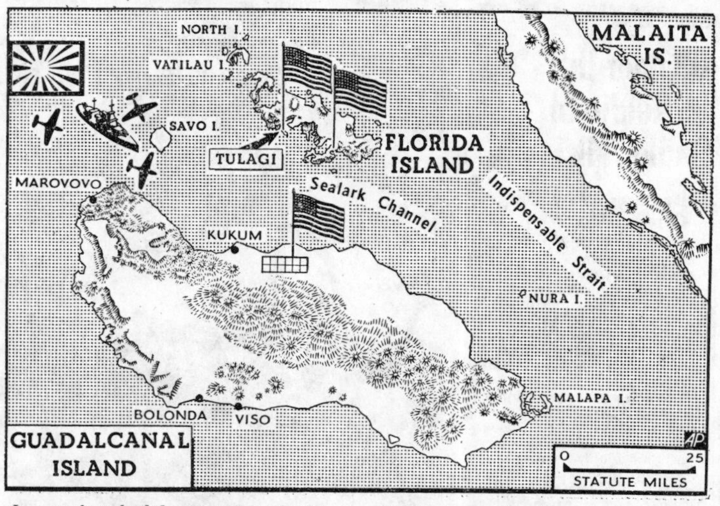

Japanese have landed more men on Guadalcanal Island under cover of darkness, but U. S. marines were reported to be holding fast after taking a toll of attacking planes and ships.

The Japs' main objective is an airport (flag) on the north shore of the island, held by the marines. U. S. forces also hold positions on Florida and Tulagi Islands.

County Pays Recount Cost

$300 Bill Paid As Result Of 2 Per Cent Vote Shift

The $300 cost of the recent recount of primary election ballots has been paid by the Board of Anne Arundel County Commissioners.

The county paid the bill because 94 ballots, previously counted by election judges, were discard on the recount, a shift of more than 2 per cent of the ballots counted. Under the election laws the county must pay if the shift of ballots exceeds 2per cent.

The recount was requested by W. W. Townshend, Sr., in the First District, and Ernest J. Hein in the Fifth District. Senator Louis N. Phipps asked a recount of the county, but the recount of the Senatorial vote was made along with the County Commissioner vote in the First and Fifth Districts. Senator Phipps requested that the recount cease after counting the Senatorial ballots alone in the six polling places of the Third District.

While making some minor changes in votes, the recount did not change the final results of the primary election.

Kiwanis Members Attend Meeting

Leave For Session Of District Convention

Six members of the local Kiwanis club left the city today to attend the three-day session of the Capital District Kiwanis International convention in Wilmington, Del.

Those in the party are Dr. William Y. Kitchin, lieutenant governor; of the district; Harry S. Kenchington and John F. Martin, president and secretary respectively of the local club; Henry Zerhusen, Jr., Harry Krause and Barney Berman.

Mrs. Kenchington and Mrs. Krause also made the trip.

GEORGE W. MILLER AT CAMP PICKETTS

Pvt. George W. Miller, 20 South Cherry Grove avenue, is now stationed at the Medical Replacement Center at Camp Picketts, Va.

His training will consist of actual maneuvers illustrating medical and evacuation problems encountered on the battlefield, as well as basic military work.

NAVY GROUP SEEKS MORE ADDRESSES FOR FILE

The Searchlight address file maintained for wives of naval and marine officers is receiving much help from wives residing in Annapolis who are furnishing addresses for names they see on the wanted list.

The Searchlight today requested that when writing in to give an address, any others that readers may have that would be of assistance be sent at the same time.

Wanted by friends are the addresses of the following:

Mrs. W. W. Anderson, wife of Lt.C., USN (CC); Mrs. Watson O. Bailey, wife of Capt., USN; Mrs. Clarissa F. Balch; Mrs. Henry E. Bernstein, wife of Lt.C., USN; Mrs. B. B. Biggs, wife of Comdr., USN; Mrs. Worthington S. Bitler, wife of Comdr., USN; Mrs. George W. Brainard; Mrs. J. A. Briggs, wife

(Continued on Page 2)

WANT GAS BOOKS RENEWED NOW

Motor vehicle operators whose "B" and "C" ration books expire this month today were urged to report to the War Price and Ration Board for renewals.

F. Marion Lazenby, chairman of the board, said these motorists should act at once as renewals are being issued two weeks in advance of the expiration date of the books. He also stressed the necessity of getting the renewals before the rush of fuel oil rationing starts.

LOST

WHITE SPITZ PUPPY
Brown Spot on Head
REWARD
Call 4112

NOTICE

Mrs. Harry Klawans of the "Leader" will return tonight after spending several days in New York on a business trip.

WANTED
MAN OVER FIFTY
Preferably retired Navy or Naval Academy Man.
Light work. Fair Hours. Fair wages
Apply
Naval Academy Officers' Club
Between 9 A. M. and 5 P. M.

WANTED
Boys for delivery on established newspaper routes.
Weekly salary. No collecting
Apply
ANNAPOLIS NEWS AGENCY
Evening Capital Building

Winning The War To Be Club Topic

Semi-Annual District Session To Be Held Here Oct 20

"Winning the War," the theme chosen for the semi-annual meeting of the Fourth District of the Maryland Federation of Women's Clubs, will be under consideration throughout the session to be held Oct. 20 in the parlor of Calvary Methodist Church.

Mrs. Alex Proskey, program chairman, has invited as guest speakers Mrs. William Parvin Starr, Federation chairman of war services, and Mrs. Harry Cottman, district chairman of war stamp and bond sales. Mrs. Starr will stress salvage and consumers' problems, while Mrs. Cottman will present a 12-point

(Continued on Page Six)

WANTED
SALESLADY
Women's Shoes
LIPMAN'S BOOTERY
172 MAIN ST.

HOME-MADE
CODFISH CAKES
5c each
J. W. BROOKS
205 MAIN ST. DIAL 4686

SERVING MAID
to serve Saturday afternoon and evening. Must have own uniform.
Call 4263

FIRST, SECOND AND THIRD CHURCHES OF CHRIST, SCIENTIST
Baltimore, Maryland
announce a Free Lecture on
CHRISTIAN SCIENCE
By
PETER B. BIGGINS, C. S. B.,
of Seattle, Washington.
Member of the Board of Lectureship of The Mother Church, The First Church of Christ, Scientist, in Boston, Massachusetts
At the Lyric Theatre
Friday evening, October 9
At 8:30 O'Clock
The public is cordially invited to attend
This lecture will be published in full in the Catonsville Herald-Argus. Any one desiring a copy of same may obtain it from the above paper at 5c a copy.

BRITISH, IN REPRISAL ACTION TO MANACLE GERMAN PRISONERS

(By the Associated Press)

Red army tank forces breaking into the fortified German left flank northwest of Stalingrad were reported today to have forced the enemy to divert veteran Prussian units, the elite of his army, from other fronts in an effort to stop the push aimed at relieving the siege of the Volga city.

The Russians, however, maintained the intiative on the steppes even as the Germans poured more and more men and machines into the holocaust. The latest official Moscow report said that German attacks were beaten off both to the northwest as well as inside the ruined city.

During the past three days, dispatches said, the Germans lost thousands of men, hundreds of trucks and armored cars and scores of tanks without compensating gains.

GERMAN SOLOMONS CLAIM

A German broadcast, heard in London, quoting what the announcer said was a Tokyo dispatch, reported that Japanese troops had made an advance against stiff American resistance on Guadalcanal island. There was nothing from any other source to confirm this report and no broadcast from Tokyo itself has been heard to make any similar claim.

Allied troops, having driven the Japanese back across the summit of New Guinea's Owen Stanley mountains, found themselves facing the same supply difficulties which the invaders encountered in their unsuccessful push toward Port Moresby. A communique said the Allies had suffered practically no losses in driving the Japanese from their advance positions near Ioribaiwa and left no doubt that the threat to Port Moresby had been smashed for the present.

Blasted by American sea and air power, the Japanese appeared to have fled from two of the three western Aleutian islands they occupied four months ago and were undergoing heavy bombardment on their remaining foothold—Kiska island. The Navy has been unable to detect signs of Japanese activity on Attu and Agattu islands.

"Rat Trap"

Probably realizing they had blundered into what a naval spokesman termed "a rat trap," the Japanese apparently left the two islands after losses thus far totaling 38 ships sunk or damaged and 40 planes destroyed.

Presumably operating from their new Andreanof islands base, Army Liberator bombers with fighters escorts dumped explosives and incendiaries on the Japanese Kiske encampment Monday, scoring hits on seaplane hangars. Six Japanese seaplane fighters which counter-attacked were shot down and all the American aircraft returned to their base.

New German penetrations of Stalingrad were reported by Berlin which said that northwest of the city "encircled enemy forces which had been split up into two parts were annihilated." A large block of houses was reported taken after a fierce fight.

Germans Anxious

Doucments taken from newly captured German prisoners emphasized again the importance the Germans attach to the Stalingrad offensive, indicating even that the Hitler command hoped to win the entire war in the east by the occupation of the Volga metropolis.

But now, according to Pravada, Moscow Communist newspaper, prisoners no longer talk of the end of the war but only express fear that the coming winter will be fatal to Germany with her forces

(Continued On Page Three)

NOTICE

Mr. Barney Berman will return tonight from a business trip in New York.

CASH
FOR YOUR
CAR
MARBERT MOTORS
261 West St. Dial 2335

WANTED!
BOY TO LEARN PLUMBING TRADE
W. T. SHAWN, INC.
WEST ANNAPOLIS, MD.

FRYERS-ROASTERS
CUT UP CHICKENS
FRESH KILLED DAILY
Buy Just The Parts You Want
J. W. BROOKS
205 MAIN STREET DIAL 4686

ANNOUNCING
THE NEW LOCATION OF
Metropolitan Life Insurance Company
68 State Circle
(Over Carr, Mears and Dawson)
Our Policyholders and the General Public Are Cordially Invited to Visit Our Office.

REDUCTION IN AUTOMOBILE INSURANCE
All bodily injury insurance premiums covering on private passenger cars, insured through our office, are subject to reductions based upon the gasoline ration book you are using.
All "A" book holders are entitled to a 20% reduction, "B" and "C" holders to a 10% reduction.
This reduction applies as of October first, but is retroactive to all policies issued from July 22, 1942. All new policies will be written at the lower rates.
Call us about your automobile insurance.
JOSEPH D. LAZENBY
(Julian Brewer and Son)
9 SCHOOL STREET TEL. 2684 — 2685

London Crowd Gathers To See Mrs. Roosevelt

Has Apartment In Bomb Shattered Wing Of Palace

LONDON, Oct. 24 (AP)—Mrs. Franklin D. Roosevelt arose early today and breakfasted alone in her apartment at Buckingham Palace as a crowd of sightseers, including many American soldiers, gathered outside the Palace, hoping to see the guest of the Royal family.

Mrs. Roosevelt's apartment in the Palace was one of those damaged by bomb blasts some time ago and its windows are partly boarded over.

After leaving the King and Queen, she spent a busy morning conferring on plans for her tour of Britain at war before leaving to give a press interview. The President's wife hopes to study the part which British women are playing in the war and visit American troops in the British Isles.

Meets Princesses

The two Princesses were not in the Palace when Mrs. Roosevelt arose this morning. They stayed in London yesterday until she had arrived by train after her trans-Atlantic flight and then went to their country home for the night. Mrs. Roosevelt had a long talk with them before they left.

Her unusually large conference, attended by more than 100 American and British reporters, was held at the United States Embassy, where she said she had been issued neither a gas mask nor a food ration card yet.

In response to British questions, she said it was "hard to say" whether or when there would be conscription of women in the United States and that she doubted whether prohibition would be brought about, although campaigners had been active since the 18-year-old draft age question arose.

Mrs. Roosevelt was greeted personally by King George VI and Queen Elizabeth yesterday on her arrival at London's Paddington station and then was taken to the Palace amid the cheers of a friendly throng.

Son Present

To make the welcome complete, Mrs. Roosevelt's son, Elliott, a lieutenant-colonel with the U. S. Army air forces in Britain, dined with the Royal family last night. He had been unable to meet his mother at the station because of official duties.

London morning newspapers did their part to extend a hearty welcome to the President's wife. Typical was a headline in the Daily Mirror, "We're Sure Glad to Meet You, Ma'am."

The Times, after expressing pleasure at Mrs. Roosevelt's arrival, said:

"We shall expect that the results of a searching but thorough observation of England at war will ultimately find their way to the President, whose insight into our affairs cannot be too penetrating for our desire."

O'Conor Hits McKeldin In Radio Talk

Declares Work On Commission Was "Lacking In Value"

Governor O'Conor declared last night that he might have selected Theodore McKeldin, his opponent for the governorship, for a defense position if McKeldin's work on the Baltimore City Redistricting Commission had not been "so lacking in value."

O'Conor, in a radio campaign address over a state hookup, reiterated that he had been impartial in appointing men to posts in the state defense organization.

"Possibly I would have appointed Mr. McKeldin to one of these positions, except for one thing," the Governor said.

"After I became Governor, I appointed him as a member of the commision to provide for the redistricting of Baltimore City, as authorized by the legislature, and his work was so colorless and was so lacking in value that I was not induced to proffer any further appointment to him."

Earlier in his address, O'Conor said McKeldin "had not pointed to a single important policy that he would adopt if elected.

"Where the Democratic statewide candidates are concerned, there need be no question in anyone's mind as to their policies," O'Conor added.

The Governor declared also that under his administration, Maryland "has been at the very front in the vanguard rallying to the assistance of the Federal government" in the war effort.

O'Conor pledged his "unqualified support" to the three sitting judges in Baltimore and asked McKeldin for his "attitude concerning their re-election.

Y.M.C.A. BOARD MEETS MONDAY

The board of directors of the Y.M.C.A. will meet at 8 P. M. Monday in the USO Club, Compromise street.

Judge Ridgely P. Melvin is president of the board.

T. ROLAND RILEY ENTERTAINS SEAMEN

T. Roland Riley gave a demonstration of hypnotism and mesmerism last night for the merchant seamen at the seamen's rest at Bay Ridge.

He entertained the seamen for about two hours.

MARINES SPLASH ASHORE ON GUADALCANAL

United States Marines wade ashore from landing barges off Guadalcanal Island during operations in the Solomons. Photo from U. S. Marine Corps Newsreel.

READY FOR THE JAPS ON GUADALCANAL

United States Marines man an anti-aircraft gun on Guadalcanal Island in the Solomons.　Photo from U. S. Marine Corps newsreel.

Friends Of

(Continued from Page One)

cept that I appreciate it. I'm the same old George Cromwell and will continue to serve you in the same old way. You can be sure if I can serve collectively or individually I will be glad to do so."

The surprise party was arranged by a group consisting of Thomas Wilmer, Edward Duvall, Mr. Dunker, Delegate Rickert, Herbert Estep, Morris Shipley and Frank Wimmer. Those invited were asked to be in the Masonic Hall at 8 P. M.

Mr. Dunker stopped at the Cromwell home and asked Mr. Cromwell to come to a small political meeting.

Was Surprised

When Mr. Cromwell entered the crowded main floor of the Masonic Hall he was greeted with "Happy Birthday to You," sung by the crowd, led by Mrs. Henry Cox at the piano. He was taken completely by surprise.

Then he was led to the speaker's platform where he was given the basket of flowers.

Delegate Rickert read a letter from Judge Ridgley P. Melvin congratulating Mr. Cromwell and pointing out that a previous engagement made some time ago prevented his attendance. He also sent a personal letter to Mr. Cromwell.

Mr. Tyler acted as master of ceremonies and presented Congressman Sasscer.

He declared the crowd gathered in the hall was " a splendid tribute to George Cromwell" and that the spirit of friendliness, kindness and true Americanism shown was typical of the spirit that would be the salvation of the nation.

Sasscer Speaks

"If George Cromwell had known about this ahead of time he would not have been here," Sasscer continued. "I served with George Cromwell in the Maryland Senate. I say him there as a man, a public servant and a legislator and I formed a deep admiration for him as a man of sound character, truthfulness and a straight shooting American.

"George Cromwell is an outstanding example of the type whose neighborhoods, communities and counties are better in many ways because they have lived."

Mr. Michaelson said he had been associated with Mr. Cromwell for many years and declared he did not "know a man in the county who has given so much of his time, day after day, for the welfare of this county. He is fair and just. He has operated his office honestly, Courteously and fearlessly."

Mr. Dulin said that the gathering "proved that service has not been forgotten.

"We are here because we want to show that he's a good fellow," he continued. " I think he is a good fellow."

Personal Time

Mr. Dunker pointed out that Mr. Cromwell had given much of his personal time to the duties of his office.

"He is not overpaid," he continued. "He could get lots more on other jobs. This is a group of representative citizens of this county. And when a group gathers like this to pay tribute to a man it is an honor."

Mr. Levay pointed out that Mr. Cromwell has served the county as a Senator, President of the Board of County Commissioners and as Register of Wills. He declared it was his belief that when the Democratic party leader, Mr. Revell, "passes on, the mantle of leadership will fall on the shoulders of George Cromwell."

Watch Presented

Officer Daniel P. Donnelly, whose birthday also fell yesterday, was introduced.

Mr. Revell was introduced as the "grand old man of Democracy of Maryland." All present stood and applauded.

He said he had known Mr. Cromwell for the last 25 or 30 years and found him always a "true gentleman."

"I am only glad that I have lived long enough to see him here tonight," he added.

Then he presented the watch.

Mr. Moss praised Mr. Cromwell's home life and his service to the county.

Lee And Welch To Judge Horses

Annapolis Hunt Club's Show To Be Held Tomorrow

C. Carroll Lee and William O. Welch will judge the 25 classes of the Annapolis Hunt Club's horse show tomorrow at Mary Helen's Riding Academy on the General's highway near Three-Mile Oak.

Special events carded include midshipman horsemanship, musical chairs (open to all riders, horses and ponies), bareback jumping, triple bar and knockdown and out.

There will be classes for ponies, thoroughbred and non-thoroughbred brood mares, green hunters, road hacks, open hunters, handy hunters, open jumpers, working hunters, ladies' hunters, pairs of road hacks and pairs of hunters.

Riders under 18 may compete in the junior horsemanship division on either ponies or horses.

Mrs. Agnes Moreland is chairman.

Navy Grid Squad Gets Contact Work

Will Be 27th Game With Penn Team

The Naval Academy football squad got down to hard work for the Pennsylvania game yesterday after a day's rest on Monday.

It will be the 27th time the teams have clashed. In the long series Penn has won 14 and Navy 10, while two have ended in ties. The series began in 1888.

Last year the midshipmen won, 13 to 2, on sustained drives before a crowd of 70,672 spectators on Franklin Field. The victory, won in the rain, was the first over the Quakers since 1935 and swept Penn from the ranks of undefeated teams.

Penn has only been defeated this year by the Georgia navy team. The Quakers have defeated Harvard, Yale, Columbia and Army, and battled out a 6-6 tie with Princeton, a team which defeated Navy 10 to 0.

An incentive for the midshipmen is the line the game will give on the relative strength of the Army team. Last week Penn ran over the West Point Cadets, 19 to 0.

Navy scouts report that Penn has two high-grade lines and twelve outstanding backs, who work together with speed, power and deception.

Comdr. John E. Whelchel plans hard work for the Navy squad today and tomorrow and will begin tapering off Friday.

Bill Crawley, back, and Fred Schnurr, tackle, are still on the injured list and it is considered doubtful if they will be ready for the Penn game.

Bert
STIFF
—PENN'S LINE-SMASHING FULLBACK
I'LL MAKE A HOLE FOR MYSELF
HE IS MORE DANGEROUS THAN EVER NOW THAT HE TOSSES SHORT PASSES OVER THE LINE
STIFF IS JUST ABOUT THE BEST LINE-CRACKER IN THE EAST
PAP
Wide World Features

"PENNS' POWER HOUSE"...by PAP

Sports Round-Up

By HUGH FULLERTON, JR. (Wide World Sports Columnist)

NEW YORK, Nov. 4 (AP)—From somewhere in the Pacific war zone Sgt. (T) Max E. R. Keiffer fires a V-mail broadside in this direction upholding the "small college" brand of basketball—particularly that played in the Kansas City National Intercollegiate Tournament over the kind supported by the "big" schools ... The range is too long to carry on a good argument, except to point out that the squad just picked for that All-Stars vs. Oshkosh game in Chicago includes five big ten players, three from other "major" conferences and the rest from colleges that definitely are "big time" basketball schools—Notre Dame, Toledo, Seton Hall, Long Island, etc ... But as a clincher, Missouri Max writes: "The second and third weeks of the second March following the end of the war, you are invited to be my house and tournament guest for the two National classics. Come out to see and decide for yourself" ... That speaks volumes for the confidence of a soldier and basketball fan and we hope we can accept.

A Friend In Need

Dick Harlow, the Harvard coach, must have had advance information about that Princeton upset last week, because Mrs. Harlow left before the game to visit her daughter, Jane, who is expecting to make Dick a grandpappy one of these days ... When she was planning the trip, Mrs. Harlow received a call from her daughter in Westminster, Md. ... "Mother," Jane said, "I really think you should stay up there in Cambridge with daddy. He needs you more than I do."

One Minute Sports Page

When the Navy called the Woodward, Iowa, High School grid coach, the town minister, the Rev. J. H. Krenmyre, took over the job. He once played end for Iowa Wesleyan ... Forty Argentine golf pros refused to play in the recent National Open championship because prexy Carlos Sojo of the Argentine Golf Association hasn't apologized for calling them "poor sportsmen" ... Fat Freddie Fitzsimmons is 12th among 32 bowlers competing in the local eliminations for the National match game championship and experts hereabouts are praising Freddie's "form" ... Vic Dellicurti, who fights Ray Robinson in the Garden Friday, became a boxer because he could outrun the cops who used to break up ball games in the street. His speed won him an invitation to join the Jefferson Boys' Club, where he became interested in boxing ... Bill Alexander, the Georgia Tech coach, has been ordered to bed ...: Trying the Notre Dame system, eh?

Today's Guest Star

Bob Stedler, Buffalo Evening News: "An All American is a fellow who don't let his team get beat, and that's Frankie Sinkwich, who [illegible] at a 10-0 score and carried [illegible] to Saturday [illegible]-star victory over Alabama.

Service Dept.

The Iowa Navy Pre-Flight School announces that the winter toughness program will include water polo with the "contact" rules tossed out ... Seems from here it would be easier to take up the old Eastern Intercollegiate League variety of water polo, banned by the colleges as too rough ... The only known rule there was to let a player go to the surface when he signalled he'd had enough ... Pvt. Larry Dew of Fayetteville, N. C., and Chanute Field, Ill., is ready to give Hank Luisetti a run for his basketball scoring money ... Playing for his squadron team, Larry recently scored 20 field goals to set the pace for an 87-10 victory ... Torger Tokle, the ski jumper, has been assigned to the new mountain infantry training center at Camp Carson, Colo., to help train the fighting mountaineers. If they copy him, the enemy will think our paratroopers have dispensed with parachutes.

Trench Mortar Survives The Blitz

Wide World Features

CHICAGO — Blitzkrieg warfare has introduced a number of new fighting weapons, but it still uses one of the oldest weapons known.

That's the humble muzzle-loading mortar. Light, maneuverable and accurate, it is employed to demolish tank traps, wipe out machine gun nests and light artillery, destroy pillboxes and small fortifications, even to lay down smoke screens.

Accuracy doesn't suffer when the mortar is set up behind a stump or wall, in a hole or trench, on a hillside or on uneven ground. Since its trajectory is arched, enemy soldiers lurking behind hills, woods, or buildings can be attacked with deadly effect.

Bowling Scores

By TIDLEY BASSFORD

Meredith-Roane experienced but little difficulty in subduing Coca-Cola on Friday night as the latter aggregation showed up with a four man team. The league leaders rapped games of 627-570 and 630 to chalk up a 1872-7664 triple, and even though it would have taken some exceptionally good rolling on the part of a fifth man to take more than one of the three contests, instances of this kind serve only to promote ill-feeling throughout the loop. Gene O'Neale continued to shoot swell duckpins for Meredith by clicking off strings of 128-149 and 112 for a 389, while Harwood Green added a nice 383 on runs of 153-96 and 134. S. Earle obliged with a timely 371.

Sadler Clicks

Sadler's Hardware, an inconsistent bunch to date, but a team which has proved that they can be mighty dangerous at times, applied the coat of white to Rogers Service Station despite some nice duckpin spilling by "Keat" Hoff who molded together a healthy set of 384. "Keat" forced yours truly, who reaped a 379, to take a back seat by flipping 140 games in the opening and closing contests but his effort was the extent to which the gas station operators arose to the occasion. "Skeeter Deale elbowed himself a noteworthy 373 in aiding the hardware boys run up a 1790 total on blasts of 601-588 and 601. Because of the fact that he's one of the "scratch" men, Bill Arnold's 369 commands attention.

Three For Myers

Led by Bill Purdy's inspiring 387 the H. B. Myers Company rolled back Snyder's Store in every game as they scored a 1743-1628 triumph over the boys from down Galesville way. Bill poked consistent games of 123-136 and 128 in leading his mates to pay dirt.

K. of C. Scores

K. of C., with three men for one game and only four men for the remaining two games, pulled the most remarkable feat in a long time by taking everything from Taylor's Service Station, even to the point of outscoring them 1638-1612. Of course, the lads from Mayo were away off stride, but even with that in consideration, it's still one for Ripley.

Coming from far off the pace to score a 595-576 triumph in the opening tilt, 7-Up went on to take a 2-1 victory at the expense of National Bohemian, losing out in total pinfall by the slim margin of five sticks, 1741-1746. Gordon Duvall kept up his sensational string of ranking sets by piling up another 383, climaxed by a 146 blast in the second game. Whacking games of 116-124 and 141 Sam Fertitta fired a 381 for the beermen to take down runner-up honors for the fray.

Rayhart Still Hot

Although American Beer dropped two decisions to Meyer's Store, their losses failed to check the recent fine rolling of Quinton Rayhart, who again emerged with a potent 392, topped off by scorching 149 in the initial go. Jerome Tarleton's 141 and 380 went quite a long way towards bringing victory to Bill Mayer's

(Continued On Page Three)

RIVALS IN 29TH ARMY-NOTRE DAME CLASSIC

LEAHY
BERTELLI
BLAIK
MAZUR
AP

Star Passer Angelo Bertelli (left) of Notre Dame and Captain Henry (Hank) Mazur (right), triple-threat Army back, will carry the brunt of the attack for their teams when the Irish and Cadets resume their intersectional rivalry on the gridiron in Yankee Stadium, New York city, Saturday, Nov. 7. Frank Leahy (top, center) coaches Notre Dame and Earl H. (Red) Blaik (bottom, center) directs the Cadets. Saturday's game will be the 29th in the series that started in 1913. Notre Dame has won 20 games, Army five and three games, including last year's scorless deadlock, have ended in ties.

Around The Radio Dial Tonight

WCAO	600K
WFBR	1300K
WBAL	1090K
WCBM	1400K
WITH	1230K
WOR, M.B.S. Key	710K
WABC, C.B.S Key	880K
WEAF, N.B.C. Red Key	660K
WJZ, N.B.C. Blue Key	770K

NEW YORK, Nov. 4 (AP)—Even the war is changing the pages in New York network headquarters. They are becoming girls and women, with the call to service depleting the roster of young men available.

Already NBC is training three women pages, and plans to put on more, while CBS has just added two girls to its staff, normally NBC employs 30 pages, while CBS has 15.

Unlike the rather colorfully-uniformed page boys, the girls and women wear their regular attire, preferably dark dresses. They are to perform the various duties of the pages, such as reception desk positions and the like.

Listening tonight: NBC—7:30 R. H. Singer on "Wartime Car Use;" 8 Thin Man drama; 8:30 Tommy Dorsey band; 9 Eddie Cantor and Charles Laughton; 9:30 District Attorney; 10 Kay Kyser hour.

CBS—8 Nelson Eddy concert; 9 Bob Burns; 9:30 Lionel Barrymore drama; 10 Great Moments in Music; 10:30 Man Behind The Gun.

BLU—7 What's Your War Job, new series, Paul V. McNutt speaker; 8:30 Manhattan at Midnight; 9 Basin Street; 9:30 Sammy Kay band; 10:15 Radio Forum, "War Nursuries."

U.S.Marines—
by Kreb
ISAAC O. PEARSON WHO USUALLY DOES HIS PITCHING FOR THE PHILADELPHIA PHILLIES MAJOR LEAGUE BASEBALL CLUB, IS NOW TRAINING TO BECOME A MARINE CORPS OFFICER.
"IKE" PEARSON
THE HOME OF THE COMMANDANT OF THE MARINE CORPS IN WASHINGTON, D.C., IS BELIEVED TO BE ONE OF THE OLDEST BUILDINGS IN THE NATION'S CAPITAL.
Tyrone POWER
FAMOUS FILM STAR WHO RECENTLY APPEARED IN THE PICTURE, "A YANK IN THE RAF," IS NOW A MARINE CORPS PRIVATE.

5:00
WCAO: Are You a Genius?
WFBR: Tick Tock Tunes.
WBAL: When a Girl Marries.
WCBM: Sea Hound.
WITH: News; Sports Special.

5:15
WCAO: Mother and Dad.
WFBR. Quaker City Serenade.
WBAL: Portia Faces Life.
WCBM: Hop Harrigan.
WJZ: Hop Harrigan.

5:30
WCAO: Landt Trio.
WFBR: Superman.
WBAL: Just Plain Bill.
WCBM: Jack Armstrong.
WJZ: The Flying Patrol
WOR: Rambling With Gambling.

5:45
WCAO: Ben Bernie's Orchestra.
WFBR: String Ensemble.
WBAL: Front Page Farrell.
WCBM: Captain Midnight.
WEAF: The Bartons.
WJZ: Secret City, sketch.
WOR: News; Melody Moments.

6:00
WCAO: News; Keyboard Capers.
WFBR: Phillip Gordon.
WBAL: News; Sports Parade.
WCBM: Don Winslow.
WITH: News; Twilight Tunes.
WOR: Uncle Don. Children Prgm.
WEAF: Funny Money Man.
WJZ: News; Sons of the Pioneers.
WABC: John Daly, news.

6:15
WCAO: Sports. Don Riley; News.
WFBR: Special edition of sports.
WBAL: Around the Dinner Table.
WCBM: Talk; Bill Dyer, sports.
WITH: Defense talk.
WEAF: News, George Putnam.
WJZ: Joe Hasel, sports.
WABC: Hedda Hopper's Hollywood.

6:30
WCAO: Keep Working, Keep Singing—America.
WFBR: Press Bulletins.
WCBM: Music A La Carte.
WOR: Press Bulletins.
WEAF: Joseph Gallicchio's Orch.

6:45
WCAO: *The World Today.
WFBR: Dinner Rhythms.
WBAL: ‡News, Lowell Thomas.
WITH: Sports Resume.
WOR: Here's Morgan, variety.
WEAF: Bill Stern, sports.
WJZ: Lowell Thomas.

7:00
WCAO: *Amos and Andy, sketch.
WFBR: Fulton Lewis, Jr., news.
WBAL: ‡Fred Waring's Orchestra.
WCBM: What's Your War Job?
WITH: News; When Lights Are Low.
WOR: Stan Lomax, sports.

7:15
WCAO: Harry James' Orchestra.
WFBR: Football Forecast.
WBAL: ‡News of the World.
WITH: South American Way.
WOR: Confidentially Yours.

7:30
WCAO: Easy Aces.
WFBR: Comm. Fund Program.
WBAL: You're in the Army Now.
WCBM: The Lone Ranger.
WITH: Musical Lingo.
WOR: Go Get It.
WEAF: Schaefer's Revue.
WJZ: That's A Fact.

7:45
WCAO: Mr. Keen.
WFBR: California Melodies.
WBAL: Optimist Club.
WEAF: News.

8:00
WCAO: Nelson Eddy, songs.
WFBR: Sizing Up the News.
WBAL: ‡The Thin Man Adventures.
WCBM: Watch the World Go By.
WITH: News, Phone Away.

8:15
WFBR: Barrie Sisters.
WCBM: Lum and Abner.
WITH: Musical Program.
WOR: Alvino Key's Orchestra.

8:30
WCAO: *"Dr. Christian"; News.
WFBR: Quiz of Two Cities.
WBAL: Tommy Dorsey.
WCBM: §Manhattan at Midnight.
WITH: Swing Class.
WOR: Red Ryder, drama.
WEAF: Dough Re Mi.
WJZ: Town Meeting of the Air.

9:00
WCAO: Arkansas Traveler.
WFBR: Gabriel Heatter.
WBAL: Eddie Cantor.
WCBM: Basin St. Chamber Music
WITH: News; Listen For Cash.

9:15
WFBR: In The Groove.
WITH: Symphony Hall.
WOR: Red Barber, sports.

9:30
WCAO: The Mayor of the Town.
WFBR: Thunder in the Sky.
WBAL: ‡Mr. District Attorney.
WJZ: T. B. A.
WCBM: Spotlight Bands.

10:00
WCAO: Great Moments in Music.
WFBR: John B. Hughes.
WBAL: ‡Kay Kyser's Musical Knowledge.
WITH: News; Interlude.
WCBM: News here and abroad.

10:15
WFBR: Invitation to the Waltz.
WCBM: National Radio Forum.
WITH: Larry London's Orch.
WJZ: Sylvia Marlowe, songs.

10:30
WFBR: World's Most Honored Music.
WCAO: News; Spotlight Review; Film Facts.
WITH: Time for the News.
WOR: News Analyst.
WABC: "The Twenty-second Letter."

10:45
WCBM: Eddie Oliver's Orch.
WITH: Musical Interlude.
WJZ: Texas Rangers.

11:00
WCAO: News of the World.
WFBR: Sports. Jack Stevens.
WBAL: News; Sports Parade.
WCBM: The Music You Want.
WITH: News; Bandland.
WEAF: George Putnam, news.
WJZ: News; Dept. Store News.
WABC: News Analyst.

11:15
WCAO: Teddy King's Orchestra.
WFBR: Musical Jigsaws.
WBAL: Hamilton Baptist Church.
WABC: "Hail the Hero."
WOR: Frank Cubel from Australia.
WEAF: Music You Want.

11:30
WCAO: Masterworks of Music.
WFBR: Karl Hoff's Orch.
WBAL: Loretta Young.
WCBM: Lou Breeze's Orch.; News.
WITH: Symphonic Swing.
WABC: Dance Orchestra.
WOR: Richard Himber's Orchestra.
WJZ: Chez Paree's Orch.
WEAF: Author's Playhouse.

11:45
WFBR: Dick Kuhn's Orch.
WBAL: Behind the Headlines.
WITH: Songs For Victory.

12:00
WCAO: News, WCAO Nocturne.
WFBR: News; Sign Off.
WBAL: All-Night Star Parade.
WCBM: News; Bob Allen's Orch.
WITH: News; Moon Nocturne.
WABC: Bobby Sherwood's Orch.
WOR: Tommy Tucker's Orchestra.
WEAF: News; Rambling in Rhythm.

12:30
WCAO: Vaughn Monroe's Orchestra.
WJZ: Bob Allen's Orch.
WBAL: Ray Mace's Orch.; News.
WCBM: Sign Off.
WOR: News, Dick Jurgens' Orches.

1:00
WITH: News; All-Night Dance Party
WCAO: News; Sign Off.
WOR: Jerry Wald's Orch.

REMEMBER THIS ONE...?

ALBERT

Stanford's Frankie Albert had been handing the ball to Kmetovic for a majority of the plays against Washington in 1941. The All-America quarterback noticed Washington's right end and tackle were pursuing Kmetovic and ignoring Albert. So he called this play late in the last quarter and ran 50 yards towards the Indians' goal.

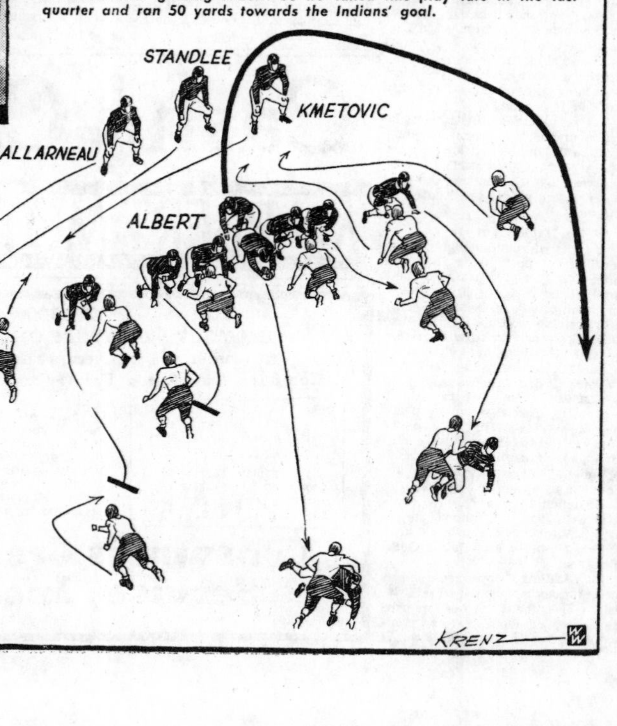
STANDLEE
KMETOVIC
GALLARNEAU
ALBERT
KRENZ

Barrett Heads

(Continued From Page One)

State Game and Inland F Commission, pointed out that members of the association can help the war effort while huntin

Save Shells

"First, use no more ammunition than is absolutely necessary; you may not get any more for the duration," he said.

"Second, save all the bra heads of your exploded shells. They are precious scrap urgently needed and may be turned over to any game warden, or any officer of the association, for proper disposal. Place a small box basket in your duckblind for this purpose and reserve a pocket in your hunting coat for empties. If they are too bulky, cut off the cardboard section, only retai the metal end.

"Finally, remember that all game is food and therefore it is vitally important that none be wasted. See that all of your game is retrieved and prope consumed.

"The armed forces need warm clothes. Save all your wildfowl feathers. They will help our boys to keep warm and comfortable while protecting our homes a lives."

Club Will Hold Citizenship Meet

Prof. Merrick To Address Session Tomorrow At USO

The American citizenship department of the Woman's Club of Annapolis and Anne Arundel county, under the chairmanship of Mrs. Edith Rawlings, will have charge of the program for tomorrow's meeting in the USO from 2 to 4 P. M.

Prof. Roderick S. Merrick, chairman on government at the Naval Academy, will speak on "American Citizenship in War and in Peace."

Mrs. Wainwright to Speak

Another speaker will be Mrs. Richard Wainwright, chairman of the camp council at Fort Meade, who will be introduced by Mrs. H. V. Hall, program chairman. Mrs. Wainwright is a charter member of the club. This will follow a brief business session at 2 o'clock and a board meeting at 1:30 called by the president, Mrs. L. Warrington Carr.

"Minute Women at War Week" will be recognized with the sale of defense stamps before and after the meeting by Mrs. G. R. Rasmussen, bond and stamp chairman of the club. In addition to Mrs. W. F. Joachim, county chairman, other club members active in its participation are Mrs. R. Gardiner Chaney, vice president of the Collere Women's Club; Mrs. E. F. L'Aigle, Legion Auxiliary president; Mrs. Conrad S. Gaw, president of the Annapolis high school P.-T.A.; Mrs. Gardiner A. Hall, matron of the Eastern Star, and Mrs. Carr.

Play Cast Announced

The cast for the play "The Neighbours" by Zona Gale, to be given at the Christmas tea on Dec. 29, includes Mrs. Gaw as "Mis' Diantha Abel"; Mrs. Alfred Wierich of the Junior Club as "Inez" with her boy-friend "Peter" taken by Mrs. Walter Hiltabidle; "Grandma," Mrs. Basil Martin; "Ezra," Mrs. Carr; "Mis' Elmira Moran," Mrs. Milton Rogers; "Mis' Trot," Mrs. Charles F. Payne; and "Mis' Carry Ellsworth," Mrs. E. E. Perkins. Rehearsal will be continued with Mrs. Helen W. Robinson of the USO staff as consultant, Friday at 2 P. M.

War Stamp Dance Tonight At USO

Service Men To Be Admitted Free

Service men will be admitted to the square dance being held tonight at 8:15, as well as the dramatic sketches and community sing on Friday in the USO, without the purchase of a 25-cent war stamp, according to Mrs. W. F. Joachim, chairman of "Minute Women at War" Week programs.

Sponsored by the Guy C. Parlett Unit No. 7, American Legion Auxiliary, under the chairmanship of Mrs. Herbert Wilson, numbers of the square dance will be called by Miss Esther McMillan, director of recreation for the Baltimore Y. W., with Miss Nellie Todd as accompanist. Informal dancing will follow.

On Friday night, members of Annapolis Chapter 46, Order of the Eastern Star, will repeat the woman-less wedding which was given recently by the entertainment committee of the Eastern Star under Mrs. Chester A. Peregoy. The cast has been augmented by several members of the Masonic Lodge 89.

The introduction of characters in blank verse will be given by Miss Margaret Wohlgemuth, and the traditional wedding music will be played by Miss Ruth Myers. The whole wedding party of 24 men will remain incognito until after the performance.

In addition to a community sing, the program on Friday also includes a radio sketch put on by Mrs. G. R. Clements called "Father Wins the Peace." The intensive drive for sale of bonds and stamps by the women of the community will climax that night, followed by the sale of defense stamp corsages in Carvel Hall after the game, under Mrs. W. T. Armbruster at booths.

Tomorrow will be known as "Housewives for Victory" day at booths throughout the city.

Hunter Killed By Own Gun

Funeral services will be held tomorrow for Francis C. Ferber, 49, vice-president of Southern Wholesalers, Washington, who was accidentally killed Saturday afternoon in a duck blind near his summer home at Sherwood Forest.

Death was instantaneous when a 12-gauge double-barrelled shotgun fell and discharged into his head.

RICKENBACKER STILL CAN GRIN

Capt. Eddie Rickenbacker's smile is still much in evidence even after three harrowing weeks afloat in the South Pacific on a rubber raft as he sets off in a jeep for a meal of soup and ice cream a few hours after his rescue and arrival at a South Pacific base. At the wheel of the jeep is Col. Robert L. Griffin, Jr., of the Marine Corps. Rickenbacker's plane was forced down at sea while on an inspection tour. Six other men were rescued but a seventh crewman died. This picture was radioed from Honolulu. (Associated Press photo from U. S. Navy.)

NORTH AFRICAN BATTLE CASUALTY

This French tank was knocked out of action on a road 18 miles south of Safi in French Morocco during the Allied offensive in North Africa. An American soldier stands guard over the tank as it rests against a garden wall. Picture by radio from London.

WAR

(Continued From Page One)

have been left enveloping the Haipong waterfront, over which supplies are believed flowing inland for a Japanese attack on Yunnan province, in Southern China.

Akyab and Magive in Burma were bombed, river steamers were machine-gunned, and Chinese bombers hit Shasi and Shayang

Lose Destroyer

News that the U. S. has lost an additional destroyer in the Nov. 13-14 battles of the Solomons was balanced by the sinking of the Japanese destroyer off Buna. The U. S. destroyer sank the night of Nov. 16 from damage sustained in the battle. The officers and crew were all rescued.

Forty-two members of a crew of 48 died when a medium-sized British merchant vessel was torpedoed and sunk in November off the northern coast of South America, the Navy announced. The ship sank in 10 seconds.

A strong force of British bombers pounded the German industrial and communications center of Stuttgart last night. Ten bombers were lost. Submarine and aircraft engine plants are located in the city.

Italian Reports

A series of roundabout and unconfirmed reports from the continent and Near East said that Adolf Hitler had sent 60,000 "tourists" and squads of Gestapo agents into Italy to prop up sagging Fascist morale and to build hurriedly coastal fortifications against a possible Allied invasion.

Reuters, British news agency, in a dispatch from Ankara said a movement for a separate peace had been started in Italy under the leadership of Marshal Pietro Badoglio, Mussolini's "unofficial opponent." According to the account a group headed by Badoglio approached the Vatican to mediate with the full knowledge of King Vitorio Emanuele, Crown Prince Umberto and Count Galeazzo Ciano.

Sir Stafford Cripps, regarded as the number two man in the British Government a few months ago, dropped from the war cabinet to become Minister of Aircraft Production at Prime Minister Churchill's request.

Russian Attack

With Germany's attention divided by the North African attacks and riflemen smashed thru biggest scale onslaught of the year. More than 28,000 Nazis have been killed or captured and Hitler's hopes of a winter line on the Volga appear to be blasted.

This was the pattern of the attack:

Germans holding positions northwest of Stalingrad were battered for an hour in a sudden, terrific artillery barrage, and Russian tanks and rifles smashed through the Nazi trench lines on a 18-mile wide front. In three days the Red army reached and occupied Kalach, on the east bank of the Don river 50 miles east of Stalingrad, and the rail line station of Krivomuzginskaya, a few miles southeast of Kalach.

Hit Nazi Column

A British force advancing along the Tunisian coast toward Bizerte inflicted heavy damage upon a German armored column and French troops held successfully despite heavy losses against Nazi at-

temps to widen their Tunisian foothold.

A Berlin broadcast heard in London suggested that Rommel had been placed in command of the Axis forces in Tunisia, and had moved there with at least part of his African Corps.

U. S. Flying Fortresses and twin-motored Lockheed P-38 fighters blasted hangars ard warehouses at Tunis Saturday and destroyed nine planes.

The Japanese were fighting back bitterly from their precarious positions on the coastal strip between Buna ard Gona, but the Allied noose was slowly drawing tight. American and Australian troops captured a new landing strip at Buna. Other Allied forces were attacking the Buna mission, one mile from Buna and the main landing field on the outskirts. The Australians are attacking Jap positions at Gona, 12 miles up the coast from Buna.

Bomb School

(Continued on Page 2)

Maj. Gen. Milton A. Reckord, commanding general of the Third Service Command.

More than 100 students representing State and city police, public utilities, railroads, public works groups, the school and fire departments, Naval Academy, Military establishments, industries and civilian defense officials, reported to witness the array of anti-aircraft shells, bombs, parachutes and similar devices.

The course of instruction includes the effect of aerial bombing, the theory of explosives, characteristics of Japanese, Italian and German bombs, problems in bomb detection, evacuation of civilian personnel from danger areas, precautionary measures to minimize damage to utilities and property and the methods of reporting unexploded and delayed action bombs after and during an aerial attack.

"This vicinity is extremely vulnerable to attacks from the air," Colonel Coff pointed out. "The junction of the Chesapeake Bay and the Severn river, the network of historic highways, the State House dome and the Naval Academy offer unmistakable guides to enemy bombers.

"The training of bomb reconnaissance agents in this community is expected to result in less loss of life and property damage if an aerial bombing of Anne Arundel county should be attempted by the Axis powers."

Gov. Herbert R. O'Conor, chairman of the Maryland Council of Defense, has announced that an exclusive showing of the authentic British motion picture, "Bomb Disposal and How the Problem is Handled in England" will be shown in the House of Delegates Chamber at 2 P. M.

Every man and woman in the city may attend the showing of this picture.

RED CROSS ANSWERS CALL FOR TRANSFUSION

In the first direct blood transfusion which the local Red Cross has been called upon to make, four donors yesterday morning volunteered their services for an emergency case at Emergency Hospital.

Answering the call for a rare type of blood were Claude M. Russell, 208 Prince George street; Walton Wiliams, 825 Chesapeake avenue, Eastport; Richard Jones, 19 Woodland avenue, and Mrs. Harry Miller, 107 Linden avenue.

The Red Cross blood bank committee, under the direction of Mrs. Winfield S. Cunningham, ordinarily sends the blood from volunteer donors to be made into plasma for use by the armed forces.

EASTPORT CHURCH GROUP TO MEET

The Woman's Society of Christian Service of the Eastport Methodist Church will hold an executive meeting at 8 P. M. tomorrow at the home of Mrs. John G. Wood, 924 Bay Ridge avenue.

1942----Picture Review Of A World At War----1942

YANKS LAND IN NORTH AFRICA—Swarming up a beach from landing barges, American soldiers go into action at Surcouf near Algiers in French North Africa. They are part of the great United Nations offensive aimed at clearing all Axis forces from the African continent. The French under Darlan have joined them.

STALINGRAD — BOMBED BUT UNBOWED—After a visit by Nazi bombers two Russian women emerge from an air-raid shelter amid the rubble that is Stalingrad. They carry blankets because the Luftwaffe hammered the Volga city hour after hour, day after day, keeping the citizens under ground. But the price paid in lives by Germany was not enough to take the city.

SUB'S-EYE-VIEW OF WAR AT SEA—Photographed through the periscope of a U. S. submarine, a Jap destroyer sinks after two torpedo hits. Men on ship are circled.

GOOD WORK, JIMMY! — After pinning the Congressional Medal of Honor on Brig. Gen. (now Maj. Gen.) James H. Doolittle for leading the raid on Tokyo, President Roosevelt shakes his hand. Lt. Gen. H. H. Arnold and Mrs. Doolittle look on.

GUADALCANAL—A FIGHT AGAINST JAPS AND JUNGLE— Sweating U. S. Marines slog through the jungle on Guadalcanal Island on their way to the front to fight the Japs. The Leathernecks captured the island's airfield just as the Japs were about to use it. It's been a tough fight ever since and the surrounding seas have thundered with history-making naval battles.

ATTACKS JAPS — Gen. Douglas MacArthur (above) commands United Nations forces in Australia-New Guinea area and is now leading troops attacking Japs at Burma.

EGYPT — BRITISH PUT ROMMEL IN REVERSE — An artillery crew (foreground) stands by as British Eighth Army infantrymen pursue Rommel's reversed Afrika Korps.

IN AFRICA — Lt. Gen. Dwight D. Eisenhower (above) commands the United Nations offensive in French North Africa aimed to rid the continent of the Axis.

CHURCHILL COMES TO AMERICA — General George Marshall (left) explains parachute tactics of a Fort Jackson, S. C., demonstration to British Prime Minister Winston Churchill during the great leader's visit to America.

ABANDON SHIP!—Hundreds of men crowd the deck of the mortally-wounded U. S. aircraft carrier Lexington as the order to abandon ship is given. Some men descend on ropes. The Lexington was lost in the Battle of the Coral Sea.

BURMA — TOO LITTLE, TOO LATE—Wreckage of an automobile (foreground) and gasoline drums standing on wall of ancient temples form a picture symbolic of United Nations' defeat in Burma, strategic land rich in raw materials of war.

LATE NEWS

Evening Capital

WEATHER
Occasional rain and not so warm today; somewhat colder tonight; gentle to moderate winds.

VOL. LIX — NO. 85. EVERY EVENING EXCEPT SUNDAY ANNAPOLIS, MD., SATURDAY, APRIL 10, 1943. SOUTHERN MARYLAND'S ONLY DAILY THREE CENTS.

FORCED SAVINGS MAY BE NEXT

Washington, April 10 (AP) — President Roosevelt's warning that the nation must be prepared to spend less and save more to "hold the line" against inflation stirred speculation today as to whether the administration is planning to recommend to Congress a compulsory lending or compulsory savings tax.

FARM LEADERS PLEDGE SUPPORT

Washington, April 10 (AP) — Keeping their powder dry, Congressional farm leaders pledged their support today to President Roosevelt's effort to hold the line against inflation with a virtual freeze of prices, wages and salaries at their existing levels.

But from farm organization leaders came outspoken criticisms of the edict, with one terming it "impossible of execution."

PRODUCE PRICES LIKELY TO BE CUT

Washington, April 10 (AP) — High government circles hinted today that poultry, egg and fresh vegetable prices may be among the first to be cut by the Office of Price Administration in carrying out President Roosevelt's order to hold or cut the cost of living.

These commodities, usually well-informed officials said, were likely to be "rolled back" at all price points from the farm to the retail grocery store. However, no official confirmation of such action was obtainable from OPA.

HOBBS BILL FACES FIGHT

Washington, April 10 (AP) — Beaten in the opening round of the first legislative labor fight of the 78th Congress, law-making champions of organized labor swung toward the Senate today in their campaign to kill the Hobbs anti-racketeering bill.

BREAK EXPECTED IN TAX DEALOCK

Washington, April 10 (AP) — With compromise plans sprouting faster than victory gardens, the House of Representatives pinned its hopes for an Easter vacation today on behind-the-scenes efforts of party leaders to break a Ways and Means Committee deadlock on pay-as-you-go tax legislation.

FIVE QUESTIONED IN HOLD-UP

Baltimore, April 10 (AP)—Police trapped five men in an automobile outside a tavern today, wounded one of them in an exchange of gunfire and took all five into custody for questioning about two tavern holdups which occurred within a space of 35 minutes.

One of the men, whom police Capt William Forrest said gave his name as Paul Black, 20, of Baltimore, was wounded in the left shoulder.

JUDGE PATIENT AT WILMER

Baltimore, Arpil 10 (AP)—Judge Samuel I. Roseman of the New York Supreme Court—an advisor of President Roosevelt and a frequent White House visitor—was a patinet in the Wilmer Institute of the Johns Hopkins Hospital today.

OPA WARNS VIOLATORS

Baltimore, April 10 (AP) — The State Office of Price Administration warned today that grocers and butchers found selling rationed foods above ceiling prices would be given administration hearings by panels of local attorneys.

FUNERAL RITES FOR MRS. ALICE V. DANIELS

Funeral rites were held yesterday at 3:30 P. M. from Taylor's Funeral Home, for Mrs. Alice V. Daniels who died suddenly on Wednesday at her residence, 97 Market street. Rev. Dr. J. Luther Neff conducted the services.

Interment was in the Naval Cemetery.

Mrs. Daniels is survived by two daughters, Mrs. L. D. Whitgrove of Portland, Ore., and Miss Frances Daniels of Annapolis.

Local Tides

TOMORROW

High water — 10:57 A. M., 0.7 feet; 10:19 P. M., 1.1 feet. Low water—4:37 A. M., 6:01 P. M.

Moon rises 11:28 A. M.; sets 1:22 P. M.

Sun rises 6:37 A. M.; sets 7:38 P. M.

MONDAY

High water—11:52 A. M.. 0.7 feet; 11:13 P. M., 1.1 feet. Low water—5:40 A. M., 6:55 P. M.

Moon rises 12:18 P. M. sets 2:09 A. M.

Sun rises 6:35 A. M.; sets 7:39 P. M.

Tides are given for Annapolis. For Sandy Point, add 15 minutes. For Thomas Point shoal, subtract 30 minutes.

STATE'S RIGHT NEED URGED BY O'CONOR IN NEW YORK SPEECH

Declares Federal Usurpation Of State Rights Would Be Great Calamity

Gov. Herbert R. O'Conor of Maryland declared that the "most vital domestic problem before the American people" was maintenance of the dual form of government, and "to have the States stripped of their powers through Federal usurption would be the greatest calamity in American history," yesterday in New York.

Maryland's executive, chairman of the National Council of State Governments, was addressing a regional meeting of council representatives from Eastern and Northeastern States.

Under the dual form of government, he said, the States and the Federal government "both as sovereign entities, must be preserved in the fullest use of their powers, in exact accordance with the pattern of the country's founders.

"Only by the fullest discharge of the States responsibilities will there be preserved the beneficial rights and freedoms which are at the core of American citizenship.

Sees Danger

"Now, when by gradual process the functions of the State government are in danger of permanent impairment and extinction, no greater obligation rests upon officials of the States than to make known to the public the danger which threatens.

"Federal encroachment can be met successfully, and repelled, I believe, only if the States justify their existence by measuring up to the requirements of the crisis."

Speaking on the topic "What is the opportunity of the States," O'Conor declared that 55,000,000 persons were engaged in war and civilian work, and that the war effort would consume 60 per cent of the national production within the year.

"Industrial activities in many sections of the States, like my own State of Maryland, are now being devoted to war production to an extent never before experienced.

"Also 12 to 15 million persons will probably be in the armed services before the end of the present conflict.

Post-War Problem

"The demobilization of industrial workers and members of the armed forces at the close of the war will present monumental and baffling problems unless we seize the opporunity now to plan for that day."

O'Conor said that post-war development and construction could not be regarded "as a monopoly of any one group or to be handled on

(Continued on Page Six)

Scoutmaster Training Class Starts Tuesday

Will Be Held Over Six Week Period

The Boy Scouts of Anne Arundel county today announced a Scoutmasters Training Course to be held on the next six Tuesday evenings beginning on April 13, at 8:00 P. M. in the Trinity Methodist Church on West street at Amos Garrett Boulevard.

This course is open to any adult interested in the boys of the county, and will teach them the proper methods of Scout leadership, the various arts and skills of the Boy Scouts the advancement and the Merit Badge education.

The director of the course is Henry Weaver, who for some years has been one of the outstanding Boy Scout leaders in the county Mr. Weaver is the Scoutmaster of the Civitan troop that meets in the old Annapolis High School. He was the first first aid instructor in the county and is well known throughout scouting circles for the work that he has done among boys. He will be aided by Scoutmasters Bernie Treat, Isaac Windsor, and Jack Wood, assistant Scoutmaster.

During the period prior to the meeting there will be demonstrations of Scout work by members of Mr. Weaver's troop who will work on the requirements that are the subject of the evenings instruction. All men who are interested in the Boy Scout Movement or desire to start troops will be welcomed for the course of instruction.

County Women Asked To Work In War Plants

Special Meeting At Linthicum April 16 To Recruit Woman-Power For Defense

Women living in the Linthicum area of Anne Arundel county will be recruited for war jobs in nearby defense plants at a special meeting to be held Friday at 8 P. M. in the Linthicum School.

Kenneth Douty of Baltimore, assistant director of the War Manpower Commission, will explain the special needs of the industries in the area, wages paid and hours required.

Judge Robert France of Baltimore, state director of Civilian Defense, will preside. A 15-minute film, illustrating women's work in war industries, will be shown.

Thousands Needed

Thousands of workers are needed by the shipyards and other defense plants which are accessible

(Continued On Page Three)

OYSTER OUTLOOK FOR NEXT YEAR IS GLOOMY

Seed Oysters Scarce As Government Orders Take Supply, Woodfield Says

Annapolitans may be enjoying the last succulent half dozen in the half shell that they will have for a long, long time. Not just because May has no "r" in it, but because oystermen can't get seed for planting for next winter's supply, and the deadline for planting is April 15.

According to Albert W. Woodfield, Maryland's representative on the Atlantic States Fisheries Commission, government order for camps are taking the supply that normally at this time of year would be used for seeding.

Even if the oysters were available the price would be prohibitive. Usually, as spring weather brings waning appetites, oyster prices drop. Last year they were selling in April from 35 to 50 cents a bushel.

$1.50-$1.85 A Bushel

But today at the big Woodfield plant at Galesville shuckers are handling shells like nuggets of gold—$1.50 to $1.85 a bushel is the price, as much as they brought at the height of the season.

Even the opening of the oyster beds off Seminary Bar, in St. Mary's river, will not relieve the situation to any appreciable extent, oystermen here say, as tonging charges and cost of freight would make the price too high for oystermen in this section.

MRS. ANNA R. GUIENOT BURIED YESTERDAY

Funeral services for Mrs. Anna R. Guienot who died on Wednesday at the residence of her sister Mrs. Edwin S. Wild of 75 Shipwright street, were held yesterday afternoon at 2 o'clock from the residence. Rev. James L. Smiley was the minister in charge.

Pallbearers were Howard B. Pyle, Frank Hladky, Arthur D. Moss, J. Lloyd Young, Frank Jewell and H. Wayne Carrick.

Burial took place in Cedar Bluff Cemetery.

John M. Taylor was the funeral director in charge.

Mrs. Guienot was the widow of John Philip Guienot. She is survived by two daughters, Mrs. Ralph Cantwell of Middle River, Md., and Mrs. W. Richard Williams of Bethesda, Md.

44 Men Leave For Army Tests

Take Physical Examinations In Baltimore

Forty-four men left the local draft board offices today to take the final physical examinations in Baltimore preparatory to entering the armed forces.

The group was in charge of Kenneth H. Moreland with Henry Lashiell LeTourneau as assistant leader.

Others in the party were:

Robert Anderson, Jack Bassford, Olin Ross Bedsworth, Jr., George Franklin Behlke, Oscar Cornelius Buser, Kenneth Joseph Carr, Louis John Carlson, Theodore R. Carroll, Earl Fred Chaney, Louis Ellsworth Clark, David Oliver Colburn, Alfred Joel Daniels, Ridgely Lee Dove, Michael Gernot Gravis, John Thomas Hall, III, Russell Randall Hall, LaRoy Lewis Hare, George Roger Hopkins, William Conrod Jarrell, Louis James Jones, Louis George Karangelen, Leonard Harold Lieberman, Elmer George Lohmeyer, Thomas Sidney McCready, Robert Gilbert Norfolk, Henry Maurice Polyanski, Mason Casper Rust, Cleveland Slight, Jr., William Augustus Small, Frank Bramble Stallings, Marion Paris Sutphin, Edward E. Taylor, Jr., Melvin Edmond Thomas, Mondell Guinn Trimble, George C. Trott, Henry Halling Trundell, Jr., George Gordon Wheeler, Samuel Louis Wilkinson, John Herbert Wlliams, John Albert Smith, Oliver Crane Hart, James Lawrence Whittington.

High School P.-T.A. To Meet

Will Be Held In School Music Room Monday

Mrs. F. W. Slaven and Miss Barbara Keyser will be the speakers at the meeting of the Annapolis High School Parent-Teacher Association, to be held 3:30 P. M. Monday, in the music room of the school.

A graduate of Goucher College, Mrs. Slaven will discuss the importance of developing in the children and youth of our nation a spirit of tolerence of the peoples of other races and nations. Miss Keyser, a graduate of Vassar, has done graduate work at Columbia. She will present the part the school may play in promoting and developing this spirit of tolerence. Miss Keyser is a member of the social studies department of our local high school.

An added feature of the program will be contributed by Mrs. Guy R.

(Continued on Page Six)

Arnold Firemen Elect Officers

Edward Balderston Elected President

The Arnold Volunteer Fire Department, Inc., has been granted its charter, and at the regular meeting of the organization held on Thursday, election of officers was held with the following results: president, Edward Balderston; vice-president, Scott Walker; secretary, Lawrence Myers, and treasurer. Oden Smith.

At this meeting application was made to the OPA to secure the necessary priorities for the purchasing of fire equipment and the remodeling of the fire engine house. It was also decided at this meeting that a board of directors would be elected, on which a representative resident of each locality served by the fire department, will be asked to serve.

A plan was also under discussion whereby each resident of the entire area, which is the Third District from Jones Station to the Severn River Bridge, would be called upon personally and asked

(Continued on Page Four)

British Eighth Army Occupies Sfax, Big German Supply Port

AXIS QUITS TWO TUNISIAN TOWNS

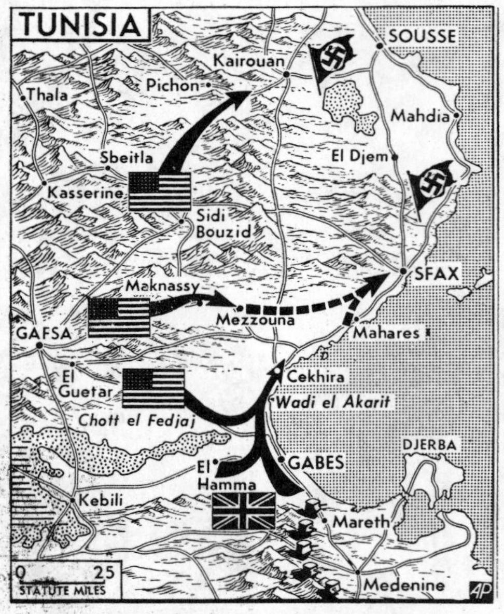

As the Allied offensive against Marshal Rommel's Axis forces progressed the enemy abandoned Mahares and Mezzouna in central Tunisia. Dotted arrows indicate line of Axis retreat; solid arrows direction of Allied drives. Today the British took Sfax.

MORE THAN 20,000 PRISONERS TAKEN IN TUNISIAN CAMPAIGN

British Troops Cover More Than 40 Miles In 24 Hours—Occupy Mahares—British First Army Has Advanced 10 Miles—Patton's Troops Occupy Pichon, North Of Fondouk—Allied Airmen Dominate Tunisian Skies—Rommel Retreating So Fast His Soldiers Cannot Lay Mines—Merchant Ship Sunk Off East Coast—RAF Bombs Duisburg

(By The Associated Press)

The British Eighth Army, moving ahead about 40 miles in 24 hours, today occupied Sfax, Marshal Erwin Rommel's key base and supply port in central Tunisia at 8:15 A. M. after routing enemy opposition.

The British had previously occupied Mahares, 50 miles north of Gabes, and now are about 150 miles south of Tunis.

Gen. Dwight D. Eisenhower's headquarters reported the British First army had advanced again in northern Tunisia and had marked up a 10-mile gain in the last four days in the Medjez-el-Bab area.

Americans of Lieut. Gen. George S. Patton, Jr., and French combined to capture high ground north and south of Fondouk, occupying Pichon, north of Fondouk, and cleaning out that area 80 miles northwest of Sfax, where a new threat to Rommel's rear appeared to be developing.

20,000 PRISONERS TAKEN

The British First army had taken 1,000 prisoners since beginning its offensive April 6 and the Americans and French captured 500 more in their advance in the central sector. This brought Axis prisoners to more than 20,000 since the beginning of the Mareth line battle.

Hurled back at all points where Allied attacks were made, the Axis was able to put up but scant opposition in the air, and Allied pilots reported that German bomber crews bailed out at the approach of Allied fighters, without even a shot being fired.

Caught in the rush of British and American forces from the south and the flank was General Mannerini, commander of the Italian Saharan group, who was taken prisoner at his headquarters when he was cut off by the junction of the U. S. Second Army Corps and the British Eighth army.

Near Rout

While the Rommel withdrawal was still too methodical to be called a route, the speed with which the Axis forces were retreating made it nearly so.

The Eighth army's vehicles were rushing ahead so fast that, for the first time, Rommel sappers had little or no time to plant mines to delay the pursuit. Today's communique, announcing the occupation of Mahares, said British advance elements were still fighting the Axis rearguard of infantry and tanks, however.

Only two enemy fighters yesterday during Allied air patrols in the central and northern sectors, and the German air force appeared to have suffered a defeat worse than that of the Axis ground forces.

The most ignominious performance of the once daring German air force occurred over a central sector, however, when a formation of 16 Stuka dive bombers was encountered by American

(Continued on Page Four)

Churches Hold Lenten Services

Special Services Planned Tomorrow

All the local churches are holding special services during this Lenten season.

At the Naval Academy Chapel tomorrow, the pulpit will be filled by the Rev. Paul Douglass, D. D., president of the American University of Washington, D. C.

Chaplain Allen A. Zaun, U. S. N. R., will be the guest preacher at the First Presbyterian church, and his subject will be "The Hunger for Goodness."

At the morning service of St. Martin's Evangelical Lutheran church, the presentation and examination of the Catechism class will be held.

"The Personal Significance of Calvary," and "The Need of Forgiveness" will be the sermon sub-

(Continued on Page Four)

Four Naval Officers Honored

Win Medals For Submarine Work

U. S. Submarine Base, New London, Conn., April 10 (AP)—Four more names were added to the submarine honor roll at ceremonies held today in the base auditorium.

Rear Admiral Freeland Daubin, U. S. N., commander of the Submarine Atlantic Fleet, presented the coveted Silver Star medal to Lt. Commander David C. White, Lt. Commander William Walker, Lieut. David Hayward McClintock, and Lieut. Guy E. O'Neil, Jr.

The citations were given in behalf of Admiral C. W. Nimitz, U. S. N., commander in chief of the Pacific Fleet.

A message from Admiral Nimitz

(Continued on Page Four)

Council Grants

(Continued From Page One)

was applied for in the first instance, not after money had been invested. Alderman Hoff and Ellington and Bernstein took a similar position.

The Adams' motion to reject was defeated 7 to 2, with Aldermen Adams and Addison voting in the affirmative. The license was granted by a similar vote.

Jury Foreman Speaks

Later in the meeting, Lieut. Richard O. Williams, U.S.N. (ret)., foreman of the grand jury, speaking as a taxpayer and citizen, on conditions generally said:

"A week ago Judge (Ridgley P.) Melvin charged the grand jury to take special pains to investigate certain places in Annapolis. I have looked into some of these places. I am a Navy man and have traveled around the world. Never in all my experience have I seen such filthy pest holes as I have seen in Annapolis."

Mr. Williams described "one place" he had visited and went into detail as to conditions citing alleged lack of toilet facilities and cleanliness.

"We feel the need of revenue," he continued. "But the City Council has got to clean up the cesspools."

He pointed out that, with the nation at war, action might be taken to place the city out of bounds if service men were maltreated or injured.

He also declared that "in a number of cases" the State law on toilet facilities is not carried out.

Cites Arrests

Mr. Williams referred to the arrests made on rioting charges as the result of a disturbance that started in the Washington hotel early Sunday and the sentencing of a group of sailors to 30 days each on rioting charges.

"This grand jury has read the report of the last April and October grand juries and thoroughly concurs with them in regard to the liquor situation," he declared.

Mayor McCready pointed out that, under the new law, the old law setting 10 rooms for hotel licenses had been abolished and 20 rooms were now required. He cited that restaurants selling beer, wine and liquor could only sell from 6 A. M. to midnight on week days and only with meals from 1 P. M. to midnight on Sundays. He said the Council was trying to clear up the situation and thought it could under the present new laws.

Mr. Williams suggested enforcement officers for liquor regulation rather than the use of the police force. He also suggested that Aldermen could enforce the law in their wards.

Fisher Comments

Alderman Fisher stressed the need of good regulation and declared that as long as liquor is sold "we're going to have fights." He declared there were still fights under prohibition.

"I came near getting killed some years ago when St. John's and Johns Hopkins students had a riot," he said. "They weren't drinking. I sat on a committee and voted to close the places up on Sunday. I thought it was all settled, but you saw what the Legislature did."

Mrs. Conrad S. Gaw suggested that the dispensary system of handling liquor in the city would bring in revenue and keep control in the hands of the Council. Alderman Fisher replied that "the dispensary form of government is my form of government, but my people don't want it and I represent the people."

When the application for the restaurant license for the Washington Hotel came up, Alderman England moved it be rejected. The motion passed unanimously.

The application of Vincent Dana for a Class B restaurant beer license was rejected on motion by Alderman Ellington.

Shore Patrols

During the general discussion several Aldermen pointed out it would help if Navy shore patrols or Army military police assisted the city police in handling service men. Several stressed the need for colored shore patrols in the Fourth Ward.

When the New York Lunch application was read, Mr. Michaelson said that when a complaint had been filed against the premises for the USO club on Northwest street some weeks ago, he had taken action which he understood was satisfactory. He said that any conditions that caused complaint would be corrected and requested the Council to give the time and consideration to allow improvements to be made that would be satisfactory to all.

"I say the place can be put in proper condition, will be put in proper condition and if it is not then don't grant the license," he said.

Conrad A. Walden opposed granting the license citing the nearness of the colored USO club and "inadequate facilities."

Pass Ordinance

After the license application had been withdrawn, former Alderman Charles Oliver asked Mayor McCready if the public could be heard at any future meeting at which the applications is brought up. The Mayor said that such hearing would be granted.

The Council, under suspended rules, passed an ordinance setting the hours for Class B, beer, on sale licenses at from 6 A. M. to midnight on week days and from 1 P. M. to midnight on Sundays. This brings them in line with the restaurant beer, wine and liquor licenses.

The following licenses were granted by the Council:

Hotel (beer, wine and liquor) on sale, generally

Carvel Hall Hotel, 186 Prince George street.

Class B (beer, wine and liquor) restaurant

The Presto Restaurant, 61-63 West street.

Wally's Hotel Inc., 79-81 West street.

The Mayfair Hotel, 115 Main street (subject approval of health officer).

Class B (on sale beer) restaurant

Jones Restaurant, 26 Clay street, Frank Jones, (subject approval of health officer).

Jim's Corner, James Leonas.

John's Lunch, 247 West street, John T. Mooseles.

Miller's Lunch, 236 West street, Harry W. Day.

Royal Restaurant, 23 West street. Steve Foundas, (subject approval of health officer).

Boston Dairy Lunch, 5 Washington street, Leroy Sisco.

Coney Island Lunch, 65 Washington street, Peter Karangelen (subject approval of health officer).

Park Lunch, 15 Calvert street.

Susie's Tea Room, 55 Calvert street, Susie Sims.

Bladen Street Station, James Konstant.

Charles Bernstein, 165 Main street.

Wardroom Lunch, 168 Main street, Pete Bounelis.

Sanitary Lunch, 108 Main street, James R. Constantine.

Mandris Restaurant, 244 Market Space.

City Lunch Room, 130 Dock street, (subject to approval of health officer) Aldermen Ellington and Walter Adams voted in negative, granted by 7 to 2 vote.

Little Campus, 63 Maryland avenue, Theodore Nichols.

Capital Restaurant, 200 Main street, Nich Bounelis.

The Candy Shop, 232 Main street, Alice Wagner.

G. A. J. Grill, 62-69 Maryland avenue, Gregory Characklis.

Class A (beer, wine and liquor) off sale

Family Liquor Store, 101½-103 Main street.

Corner Shop, 57-59 West street.

Read Drug and Chemical Company, 176 Main street, (subject approval of Counselor).

Community Market, 28-30 Market Space.

Earle's Grocery, 43 Lafayette avenue, (subject approval of health officer). Granted by 8 to 1 vote, Alderman Ellington voting in the negative.

Hopkins Pharmacy, 60 West street.

R. R. Smith Pharmacy, 110 Main street.

Taverns (beer, wine and liquor)

Samuel Lorea, 136 Dock street.

Maggie Coleman, 6 Clay street, (subject approval of health Counselor).

Dove's Tavern, 250 West street, William T. Dove.

Dixie Tavern, 58 Washington street, Henry Abrams.

Gritz's Liquors, 32½-34 West street, Bessie A. Greenfield Gritz.

Olde Towne Tavern, 132 Dock street, Henry Wahab.

Legum's Bar, 8 Market Space, Maurice Legum.

Mills Liquor Mart, 93 Main street, William O. Mills.

William Katcef, 77 West street.

Captain Dan's, 24 Market Space, M. D. G. Sanders.

Charles Alvanos, 153 Main street.

Brown's Hotel, 16 Clay street, Ulysses G. Brown.

Class B (beer) off sale

Abe Zelkowitz, 82-84 Clay street.

Class D (beer) on sale

Brunswick Billard Hall, 163 Main street.

Clubs (beer, wine and liquor)

Moose Club, 130 West street.

Annapolitan Club, 81 Franklin street.

Elks Club, Main street.

Ancient City Lodge No. 1751 I.B.P.O.E., 71 Northwest street.

Annapolis Yacht Club, Compromise and Gloucester streets.

Club (beer)

First Ward Democratic Club, 8 Martin street.

Admiral Nimitz Awards Navy Cross

Admiral Chester W. Nimitz (left), commander-in-chief, U.S. Pacific Fleet, awards the Navy Cross to Lieut. Comdr. Roy S. Benson, of Concord, N. H., at a recent ceremony at the Pearl Harbor Submarine Base. The award was won by Benson for conducting an aggressive and highly successful war patrol. (U.S. Navy photo).

BOND SALE CHART

Second War Loan—city, county goal		$2,000,000.00
SOLD		
Annapolis Banking and Trust Co.	$142,950.00	
County Trust Company	79,900.00	
Farmers National Bank	206,650.00	
Postoffice	71,876.00	
Naval Academy	103,933.35	
Annapolis at large	713,650.00	
Raised in county	114,490.50	$1,433,449.85
Short of goal		$ 566,550.15

ERROL FLYNN AND ANN SHERIDAN TO BE AT CIRCLE TOMORROW

Today at the Capitol Theatre, Bud Abbott and Lou Costello in "It Ain't Hay," will appear the last time. Tomorrow and Thursday, James Ellison and Lois Andrews will appear in "Dixie Dugan," and Randolph Scott and Claire Trevor will be featured in "Desperados" on Friday and Saturday.

Today, "Desperados" will be shown at the Circle. The rest of the week the attraction will be "Edge of Darkness," starring Errol Flyn,, Ann Sheridan and Walter Huston.

The Republic is showing William Holden and Susan Hayworth in "Young and Willing" today. On Wednesday and Thursday, "She Has What It Takes" with Jinx Falkenburg and Tom Neal will be the feature film. "Quiet Please, Murder" with George Sanders and Gail Patrick will close the week's bill.

Cartoons, specials and newsreels will be shown throughout the week at all three theatres.

State Liquor Taxes Show Big Increase

Insurance Department Taxes Also Increase

Two important sources of State revenue — alcoholic beverage and State Insurance Department taxes—have shown marked increase during the six months period ending March 31, State Comptroller J. Millard Tawes said today. As compared with the same period a year ago.

A total of $3,171,466 in alcoholic taxes has been received by the Comptroller's office since last October 1, compared with receipts of $2,843,158 for the same period of the last fiscal year.

During the first half of the current fiscal year, the State received in revenue from the State Insurance Department $2,060,027, an increase of $114,404 over the receipts from October 1, 1941, to March 31, 1942 which amounted to $1,945,623, Tawes said.

Cash on hand, including all funds, was $29,542,806 as of last March 31, an increase of $2,716,926 over the previous month and a decrease of $489,321 from the total reported a year ago for the same period.

One of the largest increases revealed by Tawes' monthly report was that of the general funds surplus, with $8,844,421 reported as of last March 31, as against $5,235830 on March 31, 1942.

A comparison of revenues for the current fiscal year and those for the same period a year ago showed decreases in the following sources of State revenue:

Motor vehicle licenses, etc., $3,942,166 for the six months period ending last March 31, a decrease of $228,626; gasoline taxes, $4,657,307, a decrease of $1,827,507; income tax, $1,796,005, a decrease of $2,050,462 from the $3,846,467 reported a year ago; Maryland Racing Commission, $800,242, a decrease of $293,801.

Tawes explained that these figures applied to the current fiscal year which started October 1, 1942, and which will end June 30, of this year. This change in the State's fiscal year was made during the recent General Assembly in order that the State's financial period might conform with that of the Federal Government.

R. P. WINTERODE, JR., ENDS ARMY COURSE

Robert P. Winterode, Jr., son of Dr. Robert P. Winterode, Crownsville, has completed his course of studies as an aviation mechanic in the Army Air Forces Technical Training School at Amarillo, Texas.

His graduation from the school fits him for airplane maintainence and he will be sent to some air base where he will assist in keeping America's Flying Fortresses in the air.

JEWISH WOMEN TO MEET WEDNESDAY

The regular meeting of the Annapolis section of the National Council of Jewish Women will be held on Wednesday at 8:30 P. M. in the Synagogue.

A board meeting has been called at 7:45 to precede the regular business of the Council. Members of the executive board are requested to attend.

A surprise entertainment and refreshments have been planned for the evening.

U. S. WARPLANES AT A GLANCE

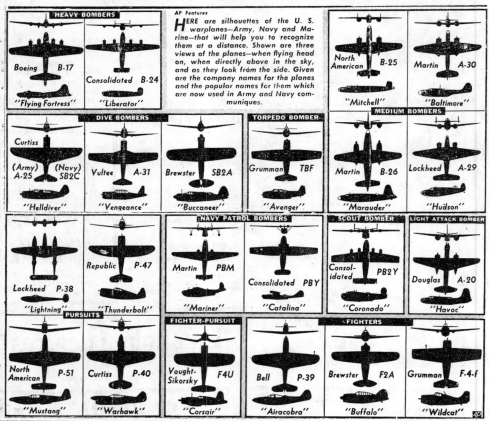

AP Features

HERE are silhouettes of the U. S. warplanes—Army, Navy and Marine—that will help you to recognize them at a distance. Shown are three views of the planes—when flying head on, when directly above in the sky, and as they look from the side. Given are the company names for the planes and the popular names for them which are now used in Army and Navy communiques.

HEAVY BOMBERS

Boeing B-17 "Flying Fortress" — Consolidated B-24 "Liberator" — North American B-25 "Mitchell" — Martin A-30 "Baltimore"

DIVE BOMBERS

Curtiss (Army) A-25 (Navy) SB2C "Helldiver" — Vultee A-31 "Vengeance" — Brewster SB2A "Buccaneer"

TORPEDO BOMBER

Grumman TBF "Avenger"

MEDIUM BOMBERS

Martin B-26 "Marauder" — Lockheed A-29 "Hudson"

NAVY PATROL BOMBERS

Lockheed P-38 "Lightning" — Republic P-47 "Thunderbolt" — Martin PBM "Mariner" — Consolidated PBY "Catalina"

SCOUT BOMBER

Consolidated PB2Y "Coronado"

LIGHT ATTACK BOMBER

Douglas A-20 "Havoc"

PURSUITS

North American P-51 "Mustang" — Curtiss P-40 "Warhawk"

FIGHTER-PURSUIT

Vought-Sikorsky F4U "Corsair" — Bell P-39 "Airacobra"

FIGHTERS

Brewster F2A "Buffalo" — Grumman F-4-f "Wildcat"

Junior Woman's Club To Meet Tomorrow

There will be a meeting of the Junior Woman's Club at the USO Club building tomorrow night at 8 o'clock.

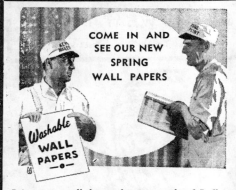

Standards Set For Nursing Scholarship

Applications Must Be Made by May 21 To Mrs. L. Warrington Carr, Chairman

Standards for the Margaret Wohlgemuth Nursing Scholarship for a high school graduate this June were set by the scholarship committee at a conference in the office of the county health department.

The standards will be based on good scholarship, physical fitness, monetary need and residence in the county. Mrs. L. Warrington Carr chairman of the committee said. The committee is composed of representatives of the different organizations contributing to the fund, with Dr. Howard A. Kinhart, principal of the Annapolis high school, and Miss Wohlgemuth as advisers.

Applications By May 21
Applications should be sent by each principal of a high school to Mrs. Carr by May 21. The scholarship fund will be turned over to an official of the State Nurses' Association, to be given to the winning student as needed for tuition, books and necesary expenses during the three year period of training.

This scholarship was inaugurated by the junior and senior divisions of the Woman's Club of Annapolis and Anne Arundel county and is shared by civic organizations of the county on an equal basis by representation upon the committee. Similar scholarships are being given throughout the country.

CALVARY QUARTERLY CONFERENCE TO MEET

The last meeting of the Calvary Methodist Church quarterly conference will be held tomorrow at 8 P. M. in the church parlor.

Dr. R. Y. Nicholson, Baltimore, district superintendent, will preside.

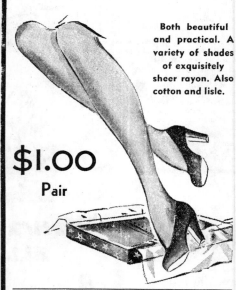

CLASSIFIED ADS

For Rent 1

FOR RENT—Furnished house. 10 rooms. Modern conveniences. Large shaded lawn. Bay Ridge Rd. H. A. Keyes, Box 31, Capital Office. m-24

FOR RENT—Furnished modern cottage, Woodland Beach. See Frank on Oldtown Road, anytime. tf

FOR RENT—Furnished room. No children. 95 Conduit Street. tf

FOR RENT—4-room bungalow on Mill Creek; four mlies from Annapolis; porch front; electric; fine well water; water-front lot; furnished. R. B. Lloyd, 5 Windsor Rd., Pikesville, Baltimore, Md. Phone, Pikesville 704. tf

FOR RENT—Bedroom suitable for two people. Call 2527. tf

FOR RENT—Bedroom adjoining bath Call 4674. tf

FOR RENT—Double room for gentlemen. Hot and cold water. Wally Hotel, 81 West street. tf

For Sale 2

FOR SALE—Dining room suite. Apply 734 Glenwood Street, Cedar Park. m-26

FOR SALE—Ford, 1932, four good tires. 16 Eastern Avenue, Eastport. tf

FOR SALE—Complete mahogany bedroom furnishings, five piece, excellent condition. Glider type swing, almost new. Other miscellaneous things. Call 6194. m-24

FOR SALE—New Saleon, 5 horsepower, 4 cycle marine engine. Call 2777. m-26

FOR SALE — ¼ acre at Wild Rose Shores, South River, with 43 ft. of waterfront and safe harbor. $1,000; $50 cash and $10 monthly. C. F. Lee, dial 2461. m-24

FOR SALE—Electric refrigerator Cold Spot about 8 cubic feet. good condition. Price $145. Call Annapolis 2611, extension 10. m-24

FOR SALE — 18 foot Sponson canoe. Square stern. $50. Phone 6020 tf

FOR SALE—Buick, 1940, 4-door sedan; heater, radio, seat covers, good tires, $750. Owner naval officer selling due to change of orders. Call Annapolis. 2826, 1 to 3 or 6 to 8 P. M. m-24

FOR SALE — City house, nine rooms. Coal furnace. Box 26 Evening Capital. m-31

FOR SALE—Metal and wood bedroom furniture. Mrs. Sanford Wally Hotel. tf

FOR SALE—Baby Walkers, Carriages, Cribs, Poster Beds, Coil Springs, Utility Cabinets, Congoleum and Fibre Rugs, Slip Covers. Radios, Refrigerators BOUGHT — SOLD — EXCHANGED — RENTED. Annapolis Furniture Co., 96 West Street. Phone 2140. m-28

FOR SALE—WATERRONT PROPERTY. EDGEWATER BEACH, Shaded sec.; on South river, exclusive colony of 21-families, Ryon Cottage, 5 r&b.; ami.; furnished, vacant; suitable all year occupancy; massive living-room, fire-place, bed-r, complete bath, elec. kitchen, 2-wide porches 1st. fl.; 2 big bed-rooms 2d fl.; closets, roof, N. & W. sides insulated, drilled well, bath-houses, material for wharf; lots 50 x 190, high, wooded; 9 minutes ride to Annapolis; quiet, restful, fine harbor, fishing, bathing; not for rent, newly paited; sunset reflection is beautiful; $5,950, $500 cash, $49 mo. 2 at Herald Harbor low price, terms. Country Specialists since 1896. See our signs. List. N. E. Ryon Co., 1216 N. Y. Avenue, Washington, D. C., Na. 7907. 7 - 9 P. M., Ge., 6146. m-24

FOR SALE—Corner dwelling, 6 rooms and bath. Occupied. Good investment. Priced for immediate sale. 800 Chesapeake Avenue, Eastport. tf

Help Wanted—Female 4

HELP WANTED FEMALE—Two salesladies, full or part time. Good salary. Apply The Leader, 162 Main St. tf

HELP WANTED FEMALE—Maid, full or part time work, three adults, no laundry. Apply 519 Sixth street, Eastport, between 5 and 8 P. M. tf

HELP WANTED FEMALE — Reliable colored woman for general housework one day a week. Call 2556. tf

HELP WANTED FEMALE — High school girl for afternoon light housework, no cooking, no laundry. Principally care for two children, five and three. Call 1 to 3, or 6 to 8 P. M. Annapolis 2826. m-24

HELP WANTED FEMALE—Only two in family. White or colored settled woman. Permanent. Phone 2765. tf

HELP WANTED FEMALE—Saleslady. ... afternoons work. Apply Ziff's, 71 West St. tf

HELP WANTED FEMALE — Lady or young lady for work in store. Pleasant surroundings. No objections to high school girl who will work evenings until graduation and steady afterward. Must be dependable, and refined. Reply stating age, education and salary expected. Box 33, Evennig Capital. tf

HELP WANTED FEMALE—Waitress for week-end work. Wally Hotel, West street. tf

HELP WANTED FEMALE — Colored girl for cleaning in bakery. York Pastry Shop, 26 Market Space . tf

HELP WANTED FEMALE—Saleslady. York Pastry Shop, 26 Market Space. tf

HELP WANTED FEMALE—Beautician, Experienced. Good salary. Phone 2444 after 6 P. M. tf

HELP WANTED FEMALE—Dishwash- Apply Mrs. Snyder, Carvel Hall. tf

HELP WANTED FEMALE—Saleslady. Apply Oscar Shacks, 37 West St. tf

Wanted 6

WANTED—Coat hangers. We will pay $1 per hundred or 10c per dozen, Colonial Cleaners and Dyers, 100 Compromise street. t-28

WANTED—Sailboat 18 to 25 ft., fully equipped. Call 6365, 7 to 8 P. M. Ask for Mr. McConkey. m-25

WANTED—Bungalow or apartment, unfurnished. Naval officer. Near Academy. Mrs. Robert G. Merritt, 3305 Woodley Road, N. W., Washington, D. C. m-25

WANTED—Short order cook, white or colored. Good wages. Apply Mandris restaurant, 2 Market Space. m-27

WANTED—Desire to rent or buy canoe. Phone 5266. m-24

WANTED—To buy or rent, house, in or near Annapolis. Write full particulars. Box 32 Evening Capital. m-24

WANTED—Wh. pay cash for your car. William J. Meyers. Call Vernon 5320 or 1708 North Charles St., Baltimore Md. tf

WANTED — Musical instruments and pianos. All kinds. Keeney's, 23 Randall street. Phone 4852. m-31

Help Wanted—Male 4

HELP WANTED MALE—Salesman for soft drink truck. Good pay. Apply Herman O. Collier. 270 West St. m-25

HELP WANTED MALE — PAINTERS. APPLY ST. MARY'S CHURCH. m-28

HELP WANTED MALE — Driver for soft drink route High Rock Ginger Ale Company. Call 2160. tf

HELP WANTED MALE—Man to help commercial photographer several hours in the evenings. No experience necessary. Apply A. N. Miller, Maryland Hotel Building. tf

Repair Work

REPAIRS — Piano Service: Tuning cleaning and repairing estimates given and liberal credit. We buy and sell all makes and styles. Keeney's, 23 Randall street. Phone 4852. m-31

Miscellaneous 12

MISCELLANEOUS — Used cars, any make, any model bought and sold. Harry's Super-Service, West and Southgate. Phone 4000. tf

MISCELLANEOUS — Paper hanging. Also stoves and furnaces repaired. Phone 4197. tf

MISCELLANEOUS — "WHEN BUILDING MATERIALS are released there will will be a great demand for home sites. Why not contract for a home site now on the easy payment plan before prices increase. I am offering some real bargains at Wardour, Horn Point, Eastport, West Annapolis, Cedar Park, West Street extended. Ferry Farms, Davidson's Farm on Mill Creek, Pendennis Mount on the Severn, Carrollton Manor on the Severn and Turkey Point on the Bay. Dial 2461, Chas. . Lee." ju-8

MISCELLANEOUS—SEPTIC TANKS, cesspools and vaults cleaned and repaired. Everything pumped and hauled. Most modern equipment. Free estimates. Telephone J. Burke, Linthicum 109. m-31

MISCELLANEOUS — We deliver anything — anywhere. Personal Delivery Service. Phone 2781. tf

MISCELLANEOUS—Septic tanks, cesspools, vaults cleaned. Everything pumped and hauled. Most modern equipment, Free estimates. Phone Arbutus. 1145 and 1294. Normile Bros., Lansdowne, Md. tf

Lost and Found 8

LOST—Two sugar ration books. Margaret V. Owens, 5 Feldmeyer Court. m-24

LOST—Pocketbook containing gasoline ration books A and B. Carrie L. Day, Severn, Md. m-25

LOST—Sugar ration book. Finder please return to Mrs. A. Alegria, 13 Cornhill street. m-24

LOST—Ration Book II. Return to Pricilla Brashears, Annapolis Neck. m-24

LOST—Ear ring, two pearls, B. & A. train arrivnig 10:40 P. M. Wednesday, or in station. Reward Mrs. Ageton, 2611, ex. 79. m-24

LOST—Cameo pin. Between Duke of Gloucester and Circle Theater. Reward. Call Mrs. L. J. O'Connor, 133 Duke of Gloucester 2457 tf

Situations—Female 10

SITUATION WANTED FEMALE — Typist wishes position mornings or typing at home. Box 34 Evening Capital. m-26

NOTICE

I hereby give notice that I will not be responsible for any bills contracted by anyone other than myself.

WILLIAM L. CLARK

—WANTED—
BOAT CARPENTERS
Helpers, Painters, Laborers, also Lathe Operator or Machinist
Call Severna 160 or apply
MODERN MARINE SERVICE
Cypress Creek, Manhattan Beach
Severna Park, Md.

BACK UP YOUR BOY 2ND WAR LOAN
Buy an Additional Bond Today

Wood Nymph

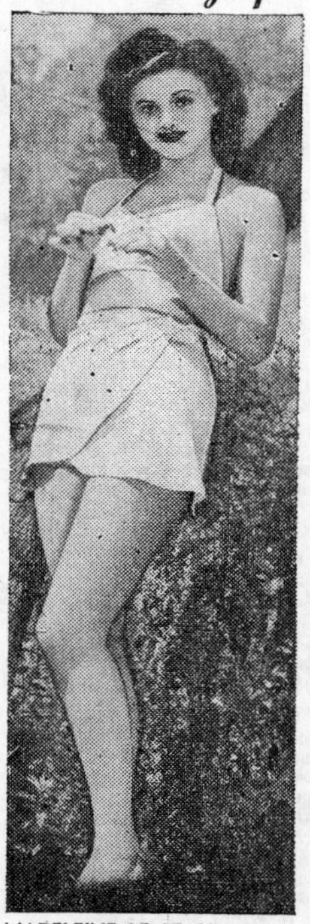

MADELEINE LE BEAU — lovely Parisian refugee—supports Humphrey Bogart, Ingrid Bergman and Paul Henreid in Warners' melodramatic romance, "Casablanca."

"THEY GIVE THEIR LIVES—YOU LEND YOUR MONEY" 2ND WAR LOAN
Buy More War Bonds Today

Rationing Calendar

FUEL OIL

No. 5 coupons, good for 10 gallons each, valid now until Sept. 30.

SHOES

Book No. 1 coupon 17 good for one pair through June 15.

SUGAR

Book No. 1 coupon 12 good for five pounds through May 31.

COFFEE

Stamp No. 23 is good for one pound through May 30.

TIRES, GASOLINE

No. 5 coupon in A books good through July 21. A, B and C coupons good for three gallons each in the East. B and C book holders ineligible to buy gasoline unless tires have been inspected.

Persons entitled to 240 miles per month gasoline rations are eligible for either grade I or grade II tires, differences in eligibility for the two grades being abolished.

MEAT, FATS, OIL, CHEESE, FISH

Red coupons E, F, G, H and J valid through May 31. Coupon J will be good through June. Coupon K valid May 30.

FRUITS AND VEGETABLES

Blue coupons G, H, and J valid through June7. Stamps K, L and M now valid.

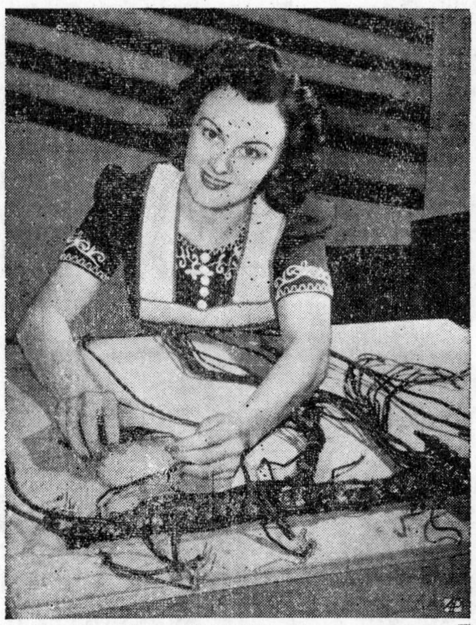

'MODEL' WAR WORKER—Once a popular model in New York City, Margaret Miller gave up that glamorous occupation to work on wire layouts for Navy combat equipment at the Westinghouse Electric Elevator Company at Jersey City, N. J.

MODEST MAIDENS

Trademark Registered U S Patent Office

"He's getting in condition for the June maneuvers!"

SCORCHY SMITH

Trademark Registered U. S. Patent Office — Just For A Lark

OAKY DOAKS

Trademark Registered U. S. Patent Office — Restless Refugees

OH, DIANA!

Trademark Registered U. S. Patent Office — Haw! Haw! It's The Law

DICKIE DARE

Trademark Registered U. S. Patent Office — War Drums

HOMER HOOPEE

Trademark Registered U. S. Patent Office — The Output On The Put-Our

THE ADVENTURES OF PATSY

Trademark Registered U. S. Patent Office — Just Where You Find It

NEIGHBORLY NEIGHBORS

HIGGINS ISN'T EXACTLY A MAN OF ACTION AND HIS INTEREST IN THOSE SPINE-CHILLING NOISES IS PURELY ACADEMIC-- BUT HE CAN'T VERY WELL BACK OUT...NOT WITH MRS. BASCOM PUSHING HIM FROM BEHIND!

THE DOOLITTLES

PLOTTING HIS FUTURE

50 Zoot-Suiters Stripped Of Garb By Servie Men

Soldiers And Sailors Stage Hunt For Zoot Suit Wearers

LOS ANGELES, June 8 (AP)—Civil and military police early today succeeded in dispersing thousands of service men and civilians in the downtown business district after a night of disorders in which zoot-suited youths were ferreted out by sailors and soldiers who divested at letast 50 of their bizarre attire.

By 1 A. M. police and sheriff's deputies had arrested 24 civilians, 11 sailors and five soldiers on charges of disturbing the peace and unlawful assembly. In three nights of Battling with service men, who maintained they and their girl friends have been "pushed around" at random by rowdies, more than 100 youths in real pleat trousers and knee-length coats were jailed on vagrancy counts.

Police Chief C. B. Horrall declared a general riot alarm last night, summoning 1,000 policemen to special duty. Navy shore patrolmen and military police, in jeeps and afoot, also toured streets teeming with service men and spectators and jammed with traffic.

Left On Sidewalks

Cars and taxis carrying bands of bluejackets and soldiers sped through the district, halting at theaters, cafes, penny arcades and dance halls in search of zoot-suiters. Victims, their clothes ripped from them, were left on sidewalks. Ambulances took three to Ememergency hospital, where they were treated and reclad. None were seriously hurt.

Order was restored after military authorities declared out of bounds the entire downtown strip of Main street, where most of the disturbances took place.

Churchill Murray, Pacific Coast Director for the coordination of inter-American affairs, said he had telephoned a report to Washington, but declined further comment. Murray made his report after touring the scene with a police captain.

International Aspect

International aspects of the disorder also were recognized yesterday at a meeting of the citizens' committee for Latin-American youth with representatives of the police and sheriff's office, after jail booking records showed Mexican names predominated among arrested zoot suiters.

Dr. George Gleason, committee member, declared it "regrettable" that small groups should bring into ill-repute the city's Mexican population.

"The great majority of these people," he said, "are law abiding, respectable and cultured."

ADMIRAL NIMITZ HOME FROM THE PACIFIC

Back on the mainland for a conference which he hopes will "carry trouble" to the Japanese, Admiral Chester W. Nimitz, commander-in-chief of the Pacific fleet, visits with his family in their Berkeley, Calif., home. In the group are Mrs. Nimitz, daughter Mary, 11, the cat Victory and the dog Freckles.

Varied Programs At Local Movies

Today at the Capitol Theatre, "Crash Dive," starring Tyrone Power, Anne Baxter and Dana Andrews, will be shown for the last time. Tomorrow and Thursday, Basil Rathbone and Nigel Bruce in "Sherlock Holmes in Washington," will be the attraction, and on Friday and Saturday "This Land Is Mine," starring Charles Laughton and Maureen O'Hara, will be shown.

At the Circle today, "This Land is Mine," is the attraction, and for the rest of the week the featured film will be, "Assignment in Brittany," with Pierre Aumont and Susan Peters.

"Mister Big," featuring Gloria Jean and Donald O'Connor, is playing at the Republic today. Lupe Valez and Michael Duane are starred in "Red Head From Manhattan," to be shown on Wednesday and Thursday. A Gene Autry "western" will be attraction on Friday Saturday.

The usual newsreels, short subjects, and cartoons will be shown at all three theatres throughout the week.

WEST ANNAPOLIS P.-T.A. WILL FORM THREE SCOUT TROOPS

Three new Scout troops—a Cub Pack for boys from 9 to 12, and a regular Boy Scout and Girl Scout Troop—will be started by the P.-T.A. of the West Annapolis School, it was decided at the P.-T.A. meeting held there last night.

Mrs. Robert H. McCready was named chairman of a committee to organize the Cub Pack, which will be the first one formed in Annapolis and the third in the county.

The troops for boys oved 12 will be formed immediately, so that members can begin scout work during the outdoor season. Mrs. Estelle Carter, principal of the West Annapolis school, is chairman of the Boys' troop committee.

A Brownie troop of Girl Scouts will be organized by a committee composed of Mrs. Edward Suitt, Mrs. Harry Weiss, and Mrs. E. M. Sames.

48 Colored Men
(Continued From Page One)

Charles Leroy Keys.
Louis Makell, John Samuel Maynard, Jacob Benjamin Moulden, Thomas Junior Moulden, Raymond Westly Mullen.
Howard Edward Nichols.
John Edward Owens.
William Albert Parker, Garfield Pinkney, Hilton Parker.
William John Smith.
Thomas Kern Turner.
Clarence Frederick Hall.
Bernard William Jackson.

Six colored men in the enlisted reserve left the local board yesterday for Fort George G. Meade and active duty in the army.

Acting corporal Howard Johnson was in charge of the group which included Arthur Wright, Allen White, Washingtotn A. Boston, William A. Snowden and Charles Ross.

WOMEN BUGLERS, TOO—Buglers have their place in women's branches of the armed services as Cadet Rosemary Kreir of Skokie, Ill., demonstrates at the Marine Corps Women's Reserve Training School, Northampton, Mass.

130 Register For Summer Trade Classes

Will Attend School At Glen Burnie

On hundred and thirty boys and girls of the Brooklyn Park and Linthicum areas have already registered for the first summer vocational classes which will start next Monday, June 14, in the old high school building in Glen Burnie, A. C. Roth, Jr., co-ordinator of vocational training for Anne Arundel county, said this morning.

Courses which will train the students for war jobs, will be offered in aircraft mechanics, welding, plumbing machine shop and radio. Girls will be admitted to the classes in acetylene welding, aircraft mechanics and in assembling radios, at which they have particular dexterity, Mr. Roth said.

Bus Transportation

Although the summer classes are particularly for boys and girls

(Continued on Page Six)

O'CONOR NAMES THREE ATTORNEYS

Governor O'Conor has re-appointed C. Walter Cole, past president of the Baltimore County Bar Association; William Curran of the Baltimore City Bar Association, and E. Paul Mason, past president of the Baltimore City Bar Association, to the commission on uniformity of legislation.

"This commission is appointed to represent Maryland in the national conference of commissioners on uniform State laws," the Governor explained, adding that the Free State ranked among the first five in the country in the adoption of such legislation.

"Much of the credit for this desirable result is due to these men whom I have appointed," he added.

CHARGE AGAINST MRS. RANDLE ON STET DOCKET

An indictment charging Mrs. Helen Aileen Randle with assault with intent to kill her husband Ulmo S. Randle, will be put on the stet docket of the Anne Arundel Circuit Court, State's Attorney Marvin I. Anderson announced this morning. He said if it should be decided later to press the charge it can be placed on the active docket.

Mrs. Randle is now serving a five year manslaughter sentence at the Women's Prison at Jessup for the fatal shooting last January of her Bay Ridge home, Randle was shot in the leg at the same time that young Willey received a wound in the abdomen.

Evening Capital

WEATHER
Cooler tonight; moderate temperature Tuesday morning

VOL. LIX — NO. 140. EVERY EVENING EXCEPT SUNDAY ANNAPOLIS, MD., MONDAY, JUNE 14, 1943. SOUTHERN MARYLAND'S ONLY DAILY THREE CENTS

Sicilians Watch For Coming Of Massed Allied Air Fleets As Lull Occurs On All Land Fronts

LATE NEWS

BUDGET BUREAU DRAWS FIRE

Washington, June 14 (AP) — The Budget Bureau and the Social Security Board drew the fire of the House Appropriations Committee today in a bill carrying $1,127,362,499 for the Labor Department, the Federal Security Agency, the War Manpower Commission, and related independent offices for the fiscal year starting July 1.

AXIS FEEL WAR IS LOST—DAVIS

Boston, June 14 (AP)—The Axis nations have reached a realization that they cannot win an affirmative and positive victory, Elmer Davis, director of the Office of War Information, said today and he predicted at a press conference that when Hitler's "people feel that he is a liability rather than an asset, they will do away with him."

OFFERS PROGRAM TO INCREASE OYSTERS

Washington, June 14 (AP) — A program intended to reverse the downward trend of the nation's oyster production, now only half as large as it was 50 years ago, went to Maryland Conservation officials today from Secretary of the Interior Ickes.

The proposal came to this:

Cultivated beds produce many more and better oysters than natural reefs, therefore there should be substituted for the present wide-spread system of free fishing on public reefs, a comprehensive system of oyster farming by private enterprise under State supervision.

FURTHER HEARINGS ON ZOOT WAR

Los Angeles, June 14 (AP)—Further hearings were docketed today for Gov. Earl Warren's special committe investigating causes of recent clashes involving zoot suiters and service men—while reinforced patrols of civil and military police reported few incidents over the week-end.

NAZI AGENTS HELPED JAPS

Washington, June 14 (AP)—The Office of War Information (OWI) reported today that German espionage agents helped the Japanese preparae their attack on Pearl Harbor and at least one of them was sentenced to death, but the sentence later was commuted.

The report said Bernard Julius Otto Kuehn, a Nazi agent, was tried before a military commission in Honolulu on charges of betraying the United States fleet in Pearl Harbor to the Japanese five day before the Dec. 7, 1941, attack. He was convicted on Feb. 21, 1942, and sentenced to be shot. On Oct. 26, 1942, the sentence was commuted to 50 years at hard labor. The basis for the commutation was not given.

COURT RULES ON FLAG SALUTE

Washington, June 14 (AP)—The Supreme Court overruled today a decision it delivered in 1940 and held that school children can not constitutionally be required to salute the American flag if they had religious scruples against such action.

Justic Jackson delivered the decision, involving a challenge by members of "Jehovah's Witnesses" of a flag-salute requirement by the West Virginia Board of Education.

HOUSE GROUP WOULD END NYA

Washington, June 14 (AP)—The House Appropriations Committee today refused to approve further funds for continuance of the National Youth Administration and ordered its liquidation not later than January 1, 1944.

DAVIS FORECASTS GOOD FOOD YEAR

Washington, June 14 (AP)—Chester C. Davis, War Food Administrator, said today that despite floods and an unfavorable spring the present outlook indicates greater farm production this year than at any time in history except last year.

TWO BILLION ASKED FOR SUBSIDIES

Washington, June 14 (AP)—President Roosevelt was reported to have urged congressional leaders at a White House conference today to provide between $1,500,000,000 in subsidies to roll back the prices of agricultural commodities to consumers.

Local Tides

TOMORROW

High water — 3:34 A. M., 1.2 feet; 3:25 P. M., 1.0 feet. Low water—10:30 A. M., 9:38 P. M.

Moon rises 5:45 P. M.; sets 3:52 A. M.

Sun rises 5:39 A. M.; sets 8:34 P. M.

Tides are given for Annapolis. For Sandy Point, add 15 minutes. For Thomas Point shoal, subtract 30 minutes.

FOUR RESCUED WHEN STORM CAPSIZES BOAT

Ferry Picks Up Two Men And Two Women Off Greenbury Point

Two men and two women were rescued late yesterday after their sailboat had turned over in the sudden gale and rainstorm which struck as they were off Greenbury Point, in the Chesapeake Bay.

The home of Mrs. Marjorie S. Gloth, Sands avenue and River Drive, Bay Ridge, was damaged by the storm. The end of the porch was blown off, the glassed in section wrecked, a steel glider blown from one end of the porch to the other, cushions and awnings hurled to the lawn, and glass in doors leading to the living room broken. Water flooded through the broken glass into the home.

Ferry Rescue

The ferry Governor Nice, commanded by Capt. Wilbert Dawsson, was running to Annapolis from Matapeake when it found the four persons whose sailboat had capsized in the water at 6:40 P. M.

They were Thomas Kenney, John Thomas Reipe, Miss Anne Coppinger and Miss Suzanne Travers, of Baltimore.

They were picked up by a boat from the ferry and taken to the galley where they were warmd, givn coffee and wrapped in blankets.

Their capsized boat was towed into Annapolis by the pilot boat.

The Reina Mercedes station ship at the Naval Academy, gives warnings of approaching storms as soon as the information is received. A recall flag—a yellow flag with a vertical blue bar through the middle is hoisted and a gun is fired to attract the attention of watermen. Watermen hearing the gun should watch the ship for signals, it was pointed out.

MRS. THERSA E. GROB BURIED YESTERDAY

Funeral rites for Mrs. Theresa E. Grob were held yesterday at 2:30 P. M. from the Hopping Funeral Home on West street. The Rev. Father George M. Powers conducted the services.

Mrs. Grob died Thursday at the residence of her daughter, Mrs Frederick J. Brown, 138 Market street. Besides Mrs. Brown, she is survived by a brother, two sisters and two grandchildren.

Assisted Japs

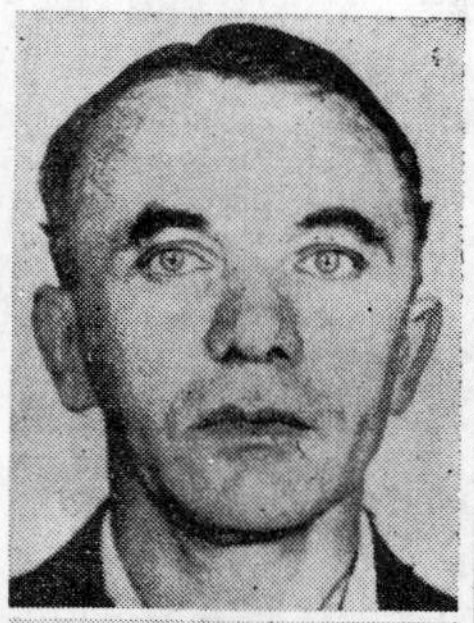

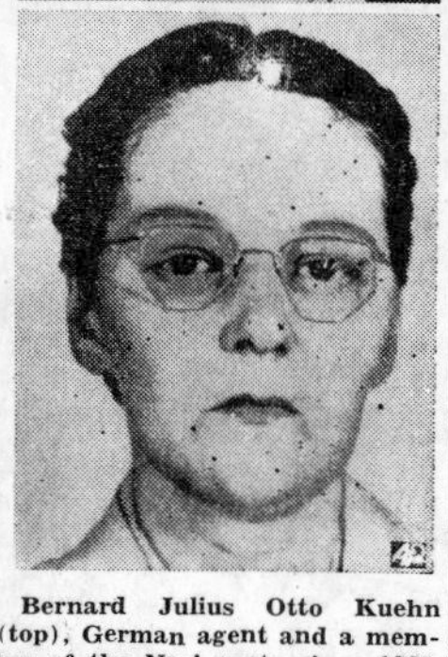

Bernard Julius Otto Kuehn (top), German agent and a member of the Nazi party since 1935, has been sentenced to 50 years at hard labor for conspiring with the imperial Japanese government to betray the United States fleet in Pearl Harbor, it has been revealed by the Office of War Information. Kuehn's wife, Friedel (below), who was arrested with him on Dec. 8, 1941, is interned for the war's duration.

Flag Day, 1943---

Banners Of 31 Nations Fly With Old Glory

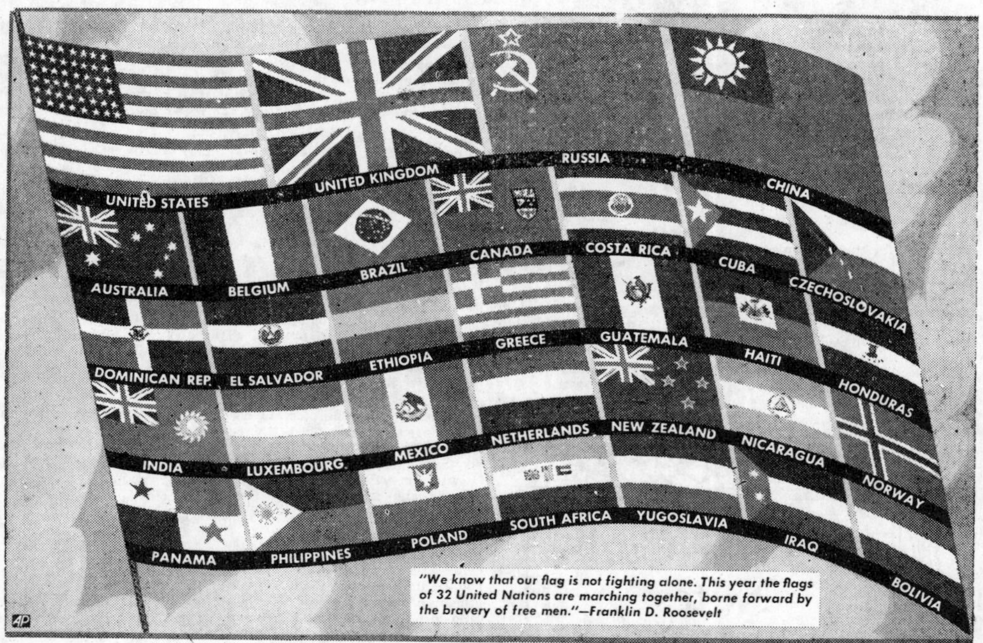

UNITED STATES
UNITED KINGDOM
RUSSIA
CHINA
AUSTRALIA
BELGIUM
BRAZIL
CANADA
COSTA RICA
CUBA
CZECHOSLOVAKIA
DOMINICAN REP.
EL SALVADOR
ETHIOPIA
GREECE
GUATEMALA
HAITI
HONDURAS
INDIA
LUXEMBOURG
MEXICO
NETHERLANDS
NEW ZEALAND
NICARAGUA
NORWAY
PANAMA
PHILIPPINES
POLAND
SOUTH AFRICA
YUGOSLAVIA
IRAQ
BOLIVIA
AP

"We know that our flag is not fighting alone. This year the flags of 32 United Nations are marching together, borne forward by the bravery of free men."—Franklin D. Roosevelt

BIG BOMBERS BATTER AIRFIELDS AT GERBINA, CATANI ON ISLAND

Allied Planes Drop 250,000 Pounds Of Bombs In Sicilian Raid—RAF Continues Battering Of Rhineland—El Salvador Recognizes New Argentine Government—American Planes Make Heavy Raids In China—Chinese Recapture Sungtze—Rabaul Hit By 30 Tons Of Allied Bombs

(By the Associated Press)

While Sicilians watched from their headlands for the coming of the massed air fleets of the Northwest African forces which already had smashed into submission all the lesser islands of Italy's guardian ring, American Liberators dumped tons of bombs on airbases of the threatened Axis stronghod, Allied dispatches said today.

Escorted by Spitfire fighters from Malta, a strong force of the four-engined bombers raided Gerbini and Catani airbases at the eastern end of Sicily yesterday, blanketing the Gerbini base where about 25 planes were seen in the target area, and leaving smoke clouds mushrooming from the hangars at Catania from the explosions of about 250,000 pounds of bombs.

RAF CONTINUES OFFENSIVE

The RAF, continuing the offensive on Germany, again struck at the Rhineland last night, but on the whole land forces from Russia to China reported an unnatural mid-June lull.

Obviously the belligerents were catching their breath and preparing for the summer's climatic offensives.

With Pantelleria, Lampedusa and Linosa in Allied hands, Sicily, at the toe of the Italian boot, appeared a logical target in the next phase of the offensive.

An Italian communique said that formations of four-engined bombers attacked Mesina, with two planes brought down by anti-aircraft fire. It asserted that three other planes were shot down over Sicily and two over Pantelleria in air duels.

The tiny isle of Linosa, 28 miles northeast of Lampedusa, raised the white flag of unconditional surrender yesterday.

Heavily Battered

The only American aerial unit composed of colored men in foreign service was among the Allied forces that bombed Pantelleria. They flew P-40 Warhawks and were under the command of Lieut. Col. Benjamin O. Davis, Jr. The colored squadron trained at Tuskegee Institute, Ala., before going overseas.

Sicilian targets have been heavily battered for two weeks by the Northwest African Air Forces and by planes from British bases on Malta and from Allied bases operating under the Middle East command at Cairo. Even before Lampedusa quit, Northwest African flying fortresses, Marauders, Lightnings, Warhawks, returned to smash at Sicily's airdromes on Saturday. Nearly 150 planes were caught on the ground at Milo, Castelvetrano and Bocco di Falco, airports and Allied headquarters said "large numbers" were riddled by fragmentation bombs.

The Fascist party directorate has recommended stricter regulation of the lives of the already regimented Italians, because of the "gravity of the moment" and the imminence of invasion, Rome broadcasts said.

Hit Rhineland

The RAF, besides bombing objectives in the Rhineland and in other parts of Germany last night, also laid mines in enemy waters, extending the virtually nonstop offensive. The specific targets were not named, nor was there any indication of the size of the raiding groups. Berlin reported that British planes were over north and west Germany, but declared no bombs were dropped.

Reuters recorded a German broadcast today saying "American" planes attacked Flushing in The Netherlands yesterday morning. Flushing was one of the targets of RAF daylight raiders Sunday.

RAF Beufighters torpedoed two supply ships and damaged four escort vessels in an attack on an Axis convoy off the Dutch coast last night.

German night raiders struck back in reprisals which caused an early morning alert in London and some damage in a northeast British coast town, which was show-

(Continued On Page Three)

War Demands Cut St. John's Teaching Staff

Seventeen Faculty Members In Armed Services Or Defense Work

With 17 members of its former faculty in the armed forces or called to war jobs, St. John's College will open its first mid-summer term on July 8 with the smallest teaching staff in a quarter of a century, president Stringfellow Barr said today.

Of the 1943-44 faculty of 16 members, only one will be new this term, Mr. Barr said. He is William I. Harper, who graduated at the Staunton Military Academy, took his B. A. at Ohio State and his M. A. at Columbia.

Four Housemasters

Mr. Harper, who has taught at

(Continued on Page Six)

3 Year Old Boy Drowned Today

Son Of Mr. And Mrs. L. C. Pasley Falls From Pier At Sherwood Forest Home

John Judson Pasley, three year year old son of Mr. and Mrs. L. C. Pasley was drowned at 8:30 A. M. today at the family summer home, 302 Robin Hill, Sherwood Forest.

The child, after playing on the pier in front of the home for about five minutes, was missed by his mother, who, on searching, found the body floating in the water. She recovered the body and telephoned the West Annapolis Fire Department, which responded immeditely with an ambulance crew.

After administering artificial respiration without result, they took the boy to the Emergency Hospital, where he was pronounced dead on arrival by Dr. Paul Sunderland, who declared the child must have struck his head and become unconscious before falling into the water.

Dr. John Claffy, county medical examiner, gave a verdict of acci-

(Continued On Page Three)

United Nations Flags Massed On State House Portico For Elks Flag Day Ceremonies

Flags of the United Nations were massed with the stars and stripes across the portico of the old State House yesterday afternoon, for the annual Flag Day exercises conducted by the Annapolis Lodge of Elks.

Although held a day before the actual date of Flag Day, which is June 14, the Elks committee, headed by Esteemed Loyal Knight James Lloyd Young, carried out the request of President Roosevelt's proclamation in which he asked that the emblem of the United Nations, representing the "massed, angered forces of common humanity," be displayed side by side with the United States flag.

"We know that our flag is not fighting alone," the President said. "The flags of 32 United Nations are marching together, borne forward by the bravery of free men. Together, they are the emblem of a gathering offensive that shall liberate the world."

All patriotic societies in Annapolis joined with the Elks in yesterday's program.

Lieut. S. W. McGovern, U.S.N., a member of the local odge, speaking from the State House portico, gave the history of the flag, and John S. White, majority floor leader of the Maryland House of Delegates, was the principal speaker. They were introduced by Exalted Ruler Howard B. Pyle.

Mrs. Eulilia L'Aigle, president of the Guy Carleton Parlett Unit of the American Legion Auxiliary, presented a flag on behalf of the Unit to Mrs. L. Warrington Carr, county chairman of Civilian War Services, for CWS headquarters.

Music was furnished by the Naval Academy band and the Police Boys' drum corps.

Flags of Four Freedoms

In celebrations in Washington today the new "flag of the four freedoms" was flown publicly for the first time, to represent all the United Nations.

Chosen by popular poll, the flag consists of a white field emblazoned with four upright bars of red, representing the principles of the Atlantic Charter: Freedom of speech, and religion, and freedom from want and fear.

MRS. O'CONOR'S TRIP UP TO RATION BOARD

Baltimore Board To Consider Circumstances

The Baltimore rationing board which issued gasoline coupons for the automobile used by Mrs. Herbert R. O'Conor on a trip to Charleston, S. C., last march will determine circumstances concerning the journey, the State Office of Price Administration announced yesterday.

Officials of the Baltimore Board

(Continued On Page Three)

CITY COUNCIL MEETS TONIGHT

The City Council will meet in regular monthly session at 8 o'clock tonight to take up routine business.

One beer license application will be considered.

Over 2,000 Here Have Paid Tax Due Tomorrow

Local Branch Of Internal Revenue Office Handling 300 A Day, Deputy Macaluso Says

More than 2,000 forehanded taxpayers have already paid their income tax installments, due by midnight tomorrow, at the local branch office of the Collector of Internal Revenue, on the second floor of the post office, Peter Macaluso, deputy collector in charge, said today.

Payments are being handled at the rate of about 300 a day, Mr. Macaluso said.

Payments must be made whether the taxpayer has received a bill or not, and must be mailed before midnight tomorrow, if not paid at the office before the 5 P. M. closing time.

Roosevelt Cites Federal, State War Cooperation

Praises State Cooperation In Letter To Governor O'Conor

President Roosevelt says the Federal, State and local governments are coordinating their efforts as never before in history toward the "one - all - important common objective—winning the war."

The President praised State cooperation in the war effort in a letter to Gov. Herbert R. O'Conor, chairman of the Governors' Conference, Council of State governments. Governor O'Conor will preside at the 35th annual meeting of the Governors' Conference beginning in Colmubus, O., next Sunday.

"America, along with the other United Nations," Mr. Roosevelt wrote, "is engaged in a worldwide struggle to determine whether the type of government which we have established and maintained here in the United States—a government dedicated to the welfare of all the people—can continue to exist."

Critical Time

The President added that "the time is critical in that everything that we have developed, everything

(Continued on Page Four)

Church Women To Hold Rummage Sale Thursday

The Women's Society of Christian Service of the Eastport Methodist Church, will hold a rummage sale at the city market on Thursday.

Mrs. Margaret W. Williams has requested that donations be sent to 815 Bay Ridge avenue, Eastport.

Jewish Women To Hold Final Summer Meeting

The closing summer meeting of the Ladies' Auxiliary of the Kneseth Israel Synagogue, will be held on Wednesday at 8:30 P. M. in the vestry rooms.

Mrs. Louis Levin and Mrs. Richard Zelko are in charge of the entertainment for the evening. Refreshments will be served at the conclusion of the meeting.

NOTICE

All garbage will be collected until further notice from all premises every Monday, Tuesday, Wednesday, Thursday and Saturday. Trash and ashes will be collected on Friday.

HARRY E. BEAN
City Commissioner

Social and Personal

by PEGGY LAZENBY

Prof., Mrs. Muller Leave On Vacation

Prof. Rene Francois Muller of Thomson street will leave tomorrow for Woodville, R. I., where he will spend a few weeks at the summer home of his parents, Dr. and Mrs. Henri F. Muller. At the same time Mrs. Muller will leave for Bernhard's Bay, N. Y. to join her parents, Mr. and Mrs. J. Bradly Vandaworker, for the rest of the summer.

* * *

Mr. Tayman To Visit Colonel Tayman

Mr. Bond Tayman, who has been visiting his grandfather, Mr. John A. Tayman, here since the close of school, will spend a few weeks with his uncle, Colonel Nelson Tayman, at his home in Cheverly.

* * *

Lieut. Comdr., Mrs. Speer Announce Daughter's Birth

Lieut. Comdr. and Mrs. John O. Speer announce the birth of a daughter, Saturday, July 17, at the Naval Academy hospital.

* * *

Hostesses Announced For USO Club

The following persons will act as hostesses at the USO Club this week:

Today—Presbyterian Church—Mrs. H. A. Buys, chairman, and Mrs. Calvin Robbins.

Tuesday—First Church of Christ Scientist—Mrs. Albert C. Cavaleer, chairman, Mrs. Ralph B. Munn, Mrs. M. Van Pelt Vucasovich, and Mrs. Harold Hallett.

Wednesday—Daughters of the American Revolution — Mrs. Charles C. Bramble, chairman, Mrs. Elmer E. Hobbs, Mrs. Charles L. Milliken, and Mrs. David G. Howard.

Thursday—Catholic Daughters—Mrs. C. H. Sherman, chairman, Mrs. William McWilliams, Mrs. Joseph S. Bigelow, Jr. and Mrs. Owen Hill.

Saturday—Mrs. G. A. Palmer, Mr. A. W. Whitney and Miss Mary Ann Hopping.

Sunday—College Women's Club—Miss Mary Louise Hicks, chairman, Mrs. H. J. Kirschner and Mrs. J. T. Norman.

Mr., Mrs. Wiegard Announced Baby's Birth

Mr. and Mrs. Paul J. Wiegard, 124 Archwood avenue, announce the birth of a daughter, Mary Martha, on Wednesday at the Emergency Hospital.

* * *

Lieut. Larned Spends Few Days Here

Lieut. Charles W. Larned, Jr., of Baltimore, is now spending a few days at Dogwood Hill with Mr. and Mrs. A. Gordon Fleet and family, before rejoining his unit in Miami, Florida.

* * *

Mrs. Riley Very Much Improved

Mrs. Helen L. Riley of 21 Market street who slipped and sprained her ankle on Friday is very much improved today.

* *

Comdr., Mr. Furlong Visiting In New York

Comdr. and Mrs. Francis M. Furlong are now visiting at the home the their daughter and son-in-law, Comdr. and Mrs. William Martin, in Geneva, New York.

* * *

Miss Brashears Spends Summer Here

Miss Patty Brashears daughter of Captain and Mrs. George Brashears, is spending the summer at the home of her mother.

* * *

Mr. Tilgham Will Leave For Blacksburg, Virginia

Tench F. Tilghman, who has been spending his vacation at the home of his mother, Mrs. Tench F. Tilghman, will leave tomorrow for the Virginia Polytechnic Institute in Blacksburg, Va., where he is a member of the faculty.

* * *

Miss Daniel Entertains Ration Board

Miss Beverly Daniel, entertained the personnel of the Ration Board at a picnic Saturday afternoon at the home of Mr. and Mrs. C. Haye Duvall, Horn Point.

Menus of the Day

BY MRS ALEXANDER GEORGE

Victory Garden Gifts

(Point-rationed foods are starred)

Four For Dinner

Devilled Veal Chops
Corn on the Cob
Enriched Bread Cherry Butter
Sparkling Fruit Salad Mold
Tea or Coffee (Hot or Iced)

Devilled Veal Chops

☆4 thick rib veal chops	¼ teaspoon celery salt
4 tablespoons flour	¼ teaspoon dry mustard
½ teaspoon salt	3 tablespoons bacon fat
¼ teaspoon pepper	4 slices tomato

Wipe off chops with damp cloth. Mix together in paper sack, flour seasonings and mustard. Add chops and coat them with this mixture. Brown chops on both sides in fat heated in frying pan. Cover and cook 10 minutes over low heat. Top with tomatoes, brush them with melted fat or some of the drippings in the frying pan. Broil 5 minutes, or until brown. Carefully turn tomatoes and brown the other side.

Corn On The Cob

2 quarts water	¼ teaspoon paprika
8 ears fresh corn	
1 teaspoon salt	

Carefully remove husks and silk from corn. Chill until ready to cook. Add to boiling water. Cover and boil gently 15 minutes, add salt and paprika and boil 2 minutes. Quickly remove corn from water. Serve hot wrapped in napkin. Never allow corn to remain in water after it is cooked or it will become water-soaked and tasteless.

Sparkling Fruit Salad Mold

1 package lemon gelatin	½ cup diced pears, fresh
1 cup boiling water or fruit juice	½ cup cubed melon
⅔ cup ginger ale	1 tablespoon lemon juice
½ cup diced peaches, fresh	½ cup cottage cheese

Dissolve gelatin in water. Cool and chill until partly thick. Stir in ginger ale, fruits, melon and juice. Chill until nearly stiff and pour over cheese placed in shallow mold rinsed out of cold water. Chill until firm. Unmold and top with mayonnaise.

Rush Expected Thursday For Vacation Gas

A rush of vacation-hungry motorists is expected at the local Rationing Board office on Thursday, when number 6 coupons become due, but at present the number of requests for vacation gas is not much above 50, Rationing Board workers said today.

The reason the Annapolis board has not been overwhelmed with requests for vacation gas, as Baltimore boards have been, is a matter of geography. Anne Arundel countians, living in a rural community, are dependent upon their A coupons for essential driving; whereas in the cities people have used public transportation lines and have sufficient A coupons left for vacation trips.

When the No. 6 cards are due July 22, many people will use that gas allowance for vacation travel, ration board officials think.

More Gas Likely

(Continued from Page One)

fear that the stamps will become invalid. B books outside of the east will be issued henceforth on a three-month basis. Individual needs will be adjusted by the ration boards by tearing out coupons not used in the three-month period, rather than giving each bookholder the same number of stamps but varying the length of time in which the coupons must be used. The east's four-month tenure of B books will be continued.

Revision of the rationing system as outlined by Ickes was hailed by Rep. Hartley (R-NJ), speaking for a congressional bloc, who said the "people of the east are reassured by the statemnts that the section is to receive fairer treatment."

Ickes said he couldn't predict what specific changes in the gas ration would be made by the pipeline flow "but in all probability it will mean some increase in the east and a decrease in the middlewest and southwest."

Eastern motorists now receive less than one and one-half gallons a week on an A card. In other areas, the card is worth four gallons a week. Eastern A card holders are under a pleasure-driving ban, as well, though OPA Administrator Prentiss Brown has declared several times he would like to see that ban lifted.

MODES OF THE MOMENT

FALL WAR BONNETS

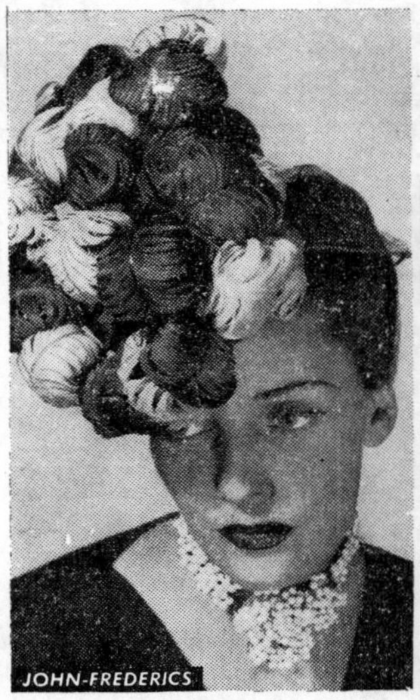

FUSS AND FEATHERS: John-Frederics presents a toque of aqua and jungle green curled feather tips on a green moire base, with matching choker.

CANDLELIGHT: A dressy dinner hat in emerald green with cushion brim, lilac velvet band and dramatic pale blue curled feathers reaching for the sky.

CHETNIK DRAPE: This is big news in the fall hat lineup. Inspired by the Yugoslav turbans, it is shown in gold beaver with tall crown and side drape.

CLIP HAT: This one clips on to the head and stays put. It's made of draped wine tie silk tilted forward and rising high in back.

By DOROTHY ROE
AP Fashion Editor

AMERICAN millners can chalk up a major victory in their first engagement with wartime restrictions.

Fall has, for the first time face to face with the WPB yardstick, emerge triumphantely as gay, untrammeled and wearable as in the piping days of unlimited fabrics.

Millinery designers, working under an entirely voluntary code of restrictions, have evolved a fall collection with no hint of wartime grimmness, crammed with new silhouettes, designed to add excitement to the basic duration wardrobe.

Biggest news of the fall collections is the fact that the new hats fit the head and stay on without benefit of either elastics or hatpins. All designers stress head-size hats, present models that stay on in a high wind.

Sally Victor makes headlnies with three new silhouettes: the Chetnik draped turban, inspired by the dashing headgear of the Yugoslaves; the "Da-Da" bonnet, which says yes in any language, and the Curvette, which is two hats in one—a halo of felt or embroidered velvet with a removable crown, to be worn all together for daytime, without the crown for evening.

John-Frederics goes Victorian with small, ladylike hats with a tin-type look. His favorite is a puffed version of the beret, prettied up with encrustations of beads or embroidery, sometimes embellished with feathers. He shows soft, casual felts with a folded paper bag look, presents a hat seamed in sections like a parachute, which ties under the chin. He shows lots of ostrich plumes, as do all the designers.

Lilly Dache likes a neat and tidy look about her hats for fall, but insists they must be feminine and gay. She shows many felts, lots of ribbon and satin hats, crochet cotton with flickers of beads, furs and barnyard feathers. She likes cloche, and the clip hat, both of which stay firmly on the head without hat pins or bands.

Florence Reichman introduces the crest hat and the milkmaid bonnet, both perfect with any hairdo, and **Walter Florell** shows small, pert fedoras and sailors in luxurious fabrics, all tipped sharply forward.

All designers feature colorful accessories to complement their hats and brighten up the new smiple dresses. There are sequin-embroidered scarfs, to be worn outside fur coats, elaborate beaded or embroided collars of felt or velvet, to match hats, and extravagant handbags made of everything from beaded felt to mink.

War bonnets of fall, 1943, add a touch of needed gaity to the wartime scene, make the basic wardrobe seem less basic.

Garden Club Notes

By Mary B. Ellershaw

Gentle, soaking rain after drouth—no sound is more dear to the ear of the gardener. All responsibility slips from his aching back and sinking into his easy chair with that book which has been lying temptingly round he relaxes into perfect peace. Let weeds flourish for the moment, nothing can be done today. Let bugs work and get soaked if they care—tomorrow is another day. With the world refreshed a new start can be made.

There are three so-called weeds blooming in great profusion now and furnishing most of the color on the fields and the garden too. The black eyed susan, the butterfly weed and the Queen Anne's lace. The old orange garden lily, both single and double forms combine with the butterfly weed, which is indeed a very handsome plant when grown in a swell drained spot and given some compost. The black eyed susans just drift here and there filling in any bare spots that offer a foothold and the Queen Anne's lace forms a graceful background of the neglected garden. If they were not so plentiful we would admire it greatly. The tiger lilies will soon take over with their great stalks of numerous orange flowers, and the phlox is beginning to bloom.

It seems only the other day we were greeting with joy the first daffodil and now the seed firms are advising the selection of bulbs for fall planting. So many of those tight-packed clumps of daffodils, too crowded to bloom, have shed their foliage and are lost in the grass, we meant to lift and separate them. It takes two years or more for the largest of these overcrowded bulbs to develop to blooming size but it is well worth the trouble to maintain and increase the planting.

Iris Borer

The iris borer is at work as is shown by the brown spots on the leaves. It is on its way down to the rhizome where it will really get in its dirty work. It can be disposed of by cutting off the leaves below the brown and burning them.

Late July and August is the best time to divide and plant. Oriental poppies. Besides the more familiar brilliant scarlet and deep red there are several other shades, salmon, pink, cerise, lavender and white, as these shades are variations from the red and scarlet some of them may be disappointing in not being entirely clear colors, but they are worth trying. If your garden soil suits these poppies they will become life long friends and there is nothing more beautiful than a planting of single white peonies, blue Siberian iris and deep red poppies. They may be divided and transplanted with as little risk as horseradish roots if this work is done during their dormant season, which is during August. If disturbed at any other season they are likely to be lost.

Root division is the best means of propagation. If the plants are three or more years old, it will be noted when the roots are dug and the soil brushed off that the roots are curiously striated, twisting strongly to the right or the left. These twists are lines of cleavage. Insert the point of a sharp knife and force it gently down the twist. Repeat the operation until each crown is separated from the others and reset immediately in the new location.

Root Cutting

Root cutting may also be made if one has a choice variety and wants to start more plants as soon as possible. The longer roots may be shortened back to three or four inches and reset and the root pieces cut off should be laid out so that one will know the upper or crown end. These pieces may then be divided again into two or three inch lengths. These may be set immediately in a specially prepared seed bed of three parts sharp sand and two parts leaf mold or good garden loam. If the bed is kept damp, but never wet, rootlets will soon form on the lower end and in about six weeks tiny leaves will form on the crown end. These little plants will sometimes bloom the next year but certainly the second year. Root divisions and root cuttings usually remain true to the variety of the parent plant, which makes it easy for the gardener to work out color plans in the garden. The seeds cannot be relied upon to come true to color.

August is also the month to lift and rest the bulbs of Madonna lilies. The loose scales may be placed in a seed bed by covering with tar paper or boards to keep out the rain—they will rot if wet—if kept dry the scales will start growth in about three weeks when the covering can be removed. If th flower stem is still green it can be gently twisted up and out of the bulb and covered with earth on the cellar floor, lying flat, and in six weeks it will show tiny bulbs along the stem to be transferred to the seed bed. These lilies being very susceptible to Botrytis blight need to be often renewed for who can spare their beauty and fragrance from the June garden?

Tulips Precious

Tulips are more precious this year because of the shortage of bulbs and any old plantings of them neglected in the garden should be taken up and stored in a cool airy place then they may be cleaned off, the larger ones set for spring blooming and the smaller put in a nursery. October is a good month to set them. All suspected of disease should be discarded. If they are planted 8 to 10 inches deep with some fertile earth below the bulb there is less tendency to divide and the bulbs are more likely to bloom each year.

If pansies are to be grown from seed it is time to order them. It pays to buy only the best. Snapdragons sown this month will make nice plants to pot up for the house in the fall. Columbine seed should also be sown to make plants big enough to winter over and bet set in the beds in the spring.

So the gardener's year moves on, study of the past, working in the present and vision of the future.

SERVICE MEN HOLD PICNIC

Continuing the celebration of a week, marking the first anniversary of the USO Club, on Saint Mary's street a picnic for men of "the other watch" will be combined with a swim tonight at Hendry's on Weems Creek.

A motor launch is providing the transportation, leaving slip 82 of the Annapolis Yacht Basin, across from the USO Club, at 6:30 P. M. Service men, their wives, and GSO members are included in the invitation, that being the date of the dedication a year ago.

Tomorrow night a 10-piece band of young women from Baltimore, who play regularly for USO dances there, known as the Harmonettes, will provide the music. They will play from 8:15 until 11:15 P. M.

Yesterday Comdr. Fred K. Elder met with the Java Club, for breakfast, and then continued his study with the group of Acts, pointing out some of the experiences of Paul as a sailor and early apostle. He has met his appointments regularly with the Java Club since its first session back in August 1942.

Last night the Junior Hadassah of Annapolis served supper, which featured a birthday celebration, in recognition of the first anniversary, with birthday cakes, a single candle on each, and appropriate decorations.

Evening Capital

VOL. LIX — No. 176 | EVERY EVENING EXCEPT SUNDAY | ANNAPOLIS, MD., MONDAY, JULY 26, 1943. | SOUTHERN MARYLAND'S ONLY DAILY | THREE CENTS

WEATHER
Continued rather warm today and tonight; scattered thundershowers this afternoon and evening.

LATE NEWS

CHURCHILL TO TALK ON ITALIAN SITUATION

London, July 26 (AP) — Prime Minister Churchill will give Commons a comprehensive picture of the Italian war situation at the next sitting, it was reported today.

EIGHT AMERICANS HELD FOR TREASON

Washington, July 26 (AP)—Eight Americans, including two women, who have broadcast regularly from Germany and Italy in behalf of the Axis war effort, were indicted today for treason, and Attorney General Biddle said they would be brought to trial when caught.

The indictments, involving a charge which carries the death penalty, were returned before Federal District Judge James W. Morris in the District of Columbia as the culmination of many months of preparation by the Justice Department.

REPUBLICANS HITS WALLACE'S SPEECH

Washington, July 26 (AP) — Vice President Wallace's bristling indictment of "isolationists" and "American Fascists" provoked a Republican charge today that he was attempting to "take the public mind off the embarrassing messes of the Administration" on the home front.

In what was regarded as a significant speech at a Detroit mass meeting yesterday Wallace charged that powerful groups "hope to take advantage of the President's concentration on the war effort to destroy everything he has accomplished on the domestic front over the last ten years."

MOSLEM LEADER IS WOUNDED

Bombay, July 26 (AP)—Mahomed Ali Jinnah, president of the All India Moslem League, was slightly wounded today by a Moslem who knifed him during an interview.

Jinnah suffered minor injuries on the chin and one hand. His assailant was arrested.

HANSEN GETS WPB POSITION

Washington, July 26 (AP) — The formal appointment of A. B. Hansen, president of the Northern Paper Mills of Green Bay, Wis., as deputy director of the War Production Board's pulp and paper division was announced today.

REDS WIN FROM PHILLIES

Cincinnati, July 26 (AP) — Two home runs by catcher Ray Mueller, each with two men on base, helped Ray Starr and Cincinnati's Reds to an 8-2 victory over Philadelphia today in an 11 o'clock game played before a crowd of 3,839 war-work swing-shifters, knothole club members and service men.

MRS. ROOSEVELT COMMENTS ON ITALY

Washington, July 26 (AP)—Mrs. Franklin D. Roosevelt declared today that the ouster of Premier Mussolini as head of the Italian government was "a break in the assurance" of the Axis powers and "might be the beginning of a crack internally."

SIX INDICTED IN COAL STRIKE

Pittsburgh, July 26 (AP) — A Federal Grand Jury investigating recent unauthorized strikes in the soft coal fields of southwestern Pennsylvania today indicted 30 persons, charging conspiracy to prevent production of coal in violation of the law.

DISCUSS STATE LABOR SHORTAGE

Washington, July 26 (AP)—Representatives from Maryland, West Virginia, Virginia and North Carolina met today to discuss plans for meeting an agricultural labor shortage which is expected, they said, to become increasingly critical as the harvest season approaches.

HOLD HEARING IN OAKES DEATH

Nassau, Bahamas, July 26 (AP) —While Nancy Oakes De Marigny, listened intently, a colored maid told today how Nancy's father, the multi-millionaire British Baronet Sir Harry Oakes, dined and played cards with friends shortly before he was bludgeoned and left to die in a blazing bed the night of July 7.

Local Tides

TOMORROW

High water — 2:39 A. M., 1.7 feet; 9:49 P. M., 8:40 P. M.

Moon rises 2:28 A. M.; sets 4:55 P. M.

Sun rises 6:01 A. M.; sets 8:25 P. M.

Tides are given for Annapolis. For Sandy Point, add 15 minutes. For Thomas Point shoal, subtract 30 minutes.

MUSSOLINI REPORTED UNDER ARREST

Ex-Dictator Said To Have Been Taken Captive Fleeing Toward Germany

LEGISLATORS PLAN SERIES OF MEETINGS

County Group To Keep In Touch With City, County Officials

The Anne Arundel county representatives in the Legislature—Senator Wilbur R. Dulin and the members of the House delegation—are planning to hold a series of regular meetings to keep in touch with legislation and check on the need for new laws.

The first meeting of the group, it was learned today, will be held early next month. Meetings will follow as the situation demands.

The legislators are planning to check up on the laws that were passed as the last session of the Legislature to see how they are working out in practice. If necessary they will prepare amendments to the laws or will draft repeal legislation.

Will Hold Hearings

They also plan to discuss problems of the county and city government with the members of the Board of Anne Arundel County Commissioners, county officials and the Mayor and City Council of Annapolis. When problems arise that require hearings, these will be held with a view of preparing needed legislation for the coming session.

This contact, it was pointed out, will make the members of the group through by familiar with the problems of the county and civic government so that they will be in a position to act on questions that arise during the Legislative session.

To Prepare Bills

The members of the delegation are planning to have all the county legislation needed ready to introduce soon after the next Legislature convenes. In this manner it can be passed and the delegates and Senator will have the time to give to larger State problems that come up in the General Assembly.

It was pointed out that during the last session of the Legislature some of the county legislation was not presented for consideration of the delegates and Senator until late in the session.

It is thought that the new plan of regular meetings will be advantageous to all concerned and facilities the passage of county and city laws, or repeal or amendment as conditions require.

ESCORT SHIP NAMED IN HONOR OF C.C. THOMAS

Mrs. Herndon B. Kelly, 16 Southgate avenue, will christen the new destroyer escort Thomas, named in honor of her first husband, Lieutenant Clarence Case Thomas, first U.S. Naval Officer killed in World War I.

The new vessel will be launched Saturday at the Dravo Corporation yards, the Fourth Naval District announced.

The vessel is designed for anti-submarine and convoy protection.

Local Officers Are Promoted

Advanced To Grade Of Commander

The promotion of a group of local Lieutenant Commanders to the grade of Commander has been approved by the President.

The officers, all on the active list of the regular navy were promoted Commander for temporary service. Those living in or near Annapolis or who are stationed here follows:

To rank from August 20: Franklin D. Karns, Jr.

To rank from September 1: John W. Bays, Thomas B. Klakring.

To rank from September 10: Charles J. Zondork, Robert V. Hull, Philip H. Ross, Bosquet N. Wev, Edward N. Teall, Jr.; Albert B. Mayfield, Jr.

To rank from September 15: Robert O. Strange, John T. Bowers, Jr.; Francois C. B. Jordan.

To rank from October 1: Knight Pryor.

FUNERAL RITES HELD FOR MRS. MALCOLM WATSON

Funeral services for Mrs. Caroline Elizabeth Watson, wife of Malcolm Watson, were held yesterday afternoon at 2 o'clock, at her late home, 118 Prince George street, conducted by the Rev. James L. Smiley.

Pallbearers were: Travers T. Brown, Harry T. LeTourneau, Dashiell H. LeTourneau, John W. Moreland, James K. Moreland, and Louis A. Hartge. Burial was in St. Anne's Cemetery.

Mrs. Watson died Thursday at her home, after a lingering illness.

Capt. Kessing Awarded Medal For Heroism

Former Graduate Manager Of Athletics At Academy Wins Citation For Action In Solomons

Capt. O. O. (Scrappy) Kessing former graduate manager of athletics at the United States Naval Academy, has just been awarded the Navy and Marine Corps medal for "heroism following an attack by Japanese bombing planes on Halavo, Solomon Islands, February 20, 1943."

Captain Kessing was first commandant of the Navy Pre-Flight School for aviators at Chapel Hill N. C., and was instrumental in putting into effect the first athletic course of toughening character developed by Commander Tom Hamilton, former football star and coach at the Academy.

Rear Admiral T. S. Wilkinson deputy commander of the South Pacific area, read the citation at the ceremony of presentation.

Captain and Mrs. Kessing formerly lived at 248 Prince George street.

ITALIAN GOVERNMENT SHIFT

VITTORIO EMANUELE III

BENITO MUSSOLINI

MARSHAL PIETRO BADOGLIO

The resignation of Benito Mussolini as head of the Italian Government, Prime Minister and Secretary of State, announced last night by the Rome radio today stirred speculation throughout the world.

King Vittorio Emanuele III has taken command of the armed forces of Italy and has appointed Marshal Pietro Badoglio, former chief of staff of the Italian army as Prime Minister, succeeding Mussolini.

Badoglio, long a friend of the King is known for his anti-Fascist and anti-German attitude. He is the conqueror of Ethiopia.

OTHER LEADERS AND CABINET OFFICERS ALSO REPORTED HELD

Martial Law Proclaimed In Italy—Blackshirts Made Part Of Italian Army—White House Withholds comment—Hull Stands On Unconditional Surrender—Allies squeeze Axis Forces In Northeastern Corner Of Sicily—Termini Occupied By Americans—Six Italian Generals, Admiral and 7,000 More Prisoners Taken—Russians Near Bryansk Railroad—Essen, Hamburg, Cologne Battered By Bombers.

(By the Associated Press)

Benito Mussolini was reported the captive of a new Italian government today following the crash of his 21-year dictatorship which threatened to topple Italy out of the war and the Axis.

Dispatches from both Switzerland and Sweden said Mussolini had been arrested. These were without confirmation from Axis quarters.

A Reuters report from Stockholm, Sweden, said officers seized the ex-dictator while he was trying to escape from Italy to Germany. A Bern, Switzerland dispatch said that he and his ministers were taken into custody.

In an NBC broadcast from Bern, Paul Archinard said that reports reaching neutral Switzerland indicated that Mussolini and several of his Fascist leaders were under arrest.

ITALY UNDER MARTIAL LAW

Martial law was proclaimed throughout harassed Italy in swift succession to the governmental shakeup which eliminated Mussolini and his Fascist cabinet and installed the conservative Marshal Pietro Badoglio as premier.

King Vittoria Emanuele made the change in the war leadership, the first major break on the Axis front and a possible prelude to an Italian bid for peace.

In Washington, the White House withheld comment on the ousting of Mussolini saying no official reports of the momentous incident had been received.

Secretary of State Cordell Hull indicated that increased military pressure to insure Italian capitulation to the Allied demand for unconditional surrender would be this country's response to the downfall of Mussolini.

He termed very timely and appropriate the ending of the former dictator's regime and said it was the first major step in the early and complete eradication of Fasism. But he emphasized repeatedly that chief reliance is on military developments.

Army Takes Over

Badoglio ordered the Italian army to take over the preservation of public order throughout the nation, forbade gathering of more than three persons, directed the people to remain at their work and empowered the troops to fire on anyone who violated the instructions.

He also issued a special order of the day stating that the voluntary Fascist militia "is an integral part of the armed forces of the nation and with them, as always, cooperates in the common work and intentions for the defense of the Fatherland."

The 250,000 Blackshirts — once Mussolini's private army—are the best equipped group among Italy's military forces of about 2,000,000 men.

The Berlin radio said Badoglio had appointed Baron Raffaele Guariglia, 54, Italian ambassador to Turkey for the las tsix months, as Foreign Minister in Italy's new government. The Foreign Ministry was among the portfolios formerly held by Mussolini. With 30 years experience in diplomacy, Baron Guariglia could have been a go-between in any negotiations for a separate peace during his residence in neutral Ankara.

"The War Continues

Confronted by some of the gravest problems that the commander of a beaten and dispirited army ever faces, with the bulk of Sicily overrun by Allied troops, with German troops and German police on Italian soil, and with mainland cities beset by bombings

(Continued on Page Four)

Italy's Surrender Seen As Opening Bloodless Second Front Overnight

Veteran Associated Press War Correspondent Lists Advantages To Allies If Italians Drop Out Of War—Northern Italian Airdromes Vital In Bombing Germany

(Associated Press war correspondent Wes Gallagher, back in this country after covering the Tunisian war as a correspondent accredited to General Eisenhower's headquarters, here surveys the possible long-range effects of Mussolini's downfall on the military situation, and future Allied strategy.)

By Wes Gallagher

NEW YORK, July 26 (AP) — Italy's surrender, apparently foreshadowed by Mussolini's downfall, would open a "bloodless" second front over night.

It would alter the whole Mediterranean strategy of the Allies and shorten the war against Germany by months and perhaps years. Some of the fruits of victory would be:

Lists Advantages

1. Allied airfields in northern Italy from which American and RAF bombers could hammer every corner of Hitler's Reich every hour of the day.

2. Certain collapse of Nazi resistance in the Balkans due to the withdrawal of the Italian garrisons, air pounding of already feeble Axis supply lines leading to Greece and similar peace moves by Hitler's war torn satellites, Hungary, Rumania and Bulgaria.

3. A bridgehead in Europe from which Allied troops might force their way into France and the Balkans.

Any Allied entry into Italy also would have its liabilities.

These would be:

1. The necessity of finding shipping and food to feed Italy's 40,000,000—a tremendous strain on American and British sea traffic.

2. The necessity of garrisoning Italy with a half million troops.

Air Gain

Perhaps the biggest gain for America and Britain would be in the air. In trying to carry out an air war against Germany from England, the Allies have been forced to fly great distances over enemy territory to reach the heart of the Reich and every foot of these distances have been bitterly contested by the Luftwaffe. The Germans have had the advantage from which direction the blows would be struck and have concentrated their fighter defenses in the west.

It is an axiom of air warfare that an air force's effectiveness increases in direct ratio to the distance it must operate from its bases.

Airfields in northern Italy would cut the distance Allied bombers would have to fly to reach Prague, home of the great Skoda munition works, from 750 miles to 300; the distance to the aircraft factories at Vienna from 800 to less than 300, and even Berlin itself from 650 miles to about 400.

Munich, center of Nazism and half way across Europe from England, is about 100 air miles from the Italian border.

Shuttle Service

Bombers flying from England could cross Germany and land in Italy returning the next night or day and the Germans would never be able to set their defenses to meet the blows. The strain on the already battered Luftwaffe would be increased 100 per cent.

Better weather conditions in the Mediterranean would increase the hours of operation.

Air men such as Air Marshal Sir Arthur Tedder and Lieutenant General Carl "Tooey" Spatz believe with such bases Ger-

(Continued on Page Six)

SOUTHERN DRAWL HIDES BEEHIVE ENERGY OF LT. COL. R. B. LUCKEY, IN SOUTH PACIFIC WITH MARINES

(The following story was written by Sergeant John W. Black, of Olnehurst, RFD, Pennsgrove, New Jersey, a Marine Corps combat correspondent.)

Somewhere In the South Pacific—(Delayed)—A pelasant southern drawl disguises the beehive of energy that is Lieut. Colonel Robert B. Luckey, U.S.M.C., 37, a native of Annapolis, who is executive officer of a Marine artillery regiment. His mother, Mrs. George B. Luckey, lives at 217 Hanover street.

Rounding out his 16th year of service with the Marine Corps, Lieutenant Colonel Luckey is probably busier now at his desk in regimental headquarters than he was at the command post of a special weapons battalion in action on Guadalcanal last year.

As is customary with high-ranking Marine officers, Lieut. Col. Luckey has had all-around training and experience as a fighting man. His duties have taken him to Nicaragua, to China, to sea for two years and to the Solomon Islands.

He was commissioned a second lieutenant in 1927, two months after receiving his bachelor of arts degree from the University of Maryland, where he had four years of activity with the university's Reserve Officers Training Corps unit.

Sent To Nicaragua

Lieut. Col. Luckey was indoctrinated at the Philadelphia Navy Yard, and his first assignment to combat duty was in Nicaragua where he remained two years.

Returning to the States, he was attached briefly to the Marine detachment at the Naval Academy From 1930 to 1932 he served aboard the cruiser, U.S.S. Rochester, based at Panama.

Next came 18 months of duty at the Norfolk Navy Yard. He

(Continued On Page Three)

GETS LETTER PRAISING SON'S WORK ON SHIPS AT PEARL HARBOR

Mrs. Madge Beach, of West Annapolis, has received from Rear Admiral William R. Furlong a letter of commendation on the work of her son, Jack Beach, an employe at the Pearl Harbor Navy Yard for the past two years. Enclosed in the letter was a window sticker bearing the words "Working At Pearl Harbor."

Rear Admiral Furlong's letter stressed the importance of the work being done by men at Pearl Harbor who are "assisting to make victory sure" by repairing damaged ships in support of the Pacific fleet.

Mr. Beach was a mechanic at the Norfolk Navy Yard before being transferred to Pearl Harbor in 1941.

CALVARY CHURCH BOARD TO MEET

The monthly meeting of the official board of Calvary Methodist Church will be held at 8 P. M. tomorrow.

The meeting is being held a month in advance of the usual date

CARD OF THANKS

The family of the late Caroline E. Watson wish to thank their many friends for their expressions of sympathy, the lovely flowers, and the use of their automobiles during their recent bereavement.

MALCOLM WATSON and FAMILY

CHARLES BOULWARE IS GRANTED PAROLE

Thirteen inmates of State penal institutions were free to report for induction into the armed forces today after Gov. O'Conor has signed commutations of sentence for them.

Eight other prisoners were granted paroles, signed by the Governor on the recommendation of director of parole and probation Herman M. Moser.

The commutations included:

Thomas Armstrong, sentenced by the St. Mary's County Circuit Court to 18 months for larceny.

Lee Saunders, sentenced by Baltimore County Circuit Court to one year for robbery.

Ivory Stringer, three years, Worcester County Circuit Court, burglary.

Paroles included:

Charles Boulware, five years, Anne Arundel County Circuit Court, second degree murder.

George Jackson, three years, Prince George's County Circuit Court, assault with intent to kill.

Frank Smith, three years, Prince George's County Circuit Court, assault with intent to kill.

George D. Wright, three years, Wicomico County Circuit Court, manslaughter.

Fred Thomas, 18 months, Harford County Magistrate's Court, larceny.

Any excuse you can give for not upping your payroll savings will please Hitler, Hirohito and puppet Mussolini.

MAC ARTHUR GREETS GEN. KRUEGER

Gen. Douglas MacArthur (right) greets Lt. Gen. Walter Krueger (left), who led U. S. forces occupying the Tobriand is ands in the South Pacific, at an advanced base in the South Pacific.

JOAN E. AVERY IN WAC SCHOOL

As the first step in preparation for a military job, Auxiliary Joan E. Avery, R.F.D., No. 3, Annapolis, has started her basic training at the Second Training Center of the Women's Army Auxiliary Corps, Daytona Beach, Fla.

Her first three days of active military duty were spent at Tent City where she lived in a wood and canvas tent. She was issued her uniform and equipment, given aptitude and physical examinations. After an interview she was classified for an army job that will release a soldier for combat duty.

Auxiliary Avery was then transferred to the cantonment area where her formal training began with classes and drill. There, with a company of approximately 150 women, she lived army style in a two-story pine barracks.

Beginning her day with reveille she finds much to keep her busy until lights out at 9:30 P. M. Basic studies include classes in military methods and procedures, military discipline and courtesy, the branches of service and first aid. Physical training and close order drill keep her in good trim.

High spots in any WAC's day are mess calls, mail calls and the ceremony of retreat at 4:30 P. M. At retreat the companies and the band march in formation on the parade ground, stand at attention while the flag is lowered and then pass in review before post officials.

Auxiliary Avery is the daughter of Mr. and Mrs. Frederick Avery of Annapolis.

JOHN D. BLAND AT NEWARK SCHOOL

John D. Bland, 31, son of Mrs. Paul V. Bland, 218 King George street, and husband of Mrs. Frances B. Bland, 126 Market steet, Annapolis, is studying aircraft mechanics in the Army Air Forces Technical Command at the Casey Jones School of Aeronautics, Newak, N. J.

Recently promoted to private first class because of his aptitude for technical training displayed in Army classification tests, Private Bland is now undergoing the second stage of his training in the New York Civilian-Schools area of the Training Command. Earlier he attended the Academy of Aeronautics at LaGuardia Field, N. Y. On completion of his third stage

of training at Roosevelt Field, L. I., N. Y., he will be graduated as a skilled mechanic qualified to take his place in the combat crew of an Army air force unit.

Bland was a post office employee here before entering the service in March.

MARRIAGE LICENSES

The Clerk of Court for Anne Arundel county this week issued the following marriage licenses:

Howard W. Schumacker, 25, Dresden, Ohio; Donna P. Hichman, 25, Cumberland, Ohio.

Leonard Neck, 29, Shady Side; Eunice Holland, 20, Sady Side.

Mathew J. Kellick, 22, Pawtucket, R. I.; Ruth Agnes Norton, 22, Providence, R. I.

Jack Allen Jackson, 23, Los Angeles, Calif; Leyenia Chapman, 22, Harwood, Md.

James Columbers Pack, 26, Severna Park; Cornelius Elizabeth Jackson, 22, Harwood, Md.

Billie J. Cunningham, 20, Bradford, Pa.; Vesta J. Smith, 20, Annapolis, Md.

James Franklin Short, 32, Annapolis; Julia Augusta Tayman, 25, Annapolis.

Elyah T. Machin, 54, Annapolis; Myrtle L. Stancil, 37, Annapolis.

Andrew H. Pupp, 22, Witherbree, N. Y.; Rosella Refer, 25, Glen Burnie, Md.

John Wesley Jones, 44, Annapolis; Viola E. Offer, 31, Parole, Md.

George LaSalle, 48, Detroit, Mich.; Margaret L. Newton, 51, Detroit, Mich.

Steve Mitchell, 17, Brooklyn, N. Y.; Rose Stanley, 21, Brooklyn, N. Y.

Kernell V. Hunt, 26, Brownswoods, Md.; Mary M. Hawkins, 21, Mulberry Hill, Md.

Bernard Elroy Tripp, Jr., 24, Rutherford, N. J.; Dprothy Margaret Gercken, 26, Rutherford, N. J.

Edward L. Pumphrey, 42, Glen Burnie; Ida K. Truitt, 45, Severn. Md.

For VICTORY
BUY UNITED STATES DEFENSE BONDS STAMPS

CLASSIFIED ADS

For Rent

FOR RENT—Newly decorated rooms for six officers Two single, two double rooms. 101 Market street. Phone: 6386. jy-31

FOR RENT—Furnished room for light housekeeping. Apply 435 4th Street, Eastport, Md. jy-31

FOR RENT—Furhised bedroom. Phone 2833. jy-31

FOR RENT—Nicely furnished bedroom for gentlemen only. Apply 609. Severn Ave., West Annapolis or phone 3254. a-3

FOR RENT—Bedroom, suitable for one or two gentlemen, 809 West St. Phone 3476 after 6:15 P. M. tf

FOR RENT—Two single bedrooms, for bachelor officers. Private entrance and bath, in walking distance of P. G. School. Phone: 3087. tf

FOR RENT—Furnished room, adults. 95 Conduit street. tf

FOR RENT—One large front bedroom, twin beds, suitable for two. Good location. 7 Dean Street. a-2

FOR RENT—Boatyard for lease on Magothy River, between Baltimore and Annapolis. Just off of Richie Highway. Formerly operated by Robert A. Stinchcomb. Marine railway, large shop, boat basin, 600 foot water front, 6 acres of land, 8-room home with bath, two-car garage. 30 boats now in storage. Phone: Annapolis 5441. tf

FOR RENT — Large furnished room [illegible], two closets, two sturdy [illegible], overlooking South River, Bay Vista 2101. tf

For Sale 2

FOR SALE—Chester White boar, 300 pounds and white sow. South Shore, 2437. a-3

FOR SALE—House, 6 rooms and bath, hot water heat, in city. Phone: 4777. tf

FOR SALE—Man's bicycle, 28 inches, in good condition. Apply between 5 and 7:30. 72 Southgate Avenue. jy-31

FOR SALE—Chesapeake Bay, dead rise, Kermath marine motor, good condition. Price $500.00. Good for fishing or oystering. Dawbert's Boat Yard, Ventnor, Pasadena, Bodkins Creek. jy-31

FOR SALE—Accordion, 120 bass, treble shift, "Brindisi". Lined carrying case. Call 6120 between 8 A. M. and 12 noon or 5 P. M. to 7 P .M a-2

FOR SALE—Houses, strictly residential section. Inspection by appointment only. D. Florestano. Phone: 2194. tf

FOR SALE — Gas range, apartment size, with oven and broiler. Phone daytime 6382. tf

FOR SALE—Young pigs, while they last. Apply Martin's Farm. Phone: 2222 or 2228. jy-31

FOR SALE—Investment property. Nice home on King George St. Will show excellent return. Price $6000.00. T. Carroll Worthington, Real Estate and Insurance, 236 Main St., Annapolis, Md. jy-31

FOR SALE—2½ acres land improved by new stucco dwelling, on bus line. Has large living room, with fireplace, 2 bedrooms, 2 baths, game room with fireplace. Holland air condition furnace, partly furnished. A good buy at $10,000.00. T. Carroll Worthington, Real Estate and Insurance, 236 Main St., Annapolis, Md. jy-31

FOR SALE—Potatoes. Phone: 2481. jy-30

FOR SALE—Hard crabs cooked or uncooked. R. E. Simmons. Phone: 6009. a-3

FOR SALE OR RENT — Waterfront property, furnished. Apply M. I. Board, 4836 McArthur Boulevard. Washington, D. C. Telephone: Emerson 4511. jy-31

FOR SALE — Strollers, Cribs, Studio Couches, Innerspring Mattresses, Carriages, Metal Beds, Springs, Wagons, Swings, Porch Rockers, Fans, Refrigerators, Slip Covers, Congoleum and Summer Rugs BOUGHT—SOLD — EXCHANGED — RENTED. Annapolis Furniture Co., 96 West St. Phone 2140. tf

FOR SALE—Used hearing aid, like new. Will sell cheap. Write box 87 Evening Capital. a-2

FOR SALE—Attractive Stieff upright piano, plain case with excellent finish. Keeney's, 23 Randall Street. tf

Help Wanted—Female 4

HELP WANTED FEMALE—Colored maid for general housework and cooking. Phone: N-271. jy-31

HELP WANTED FEMALE—White woman to take care of home. Salary and home. Apply 304 N. Linden Avenue, after 5 P. M. jy-30

HELP WANTED FEMALE—Woman for general housework. References required. Phone: 2173. jy-30

HELP WANTED FEMALE—Part or full time maid for cooking and general house work for month of August. Good pay. Call 4743. jy-30

HELP WANTED FEMALE—Girl as saleslady in record department. 78 Maryland Avenue. tf

HELP WANTED FEMALE—White or colored maid for general housework and cooking, good wages and hours. Call 4119. tf

HELP WANTED FEMALE — Sales women for full time position, Carvel Hall Gift Shop. Apply R. D. Layden, 196 Prince George street. tf

Help Wanted—Female

HELP WANTED FEMALE — Beautician, experienced, living between Annapolis and Baltimore. Phone: Glen Burnie 587. Not open on Monday. a-2

HELP WANTED FEMALE—Woman wanted to operate telephone in own home. Part time, good pay. Must have private telephone with unlimited service. Write Box 92. Evening Capital. jy-31

HELP WANTED FEMALE—Saleslady. Apply Miller's Department Store, 44 West Street. tf

HELP WANTED FEMALE — Experienced saleslady. Apply The Leader. 162 Main street. tf

HELP WANTED FEMALE — Colored waitress. Apply Wally Hotel, West Street. tf

HELP WANTED FEMALE—Maid, afternoons, general housework and cooking. Good pay. Phone: 3902. Wardour. jy-29

HELP WANTED FEMALE — Housekeeper, good wages, good hours, no laundry, three adults in family, 517 6th street, Eastport, Maryland. jy-29

HELP WANTED FEMALE—Cleaning women, just for afternoons. No cooking or laundry. Apply 601 6th St., Eastport or phone 3618. a-2

HELP WANTED FEMALE—Girl or woman for general office work with some knowledge of bookkeeping and typing. Write Box 85, Evening Capital. tf

Help Wanted—Male

HELP WANTED MALE — Essential farm labor is draft except. Available living quarters and privileges. Phone South Shore 2176, or write Box 61, Evening Capital. tf

HELP WANTED MALE—Night bar porter. Wally Hotel, West St. tf

Wanted 6

WANTED—To rent small unfurnished house with grounds, electricity and water, Phone. Annapolis 2249. a-2

WANTED—To buy man's bicycle. Good condition. Phone: 3522. a-2

WANTED—Unfurnished apartmezt or small house. Permanent tenants. Write Box 91, Evening Capital. a-2

WANTED—Naval couple desire furnished apartment or house about August 10 in or near Annapolis. Write Box 90, Evening Capital. a-2

WANTED—Garden tractor. 400 North 4th Avenue and Ritchie Highway, Glen Burdnie. jy-30

WANTED—About 2 to 12 acres with house, not over 5 miles from Annapolis. State all particulars including price. Write Box 88, Evening Capital. jy-31

WANTED — To rent small furnished apartment or partly furnished. Phone 2160. jy-31

WANTED — Electric portable singer sewing machine. Phone: 5441 jy-31

WANTED — To rent, two or three-bedroom unfurnished house in city, or on bus line, by Academy officer. Phone: 5284. tf

WANTED—Will pay cash for your car. William J. Meyers. Call Vernon 5320 or 1708 North Charles St., Baltimore Md. tf

WANTED—Used refrigerators and refrigerating equipment, any condition. Call 4791. tf

Lost and Found 8

LOST—In A and P, ration case containing two ration books No. 2; bank book; money; war savings book. Return Mrs. May Griffin, 204 King George street. a-2

LOST—Gas ration book "A". Return to Thomas B. Brown, 1208 President Street, Eastport, Md. a-2

LOST—Gasoline ration book "C". Return to Thomas W. Wilmer, Ferndale, P. O., Md. a-2

LOST—Two ration books No. 1. Return to Louise Frank Mathews, 77 Washington street. a-2

LOST—Set of false teeth. Finder call 2696 Reward 10.00. a-2

FOUND — Sailboat in Rhode River. Owner may have same on identification and paying costs. Milton Dawson, R. D. Edgewater, Md. a-2

FOUND—Rowboat. Identify to claim. Phone: 3346. jy-30

LOST—Ration Book No. 2. Minnie [illegible] Moreland, 620 Severn Ave. jy-31

LOST—Gas Ration Book "T". Return to Edward Baltz, Edgewater, Md. jy-31

LOST—Gasoline Ration Books "A" and "C". Return to Donald Shaw, 109 Revell Street. jy-30

Miscellaneous 12

MISCELLANEOUS — We deliver anything — anywhere. Peronal Delivery Service. Phone 2781. tf

MISCELLANEOUS — Used cars, any make, any model bought and sold. Harry's Super-Service, West and Southgate. Phone 4000. tf

MISCELLANEOUS — Paper hanging Also stoves and furnaces repaired. Phone 4197. tf

Help Wanted Male and Female 15

HELP WANTED MALE [illegible] FEMALE — Couple, man as caretaker, woman as cook and general house work—living quarters. Mrs. P. Miller. Phone: 4336. tf

Piano Service

PIANO SERVICE —Tuning, cleaning and repairing estimates given and liberal credit. We buy and sell all makes and styles. Keeney's, 23 Randall St. Phone: 4852 a-31

CERTIFIED PUBLIC ACCOUNTANT

To act as Budget Supervisor for Anne Arundel County with experience in office and business administration; preferably one with experience in governmental state or county budgeting. Full time required, salary $3600 to $4000 per year. Address: County Commissioners of Anne Arundel County Annapolis. Maryland on or before August 2, 1943.

Department of Public Works
State of Maryland
STATE ROADS COMMISSION
NOTICE TO CONTRACTORS
State Roads Project

SEALED PROPOSALS for the construction of a storm water sewer as follows:

ANNE ARUNDEL COUNTY—CONTRACT AA-333-1-311.

This project includes the construction of storm water sewers with inlet and manhole connections beginning at a point on the east side of Governor Ritchie Highway, approximately 385 ft. north of 11th Ave. in Brooklyn and extending south to 11th Ave., thence east along 11th Ave. for a distance of 1100 ft. PRIORITIES RECEIVED.

The employment agency for furnishing labor on the above project shall be Maryland State Employment Service, 221 Main St., Annapolis, Md.

Will be received by the State Roads Commission at its offices, 108 East Lexington Street, Baltimore, Maryland, until 12 Noon on the 10th day of August, 1943, at which time and place they will be publicly opened and read.

Qualification of bidders required.

Bids must be made upon the blank proposal form which, with specifications and plans will be furnished by the Commission upon application and cash paymet of $500, for each separate project, as hereafter no charges will be permitted.

No bids will be received unless accompanied by a certified check or bid bond payable to the State Roads Commission of Maryland, as required by Sec. 6, Chapter 761, Acts 1939, of the amount as set forth in the proposal form.

The successful bidder will be required to give bond, and comply with the Acts of the General Assembly of Maryland, respecting contracts. No refund will be made for return of specifications and plans.

The Commission reserves the right to reject any and all bids.

By order of the State Roads Commission this 27th day of July, 1943.

EZRA B. WHITMAN, Chairman
L. H. STEUART, Secretary. jy-30

Henry J. Tarantino, Attorney

NOTICE TO CREDITORS

Notice is hereby given that the Subscriber, of Anne Arundel County, has obtained from the Orphans' Court of Anne Arundel County, in Maryland, Letters Testamentary on the personal estate of

MARY G. NEVIN

late of Anne Arundel County, deceased. All persons having claims against the deceased, are hereby warned to exhibit the same, with the vouchers thereof, to the subscriber, on or before the

24TH DAY OF JANUARY, 1944

They may otherwise, by law, be excluded from all benefit of said estate. All persons indebted to said estate are requested to make immediate payment.

Given under my hand this 21st day of July, 1943.

MARCIA N. ENGLAND,
Executrix.
a-27

FOR SALE

About 1 acre on South River, near Annapolis. Beautiful modern dwelling for a home, or income producing property.

Wardour, very desirable home on large lot. Five bedrooms, two baths, two porches. Garage.

Inspection by appointment only.

FRED E. VOGES
Real Estate and Insurance
47 Maryland Avenue
Dial 4477

THREE MARYLANDERS HELD BY JAPANESE

The Navy Department announced today the names of three Marylanders who are prisoners of the Japanese in the Philippine Islands and Manchuko.

The men are:

Fern Joseph Barta, radioman, second class, whose brother, Richard Reid Barta, avaition chief radioman, U.S.N., is stationed on the Reina Mercedes, Naval Academy.

Otis Ray Bills, radioman, whose wife, Mrs. Rose Bills, lives in Baltimore.

Charles George Pearman, gunner's mate, first class, whose mother, Mrs. Anna M. Pearman, lives in Baltimore.

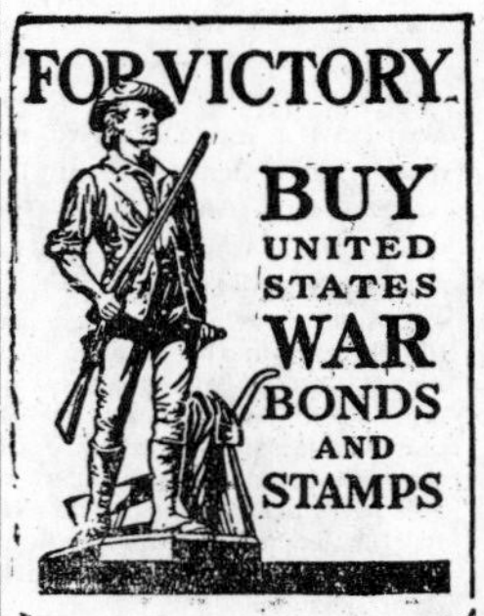
FOR VICTORY
BUY
UNITED
STATES
WAR
BONDS
AND
STAMPS

DIED

CHILDS—On July 28, 1943, at his residence, Ferry Farms, Julian Holland, beloved husband of Lucille McD. Childs. Funeral Saturday, July 31, at 11 A. M. from Taylor's Funeral Home. Interment in All Hollows Chapel Cemetery, Davidsonville, Md. jy-30

DIED

JONES—On Wednesday, July 28 at Henryton, Md., Louis Jones, beloved husband of Mary Jones, 18 Taylor Street, Annapolis, Md. Funeral services will be held Saturday, July 31, 1943, at 2 P. M., from Chew's Chapel. Interment in Church Cemetery. Remains resting at J. B. Johnson Funeral Home. jy-30

BIDS FOR COAL

Bids are invited by the County Commissioners of Anne Arundel County for approximately 85 to 100 tons of run of mine bituminous coal, 50 per cent lump, for the County Jail on Calvert Street and County Garage at Best Gate (ton of 2,000 pounds).

Bids will be opened on Tuesday, August 3, 1943, at 11:00 A. M.

The County Commissioners reserve the right to reject any or all bids.

COUNTY COMMISSIONERS FOR ANNE ARUNDEL COUNTY.
By, R. HARRY ARNOLD, Clerk.
jy-30

THE STATE TAX COMMISSION OF MARYLAND

hereby gives notice that Articles of Dissolution of the Rustic Inn, Incorporated, were received for record by it on July 1, 1943, in accordance with the provisions of Sec. 96 of Art. 23 of the Code (1939 Edition).

(Signed) Owen E. Hitchins
(Signed) Emerson C. Harrington, Jr.
Commissioners
a-6

NOTICE

Notice is hereby given that the following applications for license to sell alcoholic liquor have been filed with the Mayor, Counselor and Aldermen of Annapolis, and will be acted on at a regular meeting of the City Council, Monday, August 9.

Fleet Reserve Association, Wm. H. Busch, applicant, Class C Beer License, Fleet Reserve Association Club, Rooms, foot of Main street.

KATHERINE E. LINTHICUM
City Clerk a-2

STATE EMPLOYMENT COMMISSIONER
22 Light St., Baltimore, Md.
NOTICE OF VACANCIES

License Inspector
Caretaker; Clinical Director, Mental Disease Hospital
Instructor, Arts and Crafts
Closing date for receiving applications: August 14, 1943
MARRY C. JONES, Commissioner
a-6

MODEST MAIDENS
Trademark Registered U. S. Patent Office

"Well—he was tall and handsome, with wavy black hair, big blue eyes and . . ."

SCORCHY SMITH Trademark Registered U. S. Patent Office — On The Fence

AS THEY STRUGGLE, THE FUGITIVE SLIPS SOMETHING INTO SCORCHY'S POCKET...
FOR THE LAST TIME, HALT OR I'LL FIRE!

OAKY DOAKS Trademark Registered U. S. Patent Office — Poor Fish

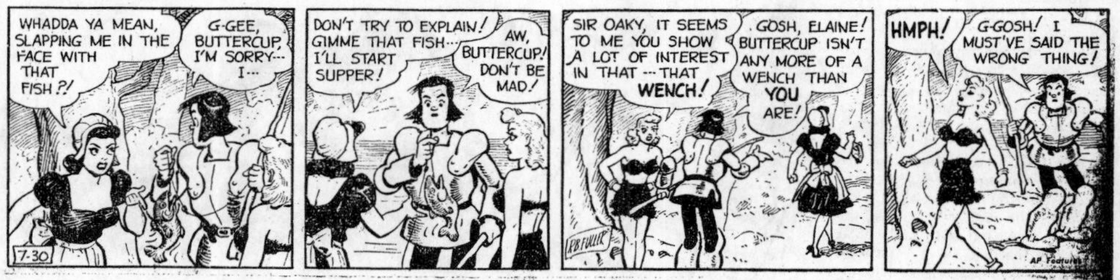
WHADDA YA MEAN, SLAPPING ME IN THE FACE WITH THAT FISH?!
G-GEE, BUTTERCUP I'M SORRY— I—
DON'T TRY TO EXPLAIN! GIMME THAT FISH— I'LL START SUPPER!
AW, BUTTERCUP! DON'T BE MAD!
SIR OAKY, IT SEEMS TO ME YOU SHOW A LOT OF INTEREST IN THAT—THAT WENCH!
GOSH, ELAINE! BUTTERCUP ISN'T ANY MORE OF A WENCH THAN YOU ARE!
HMPH!
G-GOSH! I MUST'VE SAID THE WRONG THING!

OH, DIANA! Trademark Registered U. S. Patent Office — He's Chicken-Hearted

..BUT WE'RE NOT LOOKING FOR JOBS ...YET! WE'RE TRYING TO SAVE OUR DINER.
....SAY, WAIT...!
CENTER
NEW WAR PLANT CHIEF ARRIV
From Deep South, Col. Blockbuster F To Take Contro Huge Arms Fa
....COL. BLOCKBUSTER LIKES CENTER CITY, EXCEPT THAT IT GREATLY DISTURBS HIM TO FIND NO ONE HERE ABLE TO PREPARE HIS FAVORITE DISH........ TRUE SOUTHERN-FRIED CHICKEN!
KITTEN!
WHAT DO YO' ALL WANT, HONEY CHILE?!

DICKIE DARE Trademark Registered U. S. Patent Office — Now I Lay Me—

BR-R-R- IT'S GETTIN' AWFUL COLD— GOTTA HURRY AN' GET MY BOOTS OFF
HEY, WAIT, SOMETHIN' WE ALMOST FORGOT
Y'SEE, WAGS, WE DON'T KNOW JUST WHAT'S GONNA HAPPEN TO US—I MEAN, HERE WE ARE DRIFTIN' ON AN ICEBERG —SO DONTCHA SEE— AW HECK, C'MERE

HOMER HOOPEE Trademark Registered U. S. Patent Office — Medicine Man

MY NERVES ARE UNSTRUNG FROM THE ACCIDENT! I'D LIKE TO TAKE SOME OF YOUR "SURE-FIRE HOME REMEDY," MUM!
WHY CERTAINLY, MR. POTHERS! THIS WILL RE-STRING YOUR NERVES TIGHT AS A FIDDLE.
HOOPEE, THAT STUFF IS A SURE CURE FOR THE "BUZZARD'S CURSE!"
IF YOU GAVE IT TO THE BUZZARD!
PLOP!

THE ADVENTURES OF PATSY Trademark Registered U. S. Patent Office — Homely Remedy

WELL, WELL! I THOUGHT YOU CHILDREN HAD DUG UP HALF OF TILLER'S CAVE BY THIS TIME! IT'S TOO BAD LUCIUS DOESN'T FEEL WELL!!
GREEN PLUMS! THIS CALLS FOR WARM SODA WATER AND MAYBE A DROP OF CASTOR OIL!!
THERE! YOU'LL FEEL BETTER IN A FEW MINUTES, LUCIUS—
I DONT FEEL SO GOOD EITHER, ANDREW ...BUT IF LUCIUS HAD TO TAKE CASTOR OIL I'M NOT GOING TO SAY ANYTHING ABOUT IT!!

NEIGHBORLY NEIGHBORS

DO YOU LIKE THIS BETTER, PETERS?
MYRA!! ...YOU LOOK LIKE A FIJI ISLANDER!
OH!... THIS IS TOO MUCH!! ...MYRA... OF ALL PEOPLE!!... YOU COULD HEAR PETERS IN THE NEXT BLOCK, SCREAMING ABOUT THE DUST-MOP EFFECT—!!

THE DOOLITTLES

QUIT RUSTLING THOSE BILLS EVERY TIME I MENTION A SALE OF DRESSES TO MOTHER... I'M NOT INTERESTED IN BORROWING ANY MONEY FROM YOU... NOT AT SIX PER CENT A MONTH
WOULD YA PAY ME FIVE PER CENT?
PIN-MONEY PROJECT NO. 3691

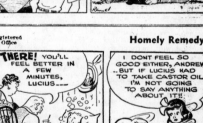

ome Clubs Are Building For Next Year

Others Seek To Strengthen Themselves This Season

By JUDSON BAILEY
Associated Press Sports Writer

The way the rivals of the St. Louis Cardinals and New York Yankees are reacting to the unimpeded sweep of these two clubs to the major league pennants is a topic that may interest the clans today.

Some still are trying to strengthen themselves for the present season, some are trying to rebuild for next year and some simply are waiting for the schedule to end.

The Washington Senators are the prize example of the first group. It would take a miracle to move the Senators ahead of the Yankees, but Clark Griffith ain't overlooking any chances. Yesterday he finally put through a deal with the St. Louis Browns for third baseman Harlond Clift and pitcher John Niggeling.

Slick Trader

The Old Fox, who was a slick trader before Branch Rickey's name became synonymous with deals, has been trying to get Clift for at least two years and if he had been able to land him to plug the Senators' gap at third base a month ago, might have managed to make a race in the American League this year.

As it is, the deal quite likely will let the Senators finish second, a jump from seventh place last year. They lost their runner-up spot yesterday, though, by dividing a doubleheader at Chicago. The White Sox nosed them out in the first game 3-2 in 14 innings, but Washington rallied to win the nightcap 4-2. The Senators made ten double plays in the two games.

The Yankees were ambushed by the Cleveland Indians 9-8 and 7-5 in morning and afternoon games and this feat enabled the Tribe to move up to second place. The second game went 14 innings before a two-run homer by Jeff Heath decided it. Heath, who had walloped a two-run homer in the first contest, also hit a triple and a single in the second game to bat in a total of seven runs for the day.

Mark Time

The Philadelphia Athletics, who stand out among the clubs that are merely marking time till the season ends, dropped their 12th consecutive game 4-0 in the face of a five-hit pitching performance by Bob Muncrief of the Browns and the Detroit Tigers nosed out the Boston Red Sox 1-0. In this game both Hal White of the Tigers and Yank Terry of the Sox pitched four-hit ball, but Detroit tallied the only run of the game in the first inning without a hit.

The Brooklyn Dodgers, who have had their whole complexion changed since the start of the season in the process of Rickey's rebuilding with young players for the future, tried out two youngsters on the mound yesterday and dropped both ends of a doubleheader to the Chicago Cubs 7-5 and 15-6.

Cards Divide

Hal Gregg and Red Barney, two youngsters who had reported from Montreal only a few hours earlier in the day, started the games for the Dodgers and each gave four hits and six walks in addition to some wild pitches before they were eliminated in the early innings.

The St. Louis Cardinals divided a mid-day doubleheader at Philadelphia, winning the first game 6-0 on Howard Krist's five-hit hurling and dropping the second 6-3 to Al Gerheauser, who succeeded in stopping Harry Walker's hitting streak at 29 games.

Cincinnati split a doubleheader at Boston, winning 5-0 for Bucky Walters after losing 4-3 and the Pittsburgh Pirates split with the New York Giants. A single by Pete Coscarart in the tenth gave Hank Gornicki his third win in two days 7-6 in the opener and Carl Hubbell won the nightcap 3-2.

Sports Round-Up

By SID FEDER

Pinch-hitting for Hugh Fullerton
NEW YORK, Aug. 19 (AP)—Billy Southworth says his St. Louis apartment is so close to Leo Durocher's, he can toss a rock in the lip's window ... But he hasn't tried it lately—he doesn't have to see Sieve Hamas, the ex-heavyweight has just written a book on "stratosphere Stamina" ... that's being distributed to all army pilots in training ... Steve's air force lieutenant now ... Vern Miller, who couldn't get below 300 playing tackle for Harvard, has shaved off 20 pounds during his basic training at Keesler Field, Miss. ...

Umps No Barney—Even In Blarney

Cable from Belfast tells about the umpire, handling a game between the 8th U. S. Air Force and a U. S. Army team tagged the North Ireland Blues, who put himself out of the game ... Seems the Blues were questioning everything from his eyesight to his ancestry ... He took it for ten scoreless frames, then announced, "it ain't worth it"—and walked out ... Another guy finished up and the Blues won 1-0, if you're interested ...

Couple of westerners in town trying to line up a Turkey Thompson-Tony Galento tea party for Los Angeles next month ... And the Jacobs Beach beachcombers are wondering if California's even far enough away for that one ... Al Sabath's Chicago horse reached Belmont yesterday ... but Alsab wasn't with them ...

Headline: 20 to 34 original! Dodgers gone

Since Rickey and the Dodgers came to Brooklyn town.
He's sliced the Dodger payroll down.
Of 34 who started out.
Just 14 Bums are still about.
If better slicers you are seekin'.
You must look far to beat the Deacon.

Hit-And-Run

Cubs scout Jack Doyle tells John (what town is this?) Carmichael, Chicago News Sports Ed, that Bill Sarni, Los Angeles' 15-year-old catcher, is farther along now than Gabby Harnett was at the same stage and age ... Incidentally, Sarni's father thought the kid should get $15,000 for signing ... but a pal of the family—and the club—straightened it out ... The Pimlico Futurity may have a $40,000 pot for the two-year olds this fall ... The Army's youngest General 35-year-old Brig. Gen. William E. Hall, was the center on Red Cagle's West Point powerhouse in the 20's ... He's the air force deputy chief of staff ...

Khaki-And-Blue Stuff

The stork dropped in on the Harry Hays (he's the ex-Tulane footballer) at Mesa, Ariz., the other day ... Since pap's in the air force, he immediately tagged the new arrival, "Roger Wilco Hays" ... Roger stands for "okay" and Wilco for "will comply" among fliers ... Billy Defoe, the old fight trainer, now is Pfc Defoe at Camp Maxey, Texas ... Couple of soldier-boy letters arrived wondering how about Billy Conn in the Joe Louis tour ... Scuttlebutt tip is that Freddie Hutchinson, who cost the Tigers $70,000 as a pitcher, is going to switch to catching when he takes off his sailor suit ... This cupid guy gets around—when a Seattle gal softball team tangled with the McChord (Wash.) Field outfit the Seattle first sacker borrowed the mitt of McChord's Private Suggs ... "And she liked it so much, she married the guy," reports the McChord tipcord ...

Knife-And-Fork Sports

One soldier correspondent writes: The mess-hall here features home cooking ... one meal, and you wish you were home cooking ...

Cunnel John Chapman, the one-time six-day bike race boss, is now farming 4,000 acres in cotton, tobacco and corn (the Garden variety) at College Park, Ga. ... Lou Little has a halfback at Columbia named Ted Meier, who is not to be confused with our AP sidekick of the same name ... Our Ted's build makes him an automatic statutory guard ...

Ben Hogan, the little guy with the long drive, and long John Winsett, the ex-Red Socker and Dodger, are air force OCS in Miami ...

"BOSTON BATTLER"...by PAP

Sal BARTOLO—The Boston featherweight is one of the best 126-pounders in action today. A natural featherweight, he has had to go out of his class to keep busy. Sal is ready for a shot at the featherweight crown. He had won over a dozen amateur championships before he turned pro in 1937.

HEADED FOR THE BROWNS

Ellis Clary (left), third baseman, tossed a glove into his bag at Comiskey Park, Chicago, as he discussed with John Miller (right), a pitcher, their transfer from the Washington Senators to the St. Louis Browns for third baseman Harold Clift and pitcher Johnny Niggeling.

Where They Play Today

Chicago at Brooklyn.
Cincinnati at Boston.
Pittsburgh at New York.
St. Louis at Philadelphia (night).

Standing Of The Clubs

	W.	L.	Pct.
St. Louis	71	37	.657
Cincinnati	61	50	.550
Pittsburgh	61	51	.545
Brooklyn	56	56	.500
Chicago	52	58	.473
Boston	49	58	.458
Philadelphia	52	62	.456
New York	40	70	.364

COL. WALLACE GETS LEGION OF MERIT

WASHINGTON, Aug. 19 (AP)—Col. William J. Wallace, U.S.M.C. of Church Hill, Queen Anne's county, Maryland, has been awarded the legion of merit medal for exceptionally meritorious conduct while stationed on Guadalcanal, Marine headquarters announced today.

Despite extremely difficult conditions and in the face of a superior number of Japanese aircraft, Col. Wallace conducted his marine aircraft group with such skill that squadrons under his command destroyed approximately 162 enemy planes and five ships during the occupation of Guadalcanal.

Col. Wallace, in the presidential citation, was commended for a most effective combat team of the units of his command.

The citation read:

"For exceptionally meritorious conduct in the performance of outstanding service to the government of the United States in command of a marine aircraft group, supporting land and sea forces in the occupation of Guadalcanal, Solomon Islands, from August 20 to September 29, 1942.

"Despite extremely difficult and hazardous conditions, and in the face of a greatly superior number of enemy aircraft, Col. Wallace conducted the operations of his group with such skill and sound tactical judgment that the squadrons under his command inflicted great losses on the enemy, destroying approximately 162 aircraft and five surface vessels, and contributing in a great measure to the success of our forces in that area."

The Standings

AMERICAN LEAGUE

Scores Of Yesterday

Cleveland, 9-7; New York, 8-5.
Chicago, 3-4; Washington, 2-4.
Detroit, 1; Boston, 0.
St. Louis, 4; Philadelphia, 0.

§Second game 14 innings.
*First game 14 innings.

Where They Play Today

Washington at Chicago.
New York at Cleveland (night).
Boston at Detroit (2 games).
Philadelphia at St. Louis (night).

Standing Of The Clubs

	W.	L.	Pct.
New York	67	42	.615
Cleveland	57	50	.533
Washington	60	53	.531
Detroit	56	50	.528
Chicago	56	54	.509
Boston	56	57	.496
St. Louis	47	60	.439
Philadelphia	40	70	.402

NATIONAL LEAGUE

Scores Of Yesterday

St.L ouis, 6-3; Philadelphia, 0-6.
Chicago, 7-15; Brooklyn, 5-6.
*Pittsburgh, 7-2; New York, 6-3.
Boston, 4-0; Cincinnati, 3-5.

*Ten innings.

Around The Radio Dial Tonight

NEW YORK, Aug. 19 (AP)—There'll be a new Henry, the third one, when the Aldrich Family returns to NBC after a summer vacation on September 2. He is 15-year-old Dickie Jones, who has been playing in the movies.

Dickie won in an audition in which several hundred aspirants made a try for the role. He replaces Norman Tokar, who succeeded Ezar Stone, creator of the role. Tokar has followed Stone into Uncle Sam's armed forces.

More changes for the fall include the transfer of the Inner Sanctum mysteries, from Sundays nights on CBS where they have been since January, 1941, to Saturday nights on CBS beginning September 4. NBC reports that after Red Skelton to his Tuesday night stand on September 14, his summer replacement, the Beat the Band quiz with Hildegarde as M. C., will be transferred to Wednesday nights. It is to replace Tommy Dorsey's show, which will close September 8.

Topics tonight: NBC—8 Blind Date; 8:30 Battle Stations in the Navy; 9 Bing Crosby; 9:30 Joan Davis variety; 10 Garry Moore show; 10:30 March of Time Returns; 11:30 Words at War, drama.

CBS—8 Mary Astor and others; 8:30 Death Valley Days; 9 Major Bowes amateurs; 9:30 Stage Door Canteen; 10 First Line, U. S. Navy; 10:30 Dr. A. Loudon on "Germans already organizing for the next war."

BLU—7 Wings to Victory; 7:30 New Eve; 8:30 Town Meeting from Chautauqua, N. Y., "Should U. S. give up foreign military bases after the war;" 9:30 Russ Morgan band; 10:30 Yankee Doodle quiz.

MBS—8 This Is Our Enemy; 8:30 Harmony Hall; 9:15 Fight night interviews; 9:30 U-Tell 'Em Club; 11:30 South American Serenade.

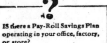

Shipping For Liberty

THIS is the Liberty ship, one of America's major replies to the submarine menace. She isn't rakish nor particularly fast, but she is a sturdy sea-going truck that hauls 9,000 tons of general cargo. First designed in 1941 as part of the Lease-Lend program, hundreds of Liberty ships have been built, hundreds more will put to sea this year. Standardized to the last small gasket, she is steam driven by reciprocating engines, is economical on fuel; has five cargo holds. These sketches show step-by-step growth.

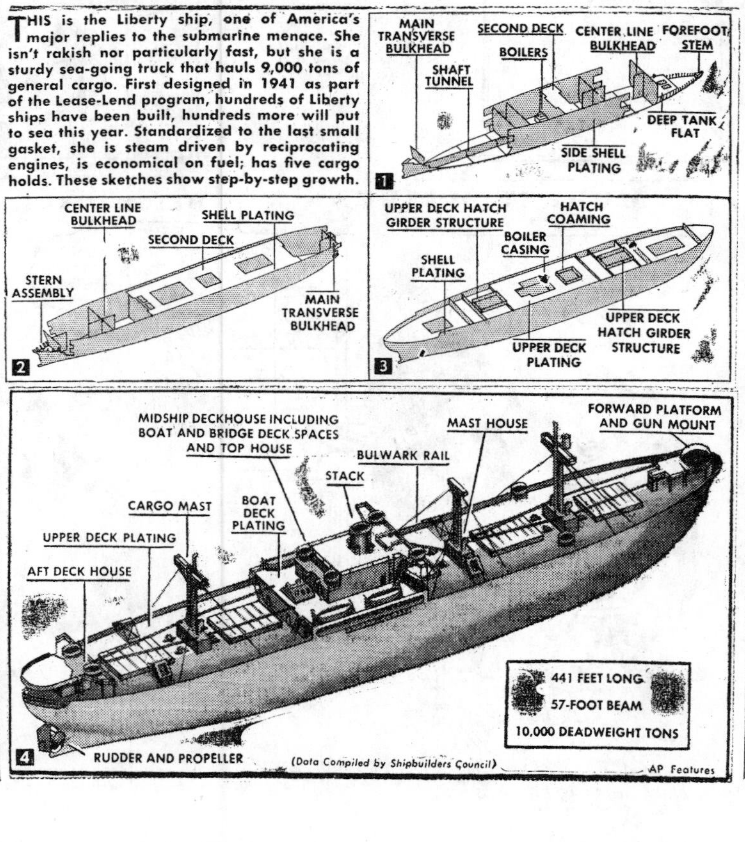

MAIN TRANSVERSE BULKHEAD   SECOND DECK   CENTER LINE BULKHEAD   FOREFOOT STEM

BOILERS   SHAFT TUNNEL   SIDE SHELL PLATING   DEEP TANK FLAT

1

CENTER LINE BULKHEAD   SHELL PLATING   SECOND DECK

STERN ASSEMBLY   MAIN TRANSVERSE BULKHEAD

2

UPPER DECK HATCH GIRDER STRUCTURE   HATCH COAMING

SHELL PLATING   BOILER CASING   UPPER DECK HATCH GIRDER STRUCTURE   UPPER DECK PLATING

3

MIDSHIP DECKHOUSE INCLUDING BOAT AND BRIDGE DECK SPACES AND TOP HOUSE   MAST HOUSE   FORWARD PLATFORM AND GUN MOUNT

CARGO MAST   BOAT DECK PLATING   BULWARK RAIL   STACK

UPPER DECK PLATING   AFT DECK HOUSE

4   RUDDER AND PROPELLER

441 FEET LONG
57-FOOT BEAM
10,000 DEADWEIGHT TONS

(Data Compiled by Shipbuilders Council)
AP Features

Evening Capital

WEATHER
Occasional light rain on the coast; cooler this afternoon; somewhat cooler tonight and Thursday.

VOL. LIX — NO. 213 | EVERY EVENING EXCEPT SUNDAY | ANNAPOLIS, MD., WEDNESDAY, SEPTEMBER 8, 1943 | SOUTHERN MARYLAND'S ONLY DAILY | THREE CENTS

LATE NEWS

DR. PILZER WINS CHEMIST'S PRIZE

Pittsburgh, Sept. 8 (AP) — Dr. Kenneth Sanborn Pitzer, 29, associate professor of chemistry at the University of California at Berkeley, today was awarded the $1,000 American Chemical Society award in pure chemistry and cited as "one of the most brilliant young chemists in North America."

The award was made at the society's 106th meeting in recognition of Pitzer's work in chemical thermodynamics, including studies of benzene and toluene.

COMMENTS ON OIL SUPPLIES

Pittsburgh, Sept. 8 (AP)—President Per K. Frolich of the American Chemical Society said today that while a shortage of natural petroleum will occur "at some future time," requiring use of synthetic products, there is "nothing to indicate hat this should result in any sudden as far as our supply and consumption of gasoline and petroleum derivatives are concerned.

11,679,000 BALE COTTON CROP FORECAST

Washington, Sept. 8 (AP) — The Agriculture Department reported today that the indicated cotton crop this year, based on Sept. 1 conditions, is 11,679,000 bales of 500 pounds gross weight.

WILL NOT WRITE OFF LEND-LEASE

Washington, Sept. 8 (AP)—President Roosevelt says it is not America's intention to write off as pure gifts the materials which are going to our Allies under lend-lease arrangements.

ARCHBISHOP SCHREMBS CRITICALLY ILL

Cleveland, Sept. 8 (AP) — Archbishop Joseph Schrembs, 77, Bishop of the Cleveland Catholic Diocese, was reported in extremely critical condition today at St. John's Hospital. Attendants said he had a "very poor" night.

78 DIED IN P. R. R. WRECK

Philadelphia, Sept. 8 (AP)—The death toll in the Labor Day wreck of the Pennsylvania Railroad's Congressional Limited stood at 78 today as a procession of men and women with dread-haunted faces filed past the rows of gnarled bodies in the city morgue seeking friends or relatives among the 23 still unidentified victims.

HOTEL DEATH TOLL RISES

Houston, Tex., Sept. 8 (AP)—Two more deaths in hospitals today raised to fifty the toll of flames which trapped screaming, frantic men in the old, three-stroy Gulf Hotel in downtown Houston yesterday.

MORE MINES BACK TO PRIVATE OPERATION

Washington, Sept. 8 (AP)—Secretary of Interior Ickes, as boss of government-controlled coal mines, announced today tnat 138 more mines, belonging to 94 companies had been returned to private operation under provision of the Smith-Connally anti-strike act.

CHURCHILL, F. D. R., MAKE NO COMMENT

Washington, Sept. 8 (AP)—President Roosevelt was seated at his momento-crowded desk in the White House offices and Prime Minister Churchill of Great Britain was busy elsewhere in the Executive Mansion when the world heard today that Italy had capitulated.

Both obviously had known the news for sometime, since the terms were agreed upon last Friday. But from neither of the leaders was there immediate formal comment.

CAPITAL JUBILANT OVER SURRENDER

Washington. Sept. 8 (AP)—Word of Italy's capitulation came to a jubilant American capital today shortly after disclosure that President Roosevelt and Prime Minister Churchill had carried their current White House conferences into this morning—apparently waiting for just such news.

ALBANIA EXPECTS ALLIED INVASION

London, Sept. 8 (AP)—Albanian guerrilla forces anticipate an Allied invasion of the Balkans within a month and the Germans are moving men and equipment from Yugoslavia into Albania to meet a possible thrust across the Strait of Otranto from the Italian heel, Istanbul press dispatches reported today.

Local Tides

TOMORROW

High water — 1:19 A. M., 1:7 feet; 1:05 P. M., 1.7 feet. Low water—8:22 A. M., 7:27 P. M.

Moon rises 4:15 P. M., sets 1:21 A. M.

Sun rises 6:41 A. M., sets 7:26

Tides are given for Annapolis. For Sandy Point add 15 minutes. For Thomas Point Shoal, subtract 30 minutes.

ITALY SURRENDERS

Gets Armistice After Signing Unconditional Surrender Pact

TERMS HAVE BEEN APPROVED BY U. S., SOVIET, GREAT BRITAIN

(By the Associated Press)

Gen. Dwight D. Eisenhower today announced the unconditional surrender of Italy in the greatest victory for Allied arms in four years of war.

He also announced that he had granted a military armistice—approved by Russia as well as Britain and the United States—to the war-sick, tottering junior Axis partner being chewed by invasion.

Adolf Hitler's "European fortress" was cracked, the way was opened for new offensives and the course of World War No. 2 immeasurably shortened.

Surrender of Italian armed forces "unconditionally" was made by the government of Marshal Pietro Badoglio, successor of Benito Mussolini, the architect of Fascism.

Thus the Casablanca "unconditional surrender" ultimatum received its first application to an entire Axis nation.

DONETS BASIN FREE OF GERMANS

Coincident with the Eisenhower announcement came a statement from Marshal Stalin from Moscow triumphantly made in a special order of the day that "The Donets basin is cleared of the Germans."

The announcement made by the Moscow radio added, "Our troops captured a number of cities, including the city of Stalino, which has been Hitler's headquarters on the Russian southern front.

The Italian surrender came five days after the British Eighth army stormed across the Messina Strait from Sicily and as Axis broadcasts asserted that American sea-borne forces were moving toward new goals.

Berlin said about 200 merchant and transport vessels with American forces aboard were about "to land somewhere."

New Landing

The German high command had acknowledged a new Allied landing at Pizzo, on the Gulf of Eufemia, 40 miles north of the British Eighth army's original bridgehead, and a Berlin broadcast added that two large Anglo-American convoys had sailed from Palermo, Sicily.

British-Canadian troops had occupied Bova Marina, 10 miles east of Melito in the south and pushed up the west coast to the Petrace river, giving the Allied force control of an area of about 100 square miles, with 76 miles of coastline.

The heavy air assaults continued yesterday, with American Flying Fortresses bombing the big airfield at Foggia, shooting down 11 out of a swarm of attacking fighters. Rome reported that Frascati and other localities in the suburbs of the Eternal City had been bombed.

Signed Friday

Dispatches from Allied headquarters in North Africa said the unconditional surrender agreement and armistice had been signed in Sicily last Friday—on the very day that Italy was invaded—and Italy, accepting all the terms, agreed that it would become effective "at the moment most favorable for the Allies."

"That moment has now ar-

(Continued On Page Six)

FLIGHT OF ARMY PLANES WILL OPEN THIRD WAR LOAN DRIVE

Fire And Church Bells Will Ring At 10 A. M. Tomorrow

The War Department is sending a flight of about 200 airplanes to sweep over the cities of Maryland tomorrow to open the Third War Loan campaign to raise $15,000,000,000 nationally and $1,700,000 in Annapolis and Anne Arundel county.

Joseph D. Lazenby, chairman of the county War Finance committee, said he had been informed that the planes would fly over Annapolis sometime in the morning.

The fire bells of the city and the bells of many churches will ring for two minutes at 10 A. M. to signal the opening of the war bond campaign. Special permission to use the bells was granted by Civilian Defense authorities.

Flag Display

Mayor William U. McCready issued a proclamation calling upon the citizens to cooperate in the campaign and urging the display of flags on all private and public buildings.

The campaign will continue through September and all bonds and stamps bought during the month will be credited to the quota.

Maryland has been assigned a quota of $196,000,000. Mr. Lazenby announced that a total of about $400,000 had already been secured toward the county quota by purchases made by various individuals and groups.

The various committees in charge of the campaign have been working for several weeks, and the official start of the drive will simply tend to intensify the effort.

"I have never worked with such an enthusiastic and interested group as the 2,000 or more committee members who are now out selling bonds and stamps," Mr. Lazenby said. "Three groups are doing splendid work—the banks under a committee headed by William J. McWilliams, the women's organization under a committee headed by Mrs. L. Warrington Carr and the block leaders under a committee headed by Mrs. Olga Plunder."

Sicilian Questioned

Desario Birancati, former vice prefect of Catania, Sicily, gestures during questioning by Allied forces which occupied the east coast port.

CAPITAL-GAZETTE THANKED FOR AID TO NAVY

Officer In Charge Of Recruiting Expresses Appreciation

Lieut. H. R. Stone, USNR, Officer in Charge of Navy Recruiting in Maryland, today expressed his appreciation of the cooperation of The Capital-Gazette Press, Inc. in securing recruits for the Navy and WAVES.

A recruiting office was opened in the Capital-Gazette Press offices, 3 Church Circle, long before Pearl Harbor and many men were enlisted. After war was declared there was a rush of enlistments and many of those who joined the Navy then have seen action.

Recently the recruiting office was opened with stress placed on the enlistment of WAVES, Seabees and 17-year-old youths.

The Capital-Gazette Press effort has been recognized by high ranking officials in the Navy Department, including Secretary of the Navy Frank Knox.

Received Citations

The Evening Capital, The Maryland Gazette, newspapers, and The U. S. Coast Guard Magazine, monthly magazine publication, all published by The Capital-Gazette Press, Inc., all have already received citations for their contributions to the war effort.

Lieutenant Stone wrote to Frank

(Continued On Page Two)

MRS. GLADYS G. SMITH NOMINATED TO HEAD LEGION AUXILIARY UNIT

Mrs. Gladys G. Smith, of Pasadena was nominated for president of the Guy Carleton Parlett Unit No. 7 of the American Legion Auxiliary last night at the regular meeting held in the Old Treasury Building.

Other officers nominated were: Mrs. Lydia Wilson, vice-president; Mrs. Helene White, second vice-president; Mrs. Helen Reed, treasurer; Mrs. Bertie Brandenburg, historian; Mrs. Minnie Gelhaus, chaplain; and Mrs. Anita Phillips, sergeant-at-arms.

The election will be held at the next regular meeting, Tuesday, October 5.

Mrs. E. F. L'Aigle, president, spoke on the recent State Convention held in Baltimore, when Mrs. Warren W. Boulden was elected Departmental President for the coming year. Mrs. Maybelle Lewis, a member of the local Unit, was elected Department Treasurer, and was presented with an orchid corsage by her Unit. Mrs. Lillie French, a page at the convention, presented the gift, and also a corsage to Mrs. Gladys Freeman of Greenbelt Unit, who was elected vice-president of Southern Maryland District, on behalf of Guy Carleton Post Unit.

Mrs. Gelhaus, Unit chaplain, received a service pin from the Department Chaplain, for the best report of activities in the State. Mrs. Gladys Smith and Mrs. White acted as color bearers. Mrs. Russell B. Howell, vice-president of the Eastern Division, was an honor guest at the convention, and said she had attended recently conventions in New York, New Jersey and Pennsylvania, but she had never witnessed a display of colors, nor a processional to compare with Maryland.

War Bond Benefit Play To Be Held At USO Saturday

Change Of Halls Announced For "Slice The Ham Thin" By Johns Hopkins Group

The comedy "Slice the Ham Thin," the first benefit affair for the Third War Bond drive to be given under the auspices of the Women's Division of the Anne Arundel War Bond Committee, which was to have been staged at the Annapolis High School auditorium Saturday night, will be held instead in the USO hall, St. Mary's street, it was announced today.

The comedy, laid in Annapolis, will be produced by the Playshop of the Johns Hopkins University which has put on many successful performances for war bond sales in Baltimore and elsewhere. Tickets to the play will cost one war bond, and may be obtained at any bond selling agency.

Committee In Charge

Saturday night's play is under the management of the "blue" section of the Women's Division. Mrs. Fred C. Thompson, regent of the Catholic Daughters of America, is chairman, and her committee includes the following members of the C.D.A.: Mrs. Henry Eiring, Mrs. James Costello, Mrs. Bernard Vallandingham, Mrs. Frank Wiegard, Mrs. Charles Sherman, Mrs. Robert Meinhold, Mrs. Charles Treadway, Mrs. John Connell, Mrs. Theodore Brady.

New First Zone Wardens Are Announced

Reorganization Plan Explained By Henry F. Sturdy At Meeting Last Night

Air raid wardens of the First Zone who recently completed the air raid course given by Civilian Defense instructors, were assigned posts last night at a reorganization meeting held in McDowell Hall, St. John's College.

The reorganization plan was explained by Henry F. Sturdy, Deputy Chief Zone Warden for the 2nd and 6th Districts, and air raid rules were discussed by the wardens with the new zone warden, John S. Kieffer, who presided at the meeting.

The new air raid organization for the First Zone, as announced by Mr. Sturdy, follows:

Wardens Announced

John S. Kieffer, Zone Warden, 245 Prince George street; Charles Crandall, Deputy Zone Warden, 50 State Circle.

Sector 1—Sector limits: St. John's campus, Bloomsbury Square, St. John's street, west side of College avenue to Bladen street.

Sector Warden, Lewis Hammond, St. John's College; senior warden, Franz Plunder, St. John's College; wardens: Scott Buchanan, 248 King George st.; Victor E. Barton, Carl H. Bruggman, Samuel B. Bird, Jr., George Brunn, John Brunn, Tristram J. Campbell, Thomas I. Fulton, John P. Gilbert, Allen Harvey, William Ross, all students at St. John's College.

Sector Two

Sector 2—Sector limits, College

(Continued On Page Six)

"NIGHT IN HAWAII" THEME OF USO DANCE TOMORROW NIGHT

A night in Hawaii, before Pearl Harbor, will be the theme of a special dance for service men of Annapolis and Fort Meade to be held at the USO Club tomorrow night.

Members of the Girls' Service Organization have worked liked beavers to transform the "upper deck" of the club into a Hawaiian paradise, and during the intermission Mrs. Katherine Campbell, former member of the Metropolitan Opera Ballet, will perform a hula dance. Even the refreshments will have a Hawaiian flavor.

The Harmonettes, an all-girl band from Baltimore, will play. GSO girls, new guest card girls and senior hostesses will act as social partners. Service men wishing to bring a guest should apply before the dance to Mrs. Samuel G. Walker, associate USO director, and ask for an admission card for this event. Only girls with proper credentials are admitted to dances.

MacArthur Directing Chute Attack

Gen. Douglas MacArthur looks out the gun port of a Flying Fortress to watch paratroopers dropping into the Markham valley to bottle up Jap forces in the Lae-Salamaua sector of New Guinea. (Picture by Signal Corps radio)

Power Squadron Plans New Class

Advanced Piloting Course To Start On September 13

The Annapolis Power Squadron will start a new class in advanced piloting on September 13 at 7:45 P. M. at the Annapolis Yacht Club. The course is open to all Power Squadron members who have received the rating of Pilot.

The Squadron plans to begin another elementary class this coming winter and notice of the time will be duly announced. This class will be open to the public and for which there is no charge other than material and books required for the course.

The Advanced Piloting Class is second year work of a four year course in navigation and piloting. From the point of view of the small boat operator, the A.P. course is probably the most immediate practical and interesting of the advanced courses, for most of its content can be put into practice aboard small boats.

Study is concentrated on charts the compass and its errors, tide and current tables, aids to navigation, current sailing, and methods of fixing positions by angles, bearings and soundings.

The United States Power Squadron was organized Feb. 2, 1914. Its stated purpose was and is to establish a high standard of skill in the handling and navigation of yachts, to encourage a study of the science of navigation, to cooperate with the agencies of the government charged with the enforce-

(Continued On Page Two)

NAVY SEEKS MORE WAVES

Recruiting Officer Will Be Here Tomorrow

Seeking more WAVES to join those already serving in the Navy, a recruiting officer will be at The Capital-Gazette Press offices, 3 Church Circle, tomorrow and every Thursday from 9 A. M. until 5 P. M.

Although placing stress on the recruiting of WAVES, the Navy also desires men with construction experience for service in the

(Continued On Page Two)

PROCLAMATION

Our government is asking Americans for $15,000,000,000 more in the 3rd War Loan to back the attack. Citizens of Annapolis will do their part in this tremendous task. All of us, no matter what walk of life we come from, are fully aware of the urgency of putting our full weight back of the invasion.

There is an intimate note back of the Third War Loan Appeal: Back the Attack With WAR BONDS. From this community come many young Americans who are doing the attacking. We would not be worthy of them and their sacrifice if we did not lend every dollar possible to our government to keep the munitions of war flowing to our fighting men.

September 9, the date set for the start of the Third War Loan Campaign, should be observed as another stepping stone toward V-day and the day when our boys come marching home.

I know I am echoing the feeling of everyone in Annapolis when I ask that the flag be displayed over all municipal buildings on September 9. I urge a similar display over all private buildings and by all homes. When we look at the Stars and Stripes on September 9, I know that all of us will be stimulated to do our duty in backing up our sons and neighbors' sons who are fighting to keep Old Glory flying. I know this community-wide display of the Star-Spangled Banner will stir us anew to do our very best as individuals and as a community in the Third War Loan Campaign to help subscribe and over-subscribe this home front objective.

Given under My Hand this 8th day of September in the year Nineteen Hundred and Forty-three.

WILLIAM U. McCREADY, Mayor.

(SEAL)

Attest:
Katherine E. Linthicum.

CARD OF THANKS

We wish to thank our friends for their kindness to us during the sickness and death of Percy Payne, for their expression of sympathy, the lovely flowers and for the use of their cars.

His wife Marcelena Payne and family

NAVY TEAM HOLDS LIGHT GRID PRACTICE

Some Players Have Colds And Injuries

The heavy downpour of rain which churned the football field into mud held the Navy football squad to light offensive and defensive drills yesterday in preparation for the crucial clash with Notre Dame.

Capt. John E. Whelchel, Navy's head coach, had other worries in addition to the weather — colds and injuries affecting several members of the Navy squad.

He refused to name the players, stating: "I won't do it. We'll just hope they recover quickly, and we'll have to take our chances on that."

45 To Make Trip

The Navy coach, however, said he had hopes that some of the sick or hurt players would be able to make the trip to Cleveland to meet the Fighting Irish.

The program calls for taking 45 members of the football squad to Cleveland, this figure being dependent upon whether the sick or injured members recover in time. The westward trip time, right now, is in the nature of a military secret, and has not been announced.

The big job facing Captain Whelchel is to spark up the Navy team so that it will start fast and not drag as in the last few games. If a team like Notre Dame gets the jump in the opening period the Middies will likely spend the rest of the day trying to catch up.

Battle Of Lines

Despite all the publicity going to the forward passing attack, the game Saturday will likely resolve itself into a battle of lines. A passer cannot function if the opposing line is charging through riding the ball back to him.

Navy's line appears to be just as big and tough as Notre Dame's, and upon the Navy linemen's ability to stop fast-breaking plays and to rush the passer may depend a national championship.

The Associated Press survey of the week puts Ben Chase of Navy among five linemen who were outstanding on the nation's college teams in Saturday's games. Navy coaches, according to the Associated Press story, declared Chase played the best of any Navy lineman against Georgia Tech, his defensive play keping the Engineers from upsetting the Middies.

Ed Sprinkle, Navy tackle, was another lineman singled out for praise.

Game Sellout

The outstanding linemen in Saturday's games were listed as Chase; Damon Tassos, Texas Aggies; Bill Ward, Washington; Bill Willis, Ohio State and Buddy Gatewood, Tulane.

The Navy-Notre Dame game was reported sold out several days ago. It will start at 2 P. M. in the Cleveland Municipal Stadium that seats more than 81,000 spectators.

The probable lineups:

Navy		Notre Dame
Channell	L.E.	Kuffel
Brown	L.T.	White
Whitmire	L.G.	Filley
Martin, J.	C.	Coleman
Chase	R.G.	Signaigo
Sprinkle	R.T.	Czarobski
Johnston	R.E.	Yonaker
Nelson	Q.B.	Bertelli
Hamberg	L.H.	Miller
Martin, B.	R.H.	Rykovich
Hume	F.B.	Mello

Sports Round-Up

By HUGH FULLERTON, JR.

NEW YORK, Oct. (AP)—The hoss racing industry, which is so big that a million bucks is hardly more than small change, seems to be all tangled up in a two-bit problem .. At least, that's the impression we get from reports of a meeting of racing secretaries from all the big tracks to consider the "claiming problem" .... The problem seems to be how to run a $2.000 horse in a $1,250 claiming race without having him claimed ...The hoss owners howl every time they lose a horse by running him for less than they think he's worth and they howl when the racing secretaries try to substitute graded handicaps or some other different method of classification ... The two-buck bettors, who don't care whether a horse is claimed or not so long as he wins some dough for them, also howl at times, so why not ignore the owners' yelps just like those of the ers? ... Racing is a howling success, anyway.

Quote, Unquote

Coach Lou Oshins of Brooklyn College (trying to keep a straight face at the football writers' lunch): "No doubt those two scrimmages the Dodgers had against our 'T' formation last week helped them make that fine showing against the Bears."

One-Minute Sports Page

The Penn State publicity department reports that transportation difficulties forced its football team to make all its trips by automobile this fall ... Yet in some towns you can't even take a taxi to a football field ... When movie director William Berke wanted a boxer for a bit in one of his pictures, he needed only to turn to his assistant cameraman, Art Lasky, a former top-flight heavyweight .... When Tulsa U. handed Utah that awful walloping Saturday, it marked the first time in Ike Armstrong's 19 seasons as Utah coach that he had lost four games in a row ... Since an Army doctor yanked out his appendix, little Roy Phillips, former Tufts U. distance runner, has decided that was what bothered him every time he ran for seven months. Roy always had figured that if Greg Rice could keep running, he wasn't going to be stopped by a few cramps.

Down in Oklahoma, reports Harold Keith, they're calling coach Henry Frank of Tulsa U. "The Alexander De Seversky of the football skyways" ... Get it? Air power ... And in England, says Schubert Dyche, ex-Montana State grid coach who now is a Red Cross supervisor, the kids call baseball "rounders gone mad."

Service Dept.

With no danger of a manpower shortage, the "Lily Bowl" football game is scheduled to be played in Bermuda, Jan. 2. Between the Army and Navy units stationed there. Uniforms have been donated by Fordham ... Pvt. Clarence Hewgley, Jr., of Keesler Field, Miss., has fought in the ring only three times but he won two championships. His first brought him the title in the Nashville, Tenn., golden gloves tournament and two bouts were all he needed to win the heavyweight crown at Keesler ... Overshadowed by the regular Norfolk Naval Training Station team during the regular season, chief specialist C. F. Burbanks' naval station All Stars won 33 games and lost eight against the strongest negro teams in the district ... A/C Artie Dorrell, who had plenty of words writtten about him when he was fighting hereabouts, is author of a piece in the post paper at the San Antonio Aviation Cadet Center. The subject is Otis Brandau, former Tennessee footballer.

NAVY'S FIGHTING CHIEFS

HIGH COMMAND: VA. R. R. Waesche, Coast Guard; VA. R. S. Edwards, Chief of Staff; Adm. E. J. King, Commander-in-Chief; VA. F. J. Horne, V. Chief Operations; Lt. Gen. T. Holcomb, Marine Corps

ATLANTIC OCEAN: Adm. H. R. Stark, Forces in Europe; Adm. R. Ingersoll, Atlantic Fleet

ATLANTIC FLEET: VA. H. K. Hewitt, Mediterranean; RA. P. L. Bellinger, Atlantic Air Force

PACIFIC OCEAN: VA. J. H. Ingram, S. Atlantic Forces; Adm. C. Nimitz, Pacific Fleet; Adm. W. Halsey, S. Pacific Area; VA. J. H. Towers, Pacific Air Force; VA. A. Carpender, S. Pacific Forces; VA. T. Kinkaid, N. Pacific Forces

AP Features

THESE are the 15 top men who rule the seven seas for Uncle Sam—five admirals, eight vice-admirals, one rear admiral and one lieutenant-general. On this Navy Day, Oct. 27, they direct the mightiest sea-going force the world has ever seen. The pictures identify them by rank and tell in what zones or operations they command. (VA stands for vice-admiral, RA, rear admiral.)

Around The Radio Dial

WITH	1230k
WOR—M. B. S. Key	710k
WABC—C. B. S. Key	860k
WEAF—N. B. C. Red Key	660k
WJZ—Blue Key	[illegible]
WBAL	1090k
WFBR	1300k
WCBM	1400k
WCAO	600k

NEW YORK, Oct. 27 (AP)—Notre Dame playing the two service teams will comprise the bulk of network football broadcasting for the next two Saturday afternoons. NBC, CBS and the BLU, each will have its gridiron expert present with a handy microphone.

This Saturday's game with Navy is coming from Cleveland with a 2:45 P. M. start, followed on November 6 from New York with the Army contest.

The MBS network will put on the Army-Penn clash this week-end at 1:45.

Sen. Claude R. Pepper of Florida, speaking on "The U. S. And The Post-War World," has been scheduled for NBC at 7:30 tonight ... Absent one broadcast because of the death of his mother, Edgar Bergen, with his Charlie McCarthy, will resume broadcasting from Hollywood on NBC Sunday night.

On the air tonight: NBC—7 Fred Waring; 8 Mr. and Mrs. North; 8:30 Beat The Band Quiz; 9 Eddie Cantor and Betty Hutton; 9:30 District Attorney; 10 Kay Kyser hour; 12:30 Navy Day program, Corpus Christi, Tex.

CBS—7:15 Harry James Band; 8 Red Barber, Sammy Kaye; 8:30 Dr. Christian starts seventh year; 9 [illegible] Barrymore, Mayor; 9:30 [illegible] Show; 10:30 Morton Gould Carnival.

BLU—7:05 The Falcon; 7:30 Lone Ranger; 8:30 Battles of Sexes; 9 Bandwagon and Freddy Martin; 9:30 Ray Andrade Band from Pearl Harbor; 10:30 Vice President Wallace on "Food For Victory and Jobs for Peace."

MBS—7:30 Hal McIntyre Orchestra; 8:30 Return of Murder Clinic dramas; 9:30 Sec. Knox in Navy Day address from Philadelphia; 11:15 Sen. Alexander Wiley on "Five Imperatives."

5:00
WCAO: "Fun with Dunn".
WFBR—News; Race Results.
WBAL: When a Girl Marries.
WCBM: Hop Harrigan.
WITH: News; Sports Special

5:15
WCAO: Bob Iula's Orchestra.
WFBR: The Black Hood.
WBAL: Portia Faces Life.
WCBM: Dick Tracy.

5:30
WFBR: Chick Carter, boy detective.
WBAL: Jus' Plain Bill.
WCBM: Jack Armstrong.

5:45
WCAO: American Women.
WFBR; Superman.
WBAL: Front Page Farrell.
WCBM: Captain Midnite.

6:00
WCAO: Quincy Howe, news.
WFBR: Dinner Rhythm.
WBAL: News; Sports Parade.
WCBM: Terry and the Pirates.
WITH: News; Twilight Tunes.

6:15
WCAO: Sports, Don Riley; News.
WFBR: Sports, Stewart Kennard.
WBAL: Around the Dinner Table.
WCBM: Talk; Eddie Fenton's Sports.
WITH: Adventures of Jimmy Allen.

6:30
WCAO: Sons of the Pioneers.
WFBR: WFBR new service.
WBAL: The Texas Rangers.
WCBM: Carroll Dulaney.
WITH: A. P. News.

6:40
WBAL: Songs Of Romance

6:45
WCAO: *The World Today.
WFBR: Velvet Strings.
WBAL—Lowell Thomas.
WCBM: Places in the News.
WITH: Harmony Caravan.

6:55
WCAO: Joseph C. Harsch, news.

7:00
WCAO: "I Love a Mystery."
WFBR: Fulton Lewis, Jr., news.
WBAL: ‡Fred Waring's Orchestra.
WCBM: Orch.; Adventures of Falcon
WITH: News; Enjoyment Time.

7:15
WCAO: Harry James' Orchestra.
WFBR: Songs of Yesterday.
WBAL: ‡News of the World.

7:30
WCAO: Easy Aces.
WFBR: Quiz of Two Cities.
WBAL: Roll of Honor.
WCBM: The Lone Ranger.
WITH: Swing Class.

7:45
WCAO: Mr. Keene.
WBAL: H. V. Kaltenborn.

8:00
WCAO: Sammy Kay's Orchestra.
WFBR: Sizing Up the News.
WBAL: Mr. and Mrs. North.
WCBM: Earl Godwin, news.
WITH: News Phonaway ,Jackpot.

8:15
WFBR: "Impact."
WCBM: Lum and Abner.
WITH: Good Listening.

8:30
WCAO: *"Dr. Christian": News.
WFBR: The Murder Clinic.
WBAL: Beat The Band.
WCBM: Battle of the Sexes.
WITH: Bing Crosby Sings.

8:45
WITH: Red Cross Show.

8:55
WCAO: Bill Henry.

9:00
WCAO: The Mayor of The Town.
WFBR: Gabriel Heatter, News.
WBAL: Eddie Cantor.
WCBM: Bandwagon.
WITH: News; Velvet Tunes.

9:15
WFBR: Gracie Field's Orch.
WITH: Symphony Hall.

9:30
WCAO: Jack Carson Show.
WFBR: Soldiers With Wings.
WBAL: Mr. District Attorney.
WCBM: Spotlight Bands.

10:00
WCAO: *Great Moments in Music.
WFBR: John B. Hughes, news.
WBAL: ‡Kay Kyser's Musical Knowledge.
WCBM: Raymond Gram Swing, News.
WITH: News; Time to Relax.

10:15
WFBR: Invitation to the Waltz.
WCBM: Listen to Lulu.
WITH: Moonlight Rhythm.

10:30
WCAO: Musical Carnival.
WFBR: The Symphonettes.
WCBM: Natl. Radio Forum.
WITH: Time for the News.

10:45
WITH: Boogy-Woogy Time.

11:00
WCAO: News; Wm .L. Shirer
WFBR: News; Race Results.
WBAL: News; Sports Parade.
WCBM: WCBM News.
WITH: News; Dave Rose.

11:15
WCAO: Jack Mayo's Orchestra.
WFBR: Tick-Tock Tunes.
WBAL: The Open Bible.
WCBM: Henry J. Taylor.
WITH: Jubilee Time.

11:30
WCAO: Invitation to Music.
WFBR: Guy Lombardo's Orchestra.
WCBM: The Music You Want.
WITH: Wax Works.

11:45
WBAL: Hasten the Day.
WITH: Songs For Victory.

12:00
WCAO: News; WCAO Nocturne.
WBAL: News; What's Playing.
WFBR: News; Sign Off.
WCBM: Tommy Dorsey.
WITH: News; Songs We All Remember.
WCBM—Glen Gray's Orch.

12:30
WCAO: Les Brown's Orchestra.

12:10
WBAL: All-Night Star Parade.

HI-Y CLUB WILL MEET SATURDAY

The regular meeting of the Annapolis Hi-Y Club will be held at 8 P. M. Saturday in the USO Club, St. Mary's street.

On Nov. 5 the club will hold an induction ceremony when 12 new boys will be taken into the club. All are from the three upper classes at the Annapolis High School.

Following the induction the club will hold its first dance of the school year. The dance will be held in the USO Club from 9 A. M. until midnight. Members of the club will begin selling tickets late this week.

Bob Muth is president of the club, and Jimmy Williams is chaplain.

TALL SOLDIER AT FORT MEADE

Army regulations say that anyone over six feet six inches in height can't join up, but John Clayton Sherrill, of York, Pa., is living proof that there are exceptions to that rule too.

Sherrill, all six-feet seven and one-half of him, made five tries over a period of nearly four years before the army finally waived the rule and allowed him in.

Now he's at Fort Meade, and looking strictly G. I., too. Authorities had told him he was too tall and that there wasn't uniforms to fit him, but within one hour after the quartermasters started throwing clothing at him he had lost all appearance of a civilian.

The largest of everything did the trick.

The Chinese word for spinach is "putsai," meaning ::the vegetable imported from Persia."

BRITAIN HAS GIVEN AMERICANS $1,174,900,000 IN LEND LEASE

President Roosevelt Files Report On Reverse Lend Lease With Congress

WASHINGTON, Nov. 11 (AP)—Congress received from President Roosevelt today a report that the British Commonwealth, through last June, had contributed $1,174,-900,000 "to the defense of the United States" through lend-lease in reverse.

The help from the Empire, in reciprocity for upwards of $5,-500,000,000 in lend-lease supplies from the United States, covered such varied items as corn-on-the-cob and socks, plane repair shops and boxing gloves.

Most of it came from the British Isles, whose total was $871,-000,000. Airports, barracks, hospitals and similar facilities for American air and land forces accounted for $371,000,000 of Britain's share, goods and services for $331,000,000 and shipping for $169,000,000.

Incomplete Accounting

The figures represent an incomplete accounting. For instance, he said, many supplies and services have been made available by the British to United States forces in North Africa, Sicily and elsewhere for which no report has been received.

Nor do they take into account anticipated exports of raw materials, commodities and foodstuffs for the account of the United States. Previously this country purchased these things, the President said, but the United Kingdom agreed last summer to put them on the basis of reverse lend-lease.

Now, without paying for them, the chief executive said, the United States will get such items as rubber from Ceylon, Trinidad, British Guiana and British Honduras, sisal and pyrethrum from British East Africa, asbestos and chrome from Southern Rhodesia, cocoa from British West Africa, tea and coconut oil from Ceylon, and benzol and tar acids from the United Kingdom.

Mayor McCready

(Continued From Page One)

ance coverage was adopted in this period than had been had in any preceding period.

Street Program

10—Our street program resulted in the following:

"The following streets have been newly graded and paved:

Granada avenue from Chase avenue to Archwood street.

Pleasant street from Clay street southerly to the railroad property.

Cheston avenue from Franklin street to within 50 feet of Spa creek.

Steele avenue from Colonial avenue to Monticello avenue.

Compromise street in front of the USO Building was made wider.

St. John's street from the southerly side of Calvert northerly along side part of Bloomsbury Square Housing development.

"The following streets have been given bituminous surface treatment:

Franklin street from Southgate avenue to Cathedral street.

Southgate avenue from Franklin street to Lafayette avenue, including both intersections.

Monticello avenue from the northerly side of Stehle street to Steele avenue.

South street from Cathedral street to Shaw street, including the latter intersection.

Charles street from Cathedral street to Shaw street, including the latter intersection.

Shaw street from Charles street to South street.

St. Mary's street from Compromise street to Duke of Gloucester street.

Obery street from Clay street to the railroad property.

Bates avenue from the southerly side of Stehle street to Academy street.

Brooke street throughout.

Colonial avenue from Southgate avenue to Steele avenue.

11—We plan to schedule all

WAR

(Continued From Page One)

and trucks. Rain, cold and fog failed to check the Russian momentum. In the Crimea, Red Marines repelled German tanks near Kerch, killed thousands and captured prisoners. Moscow said the Fourth Ukrainian army was massing at the north of the Crimea for a decisive smash. In the Nevel area of the frozen north, further gains were made within 50 miles of Latvia.

Reporting to Commons on the Moscow conference, Foreign Secretary Anthony Eden said it exceeded his hopes and "brought a new wealth and new confidence into all our dealings with our Soviet and American friends."

The Chancellor of the Exchequer, Sir John Anderson, said lease-lend "has ceased to flow in one direction only and has become a system of mutual aid."

Southwest Pacific

Powerful new reinforcements landed to support U. S. Marines invading Bougainville Island in the southwest Pacific. The tide of the jungle battle swung definitely to the Americans. "Our Bougainville operations were successful beyond our fondest expectations," Rear Admiral Robert Carney declared. Not a single U. S. ship has ben sunk, despite Japanese claims of destroying 96 including four battleships. Three U. S. destroyers announced lost by the Navy were sunk in other operations. In the Pacific air, Allied planes tumbled 67 more Japanese planes.

It was Armistice Day, but virtually nowhere in the turbulent world were men at peace.

Berlin, broadcast a Tokyo dispatch, said that a "third great aerial battle took place off Bougainville" and declared "an embittered battle is being waged between units of the Japanese fleet and American army formations."

An official Navy Department spokesman said the American fleet in the Pacific has lost no warships in at least two weeks. He said all sinkings had been announced.

Reuters reported a state of martial law in Lebanon on order of the French Committee of National Liberation.

Navy Squad Leaves Friday For New York

Will Hold Stiff Workout Before Meeting Columbia

A number of colds among the members of the Navy football team limited scrimmage yesterday to line workouts with a long practice slated for today.

The Middies will leave Annapolis, at noon tomorrow, for New York to challenge Columbia University on Saturday, athletic officials announced. The Midshipmen will not accompany the gridiron warriors of the academy to New York due to lack of transportation facilities.

No injuries were reported by Navy coaches among the Tars and they expect to have a full squad on hand for the game with Coach Lou Little's Lions.

Lions Lead Series

Navy and Columbia have played a total of 12 games with Columbia leading by six wins. Navy has won five games. One ended in a tie.

Columbia, with one of its weakest teams, has been defeated by Princeton, Yale, Army, Pennsylvania, Cornell and Dartmouth. They lost to Army 52 to 0, dropped a game to Pennsylvania 33 to 0, and were turned back by Cornell, 33 to 6.

Respect Little

Despite this record Navy coaches are taking no chances, remembering other years when a weak Columbia team has caused considerable trouble in their clash with the Midshipmen. Neither do they underrate the coaching ability of Lou Little. In addition the Columbia lineup has recently been strengthened by several V-12 Navy reserve players.

The game will start at 2:30 P. M.

The probable lineup:

Navy		Columbia
Channell	L.E.	Rock
Whitmire	L.T.	Caplis
Brown	L.G.	Kaledo
Martin, J.	C.	Allen
Chase	R.G.	Politi
Sprinkle	R.T.	McVicar
Johnston	R.E.	Gilbert
Nelson	Q.B.	Moran
Hamberg	L.H.	Gehrke
Martin, B.	R.H.	Arden
Hume	F.B.	Apel

Referee: S. H. Giangreco (Manhattan). Umpire: P. L. Meagan (Villanova). Linesman: A. Young (Pennsylvania). Field Judge; C. M. Waters (Williams). Clock Operator: C. A. Reed (Springfield).

Commissioners

(Continued From Page Twenty-e)

Treasurer and County Commissioners of Anne Arundel county to Scott Street Loan and Savings Association No. 1 of Baltimore, conveying 0.422 acres at Ridgeway in the Fourth Election District.

From same to Scott Street Loan and Savings Association No. 1 of Baltimore, conveying 2 1/4 at Mayfield in the Fourth Election District.

From same to Thomas J. F. Redmiles, conveying 5.73 acres of land in Mayfield in the Fourth Election District.

From James A. Walton, Treas-

urer and County Commissioners of Anne Arundel County to Lurty C. Lloyd and Virginia R. Lloyd, his wife, conveying lots Nos. 2978 and 2979 as designated on the plat of Woodland Beach in the First Election District.

From same to Lurty G. Lloyd and Virginia R. Lloyd, his wife, conveying Lots Nos. 1935, 1936 and 1937 of Woodland Beach in the First Election District.

From same to Lawrence L. Merrill and Ethel Merrill, his wife, conveying one lot 50x140 on the corner of Monticello avenue and Brooks street; lot number seven Brooks street and one-half of lot number eleven on Brook street, 31.47x100 in the Sixth Election District.

From County Commissioner of Anne Arundel county to Vincent Brosh, conveying five acres more or less in the Third Election District.

From same to Willie Stovall and Jennie Stovall, his wife, conveying lots 28, 29, 30, 76, 77, 78 and 79 as shown on a plat of Centralia in the Fourth Election District.

From same to William P. Byrd and Olevia M. Byrd, his wife, conveying lots numbered 38, 39, 42 and 43 all in Secton 0 as shown on a Plat of Orchard Beach in the Third Election District.

Commissioner Leatherbury moved, seconded by Commissioner Hutchins, that the board recess and sit as District Council.

Erosion Reports

The Commissioner checked all bills pertaining to erosion projects and those found correct were approved for payment.

All investigation reports submitted by the committees following appraisal of the erosion bulkheads at Arundel-on-the-Bay and Bay Ridge in the Second District; Gibson Island, Riviera Beach and Tydings-on-the-Bay in the Third District; Franklin Manor Beach, Idlewilde, Cedarhurst and Mason's Beach in the Seventh District and North Beach Park and Fairhaven in the Eighth District, were approved and filed.

It was moved by Commissioner Duvall, seconded by Commissioner Frank, that the District Council adjourn and the board convene in regular session.

Chief John H. Souers, of the County Police Department, presented specifications on two new cars for one 1942 Plymouth D.T. Sedan for use of the department and requested bids be asked for. The clerk was authorized to advertise for bids.

The board adjourned to meet on Tuesday

JAPS TRY BOUGAINVILLE "SQUEEZE"

Map shows how Japanese forces are attempting a "squeeze play" on U. S. Marines who landed on Bougainville Island in the Solomons. The featherness established a beach head in the Cape Torokina area. Heavy fighting was reported in progress. Inset map locates Bougainville (A).

"AROUND THE CLOCK" SPORTS IN A WAR PLANT

There's something in the way of sports on all the time at the Goodyear Aircraft Corporation plant in Akron, Ohio, where some 30,000 men and women produce blimps and fighter planes.

Around The Radio Dial Tonight

WITH	1230k
WOR—M. B. S. Key	710k
WABC—C. B. S. Key	860k
WEAF—N. B. C. Red Key	660k
WJZ—Blue Key	770k
WBAL	1090k
WFBR	1300k
WCBM	1400k
WCAO	600k

NEW YORK, Nov. 11 (AP)—Three games on four networks is the football fare for Saturday as the season draws near the close. Two chains, the BLU and MBS, will broadcast Notre Dame vs. Northwestern at Evanston, Ill.

The other games are divided: CBS Army vs. Sampson Naval Training at West Point and NBC Tulane vs. George Tech at New Orleans.

Intended to give young singers with talent a chance to go on a network, CBS at 9:45 A. M. Sunday is starting a weekly series as "New Voices in Song," with a different singer each time. To start things off it will be Steven Kennedy, baritone ... Roy Porter and Max Hill former war correspondents who since have turned radio commentators, are going back to their first love. Porter, who covered the earlier war days in Europe, and Hill, who was in Tokyo at the time of Pearl Harbor, will transfer their activities from the BLU to NBC. Porter goes to India and Hill to Turkey. Hill already has left the BLU, while Porter will do so later .... The MBS soldier Variety show from Ft. Dix will present its 150th broadcast Sunday afternoon. Tom Slater is the M. C.

Topics tonight: NBC—7:30 Bob Burns; 8 Fanny Brice; 9 Bob Crosby for Bing; 9:30 Joan Davis; 10 Abbott and Costello; 10:30 March of Time.

CBS—8 Mary Astor and others; 8:30 Death Valley Days; 9 Major Bowes amateurs; 9:30 Dinah Shore show; 10:30 Dick Haymes song.

BLU—7::05 House on Q Street; 7:30 Coast Guard dance; 8:30 America's Town Meeting "American British Economic Aims;" 9:30 Osborne Band; 10:30 Wings To Victory.

MBS—8 Better Half Quiz; 8:30 Human Adventure; 9:30 American Legion Armistice broadcast; 10:15 Dale Carnegie Lectures.

5:00

WFBR—News; Race Results.
WBAL: ‡When a Girl Marries.
WCBM: Hop Harrigan.
WITH: News of the Hour; Sports.

5:15

WCAO: Bob Iula's Orchestra.
WFBR: The Black Hood.
WBAL: ‡Portia Faces Life, drama.
WCBM: Dick Tracy.

5:30

WFBR: Chic Carter, Boy Dec.
WBAL: Just Plain Bill.
WCBM: Jack Armstrong.

5:45

WCAO: American Women.
WFBR: Adventures of Superman.
WBAL: Front Page Farrell.
WCBM: Captain Midnight.

6:00

WCAO: Ned Calmer-Major G. F. Eliot, news.
WFBR: Dinner Rhythms.
WBAL: News; Sports Parade.
WCBM: Terry and the Pirates.
WITH: News; Twilight Tunes.

6:15

WCAO: Sports, Don Riley; News.
WFBR: Sports, Stewart Kennard.
WBAL: Around the Dinner Table.
WCBM: Interlude; Eddie Fenton's Sport.
WITH: Adventures of Jimmy Allen.

6:30

WCAO: "To Your Good Health."
WFBR: WFBR News Service.
WBAL: Ranch Hands.
WCBM: Carroll Dulaney.
WITH: News Resume.

6:40

WBAL—Songs of Romance.

6:45

WCAO: The World Today.
WFBR: Velvet Strings.
WBAL—Lowell Thomas.
WCBM: Places in the News.
WITH: Harmony Caravan.

6:55

WCAO: Joseph C. Harsch, news.

7:00

WCAO: "I Love a Mystery."
WFBR: Fulton Lewis, Jr., news.
WBAL: ‡Fred Waring's Orchestra.
WCBM: The House on "Q" Street.
WITH: News; Enjoyment Time.

7:15

WCAO: Harry James' Orchestra.
WFBR: Invitation to Waltz.
WBAL: News of the World.

7:30

WCAO: Easy Aces.
WFBR: †Confidentially Yours.
WBAL: Bob Burns.
WCBM: Fighting Coast Guard Band.
WITH: Swing Class.

7:45

WCAO: Mr. Keen.
WFBR: Treasury Star Parade.

8:00

WCAO: Mary Astor, C. Ruggles, Mischa Auer.
WFBR: Community Fund Pro.
WBAL: Baby Snooks.
WCBM: "Watch the World Go By"
WITH: News; Phonaway Jackpot

8:15

WFBR: Your World Tonight.
WCBM: Lum and Abner.
WITH: Good Listening.

8:30

WCAO: Death Valley Days.
WFBR: Army, Navy "E" Award.
WBAL: Aldrich Family.
WCBM: Town Meeting of the Air.
WITH: Bing Crosby.

8:45

WITH: Red Cross Show.

8:55

WCAO: Bill Henry, News.

9:00

WCAO: *Major Bowes and His Amateurs.
WFBR—Gabriel Heatter, news.
WBAL: Bing Crosby.
WITH: News; Velvet Tunes.

9:15

WFBR: Grace Field's Show.
WITH: Symphony Hall.

9:30

WCAO: Dinah Shore.
WFBR: Armistice Day Program.
WBAL—Joan Davis, Jack Haley.
WCBM: Spotlight Bands.

9:55

WCBM: Listening Post.

10:00

WCAO: The First Line.
WFBR—Raymond Clapper; News.
WBAL: Abbott and Costello.
WCBM: Raymond Gram Swing, News.
WITH: News; Time to Relax.

10:15

WFBR: Little Known Facts.
WCBM: Listen To Lulu.
WITH: Stamp-A-Day.

10:30

WCAO: 'Here's to Romance.
WFBR: The Symphonettes.
WBAL: March of Time.
WCBM: Wings To Victory
WITH: Time for news

10:45

WITH: Boogy Woogy Special.

11:00

WCAO: News; Bob Trout.
WFBR: News; Race Results
WBAL: News; Sports Parade.
WCBM: Journal.
WITH: News; Wax Works.

11:15

WCAO: Jack Mayo's Orch.
WFBR: Tick Tock Tunes.
WBAL: The Open Bible.
WCBM: Commentator.
WITH: Jubilee Time.

11:30

WCAO: Raymond Scott's Orch.
WFBR: Guy Lombardo's Orchestra.
WCBM: The Music You Want.
WITH: Fred Walker Presents.

11:45

WBAL: Treasury Star Parade.
WFBR: Mal Hallet's Orchestra.
WITH: Songs For Victory.

12:00

WCAO: News; Noctnrne.
WFBR: News; Sign Off.
WCBM: Ray Heatherton's Orchestra.
WBAL: News; What's Playing.
WITH: News; Songs We All Remember.

Sports Round-Up

By HUGH FULLERTON, JR.

NEW YORK, Nov. 11 (AP)—Just when everything seemed peaceful, the furore about the major league baseball has broken loose again ... Fred (Newark News) Bendel came up with a story from a source we can't question saying that the 1944 model baseball will have a synthetic rubber core instead of balata, which is a kind of rubber anyway, but not a very popular kind last summer ... But National League prexy Ford Frick says he hasn't heard any discussion of the subject and it hasn't been listed as a topic at the major league meetings in December ... One sure thing is that minor leagues would like to have a livelier ball next season. They've missed those big batting and home run records that were very useful when it came to selling players.

Quote, Unquote

Frank Leahy, the tearful tutor of Notre Dame: "Every team that installs the T formation will do a lot of fumbling in the season. We did our fumbling last year."

One-Minute Sports Page

Latest dope on the proposed shift of the pro football playoff to Los Angeles (the Coliseum, not the Rose Bowl) is that the National League doesn't want to disappoint the fans but finds it hard to say no to the Army Air Force ... Rip Sewell was turned down by the Army after getting as far as the Camp Blanding, Fla., inducting center. His military career, it seems followed the same path as his famous blooper pitch ... Jackie Rocke, 17-year old son of the famous Notre Dame coach, is a star southpaw passer at Campion Academy, Prairie Du Chien, Wis., but he's ony a 140-pounder ... The British boardcasting will give the boys overseas a new kind of reveille on Nov. 20 by broadcasting the Beau Jack-Bob Montgomery fight at 8:55 A. M., British time.

Self Service

When coach Harold Clark of Holy Trinity High School at Trinidad, Colo., quit to join the Army Air Force, it looked as if football was out for the duration ... But 17 kids begged to play and the superintendent said okay ... The boys ran their own practices, arranged their own three-game schedule and won two out of three ... After losing 32-0 to the strong Florence team, they whipped their two traditional rivals, Holy Cross Abbey of Canon City and St. Mary's of Walsenberg by big scores ... wonder how the coach will rate when he comes back

Service Dept.

Lt. Col. "Jeenks" Gillem, former Sewanee and Birminghan-Southern grid coach, is in charge of special services of the Third Air Force in Florida ... Capt. Arthur Nehf, son of the old-time Giants' pitcher recently was appointed a Marine flight leader and was awarded the distinguished Flying Cross for his exploits over Guadalcanal after doctors had said he never would fly again because of an eye injury .... The Kearns Field, Utah, Eagles will go in for basketball this winter with a strong team. They're hoping to line up service court and boxing leagues, similar to the football setup, with teams from the Salt Lake Air Base, Fort Douglas, Bushnell Hospital, Logan Naval Training Station, Wendover Field, Hill Field and Camp Williams.

Mounting Moans

Coach Bob Higgins of Penn State puts in a claim for the season's hard-luck prize on this basis: (1) eight V-12 players declared ineligible before the season started; (2) a good Marine tackle was shipped out just for poking a fellow Marine; (3) 17 more Marines sent to boot camp in mid season; (4) his veteran fullback joined the Air Force and left the same day; (5) his best freshman back was lost because of injuries after two minutes of play, two good frosh prospects flunked out and three regulars were declared ineligible on the eve of the Cornell game and (6) to cap the climax, a premising frosh tackle borrowed a bicycle without brakes and ran smack into a delivery truck, ripping his leg open.

"THUMPING TAMI" ... by PAP'

DISCUSSING NOTRE DAME

Coach Lynn Waldorf (left) and Otto Graham (right), Northwestern's star halfback, get together for a bit of football plotting against unbeaten Notre Dame, whose eleven the Wildcats meet at Elvaton, Ill., next Saturday. With his passing, Graham is expected to be Northwestern's heavy threat. The Waukegan, Ill., gridder's record in that department shows 25 to 49 passes completed for 422 yards this season. (AP Wirephoto).

NAVY SOCCER TEAM DEFEATS SWARTHMORE, 5-1

The Navy soccer team crashed through to another victory yesterday afternoon over a hard-fighting Swarthmore team by a 5 to 1 score.

The Midshipmen took a 2 to 0 lead in the first period and were never stopped. Bill Schoeberlein, Johnny Swank and Bill Chaires sparked the Navy drive.

Swarthmore scored in the second frame when center forward Nicholson slipped through to drive one past Sam Gorsline, Navy goalie.

Art Calisto, Navy Plebe, scored two goals, one in the second and another in the fourth period.

Lineups:

Swarthmore	Pos.	Navy
McRory	G.	Gorsline
Sutor	R.F.	Eaton
Kaiser	L.F.	Reaves
Mikovsky	R.H.	Hall
Newitt..	C.H.	Chaires
Beck	L.H.	Lenschner
Deburlo	O.R.	Swank
Newberg	I.R.	Barnes
Nicholson	C.	Schoeberlein
Nunez	I.L.	Stewart
Mustin	O.L.	Bucknell

Swarthmore	0	1	0	0—1
Navy	2	2	0	1—5

Scoring: Swarthmore — Nicholson; Navy—Schoederlein, Swank, Stewart, Calisto (sub for Barnes), 2.

Substitutions: Swarthmore—Miller, Carson, Coates Mustin, Counsel; Navy — Calisto, Moul, Baldwin, Purkabeck, Demayo, Vander Wolk, Nicklas, Polk, Horgan, Griffin, Botts, Drake, Marousek, Allen, Rogers.

Sammy Baugh Shows How To Toss Record Passes

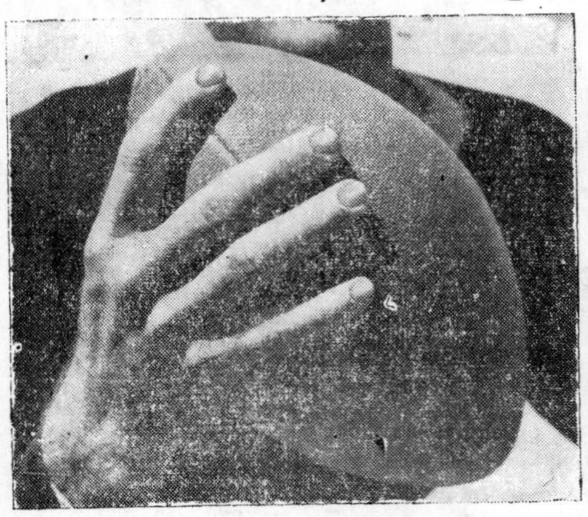

First, you grip the ball like this ...

And look for a receiver.

Ah, there he is waitiz.

So, you uncork the ball, and let it fly.

BAINBRIDGE CPO'S BOAST LONG SERVICE RECORD

If the "hash marks" of these Chief Petty Officers at the U. S. Naval Training Station, Bainbridge, Md., were laid end to end, the years they represent would reach back to the Revolutionary War. But you'd have to add in the ones which don't appear because there isn't room for all the service bars. The five veterans, each with more than a generation of service in the Navy, are (left to right): Chief Torpedoman Dennis B. Mahoney, Newcastle, Del., 41 years; Chief Turret Captain John J. Gray, Baltimore, 44 years; Chief Boatswain's Mate Frank E. McCurdy, Collingdale, Pa., 41 years; Bandmaster Wilbur J. Rasmussen, 43 years, and Chief Quartermaster Charles Krieg, 40 years. (Associated Press Photo from U. S. Navy)

Hitler Warns His New Spies Against G-Men

Counter Spy Work Reads Like Poe Story

Editor's Note: The reason why Axis spy and sabotage plots against the U. S. haven't succeeded is the FBI's system of "counter spies." Here's the story of how this war on nerves works.

By FRANK I. WELLER

WASHINGTON, Nov. 23 (AP)—Fear of the FBI counterspy caused Hitler to warn his new espionage-sabotage graduates . . . "Do not arouse suspicion of the G men! He doesn't want this gang to meet the fate of his early underground agents in the U.S.A.

German plans went into a tailspin when G-men secretly operated with Hitler's first spies and about all he got was a mess of misinformation. His agents had the dope all right, but it was FBI-doctored when it reached Germany and caused more harm than good.

It's almost an Edgar Allen Poe story the way G-men trapped 33 ranking members of the dangerous Frederick Duquesne spy ring in New York. J. Edgar Hoover says that never in espionage history did a country stand to lose more than this one.

All of Duquesne's crew were master spies. They were planted in war factories, shipyards, with-in the armed forces and in some government bureaus in Washington.

Had Data

They had details for firing ships, including the French liner Normandie (which later burned accidentally) accurate details on Chrysler tank production, airplane production, the Ford plants, defense plans of the Panama Canal, correct specifications on Sperry and Norden bombsight parts, and data on just about every war plant, communications center, American weapon, steel and munition production, convoys, and armed service training posts.

William Sebold, a German-born naturalized and loyal American citizen coerced into the Duquesne gang by the Gestapo, secretly kept G-men informed. Through him they set up a shortwave radio outfit to transmit reports to Germany . . . All of them fixed up by FBI.

Even Sebold didn't know FBI was making motion pictures and sound recordings of this interview with Nazi big-wigs.

One of the kingpins was the bald late-fortyish German Major Paul Borchardt from the last war who almost got into U. S. Army Intelligence.

Most Dangerous

Probably the most dangerous was Ulrich Von Der Osten who had worked for Hitler and Franco in Spain.

This reporter still jitters when G-men tell him that for eight days in 1941 he lived next door in a New York hotel to Von Der Osten. Well armed and ruthless, he was freehanded with good liquor, funny stories and midnight lunches and called himself Julio Lopez of Buenos Aires. I heard "Lopez" telephoning in German, Spanish and Italian after radio newscasts and once wondered aloud whether this polite, smallish, well-dressed and fiftyish gent could be a spy.

"Look, farm boy," my friend said, "people in New York often speak more than one language."

G-men had "Lopez," your correspondent and other Lopez neighbors spotted all the time.

FBI broke up a second spy plot when agents nabbed glamorous 34-year-old Grace Buchanan-Dineen, great-granddaughter of the last Count de Mun of Brittany, in Detroit and offered her jail or a job as counterspy.

Her gang had rounded up an amazing amount of fascist information on munitions and airplane factories, military and naval bases, helium gas, and the cargo and sailing date of convoys. All this she turned over secretly to FBI for "doctoring" and devious dispatch to Hitler.

Hitler His God

The Guyula Rozinek case is considered typical of hundreds of espionage-sabotage arrests. Rozinek was a captain in the German army but no one knew it in the West Coast Chemical plant that hired him. He miscued when a fellow worker badgered him into yelling:

"Hitler is my Fuehrer and my God! All Europe will be free when he wins."

J. Edgar Hoover says this FBI spying on spies is just like setting a rat trap. He baits it by pretending not to know anything about the spy and all the time secretly siphoning the danger out of his doings.

"Better," says he, "to deal with the devil you know than with the devil you don't know," meaning that a new spy might be harder to catch than the one who is known and can be picked up anytime.

Instead of swatting the hornet's nest with a single blow, the FBI collars spies one by one as they become dangerous. Authorities secretly maneuvered an excellent chemist convicted of espionage in 1917 from a Hitler-picked American war job into a place where he could be used to Allied advantage and do no harm. A German spy interned in Australia in the last war was shoved into work he could not molest.

Preventive Technique

G-men call his "preventive technique" and U. S. counter spy "war of nerves." ' In almost every instance a spy or saboteur is allowed to make his contacts, with FBI agents right beside him. Then the FBI hauls up the net and takes the whole gang.

Hoover arrested the head of Hitler's maritime spies as a "draft dodger." The Nazi had a swell chuckle about dumb cluck Americans until he finally found out why he was in jail. His buddies are there with him.

FBI captured an entire New York spy outfit by following one man all day with a motion picture truck. Sometimes a dozen G-men are on the heels of a single spy.

A tough customer tried to shake Hoover's men by threading Macy's department store, then Gimbels, Grand Central Station and the subway . . . But they were waiting

(Continued On Page Eight)

Rationing Calendar

FUEL OIL

Period 1 coupons of new ration valid through Jan. 3, 1944, worth 10 gallons per unit.

SHOES

Book No. 1 coupons 18 valid for indefinite period. Airplane coupon No. 1 in book No. 3 valid.

STOVES

Purchase certificates obtainable from Ration Board.

SUGAR

Coupon 29, book No. 4 now good for five pounds through Jan. 15.

TIRES, GASOLINE

First series of coupons in new A book, 8-A valid through Feb. 8.

Persons entitled to 601 miles per month gasoline rations are eligible for grade I tires, those entitled to 121 miles eligible for grade II tires.

C book holders must have tires inspected by Nov. 30.

MEAT, FATS, OIL, CHEESE, FISH

Brown coupons G, H, J and K valid through Dec. 4. Coupon L now valid, and M becoming valid on Nov. 28, both expire Jan. 1.

FRUITS AND VEGETABLES

Green A, B, C, stamps in ration book 4 valid through Dec. 20.

Maryland's Farm Front This Week

Newspaper advertising is being used by E. S. Valiant & Son, fertilizer dealers at Centreville, Md., and Lewis L. Dell, to urge cooperation by farmers with the Agricultural Adjustment Agency's program under which farmers are accepting soil conserving and soil-building payments in lieu of AAA cash payments. A supplemental appropriation of approximately $530,000 was recently given the Maryland AAA for the purchase of conservation materials to increase the State's yield of war foods.

War Boards Get Farm Deferments

State and County United States Department of Agriculture War Boards will negotiate future applications for draft deferment of farm labor in Maryland, Joseph H. Blandford, State War Board Chairman, announced today. The War Food Administration in Washington transferred this responsibility from the Agricultural Extension Service at the request of General Lewis B. Hershey, director of Selective Service. Until the Extension Service was given temporary jurisdiction early this month, the Selective Service acted in farm labor draft deferment cases upon the recommendation of special labor committees of the State and County USDA War Boards. P. C. Turner, Baltimore, is chairman of the State Labor Committee. To date more than 15,000 farm workers have been deferred in Maryland from military service.

Maryland now has fifteen statutory soil conservation districts serving sixteen of the State's twenty-three counties, according to Edward M. Davis, State coordinator of the Soil Conservation Service. Supervisors of the recently created fifteenth district in Garrett County are: John Beachy, Grantsville; Paul Friend, Oakland; Emerson Bishoff, Friendsville; Harry Porter, Oakland, and Foster Yost, Accident.

Soybean Meal For Livestock Feed

Livestock will be fed 90 percent of the 1943 output of soybean meal, Fred B. Sylvester, State AAA Committeeman, reported today. The War Food Administration has not set aside soybean meal for the manufacture of foods for human consumption.

Big '43 War Job For Maryland Farmers

Maryland's nationally-important crop of vegetables for processing is internationally important this year, according to Robert T. Williams, State AAA Committeeman.

Two-thirds of all the food a soldier eats in a war theater comes out of cans and Maryland farmers filled a large percentage of those cans this year. Military and war services will consume 20 percent of the nation's 1943 pack of canned vegetables.

Navy Earns Eastern Championship

NAVY FOOTBALL TEAM QUALIFIES AS ONE OF GREATEST DEVELOPED OVER YEARS AT NAVAL ACADEMY

Establishes Rank As One Of 10 Big Teams Of Nation—Rates Championship of Ivy League And Lambert Trophy—13 to 0 Win Over Army Establishes Record Of Five Straight Navy Victories —About 15,000 See Teams Clash In Michie Stadium At West Point

By RICHARD H. ELLIOTT

The Navy football team that ended an unusually successful season Saturday by defeating the Army, 13 to 0, before about 15,000 spectators and 13,000 empty seats in West Point's hilltop Michie stadium has fully earned its place as one of the few really great gridiron machines to be developed at the Naval Academy.

The team, coached by Capt. John Whelchel, not only stretched the Navy victories over Army to five in a row, but has won recognition as one of the ten leading football teams of the nation. Besides that, it nailed down its claim to the championship of the East, and in due course should win possession of the Lambert trophy which symbolizes the title.

IVY LEAGUE CROWN

By victories over Pennsylvania and Cornell it has established its right to the championship of the Ivy League, maintained intact the tradition that the Navy football team always wins when it plays at West Point, maintained the record of Navy teams is scoring two touchdowns on the Army for the fourth successive year and made the standing of the 44 service games, 19 won by Navy, 22 by Army, with three ties.

Navy has defeated the Army three times in a row in the past, in 1910-11-12 and again in 1919-20-21, but a string of five straight Navy wins sets an all time precedent. It is a precedent that may have reprecussions in the athletic setup of the Military Academy.

Army has the record of 10 games in a row over the midshipmen, during the period beginning in 1922 and running through 1933, with no games played in 1928 and 1929.

Hard Game

The midshipmen did not win their victory over Army Saturday easily. During the first half they were forced to battle every inch of the way against an aggressive, threatening Cadet team which was under pressure to break the Navy winning streak.

The West Pointers had slightly the better of the first quarter play in which both teams made four first downs. Navy only crossed midfield once in this period, moving to the Army 36 where a fumble stopped a march that had carried down field from the Navy 20 after a Cadet punt.

During the period the Army moved to the Navy 34, where a holding penalty intervened and again to the Navy 42 where a fumble and slashing play by Navy linemen stopped the march. In the period play the Army made a net of 68 yards passing and rushing, not counting punt runbacks totaling 25 yards, and lost 15 on the penalty. Navy turned in 50 yards net, rushing and passing, exclusive of 17 yards in punt runbacks.

The play was practically even during the second quarter with Navy getting to the Army 49 and West Point reaching the Middie 34 without a score. Army made three first downs during this period, one by penalty, one scored by Navy. The Army backs had a net gain of 37 yards, exclusive of a 10 yard punt return. Navy turned in a net gain of 13 yards for the quarter, and 18 yards punt return and dropped 5 yards in penalties.

Under Pressure

Throughout the period the midshipmen were under pressure of the threat of Army's fast backs, Glenn Davis, Carl Anderson, George Maxson and John Minor. It was only the fine play of the Navy line, wingmen and secondary defense that kept them in check.

Navy took over the game in the second half, and during the third period when it scored first, turned in two first downs while Army made none. Navy backs gained 71 yards passing and rushing and lost 15 on penalty. The Army ball carriers, on the other hand, failed to make any net yardage during the period, exclusive of 4 yards on two punt returns. They lost 32 yards by penalties.

The fourth period, when Army was hurling hopeful passes all over the field, brought the Cadets three first downs, a net gain of 79 yards, with 10 lost on penalties. The midshipmen made 4 first downs, one by penalty, drove over their second touchdown, made a net gain of 84 yards and lost 25 by penalties.

Hume Gains

Hillis Hume turned out to be the best ground gainer on the field with a net of 96 yards, including 25, 14 and 12 yards sprints. Maxson was next with 59 yards, including 17 gained on a pass. Harold Hamberg, who sparked the Navy's first touchdown, made a net of 39 yards rushing and returned punts 32 yards. Bob Jenkins had a net of 30 yards rushing and 23 in punt returns. Davis of Army turned in a net of 30 yards.

Soon after the opening kickoff, Navy started to march after Jenkins had run an Army punt back 5 yards to the Navy 25. He broke through the Army line for 15 yards and added 6 more, after Hume had picked up two. The former Alabama fullback then turned in gains of 6 and 5 yards and Navy had made three first downs in a row and was apparently on its way. Then Jenkins fumbled near the sideline and Army recovered to end the march on the Army 36.

Davis Run

Davis got away with an 18 yard run and Maxson followed with an eight yard gain that brought the Army downfield but a holding penalty intervened to stop this march. Later Maxson tacked together a 14 yard and 9 yard gain, with Minor contributing seven more. This ended when Maxson fumbled a Statue of Liberty play, and Tom Lombardo was tossed for an 11 yard loss.

Late in the second period Army again threatened when Davis got off a 20 yard forward pass to Ed Rafalko and Ed Kenna shot a 9 yard toss to the same player. The Cadets were on the Navy 34 when Dick Duden and Al Channell, in two plays hurled them back to Navy 40 and forced a punt.

Scoring Drive

Hamberg set up the Navy's scoring drive in the third period when he punted from his own 42 to Davis, who caught the ball on the Army 2 yard line. Hard driving Navy linemen stopped the fleet Cadet on his own 3 yard line and the pressure was on. Minor tried to batter ahead and gained five yards. Then Navy's Ben Chase took over and tossed him back for a yard and Roe Johnson followed by dropping Davis back on the Army one. This slashing line play forced Army to punt from behind its own goal and Hamberg brought the ball back 13 yards to the Army 42.

Navy was on its way. Ben Martin sliced out a yard. Hamberg contributed a 7 yard drive and then added 5 more and a first down on the Army 31. Then, Hamberg started around his own right end and, when about to be tackled, lateraled to Hume who toe danced down the right sidelines to the Cadet 6 yard line and a first down. Hume carried through tackle to the 2 yard stripe, then fumbled but recovered.

Jenkins In

The Navy coaching staff took over and Jenkins, Leon Bramlett, end and Bill Barron, back went in the game. Bramlett and Barron mousetrapped Army's Joseph Stanowicz and Jenkins roared through the hole for the score, carrying the out maneuvered Cadet linemen with him. Vic Finos made the placement and Navy had a 7-0 lead with 10 minutes of the quarter passed.

The second touchdown drive started late in the quarter after Army had been set back 32 yards on two penalties and kicked from it own 11 yard line.

Hamberg brought the kick back 10 yards to the Army 44 and Jim Pettit had it on the army 40 when the period ended. Then Hume and Pettit teamed up to make it tough for the Cadets. Hume drove 14 yards and Pettit contributed 9, with Hume going to bat again to make a first down on the Army 10-yard line. Army's Bob Dobbs trapped Hamberg for a 3-yard loss but Hume came through again, driving down to the Cadet one yard mark. Hamberg drove hard in the line and when the pile was unscrambled the ball still had six inches to go. Pettit dove over the line for the score. Army's Dick Pitzer's, end, broke up Finos' attempted placement.

The ball game was over then but Army turnd to a flurry of passing in an endeavor to score. Interference called on Navy gave them one 26 yard pass to the Navy 25 but Pettit stopped the march with an interception. Army never again got past midfield.

The win was the third scored by an Navy football team at West Point. In 1890 Navy won 24 to 0 and in 1892 12 to 4.

First Period

Brown of Navy kicked off to Anderson who took the ball on the Army 5 yard line and returned to his 31.

Maxson got 2 at center and then circled the Army right end for 13 yards and a first down on the Army 46. He was stopped by Nelson. Anderson added one in the line but Maxson was set back for nearly a yard loss in a try at Army's left tackle. Anderson circled his right end for nearly six yards being run outside by Jenkins on the Navy 48. Maxson punted to Jenkins who returned 5 yards to the Navy 25.

Jenkins crashed through Army's left tackle for 14 yards and a first down, on the Navy 39. Hume hit center for 3 yards and a first down at midfield. Jenkins picked up 5 more at center and then got three around Navy's right end on a reverse from Hume. B. Martin got one at center. Hume got another and a first down on the Army 40. Jenkins ran his right end and fumbled, Army recovering on its own 36.

Davis circled Navy's left end for 6 yards. Maxson was tossed for a two yard loss, Davis swept around Navy's right end for 18 yards and a first down on the Navy 42. Maxson got 8 more at Navy's left end but Army was penalized for holding to the Navy 49. Davis' pass to Rafalko was incomplete. Davis ran his own left end for 2 yards and Maxson punted to Hume who returned 12 yards to the Navy 24.

Hume was trapped by Hennessey for a 3 yard loss. On the next play Hume tried a lateral which went bad, Davis getting the ball, but the play was called back by the officials. Hume punted to Davis who was tossed back a yard to the Army 25.

Maxson dashed over the Army left tackle for 14 yards and a first down on the Army 39. Maxson rounded his own right end for 9 more. Maxson drove through the Army right tackle for 3 yards and a first down on the Navy 49. Minor went over the Cadet right tackle for 7 more to the Navy 42. Davis tried a Statue of Liberty play but Maxson fumbled and recovered on the Navy 49. Davis tossed a lateral to Lombardo who was tossed for an 11 yard loss on the Army 40. Maxson punted out on the Navy 18.

Hamberg replaced Jenkins in the Navy backfield. Hamberg passed to Barron for no gain. Hume picked up 6 over his right tackle. Hamberg, on a reverse from Hume, ran around Navy's right end for 12 yards and a first down on the Navy 36 as the period ended.

Second Period

Army sent a new line out to start. B. Martin got 4 at center. Hamberg stumbled as he started around his right end after a triple reverse and lost 4 yards. Hamberg then tried a Statute of Liberty pass to B. Martin but the ball was fumbled, Martin recovering for a 6 yard loss on the Navy 30. Hamberg punted dead on the Army 31. Minor got 4 at his left tackle. Lombardo fumbled a lateral from Davis but recovered for a 4 yard loss. Maxson got off a short quickkick that went out on the Navy 45.

Jenkins got 2 at his right tackle and then went through the same hole for 3 more. He failed at his left tackle and Hume punted to Davis who returned 10 yards to the Army 30.

Sprinkle and Nelson stopped Minor for no gain. Nelson dropped Davis at Navy's right end for no gain. Maxson punted to Jenkins who returned 18 yards to the Navy 30.

Hume made 4 at his right guard. B. Martin failed at center. Jenkins got away for a first down but the play was called back and Navy penalized 5 yards for offside. Navy sent in a mixed second and third string line. Hamberg punted out on the Army 35. Army sent its first string line back in the game.

Davis rounded his left end for 5 yards and then fired a forward down field to Rafalko that was good for 20 yards and a first down on the Navy 40. Navy's varsity line went back in the game. Davis passed over Anderson's head on the goal line. Anderson was thrown for a 4 yard loss when he tried Navy's left end. Kenna replaced Davis in the Army backfield. Kenna passed to Rafalko for 9 yards on the Navy 35 but Army got a first down when interference was called on Walton. Maxson made one at his right tackle. Duden tossed Maxson for a 3 yard loss on the next play and Channell dropped Lombardo who took a pass from Kenna for a 3 yard loss back to the Navy 40. Maxson punted over the goal line.

Navy started from its 20. Hume got 8 at center and Hamberg went through his own left tackle for 7 more and a first down. A long pass, Hamberg to Bramlett, was incomplete. Hamberg's fast pass to Johnston was too low. Hume reversed to Hamberg who tossed a pass down the field for Johnston but Anderson intercepted on the Army 20 and returned 11 yards.

Minor got 2 over his right guard and Davis added 7 more through Army's right tackle. Dobbs hit centre for 2 and a first down on the Army 42. Davis tossed a pass for Minor but Barron intercepted on the Navy 30.

Hamberg shot a pass to Channell who dropped the ball. Hamberg's pass to Barron was incomplete. Jenkins came in for Hamberg. Jenkins was tossed for a 5 yard loss after taking a reverse from Walton, as the half ended scoreless.

Third Period

Myslinski kicked off for Army out of bounds.

Navy started on its own 35. Hume made five around his left end on a lateral from Hamberg. Hamberg passed to Channell but the Navy captain let the ball bounce out of his arms. Navy was penalized 15 yards back to its own 25. B. Martin got five at center. Hamberg picked up three around his right end on a fake reverse. Army refused a Navy offside penalty. Hamberg punted to Davis who fumbled but recovered on the Army 25.

Maxson got a yard at center. Davis went through his right tackle for four yards. Nelson and Chanell dropped Maxson at left end for a three-yard loss. Maxson punted to Hamberg who returned 19 yards to the Navy 38. Hamberg shot two fast forward passes to Channell who dropped both. Hamberg picked up four at his left tackle and then punted to Davis who returned one yard to the Army three-yard marker.

Minor got five at his left tackle. Chase tossed Minor for a one-yard loss on his next try in the line. Johnston broke through and smeared Davis for a five-yard loss on the Army one-yard line. Davis punted from behind his own goal to Hamberg who returned 13 yards to the Army 42.

Martin got a yard at his own left end. Hamberg picked up seven more at center and then slipped through the Navy left tackle slot for five yards and a first down on the Army 31. Hamberg circled the Navy's right end and then tossed a lateral to Hume who drove down the sidelines to the

(Continued On Page Three)

Spark

HAL HAMBERG

Hamberg's kicking and passing sparked Navy's 13-0 win over the Army.

Scores!

BOB JENKINS

Jenkins scored Navy's first touchdown against Army Saturday.

TOUCHDOWN FOR NAVY

Bob Jenkins hugs the ball (arrow) as he crosses the goal line for Navy's first touchdown against Army, in the third quarter of the Army-Navy game played at West Point, N. Y. Joe Stanowicz, Army tackle, hangs on to him to no avail. The Midshipmen trounced their traditional military rivals 13-0.

Two Years Of U. S. War Pave The Way To Total Victory

JAPS TURN TO DEFENSE

By GLENN BABB
Associated Press Foreign News Editor

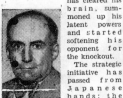

TWO years after Pearl Harbor Japan, which in the first flush of treachery dreamed of an empire embracing nearly half the human race, merely is hopeful of gaining at best a stalemate that would leave her some of her spoils.

The United States now is like a fighter who, floored by a foul blow before the opening gong, has cleared his brain, summoned up his latent powers and started softening his opponent for the knockout.

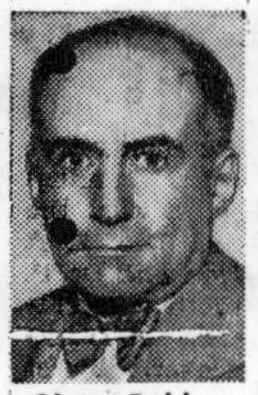
Glenn Babb

The strategic initiative has passed from Japanese hands; the Japanese know this and are girding for defensive warfare on a hemispheric scale.

The Pacific war has been largely the fight of the United States to survive that initial, tragic period of dismay and helplessness, gain time to gather its sinews and come to grips with the enemy.

In those first months, when our Pacific fleet lay crippled, Japan overran a great empire. The tentacles of the Japanese octopus slithered to the borders of India, to the shores of Australia, to the islands of the mid Pacific.

Then came Midway, Guadalcanal and the defeat of the Japanese almost within sight of Port Moresby on New Guinea. The Japanese direction was reversed.

Progress Is Slow

Still the Allies are finding progress on the road to Tokyo painfully slow. At the rate we have progressed it might take 100 years before we reached the heart of the octopus.

But it must be remembered that the enemy's power of resistance does not remain constant, nor does the striking power of the United States, which has returned the Pearl Harbor fleet to action and built another far more powerful, or of Britain.

There are factors which may be working against our enemy. Japan's industrial capacity is limited by shortages of skilled workers and of vital tools. And while she has gained much wealth it is spread over a vast expanse which can be held together only by the shipping resources of a great maritime power.

Japan was on her way to becoming such a power, but now her resources are steadily declining. Since Pearl Harbor she has suffered a net loss of 2,500,000 tons of cargo carrying capacity, according to best available estimates. All indications are that she can not replace more than half the steady attrition she is suffering.

Plan Costly Defense

There is no doubt the Japanese hope they can make the defense of East Asia and its island fringes so costly the attackers will weary of the effort and leave Japan in possession of most of the fruits of her rapine.

Whether the Japanese people can withstand the psychological and spiritual strain of this prodigious defensive fight—which offers none of the exhilaration of conquest—remains to be seen.

Orthodox American thought appears to be that they will fight to the last man; that they must be rooted out and slain one by one as they were at Attu and Guadalcanal. However, we can tell more about that when American super Flying Fortresses begin laying Japanese industrial cities in ashes and ruins.

PICTURES HIGHLIGHT AMERICA'S FIGHTING ROLE IN GLOBAL WAR

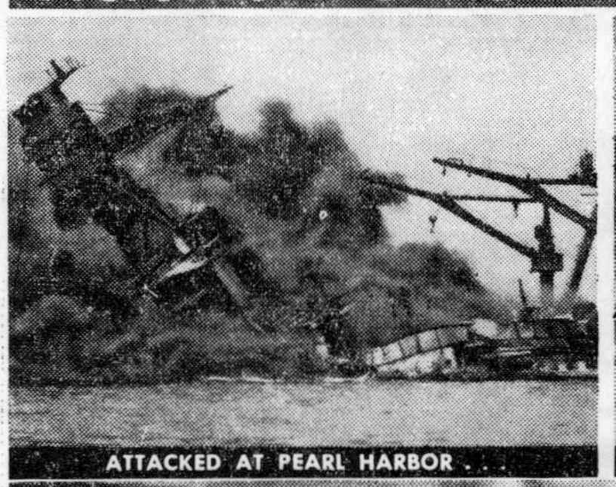
ATTACKED AT PEARL HARBOR . . .

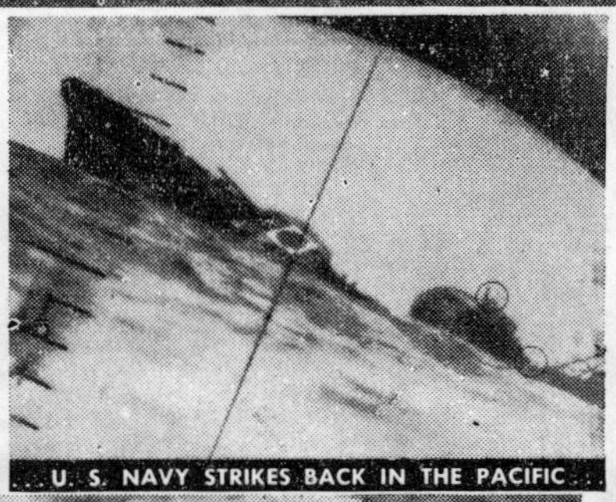
. . . U. S. NAVY STRIKES BACK IN THE PACIFIC . . .

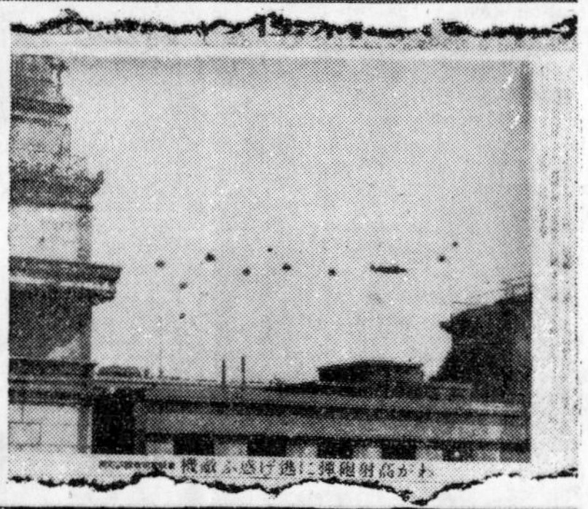
. . . DOOLITTLE'S FLYERS BOMB TOKYO . . .

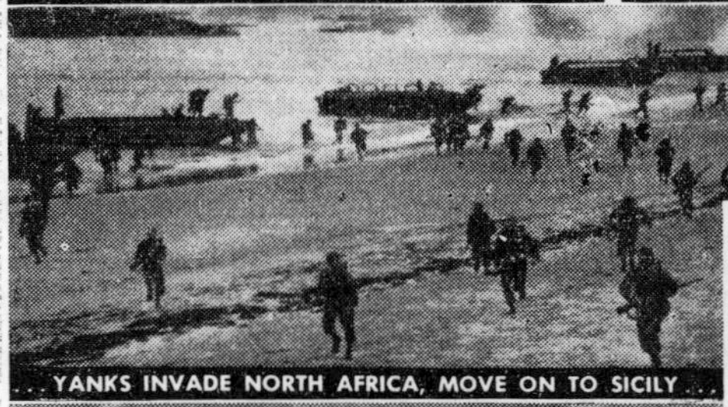
. . . YANKS INVADE NORTH AFRICA, MOVE ON TO SICILY . . .

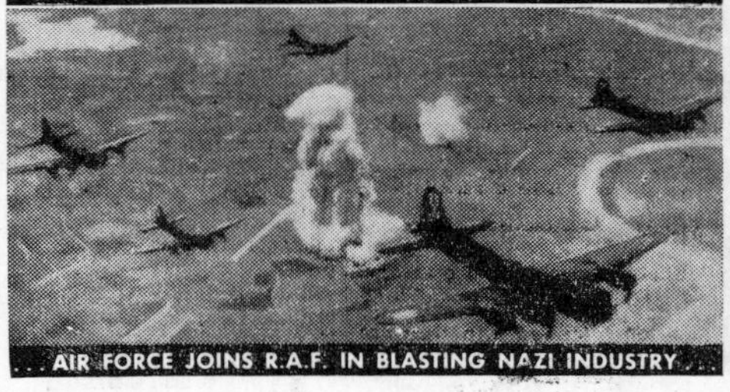
. . . AIR FORCE JOINS R.A.F. IN BLASTING NAZI INDUSTRY . . .

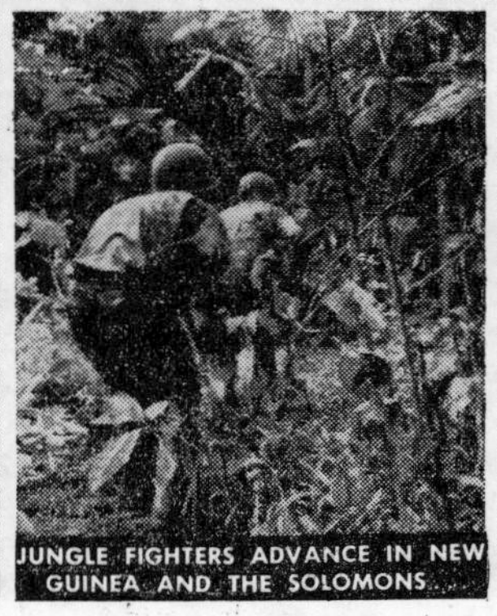
JUNGLE FIGHTERS ADVANCE IN NEW GUINEA AND THE SOLOMONS . . .

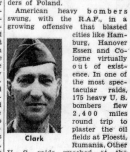

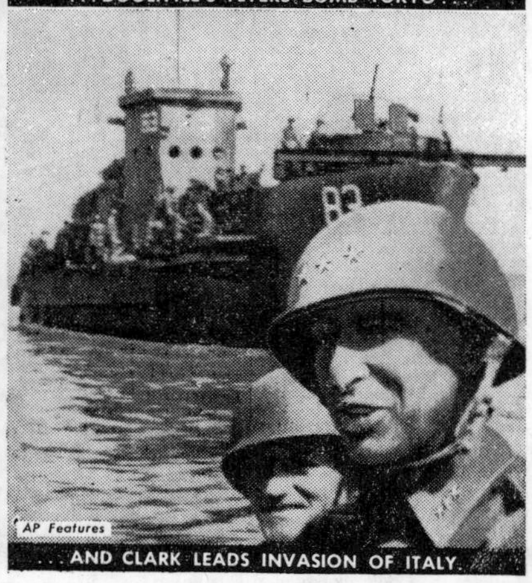
AP Features
. . . AND CLARK LEADS INVASION OF ITALY.

The Fortunes Of War, Day By Day

1941

Dec. 7—Japanese bomb Pearl Harbor, Guam and Philippines.

Dec. 8—U. S. declares war on Japan.

Dec. 11—Germany and Italy declares war on U. S.

PRODUCTION NEARS PEAK

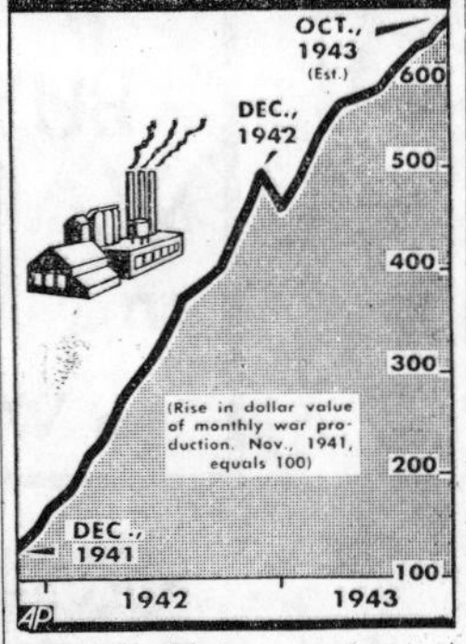
OCT., 1943 (Est.)
DEC., 1942
DEC., 1941
600
500
400
300
200
100
(Rise in dollar value of monthly war production. Nov., 1941, equals 100)
1942
1943
AP

Dec. 24—Marine garrison at Wake falls to Japanese.

1942

Jan. 1.—United Nations pact signed by 26 governments.

Jan. 2—Manila falls; Americans retire to Bataan.

Jan. 26—First U. S. troops land in northern Ireland.

Feb. 15—Singapore falls.

March 5—Japanese take Java.

March 17—General MacArthur arrives in Australia.

April 9—Bataan capitulates.

April 18 — Doolittle's flyers bomb Tokyo.

May 4-8—U. S. Navy rips Jap fleet in Coral Sea.

May 6—Corregidor falls.

June 4—U. S. Navy routs Japanese at Midway.

June 12—Japan gains toehold in Aleutians.

June 21—Tobruk falls; Germans push into Egypt.

July 3—Russia admits Sevastopol falls after eight-month siege.

July 4—U. S. Army bombers stage first raid in western Europe..

July 5—British stall Rommel's drive before Alexandria.

Aug. 8—U. S. forces land on Guadalcanal, Solomons Islands.

Aug. 9—Germans push into Caucasus.

Aug. 19—Commandos stage raid on Dieppe.

Sept. 17—Nazis penetrate Stalingrad.

Sept. 26—Japanese retreat in New Guinea.

Oct. 25—British smash Rommel's lines at El Alamein.

Nov. 8—U. S. and British forces invade North Africa.

Nov. 11—Americans capture Casablanca and Oran, end French resistance; Nazis invade unoccupied France.

Nov. 19—Russians open winter offensive at Rzhev and Stalingrad.

U.S. ARSENAL'S OUTPUT

(Total from May, '40, to Sept., '43)

AIRPLANES	123,000
TANKS	53,000
ARTILLERY WEAPONS	93,000
SMALL ARMS (Rifles, carbines, machine guns)	9,500,000
SMALL ARMS AMMUNITION	25,942,000,000

AP

Nov. 27—Most of French fleet scuttled at Toulon.

Dec. 1—Darlan becomes Chief of State in French Africa.

Dec. 24—Darlan assassinated; Giraud takes over.

1943

Jan. 13—Russians advance in Caucasus.

Jan. 18—Reds break siege of Stalingrad.

Jan. 24—British take Tripoli.

Jan. 26—Roosevelt and Churchill end 10-day meeting at Casablanca, vow "unconditional surrender" of Axis.

Jan. 27 — First all-American aerial assault on Germany made by U. S. heavy bombers.

Feb. 10—Guadalcanal cleared of Japs.

March 29—Axis defenses at Mareth Line in Tunisia collapse.

May 7—Tunis and Bizerte fall.

May 14—Americans gain foothold at Attu.

May 30—Jap garrison on Attu wiped out.

June 3 — Provisional government set up for French Empire.

June 11—Pantelleria surrenders after aerial blasting.

July 1—Allies take Rendova Island.

July 5—U. S. wins naval battle with Japs in Kula Gulf.

July 7 — Americans land on Munda.

July 9—Allies invade Sicily.

July 12—Russians open summer offensive.

July 19—Allies bomb Rome.

July 25—Mussolini is putsched; Badoglio becomes new prime minister.

Aug. 1—U. S. heavy bombers make 2,400-mile round trip to raid oil fields at Ploesti.

Aug. 15—U. S. forces occupy Kiska.

Aug. 17—Allies complete conquest of Sicily.

Aug. 28—Jap resistance ends on New Georgia Island.

Sept. 1—U. S. naval forces blasts Marcus Island.

Sept. 3—British invade Italy.

Sept. 8—Italy surrenders.

Sept. 9 — Americans land near Salerno.

Sept. 12—Mussolini freed by Nazi paratroopers.

Sept. 16—Lae falls to Americans.

Oct. 1—Allies capture Naples.

Oct. 5—U. S. Navy pounds Wake Island.

Oct. 7—Red army crosses Dnieper.

Oct. 12—Portugal gives Allies use of Azores.

Oct. 13 Italy declares war on Germany.

Nov. 1 — Americans invade Bougainville.

FIGHTING FORCES GROW

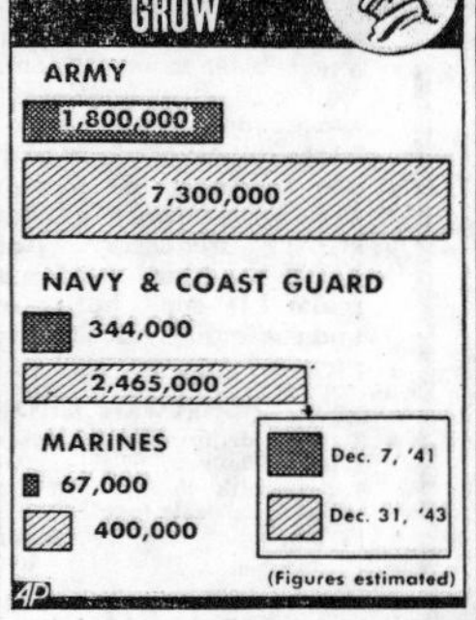
ARMY
1,800,000
7,300,000
NAVY & COAST GUARD
344,000
2,465,000
MARINES
67,000
400,000
Dec. 7, '41
Dec. 31, '43
(Figures estimated)
AP

Nov. 1—U. S., Britain and Russia announce pact.

Nov. 6—Russians take Kiev.

Nov. 20-23—U. S. Marines and Army troops capture Gilbert Islands after heavy casualties.

Nov. 27—Pacific charter agreed upon in Cairo between Roosevelt, Churchill and Chiang Kai-Shek. Japan to be stripped of all territory seized by aggression.

Dec. 3—Allied planes hit Berlin in fifth saturation raid.

Dec. 6 — Stalin, Roosevelt, Churchill announce accord in Teheran on plan to smash Germany.

AMERICA'S ARMS, MEN TURN THE TIDE IN EUROPE

By JOHN L. SPRINGER
AP Features Writer

GERMANY must realize once more that she has bitten off more than she can chew.

Many factors are responsible for Hitler's present plight—Britain's will to fight on alone even after Dunkirk and the London blitz; the willingness of the Russians to see their cities burned and seared, and to let the invader pour over their lands so long as they could keep their armies intact to strike a future blow; the fanatical resistance of the conquered peoples to Germany's "New Order."

But the clinching factor — the one that has provided the added weight now dragging down the Nazis—probably has been America's unprecedented mobilization of fighting manpower and her record-shattering production and distribution of the tools of war.

Hitler At His Peak

Two years ago, at the time of Pearl Harbor, Hitler was enjoying his greatest glories. His armies had ripped through Russia and parked for the winter within sight of the Kremlin. His submarines were winning the crucial battle of the Atlantic. His air force held control of the skies. His swastika flew across 1,500 miles in Europe, from the Arctic to Africa, from the Atlantic to the Black Sea.

For six months more, while American production feverishly picked up speed, the Axis star rose higher. Russian winter offensive which drove the Nazis from the gates of Moscow, the rebirth of British air power and the beginning of a large-scale air offensive keynoted by the first thousand - ton raid on Cologne in May, the Nazis firmly held the initiative. In southern Russia they stormed into the Crimea and headed for Caucasus oil. They battered the Soviets on the road to Stalingrad and in September entered the city, Stalin's key point on the Volga and his last strong link to the Caucasus. General Erwin Rommel's seasoned desert warriors chased the British across Africa, past Libya and into Egypt, less than seventy miles from Alexandria.

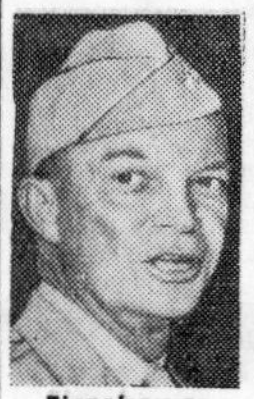
Eisenhower

War's Darkest Days

Those were the darkest days of war. If the Germans could succeed in driving south from the Caucasus and east from Egypt, they would achieve a juncture in the middle east. With enormous oil fields, rich mineral and agricultural lands in their possession, they could probably sit and hold their lines against all enemies for years—perhaps for decades.

But then the tide turned in one of the most spectacular reverses in the history of wars . . . and the Nazis have been retreating virtually ever since.

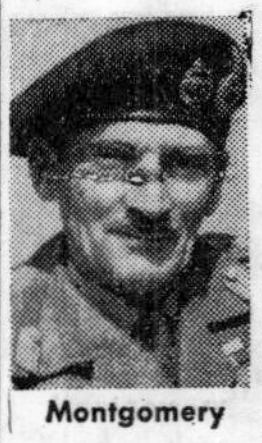
Montgomery

American lend-lease aid—tanks and guns and planes—poured into Egypt and it was with the help of this equipment that General Sir Bernard Montgomery began, on October 23, 1942, his campaign at El Alamein that was to chase Rommel back across Africa. On November 8 American forces landed in North Africa to open large-scale action for the first time. And on November 19 the Russians broke the deadlock at Stalingrad and began a drive that captured hundreds of thousands of Hitler's first-line fighters.

The second year since Pearl Harbor has been one of increasing U. S. participation—and of increasing Allied victory.

Wipe Axis From Africa

With General Dwight D. Eisenhower as commander - in - chief, Americans, British, Canadian and the newly reorganized French forces proceeded to wipe the Axis from Tunisia. The Allies went on to Sicily and Italy. Mussolini fell and Italy surrendered, and forces led by Gen. Mark Clark fought their way onto the bloody invasion beaches at Salerno, to meet finally with British forces on their way up from the boot.

In the east, strengthened by American lend-lease equipment, the Reds opened a summer offensive that merely picked up speed with winter, roared past Smolensk, Kharkov, Kiev, bottled the Nazis in the Crimea, rolled through the Ukraine to the borders of Poland.

American heavy bombers swung, with the R.A.F., in a growing offensive that blasted cities like Hamburg, Hanover Essen and Cologne virtually out of existence. In one of the most spectacular raids, 175 heavy U. S. bombers flew 2,400 miles round trip to plaster the oil fields at Ploesti, Rumania, Other U. S. raids smashed at the heart of the German war-making machine—the huge ball-bearing plant at Schweinfurt—and at the plane factory at Regansburg, where 30 per cent of the Nazis fighter craft were produced.

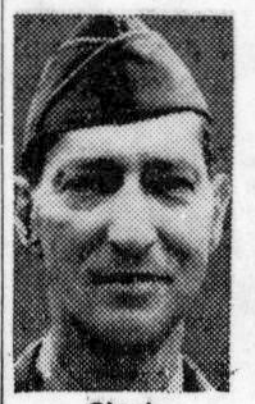
Clark

U-boats were sunk at a rate frequently of one a day. Guerrillas and underground forces—in some cases equipped with supplies from America — terrorized the Nazis in Yugoslavia, Poland, France the lowlands. On every front America's might was exerted with increasing weight. And at home the booming American war industry was reaching new peaks—turning out in the first eight months of this year, 52,000 planes, 23,000 tanks, more than 40,000 artillery pieces.

Decisive Influence

U. S. influence in the year now starting is almost certain to be decisive. The promised second front across the channel will be fought largely, it is expected, by American, of whom there will be more than ten million under arms. U. S. war production will provide the bulk of the equipment, and the U. S. shipping fleet—the greatest in all history—will carry the supplies.

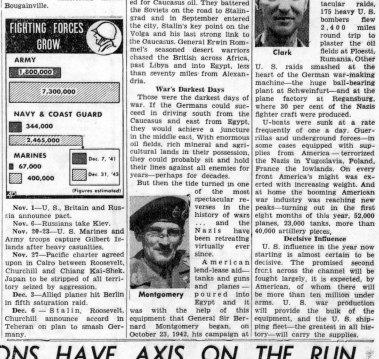

TWO YEARS AFTER PEARL HARBOR, UNITED NATIONS HAVE AXIS ON THE RUN

IN THE PACIFIC . . .

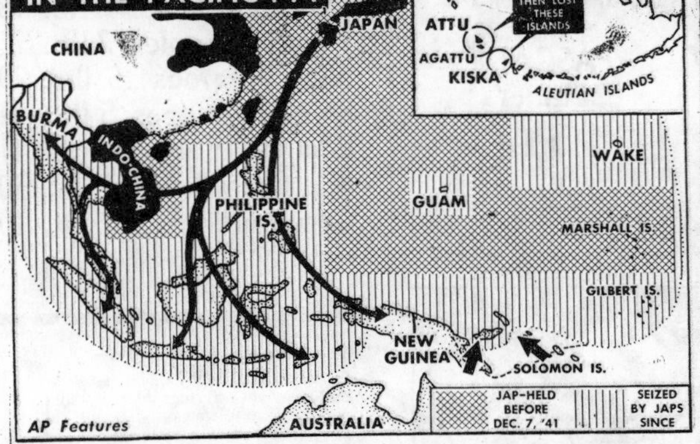
CHINA
JAPAN
ALASKA
ATTU
AGATTU
KISKA
JAPS TOOK THEN LOST THESE ISLANDS
ALEUTIAN ISLANDS
BURMA
INDO-CHINA
PHILIPPINE IS.
WAKE
GUAM
MARSHALL IS.
GILBERT IS.
NEW GUINEA
SOLOMON IS.
AUSTRALIA
JAP-HELD BEFORE DEC. 7, '41
SEIZED BY JAPS SINCE
AP Features

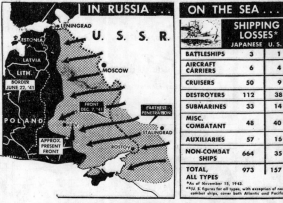

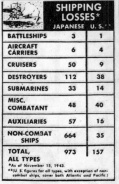

From Australia, where he retreated from besieged Bataan, General Douglas MacArthur has developed a continuing offensive that has driven the enemy from New Georgia, much of New Guinea and the Solomons, and now threatens the Japanese naval stronghold at Rabaul. The Japs have been chased from the Aleutians. U. S. naval forces have struck heavy blows at Wake, Marcus, the Gilbert and Marshall islands, and have penetrated deeper into waters invaded and controlled by the enemy after Pearl Harbor.

. . . IN ITALY . . .

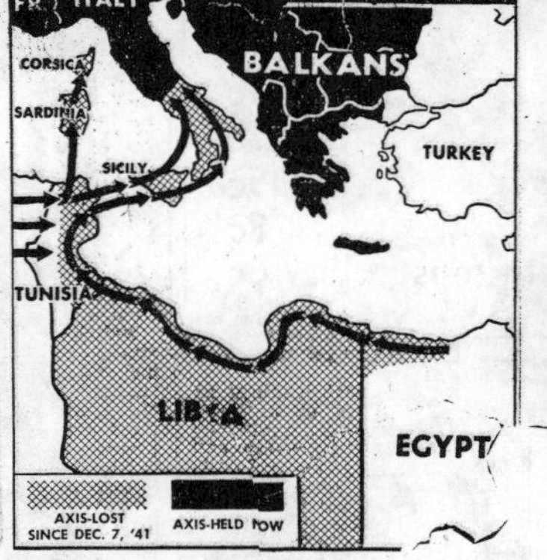
FR
ITALY
CORSICA
SARDINIA
SICILY
BALKANS
TURKEY
TUNISIA
LIBYA
EGYPT
AXIS-LOST SINCE DEC. 7, '41
AXIS-HELD NOW

Allied forces under the command eral Dwight D. Eisenhower have Axis from Africa, taken Sicily an Italy. They are pushing the Na home and have removed the Me ranean barriers to a possible second-front invasion through the under-side of France.

. . . IN RUSSIA . . .

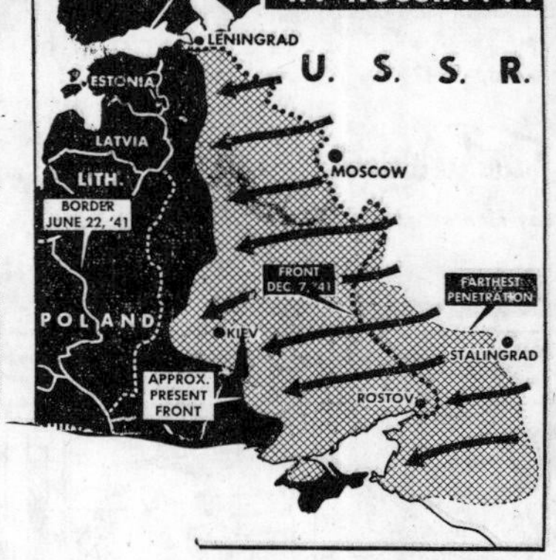
LENINGRAD
U. S. S. R.
ESTONIA
LATVIA
LITH.
BORDER JUNE 22, '41
MOSCOW
FRONT DEC. 7, '41
FARTHEST PENETRATION
POLAND
KIEV
STALINGRAD
ROSTOV
APPROX. PRESENT FRONT

recaptured about 400,000 of territory, blasted the faltering the Caucasus, the Crimea and Ukraine. In many places the and less than 100 miles from border and threaten to drive e the lands of the invader.

ON THE SEA . . .

SHIPPING LOSSES*

	JAPANESE	U. S.**
BATTLESHIPS	3	1
AIRCRAFT CARRIERS	6	4
CRUISERS	50	9
DESTROYERS	112	38
SUBMARINES	33	14
MISC. COMBATANT	48	40
AUXILIARIES	57	16
NON-COMBAT SHIPS	664	35
TOTAL, ALL TYPES	973	157

*As of November 15, 1943.
**(U. S. figures for all types, with exception of non-combat ships, cover both Atlantic and Pacific.)

The American Navy in the Pacific has successively beaten the Jap fleet and effected such heavy losses that the enemy now is hesitant to fight. The German submarine threat has been overcome in the Atlantic.

. . . AND IN THE AIR

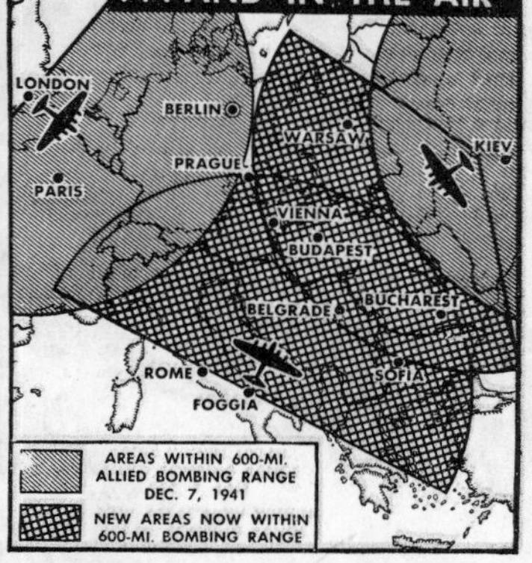
LONDON
BERLIN
PARIS
PRAGUE
KIEV
VIENNA
BUDAPEST
BELGRADE
BUCHAREST
ROME
FOGGIA
SOFIA
AREAS WITHIN 600-MI. ALLIED BOMBING RANGE DEC. 7, 1941
NEW AREAS NOW WITHIN 600-MI. BOMBING RANGE

Advances on land in Europe have opened new targets for Allied bombers and all Hitler territory now falls within a 600-mile flying range. U. S. Army warplanes have proved their superiority on all fronts, destroying more than four enemy planes for every American ship knocked out in action.

Around The Radio Dial

Station	Freq
WITH	1230k
WOR—M. B. S. Key	710k
WABC—C. B. S. Key	880k
WJZ—B. C. Red Key	660k
WJZ—Blue Key	770k
WBAL	1090k
WFBR	1300k
WCBM	1400k
WCAO	600k

By C. E. BUTTERFIELD
Eastern War Time

NEW YORK, Jan. 18 (AP)—Bond broadcasting on behalf of the Fourth War Loan Drive, now under way via networks and individual stations, has swung into a schedule that will produce numerous features over the next month.

After last night's introductory show on all networks, the entire list of BLU programs today was being directed to the campaign. Other networks will follow at about weekly intervals, with CBS and Kate Smith set for February 1, NBC for February 8 and the BLU on the concluding day of the drive. The NBC day will be in cooperation with Boy Scouts all over the country.

Simultaneously with the first half of the bond drive comes the March of Dimes campaign in connection with the infantile paralysis fund. Numerous programs are being arranged, including a special Eddie Cantor show on MBS Sunday night.

Tuning tonight: Fourth War Loan—MBS continuing all-day broadcast with these special: 10:15 to 11:35 Cleveland Symphony, Brahms' Requiem; 12 Mid to 2 A. M.—Dance Band Appeal; CBS 12:30 A. M.—Boston Hotel Rally. NBC—7:30—New series, Everything For The Boys; 9:30—Return of Date With Judy; 9:30—Fibber McGee; 10:30—Bob Hope; 10:30—Red Skelton; 11:30—Words at War, Lin Taiyi's "War Tide."

CBS—3—Big Town Drama; 8:30—Judy Canova Show; 9—Burns and Allen; 9:30—Report to Nation with Quentin Reynolds; 10—Romance Drama.

BLU—7—Awake at Switch; 8:30—Duffy's and Lauritz Melchoir; 9:30—All-American Jazz Band from Metropolitan Opera; 10:30—Radio Forum new time, Sen. Taft on "Wages, Price Control, Inflation"

MBS—8:30—New series, Pick and Pat Time; 9:15—Postponed Premier of Bob Ripley; 9:30—American Forum "Strikes;" 11:35—Sinfonietta.

5:00
WCAO: Fun with Dunn.
WFBR—News; Race Results.
WBAL: When a Girl Marries.
WCBM: Army Air Forces.
WITH: News; Sports, Bill Dyer.

5:15
WFBR: Archie Andrews.
WBAL: Portia Faces Life.
WCBM—Dick Tracy.

5:30
WFBR: Chic Carter, boy detective.
WBAL: Just Plain Bill.
WCBM: Jack Armstrong.

5:45
WCAO—American Women.
WFBR: Superman.
WBAL: Front Page Farrell.
WCBM: Captain Midnight.

6:00
WCAO: Quincy Howe, news.
WFBR: Velvet Strings.
WBAL: News; Sports Parade.
WCBM—Terry and the Pirates.
WITH: News; Twilight Tunes.

6:15
WCAO: Sports Review; News.

6:30
WBAL: Treasury Song
WCAO: To Your Good Health.
WFBR: WFBR News Service.
WCBM: Carroll Dulaney.
WITH: A. P. News.

6:45
WCAO: World Today.
WFBR: Key to Happiness.
WBAL: Lowell Thomas.
WCBM: News; Music Souvenirs.
WITH: Harmony Caravan.

7:00
WCAO: "I Love a Mystery."
WFBR—Fulton Lewis, Jr., news.
WBAL: area warings Orchestra.
WCBM: Song Parade.
WITH: News; Musical.

7:15
WCAO: Harry James' Orchestra.
WFBR: Jimmy Fidler, News.
WBAL: News of the World.
WCBM: Sweepstakes.

7:30
WBAL: Everything for Boys.
WCAO: American Melody Hour.
WFBR: Confidentially Yours.
WCBM: Metropolitan Opera.
WITH: Swing Class.

8:00
WCAO: "Big Town," sketch.
WCBM: Press Bulletins.
WFBR: Your World Tonight.
WBAL: Jinny Simms.
WITH: News; Phoneway Jackpot.

8:15
WFBR: Fulton Oursler, news.
WCBM: Lum and Abner.
WITH: Good Listening.

8:30
WFBR: Symphonette.
WBAL: A Date With Judy.
WCAO: Judy Canova Show.
WCBM: "Duffy's."
WITH: Bing Crosby Sings

8:45
WITH: Red Cross Show.

9:00
WFBR: Gabriel Heater.
WBAL: Mystery Theater.
WCBM: Famous Jury Trials.
WITH: News; Velvetones.

9:30
WCAO: Report to the Nation.
WFBR: American Forum of Air.
WBAL: Fibber McGee and Molly.
WCBM: Sportright Music.

10:00
WCAO: Romance.
WBAL: Bob Hope.
WCBM: Raymond Gram Swing, News.
WITH: Time to Relax.

10:15
WCAO: Chester Bowles, OPA.
WFBR: Cleveland Symphony.
WITH: War Bond Contest.

10:30
WCAO: Congress Speaks.
WBAL: Red Skelton.
WCBM: Radio Forum.
WCBM: America Tomorrow Forum.
WITH: Time For The News.

10:45
WCAO: Guy Lombardo.

11:00
WCAO: Quincy Howe.
WBAL: News; Sports Parade.
WCBM—News.

11:15
WCAO: Billy Arnold's Orchestra.
WCBM: Raymond J. Henle, news.
WBAL: Open Bible.
WFBR: Musical Climax.
WBAL: The Open Bible.
WITH: Vaughn Monroe Orchestra.
WITH: Jubilee Time.

11:30
WCAO: Shep Fields Orch.
WFBR: Sinfonietta.
WCBM: The Music You Want.
WITH: Fred Walker.

11:45
WBAL: Treasury Star Parade.
WITH: Songs for Victory.

12:00
WCAO: News; WCAO Nocturne.
WBAL: News; What's Playing.
WCBM: Chas. Spivak Orch.
WITH: Nite Owl Club.

SHIP NAMED FOR LATE SCREEN STAR

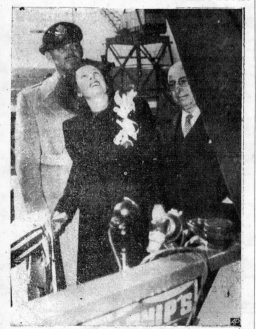

Capt. Clark Gable (left) was present at "Wilmington, Calif., at the launching of the S. S. Carole Lombard, Liberty Ship, which was christened by Film Actress Irene Dunn (cente), and named for Gable's actress-wife who was killed two years ago in an airplane crash. Louis B. Mayer (right), studio head, was a speaker. (AP Wirephoto).

Sports Round-Up
By HUGH FULLERTON, JR.

NEW YORK, Jan. 18 (AP)—Navy Lieut. Roland F. Logan, who formerly trained West Point athletic teams, has just finished constructing a nine-hole golf course at Fleet Recreation Center somewhere in the South Pacific . . . The center, which Logan says is probably the largest outside the United States, also has nine softball diamonds, two for handball, two football fields, four basketball courts and facilities for tennis, volley ball, soccer, boxing, handball, horseshoe pitching and swimming . . . The most popular sport at the Bainbridge, Md., naval training station last month was pool with 82,519 participants as compared to 24,106 for bowling and 8,325 for basketball.

Skirting Trouble

Jimmy Jamilton, former Cubs' scout and now a full-time employee of the All-American Girls Professional Baseball League, has recommended a pitcher for a tryout with the Cubs . . . But there's no need to gasp, the elbower has the definitely masculine name of Hank Stone, attends East High in Nashville, Tenn., and is a cousin of Rose Virginia Way, who coached the South Bend, Ind., team in the girls' league last season.

One Minute Sports Page

Joe Neville plans a race for three years old pacers, similar to the Hambletonian, for his Delaware, Ohio, track, and hopes to have it in the upper financial and publicity brackets a few years after its inception in 1946 . . . The favorite college sport of Prof. Philip O. Badger, National Collegiate A. A. President, is baseball—which gets very little attention from the N.C.A.A. . . . George Hass, Jr., six-foot, four-inch son of baseball's Mule Hass, is a regular on the Union College (N.Y.) basketball team and averages better than seven points a game . . . Tom Culnan, the Newark, N. J., fight matchmaker, has a bright idea for his Jan. 24 show at Laurel Garden. After the regular card he'll show 90 minutes of fight movies, featuring Joe Louis and Jack Dempsey.

Today's Guest Star

Bill Reddy, Syracuse (N.Y.) Post-Standard: "Sammy Baugh had never roped a calf until he bought a ranch only seven years ago. He has progressed so rapidly, however, that now he is in great demand at amateur rodeos . . . Well, I suppose being thrown from a horse is no worse than being knocked down by a Bear."

(Continued From Page Seven)

Service Dept.

Eddie Hiskey, former Creighton U. coach, has collected a better-than-fair basketball team among the officers at the Iowa Navy Pre-Flight School. Players include Lieut. Bob Timons, who played end for the Seahawks' football team last fall, Lieut (JG) Alton Elliott, former Syracuse captain and Ens. Ivan Hoolen, four-letter courtman at Oakland City, (Ind.) College . . . Marine Combat Correspondent Charles McKenna reports that when a Jap plane sent a torpedo through a PT boat on which he was travelling

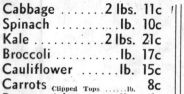

Your Federal Income Tax

No. 11

INCOME CONSTRUCTIVELY RECEIVED

In making a final return of income for Federal income and victory tax purposes, all income must be reported except those items which are specifically exempt, a list of which may be found in the instructions attached to the return form and in the next article in this series. The report of income must include income "constructively received" as well as income actually received, that is, income which becomes the property of a person during the year even though he does not have physical possession of it.

Income is constructively received when it is unconditionally credited to one's account or set apart subject to his order at any time. Thus, wages are considered as constructively received when they are credited to the account of or set apart for an employee without any substantial limitation or restriction as to the time or manner of payment or condition upon which payment is to be made, and such wages are made available to the employee so that they may be drawn upon by him at any time. Where wages are thus made available to an employee but at his request are paid to a third person, whether in payment of a personal obligation or under a vow of poverty, they are includible in his gross income just as though they had actually passed through his hands.

Similarly, interest credited on a savings bank deposit is income to the depositor when credited, even though it may not be drawn down or even entered on his pass book. Income received for a taxpayer by his agent, such as rental payments, has been constructively received when it is received by the agent.

Interest coupons which have matured, and are payable, represent income constructively received by their owner, even though they are not cashed, unless, of course, there are no funds available to pay the interest on the coupons. In the same way, dividend checks ordinarily become income when received, whether they are cashed or not. However, in the case of certain building and loan associations, dividends declared and credited may not be withdrawn by the shareholder until the maturity of the share in a future year. In such cases, the dividends do not become income during the year of the credit, but they become income in the year of the maturity of the share.

Another instance of constructive receipt of income may occur when one's debts or bills are paid by another or when a debt is forgiven. If this payment of a debt by another, or forgiveness of a debt by another, or forgivenss of a debt by a creditor, is not by way of outright gift, but in accordance with some agreement, or business transaction, then the amount of the debt paid on behalf of the taxpayer, or forgiven to him, becomes income to him in the year in which such payment or forgiveness occurs.

It often happens that a taxpayer who owns property agrees that the income from such property shall be paid to a third party, or he may contract to perform services to a second party and it is agreed that the compensation shall be paid to a third party. In each case the amount paid to the third party at the taxpayer's order is income "constructively received" by the taxpayer, and it must be reported as income in his inocme tax return.

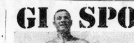

GI SPORTS GIRDLE THE . .

AP Features

Whether they be in Africa, Alaska, China, New Guinea, or somewhere in the good old U.S.A., service men and women rank sports first as a pastime. And their officers say that competition makes them more aggressive and healthier.

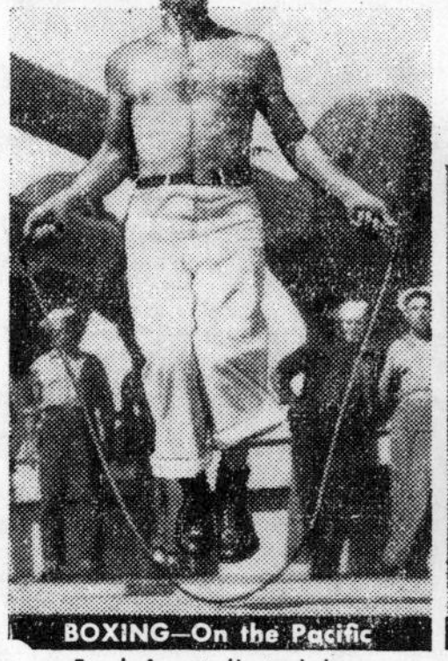

BOXING—On the Pacific

Fred Apostoli, training

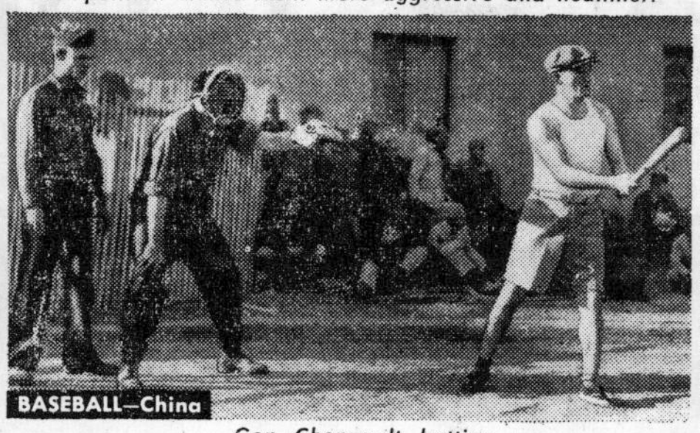

BASEBALL—China

Gen. Chennault, batting

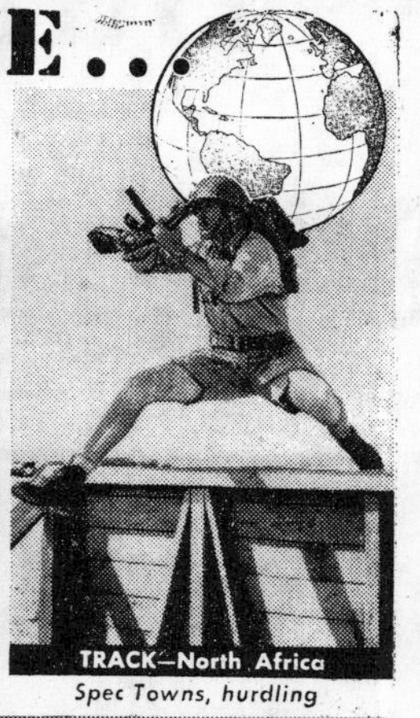

TRACK—North Africa

Spec Towns, hurdling

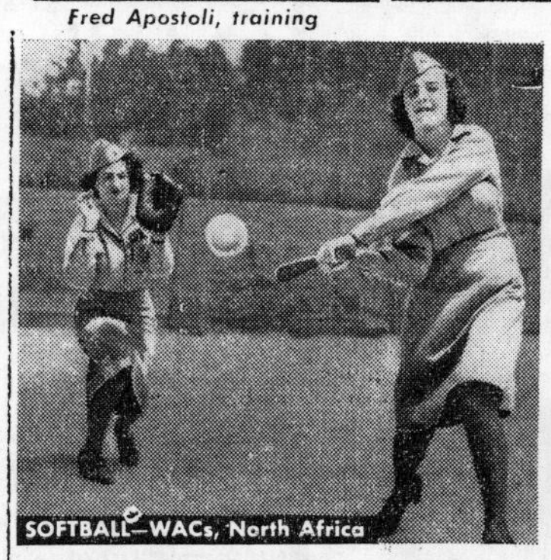

SOFTBALL—WACs, North Africa

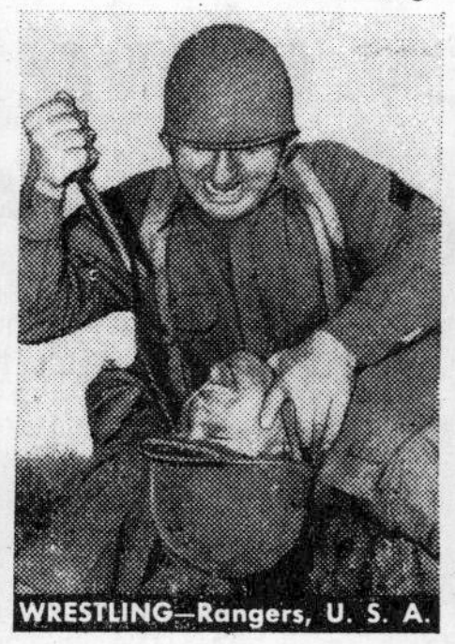

WRESTLING—Rangers, U. S. A.

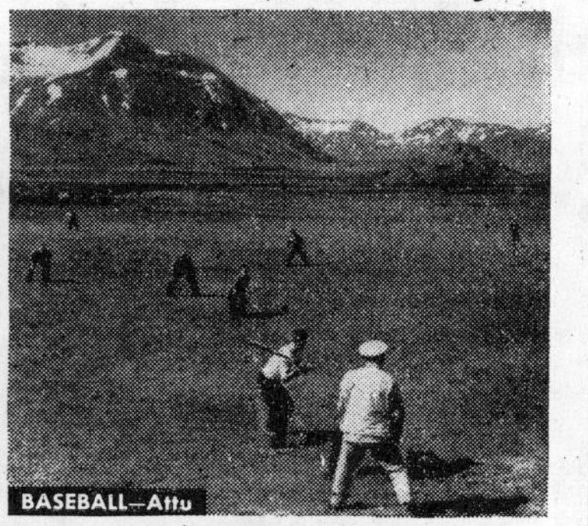

BASEBALL—Attu

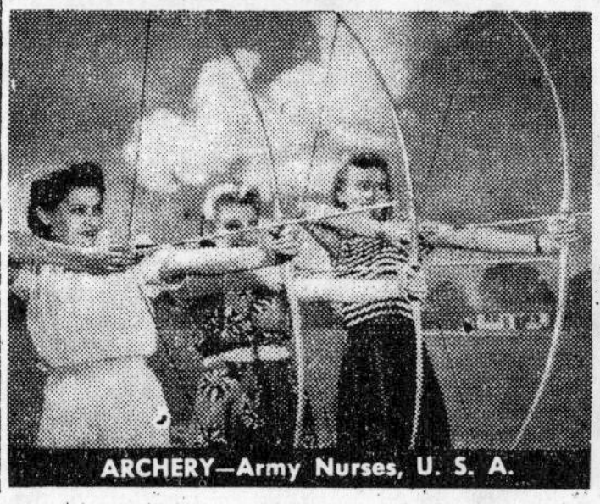

ARCHERY—Army Nurses, U. S. A.

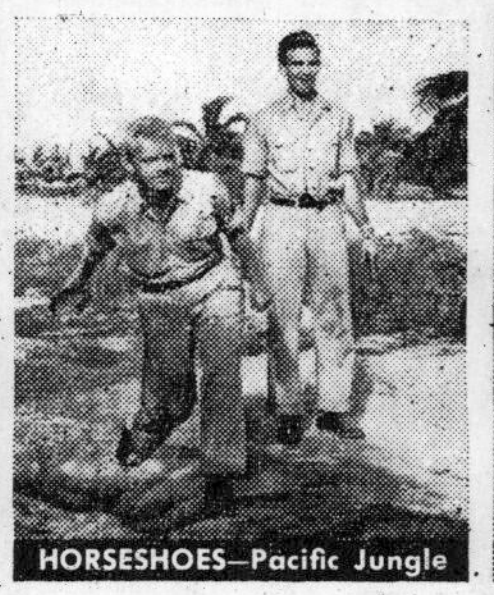

HORSESHOES—Pacific Jungle

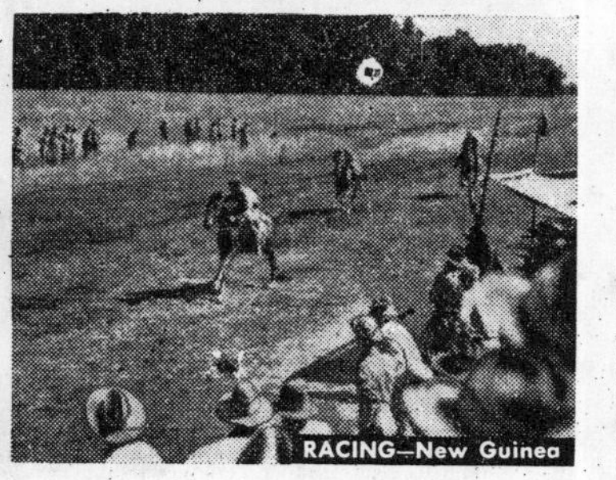

RACING—New Guinea

Around The Radio Dial Tonight

WITH	1230k
WOR—M. B. S. Key	710k
WABC—C. B. S. Key	860k
WEAF—N. B. C. Red Key	660k
WJZ—Blue Key	770k
WBAL	1090k
WFBR	1300k
WCBM	1400k
WCAO	600k

By C. E. BUTTERFIELD
Eastern War Time

NEW YORK, Jan. 19 (AP)—The first war broadcast of the Republican and Democratic National Conventions has made it necessary to think primarily of listeners fighting overseas. Arrangements for pickups of 1944 meetings are expected to include an elaborate schedule via the short waves.

Broadcasters are making plans so that the OWI operated short wave stations and the Army's radio networks will have available both comment and the actual sessions. Transmissions are expected to include both direct relays and transcribed rebroadcasts.

After Lowell Thomas transfers his 6:45 P. M. newscasts from the BLU, where it has been for more than a decade, to the same time on NBC next week, the BLU plans to continue with the identical type of program, using Henry J. Taylor. CBS has operated a like broadcast at 6:45 for several years.

Listening tonight: NBC—7:30 Rep. G. H. Bender on "Soldier Voting;" 8 Mr. and Mrs. North; 8:30 Beat The Band; 9 Eddie Cantor; 9:30 District Attorney; 10 Kay Kyser hour.

CBS—7:15 Harry James band; 8 Monty Woolley, Sammy Kaye; 9 Frank Sinatra show; 9:30 Jack Carson; 10:30 Morton Gould Carnival; 12:30 War Bond Rally at Philadelphia.

BLU—7 Connie Boswell Presents; 8:30 Battle of Sexes; 9 Dunninger's Mind Reading; 9:30 Frankie Masters band; 10:30 Star For A Night.

MBS—7:30 Halls of Montezuma; 8:30 Xavier Cugat orchestra; 9:30 Soliders With Wings; 10:15 Arch Ward on Sports..

5:00
WBAL: When a Girl Marries.
WFBR: News; Races.
WITH: News; Sports Special
WCBM: Army Air Forces.
WITH: News; Sports.

5:15
WCAO: Bob Iula's Orchestra.
WFBR: The Black Hood.
WFBR: Arche Andrews.
WBAL: Portia Faces Life.
WCBM: Dick Tracy.

5:30
WFBR: Chick Carter, boy detective.
WBAL: Just Plain Bill.
WCBM: Jack Armstrong.

5:45
WCAO: American Women.
WFBR: Superman.
WBAL: Front Page Farrell.
WCBM: Captain Midnite.

6:00
WCAO: Quincy Howe, news.
WFBR: Velvet Strings.
WBAL: News; Sports Parade.
WCBM: Terry and the Pirates.
WITH: News; Twilight Tunes.

6:15
WCAO: Sports, Don Riley; News.
WFBR: Sports, Stewart Kennard.
WBAL: Date For Sinatra.
WCBM: Talk; Eddie Fenton's Sports.
WITH: Adventures of Jimmy Allen.

6:30
WCAO: Sons of the Pioneers.
WFBR: WFBR news service.
WBAL: The Texas Rangers.
WCBM: Carroll Dulaney.
WITH: A. P. News.

6:45
WCAO: *The World Today.
WFBR: Name You'll Remember; News.
WBAL—Lowell Thomas.
WITH: Harmony Caravan.
WCBM: News; Souvenirs.

7:00
WCAO: "I Love a Mystery."
WFBR: Fulton Lewis, Jr., news.
WBAL: ‡Fred Waring's Orchestra.
WITH: News; Variety.
WCBM: Connie Boswell.

7:15
WCAO: Harry James' Orchestra.
WFBR: Heart Songs.
WBAL: ‡News of the World.

7:30
WCAO: Easy Aces.
WFBR: Quiz of Two Cities.
WBAL: Honor Roll; Music.
WCBM: The Lone Ranger.
WITH: Swing Class.

7:45
WBAL: H. V. Kaltenborn.

8:00
WCAO: Sammy Kay's Orchestra.
WFBR: Sizing Up the News.
WBAL: Mr. and Mrs. North.
WITH: News Phonaway Jackpot.
WCBM: Ray Henle, news.

8:15
WFBR: Fulton Oursler, reporter.
WCBM: Lum and Abner.
WITH: Good Lifetime.

8:30
WCAO: *"Dr. Christian"; News.
WFBR: Xavier Cugat.
WBAL: Beat The Band.
WCBM: Battle of the Sexes.
WITH: Bing Crosby Sings.

8:45
WITH: Red Cross Show.

9:00
WCAO: Frank Sinatra.
WFBR: Gabriel Heatter, News.
WCBM: Dunninger, Master Mentalist.
WBAL: Eddie Cantor.
WITH: News; Velvet Tunes.

9:15
WITH: Symphony Hall.
WFBR: Robert Ripley.

9:30
WCAO: Jack Carson Show.
WFBR: Soldiers With Wings.
WCBM: Spotlight Band.
WBAL: Mr. District Attorney.
WCBM: Vaughn Monroe Or.

10:00
WCAO: Great Moments in Music.
WFBR: Press Bulletins.
WBAL: ‡Kay Kyser's Musical Knowledge.
WCBM: Raymond Gram Swing, News.
WITH: News; Time to Relax.

10:15
WFBR: Sports Preview.
WCBM: Kay Armen, songs.
WITH: War Bond Contest.

10:30
WCAO: Musical Carnival.
WFBR: The Symphonettes.
WCBM: Star for Tonight.
WITH: Time for the News.

10:45
WITH: Boogy-Woogy Time.

11:00
WCAO: News; Film Facts; News.
WFBR: News; Race Results.
WBAL: News; Sports Parade.
WCBM: Journal.
WITH: Ray Noble's Orchestra.

11:15
WCAO: Billy Arnold's Orchestra.
WCBM: Musical Climax.
WBAL: The Open Bible.
WFBR: Eddie Howard Orch.
WITH: Jubilee Time.

11:30
WCAO: Waltz Music.
WFBR: Guy Lombardo's Orchestra.
WCBM: The Music You Want.
WITH: Wax Works.

11:45
WBAL: Hasten the Day.
WITH: Songs For Victory.

12:00
WCAO: News; WCAO Nocturne.
WBAL: News; What's Playing.
WCBM: Charles Spivak Orch.
WITH: News; Nite Owl.

12:15
WITH: Old-Time Songs.
WBAL: Piano Lessons.

12:30
WCAO: American Hotel Asso.
WBAL: Design Dancing.

1:00
WBAL: All-Nite Parade.
WITH: News; Nite Owl.

The Real McCoy

ELKTON, Md.—Feudin's over for two members of the Hatfield and McCoy clans, famous feuders of Kentucky. These two young workers at an Elkton war plant are June Hatfield (1), great-granddaughter of "Devil Anse" Hatfield, leader of the feuding clan, and Susie McCoy, great-granddaughter of Randall McCoy. The two girls are roommates.

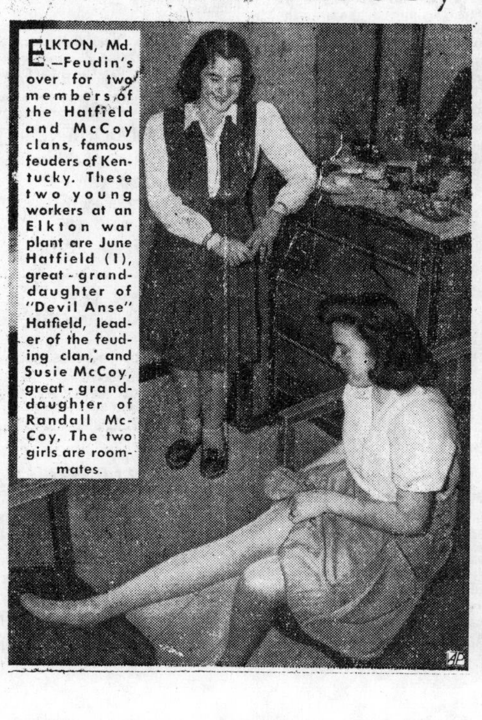

County Groups

(Continued from Page One)

It does not include some $220,000,000 worth of newspaper, radio and other advertising contributed since the bonds went on sale May 1, 1941.

Latest reports show that St. Francis county, Arkansas, has listed $114,150 in sales above its $703,000 goal; Grant County, also in Arkansas, $3,446 over its quota of $75,000 and Prairie County, Montana, listed sales totaling $67,480 compared with an assignement of $63,800.

Rural Woodstock, Conn., topped a $10,000 quota by $300 and said it would hit 200 per cent.

Downs, Kas., asked to subscribe $37,500, reported $42,500 in cash.

Larimore, N. D., said it was 39 per cent over its $43,000 quota.

Three Illinois communities also were over the top: Santa Anna Township was 15 per cent over a $132,000 quota; Goose Creek Township 15 per cent to the good on a goal of $60,000, and Garrett Township reported sales of $78,450 against a quota of $48,000.

SIX MARYLANDERS MISSING IN ACTION

WASHINGTON, Jan. 19 (AP)—The names of six additional Marylanders missing in action in the Mediterranean theatre were announced today by the War Department. They were:

Tech. 5th gr. Elmer H. Fishell, husband of Mrs. Betsy R. Fishell, Long.

Pfc. Noah P. Klinefelter, husband of Mrs. Henrietta Klinefelter, Baltimore.

Pvt. Robert L. Miller, husband of Mrs. Clara H. Miller, Baltimore.

Cpl. Charles J. Mitchell, husband of Mrs. Evelena B. Mitchell, Baltimore.

Pfc. Gilbert L. Nick, son of Mrs. Maude G. Nick, Feedysville.

Pvt. Vito E. Sinush, son of Mrs. Rose Sinush, 659 West Fayette street, Baltimore.

Navy Recruiter

(Continued from Page One)

tions and are measured for the smart uniforms which they receive only after several fittings.

Kept Busy

From the day of their arrival they are busy also with lectures, physical education and drill. They learn naval history, nomenclature and regulations, hygiene and first aid. They have gym classes and swimming lessons. Saturdays they learn to "police their quarters" and march in formation with hundreds of other girls in the weekly Captain's Inspection and Review.

Recreation in many forms is theirs, including movies, radio entertainment and appearances by leading orchestras, actors, singers and other artists. Several radio programs originate from the "USS Hunter," as the school is known, with permanent ship's company and recruits providing talent.

After completing the course, most of the WAVES, as Seaman second class, are assigned to various specialist schools for advance training. A few, because of special experience or aptitude go directly to assignments, with petty officer ratings.

Bonds For Bullets Means Victory

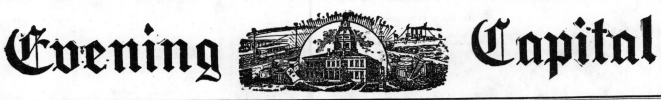

Evening Capital

WEATHER

Increasing cloudiness and not so cold tonight; Wednesday cloudy and somewhat warmer with occasional rain in west portion.

VOL. LX — NO. 17 | EVERY EVENING EXCEPT SUNDAY | ANNAPOLIS, MD., TUESDAY, JANUARY 25, 1944 | SOUTHERN MARYLAND'S ONLY DAILY | THREE CENTS

LATE NEWS

ARGENTINA MAY BREAK WITH AXIS

Santiago, Chile, Jan. 25 (AP) — Argentina is expected to break relations with the Axis before Saturday night, it was learned reliably today.

WOULD ELIMINATE INCOME ESTIMATE

Washington, Jan. 25 (AP)—Senate and House conferees on the $2,275,600,000 tax bill agreed tentatively today on a Senate amendment designed to remove the "fortune telling" element from the estimates of future income required under the pay-as-you-go law.

BRIGGS INDICTED BY GRAND JURY

Washington, Jan. 25 (AP) — George N. Briggs, suspended assistant to Interior Secretary Ickes, was indicted by a Federal grand jury today in connection with the celebrated "Hopkins letter affair." He was charged with forgery, false pretense and use of mails to defraud.

CLEMENCY HEARING FOR LOUIS LEPPKE

Albany, N. Y., Jan. 25 (AP) — A clemency hearing Feb. 2 for Louis (Lepke) Buchalter, one-time boss of "Murder, Inc." now awaiting electrocution in Sing Sing Prison, was announced today by Governor Dewey.

LAND PROMISES INVESTIGATION

Baltimore, Jan. 25 (AP) — An immediate investigation of union charges against the Bethlehem-Fairfield shipyard regarding labor and production policies was promised today by Admiral Emory S. Land, Maritime Commission chairman.

ACTION DEFERRED ON RACING REQUEST

Baltimore, Jan. 25 (AP) — State Racing Commission action on a request to increase the number of racing days over the 1943 season was deferred today pending the return of one commissioner from Florida.

SLAYING LAID TO ZOOT SUIT GANGS

Baltimore, Jan. 25 (AP) — The street slaying of a fleeing colored youth shortly after the critical wounding of another at a tavern was attributed today by police to another outbreak between Baltimore's "zoot suit" gangs.

INCREASE IN FAT COLLECTION

Baltimore, Jan. 25 (AP)—A 50 per cent increase in used household fats collections during December over November's figure was reported for Maryland today by the State Salvage Committee, which attributed the rise to the government's "meat points for fat" program.

WOMAN'S DEATH STILL MYSTERY

Chicago, Jan. 25 (AP)—The box score in the mystery-shrouded, apparently motiveless shooting of Mrs. Frank Starr Williams stood today at zero.

The only new facts unearthed by police were the account given by an unidentified army officer that he had seen Mrs. Williams, wealthy wife of an American diplomat, talking with a woman who answered the description of her assailant a few hours before the tragedy last Thursday in the Drake Hotel.

BANK OF ENGLAND GOVERNOR ILL

London, Jan. 25 (AP)—A bulletin issued by the Bank of England said today that Montagu Norman, 72, governor of the bank since 1920, is suffering from pneumococcal septemia, a form of poisoning of the blood stream following pneumonia.

PATROL BOAT CREW SAVED

New York, Jan. 25 (AP) — A Coast Guard patrol boat exploded after a fire a quarter of a mile off Princes Bay, Staten Island, today but the Third Naval District said Coast Guard fireboats and other patrol vessels removed the crew before the blast. The vessel finally was beached.

The navy did not say how many men were aboard or if any were injured.

Local Tides

TOMORROW

High water — 6:04 A. M., 0.5 feet; 7:01 P. M., 1.1 feet. Low water—0:55 A. M.—0:21 P. M.

Moon rises 9:08 A. M.; sets 7:48
Sun rises 8:19 A. M.; sets 6:19

Tides are given for Annapolis. For Sandy Point, add 15 minutes. For Thomas Point shoal, subtract 30 minutes.

Berlin Reports Allies Near Rome

Indicates They Have Taken Velletri 22 Miles Southeast Of Eternal City

COUNTY BOND SALES INCREASE TO $213,097

Ann Baxter And Nazi Messerschmidt Plane Here Friday

The Fourth War Bond campaign sale of bonds and stamps in Annapolis and Anne Arundel county rose to $213,097.50 as of Saturday, according to a report received today from the Federal Reserve Bank of Richmond.

The sales covered only E, F, and G, bonds purchased in the campaign to raise the $1,650,000 quota assigned the county.

Ann Baxter, motion picture star, and a German Messerschmitt plane shot down over Salerno, Italy, will be in Annapolis on Friday in connection with the bond campaign.

Miss Baxter, who played in "Pied Piper" and "Five Graves to Cairo" will sell bonds at the Annapolis Yacht Yard, the local company offices, the Germantown School and the Navy Experiment Station.

She will also make a short visit to the foot of Main street where the captured Nazi fighter plane will be on display from shortly after 9 A. M. until 4:30 P. M.

The Annapolis section of the National Council of Jewish Women will be in charge of the sale of war stamps and bonds at the plane exhibit. Mrs. Albert Block, is chairman of the group. Those assisting will be Mrs. Harry Woolman, Mrs. Charles Fayder, Mrs. Rubin Labovitz, Mrs. Benjamin Katcef, Mrs. Herbert Kotzin, Mrs. William Reichel and Mrs. Albert J. Goodman. They will use the stamp and bond booth at the Murphy store.

After being exhibited at Anna-

(Continued On Page Eight)

State Official Reports On Fund For Teachers

Comptroller States That Only Two Counties Have Qualified

The State Board of Public Works will meet with Governor O'Conor and representatives of the Maryland Board of Education on Thursday, at 11 A. M. in the State House to discuss the possibility of continuing "bonus" payments to public school teachers throughout the State.

Governor O'Conor said the meeting would be a closed session but a statement would be issued immediately following the conference if possible.

Only two counties of Maryland have qualified for payment of the extra State appropriation for school teachers salaries as provided by the last Legislature, officials of the State Comptroller's Office advised Governor O'Conor today.

As the result, the $115,000 State appropriation, to supplement teachers' salaries, has been diminished by only $31,617, the Governor was informed. Other counties of the State can secure their share of the appropriation by providing the sum necessary to continue the $20.00 monthly payment to school teachers until next January. Thereupon the

(Continued On Page Five)

JAMES S. KOLBE FUNERAL THURSDAY

Funeral services for James Samuel Kolbe of Weems Creek, who died yesterday at Mt. Wilson Hospital after a long illness at the age of 43, will be held Thursday afternoon at 2:30 from Taylor's Funeral Home.

Mr. Kolbe, a machinist, was formerly employed at the Navy Experiment Station, but for a number of years has been at the Washington Navy Yard.

Interment will be in Cedar Bluff Cemetery.

John M. Taylor is the funeral director in charge of arrangements.

FUNERAL RITES FOR MRS. MABEL G. BOND

Funeral services were held yesterday at 2 P. M. for Mrs. Mabel G. Bond, wife of Frank M. Bond, Deputy Register of Wills for Anne Arundel county since 1926, at 2 P. M. at her home at Pasadena. The Rev. C. Edward Berger, rector of St. Anne's Episcopal Church, officiated. Interment was in Greenmount cemetery, Baltimore.

Mrs. Bond, who was a sister-in-law of the late Chief Judge Carroll T. Bond of the Maryland Court of Appeals, was born in Baltimore, the daughter of the late Jacob and Florence Hann Her death occurred suddenly at her home at Pasadena Saturday.

MRS. MYRTLE C. BRADY BURIED YESTERDAY

Funeral services for Mrs. Myrtle Chance Brady were held yesterday from St. Mary's Church.

The Rev. Father John F. McCarthy sang the mass. Burial was in St. Mary's cemetery.

The pallbearers were James A. Brady, Ralph J. Brady, Elwood P. Brady, James A. Lloyd, Claude A. Russell and A. Lucien Brady.

Mrs. Brady died in Baltimore on Friday after a short illness.

She is survived by her husband, Bernard M. Brady, and three sons, Bernard M. Brady, Jr., U. S. Army; Charles Edward Brady and Walter Russell Brady, both in the U. S. Navy.

John M. Taylor had charge of the funeral.

Presentation Of CWS Award Is Planned

Public Ceremony Set For Feb. 1 In Houe Of Delegates Chamber At State House

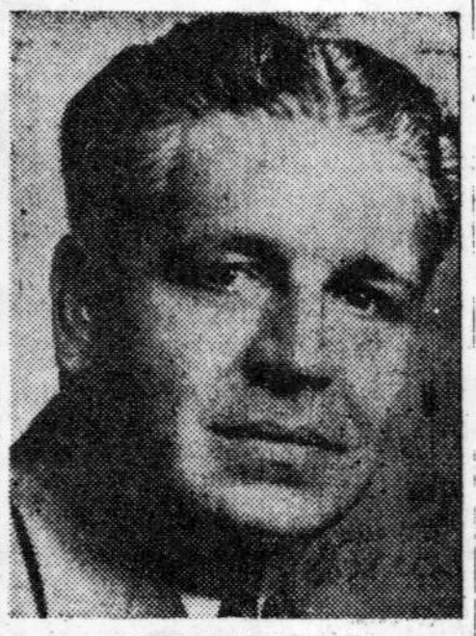

THOMAS DEVINE

Thomas Devine, assistant director in charge of Civilian War Services of the national OCD, will make the presentation of the Citation of Merit to be awarded to the Civilian War Services Division of Anne Arundel County Council of Defense, at ceremonies to be held Tuesday, February 1, at 4 P. M., in the House of Delegates Chamber, in the State House.

This is the first national OCD county wide citation, according to William G. Ewald, executive director of the Maryland Council of Defense.

Mr. Ewald explained that this award has been granted for achieving "to a high degree, the

(Continued On Page Six)

YANKS WADE ASHORE IN NEW LANDING IN ITALY

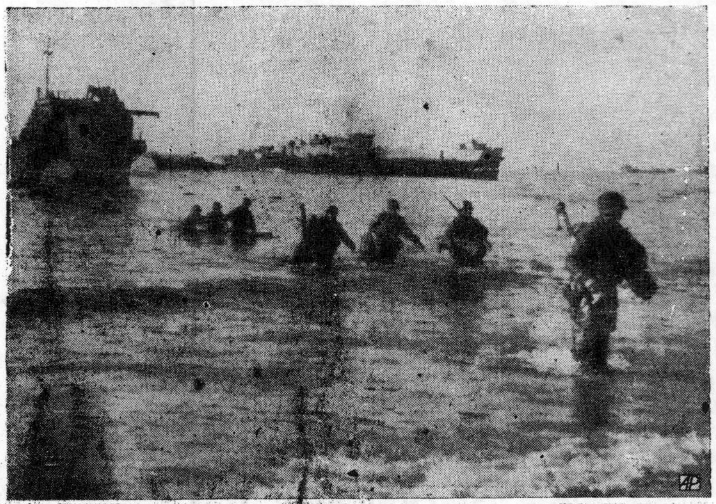

American soldiers of the Allied Fifth Army wade ashore in a new landing behind the German lines on the west coast of Italy. This is a U. S. Army Signal Corps photo via OWI radio from the Mediterranean theatre.

ALLIED HEADQUATERS ANNOUNCE TROOPS MOVED 12 MILES INLAND

Germans Claim Velletri Has Been Destroyed—Allies Dominate Appian Way and Coastal Rail Line—Battle Hastily Organized Nazi Battle Groups—German Counterattacks Slacken In Southern Italy—Allied Bombers Batter French Coast In Daylight Raids—Russians Cut Leningrad-Estonia Railroad At Smolkovo—Britain Refuses To Recognize Bolivian Government

(By the Associated Press)

The Berlin radio declared today that Velletri, on the Appian Way 22 miles southeast of Rome, had been destroyed, and indicated the Allies had captured the town.

"American troops are finding debris and ashes there after their own bombs transformed the little town into a heap of ruins," the broadcast said.

Velletri is about 18 miles northeast of Nettuno.

Allied headquarters announced only that American and British troops had advanced 12 miles inland. The Germans were reported shifting their troops from the Cassino-Garigliano front in the south to meet the new threat to Rome. A headquarters officer said Adolf Hitler, desperately needed a victory, "may decide to throw great forces into Italy and tell his generals they must produce a victory at any cost."

MEET NAZI BATTLE GROUPS

The famous Appian Way to Rome and the main coastal rail line are about 12 miles inland from the Allied Nettuno-Anzio beachhead, but it was not specified definitely that the invasion forces had reached them. It was obvious, however, that they are at least under Allied domination.

The Allied spearheads met "hastily organized battle groups" of Germans apparently moved northward from the Fifth army front around Cassino.

The Germans still were launching fierce counterattacks on the main Fifth army front at Cassino, but these blows have decreased somewhat in number and intensity in the last 24-hours, indicating that enemy forces were being pulled back to meet the invasion flanking threat.

The beachhead has been lengthened, Allied headquarters declared, without disclosing the area it covers. Reinforcements and supplies continued to pour in with little enemy interference, and the communique said the town of Anzio, bordering Nettuno to the west, had been taken.

Rail Line

The United Nations radio at Algiers said the troops striking inland were within almost a mile of the double-track Rome-Naples electric rail line.

American patrols recrossed the Rapido river to prove enemy defenses before Cassino but no counterattack was launched by the Allies to keep a force on the western bank. The Nazis, who on Sunday hurled the Americans back across the river, made no attempts to cross to the eastern bank.

French troops in the northernmost area beat back several more enemy counterattacks, and a hot battle swirled for the Mt. Croce area.

British troops kept their bridgehead across the Garigliano river on the left flank of the Fifth army line despite new Nazi counterattacks, and made some gains in the Damiano bridge area. The Germans were reported counterattacking recklessly in the Minturno and Castelforet areas.

Heavy Allied bombers blasted

(Continued On Page Eight)

MRS. EMMA A. GRAF DIED YESTERDAY

Mrs. Emma Achenback Graf died yesterday at the Emergency Hospital after a short illness, aged 89 years.

Mrs. Graf, who was born in Baltimore, came to Annapolis in her early childhood, and had lived at 81 College avenue for the last 76 years.

She is survived by one son, Albert E. Graf, 81 College avenue; one sister, Mrs. J. L. Amos, Baltimore; and one half-brother, Charles Gates, 83 College avenue.

Funeral services, Thursday at 2:30 P. M. at the Hopping Funeral Home, 170 West street. Burial in St. Anne's cemetery.

USO COMMITTEE MEETS THURSDAY

The monthly meeting of the USO Committee of Management will be held at 8 P. M. Thursday at the USO Club, St. Mary's street.

Clarence E. Tyler, chairman of the committee, will preside.

WILL HEAR PAROLE CASES THURSDAY

Herman M. Moser, State Parole Director, announced that a total of 28 parole applications were scheduled for review Thursday during the bi-weekly hearing.

Forestry Bureau Moving Here

Takes Quarters In State Office Building

The State Department of Forests and Parks was moving today from its headquarters in Baltimore here to the State Office building here. The department has maintained headquarters in Baltimore since its establishment nearly 40 years ago.

State Forester Joseph F. Kaylor transferred his office to the State capitol yesterday, but said several more days would be required to complete transferral of all office records and equipment.

The forestry department will occupy offices vacated by the State Board of Hair Dressers and Beauty Culturists and the Bureau of Mines. The Hair Dressers' Board and the Department of Correction recently left the State Office building to establish headquarters in Baltimore, and the Bureau of Mines was transferred to the space formerly occupied by the correction department.

HOLD SERVICES FOR THOMAS SEARS

Funeral services for Thomas Sears, 87, retired Best Gate farmer, were held yesterday from Edward's Chapel on the Defense Highway.

The services were conducted by the Rev. A. F. T. Raum, of the Eastport Methodist Church, and the Rev. Robert C. Wheeler, of Baltimore, a former minister. Burial was in the chapel cemetery.

The pallbearers were Albert Cranford, Howard Armiger, Ralston Sears, Benjamin Sears, John Crutchley and Webster F. King.

Mr. Sears, who was one of the oldest members of Edward's Chapel, operated a farm at Best Gate for more than 50 years. He died Friday night at his home.

He is survived by his widow, Mrs. Ida Virginia Sears, six daughters, Mrs. S. Reese Abbott, Miss Sadie Sears, Mrs. Frank T. Rawlings, Mrs. Hattie E. Smith, Mrs. Wilmer J. Lang and Mrs. Mowbray Bowen and four sons, William T. Sears, Bernard W. Sears, J. Clifton Sears and J. Edgar Sears. A sister, Mrs. Rosie E. Sclote, of Baltimore, and 17 grandchildren also survive.

John M. Taylor was in charge of the funeral.

Admirals' Thoughts On Ball Programs 44 Years Ago, Display At Library Shows

The thoughts of Admiral Ernest Joseph King, commander in chief of the U. S. fleet, and of Vice Admiral Adolphus Andrews, are very different today from what they were 44 years ago.

For in 1900 Midshipmen King and Andrews, as members of the farewell ball committee at the Naval Academy, were concerned over such matters as whether to have the two step "A Bunch of Blackberries" precede or follow the two step "Honolulu Belle."

The program for the ball which two future admirals helped arrange is one of a collection of Naval Academy dance programs on display at the Public Library. The collection which begins with an invitation to the first ball, in 1846, has been lent the library by the owner, Miss Isabella H. Claude, 22 State Circle.

Galop, Polka, Popular

When William D. Leahy, of Wisconsin, was on the program to arrange the farewell affair given by the class of '97 to the class of '96, the galop and the polka were popular. Among the numbers the orchestra played were "The Belle of Colorado," a caprice; "Hartford Post" and "The New Bully" both polkas; "Coeur de Lion" a galop; and "Arrah, Go On" a Schottische.

Midshipmen were humming the Floradora waltz in 1903, and high pompadoured Howard Chandler Christy belles decorated the program, when William Frederick

(Continued On Page Six)

Card of Thanks

The wife of Philip Ennis wishes to express her gratitude to the neighbors and friends, for the lovely flowers, the use of their cars and for their splendid cooperation during his long illness.

MRS. ELIZABETH ENNIS

FOR SALE

MIXED WOOD

$17.50 per cord—$10.00 for half a cord

Quick Delivery

PHONE 4071

NOTICE

Attention Annapolis Post No. 304 V.F.W. All members are requested to report in front of Post Office Building, Church Circle, Tuesday, January 25, 1944 at 7:45 P. M., to attend funeral services for our late Comrade Edward Horyda.

JOHN SCHAWALLENBERG,
Commander.

LOST

Either Monday or Tuesday Black and Gold Cross with pearl in center.

Liberal Reward if returned

PHONE 5142

3 Randall Court

"WOODBOURNE"
Convalescent Home
OPEN APRIL 1st
Phone W. R. 25F21 or write
BOX NO. 50
Greenock, Md.

FOR SALE

MIXED FIREWOOD

Pine and Hardwood cut any Length

$18.00 per cord delivered

Phone 2381

LOST

On Sunday a 4 months old Black Cocker Spaniel with small white streak on chest. Male. Reward if returned to owner at

12 TANEY AVENUE

Phone 2205

CASH FOR YOUR AUTOMOBILE
Andrew Krause
— Chevrolet —
900 BLOCK WEST ST.
Phone 2651

Tilghman Company
JEWELERS
WILL BE CLOSED EVERY WEDNESDAY
UNTIL FURTHER NOTICE

Have You Bought Your War Bond?

Evening Capital

VOL. LX — NO. 32 | EVERY EVENING EXCEPT SUNDAY | ANNAPOLIS, MD., FRIDAY, FEBRUARY 11, 1944 | SOUTHERN MARYLAND'S ONLY DAILY | THREE CENTS

WEATHER

Snow mixed with sleet changing to rain with slowly rising temperature and increasing winds today; cloudy, windy, and much colder tonight.

Nazis Claim Advance Below Rome

Berlin Reports Capture Of Carroceto And Declares 4,000 Allies Surrender

ROOSEVELT SAYS SITUATION IS VERY TENSE AND FIGHTING HARD

(By the Associated Press)

The Germans said officially today they had captured the railroad station in Carroceto (Aprilia), northern stronghold in the slender Allied beachhead below Rome, as the outnumbered Americans and British turned every available plane against the enemy siege lines. The town is 10 miles north of Anzio. beachead port.

The Berlin communique said 4,000 Allies had surrendered in the beachhead and that 89 tanks had been captured or destroyed. "Mopping up of the Aprilia area was continuing," the enemy added.

President Roosevelt said a very tense situation and very heavy fighting existed in the beachhead but the Allies on the whole control the seas and the air.

The Chief Executive told a press-radio conference that "we are praying for good weather, to aid sea and air operations."

The German report lacked confirmation but Algiers dispatches described the Allied aerial attacks yesterday as one of the greatest ground support operations of the war.

STORMY SKIES AID GERMANS

The Germans today were aided by stormy skies which have curtailed activity of the Allied air force and the Nazi armored units are striking southward against the British beachhead positions north of Anzio, using their tanks as mobile artillery in a deadly roving role.

It was clear and cold early yesterday but the rains cancelled much of the air support the Allies had planned for this afternoon, giving the Germans freer hand to unleash their growing power on the ground.

Americans still fighting bitterly in the ruins of Cassino on the main Fifth army front, captured five more buildings. Their artillery leveled the town prison which had been turned into a Nazi fort, but the Germans still fought tooth and nail from underground dungeons and cellars.

Countless tons of bombs smashed down on the Germans yesterday at all points ringing the bridgehead and their main operating points around Rome as heavy bombers were diverted from long range targets to join medium and fighter-bombers in furious slaps protecting the American and British troops. The planes hit Albano, Cisterna, Velletri, Campoleone and Cecchina.

But despite the fury of the air offensive, the Germans apparently retained the initiative on the ground and lashed out in many probing attacks at various points around the beachhead. Five full German divisions and a brigade were attempting to smash the Allied troops back into the sea.

All indications pointed to a main German attempt to break the Allied lines in the beachhead.

Bomb Frankfurt

American Flying Fortreses, blasted Frankfurt-on-the-Main with tons of high explosives again today, striking the already hard hit southwest German industrial and transport center for the second time in four days and the fourth time since Jan. 29.

While this assault was in progress, Liberators again operated independently of the Forts, slashing at military installations in the Pas-de-Calai area and American Marauders in their ninth operation in 11 days struck other targets in the "rocket gun" sector of northern France.

Today's operations kept the unprecendented Allied aerial assault going through yet another 24 hour cycle and followed up yesterday's mighty attacks on the German manufacturing city of Brunswick and the Gilze-Rijen air base in Holland, precipitating air fights in which the Americans were credited officially with downing 84 enemy planes. Twenty-nine

LEADERS OF KWAJALEIN ATTACK

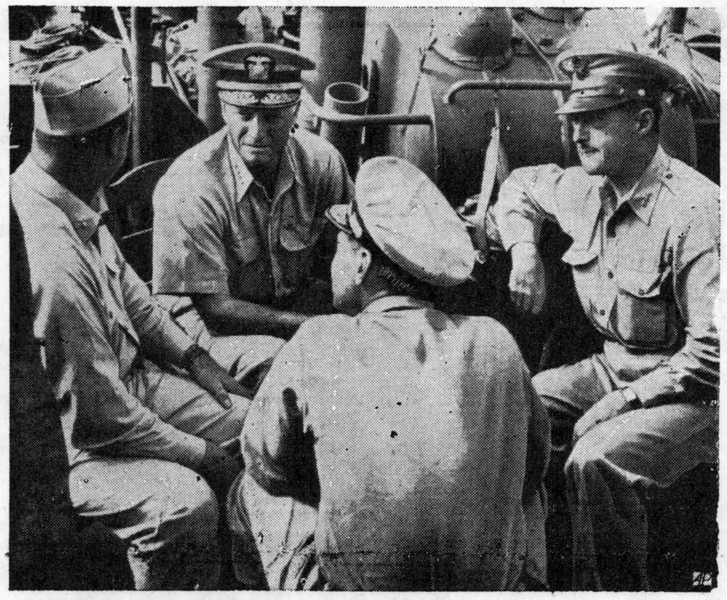

Aboard a Naval craft nearing Kwajalein Island, leaders of the successful assault on the Kwajalein atoll confer on deck. Facing the camera at left is Adm. Chester W. Nimitz, commander in chief of the Pacific fleet. At right is Lt. Gen. Robert C. Richardson, head of the U. S. Army Hawaii Department. The other two men are not identified. (AP Wirephoto.)

LATE NEWS

BRICKER WOULD LIMIT PRESIDENT'S TERM

Washington, Feb. 11 (AP)—Gov. John W. Bricker urged today a constitutional limitation on presidential tenure.

The Ohio governor, who is seeking the Republican nomination for chief executive, told a luncheon audience at the National Press Club he thought the next President should devote himself to the welfare of the nation, avoiding politics.

SNOW HITS NORTHEAST U. S.

A heavy, wind-whipped snow storm struck the northeastern part of the United States today while in a wide section of the already snow-blanketed midwest the season's most severe cold wave drove temperatures far below zero.

Eight to 12 inches of snow was predicted for New York City. An emergency storm warning was issued by the weather bureau at Boston, which forecast up to 10 inches in New England. Strong winds and increasing cold were expected to add to hazards throughout the northeast.

FEW AUTOS LEFT IN RATION POOL

Washington, Feb. 11 (AP)—Most of the new passenger cars remaining in the ration pool—estimated at less than 50,000 — will have been released to eligible buyers by July 1.

The Office of Price Administration (OPA), reporting this today, said that meanwhile monthly quotas will become smaller and eligibility requirements will be tightened.

REPORT OUSTING OF BOLIVIAN GOVERNMENT

Santiago, Chile, Feb. 11 (AP) — The newspaper La Hora said today it had received a private but unconfirmed report that the recently established Nationalist Government of Gualberto Villarroel in Bolivia had been ousted in a counter revolution and the leaders jailed.

DR. HENS GETS FIVE YEAR TERM

Baltimore, Feb. 11 (AP) — Dr. James S. Hens, former Spring Grove State Hospital staff physician and part-time examiner at the Fifth Regiment Armory induction center in Baltimore, was sentenced today to serve five years in a Federal prison for counseling a prospective inductee to evade selective service.

REVENUE BUREAU BLOCKS TAX PLAN

Washington, Feb. 11 (AP)—Representative Robertson (D-Va) said today that Internal Revenue Bureau opposition had just about stymied his proposal that the government do the mathematics on the tax returns due March 15 from some 25,000,000 small taxpayers.

24 Lost In Air Liner Crash

MEMPHIS, Feb. 11 (AP)—The Coast Guard reported today that drag lines had located part of an American Airlines Transcontinental plane that crashed into the Mississippi river with 24 persons aboard, including 3 crewmen.

A cryptic radio message from patrol boats to headquarters here said merely "piece of plane found." Later contact with the boat said it "definitely" was part of the plane.

The coast guard and U. S. Army engineers were conducting the search in a 22-foot channel 15 miles below Memphis where an employee of the engineers said he saw the ship crash and explode last midnight.

President Will Address Nation

WASHINGTON, Feb. 11 (AP) — President Roosevelt will address the nation tomorrow afternoon from 4:30 to 5 o'clock Eastern War Time.

The speech will be in connection with ceremonies attendant upon the presentation of a destroyer-escort to French naval authorities under lend-lease. The subject of Mr. Roosevelt's address was not disclosed.

Local Tides

TOMORROW

High water—7:57 A. M., 0.6 feet; 8:25 P. M., 0.8 feet. Low water—2:26 A. M., 2:15 P. M.

Moon rises 9:56 P. M. ;sets 9:57 A. M.

Sun rises 8:03 A. M.; sets 6:38 P. M.

Tides are given for Annapolis. For Sandy Point, add 15 minutes. For Thomas Point shoal, subtract 30 minutes.

INDIVIDUAL CITIZENS URGED TO LOOK UPON FOOD AS WAR WEAPON

County Canning Center Will Be Enlarged To Help Conserve Local Food

How the individual citizen can turn food into a real weapon for winning the war was explained by speakers, motion pictures, posters and exhibits, to an audience in the city council room in the Municipal Building, last night at a meeting held by the Food Fights for Freedom committee under the auspices of the County Civilian War Services.

Everybody, even city dwellers, were urged by County Agent Stanley E. Day to produce more food by planning now to plant more victory gardens this spring. Development of a synthetic nitrogen will be a help to the gardener this year, Mr. Day said.

People were urged to conserve what they grow by Lee W. Adkins, in charge of the community canning centers established by the Board of Education last summer, who said the centers will be equipped to accommodate three times as many canners this year.

The canning center at the West Annapolis school will be greatly enlarged, Mr. Adkins added and by starting earl'er in the season he hopes that 75,000 quarts of food will be canned instead of the 25,000 put up last summer.

Black Markets

Since the weapon of food can become a boomerang if it hits the black market, Burleigh Fooks, of the War Price and Rationing Board, explained how the individual can fight black markets.

"If the black market were one big market, the OPA would be able to curb it," Mr. Fooks said. "But what makes up the black market are innumerable little leaks. Many consumers themselves unwittingly help it along.

"The inability of people to recognize a black market is astounding. If a butcher offers to sell you meat without taking points, when points are required, you are aiding the black market, because it means that somebody is going to have to do without his share.

"The uncle who gave his

(Continued On Page Four)

MINUTE MEN GET SERVICE BARS FOR DRILL ATTENDANCE

Members of the Ninth Battalion, Maryland Reserve Militia, have been presented with service bars for 100 percent. attendance during the year.

The bars were presented at the Bladen street armory by Col. Caesar Aeillo, battalion commander, to members of the 900th company from Annapolis, the 901st company from St. Margaret's; the 903rd campany from Mayo and the 907th company from Glen Burnie.

Colonel Aeillo pointed out that eight companies had been organized in the county, but that four had been placed on the inactive list.

The members of the Annapolis company who received bars were Capt. Alonzo Hubbard, Capt. John Dawson, chaplain; First Lieut. Anthony Harold, Second Lieut. William Vanous; Sergeants J. David Cordell, William Buser, Louis G. Calabrese, Nicholas J. Mandris, Melvin B. Schlossman, Watler Schurr, Lloyd M. Smith, N. M. Terry, Jr., W. H. Bradford, Aaron Alshul and Privates Linwood Cantler, Thomas Espinosa and John J. Golden.

PLACES FOR NEW MEMBERS IN CHORUS

Due to the shifting of navy personnel in Annapolis, there are now places for new members in the St. John's Community Chorus, Nicholas Nabokov, the director, said today. Vacancies have occurred in the tenor and soprano sections, where new members are particularly needed, but anyone wishing to join the chorus will be welcomed, Mr. Nabokov added.

Rehearsals will be held every Monday and Friday at 7 P. M., starting next Monday. The chorus, which is in its thrid year, is preparing to give a version of St. John's Passion by Bach, for its spring concert.

School P.-T.A. Holds Play To Mark Founding

Stage "Reminiscence" At Meeting Of Organization

"Reminiscence," a dramatiza- of the founding of the P.-T. A., was staged at the meeting of the Germantown P.-T. A. yesterday, in the Germantown school auditorium.

"Emily Andrews" was skillfully acted by Mrs. John Dawson, with Mrs. C. C. Bramble portraying the part of "Mother Andrews" who attended the first meeting of the Congress of Mothers in 1897.

The story of this Congress was recounted at a Founders' Day meeting of the P.-T. A. The president, "Mrs. Jones," was delightfully characterized by Mrs. Newton Berger and the program chairman, "Mrs. Bright," was played with deftness and poise by Mrs. Forest W. Harder.

Mother Andrews

"Mother Andrews'" story of the first convention called by Alice McClellan Burney and Phebe Apperton Hurst supplied an interesting historical account of the congress.

All of the cast had made previous appearaces in amateur performances.

Assisting as the P.-T. A. group

(Continued On Page Six)

Caravan Club Reelects Officers

Mrs. Elizabeth A. Kramer Again Heads Organization

Mrs. Elizabeth A. Kramer was re-elected president at the Caravan Club which met last night. Other re-elected officers were: treasurer, Mrs. Grayce Myers, financial secretary, Mrs. Pauline Phipps, recording secretary, Mrs. Vera Engelke.

The entertainment committee consists of Mrs. Gertrude Rodgers, chairman, assisted by Mrs. Magie Tucker, Mrs. Pauline Braun, Mrs. Sadie Taylor, Mrs. Louis Phipps, Mrs. Alma Steinet, Mrs. Hilda White and Mrs. Edith Garner.

The Ways and Means committee

(Continued On Page Six)

KIWANIS CLUB AIDS IN SCRAP COLLECTION

A special committee was appointed by the Kiwanis Club at its weekly meeting to supervise the collection of scrap for salvage.

Former Judge Linwood L. Clark was appointed chairman of the committee. A truck has been donated for part-time use in gathering scrap.

The club requested all persons having 100 pounds or more of waste paper or 200 pounds or more of scrap metal to notify Mr. Clark.

The weekly session, held at Carvel Hall, was devoted to routine business. The secretary reported the proceedings of the last meeting of the board of directors.

J. M. McAllister of the Baltimore Club was a guest.

County $353,611 Below War Bond Quota

Joseph C. Harsch, Ralph Powers To Speak At Service Club Rally Tomorrow

Annapolis and Anne Arundel county were trailing $353,611 below the $1,650,000 quota assigned today with the Fourth War Bond campaign ending on Tuesday.

The Federal Reserve Bank of Richmond, Va., reported that total purchases in the city and county, through Feb. 8 were $1,296,389.

Joseph D. Lazenby, Chairman County War Finance committee pointed out that at this time in the Third War Loan campaign the city and county had purchased a total of $1,986,000 bonds and stamps. He said 10 Maryland counties had gone over the top while Anne Arundel was still struggling to make its quota.

Club Meeting

The president of all the city service clubs today requested their members to attend the war bond service club rally to be held at the Annapolis High School at 8 P. M. tomorrow.

Joseph C. Harsch, CBS news commentator and former war correspondent for the Christian Science Monitor, and Ralph Powers, who conducts the radio "Quiz of Two Cities" will speak. Both will come here from Washington.

Mrs. Katherine Ponder of Annapolis will sing. James Winship Lewis is coming here from Balti-

(Continued On Page Four)

MINUTE MEN TO HOLD GAME PARTY

A game party for the benefit of the 900th Company, Maryland Reserve Militia, will be held at the Bladen street armory at 8 P. M. February 25.

D.A.R. CHAPTER HEARS ADDRESS BY MRS. ROBERT

The necessity for serious thought and study of post-war planning was stressed by Mrs. Henry M. Robert, Jr., in her talk to the members of the Peggy Stewart Tea Party Chapter, Daughters of the American Revolution on the occasion of their Washington's Birthday celebration.

Pointing out that she could not, in one short talk, present all the post-war plans, Mrs. Robert, who is honorary president general of the national society, outlined the principal features of several plans with the purpose of stimulating the members to thought and investigation of their own. She stressed the fact that no one of these plans is complete and able to cover all necessities. Changing events and circumstances will mold the final plan, so the solution to the problem lies in the future, she stated.

She explained that the world is changing so rapidly we cannot keep up with it unless we control our thinking. We must train our thoughts to change just as fast as we are changing materially,

(Continued On Page Six)

THREE BRUSH FIRES ARE EXTINGUISHED

Three brush fires kept Eastport and West Annapolis firemen busy yesterday afternoon.

At Eastport a fire on the farm of Harry Feldmeyer for a time threatened a nearby woodland, but was extinguished after about 45 minutes.

West Annapolis firemen kept a brush fire from spreading to the garage at the home of Harry Ortland, Jr., at Wardour, and later were called to put out another at the foot of Walton street.

Y DIRECTORS TO MEET MONDAY

The board of directors of the Y.W.C.A. will meet Monday at 2 P. M. at the Y Building.

BASKETBALL
ANNAPOLIS YACHT YARD
versus
SERVICE UNIT FT. GEORGE MEADE
PW CAMP 1322
At St. John's College
Tonight 8:00 P. M.

BOOKKEEPING
And Tax Service
For any business at exceptionally low cost.
S. S. BUSINESS SERVICE
P. O. Box 88, Annapolis, Md.

RUMMAGE SALE
Sponsored by
GIRL SCOUT MARINERS
Market Space
Saturday, February 11
8 A. M. to 6 P. M.

FOR SALE
MIXED FIREWOOD
Pine and Hardwood cut any Length
$18.00 per cord delivered
Phone 2381

FOR SALE
MIXED FIRE WOOD
$17.50 per cord—$10.00 for half a cord
Quick Delivery
PHONE 4071

CARD OF THANKS

We wish to thank our friends and neighbors for their kindness during the illness and death of our mother.

MR. and Mrs. C. F. HINES

GAME PARTY
Every Friday night at 8 o'clock
ARNOLD VOLUNTEER FIRE DEPARTMENT
Two Blocks from Arnold Station
Admission 50 Cents

WANTED
GENERAL CLERK
With Typing Ability
Also Stenographer with knowledge of Shorthand
METROPOLITAN
LIFE INSURANCE COMPANY
68 State Circle Phone 2791

CASH FOR YOUR AUTOMOBILE
Andrew Krause
— Chevrolet —
900 BLOCK WEST ST.
Phone 2651

RIDE
CEDAR PARK RIDING ACADEMY
1½ Mile from Church Circle or take Arundel Bus
BEGINNERS WELCOME
Horses Bought and Sold
PHONE 6269

WE NEED AT ONCE 100
1939-40-41 Used Cars
WILL PAY
HIGHEST CASH PRICE
Marbert Motors
261 WEST STREET DIAL 2335

THIS IS BOY SCOUT WEEK
HELP THE BOY SCOUTS
Over 1½ million former Boy Scouts are serving with the armed forces. In order to expand and continue to promote this work, the Anne Arundel County Boy Scout Committee needs your financial help.
Send your contribution, of any denomination today to
66 MARYLAND AVENUE

The Fellowship Of Prayer

FIRST WEEK IN LENT

Ash Wednesday, February 23

Morally Bankrupt: "They ... became vain in their imaginations, and their foolish hearts were darkened." "Their ignorant minds became dark." (Moffatt. Read Romans 1:18-21. Psalm 51.

So St. Paul diagnosed the case of a sin-sick world and said with the stern sadness of a physician of the soul: "Thou ailest here and here." This entire chapter is sad, sad reading, for it is the acid etching of a morally bankrupt order. We blush to read it aloud—and find the same shadows darkening the headlines of today's newspapers.

Moral bankruptcy is always the final abyss; and its causes are continuously and tragically the same. Our own world is dark with death because, fundamentally, power and pride, vain in imagination and darkly ignorant in mind, asked every question in their grandiose madness, save the one simple question to which every other question is subject: Is this right?

When any civilization comes under the control of wicked stupidity, its sun has set and its cities ruined by vain imagination furnish the ashes for Ash Wednesday. This is the darkness upon which the Sun of Righteousness arose in judgment and redemption.

Prayer: Almighty and Most Merciful God, pardon, we beseech thee, our vain imaginations and our darkened hearts, in that we have forsaken thy laws and are vainly wise in our own conceits. Grant us new understanding to know thee and faithfulness to do they will that hereafter our paths may be straightforward and perfect to the end. Amen.

Agriculture supports about 90 percent of Ecuador's population.

HOW TO SHOP WITH RATION TOKENS
New System Saves Time, Trouble, Manpower and Paper

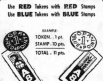
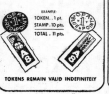

ALL RED and BLUE stamps in War Ration Book 4 are **WORTH 10 POINTS EACH**

FIVE BLUE stamps become valid beginning Feb. 27: 8A, 8B, 8C, 8D and 8E — EACH STAMP WORTH 10 POINTS

THREE RED stamps become valid beginning Feb. 27: 8A, 8B and 8C — New stamps become valid every 2 weeks — EACH STAMP WORTH 10 POINTS

Tear off ACROSS TOP of page

RED and BLUE TOKENS are **WORTH 1 POINT EACH**

RED and BLUE TOKENS are used to make CHANGE for RED and BLUE stamps only when purchase is made — EXAMPLE: TOKEN . 1 pt. STAMP . 10 pts. TOTAL . 11 pts.

Use RED Tokens with RED Stamps
Use BLUE Tokens with BLUE Stamps

IMPORTANT!
POINT VALUES of BROWN and GREEN STAMPS are NOT changed
BROWN STAMPS, Y and Z in Book No. 3 Good till Mar. 20, 1944
GREEN STAMPS, K, L and M in Book No. 4 Good till Mar. 20, 1944
TOKENS REMAIN VALID INDEFINITELY

Ration tokens come into use on February 27. The tokens, a bit smaller than a dime, will be of two colors—red and blue, corresponding to the red and blue stamps: the blue stamps in Ration Book IV for canned or processed foods and the red stamps in the same Ration Book for meats and fats. The tokens are to be given in change whenever a transaction requires change. While currently valid green and brown stamps are still good until March 20, tokens may be given in change for them, but their present point value will remain the same. However, the value of each red and blue stamp in Ration Book four will be valued at 10 points each, regardless of the figure on the stamp. These red and blue stamps will be good for about 12 weeks.

For example, on February 27, five blue stamps (A8, B8, C8, D8 and E8) in Ration Book four to be used for purchases of processed foods become valid; and a group of five blue stamps will be validated each month thereafter for 10 points each or a total of 50 points per month. Likewise, on February 27, three red stamps (A8, B8 and C8) in Ration Book four for meats and fats become valid; and a group of three red stamps will become valid every two weeks thereafter for 10 points each, which gives the consumer 30 points every two weeks with which to purchase meats, or 60 points per month.

Would Cut Committees For Special Session

Favor Retention Of Only Four Committees For Legislative Session

Abandonment of a majority of the 70 legislative committees during next month's special session of the General Assembly was proposed today by high-ranking administration officials.

The administration representatives, who declined to be quoted by name, said the ramifications of legislative organization often involved personal rivalries and delayed procedure — two conditions Governor O'Conor hopes to avoid when the session starts on March 6 or thereabouts.

These sources said they favored retention of the four major committees—Senate Finance and Judicial Proceedings, and the House Ways and Means and Judiciary groups.

They recommended also that the composition of these four committees remain the same as that during the 1943 regular session, except for changes necessitated because of a few personnel changes in the Assembly.

Presiding Officers

Election of a new Senate president and House Speaker and possibly of new majority floor leaders probably will make it necessary to name new chairmen of at least two and possibly all four of these committees.

Thus, if Sen. James J. Lindsay (D-Balto. Co.) and Delegate John S. White (D-Prince George's) become respectively Senate president and Speaker of the House—as seems possible — chairmanship of the Finance Committee and its counterpart in the House would go to two other legislators.

Sen. Joseph R. Byrnes (D-Baltimore 5th) has been prominently mentioned by administration spokesmen as Senate floor leader.

Byrnes is chairman of the Judicial Proceedings Committee and if he is made floor leader, his present post would be vacated. Another possibility is that Byrnes may remain head of the Judicial Committee and that Sen. John B. Funk (D-Frederick), a member of the Finance Committee, may advance to floor leadership.

Likewise, White's elevation to speakership would leave vacant the chairmanship of the House Ways and Means Committee.

At any rate, the administration was pictured as favoring abandonment of most of the 31 Senate and 39 House committees during the special session, since it considers the legislation scheduled for action of an emergency, State-wide nature and not requiring particular attention from the numerous other groups.

Another proposal from high administration sources was abolition during the special session of the many Assembly employees such as doorkeepers and bill clerks. The Governor was represented as hoping to keep the expense of the session to a minimum by this means.

The U. S. heavy cruiser Pittsburgh slides down the ways into the Fore River at Quincy, Mass., following launching ceremonies at the Bethlehem Steel Co. shipyards. (AP Wirephoto).

Yacht Yard Team Wins State Title

Hold Crown As Unlimited Divisional Champs Of State Basketball Association

The Annapolis Yacht Yard basketball team won the unlimited divisional championship of the Maryland Basketball Association last night by defeating the Glenn L. Martin Engineers, 56 to 32, in the Baltimore City College gymnasium.

The two teams, winners of a playoff in the Baltimore leagues, clashed before a big crowd. Both were slow in getting started but once the Boatmen began rolling they kept ahead.

Zeke Zebrowski was the high scorer of the game with 19 points, while Johnnie Schuerholz sparked the club by his feeding. Time after time he dribbled the ball through the Martin team until he found a Boatman open.

The Yacht Yard team has now won two trophies, having taken the Baltimore Commercial League crown to win the right to compete for the Basketball Association title.

The Boatmen will now represent Baltimore in a tournament to be played in New York for the benefit of the Red Cross.

During the season the Yacht Yard quint won 20 games in 21 starts. The only game they dropped was to the Naval Academy junior varsity.

The summary:

YACHT YARD	G	F	T
Bielecki, f.	5	0	10
Revell, f.	0	1	1
Schuerholz, f.	2	1	5
Bereya, f.	4	1	9
Zebrowski, c.	7	5	19
Barczak, g.	1	0	2
Blades, g.	3	2	8
Forney, g.	1	0	2
Totals	23	10	56

MARTIN ENGINEERS	G	F	T
Reppert	4	4	12
Koch	2	0	4
Parks	2	0	4
Renback	0	0	0
Hassebrock	0	0	0
Baker	0	0	0
Warner	2	0	4
Dengler	0	1	1
Knuebel	1	5	7
Meehan	0	0	0
Totals	11	10	32

Half-time score—Yacht Yard, 28; Martin Engineers, 12.

Senate Primary

(Continued from Page One)

filed yesterday for the Democratic nomination to succeed himself in the position he has held for three terms.

He was viewed as the probable winner over Charles Baden of Brooklyn Park and Vincent F. Long of Baltimore, also Democratic aspirants.

Tydings' announcement of candidacy brought to six the number of senatorial aspirants, three Democrats and three Republicans.

Contests for the Republican Senate nomination and the Democratic Congressional nominations in the first and three and, possibly, the second district shaped up as the principal primary fights. Closest balloting was predicted for the Democratic Congressional seat which Representative David J. Ward (D-Md.) of the First District now occupies.

Ward Opposed

Ward is opposed by Dudley G. Roe, former State Senator; Leon Asa Andrus, weekly newspaper publisher; and Calvert C. Merriken, members of the House of Delegates from Caroline county.

State Senator Wilmer Fell Davis (R-Caroline), minority floor leader in the Senate, was unopposed so far for the Republican nomination in the same district.

No primary opposition to three of the State's six Congressmen had been announced as the final day for filing opened, and Representative J. Glenn Beall (R-Md.) of the Sixth District had no opposition from either party.

Some Unopposed

Unopposed aspirants today were Representative Daniel Ellison (R-Md.) of the Fourth District; Representative Lansdale G. Sasscer (D-Md.) of the Fifth District; Beall; Wilfred T. McQuaid of Baltimore, seeking the Republican nomination for Congress in the Second District; and John W. Benson of Baltimore, seeking the Republican nomination in the Third District.

Three Republicans have filed for Tydings' seat: Paul Robertson, chairman of the Baltimore City State Central Committee, and Blanchard Randall, Jr., also of Baltimore; and Rives Matthews of Princess Anne.

WIN CHAMPIONSHIP

The Annapolis Yacht Yard basketball squad which last night won the championship of Baltimore City is shown above. Standing, left to right, Charles Skipper, Sr., manager; Robert Forney, Edward Barczak, Alexander Zerbrowski and Tom Bielecki. Kneeling, left to right, Raymond Krul, Milton Blades, Maxie Toy, Bennie Bereza and John Schuerholz.

"ON THE JUMP"...by PAP'

FRED SHEFFIELD—THE SOPHOMORE ACE IS THE ONLY VETERAN ON THE UTAH UNIVERSITY BASKETBALL TEAM WHICH WON THE UNOFFICIAL MOUNTAIN CONFERENCE TITLE!!

I COME FROM A LONG LINE OF HIGH JUMPERS. WELL, I'LL BE...!!

THE SHORTEST REGULAR ON THE SQUAD, THIS 6-FOOT-1 YOUNGSTER PLAYS CENTER

UTAH 29

THE LONE REPRESENTATIVE FROM UTAH IN THE NATIONAL COLLEGIATE CHAMPIONSHIPS LAST YEAR, FRED WON THE HIGH JUMP AT A LEAP OF 6FT 8IN

"JOE, JUNIOR"...by PAP'

I HOPE MY FORMULA IS HALF AS GOOD

JOE WOOD Jr.

UNLIKE HIS DAD WHO STARTED OUT AS A PITCHER AND WOUND UP IN THE OUTFIELD CONNIE BEGAN AS AN OUTFIELDER AT YALE

THE SON OF "SMOKEY JOE" IS BIDDING FOR A BERTH ON THE RED SOX MOUND STAFF IN THE UNIFORM HIS FATHER WORE WITH GREAT SUCCESS

FROM ONE DEFENSE JOB TO ANOTHER

JOE WORKED IN A DEFENSE PLANT LAST YEAR AND PITCHED FOR SCRANTON ON SUNDAYS

AP Features

Sports Round-Up

By HUGH FULLERTON, JR.

NEW YORK, March 16 (AP) — The army sometimes does things to a guy—things that are good for a guy in a peculiar business like boxing . . . Take Sgt. Lou Woods, for example, or Al Davis . . . Woods, just matched for a Chicago fight with Jake LaMotta, leading civilian middleweight, used to be one of those carefree kids who found fighting enjoyable as well as profitable and who didn't have to work hard at his trade . . . Then the army took him and eventually made him boxing instructor at Camp Grant, Ill. . . . The responsibility sobered Lou and he decided to learn more about boxing, with the result, according to reports from the midwest, that he's a lot better ringman now . . . Davis was a kid with a terrific left hook and a reputation for being a rowdy fighter that was a source of pride to him . . . "Bummy" once was banned from New York rings for roughness but was allowed to return after the army gave him a medical discharge . . . He's a lot more serious now, and determined to shed that bad boy reputation. He still has a lethal left, as he proved by stiffening Buster Beaupre and Bob Montgomery in less than three minutes of his last two fights . . . And those who have been watching him say the Davis who will fight Beau Jack tomorrow probably is a better boxing businessman than the old Davis, who had the advantages of speed and youthful enthusiasm.

Think It Over

This isn't a prediction that Woods or Davis will be a world beater when boxing makes its comeback after the war, but the chances are that men who now are serving uncle Sam will be somewhere near the top of the heap . . . Remember a chap named Gene Tunney who came out of the last war determined to become heavyweight champion? . . . H's greatest assets were determination and serious attention to his grade, and he got there.

One-Minute Sports Page

Johnny Fulton, the Stanford runner, has ended his eastern tour with no records except maybe the one he set running out on the Chicago and Cleveland indoor meets . . . Bowling Green, the dark horse of the invitation basketball tournament, is even darker after coming up with Don Whitehead, who played for Kentucky early this season, and Al Di Marco from Creighton via navy transfers . . . The Reds have sold their last minor league club, Birmingham, but boss Warren Giles says they'll be back in the farm business after the war . . . When a story about a golf tournament at Casablanca hit the wires the other day, the Chicago Daily News headlined it: "African golf meet carded, but not for crapshooters."

Dots All, Brothers

Mrs. Ward Cuff, wife of the grid Giants' veteran back, is planning to open a day nursery for pre-school children in Milwaukee while Ward is away at war . . . Her two small daughters, of course, will get in on the cuff . . . Back in 1890, the Buffalo Players' League Club, of which Connie Mack was manager and a stockholder, scored 75 runs on 73 hits in its first four games but finished the season in last place . . . How times don't change.

Through Lend - Lease, 700,000 pounds of Kentucky twist tobacco were sent to Australia troops for use as barter with South Pacific islanders.

New Guinea was named about 1545 by Spanish explorers who thought the natives resembled Negroes of Africa's Guinea coast.

Something to Blow about
F&S BEER

Fuhrmann & Schmidt Brewing Co.   Shamokin, Pa.

KATCEF BROTHERS
1-5 GOTT STREET, ANNAPOLIS   PHONE 4391

By C. E. BUTTERFIELD
Eastern War Time

NEW YORK, March 16 (AP) — Radio's quiz era, far from disappearing, seems to be still in the ascendancy. The new ones outnumber the departing Q. and A. programs.

The BLU is getting ready to present three more. One of the additions is for Saturdays at 7 P. M. Using Benay Venuta and Fred Uttal as M. C.'s, it will have wacky stunts and zany questions under the title of "Money Go Round."

While not exactly a quiz, the second new series to be conducted on Tuesday nights at 7 by Milton Berle falls in the class of audience participation. As "Let Yourself Go," listeners will be invited to the microphone to tell their secret ambitions. The program has its premiere next week after being postponed twice.

The third addition is the already announced Joe E. Brown quiz for Thursday nights at 10:30, listed as "Stop And Go."

Topics tonight: NBC—7:30 Bob Burns, Joe E. Brown; 8:30 Aldrich Family; 9 Bob for Bing Crosby; 9:30 Joan Davis; 10 Abbott and Costello; 10:30 March of Time . . . CBS—7:30 Suspense, Laird Cregar; 9 Major Bowes Amateurs; 9:30 Dinah Shore show; 10 First Line; 10:30 Here's to Romance, Harry Cool . . . BLU—7:30 Coast Guard Dance; 8:30 Town Meeting, "Foreign Oil Resources," Secretary Ickes, Senator E. H. Moore; 10:15 New time, Out Of The Shadows . . . MBS—8:30 Human Adventure; 9:30 Antonini Concert; 10:15 Dale Carnegie's Lecture.

VISIT PLANNED BY BLOOD UNIT

Residents of Glen Burnie and vicinity will be offered the opportunity about the middle of April to donate their blood to help save the lives of members of the armed forces.

It has been announced that the Red Cross mobile blood unit will visit Glen Burnie, enabling those willing to help in this most important project by contributing their blood to do so with a minimum of time and trouble.

Full details of the visit are expected to be announced next week by the chairman, Mrs. Edward Pridham.

Evening Capital

VOL. LX — NO. 65 | EVERY EVENING EXCEPT SUNDAY | ANNAPOLIS, MD., TUESDAY, MARCH 21, 1944 | SOUTHERN MARYLAND'S ONLY DAILY | THREE CENTS

WEATHER
Clearing with slowly rising temperature today; fair and continued cold tonight; Wednesday increasing cloudiness and rather cool.

Submarines Get 22 Japanese Ships

15 Are Sunk By American Submarines While Seven More Are Sunk By British

LATE NEWS

ILIAN FOOD MAY JAL LAST YEAR

ashington, March 21 (AP) — lian food supplies this year equal those of last year for commodities, War Food Adstrator Marvin Jones pre-

es told a House Agriculture ppriations subcommittee that r cent of last year's food proon was allocated to civilians, er cent to the army and 12 cent to Allied nations (ing lend lease).

K TO END STRIKE

ttsburgh, March 21 (AP)—Laand management joined with e, Federal and army officials y in negotiations seeking to a five-day strike of 600 Pennania Greyhound Lines emes which has tied up bus sportation through a large ion of the east.

VA STREAM ARS THIRD VILLAGE

Naples, March 21 (AP)—A great eam of hot lava poured out of e crater of Mount Vesuvius at speed of 40 miles an hour at on today without signs of subding, and the molten river lickl at a third village on the northvest slopes after destroying two.

After burying most of San Sebastiano and Massa Di Somma the lava stream, 30 feet high and 200 yards wide, swept on toward Cercola, below San Sebastiano. Its pace slowed as it wound down the mountain.

EARCH SNOWDRIFTS OR GIRL'S BODY

Boston, March 21 (AP) — Police re searching snowdrifts in earby Winchester today after oston Police Captain Louis Diessa quoted John L. "Limey" Wilson, who alledgedly has confessed to two slayings, as saying he picked up a girl in Medford last week and attacked her in Winchester.

PURPORTED CONFESSION TO BE USED

NEW YORK, March 21 (AP)—A flat statement that Wayne Lonergan's purported confession will be introduced as evidence at his murder trial was made by the prosecution today as selection of a jury progressed.

VICHY GUARDS EXECUTED

Algiers, March 21 (AP) — Four guards convicted of murder and brutality in the operation of the Bechar Colomb internment camp in North Africa under the Vichy regime were executed this morning by a French firing squad. . . .

15 MILLION TO PAY PART TAX BY APRIL 15

Washington, March 21 (AP) — Chairman Doughton (D-NC) of the House Ways and Means Committee said today that more than 15,000,000 of the 50,000,000 taxpayers will have to estimate their 1944 income and pay a portion of the tax on it by April 15, and that there is little hope of any last minute, legislative respite.

NO NEW PASSENGER CARS FOR YEAR

Detroit, March 21 (AP) — Emphasizing that "it takes more than raw materials alone to make automobiles" most of the nation's motorcar manufacturers believe at least another 12 months will elapse before any new passenger cars can be made.

SEES NEW CRIME PROBLEMS

New York, March 21 (AP)—Military training in the art of killing —which some 10,000,000 men now possess—will create new problems in crime prevention in the postwar period, says E. E. Conroy, spcial agent in charge of the New York FBI office.

SAYS HE CAN BACK CHARGE

Washington, March 21 (AP) — Rep. Miller (R-Mo) said today he would produce two sailors who would substantiate a story that a U. S. task force was trapped by the Japanese in Alaskan waters "because of the bungling" of the Federal Communications Commission.

Miller's assertion was made at resumption of hearings by a special House Committee investigating the FCC.

Local Tides

TOMORROW

High water — 3:50 A. M., 0.9 feet; 4:37 P. M. 1.1 feet. Low water—10:21 A. M., 10:19 P. M.

Moon rises 6:13 A. M.; sets 5:19 P. M.

Sun rises 7:08 A. M.; sets 7:20 . M.

Tides are given for Annapolis. Fort Sandy Point, add 15 minutes. For Thomas Point shoal, subtract 30 minutes.

NAVY RELIEF SHOW CAST HAS WIDE EXPERIENCE IN AMATEUR AND PROFESSIONAL THEATRICALS

Many Have Studied And Been In Productions In The United States And Abroad

The cast of "Love Rides The Rails" the 1944 Navy Relief benefit play which will have its premiere at the Naval Academy on Thursday night has had wide experience in professional and amateur theatricals.

As an example, Captain Harley F. Cope, USN, the producer, points to demure, and pretty, little Mrs. Barbara Dugdale, who has a major role in the play as the beauteous Carlotta of the Paradise Cafe. Mrs. Dugdale, wife of Lieut. William M. Dugdale (SC), has appeared on Broadway in the cast of "Sunny Rivers" by Sigmond Romberg. Earlier she studied in Hollywood, followed by two seasons with the Guild Theater, a well known stock company of Chicago. Her husband is an accomplished pianist and singer. However, Mrs. Dugdale does most of the singing for the family in "Love Rides The Rails." It is anticipated that she will be particularly remembered for her selections "Curse Of An Aching Heart" and "Sweet Rosie O'Grady."

Dance Numbers

Lieut. Frank R. Thompson, an outstanding member of the cast of last year's Navy Relief show, "Sea Legs" has designed the dance numbers and trained the dancers for the 1944 production, and in addition his dance with Mrs. Ilona Killian is likely to be a hit. Lieut. Thompson studied under Amparo Guerrero and Carlos Aguilar in Mexico and danced with Deane-Lee Ballet for three years. He has assisted in writing choreography for Carl McDonald's "Rumba" and Aaron Copland's "Salon Mexico" produced in Los Angeles in 1935. He also has assisted with dance productions at the University of California, University of Wisconsin and University of Syracuse.

Other members of the cast have had similar wide experience. For example, Mrs. Janet Ewing who depicts the role of the aged and pious widow, majored in dramatics at Finch Junior College and then studied for two years at the Leighton Rollins Studio of Acting, New York. She also spent a summer at the Bar Harbor Studio of Acting. Mrs. Ewing was last seen on a local stage in 1936 when she had a part in the Navy Relief play, "The Drunkard." Mrs. Ewing is the wife of Comdr. John L. Ewing.

Janney In Cast

The director of "Love Rides The Rails," Prof. Royal S. Pease, coached the 1933-36 Naval Academy Masquerader plays and had as one of his most adept midshipmen pupils, John Hopkins Janney. No greater tribute could be given "Jack" Janney than to use the words of Director Pease who said:

'In my many years with the Masqueraders I found him to be our most accomlished actor." Janney is now a Lieutenant Commander.

Mrs. Lucille Pederson has been a designer and producer of plays but appeared on the stage for the first time in 1940 at Rye Beach, N. H., in the role of Beth in "Little Women." She has played Mary in the "Family Portrait" followed by

(Continued On Page Three)

Red Cross Thermometer

The following shows the standing of the Red Cross War Fund campaign:

Quota	$54,500.00
Donated	15,527.34
Needed	$38,972.66

Tydings Will Address Local Commerce Group

Senator Will Speak On Economic Problems

U. S. Senator Millard E. Tydings will address the Annapolis Chamber of Commerce at the regular monthly dinner meeting to be held in Carvel Hall on Monday night.

Senator Tydings will speak on "Economic Problems, Current and Post War."

The dinner meeting will begin at 6:45 P. M. and Senator Tydings will make his address about 7:30 P. M.

Clarence E. Tyler, president of the Chamber of Commerce, said that the Mayor, Counselor and Aldermen of Annapolis, the Board of Anne Arundel County Commissioners and the members of all city service clubs would be invited to attend the meeting.

He said that any persons interested in the speech, but who did not wish to be present at the dinner, could attend after 7:30 P. M.

Mrs. Robin Redbreast Gets Cold Welcome On Return To Local Home

Mrs. Robin Redbreast, returning to the tree where she has had a nest for several years, ran into a cold reception from the snow, sleet and rain storm that heralded the first day of spring yesterday.

This particular robin has become a familiar resident in the central section of the city; she always turns up in early spring, going to the old nesting site.

Yesterday morning she arrived to find the tree covered with sleet and snow. Then she visited the back door of one of her friends in the neighborhood trying to find out what it was all about.

She was discovered, wet and cold, with rumpled feathers, chirping and hungry. So her friend brought her out a meal of breakfast cakes, most of which soon disappeared.

Then Mrs. Robin smoothed out her feathers and flew away, apparently to take shelter until she can begin her annual task of nest building in the old familiar tree.

BURNING GREASE CAUSES ALARM

A pot of burning grease called firemen to 37 West street this morning about 10 o'clock, but occupants of the house had put out the flames before the engines arrived.

LENTEN SERVICE AT CALVARY CHURCH

The fifth Wednesday evening Lenten service will be held at 8 o'clock tomorrow in the auditorium of Calvary Methodist Church. The Rev. Dr. J. Luther Neff, pastor, of the church, will introduce the guest preacher, the Rev. S. Paul Schilling, pastor of Brookland Methodist Church, Washington.

VACANCY EXISTS FOR SOCIAL EDITOR

A vacancy as social editor and general reporter will exist on the staff of The Evening Capital in the near future.

Persons interested may obtain further details by calling at the offices of The Capital-Gazette Press, Inc., 3 Church Circle, after 2 P. M.

"MERRILL'S MARAUDER S" CROSS BURMA STREAM

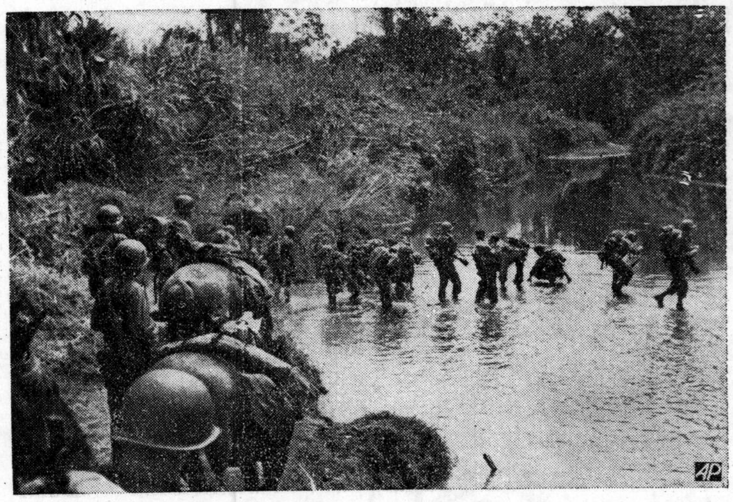

American infantry forces under Brig. Gen. Frank Merrill, known as "Merrill's Marauders," cross a stream in northern Burma as they advance against retreating Japanese troops.

COMMISSIONERS START INQUIRY INTO ESCAPE FROM COUNTY JAIL

Sheriff Joseph H. Griscom Requests Board To Make Complete Investigation Of Case

Sheriff Joseph H. Griscom today asked the Board of Anne Arundel County Commissioners for a complete investigation of the jail escape last week of Seaton Wade, colored life-termer who had been convicted of murder.

Acting immediately upon the request, members of the board, named as a committee of the whole by President John J. Levay, decided to begin the investigation during an afternoon session.

Sheriff Griscom declared that the failure to report the escape to the sheriff "constituted at least neglect of duty and gross disconcern on the part of the warden."

He also stated:

"I await the incoming April term of the grand jury."

Declaring that he didn't want to be the "goat," Sheriff Griscom presented seven reasons why he was asking for an investigation of

(Continued On Page Five)

Report Birth Of Sextuplets

MANAGUA, Nicaragua, March 21 (AP)—Sextuplets, four boys and two girls, were reported today to have been born to Paula Esquivel in Potosi, near Rivas. No confirmation was available immediately.

NAVAL ACADEMY BILL IN SENATE

A bill authorizing the Secretary of the Navy to accept gifts and bequests for the Naval Academy, passed by the House of Representatives, was back in the Senate today for concurrence in amendments.

The law now requires specific congressional authority for the acceptance of each individual gift.

Australian Journeys From Canada To See Middie, Instead Of Writing Letter

Seven years ago two school boys. Herbert Armstrong, of Atherton North Queensland, Australia, and Clayton Lewis, of Linden, Kansas, began writing to each other through an exchange correspondent's club.

All these years, letters kept going back and forth across the world between the two, although the addresses changed. Lewis' address changed from Linden, Kansas, to the U. S. Naval Academy, Annapolis, Md. Armstrong's changed from Atherton, Australia, to an air training post in Canada.

When he got as close as Canada, Armstrong, now a sergeant in the Royal Australian Air Force, decided it would be easier to slip down to Annapolis than to write a letter.

So, the other day the two met. Midshipman Lewis took Sergeant Armstrong sight-seeing around Annapolis, although, in their letters in the past, Midshipman Lewis has thought he might get to Australia first, and that his Australian correspondent would be showing him the sights of Canberra.

Seeing U. S. On Leave

Sergeant Armstrong, wearing the blue R.A.A.F. uniform with black buttons that don't have to be polished, and a single white silken wing embroidered next to the embroidered "B" for bombardier, came here from Washington which he thinks is a "beautiful city."

He is spending his leave seeing something of the eastern United State before going overseas—and he is glad he is going to England because he thinks that as soon as Germany is knocked out of the war Japan won't be hard to smash. Jap warfare has been close to him, too: they bombed an Australian town 200 miles south of his home at Atherton.

Gay Colors Surprised

When Sergeant Armstrong landed in the United States, on the Pacific coast, he was urprised at the gay colors worn by the men

(Continued On Page Three)

Boy Dies From Stove Explosion

Infant Sister Injured In Home Near Ferndale

A two year-old boy was dead and his nine-months-old sister in serious conditon today from burns suffered when an oil stove exploded in their home near Ferndale.

The boy, Jerry Bieker, son of Staff Sergt. and Mrs. Alfred Bieker, died last night at the Fort Meade Hospital. His sister Jane is a patient there.

Mrs. Bieker, who was outside the house when the explosion occurred, told police that by the time she had reached the children their crib and bedclothing were on fire. She carried them from the house, suffering burns on her hands and arms.

FIND MANY VALUABLE PEARLS

NEW YORK, March 21 (AP) — The sharp eyes of a pedestrain caught the glistening of two pearls in the brown slush on Park avenue today and a second later 63 of a $20,000 string of 88 matched pearls were found.

Public Announcement

The Annapolis Taxi Cab Association, Inc., hereby notifies the public of Annapolis and surrounding territory, that due to the reduction of their allotment of gasoline for the present quarter, that they will suspend all taxi cab operation, beginning Sunday (midnight), March 26th, until Saturday April 1, 1944. At the present time, about one-fourth of the taxi cabs of Annapolis are without gasoline, and the rest of them have only enough left to operate a few days longer this quarter. The Association has made every effort to secure the necessary gasoline to continue their 18 to 20 hour daily service for the rest of this quarter, without success.

We regret very much to discontinue this public service to the public of Annapolis for the next few days, but the drastic cut in our gasoline allotment for the present quarter makes it imperative that we take the above action.

The Annapolis Taxi Cab Association, Inc., will continue operation, beginning the new quarter, Saturday, April 1, 1944.

Signed:

THE ANNAPOLIS TAXI CAB ASSOCIATION, INC.
CHARLES A. OLIVER, President-Secretary

HENRY KIRBY, Vice-President-Gen. Mgr.

GERMANS BATTLE WAY BACK INTO KEY HOTEL IN CASSINO ACTION

(By the Associated Press)

American submarines operating in Pacific waters have destroyed another 15 Japanese ships, bringing to 642 the number of enemy craft sunk, probably sunk or damaged by submersibles, the Navy Department announced today.

The sinkings include one large and one medium transport, one large and one medium tanker, nine medium and two small freighters.

At the same time the British Admiralty announced that British submarines, operating in Far Eastern waters, have sunk seven Japanese ships, and damaged three, in action off the Nicobar islands, in the Straits of Malacca, off the east coast of Sumatra and off Sabang on the northern tip of Sumatra.

The Finnish government affirmed its continued desire for peace with Russia but declared that it could not accept the armistice terms dictated by the Kremlin.

NAZIS RECAPTURE CASSINO HOTEL

German troops fought their way back into the wrecked Continental Hotel in Cassino in Italy and enemy defenses in the southwestern part of the town and in the hills behind it stiffened as Lt. Gen. Richard Heidrich, commander of the First German Parachute Troops division, tried to make good his boast that he would throw the Allies out of the town.

New Zealanders immediately went back to their old task of trying to knock the Germans out of the Continental. The Nazis apparently moved back into the hotel during the night, and brought in more reinforcements to block the passage through the southwestern corner of the town.

Heavy German occupying forces—upwards of 100,000 men by best estimates in London—were believed to be driving into Hungary as Adolf Hitler moved swiftly to strengthen his Balkan line against Russian armies already in Bessarabia.

Hungarian Reports

Some Hungarians were reported fighting this new invader at the call of their leaders, but the Nazis retained control at the center of the country. Unconfirmed reports from Stockholm said that two Rumanian divisions were among the force the Germans had sent into Hungary and that they were being resisted stiffly by the Hungarians.

Reports that Admiral Nicholas Horty, the regent of Hungary, had been seized were not confirmed, but London saw no reason to doubt them.

A reliable, direct report from the Balkans said Hungarian troops had fought both German and Rumanian forces near the southeastern frontier around Arad. A secret Hungarian radio station broadcast a call to the nation for a general resistance to the Germans.

In Washington, diplomatic officials predicted that full German military occupation of the Balkans will end independent civil government in Rumania, Bulgaria and Hungary. Along with this will go the cherished Allied hopes that one or more of the sattelite states would make peace before Nazi divisions overran them.

Russian Front

Russian troops beating across old Rumania and old Poland at the nearest point were within 150 miles of the Carpatho-Ukraine territory which Hungary took

(Continued On Page Five)

BENEFIT DANCE
Fleet Reserve Association
FRIDAY, MAR. 24, AT ARMORY
Special Feature 2 Orchestras
Continuous dancing 9 to 1
PUBLIC INVITED
Admission 55c per person

NOTICE

TO WHOM IT MAY CONCERN
I am no longer connected with Universal Moters

Claude J. Marston

CASH FOR YOUR AUTOMOBILE
Andrew Krause
— Chevrolet —
900 BLOCK WEST ST.
Phone 2651

DR. B. H. WASKEY
Osteopathic Physician
CARVEL HALL
Office Hours 9 to 5 P. M.
Monday, Wednesday, Friday
Phone 2361—Room 112
Baltimore Phone—Forest 8308

ANOTHER SHIPMENT of REAL RUBBER TEETHERS
A "Must" For Baby
TINY TOT SHOP
185 Main Street
Dial 6382

HELP WANTED
Women Desired For
SWITCHBOARD OPERATING
Regular Employment
With Opportunity For
Salary Advancement and Promotion
No Experience Necessary
Apply 9 A. M. to 4 P. M.
THE CHESAPEAKE & POTOMAC TELEPHONE COMPANY OF BALTIMORE CITY

WANTED
Experienced Stenographer
STEADY POSITION
APPLY
Box 791
Annapolis, Md.
Annapolis Yacht Yard

IF YOU CAN'T SEE THE TREAD—SEE US!!
When your tire has the first sign of a smooth appearance, tread is worn off, that is the time to see us for prompt Recapping Service.
DON'T GAMBLE ON NEW TIRES—THEY WILL BE SCARCE
New tire production is far less than original estimate—less than one tire per car will be made in 1944. Some eligible drivers must be overlooked—A little care now will keep your car running.
AUTOMOTIVE SERVICE
RECAPPING—REPAIRING—VULCANIZING
ALL WORK GUARANTEED
Phone 2601-2602 Foot of Main St.

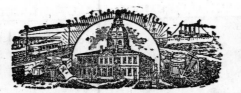

So You Want To Be A War Correspondent!

MOST people think it's easy to be a war correspondent. Artist Howell Dodd thought so, too, when he got the assignment to cover the war for AP Features. But Dodd soon discovered that the job of just getting ready for the trip abroad was one of the toughest he had ever tackled. Here he sketches some of the woes of a correspondent-to-be. You will be seeing more of Dodd's sketches in this newspaper.

1. You've got to volunteer, then sell yourself to the boss. You need years of experience, good health, and the ability to take hardship just as well as the troops.

2. Your background is thoroughly investigated by the F.B.I. and the Army. Then you equip yourself to go anywhere. That means a yard-long passport, different clothing, maybe even a tent.

3. Next comes vaccination for typhoid, yellow fever, typhus, tetanus, cholera and smallpox. Some persons are ill for days after inoculations. You must be ready to face terrible living conditions.

4. You equip yourself according to Army style, then wait perhaps weeks for transportation—wondering about the fact that chances of being killed are greater than in the Army.

Red Cross Fund Is Still Short Of $3,600 Goal

Those Still Willing To Contribute Urged To Act At Once

Unless more contributions are received without delay, the Red Cross War Fund for Glen Burnie and vicinity will fall short of the $3600 goal which has been set, it was revealed.

It was announced on Monday by Mrs. Robert Earle Smith, chairman of the campaign, that the corps of volunteer workers who have been calling on the residents of Glen Burnie and vicinity had reported almost $3,000, leaving a balance of approximately $600 to be raised. Some workers are still on the job and have yet to make some additional scattered reports, but even with these it is indicated that there will be considerable distance to go in order to win success.

An appeal to those who have not given was issued by Mrs. Smith. She said that if anyone who may have been missed by the volunteers and who wants to contribute will communicate with her by telephoning to Glen Burnie 362, she will see that they are contacted.

Seek Volunteers To Donate Blood

Many Sought For Visit Of Mobile Unit April 18

A large number of volunteers are being sought in Glen Burnie and vicinity to contribute their blood for the members of the armed forces. With the tempo of the war increasing, it is indicated that there will be greater need than ever to supply the fighting forces with more plasma than at any previous time. Stories from the battlefronts reveal the wonders that are being accomplished by the use of the plasma in saving thousands of lives.

Those on the home front, unable to take active part in the battles being fought, are being urged to rally to the aid of the men who are facing the enemy and do their part in helping to save their lives.

The mobile unit will be in Glen Burnie from 1 to 7 P. M. on Tuesday, April 18, and efforts are being made to enroll 150 volunteers. The project will be held at the Masonic Hall, where all facilities will be available for the benefit of those willing to give.

The call is for volunteers in good health between the ages of 18 and 60. They are being asked to telephone to Mrs. Frank C. Poole, Glen Burnie 686, who has charge of the enrollment. Arrangements will then be made to have them report at the Masonic Hall at the time most convenient to them.

A number of persons already have enrolled but many more are needed. Every effort will be made to reach the full number, it being pointed out that the quota in Baltimore is now being exceeded practically every week.

Mrs. Edward Pridham is chairman of the Glen Burnie project.

Anne Arundel Bldg. Permits

The Anne Arundel Board of County Commissioners this week issued building permits totalling $10,889.65 to the following:

Everet Henry, Fairfax, remodeling, $200; Charles Richards, Elvaton chicken coop, $60; Edward Duvall, Magothy, tenant house, $500; Edward Jefferson, Clearwater Beach, bungalow, $400; Charles G. Wilson, Elvaton station, dwelling, brick veneer, $1800; Frederick Brooks, Queenstown, bungalow, $500; C. H. Johnson, Crain highway, implement shed, $125; Amos C. Carr Waterbury, station, chicken house, $80; Eugene Wood, Shadyside, repairing, $400; Patapsco Park Land Co., Patapsco Park, bungalow, $100; Ernest Shepherd, Harwood P. O., $1000.

Caleb Murray, Skidmore, was granted a $75 permit to convert his garage into a dwelling, and George F. Yeager, Shore Acres, obtained a $1,000 permit for a semi-bungalow.

Other permits were issued to: The National Product Plastic Co., Camp Meade, addition to dwelling and plumbing, $500; Wm. Manning, Severna Park, addition to dwelling, $500; W. Manning, Benfield road, chicken house, $500; Clarence Crandell, Glen Burnie, garage, $400; Fred P. Magiano, West Annapolis, addition to building, $175; Cowert F. Crowder, Shoreham Beach, enclosing porch, $100; Henry J. Laque, Gambrills, dwelling $700; Mrs. Bessie McArtor, Pine Whiff Beach, addition to building, $174.65; Robert Miller, Gambrills, addition to dwelling, $100; Jacob A. Sheffett, col-

...onial Park, bungalow, $500; and Lillian and Norman Clark, Ferndale, bungalow, $1,000.

The Fellowship Of Prayer

Thursday, March 30

Citations: "Him that overcometh," "as for the conquers—" Moffatt). "Will I make a pillar in the temple of my God." Revelation 3:12. Read Revelation 3:10-13.

These passages are written, so to speak, in cipher, or more accurately, in symbolisms. A great scholar made a learned book to explain them—and left some things unexplained. Written for churches with many faults and more perils, they sound one refrain: "As for the conquerors."

This verse, from which Phillips Brooks once preached the noblest of sermons, says that the victorious who make Christ's cause their own become "pillars in God's temple." They will be the strong support of righteous causes, sustain freedoms, maintain the very structure of the Realm of God. Their strength becomes a sacrament. Their steadfastness makes the centuries secure. Their names may be forgotten; their deeds unknown. But their citations are in their own souls.

Prayer: We praise Thee O God, that "from age to age they gather, all the brave of heart and strong. In the strife with error, of the right against the wrong." As we humbly greatful for what they have done for us, may we seek to be like them in fidelities and look to thee for strength to overcome. In our Leader's Name. Amen.

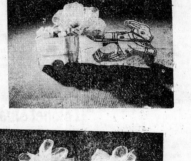

Revue Will Bring Broadway Touch To Annapolis

"Calendar Of 1944" To Be Given At High School Tomorrow For Scout Fund

Watching the colors wheel and countermarch at the closing costume rehearsal of "Calendar of 1944," which will be given at eight tomorrow evening in the auditorium of the Annapolis High School, one thought came to mind, "This really should be photographed in technicolor!" And it should. Nothing so strikingly lovely should be permitted to vanish from the scene after but one brief performance. Certain it is, only the musical extravaganzas at local movie houses give Annapolis as effectively staged dancing and massed color.

Broadway, itself, would be the first to applaud the Uncle Sam costumes, exact minature replicas of a Times Square hit now playing—blue satin tail-coat, top hat and all. Pavlowa would have nodded quick approval of the authentic costuming of the blossom and leaf-green May Pole Ballet, just to mention but two of the more than two dozen numbers presented with professional aplomb by the pupils of the Hoffman School at their yearly recital given for the benefit of the new Girl Scout camp, "Scouts Woodlands."

Mothers Busy

Mothers of tomorrow nights' stars have not been idle either, Mrs. Herbert Wilson, whose daughter, Peggy, dances blithely on toes or tap shoes in the Advanced Group, is ticket chairman; ably assisted by Mrs. Warren Bird Duckett, mother of young Kitty Bowie Duckett, whose smile alone would enslave any audience. Mrs. Walton Achenback has again achieved the impossible in coaxing forth carefully saved sugar from pantries to home-made candy kettles, Mrs. Forest Harder and Mrs. W. F. Scible are co-chairmen of the candy sale.

WAR

(Continued From Page One)

withdrawing to shorten their lines in the mountains of the main front 25 miles inland from the Adriatic.

In the Cassino area the Germans laid down artillery and mortar fire and sent over single planes to bomb and strafe Allied forward positions.

Indian Front

The British continued to drive the Japanese back from their Indian invasion and it was officially estimated that the enemy had lost 15,000 dead alone since Feb. 1 on the Arkan front of Burma, in the Imphal and Kohima areas of the Indian frontier and in behind-the-lines Chindit engagements.

The figure excludes casualties inflicted on the Japanese by Lt. Gen. Joseph Stilwell's American-trained Chinese driving down from north Burma, where figures showed 5,000 Japanese had been killed up to March 29..

The largest number of single front casualties—6,100 killed—was inflicted on the Japanese in their attempt to force the Imphal plain on the Indian frontier.

Another 1,900 Japanese soldiers have died in the Kohima sector.

General Stilwell's troops swarmed through two more villages east of the Mogaung valley in their drive on the Japanese bases of Mogaung and Myitkyina in north Burma.

Appearance of Japanese troops in the Iril valley northeast of Imphal was reported also in the announcement that British forces had captured a position eight miles east of Kanglatongby, which lies between Imphal and Kohima.

The Japanese offensive in northern Honan province assumed a scope unequalled since the Hankow campaign of 1938 as the Chinese acknowledged that enemy forces had crossed the Yellow river from Shansi province northwest of Loyang and apparently had won control of the entire Peiping-Hankow railway.

The crossing of the Yellow river, a Chinese communique said, was accomplished by the Japanese in the vicinity of Yuanchu, 45 miles from Loyang, and threatened to outflank the defenders of that ancient city, already menaced by another enemy column only six or seven miles away to the southeast.

The new Japanese thrust from Shansi not only enlarged the scope of the enemy operations but placed added emphasis on the possibility of a general westward drive toward the old walled city of Sian in Shensi province, natural gateway to Szechwan and the provinsional capital of Chungking.

The Germans asserted they had wiped out a sizable Russian bridgehead on the lower Dnestr river in a surprise attack and that their troops were still fighting in the Crimea west of Sevastopol, destroying 20 tanks there yesterday. The report was wholly unconfirmed.

The Russians announced two days ago that Sevastopol and all the Crimea had been cleared of German and Romanian troops. The latest Soviet communique told of the sinking of two 4,000 ton transports hauling enemy survivors from the devastated port.

The Russians reported no important changes yesterday on the long Eastern front.

Maj. Victor J. Koroteiev, the first correspondent to enter Sevastopol after its recapture by the Russians, said that tremendous damage had been done to the city with the center "destroyed or ruined."

Sea Fight

An armed German trawler was torpedoed and sunk and two others were damaged off the Dutch coast when light coastal forces of the British navy attacked a strong force of enemy patrol vessels while on a pre-invasion offensive sweep of the English channel. The admiralty reported that the British ships returned to harbor after suffering only superficial damage and minor casualties among the crew. One of the damaged trawlers was left burning.

A German broadcast before the Admiralty announcement told of the encounter off the Netherlands and also of one off Elba Island in the Mediterranean.

Apparently striking a mine, the 10,000 ton German freighter Odin sank last night just outside the harbor of Nravik, Norway. The vessel was carrying a cargo of Swedish iron ore to Germany, Swedish reports said.

Victim of a Nazi aerial torpedo, the 1,630-ton U. S. destroyer Lansdale sank in the Mediterranean April 20 with "moderate" casualties.

Liberation of 707 Japanese-held prisoners of war by the American conquest of north-central New Guinea was announced as fresh accounts of the enmmy's cruelty toward captives came to light.

General MacArthur said 462 of the liberated Allies were Sikhs, Indian soldiers captured in Malaya by the Japanese, 86 were Javanese and the rest Americans, Australians, Chinese, Dutch, Filipinos, Poles and Czechs. The report said 621 of the prisoners were freed in the Hollandia area and the rest at Airape.

American patrols cleaning up the Hollandia perimeter killed 62 more Japanese and captured 32, bringing the total for the entire Hollandia-Aitape invasion area up to 1,502 Japanese killed and 291 captured, as against American losses of 28 dead and 95 others wounded.

Heavy bombers returned to the Schouten Islands and hit enemy positions on New Britain and New Ireland Islands.

The importance of France's transport system in the impending invasion of western Europe was emphasized by both the Allies and Germans as the London radio urged the French to keep off the highways after the attack starts and Vichy repeated that passenger train service would be cut Monday to facilitate troop movements.

BOTTLENECK IN ENGLISH VILLAGE

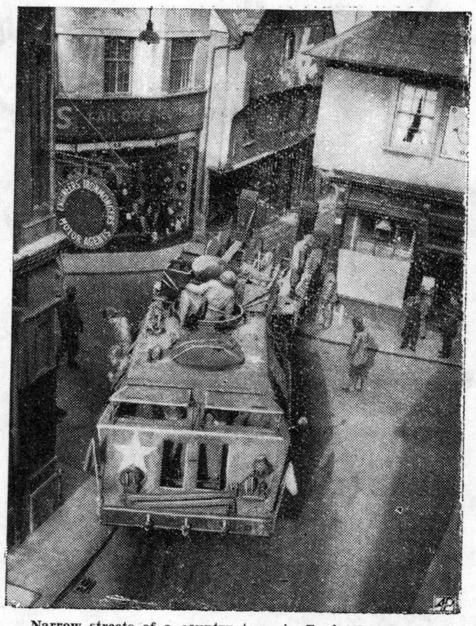

Narrow streets of a country town in England prove poorly adapted to heavy traffic such as this U. S. Army tank recovery unit en route to maneuvers.

NEW ALLIED MOVE IN BURMA

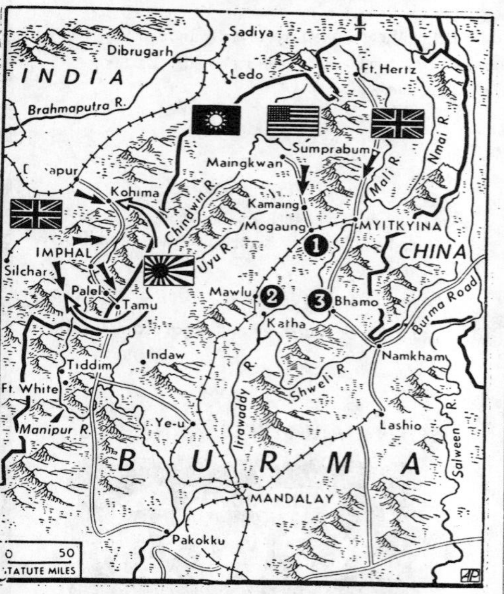

Allied forces, presumably airborne troops, were disclosed to be operating south of the Jap base at Mogaung (1) in northern Burma, supplementing previous airborne thrusts in the Mawlu (2) and Bhamo (3) areas. Black arrows indicate Allied drives; white arrows area where Jap forces have invaded India.

Salvage Collection

Collections of various types of salvage, waste paper, rubber, etc., will be made in various sections of the city as follows:

First Zone or Ward
(First Friday each month)

Bounded by Naval Academy wall, College creek to St. John's street, to North street, to State circle, to East street. East street to Fleet street, to city dock, to Spa creek. Dock, Fleet, East and North streets are collected on the first zone Friday.

Second Zone or Ward
(Second Friday each month)

Bounded by city dock, Cornhill street to State circle, around State and Church circles to South street, along South street to Shaw street to Spa creek.

Third Zone or Ward
(Third Friday each month)

Bounded by Shaw street, to South street, to Church circle, to West street. West street to old railroad line, to Division street, to Spa road to city line, to Spa creek. South street is collected in Third zone.

Fourth Zone or Ward
(Fourth Friday each month)

Bounded by St. John's street to College creek, College creek to city line, to old railroad line, to West street. West street to Church circle around circles to North street to St. John's street. St. John's street is collected in Fourth zone.

Suburban Collection

First Monday each month—Wardour, West Annapolis, Cedar Park. Second Monday—Germantown and Homewood. Third Monday, Eastport.

HALSEY IN SAN FRANCISCO

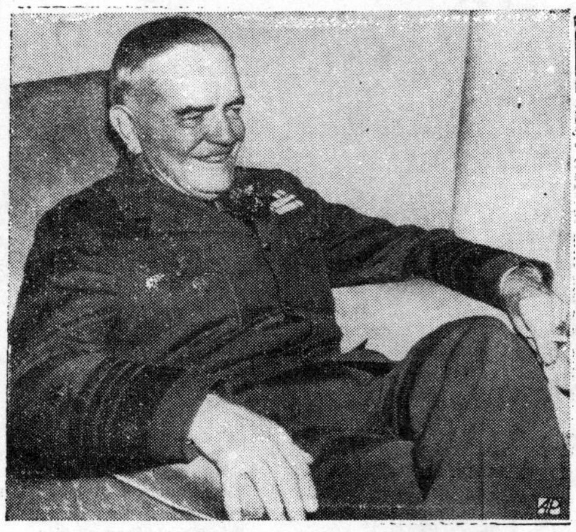

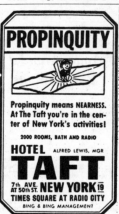

Admiral William F. Halsey, (above) commander of the South Pacific Force, who was in San Francisco May 7 for a conference with Admiral Ernest J. King and Admiral Chester W. Nimitz, told newsmen he was "having a grand time" on the west coast. (AP Wirephoto)

Colonel Stuart Wins Decoration On Bougainville

Awarded Bronze Star For Meritorious Service

(The following story was written by Sergeant Francis H. Barr, of 5534 Vickey Boulevard, Dallas, Texas, a Marine Corps Combat Correspondent.)

Somewhere In The South Pacific — (Delayed) — Marine Colonel James A. Stuart, of Annapolis, Md., recently was awarded the new Bronze Star Medal for assisting in planning jungle offensive strategy against the Japanese, and then executing the operations successfully during the Bougainville campaign.

Forty - five - year - old Colonel Stuart, a graduate of the Naval Academy, is the husband of Mrs. Sallye Cross Stuart, of 9½ Southgate avenue, Annapolis. They have three children, James A., Jr., 19, Thomas Rodney, 17, and Jerome Carroll, 15. Colonel Stuart's mother, Mrs. Effie Ann Stuart, lives at 520 North Chuctaw street, El Rone Okla.

A member of the Olympic saber team in 1924, Colonel Stuart has been stationed in Haiti and Guam, and served as a Marine officer aboard heavy cruisers.

Awarded by Admiral William F. Halsey, Colonel Stuart's citation read:

"For meritorious service as executive officer of a Marine unit in the Cape Torokina area, Bougainville, during the period from November 1 to December 28, 1943. Colonel Stuart's second judgment, outstanding professional skill, and untiring energy were of invaluable assistance to his unit commander in the planning and execution of movements and operations carried out under the most difficult conditions of jungle warfare.

"Through his excellent performance of his duties, he contributed in a large measure to the efficiency of the unit, and to its success in battle against the enemy. His outstanding devotion to duty throughout the entire campaign was in keeping with the highest traditions of the United States Naval Service.

Property Transfers

(Continued From Page Five)

wife, lot of ground on Severn avenue, Eastport in second district.

From George W. Clark to Eula R. Franks and others, lot of ground in fourth district.

From Granville H. Triplett and wife to William C. Haslup, Jr. and wife, lot of ground in fifth district.

From Rose L. Bachman and husband to Brownie Sasda and wife ,lot of ground in this county containing 51-100 acres.

From Lena Cox to Melvin H. Keil an wife, 3 lots of ground at Magothy Beach in third district.

From Magothy Homestead Corporation to Melvin H. Keil and wife, 3 lots of ground at Magothy Beach in third district.

From John A. Whitter and wife to Elmer W. Rodabaugh and wife, lots of ground at Marley Park Beach in third district.

From The Riviera Beach Development Company to Frank Chasney and wife, lot of ground at Rock Hill in third district.

From Curtis Bay Development Company to Leon David, lot of ground in fifth district containing 22-100 acres.

From Grover C. Shipley and wife to C. B. Hubbard and wife, lot of ground in fifth district.

From William B. Dixon Incorporated to Sara W. Cayonan and husband, lot of ground at Magothy Park Beach in third district.

From William B. Dixon Incorporated to James H. Williams and others, lot of ground at Magothy Park Beach in third district.

From Edward E. Clark and wife to Betsy F. Bacon, lot of ground in fourth district.

From William C. Thompson to John H. Cain, lot of ground at Powhatan Beach in third district.

From Betsy F. Bacon to Edward E. Clark and wife, lot of ground in fourth district.

From R. Glenn Prout and wife and others to Theresa B. Coleman and husband, 2 lots of ground at High View On the Bay in eighth district.

From Charles L. Tate and wife to Henry W. Duerbeck and wife, lot of ground in third district containing 3 4-100 acres.

From Charles Swansberry and wife to Dominick Duly and wife, lot of ground at Green Haven in third district.

From Gussie R. Maisel and husband to Howard Gambrill and wife, lot of ground in first district containing 2 56-100 acres.

From Waller B. Bookhultz and wife to Larry Horton and wife, lot of ground at Glen Burnie in fifth district.

From George E. Rullman Trustee to Edna Frazier and others, 2 lots of ground at Horn Point in second district.

From Edna Frazier and others to John S. Kane and wife, 3 lots of ground at Horn Point in second district.

From The Holloway Company to The Kentview Land Company, 5 lots of ground at Marley Park Beach in third district.

From Mercantile Trust Company to Anthony J. Maggio, Jr., lot of ground at Eastport in second district.

From Charles F. Lee and wife to Burton L. Parke and wife, lot of ground at Wardour in second district.

From Frankie Wilson to John G. Hager and wife—3 lots of ground at Linthicum Heights in Fifth District.

From Louis M. Vordenberge to Thayer T. Tucker and wife—4 lots of ground at Waterloo in this county.

From Frank S. Revell, Jr. and wife to Charles Kriewald and wife—lot of ground at Glen Burnie in Fifth District.

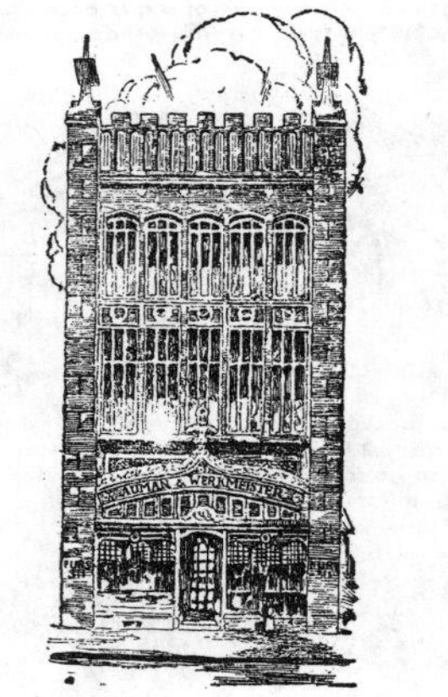

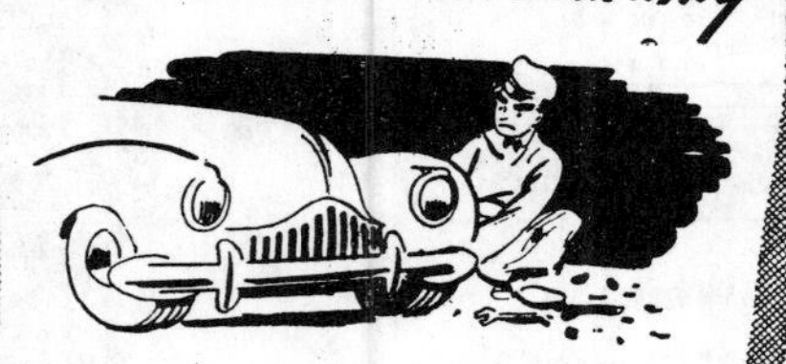

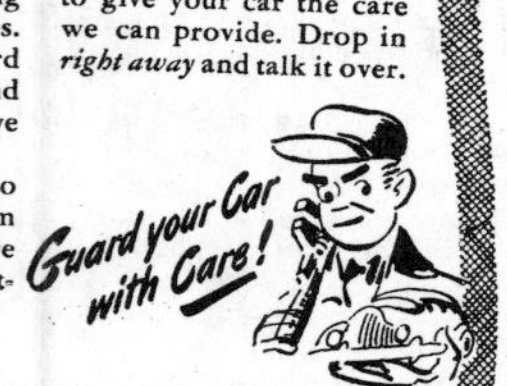

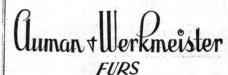

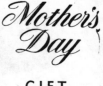

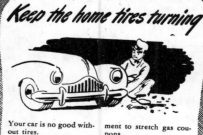

Evening Capital

WEATHER

Thundershowers today; clearing and cooler tonight; Friday partly cloudy and cooler with scattered showers in west portion.

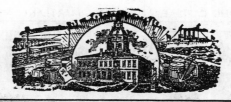

VOL. LX — NO. 91 | EVERY EVENING EXCEPT SUNDAY | ANNAPOLIS, MD., THURSDAY, MAY 18, 1944 | SOUTHERN MARYLAND'S ONLY DAILY | THREE CENTS

Cassino, Monastery Hill Captured

British Take Cassino As Poles Seize Benedictine Monastery

LAUNCH P-T BOAT BUILT FOR RUSSIA

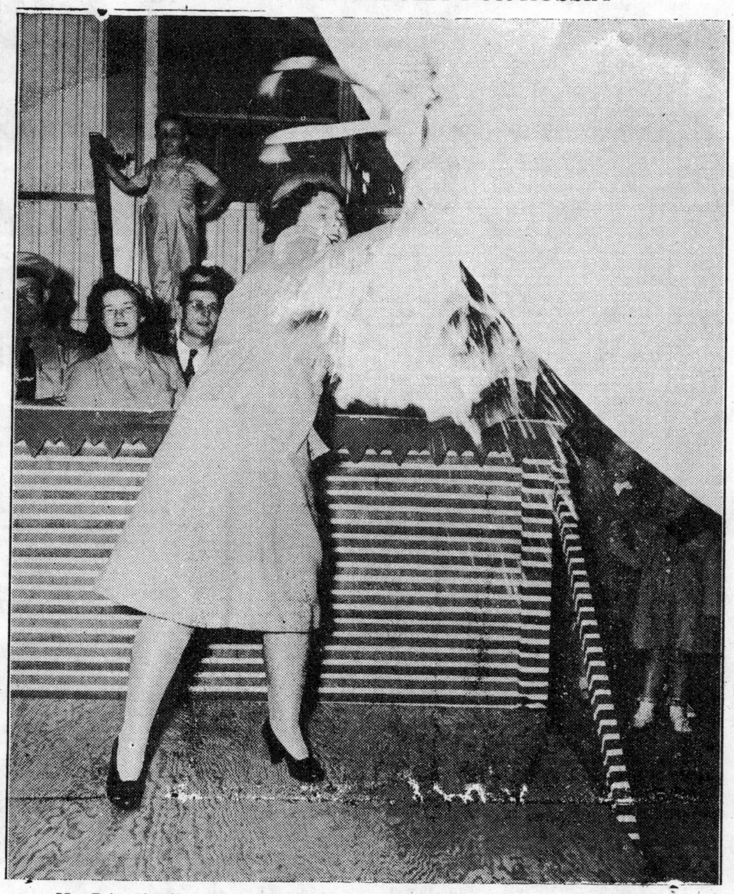

Mrs. Peter Aisquith sponsors the 30th of 100 P-T boats being built for Russia at the Annapolis Yacht Yard. The wife of a Yacht Yard worker, she was elected for the honor when her name was drawn from a hat. Four Russian naval officers attended the ceremony.

LATE NEWS

CHURCHILL WILL SPEAK MAY 24

London, May 18 (AP) — Prime Minister Churchill probably will make a statement on foreign affairs in the House of Commons May 24, opening a two-day debate, Foreign Secretary Anthony Eden announced today.

DETROIT WORKMEN RETURN TO JOBS

Detroit, May 18 (AP) — Michigan's major labor dispute appeared settled at least temporarily today as the first of 52,000 war production workers made idle by a strike of 3,300 formen began receiving calls to return to their jobs.

How soon the long assembly lines at 13 affected plants would be moving at full speed remained in doubt, but preparations were being made for an early resumption of production of aircraft parts and other war materials which top army and navy officials have termed vital to maintenance of schedules on the fighting fronts.

GANDHI TO CONFER WITH ALI JINNAH

Bombay, May 18 (AP)—Mohandas K. Gandhi, Indian Nationalist leader released recently from internment, and Mahomed Ali Jinnah, president of the All India Moslem League, will probably meet early next month to discuss settlement of political differences between Moslems and Hindus, it was learned today.

WPB APPROVES COAL PURCHASE PLAN

Washington, May 18 (AP) — A proposal that the government buy up vast supplies of soft coal to keep the mines rolling at high pitch all summer and have an adequate supply ready for homes this winter has been approved by the War Production Board, it was learned today.

FIND BODY OF MISSING STUDENT

Yonkers, N. Y., May 18 (AP) — The Hudson river's turgid waters today yielded the body of Valsa Matthai, wealthy 22-year-old Indian student missing from Columbia nearly two months, but circumstances of her death remained cloaked in mystery.

Acting Westchester county medical examiner Edwin M. Huntington said the dark-eyed Bombay, India, girl, who disappeared from a Riverside Drive dormitory during a pre-dawn snowstorm March 20 had died by drowning.

UNLOAD RED CROSS MAIL PARCELS

Barcelona, Spain, May 18 (AP)—Nine hundred Americans and Britons, exchanged for a similar number of Germans, waited today for the Gripsholm to unload about 1,600 Red Cross mail parcels for American prisoners of war in the Reich before beginning their journey home.

The diplomatic exchange ship is expected to remain here until Friday to complete the unloading. The parcels will go by rail to Germany.

TOBACCO WAREHOUSES TO REOPEN TOMORROW

Upper Marlboro, Md., May 18 (AP)—Eight Southern Maryland tobacco warehouses will reopen tomorrow following an adjustment of maximum prices by the Office of Price Administration, spokesmen for the Maryland Tobacco Growers Association said today.

FIGHT RINGWORM IN HAGERSTOWN

Hagerstown, Md., May 18 (AP)—A committee of the Washington County Medical Society made plans today to set up stations designed to aid in control of ringworm, which members said had stricken at least 500 children in the elementary schools of Hagerstown.

HARRINGTON MADE ASSISTANT ATTORNEY GENERAL

Baltimore, May 18 (AP)—T. Barton Harrington was designated today to become an assistant attorney general of Maryland on July 1, succeeding D. Heyward Hamilton, Jr.

Hamilton, who has held the position for two years, resigned to enter a private law firm.

Local Tides

TOMORROW

High water — 3:33 A. M., 1.5 feet; 3:41 P. M. 1.1 feet. Low water—10:14 A. M., 9:51 P. M.

Moon rises 4:32 A. M.; sets 5:26 P. M.

Sun rises 5:50 A. M.; sets 8:17 P. M.

Tides are given for Annapolis. For Sandy Point, add 15 minutes. For Thomas Point shoal, subtract 30 minutes.

GIRL SCOUTS WILL RECEIVE CITATION

Governor Will Speak At Ceremony On Saturday

The most colorful as well as the most stirring ceremony in which the Girl Scouts of Annapolis and Anne Arundel county have ever participated will take place on the State House steps at 11 A. M. Saturday.

The occasion will be the awarding of citations from the Treasury of the United States to Troop 8 of the Naval Academy; Troop 11 of Severna Park; Troop 24 of Jacobsville, for Girl Scout troops selling the most bonds and stamps

(Continued On Page Five)

FUNERAL RITES FOR WILLIAM G. LUCAS

Funeral services for William G. Lucas, who died at the Emergency Hospital on Sunday, were held yesterday from the residence of his daughter, Mrs. James E. Taylor, 513 Third street, Eastport.

The services were conducted by the Rev. James L. Smiley and the Rev. A. F. T. Raum. Burial was in Cedar Bluff Cemetery.

The pallbearers were Louis Senesi, Marcellus Windsor, James Smith, John Kane, Edward Kane, and James Murphy.

In addition to Mrs. Taylor, Mr. Lucas is survived by his widow, Mrs. Cora M. Lucas, three daughters, Mrs. Bessie Low, Mrs. Elsie Miller and Mrs. Dorothy White; two sons, Willard G. Lucas and Alfred L. Lucas, 16 grandchildren and seven great grandchildren.

John M. Taylor was the funeral director.

STATE PRESIDENT TO ATTEND P.-T.A. MEETING IN N. Y.

Mrs. Stanley G. Cook, of Indian Head, president of the Maryland Congress, P.-T.A., will attend the national P.-T.A. wartime conference on childhood and youth, to be held at the Hotel Pennsylvania, New York, May 22 to 24.

P.-T.A. members here will be able to hear part of the conference program when the national president, Mrs. William A. Hastings, broadcasts on Sunday from 1:45 to 2 P. M. over CBS.

Merchant Seaman Describes Life On Convoy Duty

Addresses Civitan Club In Maritime Day Observance

Frank Howard, 41-year-old merchant seaman who is at present staying at the Seaman's Rest Home at Bay Ridge told the members of the Civitan Club yesterday that Americans may rest assured "that the Merchant Marine will do its job in maintaining vital life lines" to our men overseas.

Howard, who has experienced numerous convoy trips to South America, England and Russia, described the life of merchant mariners when on active duty. He spoke in furthering the Civitan group's observance of Maritime Day on May 22.

He said that seaman in the engine room seldom know what is happening on deck during battles with Axis raiders or attacking planes. He stated that the men on the convoy route to Murmansk, Russia, often undergo the strain of air and surface attack for as long as nine consecutive days.

Seaman's Rest

Speaking at the weekly luncheon at Carvel Hall of the Civitan group, Howard said the Seaman's Rest Home at Bay Ridge was established by the U. S. Maritime Commission for Merchant seaman suffering from jangled nerves and convoy fatigue.

Howard, who served in the U. S. Navy from 1920 to 1924 said that the old-timers of the Maritime service are opposed to wearing uniforms but that the younger men now filling the ranks of the Merchant Marine are "uniform conscious." He added that uniforms are provided by the government but are optional.

In a brief question and answer

(Continued on Page Six)

MYITKYINA AIRDROME IN BURMA CAPTURED BY STILWELL'S MEN

(By the Associated Press)

The British Eighth army has captured the fortress ruins of Cassino and the battered Benedictine Monastery, and American troops, 25 miles to the southwest, have seized the coastal hinge city of Formia, the Allied command in Italy today announced.

"The Gustav line now has ceased to exist," the announcemnt declared.

The double victory toppled strongpoints at both ends of the fiercely-fought Nazi line in Italy.

British troops slammed into Cassino—which had withstood siege since January—while Poles seized Monastery hill. A substantial portion of the elite German First Parachute Division—the Green Devils—was wiped out in the two strongholds a special announcement said.

Both Cassino and the dominating height of Monastery hill were captured this morning. Other important objectives have been seized by American troops pushing westward on the Fifth army front, headquarters said, but these were not identified immediately.

GERMAN TROOPS ENCIRCLED

The German defenders of Cassino were encircled by tactics which avoided heavy casualties that would have resulted from frontal assaults, such as were beaten back two months ago.

A special Allied announcement declared "the enemy has been completely outmaneuvered by the Allied armies in Italy following the original breach of the Gustav line by the Fifth army on May 14, and the subsequent rapid advance of French and American troops through the mountains.

"Troops of the Eighth army have fought their way forward in the Liri valley and during the last 24 hours developed a decisive pincer movement which cut highway No. 6 (from Cassino to Rome) and so prevented the withdrawal of the enemy."

Earlier headquarters disclosed Polish troops had seized Hill 593, northern hinge of both the Gustav and Hitler lines.

Myitkyina Airport Captured

In a surprise attack, climaxing a spectacular forced march over rugged terrian, American and Chinese forces yesterday captured Myitkyina airdrome and are now besieging Myitkyina city, major Japanese in northern Burma.

Capture of Myitkyina is essential to the success of Lt. Gen. Joseph W. Stilwell's drive to link the new Ledo highway with the old Burma road, thus opening a direct overland supply route to China. It appeared likely that Myitkyina would fall into his hands before the coming monsoon season bogs down major operations.

Brig. Gen. Frank D. Merrill's jungle-wise American Marauders played an important role in the capture of the airdrome, a feat which will probably take its place in history as an epic of the war in the Asiatic theater. It was seized, in a surprise attack, in good condition, enabling gliders and transport planes to land there almost immediately with American engineers and Chinese reinforcements.

Myitkyina is the largest city in northern Burma and has been in Japanese hands for two years.

Merrill's men—three columns of

(Continued On Page Three)

Action Now For International Group Is Urged

Council Of Jewish Women Call On United Nations To Join Forces For Post War

Immediate action toward formation of an international organization is urged in a resolution adopted by the Annapolis Section of the National Council of Jewish Women, and made public today in observation of United Nations Council Day, May 18, as an expression of their common policy.

The statement adopted by the council follows:

"We call upon our government to co-operate now with the other United Nations in setting up a United Nations Council to proceed with the formation of the general international organization foreshadowed in the Moscow Declaration and the Connally Resolution."

Council Statement

The statement pointed out that: "At Moscow the four great powers recognized the necessity of establishing at the earliest practic-

(Continued On Page Two)

MISS FLEET TO GIVE BALTIMORE RECITALS

Miss Elizabeth Fleet, contralto soloist, will give two recitals in the Baltimore studio of George Bolek, voice teacher of Baltimore and New York.

At the first recital tonight Miss Fleet will sing a group of German songs by Franz Schubert and on May 25 she will sing a program of English songs.

Miss Fleet is the daughter of Mr. and Mrs. A. Gordon Fleet, Edgewater.

STORY HOUR AT PUBLIC LIBRARY

The Tale of the White Faced Hornet, and The Little White Goat will be the stories told at the regular Friday afternoon Story Hour at the Public Library tomorrow at 4.

BURGLARS ENTER TWO STORES

Take $25 In Change From West Street Establishments

The theft of a toal of $25 in change from two West street stores today was being investigated by the police. In each case the stores were entered from the rear.

One robbery was at Charlies West End Fruit and Produce Company, 222 West street, where $10 in quarters was taken from the cash register.

The other was at the West End Pharmacy. Here a box of change obtained from soft drink sales, containing $15, was taken from a counter.

Buddy Poppy Week Proclamation

MAY 20th To 30th, 1944

WHEREAS, The Governor of the State of Maryland has given his endorsement to the custom established that the people of Maryland wear the Buddy Poppy during the last week in May each year to Honor and Perpetuate the memory of those who served in the World Wars No. 1 and No. 2 and especially those who sacrificed their lives and sleep in Flanders fields and at home, and

WHEREAS, The Veterans of Foreign Wars and their Auxiliary of Annapolis Post No. 304, are directing the sale of Buddy Poppies in Annapolis and vicinity this year, and the Buddy Poppies to be sold have been fashioned by the hands of disabled veterans, still patients in government hospitals throughout the land, and the fund created by the sale of these Buddy Poppies will be used by the said organizations to give aid and relief to veterans in distress and their families, thereby rendering a valuable service to the community at large, serving in peace as they did in war.

NOW, THEREFORE, I, William U. McCready, Mayor of the City of Annapolis, do hereby designate the period from Saturday May 20 to Tuesday May 30 inclusive, as BUDDY POPPY WEEK, and do recommend and urge the citizens of this City to wear the Buddy Poppy during that period in order to show their gratitude for the many sacrifices made in the defense of our country and by honoring the dead and helping the living.

Given under my hand and seal of the City of Annapolis, State of Maryland, this 18th day of May, in the year of Our Lord, One Thousand, Nine Hundred and Forty-Four.

Signed:

WILLIAM U. McCREADY, Mayor.

(SEAL)

Attest:
Katherine E. Linthicum, Clerk.

THE ANNAPOLIS HUNT CLUB
WILL HOLD THEIR
ANNUAL HORSE AND PONY SHOW
—AT—
Mary Helen's Riding Academy
SUNDAY, MAY 21st
11:00 A. M.
GENERAL'S HIGHWAY NEAR 3 MILE OAK
Judges will be Mr. and Mrs. Danny Shea

PATRIOTIC CELEBRATION
— OF —
"I AM AN AMERICAN DAY"
SUNDAY, MAY 21, 1944
AT 3 P. M.
STATE HOUSE PORTICO
Presentation of Flags to Naturalized Citizens by Mrs. Henry M. Robert, Honorary President General of the D.A.R.
ADDRESS: JUDGE JAMES E. BOYLAN, JR.
MUSIC BY: U. S. NAVAL ACADEMY BAND
The Public Is Cordially Invited To Attend
BENJAMIN MICHAELSON, Chairman.

HELP WANTED
Experienced
Pantry Woman
GOOD WAGES
See Chef
CARVEL HALL

FOR SALE — BUNGALOW
Southeast corner of 3rd street and Chesapeake avenue
PRICE $3,200
For particulars see
CLARENCE E. TYLER
519 6th Street, Eastport

WANTED
YOUNG LADY
With General Office Experience
GOOD SALARY
J. LABOVITZ CO.
122-124 MAIN STREET

WANTED
JANITOR
for
Annapolis High School
For information apply at Principal's Office

on a HUNCH
enjoy a LUNCH
be one of the BUNCH
at
Charlie Snyder's
Corner Shoppe
Corner West and Cathedral Streets
featuring
HOT WEATHER
SALAD SPECIALS
Shrimp Salad
Tuna Salad
Chicken Salad
Egg Salad
fresh Garden Salad
served on crisp lettuce leaf with homemade cole slaw and potato salad
really, GRAND!

SHIPMENT OF
Ladies' Bathing Caps
LIMITED SUPPLY
J. Labovitz Co.
122-124 MAIN STREET

GAME PARTY
Every Friday Night—8 O'clock
Eastport Fire Hall
Benefit
Eastport Volunteer Fire Dept.
ADMISSION 50c
20 Games Guaranteed

FOR SALE
A limited number of Naval Academy
1945 Lucky Bags
are available at
$6.00 including mailing
Address order to
MID'N J. F. BRADLEY
Room 3238, Bancroft Hall
by Saturday, May 20th

WOMEN FOR TELEPHONE WORK
WAR JOBS TODAY—PEACE JOBS TOMORROW
Permanent work of an essential and interesting nature. Good starting pay. Frequent increases and excellent opportunities for advancement. No experience necessary. Apply at your local telephone office 8:30 A. M. to 5 P. M. Monday to Friday.
THE CHESAPEAKE and POTOMAC TELEPHONE COMPANY
of Baltimore City

WANTED
Experienced
Stenographer
APPLY
P. O. Box 791
Annapolis Yacht Yard

WE WILL CLOSE AT 1 P. M. EACH SATURDAY THROUGH SEPTEMBER 16.
OPEN 8:30 A. M. TILL 6 P. M. MONDAY THROUGH FRIDAY.
AUTOMOTIVE SERVICE
PHONE 2601 FOOT OF MAIN STREET

CUT UP CHICKENS
Just The Parts You Want
Breast, Legs, Wings, Backs, Livers and Gizards
BROILERS--FRYERS--ROASTERS
HOME MADE SALADS
J. W. Brooks
205 MAIN STREET PHONE 4686

SOCIAL and PERSONAL

Randolph-Macon Alumnae Entertained

The Annapolis Chapter of the Randolph-Macon Woman's College Alumnae Association was entertained by Mrs. George Norris and Miss Elise Ridout at their home at St. Margaret's on Saturday afternoon.

Mrs. W. H. Sewell was re-elected president of the chapter, and Mrs. C. E. Berger was elected secretary, to fill the vacancy caused by the resignation of Mrs. E. W. Thomson, who is moving to Washington.

The program was given by Mrs. R. E. Foster and Mrs. G. E. Kinney.

Among the guests present were: Mrs Byron Anderson, Mrs. Sam Hurt, Mrs. Royal R. Ingersoll, Mr. S. C. Ramage, Mrs. Earl W. Thomson, and Miss Rosa Busey, of Lynchburg, Va

• • •

Guest Of Mrs. George Lyle

Mr. William Neel, of Mount Airy, Philadelphia, is visiting his niece, Mrs. George A. Lyle, at her home, "Langtarry," Wardour.

Walter N. Noland In California

Walter N. Noland, USNR, son of Mr. and Mrs. Norman Noland, recently was graduated from the Medical Hospital Corps School, Bainbridge Training Station, Bainbridge,Md.

Mr. Noland has been promoted to the rank of hospital apprentice, first class, and has been sent to San Diego, Calif., for further training at the base hospital there.

• • •

Ensign Argue On Leave

Ensign Norman Argue, USNR, son of Mr. and Mrs. Harold Argue, of Boucher Point, Eastport, has been home on leave after his graduation from the Merchant Marine Academy at King's Point, New York.

Ensign Argue, who has had six months sea duty, has been to Africa twice, and has seen action in the Mediterranean. He has also received commendation for his cooperation during air attacks in 1943.

Lt. Robert Argue, brother of Ensign Argue, is an aviation instructor at Corpus Christi, Texas.

Lt. And Mrs. P. J. Skordas Announce Daughter's Birth

Lieut. and Mrs. Pete J. Skordas, announce the birth of a daughter, Penelope at Cochran Field Hospital, Georgia, on May 12.

Lt. Skordas, an Army avation instructor, is the son of Mr. and Mrs. John Skordas, 115 Cathedral street.

Mrs. John Skordas returned home on Friday after visiting her daughter-in-law and son in Macon.

• • •

Mrs. R. L. Neff In California

Mrs. Robert L. Neff has returned to San Diego, Calif., to join her husband, Lt. (j.g.) Neff, USNR, who is stationed there.

Mr. And Mrs. O. Basil Have Baby Boy

Mr. and Mrs. Owen A. Basil, of Munroe Court, announce the birth of a son, Charles Winger, on Wednesday, May 17 at the Emergency Hospital.

CALENDAR FOR THE WEEK

Today

8:00 P. M.—Girl Scout Leaders Club, meeting at Public Library.

8:00 P. M.—W.S.C.S. meeting at the Eastport Methodist Church.

8:00 P. M.—Women's Society fo Christian Service, Eastport Methodist Church, regular meeting in Sunday school room of church.

Tomorrow

10:00 A. M. Girl Scout County Council, Old High School building, Green street.

8:00 P. M.—Card and game party, D of A Hall, 169 Conduit street. Open to the public.

Guest Of Mr. And Mrs. Standen

Mr. Richard Hippelhouser, of Washington, is the guest of Mr. and Mrs. Anthony Standen, at the Brice House Wing, East street.

Mr. Hippelhouser has recently returned to this country from Brazil, where he spent some time on a public information mission for the U. S. government.

• • •

Mrs. Curry Home From New York City

Mrs. Duncan Curry, wife of Capt. Curry, USN, returned Friday from a week's visit in New York City.

While there, Mrs. Curry was the guest of Mrs. W. H. Ziroli, wife of Commodore Ziroli, USN, who is now on sea duty.

• • •

Hostesses Announced For USO Club

The following persons will act as hostesses at the USO Club this week:

Today: Mrs. Frank McDonald, Mrs. James Flanders, Mrs. Alvin Coleman, Jr., and Miss Mary Lou Waters.

Tomorrow: Mrs. Edward Rogers, Mrs. Clifton Russell, and Mrs. Noble Stewart.

Wednesday: Daughters of America—Mrs. Mable Schott, and Mrs. Carrie Dunn.

Thursday: Catholic Daughters—Mrs. C. H. Sherman, Mrs. Fred Thompson, Mrs. James Costello, and Mrs. Bernard Vallandingham.

Friday: Christ Child Society—Mrs. C. H. Sherman, Miss Dorothy Winchester, and Miss Patricia Winchester.

Saturday: GSO Club.

Sunday: Sunday morning—Miss Dorothea Dobson.

Sunday Afternoon: Mrs. Lucille Steiner.

Sunday night supper: College Women's Club—Mrs. Paul Reed, chairman; Mrs. David Wallace, Mrs. Herbert Bacheller, and Miss Miriam F. Parmenter.

Ensign Holland Weds Miss Watson

Miss Anne R. Watson, WAVE, of Petersburg, Va., became the bride of Ensign Willis D. Holland, USNR, of Richmond, Va., Saturday afternoon at 4:30 in St. Andrew's Chapel.

Miss Naomi Laverne Shotwell, of Washington, D. C. was the maid of honor, and Ensign Howard B. Altman, USNR, of the Post Graduate School, was best man.

The Rev. J. Luther Neff performed the ceremony.

Mr. Donald C. Gilley was the organist.

. . . . AND HE WALKED AWAY

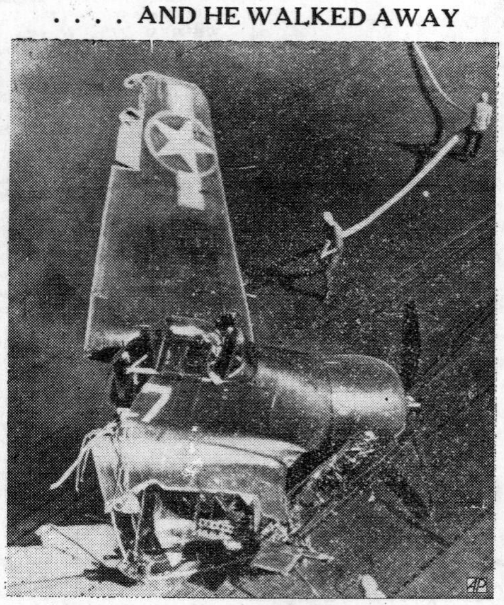

Ensign R. Black, Hellcat pilot from Brigham, Utah, is getting out of what is left of his plane after what the Navy described as one of the most remarkable carrier landings of the war. Shot up over Palau in the Caroline Islands, Black was coming in with his hydraulic system gone, flaps useless, a large hole in the right wing and his ailerons smashed when he slipped sideways and sheered off his tail and one wing on a gun turret. He still landed right side up and emerged with only a few scratches. Note deck crewmen coming up with firehose. (AP Wirephoto from U. S. Navy.)

MODES of the MOMENT

by Amy Porter

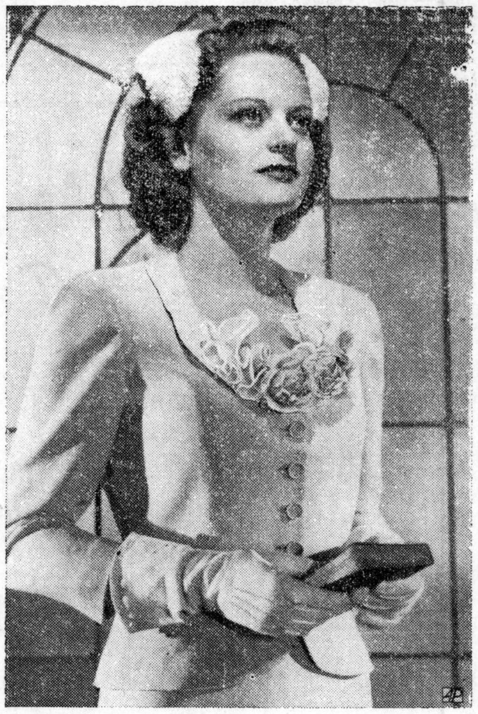

INFORMAL BRIDE: Designed for the furlough bride is this flattering young two-piece suit of pink faille, worn by film Star Alexis Smith. The jacket has a deep U-shaped neckline accented by pink and blue roses. The bride wears a charming white templet that looks like a wedding headdress, and carries a small prayer book.

Son Born To Ensign And Mrs. Barila

Ensign Bernard B. Barila, USN, and Mrs. Barila announced the birth of a son, Bernard Benedict Barila, Jr., on Thursday, May 18 at the Naval Academy Hospital.

Mrs. Barila is the former Miss Elizabeth Stevens, of Annapolis.

FIREMEN HAVE RADIO STOLEN

Fire Marshal Jesse A. Fisher told police the Water Witch Hook and Ladder quarters had been entered by a burglar over the weekend.

Entry was made through a side door. A radio was stolen.

DR. J. BURCH JOYCE DIES IN BALTIMORE

Dr. James Burch Joyce, member of an old Anne Arundel county family, died yesterday afternoon at Union Memorial Hospital, Baltimore, after an illness of a few days. He was 72 years old.

Dr. Joyce was a son of the late Cyrus N. Joyce and Eliza J. Joyce, and was born at Joyce, this county, where he maintained a summer home, living in Baltimore in the winter.

He was educated at St. John's College and the University of Maryland. He retired from practice a number of years ago.

His wife, the former Miss Flora Bolgiano, of Baltimore, died eight years ago.

He is survived by two daughters, Mrs. Frederick A. Weiss, Baltimore, and Mrs. Joseph C. Hazen, of Joyce; five grandchildren; two brothers, Cyrus N. Joyce and Dr. John C. Joyce; and one sister, Mrs. Walter C. Munroe, all of Joyce.

Funeral services will be held tomorrow at 2 p. m. at the residence 3809 St. Paul street, conducted by the Rev. Andrew H. Keese, of Grace Methodist Church, and Lt. Col. Frederick C. Reynolds, USA, chaplain at Fort Meade. Burial will be in Greenmount Cemetery, Baltimore.

CUB PACK SHOWS GARDENING ABILITY

Members of Cub Pack No. 366 showed their abilities as gardeners at their regular meeting by displaying many boxes filled with a variety of growing vegetables.

Each of the five dens presented a short program, consisting of helpful hints and poems related to gardening.

Cubs receiving achievements awards were: Bobcat pin—Bobby Baldwin, John Brooks, Stewart Moreland. Lion badge — Waverly Graham. Wolf badge — John Brooks, Stewart Moreland. Silver arrow—Bill Kenelly, Billy Cadel. Bill Purdy. Gold arrow — Jimmy Hopkins, Billy Cadell, Bill Purdy.

Sherod Earle won the Webelos badge, the highest award in cubbing.

The climax of the program was the graduation of Donald Ward and Sherod Earle from the ranks of cubbing to the Boy Scouts.

Two Glass

(Continued from Page One)

the Emergency Hospital had no facilities whatever for isolations, and there is no place now for grown people with contagious diseases.

Approximately ten cases of children with contagious diseases are turned away each year, after they have been admitted to the hospital under some other diagnosis, Miss Merrick said, and many more are refused admittance before they reach the hospital.

Double Advantage

Having the isolation cubicles of glass is a double advantage, Miss Merrick explained. It enables nurses and members of the family to watch the patient without going into the room; and by permitting the patient to see through the walls, into the ward where the other children are, it alleviates the feeling of loneliness that a child completely cut off, might have. The glass walls have the added advantage of being easily cleaned.

Funds for one of the cubicles were contributed by the Naval Academy Women's Club, and the hospital itself is paying for the other cubicle. The money was raised more than a year ago but it was impossible to get the material and equipment before.

The children's ward in which the cubicles have been built, is shut off from the rest of the building by a large glass door. The ward has a bed capacity of ten.

New Incubator

Another additional piece of equipment in the hospital is a portable incubator for premature infants, given by the Annapolis Section of the National Council of Jewish Women.

The incubator was badly needed, Miss Merrick said, for though the hospital had one incubator, which is used practically all the time, one is not enough when twins are born. There have been seven sets of twins born at the hospital during the past year, three of which were premature.

DO YOU KNOW

"The Department shall not suspend a license for a period of more than one (1) year and upon revoking a license shall not in any event grant application for a new license until the expiration of three (3) months after such revocation." Sec. 96

USO OFFICIAL GETS REPORTS ON JOB SHIFTS AFTER WAR

A post-war job shift by 27 per cent of the men in the Army, based on a representative cross-section visiting USO clubhouses in the United States, is indicated in the post-war planning section of the recently completed survey of soldier opinion made jointly by the War Department, the National Opinion Research Center and USO, according to a report received today by Clarence E. Tyler from Chester I. Barnard, president of the USO. Nearly one half of the men interviewed said they would return to their former type of work, the report added, and 15 per cent expected to go to college.

In answer to the question "are you worried or not worried about finding a good job after the war?", 72 per cent of all the soldiers said that they were "not worried at all' or "not so worried," and only about 24 per cent indicated that they were "somewhat worried' or "very worried." About half of the men indicated that they have been promised their old jobs back or expect to have their own business after the war.

Mr. Tyler, chairman of the local USO committee of management, reported that when the sample of enlisted men in USO clubs was asked, "What do you think USO clubs could do now to help with the job problem you might have after the war?", over 75 per cent of these replying made suggestions. These suggestions ranged from requests for classes to prepare men for new jobs to requests for vocational advice. The subjects suggested for the classes or discussion groups covered most major fields from social science to agriculture.

The complete survey, assembled under the title "Soldier Opinion About USO Clubs," was gahered through both questionnaires and interviews administered in 30 Army camps by the Research Branch of the Morale Services Division of the War Department, and in geographically indicative USO Clubs by the NORC. It was in this latter phase of the survey that soldier opinion of post-war prospects was obtained.

Judge Boylan

(Continued From Page One)

speak of as constitutional democracies.

List Rights

"Among our political rights, which are closely allied to our economic rights, are:

"The right to constitutional government—

"The right to choose and change the officers entrusted with the conduct of the government by orderly elections—

"Freedom of religion—

"Freedom of speech and of the press—

"Freedom to assemble for lawful purposes—

"The right to petition—

"The right to be secure in his person, house, papers and effects against unreasonable searches and seizures.—

"Protection against being deprived of life, liberty or property without due process of law, and against the taking of his property for public use without just compensation—

"The right when accused of crime, to have his accusers confront him in open court—

Quotes Taft, Lincoln

"Finally he is protected in his rights of citizenship regardless of race, color, religion, economic condition or political affiliation; and no state may deny to any person within its jurisdiction the equal protection of the law."

"President Taft said: To obey the law is to support democracy, and President Lincoln said: Let reverence for the laws be breathed by every American mother to the lisping babe that prattles on her lap; let it be taught in schools, in seminaries and in colleges; let it be written in primers, spelling books, and in almanacs; let it be preached from the pulpit, proclaimed in legislative halls, and enforced in courts of justice. And, in short, let it become the political religion of the nation; and let the old and young, the rich and the poor, the grave and the gay of all sexes and tongues and colors and conditions, sacrifice unceasingly upon its alters."

Judge Boylan concluded his address with a speech delivered by Daniel Webster at the completion of the Bunker Hill monument.

Mrs. Robert Speaks

Others on the program included Mrs. Henry M. Robert honorary president general of the Daughters of the American Revolution. Mrs. Robert's talk on "Citizenship" was addressed to those recently naturlized citizens present. Captain William N. Thomas, USN, chaplain of the Naval Academy gave the invocation and benediction. Several selections were played by the Naval Academy band under the direction of Lieut. William R Sima, including "God Bless America" and the National Anthem. Those on the committee in charge with Mr. Michaelson were: Joseph D. Lazenby, Clarence E. Tyler, president of Chamber of Commerce; Senator Wilbur R. Dulin; State's Attorney Marvin I. Anderson; R. Edward Dove, Elks; Charles L. Logan, V.F.W.; Mrs. W. H. Diefel, counselor of DA.R. and County Commissioner George E. Frank.

SISTER GREETS HERO-BROTHER

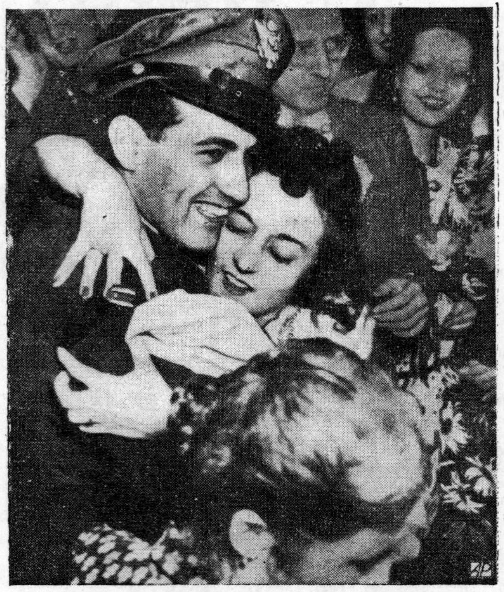

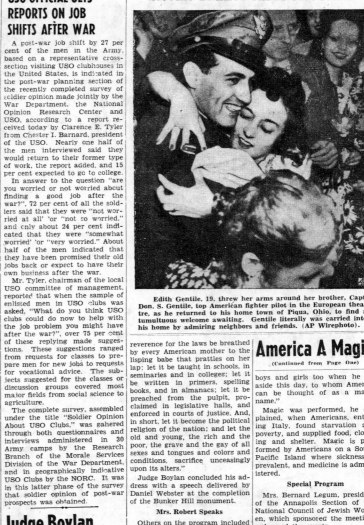

Edith Gentile, 19, threw her arms around her brother, Capt. Don. S. Gentile, top American fighter pilot in the European theatre, as he returned to his home town of Piqua, Ohio, to find a tumultuous welcome awaiting. Gentile literally was carried into his home by admiring neighbors and friends. (AP Wirephoto).

America A Magic

(Continued from Page One)

boys and girls too when he set aside this day, to whom America can be thought of as a magic name."

Magic was performed, he explained, when Americans, entering Italy, found starvation and poverty, and supplied food, clothing and shelter. Magic is performed by Americans on a South Pacific Island where sickness is prevalent, and medicine is administered.

Special Program

Mrs. Bernard Legum, president of the Annapolis Section of the National Council of Jewish Women, which sponsored the meeting, welcomed the guests.

The program also included: a recitation, "The Flag Speaks" by Marjorie Kramer; vocal solo, "I Am An American" by Jacqueline Zelko, accompanied at the organ by Jack Kahn; recitation, "The Land of Hope" by Elaine Jacobs; Howard Eisenstein led the audience in repeating the American's Creed; and a recitation "Prayer for Our Country" by Paula Saslaw, concluded the exercises. Refreshments were served at the close of the meeting.

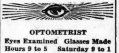

CLASSIFIED ADS

For Rent

FOR RENT — Furnished 3-bedroom house for 3 months, June 15 to September 15, $70.00 per month. Phone 2188. m-25

FOR RENT—Two furnished rooms for gentlemen on Severn River. Phone 2745. m-26

FOR RENT — Two furnished apartments, one 6-room; and one 4-room; 11 miles from Annapolis, 8 miles from Camp Meade. Call South Shore 8-3629. tf

FOR RENT—Rooms to gentlemen only. Wally's Hotel. tf

FOR RENT—Business property. Desirable office location, reasonable rent. 7 State Circle, rooms 7 and 9. For further detail see manager, Lincoln Loan Service, 224 Main street. tf

FOR RENT — Completely furnished bungalow, 12 mi. from Annapolis on Severn River at Indian Landing. Immediate occupancy. 3 double bedrooms and two single. Electric stove, refrigerator and pump. Private beach, J. William Lord, Millersville, Md. Phone South Shore 3623. m-24

FOR RENT—Furnished house, water front, including row boat, inquire James F. Collison's Store, Mayo, Md. m-27

FOR RENT—Double bedroom adjoining bath, at South River bridge also partly furnished house at Woodland beach. Phone 6021. m-24

For Sale 2

FOR SALE—Electric range, recently reconditioned, Simmons day bed, baby's bath tub, lawn mower, Child's desk, 2 metal milk stools, garden tools, tarpauli, 9 ft. x 12 ft.; child's wagon. James H. Reed, Wimbledon Farm, South River. m-25

FOR SALE—Attractive house on Southgate ave., completely furnished, grand piano, oil heat, screened thru out, weather stripped. $15,000. Write Box 72 Evening Capital. m-26

FOR SALE — Cocker Spaniel puppies, three red and three black, registered by the A. K. C. $35 each. Mrs. Barney Waldrop, Riva, Md. Sylvan Shores addition. m-26

FOR SALE—Registered Cocker Spaniel puppies. Two male, one female. Phone 3104. 160 Green street. m-27

FOR SALE—Nine room dwelling on Market street, all modern conveniences. Dial 2461 for inspection. m-26

FOR SALE—Green enamel bureau, and 3 quarter bed complete, both newly painted and table radio, all good condition. Phone noon to 9 p. m. Annapolis 4351. m-30

FOR SALE—JOHNSON'S OUTBOARD, 5 h. p. $100.00. Just overhauled. In perfect condition. Will trade smaller motor. Phone 3052. m-26

FOR SALE — Six-room house Wilson road, Weems Creek. Stucco, hot water heat. Bargain at $3250.00. House easy to heat. Apply Harry A. Reichel, 89 West street. m-27

FOR SALE—Latrobe stove. Reasonable. Telephone 3105. m-24

FOR SALE—Sellers enamel top table. Phone 6443. m-25

FOR SALE—Sixteen ft. inboard motorboat with 2 H.P. Palmer Marine engine. Call 5264. m-25

FOR SALE—Small, neat, upright piano. Reconditioned and delivered, $180.00. Others $80.00 up. Will finance. Keeney's, 23 Randall street. tf

FOR SALE—Fifty brood sows with pigs, $30.00 up. Pigs, 2 months old, $5.00 up. Thomas W. Dorsey, Gambrills, Md. Phone: Annapolis 5209. m-24

FOR SALE—Home. Best residential section of Annapolis. Occupancy in 90 days. Inquire Rear Admiral A. T. Beauregard, U.S.N., retired, 1124 G Ave., Coronado, Calif., or Lt. Comdr. P. F. Bedell, Apt. L-3, Naval Academy. m-24

FOR SALE—Steinway harpenette piano. Will finance. Keeney's, 23 Randall Street. tf

FOR SALE—Sand and gravel, excavation and hauling of all kinds. Also purebred Guernsey and Holstein calves, good grade Guernsey and Holstein milk cows. F. P. Asher, Jr., Boxwood Farm, West River, Md. Phone West River 63 tf

FOR SALE — FROZEN FOOD CABINETS, two temperature. Farm and home use. Immediate delivery. Equipment Sales Co., 3915 Market street, Philadelphia 4, Pa. m-24

FOR SALE—Model A Ford coupe. Good tires and good motor. 310 6th street. Eastport. tf

Help Wanted Male or Female 5

HELP WANTED MALE AND FEMALE—Male dishwasher and waitresses, experience not necessary. Apply G. & J. Grill, 67 Maryland avenue. tf

Wanted 6

WANTED—$20 for option or information leading to rental of furnished apartment available before Sept. 1st by Academy instructor, wife and 3-year-old daughter. Write Box 69, Evening Capital. m-26

WANTED—Will pay cash for your car William J. Meyers. Call Vernon 5320 or 1708 North Charles St., Baltimore, Md. tf

WANTED—We buy, sell, and service electric refrigerators and motors. Lorens Refrigeration Service, 205 Revell St. W. Annapolis. 4791. tf

WANTED—A Ford or Chevrolet, preferably convertible. Phone: 4435. m-25

Wanted 6

WANTED—To rent house or apartment for summer months, 2 or 3 bedrooms. Write Box 73 Evening Capital. m-26

WANTED—Sailboat for cash. Must be in A-1 condition. Give description, stating how old and price. Box 75 Evening Capital. m-26

WANTED — To buy used Waterbury similiar type watch. tf

WANTED—To buy for cash, good used vacuum cleaner. Phone 5607. m-30

WANTED—To buy Model B or A Ford in good condition. Phone 3352. m-24

WANTED—To buy for cash two or three Kapok Life Jackets. Phone 5607. m-30

WANTED—Furnished or unfurnished apartment or small house, preferably on the outskirts, within good school district. Write box 71 Evening Capital. m-25

WANTED — Naval officer, wife and baby would like house or apartment in or near Annapolis; if suitable will pay $25.00 reward. Room 212 Carvel Hall. m-27

WANTED—To buy motor scooter. Call 6352. m-24

WANTED—To rent from now until first of August, small sailboat 18 ft. or less. Call 2611 extension 135 during morning hours. m-24

WANTED—Rooms for four persons for June week. Anyone interested write to V. J. Anania, 1004 Bancroft Hall. m-24

Help Wanted—Female 4

HELP WANTED FEMALE—Cook. Apply Wally Hotel. West street. tf

HELP WANTED FEMALE—Maid with knowledge of cooking for small family. Good salary. Apply The Thrift Shop, 54 West street. m-25

HELP WANTED FEMALE — Efficient housekeeper to take complete charge of home. Three in family. Dial 3264. m-25

HELP WANTED FEMALE—SEWING IS NECESSARY—Do you know how to sew? Can you make alterations or remodel garments? Perhaps you have made a livelihood by dressmaking, if you have any or all of these qualifications give a brief outline of your experience in a note including phone number. Nationally known organization can place you in a permanent position with appropriate income in local position. Apply box 70, Evening Capital. m-24

HELP WANTED, FEMALE—Maid for general housework; live in or out. Good salary. Phone 2611—ext. 20. m-24

HELP WANTED FEMALE — Young colored woman to help serve food in kitchen. Good wages. 5½ day week. Annapolitan Tea Room, 48 Maryland ave. tf

HELP WANTED FEMALE—Business woman over 35 to work behind bar. Wally Hotel. tf

HELP WANTED FEMALE — Women desired for switchboard operating. Regular employment with opportunity for salary advancement and promotion. No experience necessary. Apply 9 A. M. to 4 P. M., Monday to Friday. The Chesapeake & Potomac Telephone Co. of Baltimore City. tf

HELP WANTED FEMALE—Maid for general house work, preferably over 25. Call Navy 2611 ext. 274. m-26

HELP WANTED FEMALE—Maid for general house work in apartment at Naval Academy. Call 2611 ext. 282. m-26

HELP WANTED FEMALE—Nurse to go to California. Leaving by train June 6. Reference. Phone 2216. m-27

HELP WANTED FEMALE — WOMEN (white), make up to $8 daily showing exclusive frocks spare time. Free dress plan. Not canvassing. Write MAISONETTE, 11 W. 29th st., Baltimore-18. m-27

Help Wanted—Male 4

HELP WANTED MALE—Short order cook. Good wages. Apply Mandris Restaurant. m-26

HELP WANTED MALE — Barber wanted. Apply Officers' Club Barber shop. Naval Academy. tf

HELP WANTED MALE—Man to drive soft drink truck. Phone: 2160. tf

HELP WANTED MALE—Man to drive tractor and trailer. Phone: 2160. tf

HELP WANTED MALE—Boy wanted to learn photo finishing and commercial photography. Apply A. N. Miller, Maryland Hotel Building. m-27

HELP WANTED MALE—Young man wanted to learn photo finishing and commercial photography. Apply A. N. Miller, Maryland Hotel Building. m-27

Miscellaneous 12

MISCELLANEOUS — Lawn mowers sharpened. Morris Rank, Best Gate road. Telephone 5570. m-30

MISCELLANEOUS—Cesspools and septic tanks cleaned. Rates moderate. Modern equipment. J. P. Devine. Phone Linthicum 170-J. tf

MISCELLANEOUS — Remodeling, repairs, painting and building work of all kinds. Estimates given freely. Call Annapolis 5520 or 5183. J. W. Palmer. m-26

MISCELLANEOUS — Used cars, any make, any model, bought and sold. Harry's Super-Service, West and Southgate. Phone: 4000. tf

MISCELLANEOUS — We deliver anything — anywhere Personal Delivery Service, Phone: 2781. tf

Situations— Female 15

SITUATION WANTED FEMALE—Care for children from 10:00 till 4:00. Phone 2504. m-26

Repair Work

PIANO SERVICE—Now is a good time to tune your piano. Tuning and repairing estimates given and liberal credit. We buy and sell all makes and styles. Keeney's, 23 Randall St. Phone: 4852. j-30

REPAIR WORK — Any home improvements, involving carpenter work. Phone: 5080. tf

Lost and Found 8

LOST—No. 3 ration book. Mrs. Anne Weems Rust, 121 Charles street. m-25

LOST—A sterling silver bracelet with a U. S. Marine insignia, between 204 Clay street and St. Mary's Hall on May 14. If found please return to Mrs. Mary Andrews, the above address for your reward. m-24

LOST—Ration book no. 4, Benjamin V. Catterton, Greenock, Maryland. m-24

LOST — "A" gasoline ration book. Charles M. Walker, 41½ Calvert street. m-24

LOST—Black billfold, containing gasoline ration book "A" and other important papers. Lt. Comdr. W. H. Berry, 20 Southgate avenue. Phone 2840. m-24

LOST—Ration book No. 4, William B. Buxton, Arnold, Md. m-26

LOST—Gasoline "E" book. Elizabeth Miller, R. F. D. No. 2, Box 414, St. Margaret's. m-24

DIED

JACOBS—Suddenly on May 22, 1944, at her residence, 157 Conduit St., Annapolis, Md., Elva S., beloved wife of Arthur Jacobs. Funeral Thursday, May 25, 1944, from the Taylor Funeral Home, 147 Gloucester St. Interment Cedar Bluff Cemetery, Annapolis, Md. m-24

NOTICE TO CREDITORS

Notice is hereby given that the subscriber, of Anne Arundel County, has obtained from the Orphans' Court of Anne Arundel County, in Maryland, letters testamentary on the personal estate of

VIRGINIA M. GARLINGER

late of Anne Arundel County, deceased.
Clerk a-20
All persons having claims against the deceased, are hereby warned to exhibit the same, with the vouchers thereof, to the subscriber, on or before the

12TH DAY OF NOVEMBER, 1944.

They may otherwise, by law, be excluded from all benefit of said estate. All persons indebted to said estate are requested to make immediate payment.

Given under my hand this 9th day of May, 1944.

ANNA MAY RUSSELL
Executrix. ju-14

NOTICE TO CREDITORS

Notice is hereby given that the subscriber, of Anne Arundel County, has obtained from the Orphans' Court of Anne Arundel County, letters of administration on the personal estate of

WILLIAM H. WOOTEN

late of Anne Arundel County, deceased. All persons having claims against the deceased, are hereby warned to exhibit the same with the vouchers thereof, to the subscriber, on or before the

12TH DAY OF NOVEMBER, 1944.

They may otherwise, by law, be excluded from all benefit of said estate. All persons indebted to said estate are requested to make immediate payment.

Given under my hand this 9th day of May, 1944.

CLARENC E. WOOTEN
Administrator ju-14

FOR SALE

Three Bedroom House at Truxton Heights. Large lot, full basement, hardwood floors. Terms. Price $5,000.00. Apply:

Joseph D. Lazenby
215 Main Street Tel. 2684

NOTICE

I will not be responsible for any debts contracted by my wife Lucy D. Burgess.

WINDSOR BURGESS.

FOR SALE

No. 1312 West St., five apts...	16,000.00
No. 23 Southgate avenue....	$18,000.00
No. 912 Monroe St..........	10,000.00
200 Acre Farm at Davidsonville	26,500.00
105 Acre Dairy Farm with all equipment	30,000.00
178 Acre Farm, with Brick Colonial Home	50,000.00
62 Acre Waterfront Farm, Brick Dwelling	30,000.00
108 Acres land, 2 bungalows and Tavern	10,000.00
18 Acres land, 2 bungalows..	8,000.00
All year waterfront home, South River	11,500.00

T. Carroll Worthington
Real Estate and Insurance
236 Main St. Annapolis, Md.

Help Wanted—Male
Permanent Position

Excellent Opportunity in Building Maintenance Dept.

Apply
CAPITAL-GAZETTE PRESS, Inc.

DIED

BROWN—Suddenly, May 22, 1944 at his home in Parole, Md., Daniel, beloved husband of the late Lottie C. Brown, father of Lydia B. Crowner and Daniel E. Brown.

Funeral services will be Thursday May 25, 1944 at 2:30 p. m. from Mt. Olivet A. M. E. Church, Parole. Rev. C. C. Brown, Pastor officiating. Interment Brewer Hill Cemetery. J. B. Johnson, Funeral Director. m-23

NOTICE

Application is made under Art. 2B Code of Maryland (1939) Supp. by Ernest Strief of Gambrills, Md. for a Class B.T.M. (Beer) and Sunday Licenses, to expire April 30, 1945, permitting him to sell the aforesaid beverage on the premises known as Ernest Strief, Defense Highway and Davidsonville Road, formerly known as Bartgis', Maryland.

Any one may speak for or against the granting of this license at a meeting to be held by this Board on Friday, June 9th, 1944 at 7:30 P. M., at 21 West street, Annapolis, by filing a written protest, signed by ten or more reputable citizens, seven days prior to the aforesaid hearing.

BOARD OF LICENSE COMMISSIONERS OF ANNE ARUNDEL COUNTY,
THOMAS W. PUMPHREY, JR.
Chairman.
HENRY J. TARANTINO, Att'y
FRANK M. DUVALL, Clerk.
m-31

NOTICE

Application is made under Art 2B Code of Maryland (1939) Supp. by James E. Ward and John L. Ward of Deale, Md. for a Class B. T. M. (Beer) and Sunday Licenses, to expire April 30, 1945, permitting them to sell the aforesaid beverage on the premises known as Herring Bay Inn, Deale, Md.

Any one may speak for or against the granting of this license at a meeting to be held by this Board on Friday, June 9th, 1944 at 7:30 P. M., at 21 West street, Annapolis, by filing a written protest, signed by ten or more reputable citizens, seven days prior to the aforesaid hearing.

BOARD OF LICENSE COMMISSIONERS OF ANNE ARUNDEL COUNTY,
THOMAS W. PUMPHREY, JR.,
Chairman.
HENRY J. TARANTINO, Att'y
FRANK M. DUVALL, Clerk
m-31

MODEST MAIDENS

Trademark Registered U. S. Patent Office

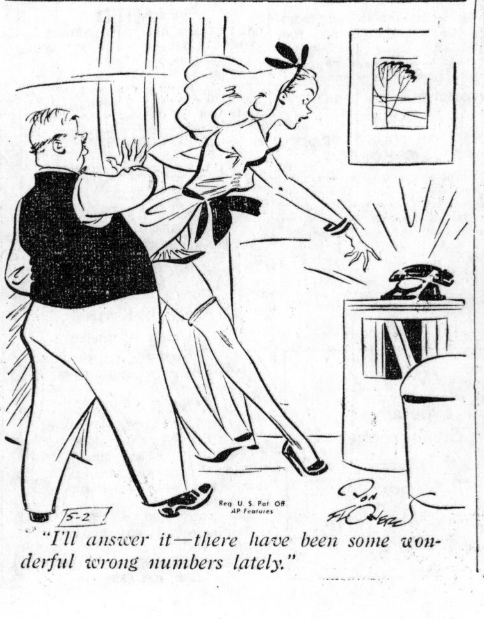

"I'll answer it—there have been some wonderful wrong numbers lately."

SCORCHY SMITH

Once Over Lightly

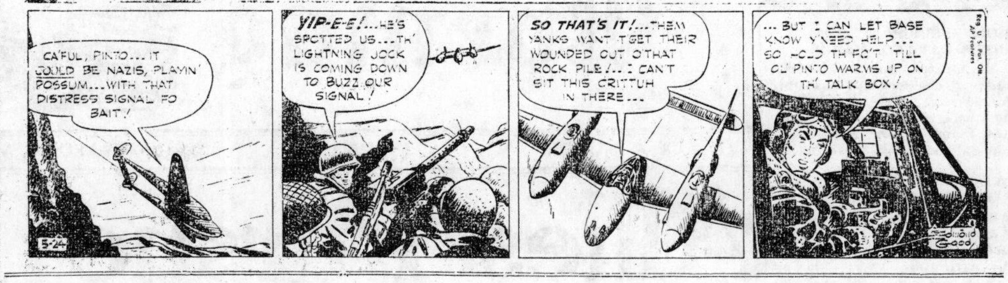
CA'FUL, PINTO... IT COULD BE NAZIS, PLAYIN' POSSUM... WITH THAT DISTRESS SIGNAL FO BAIT!
YIP-E-E!... HE'S SPOTTED US... TH' LIGHTNING JOCK IS COMING DOWN TO BUZZ OUR SIGNAL!
SO THAT'S IT!... THEM YANKS WANT T'GET THEIR WOUNDED OUT O'THAT ROCK PILE!... I CAN'T SIT THIS CRITTUH IN THERE...
... BUT I CAN LET BASE KNOW Y'NEED HELP... SO HOLD TH' FO'T TILL OL' PINTO WARMS UP ON TH' TALK BOX!

OAKY DOAKS

Trademark Registered U. S. Patent Office

Tit For Tat

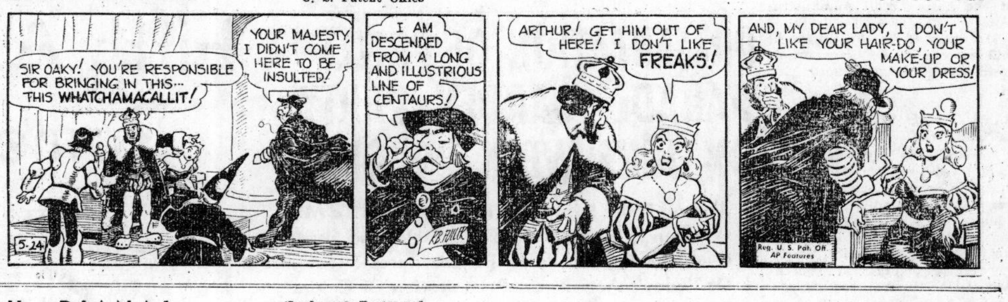
SIR OAKY! YOU'RE RESPONSIBLE FOR BRINGING IN THIS... THIS WHATCHAMACALLIT!
YOUR MAJESTY, I DIDN'T COME HERE TO BE INSULTED!
I AM DESCENDED FROM A LONG AND ILLUSTRIOUS LINE OF CENTAURS!
ARTHUR! GET HIM OUT OF HERE! I DON'T LIKE FREAKS!
AND, MY DEAR LADY, I DON'T LIKE YOUR HAIR-DO, YOUR MAKE-UP OR YOUR DRESS!

OH, DIANA!

Trademark Registered U. S. Patent Office

Bad Luck, Indeed

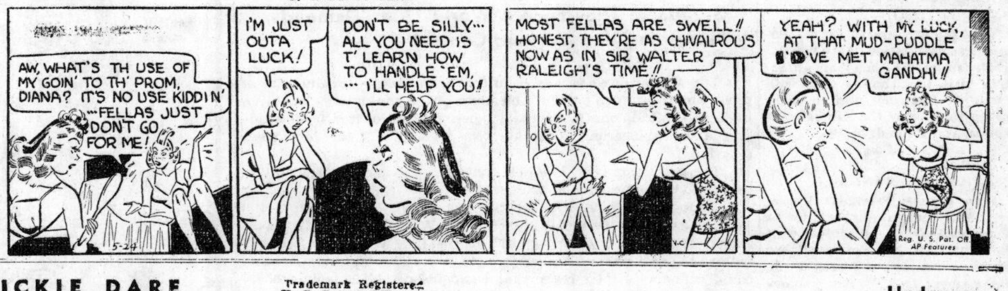
AW, WHAT'S TH USE OF MY GOIN' TO TH' PROM, DIANA? IT'S NO USE KIDDIN' ... FELLAS JUST DON'T GO FOR ME!
I'M JUST OUTA LUCK!
DON'T BE SILLY... ALL YOU NEED IS T' LEARN HOW TO HANDLE 'EM, ... I'LL HELP YOU!
MOST FELLAS ARE SWELL!! HONEST, THEY'RE AS CHIVALROUS NOW AS IN SIR WALTER RALEIGH'S TIME!!
YEAH? WITH MY LUCK, AT THAT MUD-PUDDLE I'D'VE MET MAHATMA GANDHI!!

DICKIE DARE

Trademark Registered U. S. Patent Office

Underway

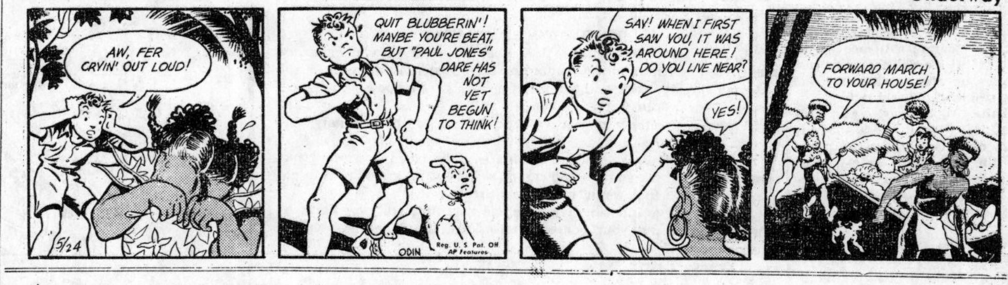
AW, FER CRYIN' OUT LOUD!
QUIT BLUBBERIN'! MAYBE YOU'RE BEAT, BUT "PAUL JONES" DARE HAS NOT YET BEGUN TO THINK!
SAY! WHEN I FIRST SAW YOU, IT WAS AROUND HERE! DO YOU LIVE NEAR?
YES!
FORWARD MARCH TO YOUR HOUSE!

HOMER HOOPEE

Trademark Registered U. S. Patent Office

Trial And Error

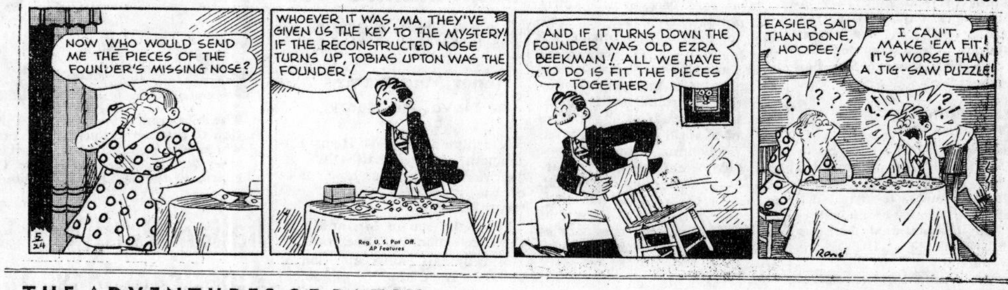
NOW WHO WOULD SEND ME THE PIECES OF THE FOUNDER'S MISSING NOSE?
WHOEVER IT WAS, MA, THEY'VE GIVEN US THE KEY TO THE MYSTERY! IF THE RECONSTRUCTED NOSE TURNS UP, TOBIAS UPTON WAS THE FOUNDER!
AND IF IT TURNS DOWN THE FOUNDER WAS OLD EZRA BEEKMAN! ALL WE HAVE TO DO IS FIT THE PIECES TOGETHER!
EASIER SAID THAN DONE, HOOPEE!
I CAN'T MAKE 'EM FIT! IT'S WORSE THAN A JIG-SAW PUZZLE!

THE ADVENTURES OF PATSY

Welcome Home!

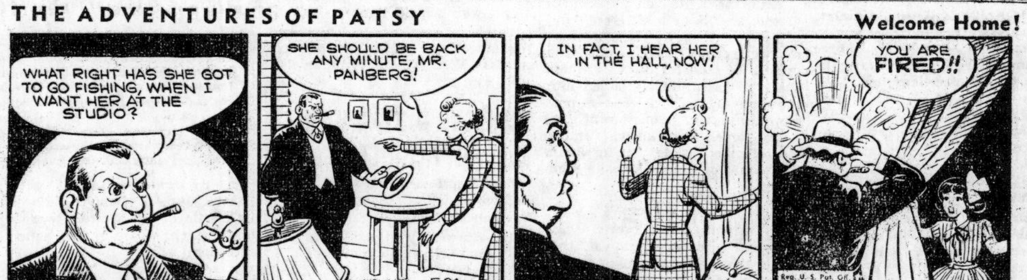
WHAT RIGHT HAS SHE GOT TO GO FISHING, WHEN I WANT HER AT THE STUDIO?
SHE SHOULD BE BACK ANY MINUTE, MR. PANBERG!
IN FACT, I HEAR HER IN THE HALL, NOW!
YOU ARE FIRED!!

NEIGHBORLY NEIGHBORS

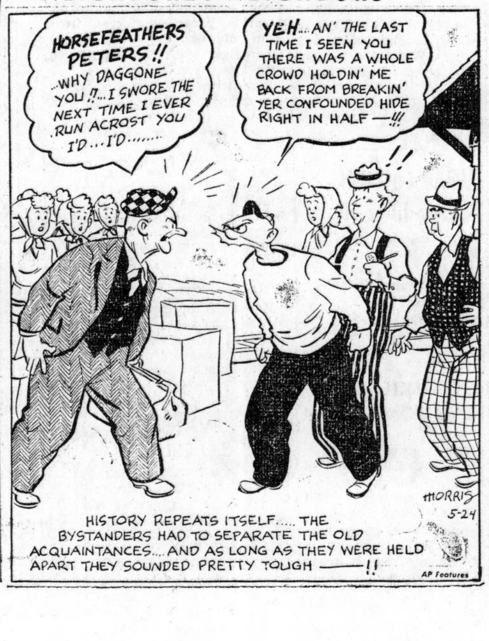
HORSEFEATHERS PETERS!! ...WHY DAGGONE YOU!!... I SWORE THE NEXT TIME I EVER RUN ACROST YOU I'D... I'D........
YEH... AN' THE LAST TIME I SEEN YOU THERE WAS A WHOLE CROWD HOLDIN' ME BACK FROM BREAKIN' YER CONFOUNDED HIDE RIGHT IN HALF —!!!
HISTORY REPEATS ITSELF..... THE BYSTANDERS HAD TO SEPARATE THE OLD ACQUAINTANCES.... AND AS LONG AS THEY WERE HELD APART THEY SOUNDED PRETTY TOUGH ——!!

THE DOOLITTLES

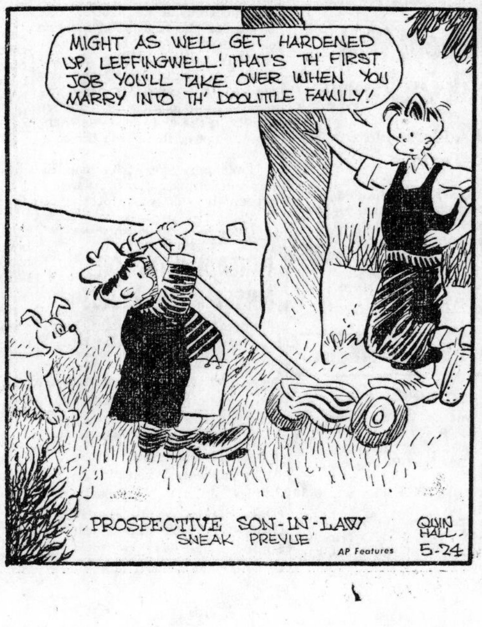
MIGHT AS WELL GET HARDENED UP, LEFFINGWELL! THAT'S TH' FIRST JOB YOU'LL TAKE OVER WHEN YOU MARRY INTO TH' DOOLITTLE FAMILY!
PROSPECTIVE SON-IN-LAW SNEAK PREVUE

Evening Capital

VOL. LX — NO. 106 | EVERY EVENING EXCEPT SUNDAY | ANNAPOLIS, MD., MONDAY, JUNE 5, 1944 | SOUTHERN MARYLAND'S ONLY DAILY | THREE CENTS

WEATHER
Considerable cloudiness and warmer with thundershowers in the mountains this afternoon; somewhat warmer tonight.

Allies Pursue Nazis Above Rome

Fifth Army Crosses Tiber And Passes Rome In Attempt To Destroy Germans

LATE NEWS

HOLD INSURANCE INTERSTATE COMMERCE

Washington, June 5 (AP)—Overruling a decision that has stood for 75 years, the Supreme Court held today that insurance is business commerce, and is subject to the Sherman Anti-Trust Act.

DUGGAN HEADS FARM CREDIT GROUP

Washington, June 5 (AP) — Ivy William Duggan of Georgia, director of the southern division of the Agriculture Adjustment Agency, was nominated by President Roosevelt today to governor of the Farm Credit Administration.

If confirmed by the Senate he will succeed A. G. Black, whose resignation was announced Mar. 3.

SAYS U. S., SOVIET CAN BRIDGE GULF

Moscow, June 5 (AP)—Eric Johnston, president of the United States Chamber of Commerce, has told Soviet trade leaders there admittedly is a "gulf" between the economic ideologies of the U.S.S.R. and the United States, but "bridges of practical cooperation can be thrown across it."

POLISH PREMIER ON VISIT HERE

Washington, June 5 (AP) — Polish Premier Stanislaw Mikolajczyk is arriving today on an official visit, to exchange views with President Roosevelt and to probe means for closing the gap between Russia and Poland.

FIGHT IN DEMOCRATIC RANKS

Even though President Roosevelt has enough support to be nominated on the first ballot at the July 19 convention if he wants to run for a fourth term, the Democrats still have something to fight about this week.

The crux of the interparty battle appears to lie in Mississippi, where Democrats will meet Wednesday to pick a delegation to cast 20 votes on the presidential and vice-presidential nominations.

"White supremacy" was advanced as a theme of a meeting expected to develop an effort to keep the delegation uninstructed and to leave the state's nine electoral college votes unpegged for future developments.

"BREATHING SPELL" IN RATIONING INDEFINITE

Chicago, June 5 (AP)—Walter F. Straub, director of the OPA Food Rationing Division, said today the nation would enjoy its current "breathing spell" in food rationing for an indefinite period, and that "no man knows" just how long it will last.

INTERNATIONAL TRAVEL PLANNED

Washington, June 5 (AP)—Senator Connally (D-Tex) unrolled a rosy post-war prospectus for ration-hobbled motor tourists today by releasing details of an agreement on international highway travel between 12 of the American Republics.

Designed, according to Secretary of State Hull, to "stimulate and facilitate motor travel among the countries of this hemisphere by simplifying certain formalities," the convention has been signed on behalf of the United States and 11 Latin-American nations but still must be ratified by the Senate

BUS SERVICE NORMAL

Washington, June 5 (AP)—Pennsylvania Greyhound bus line operations were normal today after more than a week of a tsrike more than a week of a strike which tied up traffic between Washington, Baltimore and Wilkes-Barre, Pa.

President Will Speak On Rome

Will Address Nation At 8:30 Tonight

WASHINGTON, June 5 (AP)—A fifteen-minute radio address will be made by President Roosevelt to the nation tonight on the liberation of Rome, the White House announced today.

Mr. Roosevelt will speak from 8:30 to 8:45 P. M.

Local Tides

TOMORROW

High water — 5:43 A. M., 1.7 feet; 5:41 P. M., 0.9 feet. Low water—10:52 P. M.; 0:45 P. M.

Moon rises 8:28 P. M., sets 5:45 A. M.

Sun rises 5:40 A. M.; sets 8:30 P. M.

Tides are given for Annapolis. For Sandy Point, add 15 minutes. For Thomas Point shoal, subtract 30 minutes.

PRESENTATION OF PRIZES PARADE, GARDEN PARTY ON JUNE WEEK PROGRAM

Annual Dress Parade To Present Prizes To Midshipmen Winners On Worden Field And Superintendent's Garden Party To Graduates Highlights Of Today's Activities—Presentation Of Colors Dress Parade Tomorrow—Chaplain Thomas Tells Graduates They Face A World That "Demands Everything You Are And Can Be"

The annual dress parade of midshipmen for the presentation of prizes and the garden party for members of the graduating class given by Rear Admiral John R. Beardall, superintendent of the Naval Academy, and Mrs. Beardall, today were the highlights of the June Week program.

The garden party will be held tonight, following the presentation parade to be held earlier on Worden Field.

Tomorrow at 5:30 P. M. the glamorous event of June Week—the annual color dress parade—will be held on Worden Field. Miss Mary Jessup, of Roslyn, L. I., "color girl" for the June Week exercises, will present the national and academy colors to the 20th midshipman company, winners of inter-regimental competition. Midshiman Robert Beresford Williams, Sausalito, Calif., commander of the company, selected Miss Jessup for the role.

SERMON TO GRADUATES

Capt. William N. Thomas, USN, chaplain of the Naval Academy, preached the sermon to the graduating class yesterday morning in the academy chapel, taking as his text: "To them gave he power to become sons of God." John 1:12.

Parents, sweethearts, relatives and friends of the graduates attended the services.

Chaplain Thomas told the graduates they faced a world "that demands everything you are and can be, a world that knows it must rid itself of poisons that would destroy its life."

He told the graduates they were the "architects of the world of tomorrow; you and your contemporaries are the redeemers of the world of today."

Power—Theme Word

Speaking on the words of John, Chaplain Thomas said:

"The word used by this Christian philosopher of the first century to describe the unique gift of the Man of Galilee is the theme word in every language of the globe this morning. Power, more than anything else, is uppermost in the minds of the inhabitants of a world that literally has been made into history's largest battlefield. Man-power, productive-power, striking-power, block-busters, rockets, and numerous other terms, remind us daily that power stands at the crossroads of destiny to direct the course of history.

"But the writer of the Fourth Gospel speaks of a different kind of power—the power of a life that so perfectly fulfilled all the dreams of men for life at its best that they instinctively called him the Son of God. It was a new power, unlike any cohesion of material forces ever known, unlike that of marching legions in which sheer bulk of numbers made men strong.

Inner Power

It was an inner power that made one stand against the crowd, that made goodness somehow dominant over any combination of wrong, that made truth on a scaffold more potent than evil on a throne—a power that even death could not subdue. Life began for the race of men when ears, listening for a better promise than that of victory through might in which men are but pawns of the game, heard the answer to their longing for a higher dignity in the assurance, "to them gave he power to become the sons of God."

"That may not strike you as being exciting, or particularly relevant to what you expect to be

(Continued On Page Three)

Englemann Leads Academy Class

Honor Man Named At Naval Academy

Midshipman Richard Henry Engelmann, of Cincinnati, Ohio, today was announced as honor man of the graduating class at the Naval Academy.

He is the son of Mr. and Mrs. C. A. Engelmann, of Cincinnati.

Midshipman Paul Clapp, son of Mrs. C. H. Clapp, of Missolua, Mont. won second honors.

Third place went to Midshipman William Henry Kmetz, son of Mr. and Mrs. W. J. Kmetz, of Philadelphia, Pa.

MRS. EVA P. STARNER DIES AT HOSPITAL

Mrs. Eva Pearl Starner, 16, of Edgewater, died today at the Emergency Hospital.

Mrs. Starner, who was born on Sept. 13, 1927, was a daughter o the late William Leitch and Mrs Sussane Leitch. She was a member of the Methodist Church.

Besides her parents, she is survived by her husband, Richard Starner, two sisters, Mrs. Oliver Lamb and Mrs. John Lamb and three brothers, William E. Leitch Marion F. Leitch and Calvin Leitch.

Funeral services, in charge o Benjamin L. Hopping, have not been completed.

NEW SUGAR COUPON WILL BE DUE JUNE 16

The County Ration Board announced to day that the No. 32 coupon in ration book No. 4 will become valid on June 16 for five pounds of sugar.

Under present OPA practice the coupons are made valid indefinitely.

LEGION AUXILIARY MEETING TOMORROW

The regular meeting of the Guy Carleton Parlett Unit No. 7 of the American Legion Auxiliary will be held tomorrow night in the Old Treasury Building, at 8 o'clock.

Mrs. Helene White, poppy sale chairman, requests members to bring all poppy proceeds in order to make a final report.

FUNERAL RITES FOR MRS. MARY L. L. JESS

Funeral services for Mrs. Mary Lock Lena Jess were held Saturday at 10 A. M. at her late residence, 915 Jackson street, Eastport, conducted by the Rev. James L. Smiley, vicar of St. Luke's Episcopal Chapel, of which the deceased was a member.

The pallbearers were William A. Shipley, John J. Hughes, Frederick Smith, Oden F. Smith, George W. Jess, and Albert G. Smith. Burial was in Ivy Hill Cemetery ,at Laurel, Md.

ETERNAL CITY FALLS TO ALLIES

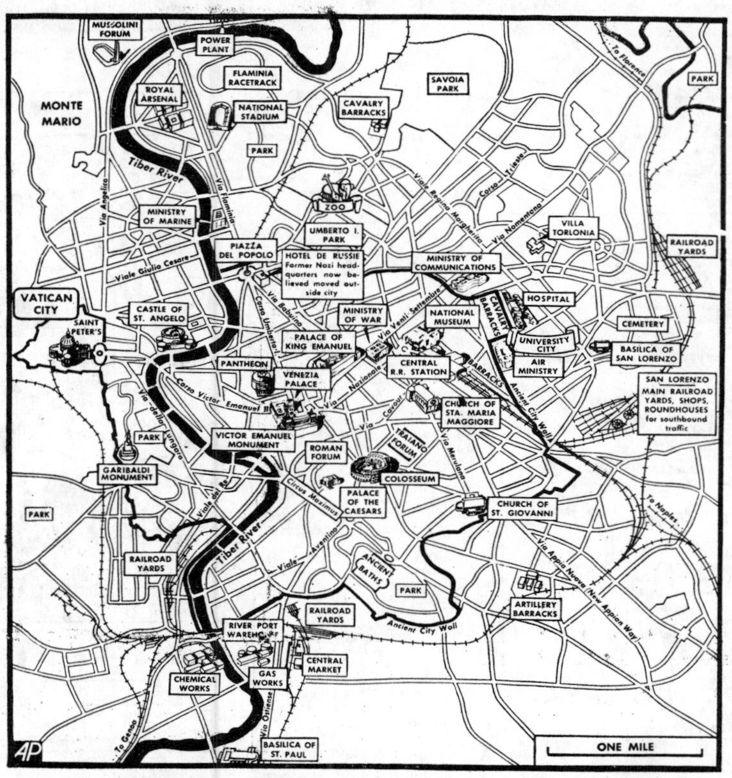

The above map shows the street plan and location of the more important features of Rome which was occupied by troops of the Fifth army last night after defeating German rearguards in the suburbs and wiping out snipers.

The Allied forces continued on through Rome and crossed the Tiber in pursuit of the German 10th and 14th armies which are retreating to the north.

ROME SPARED WAR RAVAGES JUBILANT AS IT GREETS TROOPS

Vatican Wholly Intact—Italians Crowd St. Peter's Circle—Clark Declares Parts Of Two German Armies Have Been Destroyed—About 1,250 American Planes Hit French Coast—American Submarines Sink 16 Japanese Ships—British Get 13 Axis Vessels—Tokyo Claims Japanese Ready To Launch Offensive In China

(By the Associated Press)

The American Fifth army drove swiftly through captured and intact Rome today, crossed the Tiber and made a supreme effort to overtake and destroy the fleeing and mauled German 10th and 14th armies.

Considerable numbers of the enemy appeared trapped southwst of Rome below the Tiber, the seaward bridges of which were destroyed. Prisoners exceeded 20,000. Swarms of Allied planes turned the Nazi retreat into a nightmare. Roads of retreat were blocked with wreckage of 1,200 more vehicles; lines of supply were kept cut.

Violent fighting raged northeast of Rome, the German high command said in a broadcast communique, after Adolf Hitler in two headquarters announcements had acknowledged the fall of the Italian capital despite a last-minute effort to declare it an open city.

NEAR CARNIVAL IN CITY

Rome itself, shining in sparkling sunlight and spared almost entirely from the ravages of war, gave the Fifth army troops a welcome which turned the Eternal City into a near carnival.

The Germans, the last of whom left the city last night, limited their demolitions to a few installations of no artistic or religious importance.

The dome of St. Peter's, dominating the city, bounced back the rays of sunlight and the facade smiled on columns of American troops skirting the plaza where Vatican City begins.

Otherwise there was no sign of life at the Vatican. It was wholly intact and the only remarks of a Swiss guard were that the Germans had always respected its neutrality and that he hoped the Americans would.

The great circle in front of St. Peter's had an Italian crowd in it but there were no American uniforms.

Square Open

"This square is open to the public, though German soldiers did not come into it," a Vatican guard said.

There was no special guard about the Vatican and at the portals of Vatican City, at the left of the facade, there were only a few Papal gendarmes. The Americans swooped right by but did not enter.

Mussolini's balcony hung empty in the gauzy mist of moonlight last night as Fifth army soldiers in Indian file encircled the former dictator's office at the Palazzo Venezia and thousands of Roman Partisans fanned the fires of liberation.

Godfrey Talbot, British radio correspondent in Italy reported that Pope Pius XII was "out on the balcony of the window of the Vatican this morning looking on St. Peter's square."

Germans Get News

The Germans first learned of the fall of Rome in a 7 A. M. broadcast and the Berlin press said the Allied victory "involved a loss of pestige for Germany."

The Naples radio said Lt. Gen. Mark W. Clark in a speech declared "I doubt if the 14th (German army) is any longer capable of fighting."

"We have destroyed parts of two German armies, the 10th and 14th," he continued. We have taken 20,000 prisoners, wrecked the German armies and have captured and destroyed untold quantities of enemy battle equipment.

Allied diplomatic envoys to the Holy See have returned to their old apartments in the wake of Allied occupation, a German broadcast said. Berlin sent reports of street fighting.

The main escape route of the German forces still facing the left flank of the Fifth army between Rome and the seacoast was cut when General Clark's armor and infantry crashed through the defensive screen on the outskirts of

(Continued on Page Six)

Italian Partisans Form Screen As Americans Move Into Heart Of Rome

NEW YORK, June 5 (AP)—The Allied entry into Rome received its crowning touch today when a soldier stood with one of his comrades on the marble balcony overloking the famous Palazzo Venezia where Mussolini used to harangue the Italian people and made a speech about the fallen dictator, NBC said.

A cheering crowd of Italian men, women and children stood below and although they didn't understand a word he said they laughed and cheered and waved flags.

By Daniel De Luce

ROME, June 4 (Delayed) (AP)—This cradle of the western world rocked tonight with the high wind of freedom, stirred by the Fifth Army and thousands of Italian Partisans flaunting red flags.

Behind a screen of Roman volunteers who wore hammer and sickle armbands and waved old firearms, American forces drove from suburban Centocelle to the Tiber river while half smothered with kisses and roses.

The German Wehrmacht, which once swore that Rome was an open city, fought futilely in the ancient streets to delay the American thrust.

Wherever the Americans moved today against hit and run Nazi armored forces they found Italians—of all ages and degrees of poverty—ready to die for "the liberation."

"Why were you so long coming? We expected you four

(Continued On Page Two)

Rev. Dr. J. L. Neff Reassigned To Calvary Church

Rev. R. W. Manley Succeeds Rev. John J. Dawson At Trinity

The Rev. Dr. J. Luther Neff will continue as pastor of Calvary Church and the Rev. R. W. Manley will succeed the Rev. John J. Dawson as pastor of Trinity Methodist Church, under appointments announced by Bishop

(Continued On Page Five)

CARD OF THANKS

We wish to express our appreciation for the kindness, lovely flowers and the loan of automobiles during the recent illness and death of our husband and father. Sydney Taylor.

MRS. HATTIE TAYLOR AND FAMILY.

CARD OF THANKS

We wish to thank our many friends for their kindness and sympathy, the lovely flowers and the use of cars during the recent death of our brother, Roosevelt H. Colbert.

THE FAMILY.

WANTED
SALESLADY
Prefer one having sold infants and children's clothing.
STEADY EMPLOYMENT
Excellent Salary and Commission.
J. LABOVITZ CO.
122-24 MAIN STREET
Phone 2359

WOMEN FOR TELEPHONE WORK

WAR JOBS TODAY—PEACE JOBS TOMORROW

Permanent work of an essential and interesting nature. Good starting pay. Frequent increases and excellent opportunities for advancement. No experience necessary. Apply at your local telephone office 8:30 A. M. to 5 P. M. Monday to Friday.

THE CHESAPEAKE and POTOMAC TELEPHONE COMPANY of Baltimore City

WANTED
Experienced Stenographer
APPLY
P. O. Box 791
Annapolis Yacht Yard

WANTED
CARETAKER WHITE OR COLORED FOR ESTATE ON SEVERN RIVER
Permanent Position
Caretaker's bungalow with electricity, running water and bath
Attractive salary and proposition
Apply Box No. 79 Evening Capital

JUST RECEIVED
Shipment of
FLEXEES BRASSIERES
ALL SIZES
$1.25 to $2.00
J. Labovitz Co.
122-124 MAIN STREET

ANNOUNCING
Change of address
Dr. Jean L. Kearney
Osteopathic Physician
7 State Circle
Formerly 63 Franklin Street

SUMMER SCHOOL
ANNAPOLIS BUSINESS COLLEGE
Open Wednesday, June 14th, 8:30 A. M., for beginners and advance students in shorthand and typewriting.
Classes daily 8:30 to 11:30 A. M.
Evening school continuous Monday and Wednesday 6:30 to 9 P. M.
Telephone Mrs. Hefler 3573
Evenings 5586

The BRYAN SCHOOL
P. O. Box 824, Annapolis, Md.
Course for NAVAL ACADEMY and WEST POINT Civil Service COMPETITIVE EXAMINATIONS (July 29) begins week of June 12th. Fall term for Naval Academy, West Point, Coast Guard Academy preparation begins Sept. 15th. Full information and catalog on request.
OFFICE—21 West Street, Telephone 6470
RESIDENCE—99 Monticello Ave., Telephone 2879.
ARTHUR W. BRYAN, Principal
U.S.N.A., 1922

-NOTICE-
Since Pearl Harbor we have lost five of our employees to the service. This has made it impossible for us to space the vacations for our employees the way that we would like to, so we are going to close all day each Wednesday during June, July and August for the benefit of those who are working so diligently with us in this Great Emergency.
Our Closing Hours for June, July and August will be All Day each Wednesday, 6 o'clock other week days except Saturday, we will close at 9 P. M.
We have all done our bit, now let us all DO OUR BEST.
BUY WAR BONDS AND STAMPS
Montague-Kyle and Krause, Inc.
We are a little ways out, 'tis true,
But away from high prices too.

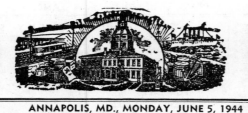

Big Chiefs Of The Second Front

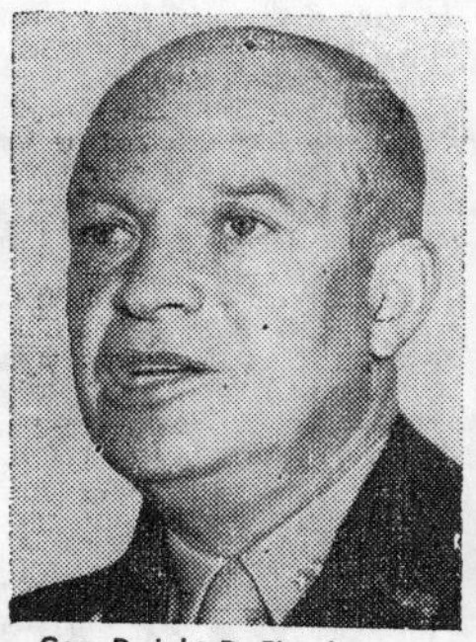

Gen. Dwight D. Eisenhower

Supreme Commander Dwight D. Eisenhower, 53, master-minded the Anglo-American drives that chased the Nazis from North Africa, Sicily, and up the coast of Italy. Texas-born Eisenhower has proved himself a master at handling details, coordinating action in many fields.

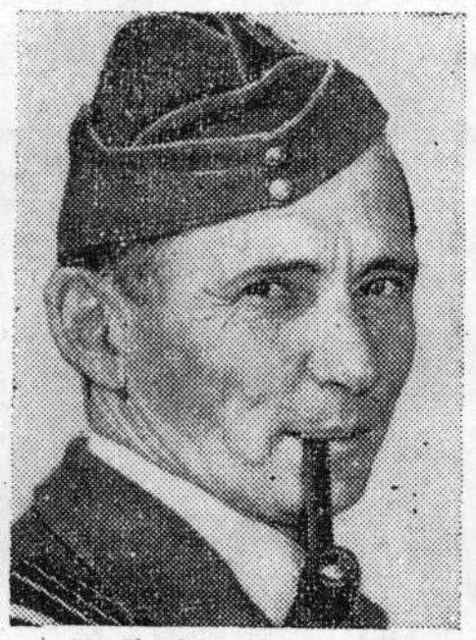

Air Chief Marshal Tedder

Deputy Commander Sir Arnold Tedder, RAF Air Chief marshal, led the air drive that helped break the Nazi line in Egypt and destroyed the Rommel myth. Short, lean, cocky, he has been a flier since World War I, researched in combat aviation between wars. He is 53.

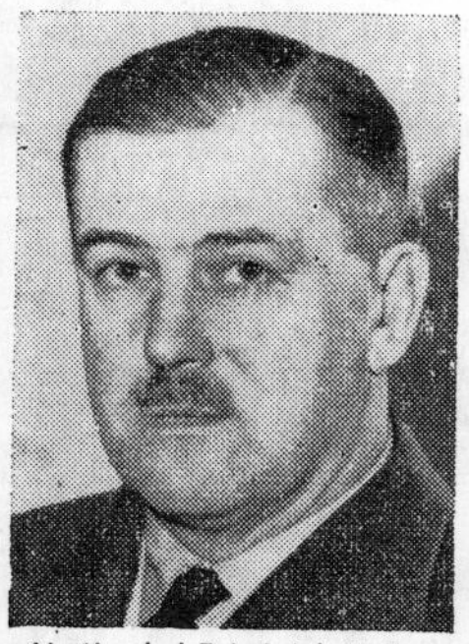

Air Marshal T. L. Leigh-Mallory

Commander of the Allied air forces, 55-year-old Air Marshal Trafford L. Leigh-Mallory helped lead the fight against the Nazi blitz on Britain, put the air umbrella over Dieppe in the commando invasion test, then headed the RAF fighter command. He is heavy-set, brainy.

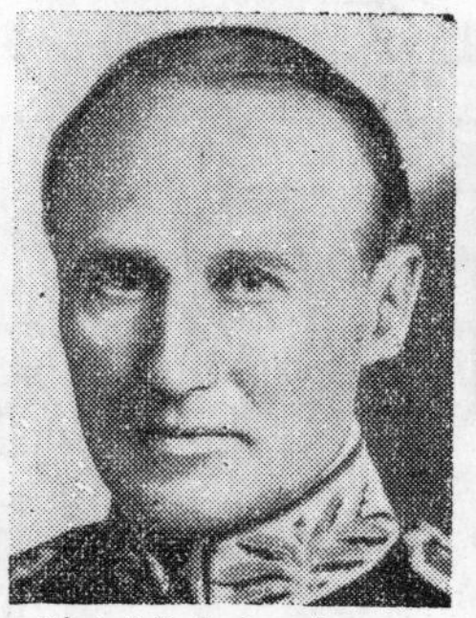

Admiral Sir Bertram Ramsay

Naval Commander, Admiral Sir Bertram Ramsay saved the day for Britain in 1940 when he directed the spectacular evacuation of Dunkerque. Former chief of staff of the home fleet, he came out of retirement when war broke, last year helped plan the invasion of Sicily. He is 60.

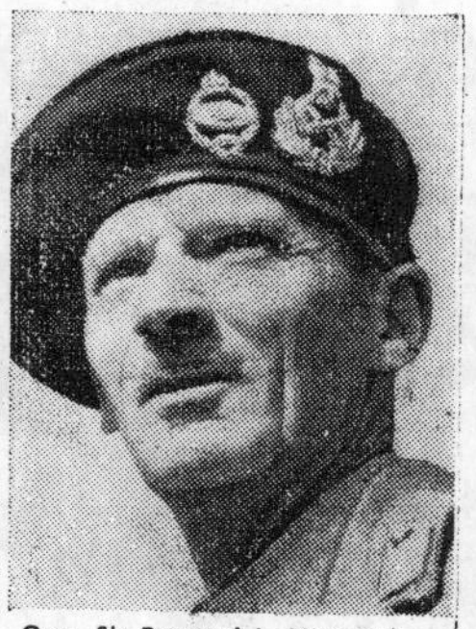

Gen. Sir Bernard L. Montgomery

Commander of the British army, General Sir Bernard L. Montgomery has scored unbroken successes against the Nazis in Africa and Italy. Non-smoking, non-drinking 56-year-old Montgomery has been a soldier since 1908. He rules his troops with a strict and Spartan hand.

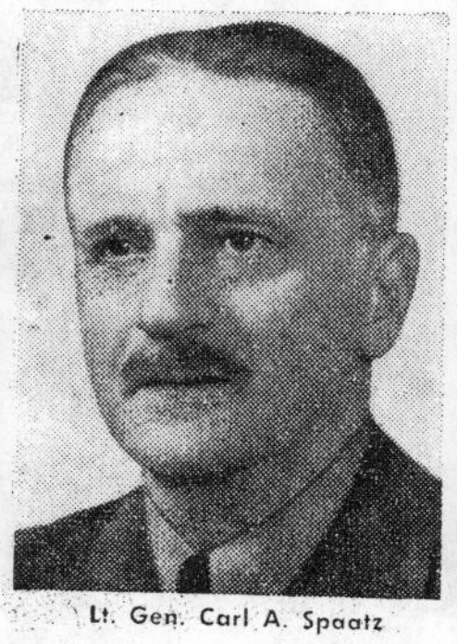

Lt. Gen. Carl A. Spaatz

Commander of U. S. strategic air forces, Lieut. General Carl A. Spaatz headed the Northwest African air forces before his new assignment. Nicknamed Tooey, he has been an airman since 1916, bulit the largest flying school of World War I. He is 52, likes jokes but is a disciplinarian.

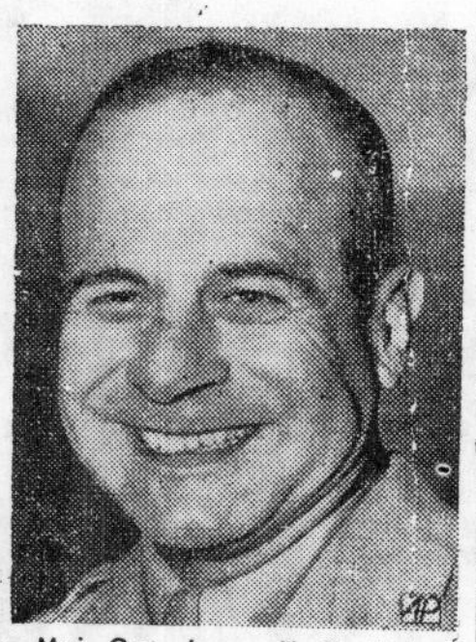

Maj. Gen. James H. Doolittle

Commander of the U. S. Eighth Air Force, California-born Major General James H. Doolittle has been flying 26 years, since he was 21. A flying cadet in the first war, he later set peacetime speed records, became America's first Tokyo-bomber, headed the Strategic Air Forces in Africa.

London Acts To Conserve Bath Water

Motto—"Scrub Once Daily—But Well"

By Hal Boyle

LONDON, June 5 (AP) — The motto of the London bath rooms now is "scrub once daily — but well."

Fear of a summer shortage led the official metropolitan water board to denounce selfish citizens who take too many baths and use water other people might need later to drink.

The supply is far below normal and Chairman Henry Berry said, in appealing for a reduction in consumption to the absolute minimum, "I have in mind the wasteful housewife, certain traders and those thoughtless people who take two baths daily."

Father Thames' pulse is unusually low. Last April the output was 106 million gallons below the flow in April, 1934, which was a drought year.

A quick witted Bobby stopped a runaway horse at Sutterton by using his amplified voice instead of the usual long arm of the law.

Unable to leap from a pursuing police car and seize the bridle of the bolting animal, the driver on sudden inspiration shouted into the car's loud speaker: "whoa."

Dobbin braked do[illegible] at once to a full stop.

Revised retail prices are giving goosepimples to gooseberry lovers. Because of spring frosts, the price has advanced to 25 cents a pound, a rise of four cents. Strawberries are up eight cents a pound to 50 cents.

Crime news, high and low.

One—Lady Irene Crawford, 38, daughter of the fourth Marquis of Camden, must serve a three-month prison sentence for stealing jewelry and clothing coupons.

Two—Someone stole a truck containing eight aircraft engines. Each engine is valued at $12,000 and weighs from 1,200 to 1,500 pounds. The only ones benefited by the theft are the Germans.

Air Marshal R. S. Soley says the British Spitfire fighter "still remains superior to every other type, including the best the Germans can produce." Some $240,000 already has been raised toward a memorial to Reginald Mitchell, designer of this plane that saved Britain.

Random Items

A widow who wrote her son about "a huge ammunition dump a hundred yards from the house," was fined $100 in a coast village on the ground she endangered the military security * * * An artillery gunner was courtmartialed in South Africa on a charge he swallowed 13 needles to make himself unfit for further service. He contended he must have swallowed the needles in his sleep.

Invasion Flashes

(Continued from Page One)

embassy to receive from ambassador Gromyko the Order of Suvorov, first degree—the Soviet Union's highest military decoration. ....

The operations section of the general staff, the signal corps message section and the military intelligence division were islands of frantic activity in the otherwise dark vastness of the Petnagon building, and officers and messengers scurried through the dim corridors relaying messages between them.

Secretary of War Henry L. Stimson was not in his office, but the assistant secretary John J. McCloy came in about 10 P. M. (EWT).

ALGIERS FRENCH FOLLOW INVASION

Algiers, June 6 (AP) — Excited Frenchmen and Allied troops listened eagerly today for every detail on the invasion of western Europe, heard first in Algiers over the German radio.

The Frenchmen hailed the beginning of the military operation as the greatese step yet taken toward liberation of their motherland.

The troops interpreted it as the greatest advance toward their final voyage back home.

* * *

MARSHAL PETAIN APPEALS TO FRENCH

London, June 6 (AP)—The Paris radio today broadcast an appeal by Marshal Peain to Frenchmen to refrain from actions "which would call down upon you tragic reprisals."

"France has become a battlefield," said the aged Vichy chief. "The circumstances of battle may compel the German army to take special measures in the battle area. Accept this necessity."

He called on officials, railwaymen, and workers to remain at their posts—where they would serve the German military machine—"In order to keep the life of the nation and in order to carry out your tasks."

"Do not listen to outside voices calling on you not to listen to our decrees," he said.

* * *

ALLIES CONDUCTED SERIES OF FEINTS

Supreme Headquarters, Allied Expeditionary Force, June 6 (AP)—It can now be revealed that the Allies have been conducting a series of feints in advance of the invasion today.

These feints were predicted sometime ago by Prime Minister Churchill, and were designed to lull the Germans so they would never know when the blow was coming.

* * *

ADD INVASION FLASHES ...

BRITISH TAKE INVASION IN STRIDE

London, June 6 (AP)—A buxom barmaid's exclamation — "thank godness, now we're beginning to get it over with"—typified the reaction of Londoners today to the news that the invasion of Europe had begun.

Although the BBC report of the German announcement that the long-awaited activity had begun was taken skeptically by those who heard it, once the news was confirmed by Allied headquarters, Londoners took it quietly.

By 11 A. M. queues formed in front of newsstands for the first editions of evening newspapers which were sold out immediately.

The news brought back to London some of the comradeship and friendliness which was expressed on all sides when the British capital was undergoing the blitz.

* * *

CAUTIONS AGAINST PREMATURE UPRISING

Supreme Headquarters, Allied Expeditionary Force, June 6 — Gen. Dwight D. Eisenhower, the the Supreme Allied Commander, went on the air this invasion day, telling the peoples of Europe the grand assault on the continent had begun and "all patriots, young and old, will have a part to play in the liberation."

He pleaded against premature uprising, saying, "be patient, prepare. Wait until I give you the signal."

He was followed by King Haakon of Norway who broadcast special orders to both organized and unorganized resistance groups in Norway but wraned his peopel not to rise up against the Germans prematurely.

* * *

DAVIS WARNS ON AXIS REPORTS

Washington, June 6 (AP)—Director Elmer Davis of the Office of War Information, advised Americans today to be wary of Axis reports on the progress of invasion fighting.

"Anything the Axis radio puts out, is in their own interest," Davis told a handful of correspondents gathered in his office in early morning hours.

As soon as General Eisenhower's first communique was received, 17 of OWI's 28 transmitters at New York began beaming it to Europe. Other transmitters, including those in London, started bombarding the airways in 22 languages.

SERTORIUS SEES GREAT CONTEST

London, June 6 (AP)—The German news agency DNB commentator, Capt. Ludwig Sertorius, declared in a broadcast early today that the "great contest between the Reich and the Anglo-Americans has begun."

"The Allied landing in the west today has put the German armed forces in the mood which they express with a laconic 'they are coming.'

"At the present moment when the Allied invasion of western Europe still is in its very first beginning nothing can be said yet about the tactical and operational developments.

"We can only stress the single-mindedness with which the German Wehrmacht is facing the enemy's onslaught, for in war ethical values are at least as important as the number of soldiers and the quantity of their equipment."

* * *

ALLIED HEADQUARTERS SECRET WAS KEPT

Supreme Headquarters, Allied Expeditionary Force, June 6 (AP)—In this military Shangri-La, cleverly hidden from snooping German spy planes, the war's greatest secret was hatched early this year.

Adolf Hitler would have squandered the lives of 10 divisions and much of his wealth to have learned it, even up to a few hours ago.

But today he was given it "free of charge." And it may cost him his life and power eventually. The secret naturally was "D-Day and H-Hour."

* * *

AMERICA RECEIVES NEWS CALMLY

(By The Associated Press)

America received news of the invasion of Europe calmly today and turned to the altars of its faiths to pray for peace with victory.

In the nation's hamlets and great cities people went to churches, temples and synagogues to mediate and to participate in the services of prayer scheduled for D-Day.

* * *

ALLIES CAPTURE SEVERAL BRIDGES

London, June 6 (AP) — Prime Minister Church announced today that Allied air-borne troops had captured several strategic bridges in France before they could be blown up and that "there is even fighting proceeding in the town of Caen."

* * *

EISENHOWER WATCHES PLANES LEAVE

Supreme Headquarters, Allied Expeditionary Force, June 6 (AP)—As the battle opening the western front raged in northern France, General Dwight D. Eisenhower occupied a lonely post on this side of the channel.

After inspecting parachute troops before they went into the fray, the director of history's greatest amphibious strike stood on the roof of a house watching the huge air armadas roar across the channel.

* * *

GEN. DE GAULLE IN ENGLAND

New York, June 6 (AP) — Gen. Charles De Gaulle has arrived in England, it was announced today in a broadcast from Supreme Headquarters, Allied Expeditionary Force. NBC monitored the broadcast.

* * *

BERLIN CLAIMS LIFE IS NORMAL

London, June 6 (AP)—German propagandists asserted today that despite the invasion of western Europe life continued normal in Berlin with "no excitement, no extra editions, no special radio announcements."

But a part of these assertions obviously were false.

From the time of the first landings a constant stream of broadcasts came from the German transmitters—many of them carrying more than an indication that Hitler's defenses along the western coast had been caught napping.

The German press chief was quoted by DNB as saying the Allies opened the invasion "on the order of Moscow."

* * *

PRESIDENT WARNS VICTORY WILL COST

Washington, June 6 (AP)—In a speech which made no reference to invasion but was delivered in the certain knowledge that the climactic hour finally had come, President Roosevelt told the nation last night that victory over Germany is certain but "it will be tough and it will be costly."

The President broadcast on the fall of Rome at 8:30 P. M. Eastern War Time,—about the time United States and Allied forces were jumping off from England for the air and water push across the channel.

Paratroopers In Van Of Attack

Many Veterans Drop Behind Hitler's Atlantic Wall

With United States Parachute Troops, June 6 (AP) — American para-troopers — studded with battle-hardened veterans of the Sicilian and Italian campaigns—landed behind Hitler's Atlantic wall today to plant the first blow of the long-awaited western front squarely in the enemy's vitals.

The Allies' toughest, wiriest men of war cascaded from faintly moonlit skies in an awesome operation.

Twin-engined C-47S—sisters of America's standard airline flagships — bore the human cargo across the skies, simultaneously towing troop-laden CG-4A gliders—to merge in a single sledgehammer blow paving the way for frontal assault forces.

Armed with weapons from the most primitive to the most modern, the paratroopers' mission was to disrupt and demoralize the Germans' communications inside the Nazis' own lines.

There was no immediate indication that their dynamite and flashing steel and well-aimed fire was not succeeding in the execution of plans rehearsed for months in preparation for the liberation of occupied Europe.

The steel-helmeted, ankle-booted warriors wore a red, white and blue American flag insignia on the sleeve and camouflaged green-splotched battle dress.

EASTPORT FIREMEN BLOW SIREN, RING BELL

The siren and bells of the Eastport Fire Department were sounded this morning at 9:30 to tell of the Allied invasion.

America's Invasion Admirals

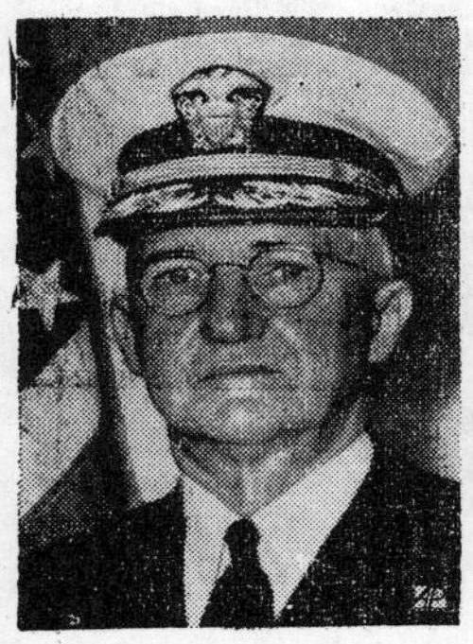

AP Features

ADMIRAL HAROLD R. STARK, director of the American invasion fleet in the Allied assault on Fortress Europe, is on old hand at battling U-boats.

Stark was aide to Adm. Sims, commander of American naval forces in European waters, in World War I, and won the Distinguished Service Medal for smothering U-boats in the Mediterraean with a flotilla of broken-down destroyers.

An advocate of quick, hard blows with the help of the Navy's own air fleet, he became an admiral in 1939 at 58. He is white-haired, mild mannered, was graduated from the U. S. Naval Academy in 1903. He was born at Wilkes-Barre, Pa.

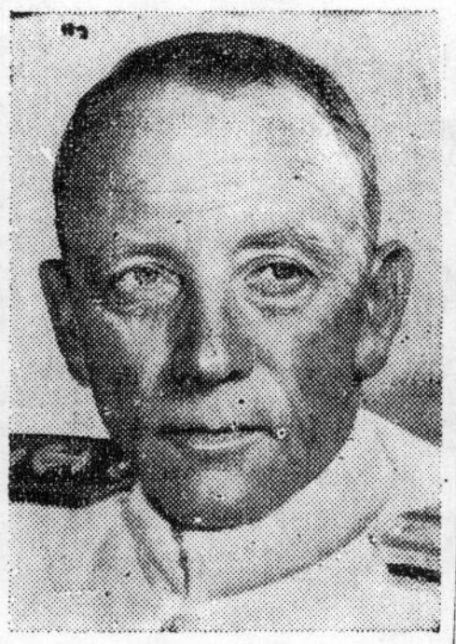

REAR ADM. ALAN G. KIRK, leader of American naval forces in the invasion of Europe, is regarded as a great sailor with a fighting heart who has spent 22 of his 55 years at sea.

Graduated from the Naval Academy in 1909, Kirk tested 14-inch naval railway guns and anti-submarine depth charges in World War I as a lieutenant at the Naval Proving Grounds.

Kirk's first great chance in this war came when he led the task force in the Sicilian invasion. He lost not a ship and won the Legion of Merit and the British Order of the Btah.

Jaunty, with dancing blue eyes, Kirk is cool and audacious under fire. He hails from Black Point, Conn.

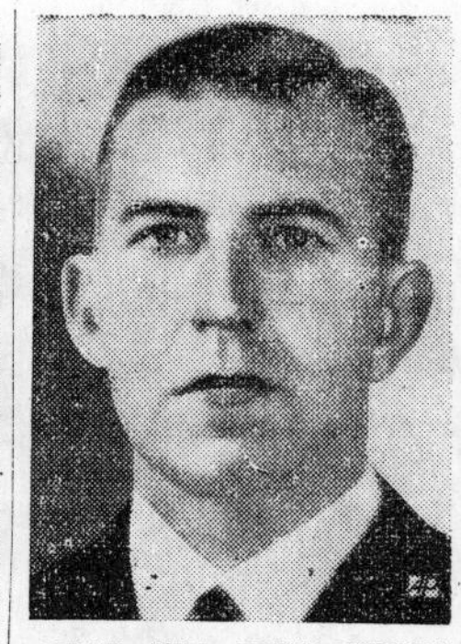

REAR ADM. JOHN WILKES, 48, a pioneer in submarines, is leader of task force units under the command headed by R. Adm. Alan G. Kirk in the European invasion.

Wilkes took to submarines shortly after graduation from the Naval Academy in 1916. He helped construct the S-47 and served as her first commander.

For heading a submarine squadron operating in the South Pacific, he recently was awarded the Distinguished Service Medal.

Striking from unsuitable bases and under constant attack, the squadron sank many Japanese warships and transports and was a bulwark in the defense of the Philippines. He is from Charlotte, N. C.

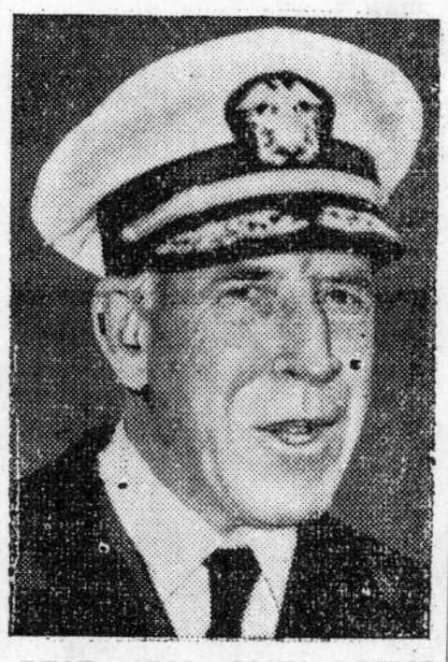

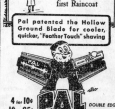

REAR ADM. JOHN LESLIE HALL, JR., 54-year-old task force unit commander in the European invasion, probably has had as many narrow escapes in this war as any high-ranking officer.

As commander of the American Sea Frontier based at Casablanca and in the assaults on Sicily and Italy, his ship has been bombed, shelled by shore batteries and attacked by submarines.

Through all this the tall, gray, slightly-stooped admiral carried himself with studied dignity. He won the Distinguished Service Medal. He served for a time with British units at Malta.

Hall was a star athlete at the academy, where he played football, basketball and baseball. His home is Charlotte, N. C.

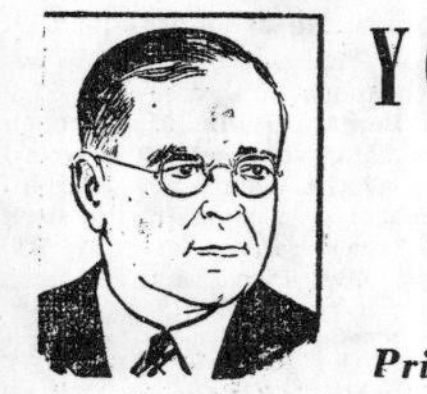

YOUR TAXES

by

HARLEY L. LUTZ

Professor of Public Finance
Princeton University

Priming the Postwar Pump

A new and more ambitious form of pump-priming has recently appeared on the horizon, completely equipped to handle our postwar fiscal problems for us. It goes under the name of Functional Finance, a misnomer as good as any to describe governmental domination of the economy.

This new manifestation of an economic panacea that failed miserably in the late departed Depression has as its bastions two so-called laws: First, that it is the responsibility of the government to keep spending exactly at such level as will absorb all the goods produced and, second, that inflation can be avoided if the government borrows the people's money when it is decided that they have too much of it for their own good.

Control Is Impossible

Even if the government should want to, it could not control the rate of spending. If the demand for goods were keen, a severer form of rationing than now exists couldly hardly hold it in check. If the demand were sluggish, then the government would have to buy up all the slow-moving stocks from the department store to the crossroads general store to maintain this false parity. And the production of goods is wholly dependent on a number of factors that the proponents of Functional Finance do not take into account at all—factors like wages, hours of employment, other governmental policies, individual initiative and the incentives to enterprise.

Suppose that the people prefer to keep their money instead of lending it to the government. Will that mean that the government (originally a group of public employees who administered services such as police and fire protection, justice, education and the like) can confiscate money? Will a paternalistic super-OPA rise out of the ashes of the present bureaus to decide just how much pocket money each of us is to have for spending? Is our pocket money allowance to be fixed by taxing away the balance of incomes when business is good and by issuing printing press money when business is dull?

No Free Lunch

One truth shines out of the murk that surrounds Functional Finance and the other current schemes for placing our economy completely in the hands of the federal government. If Americans will remember that **there is no free lunch,** then there is little chance that they will be hoodwinked by proposals so flagrantly socialistic as these.

SUN THROUGH CLOUDS AS ALLIES INVADE

LONDON, June 6 (AP)—The sun broke through heavy clouds at times in the Dover Strait area this first day of the Allied invasion of Western Europe.

After a daybreak shower there was sunshine, but later banks of heavy clouds swept up from the northwest. There were further sunny periods, although the outlook was less settled.

The wind had blown fairly hard during the night, but lost some of its strength after dawn. A moderate sea was running.

V. F. W. AUXILIARY MEETS TONIGHT

The second regular meeting of the Ladies' Auxiliary to Annapolis Post, No. 304, V.F.W., will be held tonight at the Moose Home at 8 o'clock.

Mrs. Mabel Schott, district president, will preside at a meeting of District No. 6, in conjunction with the auxiliary meeting.

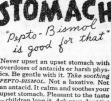

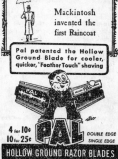

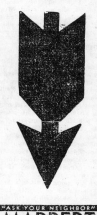

LATE NEWS

Evening Capital

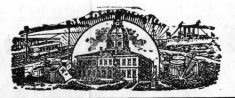

WEATHER
Fair and continued cool tonight; Friday increasing cloudiness and warmer followed by showers in west portion.

VOL. LX — NO 109 | EVERY EVENING EXCEPT SUNDAY | ANNAPOLIS, MD., THURSDAY, JUNE 8, 1944 | SOUTHERN MARYLAND'S ONLY DAILY | THREE CENTS

First Phase Of Invasion Complete

Russian Offensive Is Reported By Nazis

SEE NEW MILK CRISIS

Pocomoke City, Md., June 8 (AP)—Another possible crisis in Eastern Shore milk deliveries loomed today when a dairy operator told the Office of Price Administration that a proposed increase from 14 to 15 cents per quart of milk would not be adequate.

PRODUCTION PROCEEDS AT CUMBERLAND

Cumberland, Md., June 8 (AP)—Production proceeded quietly today at the plant of the Celanese Corporation of America following a disturbance yesterday when four girls were doused with water by men workers, plant manager Fred T. Small reported.

WOULD GIVE MILITARY TRAINING

Baltimore, June 8 (AP)—A limited number of military training units for instruction of male students over 14 years of age will be established in the Third Service Command area, command headquarters reported today.

WOULD PROBE GENERAL'S CASE

Washington, June 8 (AP) — A senatorial investigation was proposed today by Senator Chandler (D-Ky.) into the Army-reported incident of Major General Henry J. F. Miller being demoted to Lieutenant Colonel and sent home from England because he talked in advance at a cocktail party about the invasion date.

SIX COAL MINERS TRAPPED

Clarksville, Pa., June 8 (AP) — Six coal miners were reported trapped by fire in the chartiers shaft of the Emerald Coal and Coke Co. near this Greene county town today.

The U. S. Bureau of Mines said the men were at work in the 400-foot shaft last night when flames broke out among the timbers holding up the roof of one entry when a trolley wire broke, causing a short circuit. The flames quickly spread to the bituminous coal sides of the entry, blocking escape of the six men.

SEE VETO FOR OPA MEASURE

Washington, June 8 (AP)—Presidential veto of the Price and Wage Control Extension bill was considered a possibility today after the Senate voted to relieve merchants of damage liability in consumer suits if they prove that charged ceiling price violations were unintentional.

ENGINE PRODUCTION BELOW NORMAL

Production of airplane engines at the Wright Aeronautical Corporation plant in Lockland, Ohio, continued below normal today and some 15,000 of the company's employes, idle as a result of a labor dispute, were confronted with loss of their jobs if they did not return to work by tomorrow.

WOULD CHECK GOP GROUPS

Washington, June 8 (AP) — A Democrat countered renewed Republican demands for a senatorial investigation of the CIO Political Action Committee today with the threat to foster a parallel inquiry into GOP organizations active in the presidential campaign.

As Chairman Green (D-RI) called the Senate Campaign Expenditures Committee into session to consider a letter from Chairman Sidney Hillman of the CIO group, Senator Tunnell (D-Del) told a reporter the Democrats were not going to sit idly by and let the labor committee become the only object of an investigation.

POLITICAL STORM VIEWS IN SOUTH

The south hoisted new Democratic storm signals today with Mississippi joining the ranks of states determined to commit the party to a stand for "white supremacy" and Georgia Democrats barring Negroes from their July primary.

Following almost exactly a pattern set previously by Texas Democrats, the anti-administration controlled Mississippi convention voted yesterday to instruct the party's 12 electors in the state to reject the Democratic presidential nominee unless the national convention meets certain demands.

Local Tides

TOMORROW

High water — 7:52 A. M., 1.8 feet; 8:06 P. M., 1.0 feet. Low water—0:56 A. M., 3:00 P. M.

Moon rises 11:23 P. M., sets 8:25 A. M.

Sun rises 5:40 A. M.; sets 8:32 P. M.

Tides are given for Annapolis. For Sandy Point, add 15 minutes. For Thomas Point shoal, subtract 30 minutes.

82 Students Get Diplomas At Germantown

Exercises Held In Auditorium Of School

Eighty-two students of Germantown School were graduated at commencement exercises, held this morning in the auditorium of the school. Diplomas were presented by Mrs. Clarence Eason, supervisor of schools in Anne Arundel County.

Addressing the graduates, Mrs. Eason recommended for success six "Rations" that will make for a successful victory in life, long after "point rations" are forgotten. They included: preparation—live well each day for a good tomorrow; perspiration—hard work today means enjoyment of leisure tomorrow; aspiration — spiritual life dies when aspiration is gone; cooperation—only by this can victory be won; consideration—only with this may a lasting peace be made; veneration—sensing the presence of God. Those who do not sense the presence of God falter and fail. The great always know this, the near-great do not.

Salutatory Address

The salutatory address was given by Wyan Gaw, honor student, and the valedictory was given by Barbara Beavin, who won second place in the class averages. Wyan Gaw was also presented with a medal, the D. A. R. girl's Citizenship Award.

The D. A. R. boy's Citizenship Award went to Jack Tucker, who received a similar medal. Secondary awards, flag code books, were given by the D. A. R. to Marlene Stratemeyer and Sydney Francis. Presentations were made by Miss Nyce Peldmeyer, Regent of the Peggy Stewart Tea Party Chapter of the D. A. R.

Mrs. Elizabeth Carroll awarded cash prizes on behalf of the Parent-Teacher Association of the School to Evelyn Marston and Jack Tricker, who had done outstanding work on the school patrol. All members of the school safety patrol were given certifi-

(Continued On Page Two)

CALMER WEATHER IN DOVER STRAIT

LONDON, June 8 (AP)—Calmer weather prevailed in Dover Strait today with a very light but variable southwesterly breeze ruffling the surface of the sea. A light film of cloud obscured the sun during the early forenoon and sea level visibility was restricted by haze.

The barometer remained steady and the temperature hovered just above 50 degrees.

SURGICAL DRESSING WORKERS SOUGHT BY CITY BLOCK LEADERS

Volunteers to help with the big invasion quota of surgical dressings are being sought through the block system of the Civilian War Services. Mrs. I. Warrington Carr, county chairman, said today.

Mrs. Walter B. Tardy, block-chief in Annapolis, is asking all block leaders to recruit volunteers in their neighborhoods.

More than 100,000 dressings have been assigned as the monthly quota for this county alone, because of the heavy invasion needs, Mrs. Richard Wainwright Red Cross chairman, said. Twenty million dressings are needed from the eastern area this month.

Workers may go to the Red Cross headquarters in the Court of Appeals building, any time during the day that is convenient to them, without making an appointment, and may work for whatever length of time they can spare. New workers will be given instructions in making dressings. Similar arrangements may be made at county workrooms.

154 HIGH SCHOOL SENIORS TO GET DIPLOMAS TONIGHT

One hundred and fifty-four seniors, 100 girls and 54 boys, will be graduated at the annual commencement exercises of the Annapolis High School tonight, at 8 o'clock in the high school auditorium.

Dr. Theodore Halbert Wilson, president of the University of Baltimore, will deliver the address to the seniors, and diplomas will be presented by the county superintendent of schools, Dr. George Fox.

Woodfield One Of Directors In National Group

Oystermen Study New Labor Saving Mechanical-Chemical Method Of Shucking

Albert Woodfield, of Galesville, was named one of the state directors of the Oyster Growers and Dealers Association of North America, which at its meeting in Atlantic City, today was considering a mechanical-chemical method of opening oysters, which reputedly will save 35 per cent of labor in the shucking operation.

The method, which calls for getting the oysters "drunk" on carbonated water so that their muscles relax and the shells open easily, was described to oyster growers and dealers in a conference by Dr. H. F. Prytherch, of the U. S. Fish and Wildlife service.

Plant In Bay

Dr. Prytherch, who, as area coordinator of fisheries for Maryland, Virginia and North Carolina, has been conducting oyster-opening experiments for 13 years, announced plans for erection of a pilot plant in the Chesapeake Bay area "to work out the kinks" in the mechanical-chemical process.

"The carbonic acid has no bad effect whatever on the oyster," he said, adding that it had long been

(Continued On Page Two)

TERWILLIGER JOINS MERCHANT MARINE

Marvin Terwilliger, son of Mr. and Mrs. Clarence Terwilliger, 533 Second street, Eastport, left today for training in the Merchant Marines. His brother, Nile Terwilliger, has been in the navy two years, and is a signalman second class.

Their father is a chief bugle-master, now on duty at the Naval Academy. He has been in the navy for 24 years and is due for sea duty in a short time.

LED ACADEMY GRADUATING CLASS

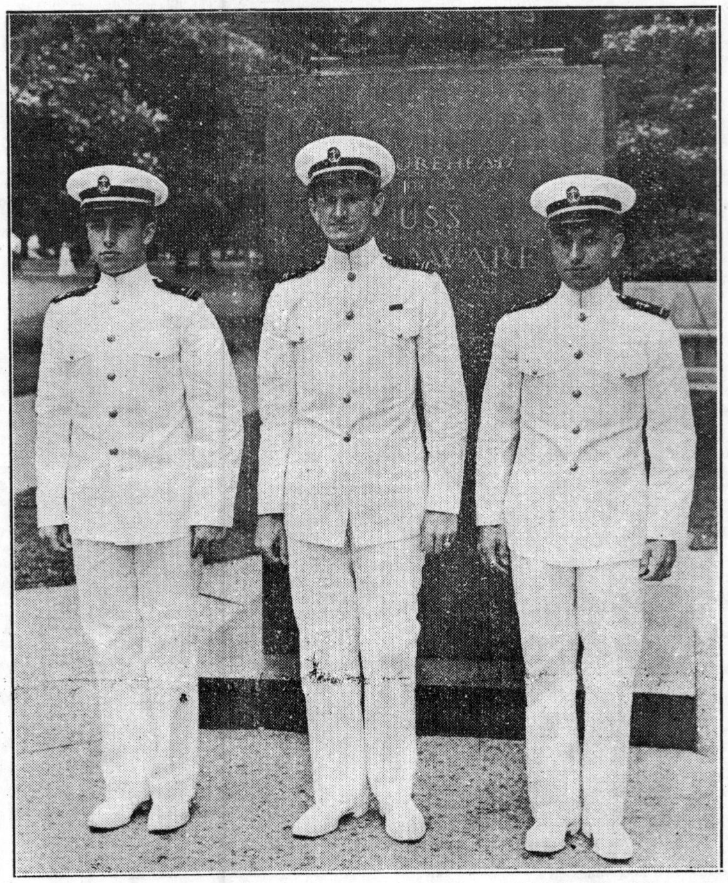

Official U. S. Navy Photograph.

Richard Henry Engelman, (center), of Cincinnati, Ohio, was the honor man of the class of 914 midshipmen who graduated yesterday at the Naval Academy. In addition to leading the class he took six prizes for proficiency in academic subjects.

Paul Clapp, (left), of Missoula, Mont., stood second in the class, with William Henry Kmetz, (right), of Philadelphia, Pa., in third place.

Colored Sailor Dies In Stabbing

Another Colored Sailor Held On Murder Charge

One colored sailor was dead today from a knife wound and another colored sailor was held on murder charges at Annapolis police headquarters.

L. Bernard Young, 21, stationed on a naval ship, was pronounced dead at the Emergency Hospital after being stabbed in the neck on Calvert street early today. Dr. J. Oliver Purvis, acting county

(Continued On Page Two)

County Man May Have Been First On French Soil

Capt. L. T. Schroeder, Jr., Of North Linthicum, Was In First Boat Beached

An Anne Arundel county man, Capt. Leonard T. Schroeder, Jr., of North Linthicum, may have been the first Allied soldier to set foot on French soil in the invasion.

According to dispatches, Schroe-

(Continued On Page Two)

Organize For Bond Drive

Three Committees Make Plans At Meeting

Committees for the Fifth War Loan to start in Annapolis and Anne Arundel county have organized at meetings held in the offices of Joseph D. Lazenby, county War Finance Chairman.

The Bankers committee, headed by George E. Rullman, made its plans at a meeting attended by representatives of local banks and building associations.

Those present included: Annap-

(Continued on Page 2)

YANKS WADE ASHORE TO START INVASION OF FRANCE

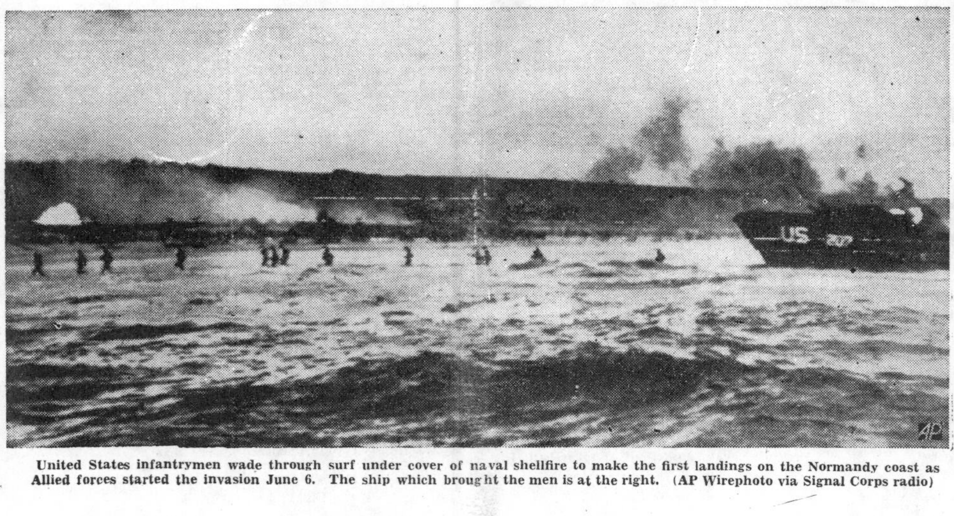

United States infantrymen wade through surf under cover of naval shellfire to make the first landings on the Normandy coast as Allied forces started the invasion June 6. The ship which brought the men is at the right. (AP Wirephoto via Signal Corps radio)

ALLIES BEGIN SECOND PHASE IN BATTLE WITH TACTICAL RESERVE

(By the Associated Press)

Allied liberating troops, with the first phase of the invasion of France accomplished, struck southward from captured Bayeux today in fierce fighting and began the second step of defeating Germa ntactical reserves thrown into battle.

A steady stream of reinforcements by sea and air strengthened the massive spearhead, and Berlin reported a pinchers threat to seize the tip of the jutting Cherbourg peninsula and its great port of Cherbourg.

The first phase of invasion, "which might be said to be securing a foothold and defeating local German reserves, has been accomplished." Supreme Allied headquarters announced.

The Allies now are begining the second phase of defeating Nazi "tactical reserves," and still ahead is the third task of crushing "strategic reserves" perhaps massing already for a strong counter-blow.

RUSSIAN OFFENSIVE REPORTED

Meanwhile, in Italy the Fifth army captured Civitavecchi, Rome's principal port, 38 miles northwest of the Eternal City, and was thrusting swiftly up the west coast to maintain contact with the retreating enemy. Secretary of War Stimson reported that a recent three-day period of heavy fighting preceding the fall of Rome cost American forces 2,379 casualties. American total casualties in Italy to May 30 included 9,964 killed, 38,554 wounded and 9,011 missing.

DNB in a Berlin broadcast announced that the Russians had launched an offensive on a broad front in the sector north of Isai, Romania.

In the Southwest Pacific, Mokmer airfield, wrested from the Japanese on Biak island, was in American hands, a prized base from which to launch air assaults against the Philippines.

Flashes From Invasion Front

GERMAN PRISONERS LAND IN ENGLAND

London, June 8 (AP) — Displaying every emotion from arrogance to bewilderment, the first large group of German prisoners from the Allied beachheads in northern France were landed last night at an invasion port in England.

A handful of high ranking Allied officials, several correspondents and the ship's crew witnessed the debarkation.

The prisoners, both officers and men, were marched to waiting trucks and moved to an undisclosed destination under an armed guard. Among the captives were four Poles, one of whom said he had been captured and drafted by the Nazis.

RUSSIANS FOLLOW INVASION NEWS

Moscow, June 8 (AP) — Russian newspapers reported on all phases of the invasion of France today, carrying maps and pictures of barges and tanks — exceptional coverage of an opereation by the other allies.

"Russian infantry will march soon across German land," Red Star promised. Izvestia observed that Pierre Laval should be sad "because he has to be hanged on the first lamp post."

COMPARES INVASION TO SICILIAN ATTACK

LONDON, June 8 (AP)—John A. Moroso, Associated Press war correspondent, reported from an invasion port today that although "the assault was widely hailed as the largest in history, it actually was no larger in its initial phases than the Allied attack on Sicily."

Moroso witnessed both the landings in Sicily and in North Africa.

"Weather prophets were the worst flops," he said. "Wind and a choppy channel almost caused disaster."

ROCKET SHIPS USED IN ATTACK

NEW YORK, June 8 (AP)—Rocket ships used in the invasion of France "discharge vast quantities of explosive onto beaches much more quickly than has ever been done before by a warship," the British Information Services said today. Use of the rocket ships was disclosed at Allied Expeditionary Headquarters.

"The rocket ships were developed as a result of experiences in the Dieppe raid," the British Agency said. "The actual destruction they

(Continued On Page Two)

American Casualties

From the start of the war, Army and Navy casualties total 217,131, an increase of 10,904 since a report on May 25. Stimson said Army casualties up to May 21 totaled 171,358. Navy casualties reported up to today amount to 45,733. The Army has 28,952 killed, 68,779 wounded, 40,084 missing and 33,543 prisoners of war. The Navy had 9,802 killed, 12,253 wounded, 9,256 missing and 4,462 prisoners.

Specific directions and progress in today's fighting in France were not disclosed, but headquarters announced that medium bombers had struck heavily at Caen, 16 miles southeast of Bayeux, starting fires. The Allies have plunged near Caen, nine miles inland on the peninsula's base.

American heavy bombers blasted railway installations at Rennes, Laval, Tours, Le Mans, Nantes and Angers, in support of the beachhead forces, flying out 750 to 1,000 strong.

A German broadcast, totally without confirmation, said 1,300 gliders used to rush in a huge airborne army, had been destroyed or captured.

Cut Railroad

Capture of Bayeux snipped the railway between Paris and Cherbourg, 45 mile to the northwest, and opened the way for a thrust deeper inland. But further west the Germans pictured Allied forces already within 20 miles of a junction that would choke off Cherbourg itself. Berlin declared house-to-house fighting raged in Ste. Mere-Eglise, 20 miles southeast of the port, and said parachutists had landed on the west coast only a score of miles southwest of Ste. Mere-Eglise.

There was no Allied confirmation of west coast landings or fighting at Ste. Mere-Eglise, on one of the two main roads to Cherbourg.

Heavy battles, with tanks and reserves sped up by both sides, flared over the peninsula. Allied beachhead troops are linking up with airborne forces dropped deeper inland, headquarters said, and improvement in adverse weather aided reinforcements from glider sky trains.

Take Villages

Field reports declared British-Canadian troops had captured a number of French towns and villages, advancing on open roads to points some miles from the coast. Infantrymen rode up to battle on bicycles and tanks to speed the advance.

Canadian and British troops have captured several hundred prisoners and shot up numerous Nazi 88-millimeter guns, field reports said.

The German high command declared the Allies had opened an attack from the bridgehead between Caen and Bayeux, and that Nazi forces had counterattacked.

(Continued On Page Two)

SOCIAL and PERSONAL

Miss Gosnell Engaged To Lieut. Morrow

Mr. and Mrs. Charles M. Gosnell, of Severna Park, Md., announce the engagement of their daughter, Miss Nancy Gosnell, to Lieut. William Berryman Morrow, USN, son of Mr. and Mrs. Norman B. Morrow of Round Bay, Md.

The wedding will take place on July 1 at the Naval Academy Chapel.

• • •

Mr. Freeman Enters Naval Academy

Mr. E. W. Freemn, Sr., publisher of the "Commercial," Pine Bluff, Ark., left here yesterday after making his first visit to Annapolis to enter his grandson, Mr. E. W. Freeman, III, in the U. S. Naval Academy.

While here, Mr. Freeman stayed at Carvel Hall.

• • •

Girl Scout Conference In Washington

Mrs. R. C. Lamb, commissioner; Mrs. G. E. Rullman, Mrs R. F. Merrick and Mrs. A. C. Hallock, of the Anne Arundel County Girl Scout Council, attended an all-day conference yesterday at the Girl Scout Little House, in Washington, D. C.

Representatives of all the Girl Scout Councils in this area, which includes Baltimore, Alexandria, Washington, Arlington, Falls Church, Westminster, Prince George's county, and Anne Arundel county attended the meeting as a planning committee to discuss needs and plans of the area for the coming year.

Mrs. O'Neal M. Johnson, of Washington, presided at the meeting.

• • •

Mrs. Joslin In Rehobeth Beach

Mrs. Royal K. Joslin and her guest, Miss Catherine Carroll, of Washington, D. C., are spending a week with Mrs. Joslin's grandparents, Mr. and Mrs. Owen Thompson, at Rehobeth Beach, Del.

Mrs. Joslin has been living with her parents, Rear Admiral and Mrs. Laurence T. DuBose, of Wardour, while her husband, Lt. Joslin, USN, is overseas.

• • •

Mrs. Smith Visiting Daughter

Mrs. W. Taylor Smith, wife of Capt. Smith, USN, is visiting her daughter, Mrs. Morrow Decker, wife of Lt. Decker, USN, of Acton Wing.

Mrs. Simth is staying at Carvel Hall.

• • •

To Attend Civitan Convention

Mr. Henry G. Weaver, president of the Civitan Club, and Mr. Oswald Tilghman, as delegates, accompanied by Mr. James Costello and Mr. Joseph Painter, as alternates, and Dr. A. K. Snyder, member, will leave here Monday to attend the Civitan National Convention at Nashville, Tenn.

The convention is scheduled for June 20 through June 22.

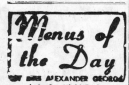

CALENDAR FOR THE WEEK

Today

9:00 P. M. to 1:00 A. M.—25th annual dance, Guy Carleton Parlett Post and Unit, No. 7, in Mirror Room, Carvel Hall.

Guests Of Mrs. Dutton

Lt. and Mrs. Pierre Cherbonnet, and baby daughter, who have spent the past week with Mrs. Cherbonnet's mother, Mrs. Benjamin Dutton, at her home, 1 Oklahoma Terrace, will leave tomorrow.

• • •

Brothers Receive Promotion

Staff Sgt. Bernard E. Bassford, son of Mrs. E. J. Bassford, of 20 Woodland avenue, has been promoted to the rank of technical sergeant.

Tech. Sgt. Bassford, a former employee of the B and A Freight Office in Annapolis, enterered the Army Air Force in September, 1941. After training at Bowling Field, he was assigned to overseas duty with the unit operating in China, Burma, and India.

His brother, Cpl. James A. Bassford, who is stationed in Washington, D. C., was recently promoted to the grade of sergeant.

• • •

American Legion Officials At Dance

Mrs. Warren Boulden, president of the department of the Maryland American Legion Auxiliary, and Dr. Herbert C. Blake, commander of the department of Maryland of the American Legion, will be guests of honor tonight at the dance to be held in Carvel Hall by the Guy Carleton Parlett Post and Unit No. 7, of the American Legion.

Other department officers of both organizations will attend from Baltimore, Washington, Elkton, Frederick, Hagerstown and Westminster.

The Stardusters will provide the music for the dance, which is open to the public.

Lawn Party Last Night

The annual benefit garden party for the Annapolis Auxiliary of the American Mission to Lepers was held last night in a beautiful setting—old trees in the lovely garden, which overlooks Spa Creek—at the home of Dr. and Mrs. George T. Feldmeyer, 2 Southgate avenue.

Assisting were the Misses Barbara Duckett, Ann Carol Armbruster, Ann Slaven, Nancy Slaven, Harriet Holt, Brooke Holt, Mary Elizabeth Kitchen, Lillie Curren, Virginia O'Neale, Charline Halpine, Jane Herring, Ann Gaw, Olga Ann Werntz, June Michaelson, Mary Bess Treat, Carol Lou Treat, Kit Willis, Sally Willis, Jane Pancoast, Patsy Weber, Sybil Godfrey and Mesdames Harry Yaggi, Stephen Duckett, W. Y. Kitchen, A. K. Snyder, Marion Ellinghausen, Albert Krapf, W. P. Harrison, Alcade Sarles, Walter Holt, Richard Heise, Otto Ortland, O. Strong and Howard A. Keith.

Mrs. John deP. Douw is chairman of the Auxiliary and Mrs. Charles C. Bramble, vice chairman.

Menus of the Day

By MRS. ALEXANDER GEORGE

Saturday Night Party

Chicken Casserole
Escarole
Corn Bread
Strawberry Fluff

(Recipes Serve Four)

Chicken Casserole

2 cups cooked chicken, cut coarsely
½ pound mushrooms
1 cup chicken stock
½ cup mushroom liquor
½ cup light cream
3 tablespoons margarine
3 tablespoons flour
Salt and pepper to taste
8 ounces macaroni, cooked
½ cup grated cheese

Peel mushrooms and remove stems. Simmer stems and peelings in a cup of water until liquid is reduced to half. Slice mushrooms and saute in a little fat five minutes. Melt margarine. Blend in flour and add chicken stock, mushroom liquor, and cream, stirring constantly until smooth and thickened. Season with salt and pepper. Add chicken and mushrooms. Line a large casserole dish with cooked macaroni. Pour chicken and mushroom mixture into center and cover whole with grated cheese. Dot with a little margarine. Bake at 400° until top is golden brown.

Strawberry Fluff

½ pint strawberries
1 cup powdered sugar
1 egg white

Wash and hull strawberries. Crush slightly. Put into a bowl with the sugar and egg white and beat with a rotary beater until the mixture is stiff enough to hold its shape. This sometimes takes as long as a half hour, but the result is worth it.

Nine Nurses'

(Continued From Page One)

the organist, Lt. A. S Jensen.

Mrs. G M. Dusinberre, vice chairman of the local Chapter of the Red Cross, presided and introduced the speakers.

Mrs. J N. Galloway, chairman of Red Cross special services, welcomed the aides to membership in the Red Cross service.

Prof. Henry F. Sturdy, the principal speaker, told of the many duties of the aides in the hospital, and what their work means to the patient. As Deputy Chief Air Raid Warden of the Office of Civilian Defense, he swore the graduates in as members of the OCD.

Dr. French Speaks

Dr Wiliam J. French, in presenting the certificates to the class, stressed the theme of cheerfulness in their contact with patients.

Mrs. Kiefer le dthe new graduates in repeating the pledge to the Red Cross.

All arrangements for the dinner and graduation were made by Mrs. Kiefer, as chairman of the nurses' aide committee and corps, and her two vice chairman, Mrs. Frederick Margraff and Mrs. Jean Champion.

The new nurses' aides who were graduated are: Mrs. Dorothy Jack, Mrs. Marion K. Brashears, Mrs. Rosalie Blouin, Mrs. Lois Boone, Mrs. Cora Cathcart, Mrs. Olive King, Mrs. Anna Swensen, Mrs Mary Burwell, and Mrs. William Millett.

MODES of the MOMENT

—by Amy Porter—

They've Gone As Far As They Can Go

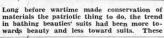

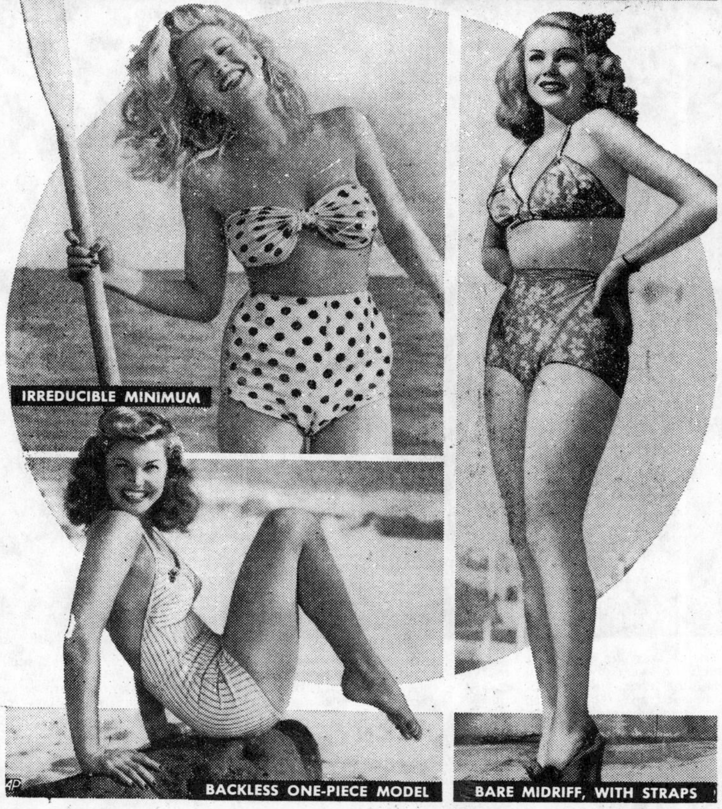
IRREDUCIBLE MINIMUM
BACKLESS ONE-PIECE MODEL
BARE MIDRIFF, WITH STRAPS

Long before wartime made conservation of materials the patriotic thing to do, the trend in bathing beauties' suits had been more towards beauty and less toward suits. These examples show however that wartime shortages or not, swim suits have gone about as far as they can go.

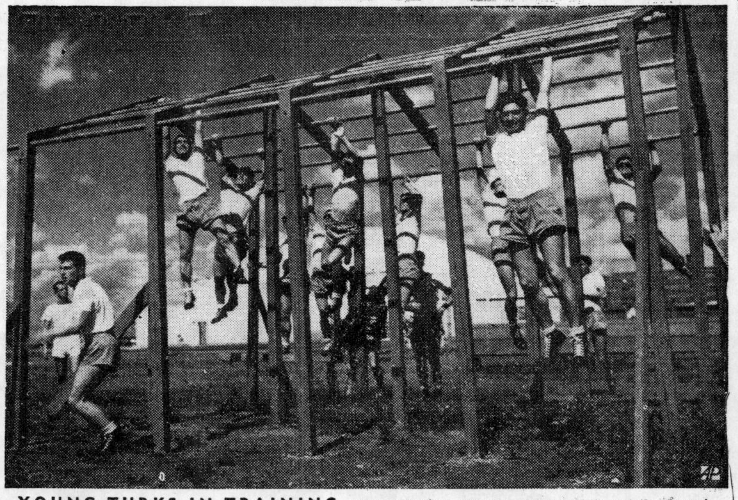

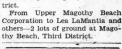

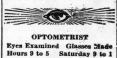

YOUNG TURKS IN TRAINING—Young Turkish officers, taking training at the Army's San Antonio, Tex., aviation cadet center, go through part of the obstacle course.

Higher Prices

(Continued From Page One)

There were less rejections by farmers and a smaller percentage of the tobacco was brought in by warehousemen than during the preceding week. This was attributed to the improved conditions of the market. The general quality of the tobacco that reached the sales floor showed little improvement.

It was estimated that approximately one third of the 1943 crop had been sold to date, the WFA said.

A gross sales figure of 7,354,513 pounds was listed by the WFA, with the first hand sales for the season at 6,725,425 pounds at an average of $48.88 per hundred pounds, and resales of 629,088 pounds.

Net farm sales this week amounted to 769,574 pounds for average of $49.26 per hundred pounds, showing a net increase of .46 over last weeks' sales.

SUPER-FORTRESS PARTS MADE BY MARTIN'S

Baltimore, June 17 (AP)—The Glenn L. Martin Aircraft Company disclosed today that "assemblies" for the giant B-29 Super-Fortress, the planes which bombed Japan Thursday, are being constructed in its Middle River plant.

The Company announcement said the local factory was "in important production of materials for B-29s."

C. AND P. WORKERS RECEIVE EMBLEMS

Mrs. Adelaide G. Henderson, an employee in the Annapolis office of the Chesapeake and Potomac Telephone Company of Baltimore City, has received a four- star emblem in recognition of twenty years of service with the company.

A three-star emblem was presented to Henry R. Froehlich for fifteen years of service, and Miss Mary E. Stehle received a two-star emblem for ten years of service.

During May, 66 employees in the C. and P. Telephone Company in Maryland were awarded emblems. They had an aggregate of 1,120 years of service.

Japanese Beetles

(Continued From Page One)

The cooperative program has for its fundamental objective the establishment of disease and parasites looking forward to ultimate and permanent relief from acute Japanese beetle damage.

Mr. Day made the following comments in discussing the disease and parasites being used in Maryland.

The milky disease is proving effective for destroying the grubs once the soil is thoroughly inoculated. The control program is attempting to establish the disease in all sections of the county. Spread and thorough inoculation of the soil is dependent upon grub population, therefore, some trouble must be expected from the beetle before permanent relief can be held. Usually two to three years are required in a heavily infested area for the disease to spread sufficiently to bring about control that is decidedly noticeable.

The parasites that are being used are effective for destroying beetle grubs, but their build-up is quite slow. Usually five to six years are required for effective results.

WAR

(Continued from Page One)

threat to the Cherbourg peninsula was a 30-mile arc from Quinville on the east coast, southwest through Montebourg and St. Sauveur and then southeast to the Carentan area. The German crisis grew more acute by the hour. The U. S. battleships Texas, Nevada and Arkansas aided the drive by bombarding German positions ahead of the Americans in the Carentan and Isigny areas.

American heavy bombers pounded half a dozen Nazi airbases in a great arc extending nearly half way around the Normandy battle zone. Fighter-bombers ranged over and beyond the beachhead attacking motor convoys, bridges, tanks, machinegun nests. RAF planes hammered a synthetic oil plant near Duisburg and targets in Berlin. Thirty-three RAF bombers were missing.

Italian Front

The Eighth Army in Italy captured Foligno, about 27 miles north of Terni. Spoleto and Trevi along the route also were seized. Allied troops also reached a point 13 miles south of Perugia. Montelcone was occupied. The Fifth Army overran Grosseto on the coast. 100 miles northwest of Rome. Allied planes destroyed 70 enemy planes yesterday, while 12 Allied heavy bombers and nine other Allied planes are missing.

Helsinki dispatches reported the compulsory of the Finnish city of Cliputi as the Russian drive rolled nearer that point. The Finns are blowing up all the bridges on two highways leading to the city.

Japanese War

Grimly fighting American invaders, after street-by-street seizure of a coastal town and capture of its airstrip, punched slowly inland on Saipan Island.

Official sources also disclosed that a task force had made the war's first official attack on the Bonin and Kazan island, destroying 47 planes, sinking two ships and damaging 10.

On Saipan, Americans won the town of Charan-Kanoa in a battle which was described as a cross between Guadalcanal and Tarawa. It was estimated that about 30,000 Japanese defended the island, but Tokyo placed the number at 15,000.

The capture of the Japanese base Kamaing, about 40 miles northwest of besieged Myitkyina in northern Burma was announced. At the same time there was a token juncture of the Chinese expeditionary force and Lt. Gen. Joseph W. Stilwell's forces with the capture by Chinese guerillas of Lauhkuan, well to the west of Hpwaw and 60 airline miles northeast of Myitkyina.

Relentless American drive and the superior weight of equipment are winning the battle of Biak island, Dutch New Guinea. Three tank-supported Japanese counterattacks were smashed.

Japan's north Pacific Matsuwa island in the Kuriles was bombed for 30 minutes on June 13 by a Navy task force which concentrated on Tagan point airfield and administrative headquarters.

Capt. Hilyer K. F. Gearing of Annapolis, commanding the destroyers, led some of his ships to cut off any Japanese vessels that might try to flee, but none were encountered.

Property Tranfers In City And County Recorded In Court

From George D. Miller and wife to Daniel J. Zacharias and wife—lot of ground in Second District.

From Mary L. Mocnik and others to Richard J. McGarry—lot of ground at Shipley Heights in Fifth District.

From Emma L. Elliott and others to Daniel Palmer and wife—lot of ground at Lusbys Corner in Second District containing 1 1/10 acres.

From County Commissioners of Anne Arundel County to George R. Carter and wife—2 lots of ground in Seventh District.

From James A. Walton, county treasurer, and others, to Willard J. Odenbeck and wife—3 lots of ground at Thompsons Farms in Fourth District.

From James A. Walton, county treasurer, and others, to Louis R. Pillsbury and wife—6 lots of ground at Glendale Terrace in Fifth District.

From James A. Walton County Treasurer and others to Martin Till and wife—2 lots of ground at Orchard Beach, Third District.

From James A. Walton County Treasurer and others to Ester M. Williams—lot of ground at Elvaton, Third District, containing 2 ½ acres.

From Harvey B. Hall and wife to Robert M. Hall lot of ground, Second District, containing 2½ acres.

From Charles W. Thomas and wife to Stanley Lee—lot of ground, Second District, containing 43 1-10 acres.

From James A. Walton County Treasurer and others to John L. Stieff and wife—4 lots of ground at Brooklyn Heights, Fifth District.

From Upper Magothy Beach Corporation to Lea LaMantia and others—2 lots of ground at Magothy Beach, Third District.

SOCIAL and PERSONAL

**Wedding In
Wayne, Pa.**

In the Wayne Presbyterian Church today Miss Virginia Lee McGinnes, daughter of Mr. and Mrs. Arthur P. G. McGinnes, of Wayne, Pa., was married to Ensign Edward Wirgate Mullinix, USNR, son of Mr. and Mrs. Howard E. Mullinix, of Round Bay.

The bride, who was given in marriage by her father, wore a bridal gown made with a tight-fitting bodice, long sleeves ending in points over the hands, and a full train. She wore her mother's headdress and wedding veil of Chantilly lace and carried a shower bouquet of gardenia and bouvardia, centered with an orchid.

The bride's attendants were her cousins, Mrs. Doak Conn, of Parkersburg, Pa., and Miss Laura Johnson, of Pen Yan, N. Y. They wore pink gowns, made with lace bodices and full skirts and carried lavender larkspur.

Mr. Mullinix, father of the groom, was best man. The ushers were: Mr. Arthur P. G. McGinnes, Jr., brother of the bride; Ensign Graut E. Nelson, USNR; Ensign Donato W. Galvin, USNR, and Ensign Thomas A. Eador, USNR.

The mother of the bride was gowned in powder blue and wore a matching hat, and the groom's mother wore a dusty rose dress and small feathered hat of the same shade. Both wore corsages of orchids.

After a wedding trip the couple will make their home in Miami, Fla., for the next few months.

* * *

**At Carvel Hall
This Week**

Spending several days at Carvel Hall are Mrs. W. T. Sithington, of Little Rock, Ark., and Lt. and Mrs. V. D. Currier, of Dilley, Texas.

* * *

**Birthday Party
For Mrs. Smith**

On Wednesday afternoon after working hours, the office force of the local Ration Board gave a surprise birthday party for Mrs. Charles Smith, secretary of the Board.

* * *

**Godfreys Return
To Annapolis**

Mrs. Vincent H. Godfrey and daughter, Miss Sibyl Godfrey, have returned to their home at 29 Southgate avenue, where they will live while Comdr. Godfrey is on duty overseas.

Miss Godfrey entertained at a party yesterday afternoon Miss Nancy Witbeck, of Nutley, N. J., who is her roommate at Fairfax Boarding School, Va.; Miss Jackie Brooks, and Miss Jane Gardner, of New Rochelle, N. Y. Miss Gardner is sister-in-law of Mrs. Dudley H. Adams, Lt. USMCR, who is on duty in Santa Barbara, California.

* * *

**Returned From
Kentucky**

Mrs. Reginald C. Lamb, and son, Charles and daughter, Katherine, have returned from a ten-day visit with Mr. Lamb's parents in Franklin, Ky.

Prof. Lamb, who also accompanied his family to Franklin, will return here after August 1.

Have Your EYES CHECKED Today

Don't let faulty eyesight cause you hours of discomfort and maybe ill health. The correct glasses for you can make all the difference between good vision and eye strain.

COMPLETE Optical Service

We are equipped to give you the best and a complete optical service. Make an appointment today.

THE Columbia Jewelry Co.

138 MAIN STREET   DIAL 3351

CALENDAR FOR THE WEEK

Today

10:30 A. M.—Story hour at the Public Library. Miss Naomi Brewer will tell "Little Toot The Dog Cantbark" and selections from "Told under the Green Umbrella" and "Winnie the Pooh."

8:00 P. M.—Stag night, contests, games, refreshments at USO.

7:00 P. M.—Cub Pack No. 334, July meeting and picnic supper at the home of Mr. and Mrs. Norman Wells at the Engineering Experiment Station.

8:00 P. M.—Lecture by Sister M. Madeleva, president of St. Mary's College, Holy Cross, on "The Frontiers of Poetry" in the Great Hall, St. John's College.

Tomorrow

Voice recordings, refreshments, at USO.

**Mrs. Valiant
At Carvel Hall**

Mrs. Joseph W. Valiant, formerly of Wardour, arrived yesterday at Carvel Hall with her grandson, Charles Carroll Dunn, and her granddaughter, Miss Fay Taylor.

Mrs. Valiant has been spending the summer in Winchester, Mass., with her daughters, Mrs. Evelyn B. Taylor, and Mrs. Charles Carroll Dunn, who will join her here on August 1 to occupy their home at 215 King George street.

**Guests Of
Mr. And Mrs. Moss**

Comdr. Paul F. Johnston, USN., and Mrs. Johnston have arrived in Annapolis and are the house guests of Mrs. Johnston's parents, Mr. and Mrs. Walter C. Moss, of Prince George street.

Comdr. Johnston has returned recently from the Southwest Pacific and will be on duty in Washington, D. C.

**Announce Birth
Of Son**

Dr. and Mrs. Walter H. Mitchell announce the birth of a son, Richard Charles, on July 27 at the Emergency Hospital.

**Mrs. Mulligan
In Norfolk**

Mrs. Charles H. Mulligan is spending two weeks at Oakdale Farms, Norfolk, where she is visiting her son, Lieut. (j.g.) Alvin E. Coleman, Jr., who is stationed there.

**Announce Birth
Of A Daughter**

Mr. and Mrs. Raymond Swartz, 3 North Cherry Grove avenue, announce the birth of a daughter, Susan Carol, at the Emergency Hospital on July 25.

**Announce Birth
Of Daughter**

Mr. and Mrs. W. Hearon Buttrill, of 271 Tyler avenue, announce the birth of a daughter, Judith Carolyn, on July 20 at the Emergency Hospital.

**Miss Anderson
In Michigan**

Miss Dorothy Ann Anderson left yesterday to spend several days with Miss Mary Ellen Compton, of Detroit, Mich., and will then join Miss Dottie Laub, daughter of Comdr. E. S. V. Laub (MC) USN., and Mrs. Laub, at Fisherman's Paradise, Bellaire, Mich., where she will remain for a week.

Ensign W. W. K. Miller, Jr., who has recently been the guest of Miss Anderson at the home of her parents, Dr. and Mrs. Albert L. Anderson, at 44 Southgate avenue, has returned to Philadelphia, and will leave from there for duty on the West Coast.

Dr. Jean L. Kearney
Osteopathic Physician

Office Hours 9 to 12 and 1 to 5
Evenings by Appointment

7 State Circle

Office—Phone 2500
Residence—Phone 2752

MODES of the MOMENT
by Ann Porter

CAREER GIRL'S WARDROBE: Clothes like these, at prices like these, are available in practically every town in America. They are (l. to r)—green gabardine jerkin costume with extended shoulder and smart hip buttoning, piped in red and worn with a white crepe blouse; gold gabardine classic shirtwaist dress with saddle-stitch trim, fly front fastening and alligator type belt; black faille evening gown with off-shoulder ruching in pink faille and tiny black velvet bows on the shirred V inset of the bodice; "Sunday-go-to-meeting" suit dress in black faille, with jet-embroidered bands on the jacket, pink faille dickey and gored skirt.

Silver Star
(Continued From Page One)

other craft for medical attention," it added.

Colonel Claude also is survived by his wife, Mrs. Emma B. Claude, of Orange, Va.

He enlisted in the Marine Corps on July 25, 1923, was commissioned a second lieutenant on Feb. 19, 1925, and was promoted to the rank he held on Tarawa on May 17, 1944.

He was 40 at the time of his death.

Text of Citation

The citation which accompanied his award:

"For conspicuous gallantry and intrepidity in action as military observer attached to the Second Marine Division during action against enemy Japanese forces on Tarawa, Gilbert Islands, November 20-22, 1943. Constantly subjected to a devastating barrage of enemy rifle and machine-gun fire while proceeding to the beach in a landing boat, Lieut Col. Claude sighted a number of previously wounded men in danger of drowning. Unhesitatingly exposing himself to the direct line of hostile fire, he valiantly plunged into the treacherous waters, repeatedly swimming distances of from 30 to 75 yards in order to bring the men back to his own boat from which they were transferred to other craft for medical attention.

"Finally gaining the beachhead after successfully completing his perilous task, Lt. Col. Claude gathered information vital to future operations before he was killed by enemy fire while proceeding on an important mission to a forward command post. His splendid initiative, great personal valor and unrelenting devotion to duty in the face of grave peril directly contributed to the saving of many lives and were in keeping with the highest tradition of the United States Naval Service. He gallantly gave his life for his country."

FIVE BLUE STAMPS
VALID ON AUG. 1

WASHINGTON, July 28 (AP)—Five additional 10-point blue ration stamps—B5 through F5—will become valid Aug. 1 for purchasing processed foods, the Office of Price Administration announced today. They will be good indefinitely.

Dewey Plans
Put On Four
Year Basis

Would End New Deal Warfare On State's Rights

ALBANY, N. Y., July 27 (AP)—Gov. Thomas E. Dewey's plans for refurbishing the federal government—if the electorate gives him the nod in November—were put strictly on a four-year basis today, with the Republican nominee calling for an end of what he classed as New Deal "warfare" on state's rights.

Listing a series of topics for study by a GOP Governors Conference at St. Louis next week, Dewey said he hoped the Republicans could fix "an area of responsibility to the people," as between federal and local governments, that would settle the problem "not permanently, but for our time, or rather, the next four years."

He stressed the four-year basis of his program at a press conference attended also by Gov. John W. Bricker of Ohio, the vice presidential nominee, but did not explain whether he was contemplating only one term if elected. More than a year ago, Bricker proposed a constitutional amendment limiting presidential tenure to one six-year term.

Wants Reorganization

The Dewey objective won immediate applause from Rep. Charles A. Eaton (R-NJ), who called after a conference with the New York Governor, for "the complete reorganization of the federal government on sound business principles."

This is necessary, Eaton said, if the United States is to assume the post-war world leadership, carrying on "tremendous economic relationships with the rest of the world." The 76-year-old ranking minority member of the House Foreign Affairs committee said he thought Dewey agreed.

The Republican nominee, meanwhile, dumped in the Governors' conference pot a wide group of subjects, including several on which the party already had taken positive stands in its platform.

Dewey said the governors would be asked to speak out on the regulation of all kinds of insurance, which the platform said should be retained by the states. He mentioned state versus federal control of the National Guard. Platform drafters urged that the guard be under state direction, with federal training and equipment.

State Control

Although he listed administration of the unemployment service as a problem, the party previously had gone on record for return of this branch to state control.

In the fields of public expenditures, federal-state taxations, health, labor relations, public works, agriculture and veterans affairs, however, the governors apparently had the widest latitude to approve policy statements that would form, with the platform, a campaign charter on domestic affairs.

Soldier Helped
(Continued From Page One)

ried the water away, left no place for the mosquitoes to breed and thus curtailed the spread of malaria," Pvt. Walker said.

There were five such crews of 25 men each—the native bushmen were civilian employees of the government — on duty with the post engineer at the Army Air Base in Accra, where Walker was stationed.

"Sometimes we dug ditches a mile in length, to carry the water far from camp.

"When we weren't doing that, we were busy dodging the mosquitoes during off-duty hours. In the barracks we covered our cots with mosquito netting tents and made certain no portion of the body could be touched the net; otherwise the pests would bite right through the mesh. We also took a spray to bed with us, spraying inside just in case a prowler sneaked in with us."

Insect Repellant

Everyone rubbed insect repellent on his neck, face and hands and even in the intense heat, wore canvas leggings or boots and kept their shirts buttoned closely around the neck, and the heads covered whenever possible.

Pvt. Walker, who is 21 years old, went overseas the first of last September. He didn't get malaria, as many of his comrades did, but the tropics had their effect on him and he was sent home in January. He was hospitalized in Florida before being sent to a redistribution center.

"I'm satisfied that I couldn't have done a more valuable job for my fellow man," he said. "No amount of sheet metal would have stopped those mosquitoes."

---

dies tomorrow, the second group to finish this year.

Thirteen of them have been studying radio engineering for two years. The remainder, divided equally into communications and aerological engineering groups, have been taking one-year courses.

---

117 OFFICERS WILL
GRADUATE TOMORROW

Naval Academy officials announced today that 117 officers would complete post-graduate stu-

---

Peekaboo... Your Toes Are Showing!

By BETTY CLARKE
AP Beauty Editor

Step up your personal efficiency by keeping your feet well groomed these summertime peekaboo toe days. You can give yourself a cooling foot bath, and by observing a few simple tips, turn out a pedicure as smart as if it was done by a professional.

Shape nails with emery board held at right angles, filing straight across nail.

Oily cuticle remover works away all excess scruffy skin around nail, between toes.

Toe tips spread apart with pads of cotton before using polish prevents smearing.

Callouses can be banished by applying cuticle remover ten minutes daily.

Beach bound in a twinkling! Polish bright as a lollipop, red against summer tan.

SUBVERSIVE FAT

Undercover work is going on these days, in some household garbage pails. Skillet scrapings, meat drippings, meat scraps and other fat bearing items are mingling unashamedly with coffee grounds and orange peels. In ordinary times this is common practice, but today when every ounce of used kitchen fat is needed for the war effort, it is deplorably wasteful. The products and by-products of used fat are so important that OPA actually allows ration points, and the meat dealer pays cash to get every ounce of used fat, and put it to work to shorten the war!

French Girls Hunt Germans

Armed Group Go Boche Hunting

By HAL BOYLE

With American Troops In Brittany, Aug. 7 (Delayed by censorship) (AP)—French mademoiselles armed with enemy Luger pistols and carrying potato masher grenades in their belts have joined Frenchmen resistance leaders in Brittany's greatest outdoor sport —capturing Germans.

Some of the women lug rifles on their shoulders and speed down secondary roads searching out isolated pockets of Germans.

"I met two of these French gals yesterday packing Luger pistols," said Lieut. Leonard Hughes of Fond Du Lac, Wis., supply officer. "We have been trying to get our hands on some of those Lugers ever since we landed — and here were these gals packing a pair of 'em. We tried to trade them cigarets for their pistols but they wouldn't do it. They wanted to keep them to kill Germans.

"Those women are amazing. They fix up old trucks and go out Boche hunting the way our girls back home set out for the movies. They get out in front and lead our supply trucks for hours, checking roads ahead to see if they are clear.

"You've got to hand it to these Free French. They're doing a wonderful job. They just go in with grenades and clean out those Germans wherever they find them."

By patroling roads over which American armor has passed, but which infantry has not mopped up, Fighting French men and mademoiselles are cutting down attacks on small American supply truck convoys. To keep our tanks supplied, our supply boys have had to fight their way up to the front.

"These isolated groups of Germans get close to roads and shoot up the trucks," said Hughes. "I have had eight of my drivers hit by snipers. They usually let most of the convoy go by, then open up with machine guns and rifles on the last few vehicles.

"But if it wasn't for the work those French gals and men are doing we would be losing a lot more men to these dirty snipers who lay low in the fields shooting at you until they get hungry, and then want to give themselves up and be fed."

Property Tranfers In City And County Recorded In Court

From County Commissioners of Anne Arundel County to George N. Mantzouris, 2 lots of ground at Herald Harbor in second district.

From James A. Walton County Treasurer and others to Harold F. Thomas, 2 lots of ground at Herald Harbor in second district.

From Emma R. Grimes to Howard S. Holzer and wife, lot of ground at Linthicum Heights in fifth district.

From Arden J. Keck and wife to Joseph B. McMillion and wife, lot of ground in fifth district.

Fram Margaret Higgs and others to Isidor Burkhardt and wife, lot of ground in third district containing 70 48-100 acres.

From Arundel Home Finance Corporation to Robert B. Riddle and wife, 2 lots of ground at Mt. Pleasant Beach in this county.

From Sunset Beach Development Company to Sadie V. Gudeman, 8 lots of ground at Sunset Beach in third district.

From Ellis Karasik and wife to Albert J. Hauf and wife, 2 lots of ground at Outing Park in third district.

From Atlantic Mill and Lumber Company to Frankie Wilson, lot of ground at Patapsco Park in fifth district.

From Daniel F. Fosher to Frank L. Talbott and wife, lot of ground at Long Point on the Magothy in third district.

From Robert L. Wilkinson and wife to Elsworth Imdorf and wife, lot of ground at Glen Burnie in fifth district.

From Frederick P. Kasmeyer and wife to David F. Walker and wife, lot of ground in fourth district containing 4 acres.

From Walter M. Bauman and wife to Frank G. Berry and wife, lot of ground at Cedarhurst on the Bay in seventh district.

From Waterfront Development Company to Frank G. Berry and wife, lot of ground at Cedarhurst on the Bay in seventh district.

From Andrew J. Harding and wife to Arthur P. J. Nordeck and wife, lot of ground at Bay Side Beach in third district.

From Benjamin Michaelson Trustee to Mary Makell and others, lot of ground on Washington street this city.

From C. Albert Hodges, Late County Treasurer to Grover C. Shipley, lot of ground at Shipley Heights in fifth district.

From Mary M. Jones to Grover C. Shipley, lot of ground at Shipley Heights in fifth district.

From Agnes E. Winchester to Albert Winchester, Jr. and wife and others, lot of ground on Conduit street this city.

From William J. Smithson and wife to Edward A. Lock and wife, lot of ground in fourth district.

From John E. Stoll and wife to George E. Gosnell and wife, lot of ground in fifth district.

From Adolph Torovsky and wife to Inez Z. Moss, lot of ground known as No. 206 Prince George street this city.

From Clara N. Naecker to Joseph F. Horning and wife, 5 lots of ground at North Beach Park in eighth district.

From Theodore N. Taylor and wife to Alden J. Buell, 2 lots of ground at Cedarhurst on the Bay in seventh district.

From Simon Kohlstein and wife to Benjamin Keyers and wife, 4 lots of ground at Mt. Pleasant Beach in third district.

From Norman W. Windsor to H. Edmund Wood and wife, lot of ground in seventh district containing 2-5 acres.

From Charles Hines Sr and wife to Evelyn Jones, lot of ground at Patapsco Park in fifth district containing 13-100 acres.

From William H. Kuhn and others to Harry C. Kenney, 4 lots of ground at Beachwood Forest in third district.

From Charles J. Mielke and wife to Walter A. Siemon and wife, 2 lots of ground at Riviera Beach in third district.

From Amy M. Rudolph to James A. Dixon and wife, 6 lots of ground at Bay Head in this county.

The District of Columbia is made up of territory which originally was part of Maryland and Virginia.

Evening Capital

VOL. LX — No. 177 | EVERY EVENING EXCEPT SUNDAY | ANNAPOLIS, MD., MONDAY, AUGUST 28, 1944 | SOUTHERN MARYLAND'S ONLY DAILY | THREE CENTS

WEATHER
Mostly cloudy with moderate temperature tonight; Tuesday fair.

American Units Are Across Marne

Russians Reported At Hungarian Border

Americans Capture Meaux And Threaten Nazi Line Of Retreat Into Germany

U. S. FLAG ENTERS PARIS

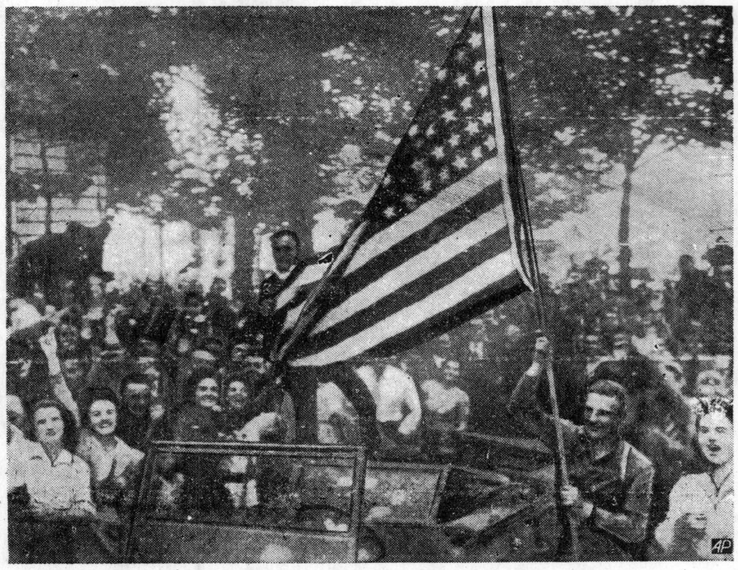

American troops carry into Paris the first United States flag taken into the French capital by the forces advancing into the city Aug. 26. Parisians wave from the curb. (AP Wirephoto via Signal Corps Radio.)

BRITISH FORCE RAIDS SUMATRA; AMERICAN PLANES HIT ANSHAN

WASHINGTON, Aug. 28—(AP)—Secretary of State Hull reported today that Bulgarian officials have been in touch with Allied governments on the question of making an armistice. He said he did not know whether American officials had been among those contacted.

In the case of Romania, which has already turned on German troops and declared its intention to fight on the Allied side, Hull said that this government had been kept advised, mainly by Russian officials, of the progress toward making armistice arrangements.

(By the Associated Press)

American troops, sweeping in a wide arc threatening German lines of retreat into the Reich, have crossed the Marne and captured Meaux in the loop of the historic river 23 miles east of Paris.

The Germans were yielding the battleground of the first World War without a fight as the Americans swept on through Meaux unchecked. Sedan, a famous battlefield in 1870 and 1940, was 105 miles, to the northeast.

Toward the sea the British established a fifth bridgehead across the Seine, swinging their forces across the river near Louviers between Vernon and Point-de-L'Arche where the Canadians have crossed.

A new French government was being set up in liberated Paris after a frenzied week-end in which Gen. Dwight D. Eisenhower was given a tumultous welcome, the Germans bombed the city, and Gen. Charles de Gaulle escaped death or injury from snipers' bullets.

RUSSIANS AT HUNGARIAN BORDER

The Paris radio in a broadcast heard in London said the city was quiet and that two additional nests of enemy resistance had been mopped up.

The German radio asserted that Russian troops have reached the Hungarian border at "one of the Carpathian passes." The broadcast seemed to indicate that the advance was through Romania to the edge of Transylvania, the Carpathian mountain province which Hitler gave in part to Hungary in 1941. However, other Russian army groups in southern Poland have been within 13 to 21 miles of five mountain passes leading into provinces which Hungary annexed from Czecho-Slovakia when that Republic was partitioned.

Surrender terms for Bulgaria probably will be handed to an envoy of that Nazi satellite in Cairo within a few days and armistice terms for Romania are expected to be signed shortly in Moscow, it was learned in London.

Raid Sumatra

A Chiasso dispatch to the Gazette de Lusanne, Switzerland, reported that German forces in Greece—cut off from the Reich by developments in Romania and Bulgaria—were preparing to abandon that country. They are expected to attempt to fight their way through Yugoslavia to Germany.

Allied bombers flying out of the east slashed at Japanese war production centers stretching 3,000 miles from Manchuria to Sumatra while American planes striking from the west maintained their incessant pounding along invasion routes to Japan and the Philippines.

Western France

For the first time in this war American troops were fighting on a battlefield of the first World War. Meaux marked the high tide of the German attempt to take Paris in September, 1914—an attempt which ended with the Allied victory of the first battle of the Marne when the Paris taxicab army stemmed the German tide. The town is 24 miles southwest of Chateau-Thierry.

The whole Allied line in western and northern France was swinging north on or across the Seine river almost the whole 200 miles from its source to the sea.

Between Paris and the English channel, Allied armies deepened their bridgeheads over the Seine and have doomed Rouen. The Allies also virtually doomed the great port of Le Havre and have opened the way intot the German's flying bomb belt in the Pas de Calais farther north.

U. S. Third army infantry was streaming into the great tank-won bulge between the Seine and the Marne forming a consolidated front 85 miles or more almost due east of Paris in a great half-wheel around the French capital. To the southeast one Amercian column was at Nangis across the

(Continued On Page Two)

LATE NEWS

HILLMAN SAYS PAC AIMS TO "GET OUT THE VOTE"

Washington, Aug. 28 (AP)—Sidney Hillman told House Investigators today his CIO Political Action Committee is obeying the laws in the campaign, doesn't wish to "capture" any party but proposes to "get out the vote" because it has faith in the judgment of most Americans.

The head of the CIO-PAC, testifying before the Anderson Committee set up to investigate 1944 campaign expenses and practices, asserted:

"We are not an appendage of either major political party * * * nor have we any desire to capture either party * * * we seek to influence thinking, the program and the choice of candidates.

"We know that when enough Americans vote, they will vote right; that their collective judgment will prove to be a sound judgment."

26 KILLED IN TRANSPORT CRASH

London, Aug. 28 (AP)—Twenty-six persons were killed early today when a large air transport crashed into a house near the trans-Atlantic military air base at Prestwick, Scotland.

The dead include seven of the plane crew, 14 passengers and five occupants of the house, which was demolished.

American soldiers and civil defenses workers labored through the darkness to recover bodies from the wreckage and still were searching this morning for any additional victims.

The plane was inbound from an Atlantic crossing.

NEWSMAN ACCUSED IN BUENOS AIRES

Buenos Aires, Argentina, Aug. 28 (AP)—Arnoldo Cortesi resumed his duties as New York Times correspondent today after spending Sunday at police headquarters because authorities questioned the accuracy of his report of an address by Vice President Juan Peron to a private session of stock exchange members.

HULL TALKED TO DULLES "LIKE A SENATOR"

Washington, Aug. 28 (AP)—Secretary Hull today summed up his conversations with John Foster Dulles, Gov. Thomas E. Dewey's foreign relation advisor, this way: I talked to him just like I would to a senator.

Hull has been conferring with senators on the Dumbarton Oaks security talks and keeping them informed of developments there.

MINERS ASKED TO SKIP LABOR DAY HOLIDAY

Washington, Aug. 28 (AP)—The Solid Fuels Administration has asked coal miners and mine operators to forego their annual Labor Day holiday because of the urgent need for added production and John L. Lewis, president of the United Mine Workers, has advised union locals that it would be proper to work on the traditional holiday.

CAPT. S. S. Janney, Jr. WOUNDED AT SAIPAN

Baltimore, Aug. 28 (AP) — Marine Captain Stuart S. Janney, Jr., who rode his own horse, Winton, to victory in the 1942 Maryland Hunt cup, was wounded slightly in the leg during the battle for Saipan, his wife said today.

VA. "REGULARS" DISTRUSTED BY F. OF L.

Richmond, Va., Aug. 28 (AP)—William F. Patrick, president of the Virginia Federation of Labor, said today the State Federation's executive board had pledged its support to the Virginia committee of 100, which has for its aim the re-election of President Roosevelt, because the regular Democratic organization "cannot be trusted to conduct a real campaign for the Roosevelt-Truman ticket."

SEEK BLONDE AND SAILOR IN DEATH

New York, Aug. 28 (AP)—All resources of New York City's police force today were called into play to find a beautiful blonde woman and a young sailor who investigators hope will be able to furnish the missing links that will lead to solution of the baffling strangulation-slaying of Mrs. Phyllis Newmark, 40-year-old wife of a Fifth Avenue importer.

Local Tides

TOMORROW

High water — 1:58 A. M., 1.7 feet; 1:33 P. M., 1.1 feet. Low water—9:08 A. M., 7:45 P. M.

Moon rises 4:41 P. M.; sets 1:37 A. M.

Sun rises 6:32 A. M.; sets 7:42 P. M.

Tides are given for Annapolis. For Sandy Point, add 15 minutes. For Thomas Point shoal, subtract 30 minutes.

WILL GIVE FREE CHEST X-RAYS AT T B INSTITUTE

Meeting Will Be Held Wednesday In State House

Free chest X-rays will be offered to the general public for the first time in Maryland Wednesday, in connection with the Institute on the Control of Tuberculosis to be held at the State House under the auspices of the Anne Arundel County Tuberculosis Association and the Anne Arundel County Health Department.

Although the Institute program does not begin until 1:30 P. M., the X-ray machine will be ready in the State House to take pictures at 9 A. M., and will be operated all day long. A technician from the Maryland Tuberculosis Association, which is supplying the equipment, will be in charge.

Other exhibits dealing with the fight against tuberculosis will also be open to the public at 9 A. M. Wednesday.

T B On Increase

The Institute itself is the first meeting of this particular character held in Maryland, and has been arranged by the County Tublerculosis Association and the Health Department because of the increased tuberculosis rate through-

(Continued from Page One)

STAR YACHT CHAMP HEADS FOR ACADEMY

Gerald Driscoll, 19-year old skipper from San Diego, Calif., who is headed for the Naval Academy, holds the 1944 International Star Class yachting championship.

Although he finished fifth Saturday in the fifth and final race of the world title series, Driscoll amassed 86 points, six more than second-place Robert L. Lippincott of Riverton, N. J. A fleet of 19 boats, piloted by veteran boatmen from throughout North America, sailed the series.

12 Hurt In Auto Accident

Truck Returning From Carr's Beach Turns Over

Twelve persons were hurt in two automobile accidents yesterday afternoon at the junction of the Carrs' Beach and Bay Ridge road.

A truck carrying a group of colored people from the beach to Baltimore, last night, failed to make the turn and upset, throwing the occupants out. Ten were injured, one suffering a broken arm and the others brush burns and bruises. They were treated at the Emergency hospital and sent home.

Elton Lee, colored, of Baltimore, driver of the truck, was charged

(Continued On Page Four)

RUSSIAN ADMIRAL'S WIFE SPONSORS PT BOAT AT YACHT YARD

A Russian touch was added to the launching party held at Carvel Hall Saturday night following the christening of a PT boat at the Annapolis Yacht Yard.

Comdr. K. Tolly, USN, who recently returned from Russia, made a speech to the Russians in their native language and then translated it in English. He said that in Russia it was the custom for the men present to sing after such a party and challenged the Russian men present to live up to their tradition.

The Russians accepted the challenge and sang two Soviet naval songs.

Mrs. Olga Yakimova, wife of Admiral Alexander Yakimova, of the Russian navy, sponsored the PT 661 which was launched prior to the dinner and dance held at Carvel Hall.

Rear Admiral Charles L. Brand, USN, of the Bureau of Ships, Washington, and Joaquim Elizalde, Philippine Commissioner to the United States attended the ceremony.

DECORATED IN ENGLAND

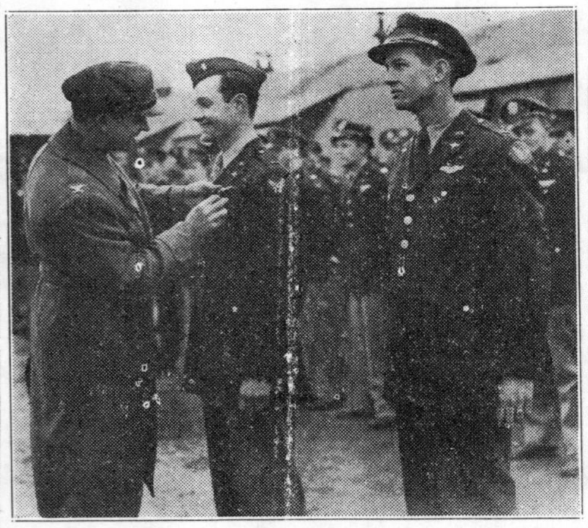

Colonel Robert Terrill, commander of a bomber group "somewhere in England" decorates Lieut. William D. James. USAAF, a member of his command and former Annapolitan with the Air Medal. Lieut. James is the son of Mr. and Mrs. Reed W. James, who made their home here for several years, Mrs. James, the former Miss Iris Cook, being a native Annapolitan. He was awarded the Distinguished Flying Cross, Three Oak Leaf clusters and the Legion of Merit, after completing 25 official and 25 unofficial combat missions and is credited with destroying three German planes.

Lieut. James graduated from Officers' Training School at Fargo, N. D. in March, 1943, and, after serving as transportation officer at Camp Livingston, La., and at Ogden, Utah, requested overseas duty. He went overseas in July, 1943, and served with a service squadron, later being made wing gunnery officer of a bomber group. He attended the Royal School of Gunnery and is one of few American officers to win the RAF gunnery wings, which he wears with the U. S. Air Corps wings. He is being sent back to the United States to the Officers' Gunnery School at Larado, Texas.

Believe Polio Has Reached Peak In County

Health Department Reports 23 Cases, No Deaths

Polio has probably reached its peak in Anne Arundel County and the Health Department expects fewer cases from now on, Dr. William J. French, County Health Director, said today.

With a total of 23 cases, but no deaths, in the county, Dr. French predicted that if there is a continuation of the present cool weather, it is likely that the rate at which cases have been reported will drop.

It is not definitely known why polio reaches its peak during hot periods, Dr. French explained, but it may be because extreme heat and humidity lower resistance.

Six Adults

The Health Department expects that mild cases which were not noticed at first will come to the attention of physicians at the county clinics from time to time during the fall months.

Polio first appeared in the county early in July. The two latest cases, both children, occurred at Eastport and at Woodland Beach, the one at Woodland Beach being the first in that section.

Six of the 23 patients are adults, ranging in age from 17 to 30; the rest are all younger children.

The fact that so far no deaths have occurred here may be largely because of early reports on cases and early hospitalization of patients most seriously affected, Dr. French said.

THE ROAD TO BERLIN

(By the Associated Press)

1—Russian front: 322 miles (from eastern suburbs of Warsaw).

2—Northern France: 495 miles (from Troyes).

3—Southern France: 545 miles (from Perly).

4—Italian front: 600 miles (from northern outskirts of Florence).

NEED FOR GOOD TEACHING IS STRESSED

Teachers' Institute Opens At High School

The importance of good teaching in the world today was stressed by speakers at the opening of the Teachers' Institute of the Public Schools of Anne Arundel county, this morning in the auditorium of the Annapolis High School, with more than 200 teachers attending.

Dr. Thomas G. Pullen, State superintendent of schools, who spoke briefly, told the teachers that "our whole form of government is based on an educated and enlightened people."

Schools will now have to train young people for world citizenship, as well as teach them to be good American citizens, said Clarence E. Tyler, in extending greeting from the Anne Arundel Board

(Continued On Page Three)

WILL HOLD RITES FOR MRS. PEARL A. LEWIS

Funeral services for Mrs. Pearl A. Lewis, of Washington, who died Friday at the Emergency Hospital, will be held at 2 P. M. tomorrow from the Lee funeral home, Fourth street and Massachusetts avenue. Northeast. Washington. Burial will be in Fort Lincoln cemetery in Washington.

Mrs. Lewis was the widow of Albert R. Lewis and the daughter of Mrs. Susie A. Brown and the late Benjamin F. Brown of Edgewater. She was a former resident of Annapolis and Edgewater.

In addition to her mother, she is survived by three sons, Albert R. Lewis, Jr., of Washington; Stanley Dewitt Lewis, with the U. S. Army Medical Corps in England, and Marvin Lewis, of Washington; two brothers, B. Herbert Brown, of Baltimore and Dewitt Brown of Annapolis, and two sisters, Mrs. Walter Purdy of Edgewater and Mrs. Rutland Beard, of Catonsville.

Seek Man Who Accosted Girl On Local Bridge

Police Report He Tried To Toss Her Overboard

County police and naval authorities today were seeking a colored man who, police reported, accosted a young woman on the Eastport bridge early yesterday and attempted to toss her over the rail, bruising her face in the effort.

Polic said Mrs. Florence Garnes, 22, of 410 Third street, Eastport, said the man was wearing a white sailor's uniform.

Sgt. Brooke Meade said Mrs. Garnes works in Washington, had returned on the last bus, and was walking across the bridge toward Eastport and her home.

"Seized Arm"

The officer said she told him the man came up to her and asked for a cigarette and then seized her arm and told told her if she did not listen to him he would throw her overboard.

He said Mrs. Garnes screamed and then, as an automobile came on the bridge from Eastport, the man let her go and ran toward Annapolis.

Sergeant Meade said Mrs. Garnes got out into the traffic lane of the bridge and ran toward Eastport, still screaming, but, after the automobile had passed, the man returned, caught her and tried to toss her over the rail.

Searched Area

He said she held on with one hand and when another automobile came on the bridge, the man again let go and started running toward Annapolis. Mrs. Garnes then ran toward Eastport, the officer said, and County Officer John Ramer, who was on duty at the police station, heard her and went out to investigate.

He summoned the police squad car, which was in Annapolis, and county and city police searched the entire area from the bridge to the Naval Academy without success.

Mrs. Terrell Dies In Auto Crash

Dies In South Baltimore General Hospital

Mrs. Ida Byars Terrell, 37 years old, wife of Allen Terrell, of Whitney's Landing, Severna Park, died at 11:20 p. m. last night in the South Baltimore General Hospital from injuries she received when thrown from her car in a collision at Benfield road and Robinson road, off the Ritchie Highway, about 9:40 p. m.

John Francis Rowley, 33, of Baltimore, driver of the other car, was this morning released under bond at a hearing before Magistrate David B. Dunker, Ferndale, on a charge of manslaughter. Rowley was arrested by Sgt. George Bolm and Officer John M. Everd, of the Mountain Road substation of the County Police.

Mrs. Terrell was thrown clear of the car, according to the police report, and her head hit the road. She was taken to the hospital in Riviera Beach Fire Department ambulance.

The body will be taken to Greenville, S. C., for burial.

HAIL DAMAGES COLORADO CROPS

DENVER, Aug. 28 (AP) — A violent hailstorm, which left hailstones stacked eight inches deep, swept through Colorado Saturday, doing damage estimated at $1,000,000. Truck crops, fruit, greenhouses and roofs in and around Denver, Pueblo and Colorado Springs were badly damaged.

JUNIOR HADASSAH MEETS TOMORROW

The Annapolis Chapter of Junior Hadassah will hold its regular meeting tomorrow night at the home of Miss Estelle Levy, 123 Cathedral street.

Will Start Free Movies On Wednesday

Weekly Shows To Be Given At Recreation Center

The free weekly motion picture performances which made such a big hit at the Glen Burnie Recreation Center last fall, winter and spring, will be launched for another season next Wednesday night, September 20.

It had been planned to resume these weekly events earlier this month but the opening was delayed for a short time in order that Charles H. England, the chairman of these affairs, could arrange to get a top-notch series of pictures.

Chairman England said this week that he has been successful in obtaining a long list of films, all of which will make a big hit. He plans to make the complete schedule known in the near future.

Under the leadership of Mr. England, the Wednesday free movies proved to be one of the leading features of the Recreation Center's regular affairs last season and it is expected that even larger crowds will take advantage of these performances this season.

Although the program of films is arranged principally for the children, the selection of subjects by Mr. England has been made with the view of also appealing to adults, many of whom attended each show last season.

The Center has excellent equipment and there are plenty of seats to take care of large crowds. Indications are that next Wednesday's performance will draw a record attendance.

The shows will get under way at 7:30 P. M. and Mr. England stressed the fact that everybody is welcome.

Announcement of other features to be held regularly at the Center is to be made by the Recreation Center Committee in the near future. This group, of which Herbert C. Estep is chairman, is holding weekly meetings to map out the program for the season.

It is expected that the Thursday night dances for the young people and the Saturday night community dances, which have continued throughout the summer, will attract increased attendance with the arrival of cooler weather.

A CAREER FOR GIRLS AGE 17 - 35

EXPERIENCE UNNECESSARY

Not Factory Work

Some knowledge of typing required

PAID WHILE TRAINING

Handling telegrams over long distance circuits Easily Learned

Apply

WESTERN UNION

TIME IS RUNNING OUT FOR TOKYO

FROM bases in the Marianas, American forces can swing the minute hand of their clock of war to the Philippines and the China coast, then to the mainland of Japan. When the minute hand hits the hour hand at midnight, the gong of doom will strike for Tokyo.

Reports Reveal That Red Cross Had Busy Year

Speakers Stress Need For Members

That the Red Cross units in the northern section of Anne Arundel county have accomplished a vast amount of work during the last year was revealed on Monday night when an important meeting was held at the Glen Burnie Recreation Center.

Reports of the work carried on by the various branches of the organization in the district were made at the meeting, at which Mrs. Charles E. Haslup, chairman for the section, presided.

Mrs. Richard Wainwright, chairman of the Annapolis and Anne Arundel County Chapter, who headed a large group of officials from Annapolis, was one of the speakers. She urged that all members of every branch of the organization keep up their work, pointing out that there will be no let-up in the demands on Red Cross services even when the war in Europe is at an end. The blood bank will have to be kept at full pace after Germany goes down to defeat and the war fund will be a necessity, she said. Mrs. Wainwright also stressed the need for continuing all the other activities.

Present Certificates

One of the features of the meeting was the presentation of certificates to a group which recently completed the Red Cross course in home nursing. The certificates were presented by Mrs. Helen B Lovell, R. N., head of the chapter's nursing service. They were awarded to Mrs. James Hopkins Mrs. Raymond Shipley, Mrs. Roy Rehm, Mrs. Albert Riddick, Mrs Kenneth Gardiner, Mrs. Robert Dilworth and Mrs. Craggs Winterson.

It was announced at the meeting that plans are being made to give a Red Cross course in nutrition in the northern section of the county if at least 20 person enroll. Mrs. Harry Baker, Ferndale Md., was appointed to take care of the enrollment. It was stated, however, that anyone desiring to enroll also may make the fact known to any unit chairman.

The importance of work in nutrition was stressed by Miss Miriam P. Parmenter, chairman of the County Nutrition Committee, a special speaker at the meeting.

A resolution on the death of Mrs. Frederick H. Pratt was passed at the meeting. Mrs. Pratt, who was treasurer of the northern section Red Cross Auxiliary, died suddenly on August 26.

YOUR NUTRITION COMMITTEE presents
Food For Folks
in cooperation with

September is Wartime Nutrition Month.

Your County Nutrition Committee is observing it by helping all organizations interested in having better school lunches in Anne Arundel county.

Figures don't lie. Of the 27 white elementary schools only nine had lunches of any kind; in five high schools, four served lunches of some kind last year. Of the 39 colored schools, 20 had school lunches. Over 15,000 children are involved. Where does your community's school show in this picture?

A Trend Is Started

Just as the Federal and State governments have done much to assure the people better mail service, or better school systems, so have they combined with interested groups throughout the nation, such as food manufacturers and parents interested in food and nutrition to improve the nation's food habits and to improve the food America eats.

Work by these groups has led to support of the community school lunch program with government participation, enrich-ment of white bread, "restoring" certain cereals by adding thiamin, niacin and iron; fortifying margarine with vitamin A, adding vitamin D to milk and adding iodine to table salt.

The school lunch program may assure the child up to one-third of his daily nutritional requirements. The plan for enriching white bread and of "restoring" cereals was designed to give you back much of the food value these commodities lose in processing. Fortifying margarine guaranteed that even though butter became short of supply, about the same amount of vitamin A could be gotten when a fortified substitue was used. Adding vitamin D to milk was another step aimed at stamping out rickets; and adding iodine to table salt to prevent simple goiter.

How About You?

Though this wasn't started by homemakers and mothers, who are closer to the problem than anyone, if you're a homemaker and mother you can join the ranks of those working for a better-fed America. This is how to go about it:

1. Continue support of the measure already started by interested groups.

2. Improve food habits of your family by taking advantage of the information nutrition specialists offer.

3. Support teaching of nutrition to every child in public schools.

And what is there in it for you? Well, there is an assurance of better health, longer life, and greater efficiency for you and your family. And indirectly, it means a stronger nation, because a nation is no stronger than its individual citizens.

Mrs. W. F. Joachim, Annapolis, is county P.-T. A. chairman of the School Lunch Committee at present, and any local P.-T. A. interested in securing better lunches in its own school should get in touch with her.

More next week about the kind of help available from governmental sources.

Have you secured your copy of the Wartime Food Guide yet?

Navajo Indians believe that Shiprock, an isolated butte which towers 1,900 feet above the plain, was once a great bird which brought the tribe to New Mexico.

Tigers, Browns Deadlocked In League Lead

Study Possibility Of Action In Tie

By Jack Hand
(Associated Press Sports Writer)

President Will Harridge had the American league constitution out for an airing today, studying the roles relating to a pennant race tie as the St. Louis Browns again settled down in first place, deadlocked with the Detroit Tigers.

The rule book said a one-game playoff would determine the winner and the site of the tilt should be determined by the toss of a coin. Both Steve O'Neill and Luke Sewell were said to be polishing up two-headed coins.

President Harridge was expected to make an announcement on the details in the near future as the possibility of a deadlock increased.

Browns Face Test

Chances were against the Brownies sticking up there as a four-game series with the persisten New York Yankees follows two more games with Boston. Detroit has Washington coming in when the Tigers finally get rid of Connie Mack's troublesome A's after two more tilts. Each team had six games to play.

In any event, the fellow who first said "they never come back" hadn't heard about the St. Louis Americans who had been evicted from their first place flat so often lately. They crawled in the back door when the Tigers nine-day sublease ran out.

Nelson Potter put the Brownies back in a tie by stopping Boston, 3-0, with two hits, singles in the third inning. Chet Laabs and Rookie Boris "Babe" Martin from Toledo, who would not be eligible for the World Series, if and when, were the hitting stars of the timely triumph.

Athletes Win

Connie Mack continues to take a hand in the race from a seventh place position. The A's, who belted the Yanks out of the lead 10 days ago, toppled Detroit, 2-1, yesterday on the four-hit chucking of lanky Russ Christopher. By the victory, Philadelphia took an 11-9 season series over the Bengals.

Rufe Gentry, who went to the hill when Stubby Overmire complained of arm trouble, saw his four-game win streak smashed.

The Yankees stuck in there, three games back, trimming Chicago, 3-1 in 12 innings and 5-4 in regulation distance behind rookies Mel Quenn and Walt Dubiel. Cleveland's "Specs" Klieman blanked Washington, 6-0, in the other American league contest.

St. Louis Cardinals scored three unearned runs to mark up win No. 102 by a 3-1 edge over Brooklyn. Buddy Kerr's leadoff homer in the ninth enabled the New York Giants to top Cincinnati, 3-2.

Pittsburgh clung to a big lead for an easy 13-8 victory over Boston in a "suspended" game from Aug. 1 but lost the regular tilt in 13 frames, 5-4. Chicago downed the Phils twice in a twi-night double, 7-6 in 10 innings and 4-1.

Standings

American League

Score of Yesterday

St. Louis, 3; Boston, 0.
Cleveland, 6; Washington, 0.
Philadelphia, 2; Detroit, 1.
*New York, 3-5; Chicago, 1-4.

*First game, 12 innings.

Where They Play Today

Boston at St. Louis, night.
New York at Chicago, night.
Washington at Cleveland.
Philadelphia at Detroit.

Standing Of The Clubs

	W.	L.	Pct.
Detroit	84	64	.568
St. Louis	84	64	.568
New York	81	67	.547
Boston	74	74	.500
Cleveland	71	77	.480
Chicago	69	79	.466
Philadelphia	68	80	.459
Washington	61	87	.412

National League

Score Of Yesterday

New York, 3; Cincinnati, 2.
St. Louis, 3; Brooklyn, 1.
*Pittsburgh, 13-4; Boston, 8-5
†Chicago, 7-4; Philadelphia, 6-1

*Second game 13 innings.
†First game 10 innings.

Where They Play Today

Chicago at Philadelphia,

twilight-night.
Cincinnati at New York, 2 games
St. Louis at Brooklyn.
Pittsburgh at Boston.

Standing Of The Clubs

	W.	L.	Pct.
St. Louis	102	46	.689
Pittsburgh	88	60	.595
Cincinnati	84	63	.571
Chicago	72	75	.490
New York	65	82	.442
Boston	61	87	.412
Brooklyn	60	88	.405
Philadelphia	58	89	.395

Lord and Master on the Links

Byron Nelson, golf's one-man blitzkrieg, is the undisputed links king of the year and the heaviest single season money winner of all time. One of the truly greats of all time, Nelson has won every big title during the course of his career. Lord Byron belongs in any golf hall of fame. These pictures tell their own story.

Here's the king of golf with his wife as they wait for the remainder of the field to finish.

Boy, what a lovely putter to bring in all that prize money.

Here's Nelson teeing off.

See how Lord Byron gets out of a sand trap.

These are only a few of the War Bonds he won.

Dewey Moves

(Continued From Page One)

ing the White House?," he demanded.

There were loud cries of "no" from the crowd.

Then, in answer to his own question, he said:

"The American people will answer that question in November. They will see that we restore integrity to the White House so that its spoken word can be trusted once again."

There were rebel yells mixed with the applause and cries of "that's right."

"He Asked For It"

Opening a smashing attack on the President with the assertion —"He has asked for it. Here it is"—Dewey said that Mr. Roosevelt had called a "malicious falsehood" the statement that he regarded himself as indispensable.

Dewey quoted Senator Harry S. Truman, the Democratic Vice-President nominee, and Mayor Frank Kelly of Chicago to the effect the nation must re-elect the President in order to attain its own "salvation" and to assure "the very future of the peace and prosperity of the world." Dewey said he had heard no presidential repudiation of either statement. Then he added:

"Let's get this straight. The man who wants to be President for 16 years is indeed indispensable. He is indispensable to Harry Hopkins, to Madam Perkins, to Harold Ickes, to a host of other political job holders.

"He is indispensable to America's leading enemy of civil liberties—the mayor of Jersey City (Frank Hague.) He is indispensable to those infamous machines, in Chicago—in the Bronx—and all others.

"He is indispensable to Sidney Hillman and the Political Action Committee; to Earl Browder, the ex-convict and pardoned Communist leader."

Declaring that it was "the simple truth that Mr. Roosevelt's record is "desperately bad," Dewey said it was no "falsification" that this nation was not prepared for war.

Quotes Marshall

He quoted Gen. George C. Marshall, army chief of staff, as saying in 1940 that the army was "only 25 per cent ready." He cited a statement of Gen. H. H. Arnold, chief of the Army Air Forces, last January 4 that "December 7, 1941 found the army air forces equipped with plans but not with planes."

"Does my opponent still desire to use the words 'falsification' and 'Goebbels,'" the Republican nominee taunted. "Does he still claim we were prepared?"

The New York governor quoted from statements by Senator Truman on the floor of the Senate that the responsibility for the then "shocking state of our defense program" must be placed on the White House. He added that Senator Alben Barkley of Kentucky, the majority leader, had said in his speech nominating Mr. Roosevelt for a fourth term that "when the treachery of Pearl Harbor came we were not ready."

Quotes President

He followed with quotations from statements of the President in 1935 and 1937 to the effect that there was no fear of American involvement in war, adding that when he, Dewey, had suggested in 1940 the creation of a two-ocean navy the President had commented that was "just plain dumb."

Dewey also took up Mr. Roosevelt's description as a "fantastic charge" the top nominee's statement the administration plans to keep men in the armed forces after the war to lessen unemployment.

The nominee quoted from a statement attributed by Stars and Stripes, army publication, to Maj. Gen. Lewis B. Hershey, director of selective service, that "we can keep people in the army about as cheaply as we could create an agency for them when they are out." The speaker pointed out that Hershey still is in office.

The New York governor contended that in March, 1940, after Mr. Roosevelt had been in office seven years, the American Federation of Labor had reported that there were 10 million unemployed.

"Is that fraud or falsehood?" he demanded. "If so, let Mr. Roosevelt tell it to the American Federation of Labor."

"By waging relentless warfare against our job making machinery," he continued, "my opponent succeeded in keeping a depression going 11 long years—twice as long as any depression in a century."

"And the somber tragic thing is that today he still has no better or different program to offer. That is why the New Deal is afraid of peace and resorts to wise cracks and villification * * *."

Women For Telephone Work

War Jobs Today—Peace Jobs Tomorrow

Permanent work of an essential and interesting nature. Good starting pay. Frequent increases and excellent opportunities for advancement. Apply at your local telephone office 8:30 A. M. to 5 P. M. Monday to Friday.

The Chesapeake and Potomac Telephone Company
OF BALTIMORE CITY

Navy Eleven Favorite To Win Duke Game

MIDSHIPMEN'S CRUSHING WIN OVER PENN STATE SENDS NAVY FOOTBALL STOCK UP IN NATION

Navy Mixed Power Plays With Good Passing To Defeat Nittany Lions By A 55 To 14 Score—Will Tackle Duke Blue Devils At 2 P. M. Saturday In Baltimore Stadium—North Carolina Pre-Flight Which Defeated Navy 21 To 14, Beats Duke, 13 To 6—Most Sport Writers Favor Navy To Defeat Southern Team

By RICHARD H. ELLIOTT

The Navy football team, by virtue of its crushing 55 to 14 win over Penn State, will enter the Baltimore stadium at 2 P. M. Saturday a favorite over the Duke squad which has been defeated by Pennsylvania and North Carolina Pre-Flight. Some 94 percent. of the sports editors of the nation forecast a Navy win.

Navy won an outstanding victory over Penn State here Saturday, using everything in the book from straight power to forwards and a little razzle dazzle, while North Carolina Pre-Flight was defeating Duke 13 to 6. This compares to the Pre-Flight 21 to 14 victory over the Navy, but the seven point advantage over Duke was earned, while the seven point margin over Navy came from a picked up fumble and run for a touchdown.

PENN GAME WILL BE TEST

It begins to look like the sport world will have to wait until the Pennsylvania game to get a real line on the strength of the 1944 Navy team as compared to other collegiate elevens. Pennsylvania has taken Duke, 18 to 7 and Dartmouth, 20 to 6.

Georgia Tech, to face Navy in Atlanta, Ga., on Oct. 21, has dedefeated North Carolina, 46 to 0. Incidentally the Cadets beat Brown, 59 to 7 Saturday.

The Navy varsity team Saturday faced a Penn State starting lineup that it outweighed five pounds to the man from end to end. While the Nittany Lions had two stalwart tackles, who more than matched their Navy opponents, the center of the Penn State line from guard to guard was outweighed an average of 23 pounds by the midshipemen center and guards. And it was through the line that Navy put on its power drive in a shattering first quarter. The two Penn State guards weighed 175 pounds each and the State center 170, compared to 190 and 195 for the Navy guards and 205 for the Navy center.

Play Improved

The Navy play against Penn State was much improved over the showing against North Carolina. There was more coordination and versatility, although there was the old fault of drawing numerous penalties that cost a total of 65 yards, and fumbles, one of which, as against North Carolina Pre-Flight, resulted in the gift of a touchdown to the oppone.

During the first quarter, when the Navy power was on at full throttle, the midshipmen backs simply tore the Penn State line to shreds. Bob Jenkins averaged 4.7 yards a rush Joe Sullivan, 4.5 yards and Jim Pettit, 18.8 yards.

In the second Clyde Scott, three times All-State fullback Arkansas and former Bullis Prep star, turned in a average of 9.6 yards every time he carried the ball, exclusive of forwards and laterals. Then R. Owen, up from the junior varsity, ffashed splendid form in rushing and pass receiving in the fourth period. Fred Earley, former blocking back at Notre Dame, showed he still had the flair. B. Smith, a member of the All-Southern Prep School team for two years, who was forced out of action after three games last year by an injury, showed plenty of in kicking, passing and running. He was a match for Harold Hamberg at passing. Ralph Ellsworth, up from Texas University, had the misfortune to see one of his fumbles turned into a touchdown, but he more than made up for this by his running and passing.

Cornell Loses

With Navy's future opponents, Cornell dropped out of the power class by losing 16 to 7 to Yale. But Notre Dame forecast its strength by defeating Tulane 26 to 0, and Purdue kept on its winning way by defeating Illinois, 35 to 19.

It took Navy just 15 plays and seven minutes to score its opening touchdown against Penn State. The power drive that carried 74 yards from the point where the initial kickoff was put into play was marked by the line plunging of Jenkins, Sullivan and Pettit, including gains of 14 and 13 yards by Jenkins, and one of 12 by Sullivan.

Vic Finos continued his splendid work in converting placements by making good on seven of eight tries, one in the fourth period being blocked by Don Miltenberger, Penn State freshmen end.

Navy's second tally came two minutes after the first when Pettit took the ball from Sullivan on a reverse and stepped down the left side of the field 74 yards for the score.

Navy with Sullivan, Pettit and Jenkins still pounding were on the Penn State 38 headed for another score when the quarter ended and a new Navy team, with Scott, Bill Barron, Hamberg and Dave Barksdale, entered the game. Penn State held and Navy was forced to kick for the first time during the game.

Keep Up Pressure

But the Navy relief players kept up the pressure, going into the air, instead of mainly along the ground. Scott, with a 13 yard gain in two plays moved them into position and Hamberg passed to John Hansen in the end zone for 29 yards and a tally.

A 12 yard punt return by Hamberg and a 23 yard end run by Scott set up the next Navy score. Hamberg passed to Charles Guy for nearly 14 yards and a first down on the Penn State 4 inch line and then bucked over for the touchdown.

Charles Kiser, Navy guard, intercepted a Penn State pass late in the second quarter to set up the next score. Scott added 23 yards in two plays and Dick Ambrogi circled end for the tally.

John Chuckran, Penn State freshman tailback, set up the first Nittany Lion score when he ran the Navy kickoff back 53 yards to the Navy 40. Bob Urion contributed a 17 yard run to the Navy 20. Interference was ruled on a pass by Elwood Petchel into the Navy end zone and the Lions had the ball on the Navy 18 inch marker. Allen Richards took it over and Joe Dragenovich converted.

Loose Play

The third quarter was marked by loose play. Jenkins fumbled and recovered forcing a Navy punt. Penn State was held and kicked. Then Sullivan fumbled and Dan Orlich recovered for Penn State but the Lions could not gain.

The Navy first string line, back in the game, then started another march that carried 96 yards for a touchdown. It was featured by a 19 yard run by Jenkins, a 10 yard plunge by Pettit and a pass, Jenkins to Leon Bramlett that gained 43 yards. Then Scott pulled a fast one, hitting tackle and shooting a lateral to Pettit who went outside on the Penn State one yard marker. Jenkins plunged over.

Ellsworth fumbled early in the fourth quarter and Al Auer, Penn State marine trainee end, picked the ball up and dashed 80 yards for the Nittany Lions' second touchdown, Drazenovich again converting.

Ellsworth stepped forth as passer a little later by shooting one to Earley who ran to the Penn State 23 yard mark, the play covering 52 yards. State held for downs and took the ball on its own 4 yard line.

After the kick and two 15 yard penalties against Navy, Bruce Smith with the ball on the Navy 43 passed to Owen who ran to the Penn State one yard line. Albion Walton went over.

Owen was the sparkplug of the final tally. He ran a Penn State kick back 31 yards, took a pass from Bruce Smith that covered 55 yards in the air and scampered over for a touchdown, the play being good for 35 yards.

First Period

Jenkins ran the Penn State kickoff back 22 yards to the Navy 26, Pettit made 4 at left tackle and Jenkins made nearly 6 at right guard. Sullivan hit left tackle for 4 and a first down. Pettit got 5 at left end. Sullivan made 5 to midfield and a first down. On a a fake reverse Sullivan failed to gain. Jenkins got 4 at right guard and then broke through center for 14 yards and a first down on the Penn State 32. Pettit picked up 8 at left end. Sullivan made 10 in two tries at center. Allen threw Jenkins for a 2 yard loss. Jenkins than hit over his right tackle for 13 yards and a first down on the Penn State 3. Jenkins picked up a yard in the line and Sullivan crashed through center for a touchdown. Finos converted the placement, Navy, 7; Penn State, 0.

Petchel ran the Navy kickoff back 21 yards to his own 34. He picked up 5 yards in two tries at center and end and then quick-kicked out of bounds on the Navy 26.

Pettit, taking the ball from Sullivan on a reverse rounded his own left end and ran 74 yards for a Navy touchdown. Finos kicked the placement. Navy, 14; Penn State, 0.

Because of a clipping penalty after the score Navy kicked off from its own 25 to Penn State who returned to its own 35. Urion made 10 yards but Petchel fumbled and recovered for a 5 yard loss. Petchel failed at center and quickkicked out of bounds on the Navy 33.

Jenkins failed at right tackle. Stoker broke through and tackled Jenkins as he tried to pass. Sullivan made 12 and a first down on the Navy 45. Jenkins got 4 and a first down at center. Sullivan got 3 more at the same point and Jenkins repeated with 2 more to the Penn State 38 as the period ended with Navy leading 14 to 0.

Second Period

Navy sent in a new team with Hamberg, Scott, Barron and Barksdale in the backfield. Hamberg's pass to Guy was incomplete and he kicked into the end zone.

Penn State started from its own 20 and failed to gain. The Nittany Lions were offside but Navy refused the penalty. They failed again in the line and Lang kicked to Hamburg who returned 12 yards to the Penn State 43, where he was stopped by Lang. Hamberg got 2 in the line and Scott made 13 in two plays and a first down on the Penn State 32. Hamberg's pass to Hansen was knocked down. Scott made 3 at left guard. Hamberg then passed to Hansen in the end zone for a totuchdown. Finos kicked the placement. Navy, 21; Penn State, 0.

Navy kicked off over the goal and Penn State started from its 20. Lang lost a yard at center. He attempted a pass that was knocked down and kicked to Hamberg who returned 12 yards to the Penn State 41.

Hamberg got 3 at center. Scott on a double reverse circled left end for 23 yards and a first down on the Penn State 15. He then hit center to the Penn State 4 but the play was called back and Navy penalized to the Penn State 15 for backfield in motion. Scott got 4 at right tackle. Ambrogi lost 3 at right tackle. Hamberg passed to Guy who was downed 4 inches from the goal. Hamberg hit center for the touchdown. Finos kicked the placement. Navy, 28; Penn State, 0.

Miltenberger returned the Navy kickoff 16 yards to the Penn State 36. Bellas got 2 in the line and Urion rounded left end for 5. Bellas made 2 more and Petchel kicked out of bounds on the Navy 15.

Ellsworth picked up 5 yards. Barksdale kicked to Petchel who returned 6 yards to the Penn State 41.

Petchel's pass was incomplete. Chuckran's pass failed. Kiser intercepted Chuckran's next pass and ran to the Penn State 30.

Scott made 13 at left tackle and then got 10 more through the line Ambrogi circled left end for a touchdown. Finos' placement was good. Navy, 35; Penn State, 0.

Chuckran ran the Navy kickoff back 53 yards to the Navy 40. He circled left end for 3 more. Urion, on a reverse from Chuckran, got 17 and a first down on the Navy 20. Petchel pass in the end zone was incomplete but officials ruled interference on Ambromitis and Penn State got the ball on the Navy 18 inch mark. Richards went over for the touchdown. Drazenovich kicked the placement. Navy, 35; Penn State, 7.

Third Period

Jenkins returned the kickoff 18 yards to the Navy 26. Pettit lost 3 at left end. Jenkins got 2 back at right tackle, fumbled on the next play but recovered for no gain. Sullivan kicked to Petchel who returned 3 yards to the Penn State 33.

Petchel gained a yard at right end but lost a yard at left tackle. Brune kicked to Petitt who returned 8 yards to the Navy 29. Navy lost 5 yards for offside. Sullivan made 19 and a first down at center. He fumbled on the next play and Orlick recovered for Penn State on the Navy 44.

Petchel's pass to Meyer was incomplete. He lost 4 on an attempt to pass to Brune and kicked out of bounds on the Navy 4.

Sullivan got 7 at left tackle. Scott added 2 at the same spot. Jenkins made two and a first down at center. Petitt lost 4 at left end. Jenkins circled right end for 19 and a first down on the Navy 30. Petitt made 10 at left tackle. Jankins passed to Bramlett for 43 yards to the Penn State 17. Jenkins made 2 at center. Scott hit left tackle and lateralled to Petitt who went out of bounds on the Penn State one yard line. Jenkins made the tally. Finos placekicked the goal. Navy 42; Penn State 7.

Petchel returned the Navy kickoff from behind the goal to the Penn State 25. Urion lost 6 but lateralled to Petchel for a yard. Chuckran's pass was intercepted by Scott on the Penn State 33.

Earley made 3 as the quarter ended with Navy leading 42 to 7.

Fourth Period

Penn State was penalized for offside. Earley failed to gain. Ellsworth passed to LaLande who lateralled to Earley to the Penn State 7, but the ball was ruled dead on the 18. Ellsworth picked up 4 yards. On the next play Ellsworth fumbled and Auer picked the ball up and ran 80 yards for a Penn State touchdown. Drazenovich converted the placement. Navy 42; Penn State, 14.

Ellsworth returned the kickoff 18 yards to the Navy 28. Barron lost 3 yards. Ellsworth's pass was incomplete, but his next pass to Earley carried 52 yards to the Penn State 23. Ellsworth made 9 in three tries in the line. Earley got 4 and a first down on the Penn State 10. Ellsworth's pass was incomplete. Penn State lost 5 yards for delaying the game. Ellsworth got a yard but Earley failed at center. Ellsworth was trapped on an attempt to pass and hit center for 2 yards.

Penn State took the ball on downs on its own 2 and kicked to its own 35. Bruce Smith passed to Hill for no gain. Navy lost 5 for offside. Bruce Smith's pass was incomplete, but another to Ambromitis went to the Penn State 27. Bruce Smith made 3 yards but Navy was set back to the Penn State 43 for holding. Navy got a yard when interference was called on a Smith pass. Navy was set back to the Navy 43 for holding. Bruce Smith passed to Owen who ran to the Penn State one yard line. Walton made the touchdown. Miltenberger blocked Finos' placement. Navy, 48; Penn State, 14.

Penn State put the Navy kickoff in play on its own 16. Richards passed to Schlesiger for 8 yards. Richards for 10 yards and a first down at left tackle. Owen intercepted Richard's next pass on the Penn State 46.

Two Smith passes were incomplete and he fumbled on the third play, recovering for a 9 yard loss. He then kicked to Muckle who returned 17 yards to the Penn State 30. Cooney dropped Richards' long pass down field. Muckle lost 2 yards and his next pass was incomplete.

Owen ran a Penn State punt back 31 yards to the Penn State 35, Bruce Smith faded deep and passed 55 yards in the air to Owen who took the ball on the Penn State 4 and scored. Finos converted the placement. Navy, 55; Penn State, 14.

Penn State put the kickoff in play on its own 28, but were penalized 5 yards for delaying the game. Muckle brought it up to the State 25 in three tries as the game ended, with Navy winning 55 to 14.

The lineup:

Navy	Pos.	Penn State
Bramlett	L.E.	Miltenberger
Whitmire	L.T.	Bush
Deramee	L.G.	Allen
J. Martin	C	Klausing
Chase	R.G.	Larson
Gilliam	R.T.	Caskey
B. Martin	R.E.	Hicks
Duden	Q.B.	Brunhn
Jenkins	L.H.	Petchel
Pettit	R.H.	Meyer
Sullivan	F.B.	Richards

Referee: H. O. Dayoff, (Bucknell); umpire, A. R. Menton, (Loyola); linesman, J. W. Coffee (Rutgers); field judge, H. C. Eyth, (Carnegie Tech.)

Score by periods:

Navy	14	21	6	14	55
Penn State	0	7	0	7	14

Scoring—Navy: Touchdowns — Sullivan, Petitt, Hansen, Hamberg, Ambrogi, Jenkins, Walton, Owen. Tries for point—Finos (7 in 8, placekicks). Penn State: Touchdowns—Richards Auer. Tries for point—Drazenovich (2 in 2, placekicks). Substitutions—Navy, backs Barron, Barksdale, Hamberg, Ambromitis, Finos, Scott, Earley, Owen, Walton, N. Smith, B. Smith, Lawrence; ends, Hansen, Carnahan, Guy, LaLande, Hill, Eagle, Markel, Siddons, Moore; tackles, DeGanahl, Larkin, McPhilips, Carrington, Coppedge, McKnight; guards, Radick, Kizer, Shofner, Brown, Bandish, Dale, Larkin, Steves; centers, Baker, Sorenson, Griffiths, Whittle. Penn State, backs, Urion, Taccalozzi, Bellas, Lang, Chuckran, Drazenovich, Meyer, Cooney, McGown, Muckle; ends, Orlich, Stoken, Auer, Schlesiger; tackles, Norton, Painter; guards, Simon, Martenis, Matthews, Dimmerling. Time of periods—15 minutes.

Statistics

	P.S.	Navy
First Downs	3	21
Rushing	2	17
Passing	1	4
Net Yards Rushing	44	353
Yards Lost	11	22
Net Yards Forwards	21	253
Forwards Attempted	14	17
Forwards Completed	5	8
Behind Line	2	0
Intercepted By	0	3
Yds. Return Inter.	0	6
Punts, Number	9	5
Returned by	2	1
Punts, Average	42	39
Kickoffs, Number	3	7
Returned by	8	6
Kickoffs, Average	54	53
Yards Kicks Ret.	189	127

(Continued On Page Six)

DARTMOUTH LINEMEN STOP PENN'S RUNNING ATTACK

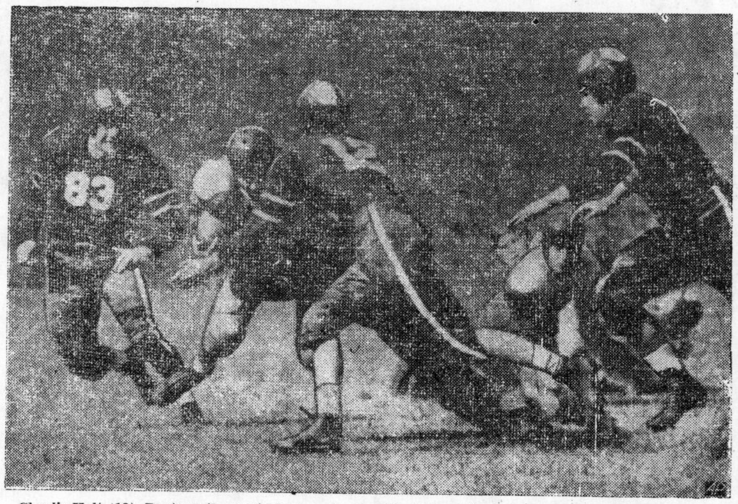

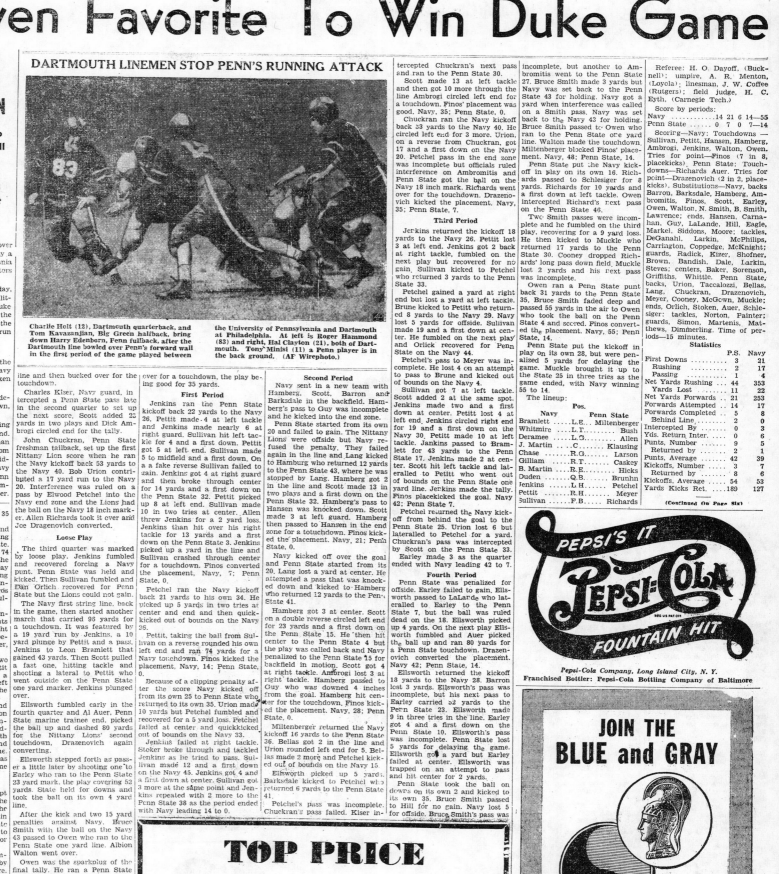

Charlie Holt (12), Dartmouth quarterback, and Tom Kavazanjian, Big Green halfback, bring down Harry Edenborn, Penn fullback, after the Dartmouth line bowled over Penn's forward wall in the first period of the game played between the University of Pennsylvania and Dartmouth at Philadelphia. At left is Roger Hammond (83) and right, Hal Clayton (21), both of Dartmouth. Tony Minisi (11) a Penn player is in the back ground. (AP Wirephoto.)

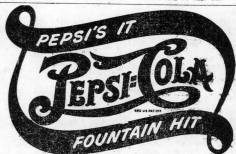

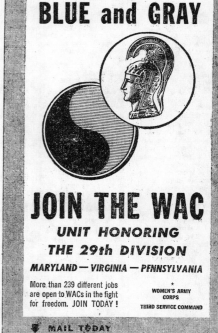

McQUINN GETS TO THIRD—BUT STAYS THERE

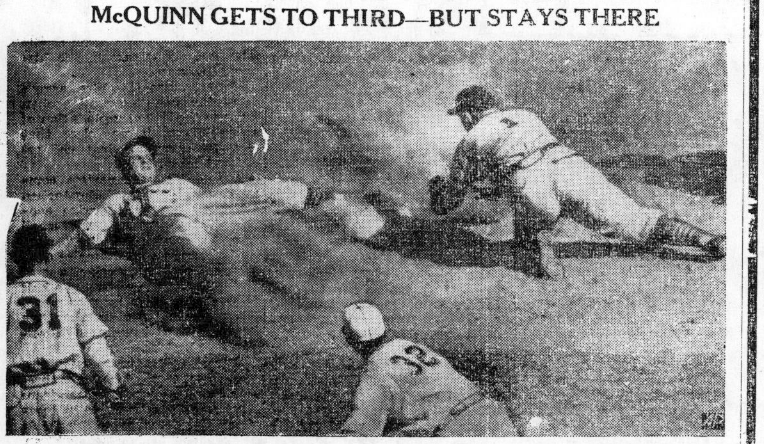

George McQuinn, Browns first baseman, slides into third base safe ahead of the throw in from the outfield on Mark Christman's single to centerfield in the second inning of the fourth World Series game in St. Louis. George Kurowski (1), Cardinal third baseman, tries to reach McQuinn with the ball. Harry Brechen (31), Card hurler, ran over to back up the play. McQuinn died on third when a double play ended the inning. Luke Sewell (32), Browns manager, is third base coach. (AP Wirephoto.)

SOCIAL and PERSONAL

Mr. and Mrs. Armbruster Celebrate 23rd Anniversary

Mr. Willis T. Armbruster, manager of Carvel Hall, and Mrs. Armbruster, who are married 23 years today, celebrated their anniversary quietly at their home in Wardour

The executive and clerical departments of Carvel Hall presented them with a tea kettle of old Sheffield silver with an attached burner and an anniversary cake inscribed with "Congratulations From Your Gang."

Mr. and Mrs. Armbruster are the parents of three children, Mrs. Alice Galloway, wife of the late Lieut. James Galloway USN., and the Misses Teresa and Ann Armbruster

* * *

Mrs. Brewer Flying To California

Mrs. Merrill Brewer has left by plane for her home in Hollywood, Calif., after a visit there with her sister, Mrs. Newton Parke, of Wardour.

* * *

Announce Birth Of Son

Mr. and Mrs. C. F. Rinehart, of Annapolis Neck Road, announce the birth of a son, Charles Francis Rinehart, Jr., on Friday, Oct. 6, at the Emergency Hospital.

* * *

Paysuers Leave For North Carolina

Marine Gunner O. J. Paysuer, Mrs. Paysuer, and two children, John and Wayne, left Tuesday for Delmont, N. C. for a visit of a week with Mr. Payseur's parents.

* * *

Officers At Carvel Hall

Among the officers spending a few days at Carvel Hall prior to reporting for duty at the Naval Academy are: Lieut. John C. Feick, USN., of Sandusky, Ohio; Lieut. and Mrs. C. A. Hill, Jr.; Lieut. O. F. Dreyer, USN.; Lieut Russell F. Moon, USN.; and Lieut. and Mrs. Daniel S. Appleton.

* * *

Miss Richardson To Leave For Pittsburgh

Miss Nancy Richardson, who has been making her home on Fifth street, Eastport, will leave Sunday for Pittsburgh where she will be employed as assistant to the Director of the Falk Foundation.

Miss Richardson has been employed for six months at the Experiment Station.

* * *

Miss Crandall Returns From Greenock

Miss Lillian Crandall, who has been visiting Mrs. Russell Moreland at Woodbourne, Greenock, Md., has returned to Annapolis.

* * *

Mrs. Varley, Jr., Enroute To San Diego

Mrs. Richard B. Varley, Jr., wife of Lieut. Varley, USN., has left the home of her parents, Mr. and Mrs. J. O. Fowler, of Edgewater for an indefinite stay with her husband's parents, Mr. and Mrs. R. B. Varley, Sr., of San Diego, Calif.

* * *

Booklovers Club To Meet Tuesday

Mrs. William A. Conrad will be hostess to the members of the Booklovers Club on Tuesday, Oct. 17 at 2:45 P. M. at her home, 121 Spa View avenue.

* * *

Mrs. Helfrich To Address JWC

Mrs. Lester A. Helfrich, president of the Fourth District Maryland Federation of Women's Clubs will tell the "Meaning of the General Federation of Clubs" to the members of the Junior Women's Club of Annapolis and Anne Arundel county at their first regular meeting of the season, at which she will be guest speaker.

The meeting is scheduled for 8 o'clock Thursday night in the East Room at Carvel Hall.

* * *

WAVES To Dine At Blue Lantern Inn

Fifty WAVES who are on duty in the Navy Department in Washington will have lunch at the Blue Lantern Inn tomorrow at noon after they have attended services at the U. S. Naval Academy chapel.

They will make a historical tour of Annapolis in the afternoon.

* * *

Wedding Guests At Carvel Hall

Mr. and Mrs. Winifred Trowbridge, of West Springfield, Mass., and Mr. and Mrs. Henry Jacob Paulsen, Sr., of Mansfield, Ohio, are among the wedding guests at Carvel Hall who are here to attend the marriage of their daughter and son, respectively: Miss Frances Winifred Trowbridge to Lieut. William Fred Paulsen, USNR, this afternoon at 4 o'clock in the Naval Academy Chapel.

A reception dinner will follow at Carvel Hall.

CALENDAR FOR THE WEEK

Today

1:30 P. M.—Junior Department of the College Avenue Baptist Church, weenie roast at the home of Mrs. W. C. Fowler, at Weems Creek.

9:30 P. M.-1:30 P. M.—Officers' dance at Officers' Mess, North Severn.

Tomorrow

9:15 A. M.—Java Club Breakfast. Comdr. Fred K. Elder, speaker, at USO Club.

6:00 P. M.—Buffet supper at USO.

7:00 P. M.—Song fest at USO.

Tuesday, October 17

2:45 P. M.—Booklovers Club, meeting at the home of Mrs. William A. Conrad at 121 Spa View avenue.

8:00 P. M.—Tuesday Pair Games of Duplicate Contract Bridge, in Card Room at Carvel Hall. Mrs. Allen Westcott, director.

Thursday, October 19

8:00 P. M.—Junior Women's Club of Annapolis and Anne Arundel County, first regular monthly meeting in the East Room at Carvel Hall. Mrs. Lester A. Helfrich, guest speaker.

Visiting Comdr., Mrs. Davis

Mrs. Henry Farrow, wife of Comdr. Farrow, USN., of Boston, Mass., is visiting her brother-in-law and sister. Comdr. R. P. Davis, USN., and Mrs. Davis, at their home, 9 Giddings avenue.

REPORT CLOTHING STOLEN FROM AUTO

The theft of clothing and other articles vauled at about $500 from an automobile parked in the rear of Carvel Hall on King George street was reported to police last night.

Patrolman W. A. Wayson said an automobile owned by J. F. Conway, of Atlantic City, N. J., had been broken open.

Among the articles listed as stolen were two ladies' coats valued at $125, a ladies' suit valued at $135, one bag of men's fishing clothes valued at $20, a carton of cigarettes, a fifth of Scotch and two fifths of rye whiskey.

ST. ANNE'S GUILD PLANS ANNUAL BAZAAR

St. Anne's Treasury Guild met last night and initiated plans for the annual bazaar and supper.

Mrs. R. Thorton Strange was elected general chairman.

THREE SAILING RACES SCHEDULED

Captain C. O. Humphreys, USN, the Director of Athletics at the Naval Academy, today announced the three races to be sailed by the midshipmen this fall.

The schedule: Oct. 14—Haverford College and University of Pennsylvania; Oct. 21—U. S. Coast Guard Academy and Oct. 28—Haverford College (at Haverford, Pa.)

SEE MORE BEEF AND LESS PORK

BALTIMORE, Oct. 14 (AP) — More beef and less pork and butter is predicted for the immediate future by State War Food Administration director Niles Baldrige.

More than 50 per cent of the total pork production is now going to the armed forces ,he said, and the WFA has ordered packers to increase the percentage allotments of each week's production to the government.

Guidepost

(Continued From Page Four)

and dependable, and that the world is a trap and inevitably a disappointment. At the last moment Dr. Scott saves her from her mother and herself by forcing her to bob her long hair, buy a new hat, taste a little of the world.

The taste leads Julia into a share of a somewhat different "triangle," and some other difficulties. There is a New York newspaperwoman and a handsome red-headed young man mixed up in the business as well as the doctor and his dying wife. I'm under the impression that Mrs. Cornwell knows more about simple people than about alleged sophisticates such as her newspaperwoman. These last are a bit out of drawing, and so is some of the villagy atmosphere, and some of the psychological tangle. Mrs Cornwell's book is good entertainment, nevertheless.

"Seventh Cross" On Circle Screen

Will Run Tomorrow Through Tuesday

At the Capitol theater tomorrow, Monday, and Tuesday, Alan Marshall and Laraine Day will star in "Bride By Mistake." "Music in Manhattan" with Anne Shirley and Dennis Day is the feature on Wednesday and Thursday. "The Seventh Cross" will be seen on Friday and Saturday with Spencer Tracy and Signe Hasso.

At the Circle theater tomorrow, Monday and Tuesday Spencer Tracy and Signe Hasso will star in "The Seventh Cross." "Bride by Mistake" with Alan Marshall and Laraine Day is the feature showing on Wednesday, Thursday, Friday and Saturday.

At the Republic theater tomorrow, Monday and Tuesday Vivien Leigh and Robert Taylor will star in "Waterloo Bridge." Rose Hobart and George McCready will be seen in "Soul of a Monster" on Wednesday and Thursday. "Swing in the Saddle" with Jane Frazee and "Red River" Dave is the feature scheduled for Friday and Saturday.

The usual news items, cartoons and featurettes will be seen at all three theaters throughout the week.

OPA Will Take

(Continued From Page One)

tors for temporary and non-recurring rations will be made to OPA local War Price and Rationing Boards rather than to ODT District Offices. These rations will be issued by local boards and any appeals from decisions of the Boards will be handled by OPA. Thus the OPA will have complete authority over the issuance of such additional rations.

It was pointed out that recommendations on temporary and non-recurring gas allotments for trucks owned by farmers will continue to be made by County Farm Transportation Committees but will be referred to OPA local boards for action instead of ODT District Offices.

Forms Available

Applications for Certificates of War Necessity or for permanent changes in CWN allotments will be handled by ODT District Offices as in the past. Forms for making such applications may be obtained at all OPA Boards, and also at ODT District and field offices and offices of County Farm Transportation Committees. ODT will continue to certify permanent commercial vehicle needs and issue Certificates of War Necessity to cover these needs.

Since the majority of current applications, according to ODT, are for temporary allocations, this new procedure will take a troublesome, but routine chore off the hands of ODT district staffs, releasing personnel to direct a greater amount of attention and effort to the transportation phases of it program such as traffic registration, organization of joint action plans, agricultural industry transportation programs and maintenance and conservation work.

Lists Conditions

There will be four conditions, under the new procedure, where local Boards will be authorized to issue a smaller ration than that allotted by ODT on the Certificate of War Necessity. These conditions are:

1. When the Board has knowledge of discontinuance or reduction in the operations of the commercial vehicle operator.

2. When the Board has knowledge of the misuse of commercial rations and such misuse indicates an overissuance. (For example, the use of commercial rations in an operator's personal passenger car.)

3. When an applicant indicates to the Board that his needs are less than those certified.

4. When an applicant fails to use all of his ration, or fails to claim his ration within a reasonable time.

If none of these four conditions apply, OPA Boards will continue to issue rations in the amount certified by ODT.

Under the amendment to the OPA gasoline rationing order commercial vehicle operators will hereafter return all unused or expired transport rations to their OPA Boards rather than to ODT District Offices as has been required in some instances in the past.

NOTICE

Mrs. Leon Strauss just returned from New York after spending 10 days buying Fall and Winter dresses for The Fashion.

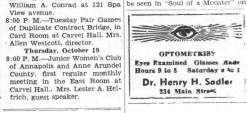

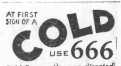

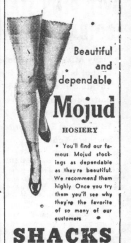

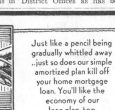

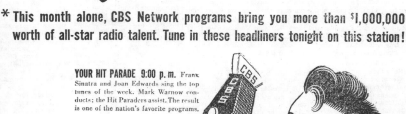

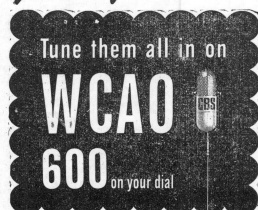

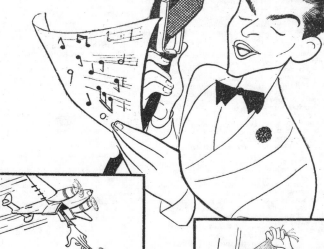

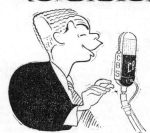

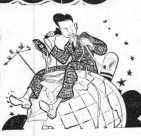

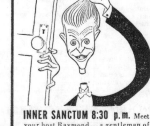

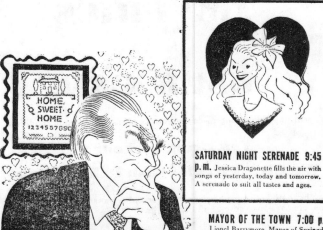

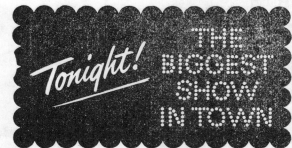

Evening Capital

VOL. LX — NO. 224 | EVERY EVENING EXCEPT SUNDAY | ANNAPOLIS, MD., WEDNESDAY, OCTOBER 25, 1944 | SOUTHERN MARYLAND'S ONLY DAILY | THREE CENTS

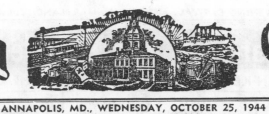

WEATHER

Fair tonight and Thursday; not quite so cool tonight.

U. S. Planes Hit Japanese Fleet

Germans Retreat On Wide Holland Front

Sink Large Carrier, Damage 2 Others, Five Or Six Battleships And Cruiser

LATE NEWS

NAVY-NOTRE DAME GAME SELL-OUT

The Naval Academy athletic office announced today a "complete sell-out" of tickets to the Navy-Notre Dame game scheduled for Nov. 4 in Baltimore stadium.

CLASHES SPREAD TO SOUTHERN SPAIN

London, Oct. 25 (AP)—Clashes between Spanish Republican guerrillas and forces of Generalissimo Francisco Franco have spread even into southern Spain, besides the guerrilla raids into northern Spain from France, an officer of the anti-Franco National Spanish Union in Paris declared today.

Madrid meanwhile said all but a handful of the Republicans striking into Spain's Navarra section from France had been wiped out.

MORE ARMS NEEDED DE GAULLE SAYS

Paris, Oct. 25 (AP)—Gen. Charles De Gaulle complained today that the French were not receiving enough arms for a large war effort

In his first press conference since he met reporters in Washington in July, the French leader commented that the "government like everyone else, is satisfied that it now is called by its right name." This was his only reference to Allied recognition.

DECORATED FOR AACHEN CAPTURE

U. S. First Army Headquarters. Oct. 25 (AP)—Lt. Gen. Omar N. Bradley, commander of the U. S 12th Army group, pinned the bronze star today on Lt. Gen Courtney H. Hodges, First army commander, for capturing Aachen the first large German city to fall into Allied hands.

CHURCHILL REITERATES SURRENDER POLICY

London, Oct. 25 (AP) — Prime Minister Churchill reiterated in the House of Commons today that "unconditional surrender in the sense of no bargaining with the enemy is still the policy of the government."

He suggested the House should bear in mind also the three-power declaration of May 12 to Axis satellites, in which they were warned to quit Germany.

ARGENTINE ATTACHE IS RECALLED

London, Oct. 25 (AP)—Argentina has recalled Col. Pablo Beretta, its military attache in London, after an invitation to visit the Allies western front was suddenly withdrawn.

BRICKER SPEAKS IN FORT WORTH

Fort Worth, Texas, Oct. 25 (AP)—Gov. John W. Bricker declared today that industry should be allowed to resume peacetime production as soon as possible and without government "shackles."

SAYS DEWEY "HIDES UNDER BED"

Chicago, Oct. 25 (AP)—Senator Harry S. Truman said in a statement here today that Gov. Thomas E. Dewey is "hiding under the bed" having "neither the courage nor the honesty" to reply to a suggestion that he call for the defeat of eight Republican senators whom the Democratic vice presidential nominee termed "isolationist."

GAME INCREASE EXPECTED

Washington, Oct. 25 (AP) — The Game and Inland Fish Commission figures indicated today that Maryland hunters could expect a considerable increase in all types of game when the season opens next month.

BALTIMORE POLL ESTIMATES

Baltimore, Oct. 25 (AP)—Baltimore election supervisors estimated today that 48 per cent of city service personnel of voting age were registered on Baltimore poll books.

Basing its figures on the only available gauge—the percentage of registered service men and women who applied for state ballots—the officials estimated that approximately 3,000 absentee voters were included in the new city registration figure of 396,745.

NO PEACE PRIZE THIS YEAR

Stockholm, Oct. 25 (AP)—The Nobel Foundation recommended to the Swedish government today that no peace prize be awarded this year. The last such award was made in 1938.

Local Tides

TOMORROW

High water — 0:48 A. M., 1.4 feet; 1:05 P. M., 0.9 feet. Low water—7:55 A. M., 7:15 P. M.

Moon rises 3:42 P. M.; sets 1:18 A. M.

Sun rises 7:27 A. M.; sets 6:18 P. M.

Tides are given for Annapolis For Sandy Point, add 15 minutes. For Thomas Point shoal, subtract 30 minutes.

BRITISH USE FLAMETHROWERS IN OFFENSIVE

Russians Driving Into Norway, East Prussia

British troops, turning flamethrowers against German bazooka nests, struck through the big Dutch road junction of 'S Hertogenbosch in mop-up operations today, and the Germans fell back in retreat on a 15-mile front above and below that key city.

'S Hertogenbosch was captured except for isolated enemy pockets, a front dispatch said, and supply roads leading north and south were snipped.

Even as the British pressed in the eastern end of the German box salient in southwestern Holland, Canadians bit deeper into the western edge, and made progress in two drives to clear the water approaches to Antwerp.

One Canadian prong hit on toward Roosendaal and Bergen op Zoom, 22 and 26 miles north of Antwerp, against strong resistance. The enemy was reported making local withdrawals below Breda and Tilburg, middle strongholds of their line across southwestern Holland from the coast to 'S Hertogenbosch.

Another Canadian column, striking westward, advanced slightly farther into the tip of South Beveland Island. German guns there and on adjacent Walcheren Island command the Schelde estuary lane to Antwerp.

Breskens Pocket

Other Canadians advanced in the diminishing Breskens pocket on the south shore of the estuary opposite Walcheren Island. Fall of Fort Frederik-Hendrik north of captured Breskens port was imminent, said a front report. Below Breskens the Canadians reached the edge of Oostburg, and cut the Oostburg-Schoondijke road.

The Canadian-British offensives threatened the whole German stand below the Maas river.

German forces endangered in western Holland are known to include patched up units of eight divisions, the 85th, 59th, 245th, 256th, 346th, 711th, 712th and 719th. About 11,000 of these are sealed off by land on the Schelde estuary islands through Canadian seizure of the neck of the peninsula in a fanout north and northeast of Woensdrecht.

The British reported the capture of 1,400 prisoners Sunday, Monday and Tuesday in the 'S Hertogenbosch sector and virtually all were from the scoring 702th division.

An Allied communique reported slight but steady Allied progress at the opposite end of the west front, and troops northeast of Epinal making further gains, including the capture of Mortagne

(Continued on Page Four)

Organize For County War Fund Campaign

Solicitation Scheduled To Start In City And County

The campaign for the National War Fund in Annapolis and Anne Arundel county is now sufficiently organized so that solicitation can start, Carl S. Thomas, general chairman, today announced.

Mr. Thomas said that, although a large number of workers were still needed that in order to keep pace with other communities in Maryland and throughout the United States, it was deemed advisable to start the solicitation in in Anne Arundel county at once.

Chief Judge R. P. Melvin has accepted the chairmanship of the Special Gifts Committee and is now busy recruiting members of this important committee who are charged with the responsibility of soliciting the large gifts in the community.

Chairmen Named

Thomas G. Basil has accepted the chairmanship of the commercial group, which solicits retail stores and business estabishments in the city. He is being assisted by Mayor William U. McCready, who will accept the re-

(Continued on Page 2)

FIRST WARD DEMOCRATS BACK PARTY TICKET

The First Ward Democratic club today announced the unanimous adoption of resolutions pledging united support of all candidates on the Democratic ticket.

The resolution also urged voters, regardless of affiliation to reelect the President of the United States in the November election.

Midshipmen Will Parade On Friday

Public Will Be Admitted To Worden Field

The Naval Academy will observe Navy Day on Friday with a parade by the regiment of midshipmen on Worden Field at 3:30 P. M.

The parade will be reviewed by Gov. Herbert R. O'Conor.

The general public will be admitted to the parade, without the necessity of having identification cards, if they enter the No. 4 gate of the academy after 3 P. M.

Because of the Navy Day parade the usual Wednesday parade scheduled for today was cancelled.

GETS LEGION OF MERIT

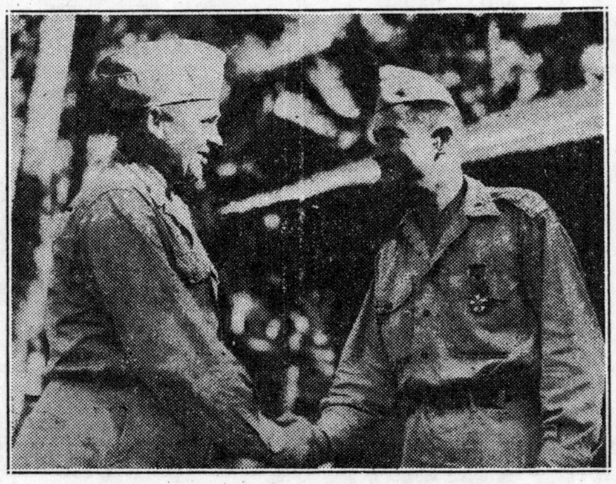

This picture taken in the Sixth army theater in New Guinea shows Col. Kenneth Pierce (right), 30 Southgate avenue, Annapolis, being congratulated by Brig. Gen. G. H. Decker, Plattsburgh, N. Y., on receiving the award of the Legion of Merit.

YANKS DRIVE ASHORE IN PHILIPPINES

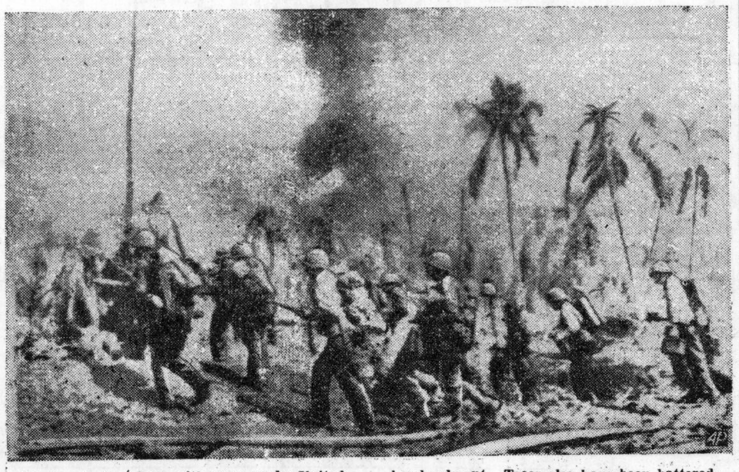

Moving up the shore with guns ready, United States troops invade the Philippines as smoke rises somewhere inland from the pre-invasion bombardment. Trees also have been battered by the shelling. (AP Wirephoto from Signal Corps radiophoto from New Guinea.)

Police Take State's Witness Back To Jail

Report They Found Him On West Street Last Night

Charls Redding, colored, held in the county jail as a State's witness in a murder case, was taken into custody on West street last night by city police and returned to the jail.

Chief William Curry and Patrolman James W. Moreland, who picked Redding up, said he told them he had got out of the rear door of the jail and climbed over the rear wall. The Officers said the colored man said he wanted to get a sandwich and had intended returning to the jail.

The officers said they recognized Redding standing on West street and followed him as he walked toward Church Circle. They said he was held as a witness in the case of Henry Washington charged with the murder of Larcona B. Young.

Tavern License Is Granted By City Council

Leonard A. Clark Gets License For 250 West Street

A tavern license at 250 West street was granted to Leonard A. Clark, 28, last night by the City Council despite a protest filed by the Board of Stewards and the minister of Trinity Mehodist Church.

Mayor William U. McCready and Aldermen Jesse A. Fisher, Charles Bernstein, Bernard Hoff, Arthur Ellington, Alphonse Addison and Walter Adams voted for the application.

Mayor McCready said the special meeting had been called after he had received a letter from Mrs. Susan Dove, owner of the property, requesting action on the application as soon as possible so the premises could be rented. The Mayor pointed out that the prem-

(Continued On Page Four)

Murder Trial In Local Court

Case Was Moved Here From Eastern Shore

The murder trial of Howard Hubbard, Sr., colored, of Caroline county, indicted for the killing of Preston, Md., restaurant owner James M. Davis, began today in the Anne Arundel County Circuit Court following the selection of a jury.

The case had been removed to Anne Arundel county after Hubbard's attorney W. Brewster Deen contended that Hubbard could not get a fair trial in Caroline county.

State's Attorney Layman J. Redden of Caroline county opened the case by explaining the circumstances surrounding the shooting of Davis on Sept. 21, 1944 in Preston, Md.

He said that "about 4:15 P. M. on the afternoon of Sept. 21, Lloyd Price of Choptank, Md., was driving through Preston when he stopped his truck because an automobile was parked "in his way in the middle of the street."

Redden said that Price started to pull out around the car when

(Continued on Page Six)

EASTPORT P.-T.A. MEETS TOMORROW

The Eastport P.-T. A. will hold its regular monthly meeting at 8 P. M. tomorrow.

Clarence E. Tyler will speak on "Community Welfare."

Mrs. William Gardner, program chairman, has arranged to have Mrs. Katherine Campbell play a few selections on the piano after the business meeting.

Mr. John Stevens, financial chairman, is completing plans for a bazaar to be held in the school auditorium on Dec. 8 from 2 to 5 P. M.

LT. TAYLOR FINISHES EDGEWOOD COURSE

Second Lieut. Harry W. Taylor, of West Annapolis, is one of the officers who was graduated at Edgewood Arsenal, after completing the unit gas officers' ground course. Before entering the army, Lieut. Taylor was a chauffeur at the U. S. Naval Academy.

State School System Needs Are Discussed

Officials Address County Council P.-T. A. Meeting

Devoting the major portion of its program to a discussion of needed changes and improvements in Maryland's educational system, the Anne Arundel County Council of Parent-Teacher Associations held its fall session at the USO Club yesterday.

Delegates heard leading educators of the county and State deplore the low standard prevailing in Maryland, which stands next to last in rank among the forty-eight states in the educational program offered its children and youth.

Wilbur Devilbiss, supervisor of high schools for the State Department of Education, in presenting its legislative program, declared that Maryland, Georgia and Virginia are the only three states in the Union which have not authorized a twelve-year school system. Three counties in Maryland and Baltimore City offer the twelve-year plan to their pupils, but the State does not provide this essential. The speaker pointed out that other states are now planning to offer thirteen or fourteen years of schooling.

Five Reasons

He cited five reasons for an extended system: (1) Changing economic conditions following conversion of war industries will leave many youths unemployed and a prey to many undesirable forces; (2) an extended system offers equal opportunities for all children in the state; (3) education is no longer regarded as only intellectual, but physical, spiritual and social as well, and the whole person must be educated by a program fitted for the task; (4) specialized programs so divided as to include elementary, junior high and senior high schools offer the best means of avoiding difficult adjustments by the students; and (5) the system so divided largely eliminates the problem of overage students.

Inviting continuing interest of the Parent-Teacher groups in the enactment of corrective legislation, Mr. Devilbiss listed as most

(Continued On Page Eight)

LIGHT CARRIER PRINCETON IS SUNK AFTER BEING DAMAGED

(By the Associated Press)

Carrier planes of the U. S. Third fleet have sunk a large Japanese carrier, damaged two other large carriers, five or six battleships, one cruiser and several other unidentified warships in a great three-pronged naval battle which is still continuing near the Philippines.

The U. S. S. Princeton, a light cruiser in Admiral William F. Halsey's force, was lost when, already badly crippled, her magazines exploded and she had to be sunk by American ships. Besides the captain, 133 other officers and 1,227 enlisted men were saved.

No mention was made in Admiral Chester W. Nimitz's latest communique of any great sea battle between American fleet units and the Japanese fleet, as claimed by the Japanese radio since late yesterday.

The Tokyo radio has admitted the loss of two cruisers and a destroyer in the action while claiming to have sunk 11 ships and damaged 5 others. The Japanese lost 150 planes.

The actions began Monday afternoon, (U. S. time) extended throughout Tuesday and general "action is continuing," Nimitz said

SUPERFORTS RAID KYUSHU

Strategic targets on the Japanese island of Kyusnu were attacked by a task force of B-29 Superfortresses of the 20th Airforce, Gen. H. H. Arnold announced at the War Department. It was the fourth raid by the sky giants on the island.

Pushing all opposition aside and crushing Japanese counterattacks, American forces liberated 14 more towns and barrioes and advxanced to the outskirts of Tabontabon, eight miles northwest of Dulag, on Leyte island, General MacArthur's headquarters announced

The advance on Tabontabon is probably the longest made by MacArthur's men since the invasion started. Advances were general along the entire line.

Capture of San Pablo airdrome, seven miles west of Dulag was also announced.

Take Third Airfield

The Americans went through dense undergrowth and mud and muck sometimes nearly up to their necks in making a circuitous march of 12 miles to capture the airfield, the third taken in Leyte The others are at Tachoban and Dulag.

Armored units of the Seventh division fanned out toward Dagami and elements of the 96th division advanced nine miles north of Catamon. Substantial gains were made west of Palo and Aacloban by units of the Tenth corps

Destruction of 64 enemy planes on Oct. 22 and 23 was disclosed by MacArthur. Six American planes were lost, but all pilots except one were saved.

The towns and barrios liberated by the Americans include Nalibunan, Calbasag, Luwan, Libeaian, Kugod, Gioabla, Rawis, Calipayan, Utap, Libras, Malayanding, Cabalracan, Julita and Tangnan.

In northern Burma, Japanese snipers and artillery were reported active against Fifth Indian Division troops moving along the Tiddim-Fort White road toward enemy-held Kennedy peak.

Tokyo Claims

Radio Tokyo claimed last night that the American invaders of Leyte island had been halted and thrown back.

Nimitz said a strong force of land-based Japanese planes attacked on U. S. task group Monday and succeeded in seriously damaging the Princeton, which is the first American carrier lost since the Liscombe Bay went down in flames off the Marshall Islands in early December 1943.

The Japanese — obviously attempting a surprise three pronged attack which they hoped would catch Halsey's force concentrating on Japanese battleships and cruisers in the Sibuyan and Sulu seas—sent a third force from Formosa.

This group included at least three carriers. However there was no indication in the communique that any Japanese carrier planes were launched against the Third Fleet which possibly achieved surprise instead in its crippling attack on the Imperial navy ships.

It was from this carrier force that Admiral Marc A. Mitsher planes sank "at least one large carrier and severely damaged two others."

Report Incomplete

Nimitz said reports of this carrier action south of Formosa ye

(Continued On Page Eight)

New Minister Installed By Presbyterians

Rev. Burnett E. McBee Also Director Of Westminster Foundation

Plans for an enlarged program of work among midshipmen at the Naval Academy were made by the Westminster Foundation at a meeting held here yesterday afternoon, the Rev. J. Maxwell Adams, D.D., national secretary of the Board of Christian Education of the Presbyterian Church, U.S.A., announced last night at the service of installation of the Rev. Burrett Eaton McBee as minister of the First Presbyterian Church.

Mr. McBee was also installed as the director of the Westminister Foundation of Annapolis at the service, which was held in the Presbyterian Church on Duke of Gloucester street, with nine visiting ministers taking part.

The Westminster Foundation is the agency through which the Presbyterian Church carries on its work among students in schools and colleges throughout the country, Dr. Adams explained. Three local members of the board of the Foundation are Prof. George R. Stephens, secretary; Prof. Howard A. Kinhart, and Prof. G. R. Clements.

"Time Of Tension"

Chaplain Robert L. McLeod, USN, who preached the sermon, declared that "we are living in a time very like the time before the advent of Christ 1945 years ago."

"It is a time of tensions," he said, "of tension among races; of tension in the economic world; of tension in education and ecclesiastical circles. The air is charged with uncertainty, expectancy and change."

It is a time which will test the sincerity of Christians, and a time which will require the leadership of Christian forces, he added.

Religion On Battlefield

Chaplain McLeod, who is in charge of the V-12 program for

(Continued On Page Eight)

SOCIAL and PERSONAL

Mrs. Christoph Hostess At Tea Aboard Reina

Mrs. Karl Christoph, wife of the commanding officer of the U.S.S. Reina Mercedes, will entertain at tea aboard ship on Thursday afternoon, Nov. 9, from four to six o'clock for the Reina Mercedes Navy Wives Club.

Invitations are also extended by Mrs. Christoph to other enlisted Navy wives who are not members of the club.

The Navy Relief Nursery, on 8 Francis street, will be open from four to six P. M. on Thursday to accommodate parents who wish to leave their children so that they will be free to attend the tea.

* * *

Capt. Vinson's Son At U. C. L. A.

Mr. Thomas N. Vinson, Jr., son of Capt. Thomas H. Vinson, USN, and Mrs. Vinson, has entered U.C.L.A. as a freshman. He was graduated from the Annapolis High School last June.

While Capt. Vinson is on duty overseas, the Vinsons are making their home in Coronado, Calif.

* * *

Miss Jordan Married To Mr. Wells

Mr. and Mrs. Warren D. Jordan, of Cedar Park road, announce the marriage of their daughter, Virginia May, to Mr. Wilson C. Wells, son of Mr. Percy Wells and the late Mrs. Wells, of Arundel road.

The ceremony was held yesterday afternoon at 4:15 at the Trinity Methodist parsonage with the Rev. Raymond Manley officiating.

The bride, who was given in marriage by her father, was attended by Miss Priscilla Manley.

* * *

Announce Birth Of Son

Ensign and Mrs. Irving M. Page, Jr., of Chicago, announce the birth of a son, James Robert, on Thursday, November 2, at the Wesley Memorial Hospital in Chicago.

Mrs. Page is the former Miss Audrey McKee, of this city.

* * *

Executive Meeting Of Junior Women's Club

Mrs. William T. Bailey will be hostess at her home, 828 Chesapeake avenue, to the executive committee of the Junior Women's Club of Annapolis and Anne Arundel county at their meeting Thursday night, Nov. 9, at 8 o'clock.

* * *

D.A.R.'s To Convene Tomorrow At Library

The Peggy Stewart Tea Party Chapter of the Daughters of the American Revolution will hold an important business meeting tomorrow at 3:30 at the Public Library, announced today by Miss Nyce Feldmeyer, regent.

* * *

Hostesses Announced For USO Club

The following persons will act as hostesses at the USO Club this week:

Yesterday—College Avenue Baptist Church (Friendship Circle) —Mrs. Mervin Pittman, Mrs. R. Heise, Mrs. H. T. Pike, Mrs. Margaret Southern, and Mrs. Ruby Bassford.

Today—Council of Jewish Women — Mrs. Marty W. Gilden, chairman; Mrs. Barney Berman, Mrs. Albert Block, and Mrs. Jack Cohen.

Wednesday — Junior Women's Club—Mrs. Powell J. Musterman, Mrs. William T. Bailey, and Mrs. Charles Meyers.

Thursday—GSO.

Friday—Marine Corps Birthday Dance—GSO Committee — Ethel Wilde, chairman.

Saturday — Trinity Methodist Church—Mrs. Robert Beall.

Sunday—Morning—Mrs. Peggy Martin; afternoon — Miss Viola Molen; evening buffet supper—St. Margaret's Lutheran Church — Mrs. Clayton Brant, Mrs. Nettie Sorgnit, Mrs. Strohmeyer, Mrs. Louise Echterhoff, Mrs. Anne Bachman, and Mrs. Caroline Taylor.

* * *

Mrs. McCombs Hostess To Sewing Group

Mrs. Charles E. McCombs, wife of Comdr. McCombs, USN, was hostess to her sewing group this afternoon at her quarters at 93 Bowyer road.

* * *

Mrs. Richardson and Daughter Visited Here

Mrs. C. G. Richardson, wife of Commodore Richardson, and daughter, Betty, returned today to Norfolk after visiting here over the week-end. While here, they stayed at Carvel Hall.

* * *

Week-End Guest Of Lt.-Comdr. and Mrs. Billing

Mr. Longstreet Hinton, of Westbury, N. Y., was the house guest for the week-end of Lieut. Comdr. Fred C. Billing, USN, and Mrs. Billing at their quarters, Naval Academy Apartments.

Mr. Hinton attended with them the Navy-Notre Dame football game.

CALENDAR FOR THE WEEK

Today

8:00 P. M.—Annapolis Chapter of Junior Hadassah, meeting at the home of Miss Rosalie Snyder, Cathedral street.

8:00 P. M.—Ladies' Auxiliary to Annapolis Post No. 304, first regular meeting of the month at Moose Home.

8:00 P. M.—Y. W. A. of the College Avenue Baptist Church, meeting at parsonage.

Tomorrow

8:00 P. M.—Dancing lessons, at USO Club.

2:00 P. M.—Loyalty Circle of the College Avenue Baptist Church, meeting at the home of Mrs. William Bradford at Weems Creek.

8:00 P. M.—Presbyterian Guild, meeting at church. Rev. Burrett McBee will address the group.

8:00 P. M.—Mid-week Hour of Power, service at College Avenue Baptist Church.

Thursday, November 9

2:00 P. M.—Severn River Garden Club, meeting at the home of Mrs. William Page Zimmerman.

7:30 P. M.—St. Anne's Society regular meeting at parish house.

3:00 P. M.—Women's Society of First Presbyterian Church, meeting at the church.

9:00 P. M.—Orchestra dance at USO Club.

Friday, November 10

8:30 P. M.—Formal dance in celebration of 169th anniversary of the Marine Corps, enlisted personnel invited, at USO Club.

Miss Calabrese Engaged To Sgt. Cannoni

Mr. and Mrs. Louis Calabrese, of 20 West street, announce the engagement of their daughter, Catherine Josephine, to Sergeant John Cannoni, son of Mr. Anthony Cannoni, and the late Mrs. Cannoni, of Charlerio, Penna.

Sgt. Cannoni is now stationed at Fort George G. Meade. No date has been set for the wedding.

* * *

Caravan Club To Meet Thursday

Mrs. Louis Phipps will be hostess to the Caravan Club at her home, 67 College avenue at their meeting scheduled for Thursday night, November 9, at 8 o'clock.

Mrs. John Kramer, president, announces that a nominating committee will be appointed at this meeting.

* * *

Christening Of Amy Morrison Gott

Amy Morrison Gott, infant daughter of Mr. and Mrs. Gilbert Gott, was baptized Sunday afternoon, November 5, at the First Presbyterian Church by the Rev. Burrett McBee.

* * *

Tea At Notre Dame College for Midshipmen

Students of Notre Dame College of Maryland, Baltimore, entertained at a tea dance on Saturday at the college following the Navy-Notre Dame football game for Midshipmen-members of the Newman Club.

JULIUS L. ROGERS NOW IN GERMANY WITH FIRST ARMY

Private Julius Laurence Rogers, son of Mr. and Mrs. John H. Rogers, of Deale, is serving somewhere in Germany with the First American Army.

He entered the army on Oct 24, 1942 and has been overseas for 19 months. He landed in North Africa and spent three months in a hospital there before taking part in the invasion of France.

Rogers is with the "galloping ghost" or the Second Armored Division, which made headlines in the dash through France to Belgium, covering 60 miles in three days and taking Beauvais and Montdider.

The division hit the Belgium frontier on Sept. 2 and streaked toward Tournai. Reconnaissance units were in Tournai several hours before it was officially announced American troops were in Belgium.

One enemy column was destroyed outside Orchies, France. The division also snapped shut the outer ring of the Falaise-Argentan pocket when it swung north to capture the ferry crossing at Elbocuf.

The division disappeared after the St. Lo breakthrough and slipped south and east to Domfront, flanking six German panzer divisions which were attempting to cut through the American lines at Avranches.

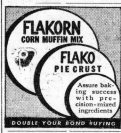

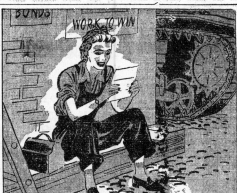

Scorecard For The Presidential Vote

YOU CAN KEEP YOUR OWN RECORD OF THE RADIO RETURNS

Electoral Votes	States & Voting Units (All figures are for precincts, except for towns in Conn., districts in Del. and R.I., and counties in Tex.)		Voting Units	First Returns Roosevelt	First Returns Dewey	Voting Units	Second Returns Roosevelt	Second Returns Dewey	Voting Units	Third Returns Roosevelt	Third Returns Dewey	Voting Units	Fourth Returns Roosevelt	Fourth Returns Dewey
11	ALA.	2,300												
4	ARIZ.	438												
9	ARK.	2,087												
25	CALIF.	14,850												
6	COLO.	1,663												
8	CONN.	169												
3	DEL.	250												
8	FLA.	1,472												
12	GA.	1,735												
4	IDAHO	845												
28	ILL.	8,737												
13	IND.	4,016												
10	IOWA	2,463												
8	KAN.	2,742												
11	KY.	4,282												
10	LA.	1,871												
5	ME.	527												
8	MD.	1,327												
16	MASS.	1,852												
19	MICH.	3,843												
11	MINN.	3,703												
9	MISS.	1,683												
15	MO.	4,519												
4	MONT.	1,175												
6	NEBR.	2,046												
3	NEV.	299												
4	N. H.	296												
16	N. J.	3,647												
4	N. MEX.	902												
47	N. Y.	9,121												
14	N. C.	1,921												
4	N. D.	2,251												
25	OHIO	8,872												
10	OKLA.	3,672												
6	OREG.	1,845												
35	PENN.	8,197												
4	R. I.	261												
8	S. C.	1,282												
4	S. D.	1,949												
12	TENN.	2,300												
23	TEXAS	254												
4	UTAH	870												
3	VT.	280												
11	VA.	1,712												
8	WASH.	3,164												
8	W. VA.	2,796												
12	WIS.	3,094												
3	WYO.	673												
531	TOTAL	130,353												

AP Newsfeatures

Price Of Peace

(Continued From Page One)

Supplies must be evenly, fairly and impartially distributed, giving the people themselves an opportunity to bring themselves back to normalcy."

Christians may most ably help by supporting UNRRA, endorsing its principles and responding generously to their calls for clothing or other needed items and by helping to rebuild devasted areas through generous contributions to the church boards, which are interested in such work, was the embodiment of a concluding suggestion of Mr. Schauer.

The Rev. Edward A. Ross, pastor of Elderslie Methodist Church at Pimlico, spoke on "economic independence in this most peculiar world, whose wonders never cease,—all civilized nations are at war, all savages at peace."

"One need have only common sense to realize that we are living in a world in which all nations are interdependent," he said. "The prosperity of one nation cannot endure unless all nations are likewise prosperous. We must have some kind of international agency if we are really going to have freedom from want. This is a problem which is not so much economic, social or political, but moral. We must be willing to get away from a narrow nationalism and self-seeking."

"Rules can be worked out with respect to international trading, shipping, tarriffs, currency, communication and aviation, just as the fine postal system has developed," Mr. Ross declared, adding that a willingness to surrender some of our economic advantages is a great part of the price we must willingly pay for a lasting peace.

Approaching the "price of enduring peace" from the standpoint of what those on the home front may contribute, the Rev. W. C. Wood, of College Avenue Baptist Church, emphasized the fact that "we must use the talents which are peculiarly our own and do our part in the place where we are."

"Our studies, meetings and activities, though often seeming futile are yet a large factor in keeping our conditions stable and our morale high," he said. "While our sons and daughters are willingly offering their lives on the field of battle, we must not be reluctant to sacrifice ourselves in lesser roles by taking a stand for our principles even in the face of almost irresistable opposition.

"One of the blights upon our national life is that men have been allowed to grow first in favor with man, rather than with God first."

"We are being inconsistent when we deplore conditions among the Hindus or Chinese or others and then fail to face and cope with our problems of race or labor which are with us. Begin by following fair practices with the maid in your home, or with conditions in your immediate neighborhood. Then only may we criticize the practices in nations afar off."

The Rev. J. Luther Neff, pastor of Calvary Methodist Church, offered the closing prayer and benediction.

Opening the session with a worship service prepared by the United Council of Church Women, Mrs. Clarence M. White, president of the Annapolis Branch, conducted the meeting. Appropriate hymns interspersed the program, with Mrs. Reese Wimbrow as the accompanist. Further assistance was given by Miss Lilliar Linthicum, Mrs. Henry Weaver and Mrs. M. Alcade Sarles.

Voters Out

(Continued From Page One)

sentatives in Congress and 31 Governors.

The total vote expected was estimated at 44,000,000 plus, including 3,369,000 soldiers and sailors. The last of approximately 2,652,000 votes cast by these service men and women which can be counted in 40 states were being sorted. Five States stopped accepting them yesterday and 35 other States will accept them through today. Eight states will accept them until various dates up to North Dakota's Dec. 5.

The voters chose between two men who have both assured them they can do the job for victory and peace—Franklin D. Roosevelt, 62-year old three termer in the White House, and Governor Thomas E. Dewey, 42, aspiring for a first term.

Republican Dewey and Democrat Roosevelt, in eleventh-hour messages to the country, agreed that no matter who wins the presidency, it is supremely important to a democracy at war to pile up a huge vote.

Last Appeals

Mr. Roosevelt summed up as goals for Americans:

"To win the war and unite our fighting men with their families at the earliest moment, to see that all have honorable jobs, and to create a world peace organization which will prevent this disaster from ever coming upon us again."

Governor Dewey likewise said "We want to make sure that this war will be the last war." He was critical again of home front measures of the Roosevelt administration and said "The great test is whether, knowing we need a new administration, we will make the change necessary to speed victory and to build the peace to come."

And thus the campaign ended, with peace-and-victory calls from both sides. There was a quiet fade-out of the more extreme accusations that have been tossed back and forth in America's big show that comes every four years.

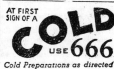

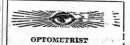

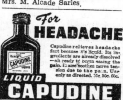

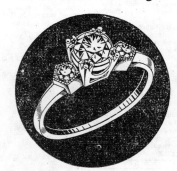

Tokyo Raid
Continued From Page One

showed. Shipping and shipbuilding yards are located in nearby Yokohoma. Early reports gave no indication of the bomb loads carried. But the Army Air Forcees said yesterday in Washington that a Superfortress can carry at least ten tons of bombs. Some B-29 flights are known to have included 100 planes.

Avoid Imperial Palace

The airmen were briefed to avoid the imperial palace, in the capital's heart, and shrines and temples.

They departed from here well aware that the raid would not be a surprise to the Japanese, long forewarned by reconnaissance flights and practice B-29 bombing missions against Truk and the Bonin islands. The flight bore little resemblance of the first thrust of 16 medium bombers, launched from a carrier, which hit Tokyo in 1942 under Lt. Col. (now Lt. Gen.) James Doolittle.

Its historic importance was underlined by General Arnold's personal report to President Roosevelt.

"This operation," he said, "is in no sense a hit-and-run raid. It is a calculated extension of our air power . . . No part of the Japanese empire is now out of our range, no war factory too remote to feel our bombs. The battle for Japan has been joined.

Preface For Invasion

"The systematic demolition of Japan's war production, begun six months ago from China bases, henceforth will be carried out with decisive force, softening up the Japanese heart for the ultimate invasion by combined United Nations land, sea and air forces. This will not be accomplished in a short time. The battle is just beginning. But today we opened against Tokyo an attack which will be carried on relentlessly from the air until the day of land-sea invasion."

Lt. Gen. Millard F. Harmon, deputy commander of the 20th Air Force under Arnold—as today's communique disclosed—said "we must and will sustain and intensify our attacks for many months to come before victory will be in sight."

French Armor
(Continued From Page One)

have crossed the Cosina river in the hills southeast of Faenza and have established five small bridgeheads against strong German resistance along a two and a half mile front, Allied headquarters announced.

German infantry was supported by heavy artillery and mortar concentrations in this critical area for the defense of the Bologna-Rimini highway strong hold, but the British captured a bridge at the riverbend and tanks crossed to aid the foot soldiers.

At another point British troops crossed the river, captured the town of Figria and proceeded to expand the bridgehead.

On the left flank Polish troops advanced a half mile north of San Biago and seized Monte Ricci overlooking the Marzeno river.

In the Adriatic coastal sector, positions along the Montone river, between Ravenna and Highway 9, were unchanged.

American troops on the Fifth Army front south of Bologna repulsed enemy raids against the outpost northwest of captured Livergnano and troops on Monte Cavalloro.

Air War

Squadrons of British Mosquito bombers dropped two-ton bombs last night on Hannover and other objectives behind German lines. Intruders shot up Nazi airfields.

Before dark, American and British bombers each dropped 500 tons of explosives on the Nordstern synthetic oil plant at Gelsenkirchen in the Ruhr in a double attack. Two British bombers and three U. S. fighters were lost to ground fire. No interceptors were seen.

German flying bombs inflicted new casualties on southern England before dawn but several were destroyed before they could cross the coast.

Yugoslav troops have captured Kotor and freed its protected harbor and the Lusica peninsula, Marsal Tito's communique announced.

Russian Front

The Russian Fourth Ukranian army was on the move again in eastern Czechoslovakia after a four week fighting lull.

Moscow announced last night the fresh drive already had ground out gains up to 16 miles on a 25-mile front west of Ungvar, Carpatho-Ukarine city which fell Oct. 27. The thrust, apparently aimed at the big highway and rail hub of Kassa (Kosice), has overrun 30 populated places as well as Csap (Cop), a railway junction 15 miles south of Ungvar.

Kassa lies about 45 miles north, northwest of the Hungarian communications center, Miskolc, itself threatened from the south and east by units of Marshal Rodion Y. Malinovsky's Second Ukarian army sweeping through Hungary.

Philippine Fighting

Mud-slogging American infantrymen lunged southward from Limon after capturing that bastion of the Japanese Yamashita line in the climax to the longest and bitterest fighting of the entire Leyte Island campaign.

The Japanese First division has been practically destroyed, Gen. Douglas MacArthur said in announcing that the Yankee 32nd had smashed into and through Limon yesterday after a typhoon-slowed battle that had remained fairly static for two weeks.

Easier country lies ahead, but it was emphasized that this does not mean the heavy fighting is over. The terrain is such that the Japanese will be able to make defensive stands and force the battleworn American doughboys to dig them out of machinegun nests and pillboxes.

General MacArthur in his communique said the American victory at Limon may result in the rolling up of the entire Yamashita line.

Japanese broadcast unconfirmed by Allied sources, claimed that two American submarines and seven warships and transports, including an aircraft carrier, were sunk or damaged in Philippine waters this week.

Only five years ago the Western Hemisphere witnessed the first successful flight of a helicopter.

Cogon, the common type of Philippine grass, is very coarse and dense, and grows to heights of three to eight feet.

Trench fever or typhus is transmitted by lice.

BULLETINS

CLOTHING COST CUT PROMISED

Washington, Nov. 24 (AP)—OPA today promised more cuts in the price of clothing and more low-priced garments on dealers' shelves.

The new, twin assault on inflated clothing prices will be followed, Price Administrator Chester Bowles said, by clamping down on the price ceilings of garment makers and tightening price rules governing retail stores.

LABOR PRESS BACKS MILITARY TRAINING

New Orleans, Nov. 24 (AP)—The Executive Board of the Eastern Labor Press Congress adopted a resolution today supporting universal military training as a permanent peacetime policy. The board met in conjunction with the American Federation of Labor.

60-POUND ROCK CAUGHT IN POTOMAC

Leonardtown, Md., Nov. 24 (AP)—Saint Mary's county fishermen reported today an abundance of rock in the lower Potomac river.

and the Chesapeake Bay off Point Lookout.

One Leonardtown fisherman told of landing 45 large rock in one day. Some of the big fish were said to weigh as much as 60 pounds.

On Thanksgiving Day, 1895, the first automobile road race in the United States was run in Illinois.

The word luxury is derived from a Latin word, luxus, meaning "superfluous abundance."

Clothing can be made out of soybean protein.

The louse is a name commonly applied to small wingless insects parasitic upon mammals and birds.

In the Fiji Islands, the human head is held to be sacred, and it is an insult to reach above the head of another person.

Rubber can be made out of soybean oil.

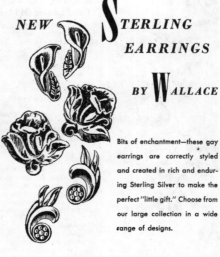

ARMY - NAVY GAME HOLDS SPOTLIGHT

Servicemen All Over World Follow Clash

By CHIP ROYAL

NEW YORK, Nov. 27 — Everyone in the United States who cares anything at all about football would like to see the Army-Navy game in Baltimore, Dec. 2. So would millions of service men beyond the shores of this great homeland.

If you've got any imagination at all, you can hear those GIs, Bluejackets and Marines all over the world rooting for their favorite team.

This is the year they've been waiting for. There hasn't been another football season like it, in the 18 falls your agent has seen around the gridirons.

It wasn't so very long ago that many fans across the country were hollering about the poor Army-Navy teams. It affected the morale of the service men, they said, because Army and Navy couldn't win at football.

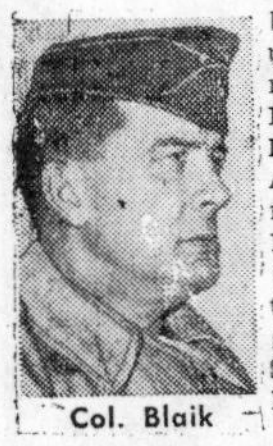

Col. Blaik

Then, things began to happen. West Point recalled Red Blaik from Dartmouth. Annapolis summoned Swede Hagberg from submarine duty. Both schools grabbed a few football players, here and there. At the start of the 1944 season, they were shouting Navy's praise. The midshipmen were tough. Then Army started to click—to make good all the promises their coach brought with him.

The banks of the Severn became quiet. The Hudson was alive with the cheers of the Cadets—all because the Navy couldn't get started, and the Army went far above expectations.

Finally, both teams settled down. By that time, it was all Army as far as the average rooter was concerned. But, many who witnessed last year's game remembered what happened — how the Navy line tore the Army forward wall to pieces, and the midshipmen went on to win.

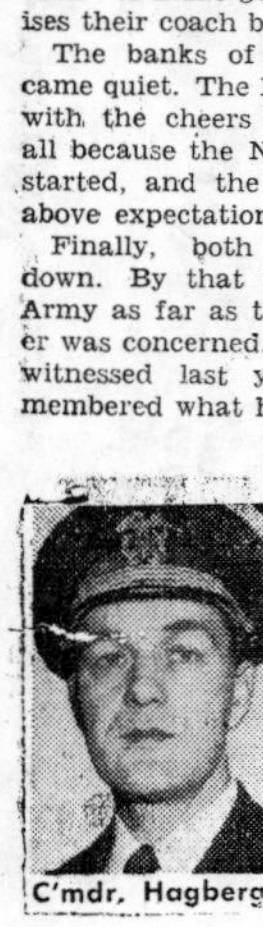

C'mdr. Hagberg

Naturally, a lot of arguments started about whether the same thing will happen this year. Someone suggested a quiz of the Notre Dame coaching staff and players might settle the issue.

The Irish should be in a position to make comparisons having been on the seat of their collective britches against both teams. what do they say?

The Notre Dame players pick the Navy because the Middy line hits harder. But, and it's another one of those big ones, the coaches say the Army because the Cadets have the most powerful backs.

After all is said and done, it won't make much difference to the boys across. As long as their Army or Navy wins the football championship they can cheer—and plenty!

Plebe Football, Soccer Teams Win Victories

Plebe Grid Teams Undefeated In Six Years

The Plebe football team ended a victorious season here Saturday by turning back the Bullis Prep School squad of Silver Spring by a 38 to 0 score.

The Plebe soccer team defeated the Sparrows Point High School team, 3 to 1.

It was the seventh straight win of the year for the Plebe grid squad and the first defeat Bullis has sustained this season.

For six years now the Plebe football teams, coached by John N. Wilson, have been undefeated.

The Plebes rolled up 19 points in the first quarter, added 13 in the third and six more in the fourth period.

Plebe fullback Dufee made two touchdowns by rounding end for long runs.

Perkins, Evans and Everngam made the goals for the Plebe soccer team.

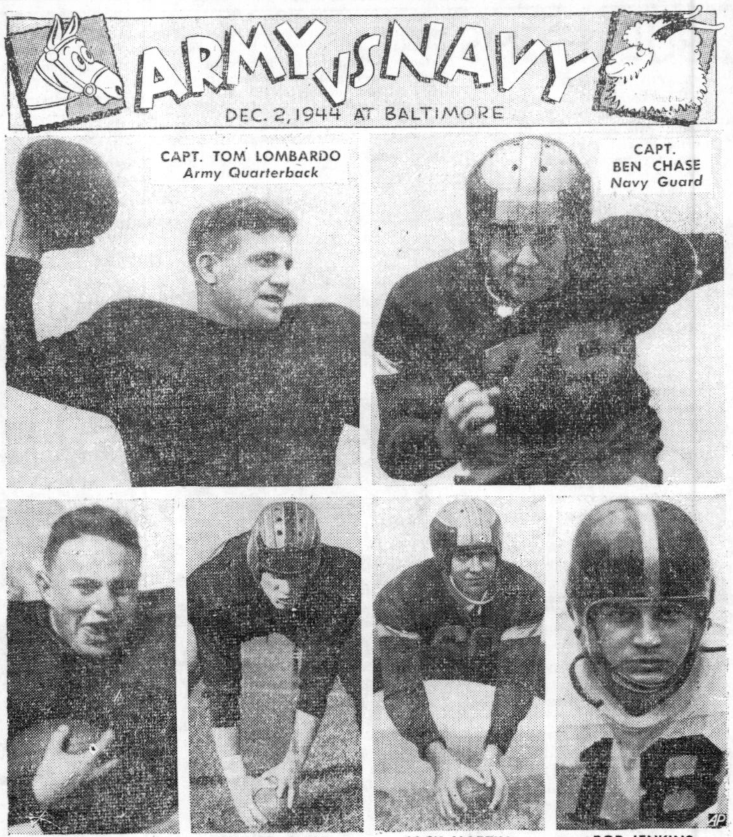

DOC BLANCHARD, Army Fullback — BOB ST. ONGE, Army Center — JACK MARTIN, Navy Center — BOB JENKINS, Navy Halfback

Sports Roundup

By HUGH FULLERTON, JR.

NEW YORK, Nov. 27 (AP)—MAN WANTED: . . . The one big task at the major league meetings two weeks hence will be to decide what to do about a successor to Kenesaw Mountain Landis as commissioner of baseball . . . It has been suggested that the major leagues might return to the old commission form of government and it seems likely that Secretary Leslie O'Connor will continue to do the work, with the two league presidents advising him, until the present agreement expires in 1946 . . . To make this setup permanent, however, would invite the same kind of trouble that led to the appointment of Landis in 1921 . . . Not since that time has baseball been in so great need of a firm guiding hand.

History Repeats

The famous Black Sox scandal which brought a new form of baseball government, came shortly after the last World War . . . . Then, as now, the big leagues still were full of young players, getting their first taste of big money, and old timers getting their last chance at it . . . The gambling wave was at flood tide and those two groups were approachable . . No one questioned the integrity of the old national commission, but it failed to prevent that scandal. Under Landis' rule no one got excited this year when the news came out that a Washington pitched had been approached to throw a game at the end of the season . . . Another good reason for appointing a new commissioner whose reputation and whose powers will at least be near those of Landis comes from the postwar problems baseball must face. A glimpse at the huge national service lists of the clubs indicates how many boys might be affected if they came back to find baseball ruled entirely by representatives of the club owners. The commissioners' first task, as Landis always saw it, was to look after the players interests . . . The magnates probably intend to be fair, but they don't always have the same ideas as the guys who work for a salary.

Guessing Game

One thing that seems certain is that neither league will invoke its right to ask the President of the United States to name a commissioner . . . To do that without presenting a list of acceptable candidates would be to invite the answer reporters got when they asked the President where the Army-Navy game would be played . . . And incidentally, it seems harder to find an acceptable candidate for the commissioner job than for any political office . . . The public might forgive a few shortcomings in a man who merely wanted to be a governor or senator, but not in one who wanted to boss baseball.

Personal Touch

In baseball's earlier time of need Hugh Fullerton, senior, wrote a piece for his paper suggesting that Judge Landis would be a good man to take charge of the game . . . Pop relates that he expected a vigorous scolding when the judge summoned him next day . . . Instead, Landis confided; "There's no job in the world I'd rather have."

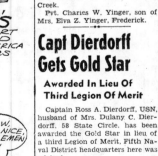

ST. MARY'S DEFEATS GERMANTOWN

St. Mary's team defeated the Germantown team by a score of 39 to 12 in a game played on St. Mary's Field. Touchdowns were made by R. Russell and R. Jones; extra points by T. Jones, C. Kimble and T. Coughlin.

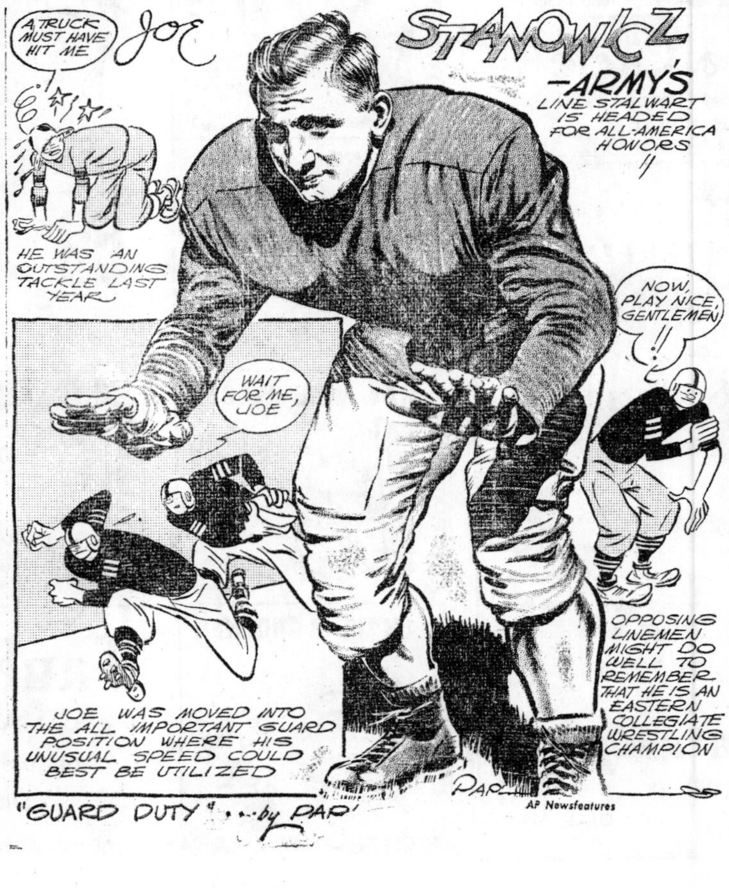

AP Newsfeatures

NAVY SOCCER TEAM DEFEATS ARMY BOOTERS

Turn Cadents Back, 1 To 0

The Navy varsity soccer team defeated the Army booters 1 to 0 Saturday before a large crowd at West Point.

George Kirk, Navy's inside right, made the winning goal in the third period.

It was one of the hardest games of the year for the Navy team which closed an undefeated collegiate season.

The Navy and Army soccer teams have meen seven times, the midshipmen holding four wins.

The two teams were evenly matched. Army played eight games this season scoring 29 points to their opponent's six while Navy played seven games, scoring 30 points to their opponents' five.

28 More State Troops Wounded

Malcolm E. Cox Of Near Annapolis, In Group

WASHINGTON, Nov. 27 (AP)—The names of 28 more Marylanders wounded in action in the European area were announced today by the War Department. They included:

Staff Sgt. William C. Bilenki, husband of Mrs. Anna W. Bilenki, Curtis Bay.

Pvt. William E. Brown, husband of Mrs. Ella E. Brown, Price.

Pfc. Terrance A. Byrnes, husband of Mrs. Lillian C. Byrnes, Frostburg.

Tech. 5th gr. Malcolm E. Cox, son of James T. Cox, Route 1, Annapolis.

Staff Sgt. John W. Graddock, son of Mrs. Alice G. Graddock, Chevy Chase.

Capt. Albin P. Dear'ng, husband of Mrs. Martha G. Dearing, Eccleston.

Sgt. Joshua L. Dryden, son of Mrs. Maude L. Dryden, Salisbury.

First Lt. Ralph G. Hawkins, husband of Mrs. Martha J. Hawkins, Smithsburg.

Staff Sgt. Paul V. Keller, husband of Mrs. Jane E. Keller, Hagerstown.

Pfc Quentin W. Kelly, husband of Mrs. Quentin Kelly, North East.

Pfc. Kenneth L. Leasure, son of Thomas Leasure, Big Lane, Midland.

Staff Sgt. Lester G. Mainhart, Jr., son of Lester G. Mainhart, New Market.

Pfc. Thomas D. Ricker, husband of Mrs. Beatrice C. Ricker, Cumberland.

Pvt. Glendon A. Ralston, son of Mrs. Nellie Ralston, Cumberland.

Pfc. William J. Robertson, husband of Mrs. Margaret V. Robertson, Cumberland.

Staff Sgt. Michael J. Sarno, husband of Mrs. Lorraine M. Sarno, Hagerstown.

First Lieut. Robert L. Stevenson, son of Louis Stevenson, Denton.

Sgt. Lake G. Todd, husband of Mrs. Frieda I. Todd, Fishing Creek.

Pvt. Charles W. Yinger, son of Mrs. Elva Z. Yinger, Frederick.

Capt Dierdorff Gets Gold Star

Awarded In Lieu Of Third Legion Of Merit

Captain Ross A. Dierdorff, USN, husband of Mrs. Dulany C. Dierdorff, 58 State Circle, has been awarded the Gold Star in lieu of a third Legion of Merit, Fifth Naval District headquarters here was advised.

His latest decoration is based upon a citation "for outstanding services as commander of a transport division and commander of a beach assault group during the amphibious invasion of Southern France last August.

"An expert seaman and leader, thoroughly experienced in amphibious warfare," says the citation, "Captain Dierdorff led an assault convoy from mounting ports in safe passage to the designated area of operations, landing troops, their equipment and supplies expeditiously and with marked skill, and thereby assisting our ground forces in the rapid extension of their beachhead.

"Upon completion of unloading activities, the ships under his capable command sailed promptly to base ports for reloading and, by their efficiency in achieving these missions, contributed essentially to the effective build-up movement of the Allied Armies in Southern France."

Captain Dierdorff was born 48 years ago in Hillsboro, Oregon.

Around The Radio Dial

WITH	1230k
WBAL	1090k
WFBR	1300k
WCBM	1400k
WCAO	600k

By C. E. BUTTERFIELD

NEW YORK, Nov. 27 (AP)—Radio contracts already have been signed for four of the New Year's Day football games.

Two of them, the Cotton Bowl at Dallas and the East-West college All-Star at San Francisco, are listed for MBS. The other two will be divided between CBS and the BLU, the former carrying the Orange Bowl from Miami and the latter the Sugar Bowl at New Orleans.

As usual NBC will detail the Rose Bowl game at Pasadena under its regular arrangement, making the day's total five.

Dialing tonight: NBC—8 Fay Bainter in "Witness For The People;" 8:30 Barlow Concert; 9 Voorhees Concert, Lily Pons; 9:30 Information Please; 10 Contented Concert ... CBS—7:30 (Repeat 10:30) Bob Hawk Quiz; 8:30 Frank Sinatra show; 9 Merle Oberon in "Dark Waters;" 10 Paulette Goddard in "You Belong To Me;" 11:30 War Bond program from Memphis ... BLU — 7 Horace Heidt time; 8:30 Blind Dating; 9 Counter Spy; 9:30 Gene Krupa band; 10:15 Ted Mlacne overseas ... MBS—7:30 Bulldog Drummond; 8:30 Sherlock Holmes; 9:30 Human Adventure.

5:00
WFBR: News; and Races.
WBAL: †When a Girl Marries
WCBM: Terry and the Pirates.
WITH: News: Bill Dyer.

5:15
WFBR: Chick Carter.
WCAO: "Evelyn Winters."
WCBM: Dick Tracy.
WBAL: Portia Faces Life.

5:30
WBAL: Just Plain Bill.
WFBR: Superman.
WCBM: Jack Armstrong
WCAO: Bob Iula Orchestra.

5:45
WCBM: Captain Midnight.
WCAO: Sons of Pioneers.
WFBR: Tom Mix Show.
WBAL: Front Page Farrell.

6:00
WCAO: Quincy Howe.
WBAL: News; Sports Parade.
WFBR: Dinner Rhythms.
WCBM: Today's Hero: Mus.
WITH: News; Twilight Tunes.

6:15
WCAO: Don Riley.
WITH: Better Music.
WBAL: Dinner Table.
WFBR: Sports Stewart Kennard.
WCBM: Interlude; Eddie Fenton's Sports.

6:30
WCBM: Carroll Dulaney.
WITH: Richard Eaton.
WFBR: Press Bulletins.
WBAL: Enjoyment Time.
WCAO: Music For Dinner.

6:45
WCAO: The World Today.
WBAL: ‡News. Lowell Thomas
WCBM: Henry Taylor, news.
WFBR: Dottie Gibson Show.
WBAL: Hillbilly Music.

7:00
WCAO: I Love A Mystery.
WCBM: Horace Heidt's Orch.
WITH: News, Enjoyment Time.
WFBR: Fulton Lewis, Jr.
WBAL: The Music Shop.

7:15
WFBR: Duckpin Derby.
WCAO: Hedda Hopper.
WBAL: News of the World.

7:30
WCBM: The Lone Ranger
WITH: Swing Class.
WCAO: Thanks Yanks.
WBAL: Great Gildersleeve.
WFBR: Invitation to Waltz.

7:45
WFBR: String Music.

8:00
WCAO: Vox Pop.
WITH: News; Phonaway Jackpot.
WFBR: Cecil Brown, News.
WCBM: Clifford Prevost.
WBAL: Cavalcade of America.

8:15
WCBM: Lum and Abner
WITH: Tommy Dorsey's Orch.
WFBR: Bond Briefs.

8:30
WFBR: Sherlock Holmes.
WCBM: Blind Date.
WBAL: Concert Orchestra.
WCAO: Frank Sinatra Show.
WITH: News, Bing Crosby.

8:45
WITH: Red Cross Show.

9:00
WITH: News; Velvet Tunes.
WCAO: Radio Theater.
WFBR: Gabriel Heatter.
WCBM: Counter Spy.
WBAL: Nelson Eddy, Orch.

9:15
WITH: Symphony Hall.
WFBR: Screen Test.

9:30
WCBM: Spotlight Band.
WFBR: Nick Carter.
WBAL: Information Please.

10:00
WITH: News; Drew Pearson.
WCAO: Guild Players.
WFBR: Henry Gladstone.
WBAL: Percy Faith Orch.; Soloists.
WCBM: Raymond G. Swing.

10:15
WITH: We The Jury.
WFBR: Texas Rangers.
WCBM: Ted Malone.

10:30
WITH: Time For News.
WCAO: Johnny Morgan.
WFBR: Symphonette.
WBAL: Dr. I. Q. Quiz
WCBM: Accent on Music.

10:45
WITH: Sports Final.

11:00
WITH: News; Dick Haymes.
WCAO: News; Films.
WFBR: News; Race Results.
WBAL: News; Sports Parade
WCBM: News Journal.

11:15
WCAO: Joan Brooks.
WITH: Music a La Cart.
WFBR: George Sterney Orch.
WBAL: The Open Bible.
WCBM: Music You Want.

11:30
WFBR: Nat Brandwynne Orch.
WITH: Concert Minature.
WCBM: Saludos Amigas.
WCAO: Sixth War Loan.

11:45
WBAL: Treasury Salute.

12:00
WBAL: News' Dave Minor.
WCAO: News; Nocturne.
WITH: News; Memory Tunes.
WCBM: Star Theater.

12:15
WBAL: Serenade.
WCBM: Gay Claridge Orch.

12:30
WBAL. Modern Moods.
WCBM: Emil Vandas Orch.
WCAO: Frank Carle Orch.

12:45
WITH: Simple Simon.
WBAL: Fairfield Four.

1:00
WBAL: The Open Bible
WITH: All Nite Show.

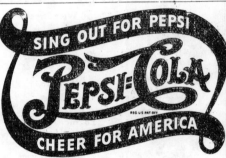

Evening Capital

ANNAPOLIS, MD.

1884--1944

TALBOT T. SPEER, President and Publisher
FRANK L. McSHANE, General Manager
RICHARD H. ELLIOTT, Editor

Published Daily Except Sunday by
The CAPITAL-GAZETTE PRESS, INCORPORATED
Telephone 2832 Subscriptions 3881

SUBSCRIPTION RATES:
Delivered in Annapolis, the United States Naval Academy, Eastport, Germantown, Homewood, West Annapolis, Wardour and vicinity by carrier for 80 cents a month. By mail in United States or Canada, $7.00 a year or $4.00 for 6 months.
Price at newsstands, 3 cents a copy.

National Advertising Representatives
INLAND NEWSPAPER REPRESENTATIVES INC.
New York—512 Fifth Ave. St. Louis—Security Bldg.
Chicago—640-2 Wrigley Bldg. Kansas City—1012 Baltimore

Entered as Second Class Matter May 28, 1933, at the Post Office of Annapolis, Maryland, under the Act of March 3, 1879.

MEMBERS OF THE ASSOCIATED PRESS

The Associated Press is exclusively entitled to the use for re-publication of all news credited to it or not otherwise credited in this paper and also the local news published herein. All rights of re-publication of special dispatches herein are also reserved.

SATURDAY DECEMBER 2, 1944

BOND HOLDINGS

With sales of War Bonds registering fair progress in the current drive, it is an interesting fact that purchases by individual investors of E bonds prior to this campaign totaled $26,800,000,000 of which $3,500,000,000 had been redeemed. That is, the small investors now have 87 per cent of all the bonds they have bought during the war.

These bonds may now be redeemed quite easily, simply by endorsing them and presenting them at a bank. Redemptions undoubtedly will increase after this drive because individuals who can not plan their future with precision and who must meet human emergencies out of the resources available to them, will need some of the money they put into the bonds. But it is probable that after the war approximately the present percentages will prevail—that is, 13 percent of E bonds will have been cashed and 87 per cent held.

From May, 1941, to September, 1944, 81,000,000 Americans have bought and kept $33,687,000,000, current redemption value, of War Bonds. That is nearly as much as the total life insurance assets of the country. It is a gigantic savings program and certainly will cushion postwar shocks for Americans.

"EDUCATIONAL TRAGEDY"

Some 2,000 delegates at a recent gathering at Columbus, Ohio, of the National Conference of Teachers of English were startled into fully realizing and protesting against a recent trend toward reducing the time allotted to their subject in high school curricula. The trend is real, and it is being promoted by apostles of the "practical" to the exclusion of what they regard as merely "ornamental."

Max J. Herzberg, principal of the Weequahic, New Jersey, High School, led the attack against lessening the time devoted to English and its literature. Mr. Herzberg who is the author of numerous school and college texts in the literary field, said:

"If English in our school curriculum were called American, there would be no hesitancy, I am sure, in seeing to it that this great subject would remain in the school schedule for every year of the student life. English teaches ideals, particularly the ideals of Americanism. It teaches the art of communication, today more than ever a great need of human beings. It would be an educational tragedy to curtail the time given to English."

A survey of American folkways, literature, tradition and heritage might well be a part of the study of English in elementary and secondary schools, Mr. Herzberg maintained. His reference to what would happen if for English were substituted the word "American" was, of course, in part fanciful, though it recognized the divergence between English as spoken in England and in the United States.

It would be, as the speaker maintained, "an educational tragedy" to restrict the time devoted to English. What can, despite its critics, be more "practical" for one starting out on the battle of life than the possession of an easy, comprehensive and correct use of the language that will be his chief means of communication all his days?

What more valuable in the hours of leisure that a mechanical age is increasingly conferring on man, than the cultivation of a taste to enjoy the best of human thought through the printed word? Deprivation of these boons is "educational tragedy," indeed.

CHANGING TACTICS

From the pattern of fighting as it develops along the Western Front the greatest danger to Germany seem to lie in the Aachen area. Berlin has admitted as much. Nazi troops have been shifted from other places in the line, while divisions of the recently organized people's army have been sent in to meet the fury of Allied advance. There have been concentrations of armor and repeated counterattacks by the enemy.

There is good reason for this concern on the part of Berlin. Here lies the gateway to the Rhine and Ruhr valleys, where is concentrated Germany's industrial strength. Cologne, for which the Allies now are battling, is in the heart of territory which Germany cannot afford to lose if the war is to be protracted.

Fighting along the Western Front is reverting to what might be termed first principles of warfare. The Germans, while still defending fixed fortifications to almost the last man, are resorting to hastily dug trenches in almost the same manner they did in the last war. After the unhappy experience at Arnhem, the Allies seem to have abandoned the paratroop idea on a big scale, although airborne troops are stil lemployed in a limited way.

As the final phases of the conflict shape up, it will be man against man, tank against tank, a deadly, bloody struggle in which nothing will count except sheer force of men and arms.

THE WAR TODAY

By DEWITT MACKENZIE
(Associated Press War Analyst)

Berlin commentators continue to insist that General Eisenhower has assigned to Field Marshal Montgomery and his 21st Army group, on the Allied northern wing, the task of delivering the assault calculated to break through the Nazi defenses and precipitate the crisis in the mattle of the Cologne plain.

Well, far be it from us to argue that point. A powerful flanking movement on that northern wing certainly may be the high "C" of the Allied offensive.

And what captain could handle it better than the great Montgomery, who won his marshal's baton as one if the war's greatest tactical experts.

What Berlin doesn't know, however, and what we don't know, is when General Ike is likely to swing his haymaker. My own idea is that it now depends largely on the weather—clear skies for the all--important air force, and frost that will tighten up the awful fields of mud.

Up to this point there have been other factors causing delay. One, of course, has been the necessity of ironing out strategical lumps in the Allied battleline as a whole, and, while there still is spade work to be done, our front seems fairly well set. Another vital factor has related to supplies, but this problem now has been solved by the opening—only four days ago—of the great port of Antwerp through which the wherewithal will be funneled to the Allied front.

That puts it up to the weather man, who's been mighty unfriendly to our side. Still, the Allied command was well aware that the old fellow was bound to be short-tempered at this time of year. Thus Eisenhower acted deliberately when he took his chances again with the elements.

The Supreme commander's reasons seem clear enough. He didn't want to stand still and so give the Germans the leeway of the winter months in which to create fresh reserves and get further set to meet the final Allied onslaught.

So today we see Nazi Field Marshal Von Rundstedt's 400-mile battle line under the fierce pressure of six Allied armies—with other Allied forces ready to come into action. He has committed about everything he can muster to the final defense.

Under these circumstances it's highly interesting to see the Soviet Embassy in Washington issue a statement that what now is needed is "a vigorous assault by the armies of the United Nations to crush Hitler Germany with the shortest delay." This has been widely interpreted as perhaps meaning that Moscow finally is about ready to stage its big drive against Hitler's powerful Vistula line in Poland, thereby putting the Fuehrer under unbearable pressure.

Be that as it may, surely the Red armies as well as those of the western Allies are in the hands of the weather man to large degree. However, this is about the time of year when the ground and rivers of Eastern Europe freeze, making possible a resumption of military operations which have been impeded by the autumn rains and mud.

Literary GUIDEPOST

"MASTERPIECES OF PAINTING FROM THE NATIONAL GALLERY OF ART," edited by Huntington Cairns and John Walker (Random; $6.50).

PEOPLE who laugh gaily at the Victorian habit of stuffing birds to exhibit them under glass bells must have forgotten that we alleged moderns have several habits as quaint. One is the publication and purchase of elaborate gift books such as "Masterpieces of Painting from the National Gallery of Art," surely a perfect example of what not to call a book.

This is an enormous book some 11 to 15 inches which must weigh more than "Anthony Adverse" and is so extensive in area that it can scarcely be held in the usual reading position. It would be most easily handled on a marble-topped "center table" and in spite of the book's beauty and the rather wonderful fact of its appearance in a war economy, it is destined for display rather than for intimate use. It is, in short, the modern equivalent of the brown thrasher under glass.

The National Gallery was established nearly a century and a half too late, by act of Congress on March 24, 1937. Even then, the building was not paid for by the nation, but by Andrew Mellon. It was opened by President Roosevelt on St. Patricks' Day, 1941, and in spite of the distressing events of the last few years it already houses one of the world's important collections of painting. This is due to no brilliance of Congress but to the charitable gifts of a number of millionaires, and there are a great many persons who have expressed emotions ranging from annoyance to nausea at the thought that the United States of America's one national gallery should thus be a memorial to a few estimable gentlemen, rather than to the nation.

For the only 4-acre book I have seen this Christmas season Huntington Cairns and John Walker have selected 85 paintings, and have dug out comment to accompany these from sources as diverse as T. S. Eliot and Leonardo da Vinci.

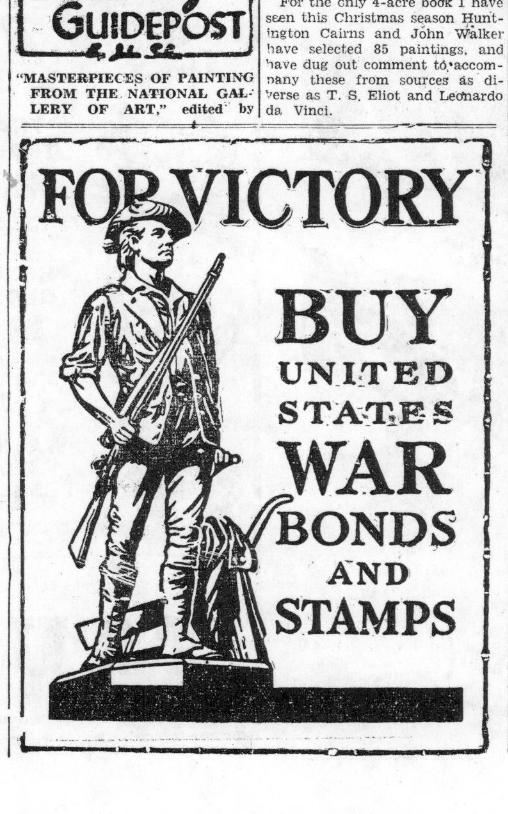

LINE OF THE MOST RESISTANCE

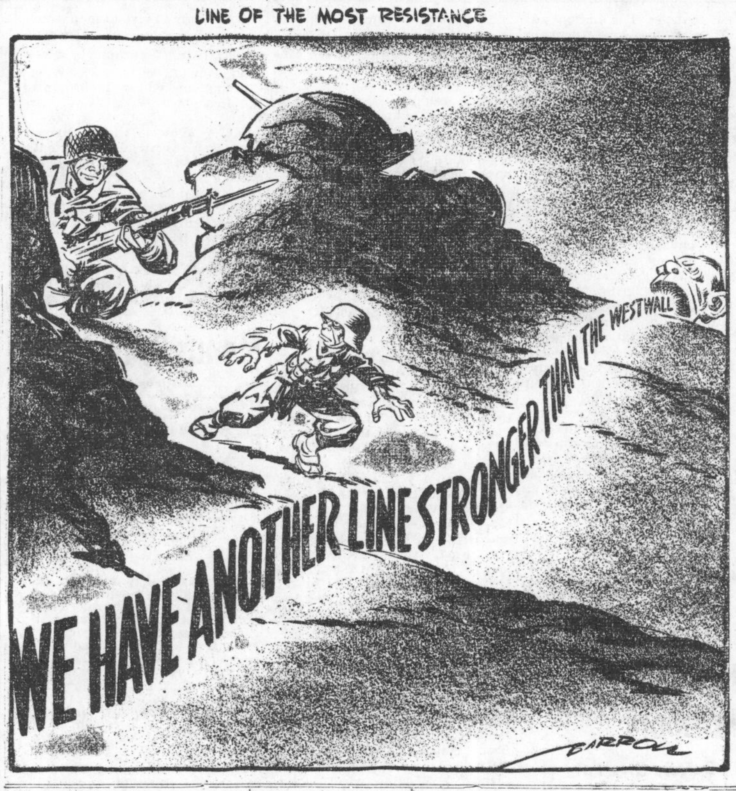

Washington Daybook

By Jack Stinnett

By JACK STINNETT

WASHINGTON — I wrote a piece not long ago about who-writes-whose speeches. The story probably never can be told in toto, for there are so many quirks that it is impossible to tell where a speech comes from.

For example, there is this story about one of President Roosevelt's very effective phrases in one of his late campaign addresses. It was a quotation from the Bible: "Thou shalt not bear false witness." It originally was written by Assistant Interior Secretary Mike Straus as a part of a speech to be delivered by "Curmudgeon" Harold L. Ickes. Ickes didn't like it, struck it out of the final draft of his speech. That draft went to the President's desk. Scanning it, the President's eye caught the deleted phrase. He liked it and incorporated it into his own campaign address.

* * *

NO DOG in history ever had the political importance of Fala, the President's Scotty. Among President Roosevelt's many "firsts" is the fact that he has been the first candidate to bring his dog into the campaign.

From the time the story was spread that a destroyer had been dispatched to pick up Fala, left behind on the Hawaiian trip, the little black Scotty was very much in the political picture. President Roosevelt denied the story.

In his Pennsylvania swing and his visit to Chicago, he had to explain why Fala wasn't along. His explanation was that Fala had had so much attention that he had a bad case of swelled head and had to be chastised by being left behind.

Fala, however, was on hand at Hyde Park for the grand finale. If he hasn't got a swelled head now, no dog knows anything. From now on Fala should be kept strictly in the doghouse, but he won't be. The most political pup in history has earned his place in the records.

* * *

IN THE weeks preceding the election, our representation to foreign countries underwent one of

Arthur Bliss Lane, one of the outstanding career diplomats in the foreign service, was named ambassador to the Polish government in exile. John C. Wiley, who had been minister to Latvia and Estonia, was shifted to Colombia.

Lebanon and Syria, which have been mandates of France since World War I, got official diplomatic recognition as "free sovereign nations" with the appointment of George Wadsworth as minister to those two states.

Jefferson Caffrey, another long-time career diplomat, was appointed ambassador to the De Gaulle government in France. Anthony J. Drexel Biddle, who has been serving as ambassador or minister to practically all the governments in exile, was superseded by the appointments of Richard C. Patterson as ambassador to Yugoslavia, Lithgow Osborne as ambassador to Norway, Charles Sawyer as ambassador to Belgium and minister to Luxembourg, and Stanley Hornbeck as ambassador to the Netherlands.

hollywood

BY ROBBIN COONS

HOLLYWOOD — Mr. Walling Keith of the *Gadsden (Ala.) Times* is director-general of the Society for Prevention of Cruelty to Southern Accents. He has just sent me a membership card for which I am duly grateful.

This gives me, I hope, an opening to suggest for membership one Joseph Cotten, who hails from Petersburg, Va., and will be forever devoted to the club's motto: "Protect and uphold the plural yawl!" Not only that, but Brother Cotten has one of those southern accents all the stage-diction teachers on Broadway couldn't eradicate if he'd let them try. Like many Dixie drawlers, Joe picks up any lost traces of it every time he visits the south and hears it as it's spoken. Recently he toured down there and wound up with a visit to his old Virginia home. "By then," he chuckles, "Ah was playin' in blackface!"

Another should-be member is Montana's Gary Cooper. Gary by protesting to a director who years ago made himself eligible wanted him to say "you-all" when addressing his leading lady in a southern drama. "Folks down south," said Gary, "never say you-all when they're talking to one person." I believe it was the first time Hollywood ever was exposed to the idea, which happily is catching on, slowly but surely.

* * *

VIVIAN BLAINE doesn't often get a call to sing in Greek, but she can if pressed, as she did during a Greek Relief drive in New York. It was in pre-movie days, when she got a job singing at a New York night spot. The piano player gave her a tip. Usually singers were retained there two weeks, but the manager was a Greek, and if she would learn a few songs in his native tongue, who could tell?

"I learned some patriotic songs, though I don't understand the words," he recalls, "and the pianist was right. That engagement lasted six months!"

* * *

MANY a youngster has worked his way through college, but Jack Skirball is the only one I know who did it by peddling movies—and wound up as a film producer. The films Skirball sold while at the University of Cincinnati will date his college days for old-time movie fans—the pictures of Francis X. Bushman and Beverly Bayne, of Olga Petrova and the late Harold Lockwood. . . .

Sylvia Sidney, during her three-year absence from the screen, toured in "Jane Eyre" and "Angel Street," both costume plays.

"I got so tired of being offered re-writes of 'Street Scene,' my first big success in pictures," she says. "Besides, I found that hiding behind a costume was a great help. Nothing builds up an actress's confidence more than wearing a train, a corset, and a lot of false hair. . ." .

She's returning in James Cagney's "Blood on the Sun". . .

The beaver, fairly plentiful in the southern valleys of Norway, was saved from extinction by government restrictions against killing.

At the outbreak of war, the Chinese in the Philippines were mostly small shopkeepers; the Japanese were farmers, craftsmen and fishermen.

NEWS From Our NEIGHBORS

SEVERNA PARK ROUND BAY and VICINITY

Luncheon guests of Mrs. Daniel H. Freeman, of Round Bay, on Tuesday were Mrs. Ralph Bruner of Louisville, Ky., who is visiting for several weeks, Mrs. Robert Fossum, Mrs. Richard L. Tubman, Miss Louise Howard and Mrs. William Arthur. Later in the afternoon Miss Howard entertained the party at tea at her home. Lieutenant Freeman and Lieutenant Bruner are shipmates.

Mrs. Byron D. Greene, on the return jounrney from West Point where she visited her son, Cadet Byron D. Greene, Jr., to her home in Arlington, was an overnight guest of Mr. and Mrs. Christian A. Lentz of Round Bay early in the week.

Mrs. James Airey of Linthicum Heights recently visited Mrs. Robert Ellenburg, of the Park.

Captain and Mrs. Irving Garcelon, of Washington, spent the week-end with Mr. and Mrs. Herbert I. Garcelon, of Round Bay.

Mrs. Henry Ledford of Mt. Sterling, Ky., is spending time with her brother-in-law and sister, Mr. and Mrs. Dudley A. Sisk, of Round Bay.

Mrs. Hannah Gilbert, of Baltimore, was the recent guest of her sister, Mrs. Charles Yentsch, of the Park.

Mrs. Elizabeth Stahl, who has been visiting at the home of her son, Mr. William Stahl, of Atlantic City, will return with her daughter and family, Mr. and Mrs. Henry Kaufmann, Henry Jr., and Billie who are joining them for the week-end.

Recent visitors at the home of Mrs. John Denues at her home on the Severn were Mr. and Mrs. John T. Denues of Stevenson, Md., Mr. and Mrs. Gifford Smith, Mr. and Mrs. Howard Ray and Miss A. Claire Spicer, of Baltimore, and First Lieutenant Margaret W. Wood, A.N.C., recently back from twenty nine months in India. Mrs Denues left early in the week on a trip to York, Pa. and recently visited in New York.

The annual Men's Club dinner dance will be held at Carvel Hall on Saturday, December 9 at 7 P. M.

GARDEN FARMS

Mumford French, USN., has returner to his base at Bainbridge, Md., after spending his furlough with his family in Garden Farms.

ST. MARGARET'S

Staff Sergeant Ray Phipps, of Bruning Field, Nebraska, returned to camp recently after spending a seven day furlough with his family.

Private Dorsey Hile recently returned to Camp Meade, after spending a furlough with his family.

Miss Doris Myers, of Severn, spent this week with her aunt, Mrs. David Pumphrey.

Mr. and Mrs. William Baker, of Roanoke, are visiting their daughter, Mrs. Benjamin Wood.

Letter To The Editor

SUGGESTS NEW SITE FOR PROPOSED AIRPORT

EDITOR, The Evening Capital
Sir:

The people of the 5th District of Anne Arundel county that live in the communities surounding the proposed "Airport Site" just south of Linthicum Heights, are beginning to realize the effect this project will have on their communities and on our country as a whole.

Of course, no one is opposed to the construction of an airport as such an attitude would be detrimental to good progress, however, it is most important that we give full and proper consideration as to the best location of this project in our country. The Baltimore Airport Commission is going to cause Anne Arundel county to take from its tax books the area that they acquire, as such will become tax exempt, hence it is fitting and proper that they try to select a site that will incur the least amount of loss in real estate values to Anne Arundel county. In this respect it is known that there are a number of highly valuable farms and homes in this area.

Many residents of the communities surrounding this area are much concerned by the methods used by the Baltimore Airport Commission. They surveyed and decided on this area without consulting or showing any consideration for these people and engaged the services of a Baltimore real estate operator of long experience to go into the area to obtain options on properties at one dollar each. A number of these property owners have been "taken in" by this operator with the hope of realizing a fancy profit. However, these options are in the name of the operator and is in no way commitment of the City of Baltimore, therefore if the price is too high they will refuse the options and proceed to acquire the property through condemnation; so these good people may not be "sitting as pretty" as they have been given to think.

In this area are two large cemeteries, one of them connected with the old established and much beloved Friendship Church, the removal of which would be a great loss to folks for miles around.

A number of public spirited residents, in and around this area, have been endeavoring to find ways and means to offset this objectionable proposal and feel that they have the solution in an area that should be more desirable to the Airport Commissoin and cause less loss to our county.

This area is just south of the one now proposed and is bounded by the Harman to Glen Burnie Road on the north, the Pennsylvania Railroad on the west, the old W. B. and A. R. R. on the east and as far south as desired. In this area are no churches or cemeteries and most of the land is idle also many property holders have been wanting to sell since the W. B. and A. service was discontinued. This area would not be as great a loss to our county tax revenue, also, there would be no churches or cemeteries demolished and no high obstructions, such as water towers, etc. to be removed. A survey of this area shows it to be of a greater average level. This area should be more desirable to all concerned for the following reasons:

1. Less loss of tax revenue to our county.
2. Acquisition cost is less.
3. Lower cost of construction because of less grading, etc.
4. No large communities bordering this area, practically eliminating any opposition.

Hence there is every reason for the Baltimore City Airport Commission and our County Commissioners to get together and try to satisfy a greater majority of our residents and cause little if any hardship on only a few.

W. H. MUHL, President
5th District Protective Ass'n.
of Anne Arundel County Box
52 Linthicum Heights, Md.

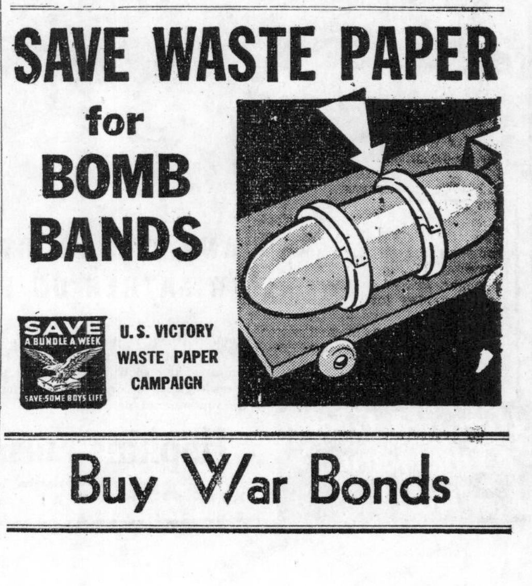

Leaves from a War Correspondent's notebook
by Hal Boyle

PARIS, Dec. 1—(Delayed)—(AP)—American soldiers, not to be outdone by Adolf Hitler's propaganda list of "secret weapons," have designed some nifty gadgets of their own.

One of the most ingenious of these novel devises was invented in the Mediterranean theater of operations by Capt. John Senseney of St. Louis, Mo. Long worried over the time lost in flight by delinquent and lazy carrier pigeons, he invented a curved metal tube.

"You just strap one end of the tube to the side of the pigeon's beak and the other end beneath his tail feathers," explained Senseney. "As he flies along, the cold wind whipping through the tube gets his tail cold and he steps on the gas to warm up. But the faster he flier the colder his tail gets—and the colder his tail gets the faster he flies.

"As soon as I get this thing in mass production I can win the war. All this pigeon loafing simply prolongs the war."

Ray Machine

More potent as a potential spreader of dismay and confusion in enemy ranks is a mysterious new ray machine being completed by a young sergeant who got the idea during a fit of depression as he was typing out one of several hundred complicated army forms.

"I suddenly realized," he said, "that armies don't march on their stomachs like Napoleon said. They march on red tape. More soldiers do paper work than carry guns.

"Take travel orders, for instance, at some headquarters you can't go from the first to the tenth floor without getting special travel orders cut to show the elevator operator. I got to thinking—and then it came to me:

"The best way to whip the enemy isn't to try to bomb them out of their foxholes. The quicker way would be to paralyze them by screwing up their red tape. That's where my new ray machine comes in.

"It can be carried and operated by one man, dropped by parachute behind the lines in the vicinity of German army headquarters.

Turns On Beam

"When he turns on the beam, it does three things: it melts paper clips on all the enemy's army documents within a 30-mile radius, thus causing them to become hopelessly mixed; it melts all typewriter ribbons and it hardens all mimeograph ink. The Germans will find it impossible to type out orders and requisitions and will be unable to mimeograph them. This mysterious ray machine of mine will paralyz all this red tape and nobody will be able to move in any direction."

Another promising secret weapon is the "champagne mortar," now being developed by an ordnance soldier who figured that since troops are drilled to salvage everything else some use ought to be found for champagne bottles broken in the rear lines.

Under his plan, supply troops would fill used C-ration cans with broken champagne bottles an explosive charges, then fire them at the German lines from mortars.

Tired Kidneys Often Bring Sleepless Nights

Doctors say that your kidneys contain 15 miles of tiny tubes or filters which help to purify the blood and keep you healthy. When they get tired and don't work right in the daytime, many people have to get up nights. Frequent or scanty passages with smarting and burning sometimes shows there is something wrong with your kidneys or bladder. Don't neglect this condition and lose valuable, restful sleep.

When disorder of kidney function permits poisonous matter to remain in your blood, it may also cause nagging backache, rheumatic pains, leg pains, loss of pep and energy, swelling, puffiness under the eyes, headaches and dizziness.

Don't wait! Ask your druggist for Doan's Pills, used successfully by millions for over 40 years. They give happy relief and will help the 15 miles of kidney tubes flush out poisonous waste from your blood. Get Doan's Pills.

134 Give Blood At Stand Held At Armory

Six Donors Give For Seventh Time At Red Cross Clinic Held Yesterday

One hundred and thirty four people gave blood yesterday at the Red Cross Blood Stand held at the State Armory. Six of the donors gave blood for the seventh time: Mrs. John H. Cooper, Mary M. Hoff, William G. Oaksmith, John Peel, Earl J. Thomson, and Capt. T. R. Wirth.

M. J. Axelrod and E. Roberts gave for the sixth time, and Lt. Comdr. T. H. Brittan, B. F. Brown, F. S. Campbell, Edna Iona Hopkins, Raymond W. Knackstet, Lt. (jg) Charles W. Seekins, Ensign R. C. Shaw, were fifth time donors.

Other blood donors were: 4th time—M. H. Boisseau, A. W. Britton, R. E. Brouse, Mrs. Carrie Casey, James V. Cherico, H. T. Chaney, Ernest Collins, T. Collison, W. F. Flood. H. J. Franklin, E .Hall, Arthur Johnson, Lt. Wm. T. Lyons, W. Matthai, A. McPherson, Wm. Mortenson, Russell Miller, Edith M. Mladoticky, W. P. Moreland, W. E. Murphy, Irene Nelson, Ralph C. Nutwell, R. A. Schreyer, Jr., Elmer Smith, Lawrence Springfield, C. W. Suit, W. J. Thomas, Alvin Trott, Jacob C. Wagner, P. J. Wiegard, Lawrence Wilde, F. W. Windsor.

Third time donors—W. Aamold, Walter Achenback, T. R. Basil, Ellis Beavin, G. W. Berry, W. Lee Burtis, Thomas Brewer, R. C. Chambers, J. B. Collins, Freddie Dean, Phylis Doddridge, J. C. Ford, Miss Regina Graham, Mrs. A. B. Griggs, J. B. Hulse, Lt. R. W. Rawson, Wm. Siwak, Mrs. A. L. Smith, Mrs. Edward B. Storm, H. B. aylor, Comdr. T. A. Torgerson, Mrs. Glendora Ward.

Second time donors—Mrs. Ottie Bassford, R. G. Beall, F. R. Boore, Georgia Bradford, W. N. Brashears, A. A. Burns, George Clark, C. DePrine, R. Fowler, C. A. Frank, Lt. H. F. Gemine, Mrs. Rosalie Jefferson, Lt. C. Elsesser, A. Landon, A. L. Lucas, Lt. Comdr. R. E. Magoffin, Comdr. Harrison McIntire, W. C. Mills, Lt. D. S. Moore, W. T. Owens, J. N. Rammacher, J. F. Roberts C. F. Runyon, Fred Segelken, Chief Yeoman G. T. Shaull, E. A. Sibley, M. L. Snook, T. G. Taylor, E. Tucker, Lt. Comdr. C. S. Walsh, Elizabeth Wetsel, B. W. Whittington, John R. Wilkie, Jr., A. L. Robinson, Ensign John K. Richter.

First time donors—Comdr. E. W. Abbot, Virginia Aiello, Marie Bowen, Aubrey Brown, Elmira Burns, O. David Colburn, J. C. Dennison, Comdr. T. H. DuBois, Helen ' Dunaway, F. A. Ehberg, Betty Felton, Lt. Comdr. A. B. Harmon, Lt. Comdr. R. Hartford, Comdr. J. W. Howard, T. Johnson, W. J. Lee, T. J. Lehres, Paul T. Ludwig, Edith Mladonicky, Lt. G. B. Rodman, Catherine Swann, Josiah Tice, Gilbert Waite, L. E. Williams, Betty Schwaler, Margaret Zang, Doris Biddle, Mrs. B. C. Pooks, Stringfellow Barr, John S. Kieffer, PhM2c Jean McMannus.

"O" TYPE BLOOD NEEDED FOR DAILY PLANE TRIP TO BATTLEFIELDS

Blood flowing in the veins of people in Annapolis one morning will be ready to give to men wounded on the European battlefields the next day, according to a new plan announced by Mrs. W. S. Cunningham, county chairman of the Red Cross Blood Donor Service.

People having the "O" type are asked to volunteer for this special blood service, as other types of blood have to be matched and cannot be used for direct transfusion on the field, which is so necessary to save the lives of the badly wounded.

A station wagon will leave the Court of Appeals building here every Wednesday morning at 8:30 beginning December 13, to take "O" type blood donors to Baltimore. Seven donors can be transported each trip, and this number has volunteered for the first one. Mrs. Cunningham said.

"O" type blood, which anybody can absorb with beneficial results, will be taken every morning at the Blood Center at 8 S. Calvert street, Baltimore and will be flown to Europe the same day, for use on the battlefields. The whole blood will keep, by a new process now in use, for 21 days.

The Baltimore Center will supply fifty pints of type "O" blood every day.

Menus Of The Day
Nutritious Biscuits

Tuna Fish and Noodle Casserole
Broccoli
Whole Wheat Baking Powder
Biscuits
Fruit Gelatin

(Recipes serve four)

Tuna Fish and Noodle Casserole

1 can tuna fish, flaked	1 cup milk
2 cups noodles, cooked	2 tablespoons parsley, chopped
2 tablespoons margarine	Salt and pepper
2 tablespoons flour	½ cup bread crumbs

Place layer of tuna fish in casserole and cover with layer of noodles. Repeat until fish and noodles are used up. Melt margarine in saucepan. Take off heat and mix with flour making a smooth paste. Return to heat and add milk stirring constantly. When mixture has thickened add parsley and salt and pepper to taste. Pour sauce over fish and noodles and top with bread crumbs. Bake at 350° for 20 minutes.

Whole Wheat Baking Powder Biscuits

½ cup unsifted whole wheat flour	2 tablespoons
¾ cup sifted all-purpose flour	½ teaspoon salt
1½ teaspoons baking powder	fortified margarine
	½ cup milk

Combine the dry ingredients and mix well. Cut the margarine into them until the mixture is the consistency of coarse corn meal. Add enough of the milk while stirring vigorously to make a soft dough that can be easily handled. Turn onto lightly floured board and knead vigorously about twenty seconds. Roll or pat into a sheet about one inch thick. Cut into rounds and place on a greased baking pan. Bake at 450° for 12-15 minutes.

CLASSIFIED ADS

For Rent

FOR RENT—7 room modern bungalow on Mago Vista Road about half mile from Jones Station. $50.00. month. Apply 1635 Ceddox street, Curtis Bay. d-11

FOR RENT—Large 6 room bungalow, all modern improvements, Edgewater, Maryland, Call Annapolis 5592 after 12 noon, Sunday afternoon only. d-11

FOR RENT — Apartment, small furnished, light housekeeping. Working couple preferred. 801 West street. d-13

FOR RENT—Two office rooms, wash room, store room and 4 car garage, located in West Annapolis. Ideal for any business that would require same. Call 4187 or 3035. d-9

FOR RENT—Furnished two bedroom apartment, Eastport. Adults only. Fred E. Voges, Real Estate, 47 Maryland avenue, Dial 4477. d-12

FOR RENT—Three bedroom furnished house on Bay Ridge road. Write Box 41, Evening Capital. tf

For Sale

FOR SALE—Man's size 38 genuine pony leather coat, excellent condition, owner in service, cost $30.00, will sell for $20.00 Dial 4060. d-9

FOR SALE—Ready built ornamental brick fireplace for use with electric logs or heater. $40.00. Also brass andirons and electric logs. Pre-war red mohair living room set. Call 5481 after 6:30 P. M. d-11

FOR SALE—40 ft. cabin cruiser. Fully equpped with Gray engine No. 6. First class condition. Dial 5279. d-9

FOR SALE—Fula Lady, cairn terrier, female, twenty months old $50.00. Also two baby males, $45.00 each. Call 6441. d-14

FOR SALE—Palmer Marine Transmission, enclosed model H-1 cond., suitable up to 50 H.P. $50.00. Phone 5256. d-11

FOR SALE—48 Base Carmen Accordian. Keeney's, 23 Randall street. tf

FOR SALE — Truxton Heights—Lots 50' x 300', only $200.00. On terms if desired. Out Spa Road, only 1 mile from Church Circle. City water available. See Mr. W. B. Monday on property, or call Annapolis 4821. xx

FOR SALE—Violin and bow, imported 19 key accordian, fine brown overcoat, size 42. Call 5386 after 6 P. M d-9

FOR SALE — Regulation size Boy's Schwinn bicycle $45.00. Dial 4206. d-9

FOR SALE—Large Doll House, carriage, kitchen cabinet, stove ice box, high chair, bed also Federal Enlarging machine. Dial 4346. d-13

FOR SALE—Hospital Bed and wheel chair, good condition. Phone 5200. d-9

FOR SALE—201 Severn avenue, 5 rooms and bath. Now rented at $42.00 monthly. Reasonable. Phone 4993. d-9

FOR SALE—Six 20 ft. high Norway Spruce, ideal for Xmas trees. Call 4794 or Box 374, Annapolis. d-12

FOR SALE—Oriole gas stove in good condition. Phone 2183 or call at 711 Severn avenue, Eastport. d-8

FOR SALE — Pedigreed Boston Bull puppies, male and female, $20.00 and $25.00. Apply 322 Adams street, Eastport. d-8

FOR SALE—One girls victory bicycle. 54 West street. Call from 6 P. M. until 9 P. M. d-8

FOR SALE — Oak, Pine and Mixed wood. Prompt delivery. Phone 5475. d-9

FOR SALE — Complete confectionery store fixtures, including fountain, restaurant range, floor cases, electric refrigerator, etc. Want buyer for entire lot. Phone 3264. tf

FOR SALE—Seasoned oak wood. Shady Oak. Call 6205. $20.00 per cord. d-19

FOR SALE — Round Bay on Severn—Round Bay Road, excellent three bedroom home; fireplace, bath, extra shower, oil heat, hot water. screened porches, garage, near beach and electric line. Unusual opportunity to obtain a comfortable and well kept home at only $8,300 in fee. Generously financed. See it today. H. M. Sandrock, Round Bay, Md. Call Severna Park 191. d-11

FOR SALE—Mixed wood. Any length. Quick delivery. Call 4071. tf

Help Wanted—Female

HELP WANTED FEMALE — Reliable maid full or part time. Apply 103 Dreams Landing. d-9

HELP WANTED FEMALE — Girl or woman, steady position, pleasant saleswork in Children's Store. Full or part time. Apply Gordon's Church Circle. tf

Help Wantd—Male 4

HELP WANTED MALE—Barber $35.00 weekly guarantee and commission. Naval Academy Officers' Club Barber Shop. Nick Florestano. d-8

HELP WANTED MALE—Man to learn Piano Repairing, steady work. Keeney's. 23 Randall street. tf

Repair Work

REPAIR WORK—Your old fur coat can be restyled with all the features of a new coat. This complete remodeling is priced from $30.00. For all particulars phone 4788. tf

Situations—Male, Female 15

SITUATION WANTED FEMALE—Efficient stenographer desires part time employment. Write Evening Capital Box 42. d-11

Wanted 6

WANTED — Two passengers, Miami Beach next week. References. Phone 4605. d-11

WANTED — Two bedroom furnished apartment or small house by December 20. Phone 4412. d-9

WANTED—$25.00 reward for information resulting in rental of house or first floor apartment, in Annapolis or Eastport. Call 2611 Ext. 2. d-9

WANTED—Late model auto in good condition, also late model house trailer. No dealer. Cash. Call 5688. d-9

WANTED — Ride to Texas or thereabouts, around December 17th. Will share expenses. Phone or write Richard Doan, Severn School, Severna Park. d-9

WANTED — Elderly lady occupyying small dwelling alone desires companion with practical nurse ability. Near Severna Park and B & A electric line. State proposition that you feel would be mutually agreeable and pleasant. Write Box 26, Evening Capital. tf

Lost and Found 8

LOST—Eight ration books No.. 3 and 4. Massie, Gene, Franklin, Kyle, Willard, Massie, Franklin, Kyle Early. Route 2, Annapolis. d-11

LOST—Two ration books No. 3 and two No. 4. Madeline Healy and William Healy, Jr. 1022 Bay Ridge avenue, Eastport. d-11

LOST—Ration book No. 4, Carolyn H. Hill, Lake Placid, New York. d-11

LOST—Black change purse, containing $10.00 bill and change, foot of Main street, Wednesday. Reward. Phone 3411. d-8

LOST—A and C gas ration coupons. Clarence Smith, Route 3, Box 759, Annapolis, Md. d-8

LOST—Ration book No. 4 belonging to Deloris Parker, 21 O'Bryan Court. d-8

LOST—Ration book No. 4. Mamie F. Bowie, 1808 Popular avenue, Sims Crossing, Parole, Md. d-8

LOST—Ration book No. 3. Alvin Hudson, Jr., 100 College Creek Terrace. d-8

LOST—Bag having identification: Miss Matilda Chase and Keys. Finder please call Annapolis 4889. d-8

LOST—Near No. 5 Maryland avenue, round beaver hat with brown suede top. If found phone reverse charges Baltimore, University 4590. d-8

LOST—Gasoline ration "A" book. Paris Anderson, 92 East street. d-8

LOST — Gas ration book. New "A." Frank Wimmer, Jr., Glen Burnie, Md. d-9

LOST — Old gasoline ration book A. Charles Cromwell, RFD No. 2, Box 551, Annapolis. d-9

LOST — Pair Black Buckle Florsheim shoes size 7½ D, delivered by mistake by Schiff's Shoe Repair Shop, Main street. Phone 4386, Lt. Lyle C. Read. d-9

LOST—Black worn cloth change purse containing $20.00 bill, 45c and two bus tokens in vicinity of upper Main street about 5 P. M. Monday. Please return to Evening Capital office. Reward from Mrs. Wm. E. Somers, RFD 3, Annapolis. d-8

Miscellaneous 12

MISCELLANEOUS—Bargain Toy Store. Opening at 20½ West street. Every Friday and Saturday until Christmas. xx

MISCELLANEOUS — Lawn mowers hand and band saws sharpened and re-toothing done by machine. Morris Rank, Best Gate Road. Phone 5570. tf

MISCELLANEOUS — We deliver anything — any where. Personal Delivery Service. Phone: 2781. tf

MISCELLANEOUS — Used cars, any make, any model, bought and sold. Harry's Super-Service, West and Southgate. Phone: 4000. tf

MISCELLANEOUS—Cesspools and septic tanks cleaned. Rates moderate. Modern equipment. J. P. Devine, Phone Linthicum 170-J. tf

IN MEMORIAM

JONETT — At his home, 74 Franklin street at 9:30 A. M., Thursday, December 7, 1944; Sautford Jonett, beloved son of the late Robert and Julia Jonett of Mt. Sterling, Ky., and husband of the late Nannie B. Jonett and father of Mrs. Louise E. Russell.

Funeral services will be held at Mt. Moriah A.M.E. Church, Sunday at 2 P. M., Rev. S. W. Williams, pastor officiating. Body will lay in state at church from 8 P. M. until 11:30 P. M. Saturday, December 9, afterwards resting at his home. J. B. Johnson mortician. d-9

IN MEMORIAM

ANDERSON—In loving memory of our dear father and grandfather, Rev. Matthew Anderson, who departed this life fifteen years ago, yesterday, December 7, 1929.

Dark and thorny was the desert,
Through it father, you made your way.
Just beyond the vale of sorrow
Were the fields of an endless day.

What peaceful hours we once enjoyed,
How sweet the memory still,
But it has left an aching heart
This world can never fill.

By his daughter, Harriet I. Adams, and grandchildren

WANTED

WOMEN 20 TO 36 TO SERVE IN THE U. S. NAVY

WAVES

ALBERT J. GOODMAN
Attorney at Law

SALE OF AUTOMOBILE
Under Chapter 417, Acts of 1924.

Notice is hereby given to George W. Mitchell, 56 Pleasant Street, Annapolis, Maryland, last address given, that we will sell for storage, repairs and other lawful charges, on the premises of the Universal Motors, 26 West Street, Annapolis, Maryland, on

TUESDAY, DECEMBER 26, 1944,
AT 2 O'CLOCK P. M.,

one 1935 Ford Tudor Sedan, Engine No. 18-2168178, left on said premises.

Terms: Cash. Immediate removal required.

WM. B. ELLIOTT, Auctioneer d-15

HELP WANTED—MALE AND FEMALE

STATE EMPLOYMENT COMMISSIONER
22 LIGHT STREET, BALTO-2, MD.

HELP WANTED

Cottage Officer	$1200	Occupational Therapist	$1300
Cottage Officer (Laundry)	1200	Mechanical Handyman	1000
Cottage Supervisor	1300	Senior Account Clerk	1500
Junior Account Clerk	1200	Vocational Instructor (Gardening and Canning)	1200

These positions are PERMANENT. Law provides 5% automatic ANNUAL INCREASE in the ENTRANCE SALARY up to five years; liberal VACATION and SICK LEAVE and RETIREMENT BENEFITS.

All meals and laundry free
Private dining room for officers
Individual room and bath
New modern attractive buildings
Full hospital insurance (allowing 21-day hospital care at $9.00 per year)
25 Minutes from Baltimore on the B. & O. Railroad.

Closing date for receiving applications: December 20, 1944

APPLY IN WRITING FOR APPOINTMENT
SUPERINTENDENT, WOMAN'S PRISON
JESSUPS, MARYLAND

HELP WANTED

MALE AND FEMALE

Permanent Employment With The State of Maryland

OPENINGS FOR WHITE AND NEGRO APPLICANTS

To men and women of good health and sound physical condition who seek future security the STATE OF MARYLAND offers permanent employment for INSTITUTIONAL ATTENDANTS AND GUARDS, and office employees such as CLERKS, TYPIST, STENOGRAPHERS and ACCOUNT CLERKS, and a WIDE VARIETY OF OTHER OCCUPATIONS, protected by its Merit System.

To qualifying applicants the State offers reasonable compensation with AUTOMATIC INCREASES, and in some occupations maintenance. Also LIBERAL VACATION and SICK LEAVE with pay, and RETIREMENT BENEFITS under the State Employees' Retirement System.

If interested in your future security through permanent employment write to or call on the undersigned giving your qualifications for any employment you desire and you will receive prompt consideration.

W. D. OWENS, State Employment Commissioner
22 Light Street, Baltimore-2, Md.

$8,950

is a lot to pay for an electric refrigerator and electric stove, but look what goes with it! One acre of ground in town, eight room modern house of unique design. Oil heat, attached garage. Two other buildings on grounds. Beautiful shrubbery and fruit trees. One half block from public service and high school buses, five blocks from grammar school. Property is attractively financed.

T. Carroll Worthington

236 MAIN STREET — DIAL 2525

MODEST MAIDENS

Trademark Registered U. S. Patent Office

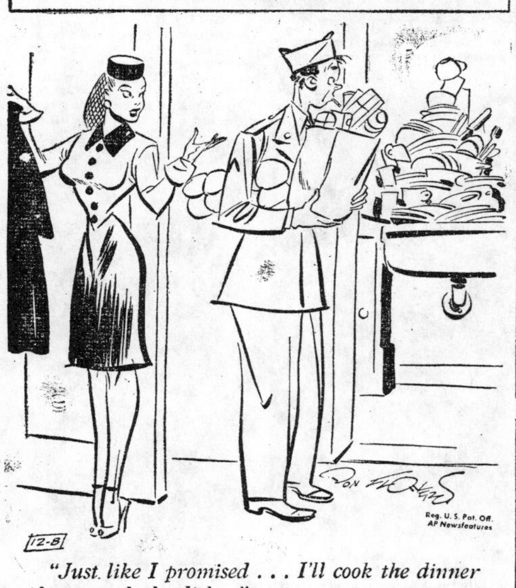

"Just like I promised . . . I'll cook the dinner if you wash the dishes."

SCORCHY SMITH

Don't Lay That Pistol Down

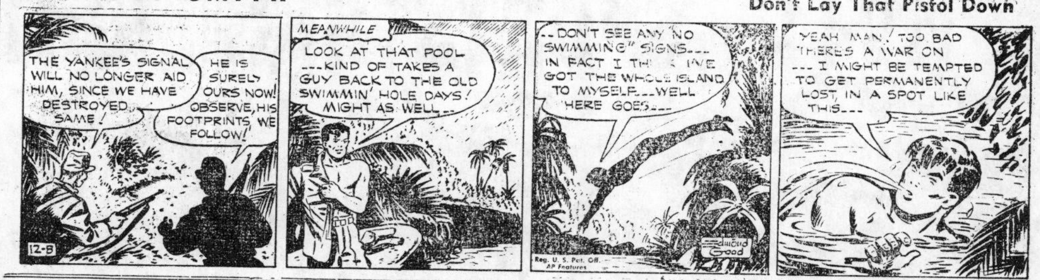

OAKY DOAKS

Trademark Registered U. S. Patent Office

Busy Butch

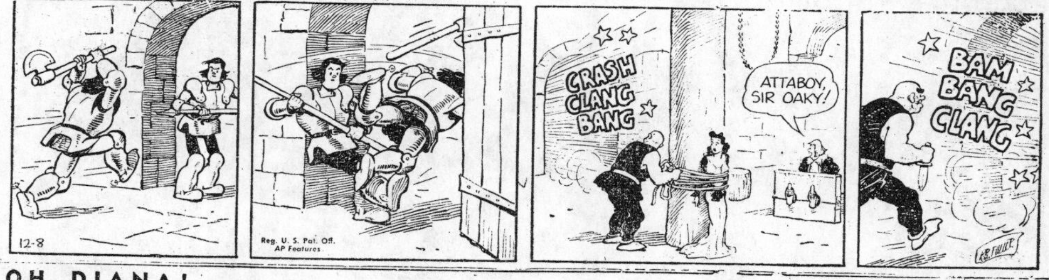

OH, DIANA!

Lost Appeal

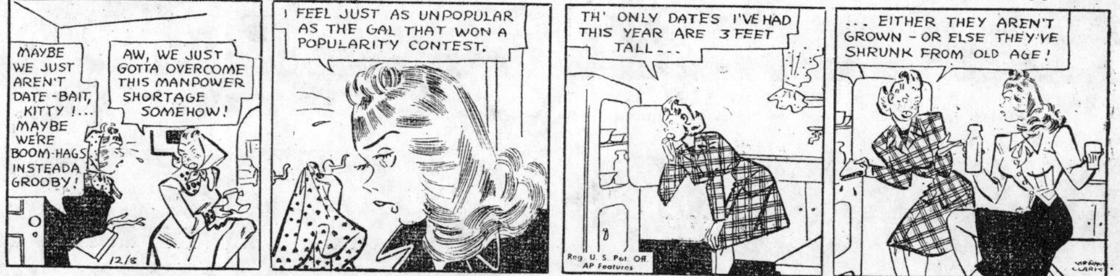

DICKIE DARE

Could Be?

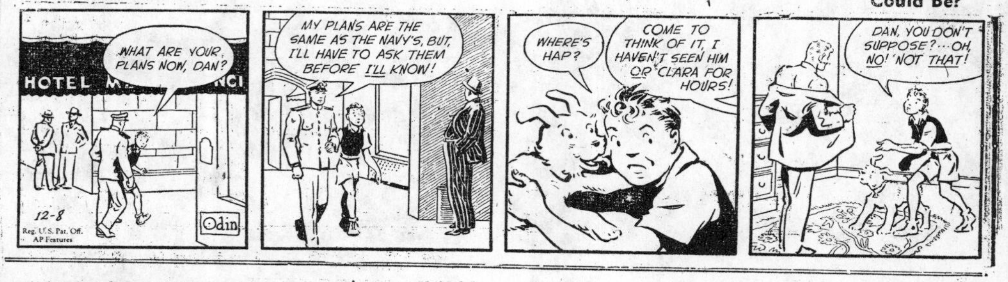

HOMER HOOPEE

Trademark Registered U. S. Patent Office

Program Notes

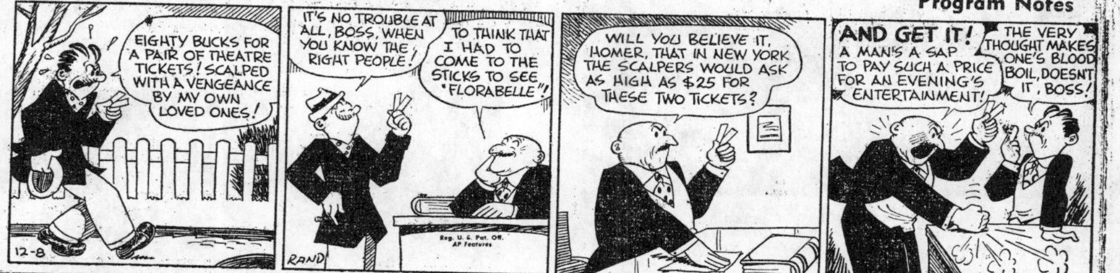

THE ADVENTURES OF PATSY

He Leads With His Chin

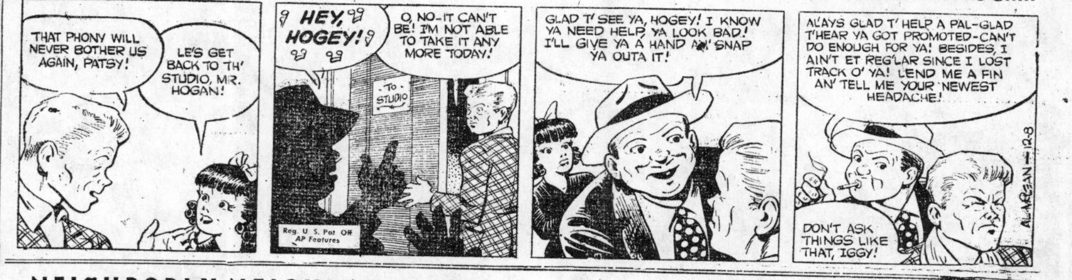

NEIGHBORLY NEIGHBORS

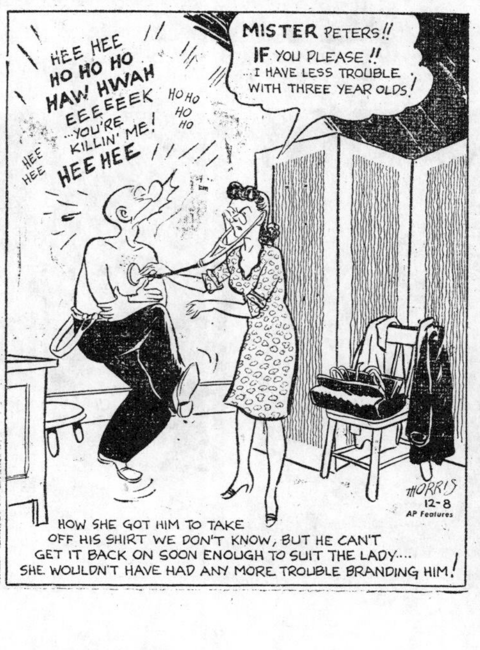

THE DOOLITTLES

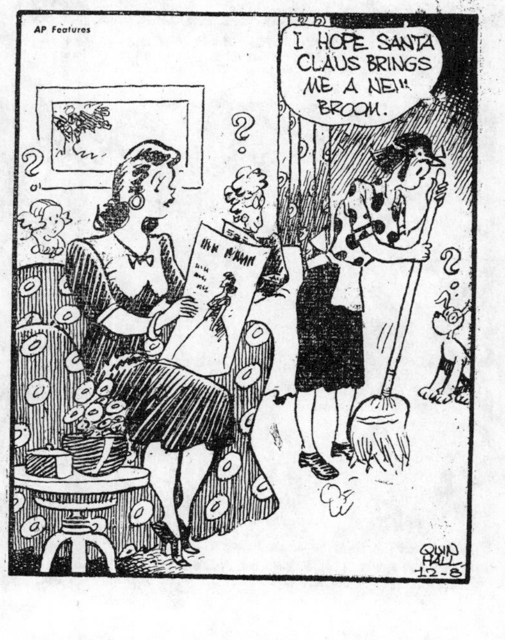

1944 - SPORTS HIGHLIGHTS OF A WAR YEAR - 1944

SUCCUMBS — Death claimed Judge Kenesaw Mountain Landis (above), high commissioner of baseball for a generation. Pending naming of a successor, Ford Frick, Will Harridge and Leslie O'Connor were chosen to administer the office.

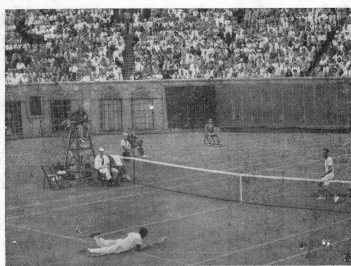

DIVE AT FOREST HILLS—Francisco Segura misses the ball and takes a dive in Forest Hills tennis match with Bill Talbert, who later lost in men's finals to Sgt. Frank Parker.

PAYOFF PLAY AS CARDS WON SERIES—The Cardinals won the world baseball series in an all-St. Louis six-game struggle with the Browns. Here Ray Sanders, Card first baseman, comes home in fourth inning rally that won final game, 3-1.

LIGHTWEIGHTS IN ACTION—With many fighters in the armed forces, boxing languished in the doldrums. One of the better title matches pitted Bob Montgomery (right) against Beau Jack in a 15-rounder won by Montgomery.

PENSIVE WINS KENTUCKY DERBY—Warren Wright's Pensive won the 70th running of the Kentucky Derby at Churchill Downs, with Broadcloth second and Stir Up third.

NO-HITTER— Jim Tobin (above), Boston Braves pitcher, won a place among baseball's elite with a no-hit game against Brooklyn April 27. Voted "most valuable" in their leagues were Tigers' Harold Newhouser and Cards' Marty Marion.

UTAH CAGERS WIN—Herb Wilinson and Arnold Ferrin of Utah, with competition from Bill Kostorfs (3) of St. John's, leap for a rebound in the Madison Square Garden basketball final which gave Utah the national title.

ARMY TOUCHDOWN ROMP — Standout football team of the year was Army, victor over all opposition, including Navy. Here John Minor runs to a score against Notre Dame, beaten 59-0.

MILER — Arne Andersson (above) of Sweden set a new world record of 4:01.6 for the mile at Stockholm July 18. Gil Dodds of Boston turned in a new indoor record, making a one-man race of the Bankers mile at the Chicago Relays in 4:06.4.

HORSE OF THE YEAR—Twilight Tear (above), three-year-old filly owned by Warren Wright, was named "horse of the year" for her string of 11 straight track victories and her triumphs in the Pimlico Special and Arlington Classic.

GRIDIRON STAR — Les Horvath of Ohio State University, shown with the Heisman trophy, was voted the outstanding college football player in a poll of 700 sports writers.

GI SPORTS IN FAR PLACES—Baseball, football and other typical American sports were seen in remote corners of the world. Here bronzed GI's play volleyball at a New Guinea camp.

THREE-TIME WINNER — Pauline Betz of Los Angeles won the women's tennis singles for the third year in succession. Above Miss Betz (left), holding the trophy emblematic of the title, talks with runner-up Margaret Osborne.

'CORN TASSEL' CLASSIC—Yankee Maid, with Henry Thomas driving, won the Hambletonian trotting classic, returned this year to its traditional site at Goshen, N. Y.

CLASSIFIED ADS

For Rent

FOR RENT—Large heated front bedroom. 329 First Street, Eastport. Phone 4413. f-15

FOR RENT—Large bungalow-Severn River, directly on water near Annapolis. Beautifully furnished. Accomodates two small families. Each apartment has two sleeping rooms with bath between. Also seperate kitchen with electric refrig., elec. range, kitchen cabinet and sink. Each family sharing large porch and large living room with huge fieldstone open fireplace which seperates the two apartments. Phone, oil burner hot water heat, garge. Splendid roads. Immediate possession. Phone Annapolis 4060. Will accept reversed phone charges to Baltimore University 7229 and Mulberry 3784. f-14

FOR RENT—One bed room apartment. Apply Box 265, Severna Park Post Office. f-13

FOR RENT—Building at Parole. Suitable for Bar-b-que or restaurant. Call 4119. f-13

FOR RENT—House for June Week. Six rooms and bath. Hot and cold water. Located at Sylvan Shores, Riva, Maryland. Mr. James Insley. Apply at same address. f-15

For Sale

FOR SALE—Five room house. Now renting $55.00 per month. Price $4500.00 Immediate occupancy. Phone 3201. f-19

FOR SALE—Latest model Remington noiseless typewriter, two iron beds and springs, one large kitchen sink. Phone 2183. f-15

FOR SALE—Brown Val A Pak and matching traveling bag, excellent condition, set $15. Also large size rain resistant man's topcoat $5.00. Telephone 3397. f-15

FOR SALE—Double metal bed, complete, $15.00. Single metal bed, complete, $15.00. Phone 6483. f-14

FOR SALE—All wool Alexander Smith floor plan rug. 9 X 18. Phone 2908. f-14

FOR SALE—Drop side crib. Adjustable spring height. Good condition. Phone Bay Vista 2142. f-13

FOR SALE—One small upright piano, $150.00, one 8 piece Rattan dining room suite, $150.00, one 7 piece Rattan living room suite, $100.00. Phone 4940. f-16

FOR SALE—19 acres of land near Lam Hass in Skidmore. Apply Benjamin Ricks, Severna Park. f-20

FOR SALE—Modern house and 6 lots at Truxton Heights. Contact William H. Cox, Weems Creek. Phone 6248. f-14

FOR SALE—Oak, pine, mixed wood. Any length. Quick delivery. Carr Brothers. Phone 3151. tf

FOR SALE—Stove and fireplace wood. Seasoned oak and pine. Quick delivery. Phone 5446. Fred L. O'Dell. tf

FOR SALE—Mixed wood. Any length. Quick delivery. Call 4071. tf

Lost and Found 8

LOST—Five number four ration books. Charles, Anna, Virginia, William and Graham Russell, 1303 West Street, Annapolis, Maryland. f-13

LOST—Black cocker spaniel puppy. Answers to name of Ricky. Reward. Phone 3816. f-15

LOST—Ration book number two. John R. Johnson, 208 Clay Street. f-15

LOST—Ration book number three. Ruth Chambers, Parole, Md. f-15

LOST—Number four ration book. Lillian Herr, 38 Maryland Ave. f-15

LOST—One gold earring with brilliant stones. Vicinity of Southgate and Lafayette. Phone 2042. Reward. f-19

FOUND—One 14 and one 16 foot bateau. Found at Beverly Beach. Write Richard Dawson, Mayo, Maryland. f-14

Help Wanted Male or Female 5

HELP WANTED MALE OR FEMALE—Store clerk, short hours, good pay. Apply Taubman's, 149 Main Street. f-13

HELP WANTED MALE OR FEMALE—Experienced pantry help. Good wages. Pleasant working conditions. Write Box 33, Evening Capital. tf

Miscellaneous

MISCELLANEOUS—Cesspools and septic tanks cleaned. Rates moderate. Modern equipment. J. P. Devine. Phone Linthicum 170-J. tf

MISCELLANEOUS—INCOME TAX — Assistance in preparing Federal and State Income Tax Returns by former Deputy Collector of Internal Revenue. Phone South Shore 3131. tf

MISCELLANEOUS — We deliver any thing — any where. Personal Delivery Service. Phone: 2781. tf

MISCELLANEOUS — Used cars, any make, any model, bought and sold. Harry's Super-Service, West and Southgate. Phone: 4000. tf

MISCELLANEOUS—Income tax returns prepared. 20 North West St.—2nd floor. 7 P. M. to 10 P. M. f-17

Personal

PERSONAL—MEN, WOMEN! OLD AT 40, 50, 60! Want to feel peppy, years younger? Ostrex Tonic Tables pep up bodies lacking iron; also contain vitamin B1, calcium. 35c taril size now only 29c. At all druggists—In Annapolis, at Read's Drug. f-15

Repair Work

REPAIR WORK—Fur repairing and remodeling. Phone 4788. tf

Help Wanted—Female 4

HELP WANTED FEMALE—HOUSEWIVES (white)—Can make $2 up an hour spare time taking orders for exclusive frocks. Free dress plan. Write MAISONETTE 11 W. 29th St., Baltimore-18. f-17

HELP WANTED FEMALE—Waitress. Good wages. Mirror Grill, 154 Main Street. tf

HELP WANTED FEMALE—Maid for general housework. References required. Phone 4226. f-16

HELP WANTED FEMALE—Experienced maid for general housework. Phone 2760. f-14

HELP WANTED FEMALE—Waitress. Good wages. Apply at Mandris Restaurant, 2 Market Space. f-19

HELP WANTED FEMALE — Maid desired. Part time. Competent. Light housework. 25 Murray Avenue. Phone 4947. f-14

HELP WANTED FEMALE—Full time maid. Experienced. Phone 3568. f-12

Wanted 6

WANTED—To rent rooms for June week. Phone Midshipman Trombola, Bancroft Hall. f-14

WANTED—To buy coach car in good condition. Phone 3454. f-17

WANTED—To Rent UNFURNISHED HOUSE with at least 3 bedrooms, in or near Annapolis. Phone 3454. f-17

WANTED—To rent or buy apartment or small house. Responsible couple. Mr. Taubman, 149 Main Street. Call 4700. f-17

WANTED — House in Eastport or Weems Creek for June week. Must accommodate 6 people. Midshipman J. L. Switzer, 5315 Bancroft Hall. f-14

WANTED—Girl checker. Apply in person. Rainbow Cleaner, 1801 West street. f-14

WANTED — Elderly lady occupyying small dwelling alone desires companion with practical nurse ability. Near Severna Park and B & A electric line. State proposition that you feel would be mutually agreeable and pleasant. ... 36, Evening Capital. tf

WANTED—Room for June Week for 3 people. Write Box 34, Evening Capital. f-15

WANTED—To buy a five drawer chiffonier and a dish cabinet. Phone 2275. f-13

WANTED—Large or small washing machine and record player. Phone 3313 f-13

WANTED—Wood lathe and jig saw. Phone 4461. f-15

Business Opportunity 25

BUSINESS OPPORTUNITIES— If you are a successful middle aged farmer, business or professional man with a major portion of your time available and are interested in earnings of from $5,000 to $10,000 per year and want to be your own boss it will pay you to communicate with us; it is helpful that you enjoy a wide acquaintance among farmers and live on a main highway within the vicinity of Annapolis. This business is established and can be conducted from your own home. For an interview write WEST'S FARM AGCY., Pittsburgh, 16, Pa. XX

FOR SALE

Complete Barber shop Equipmenet of the late Frederick C. Dreyer No. 106 West Street.

For particulars, apply to Benjamin Michaelson, Administrator, 15 School St., Phone 3551.

IN MEMGRIAM

HARRIS—In memory of my wife and mother, Mary Jane Harris, who passed away one year today, February 13, 1944.

We have only your memory, dear mother,
To remember our whole life through,
But the sweetness will linger forever,
As we treasure the image of you.
What is a home without a mother,
All things this world may send,
But when we lost our darling mother,
We lost our dearest friend.

By her husband and children.

NOTICE TO CREDITORS

Notice is hereby given that the subscriber, of Anne Arundel County, has obtained from the Orphans' Court of Anne Arundel County, in Maryland, letters of administration on the personal estate of

FREDERICK C. H. DREYER

late of Anne Arundel County, deceased. All persons having claims against the deceased, are hereby warned to exhibit the same, with the vouchers thereof, to the subscriber, on or before the

19TH DAY OF JULY, 1945.

They may otherwise, by law, be excluded from all benefit of said estate. All persons indebted to said estate are requested to make immediate payment.

Given under my hand this 16th day of January, 1945.

BENJAMIN MICHAELSON
Administrator f-20

NOTICE

Mrs. Leon Strauss of The Fashion, 53 Maryland avenue, is returning Thursday after spending ten days in New York on a buying trip.

NOTICE
THE CANDY SHOP
At 232 Main Street
Will be open all day
Wednesday, Valentine's Day
From 9 A. M. to 9 P. M.

GAME PARTY
WEST ANNAPOLIS FIRE HALL
Tuesday Night 8:15
February 13th
Benefit of
West Annapolis Ambulance Fund

Property Transfers In City And County Recorded In Court

From James A. Walton County Treasurer and others to Horace Larkins—lot of ground in fourth district containing 2 acres.

From James A. Walton County Treasurer and others to John O. Patton and wife—2 lots of ground at North Beach Park in eighth district.

From James A. Walton County Treasurer and others to David Thomas—lot of ground in fourth district containing 3 1-2 acres.

From The Solleys Business and Improvement Association to Trustees of the Marley Methodist Church—lot of ground at Stoney Creek in third district.

From James A. Lorens and wife to Amos T. Lorens—2 lots of ground at West Annapolis in second district.

From Miriam L. Gresser to Claire S. Gresser—lot of ground at Millersville in this county containing 14 8-10 acres.

From George W. Ewalt and wife to Mirian L. Gresser—lot of ground at Millersville this county containing 14 8-10 acres.

From William G. Meredith to Coca Cola Bottling Company—lot of ground in second district containing 341-1000 acres.

From Brooklyn Realty Company to Walter P. Owen and wife—lot of ground in fifth district.

From Rudy Downs and wife to John S. Strahorn Trustee—2 lots of ground at Masons Beach in seventh district.

From George E. Rullman Trustee to Robert L. Sears and wife—Property at Best Gate in second district.

From Annie A. Robertson to Carl S. Robertson and wife and others lot of ground in third district containing 80 acres.

From The Riviera Beach Development Company to Lester C. Scott and wife—2 lots of ground at Riviera Beach in third district.

From John J. Kirkness to Wilson K. Barnes and wife—lot of ground in third district containing 678908-100,000 acres.

From Warren Smadbeck and wife to Louis H. Bieligk and and others—2 lots of ground at Woodland Beach in first district.

From Elizabeth Foxwell and husband to Helen Kaifos—lot of ground near Odenton in fourth district.

From Gertrude C. Boswell and others to Marvin I. Anderson Trustee—lot of ground at Chalk Point in seventh district.

From Marvin I. Anderson Trustee to Robert M. Greenwood and wife—lot of ground at Chalk Point in seventh district.

From Dora G. Jenner and husband to William C. Heitmuller and wife 2 lots of ground at Cape Anne in seventh district.

From Lorenzo Turner and wife to Thomas Matthews and wife—lot of ground in seventh district containing 1-2 acres.

From Loranzo Turner and wife to William Pinkney and wife—lot of ground at Shady Side in seventh district containing 2 acres.

From John P. Paca, Jr. to John Morris and wife—lot of ground in fourth district.

From Jenevieve Roth and husband to John P. Paca, Jr.—2 lots of ground at Champion Forest in fourth district.

From Leora G. Schmidt and husband and others to Ada M. Gott—Property known as No. 48 Murry Avenue this city.

From Frederick W. Popp and wife to Max J. Dex and wife—2 lots of ground at Holly Hill Harbor in third district.

From Maggie Simms to James C. Simms—2 lots of ground in fourth district.

From Fred C. Conner and wife to Earl J. Leinster and wife—3 lots of ground at Herald Harbor in second district.

From Harry A. Carpenter and wife to Sidrey Williamson and wife—3 lots of ground at Dunbar Heights in fourth district.

Rationing Calendar

FUEL OIL

1944-45 heating season—Period 1, 2, 3 and 4 coupons now valid, Period 5, Mar. 1 All these coupons and the Period 4 and 5 coupons issued for the 1943-44 heating season expire on Aug. 31.

SHOES

Book No. 3, Airplane coupons No. 1, 2 and 3 good indefinitely. Loose coupons are not acceptable.

SUGAR

Coupon 34 book 4, valid for five pounds through Feb. 28. Coupons 35 good though June 2.

TIRES, GASOLINE

A-14 coupons, new book 4 valid for four gallons through Mar. 21.

B-5 and B-6 and C-5 and C-6 coupons good for five gallons.

T coupons valued at five gallons.

Motorists are required to write their license number and State of registration on face of coupons.

Eligibility for tires is based on the preferred mileage classification of the applicant

Always send in your mileage ration record when applying for any gasoline for operation of passenger automobiles. This is especially essential for furlough.

MEAT, FATS, OIL, CHEESE, FISH

Red coupons Q 5 through S 5 valid through March 31. Red coupons T 5 through X 5 valid through April 28. Red coupons, Y 5 and Z 5, A 2 through D 2 good through June 2.

FRUITS AND VEGETABLES

Blue coupons X 5 through B 2 valid through March 31. Blue coupons C 2 through G 2 valid through April 28. Blue coupons H 2 through M 2, good through June 2.

MODEST MAIDENS

Trademark Registered U. S. Patent Office

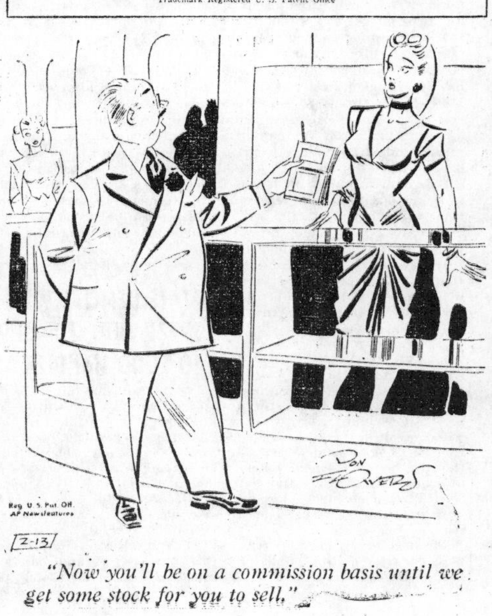

"Now you'll be on a commission basis until we get some stock for you to sell."

SCORCHY SMITH — Turned Up Missing

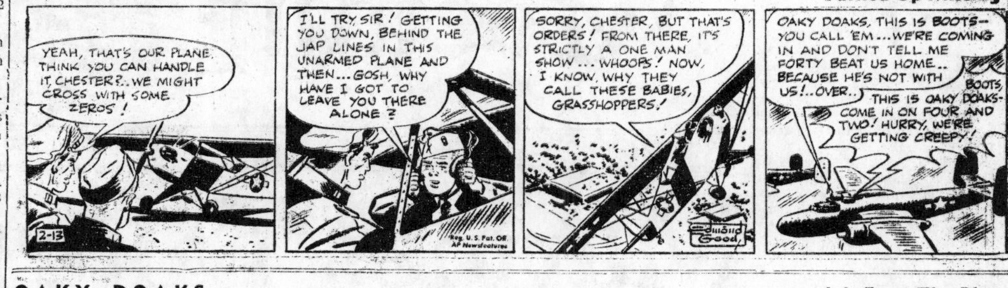

OAKY DOAKS — Jolt From The Blue

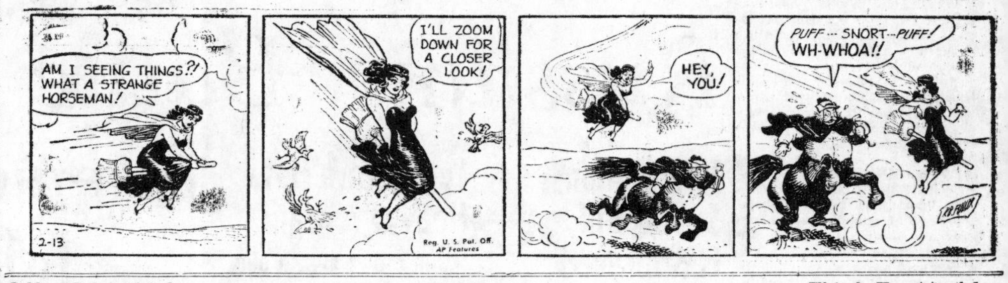

OH, DIANA! — This Is Too Much!

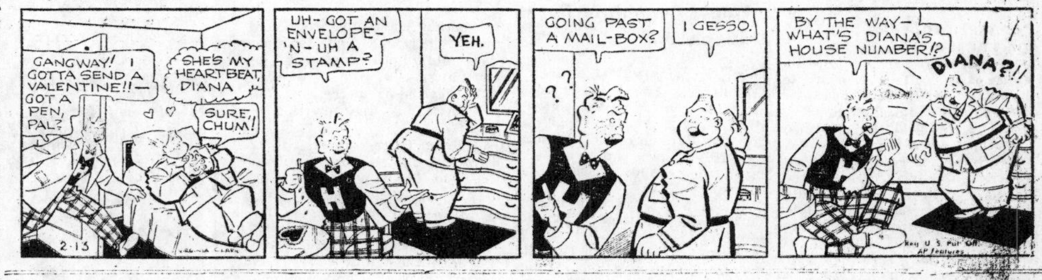

DICKIE DARE — Full Speed Astern!

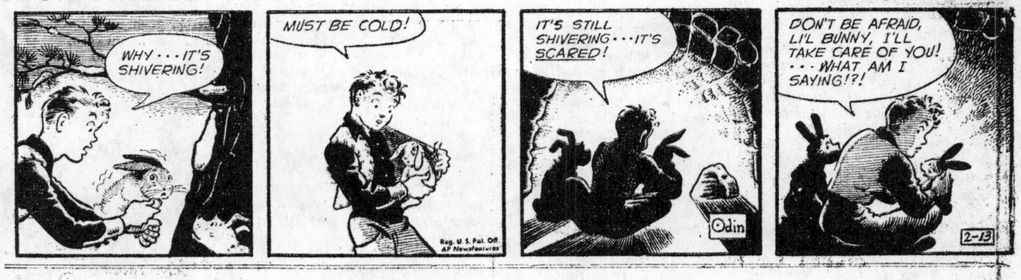

HOMER HOOPEE — Flying High

Trademark Registered U. S. Pat. Office

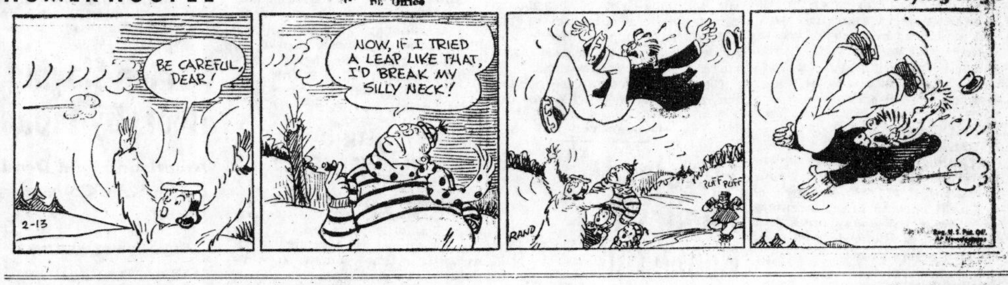

THE ADVENTURES OF PATSY — Ego Buster

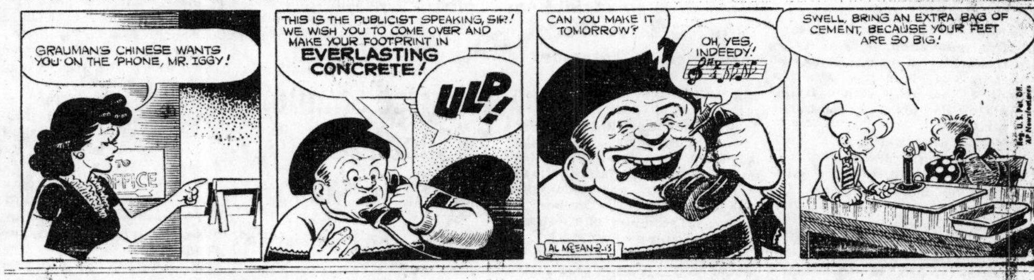

NEIGHBORLY NEIGHBORS

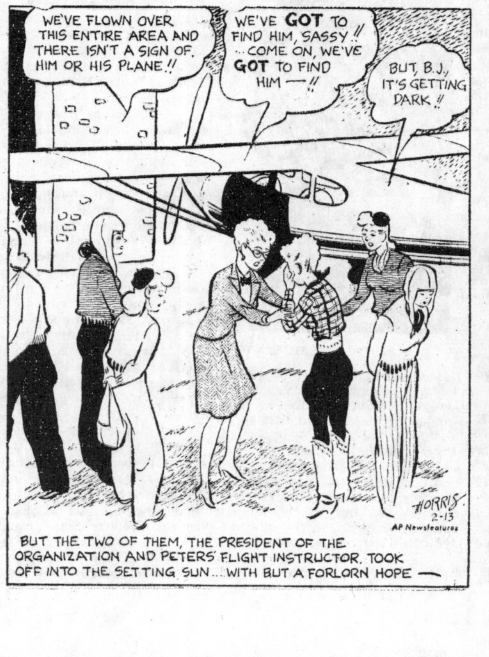

THE DOOLITTLES

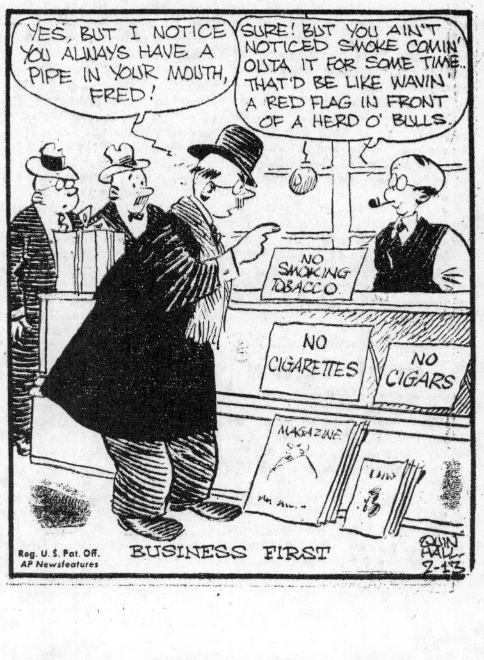

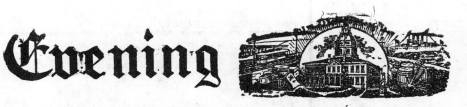

Evening Capital

WEATHER
Clear and continued cold tonight; Tuesday fair with a little warmer in afternoon.

VOL. LXI — NO. 41 | EVERY EVENING EXCEPT SUNDAY | ANNAPOLIS, MD., MONDAY, FEBRUARY 19, 1945 | SOUTHERN MARYLAND'S ONLY DAILY | THREE CENTS

Marines Take Iwo Jima Beachhead

Russians Battle Against Nazi Attacks

Veteran Invading Marines Fight Way Inland To One Of Iwo Jima Airfields

LATE NEWS

JAP FLEET WON'T COME OUT, HALSEY SAYS

Washington, Feb. 19 (AP) — Admiral William F. Halsey, Jr., paying a surprise visit to Washington, predicted today that the remnants of the Japanese fleet will not come out and fight in the current Pacific operations.

"We are going to have to dig them out," the commander of the Third Fleet told a news conference. "They have got very little left to fight with and what they have is in none too good shape."

BRIDGES DEMANDS ITALIAN TERMS

Washington, Feb. 19 (AP)—Senator Bridges (R-N.H.) came up today with a demand that the Allied authorities make public at last the Italian surrender terms.

He has a copy of purported terms, the authenticity of which neither he nor his source is sure of, which suggests a "hard peace" for the Italians

SAVINGS AND LOAN RESOURCES HIGHER

Baltimore, Feb. 19 (AP) — Resources of Maryland's insured Savings and Loan Associations increased $16,000,000 during 1944 to a year-end aggregate of $91,681,670, a report of officers showed today.

COUPON PEDDLERS GO FROM GAS TO FOOD

Washington, Feb. 19 (AP)—The Office of War Information said today that ration coupon counterfeiters, now "almost stopped" in the gasoline field, have "shifted their business to food."

"Government controls in gasoline rationing have been enforced so rigidly that recently-arrested peddlers (of bogus or stolen stamps) complained that the profiets did not equal the risk," the agency said in a report on black market dealings in a number of commodities.

COAL PRODUCTION INCREASES

Washington, Feb. 19 (AP)—Production of bituminous coal totaled 12,185,000 tons in the week ended Feb. 10, the highest since last November, the Solid Fuels Administration announced today.

Anthracite production in the week ended Feb. 10 totaled 1,117,000 tons, compared wit h842,000 tons in the previous week.

OFFICER REPORTED DEAD, IS PRISONER

Leonardtown, Md., Feb. 19 (AP)—A letter from Lt. John Hoskin Stone, who had been listed killed in action last November by the War Department, and whose death was confirmed by a friend, was received today by his mother, Mrs. Bessie L. Stone of Woodland Acres.

Lt. Stone wrote that he was a German war prisoner.

PACKINGHOUSE STRIKE THREATENED

Washington, Feb. 19 (AP) — The CIO-Packinghouse Workers Union, representing 125,000 employes of top meat packing firms, threatened a strike call today unless the WLB releases a long-delayed wage decision before noon.

CONFESSES BEATING MOTHER TO DEATH

Detroit, Feb. 19 (AP)—Prosecutor Gerald K. O'Brien of Wayne county announced today that 16-year-old Elvin Kent had confessed that he beat his mother, Mrs. Ida Kent, 43, to death with a frying pan Thursday night in resentment at a rebuke.

O'Brien, who said he would seek a first degree murder warrant, asserted Elvin, a tall, athletic youth ascribed his motivation to an "Act Of God."

FISHERY BILL OPPOSED BY COMMISSION

Baltimore, Feb. 19 (AP)—Chairman Edwin Warfield, Jr., of the Tidewater Fisheries Commission declared today that a bill to alter the present fishery management law by permitting unlimited fishing would "nullify the gains already made toward conservation and rehabilitation."

As a result, Warfield said, the commission's opposition to the measure (H B 170) will be expressed to State legislators at a hearing before the House fish and fisheries committee tomorrow in Annapolis.

CHURCHILL BACK IN ENGLAND

London, Feb. 19 (AP)— Prime Minister Churchill returned to England today from the Crimea conference after stops at Athens and Cairo.

Local Tides

TOMORROW

High water — 11:58 P. M. 0.4 feet; 1:12 P. M., 0.9 feet. Low water—6:23 A. M., 8:08 P. M.

Moon rises 1:08 A. M.; sets 3:02 P. M.

Sun rises 7:54 A. M.; sets 6:47 P. M.

Tides are given for Annapolis. For Sandy Point, add 15 minutes. For Thomas Point shoal, subtract 30 minutes.

Nine Billion Supply Bill Is Approved

House Committee Backs Supply Bill

WASHINGTON, Feb. 19 (AP)—Highlighted by a $4,500,000,000 item for interest on the National debt, a $9,163,071,163 supply bill for the Treasury and Postoffice Departments was approved today by the House Appropriations committee.

It is to finance two agencies during the 12 months starting next July 1.

Only $1,342,813,090 of the total are direct appropriations, for actual operations of the two agencies, the balance consisting of so-called permanent and indefinite appropriations for such things as debt interest and tax refunds.

The $4,500,000,000 interest estimated for 1946 is an increase of $750,000,000 over estimated current year payments for that purpose. It assumes that the national debt will be $292,000,000,000 by June 30, 1946, an increase of $58'000,000,000 over the present debt.

The Treasury's share of the total direct apprORiations is $285,76,800, a reduction of $10,748,300 from budget estimates and $4,688,497 below appropriations for the present year.

Postoffice Department

For the Postoffice Department, the bill carries $1,057,049,290 in direct funds, a reduction of $8,486,430 from budget estimates and a decrease of $55,185,232 from current year appropriations.

However, the committee pointed out, neither fund provides for ov-

(Continued On Page Six)

Cleveland Replies To Boone Bill

Improved Financial Condition Of St. John's Outlined In Statement

A statement showing the improved financial condition of St. John's College, which has received gifts of more than a million dollars since the present administration took over the affairs of the institution in 1937, was made public today by Richard F. Cleveland, of Baltimore, secretary of the board of visitors and governors.

The statement was made in answer to a bill introduced in the Legislature recently by Delegate Bertram L. Boone, 2nd, of Baltimore, which called for a commission to study St. John's with a view to making it part of the State educational system.

In explaining his bill at the time he introduced it Delegate Boone said the college was "going to pot" and that the state, which has appropriated funds for the college since 1911 in return for scholarships, was not getting a fair return for its investment.

Finances Outlined

Mr. Cleveland's statement follows:

"Mr. Bertram Boone's proposal to the House of Delegates that a committee be formed, in effect, to provide decent burial for St. John's College, because, in his reported phrase, 'the thing has gone to pot,' requires thorough consideration. As secretary of the board of visitors and governors of the college, I submit brief facts and a constructive proposal.

"Before the present administration took over the affairs of St. John's College in July, 1937, it owed $300,000, plus interest, on an overdue mortgage: it owed $50,000, unsecured, to a New York bank, and was several months in arrears to the extent of about $18,000 to trade creditors.

"Morale was very low, for finan-

(Continued On Page Two)

Legislature Has Heavy Program

"Jim Crow" Repeal Bill In House Committee

Another heavy program of committee hearings and expanded floor work on a number of important issues are in store for State legislators in the new General Assembly week starting tonight.

A lower House committee likely will start preliminary work on the "Jim Crow" repeal bill which passed the Senate 20 to 9 last Thursday, budget hearings featuring State Department heads will be continued in the Senate Finance and House Ways and Means Committee, and another of the "home rule" bills will come up for a public airing.

Just which committee will get the "Jim Crow" measure is unknown, since it has yet to be sent over by the Senate, but it probably will be the judiciary headed by Delegate Milton Tolle (D-Baltimore Co).

The Senate Judicial Proceedings Committee is set to send an unfavorable report to the floor on a bill which would place regulatory control of building and loan associations in the State Banking Commission.

REBEKAH LODGE MEETING TONIGHT

Annapolis Rebekah Lodge Number 73, I.O.O.F., will hold a meeting tonight at 8 o'clock in the Daughters of America Hall on Conduit street. The deputy, Mrs. Lillian Mack, of Glen Burnie, and several visitors will be present and refreshments will be served.

FERRY LINK OUT FOR SIX WEEKS

The State Roads Commission says that service on the Romancoke-Claiborne ferry probably will not be resumed for about six weeks—the time required to overhaul the three boats.

An emergency schedule now is in effect for the Sandy Point-Matapeake run. One of the vessels normally assigned to that route is being repaired.

Maurice Samuel To Speak At Forum Tomorrow

Author And Publicist To Give Lecture

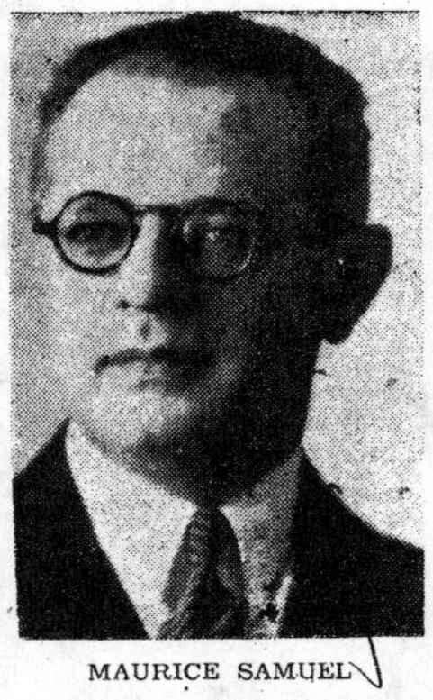

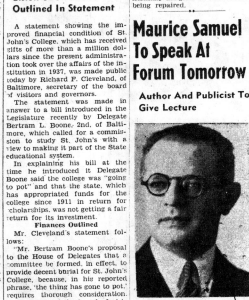

MAURICE SAMUEL

Maurice Samuel, author, traveller and publicist will speak at the Jewish Community Center Forum, 17 West street, at 8:30 P. M. tomorrow on "The Hope of our People for the Future."

Mr. Samuel occupies a unique position in American Jewish life. For the last twenty-five years he has served, through the written and spoken word, as the interpreter of Jewish values both to the

(Continued On Page Six)

THE EVENING CAPITAL ON GUADALCANAL

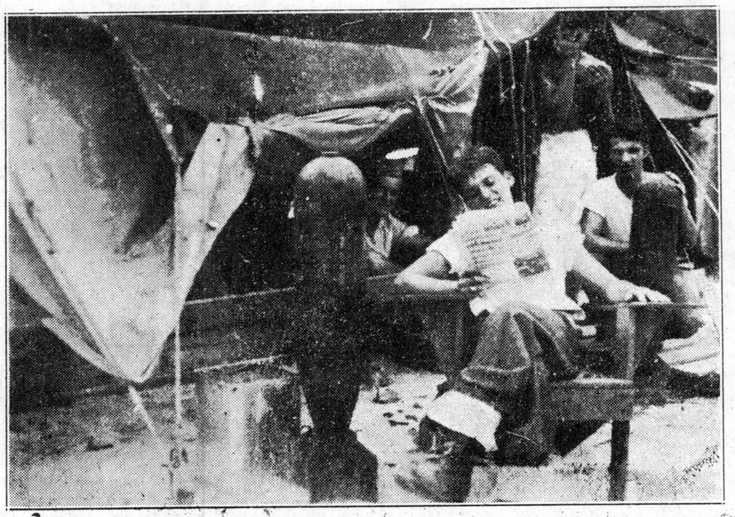

Seaman James E. Williams, first class, Seabee, son of Mr. and Mrs. Joseph W. Williams, 533 Tyler avenue, Eastport, catches up with the home town news through the pages of The Evening Capital as he relaxes on Guadalcanal.

KILTED SCOTS BATTLING NAZIS IN CENTER OF FORTIFIED GOCH

(By the Associated Press)

Invading American Marines have established a secure beachhead on Iwo Jima island, fought their way to one of the island's airfields and penetrated its defenses Admiral Chester W. Nimitz announced today.

Veteran Fifth Corps Marines of America's oldest amphibious outfit established a 4,500 yard beachhead to an average depth of 500 yards and drove inland to the edge of the airfield under increasing Japanese artillery and mortar fire.

Advance units of the attackers had reached the southern end of the airfield and penetrated the field's defenses east of the airstrip.

The beachhead extends for nearly two and a half miles northward from the volcano at the southern tip of the air-base island.

MARINE CASUALTIES "MODERATE"

Nimitz credited B-29s and submarines with helping pave the way for this morning's invasion of the island whose seizure will step up the air offensive against Tokyo where the Fifth Fleet air arm destroyed or damaged 36 ships and 759 planes in two days before withdrawing.

Thousands of rockets raked the southern Iwo beaches climaxing the heavy naval bombardment which included batteries of such ancient battleships as the Nevada, sunk at Pearl Harbor and resurrected to help pave the way for the invasion of Normandy and now a stepping stone to Tokyo.

Marine casualties "are moderate," Nimitz said.

Two "light units" of the navy supporting fleet of more than 800 ships which prepared the way for the 9 A. M. invasion were damaged.

Resistance was originally light but Japanese counterfire, at first sporadic, steadily intensified as the Marines smashed against the enemy entrenched in ridges and burned them out of pillboxes with flamethrowers.

Warship Support

Warships, which Tokyo said encircled the island, furnished artillery support while swarms of carrier planes dived on the Japanese in front of the Marines' path.

Several hours after the initial landing, Webley Edwards, representing the combined radio networks, flew over the beaches and reported "there's a whale of a scrap still going on."

The immediate objective was Iwo's two main airfields from which land-based American fighters and medium bombers will be able to strike the Nipponese homeland for the first time.

Battleships, including new 45,000 tonners and cruisers poured murderous shellfire into the eight-mile square island since Friday to soften the coastal defenses. Iwo had undergone the most intensive neutralization campaign in the Pacific war.

An aerial observer said that the Japanese were fighting back from underground defenses.

Sizzling Pork Chop

"Smoke and dust covered the entire island," he continued. "Iwo itself looked like a fat pork chop sizzling in the skillet as the carrier planes swept in under us, strafing and bombing every installation they could find."

One fighter crashed in flames just inland where the Marines fought. In the calm waters off the island, hundreds of ships maneuvered endlessly with the old pre-war battleships, including the New York, Arkansas, Idaho and

(Continued On Page Six)

Wanton Slaying Of 60 Priests And Others By Japanese Is Revealed

Americans Find Dead In De La Salle College In Manila.

By RUSSELL BRINES

MANILA, Feb. 18 (Delayed) (AP)—The wanton slaying of at least 60 priests and women and children refugees in the De La Salle College in Manila's Malate district by Japanese soldiers was revealed today with recovery of the mutilated remains.

Of 70 persons caught in the college only eight survived, said one of them, the Rev. Francis J. Cosgrave, 47, a Redemptorist Father of Sydney, Australia.

Father Cosgrave, recovering from two bayonet wounds in Santo Thomas Hospital, filled in details of the terrible afternoon last Monday.

One Japanese officer and 20 enlisted men shot and bayoneted the American, Filipino, German, Irish and Spanish religious brothers and Filipino refugees.

The bodies, serving as mute and ghastly evidence, were discovered today when the United States 148th Infantry Regiment captured the college area.

Storm Room

Father Cosgrove said the Japanese garrison had remained in one wing of the college, while permitting the priests and refugees to occupy another.

Monday, another tense day on the fringe of the battle area, the Japanese stormed into the priests' room, Father Cosgrave reported. He said the religious group and refugees were just finishing a simple lunch.

The officer screamed something, then fired pointblank with a pistol. Then the Japanese soldiers charged into the sobbing, terrified throng of victims, firing guns and slashing right and left with their bayonets.

Today the bodies lay as they fell in the blood-smeared interior of what once was a modern college near the Rizal stadium.

They were lying in grotesque helplessness, these slashed and smashed bodies. Some, caught in the first volley, tumbled in the

(Continued On Page Six)

BOOKLOVERS' CLUB MEETS TOMORROW

The Booklovers' Club will meet at 2:30 P. M. tomorrow at the home of Mrs. Eugene S. Mayer, 115 Spa View avenue.

Two papers will be read. Mrs. Alexander Dillingham will give a paper on "Ancient History," and Mrs. Lyman Kells one on "Woodrow Wilson."

Douglas White Gets Air Medal

Local Sergeant Decorated For Meritorious Achievement

FIFTEENTH AAF IN ITALY, Feb. 19—Sgt. Douglas O. White, 26, ball-gunner in a B-24 Liberator of a 15th Air Force group at an airbase overseas, formerly of 109 McKendree avenue, Annapolis, Md., has recently been awarded the Air Medal "for meritorious achievement in aerial flight."

He is a veteran of numerous combat missions against vital axis-targets in the German network of industrial sectors throughout southern Europe.

Sgt. White attended high school in Annapolis for three years and prior to his entry into the service June 6, 1942, was employed by the U. S. Post Office in Annapolis.

He is married to the former Helen Jean Ward. Also serving with the armed forces is a brother, M/Sgt. Robert G. White, in an ordnance company.

TO GIVE PLAY AT P.-T. A.

Mrs. Lester Wood, chairman of the program committee of the Annapolis Grammar School P.-T. A. will present a play in honor of the P.-T. A. Founders' Day, at the meeting to be held tomorrow afternoon at 2:30 in the music room of the school. A short business meeting will precede the play.

The meeting is open to friends and parents of the pupils. Refreshments will be served.

Savings Bonds Mature On Mar. 1

Federal "Baby Bonds" May Be Reinvested

Secretary of the Treasury Morgenthau today reminded bond buyers that Series A Savings bonds—those sold in 1935, when they were known popularly as "baby" bonds—will begin maturing on March 1. The Secretary said that as the bonds mature the Treasury will pay them off in cash at the rate of $4 for every $3 originally invested. However, if individuals desire they may reinvest any part of the proceeds of their Series A bonds, up to such denominational amount as the proceeds will fully cover, in Series E War Bonds.

Individuals who are the registered owners or co-owners of maturing Series A bonds may present them for payment to any incorporated bank or trust company that has qualified as a paying agent. This includes practically all banks and trust companies throughout the country. Payment will be immediate, provided the owners or co-owners have satisfactory identification.

Individuals also may make their reinvestment in Series E. bonds at practically all banks and trust companies, through the established payment and issue procedure. This must be accomplished concurrently with surrender of the

(Continued On Page Four)

STATE OFFICIAL WILL SPEAK HERE TOMORROW TO FOOD HANDLERS

A. L. Sullivan, state food and drug commissioner, will be one of the speakers at a meeting of food handlers to be held by the Anne Arundel County Health Department, tomorrow night at 8:30 p. m., at the Green street laboratory.

Dr. Alice B. Tobler, assistant county health officer, will be the other speaker.

The meeting is for all restaurant proprietors and handlers of food at all public eating places.

EARLEIGH HEIGHTS TRUCK IN COLLISION ON WAY TO FIRE

Three people were cut by flying glass when the Earleigh Heights fire truck and a truck driven by Walter Shananberger of Robinsson, were in a collision during the snow storm Saturday, at the intersection of the Ritchie Highway and the Earleigh Heights road.

Shananberger, blinded by snow on his windshield, failed to see the fire truck, which had stopped to take on two firemen.

Shananberger, his wife and small boy were cut by glass. None of the firemen was hurt.

The fire truck was delayed about five minutes on the call it was answering from Lake Waterford. The person giving the alarm said there was a house fire, so Earleigh Heights, Riviera Beach and Arnold were all called, but it turned out to be only a chimney fire, which did little damage.

The left front fender and wheel of the fire truck, which was driven by George Daniels, was slightly damaged and the front of Shananberger's truck was smashed.

ROAST PORK WITHOUT POINTS IS TREAT AS MEAT HOUSE BURNS

Some Herald Harber firemen and neighbors of Charles Trawitz enjoyed a roast pork dinner without benefit of ration points, when the meat of six butchered hogs was half-baked in an early morning fire that destroyed Tarwitz' meat house at Beazley's Corner.

About two-thirds of the hams, shoulders and bacon was saved while still in edible condition, firemen said, but since it had to be cooked and eaten at once, Trawitz gave it away. What wasn't edible for human beings made a feast for the neighborhood dogs.

Firemen said it was supposed that the blaze started from grease from the meat.

Herald Harbor had another unusual call when a motorist notified them of a fire along the road near Dorr's Corner. They discovered that an aged colored man, walking to Baltimore, had sat down to rest and lighted an old automobile tire to get warm. Firemen put out the fire and got the man a ride to Baltimore.

MRS. J. V. POLYANSKI DIES AT HOME HERE

Mrs. Josephine V. Polyanski died Saturday at her home, 14 Munroe Court, after an illness of several months. She was born in Poland April 19, 1874. She was a member of St. Mary's Catholic Church.

Surviving are one son, Reuben J. Polyanski, and two daughters, Mrs. John J. Stehle and Mrs. Howard C. Cushman, and nine grandchildren and three great-grandchildren.

The funeral will be held tomorrow at 9:30 A. M. from the Hopping Funeral Home, 172 West street, with requiem high mass at St. Mary's Catholic Church at 10 A. M. Interment in St. Mary's cemetery.

Martin Named To Command Midshipmen

Will Take Over Regiment On Sunday

Midshipman B. S. Martin, Prospect Park, Pa., today was named regimental commander, of midshipmen in the final group of midshipmen officers and petty officers to take command on Sunday.

Rear Admiral John R. Beardall,

Women For Telephone Work

War Jobs Today—Peace Jobs Tomorrow

Permanent work of an essential and interesting nature. Good starting pay. Frequent increases and excellent opportunities for advancement. No experience necessary. Apply at your local telephone office 8:30 A. M. to 5 P. M. Monday to Friday

The Chesapeake and Potomac Telephone Company
OF BALTIMORE CITY

---

superintendent of the academy, announced the final list under the acaedmy plan of rotation of command. One group of midshipmen held command assignments from Sept. 30 to Dec. 14 and a second group took over on Dec. 15. The final group, selected from the first two on proven efficiency, will be in command during June Week.

Regimental Staff

Serving with Martin will be: W. N. Culp, Jr., Birmingham, Ala., regimental subcommander. P. W. Barcus, West Los Angeles, Calif., regimental adjutant. R. O. Welander, Bellerose, N. Y., regimental plans and training. J. W. Enyart, Macon, Mo., regimental supply and commissary. A. M. Masich, Winston Salem, N. C., regimental intelligence officer. L. E. Mayes, Moore, Okla., regimental communications officer. A. J. Allen, Atlanta, Ga., regimental chief petty officer. J. V. Houston, Mooresville, N. H., national color bearer. P. H. Allen, Easthampton, Mass., regimental color bearer.

Battalion Commanders

The new battalion and sub commanders are:

First battalion, D. G. Iselin Racine, Wis., commander; J. E. Langille, 3d., Leesburg, Fla., sub commander.

Second battalion, H. A. Watson, San Antonio, Tex., commander; G. M. Bard, 2d., Washington, sub commander.

Third battalion, R. C. Duncan,

(Continued On Page Four)

Annexation

(Continued From Page One)

members of the City Council, the county representatives in the Legislature, Chamber of Commerce and other groups to attend.

C. Carroll Lee, chairman of the committee, said the idea was to hold a general discussion of the subject.

DR. FOSTER TO ADDRESS D.A.R.

Dr. James W. Foster, director of the Maryland Historical Society of Baltimore, will speak to the Peggy Stewart Tea Party Chapter, Daughters of the American Revolution at 8 P. M. tomorrow in the east room of Carvel Hall.

He will discuss "Two Forgotten Episodes of the Revolution."

Dr. Foster said he had just "done some exploring and have uncovered some fascinating information, one about the express riders who brought the news of the battle of Lexington to New York and the southern colonies, and the other is about the response here in Maryland to the call when Cresap and his men marched to join Washington."

Mrs. R. H. Langdon is chairman of the hostesses who include Mrs. Edward Sibley, Mrs. J. L. Hill, Mrs. R. F. Frellsen, Mrs. C. H. Rawlins, Mrs. F. E. La Cauza, Miss Betty Carson and Mrs. D. F. Rex.

Retreating Japs

(Continued From Page One)

ous hits on the Ludendorff bridge at Remagen, sometimes momentarily halting the flood of men, tanks and guns comprising four divisions which the enemy said already had crossed the span. The bridge still stood and still was in use. Assault coats plied the Rhine as if it were the Mississippi; the Germans said pontoon bridges had been thrown across.

Soviet troops are attacking powerfully north of Frankfurt in an attempt to expand their bridgeheads over the Oder river, the German high command said after Moscow announced capture of the east bank fortress of Kuestrin.

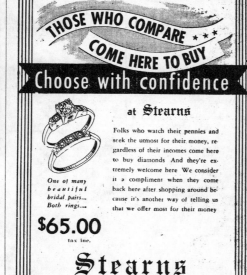

HITLER VISITS ODER FRONT

Adolf Hitler (right) returns a salute from his Nazi soldiers during a visit to division headquarters on the Oder River front east of Berlin, according to German caption accompanying this photo distributed by the Swedish picture agency Pressens Bild. (Picture by radio from Stockholm to New York.)

The Nazi command said the Russian assaults were held, and declared Germans still were fighting in the southern fringe of Kuestrin, 38 miles north of Frankfurt and one miles north of Berlin, one of the three biggest fortresses guarding the German capital.

Moscow Silent

Moscow still had not officially reported any crossing of the Oder, but dispatches said three Red Army groups apparently were being disposed for an assault on the German capital. Kuestrin, churned to rubble, fell after five days of hand-to-hand battle, the Russians said.

The German communique told of local breaches by Red Army troops beating toward Stettin from the north.

The second White Russian Army of the northeast battled within sight of the sharp church spires of Danzig where the war began. Part of the civilian population and military garrison of Danzig has been evacuated by sea Moscow dispatches said.

But Red Army planes now had blocked sea escape lanes, and a Soviet correspondent said "the end of German divisions trapped on the Danzig coast is drawing near." Some accounts said the Germans were fleeing in panic.

Farther east, the siege tightened on Koenigsberg, East Prussian capital. A large portion of the population apparently had escaped.

Tank-led 41st Division Infantrymen captured Zamboanga town and seized four more villages as they pursued retreating Japanese toward the hills of Mindanao island, headquarters announced, while other Doughboys pressed the cleanup of southern Luzon island.

The 41st seized four villages on the highway about two miles north of Zamboanga as engineers were reconditioning a captured, nearby bomber airdrome, 215 miles from Borneo. The Japanese abandoned formidable fixed positions before the town and around the airdrome and field northward into the hills dominating fabled Zamboanga.

Against similar light opposi-

---

tion on Luzon the 11th Airborne Division captured Los Banos, former prison town, and Batangas, tenth provincial capital on the island to be liberated.

No opposition was encountered at Batangas, about 25 miles south of Los Banos, on the southwest coast of Luzon.

Driving foot by foot against bitter resistance, Maj. Gen. Keller E. Rockey's Fifth Marine Division pushed the Japanese closer to the sea and destruction in a narrowing triangle around Kitano Point, northern extremity of Iwo, Monday.

There were indications that the enemy is weakening steadily even though resistance remains stiff.

Today's morning communique, covering action up to 6 P. M. Monday, said Maj Gen. Graves B. Erskine's Third Marine Division in the center and Maj. Gen. Clifton B. Cates' Fourth on the right are mopping up along the northeast coast.

In the Fourth's sector near Tachiwa Point, where Iwo's bulge makes its greatest extension eastward, a small Nipponese pocket still held out.

Fifth army troops in Italy blasted the Germans from 590-foot Monte Spigolino, in the forbidding mountain country 14 miles northwest of Pistoia, and repulsed enemy counterattacks upon the peak, Allied headquarters announced.

The activity flared in a section southwest of Monte Belvedere, which the Americans hold. Monte Spigolino is about three miles east of Piansinatico, on Highway 12 running from Lucca to Modena.

Like the action in the Belvedere region, the advance apparently was designed to guard Fifth Army positions for whatever may be in store on the Italian front in the coming months.

CRUISER HELENA GETS CITATION

The light cruiser Helena, sunk in the battle of Kula Gulf has received the first new Navy unit citation issued by Secretary of the Navy James b. Forrestal.

The citation, which entitles all members of the crew serving on and during the period covered to wear a citation ribbon was for heroism of the crew displayed in battles in the Solomons and New Georgia area in 1942 and 1943.

Comdr. John L. Chew, USN, son of Mrs. John L. Chew, 15 Southgate avenue, now on duty at the academy, was on duty on the Helena from the time of commissioning until the warship was sunk. He took part in 13 battles.

Major Perkins

(Continued From Page One)

vices as officer-in-charge of the electrical and instrument shops of a strategic air depot of the Eighth Air Force, in England.

Col. James F. Early, Air Corps, said that from Jan. 1943 to Dec. 1944, Major Perkins demonstrated exceptional skill in constantly developing new and improved methods to increase the productivity of his departments. In addition he discovered the cause of aircraft retractable landing gear failure and took steps to correct it.

"Major Perkins' foresight, inventive ability and untiring effort reflect highest credit upon himself and the armed force of the United States," the citation continued.

YOUNG OAKS BURNED IN WOODS FIRE

A woods fire burned over half an acre of young oak trees near the Wilhelm residence on the Benfield road, yesterday afternoon. Earleigh Heights firemen responded to the call.

BARR SPEAKING AT LYNCHBURG FORUM

Stringfellow Barr, president of St. John's College, has gone to Lynchburg, Va., to speak today at the Lynchburg Forum on the subject "Post War Education."

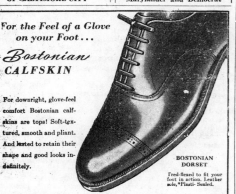

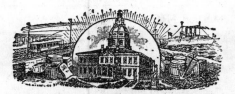

Evening Capital

WEATHER
Fair and continued warm tonight; scattered showers and a few thunderstorms Saturday.

VOL. LXI — NO. 88 | EVERY EVENING EXCEPT SUNDAY | ANNAPOLIS, MD., FRIDAY, APRIL 13, 1945 | SOUTHERN MARYLAND'S ONLY DAILY | THREE CENTS

Truman Takes Over Government

Ninth Army Within 45 Miles Of Berlin

LATE NEWS

TOMORROW DAY OF MOURNING

Washington, April 13 (AP) — President Harry S. Truman proclaimed today that tomorrow should be a day of mourning for Franklin D. Roosevelt throughout the United States.

MESSAGES POUR IN TO WHITE HOUSE

Washington, April 13 (AP)—Telegrams by the thousands poured into the White House last night and today from dignitaries and plain people all over the world.

"MORE SORRY FOR THE PEOPLE:" MRS. ROOSEVELT

Washington, April 13 (AP) — Eleanor Roosevelt's words on learning of the death of her husband, the nation's chief executive: "I am more sorry for the people of the country and the world than I am for us."

She spoke them to Presidential Secretary Stephen Early after he had called her to the White House from a meeting a few blocks away.

REPUBLICANS PLEDGE "FAITH AND TRUST"

Washington, April 13 (AP) — The Republican Senate conference representing 40 of the body's 96 members pledged their "faith and trust" in President Truman today.

They gave their pledge as grief-stricken Congressional leaders cancelled routine business and met instead to arrange memorial services to the memory of President Roosevelt.

A joint session of both the Senate and House will be held probably next week.

The House was in recess today.

STATE MOURNS ROOSEVELT

(By The Associated Press)

Flags at half-staff, cancellation of numerous social and business functions, special exercises in schools and intervals of meditation and silent prayer in factories bore witness today to Maryland's deep mourning in the tragic death yesterday of President Roosevelt.

To many Marylanders, the President was a friend or acquaintance through political connections dating back 33 years and business associations a quarter of a century old.

His business connections, which continued until he became President, started in December 1920, when he became vice president of the Fidelity and Deposit Company of Maryland, director and head of its New York office.

Roosevelt made numerous official, political and vacation appearances in Maryland during his Presidential tenure.

SENTENCED ON OPIUM CHARGE

Baltimore, April 13 (AP)—A 55-year-old citizen of China, Lee Chung Ping, was sentenced to three years imprisonment and fined $1,000 today by Federal Judge William C. Coleman for importing gum opium into the United States.

MORE MEN 30-38 TO BE DRAFTED

Cumberland, Md., April 13 (AP)— More men between the ages of 30 and 38 will be drafted in the next few months because most of the younger men between ages of 18 and 30 have already been inducted into the armed forces, local draft board officials predicted.

Officials said that fathers will be given more consideration for occupational deferment in the 30 to 34 age group than non-fathers.

TORNADO DEAD: 71

Oklahoma City, April 13 (AP) — Oklahoma counted its tornado-dead at 71 and the homeless in hundreds today after twister bounced crazily over the state to spread destruction in a dozen cities and rural communities.

The storms swept on into Arkansas, killing three, and two persons were reported missing in storm at Morrisville, Mo.

SCREEN ACTRESS FOUND DEAD

Beverly Hill, Calif., April 13 (AP) — The body of Peggy O'Neill, 21, blond screen actress, was found early today in the apartment of Albert Mannheimer, a screen writer, and Sheriff's Lt. A. L. Hutchison said she died of sleeping tablets she had taken after a lover's quarrel.

Local Tides

TOMORROW

High water — 7:23 P. M. 1.6 feet; 7:43 P. M., 0.9 feet. Low water—0:53 P. M., 2:04 P. M.

Moon rises 8:42 A. M.; sets 10:32 P. M.

Sun rises 6:32 A. M.; sets 7:43 P. M.

Tides are given for Annapolis. For Sandy Point, add 15 minutes. For Thomas Point shoal, subtract 30 minutes.

CROSS ELBE RIVER ON WIDE FRONT

Within 90 Miles Of Russian Siege Lines

The Ninth Army closed within 45 miles of Berlin today in a 60-mile armored advance which reached the already-crossed Elbe river on a wide front.

Nearly a hundred miles of the Elbe banks were patrolled by Ninth Army troops tonight. They stood within 90 miles of Russian siege lines east of the sprawling, ruined capital.

The nearest approach to the capital was in a bend of the river just south of Tangermuende, where the harried Germans blew the bridge.

Duisburg, Europe's greatest inland port and Germany's 14th city, fell to the Ninth Army in the shrinking and bypassed Ruhr pocket. The Third Army captured Erfurt, reached the streets of Jena and were 18 miles from Leipzig and 34 from Czechoslovakia.

Near Leipzig

Between these charging forces of Lts. Gen William H. Simpson and George S. Patton, Jr., First Army tanks broke into a 35-mile run across the "Golden Meadows" to within 17 miles of Leipzig, largest city in Saxony. Lt. Gen. Courtney H. Hodges' shock troops reached the Weisse river, two miles west of Zeitz, a town already within light artillery range of the Third Army.

The Hell On Wheels (Second) armored division, which crossed the Elbe at Madgeburg yesterday, was meeting stiff opposition on the eastern bank of that last river barrier before Berlin. Reinforcements and supplies poured across the Elbe as the tank troops gathered strength for the final push on Berlin, expected to start within a day or so.

The Ninth Army dash to the Elbe outflanked all Denmark, and the German ports of Hamburg and Luebeck.

Canadian First Army

The First Polish armored division of the Canadian First Army advanced to within 16 miles of Emden and almost to within sight of the North Sea. Gen. Henry Crerar's army drove another westward crossing over the Dutch river of Issel near Arnheim and expanded its original bridgehead between Deventer and Zutphen to a depth of six miles and a width of four. British troops under Canadian command (probably the 49th Division) stormed Arnhem ancient capital of Gelderland on the Rhine 50 miles southeast of Amsterdam. The Issel meets the Rhine at Arnhem.

Crerar's Second Infantry Division pushed 12 miles farther into northern Holland to the outskirts of Assen, 15 miles south of Groningen (120,000).

The bottom of the German sack southwest of Bremen was pinched in the vicinity of Cloppenburg. Canadians pushed in from the west in gains up to seven miles. Vechta, a road hub 14 miles south east of Cloppenburg, fell to the 51st Highlanders.

Russian Front

Russian troops were moving today on the Czechoslovak city of Bruenn (Brno), 68 miles north of Vienna, after cutting the last lifelines between the two cities in attacks that doomed the remaining Nazi forces in the historical Austrian capital.

Moscow said Soviet spearheads burst within 33 miles of Bruenn in an invasion over the southern Moravia border.

Inside Vienna, fall of which has been expected hourly, there was bitter house-to-house fighting as Marshal Feodor I. Tolbukhin's Third Ukrainian Army yesterday seized 60 blocks of the Jewish quarter of Leopoldstadt, between the Danube and the Danube canal.

The Nazis have concentrated their Vienna forces for a final

(Continued On Page Six)

A PRESIDENT PASSES—SUCCESSOR TAKES OFFICE

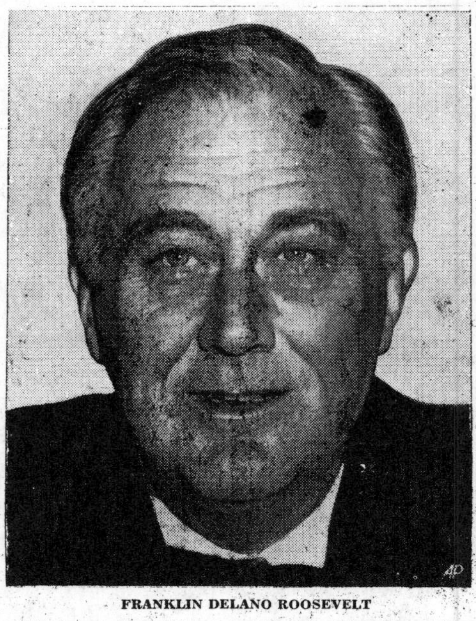

FRANKLIN DELANO ROOSEVELT

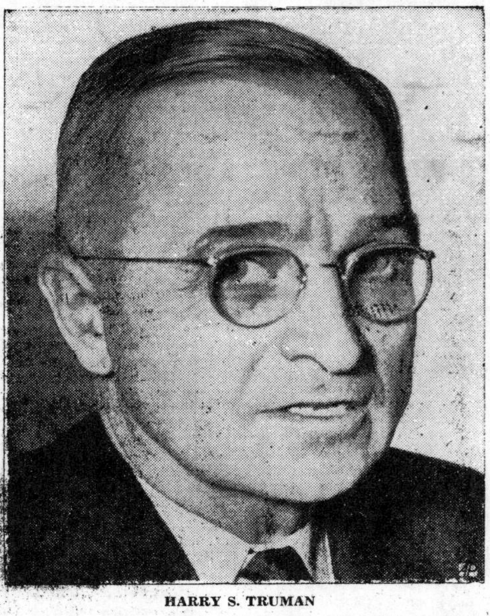

HARRY S. TRUMAN

The long and colorful career of Franklin Delano Roosevelt, 31st president of the United States, came to an end at 4:35 P. M. yesterday at Warm Springs, Ga., when the only Chief Executive of the nation to serve more than two terms died on the eighty-third day of his fourth term of a cerebral hemorrhage. Harry S. Truman, elected as Mr. Roosevelt's vice president in November, became the 32nd President of the United States at 7:09 P. M. last night.

NEW PRESIDENT DECLARES HE WILL CARRY ON AS HE BELIEVES ROOSEVELT WOULD HAVE DONE

Body Of Former President Due In Washington At 10 A. M. Tomorrow—Funeral Services Will Be Held At 4 P. M. Saturday In The East Room Of The White House—Burial Will Be In The Family Garden At Hyde Park At 10 A. M. Sunday—Mrs. Roosevelt Uses Army Plane To Reach Warm Springs

(By the Associated Press)

With the long and eventful career of Franklin Delano Roosevelt ended suddenly by death, his successor, President Harry S. Truman arrived at the White House at 9 A. M. today and called the nation's top military chiefs into conference on the war situation—taking up the reins of government.

Solemn groups, which had gathered near his residence and in the vicinity of the Executive Mansion watched him as he made the trip from his apartment at 4701 Connecticut avenue. There were no cheers, only waves of greeting.

Stunned by the shock of its leader's passing, a mourning nation gave solid backing to the gray-haired man in the gray business suit who became President of the United States at 7:09 o'clock last night.

TO CARRY ON ROOSEVELT POLICIES

Mr. Roosevelt died at Warm Springs, Ga., just two hours and 34 minutes earlier.

The new President himself announced simply that he would try to carry on as he believed President Roosevelt would have done. Then, swiftly, he asked the Roosevelt cabinet to stay on, gave assurance that the United Nations conference would open in San Francisco April 25, on schedule and issued a statement that the war would be prosecuted to the utmost on all fronts, east and west.

To the 60-year-old, thinly complexioned new President fell the immediate and sorrowful task of burying a Chief Executive for whom he had boundless admiration and unfaltering loyalty.

Pledges of support came for Mr. Truman's regime.

Roosevelt's Death

The career of Mr. Roosevelt was halted abruptly by a tragic though painless death yesterday as the nation's 31st President seemingly was about to see the fruition of his plans for bringing about lasting peace to a war-ridden world. He was 63 last January.

Death came unexpectedly at 4:35 P. M. (EWT) in a simply furnished bedroom of his Pine Mountain cottage. The cause: a "massive" cerebral hemorrhage.

Mr. Roosevelt went there March 30 for one of his periodic visits to seek rest and to bask in the sun. He had planned to stay another week, then return to Washington, spend a day and start out again for a cross-country trip to San Francisco to open the World Security conference April 25.

All this now is up to his successor.

The President's body, prepared during the night, was to be taken back to Washington by special train on the Southern Railroad. The train will reach the National Capitol at 10 A. M. (EWT) Saturday.

Mrs. Roosevelt arrived last night from Washington. She flew in an army plane to Fort Benning at nearby Columbus with Stephen T. Early, White House secretary, and Vice Admiral Ross T. McIntire, White House physician and Navy surgeon general.

Funeral Services

Funeral services are to be held at 4 P. M. (EWT) Saturday in the historic East Room of the White House.

The body will not lie in state.

Burial will be at the family home at Hyde Park, N. Y., Sunday.

Presidential Secretary William D. Hassett said the funeral services would be of the same "utmost simplicity" the President decreed for his mother, who died in 1941.

Burial will be at 10 A. M., in the family garden between the rambling stone and stucco house and the Roosevelt library at Hyde Park.

Members of the cabinet and Supreme Court, heads of Federal agencies, a representative group of senators and representatives, members of the family and friends will accompany the funeral party.

The East Room services will be conducted by Bishop Angus Dun of the Washington Episcopal Cathedral; Rev. Howard S. Wilkinson, of St. Thomas Episcopal Church, and Rev. John G. Magee of St. John's Episcopal Church.

Conducting the burial service at the graveside in Hyde Park will be Rev. Dr. George W. Anthony, new rector of St. James Episcopal Church where the President was senior deacon.

Mrs. Roosevelt, Early and McIntire were driven immediately to the President's cottage after they arrived by car from Fort Benning shortly before midnight.

Mrs. Roosevelt was described by officials as bearing up "very nobly —heroically."

Warm Springs Shocked

Warm Spring village and its nearby foundation for after-treatment of infantile paralysis—which Mr. Roosevelt helped found after he had been stricken and crippled by the disease— were stunned by the news of the passing of the nation's 31st president and its first chief executive to serve more than two terms.

He was elected to a fourth term

(Continued On Page Three)

ROOSEVELT REACTION

CHURCHILL ADJOURNS HOUSE OF COMMONS

LONDON, April 13 (AP)—Prime Minister Churchill came before a hushed House of Commons today and asked that it adjourn out of respect to a man of "immortal renown," the late President Roosevelt.

Speaking with considerable emotion, Churchill said:

"It is not fitting that we should continue our work this day. I feel that the House will wish to render a token of respect to the memory of this great departed statesman and war leader by adjourning immediately."

* * *

EISENHOWER SETS MOURNING PERIOD

LONDON, April 13 (AP) — Gen. Eisenhower issued a general order today decreeing 30 days of mourning for American troops in the European theater in connection with the death of President Roosevelt.

* * *

KING GEORGE EXPRESSES GRIEF

LONDON, April 13 (AP) — King George VI expressed his grief and shock over the death of President Roosevelt in a message to Mrs. Roosevelt today.

"The Queen and I are deeply grieved and shocked by the news of President Roosevelt's death," he wrote. "In him humanity has lost a great figure and we have lost a true and honored friend.

"On behalf of all my people I send our most heartfelt sympathy to you and to the members of your family."

BRIG. GEN. ROOSEVELT LEAVES FOR WASHINGTON

LONDON, April 13 (AP)—Brig. Gen. Elliott Roosevelt set out for Washington today by air and expected to arrive in time for his father's funeral Saturday.

Commander of an Eighth Air Force photo reconnaissance wing, he was visiting friends in London when he heard the news in the midnight broadcast by BBC.

Another officer said he was stunned and sat quietly for some time, then repeated over and over: "It just can't be true."

Before leaving the airbase on a special Army plane he received a cablegram from his mother, telling of the President's death.

(Continued On Page Six)

CITY MOURNS FOR PRESIDENT

Social Events Cancelled —Memorial Services Planned—Sports Curtailed

Annapolis mourned its dead President today.

Stunned by the suddenness with which tragedy struck a nation on the verge of victory, national state, county and city officials this morning arranged memorial observances in honor of the man whom the people chose four times to lead them through the most perilous years of the country's history.

Events Cancelled

The Naval Academy immediately cancelled all social events and lowered its flags to half mast for a thirty day period of mourning.

The Musical Clubs shows scheduled for tonight and tomorrow night, the midshipmen's dance and officers dance for tomorrow night, were cancelled. All Saturday sports events set for later than 1:30 were changed to begin at 1:30 and all sports will be suspended at 4 p. m. tomorrow, the time of the services at the White House.

Memorial services will be held in the Naval Academy Chapel at 10:30 Sunday morning.

The firing of saultes and the wearing of mourning bands by officers, which would take place in normal times, will not be done because of the war, Academy officials announced.

State House Draped

Governor O'Conor, who issued a statement on the President's death from Hot Springs, Va., ordered the State House to be draped in mourning, and all State offices to be closed tomorrow. The Governor asked all county and municipal offices to be draped in mourning tomorrow, during the services at the White House, and ordered all State Police to wear mourning bands Saturday and Sunday.

College Bell To Toll

Last night the regular College meeting and all seminars were cancelled at St. John's College, in

(Continued On Page Six)

ANNEXATION FACTS EXPLAINED AT MEETING HELD IN EASTPORT

TEXT OF LAZENBY ANNEXATION SPEECH

I will try to discuss annexation plainly and simply as I see it, and when I finish I hope you'll agree that the title I have given this talk "Annapolis Is Going To Town," is a good one.

A vote for annexation is the surest way to dress up the city we love so much, and send it to town in a big way.

After a topic such as annexation gets talked about for a few months the beginning of the proposition is often lost sight of, and the issue becomes clouded with a lot of extraneous matter, that has little bearing on the subject. Therefore lets go back to the beginning, and see where it all started.

Talk of annexation started in the Board of Directors Meeting of the Annapolis Chamber of Commerce, over a year ago. This Board of Directors is made up of the following men: Clarence E. Tyler is the president of the Chamber of Commerce and chairman of the board, we all know that Mr Tyler is an eminently respected resident of Eastport. The other directors are Willis T. Armbruster, who incidently lives in the county, and who is manager of Carvel Hall, E. E. Bangert, who is head of the Community Market, J. W. Basil, of the Coca-Cola Company, Alton S. Bell, of the Parsons Company. Barney Berman, whom we all know on Main street, Captain Morris Gilmore, of the Navy Athletic Association, and chairman of the Board of the Annapolis Banking and Trust Company.

Gardiner A. Hall, a county man, of the City Awning Company, Irving P. Hall, who is also a county man, of the Automotive Service Company, Benny Holiday, of the Annapolis Banking and Trust Company, Frank McShane, of The Evening Capital, Carey L. Meredith, the president of the Farmers National Bank, Churchill Murray, a county man, who we all know as insurance exclusively, Walter H. Myers, a county man, of the Henry B. Myers Company, Chris B. Nelson, a county man, of the Annapolis Yacht Yard, T. Os-

(Continued on Page 3)

Another Meeting To Be Held At 8 Tonight In Eastport School

The suburban areas, if annexed to Annapolis, will sooner or later actually control the entire Greater Annapolis, Joseph D. Lazenby, Chamber of Commerce representative, told the people of Eastport last nite at an annexation meeting held in the Eastport school.

Mr. Lazenby pointed out that there are probably about 100 building sites left in Annapolis and that any growth will necessarily take place in the annexed areas.

"Therefore in a short time the majority of voters will be in this area," he said. "However, I do not feel that Annapolis is at all worried about this, nor do I think you would be worried about it, because we are one community, with one community of interest. The world regards us as one place, and that place Annapolis, and certainly including in the city an area containing the highest type of residents can do nothing except benefit the community."

Meeting Tonight

C. Carroll Lee, chairman of the Citizens' Annexation Committee, presided at the meeting, the first to be held in the outlying sections. The group will meet again at 8 o'clock tonight at the Eastport school to discuss annexation with the residents of Eastport living between Sixth street and Forest Hills.

Mr. Lee read the resolutions on annexation which have been adopted by the City Council and listed saving in tax rates and by elimination of the 21 cent front foot Sanitary Commission assessment. (These appear elsewhere in this edition.)

Mayor William U. McCready, asked to give a review of the financial position of Annapolis, declared that the city's total indebtedness was $113,700, with a water company bonded indebtedness of $98,000 by the last auditor's report. He said that this year, $25,000 had been cut from the city debt and said that another $10,000 would be paid off on June 1. He contrasted this with the indebtedness of Eastport which is $186,000.

Tax Assessments

Answering a question about as-

(Continued On Page Three)

MRS. VIRGIE L. SMITH DIED YESTERDAY

Mrs. Virgie L. Smith, of Conduit street, wife of William A. Smith, died at her home yesterday after a lingering illness. She was a member of Calvary Methodist Episcopal Church and the Annapolis Chapter 11, 46 of the Eastern Star.

She is survived by her husband, a daughter, Mrs. Edythe Mae Robinson, two sons, William J. Smith and John Burton Smith, of Washington, D. C. Three sisters, Alma Cunningham, of Carona, Calif., Mrs. Elizabeth Hatchel, Mrs. R. E. Simmons, a brother, Edward A. Lee, all of Annapolis, and six grandchildren also survive.

Funeral services will be held Sunday at 3 P. M. at the Taylor Funeral Chapel, 147 Duke of Gloucester street. Interment will be in Cedar Bluff Cemetery.

MRS. CLARENCE NEWTON DIES SUDDENLY

Mrs. Anne C. Newton, wife of Clarence Newton, was found dead in bed this morning at her home, 114 Archwood avenue.

Dr. John M. Claffy, County medical examiner, said death was due to a heart attack.

Besides her husband, Mrs. Newton is survived by a son and daughter, her mother, who lives in Washington, and several brothers and sisters.

Evening Capital

WEATHER
Mostly cloudy and cooler tonight and much cooler Sunday.

VOL. LXI — NO. 89 | EVERY EVENING EXCEPT SUNDAY | ANNAPOLIS, MD., SATURDAY, APRIL 14, 1945 | SOUTHERN MARYLAND'S ONLY DAILY | THREE CENTS

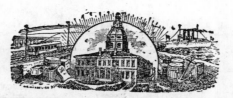

Funeral Rites Held For Roosevelt

Ninth Army In Outer Defenses Of Berlin

LATE NEWS

OPEN GRAVE AT HYDE PARK

Hyde Park, April 14 (AP)—The earth of Hyde Park, warmed by spring sunshine, was laid open today to receive the body of Franklin Delano Roosevelt.

In a rose garden, shielded by an ancient cedar hedge, a grave was prepared for the burden it will receive Sunday morning when a white-haired, white-bearded clergyman recites:

"Unto Almighty God we commend the soul of our brother departed, and we commit his body to the ground, earth to earth, ashes to ashes, dust to dust; in sure and certain hope of the resurrection unto eternal life."

Daffodils blossomed in the garden, hidden between the Roosevelt Manor house overlooking the Hudson and the Franklin D. Roosevelt library, and rose bushes weere leafing near the freshly-turned earth.

The village of Hyde Park, still bewildered by the sudden death of its first citizen, mourned quietly and proudly.

EDEN. ATHLONE REACH WASHINGTON

Washington, April 14 (AP)—The Earl of Athlone, Governor General of Canada and uncle of King George of England arrived in Washington at noon today tot represent the British Royal family at the Roosevelt funeral.

The Governor General came in at the National Airport in a Royal Airforce Liberator bomber.

British Foreign Secretary Anthony Eden arrived at the same airport a short time later to represent the Churchill government at the funeral.

BUSINESS IN STATE STOPS IN TRIBUTE

(By The Associated Press)

In tribute to President Roosevelt, Marylanders called off today various scheduled activities, closed up many amusement and business places and held memorial services in colleges and churches.

All taverns and night clubs were requested by the Board of Liquor License Commissioners to remain closed during the day.

The Maryland Restaurant Association asked its members to close between 3 P. M. and 5 P. M. today.

State and city offices and courts were closed. Federal offices were open half the day.

The Baltimore Stock Exchange and Grain Market was closed today, but produce markets continued business as usual.

War plants throughout the State operated at full schedule but many moments of meditation and prayer were observed.

OVER 300,000 WATCH CORTEGE

Washington, April 14 (AP)—The Metropolitan police estimated the largest crowd ever assembled in Washington—between 300,000 and 400,000—saw President Roosevelt's body borne today from the Union Station to the White House.

Maj. Edward D. Kelly, police superintendent, said the number of persons lining the two-mile long procession route surpassed even the largest Presidential inaugural crowds.

ROOSEVELT MESSAGE READ TO UNION

Washington, April 14 (AP) — President Roosevelt prepared before his death a message stating that "the maintenance of lasting peace in the Americas is bound up with the maintenace of lasting peace throughout the world."

President Harry S. Truman today sent it to the meeting of the governing board of the Pan-American Union which met in honor of Pan-American Day.

Mr. Truman accompanied it with a message of his own in which he said "I wholeheartedly subscribe" to the good neighbor policy.

JAP PREMIER EXTENDS SYMPATHY

San Francisco, April 14 (AP) — Premier Adm. Baron Kantaro Suzuki of Japan, has extended his "profound sympathy" to the American people on the death of President Roosevelt, the Japanese Domei news agency said today in a broadcast recorded by the Federal Communications Commission.

Local Tides

TOMORROW

High water — 8:17 A. M., 1.6 feet; 8:33 P. M., 0:8 feet. Low water—1:39 A. M., 3:11 P. M.

Moon rises 8:56 A. M.; sets 11:43 P. M.

Sun rises 6:31 A. M.; sets 7:44 P. M.

MONDAY

High water — 9:12 A. M., 1.5 feet; 9:26 P. M., 0.8 feet. Low water—2:27 A. M., 4:11 P. M.

Moon rises 9:43 A. M.

Sun rises 6:29 A. M.; sets 7:45 P. M.

Tides are given for Annapolis. For Sandy Point, add 15 minutes. For Thomas Point shoal, subtract 30 minutes.

FIRST AND THIRD ARMY TANKS MOVE PAST BESIEGED LEIPZIG

(By the Associated Press)

The American Ninth Army won a second crossing over the Elbe river today and fought slowly forward on the outer defenses of Berlin. First and Third Army tanks hurtled well past besieged Leipzig, neared the Russian lines and advanced into the Nazi mountain stronghold of Bayreuth.

The flanking sweep past Leipzig carried deep into Saxony to within ten miles of Chemnitz, 88 miles from the Russian lines and 38 from Dresden.

To all practical purposes, Germany was virtually bisected for the last direct communications from Berlin south—including the superhighway to Munich—were cut. The Third Army was within 25 miles of Czechoslovakia and had bypassed the northwest tip of that republic.

Gen. Omar Bradley's armies by-passed Leipzig and tightened the siege arc around the great Saxony city where 1,000,000 German civilians have been reported awaiting the Americans. The closest troops last were reported four miles away.

Near Dresden

The Third Army plunged into Bayreuth and onto the approaches of Dresden and neared the great traffic center of Chemnitz.

The First and Ninth Armies virtually eliminated the Ruhr pocket, taking 114,000 prisoners from the 150,000 orginally estimated as trapped.

The nearest Ninth Army troops last were reported 45 miles from Berlin. Those east of the Elbe were encountering profuse fire from flak batteries guarding the capital and making slow progress on the flat Brandenburg plain.

Third Army troops were 88 miles or less from Russian lines and within 25 of the Czechplovakia frontier. Their drive across southwest Germany to within 10 miles northwest of the Saxony industrial city of Chemnitz (335,000) carried Lt. Gen. George S. Patton's troops 25 miles past the northwestern tip of Czechoslovakia and into the rear zone of German lines in the east.

Dresden, capital of Saxony, was 38 miles from Patton's swift armored columns.

Skoda Works

His men moved within 85 miles of the Skoda munitions works at Pilsen and 96 of the Czechoslovak capital of Prague.

The places captured were the aircraft center of Brunswick (201,306), the Napoleonic battle city of Jena (60,000), Zeitz (35,300), Saalfeld (16,000), Rudolstadt (16,000) and the Dutch stronghold of Assen (20,000).

Canadian troops fought inside or at the edge of the Dutch cities of Groeningen (120,000), Arnhem (89,000), Appeldorn (71,158) and Zwolle (42,000).

The Americans fought within Madgeburg (334,358), Dortmund (537,000), Bayreuth (41,000) and Gera (75,000). The British besieged Germany's second port of Bremen and menaced and outflanked Hamburg, the largest port. The French were nine miles from Stuttgart.

V-E Day

The German army, still fighting fiercely in the east, no longer has either a cohesive front nor a coherent command in the west. The long-awaited Allied linkup severing the Reich in the middle is near—but that does not mean that the war in Europe will end at that time.

There might still be military fighting on into next winter, but it was not likely that it would still

(Continued on Page Six)

Board Of Visitors To Start Inspection Here Monday

Will Be At Naval Academy Until Thursday

The Board of Visitors, appointed by the President, Vice Presideent and Speaker of the House of Representatives, will begin their annual inspection of the Naval Academy on Monday.

The members of the board will assemble at 11 A. M. at the Naval Academy Officers' Mess and will appoint committees and formulate plans.

After luncheon and an inspection of the Naval Academy they will attend a reception at the superintendent's quarters. A night session of the board will follow.

The inspection will continue through Thursday morning.

Board Members

Members of the board are:

Appointed by the President: Dr. Franklyn B. Snyder, president Northwestern University; Col.

(Continued on Page Six)

LAST TRIP TO WHITE HOUSE

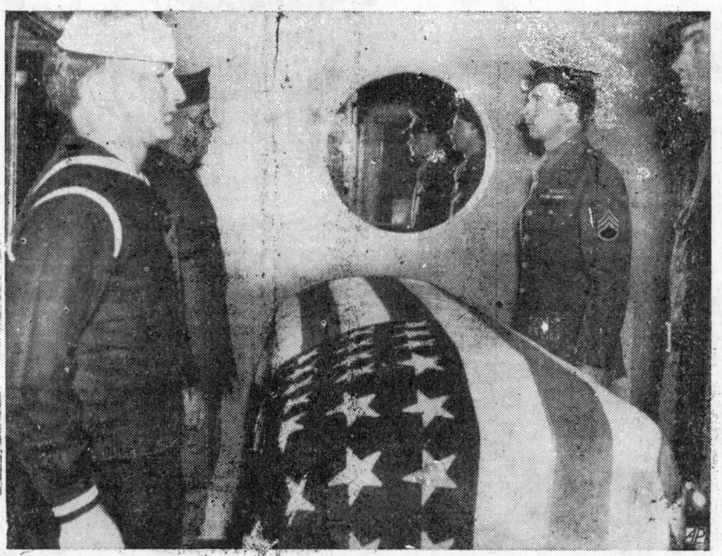

Service men standing guard over the bier of the late President on the train which brought his body back to Washington.

ST. MARY'S MOURNS DEATH OF PRESIDENT

The Parish societies and school children of St. Mary's paid a tribute of prayer and devotion to President Roosevelt this morning at services conducted at 8 o'clock.

The Very Rev. Augustine J. Smith, C.SS.R., rector of St. Mary's, delivered a brief testimonial of praise for the immense personal courage and devotion exercised by the late Chief Executive, Father Smith declared that it is now encumbent upon the nation that he served so faithfully, to intercede with Almighty God the peaceful repose of his soul. He thus introduced the recitation of the Rosary, during which the church bells of St. Mary's were tolled, in keeping with ancient custom for the passing of the head of the State.

This evening at 7:30, the regular Saturday night services, consisting in the recitation of the Rosary and Benediction will likewise be dedicated to the memory of the lately departed President.

President Roosevelt will be prayed for at all the Masses on Sunday morning, at St. Mary's. At ten o'clock, a special memorial will be made for the deceased head of the nation. This service will be attended by parishioners of St. Mary's, as well as officials of the State. the Naval Academy, a section of midshipmen from the Catholic Church party, and a contingent of enlisted men. A short sermon will be preached by the rector of St. Mary's, the Very Rev. Augustine Smith, C.SS.R.

GREY LADIES, NURSES' AIDES TO SELL HOSPITAL TICKETS

The Grey Ladies and Nurses' Aides will occupy booths on Main street from May 4 to May 12 for the sale of tickets to the ball and game party to be held on Florence Nightingale's birthday at Carvel Hall by the Hospital Day Club, it was announced at the meeting of the club last night at the Nurses' Home.

Mrs. J. B. Pollard, chairman of the Grey Ladies, announced the group's support and assistance for the drive to raise funds for the Emergency Hospital at the meeting at which Mrs. Amelia D. Florestano, chairman of the Hospital Day Club, presided.

Plans were also made last night for another card party to be held in conjunction with the drive on Wednesday, April 25, at he Nurses' Home.

Mrs. B. Marshall mentioned that the P.-T.A. of Deale, of which she is president, will sponsor a game party for the benefit of the Emergency Hospital.

HONOR ROOSEVELT

Business Stops As City Mourns

As the earthly remains of the man who was probably the best loved and the most hated President in the history of the United States were brought home to the White House he had occupied for a precedent - shattering twelve years, Annapolis today paid tribute to his memory.

In this city which Roosevelt had often visited, both during his years as Assistant Secretary of the Navy and later during his first three terms as President, foe joined with friend in calling him "great" as memorial services were held, and others planned, in honor of his memory.

Stores Close

Business operations were suspended as far as possible, all stores with the exception of groceries and drug stores, being closed all day, while the food stores and drug stores announced a closing at four o'clock, for the remainder of the day.

Moment of Silence

The C. and P. Telephone Company announced that, with the rest of the nation, telephone service would be suspended momentarily at four o'clock, the hour of the funeral services at the White House.

Theaters Closed

All theaters in the city were closed after the last showing last night and will remain closed until 5 P. M. today.

First Service At St. Anne's

A series of memorial services for Franklin Delano Roosevelt began last night when a large congregation attended St. Anne's Episcopal Church and heard the rector, the Rev. C. Edward Berger, briefly eulogize the late President as "a very great man."

"It is too early to appraise the worth of the work of our President," said Mr. Berger. "History will make that clear. But we know already that we have been in the company of a very great man. It seems invariably to be true that great men make enemies an it is no news that Mr. Roosevelt made them.

"Among Greatest"

"Today even his enemies are admitting his greatness. When the histories are written he will be numbered among the greatest of our great men.

"It was my privilege this morning to participate in a memorial assembly at the high school. An air of grief pervaded the atmosphere, and it was easy to discern what was in the minds and hearts of the students, for what was in their hearts was written in their faces. They were shocked and they were saddened. It seemed to me that they reflected the attitude not only of their families but of their nation and of the people of the whole world as well.

"It appears that Mr. Roosevelt died at the worst possible time; so much hangs in the balance.

"But it seems that God raises up men and endows them with the ability to meet the needs of the hour. A great task often makes a man great."

Special Prayer

During the service the rector read a prayer written especially for the occasion, which was in part: "Oh God, who rulest over all the kingdoms of the world, we yield Thee hearty thanks for the wisdom, strength and courage with which Thou didst visit our late President. We praise Thee for his love of humanity and for the grace by which Thou didst lead him fearlessly to contend against evil and to make no peace with oppression and we humbly beseech

(Continued on Page Six)

GEORGE B. STINCHCOMB DIES AT SEVERNA PARK

George B. Stinchcomb, retired farmer of Severna Park, died this morning at Emergency Hospital.

He is survived by his widow, Mrs. Ann Eleanor Waring Stinchcomb, one daughter, Mrs. George A. Jenkins, of Pasadena, Md.; two sons, Theodore F. Stinchcomb and Waring Stinchcomb, one grandson, Waring Stinchcomb, and a sister, Miss Sally Stinchcomb, all of Annapolis.

Funeral arrangements have not been completed.

SGT. GREEN DUE BACK FROM PACIFIC

M/Sgt. John H. Green, of the Quartermaster Corps, is expected to arrive at Fort George G. Meade from the Pacific theater of operations where he served 36 months. He will visit his parents at 4 College Creek Terrace, Annapolis.

CHRISTIAN SCIENCE SERVICE

A half hour memorial service will be held at 8 p. m. tomorrow at the First Church of Christ, Scientist.

ELIMINATION OF SANITARY TAX STRESSED AS INDUCEMENT FOR EASTPORT JOINING WITH CITY

Annexation Meeting At West Annapolis At 8 P. M. Monday

Elimination of the Annapolis Sanitary Commission's method of taxation was urged as an inducement for annexation last night at a meeting of Eastport residents, living between Sixth street and the Forrest Hills area, held in the Eastport school.

The Citizens' Annexation Committee returned to the school for the second night in succession. On Monday at 8 P. M. the committee will be at the West Annapolis school and on Tuesday at 8 P. M. a meeting will be held in the Germantown school.

Mayor William U. McCready, C. Carroll Lee, chairman of the com-

(Continued On Page Three)

WILL HOLD RITES FOR MRS. ANNE C. NEWTON

Funeral services for Mrs. Anne C. Newton, who died suddenly yesterday at her home, 114 Archwood avenue, will be held tomorrow at 2:30 P. M. at the Hopping Funeral Home, 172 West street with interment in Cedar Bluff Cemetery.

Mrs. Newton was born in Boston, the daughter of Christine B. Cromar and the late Theodore J. Cromar. She was a member of St. Anne's Episcopal Church.

Surviving are her husband, Clarence O. Newton; one daughter, Miss M[illegible]an C. Newton; one son, John C. Newton; her mother, Mrs. Cromar; two brothers, Theodore Cromar, of Annapolis, and Charles Cromar, of Richmond; and one sister, Mrs. Stanley Herr, of Washington.

MOURNING WASHINGTON GIVES LAST TRIBUTE TO ITS FIRST CIIZEN OF A DOZEN YEARS

Services Held In White House At 4 P. M.—Body Of Dead President Reached Washington Shortly Before 10 A. M.—Taken To White House On Army Caisson Drawn By Seven White Horses—Services Held In East Room—Private Burial Services At Hyde Park At 10 A. M. Tomorrow

(My the Associated Press)

Wartime Washington, steeped in sorrow, offered a last sad farewell today to Franklin Delano Roosevelt—its first citizen for a dozen dramatic years.

It was a capital clad in mourning—a hushed, somber contrast to the carnival atmosphere of other Roosevelt homecomings.

The body of the dead President reached the sorrowing capital shortly before 10 A. M.

President Truman and members of the cabinet were at the Union Station a few minutes before the train pulled in at 9:50 A. M. (EWT), waiting to lead a mournful procession to the White House.

FUNERAL AT 4 P. M.

Members of the Roosevelt family were the first to enter the funeral train, followed by President Truman. Brig. Gen. Elliott Roosevelt and his wife and Mr. and Mrs. John Boettiger went aboard. They were followed by Admiral William D. Leahy, who was President Roosevelt's chief of staff, by Bernard Baruch, James F. Byrnes, and War Mobilization director Fred M. Vinson. Members of the Supreme Court and their wives, and cabinet officers and their wives, also entered the train.

The Marine Band played softly "Hail to the Chief" and the national anthem.

The funeral train was parked on a Union station siding near a bustling freight depot. Crowds thronged as close as police would let them to the train.

The body was lifted to a huge Army cassion drawn by seven white horses and the procession moved slowly to the White House where the funeral services were held. Virtually every high dignitary of the government rode in the procession as it wended its way through the city. Two sharp notes of a sailor's pipe signaled the start of the long cortege.

Thousands Line Streets

Thousands of persons who lined the streets of the procession murmured only in whispers as the casket passed. Before the caisson marched a guard of all military services. A light bomber, gleaming in the sun, circled overhead.

Many along the route were in tears.

The caisson halted before the White House and the casket was borne inside by uniformed members of the armed services. Mrs. Roosevelt and members of the family slowly followed.

The silence was so deep that even the chirping of the birds on the White House lawn could be heard distinctly.

Within the White House, the casket was placed on a carrier and wheeled straight across the bronze seal embedded in the lobby floor, into the famed East Room.

Younger In Death

An altar stood before the double doors in the center of the east wall and the casket was put at rest immediately before it. Flowers banked the whole long expanse of the east wall and overflowed into the corners of the room. Looking down upon the casket were the pictures of George and Martha Washington.

There were no flags. The red drapes of the room were not drawn.

Resting beneath the glass enclosure of the casket, the body of Franklin Roosevelt was dressed in a greyish blue business suit, a greyish blue fore-in-hand tie and a white, soft-collared shirt. He looked younger in death than when last seen by friends in Washington where his office weighed so heavily. Outside on the lawn, a service band played an old hymn "Abide with me."

The little dog he loved, Fala, was brought in on a leash.

Rites Simple

Funeral rites impressive in their simplicity were held at 4 P. M.

The Episcopalian order for the burial of the dead was the funeral service for the White House ceremony, attended only by the family and those associates and friends who could be accommodated in the East Room.

There will be no state funeral.

"Unto God's gracious mercy and protection we commit you." read the prayer offered by Bishop Angus Dun of Washington Episcopal Cathedral.

"The Lord lift up his counten-

(Continued on Page Six)

800 MIDSHIPMEN IN FUNERAL ESCORT OF LATE PRESIDENT

Eight hundred Midshipmen from the Naval Academy left for Washington today to serve as a section of the escort for the body of the late President Roosevelt.

The Midshipmen, representing one fourth of the Annapolis regiment, will participate in the escort of the President's body from Union Station to the White House, officers at the academy said.

Commanded by Midshipman Ben S. Martin, the 800 were accompained by the regimental staff, officers said.

Predicts Navy Relief Show Will Be Success

Will Be Presented On April 27, 28 and May 4, 5

After weeks of rehearsals Lieut. Charles J. McGaw, director of the play, "The Man Who Came To Dinner," has finally told the cast that he is confident the show will be a success when presented here the nights of April 27, 28 and May 4 and 5. The play will be presented as the 1945 Navy Relief benefit and details on ticket sales will be announced shortly by Capt. A. P. Randolph, chairman of the production.

Last week the director put all the acts together in sequence for the first time and allowed the cast to go through the entire play wihout interruption. The performance had some rough spots but Lieut. McGaw was enthused over recent progress.

Feminine Role

Virginia Bays in the leading feminine role of Maggie Cutler gave a talented and well received interpretation of her part to keep pace with the most important member of the cast, Lieut. John Curtis Reed who, as Sheridan Whiteside, portrays the part of "The Man Who Came To Dinner."

(Continued On Page Three)

THE ROAD TO BERLIN

By The Associated Press

Eastern front—18 to 20 miles (from near Ederswalde) German report.

Western front—45 miles (from Tangermuende).

Italian front—530 miles (from Menate):

SCHOOLS TO CONTINUE WORK V-E DAY

V-E Day will be observed in county schools, authorities stated today, but there will be no holiday. Each school in the county is preparing a patriotic-religious program to be given on that day which will be marked by solemnity. The program will be the only interruption of regular class work.

So you guess you will have

ANOTHER DRINK?

ATTENTION!

★

Boy Scouts Will Collect Waste Paper On Saturday, April 21

★

Residents of the following sections are requested to cooperate:

ANNAPOLIS, EASTPORT, GERMANTOWN, WEST ANNAPOLIS, WARDOUR, FAIRFAX, HOMEWOOD

★

LINTHICUM HEIGHTS, FERNDALE, SHIPLEY, RIVERIA BEACH, ORCHARD BEACH, ARNOLD, BROOKLYN PARK AND NORTH LINTHICUM

★

Have your paper on your front porch by 9 A. M. on Saturday, April 21, and a Boy Scout or Cub will pick it up.

This is the General Dwight D. Eisenhower Campaign to collect 150,000 tons of paper during the months of March and April.

★

HELP THE GENERAL, THE NATION, THE SCOUTS AND YOURSELF

GET YOUR PAPER READY FOR COLLECTION THIS MEANS ALL TYPES OF WASTE PAPER

For Summertime

Rocker, illustrated $3.19

Folding Chair, not illustrated . . $2.98

Adjustable. Perfect for lawn or beach. These chairs have strongly constructed hard wood frames. Gaily striped canvas covers.

Child's Sturdy See Saw $6.95

SAND BOXES

Brightly colored, adjustable awnings shade the youngsters when they play in these strongly built sand boxes.

$8.95 to $11.95

Economy Auto Supply Co.

25 WEST STREET   DIAL 4131

Barr Speaks

(Continued From Page One)

by another method, a means by which men have come together and set up a government of self-discipline. This is the second way in which governments are formed.

"We do not know of any way whereby people have been able to live together peaceably without government or law. We sometimes forget this. We are now in the most difficult situation that has confronted any generation in history. As far back as history runs, we have had wars, but never before in the history of the whole human race has the world been one community.

Sovereign Nations

"We are not going to have peace as long as we are living as long as we have many sovereign nations. It has been asked, "What would George Washington say to the idea of 'hauling down our flag' by relinquishing our sovereignty?' The answer is found in what he did. He lived under the sovereignty of Virginia and saw it would not succeed, so he pulled down the old flag to bring about the union.

"The Federal government is not responsible to the States, but to the individual. Most of the laws under which the citizen lives are local laws, but there are some powers the state and local governments have relinquished. One of them is the right to make war.

"The existence of civilization is threatened by the next war. Nations making of themselves an armed camp cannot afford perfect freedom. They will be assailed by other armed camps. If we do not want that situation, we want world government, whether we have discovered it or not. The problem is in our laps—not like a lap robe, but like a time-bomb. The time-bomb has a long fuse and a long one, but the fuse is lighted and we have the only one means of extinguishing it," Mr. Barr continued, and declared that we must have a strong world government. It was Hamilton who said that the first requirement of a good government is strength — after that, you make it responsible."

Dumbarton Oaks

The Dumbarton Oaks is nothing but proposals and it was the speaker's opinion that these alone would not be able to enforce peace. Exhaustion will prevent war for a decade and Dumbarton Oaks may prevent it for three decades and in that time we may discover that what we need is a government. This, said Mr. Barr, may have been the dream of President Roosevelt.

"The several conferences, Bretton Woods, etc., may have been planned to present problems and help the nations to come to the realization that these problems are so large that only through world government can they be solved," Mr. Barr continued. "I believe that, Commander Stassen sees this more clearly than any statesman at the moment and I think it was for this reason that Mr. Roosevelt appointed him a delegate to San Francisco.

"Contributing largely to the propagation of the world government idea," said Mr. Barr, "are: (1) Clarence Streitt, author of Union Now with Britain, and president of Federal Union Incorporated; (2) Robert Lee Humber, who authored the Declaration of the Federation of The World and succeeded in getting the legislature of North Carolina to memorialize Congress on World Federation. New Jersey followed North Carolina, as did Maryland and 12 other state legislatures; (3) E. B. White, who writes for the "New Yorker," and who was described by Barr as the "best political scientist we have operating at the moment"; (4) Commander Stassen who is convinced that if the San Francisco delegates will pass one law — no government shall take the life of any citizen in time of peace without trial by law—then there will come a demand for world government.

World Government

Mr. Barr pointed out that Dumbarton Oaks is the first step toward world government and that in the building of a bridge you have to hit both sides. "If you have only half the bridge, you still have something on which to build and there is always the chance that the bridge may be finished," he said. "Dumbarton Oaks Economy and Security Council as proposed, gives us a chance to learn 'what the score is' and to live as adult people. If you want peace, this is the price of admission."

Following his talk, Mr. Barr answered numerous questions put by his hearers.

Replying to the question, "Are a large army and navy and compulsory military training trends in conformity with the spirit of Dumbarton Oaks?" Mr. Barr said that these trends are not contrary to the league. "Dumbarton Oaks says that we are a sovereign government, retaining the obligation to protect you and if we should this federation we are about to enter break down," he said.

Answering the question: "Could Federal Union be brought about at San Francisco from the Dumbarton Oaks proposals?" Mr. Barr said that "I wouldn't want to say it could be but I believe that it is possible that nations might discover that world government is the only solution."

In introducing the speaker, Dr. Howard A. Kinhart declared that Mr. Barr has been one of the first to recognize the problem confronting us as war in Europe seems to draw near the end. The problem involved is what shall be done after the war in the way of maintaining peace. Dr. Kinhart pointed out that the speaker has been a potent force in education along this line.

Mrs. Joachim, president of the association, opened the meeting with a brief prayer and the girls' chorus of the school sang two well-chosen numbers — "Lift Thine Eyes" from Mendelssohn's oratorio "Elijah"; and "Like As A Father" by Cherubini.

Officers for the coming year were elected and will be installed at the next meeting. They are: Mrs. W. F. Joachim, president; Mrs. Raymond Swartz, 1st vice president; Mrs. Lee F. Clemens, 2nd vice president; Dr. Howard A. Kinhart, recording secretary; Mrs. Conrad S. Gaw, recording secretary; Mrs. Alfred Erickson, corresponding secretary and Lieut. Comdr. Elmer M. Jackson, Jr., treasurer.

The May meeting will be a social one, with refreshments served by the hospitality committee, of which Mrs. Dorsey Duvall is chairman. Mrs. Lee Clemens, attendance chairman, with her committee, registered those attending last night's meeting.

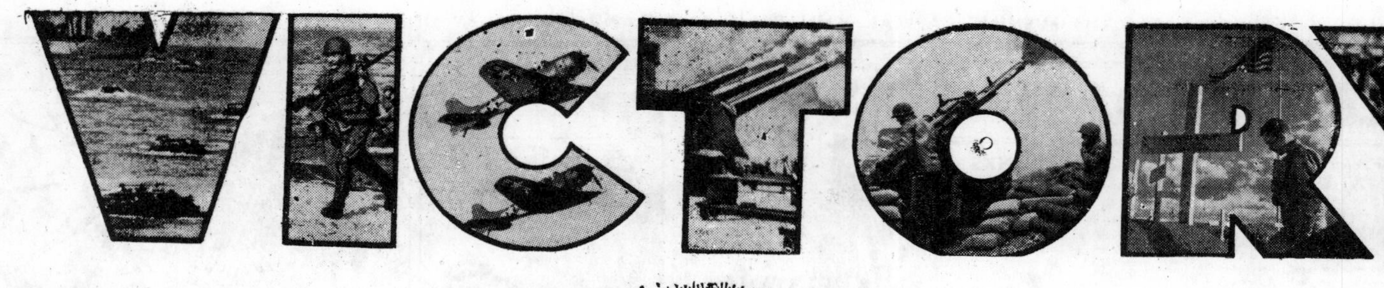

Evening Capital

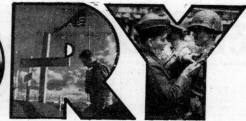

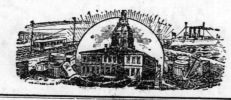

WEATHER
Increasing cloudiness and not so cool tonight, Tuesday, showers followed by cooler.

VOL. LXI — NO. 108 | EVERY EVENING EXCEPT SUNDAY | ANNAPOLIS, MD., MONDAY, MAY 7, 1945 | SOUTHERN MARYLAND'S ONLY DAILY | THREE CENTS

Germany Surrenders Unconditionally

LATE NEWS

CHURCHILL BROADCAST 9 A. M. TOMORROW

London, May 7 (AP)—The British government announced that tomorrow will be celebrated as V-E Day. Prime Minister Churchill will broadcast at 9 A. M. Eastern War Time and King George VI at 3 P. M., EWT.

BIG THREE TO MAKE SIMULTANEOUS ANNOUNCEMENT

Washington, May 7 (AP)—President Truman said today he had agreed with the London and Moscow governments that he would make no announcement on the surrender of enemy forces "until a simultaneous announcement can be made by the three governments."

U. S. TO RETAIN AIR ARM IN EUROPE

London, May 7 (AP)—All indications here point to the fact that the U. S. Army is preparing to retain a strong air arm in Europe for police and transport duties long after the end of the war.

While there has been no official announcement concerning the size of the Allied occupational air force, it is estimated unofficially that it probably will require a total of between 75,000 and 100,000 men in the ground crews alone. The force will be composed of both American and British planes and personnel, though not necessarily in equal numbers.

Presumably the American contingent will be drawn from both the Eighth and Ninth Air Forces.

NAVY PLANE CRASHES IN VA.

Ewing, Va., May 7 (AP)—Four service men were killed when a navy plane, enroute from Anacostia, D. C., to Dayton, Ohio crashed against a mountainside near here Friday night and burned.

The dead, identified by the Potomac River Command included Lieut. Col. J. F. Walters, USMC 34, Rockville, Md.

WPB PREPARES WAR PRODUCTION CUTBACK

Washington, May 7 (AP)—WPB prepared today to abandon its civilian production freeze which has been in force through the phases of military stalemate, setback and imminent victory in Europe.

Indications came also that this week would bring cutbacks in war production for the Army ground forces—cuts which originally were to have awaited an official V-E Day Proclamation.

DEALINGS QUIET ON WALL STREET

New York, May 7 (AP) — The Stock Market celebrated the German surrender today by a brisk but selective rally after early profit taking had put most leaders in moderately lower territory.

"Busines as usual" was the rule at the opening and, while selling soon cropped up, dealings were relatively quiet. Bids began to arrive before midday and early losses running to a point or so were reduced or converted into gains of as much. The ticker tape picked up speed on the comeback.

GOEBBEL'S BODY REPORTED FOUND

London, May 7 (AP)—Reuters in a Moscow dispatch said today that it was reported without confirmation that the bodies of German propaganda minister Joseph Goebbels and his family had been found in an air raid shelter near the Reichstag building in Berlin.

MINERS DEFY WORK RETURN ORDER

Wilkes-Barre, Pa., May 7 (AP)—Pennsylvania's 72,000 anthracite miners defied the government's orders to return to work today at 363 operations which were seized last Thursday by Secretary of Interior Ickes under presidential direction.

The miners said they had received no instructions to report back to their jobs from John L. Lewis, president of the United Mine Workers.

BALTIMORE WAR PLANTS STAY ON JOB

Baltimore, May 7 (AP)—Baltimore's war workers stayed on their posts as news of Germany's unconditional surrender seeped into war plants this morning.

Major industries in and around Baltimore withheld the official announcemnt of the European capitulation from their workers pending a statement from the White House that one phase of the war was actually over.

Local Tides

TOMORROW

High water — 2:51 A. M., 1.3 feet; 3:08 P. M.; 1.1 feet. Low water—9.25 A. M., 9:25 P. M.

Moon rises 4:23 A. M.; sets 4:22 P. M.

Sun rises 6:02 A. M.; sets 8:06 P. M.

Tides are given for Annapolis. For Sandy Point, add 15 minutes. For Thomas Point shoal, subtract minutes.

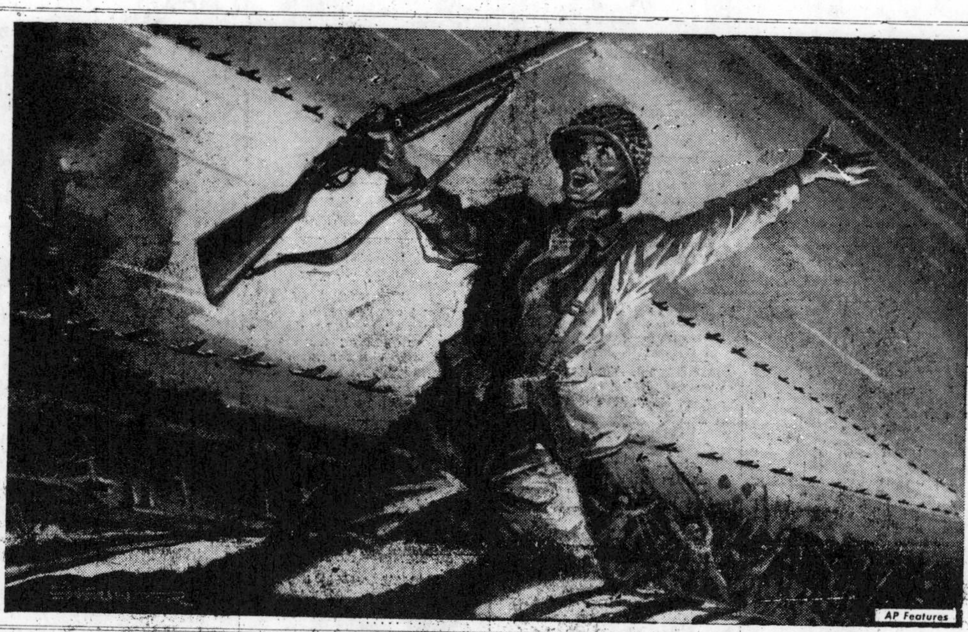
AP Features

Yank Bombers Sink 35 More Jap Ships; Damage 17

Tenth Army Resumes Offensive On Okinawa

(By the Associated Press)

American bombers reaching out from the Philippines and Okinawa, where Yank ground forces killed 23,221 Japanese in ten days, have sunk 25 more Nipponese and damaged 17 others, U. S. "On-to-Tokyo" commanders announced yesterday and today.

A Japanese breakthrough in central China to within 35 miles of the U. S. air base at Chihkiang was the only blight on Allied ground offensives as Washington reports said 6,000,000 Americans would be thrown against Japan after V-E day.

The U. S. Tenth Army resumed its general offensive on Okinawa after killing 3,000 Japanese in last Friday's counterattack.

In the Philippines the 25th Division captured the last hill mass controlling the Balete Pass entrance to fertile Cagayan valley of northern Luzon in a four day bat-

(Continued On Page Three)

FUNERAL SERVICES HELD FOR JOHN A. JACOBSEN

Funeral services for John A. Jacobsen, 117 Conduit street who died Friday, were held today at 2 P. M. from Taylor's Funeral Capel. The Rev. Charles E. Berger, rector of St. Anne's Church, read the last rites.

Survivors are his wife, the former Miss Edith May McCaffrey; a daughter, Mrs. Samuel W. Crouch of Baltimore; a brother, Joseph Jacobsen of Baltimore; and one granddaughter.

Pallbearers were William U. McCready, William A. Strohm, Chester Cromwell, Senattor Wilbur R. Dulin, Charles O. Dulin, and A. Guy Miller.

Interment was at Loudon Park Cemetery, Baltimore.

MOTH BOAT RACES BEGAN YESTERDAY

A cold stiff wind yesterday brought four moth boats to the Langan dock at the end of the first race of the weekly spring series of the Spa Creek Moth Boat Club.

In the order of their entry Dicky Kavanaugh in his "Sicum" was first; Bobby Joe Kavanaugh in "Red Bird," second; Ralph Brady in "Boogie" third, and Tick Coughlin, in "Little Miss" fourth.

The skipper of "Little Miss" was the winner of a boat whistle for out-fitting his boat first. Prizes were donated by Thomas Langan and Arcady Semenoff. Mrs. Langan is sponsor of the club, membership to which is open to any boy or girl that owns and navigates a moth.

Annapolis Coast Guardsman In Ryukyu Operation

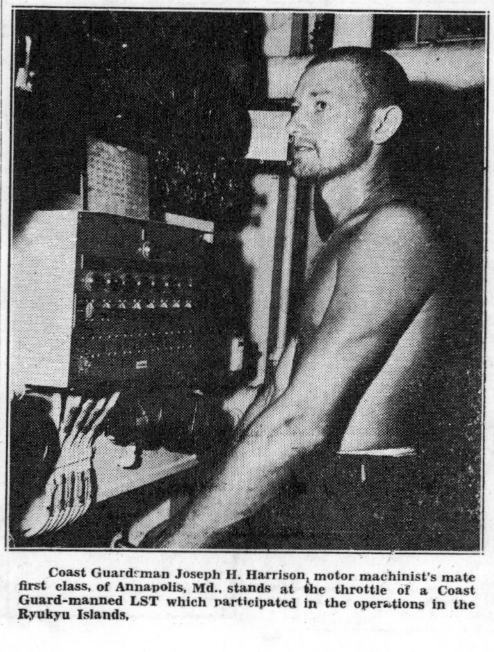

Coast Guardsman Joseph H. Harrison, motor machinist's mate first class, of Annapolis, Md., stands at the throttle of a Coast Guard-manned LST which participated in the operations in the Ryukyu Islands.

Grocers Ask Revision Of Price Control

Food Distributors Meet At Carvel Hall Sunday

Retail grocers of the state of Maryland have petitioned for revision of OPA policies on food commodities by Congress stating they cannot continue to handle such commodities at a loss and that correction of the policies must be made by Congress rather than administrative action.

A meeting of the Independent Retail Food Distributors was held at Carvel Hall Sunday when discussion of post-war plans took paramount place with their resolutions on OPA policies.

E. E. Bangert, of Annapolis, was elected president of the Independent Retail Food Distributors for the coming year, Herman Lissy, Baltimore, first vice-president; Fred A. Fique, Baltimore, recording secretary; William H. Stellhorn, treasurer; Harry W. Walker, Baltimore, secretary-manager.

The meeting Sunday included dinner at which Lansdale G. Sasscer, of Upper Marlboro, Congressman from this district, spoke and a business meeting at which

(Continued On Page Three)

LT. ELUSTKA TO BECOME NAVAL AVIATOR

After forty months aboard the battleship, USS North Carolina, Lt. Robert J. Elustka, has returned from the Fleet to the states for aviation training. He has successfully completed naval air primary training at the Naval Air Station, Ottumwa, Iowa, and has been transferred to the Naval Air Station, Pensacola, Fla., for intermediate training.

A graduate of the Naval Academy in the class of 1941, Lt. Eluska wears the American Theater, America Defense, Expert Pistol, and Pacific ribbons with eleven combat stars.

After completion of intermediate training he will be designated a naval aviator. Lt. Elustka's home is R.F.D. No. 3, this city.

The comic section of the Evening Capital was not printed today because of delay in the mails. It will be resumed tomorrow.

City Awaits V-E Day In Quiet

Governor And Mayor Will Proclaim Day After Official Confirmation

In a nation seething with excitement over an unconfirmed V-E Day Annapolis remained calm and quietly awaited proclamation by President Truman that the day has arrived officially. Surrender Day had come and the news was definite that all German armies had surrendered but Annapolis delayed observance for one real thing—V-E Day.

Governor O'Conor announced he would not proclaim V-E Day until President Truman had issued a statement and Mayor William U. McCready concurred in this decision when he said he would not call for any commemoration until official word from the President was received.

Business proceeded as usual, stores and bars remained open although proprietors and em-

(Continued On page four)

MRS. COATES DIED AT RESIDENCE SATURDAY

Mrs. Mary M. Coates died Saturday at her residence, Cedar Park, after a lingering illness. Mrs. Coates was born in Davidsonville, Md.

She is survived by her husband, R. Leonard Coates, three daughters, Mrs. Thelma Peabody, Mrs. Mary Catherine Eskew, and Mrs. Helen Christine O'Daniels, and one son, Joseph L. Coates with the U. S. Army overseas.

Funeral services will be held Tuesday morning at 9:30 from her late residence with Requiem Mass at St. Mary's Catholic Church, 109 Gloucester street, at 10 A. M.

Interment will be in St. Mary's Cemetery.

Russia Asked To Give Grounds For Polish Arrests

U. S. And Britain Demand Evidence On Underground Leaders

By JOHN M. HIGHTOWER

Associated Press Diplomatic News Editor

SAN FRANCISCO, May 7 (AP)—The United States and Britain were reported by United Nations conference officials today to have demanded of Russia that she supply her evidence against the 16 arrested leaders of the Polish underground.

The aim is to break the latest Big-Three deadlock over Poland. It is part of a strategy sidetracking the Polish row from the main line of the conference in order that the Big-Three may try for maximum unity in designing a world organization for future peace.

President Truman and Prime Minister Churchill are reported to have intervened directly with Marshal Stalin.

Russian Foreign Commissar Molotov is now slated to quit San Francisco for Moscow around midweek. So long as he is here, speculation continues that Russia may give the conference a sensation by making known her future plans toward Japan.

On the main line of conference developments, word spread today that Stalin may have replied favorably to Molotov's request for instructions on the review and regional arrangements amendments to the Dumbarton Oaks charter.

Perhaps the greatest developing isue now is the demand of the Latin American countries that the Pan-American Security System be allowed to be independent of the proposed World Security Council in using force to block aggression.

The Latin American nations also reported upset by a Big-Power amendment which says says that in selecting the six non-permanent members of the security council, the world assembly may take into account their ability as

(Continued On Page Three)

FINAL CAPITULATION MADE AT EISENHOWER'S HEADQUARTERS

LONDON, May 7—(AP)—E. P. Stackpole, Press Association correspondent in the Parliament lobbies, wrote today that "Although the war is over, I understand there will be no official announcement of this until tomorrow afternoon."

The Exchange Telegraph Company's political correspondent wrote:

"The war in Europe is over.

"The official announcement of that fact has been delayed and will not be made, it is understood, until tomorrow afternoon.

Press Association said that "as Parliament will be sitting tomorrow, Mr. Churchill may make the announcement first in the House of Commons."

Press Association declared that the delay in announcing V-Day "is occasioned by an agreement which has been reached between Mr. Churchill, President Truman and Marshal Stalin that the announcement, when it comes, shall be made simultaneously in London, Washington and Moscow.

LONDON, May 7, — The greatest war in history ended today with the unconditional surrender of Germany.

The surrender of the Reich to the western Allies and Russia was made at Gen. Eisenhower's headquarters at Reims, France, by Col. Gen. Gustaf Jodl, chief of staff for the German Army

This was announced officially after German broadcasts told the German people that Grand Admiral Karl Doenitz had ordered the capitulation of all fighting forces, and called off the U-boat war.

The surrender took place at a little red school house which is the headquarters of Gen. Eisenhower.

The surrender which brought the war in Europe to a formal end after five years, eight months and six days of bloodshed and destruction was signed for Germany by Col. Gen. Gustav-Jodl.

It was signed for the Supreme Allied Command by Liqenan General Walter Bedell Smith, chief of staff for General Eisenhower.

It was also signed by General Ivan Susloparoff for Russia and by General Francois Sevez for France.

After signing the full surrender, Jodl said he wanted to speak and was given leave to do so.

"With this signature," he said in soft-spoken German, "the German people and armed forces are for better or worse delivered into the victors' hands."

General Eisenhower was not present at the signing, but immediately afterward Jodl and his fellow delegate, General Admiral Hans Georg Friedeburg, were received by the Supreme Commander.

They were asked sternly if they understood the surrender terms imposed upon Germany and if they would be carried out by Germany.

They answered yes.

America Greets

America greeted announcement of Germany's unconditional surrender with a mixture of emotions.

Hilarious gayety, solemn prayer in the streets, a partial stoppage of business and an electric feeling excitement swept from coast to coast.

New York city's reaction was a snowstorm of wastepaper that cascaded from buildings as people shouted and sang in the streets. Others openly wept and prayed on sidewalks.

Police roped off Times Square and all vehicular traffic was stopped in the financial district. Thousands left their jobs to parade with flags and banners.

"Business as usual," was the reaction from the New York Stock Exchange.

In Washington, President Sergio Osmena of the Philippines termed the German surrender "a decisive step" along the road to final victory but emphasized that the United Nations must not rest until "Japan is likewise completely crushed."

White House Ready

The White House marked time today on a momentarily expected victory in Europe proclamation—but arrangements were complete for President Truman to go on the air when it is issued.

Broadcasting equipment was readied for use in the White House diplomatic room, usual site of Presidential addresses.

Shortly before noon, boxes of sandwiches were carried into the office of Jonathan Daniels, Presidential press secretary, indicating no one planned to go out for lunch. The usual parade of official

(Continued On Page Three)

Taxes Reduced By Annexation Mayor Says

Westervelt Statement On Assessment Answered

Mayor William U. McCready announced today he had received through the mail a postcard from E. H. Westervelt on which the latter states that annexation would increase rather than reduce his taxes. The mayor who expressed his belief that "these cards have been sent out to a great number of people" has issued a statement of answer and explanation.

The explanation follows:

Mr. Westervelt states that 'I personally figure that annexation, under the present setup would not reduce my taxes, but would cost me at least $10.00 per year more.' Mr. Westervelt is not assessed for any real estate in Anne Arundel county but Mrs. Thelma Westervelt is assessed for a house and a 70 foot lot on Glenn avenue in Homewood $3010.00.

Using this basis at present in the county the tax is $91.49: A. A. County Sanitary Commission Tax, $4.90: Minimum Charge, $2.00 for a total of $98.39.

The same assessment in the city would be: City Tax rate $1.00 per $100.00, $30.10; Metropolitan Sew. Comm. Tax rate, 34c per $100.00, $10.23; County Tax rate $1.54 per $100.00, $46.35; State Tax rate, 12c

(Continued on Page Three)

CLASSIFIED ADS

or Sale

OR Sale—1936 Pontiac 2 door sedan, $345.00. Within O.P.A. ceiling price. Front rebushed and new bolts. All reconditioned motor from factory. All new gears in housing and one in rear. Extra good rubber. Two new tires. New clutch. Good upholstering. Phone 4460.

OR SALE—Two stories and attic—4 bedrooms and bath, living room, dining room and kitchen, all large rooms. Good condition. City conveniences, near boat harbor. Immediate possession. Large lot. Terms. Write Box 5, Evening Capital.

OR SALE—Portable washing machine with hand wringer. Call 5867 before 1 o'clock noon.

OR SALE—1½ acres bordering on Weems Creek above the bridge running back to solid road. About 100 feet fronting on water. Very desirable neighborhood. Price $1500.00. Will finance liberally. Apply Box 6, Evening Capital.

OR SALE—Man's victory bicycle with stand. Excellent condition, $30. Phone 5157.

OR SALE — Truxton Heights—Lots 50' x 300', only $200.00. On terms if desired. Out Spa Road, only 1 mile from Church Circle. City water available. See Mr. W. B. Monday on property, or call Annapolis 4821.

OR SALE — Pre-war gas range. Practically new. Phone 3422.

FOR SALE—Console R.C.A. Magic Voice radio, $60.00. Call 3761.

OR SALE—Pines-on-Severn, 6 rooms, permanent home, oil heat, full cellar, stationery tubs, short walk from B & A station. Call 4978.

FOR SALE—2½ acres, 500 feet waterfront, 7 room house with conveniences, outbuildings, tennis court, fruit trees etc. Price $11,500. Possession Sept. 1st. Dial 2461, Charles F. Lee.

FOR SALE—1942 Buick 4 door sedan. Model 41. Radio and heater. Price $1596.00, within O.P.A. ceiling price. Phone Annapolis 2341 before 6 p. m. or 4508 after 6.

FOR SALE—Soy beans, corn, seed potatoes, horse, cow. Also wood and coal stoves and furniture. To settle estate. Phone 5608.

FOR SALE—Fine carved Monarch upright grand piano. Excellent tone. Must sell quickly to settle estate. Phone 5608.

FOR SALE—McCormick-Deering tractor, tractor plow, and double disk harrow. Also corn planter, potato planter, team plow, potato hiller, cultivator, gas engine, saw rig, horse, cow, and all small farm tools. Must sell everything immediately due to sudden death of Alex Anderson. Phone 5608.

FOR SALE—Old English Boxwoods and other plants. Reasonable. Boxwood Gardens, 334 First street Eastport.

FOR SALE—Quantities of unshelled yellow corn. 1113 Tyler avenue, Eastport. Crosby Stokes. Nothing less than barrel quantities.

For Rent

FOR RENT—Office, 47 Maryland avenue. Dial 5013.

FOR RENT — Bay Ridge — Stucco Bungalow, year round containing Living and Dining room, four Bed Rooms, Kitchen, Bath, 2 screened Porches, Basement and 2 car garage, located on Lot 100 ft. x 250 ft. overlooking Chesapeake Bay. Furnished. Will Repair and Improve. Inspection by appointment contact C. C. Hartman, 227 St. Paul street, Baltimore, Md., Telephone: Lexington 4830.

FOR RENT—Furnished—Two rooms, Elec. kitchen, bath, and porch, private entrance. Newly decorated. Annapolis 5696 after 7 P. M.

FOR RENT—Two sleeping rooms for June Week, 12 N. Locust avenue.

FOR RENT—Four bedrooms for June Week with conveniences of private home. Adults only. Phone 4351.

OR RENT—Gentlemen only. Two bedrooms and private bath. Phone 4674.

Help Wanted—Female

HELP WANTED FEMALE—Cook and light house work, Home at Bay Head near Annapolis. References. $100.00 per month. Call Annapolis 5421.

HELP WANTED FEMALE—First class cook. Good wages. Short hours. If interested phone 3816.

HELP WANTED FEMALE—Experienced cook for home in country. Five minutes from Annapolis. Phone 4797.

HELP WANTED FEMALE—Beautician. Apprentice wanted. Richard's, 233 West street.

HELP WANTED FEMALE—Waitress, good wages. Apply Mirror Grill, 154 Main street.

HELP WANTED FEMALE—Special waitress for June Week. Apply The Annapolitan, 48 Maryland avenue.

Help Wanted Male and Female   15

HELP WANTED MALE AND FEMALE—Couple Wanted: Moving to South River June 15th Desirous of engaging couple on permanent basis. 2 large rooms and bath for living quarters. One child, five. Address: Mrs. Wood, 2129 S street, N. W., Washington, D. C.

Help Wanted Male

HELP WANTED MALE — Salesmen Wanted: Better than your own business. No capital expenditure. Handle a guaranteed line of roof material. Thirty-nine year old reliable firm. Big demand—large earnings. Merchandise sold direct to consumer—factories, mills, warehouses and farm property. Write: The American Oil & Paint Co., Cleveland 5, Ohio.

HELP WANTED MALE—Man to work full or part time for outdoor work. Phone 4797.

HELP WANTED MALE—Mechanic and helper. Apply Maryland Garage, 170 Conduit street.

HELP WANTED MALE — Experienced fireman. Apply Arundel Laundry, West street.

HELP WANTED MALE—We are willing to pay good money to those who will work and produce. We place no ceiling on earnings. We want only men who are interested in real money and a permanent position. Apply Wednesday 2 to 6, Saturday 10 to 4, American Life Insurance Company, 92 West street.

Wanted   6

WANTED—To rent unfurnished house or apartment. Must be in Annapolis or close to bus line. Phone 2506.

WANTED—Waterfront bungalow with modern conveniences, on South River between Edgewater and Bay. Write Box 3, Evening Capital.

WANTED—To buy 100 locust fence post, 7½ feet long, delivered. Phone 4069.

WANTED—To buy a radio that works. Please reply giving full particulars. Box number four, Evening Capital.

WANTED—To buy 2 paint spray guns. Globe Furniture, 16 Market Space. Phone 2733.

WANTED—Ride to California. Will share expenses. Able to drive. One gentleman. Phone 4700.

WANTED—Elderly couple would like to rent an unfurnished first floor apartment or bungalow. Phone 4305.

WANTED—To buy old guns. Any condition. Pistols, Revolvers, Rifles, and Shot guns. Hartman's Gun Shop, 526 Sixth street, Eastport. Hours 6 to 11 p. m. daily.

WANTED—Elderly colored man to feed hogs. Apply Thomas W. Dorsey, Annapolis 5300.

WANTED—High cash prices for your old sewing machine. Singer Sewing Machine Company, 139 Main street. Phone 3181.

Miscellaneous

MISCELLANEOUS—We deliver anything—any where. Personal Delivery Service. Phone: 2781.

MISCELLANEOUS—Used cars, any make, any model, bought and sold. Harry's Super-Service, West and Southgate. Phone 4000.

MISCELLANEOUS — Lawnmowers, saws sharpened by machine. More precise work. Rank, Best Gate Road. Telephone 5570.

MISCELLANEOUS—Supervised playground-children 2 to 5 years. Swings, seesaw, sandbox. Tuesdays and Thursdays, 9:00 to 5:00. Saturday mornings, 9:00 to 12:00. 25c. per hour. Mrs. C. L. Allen, 5 Cumberland Court, Annapolis 2780.

MISCELLANEOUS — Cesspools and septic tanks cleaned. Rates moderate. Modern equipment. J. P. Devine, phone Linthicum 170-J.

MISCELLANEOUS—We deliver anything, anywhere, anytime. Low rates on all deliveries. Beasley's Delivery Service. Phone 6250.

MISCELLANEOUS — At stud—three male cocker spaniels, solid colors, to approved females only, at $25.00. Call 4351.

Lost and Found   8

LOST—Lady's purse on Main street, containing identification and money. Reward. Phone South Shore 2364.

IN MEMORIAM

STINE—In loving memory of my son, Roger N. Stine, who died 6 months ago December 3, 1944.
A broken circle, a vacant chair,
We seem to miss you everywhere;
But in our lonely hours of thinking
Thoughts of you are ever near.
Peaceful be thy rest, dear son,
Our hearts are filled with pain,
A place is vacant in our home,
which never can be filled again.
Mother and Sisters.

CARD OF THANKS

I wish to express my appreciation and thanks to friends, relatives for their messages of sympathy, floral designs, and use of automobiles during my bereavement.
Also the West Annapolis Fire Department and Anne Arundel County Police.
Mrs. Ethel Miller   J-2

FOR SALE

A delightful little bungalow at Wild Rose Shores. 300 feet on the water—1.12 acres—4 roms and bath—modern—year round. Price $6,000.00. Apply:
Joseph D. Lazenby
215 MAIN STREET
Telephone 2684

Rationing Calendar

FUEL OIL

1944-45 heating season— Period 1, 2, 3, 4 and 5 coupons valid through August. All these coupons and the Period 4 and 5 coupons issued for the 1943-44 heating season expire on Aug. 31.

SHOES

Book No. 3, Airplane coupons No. 1, 2 and 3 good indefinitely. Loose coupons are not acceptable. New stamp valid Aug. 1.

SUGAR

Coupon 35 good through June 2. Coupon 36 good for five pounds through Aug. 31. Next stamp valid Sept. 1.

TIRES, GASOLINE

A-15 coupons, new book 4 valid for four gallons through June 21. B-6 and B-7, and C-6 and C-7 coupons good for five gallons. T coupons marked second quarter, 1945, valid through June 30.
Motorists are required to write their license number and State of registration on face of coupons.
Eligibility for tires is based on the preferred mileage ration record when applying for any gasoline for operation of passenger automobiles. This is especially essential for furlough.
Always send in your mileage ration record when applying for any gasoline for operation of passenger automobiles. This is especially essential for furlough.

MEAT, FATS, OIL, CHEESE, FISH

Red coupons Y-5 and Z-5, A-2 through D-2 good through June 2. E-2 through J-2 good through June 30. K-2 through P-2 valid through July 31. Q-2 through U-2 valid May 1 through Aug. 31.

FRUITS AND VEGETABLES

Blue coupons H-2 through M-2 good through June 2. Blue coupons N-2 through S-2 good through June 30. Blue coupons T-2 through X-2 valid through July 31. Y-2 Z-2 and A-1 through C-1 good May 1 through Aug. 1.

MODEST MAIDENS

Trademark Registered U. S. Patent Office

"Well... one of the neighbors told me to go fly."

SCORCHY SMITH   Up—And Away

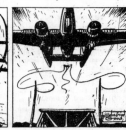

OAKY DOAKES   A Royal Decree

OH, DIANA!   Misplaced Ambition

HOMER HOOPEE   Lemonade Or First Aid

DICKIE DARE   Anchors Aweigh

THE ADVENTURES OF PATSY   Vacation For The Boys

NEIGHBORLY NEIGHBORS   THE DOOLITTLES

Evening Capital

WEATHER
Fair with moderate temperature today, tonight and Friday.

VOL. LXI — NO. 187 | EVERY EVENING EXCEPT SUNDAY | ANNAPOLIS, MD., THURSDAY, AUGUST 9, 1945 | SOUTHERN MARYLAND'S ONLY DAILY | THREE CENTS

Reds Battle Japanese In Manchuria

LATE NEWS

TRUMAN CALLS ONFERENCE ON BOMB

Washington, Aug. 9 (AP)—President Truman called in top miliary, diplomatic and scientific advisers today to discuss the atomic bomb whose terrific destructive effect twice has been felt by Japan.

WEDEMEYER CONFERS WITH RUSSIANS

Chungking, Aug. 9 (AP)—Lt. Gen. Albert C. Wedemeyer, commander of U. S. forces in the China Theater, conferred with Russian military representatives today shortly after the announcement of the Soviet Union's delaration of war upon Japan.

RUSSIANS ADOPT EW WAR CRY

Moscow, Aug. 9 (AP)—A new war slogan: "Death to the Japanese Samurai!" caught on quickly in Moscow today, replacing the long-familar: "Death to he German Invader!" war-cry of he fight against the Nazis.

CHIANG-KAI-SHEK WIRES GRATIFICATION TO STALIN

Chungking, Aug. 9 (AP)—Generalissimo Chiang-Kai-Shek wired Premier Stalin today his "sincerest admiration and most proound gratification" at Russia's declaration of war aginst Japan, which, he said, greatly heartened he entire Chinese nation.

JAP AIR FORCE ATTACKS THIRD FLEET

With Adm. Halsey's Third Fleet, off Japan, Aug. 9 (AP)—Japanese planes attempted an attack on Admiral Halsey's Third Fleet today for the first time since it started its marauding operations along the coast of Nippon more than a month ago.

YUGOSLAVIA WANTS $61,000,000 REPARATIONS

Belgrade, Aug. 9 (AP)—Yugoslavia will demand $61,000,000 in reparations from Germany and industrial equipment including "some complete factories," Marshal Tito announced yesterday.

CARRIER PLANES HIT JAPAN

Guam, Aug. 9 (AP)—More than ,200 U. S. Third Fleet and British carrier planes opened rocket and bomb attacks at dawn today on Japan after the Navy had told Nippon the day before to expect the attack—and the fleet noisily moved into position with daily gun practice.

TO STUDY PROPOSALS ON COMPENSATION LAWS

Baltimore, Aug. 9 (AP)—CIO proposals for liberalizing Maryland's unemployment compensation statute as a safeguard against possible postwar economic crises were earmarked today for study by a legislative council subcommittee and the Maryland Unemployment Commission.

"CANNED GUNS" TO BE USED IN FUTURE

Baltimore, Aug. 9 (AP)—Important areas of the country may be defended in a future war by guns "canned" and stored under the open sky during this year and next.

ALLIED POWER HITS SUMATRA, LOWER BURMA

Calcutta, Aug. 9 (AP) — Widespread Allied air action against targets in Sumatra, in lower Burma and along the Bangkok-Singapore railway was announced today by Southeast Asia Command headquarters.

JAP AMBASSADOR UNDER GUARD IN MOSCOW

Moscow, Aug. 9 (AP)—Japanese Ambassabor Noatake Sato and his staff as well as at least two Japanese newspaper correspondents were confined to the gardens of the Japanese Embassy today. Smoke rose from the chimneys, supposedly from burning papers.

JAP CABINET HOLDS EMERGENCY SESSION

London, Aug. 9 (AP)—The Australian radio, quoting a Domei broadcast, said the Japanese Cabinet held an emergency session today to discuss the Russian declaration of war.

OFFER JAPS VESSEL FOR RELIEF SHIP

Washington, Aug. 9 (AP)—The State Department has offered the Japanese an 11,758-ton vessel to replace the relief ship Awa Maru, sunk by mistake by an American submarine.

Local Tides

Tomorrow

High water — 7:30 A. M., 1.6 feet; 7:56 P. M., 1.3 feet. Low water—1:13 A. M., 2:19 P. M.

Moon rises 8:41 A. M.; sets 9:58 P. M.

Sun rises 6:12 A. M.; sets 8:09 P. M.

Tides are given for Annapolis. For Sandy Point, add 15 minutes. For Thomas Point shoal ,subtract 0 minutes.

NAGASAKI, SEAPORT AND RAIL CENTER, TARGET OF NEW ATOMIC BOMB STRIKE

Details Lacking As To Number Of Planes Involved In Attack

GUAM, Aug. 9—(AP)—The world's most destructive force—the atomic bomb—was used for the second time against Japan today, striking the important Kyushu island city of Nagasaki with observed "good results."

More than one bomb may have been dropped in this second attack and it might have been of a different size than the first one which destroyed 60 per cent of Hiroshima. The carefully worded communique said only that the second use of the atomic bomb had occurred, leaving to speculation all other details.

The bomb was dropped at noon, Japanese time—about nine hours after Tokyo radio reported Red Army troops supported Russia's declaration of war on Japan by attacking enemy forces in eastern Manchukuo both by land and by air, and while four other Japanese cities still burned from round-the-clock B-29 incendiary and demolition attacks.

IMPORTANT MILITARY TARGETS

Nagasaki, western Kyushu seaport and railroad terminal with an estimated 255,000 population in its 12 square miles, was a far more important military target than Hiroshima, first atomic bomb target.

The double blow, coupled with renewal of Halsey's Third Fleet carrier aids and stepped up B-29 attacks, could not fail to hit hard at Japanese morale.

Nagasaki contained three Mitsubishi plants—ordnance, a steel and arms works, and an electric manufacturing company.

Crewmen who dropped the mighty atom on Nagasaki immediately flashed "good results" via radio to Spaatz' headquarters. His communique did not say whether only one bomb was dropped, or only one plane went over the target.

Nagasaki, although having only about 70 percent of Hiroshima's population, was considered more important industrially. Its buildings were so close together that it was referred to as "a sea of roofs."

It was vitally important for the shipment of military supplies and embarkation of troops to Japan's operations in China, Formosa, Southeast Asia and the Southwest Pacific.

Immediately before issuing his Nagasaki - atom bomb communique, Spattz had reported that 402 Superforts carrying 2,300 tons of incendiaries and demolition bombs had achieved excellent results in attacking four other major targets yesterday and early today.

Widespread fires raged in the industrial areas on Fukuyama, 42 miles northeast of Kure, after 92 Superforts spilled more than 500 tons of incendiaries there.

Two Superforts were lost in a 1,400-ton demolition raid in Japan's big steel center, Yawata. The heavy explosive load was unloosed by 233 B-29s.

To Promote Soil Conservation

State Roads And Soil Conservation Commissions To Work Together

The State Roads Commission and the State Soil Conservation Committee have concluded an agreement for the promotion of cooperative soil work conservation between the two agencies, Governor O'Conor disclosed today.

Both Maj. Ezra B. Whitman, chairman of the State Roads Commission, and Dr. T. B Symons, director of the Maryland State Soil Conservation Committee, are convinced, the Governor said, that the arrangement worked out will be beneficial to the Roads Commission in highway maintenance as well as to abutting land owners.

The Chief Executive pointed out that it was mutually agreed by both agencies that control of soil erosion and proper disposal of rain water along the highway is a matter of mutual concern, and the purpose of the agreement is to develop the closest possible working relationship between the departments.

In a joint memorandum going out to all soil conservation districts, as well as to district and

(Continued On Page Three)

AWARDED SILVER STAR

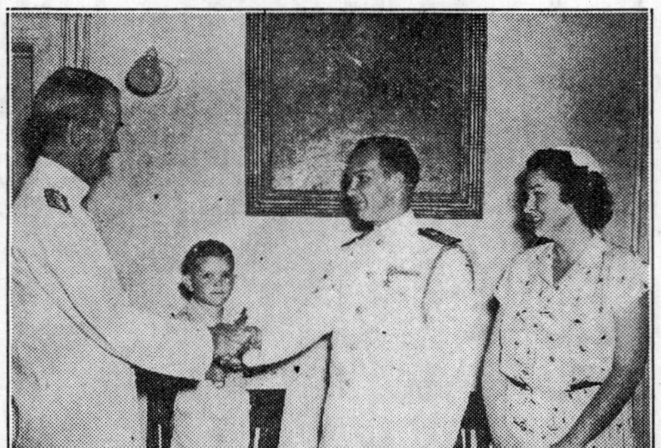

Official U. S. N. Photo.

Comdr. Richard S. Craighill, U. S. N., aide to Rear Admiral Beardall, superintendent of the Naval Academy, is shown receiving the Silver Star from Adm. Beardall. The medal was awarded for Comdr. Craighill's wife, Mrs. Craighill and their son, Richy. gallantry as commanding officer of a destroyer in action against the enemy in the Southwest Pacific.

TRUMAN ANNOUNCES RUSSIAN WAR ON JAPAN

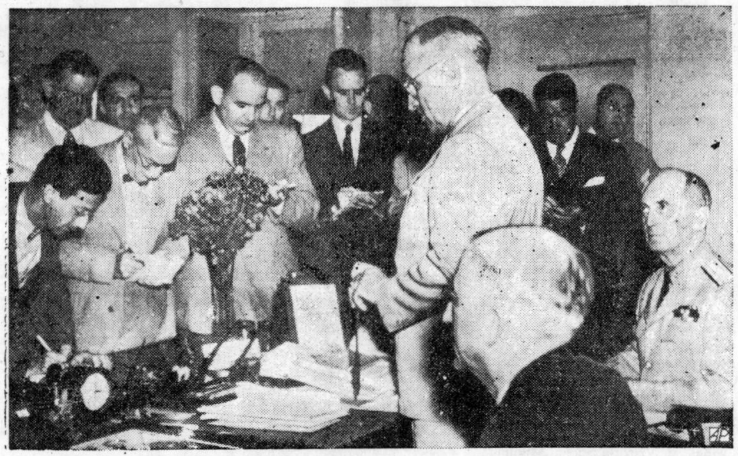

President Truman announced today August 8th that Russia has declared war on Japan. Secretary of State James F. Byrnes is seated in the fore ground and to the right of Truman is Adm. William D. Leahy. Newsmen are at left in this confercene scene in the President's White House office. (AP Wirephoto)

RUSSIAN WAR MAP

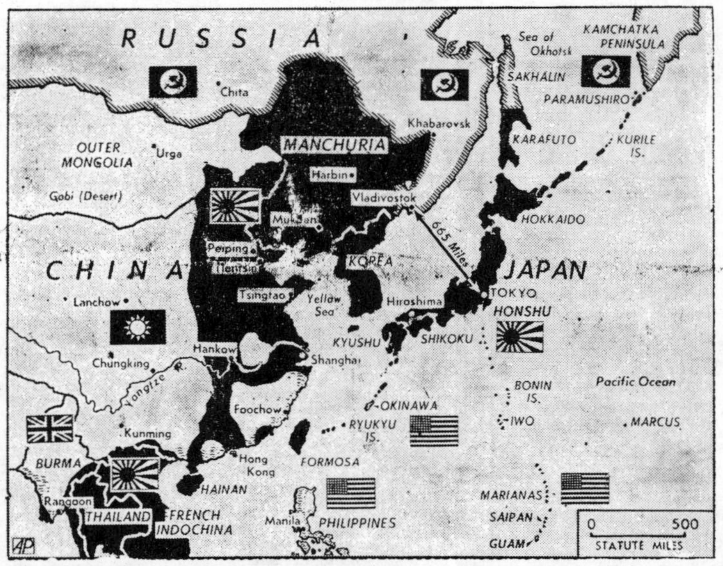

Russia entering the war against Japan completes the ring. Map locates Russian territory .(shaded areas) bordering Japan and Jap-held areas on the north as Soviet declaration of war on Japan today completed the Allied ring around the Japs. Distance is from Vladisovtok area bases to Tokyo, now under threat from the north as well as the south. Black areas are Jap-held.

BOARD OF EDUCATION PREFERS PAY - AS - YOU - GO POLICY FOR NEW PROGRAM

Junior High School Goes Into Operation In County This Fall

A pay-as-you-go policy is advocated by the Board of Education of Anne Arundel County in preference to a school bond issue to pay for the additional building required to carry out the 12 year system of schooling that, by act of the General Assembly this year, replaced the 11 year system in the state.

By 1949 the county must have additional facilities for approximately 1,400 children in the junior high school ages. To meet the cost of the necessary building program the Board favors a tax increase.

Superintendent George Fox has stated in behalf of the Board that "by raising the school tax to $1.15 per $100 the budget will provide $215,000 for new buildings. This would be an increase of 20 cents in the school tax and would cost the average property owner $12 per year."

The additional year will be the eighth grade, a year of schooling between the elementary grade and high school, planned with the purpose of extending the general education of children before they have reached the senior high school age of specialization. This new grade will be in the junior high school category.

Junior High School

(Continued On Page Two)

1945 Birth Rate Higher Than 1944

Increase Of 189 In Six Month Period To July 1

Births in Anne Arundel county have not taken the decline always predicted in the wake of war. Despite the end of the European war the births for the six month period, January 1 to July 1, 1945 numbered 189 more than the same period of 1944. Both periods are above the normal rate for the county, Dr. William J. French, County Health Officer eports.

In 1944 the total births for the first six months were 920, of which 718 were white and 202 colored. This year for the same period births numbered 1,109 of which 887 were white, 321 colored and one yellow.

The year's total of 2,017 (1,613 white, 404 colored) in 1944 may be expected to be exceeded in the current year.

The wartime birth rate is always high, Dr. French explained, and in addition the population of the county has increased fom 6r8,000 to 75,000. He does not attribute the increased rate to the increase in population but believes it has been due to men leaving for service in

(Continued On Page Seven)

Academy Band Leader For 30 Years Dies

Adolf Torovsky, 78-year-old leader of the Naval Academy band until his retirement 20 years ago, died last night of a heart ailment at his home 79 Franklin street.

He had been a member of the band 30 years.

Torovsky, whose musicianship was recognized in this country and abroad, died unexpectedly last night at 6:30 P. M. while waiting in the kitchen of his home for dinner to be prepared. He had been in ill health for several weeks but had been able to be about.

Born in Czechoslovakia, he studied under Johann Strauss II in Vienna where he was a member of the 26th Hungarian Regiment band. He came to this country in 1892 when his enlistment had expired and joined the Naval Academy band as a trumpet player.

He was proficient on every instrument in the band and was also an accomplished linguist. He quickly became second leader and subsequently first leader of the academy band.

In 1922 the year he retired, Torovsky accompanied H. L. Mencken critic and author, to Czecho-

(Continued On Page Three)

ATTACK LAUNCHED AT MIDNIGHT ON EAST BORDER OF MANCHURIA

(By the Associated Press)

Red Army troops slashed across the eastern and western frontiers of Japan's stolen Manchuria early this morning shortly after the Russian declaration of war became effective, and sharp fighting now is in progress in all invaded areas, the Tokyo radio announced today.

A broadcast Domei dispatch said Russian forces had battered across the eastern frontier of Manchuria at "several points" along a 300-mile line extending southward from Hutou to Hunchun. Hutou, just across the Soviet-Manchuria border, is 350 miles east of Harbin, and Hunchun is about 240 miles southeast of that key industrial and communications center, regarded as a prime Russian objective.

A Japanese Imperial Headquarters communique said the Russians struck across both the eastern and western frontiers, beginning shortly after midnight. This suggested a vast pincers movement against the crack Kwantung army, pride of the Emperor Hirohito's forces, believed massed in Manchuria.

REDS HURL AIR ATTACKS IN MANCHURIA

At the same time, the enemy communique said, Soviet planes raided targets in northern Korea and northern Manchuria in separate actions.

Domei said the targets of the Soviet planes included Harbin and Kirin, capital of Kirin Province, 270 miles southwest of Vladivostok; Rashin, a Japanese naval base in Korea, and Genzan, (Wonsan) a port of the eastern coast of Korea. Other points also were attacked by the Russian planes, the dispatch said.

The enemy bulletin declared puppet Manchurian troops had joined the Japanese in counterattacks.

"At the same time," the dispatch said "the Government called an extraordinary meeting of the State Council and took steps for giving immediate full play to the nation's power, thereby putting in order the government and people's front for repulsing the Red Army."

The Tokyo radio said Soviet ground forces launched a sudden attack at the eastern Soviet-Manchuria border early this morning. The broadcost, quoting a communique of the Japanese Kwantung army, also said a small number of Soviet aircraft bombed Manchurian territory, but gave no precise location.

Soldiers Sing

Columns of singing Red Army men, fresh from the victory over Hitler's Germany, tramped through the heart of Moscow just 45 minutes after the Soviet radio announced the news to the people.

Crowds poured from buildings and cheered the marching men. But the people were not surprised by the announcement. Aware of Russia's long enmity for the Nipponese, they had been prepared for the news for some time.

In fact, people seemed to take it as calmly as Soviet Foreign Commissar Vyacheslav Molotov announced it to newsmen.

The Foreign Commissar disclosed the dramatic news in a casual, almost nonchalant fashion at a press conference in the brilliantly illuminated conference room at the Soviet foreign office Three and a half hours before, at 5 P. M., (Moscow Time) he had summoned Japanese ambassador Naotake Sato to the Kremlin and handed him the declaration, to be effective at midnight, seven hours later.

Sato was permitted to send his last telegram to Tokyo with the announcement. The ambassador remained at the Japanese embassy in Moscow last night, with his staff gathered about him.

The Tokyo radio in an English-language broadcast to North America, said no official message had been received up to 2 P .M., Tokyo Time, from Sato. The broadcast recorded by the FCC, came after other Tokyo radio reports quoted Moscow broadcasts as saying Sato had been informed of the declaration.

An hour and 30 minutes after newsmen were told the news, the Soviet radio proclaimed if from one end to the vast Soviet Union to the other.

To Bring Peace

Molotov, asserting the declaration of war was a move to join the Allies in bringing peace to a war-weary world, disclosed that Emperor Hirohito had asked the Soviet Union to mediate in the Pacific war. This was in "mid-July."

Britain and America were informed he said.

He added that Toyko's rejection of the Potsdam unconditional surrender ultimatum left the Japa-

(Continued On Page Five)

EXHIBITS BY CHILDREN TO CLOSE REREATION PROJECT TOMORROW

The Annapolis Grammar School playground will close tomorrow for the season of recreation sponsored by the Anne Arundel County Board of Education. The programs at the West Annapolis, Germantown and Eastport schools closed earlier with an exhibits of handicrafts and demonstrations of games displayed at the different schools.

Another exhibit will complete the entire project tomorrow when the handiwork of all children who attended all the playgrounds will be showed in the assembly room of the old high school on Green street.

Civitan Club Favors Expanding Academy Here

R. H. Elliott, past president, was welcomed by members of the Civitan Club assembled for the regular luncheon meeting at Carvel Hall yesterday.

In a discussion of the projected Naval Academy expansion on the property of St. John's College emphasis was laid on the importance of retaining the institution in the city of Annapolis. The Navy Department is faced with the necessity of seeking expansion elsewhere unless its program is carried out here.

Members stressed that those charged with the final responsibility of the transaction should understand the overwhelming sentiment in Annapolis for expansion in accodance with the Navy plans.

WORK MAY START ON NEW FIELD HOUSE THIS YEAR

Sometime during the year begining July 1, 1945, work should start on the long delayed field house at the Naval Academy. The Navy Department appropriation bill for the fiscal year 1946 carries an appropriation for $1,500,000 for purchase of land, accessories, and construction of the field house. The work will be started in that year only if manpower and materials are available.

The Senate Committee on Appropriations, in its report on this subject, pointed out that the Naval Academy indoor athletic space averages only 13 square feet per student, while the American school standard is 50 square feet.

While other buildings are necessary at the Academy, this, in the opinion of the Navy, is the most important and pressing of all," spokesmen of the committee said.

The new field house would serve as space for indoor winter drills, and as a temporary auditorium.

SPIES TURNED ON NAZIS

WASHINGTON, Aug. 9 (AP) — The FBI said today that five German spies sent to the United States after 1939 to learn of atomic bomb developments were persuaded to double cross the Nazis and work as counter espionage agents.

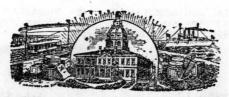

SOCIAL and PERSONAL

Son Born To Mr. And Mrs. Coleman

A son, Robert Deloraine Coleman, was born to Mr. and Mrs. Robert E. Coleman at Emergency Hospital, Friday morning, August 3. Mr. Coleman is manager of the Safeway Grocery Store.

Mrs. Wilson And Son Visit In Annapolis . .

Mrs. Nathan C. Wilson, Sr., and son, Nathan, Jr., have been visiting Mrs. Wilson's brother-in-law and sister-in-law, Mr. and Mrs. J. T. Basil, 22 Madison street, and Mrs. Betty Cook, 109 Chesapeake avenue, Eastport.

Mrs. Wilson, her son, Nathan, and daughter, Louise of Washington, will leave tomorrow for a weeks visit at Kennyville, Md., on the Eastern Shore, with Mr. and Mrs. Clarence Kelly.

Mrs. Wilson, who spent the past two years in Virginia, will again occupy her former residence, 507 Burnside street, Eastport, in the early fall.

Miss Decker To Wed At Naval Academy Chapel

Miss Suzanne DuPuy Decker, daughter of Comdr. Walter Bordman Decker, USN, (ret.), and Mrs. Decker, 7650 Maury Arch, Lockaven, Norfolk, Va., will become the bride of Lt. H. A. I. Sugg of 214 Prince George street Saturday afternoon at 4:00 P. M. The wedding will take place at the Naval Academy Chapel. A small reception at Carvel Hall for the wedding party and out of town guests will follow the ceremony. Lt. Sugg is the son of Mr. and Mrs. A. I. Sugg, Missouia, Montana.

* * *

Wedding At Baptist Church

Yesterday afternoon at 3:30 P. M., Mrs. Jane Pomeroy Sturgis, daughter of Mr. and Mrs. John Pomeroy of Miami, Fla., was married to William E. Dunt at the College Avenue Baptist Church. The Rev. W. C. Wood, pastor, officiated. The bride was attired in a powder blue suit with white accessories, and carried a gardenia corsage.

After a short honeymoon the couple will reside in Dundalk. Mr. Dunt is the golf professional at Sherwood Forest, but is now doing war work in Baltimore

* * *

Daughter Born To Myers

Pfc. and Mrs. John A. Myers announce the birth of a daughter, Gale Cecilia, at Emergency Hospital last Monday. Mrs. Myers is the daughter of Mr. and Mrs. Robert G. Middleton of Eastport. Pfc. Myers is at present stationed in Panama.

CALENDAR FOR THE WEEK

Today

2:00 P. M.—Meeting of Severn River Garden Club at the home of Mrs. Frederick A. Weiss, Jr., at Joyce.

8:00 P. M. — Meeting of the executive committee of the Junior Women's Club at the home of Mrs. Everett Henry, Fairfax.

8:30 P. M.—Orchestra dance at the USO.

Tomorrow

Refreshments served at USO by St. Luke's Chapel.

Celebrates Fifth Birthday

The fifth birthday of Bobby Landers, son of Mr. and Mrs. R. B. Landers, 4 German street, was celebrated Tuesday afternoon with a birthday party attended by numerous guests. Games and contests, with appropriate prizes, preceeded the serving of refreshments.

Among the children present were Dick Gott, George and Jimmy Clark, Frankie B. Walsh, Henry and John Ciccaroni, Eddie Chambers, Freddie Rawlings, Ethel Jones, Joan Deale, Eleanor and Sheron Gott, Judy Phipps, Patsy Heller, Sally Hendricks, Kyra Landers, Sally Basil, Mary Anne Morgan, Teaty Housely, Patsy Shaw and Norman Cook.

Adult guests were Katherine Walsh, Reba Basil, Helen Popham, Joris Newton, Hattie Newell, Clara Lloyd, Ida Eken, Elizabeth Ciccaroni, Florence Morgan, Evelyn Sisson, Abel Hendricks, Marion Heller, Francis Cook, Dorothy Gott, Dorothy King, Katherine Mooseles, Ray Landers, Eddie Lloyd, Jack Morgan, Gus Leonos and Frank Walsh.

The birthday party was followed by a cocktail party in the evening for the adult guests.

* * *

Visiting Mrs. McIntosh

Mrs. Marian C. Davis of Gloversville, New York is spending the week visiting Mrs. Rose E. McIntosh at her residence, 8 Maryland avenue. Mrs. Davis is the mother of Mid'n. Ted Davis, a first classman at the Naval Academy.

Meeting Tonight At 8 O'clock

The executive committee of the Junior Women's Club will meet at 8 P. M., this evening at the home of Mrs. Everett Henry of Fairfax.

Mrs. Bassford Returns Home

Mrs. C. M. Bassford, 50 Franklin street, who has been spending some time at Ocean City, N. J., has returned to her home in Annapolis.

THEY DROPPED ATOMIC BOMB ON JAPS

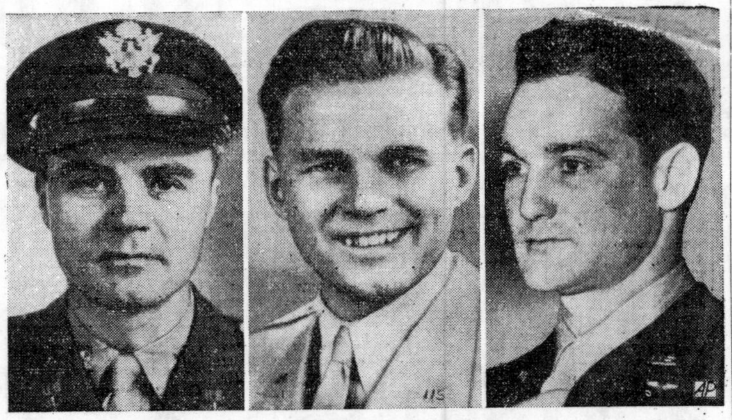

Col. Paul W. Tibbets, Jr., (left) of Miami was pilot, Capt. Robert A. Lewis (center) of Ridgefield, N. J., co-pilot, and Maj. Thomas W. Ferebee (right) of Mocksville, N. C., bombardier of the Superfortress Enola Gay which dropped the first atomic bomb on the Japanese city of Hiroshima August 6.

Married In Texas

Miss Mae Catherine Ray became the bride of Second Lieut. Edward J. Libotte, AAF., son of Mrs. Mary Libotte, 809 Chesapeake avenue, Eastport, on July 28. The ceremony was performed by the Rev. Hugh B. Warner, pastor, at the First Christian Church, Sweetwater, Texas.

Lt. Libotte, a graduate of Annapolis High School, is at present stationed at Abilene Army Air Field awaiting reassignment. He is a post graduate of the Second Army Air Force 72nd Fighter Wing pilot crew training program. He was commissioned and received his wings at Victoria Field, Mission, Texas, June 28, 1944. Before entering the armed forces, Lt. Libotte was a member of the Engineering Department at the Naval Academy.

* * *

Capt. Miller Leaves For Pacific

Capt. Wallace J. Miller, USN, 141 Lafayette avenue, has left for duty in the Southwest Pacific, after spending a six week leave with his wife, Mrs. Miller, and daughters, Betty Sue, and Mrs. Herbert F. Mills.

Atomic Bomb

(Continued From Page One)

nese proposals without significance.

Molotov's announcement said Russia entered the Japanese war as her "loyal Allied duty" on the request of the United States, Britain and China. He reminded the Japanese that after the defeat and capitulation of Germany, Japan was the only great power "which still insisted on the continuation of war."

After Japan's refusal to capitulate, he continued, the Allies asked the Soviet Union to join "against Japanese aggression, and by this shorten the war, to reduce the number of casualties and to speed the restoration of universal peace."

"Loyal to its Allied duty the Soviet Union has accepted the proposal of the Allies and has joined in the declaration of the Allied powers of July 26. (The Potsdam declaration demanding unconditional surrender).

"The Soviet government considered that this policy is the only means able to bring peace nearer, free the people from further sacrifice and suffering and give the Japanese people the possibility of avoiding the dangers and destruction suffered by Germany after her refusal to capitulate unconditionally," the statement said.

Calvert County

The Maryland Gazette wants news from every community in Calvert County. Phone or mail all items to Miss Sadie Gray, Telephone Prince Frederick 12-J.

Mrs. John W. Williams, Jr., and infant daughter are spending some time with Mr. and Mrs. John Wright Williams at their home in Prince Frederick. Mrs. Williams is hoping that her husband, Lieut. John W. Williams, Jr., will shortly be home on furlough. He was in France when last heard from.

Guests of the Misses Gray at Linden this week and the past week-end include Mrs. Charles K. Duce, Mr. and Mrs. John Peterson, Mr. J. Edward Harrison, of Baltimore; Mrs. Turner and Miss Maude Roberts, of Annapolis, and Mrs. Robert Rector and Mrs. John Baden, of Baltimore.

Dr. and Mrs. R. L. Silvester, of Washington, are spending some time at the home of Mr. and Thomas B. Mackall.

Mrs. Arthur A. Harkness and Mrs. John Cassell are spending a couple of weeks at Braddock Heights.

The Rev. W. E. Thomsen, Mrs. Thomsen and their two children, Bill and Nancy Jane, visited friends in Calvert last week.

Miss Agnes Tate, of Baltimore, spent several days last week at the home of Mrs. Everard Briscoe.

Linden O'Neill has recently received a transfer in connection with his work with the Merchant Marine, in which service he has been for one year. He is now located in Baltimore and is able to spend the week-ends with his family at their home in Prince Frederick.

Dr. I. N. King spent a couple of days last week in Washington, returning to Calvert on his yacht with his son and daughter-in-law, Mr. and Mrs. Roland King. Mr. and Mrs. King were aboard the yacht recently at Solomons for a week and this week they are entertaining friends on her at West River, in Anne Arundel county.

Mrs. Frances Dorsey, secretary to the Welfare Board, has returned to her work after spending her vacation with friends in Baltimore and Ocean City.

Property transfers in Calvert last week were the following: A. Louis Espey and Arnie L. Espey to Donald M. and Helen F. Swats, 6 lots at North Beach; Mary F. Russum to Kenneth and Mary Jane Parker, 4½ acres near St. Leonards; M. E. Rockhill to J. Bryce and Carlotta L. Weaver, 2 lots at Long Beach; Lam Latjrun and Martin F. Ries to Alden H. and Mary H. Sisson, lot at North Beach; Hannah J. Sanders to Phillip and Nellie Mae Herrmann, lot at North Beach; Marvin E. and Thelma West to Phillip and Nellie Mae Herrmann, 2 lots at North Beach; Ernest and Katherine V. Zimmerman to Steve Manthon, lot at North Beach; Anna M. and Charles M. Russell to Vada K. Russell, lot at North Beach; Vada K. Russell to Anna M. and Virgnia Russell, lot at North Beach; Stanley H. and May B. Colburn to Eugene C. and Lorenzo W. Guthrie, lot at Dares Beach; James E. and Lula Lusby to Earle S. Coster, lot of land near Olivet; Benjamin Hance and wife to Mary and Dorothy M. Hurley, 7 acres near Adelina; Samuel G. and Helen Ruth Barnard to Joseph O. and Mary T. Dean, lot at Barnard's Point on Battle Creek; Sarah E. Webster to Charles R. and Della I. Olsen, lot on Back Cover; Sarah J. Tongue to Jean Hamilton and H. H. Richardson, 1.4 acres near Coster; Aaron Toy, et al to Olive and Florence Sherbert, 1.36 acres near Barstow; Marie and Grant Ridgely to T. C. Warner Ayers, lot at Cove Point.

On August 3rd the Clerk of Court issued a marriage license to James Robert Conner and Henrietta Buckler, both of Adelina; and on August 6th to Julio Philip Fernandez, U.S.N., of New Orleans, La., and Mildred Anselma Barcal, of New Orleans.

On Saturday July 14 Joan Johancen and her cousin Ruth Clark of Baltimore celebrated their birthdays together at Joan's home in Ferndale. Ruth's birthday was July 12. Her father is a ensign in the United States Navy and is stationed somewhere in the South Pacific. The two girls guests were Gail Clark, Pauline Pumphrey, Claudette Boven, Joan Baker, Adriane Knight, Patsy Oliver, Teresa Oliver, Charles Harding, Barbara Stunburgh, Richard Lohrman, Harry Rae, Jinny Prhoff, Mrs. Walter Clark, Mrs. Mabel Tufel, Mr. and Mrs. John Neubert, Mr. and Mrs. Edmund Phaff, Mrs. George Behm, Mr. and Mrs. John Crambett, Mrs. Lily Miller, Mr. and Mrs. Robert Harding, Miss Alice M. Johancen, Miss Thelma Miller, Mr. and Mrs. Paul M. Johancen. An enjoyable time was had by all playing games and singing songs. Both girls had a birthday cake with their name on it.

Mr. and Mrs. N. E. Bexter, Master Edmund Baxter, Mr. and Mrs. C. Albert Woods, Miss Adrienne Woods, Mr. William Utz, Mrs. J. Moritz Smith, Miss Myrna Lee Smith, Mr. and Mrs. Leroy Brown and Mrs. Katherine Parsons were the Sunday guest of Mr. and Mrs. Richard B. Fones. Also Mr. George H. Smith and Mrs. George H. Smith who is convalescing.

ANNE ARUNDEL SAYS:

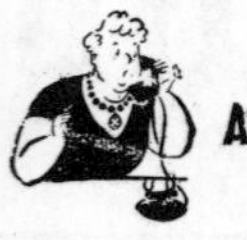

Have you heard about Teaneck, N. J., the crimeless, juvenile delinquencyless town? At least Teaneck is the nearest thing to a crimeless city in this country although it has a population of 3,000 and is next door to New York City and New Jersey centers.

Just nine names of juveniles were entered in the police department book of Teaneck in 1944. Only two of these actually committeed a crime and those two came from another town. On the records of the others were such dark deeds as accidentally smashing a window.

Entries of adult crimes are equally inocuous and include items like eavesdropping and detaining a homing pigeon.

Teaneck has attained its vaccuum of juvenile delinquency by a community government in the counsels of which youth's voice may be heard.

When teen-agers get an idea the entire town pitches in to do something about it, that is, if it's a good idea For instance, a group of high-school students thought an outdoor party in the town's central park was in order. So did the Recreation Superintendent.

So — students selected their own chaperons, the police safety bureau built a dance floor, the fire department set up floodlights and built a safe bonfire and the highway department contributed trucks for transportation.

Teen-agers of Annapolis aren't going to get any idea about a central park outing since there is no central park nor do they have a Recreation Superintendent with whom to consult. But the way Teaneck citizens keep their books clear of juvenile crime is something for Annapolis to think about, isn't it?

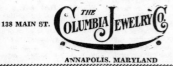

Neighborhood News

(Continued From Page Four)

sired. At 8:15 P. M. the Southern States annual meeting will be held. Mr. Raymond Armstrong, chairman of the advisory board will preside over the business session. An interesting program will be presented.

Sunday school next Sunday at Old Mt. Zion Church will be at 10:30 A. M., and Epworth League at 8 P. M.

The condition of Mrs. Lydia H. Sutton, who is suffering a heart condition, at the Emergency Hospital, is considered favorable.

Miss Norma Sutton, daughter of Mr. and Mrs. Norman Sutton, underwent an appendictomy, on Friday at the Emergency Hospital. She is recovering nicely.

CROWNSVILLE and WATERBURY

At a meeting of the Ladies' Aid Society of the Union Protestant Church in Herald Harbor Wednesday, August 1, the following officers were elected for the coming year: President, Mrs. Lottie Schone; vice-president, Mrs. Eva Stitt; secretary, Mrs. Ralph Smith; treasurer, Mrs. Carolyn Sanderson. The last meeting was held at the home of the treasurer, Mrs. Carolyn Sanderson, on Wednesday afternoon.

Chaplain Foss, of Fort George G. Meade, conducted the services on Sunday evening at the Union Protestant Church in Herald Harbor.

Nineteen guests attended a dinner in honor of Pvt. William John Haacke, at the home of his grandmother, Mrs. Ida Bruning, recently.

Master Danny Beazley has returned to his home in Saluda, Middlesex County, Va., after visiting his grandparents, Mr. and Mrs. George E. Beazley, Sr., at their home on Bonaparte road, Herald Harbor.

Mrs. Minnie Stitt is recuperating from a fall recently.

Announcemen

The American Piano Company has granted Oliver C. Keeney & Sons exclusive franchise for the Chickering & Marshall-Wendel Pianos.

These instruments are outstanding in reputation, appearance and performance and are definitely best grade pianos.

In an endeavor to improve the music store the firm of Oliver C. Keeney & Sons feel deeply grateful in being granted this franchise in times like these.

There is no doubt that better things, musically, are in store for people of Annapolis.

Keeney's hope for floor samples in the very near future.

O. C. KEENEY & S
Sheet Music and Musical Instruments
23 Randall Street, Annapolis.

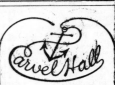

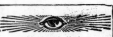

Our war with Japan lasted 1,346 days after the Pearl Harbor attack.
The European war lasted 2,075 days after Hitler struck Sept. 1, 1939.
For the Chinese, peace came after 2,946 days of uninterrupted warfare with the Japanese.

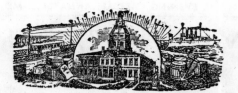

Evening Capital

WEATHER
Partly cloudy and cooler. Thursday fair and moderate temperature.

VOL. LXI — NO. 192 | EVERY EVENING EXCEPT SUNDAY | ANNAPOLIS, MD., WEDNESDAY, AUGUST 15, 1945 | SOUTHERN MARYLAND'S ONLY DAILY | THREE CENTS

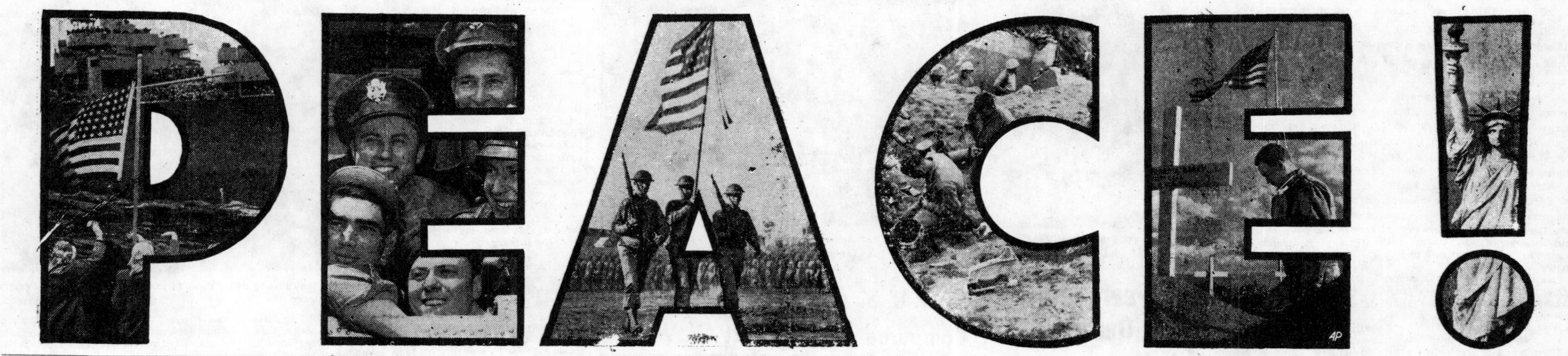

PEACE!

SEES NEED FOR ACADEMY EXPANSION

Sasscer Warns Of Threat To Academy; Advocates Acquisition of St. John's

Congressman Lansdale G. Sasscer, decrying the attempts to establish a Naval Academy on the west coast and seeing in them an imminent threat to the very existence of the Annapolis academy, is advocating its expansion on the St. John's property as the only possible site in this vicinity.

The representative from the Fifth District, Maryland, of which Anne Arundel county is a part, declared views in letters to persons, among them Mrs. Marden Rigg, chairman of the committee of the hundred women, who have written him in opposition to the acquisition of St. John's and sent a copy of his reply to J. Marion Lazenby, member of the Citizen's Committee for the retention of the Academy in Annapolis.

Two Academies

If an attempt is made to establish two academies Sasscer wrote he had "almost a moral certainty" that the Annapolis school would become only a specialist or postgraduate school."

Expressing his "strong personal sentiment for St. John's" he stated his belief that "we are at the crossroads of decision" and must press for expansion, which includes "the taking of St. John's" or lose the Naval Academy, which he termed a "tremendous asset and advertisement not only to Anne Arundel county but our state."

No Alternative

He wrote that the possibilities of alternative available land had been fully explored and said the belief held by the "Committee" (presumably the House Naval Affairs Committee) was that there is no alternative.

Reviewing the position taken by the college Board of Visitors and Governors he stated his conclusion that the college will continue to be handicapped as it admittedly has been, in enrollment and endowment, as long as the question of acquisition of the property is agitated.

Sasscer expressed his hope that Maryland may retain both an enlarged academy and also St. John's College.

Text Of Letter

The text of his letter follows:

I received and carefully read your letter with reference to the important Naval Academy-St. John's controversy and am glad to outline the situation as I see it.

The united effort of the federal and state officials, civic organizations, etc. on the West Coast capitalizing the wide disparity of feeling and disunion over the issue in this area, aided by a daily crusade of one of the leading Washington papers for a Pacific Coast Acad-

(Continued on Page Six)

Local Tides

TOMORROW

High water — 12:13 A. M., 1.5 feet; 11:24 P. M., 1.1 feet. Low water—7:01 P. M., 5:59 A. M.

Moon rises 2:30 A. M.; sets 2:11 A. M.

Sun rises 6:14 A. M.; sets 8:00 P. M.

Tides are given for Annapolis. For Sandy Point, add 15 minutes. For Thomas Point shoal, subtract 30 minutes.

THE TOWN WENT WILD

The tranquil inertia of Maryland's capital joyously exploded when news of Japan's surrender flashed last night.

The first hours of peace flowed like a river—a mighty, turbulent stream of shouting, laughing humanity—shattering the colonial calm of Annapolis.

The city went wild. Old residents state that nothing to equal the demonstration had ever been seen in the ancient streets in all its history.

Two minutes after official announcement of acceptance Japan's unconditional surrender sirens blasted, church bells tolled and cars began an incessant parade with blaring horns through the streets and around the old circles.

For hours a bumper-to-bumper line continued down Main street and West street. Confetti and shreds of paper fell like snow, tin cans dragged from automobiles, children beat any article that would make a noise, sailors arm-in-arm in street-wide lines wound across Church Circle somehow managing to wedge between cars without being run down.

Three sailors went into St.

(Continued On Page Three)

METHODIST SERVICES TONIGHT

The Eastport Methodist Church will hold Victory Day Services this evening at 7:30 P. M., it was announced today.

CALVARY CHURCH V-J SERVICE TONIGHT

In celebration of V-J Day, the Calvary Methodist Church will be open all day for persons desiring to offer prayers. And at 8 P. M. a Peace Thanksgiving Service will be held.

In the absence of the pastor, Dr. J. Luther Neff, the Rev. Dr. James B. Clayton will conduct the service and the the Junior Choir will join the senior choir for the singing of patriotic hyms. Mrs. John W. Dudley, Jr., leader of the Junior Choir will accompany at the organ.

PRESIDENT READS JAP MESSAGE TO CABINET

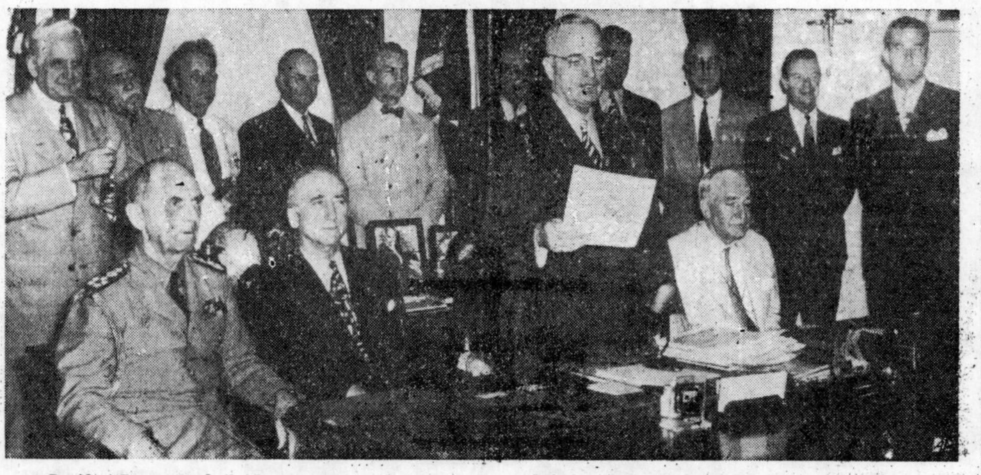

President Truman reads the Japanese message, to members of his cabinet in his office at the White House. Seated beside him are Adm. William D. Leahy, (left), Sec. of State James Byrnes (second from left) and former Sec. of State Cordell Hull (white suit). Cabinet members standing in background are (l to r) WPB Chief J. A. Krug, Foreign Economic Chief Leo Crowley, Maj. Gen. Philip Fleming of Federal Works Adminstration; Economic Stabilizer William H. Davis, Reconversion Chief John W. Snyder, Sec. of Navy James Forrestal, Sec. of Treasury Fred Vinson, Attorney General Tom Clark, Sec. of Labor Lewis Schwellenbach, National Housing Chief John B. Blandford, Jr., Postmaster Robert Hannegan. (AP Wirephoto)

Academy Explodes Into Maelstrom Of Celebration At Victory Word

All of a nation's glory in victory was concentrated last night at the U. S. Naval Academy when 2,000 midshipmen, on yard liberty, at the word ENE let lose with all they had from lusty lungs and strong arms that beat the Japanese gong and tossed thousands of rolls of paper to serpentine over the milling throngs.

Midshipmen bounded into an orgy of youthful exultation—like a flock of white birds released from captive hands. Beatific-faced teen-age lads received the nod to "sound off" from their skipper, Rear Admiral J. R. Beardall, Academy Superintendent, and the regiment surged into Navy cheers and wild hurrahs for their elder brethren manning victorious American fleets against Japan.

2,000 Celebrate

More than 2,000 Midshipmen celebrated victory in typical American youth fashion—they took up the slack and let loose with every Navy and non-regulation yell known to exuberant sailor spirit, punctuated with handsprings, songs, snake dances and extemporaneous shouts of sheer abandonment.

The deep-throated siren on the powerhouse moaned for more than an hour the chapel bells chimed in soft, mellow melody.

The future officers manned the cornices and roofs of Bancroft Hall let fly with thousands of

(Continued On Page Four)

POST OFFICE CLOSED TODAY, TOMORROW

Postmaster William A. Strohm announced today that in conforming with Presidential order, all divisions of the Post Office will be closed today and tomorrow.

There will be no delivery of mail by foot or rural carriers today and tomorrow. Patrons having Post Office boxes will receive their mail as usual. All special delivery and perishable matter will be delivered immediately upon receipt.

Collection of mail in the city and outlying districts will be at 3:00 P. M. and 11:00 on both days. All mail deposited at the main Post Office will receive the usual week day dispatch.

V-J SERVICES

V-J Day services will be conducted at the Asbury Methodist Church this evening at 8 P. M., it was announced this noon.

ATOMIC BOMB CARRIER SHIP GOES DOWN

GUAM, Aug. 15 (AP)—Two great explosions flashed out of her slim bow at 12 minutes past midnight. Flames streaked through her shock-darkened passageways, searing the piled bodies of her crew into shapeless masses. Within 15 minutes she plunged headfirst into the sea.

That was the end of the proud cruiser Indianapolis — torpedoed 450 miles off Leyte July 30 with 883 dead and missing, after she had finished a record speed run from San Francisco to Guam to deliver the first atom bomb to the

(Continued on Page Six)

THE FRUITS OF PEACE ARE NOT RATIONED

WASHINGTON, Aug. 15 (AP)—OPA today announced immediate termination of the rationing of gasoline, canned fruits and vegetables, fuel oil and oil stoves.

Price Administrator Chester Bowles said that meats, fats and oils, butter, sugar, shoes and tires will stay on the ration list "until military cutbacks and increased production brings civilian supplies more nearly in balance with civilian demand.

"Nobody is any happier than we in OPA," Bowles said, "that as far as gasoline is concerned, the day is finally here when we can drive our cars wherever we please, when we please and as much as we please."

The OPA chief said "right now it's impossible" to estimate when other commodities can be removed from rationing.

Paper Collection Thursday

Citizens of Annapolis who didn't have their newspaper and tin cans picked up at Wednesday's collection are urged to place them on the streets Thursday as all districts not covered by the pick-up truck Wednesday will be visited Thursday, it was announced today.

WAR WEARY NATION HITS HEIGHTS OF CELEBRATION AS OFFICIAL WORD COMES

WASHINGTON, Aug. 15—(AP)—The world entered a new era of peace today.

Along the enormous battlefronts of the Pacific and Asia the mightiest forces of destruction ever assembled rolled to a victorious halt around the prostrate, vanquished Empire of Japan.

Throughout the Allied world, wracked by war or threat of war since Germany struck Poland on Sept. 1, 1939, it was a time for rejoicing and celebration. But already the problems of peace were beginning to pile up.

"We are faced with the greatest task we ever have been faced with," said President Truman.

He announced Japan's capitulation at 7 o'clock, Eastern War Time, last night. The act marked the beginning of a truce that will last a few days until General of the Army Douglas MacArthur, as Supreme Allied Commander, can accept formal Japanese surrender on the basis of the Potsdam declaration.

More than four hours after Mr. Truman announced the surrender, the war was still on in the Pacific. A communique from Guam early today reported that units of the U. S. Third Fleet in the vicinity of Honshu were being approached by Japanese aircraft.

"Those that do so are being shot down," the war bulletin said.

Radio Tokyo, however, waited another hour, until 1 P. M., Japanese time, to tell its troops of the surrender.

The broadcast said: "We have lost, but this is temporary," it added.

Domei News Agency reported that Emperor Hirohito, addressing his nation for the first time by radio, blamed surrender on two main fac...

1. That the trend of the world was against Japan.
2. On the atomic bomb—which went into action only nine days ago and was used against only two cities.

Many Japanese who played leading rolls in the war were expected by officials here to commit hara-kiri as a result of the defeat. Domei reported from Tokyo early today that the Japanese War Minister, Korechika Anami, had killed himself to "atone for his failure."

Mr. Truman announced the surrender at a two-minute news conference. He released at the same time the text of an acceptance note which the Japanese government had sent to Washington through neutral Switzerland yesterday afternoon.

"I deem this reply a full acceptance of the Potsdam declaration which specifies the unconditional surrender of Japan," Mr. Truman said.

With the President's announcement came a flood of orders:

1. General MacArthur was designated formally as Supreme Commander for all Allied powers—the United States, Russia, Britain and China—to accept the formal Japanese surrender.
3. Allied armed forces were ordered to suspend offensive action.
4. Today and tomorrow were proclaimed by the President as holidays, although V-J Day awaits the formal surrender.

At Manila MacArthur declared "I shall at once take steps to stop hostilities and further bloodshed."

But no steps taken anywhere could make up for the losses of life and treasure already lost in mankind's most frightful conflict.

The United States alone could count nearly 1,000,000 dead and wounded and a money cost estimated at $300,000,000,000.

The nations of the world altogether suffered incalculable casualties; some persons put the total at more than 23,000 killed and wounded exclusive of air raid and starvation losses that never can be known.

(Continued On Page Six)

The Key Men In The Drive To Tokyo

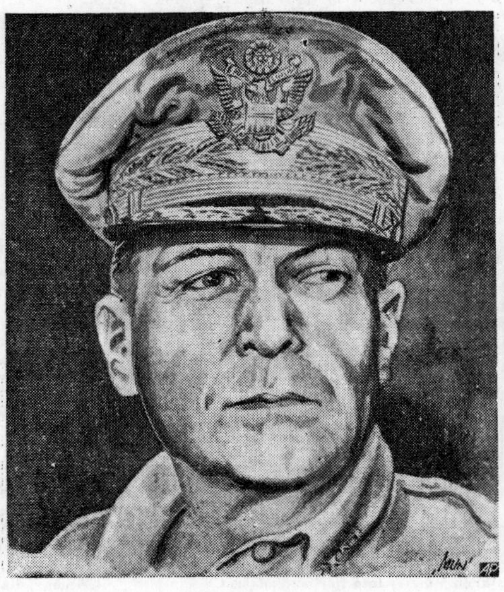

GEN. DOUGLAS MacARTHUR

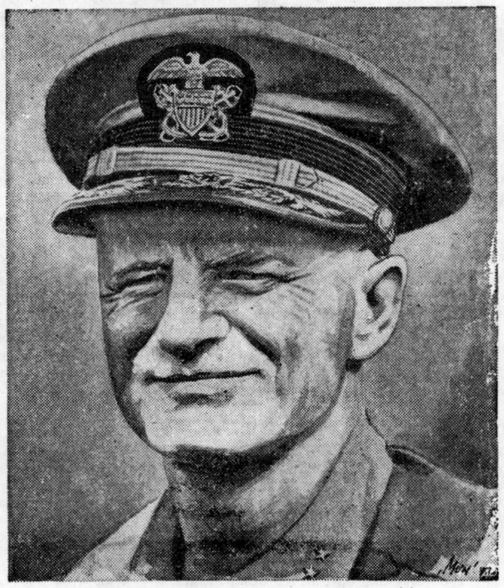

ADM. CHESTER W. NIMITZ

PLACE: Pearl Harbor: TIME: Dec. 7, 1941 -- A Date To Live In Infamy

THUNDER OF BOMBS BROUGHT AMERICA INTO WORLD WAR II

By JOHN L. SPRINGER
AP Newsfeatures Writer

PEARL HARBOR was awakened on the morning of Dec. 7, 1941, by the thunder of bombs and the crumbling of steel. Drowsy seamen and soldiers looked up to see a fleet of Japanese fighter, bomber and torpedo planes raining blows on the core of the U. S. Pacific fleet, resting helplessly in the harbor.

It was the "sneak punch," thrown without warning that plunged America into World War II.

At 7:50 that morning, as on hundreds of Sundays before, seven great battleships rode easily at anchor. Cruisers, destroyers and smaller ships rested in snug rows. On nearby Hickman, Wheeler and Bellows Fields, planes sat peacefully in their hangars or out on the open runways.

Five minutes later the Japanese came. More than 150 planes, from aircraft carriers which boldly had moved close to Hawaii, droned over the island of Oahu.

Harbor In Flames

There was one great blast, steadily more until the whole harbor was enveloped in flames and smoke. The battleship Arizona blew up and its twisted, smoking wreckage settled into the sea. Other ships capsized. Flames poured from the airfields, where planes and hangars were riddled with holes. As men raced from their barracks, machine gun fire from strafing planes shot them down.

By 9:45 the attack was over. Every warship in the harbor had been stricken. Eight of the 17 battleships in the entire U. S. fleet had been put out of action — two so severely wounded they could never be used again; the others so battered they would need many months of repairs. Three cruisers, a seaplane tender and repair ship were damaged; two destroyers and a mine layer were sunk. Another destroyer, which was sunk, was later repaired.

The Navy had sunk three submarines. Desperate anti-aircraft fire had downed 28 enemy planes and the few U. S. aircraft that had got into the sky had knocked out 20 of the attackers. But when U. S. losses were tallied, the destroyed American planes totaled 177. A total of 2,343 Navy and Army men were killed in the boiling, oil-covered waters of the harbor, or in the holds of ships, or on the blistered airfields. There were 1,272 wounded.

It was the worst defeat—and the greatest humiliation—America's Navy had eever suffered.

Who Was To Blame?

The question of blame for this defeat recurred again and again throughout the war. An investigating committee named by President Roosevelt pointed at Adm. Husband E. Kimmel, commander in chief of the Pacific fleet, and Maj. Gen. Walter C. Short, commanding general of the Hawaiian department. This committee's report said the secretaries of Wa and Navy had warned of the possibility of war and had ordered precautions. Steps taken by Kimmel and Short, the report said, were inadequate. The two men were relieved of their post and threatened with later court martials. But in December, 1944, the Army and Navy announced no grounds had been found for courtmartial proceedings.

There also was much reason to think that many Japanese, given freedom to pry around the island, had stuffed Tokyo with vital military information.

While the Japanese struck at Pearl Harbor, other planes of the Rising Sun swooped over the Philippines, Wake, Guam and Hong Kong.

But while ships still blazed, the Navy began to rebuild at Pearl Harbor. Within a year it could announce that virtually all the damage had been erased forever.

A VICTIM OF INFAMY—This mass of twisted, burning wreckage is what remained of the once mighty U.S.S. Arizona after the treacherous Japanese attack on Pearl Harbor.

FROM ABOVE—A Japanese bomber flies over an airfield at Oahu while fires rage below. This photo of the attack on Pearl Harbor was made from another Nipponese raider.

FROM BELOW—An explosion sends a cloud of smoke and flame high into the sky after a bomb hit at the Naval Air Station at Pearl Harbor. Grounded Navy men watch futilely.

Pearl Harbor Quotation

AP Newsfeatures

JAPAN'S attack on Pearl Harbor led by many memorable quotations. Among them: :

President Roosevelt: "Dec. 7, 1941 . . . a date which will live in infamy."

Winston Churchill: "It only remains for two great democracies to face their task with whatever strength God may give them."

Sen. Burton K. Wheeler (D. Mont.), Roosevelt's foreign policy foe: "The only thing now is to . . . lick hell out of them."

President Manuel Quezon of the Philippines: "The flag of the United States will be defended until the last round of ammunition has been fired."

Emperor Hirohito of Japan: "The hallowed spirits of our imperial ancestors . . . give us confidence."

Adolf Hitler: "That Japan took this step must fill all decent people with profound satisfaction."

Attache at New York Japanese consulate, clearing out his belongings: "This is a special Sunday."

Cordell Hull, Secretary of State: "Japan has been infamously false and fraudulent."

Gen. John J. Pershing, commander of the A.E.F. in World War I: "All Americans today are united in one ambition—to take whatever share they can in the defense of their country."

How U. S. And Japanese Strength Compared At The Start Of War

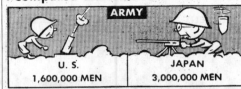

ARMY

U.S.	JAPAN
1,600,000 MEN	3,000,000 MEN

NAVY

U.S.	JAPAN
344 WARSHIPS	262 WARSHIPS
17 Battleships	12 Battleships
7 Aircraft Carriers	8 Aircraft Carriers
37 Cruisers	46 Cruisers
170 Destroyers	125 Destroyers
113 Submarines	71 Submarines

AIR FORCE

U.S.	JAPAN
3,000 PLANES (1,157 suited for combat)	3,600 PLANES (Including all types)

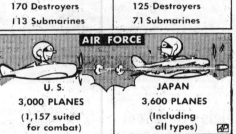

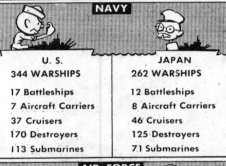

FROM PEACE TO WAR IN A FLASH

By TRUDI McCULLOUGH
AP Newsfeatures Writer

TO A U. S. that has fought total war around the globe a flashback of American receiving and trying to comprehend the news of Pearl Harbor seems as unreal as ancient history.

At approximately 2:20 P. M. on Dec. 7, 1941, in Washington, D. C., three newsservice men were laying out their wire reports. The telephone rang in all three offices. They picked up the phones and hard a voice say, "This is Steve Early. I have a statement here which the President asked me to read." Then Early read that Hawaii was being bombed.

For the first half dozen reporters to reach the White House Steve Early had more news: The first attacks on Hawaii and the Philippines had been made wholly without warning and even as Japanese diplomats paid a peaceful call on Secretary of State Cordell Hull. The President was with the Secretaries of War and Navy. He had ordered all previously prepared defense measures invoked.

Thermometer Rises

From then on the thermometer of news rose higher and higher: "Both attacks are believed to be still in progress."

"An American ship only 700 miles out of San Francisco has radioed distress signals."

"The Navy has just advised the President that Guam has been attacked."

All over the country, whether in Norfolk where it was the coldest day of the year, to Boston where the Sabbath calm prevailed, to Kansans finishing a heavy noonday dinner, to New Yorkers at a football game or the movies, the first question was "Where was our Navy?" Almost as universal was the second reaction: "Those Japs must be crazy."

Little People Speak

Stunned but with unquestioning confidence, the little people all over the country spoke. A Chicagoian said: "How terrible for the Japanese. It's mass suicide. Well, we've got to whip the whole world, and we can do it."

In Topeka a woman called the Capital agitatedly reporting that a Japanese plane had just dived over her house. In Nebraska a soldier said to another, "Boy, take your last look at Omaha for a long time. Which way's the war?" People had only enough oil for a year.

In Detroit hotel lobbies were deserted as people stayed with their ears glued to the radio. The radio everywhere told servicemen to report for duty at once, announced recruiting stations would be open at 8 A. M. In Pittsburgh five young men out for a carefree afternoon changed their talk to "enlisting tomorrow." In Cleveland someone recalled how the Japanese Navy had struck at Port Arthur while the Japanese Ambassador was attending a Russian Court ball. There too 80 specialists on Pacific Relations sat around a conference table arguing. In one second, when the flash came, their differences were resolved.

Unity Blossoms

All over the U. S. their reaction was duplicated. Nothing else could have united America so immediately and so completely.

Back in Washington, reporters discovered the mild mannered police who used to patrol the munitions building had been replaced by fully equipped G. I.'s with live ammunition. The high command changed from mufti to uniforms. And in the press room Steve Early's assistant gave a preliminary report on casualties: 300 military wounded, 104 military fatalities. They were the first of the dead.

RUSH TO THE COLORS—Outbreak of war brought a flood of volunteers to the armed forces. This enlistment scene, at the U. S. Marine recruiting office in New York the day after Pearl Harbor, was duplicated throughout the nation.

SUDDEN JAPANESE ATTACK ON HAWAII CLIMAXED TEN YEARS OF AGGRESSION

By THOMAS A. BOYNTON
AP Newsfeatures

JAPAN'S seizure of Manchuria in 1931 began what the U. S. State Department has termed "the fateful decade" — ten years of "ruthless development of determined world domination" by the Axis.

The decade ended in war with the United States, when the Japanese suddenly attacked Pearl Harbor and other American bases in the Pacific Dec. 7, 1941. For Japan, this attack was the greatest of a long line of aggressions made to establish a "new order," the "Greater East Asia Co-Prosperity Sphere."

This is the background of the conflict that now has led to disaster for Japan:

She was a newcomer among world powers. In 1853, after two and a half centuries of virtual Japanese seclusion, Commo. Matthew C. Perry entered the empire's home waters with a U. S. naval force. Until then, Japan's foreign commerce had been meager. From 1625 until the 1840s island waters had been closed completely to outsiders, and then certain ports were opened for limited trade, mainly with the English and the French.

It was Perry who opened the door to Japan, and in 1855 Japan signed a commercial and settlement treaty with America — her first with a major western power.

Face To Face

Between 1894 and 1898, however, the United States and Japan wung face to face in the Pacific. In 1894-5 Japan defeated China and took Formosa, stepping stone to the rich southwest Pacific. The United States won a war over Spain in 1898, acquiring the Philippines and annexing Hawaii.

During Japan's 1904-5 war with Russia, a sympathetic United States actually floated Japanese war loans. Peace was signed at Portsmouth, N. H., at the invitation of President Theodore Roosevelt. Japan won supreme rights over Korea and authority over Manchuria's great Changchung railway. In 1906, Port Arthur became a Japanese naval station.

This Asiatic anchor planted, Japan made 21 demands upon China in 1915, seeking to further her continental supremacy. Washington objected, recalling Japan's earlier commitment to an "open door" policy in China. Pre-World War I friction also developed as U. S. citizens sought relief from mass immigration of Orientals, but this matter did not come to a head until 1924, when Congress passed the Asiatic Exclusion Act, bitterly denounced by Japan as discriminatory.

Fought With Allies

Yet Japan fought on the Allied side in World War I, and increased her ocean empire by taking over former German islands.

When Japan wrenched Manchuria from the Chinese in 1931, the United States refused to recognize the conquest. Despite vigorous protests by Secretary of State Stimson, the Manchurian drive soon spilled over into Jehol, North China. Japan said she would go no further.

Yet she withdrew from the League of Nations in 1933, after the league condemned this aggression. And in 1935-36 she rejected the London Conference decision of Britain, France and the United States to hold to naval equality unless threatened, then renewing her naval race. Then, on Nov. 25, 1936, Japan signed the anti-Comintern pact with Germany.

Attack Marco Polo Bridge

The United States hoped to prevent widespread warfare after Japanese troops attacked the Chinese at the Marco Polo Bridge July 7, 1937. Secretary Hull offered his "good offices" to help settle the issue. Japan just intensified her campaign. President Roosevelt clamped the Neutrality Act on both powers, stopping war shipments in U. S. vessels.

In September, 1940, Joseph C. Grew, ambassador to Tokyo, cabled Secretary Hull that German victories, "like strong wine," had gone to Japanese heads, and military factions thought Japan should consolidate its Greater East Asia position while the Reich still was agreeable.

Even before the Franco-German armistice of June, 1940, Japan put pressure on the French in Indo-China. Hull observed it was clear that Japan's leaders were "bent on the conquest by force of all worthwhile territory in the Pacic ocean area."

A blow to the Japanese was passage of the Lend-Lease act in January, 1941, under which President Roosevelt promised "all out aid" to China. From Tokyo, Ambassador Grew reported Japanese plans to attack Pearl Harbor in case of "trouble" with the United States.

Discussions Grow Tense

Discussions between the new Japanese ambassador, Naokuni Nomura, and Secretary Hull became more and more tense as Japanese aggression pushed on. In June 1941, Hull handed Nomura a formula for peace, containing these points:

Both governments should affirm their national polices as directed toward lasting peace and cooperation; the United States would suggest to China that China and Japan enter peace negotiations, provided Japan first communicate to and discuss with the United States the general terms; mutual trade and commerce agreements would be made; and the two countries should discuss proposed neutralization of the future independent Philippines.

However, Japan's next move was occupation of Indo-China un-

COMMO. MATTHEW PERRY
. . . He Opened The Door . . .

PREMIER-GEN. HIDEKI TOJO
. . . He Slammed It Shut . . .

der Vichy French permission. Roosevelt made a futile appeal to stop the move, then froze Japanese assets in the United States.

Japanese Plans Cited

In August, the State Department told the British embassy the Japanese planned to invade the Indian ocean area, isolating China, and probably move to block Suez and the Cape of Good Hope on the British trade routes. That same month President Roosevelt warned Nomura that "if the Japanese government takes any further steps . . by force or threat . . the United States will be compelled to take immediately any and all steps which it may deem necessary . . for safety and security."

Saburo Kurusu joined Nomura in Washington early in November. The two decried the "encirclement" of Japan and Lend-Lease aid to Chiang Kai-shek as well as the economic blockade. But they made it evident that Japan insisted on a "victor's peace" in China, with U. S. assent and continued Japanese occupation. Japanese troops continued to flood Indo-China.

On Dec. 6, President Roosevelt cabled Emperor Hirohito and asked that peace be preserved. At 7:55 A. M., Honolulu time, Sunday, Dec. 7, Japanese carrier planes attacked Pearl Harbor. In Washington, an hour later Nomura and Kurusu called on Secretary Hull with a memorandum. It said the United States had prevented peace in China, had blocked Japan's co - prosperity plan, had shown no conciliation in discussions, had planned war with Germany and Japan, and was party to an anti-Japanese conspiracy with Britain and other countries.

To Nomura and Kurusu, Hull snapped: "I have never seen a document that was more crowded with infamous falsehoods and distortions—infamous falsehoods and distortions on a scale so huge that I never imagined until today that any government on this planet was capable of uttering them."

At 11 A. M., Dec., Tokyo time (9 P. M., Dec. 7, E.W.T.), the U. S. Embassy at Tokyo received a communication from the Japanese Foreign Minister advising "that there has risen a state of war between Your Excellency's country and Japan beginning today."

THE FIRST WEEK OF WAR

AP Newsfeatures

THE Japanese got their war off to a fast start with their attack on Pearl Harbor and other U. S. possessions in the Pacific. Within a week they had established themselves on the Philippines and Guam and had begun their drive down through the jungles of Malaya.

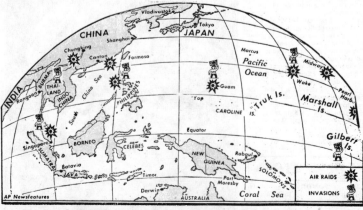

DEC. 7 — Japanese planes attack Pearl Harbor, Wake, Guam, Philippines, Malaya and Hong Kong. Japanese invade Thailand.

DEC. 8 — United States declares war. Japanese attack Midway, Thailand capitulates. Enemy moves into Northern Malaya.

DEC 9 — Japanese occupy northern Gilbert Islands, blast Burma Road from the air.

DEC. 10 — First landings made in the Philippines. British lose battleship Prince of Wales and battle cruiser Repulse off Malaya.

DEC. 11 — Japanese forces attack Wake. Germany, Italy declare war on United States.

DEC. 12 —Japanese occupy Guam.

Evening Capital

VOL. LXI — NO. 193
EVERY EVENING EXCEPT SUNDAY
ANNAPOLIS, MD., THURSDAY, AUGUST 16, 1945
SOUTHERN MARYLAND'S ONLY DAILY
THREE CENTS

WEATHER
Fair tonight and Friday. Slightly cooler tonight.

Admiral Fitch Installed At Academy

LATE NEWS

SUNDAY, AUG. 19, TO BE DAY OF PRAYER

Washington, Aug. 16 (AP)—Next Sunday, Aug. 19, has been set aside by President Truman as a day of prayer to God to "support and guide us into the paths of peace."

U.S.-BRITISH DISCUSS PALESTINE PROBLEM

Washington, Aug. 16 (AP)—President Truman disclosed today that his government is discussing with the British a Jewish national state in Palestine.

CHURCHILL CREDITS ATOMIC BOMB WITH ENDING WAR

London, Aug. 16 (AP)—Winston Churchill, who guided Great Britain through all but the last days of the war, told Commons today that the atomic bomb "more than any other factor" brought about the "sudden and speedy ending of the war against Japan."

ESTIMATE YEAR NEEDED TO REPLENISH CANNED FOOD

Baltimore, Aug. 16 (AP)—Baltimore canners estimated today that it would take a year's pack of fruits and vegetables to replenish retail food store and market stocks.

JAP PUPPET REGIME IN CHINA DISSOLVES

(By The Associated Press)
Tokyo broadcast of Domei agency dispatch today saying that the Japanese-dominated "national governmen of China," at Nanking had decided to dissolve.

CHINESE REDS CONTINUE SPORADIC CIVIL CLASHES

Chungking, Aug. 16 (AP)—Unofficial reports today said Chinese Communist troops, apparently bent upon seizing control of all key cities north of the Yellow River when Japanese lay down their arms, had clashed with central government guerrillas at several points near Tsingtao and Tientsin.

INDUCTEES TO BE CHIEFLY 18-YEAR-OLDS

Baltimore, Aug. 16 (AP)—State Selective Service headquarters reported today that virtually all future inductions into the armed forces from Maryland would be youths just reaching 18 years of age.

UNRRA DELEGATES ACCEPT REFUGEE PLAN

London, Aug. 16 (AP)—Delegates to the third UNRRA conference accepted today the British-sponsored principle of helping refugees who refuse to return to their homelands.

JAPS STILL FIGHT ON LUZON

Manila, Aug. 16 (AP)—Scattered fighting continued in Northern Luzon's mountains today.

American commanders spurred efforts meanwhile to reach all isolated Japanese of Emperor Hirohito's surrender and to persuade them to lay down their arms.

HOSTILITIES END IN BURMA

Rangoon, Aug. 16 (AP) — The cease fire order went out from 12th Army headquarters to Allied troops late last night, ending offensive hostilities in Burma.

8,000 BALTIMORE WORKERS FACE JOB DISCHARGE

(By The Associated Press)
Three thousand Bethlehem Fairfield Shipyard workers will be discharged tomorrow and Saturday, a company source said today. This raises to more than 8,000 the number of war workers facing immediate unemployment in the Baltimore area.

TRUMAN TO ASK PEACETIME DRAFT

Washington, Aug. 16 (AP) — Enactment of a peacetime military training program will be recommended by President Truman as soon as Congress reconvenes on Sept. 5.

Local Tides

TOMORROW

High water — 1:07 A. M. 1.1 feet; 12:19 P. M. 1.0 feet. Low water—8:13 A. M., 6:49 P. M.

Moon rises 3:29 A. M.; sets 12:44 P. M.

Sun rises 6:19 A. M.; sets 7:59 P. M.

Tides are given for Annapolis. For Sandy Point, add 15 minutes. For Thomas Point shoal, subtract 30 minutes.

"Fill 'Er Up" Motorists Storm Gasoline Stations

Annapolis Will Be Gasless Friday Unless Supplies Arrive

That familiar cry, "Fill 'er up" heard so often at gasoline stations in the good old days but unsung in recent years, echoed again yesterday all through Annapolis.

When official announcement from the nation's capital disclosed that gas was no longer a rationed item motorists began flocking to their filling stations.

"Fill 'er up" was the unrestrained demand of Annapolis motorists, almost without exception, all day Wednesday and up to noon today, as they rejoiced in the lifting of one of the most irksome of wartime restrictions.

Local petroleum dealers had not received any official communications but they understood to a man their duty—and they did it. They gave happy citizens all the gas they wanted and laughed off the long endured headache of coupons.

However, the gas rush caught the dealers unprepared and some of the gas stations here are already out of gas. Others will be out by this evening, and the entire city will be gasless by noon tomorrow, unless shipments of gas arrive shortly.

Officials of the Arundel Bus Company here, and the Baltimore and Annapolis Railroad have stated that there is no way of determ-

(Continued On Page Three)

25TH WEST ANNAPOLIS CARNIVAL OPENS FRIDAY

The curtain will go up on the 25th annual West Annapolis carnival tomorrow night commencing at 7 P. M. with officials hailing this year's show as the largest one ever presented in the 25 year history of the event.

The carnival is sponsored by the West Annapolis Fire Department with all proceeds going toward the upkeep of the fire department ambulance and other fire apparatus.

Fire Chief Howard Thomas has announced that the carnival that commences Friday will run through August 25, with special amusements being featured for the children A Merry-go-round, a small kiddy train and ponies are a few of the features lined up for the younger generation.

Mikado's Cousin To Set Up New Jap Cabinet

(By The Associated Press)
Emperor Hirohito told General MacArthur today it would be impossible to send envoys to Manila tomorrow to receive the surrender terms and that it would take 12 days for his "cease fire" order to reach all fronts.

Emperor Hirohito ordered his defeated forces to stop fighting today, Japanese broadcast reported, and simultaneously named a royal-blooded General to head Japan's peacetime government.

The Mikado's belated "cease fire" order was issued only after General MacArthur, Supreme

(Continued On Page Three)

4,000 Graduated From Academy During War

Additional 5,500 Graduate As Reserve Ensigns

An appraisal shows these outstanding results of the Naval Academy's war effort:

The academic course for regular War midshipmen was stepped up in order to meet the demand for officer personnel in the rapidly-expanding Navy, with the result that six classes, totaling more than 4,000 were graduated, most of whom were assigned to duty in the Pacific war area.

The Academy also undertook the task of giving special courses of training to reserve midshipmen over periods of four months. The 12th and final class, to be sent forth Aug. 24, will bring to a total of approximately 5,500 graduated as reserve ensigns. The majority of these have likewise been detailed to Pacific service.

Scores of WAVES performed service in laboratories and along other lines at the Academy, the experiment Station and in other activities of the Severn River Naval Command.

And finally, hundreds of men and women were given employment in clerical and other capacities, not a few accepting work as mechanics, helpers.

The number of young officers, ranging in rank from Ensigns to Lieutenant-Commanders, taking special courses in postgraduate work, was more than doubled, and hundreds of graduates were given special assignments with the fleets.

Demobilization Of Services To Start Shortly

Tentative Plans Of Armed Forces Set Up For Releases

WASHINGTON, Aug. 16 (AP) — If the Japanese behave, if transportation permits and if the draft act remains in effect, the Army plans to let, 5,000,000 soldiers become civilians in the next year.

The Navy, with a newly-announced point system, will free 1,500,000 to 2,500,000 in the next 12 or 18 months.

The Marine Corps has adopted the Army point system for discharges but makes no estimate of the number affected.

The Army probably will not cut the number of points required for discharge below the present 85 for two months or more. WACs need 44.

The War Department has 471,000 men with 85 or more points waiting to be released.

Over 38

In addition, on order yesterday directed release of enlisted men and women over 38 who apply in writing for a discharge. Applicants must be released immediately if replacements are available and in no case may they be held for longer than 90 days after application. Maj. Gen. Stephen G. Henry, assistant chief of staff, estimated 300,000 are affected by the order. This includes, however, some of

(Continued On Page Five)

CIVITAN MEMBERS OFFER PRAYERS FOR VICTORIOUS PEACE

Members of the Civitan Club offered prayers of gratitude for victory at the weekly luncheon meeting held at Carvel Hall yesterday.

Howard Hayman, vice president, who conducted the meeting in the absence of T. O. Tilghman, president, called upon each member to offer a prayer.

The members stood and recited their prayers in turn. In addition to thanks for the victorious end of the war, they prayed that the men and women who died may never be forgotten and that future generations may enjoy peace.

The club went on record as favoring the Chestnut street property, owned by the city, as a recreational park The property is adjacent to the USO Club and the school grounds along Compromise street. The Council, at the Monday night meeting, held up public sale of the property for a year.

INCOMING SUPERINTENDENT

VICE ADMIRAL A. W. FITCH

Departing Superintendent

REAR ADMIRAL BEARDALL

Price Of Victory Comes High

Families Notified Of Death Of Lt. Ray And S/Sgt. Seipp

Although hostilities on the Japanese front have ceased, the report of American soldiers killed in that area will continue to pour into the Navy and War Departments for sometime to come.

A good many American citizens who only so recently joined in the mass celebrations staged throughout the different cities in this country of the complete and utter defeat of the last aggressive nation, will now face the stern realization that their sons, brothers,

(Continued On Page Three)

New Aides Designated By Admiral Fitch

Vice Admiral Aubrey W. Fitch, who today became superintendent of the Naval Academy, designated Commander Russell Burke, USN, and Commander James Gray, USN, to replace Commander Richard S. Craighill and Commander Glover T. Ferguson as aides to the commandant and public relations officers.

NO DAMAGE CAUSED BY FIRE AT CARNIVAL

Flames enveloped the tractor of the ferris wheel operating at the Eastport Firemen's Carnival and temporarily stranded a number of passengers, who were principally children, in mid-air last night at 10 P. M.

The ferris wheel was about three-fourths occupied when the tractor suddenly caught on fire. While men fought the flames by throwing dirt on the tractor the wheel jerked and started to turn and children tried to scramble from the cars in which they were riding. Some were successful in making the jump but others were prevented when the wheel jerkily moved again.

One small boy climbed down the framework from a height of about 20 feet.

Mothers waited nervously. Some, not sure whether their children were on the ride ,were straining to see to the top of the wheel.

There was no panic on the grounds, however, and passengers and crowds below remained calm.

The Eastport Fire Department responded to a call but the flames had been brought under control by the time firemen reached it. They used CO2 fire extinguishers to make certain the fire could not smoulder and break out again.

Passengers were brought down when attendants revolved the wheel by hand.

RELIEVES REAR ADMIRAL BEARDALL IN CEREMONIES HELD IN TECUMSEH COURT

Vice Admiral Aubrey Wray Fitch took command of the United States Naval Academy today.

In a ceremony in Tecumseh Court attended by heads of the departments, the regiment of regular and the battalion of reserve midshipmen the first three-star admiral in 80 years and second in the school's history became the 34th superintendent of the Naval Academy.

Admiral Fitch, a veteran of 39 years of naval service, read orders directing him to assume the joint command of superintendent and commandant of the Severn River Naval Command following rendition of Admiral's honors by the Academy band.

The departing superintendent, Rear Admiral, R. J. R. Beardall, head of the naval school since Jan. 31, 1942, then read orders directing him to take command of the 15th Naval District and the Panama Sea Frontier.

THREE STAR FLAG

Following reading of orders, the two-star flag of Rear Admiral Beardall was lowered and the second three-star Vice Admiral's burgee in the Academy's 100-year-old history—the first was that of David Dixon Porter in 1865—broke from the mast of the station ship "Reina Mercedes."

A native or St. Ignace, Mich., the new superintendent served as Deputy Chief of Naval Operations for Air until came to the Annapolis command last month by Secretary of the Navy Forrestal.

The Naval Academy grounds where officially assumed charge of today were not new to "Jake" Fitch, as he is known throughout the Navy. Entering the Academy in 1902, he was commissioned an ensign upon graduation four years later.

New Superintendent

During World War I, Fitch was gunnery officer on the USS Wyoming—later used for many years as a midshipmen's cruise ship. He learned to fly at Pensacola, Fla., in 1929, and from then until his new assignment was connected with Naval Air Forces. He still flies though 62.

White-haired and baldish, his scalp dotted with freckles from South Pacific suns, he flew his flag from the carrier Lexington during the Battle of Coral Sea in May, 1942. In that engagement in which he won the Distinguished Service Medal, his airmen outfought two Jap task forces, but the Lexington was fatally hit.

Turning to the flattop's skipper, Capt. Fredrick Sherman, Admiral Fitch displayed a "coolness credited with saving the crew of the carrier. His only comment was, "Well, let's get the hell off the ship!"

He also commanded another carrier, the Saratoga, and during his two years as commander of Naval Air Forces in the Pacific, he led fliers who accounted for at least 3,104 Japanese planes.

Eight Decorations

Admiral Fitch was awarded the Army Distinguished Flying Cross for "numerous hazardous flights" in Pacific combat zones. He received the Gold Star Medley in lieu of the second Distinguished Service Medal for service as commander of South Pacific Air Forces All told, he holds eight decorations.

Fitch is rated a crack tactician and a stickler for detail and physical conditioning, himself engaging in such sports as crew and crack during his plebe year and boxing and gymnastics in all of his four years at the Academy.

Admiral of the Fleet Chester Nimitz, commander in chief of the Pacific Naval Forces, never won his wings—but his success in combining surface and air strength sprang from counsel received from his flying officers. Such admirals as "Bull" Halsey, "Fuzz" Sherman and "Jake" Fitch argued — and won—the case of the carrier-cruiser task force.

High command of the Naval Academy is now in the hands of aviators—both the new superintendent and the commandant of midshipmen, Capt. I. H. Ingersoll—wear the gold wings of Navy fliers.

Departing Superintendent

The departing superintendent, Rear Admiral Beardall, succeeded Rear Admiral Russell Willson as head of the school. He wore no four stripes when appointed, being the first captain named to the Academy helm since Capt. Archibald H. Scales became superintendent in 1919. Beardall wore Rear Admiral's braid on assumed command of the Academy having won promotion during the 30-day interim.

The Naval Academy, during its century of existence, has been commanded by six commander 12 captains, 12 rear admirals, two commodores and two vice admirals.

Southern High Students May Come To City

Members of the Anne Arundel county Board of Education may agree on the wisdom of making Southern High School a junior high school and to transport senior high school students (10th, 11th and 12th years) to Annapolis beginning September, 1946.

The Board reached this conclusion, still subject to change if residents of the district do not favor it, because many families of the area wanted to send their children to a larger high school with the added opportunities and equipment that size gives to a school.

The move is also contemplated

(Continued on Page Two)

LAST RITES TO BE READ FOR MISS AGNES GERACI

Miss Agnes Maria Geraci, a life long resident of Annapolis and for a number of years employed at the U. S. Naval Academy, died Wednesday afternoon at the Emergency Hospital after a short illness.

Miss Geraci had long been active in Red Cross work and all civic activities and was a member of the Junior Women's Club in Annapolis.

Funeral services will be conducted Saturday morning from the Taylor Funeral Chapel at 9:30 A. M., with Requiem Mass at St. Mary's Catholic Church to be sung at 10 A. M. Interment will be in St. Mary's Cemetery.

Miss Geraci is survived by her mother and father, Mr. and Mrs. Frank B. Geraci; and three brothers, Lt. Col. P R. Geraci, USMC T/Sgt. Thomas K. Geraci, USA and Alvin J. Geraci.

JAMES DANIELS RITES TO BE SATURDAY

James Earnest Daniels of 314 Adams street, for a number of years an employe of the Baltimore and Annapolis Railroad here, died at his home after a long illness Tuesday evening. He suffered a heart attack

A Veteran of Foreign Wars, Daniels served a year and a half overseas during the first World War. He is well known as a sportsman whose principal interests in that line were fishing and hunting.

Last rites will be held Saturday afternoon at 2 P. M., from the late residence with interment in St. Mary's Cemetery.

Survivors are his wife, Mrs. Sarah F. Daniels, two daughters, Helen C Daniels and Dorothea J. Daniels, and Mrs. Walter Ward, a sister.

O.D.T. Approves Annual Labor Day Horse Show

Proceeds Of Show Will Go Toward Upkeep Of Church

Given the green light by the O.D.T. Convention Bureau, the annual Labor Day Horse Show staged at the St. Margaret's Hunt Club grounds will be conducted this year as usual, it was learned today from representatives of the St. Margaret's Church, sponsors of the show.

Miss Geraci had long been active this year as usual, it was learned adjacent to the USO Club and the today from representatives of the St. Margaret's Church, sponsors of the show.

The annual show has been sponsored for years by the St. Mar-

(Continued On Page Eight)

Tax Drop Seen Likely After First Of Year

WASHINGTON, Aug. 16 (AP)—All Americans seem likely to get a cut in their income taxes after January 1. Perhaps several million will have to pay no income taxes at all next year.

Congress is coming back September in a tax-cutting mood. Some of the best-informed tax experts in Washington think a reduction in personal income taxes will be enacted before Christmas—with administration approval if the cut isn't too drastic.

People in the lowest income group would be the ones whose income taxes might be wiped out entirely.

A survey of Congressional and

(Continued On Page Three)

MIDDIES CELEBRATE VICTORY

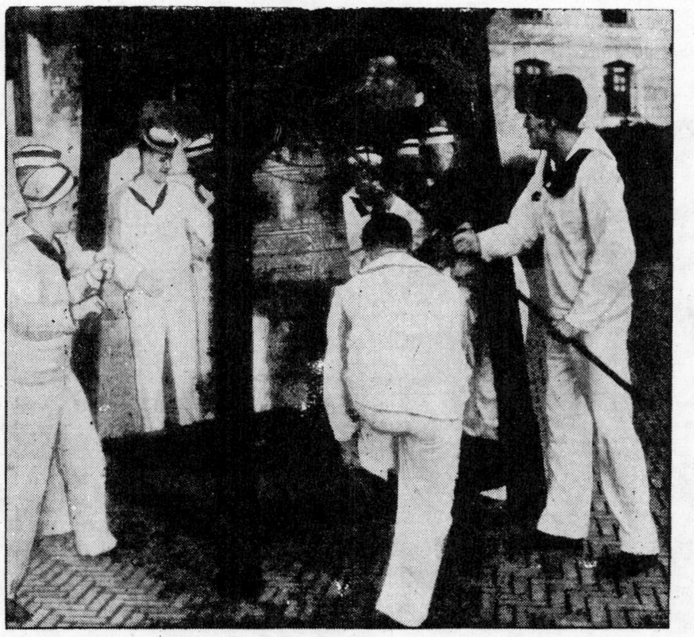

Naval Academy midshipmen, 2,000 strong, used everything handy to beat a victory tattoo on the Japanese bell brought back by Commodore Perry in 1854. Here one uses a rake. The bell had NOT been rung since Pearl Harbor.

"In Keeping With The Highest Traditions ★ ★ ★ ★ Of The United States Navy"

Captain S. H. Ingersoll, USN, commandant of midshipmen at the Naval Academy, presents the Croix de Guerre with Silver Star to Commander George D. Hoffman, USN. The medal with citation of the Order of the Division, was awarded by General de Gaulle, President of the Provisional Government of France for Commander Hoffman's service in the liberation of France.

Lieut. Commander Robert W. McNitt, USN, receives a Gold Star in lieu of a second Silver Star medal, for gallantry and intrepidity in action as assistant approach officer on a submarine on war patrol.
The award was made by Captain H. A. Spanagel, USN, head of the Postgraduate School.

For meritorious service in action as a submarine officer on war patrol, Lieut. Commander Roy G. Anderson, USN, has been presented the Bronze Star medal.
Captain H. A. Spanagel, USN, head of the Postgraduate School made the presentation.

Commander Ernest W. Longton, USN, is shown receiving the Croix de Guerre in a presentation by Captain T. J. Ryan, Jr., USN, of the Department of Ordnance and Gunnery of the Naval Academy. Commander Longton also holds the Silver Star, the Bronze Star, and the Gold Star in lieu of a second Bronze Star.

Lieut. Benjamin E. Noyce, USN, (right) receives a Commendation Ribbon from Comdr. R. E. Bengston, UEN, in a ceremony at the U. S. Naval Auxiliary Air Station, Camp Kearney, San Diego, Calif.

Commander Charles L. Frazer, USN, is presented the Bronze Star for meritorious service as gunnery officer of the USS Agusuta during the amphibious assault on the coast of France on June 6, 1944.
The presentation was made by Captain H. A. Spanagel, USN, head of the Postgraduate School.

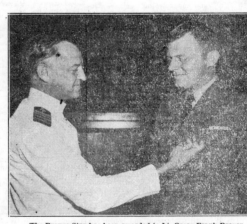

The Bronze Star has been awarded to Lt. Oscar Frank Dreyer, USN, for distinguishing himself in operations against the enemy while serving as executive officer of a destroyer with Task Force 58.
Lt. Dreyer received his decoration from Captain Spanagel of the Postgraduate School.

Captain T. J. Ryan, Jr., head of the department of Ordnance and Gunnery at the Naval Academy, presents the Bronze Star Medal to Commander Ernest W. Longton, USN. The Bronze Star was awarded Commander Longton for meritorious achievement as commanding officer of the U.S.S. Ellyson during the invasion of France.

Lieut. Commander Charles C. Hoffman, USN, has been presented the Presidential Unit Citation which was awarded to members of Patrol Squadron 22 for extraordinary heroism in action against the enemy in the Pacific Theater of War.
Captain Spanagel of the Postgraduate School made the presentation.

"For distinguishing himself by extraordinary heroism in the line of his profession as commander of a squadron of ships in the naval action in the Southwest Pacific area," Captain Kenmore M. McManes, USN, has been awarded the Navy Cross. For performances of outstanding service in the Southwest Pacific, he has received the Legion of Merit medal.

The presentations were made by Adm. Harold R. Stark.

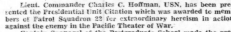

THE MIGHTY MISSOURI FIRES A SALVO

ANNAPOLIS' 100th Birthday

JUNE WEEK: MIDSHIPMEN PASS IN REVIEW

FOUNDER

SEC'Y OF NAVY GEORGE BANCROFT

FOR 47 years after the establishment of the U. S. Navy department in 1798, education of midshipmen was carried on in navy yards and at sea. In 1845, shortly after his appointment as Secretary of the Navy by President Polk, author, historian and diplomat George Bancroft saw the immediate need for a permanent establishment to train naval officers and took immediate steps to bring it about. Old Fort Severn, beautifully situated on the banks of the Severn at Annapolis, Md., was chosen as the site, repairs were made to the few buildings, and on October 10, 1845, the doors of the academy were opened to the first students, most of them veterans of five years' service with the fleet. Commander Franklin Buchanan, an officer of 30 years' service, was named as the school's first superintendent. Since that historic date, more than 17,500 midshipmen have passed through the Academy, and the few small buildings of 1845 have given way to an academy of numerous halls, laboratories and dormitories, second to none in the world.

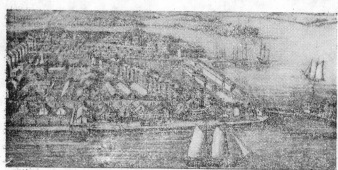

NAVAL ACADEMY BUILDINGS converted into an Army hospital during Civil War. Steamer Baltic took officers, professors, equipment to Ft. Adams at Newport, R. I.

NAVAL ACADEMY BALL at Annapolis, Jan. 8, 1869. Vice Admiral David Dixon Porter, superintendent at close of Civil War, developed social life and encouraged athletics.

MIDSHIPMEN hard at their studies at turn of century. Seven-year course, including four years at sea, soon after founding of school was changed to four years in 1851.

MIDSHIPMAN Chester W. Nimitz, class of 1905.

ADMIRAL NIMITZ, who led fleet to victory over Japs.

MIDSHIPMAN William F. Halsey, Jr., class of 1904.

ADMIRAL HALSEY, commander of Pacific's Third Fleet.

40 YEARS AGO   AND TODAY   THEN   AND NOW

PLANNING THE SITE OF THE U. S. NAVAL ACADEMY AT ANNAPOLIS, 1845.
LEFT TO RIGHT: NAVY SECRETARY George Bancroft, Brevet Major John Lane Gardner, War Secretary William Marcy and Commodore Lewis Warrington.

HEAVE ON THE HALYARD. Midshipman William George gives sharp tug on halyard of his sailing craft while on a training sail.

A PLACE FOR EVERYTHING. There's no such thing as sweeping the dirt under the rug. Two middies stand at attention when their room is being inspected.

1ST SUPT

COMMANDER Franklin Buchanan served from 1845 to 1847.

33D SUPT

VICE ADMIRAL Aubrey Wray Fitch took post on August 16, 1945.

MODERN CLASSROOM. Instructor Commander William Vanous teaches ship maneuvering to class of reserve officers undergoing one-year General Line Officer course.

CUSTOM. Ensign Richard Vaill is kissed by Sheila Edwards after graduation.

NAVAL ACADEMY CENTENNIAL EDITION

October 10, 1845
Annapolis

Evening Capital

October 10, 1945
Maryland

"WELL DONE"

The United States Naval Academy, as it celebrates the 100th anniversary of its founding today, can look back on the brilliant service of its sons, who have proven in war that their alma mater has accomplished its mission of providing leadership for a fighting fleet.

The accomplishments of the Navy in the war just ended have justified the vision of George Bancroft, and the small group of officers and representative citizens, who in 1845 founded a school on land to teach the art of handling and fighting ships at sea. It was considered a novel idea then—in the days of the old frigates and of "iron men and wooden ships." Many experienced officers of the Navy of that day were skeptical, to say the least, of training officers on shore.

The academy motto—Ex Scientia Tridens—has been tried in the fire of battle. The roaring guns of the fleet and the fighting planes that rose from carriers to sweep the skies dominated the oceans of the world and established beyond all question that out of knowledge comes seapower.

There is more to the Naval Academy than the huge granite buildings, rising from their setting of grass and foliage, against the background of sparkling blue waters of the Severn river. That is the mere physical plant, but there is a force unseen but potent that has stamped the academy graduate. This is the tradition of the service that finds its way into the heart and soul of the midshipmen during their stay in Annapolis.

John Paul Jones, the Father of the Navy, sleeps beneath the academy chapel, but his immortal words: "I have not yet begun to fight" have become the foundation of the great tradition of the American Navy. The exploits of Stephen Decatur, and the intrepid officers of the Tripolitan War period; the dying word of Master Commandant James Lawrence: "Don't give up the ship"; Admiral David Farragut's: "Damn the torpedoes", coupled with his orders to "go ahead" have become just as much a part of the academy curriculum as seamanship.

These men were not products of a Naval Academy—they were trained on the high seas—but their spirit and determined courage set the standard of conduct that has been interwoven into the fabric of the great national institution that today can scan with pride the span of a hundred years of history.

The men who have taken the fleets of this nation into battle—the men of a later period who were graduates of the academy—have gloriously upheld this tradition. Admiral George Dewey used to relate that as he steamed his warships into Manila Bay to destroy the Spanish fleet there, he had come to the decision by asking himself. "What would Farragut do?"

When Comdr. H. W. Gilmore, mortally wounded on the conning tower of his submarine by Japanese bullets, turned to his junior officer and ordered: "Take her down!", he was giving his life to save his ship. Thus does naval tradition flower through the years. Buildings at the academy, studies, weapons and methods of making war may change, men pass on, but the great tradition continues eternally.

It was this tradition of a fighting service that brought the Navy from its low point after the Japanese sneak attack on Pearl Harbor to the greatest Navy in world.

The men of the Naval Academy, imbued with its spirit and training, supplied the leadership — they

PRESENT NAVAL ACADEMY

Airplane view of the Naval Academy showing the 224 acres and buildings, with an estimated present day value of about $100,-00,000. Work on the present building began in 1899 under plans prepared by Ernest Flagg. New York architect.

were the steel framework that gave strength to the great fighting force that was mustered out of the power of America.

Admiral Ernest J. King with Fleet Admirals Chester W. Nimitz and William D. Leahy and Admirals Frederick W. Halsey, Jr., Raymond A. Spruance, Thomas Cassin Kinkaid and Henry K. Hewitt, headed a group of comanders who solved the greatest problem of naval warfare in history.

Under their leadership, the German submarines were nullified, the Japanese fleet battered out of existence and thousands of men and millions of tons of supplies convoyed across the Atlantic and Pacific. The end came when Japan surrendered on the battleship Missouri in Tokyo Bay.

The great victory thus won was, in large part, the product of men who were cradled at the academy and is a shining jewel fit to crown its splendid record of a hundred years.

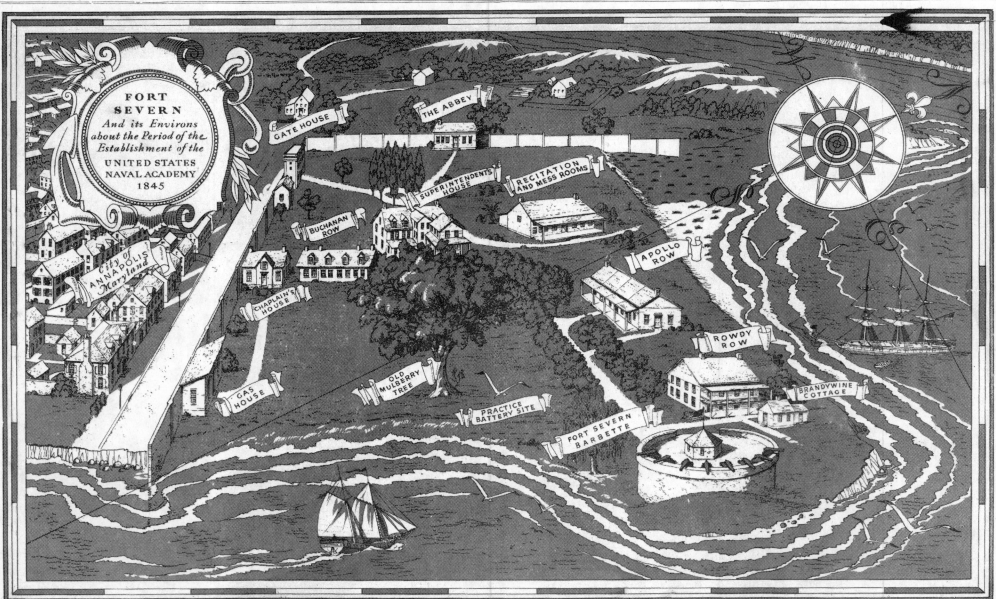

FORT SEVERN
And its Environs about the Period of the Establishment of the UNITED STATES NAVAL ACADEMY 1845

Scott street, now part of the Naval Academy, is shown at the left running along the wall of the original Academy. Comdr. Franklin Buchanan, the first superintendent made his home in the old Dulany mansion. Midshipmen were quartered in Apollo Row, Rowdy Row, Brandywine Cottage, the Abbey and the Gas House.

(Courtesy 1945 Lucky Bag)

BRONZE REPLICA OF TECUMSEH, "MIDSHIPMEN'S GOD OF 2.5" CONTAINS "BRAINS" AND "FIGHTING HEART" OF WOODEN BUST THAT WAS ONCE FIGUREHEAD OF SHIP OF THE LINE DELAWARE

Tecumseh, the midshipmen's "God of 2.5," the bronze bust of an Indian chief, mounted on granite facing the entrance to Bancroft Hall, is a replica of the wooden figurehead of the Ship of the Line Delaware, sunk during the Civil War in the attack on Norfolk, Va.

When the ship was raised after the war, the figurehead was removed and sent to the Naval Academy. Apparently because it was carved from wood the bust came to have a tradition for potent influence in behalf of midshipmen seeking to make the passing mark of 2.5 in academics

The "wooden man" among the midshipmen is one who has difficulties in mastering the academic subjects and who lives in fear of not making the passing mark. Therefore, the tradition that if the "wooden" midshipmen placated the wooden bust, they would be blessed with good luck.

The bust is named after the war-like Chief Tecumseh, but it was intended to represent the Indian Chief Tamenend, friendly chief of the Delawares, friend of William Penn and a lover of peace, who was known as "Saint Tamenend' in the early days of the colonies. Tammany Hall was named after him, Tammany being a corruption of Tamenend.

After being exposed to the weather for many years the wooden bust began to deteriorate and in 1930 the Class of 1891 took upon itself the task of perpetuating it in bronze.

In order that the "God of 2.5" would lose none of the potent power with which generations of midsipmen had endowed the wooden bust, the "wooden brains" and "fighting heart" of the wooden chief were cut from the original bust and encased in the bronze replica. In order further to insure the potency of the bronze bust, the following were placed in the replica: original tomahawk and arrows, peace pipe, a roster of the Class of 1891, with a short history of each man, photographs of the wooden bust and the bronze replica and a design of the Delaware

1890 MIDSHIPMEN AT WORK AND PLAY

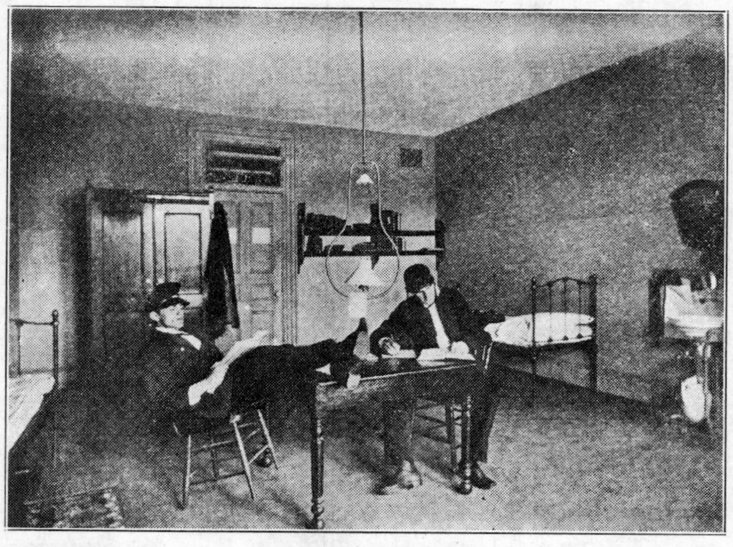

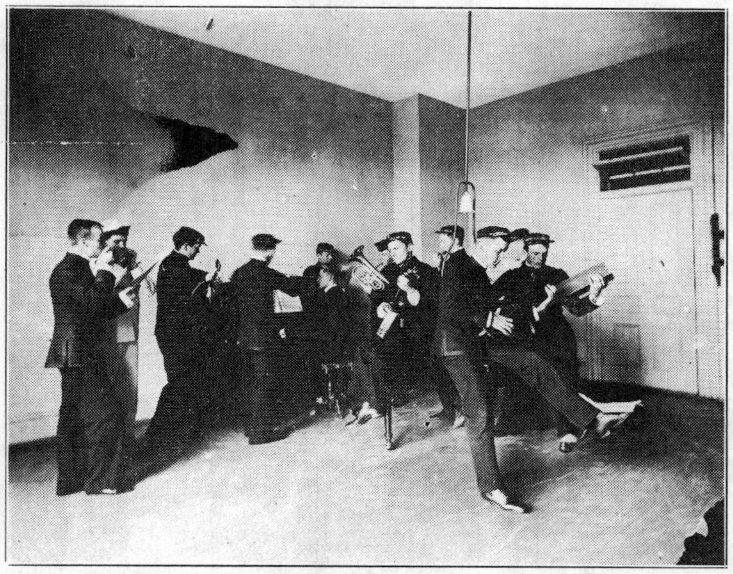

They may not have caled it jive, nor have even heard of jitterbugs, but the midshipmen of 1890 had the spirit as shown by the lower picture of a "jam session" staged in one of the few periods they had free from studies and drills. One of the midshipmen is wearing "white works", somewhat similar to the present uniform of that name.

Two midshipmen of the same period are shown in the top cut busy with studies in their room. The old fashioned light fixture over the study table is of interest.

MICHAELSON MADE FIRST EXPERIMENTS AT NAVAL ACADEMY

Albert Abraham Michaelson, noted scientist, who won the Noble Prize in physics in 1907, made his first experiments in measuring the speed of light while on duty at the Naval Academy.

Michaelson, who died in 1931, graduated from the academy in 1873. As an Ensign, and later as a professor, he taught from some years in the Department of Physics and Chemistry.

His experiments were made on the sea wall of the academy and were the beginning of his work in physics which later was to bring him world-wide recognition and gain the Nobel Prize of $40,000.

It is of interest that his first experiments on the speed of light were accurate within one-thousandth of one percent.

Some of the records of Michaelson's experiments are now preserved in the academy museum, along with other historic relics of the academy.

JAPANESE SURRENDER SWORD AT ACADEMY

The surrender sword of the commander of the Japanese Imperial Naval Forces in the Philippines, Vice Admiral Okochi, is on display in the Naval Academy museum.

MUSICAL NOTE!

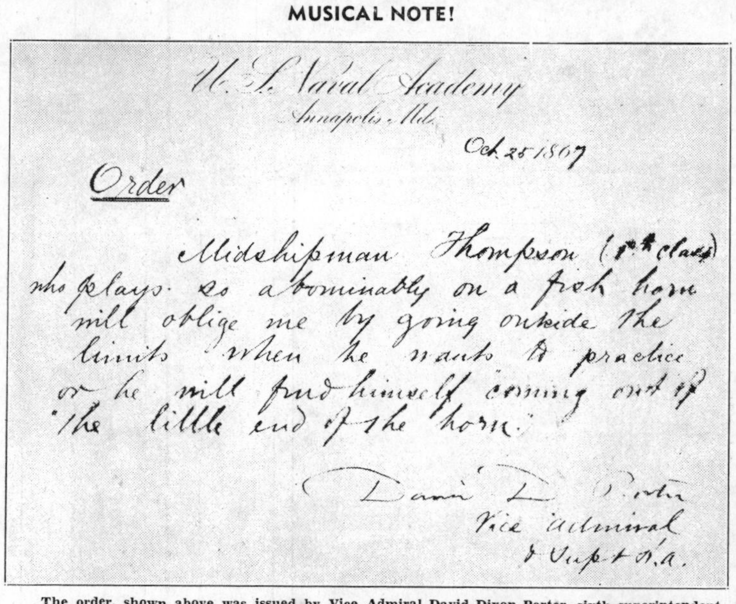

U. S. Naval Academy
Annapolis Md.
Oct 25 1867

Order

Midshipman Thompson (1st class) who plays so abominably on a fish horn will oblige me by going outside the limits when he wants to practice or he will find himself coming out of the little end of the horn.

David D. Porter
Vice Admiral
& Supt N.A.

The order, shown above was issued by Vice Admiral David Dixon Porter, sixth superintendent of the Naval Academy, who became the Navy's second Admiral after the death of Admiral David Farragut. It is characteristic of the dynamic Porter, who rebuilt the academy after the Civil War. Midshipman Robert Means Thompson, whose fish horn annoyed the Admiral, in later life as Colonel Thompson became one of the greatest benefactors of the academy. He engaged Ernest Flagg, the architect who designed the present academy. The Thompson stadium is named in his honor.

"Don't Give Up The Ship" Flag, Flown By Perry At Battle Of Lake Erie, Now Inspires Midshipmen

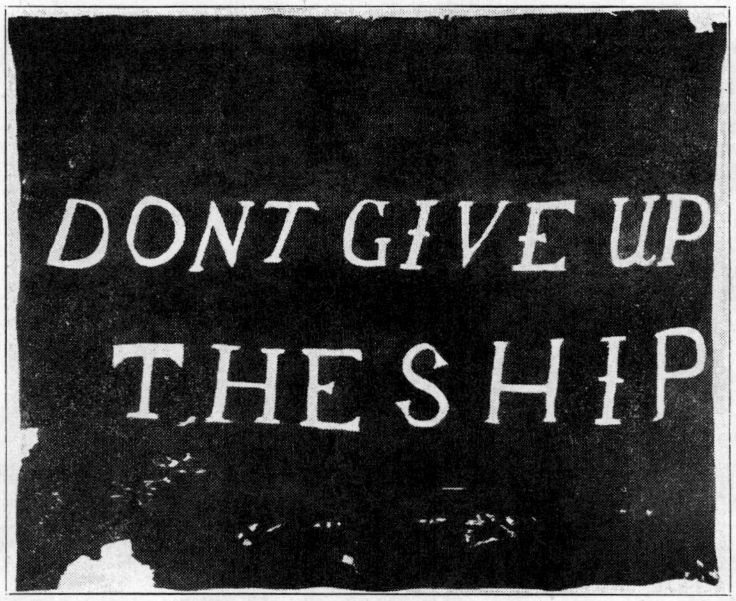

Protected in a glass case, mounted high on the wall of Memorial Hall at the Naval Academy, is a tattered blue flag, with sprawling, uneven white letters, spelling out this order:

"DON'T GIVE UP THE SHIP"

Every summer young men, fresh from home and civilian life, assemble in the hall, and with their eyes fixed on the flag, swear allegiance to the United States, and become midshipmen, in the United States Navy.

Potent Influence

This blue flag, potent in its inuence, with a history dating back to 1813, is open to inspection of visitors attending the centennial celebration of the Naval Academy.

The words, on the flag, now a fundamental slogan, of the Navy, were repeated again and again by the dying Master Commandant James Lawrence, fatally wounded when his ship the Chesapeake was defeated by the British frigate Shannon on June 1, 1813 off Boston harbor.

Used By Perry

The flag is the one that flew from the masthead of the brig, Lawrence, when Master Commandant Oliver Hazard Perry, won the battle of Lake Erie on Sept. 10, 1813, sweeping the British from the lakes and winning the control of the Detroit and Michigan territory back to the United States. The territory had been lost to the British in land fighting in the summer of 1812.

Lawrence, after successful voyages in the Hornet, was promoted to captain and given command of the Chesapeake, with orders to destroy the British fisheries on the Grand Banks. When he attempted to run the British blockade out of Boston in 1813, his first lieutenant was ashore with pneumonia, two other officers were on leave, and a new crew was unorganized.

Lawrence Wounded

The Shannon, under Captain Broke, was a crack ship and, soon after the fight began, caught the Chesapeake at a disadvantage, pouring in a broadside, fatally wounding Lawrence. Captain Broke was nearly killed by a cutlass stroke as he led boarders to the gundeck of the Chesapeake. During the four days that Lawrence lay in delirium he kept crying: "Don't give up the ship."

When Perry set out later in the year to meet the British fleet on Lake Erie he had the flag with Lawrence's dying words made, and flew it throughout the battle. It was after this battle that Perry sent his famous dispatch to General Harrison: "We have met the enemy and they are ours—two ships, two brigs, one schooner, and one sloop."

It was written on the back of an old letter.

NAVAL ACADEMY SUPERINTENDENTS

The superintendents, in the order in which served, follow:

1. Comdr. Franklin Buchanan, USN., died 1874, superintendent from 1845 to 1847. During Civil War served in Confederate Navy with rank of Admiral.

2. Comdr. George P. Upshur, USN., died 1852, superintendent from 1847 to 1850.

3. Comdr. Cornelius K. Stribling, USN., died 1880, superintendent from 1850 to 1853.

4. Comdr. Louis M. Goldsborough, USN., died 1877, superintendentdent from 1853 to 1857.

5. Capt. George S. Blake, died 1871, superintendent from 1857 to 1865. Took Naval Academy to Newport, R. I. during Civil War.

6. Admiral David Dixon Porter, USN., died 1891, superintendent from 1865 to 1869. Academy returns to Annapolis.

7. Commodore John L. Worden, USN., died 1897, superintendent from 1869 to 1874.

8. Rear Admiral Christopher Raymond Perry Rodgers, USN., 1874 to 1878, also served for short period in 1881.

9. Commodore Foxhall A. Parker, USN., died 1879, superintendent from 1878 to 1879.

10. Rear Admiral George Beall Balch, USN., died 1908, superintendent from 1879 to 1881.

11. Capt. Francis Munroe Ramsay, USN., died 1914, superintendent from 1881 to 1886, first academy graduate to hold the office.

12. Comdr. William Thomas Sampson, USN., died 1902, superintendenet from 1886 to 1890.

13. Capt. Robert L. Phytian, USN., 1917, superintendent from 1890 to 1894.

14. Capt. Philip H. Cooper, USN., died 1912, superintendent from 1894 to 1898.

15. Rear Admiral Frederick C. McNair, USN., died 1900, superintendent from 1898 to 1900.

16. Rear Admiral Richard Wainwright, USN., died 1926, superintendent from 1900 to 1902.

17. Capt. Willard H. Brownson, USN., died 1935, superintendent from 1902 to 1905.

18. Rear Admiral James H. Sands, USN., died 1911, superintendent from 1905 to 1907.

19. Capt. Charles J. Badger, USN., died 1932, superintendent from 1907 to 1909.

20. Capt. John M. Bowyer, USN., died 1912, superintendent from 1909 to 1911.

21. Capt. John H. Gibbons, died 1944, superintendent from 1911 to 1914.

22. Capt. William F. Fullam, USN., died 1926, superintendent from 1914 to 1915.

23. Capt. Edward Walter Eberle, USN., died 1929, superintendent from 1915 to 1919.

24. Capt. Archibald H. Scales, USN., superintendent from 1919 to 1921.

25. Rear Admiral Henry Braid Wilson, USN., superintendent from 1921 to 1925.

26. Rear Admiral Louis McCoy Nulton, USN., superintendent from 1925 to 1928.

27. Rear Admiral Samuel S. Robinson, USN., superintendent from 1928 to 1931.

28. Rear Admiral Thomas S. Hart, USN., superintendent from 1931 to 1934.

29. Rear Admiral David Foote Sellers, USN., superintendent from 1934 to 1938.

30. Rear Admiral Wilson Brown, USN., superintendent from 1938 to 1941.

31. Rear Admiral Russell Willson, USN., superintendent from February to December, 1941, leaving to serve on Admiral Ernest King's staff after Pearl Harbor attack.

32. Rear Admiral John R. Beardall, USN., superintendent from January 31, 1942 to August 16, 1945.

33. Vice Admiral Aubrey Wray Fitch, USN., became superintendent on Aug. 16.

LIFE RAFT, GIG, RECALL FIGHT OF MEN AGAINST SEA

The drama of "men against the sea" during the recent war and in the Navy are recalled by a modern life raft, now in the Naval Academy museum, and the battered cockleshell of a boat, canvas decked and strained by ocean water, which is kept at the head of the second floor stairway in the gymnasium.

In the modern raft, three men—Anthony J. Pastula, Aviation Chief Machinist's Mate Harold F. Dixon and Gene D. Aldrich, drifted 1,200 miles in the Southwest Pacific after their bomber was forced down during the war just ended.

The boat is the gig of the ill-fated steam-sloop Saginaw. In it five men made a cruise of 1,500 miles seeking aid for their shipmates when the Saginaw was wrecked on a coral reef of Ocean Island, in the North Pacific Ocean September 29, 1870, and broke in two. Four of the volunteers that manned the gig died in the effort, but the fifth sent a rescue ship to the Saginaw.

Marble Tablet

In Memorial Hall, where the Navy remembers its heroes, a marble tablet commemorates the men who died, reviews their feat and concludes with the quotation "Greater love hath no man than this, that a man lay down his life for his friends."

The Saginaw was sent from San Francisco to the Sandwich Islands, now known as Hawaii, in 1870, to keep in touch with contractors who were building a harbor and coaling station on Midway Island. This task done, Lieut. Comdr. Montgomery Sicard, commanding the Saginaw took the workmen aboard and headed for Ocean Island about which he had been ordered to make a report. His ship, including crew, had 90 men in its complement.

Hit Reef

A strong ocean current drew the Saginaw out of her course and about 3 A. M. September 29, 1870, she struck on the reef, while breakers curling over the bulwarks, tore out the smoke stack and the mainmast. Officers and men toiled to abandon ship dragging what food and belongings they could ashore on the low sand spit that was Ocean Island.

They had no fresh water, but an officer rigged up a boiler and some rubber hose to serve as a condenser able to provide 40 or 50 gallons daily. Fuel for the condenser was supplied by the bleached timbers of a wrecked whaler. Food was doled out at quarter rations, fish and seal meat supplementing the diet.

Desperate Position

Far out of the ship's path and with no means of communicating with authorities, the position of the crew was desperate. Commander Sicard determined to fit out the gig and sent her with a volunteer crew for assistance. The 26-foot boat was decked with painted canvas, leaving an open cockpit. A few navigating instruments, 25 days provisions and 90 gallons of water were but aboard.

Lieut. John G. Talbot, volunteered to command the venture. Peter Francis, quartermaster; John Andrews, coxswain; James Muir, captain of the hold, and William Halford, coxswain, volunteered to accompany him.

They set sail for Honolulu on November 19. After five days heavy seas put out the little fire they kept on board and most of their bread. Their flint and steel were lost and for the rest of the voyage food had to be eaten raw and soggy with salt water, with the result that they were sick for days.

Hard Gales

Still they pushed on, the weather growing worse, the waves pounding leaks in the canvas decking. Twice they were forced to lie to with an improvised sea-anchor to keep from being swamped. Three hard gales were encountered. On December 16 they sighted land, but the wind shifted and they could not make shore.

They beat about until the night of December 19, when the gig was caught in the current and was sucked in among the breakers on the shore of the Island of Kauai. The gig rolled over tossing the sick men into the surf. Only Halford was able to stumble ashore.

Reached Honolulu

"After I reached the beach I must have fallen down and slept for the next thing I remember was the sun shining in my eyes. People were coming towards me and we found Muir, dead, further down the beach," Halford said.

From Kauai Halford went to Honolulu and soon afterwards the isolated sailors on Ocean Island were picked up by a rescue ship.

NEW AND OLD CHAPELS

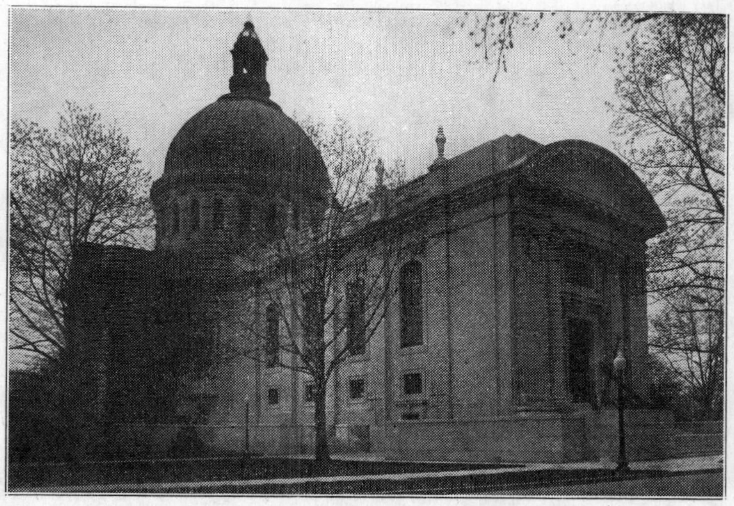

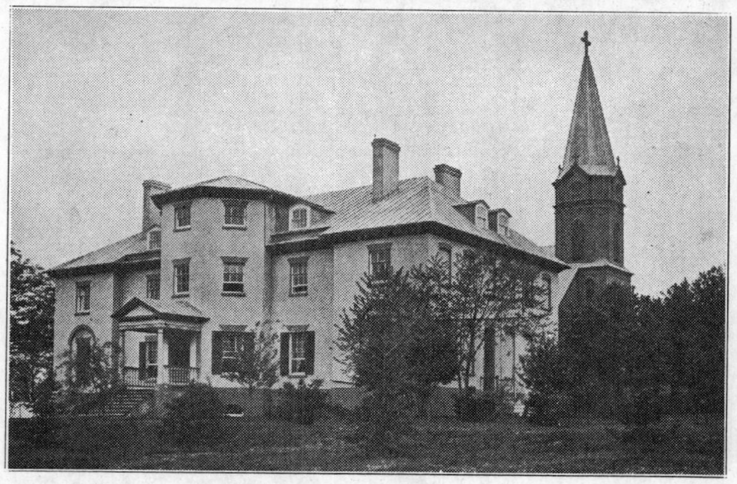

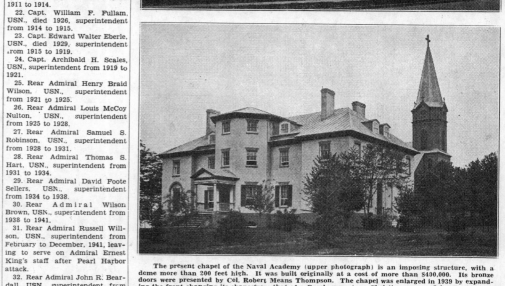

The present chapel of the Naval Academy (upper photograph) is an imposing structure, with a dome more than 200 feet high. It was built originally at a cost of more than $400,000. Its bronze doors were presented by Col. Robert Means Thompson. The chapel was enlarged in 1939 by expanding the front changing its shape from that of a Greek cross to a Christian cross. John Paul Jones, Father of the American Navy, is buried in the crypt beneath the chapel.

The lower photograph shows the second chapel, which preceded the present building. The steeple shows over the old Colonial Government House, residence of Maryland governors until 1868, which was taken into the academy and torn down in 1902. First services were held in the second chapel on May 24, 1869. The first chapel used by the midshipmen was in the old Lyceum building. Before that services were held in a classroom.

Pictorial Record Of Academy's Past

Midshipmen and officers dance at a naval ball held in Fort Severn on Jan. 8, 1869. For many years it was the custom to hold a social affair at the academy about the first week of the New Year.

The historic frigate Constitution, shown under sail, was assigned to the Naval Academy as a school and station ship from August, 1860 until 1871 when it was transferred to Philadelphia. It took the midshipmen to Newport, R. I., soon after the outbreak of the Civil War.

The Naval Academy during the Civil War, when the midshipmen were in Newport, R. I., and the grounds were occupied by U. S. Army Base Hospital No. 1. Temporary hospital buildings are shown in the foreground, grouped around the old mulberry tree.

The second chapel built at the Naval Academy during the administration of Superintendent Porter is shown on left. The first services were held here on May 24, 1869. It was located about halfway between the present chapel and the superintendent's quarters. Blake Row, officers' quarters, flanked the chapel.

View of the Naval Academy library, about 1894, when it was on the first floor of the old Colonial Government House, residence of Maryland governors. The building was taken into the academy in 1866 and was torn down in 1902.

Quartermaster Richard Knowles, who lashed Admiral Farragut to the rigging of the Hartford when that intrepid officer stormed into Mobile Bay. Knowles, holding a cutlass, was stationed at the Naval Academy about 1875.

The ferry that used to run across the Severn is shown, upper right, leaving its dock at the foot of Severn, now Wagner street. The Naval Academy, before it expanded to take in what is now the Worden field area, is shown in the foreground. Beyond the wall—torn down about 1895—is Lockwoodville, a section of the city that was in the Worden field section.

One of the post Civil War classes at the Naval Academy, gathered around the monument erected in memory of Comdr. William L. Herndon, who went down with his ship off Cape Hatteras on Sept. 12, 1857.

Midshipman Stephen B. Luce when he was about 15 years old, wearing the uniform of 1845 when the Naval Academy was founded, including straw hat. Luce later became a Rear Admiral and an authority on seamanship. Luce Hall, the Seamanship Building at the academy, bears his name.

View of a section of Annapolis taken into the Naval Academy between 1867 and 1891. This was in the Worden Field area, known to midshipmen as Oklahoma. Three high hills were cut away to make the present parade ground of Worden Field.

New Quarters of the midshipmen, finished in 1869, and used as a dormitory until 1904. They located parallel to Maryland avenue between the present Officers' Club and Sampson Hall. The Old Quarters of the midshipmen were located in Stribling Row.

ALL BUT TWO PRESIDENTS SINCE FILLMORE HAVE MADE OFFICIAL VISITS TO NAVAL ACADEMY

King, Queens, Princes, Generals And Admirals Have Seen Midshipmen At Work And Play

During the 100-year history of the Naval Academy it has been visited by every President of the United States since Millard Fillmore, with the exception of Benjamin Harrison and Grover Cleveland.

President James K. Polk, during whose administration the academy was founded, did not visit the naval school. Neither did his successor Zachary Taylor.

But from Fillmore on the Presidents have come to Annapolis by horseback, cariage, train, and automobile or used the water route in sailing and steam vesels.

MET COMMODORE PERRY

President Fillmore came to the young Naval Academy on Nov. 8, 1852 on a historic mission—to confer with Comodore Matthew C. Perry who was about to leave for the Far East to open Japan to world commerce. The President, accompanied by his Secretary of the Navy, was received at the old West stret railroad station by officers in full dress. He was greeted with a 21-gun salute when he reached the academy where he boarded the tender Engineer which took him to the steam warship Mississippi, lying off Annapolis. He remained on the vessel over night in conference with Perry, landing the next day on the return trip to Washington.

Frequent Visitor

President Franklin Pierce was a frequent visitor. On April 18, 1856 he attended a naval ball given by Capt. Louis M. Goldsborough in Parade Hall. The next day the midshipmen were drawn up under arms, and a 21-gun salute fired, as the President went aboard the steam warship Merrimac. He left for Washington at 3:30 P. M. that day. The Merrimac was destined to be captured by the Confederates during the Civil War and became the Southern ironclad of the same name that fought the history making battle with the Monitor in Hampton Roads, Va.

President Pierce landed at the academy, on Oct. 16, 1856, from the U.S.S. Wabash, which had been cruising off Annapolis. On Oct. 24, all midshipmen were required to visit the Wabash. The President left for Washington that afternoon.

Lincoln Here

President Abraham Lincoln visited the academy during the Civil War when it was a Federal army hospital. General U. S. Grant and his staff came here on a similar mission.

On Jan. 10, 1873, President Grant, accompanied by the Secretary of the Navy, Admiral D. Porter, and other officers attended a ball at the academy. The journal of the officer of the day noted: "at midnight the ball was still in progress."

Officers and professors at the academy, in full dress assembled in the library, on June 10, 1876, to meet President Grant, who made an official visit. He received a salute of 21-guns from the old frigate Santee. Two days later the President came to the academy by water and was greeted at the wharf. The yards of the Frigate Constellation were manned in his honor.

Garfield Eloquent

President James Garfield was a visitor during the 1881 June Week. He spoke to the graduates, assembled in the chapel, on "The Possibilities of Youth." His address was so eloquent that the midshipmen rose in wild applause some even standing in their seats to cheer. A month later Garfield was mortally wounded by an assassin.

President Chester A. Arthur made an inspection trip to the academy on April 19, 1882, coming from Washington by special train. He left the institution at 4:15 P. M. the same day.

In April, 1897, President William McKinley came to the academy on a visit. He was caught in a heavy rain and spent the night. At the Officers' Club he told stories, smoked cigars and read the newspapers, remarking he had visited the academy previously while a Congressman.

Theodore Roosevelt

President Theodore Roosevelt made his famous remark "the shots hit are the shots that count when he addressed the graduating class on May 6, 1902. He then went to the Naval Hospital where he presented a diploma to Midshipman E. S. Land, who was ill. After watching evolutions of the submarine Holland, he returned to Washington. Midshipman Land is now Rear Admiral, USN., (ret), chairman of the U. S. Maritime Commission.

On June 30, 1905, President Theodore Roosevelt again made the graduation address. On April 24, 1906 he spoke at commemorative exercises held at the academy for Jonh Paul Jones, whose body had been returned from France.

President William H. Taft was the graduation speaker on June 7, 1912.

Woodrow Wilson

President Woodrow Wilson addressed the graduates on June 5, 1914. He attended the 1916 graduation when the then Secretary of the Navy Josephus Daniels handed out diplomas.

On June 2, 1921, the graduates heard an address by President Warren G. Harding. President and Mrs. Harding while cruising on the yacht Mayflower in the spring of 1922, stopped at the academy and attended a baseball game.

President Calvin Coolidge spoke to the graduates on June 4, 1925.

President Herbert Hoover was a frequent visitor to the academy, attending football games and embarking at the wharf on fishing trips in the Chesapeake.

Franklin D. Roosevelt

President Franklin D. Roosevelt also made many trips to the academy to board vessels for fishing trips and cruises. He addressed the graduating class in 1933. Two years later he returned to watch his son, Franklin, Jr., row in a Harvard shell during a crew regatta on the Severn. On May 30, 1935 he was the guest of Rear Admiral and Mrs. Sellers, at a water carnival, which included a reproduction of the burning of the Frigate Philadelphia after she went aground in Tripoli harbor.

Besides the Presidents, the great of the world in war and peace have visited the academy during its century of history. Don Pedro II, last Emperor of Bazil, came in 1875, Prince Henry of Prussia in 1902, Edward, Prince of Wales, later to abdicate the British throne was here in 1919. Among the hundreds of great names was Marshal Foch, Viscount Jellicoe, General Haller, of Poland. Cardinal Mercier, King Albert of Belgium, Queen Marie of Romania and recently General deGaulle of France.

HISTORIC RELICS ARE DISPLAYED IN MUSEUM

Historic relics and treasures of national significance, covering the naval history of the nation over the period of the last century, are on exhibition at the Naval Academy in connection with the centennial anniversary.

Flags, swords, weapons and other relics from the present war mingle with those of past wars in the approximately 45,000 items housed in the museum and other buildings. Among these is the sword carried by John Paul Jones, which is displayed in the crypt of the academy chapel where the body of the naval hero is interred.

There is preserved an 18-foot flat bottomed boat used by General W. T. Sherman afer he had completed his march to the sea through the South during the Civil War to report his accomplishment to the Federal fleet, which blocked the southern coast line.

The museum has the only existing complete collection of Naval Academy class rings.

2,962 MIDSHIPMEN ENROLLED AT ACADEMY

The approximately 50 midshipmen who were enrolled when the Naval Academy started 100 years ago today have grown to 2,962 making up a brigade consisting of two regiments.

There are 1,109 Plebes, or Fourth classmen; 849 First classmen; 516 Second classmen and 488 Third classmen, or youngsters.

The Second and Third classmen, except for the war, would have been the Class of 1948, but because of the emergency and the three year course, to be returned to four, they were divided according to their merit ratings.

The small group of instructors who took up their duties on Oct. 10, 1845 has been followed by a staff of 468 officers, in addition to a number of civilian professors, assistant professors and instructors.

A total of 18,559 midshipmen have been graduated since the academy was founded.

FIRST NAVAL ACADEMY SUPERINTENDENT

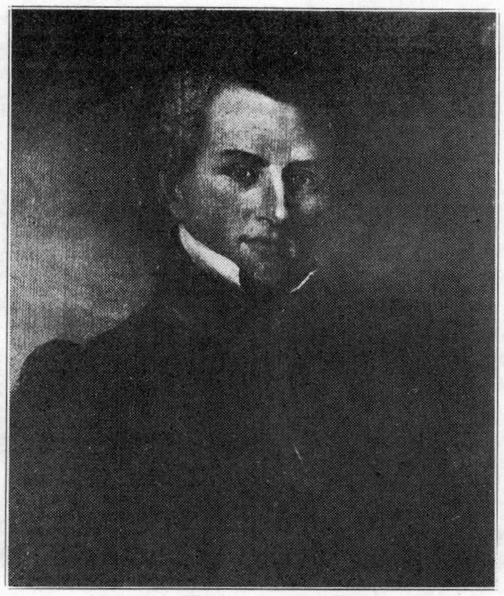

COMMANDER FRANKLIN BUCHANAN

Comdr. Buchanan, First Academy Head, Was Destined To Turn Guns On Midshipmen He Had Trained

Maryland Officer Became Admiral In Confederate Navy

Commander Franklin Buchanan, the first superintendent who opened the Naval Academy on Oct. 10, 1845. was a distinguished son of Maryland.

He was destined to leave the Federal Service in the Civil War to become the highest officer in the Confederate Navy, and then climax his career by serving as president of the Maryland Agricultural College, now the University of Maryland.

Born in Baltimore on Sept. 17, 1800, Buchanan, after a dramatic and eventful life, during which duty required him to turn his guns on officers he had trained as midshipmen, died at his home, "The Rest," on the Miles River, near Easton, Md. He died on May 11, 1874 and was buried at Wye House.

Commanded Merrimac

During his career as an officer of the Confederate Navy, Buchanan inaugurated a new era of naval warfare when he took the iron clad Merrimac into action in Hampton Roads, Va. Later he commanded the Confederate ironclad and ram, Tennessee, which fought the fleet of Admiral Farragut at Mobile Bay.

Buchanan's life was closely interwoven with Maryland. His great-grandfather, Dr. George Buchanan, settled in Baltimore in 1723 and founded an estate of about 600 acres now part of Druid Hill Park. The estate was called "Auchentorolie." Today a Baltimore street—Auchentoroly Terrace—perpetuates the name.

His father, Dr. George Buchanan was one of the founders of the Medical Society of Baltimore, and a charter member of the Medical and Chirugical Society of Maryland, organized in 1799.

Married Here

Buchanan was married on Feb. 19, 1835, to Miss Anne Catherine Lloyd, daughter of Gov. Edward Lloyd of Maryland, in the Chase Home in Annapolis. The cemetery where he is buried is the ancestral home of the Lloyds.

Entering the Navy as a midshipman on Jan. 28, 1815, young Buchanan was assigned to the Frigate Java and received his early training under Capt. Oliver Hazard Perry. He was a commander on Oct. 10, 1845 when he put the Naval Academy into commission in Fort Severn, Annapolis.

Secretary of the Navy George Bancroft, founder of the academy, in speaking of the first superintendent, said:

"Commander Buchanan, to whom the organization of the school was entrusted has carried his instructions into effect with precision and sound judgment and with a wise adaptation of a simple and moderate means to a great end."

Restive when the Mexican War broke out, Buchanan applied for sea service, and, on March 8, 1847. left the academy to command the sloop Germantown. Later, in command of the steam frigate Susquehanna, he accompanied Commodore Matthew C. Perry on the voyage which opened Japan to the world in 1854.

Resigned From Navy

Buchanan was a captain in command of the Washington Navy Yard when the Civil War broke out. The day after Massachusetts troops were mobbed in the streets of Baltimore, he submitted his resignation from the Federal service, apparently expecting Maryland to secede from the Union.

On Sept. 5, 1861, he was appointed a captain in the Confederate Navy and Chief of the Office of Orders and Details in Richmond, Va. The following February he was placed in command of the naval defense of the James river, where the ironclad Merrimac was built.

With Buchanan in command, the Merrimac, on March 8, 1862, steamed down the Elizabeth river into Hampton Roads, throwing consternation into the Federal blockading fleet. The Federal cannon balls bounced off her iron sides as she rammed and sunk the Cumberland and ran the Congres ashore, setting her on fire with hot shot.

Brothers Opposed

Lieut. Joseph B. Smith, commander of the Congress, who died under the Merrimac's fire, had been a midshipman under Buchanan. McKean Buchanan, brother of the Confederate captain, was a paymaster on the Congress fighting the guns on her berth deck.

Buchanan was shot through the leg in the action, otherwise he would have commanded the Merrimac when she fought her historic battle with the Monitor on March 9, 1862, the first clash of ironclads in history.

Made an Admiral of the Confederate Navy on Aug. 19, 1863, Buchanan was sent to organize the defense at Mobile Bay. When Farragut's fleet stormed into the bay on Aug. 5, 1864, the Tennessee attempted to ram the ships out being hard to handle was unsuccessful. She retired under the guns of Fort Morgan.

Battled Farragut

Soon along the Federal ships the word passed:

"Old Buck's coming out!"

The Tennessee moved out from under the protecting guns of the fort to engage the entire Federal fleet. Farragut sent his ships into the battle 'bow on." In the first encounter the smokestack of the Tennessee was broken off and smoke filled the vessel. Buchanan's leg was broken by a flying bolt, and Captain Johnson, who succeeded to command, surrendered.

Buchanan recuperated on the Federal ship Metacomet. He was exchanged on March 4, 1865, and returned to Mobile. When Federal forces occupied the city he was paroled and returned to his home.

He served as president of the Maryland Agricultural College for a year.

RESERVE OFFICERS WERE TRAINED AT ACADEMY

During the first and second World Wars the Naval Academy instituted courses for the training of reserve officers.

Temporary buildings were erected to house these trainees during World War I, but during the war just ended the Reserve Midshipmen were quartered in Bancroft Hall.

Since Pearl Harbor the Academy has sent 6,123 Ensigns and Marine Corps Second Lieutents into the service. Included were 2,812 regular graduates of the academy.

PRESENT SUPERINTENDENT

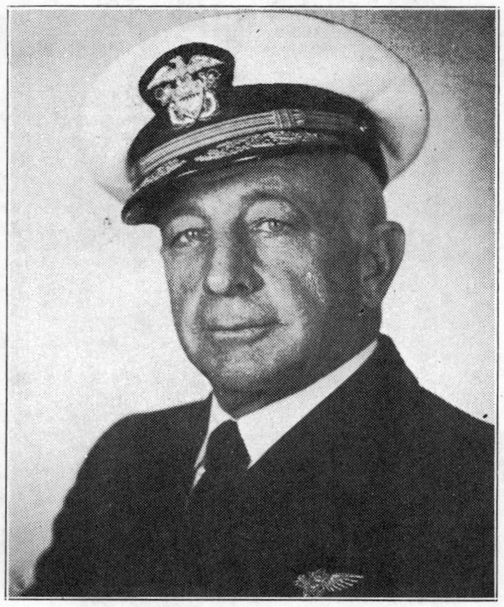

VICE ADMIRAL A. W. FITCH

ADMIRAL A. W. FITCH, PRESENT SUPERINTENDENT, COMMANDED AIR FORCES IN PACIFIC AREA

Is Highest Ranking Officer To Hoist Flag Over Academy

Vice Admiral Aubrey Wray Fitch, veteran commander of air operations in the Pacific combat zone, became the thirty-third superintendent of the Naval Academy when he succeeded Rear Admiral J. R. Beardall on Aug. 16.

He was the first superintendent to hoist the three-starred flag of a Vice Admiral on taking command of the academy. David Dixon Porter, the sixth superintendent, was made a Vice Admiral during his term of superintendent.

Admiral Fitch, who is a native of St. Ignace, Mich., served as Deputy Chief of Naval Operations for Air in the Navy Department, prior to becoming superintendent.

The Naval Academy grounds he officially assumed charge were not new to "Jake" Fitch, as he is known throughout the Navy. Entering the academy in 1902, he was commissioned an ensign upon graduation four years later.

Learned To Fly

During World War I, Fitch was gunnery officer on the USS Wyoming—later used for many years as a midshipmen's cruise training ship. He learned to fly at Pensacola, Fla., in 1929, and from then until his new assignment was connected with Naval Air Forces. He still flies, though 62.

White-haired and baldish, his scalp dotted with freckles from South Pacific suns, he flew his flag from the carrier Lexington during the Battle of Coral Sea in May, 1942. In that engagement in which he won the Distinguished Service Medal, his airmen outfought two Jap task forces, but the Lexington was fatally hit.

Turning to the flattop's skipper, Capt. Frederick Sherman, Admiral Fitch displayed a coolness credited with saving the crew of the carrier. His only comment was, "Well, let's get the hell off the ship!"

He also commanded another carrier, the Saratoga, and during his two years as commander of Naval Air Forces in the Pacific, he led fliers who accounted for at least 3,104 Japanese planes.

Eight Decorations

Admiral Fitch was awarded the Army Distinguished Flying Cross for "numerous hazardous flights" in Pacific combat zones. He received the Gold Star Medal in lieu of the second Distinguished Service Medal for service as commander of South Pacific Air Forces. All told, he holds eight decorations.

Fitch is rated a crack tactician and a stickler for detail and physical conditioning, himself engaging in such sports as crew and track during his plebe year and boxing and gymnastics in all of his four years at the academy.

Admiral of the Fleet Chester Nimitz, commander in chief of Pacific Naval Forces, never won his wings—but his success in combining surface and air strength sprang from counsel received from his flying officers. Such admirals as "Bull" Halsey, "Fuzz Sherman and "Jake" Fitch argued — and won—the case of the carrier cruiser task force.

High command of the Naval Academy is now in the hands of aviators—both the new superintendent and the commandant of midshipmen, Capt. I. H. Ingersoll—wear the gold wings of Navy fliers.

Hanging Of Instructor In Effigy By Midshipmen Brought Increased Pay And Prestige For Professors

Congress Gave Teachers Officer Rank And $400 A Year Boost In Salary

The hanging of an instructor in effigy by the midshipmen in the early days of the Naval Academy resulted in the Congress giving the corps of teachers more prestige and increased pay.

The instructor who figured in this all but forgotten episode, was one of the most versatile of the foundation builders of the academy—Professor Henry Hayes Lockwood, instructor in Natural Philosophy, a graduate of West Point, who was to command a brigade of Federal troops during the Civil War.

Lockwood, who taught mathematics and lectured on astronomy, in addition to instructing in natural philosophy, took over the gunnery department and attempted to drill the midshipmen in light artillery.

Midshipmen Opposition

The midshipmen did not take kindly to this soldier drill. They had a slogan: "A messmate before a shipmate, a shipmate before a stranger, a stranger before a dog, but a dog before a 'sojer.'"

They did everything they could to discourage Lockwood, but the instructor was made of stern stuff. Once he marched a gun battery, including field pieces, into the Severn river, as he was trying to stammer out the command "Halt"

The midshipmen did not give in easily. Linch pins from the field pieces were stolen and tossed into the river, the guns were dismantled and the parts hidden. Lockwood had to put up with severe heckling.

Unusual Position

The instructors occupied an unusual postion at the time in that they were not rated as officers and therefore were from a military viewpoint subordinate to the midshipmen.

The situation came to a climax on St. Patrick's Day when the midshipmen hanged Lockwood in effigy from the flagstaff of the academy.

This action stirred the authorities to action and a court-martial was convened to try the ringleaders for insulting a superior officer.

The defense of the midshipmen involved was that as the professors were not officers they were not superior to the midshipmen. That brought Congressional action. The instructors were given officer rank and had their pay increased $400 a year.

With this development the midshipmen held that Lockwood should not mind being hanged every year.

Interesting Character

Lockwood was one of the most interesting characters in the early group of instructors. He had attended Dickinson College before graduating from West Point and served as an army officer in the Second Seminole War in Florida in 1836-37. He resigned from the army because of slow promotion and farmed in Delaware for four years. His brother, John A. Lockwood, later to become the first surgeon at the academy, persuaded him to become a professor of mathematics in the Navy. During this time he served as adjutant of landing forces from the Frigate United States in the premature capture of Monterey.

Jackson's "Head" Was Severed From Old Constitution

Political heads fell under the administration of President Andrew Jackson when he enunciated his famous principle, 'To the victor belongs the spoils'. But Jackson's head also fell in effigy when his likeness in the form of a wooden figurehead on the bow of the Frigate Constitution was sawed from the torso by an indignant Whig partisan in the harbor of Boston.

The completed figurehead with the decapitation restored is now part of the museum collection of the Naval Academy and of interest to visitors in connection with the centennial observance.

Other Figureheads

The figurehead of Jackson was not the first one carried on the bow of the Constitution. The first one, a figure of Hercules, was shot away in the War with Tripoli and the second one, Neptune, met a similar fate, but in 1834 the Constitution was laid up in the Charlestown Navy Yard in Boston and the placement of the new figurehead was in order.

At this time, President Andrew Jackson visited Boston and Captain Elliott, then in command of the Navy Yeard, conceived the idea of placing the President's likeness on the Constitution as its figurehead. Apparently Captain Elliott was greatly misled in his estimate of the popularity enjoyed by Jackson in New England. The news of his purpose created a hue and cry in Boston and handbills were distributed calling upon the citizenry to "save this Boston built ship from this foul disgrace." Prominent Whigs offered the sculptor a bribe if he would refrain from executing the commission, but the figurehead was finally completed and secured in place on the famous old ship.

Removed During Night

The ship remained for some time in the harbor between two men-of-war for further protection from the outraged citizenry and the exictement was just about dying out when one morning Boston awoke to find the head had been completely severed from the figure of Andrew Jackson.

According to the story, the captain of a sailing vessel, a young man named Dewey, in the employ of wealthy Whig merchants, had undertaken the decapitation for a wager of $100. The deed was accomplished during a terrific thunderstorm and the sawing of the head was done by the light of blinding flashes of lightning.

V-J DAY CELEBRATED

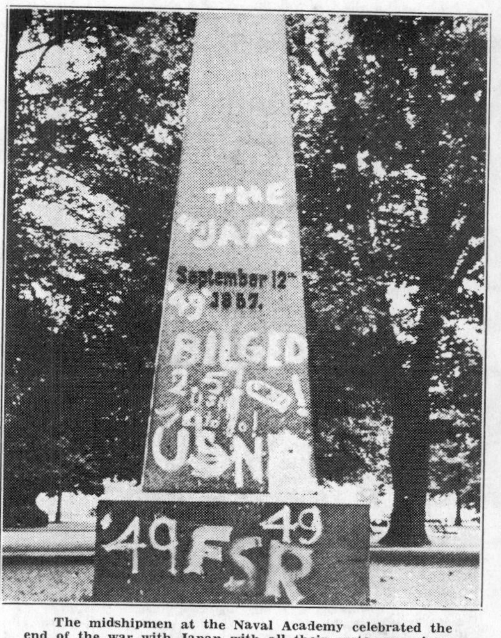

The midshipmen at the Naval Academy celebrated the end of the war with Japan with all their customary vigor. When they finished the Herndon monument was decorated with Navy slang terms that left no doubt that the Japs had been defeated or "bilged" as the Middies expressed it.

OLD TIME ATHLETES

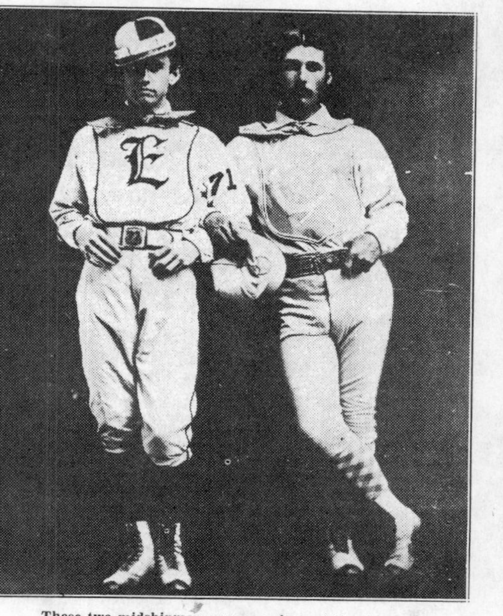

These two midshipmen were members of the Essex Club, and the Naval Academy Class of 1871. They had their picture taken wearing the uniform of their athletic teams.

Come to Church

ST. ANNE'S PARISH

(Protestant Episcopal; Founded 1692)
The Rev. C. EDWARD BERGER
Rector
The Rev. Max H. Rohn, Curate
ST. ANNE'S CHURCH
Church Circle

Sunday, November 4
23rd Sunday after Trinity
7:30 A. M.—Holy Communion.
9:30 A. M.—Church school at church for persons 11 years of age and over, at parish house, 201 Duke of Gloucester street, for children under 11 years of age.
11:00 A. M.—Holy Communion and Sermon.
5:00 P. M.—Evening prayer service and sermon by the curate.
Thursday, November 8
7:30 A. M.—Holy Communion.

ST. LUKE'S CHAPEL
THE REV. JAMES L. SMILEY,
Vicar
Chesapeake ave. and Second st. Eastport
10:00 A. M.—Sunday School.
11:00 A. M.—Morning prayer and Sermon.

NAVAL ACADEMY CHAPEL

Sunday, November 4
9:00 A. M.—Holy Communion.
10:30 A. M.—Morning worship.
11:45 A. M.—Sunday School

ST. MARY'S PARISH

Rev. John J. Hosey, C.SS.R., Rector
St. Mary' Church: Sunday Masses—6, 7, 8, 9, 10, 11, and 12 o'clock.
Sunday School for the children of the public schools—after the 9 o'clock Mass.
Weekday Masses—6:30, 7 and 8 o'clock.
Evening Devotions at 7:30 on Sunday, Wednesday and Saturday.
Perpetual Help Devotions Wednesday after the 8 o'clock Mass, and Wednesday evening at 7:30.
Special devotions for the month of November: every evening during the month at 7:30: Rosary Litany, Prayer to Saint Joseph and Benediction.
Confessions are heard weekly:
Saturday afternoon 4:30 to 6 o'clock; Saturday evening 7:30 to 9 o'clock; and Sunday morning before the 6:30, 7, and 8 o'clock Masses.

FIRST PRESBYTERIAN CHURCH

Rev. Burrett E. McBee, Minister
Duke of Gloucester Street
Lt Comdr. Robert D. Bass
Superintendent of Sunday School
Mrs. Burnett F. Treat
Superintendent of Primary Dept.
9:45 A. M.—Sunday School.
10:45 A. M.—Morning service. Sermon by the minister.

COLLEGE AVENUE BAPTIST CHURCH

College Ave. and St. John's St.
Rev. W. C. Wood. Pastor
Sunday, November 4
9:45 A. M.—Bible School.
11:00 A. M.—Morning worship.
6:45 P. M.—Training Union.
8:00 P. M.—Evening worship.
Wednesday November 7
7:00 P. M.—Junior choir practice.
8:00 P. M.—Hour of Power.
9:00 P. M.—Choir practice.

CALVARY METHODIST CHURCH

State Circle At North Street
THE REV. J. LUTHER NEFF, D. D.
Minister
9:45 A. M.—Church School.
11:00 A. M.—12:00 A. M.—Nursery Hour for children of parents desiring to attend morning service.
11:00 A. M.—Communion Service.
8:00 P. M.—"The Empty House."
Wednesday
8:00 P. M.—Prayer Service.
9:00 P. M.—Official Board meets.

ST. MARTIN'S EVANGELICAL LUTHERAN CHURCH

39 Francis Street
Rev. Homer W. Koch, Jr., pastor
Henry G. Weaver,
Superintendent of Sunday School
9:45 A. M.—Church School.
11:00 A. M.—Worship service. At this service, the new pastor will be installed.

TRINITY METHODIST CHURCH

Rev. WILLIS P. FRYE
9:45 A. M.—Church School, classes for all ages.
11:00 A. M.—Morning worship.
8:00 P. M.—Evening service.
Wednesday
8:00 P. M.—Mid-week prayer service.

EASTPORT METHODIST CHURCH

REV. A. F. T. RAUM, Pastor
Chesapeake Ave and Sixth St.
Eastport
SUNDAY SERVICES
:45 A. M.—Sunday school for all ages. Wm. H. Moreland, supt.
00 A M.—Morning worship. Holy Communion. William F. Miller, guest speaker.
8:00 P. M.—Evening worship. Music by Wesleyan Service Guild. The Rev. F. C Reynolds, district supt., guest speaker.
Monday
8:00 P. M.—Youth Fellowship meeting.
Wednesday
8:00 P. M.—Mid-week prayer and Praise service Study of Genesis.
Thursday
8:00 P. M.—Wesleyan Service Guild meeting at church.
Friday
8:00 P. M.—Christmas sale by WSCS.

SEVERN PARISH

The Rev. Jesse Woodrow, Rector
Crownsville
St. Paul's Chapel, 7:30 a. m. (Crownsville).
St. John's Chapel, 9:15 a. m. (Gambrills).
St. Stephen's, 11 a. m. (half way between Millersville and Crownsville).

FIRST CHURCH OF CHRIST, SCIENTIST

Maryland Ave. and Prince George St.
9:45 A. M.—Sunday School.
11:00 A. M.—Sunday Service. Subject of the Lesson—Sermon: "Probation after Death."
8:00 P. M.—Wednesday evening meeting including testimonials on healing in Christian Science.
The reading room, also on Maryland avenue and Prince George streets, is open every day from noon to 5 P. M., except Sunday and holidays where all authorized Christian Science literature may be read, borrowed, or purchased. Works in the Braille System are also available.
ALL ARE CORDIALLY WELCOME

EASTPORT CHURCH OF THE NAZARENE

Severn Ave. near Burnside
THE REV. HARRY J. FELTER
Minister
'The Church with a Friendly Welcome'
SERVICES
10:00 A. M.—Sunday School.
11:00 A. M.—Morning Worsh'p.
6:45 P. M.—Junior Society meeting.
6:45 P. M.—Young People's Fellowship.
7:30 P. M.—Praise and Testimony.
8:00 P. M.—Evening Evangelistic Service.
Wednesday, 7:45 P. M.—Prayer meeting.

EDWARD'S CHAPEL

METHODIST CHURCH
REV. A. F. T. RAUM Pastor
Riva Road, Parole, Md
9:30 A. M.—Morning worship. John Niemiller, guest speaker.
10:45 A. M.—Sunday School rally—Joseph O. H. Fowler, Supt.
Thursday
8:00 P. M.—Meeting of the Wesleyan Service Guild.

ST. MARGARET'S CHURCH

4 Miles Northeast of Annapolis.
REV. HENRY POWERS, Rector.
Protestant Episcopal—Founded 1692
10:00 A. M.—Church school.
11:00 A. M.—Morning worship and sermon.
Holy Communion first Sunday of each month.

LATTER DAY SAINTS

(Mormon)
ALTON B. MOODY, Presiding Elder
K. of P. Hall — School Street
10:00 A. M.—Sunday School.
11:00 A. M.—Church Service.
Meeting in K. of P. Hall, School St. Public invited.

WOODLAND BEACH COMMUNITY CHURCH

REV. ORRA N. BRANT, Pastor
Sunday, November 4
11:00 A. M.—Worship Service. Fellowship in the Church—Text: Rom 12:5— "So We, Being Many, Are One Body in Christ."
Everybody welcome.

ALL HALLOWS' PARISH

Founded 1692
REV. VICTOR S. ROSS, Rector
ALL HALLOWS' CHURCH
Birdsville
Holy Communion—2nd, 4th and 5th Sundays—11:00 A. M.
1st and 3rd Sundays—9:00 A. M.
Sunday School—10 A. M. every Sunday
ALL HALLOWS' CHAPEL
Davidsonville
Holy Communion—1st and 3rd Sundays —11:00 A. M.
2nd, 4th and 5th Sundays—9:00 A. M.

FULL GOSPEL CHURCH (Assemblies of God)

J. F. SHORT, Pastor
Revell and Severn Sts., West Annapolis
9:45 A. M.—Sunday school.
11:00 A. M.—Morning Service.
8 P. M. Thursday and Sunday, Evangelistic Service

MARLEY CHARGE METHODIST CHURCH

THE REV. BENJAMIN A. BRYAN, Pastor
MARLEY: Combined worship service and church school at 10 A. M.
ARUNDEL: Church school, 10 A. M Worship service 7:30 P. M.
RIVIERA BEACH TRINITY CHURCH Church school, 9:45 A. M.; worship service, 11 A. M.

ASBURY METHODIST CHURCH

Arnold, Maryland
REV. WILLIAM C. WARNER, Minister
SUNDAY
10:00 A. M.—Church school with classes for all ages.
11:00 A. M.—Morning service. Sermon by the minister.

EASTPORT BAPTIST CHURCH

REV. ALDEN F. NORRIS, Pastor
10:00 A. M. — Sunday School, Supts. John E. Stokes and Maurice E. Meade.
11:00 A. M.—Morning worship. Sermon by the minister: "Gospel of the Grace of God."
Nursery class will be held during the 11:00 o'clock service. Parents invited.
6:45 P. M.—B. T. U.
8:00 P. M.—Evening service: "TThe Hungry and Thirsty."

KNESETH ISRAEL SYNAGOGUE

Prince George and East St.
Rabbi Morris D. Rosenblatt
5:00 P. M.—Friday—Evening Services at sundown.
8:30 A. M.—Saturday sermon by Rabbi Rosenblatt.
4:00 P. M.—Saturday afternoon class in Bible Study, Led By Rabbi Rosenblatt.
:00 P. M.—Minchah.
5:00 P. M.—Minchah.
9:00 A. M.—Sunday morning service.
9:45 A. M.—Serviceman's worship, conducted by Rabbi Abraham D. Shaw of Baltimore.
10:00 A. M.—Sunday School in Community Center.

EDGEWATER METHODIST CHURCH

Edgewater, South River
REV. H. L. WEAVER, Pastor
10:00 A. M.—Sunday School.
7:30 P. M.—Evening Service.

SEVENTH DAY ADVENTIST

HAROLD E. METCALF, Pastor
Pythian Hall, School Street
"The Church of the Open Bible"
Sabbath (Saturday) services.
2:30 P. M.—Sabbath School.
3:30 P M.—Preaching.

SALVATION ARMY

47 Randall street
MAJOR ANNA SANDQUIST
Public Services
10:00 A. M.—Sunday school.
11:00 A M—Holiness meeting.
6:30 P. M—Young People's meeting.
8:00 P. M.—Salvation meeting.
Y. P. Activities and sectional meetings announced each Sunday
7:30 P. M.—Open air meeting.
Sunday Scho 1:45 A M

SEVERN METHODIST CHURCH

10:00 A M.—Sunday School and Adult Bible Classes.
11:00 A M.—Preaching by the pastor.
THE PUBLIC IS INVITED

ST. PAUL'S LUTHERAN CHURCH

(Missouri Synod)
Third Ave. & A St., Glen Burnie
REV. EDWARD G. COLLINS. pastor
8:00 P. M.—Vesper Services
10:00 A M.—Church School.
11 15 A. M.—Divine Services

CHURCH OF GOD

REV. THOMAS ASHER, pastor
Miles north at Iglehart on Route 178
10:00 A. M.—Sunday School.
11:00 A M.—Morning Worship.
7:30 P. M.—Y. P. E. Services.
8:00 P. M.—Evangelistic service.
Thursday, 8 P. M., Evangelistic service.

ST. PHILIP'S CHURCH

(Protestant Episcopal)
REV. DAVID H. CROLL
Priest in Charge
Holy Communion:
7:30 A. M., 9:30 A. M., 11:00 A. M. (1st and 3rd Sundays)
Morning Prayer:
11:00 A. M. (2nd and 4th Sundays)
Evening prayer:
7:30 P. M. every Sunday.

UNIVERSAL SPIRITUAL GOSPEL TABERNACLE

63 SPA ROAD
(Basement)
Services Thursdays & Sundays, 8 P. M.
Sunday School, 2:30 P. M.
Thursday, 8:45 P. M.—Prayer Services.
11:30 A. M.—Morning Services.
Rev. Mother Eva S. Jefferson, Pastor.

FIRST BAPTIST CHURCH ANNAPOLIS, MD.

(COLORED)
41 Washington Street
REV. LEROY BOWMAN, Pastor
DANIEL B. SAMPLE, Church Clerk
J. B. JOHNSON, Chairman of Official Board.
10:30 A. M.—Sunday School, James Marchbund, superintendent.
11:45 A. M.—Morning worship.
6:00 P. M.—B.T.U.
8:00 P. M. — Evening worship. Holy Communion first Sunday of the month.
Public invited.

WAYSIDE SPIRITUAL TABERNACLE

12 TAYLOR STREET
The Rev. Wilson Dyson, Pastor
(Colored)
Sunday Services:

MOUNT OLIVE A. M. E. CHURCH

Camp Parole, Md.
REV. C. C. Brown, Pastor
Sunday School—9:30 A. M., John A. Makell, superintendent.
Morning Service—11 A. M.
A.C.E. League—6:30 P. M.
Evening Worship—8 P. M.

ASBURY METHODIST CHURCH

West Street
(COLORED)
REV. ISAAC R. BERRY. pastor
9:30 A. M.—Church School, Mrs. Freddie Smith, superintendent.
11:00 A. M.—Morning worship. sermon by the minister.

MT. MORIAH A. M. E. CHURCH

REV. S. W. WILLIAMS, Pastor
Mrs. Cecelia B. Green
Supt. of Sunday School
9:45 A. M.—Sunday school.
11:00 A. M.—Morning Worship.
8:00 P. M.—Evening Worship.

SECOND BAPTIST CHURCH

(COLORED)
Larkin Street
REV. NORRIS H. MORGAN. Pastor
Mrs. Mary Ann Green. church clerk.
Services for Sunday:
11:30 A. M.—Worship and sermon by pastor.
1:00 P. M.—Sunday School.
Mary Ann Green, supt.
3:30 P. M.—The Rev. Leroy Bowman, his choir and congregation to worship also.
8:00 P. M.—The Rev. Robert Lane will preach the Rally service.

Church of God And Saints of Christ

ELDER ROSWELL ROLES, JR., Pastor
62-64 Clay Street
(Colored)
10 A. M.—Testimonials.
11:45 A. M. Sermon by the pastor:
3:00 P. M.—Sabbath School.
7:30 P. M.—Testimonials.

MT. ZION M. E. CHURCH

Colored—Eastport
REV. L. C. CHASE, Pastor
9:30 A. M.—Church School. J. Luner, Superintendent.
11:30 A. M.—Sermon by pastor.
8:00 P. M.—Program and Sermon.
8:20 P. M.—Program and Sermon.

RADIO

WITH	1230k
WBAL	1090k
WFBR	1300k
WCBM	1400k
WCAO	600k

By C. E. BUTTERFIELD

NEW YORK, Nov. 3 (AP)—The celebration—that is the seven-day observance of 25 years of broadcasting—starts tomorrow. Various regular programs are taking cognizance of the event throughout the day, with others and added specials to join in as the week proceeds.

Coming up: Tonight—NBC 7:30 Announcement of 13th annual H. P. Davis Memorial Awards to announcers of stations on NBC, five to be presented in addition to four honorable mentions. Ben Grauer, 1044 national winner, guest.

Sunday—CBS 2:30 P. M. Bataan Memorial program from Ft. Riley, Kan.

On Saturday night list: NBC—7 Foreign Policy from Paris; 8 Life of Riley; 9:30 Can You Top This; 10:30 Grand Ole Opry ... CBS—7 Helen Hayes in "My Little Boy;" 8:30 Lionel Barrymore, Mayor; 9 Hit Parade; 10:15 Report To Nation; 10:45 Norman Thomas on "Are We Aiming Against Russia" ... ABC—8 Woody Herman show; 8:30 Man From G-2; 9:30 Boston Symphony; 10:30 Hayloft Hoedowners ... MGS—8 Whisper Men at new time; 9 Leave It To The Girls; 10 Chicago Theater, "Bittersweet."

Sunday Forums: MBS 11:30 A. M. Reviewing Stand "A Place To Live;" NBC 1:15 America United "Fruit and Vegetable Marketing;" NBC 1:30 Chicago Roundtable "Revolt In South Pacific."

Other: NBC—2:30 John Charles Thomas; 4 Army half-hour; 5 Toscanini and NBC Symphony; 8:30 Gildersleeve; 7 Jack Benny; 8 Charlie McCarthy; 8:30 Fred Allen; 10 Phil Spitalny Girls' tenth anniversary ... CBS—2 Paul Lacalle Concert; 3 N. Y. Philharmonic; 5 Patrice Munsel time; 6:30 Fanny Brice; 7:30 Blondie; 8:30 Crime Doctor; 9 Request Performance; 10 Paul Baker quiz; 10:30 We The People, Gen. Wainwright ... ABC— 12:30 Friendship Ranch; 1:30 Sammy Kaye serenade; 5 Mary Small Revue; 6 Hall of Fame, Milt Berle and and others; 7:30 Quiz Kids; 8 Sunday Eevning Hour, Jeanette MacDonald; ;9:15 Hollywood Mystery; 10 Martha Scott in "Storm Over Patsy." ... MBS—10:30 A. M. Pro Arte String Quartet; 3 P. M. Roosty of AAF; 5 The Shadow; 6 Quick As A Flash; 7 Opinion Requested; 8 Mediation Board; 9 Human adventure, X-Rays; 9:30 Double or Nothing; 10:15 Name Of Song quiz.

5:00
WITH: News; Bill Dyer.
WCAO: Philadelphia Orch.
5:15
WCBM: Sports Parade
5:30
WITH: Sports Special.
WBAL: John W. Vandercook.
WFBR: Concert Orchestra
5:45
WBAL: Tin Pan Alley.
WCBM: Gene Krupa's Orch.
6:00
WFBR: Health Players
WITH: News; Voice of Love
WBAL: News; Sports Parade.
WCAO: Frank Fan
WCBM: Eddie Fenton
6:15
WBAL: Dinner Table.
WITH: Better Music.
WCAO: Don Riley, Sports
WFBR: Sports Program
WCBM: Louis Jordan Orch
6:35
WFBR: Press Bulletins.
WITH: Richard Eaton, News.
WCAO: Jimmy Carroll
WBAL: Bonnie Gay; Living
WCBM: Hawaii Calls
6:45
WFBR: Labor, U.S.A.
WCAO: World Today.
WBAL: Saturday Edition.
WITH: Md. Quintette
7:00
WFBR: Betty Wells
WITH: News; Enjoyment Time.
WOR: Guess Who?
WCBM: Sinfonietta
WCAO: Helen Hayes
WBAL: Own Foreign Policy
7:15
WFBR: Reporters Abr.
7:30
WITH: Swing Class
WFBR: Dick Tracy
WCAO: The First Nighter
WBAL: Tuneful Trolley
WCBM: Scholastic Sports
7:45
WCBM: Sports Program
8:00
WITH: Phoneaway
WBAL: Life of Riley
WCAO: D. Haymes Show
WFBR: Woody Herman Show
WCBM: Victory Bonds
8:15
WITH: Name Bands
WCBM: Pratt Library
8:30
WCAO: Mayor Of The Town
WITH: News; Crosby
WBAL: Consequences
WCBM: Let's Finish the Job
WFBR: Boston Blackie
8:45
WITH: Red Cross Vets
9:00
WCAO: Your Hit Parade.
WBAL: National Barn Dance.
WCBM: Leave It To Girls
WFBR: Gang Busters
WITH: News-Ray Block
9:30
WBAL: Can You Top This
WCBM: Operetta
WFBR: Boston Symphony
WOR: The Conspirators
WITH: Catholic Book Week
9:45
WCAO: Night Serenade
WITH: Treasury Salute
10:00
WCBM: Chic. Theater
WOR: Chicago Theatre of the Air
WITH: D. Pearson Col.
WBAL: Judy Canova Show
10:15
WITH: Personal Problems
WCAO: Report To Nation
10:30
WITH: Time for the News
WBAL: Grand Old Opry
WFBR: Invitation to Waltz
10:45
WCAO: OPA Mail Bag
WITH: Some Like It Hot
WFBR: Hayloft Hoedown
11:00
WITH: News; Dance Party.
WFBR: Press Bulletins.
WCAO: N. Calmer, news
WBAL: News; Sports Parade
WCBM: Night News Journal
11:15
WBAL: Dance Time.
WCBM: Final Sports Rally
WCAO: Entertainment
WFBR: Let's Spin It
11:30
WFBR: Tony Pastor Orch.
WCAO: Saturday Frolic.
WBAL: Church of Nazarenes.
WCBM: Charles Spivak Orch
11:45
WBAL: Melody Keys
12:00
WCAO: News; Night Frolic
WITH: News; Dance Party.
WBAL: News; Modern Moods
WBFR: Gay Claridge Orch

Sunday

7:00
WBAL: Gospel Tabernacle
7:30
WBAL: Music for Sunday
7:45
WBAL: Church of Christ
8:00
WFBR: The Gospel Hour
WBAL: The Calvary Hour
WCBM: Morning Melodies
WCAO: Press News
8:05
WCAO: Organ Fantasies
8:30
WCAO: The Jubilaires
WBAL: Rev. Rittenhouse
WCBM: The Week in Review, News
8:45
WCAO: Harry Winston Ensemble
WCBM: Morning Glories
9:00
WCBM: Christ Episcopal church
WBAL: World News Roundup
WCAO: News of the World
WFBR: WFBR News Service
9:10
WFBR: Chestertown News
9:15
WBAL: Christian Science Program
WCAO: E. Power Biggs—Organist
WFBR: Frank and Ernest
9:30
WCBM: Echoes of Poland
WOR: The Navy Goes To Church
WBAL: Eternal Light
WFBR: The Voice of Prophecy
9:45
WCBM: Italian Program
WCAO: New Voices in Song
10:00
WBAL: Latest News
WCAO: Church of the Air
WCBM.: Jewish Radio Hour
WFBR: Message of Israel
WOR: Brownstone Theatre
10:05
WBAL: Sunday Morning Roundup
10:15
WCBM: Jewish Radio Hour
10:30
WCAO: Legend Singers
WFBR: The Southernaires
WBAL: World News
WCBM: Jewish Radio Hour
10:35
WBAL: Sunday Morning Roundup
11:00
WCAO: Warren Sweeney and the News
WFBR: Emmanuel Lutheran Church
WCBM: Christ Lutheran Church
WBAL: Gospel Tabernacle
11:05
WCAO: Blue Jacket Choir
11:30
WCAO: Invitation To Learning
12:00
WBAL: News Reporter

FIRST 1946 FORD IN ANNAPOLIS

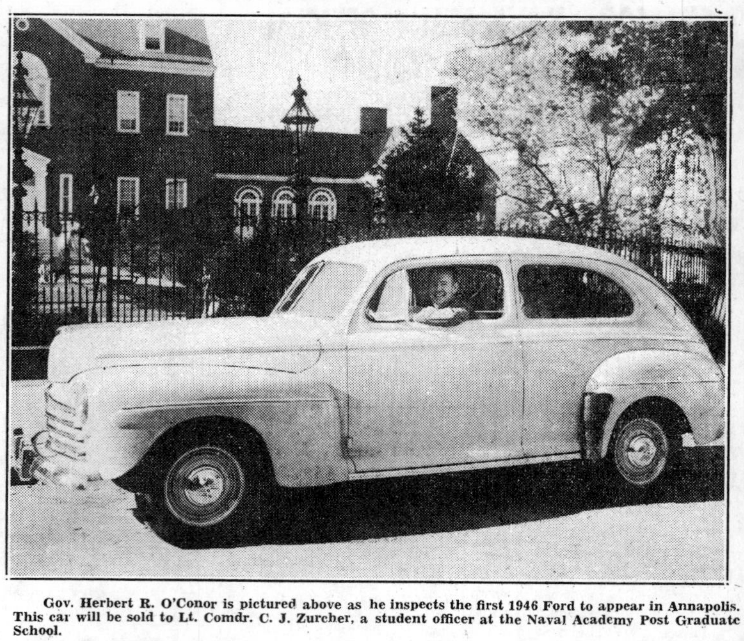

Gov. Herbert R. O'Conor is pictured above as he inspects the first 1946 Ford to appear in Annapolis. This car will be sold to Lt. Comdr. C. J. Zurcher, a student officer at the Naval Academy Post Graduate School.

The first of the postwar cars—a 1946 Ford—to be purchased in Annapolis, will be sold by Universal Motors, 26 West street, to Lt. Comdr. C. J. Zurcher, 11 Dogwood street, a student officer at the Navy Post Graduate school, L. H. Green, Sales Manager said today.

The last automobile was sold on December 31, 1941.

Official announcement of the OPA price ceiling on new cars is expected to be forthcoming this week.

The first 1946 Ford model arrived in the city early last week and was placed on display at the Universal Motors on Friday. About 2,000 people have viewed the automobile.

Applications

Applications for the 1946 Ford have been accepted since Oct. 1, and there is a backlog of 115 applications. The first 40 of this group, have already made a down payment on the new vehicles.

Release of the new cars from the production line will be slow. It is expected the full production peak will be reached about July.

The price of the 1946 Ford has not been announced officially by the OPA, but Green asserts that he believes it will be in the neighborhood of $1,125, a slight reduction over the 1944 selling price.

An Annapolitan and a discharged service man, Russell Lacey, 18 Murray avenue, is second in line to receive a new car. Lt. Comdr. Joseph H. Rayburn, 11 Sylvan Circle, Lt. Comdr. E. J. Fruechtl, and Garnett Clark, of South River, compose the remainder of the first five on the application list.

A number of added attractions will feature the 1946 Ford model. A few of which will include a new desk lid ornamentation, a deluxe grille, parking lights, wider hood, interior, rear lateral stabilizer, voltage control regulator and many others too numerous to name.

Another Ford product, the Mercury automobile is expected to reach the dealers around December 1, in limited guantity.

The first of the 1946 Ford trucks, the 158 inch Ford long wheel base chasis arrived today.

Oddly enough, Green said, they do not have any takers for this type of truck at the present, although there is a long waiting list for various other kinds of Ford trucks.

WCAO: News Bulletins
WCBM: Pilgrim Hour
WFBR: Moreland Chime Concert
12:05
WBAL: Parade of Stars
WCAO: Modern Moods
12:15
WFBR: Guardians of Victory
WBAL: Listen Motorists
12:20
WBAL: Music for Sunday
12:25
WBAL: Stay Out of Court
12:30
WFBR: Friendship Ranch
WBAL: Midday Jamboree
WCBM: Lutheran Hour
WCAO: Musical Memories
12:45
WBAL: Ranger Joe's Ranch
1:00
WCAO: Church of the Air
WBAL: Latest News
WOR: Paul Schubert, William Hillman, Leo Cherne
WFBR: Singing Lady—Ireene Wicker
WCBM: Know Your Songs
1:15
WFBR: Chinese Informelodies
WBAL: America United
WCBM: Ilka Chase
1:30
WCBM: Sweetheart Time
WCAO: "Your Maryland"
WBAL: Man and His Music
WFBR: Sammy Kaye Serenade
1:45
WCBM: Sweetheart Time
WBAL: Sen. Tydings Weekly Report
WCAO: Edward R. Murrow
1:55
WFBR: Sunday News Extra
2:00
WBAL: Harvest of Stars
WCBM: Personal Affairs Clinic
WFBR: Victory Garden Club
WCAO: Stradavari Orch.
2:30
WCBM: Bill Cunningham—News
WFBR: Hour of Song
WBAL: John Charles Thomas
WCAO: "Next Week"
2:45
WCBM: Little Known Facts About Well Known People
2:55
WCAO: CBS Presents Olin Downes
3:00
WOR: Quiz of Two Cities
WBAL: World Parade
WCAO: New York Philharmonic-Symphony Orchestra
WCAO: New York Philharmonic Symphony Orchestra
WCBM: Showers of Blessing
WFBR: Know Your Songs
3:15
WFBR: Galilee Singers—Quartet
3:30
WOR: Return To Duty
WBAL: One Man's Family
WFBR: Orson Wells' Almanac
WCBM: Memory Lane
3:45
WFBR: Jean Tighe & Bob Johnson—Songs
4:00
WFBR: Darts for Dough
WBAL: The Army Hour
WOR: Murder Is My Hobby
WCBM: Murder Is My Hobby
4:30
WCBM: The Nebbs
WFBR: Jones and I: Natl. Safety Council
WBAL: Woman of the Week
WCAO: Electric Hour—Nelson Eddy
WOR: The Nebbs
4:45
WCBM: The Nebbs
5:00
WCAO: Family Hour
WFBR: Mary Small Junior Miss Revue
WCBM: The Shadow
WOR: The Shadow
WBAL: Symphony of the Air
5:30
WCBM: Nick Carter
WCAO: Gene Autry—Songs
WFBR: Charlotte Greenwood Show
WOR: Nick Carter
5:45
WCAO: William L. Shirer and the News
6:00
WBAL: The Catholic Hour
WOR: Quick As A Flash
WCBM: Quick As A Flash Hour
WCAO: Adventures of Ossie and Harriet
WFBR: Hall of Fame; Paul Whiteman's Orch.
6:30
WFBR: Quiz-Teen Time
WBAL: News Reporter
WCBM: Cedric Foster, News
WCAO: Fannie Brice—"Baby Snooks."
6:35
WBAL: Song Parade
6:45
WCBM: Fulton Lewis, Jr.
WBAL: Music Preferred
7:00
WBAL: Jack Benny
WCBM: Opinion Requested
WCAO: Adventures of the Thin Man
WFBR: Drew Pearson
WOR: Opinion Requested
7:15
WFBR: Don Gardiner—News
7:30
WCBM: California Melodies
WFBR: The Quiz Kids
WBAL: Band Wagon Starring Cass Dailey
WCAO: Blondie
8:00
WCAO: Beulah Show
WBAL: Charlie McCarthy
WFBR: Sunday Evening Hour
WCBM: A. L. Alexander Mediation Board
WOR: A. L. Alexander's Mediation Board
8:30
WBAL: Fred Allen
WCAO: The Crime Doctor
8:45
WCBM: Gabriel Heatter—News
8:55
WCAO: Ned Calmer and the News
9:00
WCAO: Request Performance
WFBR: Walter Winchell
WCBM: The Human Adventure Drama
WBAL: Manhattan Merry Go Round
9:15
WFBR: Hollywood Mystery Time
9:30
WBAL: American Album of Familiar Music
WCAO: Star Theatre—James Melton
WCBM: Double or Nothing
WOR: Double or Nothing
9:45
WFBR: Jimmy Fidler
10:00
WCAO: Take It Or Leave It
WFBR: Theatre Guild on the Air
WCBM: Operatic Revue
WBAL: Hour of Charm—Phil Spitalny Orchestra
WOR: Operatic Revue
10:30
WCAO: We, The People
WCBM: What's The Name of That Song
WBAL: Meet Me At Parky's
11:00
WBAL: News Summary
WCBM: Night News Journal
WFBR: Late News Reports
WCAO: Ned Calmer and the News
11:10
WCAO: Larry LeSoeur— News Analysis
11:15
WBAL: The Open Bible
WFBR: Let's Spin It
WCBM: Mood Matters
WCAO: Entertainment
11:30
WFBR: Jerry Wald's Orch.
WCAO: Vaughn Monroe's Orch.
11:45
WCBM: The Music You Want
12:00
WFBR: Station Sign Off
WCBM: Weather, Sign off
WCAO: Press News
WBAL: News
WCBM: Weather, Sign Off
12:05
WCAO: Tommy Dorsey's Orch.
12:15
WBAL: Fairfield Four
12:30
WCAO: Sign Off
WBAL: News
12:35
WBAL: Sign Off

50 NEW MEMBERS TAKE HOLY NAME SOCIETY PLEDGE

The Feast of Christ the King was brought to a fitting close in St. Mary's Catholic Church on Sunday evening, October 28, with the reception of 50 members into the Junior and Senior Holy Name Society.

A very inspiring talk was given by the Spiritual Director of the Society, Rev. John Hosey, the rector of St. Mary's Church, stressing the importance of living up to the ideals of the Holy Name Society, especially in these days of reconstruction. Father Hosey spoke of the value of the good example of the men receiving Holy Communion in a body on the second Sunday of the month.

After reciting the Holy Name pledge of allegiance to God and country, each new member was called to the altar rail and presented with the Holy Name manuel and button by Father Hosey, assisted by the president of the society, Joseph P. Leary.

Solemn benediction of the Blessed Sacrament concluded the ceremony.

Census cards were distributed to the new members and the hundred new members present, to be returned at the next meeting.

The officers of the Holy Name Society, seated in the sanctuary during the ceremony, were Yalter Gies, president of the Holy Name section for Anne Arundel county; Joseph P. Leary, president of the Annapolis branch; Ferdinand Dammeyer, vice-president; Walter B. Smith, Jr., secretary, and Stephan Vanyo, treasurer.

The drive for new members will continue until January, when the next reception will take place. The Holy Name Society is being reactivated, due to the return of many of the men who have served in the armed forces.

HEIDELBERG, Germany, Dec. 11 (AP)—Gen. George S. Patton, Jr., was reported rallying tonight, with some improvement from the paralysis resulting from the fracture of his neck.
His wife flown from the United States today reached his bedside.

Evening Capital

WEATHER
Clear and cooler tonight. Wednesday fair and continued cold.

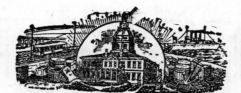

VOL. LXI — NO. 291 | EVERY EVENING EXCEPT SUNDAY | ANNAPOLIS, MD., TUESDAY, DECEMBER 11, 1945 | SOUTHERN MARYLAND'S ONLY DAILY | THREE CENTS

S.P.C.A. To Enforce County Dog Law

LATE NEWS

DOUBT JAP MAY BE CALLED IN M'VAY TRIAL
Washington, Dec. 11 (AP)—The Judge Advocate in the courtmartial of Capt. Charles V. McVay, 3rd, said today he was not certain whether he would call a Japanese submarine commander to testify on the sinking of the USS Indianapolis.

O'CONNOR REAPPOINTED HEAD OF RED CROSS
Washington, Dec. 11 (AP)—President Truman today reappointed Basil O'Connor of New York as National Chairman of the American Red Cross.

ARABS SAY U. S. HAS NO RIGHT TO INTERFERE
Cairo, Dec. 11 (AP)—A committee representing all Arab parties in Palestine declared today the United States had no right to interfere in the Palestine question, saying it was essentially a matter for Britain and Palestine alone.

ORDERED U. S. FORCES TO WAIT FOR JAP MOVE
Washington, Dec. 11 (AP)—Gen. George C. Marshall said today President Roosevelt personally ordered included in prewar warning messages to American commanders instructions to wait for an overt act by Japan.

RELEASE DATE ADVANCED FOR NAVY PERSONNEL
Washington, Dec. 11 (AP)—Navy men and women in this country who under previous rules would be eligible for release by December 31 now may be discharged immediately.
Announcing this last night, the Navy said the plan is to let as many as possible arrive home for Christmas.

REDS AND CHINESE AGREE ON TROOP ENTRY
Chungking, Dec. 11 (AP)—The official Central News Agency reported today that Moscow and Chungking had concluded an greement on problems of flying entral Chinese Government oops into Manchuria.
The announcement said that eement also had been reached the procedure for Chungking to e over local administrations oughout the vast territory.

UMAN ASKS LINQUENCY DRIVE
Miami Beach, Fla., Dec. 11 (AP)—President Truman in a personal message called today on the nation's police officials to organize a country-wide crime prevention drive aimed at the roots of juvenile delinquency.

Commission Calls Two More Trainers

BALTIMORE, Dec. 11 (AP)—The Maryland Racing Commission called before it today two more thoroughbred trainers for hearings on stimulation charges as a horseman's group contended the commission would destroy the sport in Maryland 'in its enthusiasm and zeal to protect the racing interests of the State."

Summoned for hearings were E. A. Christmas, trainer for W. L. Brann, and R. F. Curran, who handles the E. D. Talbert string. A hearing was held yesterday for another trainer and two more have been summoned to appear tomorrow.

The commission said a chemist's test showed the presence of a stimulant in the saliva of Brann's New Challenge, Pimlico winner Nov. 19, and in Weathercock, another Brann horse, which ran second at the track Nov. 27. It charged that tests taken from Talbert's One Only, which ran fifth at Pimlico Nov. 17, also showed stimulation.

Yesterday's hearing for Clay Sutphin of Annapolis, Md., trainer for S. W. Labrot, Jr.'s Shako, was continued for a week or 10 days so that additional defense witnesses and testimony can be assembled.

Local Tides

TOMORROW

High water — 10:20 A. M., 0.9 ft.; 10:49 P. M., 0.6 ft. Low water —5:08 A. M., 4:54 P. M.

Moon rises 12:54 A. M.

Sun rises 7:17 A. M.; sets 4.43 P. M.

Tides are given for Annapolis. For Sandy Point, add 15 minutes. For Thomas Point shoal, subtract 30 minutes.

Date For Nation - Wide Steel Strike May Be Settled By Committee Today

PITTSBURGH, Dec. 11—(AP)—The CIO-United Steelworkers' 175-man wage policy committee gathered here today to decide what one USW spokesman termed "the date of a nationwide steelstrike."

The spokesman, who declined to allow use of his name, said the strike announcement probably would be made during the day and that the walkout might be called for "sometime in January."

He said there was no foundation to rumors that the USW planned to call a series of strikes, hitting first one company, then another.

Union members in 27 states have by vote authorized calling a strike to suport their demand for a $2 a day wage increase. The wolkout would affect approximately 700,000 steelworkers.

DETROIT, Dec. 11—(AP)—A union plan for curbing "wildcat" strikes and slowdowns paved the way today for wage talks with the Ford Motor Company, only member of the automotive "Big Three" still under union sontract.

The Ford company's favorable reaction to the proposal also raised the possibility that some similar method might be used in solving other car industry labor deadlocks, such as the strike idling 213,000 General Motors employes.

Countering a management demand for "company security, the CIO United Automobile Workers offered to subject instigators of unauthorized work stoppages in Ford plants to discharge and participants in such action to fines.

State's First General Snow Slows Traffic

Snow blanketed Annapolis for the first time this winter, and Chief of Police William Curry declared war—on old man winter and careless drivers.

Safety experts claim that the present winter with its ice and snow will be one of the greatest traffic accident years in history.

Warns Motorists

"Motorists driving in Annapolis are warned that they should be especially careful during the current bad driving spell while there is snow and ice on the streets," Chief Curry said. "Failure to comply with traffic regulations will result in fines, and a continual neglect will result in more drastic steps being taken."

Curry outlined a few safe driving tips which he said are based on National Safety Council research, and are aimed at reducing absenteeism due to winter transportation difficulties.

Maintain Visibility

He said that drivers should always maintain visibility, that they must see a hazard to avoid one. Drivers should always check their windshield defrosters and wipers, headlights, and keep their windshields clean, he explained.

"The rate of speed should be reduced when there is snow and ice on the pavements," he declared. It is a good thing to remember that it takes three to 11 times the normal distance to stop on snow or ice without tire chains.

Anti-Skid Chains

He urged that drivers put on anti-skid chains whenever snow or ice covers streets. Tire chains reduce the braking distance 40 to 50 per cent.

The police chief pointed out several reasons why it is vital this year to prevent auto accidents.

"The traffic accident fatality rates for recent winters were 24 to 53 per cent higher than the summer rates, and the combination of

(Continued on Page Six)

Undiscouraged, Vet To Rebuild Fire-Razed Store

A veteran discharged three weeks ago, this morning found his brand new electrical appliance store at the South River bridge and all its stock burned to the ground, but he plans to build another store "right away."

Matthew A. Wilmer, of Edgewater, three weeks out of the Navy in which he was Radioman second class, didn't even find out until 8:30 A. M. today about the total loss of his store which burned last night.

Wilmer said this morning that the Eastport Fire Department had been summoned last night by a man whose name he didn't know who lived near the store, shortly after the place caught fire at 3 A. M. but that no one notified him although he has a telephone and lives less than two miles away. He learned of it only this morning.

Origin of the fire was at first believed to be an oil stove, he said, but he declared there was no fire in the stove and that the cause was unknown.

The store and all it contained was demolished at a loss approximately $5,000, but was fully insured, he said, Wilmer's father, M. J. Wilmer, contractor and builder erected the building for his son and when the latter returned from the service he had bought the stock, specializing in home and automobile radios, and established his dealerships.

Wilmer served three years on duty in the Atlantic in the Navy. He plans to build another store in the immediate future.

SALVAGE COLLECTION TOMORROW

Papers and tin cans placed at curbing of the street will be collected tomorrow throughout the city. Householders are asked not to forget to pile their salvage ready to be picked up.

Concentration Camp Inmates Used As Guinea Pigs In Developing Poison Gas

WASHINGTON, Dec. 11, (AP)—Senators heard from a military government official today that Germany "developed the deadliest poison gas in the world" by testing it on concentration camp inmates.

The testimony came from Col. Bernard Bernstein, director of the Division of Cartels and External Assets, U. S. Military Government in Germany. He submitted a statement to a Senate military subcommittee headed by Senator Kilgore (D., W. Va.).

Bernstein also offered what he said was a German denial of a Standard Oil Company of New Jersey contention that the United States benefitted, rather than suffered, through Standard's prewar relations with the big German dye trust, I. G. Farbenindustrie.

On the poison gas matter, he said that many plants and all stocks of poison gas were destroyed by order of the German government before occupation by the Russians. Bernstein continued: "But at least one of the terrible secrets which the Germans hoped to save for the next war was uncovered.

"Our investigation has disclosed that an I. G. Farben official at Wuppertal - Elberfeld developed the deadliest poison gas in the world. This gas, unknown to the military authorities of the Allied Nations, could have penetrated any gas mask in existence.

"I. G. originally carried out its poison gas experiments on monkeys; later on human beings. . . . These gases were not only used on helpless people during the stages of experimentation, but were later used with full knowledge and acquiescence on the part of Farben to exterminate whole groups in concentration camps such as Auschwitz."

DROP ACADEMY EVENTS AS COLDS SHOW INCREASE

Basketball practice, drills, exercises, recreation and town liberties at the Naval Academy were ordered discontinued until further notice yesterday by the Commandant of Midshipmen, Rear Adm. S. H. Ingersoll, because of colds at the Academy. Visitors are not allowed at Bancroft Hall.

Following this announcement it was learned that Dick Duden, an All American end in football, and a star of the Navy basketball team had entered the Naval hospital with an inflamed right thumb.

Hospital Crowded

Hospital wards are crowded to capacity, and makeshift beds have been set up in the corridors of the hospiital and the visiting team's dormitory in Bancroft Hall.

Approximiately 120 midshipmen are confined in the hospital wards and another approximate 130 in the visiting team's dormitory in Bancroft Hall, an official said.

Fitch Ill

Vice Admiral Aubrey Wray Fitch, academy superintendent, has also suffered from the present siege of colds and has been confined to his quarters.

A spokesman at the academy said that the steps taken by the Commandant of Midshipmen were a precautionary measure to insure against the spread of the colds.

The restriction is expected to be rescinded within three to four days, he said.

Basketball Players

John N. Wilson, head basketball mentor at the academy, reported that none of the basketball players have been affected. He said that all the players were in top physical condition, with the exception of Duden.

The coach said that he hoped that the restriction woud be lifted within a few days.

(Continued on Page Six)

PLANES STILL MISSING NAVY CALLS OFF HUNT

MIAMI, Fla., Dec. 11 (AP)—The mysterious disapparance of six Navy planes and 27 crewmen remained unsolved today as the Navy called off one of the most intensive searchers of its kind ever conducted along the Atlantic seaboard.

As dusk settled last night, the Navy announced that its great hunt which had sent hundreds of planes and vessels over thousands of square miles of land and sea was ended.

At the same time, the Navy asked ships and aircraft operating in the area between Key West and Jacksonville to continue to keep a lookout for any possible clues.

Fourteen of the missing airmen were aboard five Avenger torpedo bombers which failed to return to their base at Fort Lauderdale from a navigational training flight last Wednesday. The other 13 were lost when a Martin Mariner patrol bomber disappeared while hunting for the five.

HOUSE COMMITTEES ALIGNED AGAINST SERVICE MERGER

WASHINGTON, Dec. 11 (AP) — Leaders of the powerful House Military and Naval Committees aligned themselves firmly today in opposition to any merger of the Army and Navy.

Proposing instead that an independent air force be created, chairman Andrew J. May (D-Ky) of the military and Carl Vinson (D-Ga) of the naval committees delcared "unification of the Army and the Navy is not the answer to the problem of national defense under modern methods of warfare."

Some Congressional quarters interpreted the May-Vinson action as a move to split the Army in its support of merger plans by lining up the Army Air Forces behind the new proposal.

Sources close to both May's and Vinson's committees told newsmen the measures could be regarded as "the Navy's answer to demands for unification." Both May and Vinson, however, said the identical bills they introduced were the producct of their joint efforts.

PARKING METERS TO BE INSTALLED ON CITY STREETS

Parking meters will be installed on the business streets of Annapolis, under a contract made early in 1942, the City Council was informed last night at the regular monthly meeting.

The city, on Jan. 26, 1942, entered into a contract with the meter corporation for the installation, but work was held up by the war. The corporation is ready to go ahead with the installation at the original contract rates, and expects to have the meters in place between February 15 and March 1.

Mrs. G. R. Clements, on behalf of the Anne Arundel County League of Women Voters, presented a resolution urging the Mayor and City Council, and the Board of Anne Arundel County Commissioners, to consider establishment of a community recreation department and to take over the USO Club for this purpose. Also urged was the appointment of a recreation director.

Alderman Jesse A. Fisher, who presided in place of Mayor William U. McCready, said he was heartily in favor of recreation, "and hope we can get an organization to take over the building and operate it without expense to the taxpayers."

"I don't see why the Chamber of Commerce can't use the buildinig," he continued. "I am opposed to turning it over to any one particiular organization."

The Council voted to pay a bill for $1,500, submitted by George B. Woelfel, City Counselor, for professiional services rendered in the case of Harry Abrams vs. William U. McCready, Bernard C. Hoff and the Mayor, Counselor and Aldermen of the city. Woelfel reported the case had been successfully concluded in Baltimore City.

Accompanying the Woelfel bill was a statement signed by practically every member of the Anne Arundel County bar, declaring they were familiar witih the work done by Woelfel and "firmly believe that his fee of $1,500 in the premises is a fair and reasonable one." Abrams had brought suit against McCready, Hoff and the Mayor, Counselor and Aldermen for $50,000 damages.

Alderman Arthur Ellington pointed out that Woelfel rendered the services prior to July 1, when he was retained on a "pay as you work basis."

The Council voted $25 to decorate the Municipal Building for Christmas. Alderman Arthur T. Elliott made the usual Santa Claus motion to pay the December salaries of all monthly and semi-monthly city employes on December 15.

The Police Department Committee, headed by Alderman Elliott, reported the police radio in bad condition, and recommended the purchase of a new radio set that would conform to the State police system. The matter was referred to the Mayor and Police Committee, with power to act.

The committee also pointed out that the Police Commissiioner wished to employ a finger print expert and thought that a change in the city code may be necessary.

(Continued On Page Six)

EIGHT INJURED AS BUS AND AMBULANCE CRASH

FORT GEORGE G. MEADE, Dec. 11, (AP)—A school bus-Army ambulance collision yesterday on the Crain highway near here, led to the hospitalization yesterday of six soldiers and injuries to two of the 28 children in the bus, the post public relations office announced.

Two of the soldiers were patients being transported from Camp Pickett, Va., to the Valley Forge (Pa.) General Hospital.

The children were returning to the Leonard Hall Junior Naval Academy for boys at Leonardtown, Md., from the Baltimore area, after an unexpected school holiday, brought about when a boiler at the school exploded, depriving some of the buildings of heat.

The injuries of the two children, Robert Leach, 11, and Wiliiam Lombard, 12, both of Baltimore, were described as minor.

DOG WARDEN AT HEARING

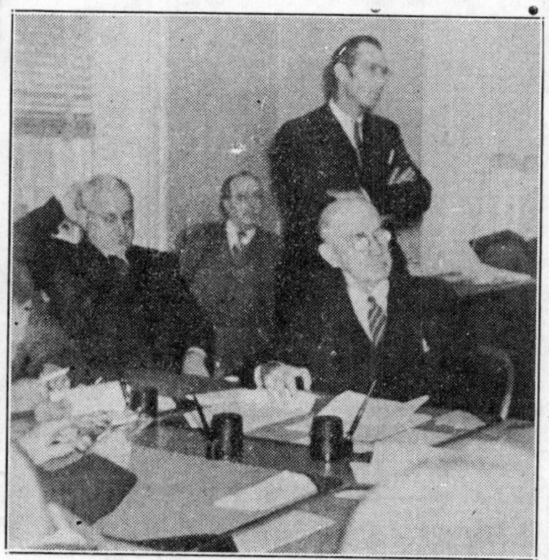

James L. Duncan, dog warden in the Fifth district, stands with folded arms, while the Board of Anne Arundel County Commissioners hears charges of cruelty to animals filed against him for shooting dogs. Duncan contended that under the quarantine law dogs found loose are required to be destroyed. Benjamin Michaelson, counsel to the commissioners, is shown seated at the extreme left. Dr. Granville Triplett, budget supervisor, seated in the center background. Harry Arnold, clerk to the commissioners, is seated in front of Duncan.

FEDERAL INCOME TAX PAYMENT DUE JAN. 15

Federal income tax payers have two chores to perform on or before Jan. 15.

By that date the balance of any tax due on 1945 estimated income must be paid, and an amended estimate of the 1945 income, if there have been changes from the original estimate, filed. It the completed 1945 tax return can be filed with the final payment by Jan. 15, it will not be necessary to amend estimated income.

The estimate income for 1946 must be filed by March 15. The corporation tax for 1945 also must be paid by this date.

Conservation Vote Proceeding Slowly

Ballots on the creation of a soil conservation district in Anne Arundel county are coming in slowly at the office of County Agent Stanley E. Day, he reported today. If farmers do not vote by Friday their ballots cannot be counted. Those who wish to vote secretly may do so at the office of the agent Friday, Dec. 14, between 9 A. M. and 4 P. M.

If farmers want the conservation district it is up to them to vote, Day pointed out, since 400 ballots are required before a district may be formed. All farmers who did not return their ballots are urged to vote in the county agent's office, Friday, Dec. 14.

STRANGE RE-ELECTED PRESIDENT EASTPORT FIRE DEPARTMENT

L. E. Strange was re-elected president of the Eastport Fire Company at an election of officers held in the fire hall, 433 Second street, Eastport, last night. Others re-elected were E. G. Bowen, Jr., treasurer; G. M. Elliott, secretary; and W. R. Blades and J. C. Dove, members of the board of directors.

Newly elected officers were J. G. Meiser vice president; F. A. Willford, assistant secretary; T. C. Stephen, chief; D. G. Lucas, captain; H. L. Barry, W. L. Belcher, and G. S. Tarrick, as members of the board of directors.

Town Meeting Tonight

A Town Meeting for a discussion of recreation program in the community is scheduled for 8 P. M. tonight at City Council Chamber. All interested citizens are invited to hear the views and projects of service organizations and of youth of the city.

SLOWDOWN CALLED IN WESTERN ELECTRIC PLANTS

NEW YORK, Dec. 11 (AP) — A spokesman for the Western Electric Employes Association, Independent Union, said a slowdown was underway in 21 Western Electric plants in New York and New Jersey and that the union would decide today whether to call a strike immediately.

M'Carthy Gives Plans For New Animal Shelter

James L. Duncan, dog warden in the Fifth District, today was exonerated of a charge of cruelty to animals, growing out of the shooting of dogs, by the Board of Anne Arundel County Commissioners. He was admonished against the indiscriminate shooting of dogs in congested areas.

The S. P. C. A. of Anne Arundel County today was given the enforcement of the county dog law by the Board of Anne Arundel County Commissioners, as of Jan. 1, 1946.

The offer to take over the enforcement was made in a letter from Albert H. MacCarthy, president of the society, to the commissioners.

Outlines Plans

MacCarthy outlined the plans for the new building, exhibiting a sketch to the Commissioners. An isolation ward is provided in the cinder block building. There would be quarters on the second floor for the pound keeper.

He said the plans were taken from a new building in Brooklyn, N. Y.

He said the policy would be to continue dog wardens who had carried out their duties efficiently, but that there would be a change in salary, as the society would relieve the wardens of the care of dogs.

"Our policy would be to make it as easy as possible for dog owners to get their licenses," he said. "As to dog wardens, the salary would depend entirely on the amount of work done. We could carry liability insurance.

Adopted Unanimously

Commissioner George Frank moved that the SPCA offer be accepted. The Commissioners voted for the motion unanimously.

The offer submitted by MacCarthy follows:

"Our Society has now reached the blueprint stage of its building operations and must decide whether to erect a shelter building to be used as a public pound or a new boarding kennel to supplement its present kennels.

"Should your Board wish the Society to act as the license enforcement agency for the county, the Society would be ready to begin that work under contract on January 1st by the temporary use of its present buildings until the new sanitary masonry shelter building is available at the site now completed and located in the woods remote from the highway.

(Continued On Page Six)

GENERAL PATTON AND HIS CHIEF OF STAFF

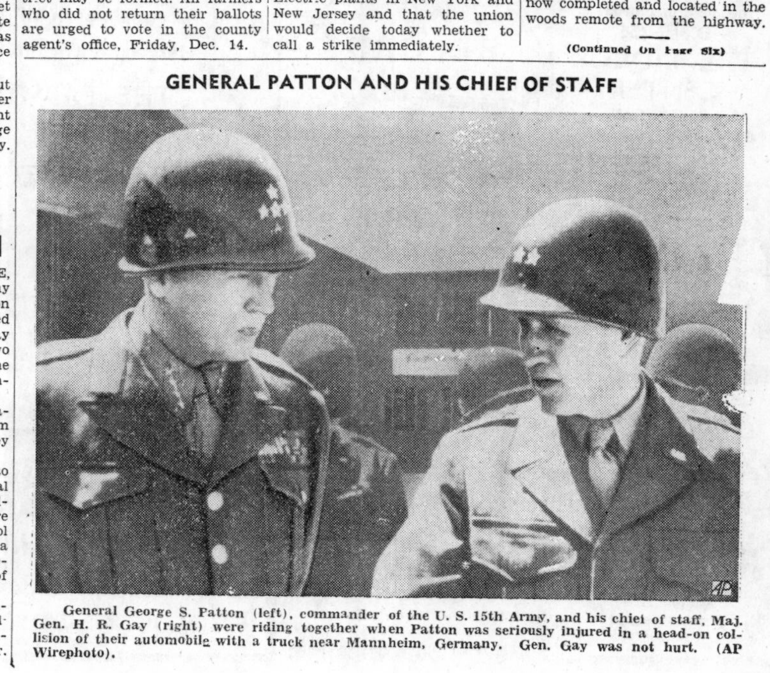

General George S. Patton (left), commander of the U. S. 15th Army, and his chief of staff, Maj. Gen. H. R. Gay (right) were riding together when Patton was seriously injured in a head-on collision of their automobile with a truck near Mannheim, Germany. Gen. Gay was not hurt. (AP Wirephoto).

Dick And Clyde Scott Win Honors

Dick Scott, Navy center, was selected for the All America second team, in the Associated Press poll.

Clyde Scott, Navy halfback, was selected for a similar spot in the All-America team backfield.

Other members of the second team are: Max Morris, Northwestern and Henry Foldberg, Army, ends; Thomas Dean, Southern Methodist and Jim Kekeris, Missouri, tackles; John Mastrangelo, Notre Dame, and Joseph Dickerson, Penn, guards; Frank Dancewicz, Notre Dame; Harry Gilmer, Alabama; Peter Pihos, Indiana; and Ollie Cline, Ohio State, backs.

The third team consists of: Henry Walker, Virginia and Neill Armstrong, Oklahoma A & M., ends; Clarence Esser, Wisconsin and George Savitsky, Penn, tackles; Al Sparlis, UCLA and Jim Lecture, Northwestern, guards; Ralph Jenkins, Clemson, center; George Taliaferro, Indiana; Scott, Stan Kislowski, Holy Cross and Robert Evans, Penn, backs.

Navy players who won honorable mention are Bramlett, Navy, end; Coppedge, Navy, tackle; Carrington, Navy, guard; Kelly, back.

1945 ★ ALL- AMERICA

JOHN GREEN
Army

DEWITT COULTER
Army

FELIX BLANCHARD
Army

GLENN DAVIS
Army

ALBERT NEMETZ
Army

HERMAN WEDEMEYER
St. Mary's

RICHARD DUDEN
Navy

WARREN AMLING
Ohio State

VAUGHN MANCHA
Alabama

HUBERT BECHTOL
Texas U.

ROBERT FENIMORE
Oklahoma A. & M.

Hagberg Missed Main Ambition -- To Beat Army

The nation's "school of the sea" will soon see the departure of its head football mentor—Comdr. Oscar E. Hagberg, who will return to sea duty shortly after the New Year.

Never Beat Army

However, one of Hagberg's biggest ambitions, that of licking the Army, was never realized. In 1944, the Middies absorbed a 23 to 7 loss from the Cadets and in the season just completed they were vanquished by the West Pointers, 32 to 13.

Only nine times before in the history of Navy football which dates back as far as 1882, when Midshipman Vaulx Carter organized the first gridiron team on the banks of the Severn, has a Navy eleven surpassed Hagberg's team of 1945.

In 1897, the Middie team of that year won seven and lost one; in 1905 they won 10 and lost one, and tied one; in 1907 and 1908 they won nine, lost two and tied one; in 1910 they won eight, lost none, and tied one; in 1917 they won seven and lost one; in 1926 they won nine, lost none, and tied one; in 1934 they won eight and lost one.

Equaled Twice

The record of this year's team was only equaled twice before in the 63 year football history at the Academy. In 1913 and 1941, the Navy teams triumphed seven times, lost one, and tied one.

An overall picture dating from the autumn of 1897 when football came into its own at the Academy, gives the Navy 291 victories, 126 defeats, and 36 ties for an average of .698.

Hagberg, a native of West Virginia, was born in 1908 and entered Bethany College in 1926. He came to the Naval Academy in 1927 and graduated with the class of 1931.

While a plebe at the Academy, Comdr. Hagberg was an active sport figure in football, basketball and lacrosse. During the 1928 football season, "Hag" suffered an injury to his shoulder and did not see much play that year.

In football Hagberg, a versatile athlete, performed at end, tackle, and fullback. He also did a good deal of punting for the Navy during those years.

Graduated In 1931

After his graduation in 1931, Hagberg played on and coached several championship fleet teams. He returned to the Academy in 1933 to coach the junior varsity squad. In 1934 he became end

'Continued On Page Three'

In climaxing two years of coaching at the Naval Academy, Hagberg's teams have annexed 13 wins, tied one, and lost four for an overall average of .765.

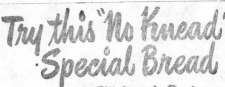

Know somebody special who'd really appreciate a book-full of memories?

From Annapolis, MD?
Or Burlington, VT?
Or Cape Cod, MA?
Or Holyoke, MA?
Or Meriden, CT?
Or New Bedford, MA?
Or New Milford, CT?
Or Pawtucket, RI?
Or Rutland, VT?
Or Warwick, RI?

Order them their personal copy of an exciting, 11"x14" coffee-table book like this one, complied from full front and inside pages of back issues of the local newspapers from these communities.

Order a copy for them today! Fill in, tear out and mail the Order Form, below. Include the payment show <u>plus</u> $2.94 shipping for each book ordered. (New York Residents add 5.75% Sales Tax.

If you'd like it shipped as a gift, enter the name of the person you wish it sent to in the section marketed "SHIP TO:". We'll be happy to sign your name to it, and send it directly to them at no additional cost.